ISLAM IN THE SOVIET UNION

YAACOV RO'I

Islam in the Soviet Union

*From the Second World War
to Gorbachev*

Columbia University Press
New York

Columbia University Press
New York

© 2000 by Yaacov Ro'i
Printed in India

Library of Congress Cataloging-in-Publication Data
Ro'i, Yaacov.
    Islam in the Soviet Union : from the second World War to Gorbachev
by Yaacov Ro'i.
      p.   cm.
    Includes bibliographical references (p.   ) and index.
    ISBN 0-231-11954-2 (cloth). — ISBN 0-231-11955-0 (pbk.)
    1. Islam—Former Soviet republics—20th century.   2. Islam—Russia
(Federation)—20th century.   I. Title.
BP63.A34R65   2000
0007'.0947'09045—dc21   99-41848

BP
63
A34
R65
2000

CONTENTS

v

Contents

Contents

PREFACE AND ACKNOWLEDGEMENTS

This book is designed to fill a gap in the historiography of the Soviet Union. There is so far no academic study of Islam in the period following World War II, without which it seems impossible to understand one of the more intriguing and complex aspects of the Soviet domestic scene. With the opening of Soviet archives, the present author resolved to try making good this lacuna.

This has been no easy task. In the first place, not all the requisite archives have been placed at the disposal of the foreign researcher. Secondly, those archives which have opened their doors have a great wealth of material, which it is beyond the powers of a single scholar – at least of this one – to wade through. Thirdly, the material is singularly one-sided and presupposes certain ideological perceptions which permeate almost every sentence, although it is intended to be informative so as to comprise a basis for policy-making. I am acutely aware of the fact that this study is not the last word on the subject, but trust that it will provide a starting-point which will facilitate subsequent research. And while the reader's patience may be taxed by so much detail, the importance of bringing the information to light for the first time has been uppermost in my mind.

The archival material, which constitutes the mainstay of this study, is primarily that of the Council for the Affairs of Religious Cults, the Soviet government organ set up in 1944 to deal with all recognised religions other than the Russian Orthodox Church, and of its successor organisation, the Council for Religious Affairs, established at the end of 1965 to deal with all religions. In Moscow I also had access to the party archives, specifically to material of the Central Committee Department of Propaganda and Agitation; and in Tashkent to the Uzbekistan State Archives, from which I received materials of the apparatus responsible to the Uzbek SSR Council of Ministers for the implementation of policy regarding religion. I endeavoured to reach other archives in republican capitals including those of one or two of the Muslim Spiritual Directorates, but had no success. I was not able to discover documentation belonging to any single religious society or mosque, and it is not clear to me whether this was because no such material exists, which is what I was repeatedly told, or whether, being a foreigner, I had no reason to expect I might be allowed to see it.

The book deals with Islam inside the Soviet Union. Its intention is to portray the developments which occurred within Soviet Islam over a period of more than four decades in order to enable an understanding of how it survived under an authoritarian, if not always totalitarian, atheistic regime ideologically committed to the extermination of religion even while accepting the political necessity of allowing it a temporary, truncated existence. This study tries to do this by showing both the strengths and the weaknesses of the 'Muslim religious movement', to use Soviet terminology, and by surveying the various components of the Islamic mosaic.

Foreign policy aspects are touched upon only cursorily, and then solely in order to illuminate some of the domestic questions to which they are pertinent. It seems to me that while Soviet Islam undoubtedly has important foreign policy implications, this is a totally distinct topic and one that is not intrinsic to a study on Islam within the country. Nor does this book examine atheistic propaganda, except for a number of perfunctory references which appeared relevant to the general question under study, again not because this is a negligible issue, but because it seems to be extraneous to the understanding of the essence of Soviet Islam. (I have, of course, made occasional use of propaganda material, specifically of some articles which appeared in propaganda publications, in order to cite facts that I did not find elsewhere.) Finally, this work does not touch upon all those many sides of the life of the Soviet Union's Muslim nationalities which do not have a direct bearing upon Islam as such.

Muslim peoples inhabited rather disparate areas of the Soviet Union. Their largest concentration – by the end of the Soviet period, approximately two-thirds – was in Central Asia. The remainder were split almost evenly between the Caucasus, on the hand, and the Volga region, the Western Urals and the large cities of the RSFSR on the other. By 1989, the year of the last Soviet population census, they accounted in all for some 54 million people, nearly 20 per cent of the country's entire population.

Apart, however, from the fact that they had adopted Islam at some time in the past, the Muslims did not comprise a homogeneous group. In Central Asia and the Caucasus they consisted of many ethnicities. The former region had five major ones – the Uzbeks (about 30 per cent of all the USSR's Muslims), Kazakhs, Kyrgyz, Tajiks and Turkmen – and a plethora of smaller ones, some of whom had lived there for centuries, like the Karakalpaks. Others had arrived in the last century or so, such as the Uighurs and Dungans, and the Tatars, who had come in various capacities in the wake of the Russian conquest. The Caucasus were even more motley in their ethnic make-up. Apart from *c.* 6 million Azerbaijanis, the largest group were the Chechen with approximately 1 million at the end of the Soviet era, while two other groups, the Avars (all Muslims) and the Osets (only partly so), topped 500,000 and not all of them were in fact Muslims. Of the forty-old relevant ethnic groups listed in the 1979 census, well over half were indigenous to the Caucasus. Only in Russia proper could the Muslims be grouped together, for they were mostly Tatars of one sort or another (over 6 million in the postwar population censuses) or Bashkirs, who are kindred to the Tatars.

The difference between the nationalities, even within the main regions, expressed itself linguistically and culturally, as well as in terms of sheer ethnicity. The dissimilarity reflected diverse life-styles, traditions and extraneous influences among other differences, in addition to unrelated historical experience both before and after the Russian conquest. The duration of the group's subservience to Russian rule, in particular, often served as a criterion for the measure of its assimilation or acculturation to the dominant super-culture. Already before 1917 the Tatars, who had endured three and a half centuries of Russian influence (since the conquest of the khanates of Kazan and Astrakhan by Ivan IV), were manifestly more westernised, secular and urban than most of the country's Muslim peoples whose territories had been annexed for the most part since the latter part of the eighteenth century and, in the case of Central Asia, within the last half-century.

These factors inevitably made an impact upon the nature and intensity of Islamic practice among the peoples concerned. In the traditionally sedentary parts of Central Asia, among those known in the Soviet period as Uzbeks or Tajiks, there were significant differences between the urban and rural communities, not to mention variations that existed between populations which had been settled for centuries and those which, well into the Soviet period, persisted in a semi-nomadic way of life. Similarly crucial in determining the extent of Islamic influence on any given collective was the span of time that had passed since its conversion to Islam, together with the character and instruments or agents of its conversion. Islam was a much more innate component of the culture and society of populations whose ancestors had become Muslims in the seventh or eighth century, like the oasis-dwellers of Central Asia and some of the Dagestani peoples, than it was among those who became islamicised in the eighteenth or nineteenth century, such as the Kazakhs and Kyrgyz of the steppe, whose traditions continued to highlight traces of their earlier shamanism. Similarly, populations converted largely by Sufi adepts tended to retain Sufi influences of one sort or another, even if they no longer perceived themselves as followers of this or that Sufi order.

Given the above, it may seem artificial to discuss the various aspects of Islamic life in the Soviet Union, as if one could speak of a Muslim community of corporate identity in any sense. However, since the Soviet regime and, to an extent, Soviet society viewed its Muslim citizens as a differentiated group – although expectations regarding the behaviour of, for example, the Tatars of the RSFSR's urban centres and the Chechen and Avars of the North Caucasian mountain areas were evidently disparate – and since Muslims throughout the country possessed, or aspired to possess, similar institutions and attributes of collective conduct, Soviet Islam is being treated in this study as a single entity. This does not imply that one can ignore the diversity of the Muslim ethnicites and regions; indeed, many of the manifestations depicted relate to a specific area or people. But the perception of Soviet Islam as a theme unto itself does indicate that, notwithstanding the peculiar features of any given republic or oblast', it could rightly be addressed as a distinct phenomenon. It was distinct from other aspects of Soviet society in its Muslimness, and from Islam in other countries in that it existed within the confines of the Soviet Union and bore the imprint of Soviet reality.

For the sake of convenience this book uses place names that were in vogue in the period with which it deals, for example, Kirgiziia, not Kyrgyzstan. Some of these were even changed in the course of the decades under study – such as Molotov and Chkalov which reverted to being Perm' and Orenburg – yet I have adhered throughout to the names as they appear in the source material.

As to orthography, I have felt obliged to make a number of compromises in order to make reading somewhat easier. Russian words and names are rendered in accordance with the accepted transliteration from Cyrillic. Terms and names taken from the languages and regions of the Muslim peoples of the former Soviet Union have in some cases been simplified, while remaining faithful as far as possible to the original spelling and sound. Thus Amu-Darya, rather than Amu-Dar'ia, as it appears in Russian, and *chaikhona*, rather than the Russian *chaikhan*. For Arabic words and names I have dispensed with diacritical and vowel-length marks. Mostly, again for the sake of simplicity, I have tended to render plural forms of foreign words by adding an 's', instead of the form used in the language of origin, thus *aksakals*. The exception to this is words appearing very frequently; therefore, oblasti, kolkhozniki, *upolnomochennye*.

Acknowledgements

The author owes a debt to a great many colleagues who have given him major assistance in this research. Before mentioning individuals, it is my pleasure to thank St Antony's College, Oxford, which awarded me a fellowship for the academic year 1995 6. The various facilities which St Antony's put at my disposal and the congenial atmosphere of Oxford enabled me to do the bulk of the spade work at a convenient distance from the chores of my home university. Keston College, also in Oxford, put its ample source material at my disposal, and I owe a particular debt of gratitude to its librarian, Malcolm Walker, who went to considerable pains to cater to my needs. I also wish to thank the staff of the Cummings Center for Russian and East European Studies at Tel Aviv University for sundry services, and particularly Deena Leventer, who has graciously given me much of her precious time to help make the manuscript a little more readable. Among my fellow academics, my first bout of thanks must go to Michael Zand, who was also kind enough to give me much of his time and without whose erudition I would have hesitated to submit my manuscript at all. I also wish to name Moshe Gammer, who assisted me with Chapter 6, sharing with me some of his knowledge of the Northern Caucasus; Ted Friedgut, who gave me essential bibliographical advice for Chapter 11, read through my draft of that chapter and supplied me with a host of comments of which I hope I have made good use; and Meir Litvak and Michael Winter, who helped me with their expertise in Islam. And most of all, I owe a debt of gratitude to my wife, who has suffered my total commitment to this study for three full years with incredible patience and given me much-needed support.

Tel Aviv   Y. R.
June 1999

GLOSSARY

abstashi, abstai   lit. older sister; used for female religious figure or mulla's wife, who would give religious instruction to girls

adat   local or tribal custom

adhan   see *azan*

akhun, akhund   leading religious figure in Shiite mosque. (Originally, in Western Turkestan title given to scholars, '*ulema* of high rank, and in Kazan' to a settlement's leading imam)

aksakal   lit. white beard; elder

aktiv   the most active members of a public group or organisation

alowkhona   lit. house of fire; Tajikistan, meeting-place for menfolk in republic's mountain villages

artel   co-operative association of workers

Ashura   10th day of Muslim month of Muharram; major day of mourning for Shiites

atombo, atynbu   Kirgiziia; female religious figure who gives religious instruction to girls and performs rites for women

aul   Caucasian or Kazakh village

avliya, ovliya   Turkmenistan; saint

ayat   see Qur'an

azan   call to prayer, consisting of seven formulae, sounded from mosque roof or minaret

bai, bay   wealthy person

bakhshi, bakshy   male or female sorcerer who cures illness by driving evil spirits out of the body

bata   raising hands to face after food, symbolising thanksgiving to God

bey, biy   aristocratic rank among Turkic nomads, head of clan

bibiotun   female religious figure

CPSU Central Committee   its apparatus, headed by its Secretaries, comprised the permanent cadres of party *apparatchiki*; under Brezhnev constituted 22 departments

chachvan   veil covering woman's face, used by married women and girls after reaching puberty, customary in lowlands of traditionally sedentary parts of Central Asia

chador, chadra   veil, see *chachvan* (Russian sources frequently confuse between the *chador* and the *paranja*)

chaikhona   Central Asia; tea-house

chilla   40-day period of mourning, or seclusion – for purpose of reading

Qur'an or, among Sufis, to meditate, during which a person is cut off from worldly things

dawra   expiation of sins of deceased after interment, or monetary donation for expiation of sins

dehqan   peasant in traditionally sedentary parts of Central Asia

dervish, *darwish*   member of Muslim order or sect who takes upon himself vows of poverty and austerity, often functions as an itinerant preacher

dhikr   see *zikr*

domullo   a learned person; orig. a person steeped in Islamic learning

druzhinniki   members of 'volunteer' civil guard set up in the Khrushchev period to aid the local militia, part of effort to activate the population in preservation of law and order and maintenance of labour discipline

duakhon   person who recites the *du'a* or *doga* (a personal supplication or invocation, usually on behalf of someone sick or deceased), i.e. healer by means of prayer

dugashi   Kazakhstan; see *duakhon*

dvadtsatka   the twenty people who undertook responsibility for the upkeep of a prayer-house and the observance of the law within the religious association attached to it

efendi   N. Caucasus; religious figure, equivalent to imam

elat   Khorezm, Karakalpakiia; community

fatiha   first *sura* of Qur'an, prefaced to Qur'an as a sort of introductory prayer, an indispensable component of prayer ritual recited at least seventeen times a day (at the beginning of every *rak'a* and at other ceremonies)

fatwa, fetwa   interpretation of dogma based on Qur'an and Hadith, tantamount to a legal opinion

fidiyya   expiation of sins of deceased person

fiqh   Islamic jurisprudence

fitr   payment made in money or kind during the fast of Ramadan for the clergy and needy; if not paid during the fast, has to be paid on 'Id al-fitr (Uraz-Bayram)

folbin   category of irregular clergy; fortune-teller

gazavat, ghazavat   N. Caucasus; holy war, religious war against the infidel, to liberate Muslim lands from non-Muslim yoke

glavizdat   government publishing agency

gorispolkom   municipal executive committee, municpality

gorkom   city or town party committee

gorkomkhoz   municipal administration

gorsovet   town soviet or council

Guli-surh   Uzbekistan; lit. festival of the ripening of the red flower, popular spring festival

hadith   tradition, the account of what the Prophet said or did, second in authority after the Qur'an

haftiaq   collection of *suras*, one-seventh of the Qur'an

hajj   annual pilgrimage to Mecca and Medina, one of five pillars of Islam

iftar   collective repast upon breaking of fast every day during Ramadan

ijtihad   independent judgment in a legal or theological question based on interpretation of the Qur'an and *hadith*

imam   prayer-leader (Sunni), one who stands in front of the congregation, religious dignitary whose presence is essential for collective prayer; by definition has to be male, educated and of good repute

imam-khatib   imam who also fulfils role of *khatib*

ishan, ishon   lit. they, someone addressed in third person plural out of respect; in Central Asia, a Sufi teacher or leader

ispolkom   executive committee, usually denotes leading executive organ of city or oblast' soviet or council (see *gorispokom, oblispolkom*); also of registered religious society

jinaz   Muslim burial service

jum'a-namaz   collective Friday prayer

kaitarma   return of bride to her family after consummation of marriage, until groom's family completes payment of *qalym*

khalifa   lit. successor; among Ismailis, a religious leader, substituting for a higher authority, the *pir*; among Sufis, person who maintains contact between the *ishan* and his *murids*, when the former is prevented from travelling freely; in regular Sunni community, substitute for mulla

khatib   person who delivers Friday sermon (*khutba*), usually therefore conducts the Friday prayer (*jum'a-namaz*)

khatm-i Qur'an (sometimes, *khatim* or *khitma-Qur'an*)   lit. concluding the Qur'an, recitation of entire Qur'an from beginning to end; sometimes used just for reciting excerpts from the Qur'an

khoja   descendants, or reputed descendants, of the Arabs who conquered and islamicised Central Asia or of those whom they converted to Islam

khutba   Friday address or sermon by *khatib* who conducts collective prayer-service; reading from sacred writings

kishlak   traditionally sedentary parts of Central Asia; rural settlement, village

kolkhoz (pl. *kolkhozy*)   collective farm

kolkhoznik (pl. *kolkhozniki*)   kolkhoz member

Komsomol   Young Communist League, Communist Party youth organisation

komsomolets (pl. *komsomol'tsy*)   Komsomol member

krai   administrative division, retained only in a few cases

kulak   well-to-do peasant; the main victims of repression during collectivisation

Lailat al-qadr   lit. the night of power; the occasion of the first revelation, the 27th day of Ramadan

magnitizdat   recording illicit materials on tapes and distributing them

mahalla   Central Asia; neighbourhood of traditional urban settlement

marsiyya   Shiite, Azerbaijan; elegy or prayer containing stories of the martyrdom of the third imam, Husayn, and read in his memory

marsiyyakhan   Azerbaijan; person who sings these elegies, hence Shiite preacher

Mavlud, Mawlid   a. birthday of the Prophet, Mawlid an-Nabi, sometimes celebrated for an entire month; panegyric of a legendary character relating to the life of the Prophet, originally read on Muhammad's birthday, but often part of ceremonial marking rites of passage, especially on seventh day after death, or fulfilment of vows

mazar   Central Asia; holy tomb or shrine visited for purposes of prayer, supplication or healing

medrese, madrasa   advanced religious school

mehmankhona, mihmonkhona   rural Tajikistan; lit. guest-room, sometimes village inn, construct where men gather in winter to spend their leisure-time

mekteb, maktab   elementary religious school, originally attached to mosque

mihrab   niche in wall of mosque facing Mecca where mulla preaches

muezzin, *mu'adhdhin*   person who calls to prayer from mosque roof or minaret, (see *azan*) serves as assistant to clergy

mufti   Russia and Soviet Union; head of Muslim spiritual directorate

Muharram   first month of Muslim year, includes three fast days observed by Shiites, most notably the Ashura

muhtasib   orig. person who supervised believers' behaviour, for example checking normative conduct in local market; in tsarist period each *uezd* would have a *muhtasib*, in period under study regional representative of spiritual directorates

muhtasibat   office of *muhtasib*

mulla   Muslim religious figure; often senior clergyman in a mosque (the *khatib* among Sunnis, the *akhund* among Shiites

murid   Sufi novice or adept; strictly speaking, one who studies with the shaykh or *murshid* in order to become a mystic, and perhaps eventually a shaykh or *murshid*; more loosely used for all followers or adherents of a shaykh or *murshid* who accept his authority as a leader or even as a mediator between them and God

murshid (equivalent of *ustadh*; shaykh; or *pir*)   Sufi spiritual guide or mentor qualified to direct the aspiring novice (the *murid*)

mutawali   president of registered religious society, chairman of its executive organ, sometimes called *mutawaliyyat*

namaz   (*salat*), the basic prayer, recited five times daily, one of the five pillars of Islam

nazir, nazr   orig., payment made on fulfilment of vow; religious tax

nikoh   religious wedding ceremony

oblast' (pl. *oblasti*)   administrative region within larger union republics

oblispolkom   oblast' executive committee

obkom   oblast' party committee

okrug   in early Soviet period, territorial division for administrative purposes, later retained for military districts

otyn   female religious figure who gives religious instruction to girls and performs rites for women

paranja (*faranji*)   woman's garment which covers her from head to foot

pir   (i). Caucasus; holy tomb (*mazar*) (ii) old person or elder (Persian), corresponding to Arabic shaykh or Turkic *baba*; in Islamic law used for persons in their fifties, or even forties, in Sufi terminology the *murshid* or mentor

poselok (pl. *poselki*)   administrative; urban type settlement

qalym   bride-money paid by the groom or his family to bride's parents

qari   lit. reader of Qur'an; person who performs recitation of the Qur'an, often done by heart

qazi, qadi   orig. person who sits in judgment in Islamic court; in Central Asia learned theologian who interprets Shari'a law, sometimes used for regional representative of spiritual directorates

Qur'an   Muslim holy book, divided into 114 sections of varying length called *suras* that are often loosely connected; the *suras* are sub-divided into verses, *ayats*

qurban   sacrifice of an animal, normally a sheep, but sometimes a goat, cow or camel, obligatory for every Muslim who can afford it on festival of Qurban-Bayram

Qurban-Bayram ('Id al-adha)   Feast of the Sacrifice, also known as the Great Festival, occasion for the *hajj*

qurultay   convention

raiispolkom   raion executive committee

raikom   raion party committee

raion (pl. *raiony*)   administrative district, both rural and municipal

rak'a   lit. bowing or bending, prostration; involves utterance of *takbir* and *fatiha*, then the bending of the body from an upright position and two prostrations, an integral part of each *salat* or *namaz* (every *salat* containing a fixed number of *rak'as*)

religiozniki   Russian; in Soviet usage, derogatory term for pious people, 'fanatics'

revkomissiia   inspection or auditing commission

ruzakhan, rozakhan Shiite; person who recites elegies, *marsiyyas*, hence preacher

Saban-tui Tatar festival; Festival of the Plough, originally, but no longer, connected with 'Id al-fitr

sadaqa voluntary alms; in some verses of the Qur'an there is confusion between *sadaqa* and *zakat*, which are used interchangeably

salat see *namaz*

samizdat the circulation of materials not submitted to censorship in accordance with Soviet law

seid, seyyid descendant of Muhammad

sel'sovet soviet of one or several villages

shahada testimony or profession of faith; statement that there is no God other than Allah and that Muhammad is His Prophet or messenger; one of five pillars of Islam

shahsei-vahsei Russian term for Shiite Ashura ceremony involving street processions and self-torture, when the mourners wail *Shah Husayn, Va Husayn* (Shah Husayn, Woe Husayn)

Shari'a Muslim code of law

shaykh lit. old man; a.religious figure serving at place of pilgrimage; b.Sufi, head of order

sobornaia mosque major mosque; orig. mosque where Friday prayers were held, as against the smaller *mahalla* mosque where people came to pray five times a day (borrowed from Russian *sobornaia*-cathedral [in adjectival sense]

sopi a. Kirgiziia, muezzin; b. Turkmenistan, Khorezm, Sufi *murid*

Sufi Muslim mystic

sunnat lit. custom, as distinct from an obligatory precept; circumcision, i.e. rite practised in accordance with the Sunna

sura see Qur'an

tabib practitioner of popular medicine

tafsir commentary on the Qur'an

takbir formula preceding, and repeated several times during, each prayer, or *salat*, testifying to greatness of God

tamada N. Caucasus; lit. master-of-ceremonies; representative of *tariqa* at district level, roughly corresponding to Central Asian *ishan*

taqiyya lit. guarding oneself; doctrine of precautionary dissembling, or dispensation from the requirements of Islam, to avoid detection or punishment

tarawa, tarawih evening prayer during Ramadan

tariqa (pl. *turuq*) lit. way or path; mystical method, school or system of guidance for traversing the Sufi path, hence Sufi order

taziyya Shiite, rites of mourning for Imam Husayn during Muharram

tekke, or *husayniyya* Azerbaijan; meeting place for performance of religious duties; in Soviet period, illegal religious assembly *toi, tuy*   Central Asia; entertainment, celebration, usually in connection with circumcision (*toi-khutna*) or wedding

tserkovniki   Russian; lit. ministers of religion (derogatory, used in Soviet period to describe religious officials in non-Christian faiths as well)

tu   flag or banner

turkkh   N. Caucasus; assistant of *tamada*, person responsible for organising collective prayer and *zikr* at village level; also one who officiates at places of pilgrimage.

uezd   administrative unit (abolished 1929)

'ulama, 'ulema   plural of *'alim*, scholar of Shari'a law

umma   universal community of Islam, embracing all believers

upolnomochennyi (pl. *upolnomochennye*) CARC or CRA representative in each union and autonomous republic and *oblast'*

uraz   from Turkish *uruç* (fast); fast of Ramadan, one of five pillars of Islam

Uraz-Bayram, sometimes Uraz-hait   'Id al-fitr; or Little Festival, celebrating end of 30-day fast of Ramadan

ushur, ushr   tithe, levied for public assistance, frequently used in sense of *sadaqa*, the Shari'a drawing no strict line between *ushur* and *zakat*

ustadh   Sufi mentor; see *murshid*

vekil   N. Caucasus; regional representative of shaykh or head of Sufi order; in case of Kunta Haji, head of order

wird   lit. the special litany given the adept by his *ustadh*, used to denote a sub-division of the Sufi *tariqa*

yashmak   Turkmenistan; scarf covering lower part of face

yasin-sura, surat-yasin   *sura* of the Qur'an (no.36), recited especially for the dying

zakat   obligatory alms, purification of riches by giving, a communal tax contributed to the community treasury

ziyafat   entertainment of guests with food and drink

ziyarat   lit. visitation; hence, Muslim holy shrine (N. Caucasus)

zikr, dhikr   lit. remembrance; remembrance or glorification of God with certain fixed phrases, repeated in ritual order and co-ordinated with particular movements or breathing technique, integral part of ritual of all Sufi or dervish orders

ACRONYMS AND ABBREVIATIONS

agitprop AUCP(b)/CPSU Central Committee Administration (until 1948) or Department (as of 1948) of Propaganda and Agitation. In 1966 renamed Department of Propaganda. (Lower level – republican, oblast', etc. – party organisations had their own agitprop)

AO autonomous oblast'

ASSR autonomous soviet socialist republic

AUCP(b) All-Union Communist Party (bolsheviks), official designation of Soviet ruling party from 1936 to 1952

CARC Council for the Affairs of Religious Cults

CAROC Council for the Affairs of the Russian Orthodox Church

CRA Council for Religious Affairs

Cheka acronym for Extraordinary Commission, set up by Lenin in December 1918 to combat counter-revolution, the first security police organ of the Bolshevik regime

CP Communist Party

CPSU Communist Party of the Soviet Union, official designation of Soviet ruling party as of October 1952

d., delo archival, file

DUMES Spiritual Directorate of the Muslims of European Russia and Siberia (until 1948 TsDUM)

DUMSK Spiritual Directorate of the Muslims of the Northern Caucasus

DUMZ Spiritual Directorate of the Muslims of Transcaucasia

f., fond archival, record group

GARF Gosudarstvennyi arkhiv Rossiiskoi Federatsii, State Archive of the Russian Federation (formerly TsGAOR, Tsentral'nyi gosudarstvennyi arkhiv Oktiabr'skoi Revoliutsii)

JPRS Joint Publication Research Service

KGB Committee of State Security, set up 1954

l., list archival, page

MGB Ministry of State Security, 1946-53

MVD Ministry of Internal Affairs, amalgamates with MGB in 1953 until establishment of KGB in 1954

NKVD People's Commissariat of Internal Affairs, as of 1934 united functions of security police and internal affairs apparatus, until formation of NKGB in 1943

o., *opis'*   lit. inventory; large archival *fonds* may be split up into so many inventories

ob., *oborot* obverse side of page (archival reference)

p., *papka* archival, box, containing several files

PRO   Public Record Office

r., *rolik*   archival, microfilm

RCP(b)   Russian Communist Party (bolsheviks), name of Soviet ruling party 1918-1936

RL   Radio Liberty research bulletin

RTsKhI-DNI   Rossiiskii tsentr khraneniia dokumentov i izucheniia noveishei istorii, Russian Centre for the Preservation and Study of Documents of Contemporary History

SADUM   Spiritual Directorate of the Muslims of Central Asia and Kazakhstan

SNK, Sovnarkom   Council of People's Commissars, as of 1946 Council of Ministers (government of USSR)

SSR   Soviet Socialist Republic, used for USSR's fifteen union republics

SWB   BBC Summary of World Broadcasts

TsDUM   Central Spiritual Directorate of the Muslims of Inner Russia and Siberia (in 1948 renamed DUMES)

TsGAUz   Tsentral'nyi gosudarstvennyi arkhiv Uzbekistana, Central State Archive of Uzbekistan

TsKhSD   Tsentr khraneniia sovremennoi dokumentatsii, Centre for the Preservation of Contemporary Documentation

VTsIK   All–Russian Central Executive Committee of the Soviets, as of 1936 USSR Supreme Soviet

ZAGS (*otdel zapisi aktov grazhdanskogo sostoianiia*)   civil registry office, for births, marriages and divorces, and deaths

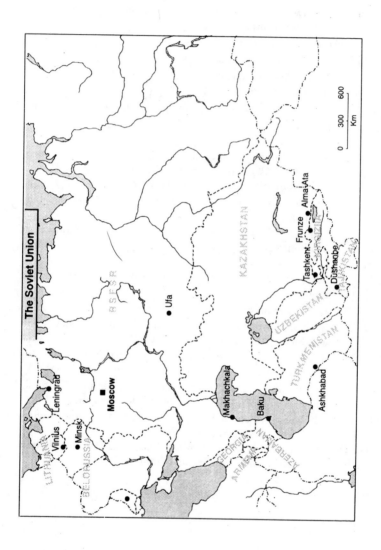

The Soviet Union

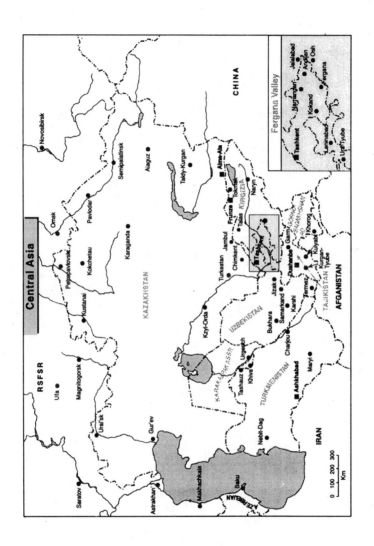

Central Asia

RSFSR

CHINA

KAZAKISTAN

UZBEKISTAN

KARAKALPAK ASSR

TURKMENISTAN

KIRGIZIA

TAJIKISTAN

AFGANISTAN

IRAN

AZERBAIJAN

Fergana Valley

Novosibirsk
Omsk
Petropavlovsk
Kokchetau
Kustanai
Semipalatinsk
Pavlodar
Aiaguz
Karaganda
Magnitogorsk
Ufa
Ural'sk
Saratov
Astrakhan'
Gur'ev
Makhachkala
Baku
Nebit-Dag
Ashkhabad
Maryi
Charjou
Urgench
Khiva
Tashauz
Bukhara
Karshi
Samarkand
Jizak
Kzyl-Orda
Turkestan
Chimkent
Jambul
Talas
Frunze
Tokmak
Naryn
Alma-Ata
Taldy-Kurgan
Tashkent
Dushanbe
Garm
Khorog
Kulyabi
Kurgan-Tyube
Termez

Tashkent
Namangan
Jalalabad
Andijan
Osh
Kokand
Leninabad
Fergana
Ura-Tyube

0 100 200 300
Km

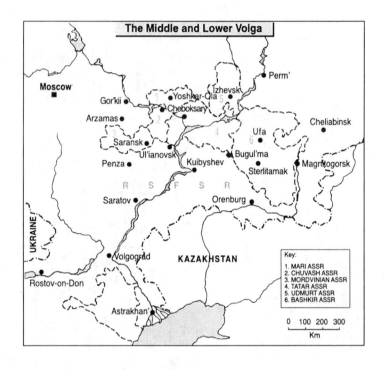

The Middle and Lower Volga

Moscow

Gor'kii
Arzamas
Yoshkar-Ola
Cheboksary
Izhevsk
Perm'

Cheliabinsk

Saransk
Ul'ianovsk
Penza
Kuibyshev
Ufa
Bugul'ma
Sterlitamak
Magnitogorsk

Saratov
Orenburg
R S F S R

UKRAINE

Volgograd
KAZAKHSTAN

Rostov-on-Don

Astrakhan'

Key:
1. MARI ASSR
2. CHUVASH ASSR
3. MORDVINIAN ASSR
4. TATAR ASSR
5. UDMURT ASSR
6. BASHKIR ASSR

0   100 200 300
Km

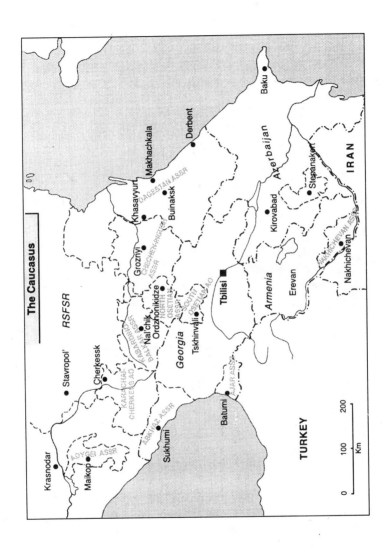

The Caucasus

RSFSR

Krasnodar
Maikop
Sukhumi
Batumi
Stavropol'
Cherkessk
Nal'chik
Ordzhonikidze
Tskhinvali
Grozny
Khasavyurt
Buinaksk
Makhachkala
Derbent
Baku
Tbilisi
Kirovabad
Erevan
Stepanakert
Nakhichevan

Georgia
Armenia
Azerbaijan

ADYGEI ASSR
KARACHAI-CHERKESS AO
KABARDIAN-BALKAR ASSR
NORTH OSETIAN ASSR
SOUTH OSETIAN AO
ABKHAZ ASSR
AJAR ASSR
CHECHEN-INGUSH ASSR
DAGESTAN ASSR
NAKHICHEVAN ASSR

TURKEY

IRAN

0   100   200
Km

NOTE ON METHODOLOGY

The majority of the documentation on which this study is based comes from the archives of the Council for the Affairs of Religious Cults (CARC) and the Council for Religious Affairs (CRA)[1] preserved in the State Archive of the Russian Federation (GARF). This material is drawn from all the general documentation for the years 1944-74, but not from all the files for republics and oblasts, as this was physically impossible. I therefore chose a number of what seemed to be more interesting areas: Osh for the years 1945-57, Tajikistan, the Chechen-Ingush and Kabardino-Balkar ASSRs for the years 1960-5, so that a disproportionate number of examples relate to these parts. (The reader must not draw any conclusions from the smaller quantity of references to occurrences in other parts.) Other documents come from the archive of the Department for Propaganda and Agitation of the CPSU Central Committee (Agitprop)[2] preserved in the Russian Centre for the Preservation and Study of Documents of Contemporary History (RTsKhIDNI) until 1952 and the Centre for the Preservation of Contemporary Documentation (TsKhSD) as of 1953. The third major group of materials come from the archive of the representative of the above councils at the government of the Uzbek SSR in the Central State Archives of Uzbekistan (TsGAUz) in Tashkent.

On the face of it, this should be the optimal material for our study since it represents first and foremost the reports of the two councils to the top leadership in the party and government and

---

1. For the two councils, see pp.11-12.

2. CARC and the CRA also maintained sporadic contacts with other Central Committee departments, such as the Department of Science and Culture and the Department of Party-Organisational Work. P. A. Tarasov, who was the addressee of a number of letters in the mid 1950s, worked in the former, and A. M. Vasil'ev, who received letters from the CRA in the early 1970s, worked in the latter. They also cooperated with the Department of Administrative Organs when it came to preparing drafts for legislation or government resolutions regarding religion (interview with T. S. Saidbaev, 8 Feb. 1998).

1

the reports of its officials, or *upolnomochennye*,[3] in the various republics and oblasts of the Soviet Union. The *upolnomochennyi* had to report regularly to CARC and the regional (republican, oblast' or krai) authority to which he was attached, just as he had to coordinate all issues of principle with both of them.[4] He was to report to CARC at least once every three months on a wide variety of issues: the number of applications received to open prayer-houses and register religious societies, including those which had been rejected and the reasons for their rejection; questions of principle raised by clergy; violations of legislation, especially the unauthorised opening or closing of prayer-houses, holding religious rites in the open and instigation or provocation to anti-Soviet pronouncements; complaints regarding actions by local officials, particularly inequitable imposition of taxes upon clergy; cases of bringing clergy to justice and attempts by clergy to discredit certain officials or conceal revenues.

When I first began working in the former Soviet archives, my naive assumption was that this material would be essentially reliable, devoid of even the problems of departmental interest which often colours Western governmental material. But the more I worked with these documents, the more difficulties arose. This does not mean that a historian of the Soviet Union can afford to disregard the archival materials which have been declassified and put at the disposal of the researcher. But he must beware of assuming that since these are internal reports, intended *a priori* as part of the input on which policy-making was based, the data provided in them represent hard facts. In some cases at least, the contrary – distortion of the truth – would seem to be the rule rather than the exception. CARC itself was constantly checking up on the reporting of its *upolnomochennye*.

There seem to be four basic types of inaccuracy, all of which constitute, in one way or another, conscious deceit or fabrication. The first relates to reporting that was designed to correspond to the expectations of one's superior. True, this happens to an extent in every administration or governmental system and must surely

3. The Russian term is sometimes rendered in English 'plenipotentiary'. But finding this and other options – representative, commissioner – unsatisfactory, I have retained the Russian throughout.
4. CARC instructions to *upolnomochennye*, 15 May 1946, TsGAUz, f.2456, o.1, d.65, 1.20.

be expected in an authoritarian regime like that of the Soviet Union. Yet, there seems to have been a systemic lack of compunction about mis- and dis-informing at all levels. The dimensions and systematic nature of the distortions are simply astounding. One can only conclude that the medium and low-level official or the representative in the field of government institutions did not perceive his task as transmitting accurate information so that the higher organs could mould their policy on the basis of real data. Rather, he saw his assignment as the composition and dispatch of reports which conformed to a predetermined line. Nor perhaps was he far from the mark. In 1955 CARC wrote to its representative in Tashkent: you write that the influence of religion has grown of late in Uzbekistan, but we cannot accept this conclusion, for this cannot be the case in Soviet reality.[5]

Nor was it only Moscow that local officialdom sought to mislead. Raion officials reporting to the republican capital were similarly motivated. In September 1969 the Azerbaijan CP Central Committee's Agitprop department heard a report by second secretary of the Sheki *gorkom* who told how twenty seven unregistered mullas had given notice of their repudiation of all religious activity, how an empty mosque had been transferred to an industrial complex as a warehouse, and how a holy place had stopped functioning. Yet when the republican *upolnomochennyi* visited Sheki a month later he found none of this to be true: the mosque was still in the possession of believers and the shrine was operating as a place of pilgrimage. As to the unregistered mullas, on returning from Baku in September the *gorkom* secretary had issued instructions to make the unregistered clergy sign documents stating that they had indeed renounced their religious activity. The *gorispolkom* chairman had authorised the head of the financial department to organise this: an appropriate form was elaborated and duplicated and the local imam instructed to fill in the forms and gather the requisite signatures, which he did at prayers on the following Friday. He thus obtained documentary evidence of the struggle waged by the local organs of government against clergy who functioned illegally. But

5. I. V. Polianskii to Kh. N. Iskanderov, 17 Aug. 1955; TsGAUz, f.2456, o.1, d.175, l.25. Polianskii sought to explain the apparent religious upsurge in many ways, attributing it in particular to technical changes, such as the improved organisational work of the religious establishment. For this instance, see p.564.

the mullas in question went about their religious activity unperturbed.[6]

The second type of misrepresentation is reporting that claimed
to provide a comprehensive picture of events, developments or
situations and in fact did not do so at all. The reasons for this
were often technical, the result of constraints and limitations which
were known to all concerned – the official who wrote the report
and his superiors. For example, an official would have details
about what happened in one mosque, or in one or two raiony,
which he had perhaps visited. He would then extrapolate from
his firsthand information regarding all the other mosques in his
area of jurisdiction, and would present his information as pertinent
to the entire oblast' or autonomous republic for which he was
responsible. Or, even more commonly: CARC representatives in
the localities were instructed to report the level of religiosity.
They were provided with special forms and questionnaires for
this purpose. Apart from participation at religious services in the
various prayer-houses on Fridays, they were to provide data for
life-cycle rites (name-giving, circumcision, religious marriages and
burials). It was known to all that, on the one hand, religious
ceremonies were registered only when they took place in a registered
prayer-house and that, on the other hand, most of these ceremonies
were performed in private homes.[7] Yet the forms were filled in
and their findings became the basis for reports by CARC in Moscow
to the Central Committee and the Council of Ministers on the
extent of the population's observance of the traditional way of
life. No attempt was made by any level of officialdom, including
the very top level, to obtain a true picture. It was apparently
convenient for all concerned to contend that the dimensions of
religiosity on the individual level were far less than they in fact
were. Only when the Soviet regime began to avail itself of sociological surveys towards the end of the 1960s did the true picture

6. A. Ahadov, Report, undated [probably early Nov. 1969]; GARF, f.6991,
o.6, d.220, ll.15-22.

7. The *upolnomochennye* in Kazakhstan suggested to the CRA in 1970, for example,
to simply remove the item in the form it distributed which asked about the
extent of circumcision, on the grounds that it was performed not by registered
clergy but clandestinely by unregistered mullas and sometimes even by surgeons
in hospitals, and there was no way of knowing how many circumcisions had
been performed over any given period – K. Kulumbetov to V. Kuroedov, 18
Dec. 1970; GARF, f.6991, o.6, d.290, ll.39-41.

begin to emerge. And not a few Western observers and students have fallen into the trap and contended that the population started observing these rites only as of the late 1960s or early 1970s.

The third category of deception relates to reports that were specifically intended to deceive the establishment in Moscow, not in order to toe a particular line, but in order to provide a cover-up for the local bureaucracy or social system. The CARC *upolnomochennyi* had to report periodically on the 'religious movement' in his area, on the existence and activities of registered and unregistered communities and clergy. Although officially a representative of CARC, he was an appointee of the local *oblispolkom* or republican government and often fulfilled assignments for it simultaneously with his duties to CARC. In the Muslim areas – as probably elsewhere as well – he was a representative of the local elite and belonged to the titular nationality. His loyalty was, accordingly, first and foremost to the local government organs, and in the case of a number of Muslim peoples to the clan or tribe that traditionally controlled the area. This loyalty was a central value and a guarantee of the continuance of local tradition and the tribal ethos. The authorities in Moscow were the other side, to whom he owed nothing and of whose machinations he and his peers had constantly to beware. All CARC representatives were party members, usually of long standing, a fact which Moscow hoped would ensure that they had imbibed party values, but which in practice made little or no difference.[8] Thus, the CARC *upolnomochennyi* in the Chechen-Ingush ASSR, which was thought to be the most religious of all Muslim areas, reported in the mid 1960s, several years after the return of the Chechen and Ingush from deportation, that there were no religious communities there at all. It was true that there were no registered communities, for reasons to which we shall return, but there was a great deal of other, unregistered activity.

Similarly, the CARC *upolnomochennyi* in Fergana Oblast' in Uzbekistan had reported – not verbally to the *obkom* but in writing to the republican *upolnomochennyi* in Tashkent, with a copy to CARC in Moscow – instances of inappropriate behaviour on the part of two officials of the Fergana Obkom, who had tried to

8. For local government, its loyalties, dilemmas and general characteristics, see Chapter 11.

exert pressure or influence on believers. He was accordingly hauled over the coals by the *obkom* third secretary:

> How long have you been a party member? Are you acquainted with party policy? If so, why did you write an anti-party document? You wrote nonsense, you wrote a calumny. For that we are going to dismiss you. To what organisation do you belong, that obliges you, if *obkom* or *oblispolkom* officials commit mistakes, to immediately report this to Moscow? We appointed you to the job, so why do you act on your own without our consent?[...]You cannot be trusted[...]What are you, an *upolnomochennyi* of the Central Committee of the CPSU?[9]

Our last category is the half-truth, the information the official on the spot received incidentally or from some interested third party and did not bother to check. This was something the centre was constantly warning against and was clearly widespread. The *upolnomochennyi* did not usually have a car at his disposal nor did he have sufficient funds, and it was burdensome, uncomfortable and expensive to travel around his entire oblast' or autonomous republic.[10] It was far easier to simply believe or at least pass on anything he might be told by whomever it might be. This negligence led to major discrepancies in reporting. Inherent contradictions of this nature abound in the material. On one occasion CARC Chairman Polianskii reprimanded the republican *upolnomochennyi* in Uzbekistan for giving in two separate reports totally different figures regarding attendance and donations at the very same prayer-service.[11]

In addition, whereas the *upolnomochennyi* was generally able to win the confidence of some members of the *aktiv* of registered mosques, this was far from being the case in regard to unregistered associations. As a result, while reporting on the former tended to

9. U. Mangushev to I. Polianskii, 15 Jan. 1955; GARF, f.6991, o.3, d.113, ll.86-9.

10. For the work conditions of CARC's *upolnomochennye*, see pp. 13-4 and 614-5.

11. Reporting in 1953 on the number of worshippers in one of Tashkent's mosques, he had said there had been 10,000 worshippers on the festival of Qurban-Bayram and that they had given donations to the value of 10,250 rubles; yet a year later referring to the same occasion he said there had been 3,000 worshippers who had given 3,750 rubles – I. Polianskii to Kh. Iskanderov, 25 Sept. 1954; TsGAUz, f.2456, o.1, d.166, l.93.

be fairly truthful, even if selective, information transmitted concerning the latter was suspect almost by definition. Since the members of these groups knew that once their existence was exposed, they were likely to be shut down, their leaders and other representatives could not trust the *upolnomochennyi* and refrained from providing him with accurate information. And where there was not even such a group, but just the conduct of rites by itinerant and 'mosqueless' mullas, these would simply deny that they engaged in satisfying the religious needs of local believers, who likewise covered up for them and refused to make any statement whatever. Even the *sel'sovet* or kolkhoz officials supplied no data, since they, too, were mostly believers.[12] This situation did not prevent the *upolnomochennye* from including in their reports a section on the unregistered groups and clergy, more often than not ignoring the equivocal nature of the information it contained.

A historian looking at any document must always bear in mind its general circumstances and specific purpose and find out what he can about both its author and addressee. Here we come face to face with, on the one hand, local officials intent, on the whole, on impressing Moscow with their efficiency and achievements, and, on the other hand, officials at the centre, aware at one and the same time of their dependence on the quality of the information they were obtaining from the provinces and of the extreme partiality (in both senses) of the reporting.

To all the above it is incumbent upon us to add that both the *upolnomochennye* in the various localities and the officials of CARC and the CRA in Moscow were not for the most part people who had studied Islam or the national culture of the USSR's Muslim ethnicities. There are, as a result, frequent unintentional inaccuracies arising from sheer ignorance of the subject matter. One CARC *upolnomochennyi*, for instance, contended that marriages of returning soldiers of Muslim nationalities were being performed in large numbers in the year following World War II, because Muslim law demanded that a couple separated for over forty days had to have its marriage consummated anew. This was almost certainly the story he was told by Muslim clerics, relying – with justification

12. H. A. Akhtiamov, Address, Instructional conference of CARC's Central Asian *upolnomochennye*, Tashkent, 17-20 1949; GARF, f.6991, o.3, d.67, ll.123-4; and U. Abdullaev, Report, Instructional meeting of CARC *upolnomochennye* in the Uzbek SSR, 15-17 March 1956; TsGAUz, f.2456, o.1, d.183, l.58.

– on his lack of knowledge of Muslim custom in order to provide an explanation for what was happening in fact.[13] Many technical terms describing customs of one sort or another appearing in the documents are used imprecisely.

The discourse which emerges from the archival material between Moscow and the periphery, and between the professional bureaucrats and the top party bosses is an interesting and important topic unto itself. But even for those who do not address it per se, it is essential to constantly remember its existence, to try to understand the guidelines it set for both sides as they conveyed information – or misinformation – and directives or recommendations to each other, and to read the documents with the most extreme care. The problem was of course a general one, and one of the run-of-the-mill assignments of party comptrol commissions was to verify, check and counter-check reports that were received from the field, for which they had a variety of mechanisms. But, despite their awareness of the faultiness of incoming materials, the authorities in Moscow, like scholars today who have access to the same documentation, had to depend in the main on what they were told by their subordinates and by local bureaucracies. We can only hope that our historical research will have better results than the policy-making efforts of the Soviet leadership.

I have endeavoured in this book not to take at face value information contained in the documentation which aroused my suspicions for one reason or another. While my efforts were presumably not always entirely successful, I believe that the picture presented here is as a whole correct, even though it will require supplementing when new archives are opened. Perhaps, too, scholars from the areas and ethnic groups concerned will be able through personal interviews with religious activists in the Soviet period to add a dimension that I was unfortunately not able to provide.

13. See p. 534.

Part I. THE SETTING

1

SOVIET RELIGIOUS POLICY AND ITS IMPLEMENTATION

The status of Islam in the Soviet Union in the period from World War II onwards derived from two main factors: trends and developments within the Muslim community and the prevailing laws and decrees on religion.[1] Since the latter comprised the terms of reference within which all the players on the religious scene had to operate, it is incumbent to look at these prior to studying the specifics of the Muslim scene. True, most of the decrees on religion were not published, but their general content and sometimes even their texts were known to those concerned. They would be transmitted by the authorities at the centre to their representatives in the localities and/or to republican and local government institutions. These, in turn, informed the religious personnel with whom they maintained contact.[2]

1. It was also influenced by the position of religion as a whole and of the Russian Orthodox Church in particular, which in many ways paved the way for the other faiths. This topic has been studied elsewhere and cannot be surveyed here; see, especially Ellis, *The Russian Orthodox Church*, and Pospelovskii, *Russkaia pravoslavnaia tserkov' v XX veke*. As one CARC *upolnomochennyi* said, it was impossible to discuss the religious movement of the various faiths without relating to the Russian Orthodox Church, which both influenced the dynamics of the other faiths and filled a leading role in the restoration of the population's religious feeling – A. Saltovskii, *upolnomochennyi* for Alma-Ata Oblast', Report, Conference of CARC *upolnomochennye*, 30 Sept. 1946; GARF, f.6991, o.3, d.41, l.86.

2. CARC Chairman A. A. Puzin wrote to the council's *upolnomochennye* – 24 July 1961; GARF, f.6991, o.3, d.1368, l.193 – that texts of resolutions and legislation on religion were not to be let out of state offices, but their content was to be transmitted to members of the executive organs and inspection committees

Before reviewing the legislative framework, it is perhaps worthwhile dividing the four decades or so that this study surveys into subperiods from the point of view of Soviet policy towards religion. The years 1943-7 saw what seemed to be a legitimisation of religion within the Soviet regime's general effort to acquire maximum support from the population during the tribulations of World War II and its immediate aftermath. In the following period, 1947-54, the authorities, apparently alarmed at the religious revival let loose by the war, on the one hand, and by their own concessions, on the other, resolved to start closing prayer-houses, without, however, resorting to the repressive measures of the 1920s and 1930s. Then came a further 'liberalisation' in the years 1955-8, which saw new attempts to somehow bring religion within the scope of the wider 'thaw' and de-stalinisation. But such a line became incompatible with the party leadership's renewed efforts to promote the country's 'socialist construction' and to implement Khrushchev's promise to put the Soviet Union on the path of attaining true communism within the foreseeable future. This led to the anti-religious campaign of 1958-64 associated with the First Secretary's name, during the course of which religious activity was seriously repressed. And, finally, came a period of 'normalisation' from 1965-85, in which the regime sought to find a *modus operandi* that would enable it to co-exist with religion, making it clear, however, that religion was being tolerated as a necessary evil and not encouraged.

The basic pieces of religious legislation remained throughout the post-World War II period the decree of 1918 separating the church from the state and the school from the church and the 1929 law on religious associations, which laid down the regulations for the operation of communities and clergy of all denominations.[3] The Soviet constitution also included an article on religion which

---

of the religious societies, representatives of believers' groups, heads of the religious centres and clergy. Prior to 1958, it was general practice not to publish either laws of the Supreme Soviet or decrees and regulations of the Council of Ministers; in 1958 a law was published that all laws and decrees that had 'general significance' or were of a 'normative character' be published either in the Journal of the Supreme Soviet or the Collected Decrees of the Government of the USSR –Berman, *Justice in the U.S.S.R.*, pp.76-7. Insofar as this law was enforced, it does not seem to have applied to religion.

3. These documents have been printed in full in Pospielovsky, *A History of Marxist-Leninist Atheism and Soviet Anti-Religious Policies,* pp.133-5 and 138-46.

recognised freedom of conscience and religious practice.[4] Altogether, most of the motifs which characterise the line pursued by the regime in the postwar period can be found in the prewar years as well, although emphases changed, as they did within the four decades under study. In fact the period beginning 1944 and ending with the advent of perestroika saw a considerable number of new decrees of both the party and the government which stipulated the latest emphases and concerns of the regime. Although, like the legislation of the prewar period, their fundamental underlying assumption was that religion would die out with the ultimate construction of a socialist society, and their chief purpose was to facilitate and precipitate this process, these decrees were of a variegated nature and indicated the differing moods which prevailed among the ruling élite over these four decades. For example, the enactments of the years 1944-6 and 1954-6 offered a certain leeway regarding religious activity and entailed an implicit criticism of the extreme anti-religious activity of the pre-war years. Indeed, officials occasionally insinuated or even stated pointblank that the excesses of the 1920s and 1930s had had a negative impact for which the regime continued for years to pay the price.[5] The legislation of Khrushchev's latter years, on the other hand, was manifestly designed to seal any cracks that might have appeared in the regime's general anti-religious stand and to actively curtail religious activity.

The first major document which must be examined is the statute of the Council for the Affairs of Religious Cults (CARC), formed

---

4. Article 124 of the 1936 (Stalin) Constitution read: 'In order to ensure its citizens freedom of conscience, the church in the USSR is separated from the state, and the school from the church. Freedom of religious worship and freedom of anti-religious propaganda is recognised for all citizens.' The relevant article – No.52 – of the 1977 (Brezhnev) Constitution, which superseded that of 1936, read: 'Citizens of the USSR are guaranteed freedom of conscience, that is, the right to profess or not to profess any religion and to conduct religious worship or atheistic propaganda. Incitement of hostility or hatred on religious grounds is prohibited. In the USSR the church is separated from the state, and the school from the church' – quoted in Lane, *Politics and Society in the USSR*, pp.549 and 564.

5. For example, V. I. Gostev, 'Theses of an instructional address at a convention of [CARC] *upolnomochennye* in the Ukrainian SSR', Minutes, CARC session No.1s, 6 Jan. 1955, and A. Budov to A. A. Puzin, 12 June 1965; GARF, f.6991, o.3, d.110, l.6, and d.1486, l.21.

by a special decree in May 1944.[6] A Council for the Affairs of
the Russian Orthodox Church (CAROC) had been set up in
1943 under the auspices of the Soviet government (the Council
of People's Commissars – SNK), headed by Georgii Grigor'evich
Karpov.[7] In December 1965 the two councils were combined in
a single Council for Religious Affairs (CRA), headed by Vladimir
Alekseevich Kuroedov, who had succeeded Karpov in 1960.[8]

Established under the auspices of the government, CARC's
principal task was defined as 'implementing the link between the
Government of the USSR and the leaders of religious associations
of the Gregorian Armenian, Old Believer, [Roman] Catholic,
Greek Catholic and Lutheran churches and of the Muslim, Jewish,
Buddhist and sectarian faiths on questions of these faiths that require
resolution by the USSR Government'.[9] This was elaborated upon
in the CARC statute, which said that the Council was to give
these questions 'a preliminary review'; to elaborate drafts of laws
on questions relating to the above-mentioned religions and instructions regarding the application of laws, and submit these to
the government; to 'supervise the correct and timely implementation'
of laws and decrees regarding religion throughout the country;
to present SNK with its conclusions on questions put by these
religions; to inform the government promptly of the countrywide
situation of the religions in question and their position and activity
in the various localities; and to provide 'a general reckoning of
churches and prayer-houses and comprise statistical reports on the
basis of data supplied to CARC by local soviet organs'.[10]

CARC was headed by Ivan Vasil'evich Polianskii, until his
death in 1956, and had in its early days a total staff in its Moscow
office of forty-three, of whom thirteen were senior officials. It
was divided into departments, one of them, headed by a member
of CARC's collegium and with two inspectors, to deal with the

6. CARC was set up by Decree No. 572 of the USSR Council of People's
Commissars (SNK), 19 May 1944; GARF, f.6991, o.4, d.1, l.1.

7. See Pospelovskii, *Russkaia pravoslavnaia tserkov'*, ch.7.

8. For the CRA's organisational structure, see Luchterhandt, 'The Council for
Religious Affairs', pp.60-2. For the merger, see also below.

9. Decree No. 572 of the USSR Council of People's Commissars (SNK), 19
May 1944; GARF, f.6991, o.4, d.1, l.1.

10. USSR SNK Decree No.628, 29 May 1944, Appendix No.1; GARF, f.6991,
o.4, d.1, ll.4-5.

affairs of the Muslim, Jewish and Buddhist faiths.[11] In order to be effective CARC was to have representatives (*upolnomochennye*) at every union and autonomous republic SNK and at oblast' *ispolkoms*.[12] These *upolnomochennye* were appointed by the responsible organ in the republic or oblast', whose executive organs determined and paid their salaries. Inevitably the loyalty of the *upolnomochennyi* to CARC was often in question. He reported both to CARC and the republican or oblast' leadership, and often the information sent to the latter was a more truthful and candid version than the one transmitted to Moscow.[13] Another result of the subordination to the local government apparatus was that the *upolnomochennye* were frequently sent on assignments on its behalf, which prevented them for protracted periods from addressing themselves to their duties as CARC *upolnomochennye*.[14] Yet, although the connection with the leadership at the level of the republic and/or oblast' was designed to create a *modus operandi* which would entail its involvement in the implementation of religious policy, this intent frequently miscarried. As Polianskii told the Soviet

11. *Ibid.*, Appendix No.2, and I. V. Polianskii to L. P. Beriia, J. V. Stalin, V. M. Molotov and K. E. Voroshilov at the Council of Ministers, and A. A. Zhdanov, N. S. Khrushchev, A. A. Kuznetsov, N. S. Patolichev and G. M. Popov at the AUCP(b) Central Committee Secretariat, 27 Feb. 1947; GARF, f.6991, o.4, d.1, ll.6-7, and o.3, d.47, l.96. The Council had five full members (the chairman and vice-chairman, the senior secretary, and two department heads), one further department head, three instructors and four inspectors, each responsible for a different faith.

12. *Ibid.*, Appendix No. 1; GARF, f.6991, o.4, d.1, ll.4-5. The oblast' was the highest administrative unit after the union republic in the larger union republics. Each administrative unit – the oblast' or krai, the raion (each oblast' or, alternatively, union or autonomous republic or autonomous oblast' was divided into raiony, as were the larger cities) and each city or town – had its own executive committee, *ispolkom*; for the benefit of simplicity and accuracy, I shall use the Russian terminology both for the administrative units and their governing organs. In practice CARC did not, for a variety of reasons, always have *upolnomochennye* in every oblast'; see p.624.

13. Author's interview with a former CRA official who has asked to remain anonymous. According to this official, the CRA, and presumably also CARC, sought to procure other sources of information in order to verify the authenticity of what it heard from the *upolnomochennye*, and had to be careful not to reveal these sources. For the issues on which the *upolnomochennye* reported, see Note on Methodology.

14. In the cotton-growing areas of Central Asia, for example, these assignments would often be connected with work in the cotton-fields and cotton-harvesting.

leadership early in 1947, local officialdom knew neither the situation regarding religion in their territories nor the laws on religion; indeed, they were not interested in religion and left everything to the *upolnomochennye*.[15]

CARC explained that its formation and that of CAROC did not represent any fundamental change in regime policy toward religion. In fact, in many respects they were the heirs of the Standing Commission on Questions of Religion at VTsIK, created in 1929 and dissolved in 1938. Like it, they reflected what have been described as 'the basic dilemmas' of the Stalinist, indeed of the Soviet, system. These included dealing with local officialdom, that 'eternal problem' in Russian history, and finding a *modus operandi* between the fulfilment of ideological goals, that sought the achievement of communism, and the demands of political reality. Like the Commission, too, the two councils, despite their seemingly 'prestigious mandate', did not make the real decisions. The official representatives of the regime, supposed to preserve the goodwill of the believer community and hear its demands and complaints, the Commission – and the Councils – became paradoxically guardians of the religious organisations. It was their interest 'to restrict the most obvious and brutal violations of Soviet law' directed against religion, not out of any 'benign feelings' but as a result of the desire to facilitate the operation of government.[16]

The leadership of the two councils claimed they had been set up because the leaders of the various religious organisations had changed tack, recognising the Soviet regime, which itself could neither remain indifferent to this turnabout nor ignore the fact that a rather considerable portion of the 'toiling masses' were still believers, and belief in God dictated the performance of religious rites and therefore the existence of prayer-houses and clergy. Thus, it was the new, 'patriotic' position of the religious leaders, which had begun to emerge before the outbreak of the war and was highlighted in the war years, that engendered a demand to create

15. I. V. Polianskii to L. P. Beriia *et al.*, 27 Feb. 1947; GARF, f.6991, o.3, d.47, ll.100-2.

16. Luukkanen, *The Religious Policy of the Stalinist State*, pp. 180-7. Prior to the establishment of the Standing Commission a number of organizations had existed to deal with religious affairs and implement regime policy on religion. They were attached first to the People's Commissariat of Justice and subsequently to VTsIK and the RCP(b) Central Committee – Corley, *Religion in the Soviet Union*, pp.50-1.

a special organ to implement the link between them and the state leadership, to normalise church-state relations and regulate the activity of the various faiths and its dimensions. The regime had to address 'methods and forms of religious propaganda,' the religious education of children, and 'questions connected with the church's influence upon the socio-economic activity of the workers'. Considerations of state policy and expediency had been behind all resolutions and laws on religion issued prior to the formation of CARC and continued to guide CARC's own directives and instructions.[17] Whatever the underlying assumption, it was now clearly not government policy to actively seek the elimination of religion and religious activity. As Polianskii repeated several times at sessions of his staff, conveying the words of his superiors: 'We are not firemen and it is not our task to put out the religious fire.'[18]

Nonetheless, regime policy regarding religion was often opaque. CARC itself complained to the Soviet leadership that the legislation on religion did not correspond to contemporary conditions. Its chairman noted shortly often the war that many people held the view that the government's more relaxed, pragmatic attitude to religion was solely temporary, the outcome of the situation that had arisen during the war. Some thought the time had come to renew pressure, others that the church must be used in the service of the state, as in capitalist countries. Polianskii himself suggested a review of existing legislation – a demand that was to be reiterated periodically in the ensuing years and decades – in order to regulate the most basic religious activity and clarify apparent contradictions.[19] It is not clear whether the Soviet leadership actually intended engendering a state of general obfuscation, or whether the situation reflected genuine indecision or simply a failure to take the necessary decisions.[20]

Over a decade later CARC's second chairman, Aleksei Aleksandrovich Puzin, said that the state's functions in regard to the

17. Report, Conference of CARC *upolnomochennye*, Rostov-on-Don, 14 June 1946, and Minutes, CARC Session No.13, 10 July 1947; GARF, f.6991, o.3, d.38, ll.9-11 and 17-8, and o.4, d.19, l.442.

18. L. A. Prikhod'ko, Notes, 20 Nov. 1958; GARF, f.6991, o.3, d.164, l.86.

19. I. V. Polianskii to L. P. Beriia *et al.*, 27 Feb. 1947; GARF, f.6991, o.3, d.47, ll.100-1.

20. A study on the prewar period also noted that 'the whole picture of Soviet religious policy seems to have been more confused then coordinated' – Luukkanen, *The Religious Policy of the Soviet State*, p. 22.

religious associations consisted primarily of ensuring the freedom of religious worship and the resolution of practical questions which arose 'in connection with the creation of normal conditions for the satisfaction of believers' religious needs'. As these problems could not be solved independently by the religious organisations, but required some sort of involvement on the part of the state, the government had set up the two councils, CAROC and CARC.[21] Apologetics notwithstanding, their creation impressed the faithful of all religions, and even other sectors of society, that a change had occurred in the attitude of the regime to religion. One CARC representative said in the late 1950s that formerly people had been sent to Siberia for religious convictions; since CARC came into being a series of measures had been taken to actually protect religious dogma.[22]

CARC reported the state of the various faiths under its juris-diction to the government and the CPSU Central Committee apparatus. It also received instructions from both these bodies, usually it seems by word of mouth, often even by telephone.[23] The CARC leadership transmitted these directives to its own medium and lower level apparatus in Moscow and to its *upol-nomochennye* in the field. Officially attached to the government, in the earlier years at least its leaders met frequently, if not regularly, with senior government officials. It appears from the documentation that for the most part the initiative for broaching issues laid with CARC which, having received information concerning trends and events within the various faiths then approached the relevant party or government organ in order to learn how to deal with them.

In the course of time, the link with the Council of Ministers diminished and the CPSU Central Committee became to all intents and purposes the sole leadership organisation with which CARC, and later the CRA, maintained regular contact, although the formal designation – attached to the Council of Ministers – remained.[24] Within the Central Committee the Council related first and

21. A. A. Puzin, Information, sent to Novikov at the USSR Supreme Soviet, 29 July 1957; GARF, f.6991, o.3, d.146, l.126. Puzin chaired CARC from 1957 until the creation of the CRA in December 1965.

22. Minutes, CARC session No.4, 25-26 Feb. 1959; GARF, f.6991, o.3, d.183, l.118.

23. See Chapter 10, n. 6.

24. Interview with T. S. Saidbaev, 8 Feb. 1998. Saidbaer was deputy head of the CRA Department for Islam and Buddhism from February 1966 until 1970.

foremost, but not solely, to its Department of Propaganda.[25] It also referred periodically to the Department of Administrative Organs and occasionally to other branches of the party machinery. It is important, however, to note that religion was not a major issue in the Propaganda Department. For a great part of the postwar years – certainly from the late 1960s until the end of our period – it seems to have had just one official to deal with religion altogether, although at one stage there were two, one responsible for the RSFSR, the other for the national republics.

In addition to the Central Committee ideologists, there were bodies within the government apparatus, besides CARC and the CRA, which had a direct and permanent connection with religion and with which the councils had a more or less permanent relationship. These included the security organs, especially the KGB, or at the beginning of our period the NKVD, which were involved in various aspects of religious policy implementation – and at certain periods perhaps even of decision making. Some of the reports of these organs reached CARC, and they in turn received materials from the Council.[26] Although the Western student has no access to KGB archival material, there are indications of that organisation's intentions, operations and scope of activity which from the earliest Soviet period included ecclesiastisal affairs. Both Karpov and Polianskii were senior NKVD officers.[27]

25. Until 1948, when all Central Committee administrations became departments, the department was called the Administration of Propaganda and Agitation. It then became the Department of Propaganda and Agitation until 1966, when its name was changed to the Department of Propaganda. Popularly, however, it continued to be called Agitprop.

26. Thus in 1952 Minister of State Security S. D. Ignat'ev received CARC's report on the situation and activity of the various faiths in 1951 – RTsKhIDNI, f.17, o.132, d.497, l.48. The report was also sent to Central Committee Secretary M.A. Suslov and the Council of Ministers Presidium Bureau.

27. The NKVD like its forerunners – the Cheka and OGPU – had a special subsection that dealt with religion. The head of this subsection from 1922-39, Evgenii Tuchkov, was a member of CARC's predecessor, the Standing Commission on Religious Questions – Luukkanen, *The Religious Policy of the Stalinist State*, pp.35 and 68. Probably the most comprehensive scholarly work on the KGB – Knight, *The KGB: Police and Politics in the Soviet Union* – which provides considerable insight into that organisation's structure and functions makes no mention of its intervention in religious affairs in the late and post-Stalin period. According to one source, Polianskii had the rank of NKVD colonel – Bociurkiw, *The Ukrainian Greek Catholic Church and the Soviet State*, p. 69.

In the 1920s and 1930s the NKVD had had a major role in the administration of religious policy[28] and not a few of the personnel of CARC and CAROC, including Karpov himself, who was a major-general in the NKVD, came from that organisation.[29] While this may have helped establish contact between the new formations and the secret police, a certain measure of competition seems to have developed between them; undoubtedly·some of the assignments meted out in the earlier period to the security organs now fell within the jurisdiction of CARC.[30] At the same time, there were grey areas regarding which it was not clear who exercised responsiblity; whereas activity that was undisputably 'anti-Soviet' and 'underground' fell into the sphere of the secret police.[31]

The terms of reference of the security apparatus in the postwar period included exposing and punishing violations of the law by religious personnel, especially by non-conformist and sectarian groups;[32] gathering material on groups or individual citizens who occupied positions of responsibility yet persisted in religious activity; as well as checking up on people appointed to positions within the clerical hierarchy and on religious personnel selected to travel abroad or meet with foreign delegations that came to the Soviet Union.[33] In one instance the republic's KGB apparatus informed

28. See Corley, *Religion in the Soviet Union*, passim.

29. For Karpov, see Pospelovskii, *Russkaia pravoslavnaia tserkov' v XX veke*, p.188, and Corley, *Religion in the Soviet Union*, pp.203-4.

30. For instance, in 1923 the RSFSR OGPU had ratified the charter of TsDUM –I. V. Polianskii to K. E. Voroshilov, 13 Aug. 1948; GARF, f.6991, o.3, d.54, l.177.

31. CARC deputy chief Iu. V. Sadovskii, pointed out at a CARC session in 1948 that most believers were ordinary Soviet citizens preoccupied with constructing socialism. These had to be distinguished from the small group of anti-Soviet 'fanatics', whose activity was dealt with by the security organs – CARC session No.9, 10 June 1948; GARF, f.6991, o.4, d.22, l.139.

32. The Christian sects which had broken away from the official church in the sixteenth and seventeenth century had been regarded by the tsarist government as endangering not only conformism and solidarity within the church, but also the authority of the state, of which the Russian Orthodox Church was a main bulwark. Sectarianism in other faiths was categorised similarly from the point of view of its political implications. As the Soviet authorities began seeking a *modus vivendi* with the country's major religions, they continued to perceive the sects as a source of inherent disloyalty.

33. See, for example, the KGB investigation of religious practices among the intelligentsia – Corley, *Religion in the Soviet Union*, pp.210-11.

a CARC official visiting in the republican capital that it had no confidence in the Council's *upolnomochennyi* and was dissatisfied with his work.[34] The secret police not only had constant contact with CARC and the CRA; it penetrated religious organisations and had connections with a number of clergy. Throughout the Soviet period it had a special section 'whose job was to monitor and control religious groups'. As of the late 1960s it was the 4th Department of the 5th Directorate.[35]

CARC and, as of 1966, CRA prepared annual reports for the party and government apparatus on the situation of the various faiths. These incorporated, among other data, the number of prayer-houses and clergy, official and unofficial – the figures for the un-official ones were at best approximate; information concerning all aspects of the implementation of the legislation on religion (CARC and the CRA had a legal department with professional experts); and details of the clergy's preaching activity. Those who prepared these reports thought – in the words of one of them, 'perhaps naively' that they reached the top level of the leadership, who would draw practical conclusions from them, realising that the situation required policy changes.

There is evidence that CARC and the CRA did not always see eye to eye with the Central Committee Department of Propaganda. In the words of one senior CRA official, the ideologists had to safeguard their own 'canons' and convictions, while the CRA's task was to ensure implementation of the legislation on religion. Consequently, its positions not infrequently contradicted those of the department, and this resulted in violent discussions and other unpleasantnesses. For example, the Constitution spoke of freedom of conscience and the law stipulated that every group of twenty believers might form a religious association; yet – char-acteristically for Soviet enactments recognising civil rights – the very same law imposed obstacles which were extremely hard to overcome. This meant that the process of implementation abounded with difficulties which the party apparatus tended on the whole not to appreciate and refused to understand.[36]

34. L. A. Prikhod'ko to I. V. Polianskii, 5 May 1956; GARF, f.6991, o.3, d.217, l.56.

35. Corley, *Religion in the Soviet Union*, pp.360-1.

36. Author's interview with a former CRA official who has asked to remain anonymous. For differences of opinion between CARC and Agitprop see p.33.

The very establishment of CARC was an indication that the regime was addressing itself to the country's religions from a more constructive point of view than had characterised its attitude in the 1920s and 1930s. Toward the end of 1944 came an even more auspicious decree, 'On the Procedure for Opening the Prayer-Houses of Religious Cults', its very title promising a new era in religious life. This decree laid down that every application to open a prayer-house had to be signed by twenty local adult citizens who had not been deprived of the franchise – the *dvadtsatka* – and addressed to the local governing authority.[37] The application would be looked into, checked and verified by the relevant CARC *upol-nomochennyi* to whom it would be sent by that authority with any supplementary information that might be deemed necessary.

In instances when the local authorities considered it 'expedient and possible' to comply, all the material relating to the application would be sent to CARC. That body would address itself in its decision to the following information: did the signatories of the application answer all requirements and were they indeed representatives of a larger group or did they perhaps comprise the entire group; what was the condition of the prayer-house which they were asking to open and what function was it currently fulfilling; when and by whose decision had it been closed; how many prayer-houses of the same faith existed in the raion or town and what was the distance from these prayer-houses to the settlement of the applicants? Insofar as CARC concurred with the local authority regarding the opening of the prayer-house in question, it was to present its decision to the All-Union government. Once the government had also given its approval, CARC would inform the local authority, who would then proceed to register the new religious society and legalise the transfer to it of the prayer-house. In the event of the rejection of the application by the local authorities, they were to elaborate their reasons and inform both CARC and the applicants.[38]

In addition to its minister or ministers of religion, appointed or confirmed by the relevant religious centre, and the *dvadtsatka,*

---

37. The 1929 VTsIK decree on religious associations stipulated that the *dvadtsatka* (lit. twenty) be considered the founders of the religious association. This body was responsible before the law for the upkeep of the actual prayer-house and for the maintenance of law and order within the association.

38. SNK Decree No. 1603, 19 Nov. 1944; GARF, f.6991, o.4, d.1, ll.10–12.

each religious society had by law to have an executive organ, and an auditing or inspection committee (*revkomissiia*), the former comprising three to five people[39] and the latter three. These two bodies were elected by a general meeting of the religious society, and their members seem mostly to have been chosen from the ranks of the *dvadtsatka*. If for one reason or another, usually as a result of death, the numbers of this lay *aktiv* were depleted, it was incumbent upon the religious society to supplement the remaining members with new ones.[40]

These lay officials were charged with conducting the financial and economic life of the religious society, as well as its general administration, fields of activity specifically not included in the jurisdiction of the clergy. CARC itself had no authority regarding the financial affairs of religious societies, at least in the initial period: in 1947 Polianskii made clear to his subordinates that the Council was categorically forbidden to become involved in their financial activity so as not to fall foul of them, as they and the religious centres would see in this direct interference in the affairs of the church. (The sole exception was if believers approached its officials with a complaint that the clergy embezzled money and a request that they be brought to justice.)[41]

Yet a further decree of early 1946, entitled 'Prayer-Houses of the Religious Cults', seemed to guarantee their existence and operation in face of possible trouble from local officialdom. It

39. As of November 1958, the executive organ's number was restricted to three –Conference of CARC's Central Asian *upolnomochennye*, Tashkent, 5 June 1959; GARF, f.6991, o.3, d.186, l.5.

40. Many religious societies did not do this automatically and sometimes, when an *upolnomochennyi* awoke to the fact that the quotas were not fulfilled, for example if he had to fill in forms regarding the lay personnel of registered mosques, several had to be elected at one stroke – for example, U. Mangushev, *upolnomochennyi* for Fergana Oblast', to Kh. N. Iskanderov, 30 Jan. 1954; GAU, f.2456, o.1, d.170, l.1. In 1959 CARC decided that the *dvadtsatka* had become a different institution from what had been originally contemplated. Intended to comprise a group of founding members, it had been transformed into a sort of enlarged religious *aktiv*, which took a constant part in the running of the religious society. As part of its policy to cut down the religious *aktiv* of all faiths on a countrywide level, CARC resolved to restore to the *dvadtsatka* its pristine role –A. Puzin to all CARC *upolnomochennye*, draft, undated, prepared for CARC session No.26s, 16 Oct. 1959; GARF, f.6991, o.3, d.185, ll.112-13.

41. I. V. Polianskii, Minutes, CARC session No.9, 3 June 1947; GARF, f.6991, o.4, d.19, l.279.

forebade the closing of prayer-houses that were being used by religious societies or the refurbishing of non-functioning prayer premises for other uses without permission from CARC. It laid down that the demolition of prayer-houses could take place upon the instruction of the republican SNK or the oblast' or krai *ispolkom* only in exceptional cases (such as danger of collapse); even then only after the issue of a technical deed – a statement of a technical commission that examined the state of public buildings – and with the confirmation of the CARC *upolnomochennyi.* The decree similarly established that the construction of new prayer-houses would be permitted 'in individual cases with the labour and means of believers'. It suggested to republican and oblast' authorities to take into account, when planning the distribution of building materials, their allocation for the repair of prayer-houses, not to obstruct the use of church bells, and to permit the muezzin to call Muslims to prayer from the roof or minaret of mosques.[42]

Even the decree 'On the Procedure for Imposing Taxes on Religious Clergy' seemed to be a step forward, for it implied or even entailed the legalisation of the clergy's activity. (Indeed, as we shall see, some financial organs refrained from taxing unregistered clerics on the pretext that by doing so they would be giving them legitimacy.) According to this document, clergy receiving income from the performance of religious rites, whether through the diocese or parish or directly from believers, either in money or in kind, and also from work in construction or agriculture, should be taxed as per Article 19 of the edict on income tax of the USSR Supreme Soviet of 30 April 1943; in rural areas they would thus be taxed like people in the agricultural sector who had additional unearned income. This was to apply, too, to persons who were not actually clergy but who received income from performance of religious rites, and to members of executive organs, insofar as they received remuneration for their duties, as well as to the religious societies' service personnel.[43] This did not necessarily mean that the relevant

42. SNK Decree No.232-101s, 28 Jan. 1946; GARF, f.6991, o.3, d.34, ll.1-2. Most minarets seem to have been destroyed in the 1920s and 1930s.

43. Decree of the USSR Council of Ministers (SNK had been renamed the Council of Ministers in March 1946) No. 2584, 3 Dec. 1946; GARF, f.6991, o.4, d.1, ll.24-26. For the instructions issued by Finance Minister A. Zverev to financial organs throughout the country in accordance with this decree, see A. Zverev to ministers of finance of union and autonomous republics, krai, oblast', okrug, uezd, municipal and raion financial departments, 13 Dec. 1946; GARF,

local financial organs operated in conjunction with the law, many aberrations being reported, or that all clergy reported their incomes correctly or at all.[44]

CARC's basic assignments, as well as the three pieces of legislation which followed CARC's formation, presupposed the existence of a religious establishment which maintained an institutionalised link with government organs at the centre and in the periphery. Its component parts were registered with the authorities; indeed, the approval of the latter was often a prerequisite for their formation and existence. Following from this connection, the establishment's actions and activities were under constant scrutiny and were expected to comply with certain norms and criteria.

The religious establishment essentially comprised two interconnected institutions: the religious centre and the individual house of worship.[45] Together they formed a sort of hierarchy, in which the latter was formally subordinate to the former. The religious centre whose function it was to control the life and activity of the religious communities,[46] was the organisation through which the government intended exercising its dominance over religion and religious activity. Throughout the 1940s and into the early 1950s, the CARC leadership was of the opinion that the higher the prestige of the religious centres and the better their organisation, the easier it would be for the Council to regulate the processes taking place within the various faiths. The greater the centre's authority over the parish, the prayer-house and the clergy, the better it would serve its purpose from the point of view of the central authorities in Moscow.[47] Given this basic assumption,

---

f.6991, o.4, d.1, ll.27-28.

44. See, for example, a letter, probably a circular, signed by USSR Deputy Finance Minister F. Uriupin, 17 June 1946; GAU, f.2456, o.1, d.83, l.6.

45. Not all faiths had such a centre: those that did were the Russian Orthodox Church, the Gregorian Armenian Church, the Evangelist Christian Baptists (ECB), the Lutherans, and the Muslims, who had four – see Chapter 3. The Roman Catholics and the Jews had no centre.

46. See, for example, I. V. Polianskii to V. M. Molotov, 7 Dec. 1945; GARF, f.6991, o.3, d.10, l.139.

47. I. V. Polianskii to G. F. Aleksandrov, 1 July 1947; RTsKhIDNI, f.17, o.125, d.506, l.113. Even within CARC, however, there were people who had doubts as to the expediency of the religious centres; in 1952, voices were heard suggesting a severe restriction of their rights and role – I. V. Polianskii to G. M. Malenkov, 29 Nov. 1952; GARF, f.6991, o.3, d.85, ll.241-3.

CARC condoned requests to enable the religious centres to publish religious materials, maintain seminaries for the preparation of religious cadres and establish contacts with kindred religious organisations abroad.[48] The relationship between the two parties – the religious centre and the individual religious association – was elaborated in the centre's charter, which in turn was finalised in accordance with directives from the government body empowered to supervise the religion in question, in the case of Islam, CARC (and as of December 1965, the CRA). The centre appointed the clergy of all registered mosques, or other prayer-houses, sent them periodic instructions and interpretations of religious dogma and received a considerable portion of their revenues.[49]

There do not seem to have been any further major pieces of legislation in the late Stalin period. Yet, the relatively constructive approach of 1944-6 underwent a manifest change in the following years. If the main activity of CARC in its first three or so years centred on opening prayer-houses and registering religious associations, this changed after a Central Committee decision or instruction in summer 1947 to slow down the process, which in fact brought it to a virtual halt by 1948. The final years of Stalin's rule saw a clear move to close down prayer houses and withdraw religious associations from registration (to use Soviet terminology), in other words, to deprive them of their documents of registration.

This change was reflected in CARC's letters of instruction to its *upolnomochennye*, of which at least nine were sent between January 1945 and December 1948. The first of these was devoted to the *upolnomochennyi's* assignments, beginning with the opening of prayer-houses. The letter dealt at length with stipulations regarding applications to this end. True, it spelled out, among others, grounds for the rejection of applications, specifically: if the signatories' names were used without their knowledge and consent; if the building intended for use for prayer purposes was unsuitable or did not meet the required technical, sanitary and anti-incendiary conditions; and if it were impossible to vacate the building in view of its use for other purposes although if it served as a storehouse this qualification did not apply.[50]

48. Draft, Instructions to CARC, undated [June 1948]; GARF, f.6991, o.3, d.53, ll.40-41.

49. For details, see pp. 105-8 and 125-30.

50. In rural areas in particular the great majority of former mosques in fact

Nor was it only this last qualification which indicated the generally positive approach. Thus, for example, it was stated that should the prayer-house under consideration not be appropriate or available, prayers could be conducted in houses belonging to private individuals or communally owned premises that might be rented for the purpose.

The *upolnomochennyi's* second task was to register religious societies, their executive organs and clergy. A religious society, it was stipulated, could only be registered after CARC had authorised the opening of the prayer-house in question. Requests of this nature had to be addressed to the local *ispolkom*, which would review them, check all the data included in them, verify the condition of the prayer-house, make sure it was not being used for other purposes or, if it was, that there would be no major problem in vacating it, and then make its decision. In the event of a positive decision, the local authority then had to transmit all the documentation to the *oblispolkom*, if the republic was divided into oblasti,[51] or the republican council of ministers. This level, again if it ratified the decision, passed all the material to the local *upolnomochennyi*, who also had to verify the content of the application and then reach his own conclusions which, if they were positive, he transmitted to CARC.[52]

The registration of prayer-houses was perceived in government documentation as beneficial to regime and believers alike. On the one hand, it served as a means of regulating religious life, including it in the orbit of official control. On the other hand, a prayer-house and religious society which had registered existed legally and, in theory, provided they complied with the exigencies of the legislation on religion, could not be molested, whereas those which were not registered were exposed *a priori* to every sort of harassment. In the words of CARC Chairman Puzin in the mid-1960s, registra-

---

served as storehouses.

51. See n.12 above. All the Muslim union republics except Azerbaijan, as well as the RSFSR, were so divided; the autonomous republics were not.

52. For the decree on which these instructions were based, see p.20 above. The All-Union government – to which CARC transmitted its decision – would issue a special instruction (*rasporiazhenie*) approving the opening of a group of prayer-houses, see, for example, eight such instructions issued in 1945 – GARF, f.6991, o.3, d.32, ll.5,9–10,14–15,19–20,25–6,34,42–4 and 50–1. A February 1955 decree (see pp.39–40 below) omitted the need to refer to the all-union level and the final decision was henceforth taken by the republican council of ministers.

tion implied that the authorities permitted the activity of the religious society and that the believers recognised and observed the laws of the state and acknowledged the control of their activity by the organs of state.[53]

At the same time, there were several stipulations in CARC's first letter of instruction which could hardly be encouraging to believers. The signatories of the application had to provide information regarding their citizenship, workplace, age and place of residence and state whether they had ever been convicted by a Soviet court. Once an agreement had been concluded for the transfer of a building to the religious association, it had to give the *upolnomochennyi* a list of the members of its executive organ and inspection commission. The association's cleric or minister had also to complete a questionnaire giving his full name, religious rank or office, year and place of birth, details of previous places of service or work and residence, and information regarding his occupation under the Germans if he had lived in occupied territory and any previous conviction. Neither he nor the religious association might begin functioning prior to receipt of a document of registration from the *upolnomochennyi*.[54]

This first letter of instruction went on to discuss other assignments of CARC and its *upolnomochennye*. These included taking stock of all prayer-houses, both functioning and non-functioning ones, the former category including those opened following a believers' application filed in accordance with the new procedures and prayer-houses which had operated previously but had also to be registered.[55] A further responsibility was the correct and timely implementation of laws and decrees on religion, namely the limitation of religious

53. Minutes, CARC session, 17 March 1965; also A. A. Puzin, 'Leninist principles regarding the attitude to religion, the church and believers', 5 Aug. 1965; GARF, f.6991, o.4, d.168, l.99 and o.3, d.1483, ll.94–5.

54. As laid down in the 1929 Law on Religious Associations.

55. It is evident from the documentation that there was some uncertainty regarding the date prior to which a prayer-house had to have operated in order to be registered as a *de facto* functioning one, which – provided it fulfilled all the stipulated requirements – did not need to go through the protracted process of filing an application and awaiting the permission of CARC in order to begin conducting prayer services. Certainly those which had operated at the time CARC was set up in May 1944 entered into this category. The non-functioning prayer-houses were those which had been shut down in the 1920s and 1930s and, for the most part, requisitioned for other purposes; see below.

instruction to authorised religious seminaries; the restriction of the activity of the religious society[56] and clergy to strictly religious purposes; confining the activity of the 'religious centre' to the territory given over to its leadership and of the religious society to the place of residence of its members and the location of its prayer-house. The conduct of prayer meetings within the prayer-house did not require special permission nor did the collection of donations in money or kind both inside the prayer-house and outside it, but the collection had to be from believers of the religious society in question and be intended for purposes connected with managing the prayer-house, hiring clergy or maintaining the executive organ or with the society's patriotic activity.[57] Under no circumstances might there be membership dues or any other form of obligatory fund-collecting. Religious rites or ceremonies might not be conducted in the open (apart from those that were an essential component of the prayer service) without written permission from the local *ispolkom*, but the society or clergy might perform individual rites – as distinct from communal prayer – in private homes.[58] The religious society was not a juridical person and could not own property or engage in productive, commercial or educational activity; it could not, for instance, set up a mutual assistance fund, an almshouse or shelter, or a funeral fund, or give assistance to individual members.[59]

The *upolnomochennyi* was also to review and submit to CARC all materials concerning the closure, construction or refurbishing of prayer-houses. Closing a prayer-house could take place if two-thirds of the society's founders (the twenty or more who had

56. The Russian text uses several words which would seem to denote one and the same thing. I have tried throughout to translate the particular term used in the original text, i.e. association, society, community or group.

57. During the war and in its immediate aftermath religious societies collected sums for various purposes connected directly with the war effort or with some of the pressing social and other problems created in the wake of the war; see below for a number of examples. One CARC circular said a religious society might collect money for official and social causes – Instructions of CARC to its *upolnomochennye*, 15 May 1946; GAU, f.2456, o.1, d.65, l.13.

58. *Ibid.*, l.14. The 1929 law stated explicitly – in the wake of the 1924 Constitution that the holding of prayer-services outside the building allotted to a religious association for that purpose required such permission.

59. The majority of the stipulations of the decrees of this period had been laid down in the 1929 Law of Religious Associations.

signed the original application to register) asked for their signatures to be taken off the document of registration and others were not found to undertake the implementation of the agreement by which the society had received its prayer-house, or if the religious society violated the existing legislation on religion or that same agreement.[60] Another document added that a further cause for withdrawing a religious society from registration, a measure that normally accompanied the closure of a prayer-house, was its disbandment. If a prayer-house which had not been closed by the authorities had not operated for one reason or another for more than one year, it was to be considered non-functioning and in that event the religious society would be withdrawn from registration, and considered as having disbanded.[61] A non-functioning prayer-house, like a functioning one or a religious society, could not be demolished without CARC's consent.

Finally, the *upolnomochennyi* was charged with receiving representatives of religious societies and clergy who had questions requiring government resolution or which might be solved on the spot;[62] receiving and reviewing complaints relating to religion, which he would pass on to the relevant administrative authority with his recommendations; travelling to 'the localities' to give instructions to, and check the work of, *raiispolkoms* and municipal soviets in the sphere of religion, inspect prayer-houses and verify statements and complaints.[63]

60. There were other eventualities in which a prayer-house could be shut down, which related to the time of the German occupation. These were basically irrelevant to the study of Islam, only a very few areas (in the Northern Caucasus) which had a Muslim population having fallen under the Germans during the war. The great plethora of religious institutions set up by the Germans as part of their endeavour to win over the population was, from the viewpoint of the Soviet authorities, one of the difficult legacies of the occupation.

61. CARC instructions to its *upolnomochennye*, 15 May 1946; GAU, f.2456, o.1, d.65, l.4.

62. These concepts, government resolution and solution on the spot, as far as I can find, were nowhere explained.

63. I. V. Polianskii, Instructions for CARC *upolnomochennye*, ratified by CARC, 17 Jan. 1945; GARF, f.6991, o.4, d.2, ll.9–28. The letter included six appendices: a form of registration of a religious society; a model agreement for use of a prayer-house; a form of registration of the executive organ and inspection commission, and of clergy; and forms providing specific information concerning functioning and non-functioning prayer-houses and clergy in the area under the *upolnomochennyi's* jurisdiction – *ibid.*, ll.29–36. It was apparently not the first such

The letter which accompanied the letter of instruction suggested that the *upolnomochennye* proceed forthwith to the registration of functioning prayer-houses together with the clergy and executive organs of the religious societies so as to place their activity in an organised framework.[64] The issue of registration, however, was a thorny one and full of pitfalls, as became clear upon receipt of the *upolnomochennye's* first quarterly reports in April 1945. This led to the CARC chairman clarifying a number of points. He reprimanded both those *upolnomochennye* who simply noted the existence of functioning religious organisations and waited passively for believers to take the initiative regarding registration and those who saw their task as unmasking religious societies and taking measures to legalise religious activity. They were in fact to be active in registering religious societies which met requirements, that is, had a prayer-house, a cleric and an executive organ, and to disband those that did not. If a community did not want to register for one reason or another, its leaders should be told none-theless to submit a written statement saying they wished to register, and if this was not forthcoming within the stipulated period, its activity was to be terminated. So, too, was that of all unregistered groups which local officials allowed to hold occasional prayer ser-vices, the law specifying that no religious association might proceed to operate without registering with 'the organs of state power'. (Beyond this there was no clear stipulation regarding the legal status of unregistered communities. Some officials perceived these as functioning illegally by definition, even as a sort of religious underground, while others did not concur with this interpretation. This was not, for instance, the opinion of CARC's legal advisor in the mid-1940s, who insisted that a religious society was illegal only if it violated a specific law. 'If it exists and operates while being unregistered,' he maintained, 'this does not mean that it exists illegally.'[65] The CARC leadership, too, stated specifically

circular, for some republican *upolnomochennye* were sending similar letters to the oblast' *upolnomochennye* under their jurisdiction several months before – see I. Ibadov to oblast' *upolnomochennye*, 6 Oct. 1944; GARF, f.6991, o.3, d.4, ll.71-5 – and they presumably based their instructions on materials from the centre. But this seems to be the first comprehensive document embracing the sum total of the *upolnomochennyi's* duties.

64. I. V. Polianskii to *upolnomochennye*, 14 Feb. 1945; GARF, f.6991, o.3, d.11, l.1.
65. Iu. Sadovskii and N. Peshekhonov to I. Ibadov, 20 Feb. 1946; GAU, f.2456, o.1, d.90, l.10.

in a closed forum of its own staff that it was incorrect to identify 'religious underground' with unregistered religious associations.)[66]

Somewhat later (1948) CARC Chairman Polianskii specified the main reasons for religious societies not in fact registering. These were, on the one hand, the opposition of local organs of government and, on the other, reluctance on the part of their own leaderships, who hoped in this way to evade both the control of the religious centres and the imposition of income tax. While still claiming to seek the registration of certain societies, he admitted – in line with the more stringent atmosphere of 1948 – that every newly registered community became a hub of religious activity which bolstered the religious atmosphere much more extensively, and had many more adherents, than could any religious association operating at its own risk and in a state of fear.[67]

As to the registration of clergy, it was not the affair of the *upolnomochennyi* whether a cleric had or did not have a satisfactory religious training. This was the affair of the religious organisation and of the religious centre which appointed him.[68] The *upolnomochennyi* could and must reject clergy who were unsuitable from a political standpoint only or who were not attached to a specific community, so-called 'itinerant preachers'.[69] The registra-

66. I. V. Polianskii, Address, Conference of CARC *upolnomochennye*, 11-13 June 1946; GARF, f.6991, o.3, d.39, ll.81-3. In 1959 when one *upolnomochennyi* suggested that the obfuscation should be overcome by a specific article in the criminal code saying that unregistered clergy engaging in religious activity should be punished by law, CARC Chairman Puzin expressed a contrary opinion. Such a law, he maintained, would necessitate a concomitant one, stipulating the bringing to book of those Soviet organs which did not register these itinerant clergy and unlawfully functioning mosques unless they violated Soviet law, there being no other lawful pretext for refusing to register them – Conference of CARC's Central Asian *upolnomochennye*, 5-6 June 1959, and A. A. Puzin, 'Leninist principles regarding the attitude to religion, the church and believers', 5 Aug. 1965; GARF, f.6991, o.3, d.186, ll.200-1, and d.1483, l.95. In the latter document Puzin admitted, however, that being beyond the control of the organs of power, unregistered associations were prone to violate Soviet law and were often able to do so without being punished.

67. I. V. Polianskii to the Council of Ministers Cultural Bureau, K. E. Voroshilov, M. A. Turkin, M. A. Suslov and A. A. Kuznetsov, 10 June 1948; GARF, f.6991, o.3, d.53, ll.20-1.

68. In faiths which had no religious centre, the community elected its own cleric.

69. Letter of Instruction No.1, 29 May 1945; GARF, f.6991, o.3, d.11, ll.19-23. As we have seen, there had been a previous letter of instruction which was not

tion of clergy and communities was the burning question in the next letter of instruction as well, in which Polianskii took the *upolnomochennye* to task for not speeding up the process. From all sides CARC was being informed that religious activity was mounting. This trend was reflected not only in increasing numbers of applications to open and register prayer-houses, but particularly in the activity of a large number of functioning unregistered formations discovered in the process of the *upolnomochennyi's* practical work, which showed no particular interest in registering and often even refused to do so. This was unacceptable; by the end of the second quarter of 1945, of 6,922 religious societies (belonging to all the religions under CARC's auspices) which had been exposed and taken stock of, only 17 per cent were registered.[70]

Another concern was the fate of non-functioning prayer-houses and particularly those which had remained empty and were not in use as 'cultural-educational' institutions, economic enterprises or residential homes. The usual rule was that the refurbishing of non-functioning prayer-houses required CARC's consent. But empty prayer-houses could be handed over by republican governments or oblast' and krai *ispolkoms* with the preliminary consent of the local *upolnomochennyi* for temporary use by state or public institutions or enterprises – without the right of interior or exterior refurbishing – if they gave a commitment to vacate the buildings within a month of a demand to do so.[71] (The 1918 law separating church and state had decreed all prayer-houses public property.)[72]

Perhaps a first indication of the change of direction that characterised Stalin's last years was a circular signed by CARC Deputy Chairman Iurii Sadovskii. True, even earlier documents had entailed a mixed bag, but the primary message was that the powers-that-be were acknowledging the 'religious movement', as they called it, and were seeking to respond to it, not by indiscriminate repression but by control and regulation. This was to be accomplished through formalising the existence of religious societies which fulfilled certain conditions and permitting the opening of a number of additional

---

numbered; the following letters of instruction until Dec. 1948 are thus Nos.2-8.

70. Letter of Instruction No.2, 6 Oct. 1945, GARF, f.6991, o.3, d.23, ll.72-3.

71. CARC instructions to its *upolnomochennye*, 15 May 1946; GAU, f.2456, o.1, d.65, l.18.

72. SNK Decree of 21 Jan. 1918, Art.13 – Pospielovsky, *A History of Marxist-Leninist Atheism and Soviet Anti-Religious Policies*, Appendix, pp.133-4.

prayer-houses. In August 1946 Sadovskii announced that the former assignment, the registration of functioning religious societies was on the whole completed, in other words, communities that had not yet taken advantage of the regime's readiness to register such of them as had been operating prior to 1944 could no longer do so, although Sadovskii went on to say that the opening of new prayer-houses would continue as per established procedure.[73]

As early as 1946-7 differences of opinion were beginning to surface regarding the policy which should be followed *vis-à-vis* the 'religious movement'. CARC, or at least its chairman, clearly believed that a fair number of religious societies should be registered in order to enable some sort of control of religion. In a letter to Deputy Chairman of the Council of Ministers Viacheslav Molotov in mid-1947 he seemed to negate the distinction between the registration of functioning prayer-houses and religious societies and the opening of new ones. The latter process, too, he pointed out, in fact simply denoted the legalisation of the most dynamic remnants of former religious organisations which had never ceased existing but had carried on their activity clandestinely and so had not been subject to control or supervision. In Polianskii's view, it was expedient from purely state considerations to register a certain number of communities so as to make such control possible.[74]

Polianskii laid down his position even more poignantly in a letter to the head of the Central Committee's Propaganda Administration under whose jurisdiction religion fell and another to Central Committee Secretary Andrei Zhdanov. He differentiated between the Russian Orthodox Church, which was a home-grown institution, and the other religions which had mostly been imported from abroad. The former traditionally sided with the state, followed its lead, and depended very much on the state's attitude to it. Moreover, due to its more strictly hierarchical stucture, it was easier to control effectively. Among the latter there were faiths that were inherently antagonistic to the Soviet regime, namely some of the Christian sects; others which were generally disloyal (the majority of Roman Catholics and some Lutherans); and a third group, which were not only fundamentally loyal but saw

73. Iu. Sadovskii, Circular to all *upolnomochennye*, 8 Aug. 1946; GARF, f.6991, o.3, d.35, l.29.
74. I. V. Polianskii to V. M. Molotov, 10 June 1947; GARF, f.6991, o.3, d.47, ll.196-8.

themselves as participants in 'socialist construction'. It was unquestionably preferable that these religions conduct themselves openly and in organised fashion and be susceptible to CARC's influence rather than being amorphous, secret and inaccessible to control. During the three years of its existence CARC had striven to attain one basic aim: the channelling of religious activity into an organised framework, subjecting it to the requisite supervision and regulation necessary for observance of the legislation on religion and for political expediency. This had, on the whole, been achieved, the dimensions of 'the religious movement' established – the number of religious communities having attained a natural limit and its increase stunted – and the aspirations of the clergy and religious societies to extend their influence over the believers' social existence curtailed.[75]

In a letter sent earlier in 1947 to the country's leaders, Polianskii had described the 'political' role enjoyed by religious associations, which had been enhanced by the war, as anachronistic and contradictory to the very structure of the socialist state. CARC perceived the elimination of any political slant or direction from the activity of the religious associations and its restriction to the actual performance of religion as one of its central assignments. Since, however, this could only be achieved over time, this orientation should in the meanwhile be used in the interests of the Soviet Union both in the domestic context and in foreign policy. CARC had accordingly influenced the activity of the religious associations and the clergy, bringing it into line with the stringencies of Soviet policy and the country's economy, eliminating religion's most harmful manifestations and conducting a struggle against anti-social moods and the more reactionary clergy.[76]

The propaganda and agitation administration apparatus was of a different opinion from that voiced by Polianskii. Its deputy chief, Dmitrii Shepilov, wrote to Central Committee Secretary Mikhail Suslov that Polianskii had given a 'totally incorrect, distorted description of the religious movement', which he had described

75. I. V. Polianskii to G. F. Aleksandrov, 1 July 1947, and to A. A. Zhdanov, 7 July 1947; RTsKhIDNI, f.17, o.125, d.506, ll.110-33 and 144-63.
76. I. V. Polianskii to L. P. Beriia, Stalin, V. M. Molotov and K. E. Voroshilov at the Council of Ministers and to A. A. Zhdanov, N. S. Khrushchev, A. A. Kuznetsov, N. S. Patolichev and G. M. Popov at the AUCP(b) Central Committee Secretariat, 27 Feb. 1947; GARF, f.6991, o.3, d.47, ll.75 and 96.

as having been markedly curtailed, whereas in fact it had grown. Shepilov took exception to Polianskii's stand on the Russian Orthodox Church, the general loyalty of the religious establishment and the consequent political insignificance of 'the religious movement'. This appraisal of the role of religion and the religious organisations merely helped the growth of religious activity; CARC was joining hands with ministers of religion and indulging fanatics.[77] Shepilov wrote in similar vein to Zhdanov.[78]

It seems that in June or July 1947 CARC received instructions confining any future opening of prayer-houses to just four of the religions under its auspices (Old Believers, Muslims, Gregorian Armenians and Buddhists). Regarding the others, prayer-houses might be opened only 'in special, exceptional cases'.[79] Yet, within the following months the restriction was evidently extended to all faiths, for to all intents and purposes the opening of prayer-houses ceased in 1948. Nonetheless, it appears that the government did not actually issue any instruction not to open any more prayer-houses. The procedure was that each individual application had to be rejected on the spot by the local *upolnomochennyi*. The following years actually saw a clear tendency to close prayer-houses and remove religious societies from registration. Altogether 1,237 registered prayer-houses of the various faiths were shut down between 1948 and 1954.[80] At the very end of the 1940s, however, one of CARC's republican *upolnomochennye* pointed out that regulating religious activity meant registering religious societies permitted by CARC to register and disbanding those which came into existence without authorisation; yet this did not imply even now

77. D. Shepilov to M. A. Suslov, undated; RTsKhIDNI, f.17, o.125, d.506, ll.134-5. Shepilov used derogatory words for the clergy and the religious which have no equivalent in English (*tserkovniki* and *religiozniki*).

78. [D. Shepilov] to A. A. Zhdanov, undated; RTsKhIDNI, f.17, o.125, d.506, ll.164-6.

79. Directives regarding the work of the Council for Religious Cults at the USSR Council of Ministers – RTsKhIDNI, f.17, o.125, d.506, l.183 – included as Appendix No.1 to a draft Council of Ministers' decree, apparently sent by Polianskii to Minster of Culture S. Kaftanov, G. F. Aleksandrov, and State Security Minister V. A. Abakumov, 26 July 1947; GARF, f.6991, o.3, d.47, ll.299-306.

80. Minutes, CARC session No.26, 1-2 Dec. 1949, and Information on the applications of believers of the religious cults to open prayer-houses (Appendix to G. G. Karpov and I. V. Polianskii to the USSR Council of Ministers, 5 Feb. 1955); GARF, f.6991, o.3, d.60, l.103, and d.113, l.116.

that *upolnomochennye* should refrain from recommending the registration of those religious societies which they thought required registration.[81]

Prayer-houses, Polianskii explained, were not to be closed *en masse*, as a 'campaign', but wherever this might be called for out of considerations of state or if local conditions might 'dictate' it. Before a decision to close a prayer-house was taken, all the pros and cons had to be carefully weighed. Nor was closure to be accompanied by 'administrative' action.[82] Just as in the period 1944-7 the most recurrent theme in the minutes of CARC sessions was the review of applications to open prayer-houses, so in the years 1949-53 it was the ratification of decisions of local government organs to close prayer-houses and withdraw religious societies from registration.[83] Only occasionally did CARC decline to concur with such a decision, usually, in this event, postponing discussion until fuller information might become available rather than categorically refusing to put its seal on the proposed closure.

In the late Stalin years CARC increased its efforts to direct the activities of the registered religious associations so as to minimise their dimensions and influence and ensure a maximum observance of all the relevant laws and decrees. It sought to supervise the religious centres unremittingly in order to forestall, mitigate and eliminate the more harmful manifestations of religion and oppose the activities of religious communities which had come into being and continued to exist illegally or were of a 'mystic' or 'fanatic' character.[84] It allowed, however, the formation and maintenance of international ties insofar as they were necessary from the point

81. H. A. Akhtiamov, Address, Conference of CARC's Central Asian *upolnomochennye*, 17-20 Dec. 1949; GARF, f.6991, o.3, d.67, ll.125-6.

82. Concluding remarks by I. V. Polianskii, Minutes, meeting of CARC inspectors, No.26, 1-2 Dec. 1949; GARF, f.6991, o.3, d.60, ll.103-4. Polianskii specified a number of reasons that might be given by the *upolnomochennyi* for rejecting an application to register, adding that this must be done in a way that made it clear to the believers that the application was being refused and that left no option other than concurring. 'Such reasons,' he was adamant, 'can always be found.' Polianskii then listed arguments which might serve as grounds for shutting down prayer-houses – *ibid.*, l.104. For administrative action, see n. 94.

83. See GARF, f.6991, o.4, dd.24,25,26,28,30, *passim*.

84. The terms 'fanatics' and 'fanaticism' were frequently used in Soviet jargon – as in that of the tsarist period – to describe religious activists or activism. Needless to say, these words were used in wholesale fashion and did not denote objective reality. ('Mystic' was a less relevant term in the context of this study.)

of view of propaganda regarding freedom of worship in the Soviet Union.[85] Altogether, CARC received recurrent instructions from the party Central Committee not to proceed forcefully in terminating religious activity, but rather to 'combine persuasion with compulsion', first applying the former and only when that failed, the latter.[86] It nonetheless sought with the help of the republican and oblast' organs of government to wage a sustained struggle against unregistered formations which conducted religious rites in an 'organised and systematic' fashion.[87]

Meanwhile, the Central Committee Department for Propaganda and Agitation (Agitprop) was concerned with the issue of atheistic propaganda. Continuing to hold the view it maintained in 1947 that religion was going from strength to strength, it sought to enhance and improve the propaganda effort. Atheistic propaganda had in fact disappeared completely from the scene in the war years, when the League of the Militant Godless was disbanded,[88] and, not unnaturally the department contended that the success of religion was due first and foremost to neglect of the propaganda front. In September 1944 the Central Committee had issued a first decree seeking to reanimate atheistic propaganda,[89] which apparently was not being adequately implemented. In 1947 Shepilov called for an improvement in propagating 'natural-scientific knowledge among the population', setting up in every town and raion 'an *aktiv* of propagandists comprising lecturers, teachers, agronomists and doctors', and preparing and publishing model lectures on natural-scientific questions.[90] In the same year, the

---

85. Memorandum, sent to G. M. Malenkov and K. E. Voroshilov, 23 April 1949; RTsKhIDNI, f.17, o.132, d.111, l.45 and GARF, f.6991, o.3, d.61, ll.36-8. Also minutes, CARC session No.13, 26 June 1951; GARF, f.6991, o.3, d.74, l.172.

86. Minutes, CARC instructional convention No.26, 1-2 Dec. 1949; GARF, f.6991, o.3, d.60, l.97.

87. I. V. Polianskii to K. E. Voroshilov, 4 Feb. 1950; RTsKhIDNI, f.17, o.132, d.285, ll.21-3.

88. Set up in 1925 as the League of the Godless (*Bezbozhniki*), it was closed down in 1941 and all atheist publications stopped as part of the effort to mobilise maximum support among the population for the war effort – Corley, *Religion in the Soviet Union*, pp.16 and 130.

89. 'The organisation of scientific-educational propaganda', 27 Sept. 1944 in *O religii i tserkvi*, pp.67-9.

90. [D. Shepilov] to A. A. Zhdanov, undated (approximately 10 July 1947), RTsKhIDNI, f.17, o.125, d.506, ll.165-6.

All-Union Society for the Dissemination of Political and Scientific Knowledge [91] was formed under the auspices of the Central Committee propaganda apparatus, which, among other assignments, was directly responsible for the implementation of atheistic propaganda.

In 1949 Agitprop prepared a draft Central Committee resolution 'On measures for enhancing the propagation of natural-scientific knowledge'. It stated that the Central Committee

considers that the revival of religious ideology is the result of many local party organisations having in recent times weakened, and in some cases having completely ceased, the propagation of natural-scientific knowledge and adopting a non-Bolshevik position of neutrality in regard to religious ideology, thus facilitating the activity of the ministers religion (*tserkovniki*).

The draft enumerated all the shortcomings of the various bodies which should have been mounting an effective propaganda campaign. It also censured those who believed that 'it is now possible not to conduct anti-religious propaganda and that religion will die of its own accord'. Finally, it suggested a series of measures designed to initiate a major anti-religious propaganda campaign.[92]

The post-Stalin period was indeed ushered in with two major resolutions of the CPSU Central Committee relating to atheistic propaganda, the first of July 1954 and the second of November of the same year. The former noted that this aspect of ideological work was being neglected and that the churches and sects had 'revitalised their activities, strengthened their cadres and, adapting flexibly to modern conditions, are ardently disseminating religious ideology among backward sectors of the population'. This had led in turn to 'an increase in the number of citizens observing religious holidays and performing religious rituals, and a revival of pilgrimages to so-called "holy places"'. The celebration of religious holidays, which was frequently accompanied by drunkenness and the 'mass killing of cattle', was causing 'major damage to the

91. Later known simply as Znanie (knowledge).

92. Draft of a resolution of the AUCP(b) Central Committee, unsigned and undated (sometime between 25 April and 1 June 1949); RTsKhIDNI, f.17, o.132, d.10, ll.19-24. A further letter from D. Popov and P. Liashenko (apparently Agitprop officials) to Suslov, 10 May 1950 (RTsKhIDNI, f.17, o.132, d.286, ll.3-4), called for steps to improve arrangements for the publication of anti-religious literature.

economy and drawing thousands of people away from work... Religious prejudices and superstitions are poisoning the consciousness of Soviet people and interfering with their conscious and active participation in the building of communism.'[93]

The campaign unleashed by this obviously stringent resolution that was intended to place constraints on all religious activity was called off by the second resolution – without any explanation. In notes compiled by CAROC Chairman Georgii Karpov and Polianskii and apparently sent to the Central Committee on a draft of the second resolution that they were shown early in October, these officials contended that the July resolution had been interpreted by the media as an indication to let loose a vicious attack upon clergy and church-goers in the tradition of the late Stalin years and by local government organs as a blanket to condone 'administrative' interference in the activity of the church[94] as well as 'a crude attitude to clergy and believers who perform religious rites'. Propaganda, they insisted, should be directed against religious ideology and not against the church or clergy as such and it should seek to instil 'correct, scientific notions' that would promote 'a well-balanced dialectic-materialist worldview'. The 'errors and distortions' engendered by the July resolution had led to the drawing of 'provocative' (presumably anti-Soviet) deductions among church figures in Eastern Europe and caused embarrassment to representatives of Soviet churches who were in constant contact with foreign delegations or went abroad on church or other public missions.[95] (The last contention was a sign of the times, the Iron Curtain having been markedly mitigated by the post-Stalin leadership, and the argument that this or that measure might have deleterious effects on foreign countries or populations was to be-

93. 'On major shortcomings in scientific–a theistic propaganda and measures for improving it,' 7 July 1954 in *O religii i tserkvi*, pp.69-75.

94. The Russian term *administrirovanie* (administrative action) had a clear connotation in the context of the discussion in the Stalin period regarding the legitimacy of measures taken by government organs without due reference to legal procedure. *Administrirovanie* was the opposite of the 'socialist legality' which served as the guiding slogan of the post-Stalin leadership.

95. G. G. Karpov and I. V. Polianskii, Notes and additions to the draft of the CPSU Central Committee resolution 'On mistakes in the conduct of scientific-atheistic propaganda among the population', 4 Oct. 1954; GARF, f.6991, o.3, d.312, ll.313-6.

come a common feature of the debate that went on in the Soviet Establishment regarding its policy on religion.)[96]

Unquestionably, the resolution of 10 November 1954 ushered in a period that was in many ways reminiscent of the years 1944-6. In a society in which the utterances and actions of the leadership were under constant and pedantic scrutiny, a Central Committee resolution that appeared to castigate the extremities of the anti-religious campaign unleashed in July, which talked of the need to refrain from violating believers' feelings and of impermissible instances of administrative interference in the affairs of religious societies, and pointed out that many believers were loyal citizens who participated actively in socialist construction,[97] could have only one interpretation: the shoe was now on the other foot. In a speech at a meeting of CARC *upolnomochennye* in Belorussia within days of the passing of the resolution, Polianskii was once more addressing the question of opening prayer-houses. It was obvious to him that the clergy and believers would interpret the resolution to mean that they could go farther than was intended, that they would come forth with 'requests and applications' especially in regard to the opening of prayer-houses, and he called upon the *upolnomochennye* to be tactful and firm, neither repelling these approaches nor being unduly permissive.[98] Indeed, Karpov and Polianskii addressed a letter to the USSR Council of Ministers stressing that the situation in which not a single prayer-house had been opened since 1948 represented an abnormality and was politically harmful.[99]

The next stage was in fact the decree of the USSR Council of Ministers of 17 February 1955, which introduced a number of procedural changes in the opening of prayer-houses. For example, approval of registration had henceforth to be given by the republican,

96. A certain lifting of the Iron Curtain and a beginning of increased contact with the outside world had begun before Stalin's death in the wake of the establishment of the World Peace Movement, in which Soviet religious leaders played a considerable role. These contacts acquired new dimensions and included much higher levels following Stalin's death.

97. 'On mistakes in the conduct of scientific-atheistic propaganda among the population' in *O religii i tserkvi*, pp.75-80.

98. Minutes, Session No.2s of BSSR *upolnomochennye*, 18-19 Nov. 1954; GARF, f.6991, o.3, d.101, ll.193-8.

99. G. G. Karpov and I. V. Polianskii to the USSR Council of Ministers, 5 Feb. 1955; GARF, f.6991, o.3, d.113, ll.110-11.

rather than the all-union, council of ministers, thus notably simplify-
ing bureaucratic procedures. Its most important facet was that
religious associations which for one reason or another had not
yet registered but which had a prayer-house on the above date
were given the right to register.[100] In the wake of this decree the
numbers of functioning prayer-houses began once again to mount
and closures became rather rare. As one CARC official pointed
out, CARC's personnel in Moscow and the periphery had come
to the conclusion that they should no longer close prayer-houses
and disband religious societies without taking into consideration
the political expediency of such measures.[101] According to the
November 1954 decree, it was stressed, administrative interference
even in the activity of unregistered groups and a crude attitude
to unregistered clergy contradicted CPSU policy, as did all ground-
less opposition to registering such groups.[102]

The discussion opened up by this rather precipitous turnabout
in religious policy and the testimony it offered regarding the significance the CPSU Central Committee attributed in these years
to religion and the means of conducting the struggle to overcome
it, bore out CARC's frequently reiterated contention that its work
was distinctly political. Polianskii himself dwelt on this theme
time and again, insisting that the official separation of church and
state was irrelevant to this evaluation.[103] So, too, did other members
of his apparatus both in the centre and in the periphery. One of
the latter pointed out to the Council's *upolnomochennye* in Uzbekistan
that if they did not acknowledge the political import of their role

100. Polianskii to *upolnomochennye*, 22 March 1955; GAU, f.2456, o.1, d.178,
ll.133-4. Polianskii made clear that a prayer-house was a building built as such
or rented for the purpose of conducting prayers and adapted accordingly, but
not residential premises provided by private individuals for the conduct of prayer
services by unregistered groups of believers, i.e. without a certified agreement
or contract. (Religious associations of faiths other than the Russian Orthodox
Church were not permitted to purchase buildings to serve as prayer-houses
–Polianskii to USSR Council of Ministers, 26 Aug. 1955; GARF, f.6991, o.3,
d.114, l.125. Polianskii described this discrimination as a violation of the 1918
decrees which had stipulated the equality of status of all religions.)

101. Address of L. A. Prikhod'ko, Minutes, CARC Instructional meeting No.12s,
26-28 July 1955; GARF, f.6991, o.3, d.110, l.196.

102. Minutes, CARC session No.7s, 21 March 1957; GARF, f.6991, o.3, d.145,
l.47.

103. For example, I. V. Polianskii to G. F. Aleksandrov, 1 July 1947; RTsKhIDNI,
f.17, o.125, d.506, l.118.

and feel responsibility for fulfilling the assignments given them, 'we shall be poor helpers of the party and government in taking appropriate steps on the ideological front'.[104]

Of all the years from the end of the war down to *perestroika*, the period 1955-8 probably saw a closer rapport between religious groups of the various faiths and the authorities than any other.[105] At the same time, even in this period there were sundry instances of local government organs repressing and persecuting religious societies.[106]

But this period was merely an interlude. Analysing the whys and wherefors of these chops and changes in the context of the wider political picture is a topic far removed from our theme.[107] However, the thrust of the ideology which underpinned Khrushchev's building of communism could clearly not tolerate any compromise with religion as one of the more 'reactionary' and 'backward' holdovers from capitalism. By 1957 statements were being made that the November 1954 resolution had been misunderstood and was 'mistakenly evaluated as a call to stop the systematic struggle with religious ideology'.[108] A year later CARC officials were explaining that the whole country was now striving to restore 'socialist legality'.[109] CARC and its *upolnomochennye* had the task of ensuring that the clergy and religious societies imple-

104. Minutes, Instructional meeting of CARC's *upolnomochennye* in the Uzbek SSR, 15-17 March 1956; GAU, f.2456, o.1, d.183, l.60.

105. The period abounds in documentation relating to the reception of religious personnel by government officials and of requests, applications and complaints lodged by the former with the latter. See, for example, G. F. Frolov to V. I. Gostev, 27 March 1956; GARF, f.6991, o.3, d.127, ll.32-7.

106. See, for example, Memo on the activisation of religious associations and groups, sent by A. A. Puzin to K. E. Chernenko, Central Committee Department of Propaganda and Agitation, 25 Nov, 1957; GARF, f.6991, o.3, d.148, ll.37-9.

107. Some attempts have been made to do this, notably in Anderson, *Religion, State and Politics*, Chapter 2. Anderson has shown that fathoming the considerations that lay behind the changes and, even more so, the personalities who sought to sway the balance one way or another, is no simple matter and will probably remain unresolved until the Presidential Archives in Moscow are opened.

108. This statement, made by M. B. Mitin, head of Znanie, is quoted in Anderson, *Religion, State and Politics*, p.11. Mitin noted that as a result the number of atheist lectures given by Znanie had decreased by one-third from 1954 to 1956.

109. For Soviet law reform in the post-Stalin period, which was based on the understanding that under Stalin there had been serious 'violations of socialist legality', see Berman, *Justice in the U.S.S.R.*, Chapter 2.

mented the laws on religion in timely and correct fashion. Indeed, ensuring the observance of these laws was now said to be the main assignment of CARC and its *upolnomochennye*.[110] In this context they had to distinguish between clergy, who were 'parasites' seeking to use religion for their own personal enrichment, and ordinary believers who, according to the Party's injunctions, were not to be offended in the course of the struggle against religion.[111]

During the following years a plethora of newspaper articles attacked religion,[112] and to curtail religious practice, anti-religious legislation was passed which was accompanied by a series of practical measures with the same end, notably the large-scale closure of prayer-houses. This last step affected particularly the Russian Orthodox Church, which lost over 40 per cent of its registered churches between 1 January 1958 and 1 January 1964, and Ukraine, where about 54 per cent of all the USSR's registered prayer-houses were to be found, but nearly all religions and most union republics were adversely affected by the closures.[113] Characteristically, in order to enhance the hold of government organs over religious societies and facilitate closures, a point was now made of emphasising the role of their executive organs, whose members could be dismissed by representatives of the secular power and otherwise influenced by it more easily than the clergy, who were appointed by the religious centres and were committed to implementing their policy.[114]

110. A. Puzin to all republican and oblast' *upolnomochennye*, 6 Aug. 1957; GARF, f.6991, o.3, d.145, 1.81.

111. L. A. Prikhod'ko, Address, All-Union conference of CARC *upolnomochennye*, 25-27 Nov. 1958; GARF, f.6991, o.3, d.165, ll.110-1. For anti-parasite legislation, see p.350.

112. Anderson quotes at length from a *Pravda* editorial of 21 Aug. 1959 (Anderson, *Religion, State and Politics*, pp. 19 and 32) and refers to a number of articles by L. F. Il'ichev, head of the Central Committee Department of Propaganda and Agitation, in *Kommunist* and *Nauka i religiia* (*ibid.*, pp. 17 and 20).

113. See *ibid.*, pp.55-9. According to one authoritative source, on average, 420 Orthodox churches were closed per year over the period 1950-64 – V. Garadzha, 'A Re-Interpretation', *Nauka i religiia*, 1 (1989), p.3. The large number of prayer-houses in Ukraine was a vestige of the German occupation, and the large number of Russian Orthodox churches there reflected the transfer to the Russian Orthodox Church of the Uniate churches when that confession was outlawed in 1946. And see Chapter 2, n.34.

114. H. Akhtiamov, Address, Conference of CARC *upolnomochennye*, 5-6 June 1959; GARF, f.6991, o.3, d.186, ll.53-4.

The party and government anti-religious decrees and resolutions from 1958 until Khrushchev's fall in 1964 were numerous and covered a broad spectrum of religious life. The year 1958 saw, a first batch of decrees, including a Central Committee resolution on 4 October on enhancing atheistic work among the population and another, on 28 November, 'On terminating pilgrimages to so-called "holy places"'.[115] The superstitions connected with these holy places were considered especially pernicious and obscurantist. CARC, its *upolnomochennye*, the organs of local government and broad circles of the public were to take all necessary measures to unmask the 'deceit' practised at shrines, to put a stop to the 'extortion of material benefit' from the spread of superstition and to pilgrimages, and to close down these sites. The religious centres and clergy were to be warned that the government would no longer tolerate all this 'hysteria and exploitation'. Propaganda and explanatory work were to be conducted among the population with an end to building up a body of public opinion to apply pressure for the closure of holy places. Administrative measures might also be applied, but only as a last resort. Altogether, this operation had to be conducted carefully and thoughtfully, always bearing in mind the conditions and atmosphere in the various localities.[116]

The Central Committee Department of Propaganda and Agitation took the opportunity to lash out at CAROC and CARC, accusing them of not fulfilling their functions satisfactorily, among others, of succumbing to the clergy and sustaining unfounded demands put forward by them. The councils' work in the subsequent period was directed at correcting their mistakes, in particular, at enhancing their control of the activity of the religious associations and clergy, so as to ensure that they in fact observed the laws on religion.[117] In January 1960 the Central Committee issued a further resolution, 'On measures for eliminating violations by the clergy of Soviet legislation on religion'. Among the violations it mentioned specifically were fomenting nationalist feelings, teaching religion

115. Neither of these was published, but both were mentioned recurrently in the subsequent period, as they constituted terms of reference for CARC's instructions and activity.

116. A. A. Puzin, Lecture, All-Union conference of CARC *upolnomochennye*, 25-27 Nov. 1958; GARF, f.6991, o.3, d.165, l.24ob.

117. A. A. Puzin, Address, All-Union conference of CARC *upolnomochennye*, 18-20 April 1960; GARF, f.6991, o.3, d.208, l.6.

to children, organising pilgrimages and initiating charitable activities.[118]

Nor were all constraints spelled out explicitly in official party or government resolutions. In January 1958 CARC instructed its *upolnomochennye* not to continue allowing the conduct of religious rites in private homes. Until then, on the basis of an instruction of the Standing Commission on Questions of Religion at the VTsIK Presidium, 'On the procedure for implementing legislation on religion', CARC had allowed the conduct of certain rites in believers' homes at their request. As of the above date the conduct by registered clergy of any rites or of 'religious propaganda' outside the prayer-house was strictly prohibited, the performance of certain rites being considered by the authorities as constituting a form of religious propaganda. By December 1960 CARC was proposing that this restriction be qualified so as to exclude rites performed at the request of the dying or seriously ill.[119]

This qualification was indeed included in the 1961 Instructions for the application of legislation on religion issued by CARC and CAROC conjointly. Despite its generally restrictive nature, this document stressed that all local government organs and the *upolnomochennye* of the two councils must ensure that citizens enjoy the freedom of conscience proclaimed by the Soviet constitution. Nor might they allow 'the adoption of administrative measures in the struggle against religion (the illegal closure of prayer-houses, etc.), administrative interference in the activity of religious associations or a crass attitude to the clergy, or any violation of believers' sensitivities'. Yet a prayer-house could be closed if the religious association using it were 'withdrawn from registration' –which, in turn, was possible if that association violated the laws on religion – or if it had to be demolished in connection with local reconstruction work or owing to it being in dilapidated condition.[120] At the time of Khrushchev's anti-religious campaign the interpretation of 'violations of legislation' was undoubtedly very broad. In any case, local government organs were empowered to deprive a registered religious sociey of its prayer-house and

118. Anderson, *Religion, State and Politics*, p.33.

119. V. Riazanov, CARC deputy chairman, to L. F. Il'ichev, 15 Dec. 1960; GARF, f.6991, o.3, d.210, ll.65-6.

120. GARF, f.6991, o.4, d.120, ll.1-9; this document is reproduced in Kuroedov and Pankratova (eds.), *Zakonodatel'stvo o religioznykh kul'takh*, pp.77-87.

use it for other ends, deciding in accordance with the specific conditions pertaining in their area whether or not to provide alternative premises.[121]

In March 1961 the government issued a decree, 'On enhancing control of the implementation of the legislation on religion', which opened with the statement that of late local government organs had loosened their control over the implementation of legislation on religion, thereby facilitating its violation by the clergy. It obliged them 'to take the necessary measures to eliminate violations of this legislation by the clergy and religious associations'.[122] The key role of local government in implementing the anti-religious decrees of these years was highlighted in a letter sent by Puzin to the CPSU Central Committee demanding that it take measures to enhance the responsibility of local organs and officials in making the decrees effective.[123]

These local government bodies were to be helped in this task by 'commissions of assistance', composed of party and state workers, educational personnel, pensioners and others who would be attached to the *raiispolkom* and chaired by its deputy chairman. They were to monitor the activities of the religious associations and do all in their power to weaken these activities. These commissions were typical of the 'social organisations' used in the Khrushchev period to mobilise society to aid in policy implementation and to show the popularity of the regime's policy and the identification of the masses with it.[124] The commissions of assistance continued to be active well into the Brezhnev era and are referred to recurrently in this period in connection with decrees on tightening control over the implementation of religious legislation.[125]

121. N. I. Smirnov, Reception of Kh. Sh. Siuniakov, 6 July 1961; GARF, f.6991, o.4, d.121, l.14.

122. GARF, f.6991, o.4, d.1, ll.45–6.

123. A. A. Puzin to the CPSU Central Committee, 22 Dec. 1962; GARF, f.6991, o.3, d.1390, ll.108–11.

124. The origins of these commissions go back to the 1920s when, too, the regime was seeking to mobilise society to participate in its major campaigns, to which category the onslaught on religion clearly belonged. They had then fallen into disuse, and returned in the early 1960s. For the legislation in the 1960s concerning the commissions of assistance, see *Zakonodatel'stvo o religioznkyh kul'takh*, pp. 88–94.

125. For example, in the wake of the 24 July 1968 decree, see below; GARF, f.6991, o.6, d.217, ll.134–6.

The changes in existing legislation stipulated by these various decrees and resolutions, which reflected the *de facto* state of affairs, were officially ensconced in the law by a December 1962 decree of the presidium of the RSFSR Supreme Soviet introducing the relevant changes in the 1929 Law on Religious Associations.[126] It is not easy to gauge how effective these various measures were and almost certainly their impact varied according to the general atmosphere in any given period and in the different localities. Some *upolnomchennye* sought to give the impression that in fact these edicts restricted the activity of the registered religious societies and effectively regulated procedures connected with the management of their administrative affairs.[127]

One component of the general repression of religion in these years was the reference to the judicial system of transgressors against legislation on religion. The criminal codes of the RSFSR and other republics, which were revised under Khrushchev,[128] contained articles specifying punishment for those who practised 'deceit with an aim to evoking superstition among the masses in order to elicit material profit' for themselves from such actions.[129] They also included articles giving blanket authority to the procuracy to initiate proceedings against almost all religious activity apart from the actual conduct of worship in registered prayer-houses.[130] At the

126. GARF, f.6991, o.4, d.119, ll.3-10.

127. For example, M. Miragzamov, *upolnomochennyi* for Uzbekistan, to M. Kh. Khalmuhamedov, 22 Oct. 1966; GARF, f.6991, o.6, d.11, ll.63-5.

128. For the legal reforms of this period, see Berman, *Soviet Criminal Law and Procedure*. In December 1958, the USSR Supreme Soviet enacted Fundamental Principles of Court Organisation, of Criminal Legislation, and of Criminal Procedure, on the basis of which in 1960 the RSFSR and the other union republics enacted a new Criminal Code, a new Code of Criminal Procedure and a new Law on Court Organisation. In subsequent years new crimes were added and, perhaps more pertinently to the discussion of religion, changes in what constituted a crime under a pre-existing article resulted in a substantial expansion of its scope – *ibid.*, pp.19, 46 and 73.

129. A. A. Puzin, Lecture, All-Union conference of CARC *upolnomochennye*, 25-27 Nov. 1958; GARF, f.6991, o.3, d.165, l.23ob.

130. For relevant excerpts from the criminal codes of the RSFSR, the Uzbek, Azerbaijani, Tajik and Turkmen SSRs, see *Zakonodatel'stvo o religioznykh kul'takh*, pp.197-202. For excerpts from the Tajik SSR Criminal Code, of 17 Aug. 1961, and changes introduced by the decree of the republican Supreme Soviet Presidium on 28 May 1966 in the wake of the All-Union Supreme Soviet Presidium decree of 18 March 1966, see GARF, f.6991, o.6, d.220, ll.222-5.

beginning of 1962 the Central Committee Secretariat approved 'proposals' of the two chambers of the USSR Supreme Soviet that religious organisations actually fostering the practice of religious rites be held criminally liable.[131] The main brunt of criminal proceedings initiated against religious activists was directed against some of the Christian sects that were considered inherently anti-Soviet, but they had implications for fringe groups at least of other faiths.

Another component of the repression connected with the anti-religious campaign was the initiation of secular rites to replace religious ones. These were intended first and foremost to restrict the practice of religious life-cycle rites (baptism, name-giving, circumcision, marriage and burial), but also the celebration of religious festivals. As of 1958-9 the new rites, as they were called,[132] were discussed increasingly in the press and at atheist conferences and seminars. In 1962 the issue of religious and secular rituals was raised at the bureau of the RSFSR party organisation, and in 1963 the Central Committee's Ideological Commission called for 'the more active introduction into the life of the Soviet people of non-religious festivals and rites'.[133] In February 1964 the RSFSR Council of Ministers issued a decree 'On the introduction of new civil rites into the life of Soviet people'. This decree set up a council under the Council of Ministers' Juridical Commission to prepare the inauguration of these rites, in particular procedures for the registration of children, the issuing of internal passports (at age sixteen) and marriage.[134] According to one source, the reason for introducing secular holidays and rites was to undermine the contention that the origins of religious festivals and rites were popular and national. In order to divest these ceremonies of their religious form, it was resolved to provide an alternative spring and harvest festival, a day to commemorate the dead, a ritual for registering the new-born, and so on.[135]

131. Anderson, *Religion, State and Society*, p.24.

132. The description was somewhat misleading, for the regime had instituted certain rites as early as 1918, when a Red Calendar was introduced to oust the holidays connected with the old regime and social order and replace them with new ones. Certain life-cycle rites were also brought in in these early years, but did not take root – Lane, *The Rites of Rulers*, pp.75 and 154.

133. Anderson, *Religion, State and Politics*, p.48.

134. Decree No.203, 18 Feb. 1964; GARF, f.6991, o.4, d.119, ll.13-13a.

135. Anufriev and Kobetskii, *Religioznost' i ateizm*, p.55.

Some of the more extravagant excesses of the anti-religious campaign of Khrushchev's last years were severely criticised in the year or so after his removal in October 1964 as violations of legality, and generally abandoned (although the new regime persisted in prosecuting sectarians perhaps within the framework of its crack-down on political dissent).[136] In January 1965 the presidium of the USSR Supreme Soviet issued a decree 'On some cases of the violation of socialist legality in regard to believers'. This was followed a few months later by a CARC circular asking its *upolnomochennye* what measures they had taken to implement this decree, what measures had been taken by republican, oblast' and other organs to terminate administrative excesses *vis-à-vis* believers and to correct mistakes that had been permitted in the past, whether there had been cases of administrative action in the current year and what steps had been taken to maintain believers' rights and interests. And finally, CARC sought information concerning the commuting of sentences by the courts.[137]

The year 1965 also saw a major effort to take stock of all religious associations, both registered and unregistered, including those which met irregularly and did not have permanent prayer premises, and all 'holy places' and tombs to which pilgrimages took place.[138] In the course of the year, too, a first conference of CARC officials with the participation of scientists took place,

136. Minutes, CARC session, 17 March 1965; GARF, f.6991, o.4, d.168, ll.70-150, and Anderson, *Religion, State and Politics*, pp. 68-74. The new leaders' attitude to sectarians should probably be seen in the context of the general onslaught against dissidents of the mid 1960s. Members of the Christian sects continued, for example, to be the main victims of efforts to bring to book transgressors of legislation on religion, see V. Kuroedov to *upolnomochennye*, 13 Jan. 1969, and the accompanying survey by the CRA legal department 'On the practical application of the decrees of the presidiums of union republic supreme soviets 'On administrative responsibility for violation of the legislation on religion' " –GARF, f.6991, o.6, d.217, ll.1-10.

137. A. Puzin to all *upolnomochennye*, June 1965; GARF, f.6991, o.4, d.170, l.14a. The review of sentences for offences in the realm of religion had begun already prior to Khrushchev's dismissal.

138. CARC session No.37, 13 Nov. 1964, and A. A. Puzin to *upolnomochennye*, draft, 5 May 1965; GARF, f.6991, o.4, d.170, ll.2-5. Already in 1961 forms requiring details of all prayer-houses, their clergy and lay leadership had been sent to all CARC *upolnomochennye* –A. A. Puzin to *upolnomochennye*, 20 and 24 July 1961; GARF, f.6991, o.3, d.1368, ll.163 and 193 –but they seem to have been completed in a haphazard and sporadic fashion.

Puzin emphasising that policy must be the connecting link between science and practice, for, while it had to be based on scientific data, practice had to follow from its stipulations. He bemoaned the great gap existing between legislation and party decrees on religion and their implementation in the localities. He pointed out that the time had come, not for a change in policy, but for a change in the methods of struggle against sectarian faiths. It should become possible for some of them to register in certain circumstances, which meant permission for their activity and, at the same time, recognition and observance of the law on their part and their acknowledgement of state control of religious activity. Registered religious associations, Puzin reiterated the usual contention, perpetrated less violations of legality and it was possible to control their leadership, which was out of the question regarding unregistered groups.[139] Finally, in December 1965, the fusion took place of CAROC and CARC into a single Council for Religious Affairs,[140] the functions of which were in principle the same as those of the two councils.[141]

Among the activities undertaken by the CRA in its early years was a study of the 'content, form and methods of religious organisations' influence on children and youth', and the elaboration

139. CARC session, 17 March 1965; GARF, f.6991, o.4, d.168, ll.70-82. The focus of this particular session was sectarianism, and the initiative for its convention came from Chairman of the Supreme Soviet Presidium Anastas Mikoian.

140. The idea of a fusion had been discussed at least since 1954. At a joint meeting of the leadership of the two councils in 1954 in connection with Malenkov's attempt to enhance the efficiency of government institutions, CAROC Chairman Karpov and member G. T. Utkin proposed a merger; they noted that this issue had been debated four times already, the last time by the Central Committee just a few months previously – Minutes, Joint session of CAROC and CARC, 29 June 1954; GARF, f.6991, o.3, d.101, l.68. Almost a year later the CARC leadership wrote to the Central Committee that the differences between the position of the Russian Orthodox Church and that of all other faiths was one of principle, that as a result of these differences the two councils were preoccupied with totally different issues and the tactics employed by the state *vis-à-vis* the Russian Orthodox Church, on the one hand, and all other faiths, on the other, were also basically dissimilar. In view of all these political considerations there was need for two distinct organisations – I. V. Polianskii, V. I. Gostev, L. A. Prikhod'ko and P. A. Zadorozhnyi to the Central Committee, 20 May 1955; GARF, f.6991, o.3, d.113, ll.190-5.

141. See its charter, ratified by Council of Ministers Decree No.361, 10 May 1966; GARF, f.6991, o.6, d.1, ll.12-3.

of recommendations for 'protection of the rising generation from the influence of religion'.[142]

In mid 1968 the RSFSR Council of Ministers issued yet another decree, 'On tightening control over the implementation of legislation concerning religion'. This time the emphasis was on actual violations of the law by the local organs rather than on their failure to ensure adherence on the part of the clergy. Certain autonomous republic councils of ministers and oblast' and krai *ispolkoms* had not reviewed believers' applications and complaints for a long period, refused without grounds to register religious associations, and obstructed their use of premises for prayer. Nor were they taking the requisite steps regarding religious organisations which declined to register. The decree obligated the abovementioned government organisations to regulate the registration procedure, to investigate each unregistered association and determine which of them were subject to registration in accordance with the law, and to take the necessary measures in conformity with established procedure regarding associations which refused to register.[143]

On the whole, the post-Khrushchev era saw little that was new in the way of either legislation or ideas as to how to tackle the issue of religiosity. There was enhanced concern at the overlap between religion and nationalism, first and foremost among the Russians themselves, and at growing evidence of religious observance among people with higher education and the younger generation. The interconnection between religion and nationalism was given expression in much of the creative, artistic and academic work of the intelligentsias of most if not all the nationalities of the Soviet Union: in the plastic arts, in theatre and literature, in historiography, in the growing interest in historical monuments and ethnography.[144] (From the early Bolshevik period the terms historical, cultural or architectural monuments were used as euphemisms for former prayer-houses and other religious sites and

142. An undated draft plan for this study, drawn up probably in mid-1968, is in GARF, f.6991, o.6, d.149, ll.4-6.

143. Decree No.494, 24 July 1968; GARF, o.6, d.146, l.14.

144. There is an extensive literature on this topic, for example the works of John Dunlop regarding the Russians, of Bohdan Bociurkiw on the Ukrainians, of V. Stanley Vardys on the Lithuanians. Its implications for the Muslim nationalities are discussed in Chapter 12.

buildings.) But the prevalent view seems to have been that these manifestations could not be tackled by legislation. Not a few voices were heard contending that the harsher line followed at times had a negative feedback, driving believers underground and making them ever less conducive to control and influence.

Under Brezhnev the top leadership does not seem to have been particularly concerned with religious issues, despite recurrent attempts to invigorate ideological work in general. However, one Central Committee resolution was passed in July 1971 which noted once again that 'party organisations and ideological institutions have weakened their attention to the atheistic education of the population and have frequently permitted a compromising attitude to the spread of religious views'. It noted also the participation of communists in religious rites and the idealisation of religious customs in some artistic and literary works.[145] This disinterest changed somewhat at the end of the 1970s, with the election of the Polish Pope John Paul II in October 1978, the Khomeini revolution and the establishment of an Islamic republic in Iran, and perhaps also the growing authority and influence of KGB chief Iurii Andropov. Calls for toughening up on ideology increased and at the June 1983 Central Committee plenum devoted to ideology, the first since 1963, Central Committee Secretary Konstantin Chernenko made a number of important references to different aspects of religion.[146]

In the sphere of legislation there was also very little of note. The 1977 'Brezhnev Constitution' changed the article on religion only slightly, guaranteeing, rather than merely recognising, freedom of conscience and speaking of the right of atheistic rather than anti-religious propaganda. And in 1975 the 1929 Law on Religious Associations was officially amended, although this was for the most part a reiteration of the changes incorporated in the RSFSR Supreme Soviet decree of 1962.[147]

Much was written about the need to improve the level both of the study of religion and of atheistic propaganda. The 'measures to enhance the atheistic education of the population' elaborated

145. Anderson, *Religion, State and Politics*, p.109.

146. *Pravda*, 15 and 16 June 1983.

147. The greater part of the amended law was published in *O religii i tserkvi*, pp.126–39. For the article in the 1977 constitution, see n.4; for the 1962 decree, see p. 46.

by the Central Committee Ideological Commission in 1963 included a decision to set up an Institute of Scientific Atheism at the Central Committee Academy of Social Sciences and a host of other steps designed to place atheistic work on a scientific footing with the help of more qualified cadres; atheistic education was even to become a part of political education in institutions of higher learning.[148] A 1971 *Pravda* editorial stressed the need for the establishment to avail itself of sociological surveys and research in order to enhance the effectiveness of atheistic education.[149] The constantly reiterated reference to the poor quality of atheistic cadres and the immense numbers of lectures delivered would suggest that very little was in fact achieved. The CPSU Central Committee decree of 1979, 'On the further improvement of ideological and political-educational work'[150] conceded that notwithstanding the intensity and duration of propaganda work, much still had to be done in order to educate *homo sovieticus*. In some regions, among them the Muslim areas, the main emphasis of the campaign that followed the decree was an anti-religious one.[151] One of the techniques which was highlighted as of the second half of the 1960s was work with individual believers, which in spite of difficulties claimed to have had marked successes.[152]

As to the media, they increasingly stressed not only the greed and economic motives of religious figures, a contention which had been widely used in the Khrushchev years and, indeed, since the early years of the Soviet regime. They also dwelt on the link of religious dissenters with their foreign masters and on the fringe nature of those religious 'extremists' who were the root of so much trouble. As time went on, such criticism spilled over from the dissident or outlawed groups to other, more mainstream ones.[153]

While the authorities seem to have been generally ineffective

148. See *O religii i tserkvi*, pp.82–89. The document was first printed in *Partiinaia zhizn'*, 1964, No.2.

149. *Pravda*, 18 Aug. 1971. The article referred specifically to surveys conducted in the Chechen-Ingush ASSR and a number of oblasti of the RSFSR (Voronezh, Penza, Orel and Omsk).

150. Published in *O religii i tserkvi*, pp.92–100.

151. See my article, 'The Task of Creating the New Soviet Man: "Atheistic Propaganda" in the Soviet Muslim Areas'.

152. Anderson, *Religion, State and Politics*, p.116.

153. *Ibid.*, pp.117–19.

in their efforts to curb the practice of religion and the extent of religiosity, they did exert considerable pressure on and control over the religious establishment. This had the effect, among others, of widening the gap between institutionalised religion and the mass of believers, who thus became less conducive to control both by their own religious leaders, whom they saw as compromised, and by the powers-that-be. The situation differed somewhat from faith to faith, depending on a complex of factors, with some religious leaders trying to fight a rearguard action in order to retain their sway and even being caught up to an extent in the militancy of their constituents.[154]

Perhaps nowhere was the lack of a consistent policy more evident than in the realm of opening and closing prayer-houses. On the whole, closures continued in the first post-Khrushchev decade (1964-74), although in these years some prayer-houses were also opened. The following decade saw a more meaningful upswing in the number of openings, published figures speaking of a total of 12,427 prayer-houses in 1986 as against just over 11,600 in 1964. Again, there were major differences in the various faiths. Despite some concessions to the central church organisation, the Russian Orthodox Church probably suffered the most.[155] Some confessions remained static, while others, notably several Protestant ones and the Muslims, saw the main gains.[156] It seems that the greater flexibility shown to some communities, such as the Baptists, the Seventh Day Adventists and the Mennonites, emanated from considerations of social and political expediency, within the more general assumption by which the CRA was guided: that a registered community was more easily influenced and controlled.[157]

* * *

154. For instance, among the Roman Catholic hierarchy in Lithuania.

155. According to the director of the Central Committee's Academy of Social Sciences Institute of Scientific Atheism, the Orthodox lost on average forty-eight prayer-houses per year over the period 1965-74 and twenty two between 1975 and 1987 – V. Garadzha, 'A Re-Interpretation', *Nauka i religiia*, 1 (1989), p.3.

156. For further details regarding the Muslim data, see p.61.

157. See, for this entire paragraph, Anderson, *Religion, State and Politics*, pp.126-32.

In conclusion, the situation of religion changed quite remarkably in the four decades covered by this study. Religion surfaced in the war years after a period in which its existence had been officially almost liquidated. While the party continued to be committed to its total elimination, certain state and government institutions sought to regulate and control retigious activity believing that this was not only possible but also likely to be beneficial, since the liquidation of religion was clearly not going to be achieved in the foreseeable future. At different times and in varying degrees religious leaders took advantage of the dichotomy within the policy-making élite in order to expand their respective establishments. At the local level the religious communities were often influenced as much, if not more, by the position adopted by the officialdom which was immediately responsible for keeping them within the bounds of the law than by the policies announced at the centre, although strictly speaking, of course, these were universally binding.

At the same time, the situation of religion was not just the outcome of policy and decision making in either Moscow or the periphery. It was influenced by general social and cultural trends, such as the growth of nationalism, with which it naturally interacted. It was also affected by the basic attitude of the population to the Party and state, more consciously so among the more highly educated, but perhaps more significantly so among the less enlightened rural community. Until the 1970s at least, the former, who had imbibed the fundamental message of secularisation with which their education had been impregnated and which was an inherent ingredient of their socialisation, were on the whole estranged from religion in any form. The latter tended to regard religion with more affinity as part of their everyday lives, especially its life-cycle rites, and had less motivation to become estranged from it. It was, then, mostly the less educated who kept religion alive and, paradoxically, it was from them that their more educated fellows took the lead as they fell increasingly under the sway of national tradition.

This was perhaps nowhere more evident than in Islam. While its lot was in every way subject to the fate of religion as a whole, it, like every faith, had its own special features. One of these, the one most pertinent to it as a religion, was its essence as a way of life rather than as a belief system. This gave it deeper roots and made it harder for the authorities to control, let alone eradicate. Another was the respect in which elders were held in Islam, making it more difficult for the younger generation to break away from tradition, for this also entailed estrangement from their families. A third factor was the close-knit extended family that was intrinsic to the national existence of most of the ethnicities which had traditionally observed Islam, especially in the rural areas, where the majority of them lived right down to the end of the Soviet period.

We shall be looking at these and other features of Soviet Islam in the following chapters, starting with the most complex issue of all, its dimensions and scope. Although the aggregate population of the nations that had in the past practised Islam was second in size to the Russian population, for a variety of reasons that we shall enumerate and analyse the number of prayer-houses at their disposal was always relatively small, when compared not only with the number of Russian Orthodox churches, but also with the prayer-houses of the Roman Catholics or Evangelical Christian Baptists. Consequently, any study of Islam must pay due attention not only to its establishment but also, and perhaps even more so, to its non-establishment facets. The fact that these are less tangible and less well documented and tend to be prevalent in more out-of-the-way areas does not diminish their centrality to the understanding of the general picture. Their dimensions, even if they cannot be accurately measured, were, according to all accounts, significant, if not truly impressive.

2

THE DIMENSIONS OF ISLAM

When one talks of the scope of Islamic activity in the Soviet Union one is referring to a variety of components: the number of registered mosques, of unregistered communities and groups, and even of non-functioning mosques; the tally of clergy and other religious 'activists', both registered and unregistered; the size of mosque attendance and the extent of belief and religious practice. While today we know the numbers of registered prayer-houses and clergy in the country at large and in any given area throughout the postwar period,[1] other statistical data are more questionable, based as they often were on extrapolation or encompassing only a small portion of the relevant data. Nevertheless, since gauging the extent of Muslim activity seems a *sine qua non* for any study of Islam, the endeavour will be made to undertake some estimates and reach some conclusions.

The overwhelming majority of Soviet Muslims were by tradition Sunnis of the Hanafi school (*mazhab*). These included all the largest ethnic groups with the exception of the Azerbaijanis, namely the

---

1. Even here there are some small discrepancies for reasons that are not always clear, perhaps because there would be the odd registered religious association which did not have a mosque, that is one set of figures might have related to actual prayer-houses, while another recorded the number of religious associations. Officially there could not be a registered religious association without a prayer-house, but, for instance, after the 1966 earthquake in Tashkent in which two mosques were utterly destroyed the religious societies associated with them continued to exist for a year or so – GARF, f.6991, o.6, d.21, l.177 – until withdrawn from registration for want of a prayer-house. The identical thing happened when two mosques were burned down. CARC's statistical report for 1 Jan. 1964 noted that the Muslims had 309 registered prayer-houses and 312 religious societies, and the discrepancy was even larger for most of the other faiths – GARF, f.6991, o.4, d.430, l.1. Or conceivably, prayer-houses that were not in nationalised or municipally owned buildings but in privately owned ones might not be included. I have found instances of both. In any case the difference is usually not more than three or four.

Uzbeks, Kazakhs, Kyrgyz, Tajiks, Turkmen, Volga (or Kazan') Tatars and Bashkirs, as well as a host of smaller ones. Of the Dagestanis, the majority belonged to the Shafi'i school. Probably less than ten per cent of the Muslim population were Shiite (mostly Twelver Shiites), including about two thirds of the Azerbaijanis. There were also a few small groups belonging to a variety of sects.[2]

The Soviet Union published no statistics on the religious affiliation of its various ethnic groups, and one of the sources of the lack of clarity regarding total numbers of Islam's adherents was the uncertainty over how far all members of the Muslim nationalities could or should be considered Muslims. The population of those nationalities that had traditionally adhered to Islam (as they were described in Soviet jargon) was from the point of view of size second only to the population which had traditionally professed Russian Orthodoxy. The documentation speaks throughout of the Muslims being the largest contingent of believers in the country after the Orthodox Church.[3] The usual figure given in the early period is of 20 million Muslims: 17 million Sunnis and 3 million Shiites;[4] by 1949 Voroshilov was talking of no less than 30 million.[5] The Soviet census of 1979 revealed some 43 million citizens belonging to Muslim nationalities and that of 1989, 54 million.

CARC itself sought to gather statistical information from its *upolnomochennye* in the field that would enable it to clarify all the

2. For some figures, see Bennigsen and Lemercier-Quelquejay, 'Islam in the Soviet Muslim Republics', pp.132-6. The authors noted that just a few of the nationalities traditionally perceived as Muslim also had some Christian members: two communities among the Volga Tatars converted in the sixteenth and eighteenth century, many of whom, however, re-converted to Islam after 1905; while about one-half of the Abkhaz and two-thirds of the Osets never became Muslims. In addition, somewhere between 25,000 and 50,000 of a Kurdish population of 116,000 in 1979 belonged to the Yezidi religion. Similarly, there were some Muslim groups among nationalities with a Christian majority, such as the Muslim Georgians (Ajars and Ingilois) and the Chuvash.

3. E.g., CARC Chairman Polianskii, Address at Moscow conference, 11-13 [June] 1946, and CARC inspector N. I. Abushaev, Information, 17 Nov. 1949; GARF, f.6991, o.3, d.39, l.59, and d.61, l.119.

4. For example, Minutes, CARC session No.4, 29 Jan. 1947; GARF, f.6991, o.4, d.19, l.80.

5. See Chapter 4, n. 80.

above-mentioned points.[6] Although aware of the problems involved
in evaluating the dimensions of prayer attendance, for example,
CARC and its *upolnomochennye* periodically endeavoured to estimate whether it was growing, static or falling off. From the
earliest stages and right through the years for which archival material
is available, CARC and the CRA issued precise instructions as
to the points they wanted elucidated and distributed a variety of
forms to ensure as far as was possible that they receive the requisite
data. The officials in Moscow collated and sifted the material and
sent it on with their own comments and interpretations to the
party Central Committee and the Council of Ministers.

On the eve of the October Revolution there had been over
20,000 mosques in the Russian Empire.[7] Most of these seem to
have been closed down in the 1920s – less than 4,000 were reported
to have been still functioning in 1929[8] – and nearly all the rest
by the outbreak of the Great Patriotic War in June 1941.[9] There
appear to be no figures, at least not in the post-1944 documentation,

6. This was one of the assignments laid down in its founding statute see p.12.

7. A detailed account of the number of parishes in each *guberniia*, claims there
were 24,582 – Archival information, prepared by acting head of TsGIAL (Central
State Historical Archive in Leningrad) Golova and senior scientific worker Kovalev,
30 Nov. 1944; GARF, f.6991, o.3, d.33, ll.26-7. Bennigsen similarly speaks of
some 25,000 – 'Muslim Conservative Opposition to the Soviet Regime: the Sufi
Brotherhoods in the North Caucasus', p.335 – whereas the head of CARC gave
the number of 21,873 – I. V. Polianskii to G. F. Aleksandrov, 1 July 1947;
RTsKhIDNI, f.17, o.125, d.506, l.129. True, one Soviet source said there had
been just 17,037 (Statistical information of prayer-houses of the religious cults
in the USSR on 1 April 1946; GARF, f.6991, o.4, d.106, l.1), perhaps not
including the mosques in the two autonomous khanates of Bukhara and Khiva.

8. G. F. Frolov, Memo of number of registered prayer-houses functioning in
1929, 1948 and 1955, 24 June 1955; GARF, f.6991, o.3, d.114, ll.87-91. The
exact number given was 3,697; at the same time, Frolov added a note saying
that the data for 1929 had been collated from a variety of sources and should
be considered approximate.

9. In Kirgiziia, for example, CARC *upolnomochennyi* Akhtiamov reported that
there had not been a single functioning prayer-house of any denomination by
1941, although he later discovered that one had been operating since 1938 – H.
Akhtiamov to CARC, 10 July and 15 Dec. 1945; GARF, f.6991, o.3, d.29,
l.124, and d.30, l.248. In the Karachai-Cherkess AO seven mosques were still
functioning in 1940 – Minutes, meeting of CARC instructors, No.17, 20-22
Dec. 1950; GARF, f.6991, o.3, d.66, l.123 – which in all probability were still
functioning the following year. In the remoter areas of Uzbekistan, Tajikistan
and the Chechen-Ingush ASSR, many mosques seem never to have formally
closed down; see pp.289-90.

to indicate how many mosques operated in the years 1941-4.[10] In other words, when, in the latter half of 1944, CARC began registering mosques that were already functioning, nobody probably had any clear indication of how many of these there in fact were.[11]

While none of the mosques that had remained open seem to have been officially registered prior to 1944, once CARC launched its campaign to register and open prayer-houses,[12] functioning mosques began to be divided into two distinct categories: those registered with the local organs of government, and those which for varying reasons were not. From the point of view of the statistics provided by CARC, at least as of spring 1946,[13] the former comprised a category unto themselves.

Although the numbers for Muslim prayer-houses were not large, the procedure for registering functioning prayer-houses and even more so for opening new ones – which would of course be registered, having been opened by consent of the local and central authorities – was cumbersome and protracted. In April 1946, just shortly before the decision not to continue registering prayer-houses on the basis of having functioned earlier, CARC was still of the

10. We have documentation, however, for some oblasti, although it too may well be partial. Of 172 prayer-houses reported to have been operating in Andijan Oblast' at the end of 1945, two had been operating since 1930, two since 1935, one since 1938, five since 1939, three since 1940, one since 1941, six since 1942 and 13 since 1943; all the rest began functioning in 1944 or 1945. Of 49 operating in Fergana Oblast', two had begun operating in 1943 and all the others in 1944 – TsGAUz, f.2456, o.1, d.71, l.13, and d.46, ll.50-1. A few mosques in the Northern Caucasus were closed down as late as 1943 (just prior to the deportations), e.g. seven in the Chechen-Ingush ASSR; whereas in Kirgiziia at least two rural mosques – both in Frunze Oblast' – began functioning in 1942, and several others in 1943 – GARF, f.6991, o.4, d.319, ll.2-8, and d.19, l.244.

11. In early 1946 CARC Deputy Chairman Iu. V. Sadovskii explained that his organisation still had no information on this score – Information, 24 Jan. 1946; GARF, f.6991, o.3, d.34, l.28.

12. See p.20.

13. The report by Sadovskii in early 1946 does not make the distinction, merely saying that 495 mosques had been taken count of as functioning prayer-houses, 52 of which had been opened by CARC – Information, 24 Jan. 1946; GARF, f.6991, o.3, d.34, l.28. Statistical information prepared at the end of the first quarter of 1946, giving data for prayer-houses divides functioning prayer-houses into two columns: opened by CARC and 'registered as having functioned before' –GARF, f.6991, o.4, d.146, l.1. By the time the statistical information was drawn up just two years later, these two groups had been combined under the heading 'functioning registered mosques' – GARF, f.6991, o.4, d.212, l.1.

opinion that it would be registering quite a lot more than it in fact did.[14]

By 1 January 1947 the number of registered mosques was 345,[15] by 1 June 385, of which 124 had been opened by CARC,[16] and by 1 April 1948 it had reached 411.[17] This number remained stable for about one year, the 416 mosques registered at the beginning of 1949 representing the peak from the point of view of quantity for the entire postwar period, at least until 1989. The last years of Stalin saw a gradual decrease, reaching a low of 337 at the beginning of 1955.[18] Numbers then began to mount, sixty mosques being registered within a space of three years, reaching a total of 398 in 1957, and apparently just topping the 400 mark by early 1958.[19] In the process of the anti-religious campaign of Khrushchev's last years, they declined once more, reaching an all-time low for the postwar era of 309 in early 1964.[20] The

14. Polianskii wrote to Voroshilov – 5 April 1946; GARF, f.6991, o.3, d.34, l.43 – that account had been taken of 545 mosques, 62 of which had been opened by CARC, 226 registered as having functioned earlier, and 319 were still subject to registration, as having in fact been in existence before the crucial date.

15. I. V. Polianskii to I. V. Stalin, L. P. Beriia, V. M. Molotov and K. E. Voroshilov at the Council of Ministers, and to A. A. Zhdanov, N. S. Khrushchev, A. A. Kuznetsov, N. S. Patolichev and G. M. Popov at the Central Committee, 27 Feb. 1947; GARF, f.6991, o.3, d.47, l.77. 118 of the 345 had been opened by CARC.

16. Information on opened, registered and factually functioning (unregistered) religious societies on 1 June 1947; GARF, f.6991, o.3, d.47, l.201.

17. I. V. Polianskii to the Council of Ministers Cultural Bureau, K. E. Voroshilov, M. A. Turkin, M. A. Suslov, and A. A. Kuznetsov, 10 June 1948; GARF, f.6991, o.3, d.53, l.16. (The letter to Kuznetsov was dated 19 June.)

18. By 1 Jan. 1950 the 416 had gone down to 385, by 1 Jan. 1951 to 374, by 1 Jan. 1952 to 357, by 1 Jan. 1953 to 349, and by 1 Jan. 1954 to 340 – I. V. Polianskii to K. E. Voroshilov, G. M. Malenkov, M. A. Suslov and V. A. Abakumov, 17 March 1951, and to the Bureau of the Presidium of the Council of Ministers, M. A. Suslov and Minister of State Security S. D. Ignat'ev, 5 April 1952, G. F. Frolov, Report, 6 May 1953, L. A. Prikhod'ko, V. D. Efremov and P. A. Basis, Report, 8 May 1954, and Statistical report, 1 Jan. 1955; GARF, f.6991, o.3, d.91, l.212, and d.100, l.32, and o.4, d.255, l.1, and RTsKhIDNI, f.17, o.132, d.497, l.28.

19. A. Puzin to K. U. Chernenko, Dept. of Propaganda and Agitation, undated; GARF, f.6991, o.3, d.148, l.10, and Anderson, Religion, State and Politics, p.55.

20. Statistical report, 1 Jan. 1964; GARF, f.6991, o.4, d.430, l.1. Another report of the same year gave the figure as 325 – Statistical report, 1 Jan. 1964; GARF, f.6991, o.4, d.146, l.170. Anderson gives the number for 1 Jan. 1964 as 312

following decade saw a very slight growth in numbers and then a more meaningful one in the years 1977-83, and by 1985 the number had climbed back to 392.[21]

The distribution of these mosques according to union republics was not even throughout the postwar period, and in times of closures certain areas would be particularly targeted and tended to suffer more. The RSFSR usually had nearly half of the country's registered mosques. It boasted not a few meaningful enclaves of traditionally Muslim populations, including some autonomous republics in which the titular nationality was one such population – the Tatar, Bashkir and Kabardinian ASSRs until 1957 and after the restoration of the administrative units of the North Caucasian peoples deported by Stalin in 1944 also the Chechen-Ingush ASSR[22] – not to speak of Dagestan, where all the indigenous nationalities belonged to this category.[23] But perhaps precisely because they were enclaves, that is areas where they comprised a minority in the entire population, they were more vulnerable and bore the brunt of Khrushchev's closure campaign. Thus, while the RSFSR had 187 mosques in 1948, 172 in 1955 and 182 in 1957, the number was down to 139 in 1965.[24] On the other hand, Uzbekistan

---

– *Religion State and Society*, p.55. (According to the former statistical report, this was the number of registered religious societies.)

21. Anderson, *Religion, State and Society*, p.130. 57 Muslim religious societies were registered between Jan. 1980 and Jan. 1985 – Corley, *Religion in the Soviet Union*, p. 295.

22. The 1957 decree which allowed these peoples – the Chechen, Ingush, Balkars, Karachais and Kalmyks – to return to their homes and restored their names to the administrative units which they had previously inhabited, left two Muslim peoples in Central Asia without the right of return: the Crimean Tatars and the Meskhetian Turks (as well as the Volga Germans). Even where they constituted the eponymous nationality, most of these Muslim peoples did not comprise a majority of the population in their national region (autonomous republic or oblast').

23. The Dagestan ASSR's 41 raions were divided as follows: 15 Avar, 6 Dargin, 7 Kumyk, 8 Lezgin, 3 Lak, 1 Tabasaran, 1 Turk (i.e. Azerbaijani) – I. Zakaryaev, Report, June 1946; GARF, f.6991, o.3, d.38, l.62.

24. I. V. Polianskii to the USSR Council of Ministers Cultural Bureau, K. E. Voroshilov, M. A. Turkin, M. A. Suslov and A. A. Kuznetsov, 10 June 1948, and Information, undated [1965]; GARF, f.6991, o.3, d.53, l.18, and o.4, d.436, l.2. Of the 43 mosques closed in the RSFSR, 13 were in the Bashkir ASSR which had had a relatively large number of mosques when the campaign began (29); the other 'Muslim' autonomous republics went unscathed, the 30 remaining mosques being in Tatar communities in 'Russian' oblasti (Kuibyshev, Orenburg,

and Tajikistan were the foci of the closures of the late Stalin period, the number of registered mosques dropping between 1948 and 1953 from 101 to sixty in the former and in the latter from forty-one to twenty-six.[25]

Nor was the distribution of registered mosques within the various union republics ordained by considerations of the size of the believer population in any given area. As one report said point-blank, the way mosques were allocated was completely incidental, without any reference to satisfying the needs of believers. Thus of the sixty registered mosques in Uzbekistan in 1953, no less than thirty-seven were situated in Tashkent and Tashkent Oblast', whereas Bukhara Oblast' had only three, all in the town of Bukhara, Samarkand Oblast' just one, and two oblasti, those of Surkhan-Darya and Kashka-Darya, none at all. The fact that Kazakhstan had in its entire territory no more than twenty mosques and Turkmenistan four in all again left vast areas without a registered mosque to which believers could have resource. Since the quantity of mosques could not satisfy the needs of believers, they fell back on the services of unregistered clergy for the conduct of religious rites.[26]

The general lack of clarity regarding the potential and actual number of Muslim believers was made all the more acute by the lack of any accepted criteria for gauging the true figures for the believer population. These were impossible to estimate for any single union republic or other administrative unit, let alone for the country as a whole. The optimal yardstick, it seemed to experts, was attendance at prayer-service on Uraz-Bayram, when every Muslim considered it his duty to participate in collective prayer.[27]

Penza, Ul'ianovsk, etc.). Two mosques had existed in each of the following republics in 1952: Armenia, Georgia and Belorussia, and one in Lithuania; by 1965 the two in Belorussia had disappeared, but the others remained.

25. I. V. Polianskiii to the Council of Ministers Cultural Bureau *et al.*, 10 June 1948, and L. A. Prikhod'ko, V. D. Efremov and P. A. Basis, Report, 8 May 1954 – GARF, f.6991, o.3, d.53, l.18, and d.100, l.33. It was clearly felt that too many mosques had been allowed to register in Uzbekistan: Sadovskii's 1946 report noted that 202 of all the country's 495 functioning mosques were in that republic as against just 10 in Azerbaijan, 18 in Kazakhstan, 14 in the Bashkir ASSR and 12 in the Tatar ASSR – Information, 24 Jan. 1946; GARF, f.6991, o.3, d.34, l.28. (Two of Tajikistan's registered mosques were destroyed by an earthquake: K. Hamidov, Report, 14 Dec. 1949; GARF, f.6991, o.3, d.67, l.94.)

26. L. Prikhod'ko, Report, 20 May 1953; GARF, f.6991, o.3, d.91, ll.253-4.

27. *Ibid.*, l.255.

Yet, even this was not foolproof, for many believing Muslims, including, at least in Central Asia's traditionally sedentary areas, all women, never attended collective prayers. Moreover, certain rites were observed even by people who never attended mosque: 'most of the population' of the relevant nationalities circumcising their sons and burying their dead in accordance with religious custom.[28]

When comparing the number of mosques with that of prayer-houses of other faiths under CARC's auspices, it is impossible not to notice that it does not reflect the extent of their potential worshippers. On 1 January 1949, the 416 registered mosques were fewer than the Lutheran or Old Believer prayer-houses[29] and many fewer than those of the Roman Catholics and the Evangelical Christian Baptists.[30] These were faiths which were widespread in the areas annexed by the Soviet Union in the context of World War II and which had been under Nazi occupation. The Nazis had made a point of opening prayer-houses in order to gain the sympathy of the population and when Soviet rule was restored, Moscow was faced with a major dilemma in order at one and the same time not to alienate the inhabitants and to eradicate or at least curtail religious activity.[31] The only Muslim areas in which this problem existed were in the Northern Caucasus, namely the Cherkess AO, where in fact sixty-two mosques existed at the time of CARC's formation in May 1944,[32] and the Kabardinian

28. *Ibid.*, l.256. For further detail, see Chapter 9.

29. They had 504 and 439 respectively – V. I. Gostev, Information, 15 Nov. 1950; RTsKhIDNI, f.17, o.132, d.285, l.204.

30. These had 1,400 and 2,548 respectively – *ibid.* In 1947 Polianskii had noted that altogether the number of functioning prayer-houses comprised 17 percent of all the prayer-houses of the pre-revolutionary period – I. V. Polianskii to G. F. Aleksandrov, 1 July 1947; RTsKhIDNI, f.17, o.125, d.506, l.111. The most the Muslims ever attained was approximately 2 per cent, whereas the Roman Catholics and Evangelical Christian Baptists had in mid 1947 well over 50 percent (1,475 as against 2,510 and 2,678 as against 4,521 respectively).

31. This was almost certainly the reason that over one-half of all the Soviet Union's prayer-houses, including those of the Russian Orthodox Church, were in Ukraine (54 per cent in 1958) – Anderson, *Religion, State and Politics*, p.56. And see Chapter 1, nn. 60 and 113.)

32. V. V. Bulatov, *upolnomochennyi* for Stavropol Krai, told a CARC session in 1950 that before 1917 there had been 68 mosques in the krai, but in 1940 only seven were functioning. In 1942 under the Nazis 60 had renewed activity, 52 of them in the Cherkess AO, sometimes two or three in a single aul. This

ASSR, where a number of mosques opened under the Nazis in 1942 were also still in operation at this time.[33]

This discrepancy between the large number of believers and the relatively small number of prayer-houses highlights the point that the existence, registration and opening of prayer-houses were not related to the total number of believers in the population, but to extraneous historical circumstances. And even though the postwar closures affected first of all the Greek and Roman Catholics[34] and most of the other large Christian denominations more than Islam, the latter remained with but a small proportion of the total number of prayer-houses under CARC's auspices (which was 6,657 in early 1946, 5,237 in mid 1950 and 4,127 in 1964).[35] CARC appears to have sought to amend this disproportion to an extent by giving relatively more positive replies to applications from Muslim religious associations to open prayer-houses in the 1944-7 period than to others,[36] but this was but a drop in the ocean.

---

number had decreased in the process of registering religious societies and clergy after Soviet rule was restored – perhaps in connection with the deportation in late 1943 of the Karachai – and by 1 Jan. 1947 just 23 remained – Minutes, Instructional meeting No.17, 20-22 Dec. 1950; GARF, f.6991, o.3, d.66, l.123.

33. Z. Kumekhov, Chairman of the Kabardinian ASSR SNK, to I. V. Polianskii, 1 July 1944; GARF, f.6991, o.3, d.6, l.2. The first CARC *upolnomochennyi* in the Kabardinian ASSR registered eight such mosques in 1945 – Report of Geshov, conference of CARC *upolnomochennye*, 14 June 1946; GARF, f.6991, o.3, d.38, l.173. The other Muslim administrative unit the Germans had overrun was the Crimea, from which the Tatars were deported in May 1944 for collaborating with them and no functioning mosques remained.

34. The Greek Catholic Church was outlawed in 1946 and its churches taken over by the Russian Orthodox Church; on 1 Jan. 1949 just 327 remained of the 2,290 there had been just three years earlier and these too had disappeared by 1 July 1950. The number of Roman Catholic churches fell over the same period from 1,671 to 1,251, many parishes simply disbanding in the wake of the repatriation to Poland of 1945-49. By 1 July 1950 the Evangelical Christian Baptists were by far the most numerous from the point of view of prayer-houses, with 2,288. The Buddhists also lost most of their prayer-houses, remaining with just two out of 238, following the Japanese repatriation from South Sakhlin –V. I. Gostev, Information, 15 Nov. 1950; RTsKhIDNI, f.17, o.132, d.285, pp.202-5.

35. All these figures exclude the Russian Orthodox Church which claimed well over two-thirds of all registered prayer-houses at the beginning of the Khrushchev repressions and rather less than two-thirds at their conclusion.

36. By mid-1947 CARC and its *upolnomochennye* had reviewed 2283 applications, of which only 320 had been approved – I. V. Polianskii to G. F. Aleksandrov, 1 July 1947; RTsKhIDNI, f.17, o.125, d.506, l.116. Of these, 124 came from

The registration process is well illuminated by the numbers of applications to open new prayer-houses – as distinct from the registration of those that had been functioning before the critical date – which were received by the local authorities. These reflected very closely the inclination of the powers-that-be to respond positively to at least some of these overtures. In 1946 Muslim believers filed no less than 562 such applications, in each of the years 1947 and 1948 close to 400,[37] in 1949, 122 and in the years 1950-2 less than forty each year.[38] It was perfectly clear that groups of believers were not prepared to take the risk of exposing themselves to the authorities unless they thought that they had a reasonable chance of succeeding. Thus, while in the course of 1947 of 323 applications that were reviewed forty-eight were approved, of the 116 reviewed in the first seven months of the following year not a single one met with a positive reply.[39] Applications began to proliferate anew as of the February 1955 decree.[40] In the years of Khrushchev's anti-religious campaign once again no prayer-houses seem to have been opened or registered; the form distributed

---

Muslim religious associations, as against just 388 which had been refused – *ibid.*, Appendix, No.1.

37. The exact figures were 373 and 378. Of the latter figure 157 were filed in the first quarter of the year. All 98 actually reviewed in these three months – as indeed all applications filed for other faiths as well – were rejected – Information, First quarter, 1948, GARF, f.6991, o.4, d.215, l.2ob, and V.I. Gostev, Information, 15 Nov. 1950 – RTsKhIDNI, f.17, o.132, d.285, ll.205-6.

38. *Ibid.*, ll.206-7; Report, 8 May 1954 – GARF, f.6991, o.3, d.100, l.35. The exact figures for 1950-52 were 33, 37 and 22. We have no aggregate for 1945, but it was probably no lower than 1946. In Dagestan alone we know there were 67 applications – I. Zakaryaev, Report, June 1946; GARF, f.6991, o.3, d.38, l.62; in Tashkent, over 100 applications were filed in 1944-45 to open 96 mosques and *mazars* – Address of Nasretdinov, Minutes, Conference of CARC *upolnomochennye* in the Uzbek SSR, 9 Aug. 1948; TsGAUz, f.2456, o.1, d.120, l.4.

39. G. F. Frolov, Information, undated; GARF, f.6991, o.3, d.59, ll. 5 and 18. We have seen that by 1948 instructions had apparently been issued not to open any prayer-houses (see pp.34-5), and the number of applications from Muslim groups was by now larger than for any other – *ibid.*; see also GARF, f.6991, o.4, d.215, l.2ob.

40. In Uzbekistan alone 99 applications were filed in the years 1956-58 – Address by N. I. Inogamov at all-union conference of *upolnomochennye*, 25-27 Nov. 1958; GARF, f.6991, o.3, d.165, l.37. The *upolnomochennyi* for the Bashkir ASSR pointed out on the same occasion that in 1954 just three applications had been sent in and in 1958 – 17 (*ibid.*, l.93).

to the *upolnomochennye* for their statistical reports in this period has a column for prayer premises closed in the current year, but none for those opened.[41]

The number of registered clergy was usually somewhat larger than that of the registered religious associations, as their ranks included members of the four spiritual directorates[42] and some mosques had more than one cleric.[43] Thus, as of 1 April 1948 there were 457 registered Muslim clergy (as against 411 mosques)[44] and, although their number was reduced even more drastically in the late Stalin period than that of the mosques,[45] by 1961 there were 537 clergy to 373 mosques and at the beginning of 1963, 407 (as against 322 mosques).[46] Although the number of registered mosques was actually smaller (314), by 1970 there were said to be 543 clergy.[47] The reason for the considerable growth as of

41. See, for instance, GARF, f.6991, o.4, d.430, l.1.

42. These directorates will be discussed in the next chapter.

43. This seems to have been true especially in Uzbekistan where of 77 mosques registered by the end of 1946, 8 had 3 clerics and 17 had 2 – TsGAUz, f.2456, o.1, d.83, ll.16-21. In 1954 there were 242 registered clerics in Central Asia for 142 mosques, contrasting sharply with the situation in the RSFSR: of the mosques subordinate to DUMES 18 had no cleric at all. The age distribution of the Central Asians was also much more favourable, 16 being under 40 and 130 between 40 and 49 – Report, 8 May 1954; GARF, f.6991, o.3, d.100, ll.39-40. By 1956 Uzbekistan's 72 registered mosques had 132 clerics between them, excluding the muezzins – The composition of the clerical personnel of mosques and mausolea in the Uzb.SSR on 30 Sept. 1956; TsGAUz, f.2456, o.1, d.184, l.58. A year previously a report by Iskanderov to the head of Uzbekistan's Communist Party's Central Committee Propaganda Department, U. Yusupov, had given 185 clerics for the republic's 61 mosques and 6 registered *mazars*, 23 June 1955; TsGAUz, f.2456, o.1, d.179, ll.89-91. Yet by the end of Khrushchev's anti-religious campaign Uzbekistan's 66 registered mosques had just 68 clergy –M. Miragzamov to M. Kh. Khalmuhamedov, 22 Oct. 1966; GARF, f.6991, o.6, d.11, l.63.

44. Statistical information on clergy of religious cults at prayer-houses in USSR on 1 April 1948 – GARF, f.6991, o.4, d.215, l.2.

45. The number of clerics attached to mosques had been 436 on 1 Jan. 1948 and it decreased annually over the next four years to 420, 412, 371, 358 – I. V. Polianskii to M. A. Suslov, 5 April 1952; RTsKhIDNI, f.17, o.132, d.569, l.93.

46. A. A. Puzin to the CPSU Central Committee Department of Propaganda and Agitation, 7 June 1961, and Statistical report on registered religious societies, prayer premises and clergy on 1 Jan. 1963 – GARF, f.6991, o.3, d.1363, l.97, and o.4, d.429, l.1ob.

47. CRA, Information sent to the CPSU Central Committee, 22 May 1970; TsKhSD, f.5, o.62, d.38, l.4.

the late 1960s is explained at least in part by the registration of clergy in places without registered mosques by affiliation to the nearest registered prayer-house (especially apparently in Azerbaijan and Kazakhstan); perhaps the muezzins, too, whose primary function was summoning believers to prayer, but who served in effect as assistants to the imam, were now being included.[48] By the beginning of 1983 the proportion of clergy to mosques had gone up even further, with about 1,000 of the former (as against 374 mosques), and it continued growing, reaching about 1,540 (as against 392 mosques) by early 1985.[49]

When the composition of the clergy is broken down for purposes of statistical assessment, it is usually done by age and education. On just one occasion we find a classification by rank. In 1947 there were said to be twenty-five higher, 302 medium and eighty-three lower clergy.[50] By 1963 the great majority of registered clergy were people who had become mullas after 1941 although over sixty years old;[51] in other words, they were not trained to

48. In 1946 the muezzins had already been included in the list of clergy in Dagestan – Statistical information, 10 June 1946; GARF, f.6991, o.3, d.38, l.66, but this seems to have been an exception. In Uzbekistan nearly every registered mosque had a muezzin, see list of 62 muezzins in the republic's various oblasti, undated – probably late 1950 or early 1951 – drawn up by senior inspector I. A. Shalaev of the republican *upolnomochennyi's* apparatus; TsGAUz, f.2456, o.1, d.137, ll.5-7. But these muezzins were not included in lists of clergy; see, for example, Information from questionnaires of clergy in the city of Tashkent as of 20 March 1955; TsGAUz, f.2456, o.1, d.184, ll.77-86. For the registration of clergy by affiliation to registered mosques, see pp.216-7.

49. CRA memo, 'The situation of religions in the USSR and the observance of legislation on religion in 1982', 2 June 1983-TsKhSD, f.5, o.89, d.82, l.37; and Corley, *Religion in the Soviet Union*, p. 298. According to the latter source, 558 Muslim clergy had been registered 'since 1980.'

50. I. V. Polianskii to G. F. Aleksandrov, 1 July 1947; RTsKhIDNI, f.17, o.125, d.506. l.131. Presumably the first category includes the heads of the four spiritual directorates and their qazis or *muhtasibs* (see Abushaev, Information on the Muslim religion, 17 Nov. 1949; GARF, f.6991, o.3, d.61, ll.119-20), the second and third imams and *imam-khatibs*. In any case, only the senior cleric in each mosque seems to be included, for the aggregate of the second and third categories is identical to the total number of registered mosques.

51. In 1948 too most of the mullas had begun functioning as such after 1941: 52 had begun before 1916, another 34 before 1941, 98 between 1941 and 1945, and 272 after 1945; their general age was a little younger than in 1963: although there was not a single mulla under 40, 134 were under 55; indeed, 160 of them were still engaged in 'productive work'. Some, at least, of the data even regarding these registered mullas are doubtful: in the All-Union statistics identical

be mullas but on retiring had been chosen by their fellow believers to lead the community because they knew the rites and could probably recite parts of the Qur'an by heart. Only fifty-six were people with higher religious education, some of whom had been trained at the theological seminary in Bukhara, but the majority of the others had had some religious education: about one-half had had secondary religious education, that is had studied at one of the *medreses* which had abounded in pre-revolutionary Russia, not to speak of the khanates of Bukhara and Khiva; rather less had elementary religious education, having presumably attended a *mekteb*, the elementary school which had existed at almost every local mosque; only thirty-eight had had no religious education at all.[52] Neither the age ratio nor the level of education improved over the years.[53]

The data regarding the actual numbers of registered mosques and clergy were generally reliable, based, as they were, on prayer-houses and clerics registered with the authorities and so accounted for officially.[54] The computation of their revenues and expenditures

figures are given for the mullas' religious and secular education, and almost certainly the former are erroneous; in the RSFSR statistics 59 mullas are registered as having begun working between 1917 and 1941, i.e. more than for the USSR as a whole, so one figure is clearly wrong – GARF, f.6991, o.4, d.215, ll.2 and 3.

52. The document informs us that just 33 had been mullas since before 1917, 64 since before 1941, and the remaining 310 had begun functioning as mullas after 1941, although 303 were over 60 years of age and just 13 under 39. Not a single mulla had higher general education, 48 had had secondary education and the remaining 359 only elementary education. Of the 56 who had higher religious education, a few might have had higher religious education from an earlier period. (Of the clergy in 1947, before anyone could have graduated from the Bukhara *medrese*, 25 had had higher religious education – I. V. Polianskii to K. E. Voroshilov, S. V. Kaftanov, G. F. Aleksandrov and V. S. Abakumov, 1 July 1947, Appendix No.3; RTsKhIDNI, f.17, o.125, d.506, l.131 – some of whom had since died). 182 had had secondary and 131 elementary religious education. The breakdown by age and education in 1971 is generally similar, although by then there were a few more who had had secondary general education, and there were more who had had elementary than secondary religious education. For the Bukhara seminary, see pp.161-3.

53. Of the 543 clergy in 1970, 448 were over 60 and just 24 under 40, 452 had elementary and 75 secondary secular education, and 233 had elementary, 199 secondary and 29 higher religious education – CRA, Information sent to the CPSU Central Committee, 27 April 1971; TsKhSD, f.5, o.63, d.89, l.98.

54. Even here there were incongruences. The *upolnomochennyi* in Osh Oblast' in his report for the first quarter of 1949 reported that there were 14 imams in his oblast', yet when he broke them down by the year when they began

was also relatively pedantic, at least as of the mid 1950s, but these figures are only of secondary importance from our point of view,[55] as they tell us more about the financial circumstances of the community than about their religiosity. Certainly, they do show a meaningful upward trend,[56] which is only partly explained by inflation. At the same time, the various payments reflected, like nearly every other aspect of religious life, the general atmosphere surrounding religion. Thus, the *fitr* was down by half a million rubles in the first year of Khrushchev's anti-religious campaign.[57] This payment made by, or on behalf of, every adult Muslim during the *uraz* or at latest at its conclusion on Uraz-Bayram, was indeed an indicator of the extent of 'the Muslim religious movement'. Just in one raion in Kirgiziia's Talas Oblast' the *upolnomochennyi* found that the *fitr* was paid in every kolkhoz by large numbers of people.[58] But the sums recorded in the books of the

operating as clergy, he said that 3 had been initiated before 1916, 6 between 1918 and 1930, 3 between 1930 and 1941, 11 between 1941 and 1945, and 13 since 1945, giving a total of 36 – H. Akhtiamov to I. Halimov, 13 April 1949; GARF, f.6991, o.3, d.454, l.16ob.

55. The Soviet government organs, on the other hand, paid a great deal of attention to the financial aspect of religion, partly undoubtedly in order to indicate how clergy exploited believers.

56. See, for example, Information on sums received on Idi Ramazan ['Id al-fitr] for the republics of Central Asia and Kazakhstan prepared by the SADUM bookkeeper, 14 July 1952, which showed a growth from 1950-1952 from 555,612 rubles to 719,441 rubles – TsGAUz, f.2456, o.1, d.144, l.157. On the same festival in the peak years of the mid 1950s the figures soared: 806,000r. were collected in Uzbekistan alone in 1955, about 1 million rubles in 1956, 2 million in 1957 and 2.5 million in 1958 – Address by Inogamov at all-union conference of *upolnomochennye*, 25-27 Nov. 1958; GARF, f.6991, o.3, d.165, ll.35-6. The hard years of Khrushchev's campaign over, the revenues of the registered mosques increased again, mounting annually from 1966-1970 from 1,752,547r. to 2,819,400r. – CRA, Information sent to the Central Committee, 27 April 1971; TsKhSD, f.5, o.63, d.89, l.100. There were from time to time exceptions to the general trend, due usually to local or incidental circumstances, but on the whole it is unmistakable.

57. This was revealed by the chairman of SADUM, Ziyautdin Babakhanov, to Puzin when the latter received him on 25 April 1959; GARF, f.6991, o.4, d.100, l.50.

58. In one kolkhoz no less than 1,240 people paid the *fitr*, in another 696, in a third 320, in a fourth 240, and so on. In one village in Frunze Oblast' with 273 households *fitr* was paid by 1,400 people – V. I. Gostev to P. A. Tarasov, 4 Jan. 1954; GARF, f.6991, o.3, d.102, l.9. For further discussion of the *fitr*, see pp. 486-8.

registered mosques never revealed the full picture, for the *fitr* was not necessarily given to a registered mosque: it could equally be donated to unregistered clergy or even to indigent relatives or neighbours.

It is also interesting to learn how both revenues and expenditures were broken down. In Osh Oblast' in 1963, for example, the eighteen registered mosques received just under 35,000 rubles for the performance of rites and as ritual payments; their income was considerably less than their expenses. This indeed may have reflected the anti-religious campaign which was then in full swing in that, on the one hand, believers felt they would be well advised to pay less, and, on the other hand, the religious associations thought they could assuage the authorities and prove their value to the state by paying more into funds which were considered important for the country as a whole.[59] By the early-mid 1970s the eight registered mosques of Andijan Oblast' in Uzbekistan had a total income of over 125,000 rubles and expenses of approximately the same rate.[60] The aggregate income of the country's registered

---

59. The income for Osh's mosques reached just over 50,000 rubles (7,026r. as *fitr*, 3,137r. from Uraz-Bayram, 2,361r. from Qurban-Bayram, 1,672r. from Mavlud, 216r. for funeral services, 2,756r. for performance of marriages, 17,699r. for circumcisions, and 16,778r. 'other'). Expenses, on the other hand, were over 86,000r. of which more than 10,000r. were taken out of reserves, but this does not account for the difference, so that one must presume there is a mistake in the income. Certainly, for instance, the income from funerals looks extremely low. Of the 86,033r. spent by the mosques, the largest item was salaries (36,481r.); the other two fairly large items were the Department for international relations of the USSR's Muslim organisations (23,274r.) and SADUM (15,426r.). Only 7,715r. were spent on the upkeep of the mosques (repairs, etc.) – I. Shadiev, Information for 1963; GARF, f.6991, o.4, d.435, ll.50-1.

60. Their revenues were broken down as follows:

1.for performance of *nikoh*	8,628r.
2.for performance of *jinaz*	13,789r.
3.for performance of other rites	38,921r.
4.*fitr-sadaqa* during month of *uraz*	32,151r.
5.voluntary donations on Uraz-Bayram	12,782r.
6.voluntary donations on Qurban-Bayram	6,386r.
7.other revenues	10,087r.
8.revenues from no. of *imam-khatibs*	3,957r.
Total	126,701r.
(Reserve 1.1.73	34,685r.)

Expenses:

1.For maintenance of clergy [salaries]	9,860r.
2.For maintenance of service personnel	11,609r.

mosques was by now over 2.8 million rubles, most of it from voluntary contributions and less then one-quarter from the conduct of rites. Of this nearly 600,000 rubles went to the spiritual administrations, just under 500,000 to repairs and maintenance costs, 400,000 to the peace fund, 325,000 to salaries of clergy, 281,000 to the salaries of service personnel and 150,000 to payments to members of executive organs.[61]

Other data regarding the registered religious associations, even though they should not be taken too literally, also provide a certain interest. Thus, the documentation abounds in information regarding mosque attendance. Certainly, estimates of attendance in and around a major prayer-house on religious festivals, are inherently problematic, as large crowds are difficult to assess.[62] Unquestionably, too, numbers were often contrived, in order to prove this or that point.[63] The local government officials, for instance, who provided most of the information must often have been prone to underestimate so as not to invite trouble from the centre.[64] The *imam-khatib* and *mutawali* of a registered mosque in

---

3.For maintenance of executive organ	7,331r.
4.Transmitted to Peace Fund	28,500r.
5.Transmitted to preservation of historical monuments	15,500r.
6.Transmitted to SADUM	28,446r.
7.Transmitted to municpality financial department for rent	1,567r.
8.Acquisition of building materials and payment for repairs	14,392r.
9.Maintenance of premises (electricity, water, gas)	9,300r.
10.Domestic expenses	542r.
11.Other expenses (post, telegraph, assignments)	801r.
Total	127,848r.
(Reserve 1.1.74	33,538r.)

Shamnonov, *upolnomochennyi* for Andijan, to K. Ruzmetov and CRA, 3 Jan. 1974; GARF, f.6991, o.6, d.567, l.24.

61. CRA, Information, sent to the Central Committee, 27 April 1971; TsKhSD, f.5, o.63, d.89, l.101. Not all executive organ members were paid for their services; for further details on this institution, see pp. 279-85.

62. In a report on the numbers who gathered on Uraz-Bayram in 1951 at Osh's Takht-i Sulayman, the *upolnomochennyi* for Osh Oblast' said there were about 20,000, but some estimated that there were about 30,000 and others said just 12-15,000 – I. G. Halimov to CARC, 27 July 1951; GARF, f.6991, o.3, d.454, l.139.

63. For example, a paucity of worshippers might be used to indicate that the continued existence of a religious association was no longer justified and therefore should be formally considered as having disbanded.

64. For local government, see Chapter 11.

Bukhara issued a document stating that on Qurban-Bayram in 1961 just ninety worshippers had attended their mosque, whereas attendance had in fact been 850; they claimed they had been instructed by a local functionary to provide an underestimate.[65] A similar tendency probably characterised mosque executive organs when it came to festival attendance, for giving large figures might raise eyebrows and have unsalutary results.[66]

To take a case in point: in summer 1951 CARC prepared a detailed list for registered mosques throughout the Soviet Union.[67] The information provided included: locality and address; date and form of registration; date of construction and type of building; whether it was an historical monument; whether the building belonged to the state or municipality or was privately owned; the distance from the nearest mosque; some minimal data on the clergy; and, finally, the extent of attendance.

Unfortunately, data for attendance in this document are not homogeneous, that is, they do not fit under a single rubric, some *upolnomochennye* giving figures for Fridays only, others for ordinary weekdays and some just for festivals. What is instructive is that six of Uzbekistan's sixty-five mosques had regular Friday attendance of over 1,000 (four of them in Tashkent and the other two in Andijan and Samarkand) and a further ten had an attendance of 500 and over. In Kazakhstan, where mosques were much farther apart, several mosques had at least 2,500 on Fridays (in Alma-Ata, Akmolinsk, Jambul, Karaganda, Semipalatinsk, Chimkent and Turkestan) and another four had an attendance of at least 1,000. In Kirgiziia too there were six mosques with a Friday attendance of 1,000 and more and another seven which had an attendance

65. Sh. Shirinbaev, Information, sent to Deputy Head Uzbekistan CP Central Committee Department of Agitation and Propaganda K. G. Gulamov, 27 May 1961; TsGAUz, f.2456, o.1, d.290, l.107.

66. Thus, a mosque in Tashkent, which was unable to accommodate all worshippers within its precincts in the early 1950s and so held its festival prayer services in an open square, reckoned the number of worshippers who attended them to be approximately 1,000, whereas the local CARC *upolnomochennyi* gave the figure as 3,500 to 4,000 – Almaev, Memorandum, 12 July 1952; TsGAUz, f.2456, o.1, d.142, l.13.

67. Unfortunately, the lists which have been preserved do not include any of the mosques under the jurisdiction of DUMZ, many of those subordinated to DUMSK, or mosques in Tajikistan.

of over 1,000 on the two major festivals (for Uzbekistan and Kazakhstan figures for festival attendance were not provided).[68]

Another list with an identical title prepared by the republican *upolnomochennyi* for Uzbekistan, just a few months later provides far larger numbers. In all it appears that on festivals some 150,000 attended prayer-services in Uzbekistan's registered mosques in 1951.[69] Six years later the number of worshippers in Uzbekistan's mosques on Qurban-Bayram was said to have been 200,000, or, according to one report, as many as 315,000.[70]

Most of the mosques in the RSFSR had a much smaller attendance, some of them very small indeed, especially in rural areas. In 1949 rural mosques in the Tatar ASSR were said to have an approximate Friday attendance of 35-50.[71] A few, however, had a festival attendance in the early 1950s of over 2,000 (the two functioning mosques in Astrakhan' and in Ufa and the one in Orenburg) and one or two more of about 1,000 (in Novosibirsk and Omsk); while the sole Moscow mosque had an attendance

68. List of functioning registered mosques subordinate to the Spiritual Directorate of the Muslims of Central Asia and Kazakhstan (SADUM) as of 1 June 1951; GARF, f.6991, o.4, d.27, ll.67-88. (Turkmenistan's four mosques were reported as having 'on average' a very low attendance.)

69. Kh. N. Iskanderov, List of functioning registered mosques subordinate to SADUM, 15 Oct. 1951; TsGAUz, f.2456, o.1, d.137 (pages unnumbered). This list reported that the mosque in Andijan which the former list had said had an attendance of 1,000 on Fridays boasted 3,500-4,000 on Fridays, and two mosques in Namangan for which the former had given a Friday attendance of 200 and 500 respectively had 3,000-3,500 and 5,000-6,000 apiece, while the four registered mosques in Fergana Oblast' which had appeared in the first list as having on Fridays between 150 and 300 worshippers, were registered in that of Iskanderov as having: one Margelan mosque 3,500-4,000 on Fridays and 8,000 on festivals and the other 1,000 on Fridays and 1,500 on festivals; the one in Fergana 500-600 on Fridays and about 2,000 on festivals; and the mosque in Kokand 2,000-2,500 on Fridays and 5,000 on festivals. The second list also provided almost full data for festivals. It would appear that Iskanderov's figures persuaded CARC, which wrote up the list for Uzbekistan a second time, giving these as the correct ones – GARF, f.6991, o.4, d.27, ll.31-8.

70. K. F. Tagirov, Memo, 23 Aug. 1957, who gave the lower figure, and N. I. Inogamov, Address, All-Union conference of CARC *upolnomochennye*, 25-27 Nov. 1958; GARF, f.6991, o.4, d.73, ll.74-8, and o.3, d.165, ll.35-6.

71. N. Abushaev, Information, 17 Nov. 1949; GARF, f.6991, o.3, d.61, l.121. The weekday attendance was even less (see List of functioning registered mosques subordinate to DUMES as of 1 May 1951; GARF, f.6991, o.4, d.27, ll.1-29), notably in the Tatar ASSR and Ul'ianovsk Oblast'.

of 900–1,200 on Fridays and on festivals of 5,000–6,000 and the one in Kazan' was attended on festivals by about 4,000 worshippers.[72]

The very meagre attendance on ordinary weekdays made it impossible to gauge how many people actually observed the daily *salat*, or *namaz*, as it was called in the Soviet Union, one of the five pillars of Islam. It was generally assumed that most working people were unable to do so. Surveys conducted in a few areas in the second half of the 1960s and the early 1970s showed that among Tajikistan's rural, *dehqan*, population it was chiefly pensioners who prayed five times a day, but 30 percent of believers aged 40–60 prayed two or three times. Of some 2,500 believers questioned in the Karakalpak ASSR 60 per cent did not pray daily, 25 per cent prayed as prescribed and 12 per cent did so once or twice a day.[73]

Statistics of festival attendance by oblast' in the mid 1960s give the aggregate total number for registered and unregistered associations. Thus, 131,947 attended Uzbekistan's sixty-seven registered and eighty unregistered mosques on Uraz-Bayram in 1963,[74] considerably less than had come in the period prior to Khrushchev's anti-religious campaign;[75] 78,200 attended Kirgiziia's thirty-three registered and 295 unregistered mosques on the major festivals (Uraz-Bayram and Qurban-Bayram) in the same year, over half of them in Osh Oblast';[76] 34,700 worshippers came to Kazakhstan's twenty-five registered and eighty-six unregistered mosques; 25,000

72. List of functioning registered mosques subordinate to DUMES as of 1 May 1951; GARF, f.6991, o.4, d.27, ll.1–26. For the Kazan' mosque the figure of 600 was given for Friday prayers, and someone added by hand 1,000–1,500. It seems this was intended as a correction, not as signifying the attendance on festivals. Another similar list, as of 1 Jan. 1953 – GARF, f.6991, o.4, d.29, ll.1–24 –noted specifically that the larger numbers for Astrakhan' and Ufa were on festivals (the first list had simply spoken of 'approximate number of worshippers attending the mosque'). This document is the source, too, for the festival attendance in Moscow and Kazan'. Most of the data are basically the same in both lists.

73. *Islam v SSSR*, p.71. For a further discussion of mosque attendance, see pp. 218–25.

74. Information on factually functioning religious associations as of 1 Jan. 1964; GARF, f.6991, o.4, d.435, l.39.

75. Beginning apparently in 1959 the numbers showed a decline: 200,700 in 1959; 157,150 in 1960 (Sh. K. Shirinbaev, Address, All-Union conference of CARC *upolnomochennye*, 18–20 April 1960; GARF, f.6991, o.3, d.80), and so on.

76. 34,400 attended the oblast's 18 registered mosques alone – I. Shadiev, Information for 1960–63 inclusive, undated; GARF, f.6991, o.4, d.435, l.52.

to Moscow's one registered and one unregistered mosque;[77] 15,000 to the Bashkir ASSR's eighteen registered and eighty-seven unregistered ones; and 20,000 to the Tatar ASSR's nine registered and 496 unregistered ones.[78] In Derbent in the following year over 6,500 Shiites worshipped in the town's mosque during the ten major days of mourning (as against 11,000 who attended Dagestan's twenty-seven registered Sunni mosques on Uraz-Bayram and over 7,000 on Qurban-Bayram).[79]

The fall in mosque attendance in the early-mid 1960s was not, of course, peculiar to Uzbekistan. There tended to be a clear correlation between, on the one hand, mosque attendance and donations given by believers to the mosques and, on the other, regime policy, although it is impossible to know whether this was the direct result of an enhanced atheistic propaganda effort, as the authorities contended, or of actual pressures on the part of the local organs of government, or simply of a popular sense that for a while it might be advisable to refrain from attending mosque. From comparative statistics for the years of the Khrushchev antireligious campaign it actually appears that in certain areas at least festival attendance at registered mosques increased.[80] Perhaps this was because people felt safer celebrating there, despite the surveillance, than in unregistered groups, which were more exposed to coercion by the authorities and even retribution. All in all, in

77. By the end of the decade 40,000 worshippers were reported as gathering at the Moscow mosque on festivals – CRA report, 22 May 1970; TsKhSD, f.5, o.62, d.38, l.34.

78. Information on factually functioning religious associations as of 1 Jan. 1964; GARF, f.6991, o.4, d.431, ll.8,73,97; and d.435, ll.1, 47-8. All the evidence points to the fact that although there were much larger numbers of unregistered groups in some areas, the few registered mosques attracted the great majority of worshippers; thus we are informed that 6-7,000 attended the two mosques in Ufa just two years previously (and presumably the numbers did not change markedly over this short period) – GARF, f.6991, o.4, d.300, ll.7,9. In Kazakhstan in 1973 it was said specifically that about 24,000 worshippers attended the republic's 26 registered mosques and some 4,500 the 28 unregistered ones – GARF, f.6991, o.6, d.557, l.54. In some areas the numbers for unregistered groups were only partial, including only those accounted for by the relevant *upolnomochennyi*.

79. Minutes, CARC session No.24, 27 Aug. 1964; GARF, f.6991, o.4, d.147, l.80.

80. For example, in Osh Oblast' attendance grew steadily every year from 1960-63 for each of the two major festivals – I. Shadiev, Information for 1960-63 inclusive, undated; GARF, f.6991, o.4, d.435, l.52.

both the registered religious associations throughout the entire Soviet Union, 602,000 were reported to have participated in prayer-services on a single major festival in 1962.[81] And festival attendance in registered mosques remained at over half a million over the following years,[82] as against 150,000 on Fridays.[83] In the mid 1970s, however, the aggregate of worshippers in registered mosques throughout the country was given as over 300,000, about 130,000 of them people of working age.[84] This aggregate looks unreasonably low, provided, that the half-million figure is correct, given the sense of all the evidence from the field that the numbers of worshippers on the main festivals were on the increase. Nor has any testimony been found suggesting that the trend was downward. In years when festival fell on an ordinary weekday the number of people of working age grew notably.[85]

One aspect of festival celebration which was carefully chronicled was that of animals slaughtered as 'sacrifices' on Qurban-Bayram.[86] This was one of the issues where the statistics showed a marked decline over the years[87] except in the Northern Caucasus.[88] Yet

81. Statistical data on the activity of the church in the USSR on 1 Jan. 1963; GARF, f.6991, o.4, d.146, l.170. The numbers thought to have prayed in each of the two categories is not specified.

82. CRA report, 22 May 1970; TsKhSD, f.5, o.62, d.38, l.5.

83. A. Barmenkov, Theses of lecture, sent to the CPSU Central Committee, 19 June 1968; GARF, f.6991, o.6, d.147, l.11.

84. A. Barmenkov to CPSU Central Committee Department of Propaganda 13 March 1974; TsKhSD, f.5, o.67, d.115, l.3. Of the over 300,000, well over one third – 127,000 – were in Uzbekistan, where an additional 20,000 were recorded as having particpated in prayer-services conducted outside the registered mosques.

85. A. Barmenkov to the Central Committee Propaganda Dept., 17 June 1971; GARF, f.6991, o.6, d.361, l.38.

86. In 1949 in Bukhara Oblast' 650 animals were slaughtered, in Petropavlovsk, 380, in 23 settlements in the Bashkir ASSR approximately 850, in the rural raiony of Azerbaijan between 400 and 500 – N. Abushaev, Information, 17 Nov. 1949; GARF, f.6991, o.3, d.61, l.122. Polianskii added further figures and slightly augmented those of Abushaev in a report on Qurban-Bayram to Suslov and Voroshilov, 13 Dec. 1949; RTsKhIDNI, f.17, o.132, d.109, l.129.

87. See, for example, L. Prikhod'ko, Report, 31 Jan. 1953; GARF, f.6991, o.3, d.91, ll.22-3.

88. In the early 1960s meaningful numbers of livestock were still being slaughtered, for example, in Dagestan – M. S. Gajiev, Report, Minutes of CARC session No.1, 7 Jan. 1964; GARF, f.6991, o.4, d.146, l.15. A report on Qurban-Bayram in 1971 noted that although the prices of sheep and goats went up as the festival

still in 1974 it was reported that over 6,000 livestock were 56 slaughtered on Qurban-Bayram, and CRA chairman Vladimir Kuroedov noted that this figure did not present a full picture since it was based on hides given to registered mosques, which was not done by everyone who performed the ritual.[89] On the contrary, most of the sacrificial animal seem to have been slaughtered at cemeteries or in private homes by unregistered clergy, and the hides, and sometimes part of the meat, given to them.[90] Moreover, many people offered animals from the small personal stock they were allowed to retain, augmenting the difficulty of gauging numbers with any accuracy.[91]

Another factor CARC studied with interest was the participation in collective prayer of women and youth, which would be recorded separately from the figures for general attendance at prayer-services. Attendance of women in mosques on festivals was common in the urban mosques of the RSFSR and in Kazakhstan. At the very end of the 1940s Polianskii pointed out that in Akmolinsk (Kazakhstan) at least 1,000 of the approximately 2,500 who attended prayers on Qurban-Bayram were women, as were over 500 of the 3,300 in Ufa, and that they comprised about 10 per cent in one mosque in Andijan Oblast' and at least 15 per cent in Alma-Ata.[92] By 1950 in Moscow special prayer services were being organised for women on festivals, which in that year drew an

---

approached in the Ajar ASSR, Dagestan, the Karachai-Cherkess AO and some other regions, about 1,000 more livestock were slaughtered than in the previous year, reaching a total of 13,267 – A. Barmenkov to the Central Committee Propaganda Dept., 17 June 1971; GARF, f.6991, o.6, d.361, 1.37.

89. V. Kuroedov to the Central Committee Propaganda Dept., undated; GARF, f.6991, o.6, d.622, 1.40. Of the 6,000, about 2,600 had been slaughtered in Uzbekistan, about 500 in Kirgiziia and 600 in the Ajar ASSR. As early as 1953 it was noted that since most believers slaughtered the animals in their own courtyards rather than in those of the mosques, it was extremely difficult to estimate the number of livestock involved – I. V. Polianskii to G. M. Malenkov and N. S. Khrushchev, 2 Oct. 1953; GARF, f.6991, o.3, d.93, 1.244.

90. I. V. Polianskii to the CPSU Central Committee and the USSR Council of Ministers, 20 Sept. 1955, and L. Aisov to CARC, 6 Jan. 1965 – GARF, f.6991, o.3, d.114, 11.200-1, and d.1609, 1.13; and I. A. Shalaev to Kh. G. Gulamov, G. S. Sultanov and I. V. Polianskii, 11 Nov. 1955 – TsGAUz, f.2456, o.1, d.174, 11.92-3. For the ritual sacrifice of Qurban-Bayram, see pp.494-7.

91. I. V. Polianskii to M. A. Suslov, 27 Dec. 1951; GARF, f.6991, o.3, d.76, 1.186.

92. I. V. Polianskii to M. A. Suslov and K. E. Voroshilov, 13 Dec. 1949; RTsKhIDNI, f.17, o.132, d.109, 1.127.

attendance of 4,000 on Uraz-Bayram and 3,000 on Qurban-Bayram.[93] In 1958 Puzin noted that in Kazakhstan 40 per cent of all worshippers on the major festivals were women.[94] But this figure, too, was not undisputed: not long after the percentage was said to be exactly half that figure.[95] In Derbent, where most of the community were Shiites, women comprised about one half of the worshippers on Ashura in the mid 1950s.[96] For the most part, women did not participate in prayer-services in Central Asia proper, although on the major festivals they often gathered in the mosque courtyard or in the street outside as 'spectators'. Since it could safely be assumed that the number of women believers was not smaller than that of the men, this meant that, in the words of one *upolnomochennyi*, insofar as one used mosque attendance to estimate the dimensions of the believer population, the findings had simply to be doubled.[97]

Nor did the proportion of youth – usually defined as 'the 18 – 30 age-group – who participated in festival prayers fall over the years. In 1949 in Andijan at least 600 were youth between the ages of eighteen and twenty-five, as were at least 1,000 out of 4,300 in Chimkent. This group also comprised 20 per cent of worshippers in Alma-Ata, 12 per cent in Turkestan (Kazakhstan), 30 per cent in Kazan', 20-25 per cent in Petropavlovsk, 10 per cent in Moscow and 5 per cent in Ufa.[98] On Qurban-Bayram in 1954 young people were said to have comprised 25 – 30 per cent of all worshippers throughout the country.[99] In 1956 in Samarkand on the same festival young people under twenty-five constituted one-half of the 12,000 worshippers.[100] In two mosques in Dushanbe

93. A short report, undated; GARF, f.6991, o.3, d.81, l.90.

94. A. Puzin, Address, All-Union conference of CARC *upolnomochennye*, 25 Nov. 1958; GARF, f.6991, o.3, d.165, l.19ob.

95. Information, sent to A. I. Aleksandrov at the CPSU Central Committee, 14 Feb. 1962; GARF, f.6991, o.3, d.1389, l.11.

96. Khabilov to I. V. Polianskii, 4 June 1954; GARF, f.6991, o.3, d.102, l.127; see also n.168 below.

97. H. Akhtiamov, Short report, Conference of CARC's Central Asian *upolnomochennye*, 17 Dec. 1949; GARF, f.6991, o.3, d.67, l.101.

98. I. V. Polianskii to M. A. Suslov and K. E. Voroshilov, 13 Dec. 1949; RTsKhIDNI, f.17, o.132, d.109, l.127.

99. I. V. Polianskii to the CPSU Central Committee, 27 Sept. 1954; GARF, f.6991, o.3, d.102, l.300.

100. Gitlin, *Natsional'nye otnosheniia v Uzbekistane*, p.217.

in the early 1960s young people accounted respectively for 20 and 25 per cent of worshippers,[101] and for between 10 and 20 per cent in not a few areas in the mid 1970s.[102] The involvement of young people, moreover, was not restricted to presence in the mosque, other facets of the observance of the fast and the festivals sometimes attracting and including young people. For example, the *iftar*, the collective repast at the end of the day-long fast throughout the entire month of Ramadan, would be held in private homes and adolescents and even children would join in.[103] Allowing children under eighteen to attend mosque was deliberately flouting the law and so information on this score is sparse, although some does exist, as well as occasional figures for non-attendance at school on Muslim festivals.[104]

A further question of interest for the authorities was absenteeism on religious festivals, which was much more marked in rural than in urban areas: in some kolkhozy people either did not go to work at all or arrived late.[105] On the whole, the figures regarding these

101. A. A. Puzin to the CPSU Central Committee Department for Propaganda and Agitation, 7 June 1961; GARF, f.6991, o.3, d.1363, l.96.

102. They comprised 18.2 per cent of worshippers on Qurban-Bayram in January 1974 in Dagestan, 11 percent in Kirgiziia, 14.7 per cent in Uzbekistan – V. Kuroedov to the Central Committee Propaganda Dept., undated; GARF, f.6991, o.6, d.622, l.38. For mosque attendance of women and youth, see pp. 223-5.

103. In the town of Samarkand in 1972, 300 children and adolescents were reported to have taken part in such *iftars*, and in the following year throughout Samarkand Oblast' about 400 people aged 20-30 took part in *iftars* conducted by clergy of the registered mosques – A. Barmenkov to Komsomol Central Committee Secretary L. I. Matveev, 15 Jan. 1974, and to the Central Committee Propaganda Dept., 13 March 1974; GARF, f.6991, o.6, d.622, ll.7 and 10. For these occasions, see pp. 483-5.

104. In 1951 in one secondary school in Frunze on Qurban-Bayram just half the students attended and approximately the same number in a rural school also in Kirigziia, whereas 30 children failed to attend school in Petropavlovsk and 35 in Osh – I. V. Polianskii to M. A. Suslov, 27 Dec. 1951; GARF, f.6991, o.3, d.76, l.185. In the early-mid 1970s a particularly large number of children were reported to have attended festival services in Andijan Oblast' and in Tashkent – A. Barmenkov to CPSU Central Committee Department of Propaganda, 13 March 1974; GARF, f.6991, o.6, d.622, l.12. For absenteeism in schools on festivals, see pp.493-4 and 501.

105. I. V. Polianskii to G. M. Malenkov and N. S. Khrushchev, 2 Oct. 1953; GARF, f.6991, o.3, d.93, l.245. For violations of work discipline in connection with the festivals, see pp.434 and 448.

violations of work discipline showed a decrease as time went by.[106]

CARC followed closely the observance not just of the two main festivals but also of the month-long fast, the *uraz*. Sometimes its *upolnomochennye* reported actual figures of those who fasted. These seem to refer to members of registered religious associations, as was indeed stated specifically in one report,[107] there being no way to obtain such data for other groups. At the same time, a few accounts from individual kolkhozy told of workers fasting and consequently unable to keep up their normal production level.[108]

It was reported repeatedly that in many areas only the elderly fasted. Nevertheless, in some rural regions in the late 1940s observance of the fast was almost total.[109] And in the early 1950s, 70-75 per cent of the adult population were reported to have fasted in the rural areas of Dagestan and 75-80 per cent in those of the Kabardinian ASSR.[110] A few years later we hear that in some villages in the Tatar ASSR, as well as in villages in Kazakhstan with Dungan, Karachai, Ingush and sometimes Uzbek populations 50-60 per cent of the entire adult population fasted, including students and some members of the local soviet apparatus.[111] The

106. For example, K. F. Tagirov, Information, 23 Aug. 1957; GARF, f.6991, o.3, d.73, l.72.

107. One report noted that in five registered mosques in Bukhara Oblast' about 800 observed the fast, in Chimkent at least 3,400, in Turkestan 3,000, in the Bashkir ASSR's 23 mosques over 4,500, in Chistopol' at least 700, in Novosibirsk −500, in the Moscow community about 4,000 and in nine Tatar settlements in the Mordvinian ASSR with a total adult population of 1,250, 726 people fasted – Annual report of CARC activity for 1950, ratified at CARC session No.13, 26 June 1951; GARF, f.6991, o.3, d.74, ll.149-50.

108. See, for example, L. A. Prikhod'ko and N. I. Abushaev, Short survey, draft, 16 March 1950; GARF, f.6991, o.3, d.63, l.88. For the effect of the fast on the work force, see pp.480-3.

109. For example, N. I. Abushaev, Information, 17 Nov. 1949; GARF, f.6991, o.3, d.61, l.122.

110. L. A. Prikhod'ko, A short report, 4 April 1952; one CARC official at least, N. V. Kol'tsov, did not believe that so many people observed the *uraz* in these two autonomous republics or that the figures were authentic – Minutes, CARC session No. 10, 11-12 April 1952; GARF, f.6991, o.3, d.81, ll.85-6, and d.83, l.163.

111. I. V. Polianskii to G. M. Malenkov (with a copy to P. N. Pospelov at the CPSU Central Committee), 8 Aug. 1953; GARF, f.6991, o.3, d.93, l.182. The Karachai and Ingush were among the peoples deported to Central Asia

Ajar ASSR in the early 1970s boasted some 45,000 who observed the fast, most of them women and 8,000 of them young people, in all approximately 30 per cent of the adult population.[112] In Tajikistan it was assumed in the early 1980s (on the basis of 'observation, conversations and questioning') that 15 per cent of the local nationalities' urban, and 25-30 per cent of their rural, population observed the fast in its entirety.[113]

During the fast, too, mosque attendance mounted; tables comparing Friday attendance prior to the beginning of the *uraz* and during that month invariably showed an increase, sometimes a very meaningful one. The special evening-prayer held during the fast, the *tarawa-namaz*, when the Qur'an would be read, also drew considerable numbers.[114] The *iftar* was likewise very popular, especially in certain parts: in 1973, 2,000 *iftars* were held in Tashkent Oblast' alone and 2,500 were held under the auspices of Osh Oblast's eighteen registered associations.[115]

Statistical information on the conduct of religious life-cycle rites, or rites of passage as they are sometimes known, and of other rites performed at the request of individual believers, covers just a small fraction of all such rites. In the first place, they relate *a priori* only to rites performed by registered clergy. Consequently, no rites at all were recorded for the Chechen-Ingush ASSR subsequent to the return of the Chechen and Ingush from their places of exile, for it had no registered mosques. However, the *upolnomochennyi* in this republic reported that from his personal observations about 90 per cent of Muslims who married did so

and Kazakhstan in 1943-4. The Dungans had come from China to what later became Kazakhstan and Kirgiziia after the anti-Manchu Muslim rising of 1862-77.

112. A. Barmenkov to the CPSU Central Committee Propaganda Department, 13 March 1973 and 13 March 1974; GARF, f.6991, o.6, d.537, l.15, and TsKhSD, f.5, o.67, d.115, l.3.

113. *Islam v SSSR*, p.72. In one oblast' of the republic, for instance, that of Kurgan-Tyube, research showed that 29 per cent of the men and 33 per cent of the women fasted – *ibid.*, p.78. (It is not clear whether or not this is the statistic upon which the figure for the entire republic is based.) For further statistical data concerning the fast, pp.476-9.

114. In 1950-52 in the Kabardinian ASSR usual Friday attendance was 200, 160 and 145, during *uraz* – 850, 690 and 620; in Dagestan 135, 110 and 110 on regular Fridays and during *uraz* 1,520, 2,110 and 2,190 – L. Prikhod'ko, Report, 31 Jan. 1953; GARF, f.6991, o.3, d.91, l.14. See also pp. 222 and 472-3.

115. A. Barmenkov to the Central Committee Propaganda Department, 13 March 1974; GARF, f.6991, o.6, d.622, ll.9-10.

according to Muslim ritual, 99 per cent of the dead were given religious funerals, and 98 per cent circumcised their sons.[116]

Secondly, in some areas, for example in Dagestan, still in the 1970s the registered mosques did not record rites at all.[117] Finally, those mosques which did keep records may well have done so only partially, for the clergy had a clear interest in concealing some rites so as not to declare their entire income for tax purposes.

Yet even these data, for all their lacunae, are informative. Thus, one cannot but note the high proportion of religious burial services, although it is not clear whether this was because more people in fact buried their dead according to religious custom than, for instance, performed religious marriages or circumcised their sons, or because more people turned to the registered clergy for this specific rite, or because the latter were least afraid to report conducting burial services. Whatever the reason, the percentage of religious services conducted in connection with life-cycle rites registered in the official registration bureau (ZAGS) in 1963 indicates that for burials these were 90-95 per cent in the Kabardino-Balkar ASSR, and that while in the city of Semipalatinsk they accounted for just 42.5 per cent, there were twice that figure in Semipalatinsk Oblast's smaller towns.[118] In Ul'ianovsk Oblast' in the same year percentages were 23.8 for name-giving, 24 for marriages and 45 for burial services.[119] In the eighteen registered mosques of Osh Oblast' for which there are relatively full data for 1963: 17,547 believers paid the *fitr*, while there were 626 religious burials, 561 religious marriages, 3,092 circumcisions and, rather peculiarly, exactly the same number of *khatm-i Qur'ans*.[120] In 1959 over 90 per

---

116. A. Asaulka, statistical report, 14 Jan.1967; GARF, f.6991, o.6, d.21, l.91.

117. See p.647.

118. Information, undated; GARF, f.6991, o.4, d.431, l.27, d.435, l.3. The only two registered mosques in the entire oblast' outside Semipalatinsk were in Aiaguz, where the percentage was 83.3 and Zhana-Semei where it was 93.4. In Alma-Ata it was just 3.4 – *ibid.*, l.4. It is not quite clear how the percentages were worked out, for, as the *upolnomochennyi* for Uzbekistan pointed out, the ZAGS forms not including data by religion, it was impossible to establish percentages – Sh. Shirinbaev, Information, undated; GARF, f.6991, o.4, d.435, l.39. Conceivably, the percentage is of all burials conducted for citizens belonging to traditionally Muslim ethnic groups.

119. GARF, f.6991, o.4, d.431, l.107. These were relatively high figures for the RSFSR. For name-giving, see p.529.

120. I. Shadiev, Information, undated; GARF, f.6991, o.4, d.435, l.50.

cent of the marriages performed in Tashkent were conducted in accordance with religious practice.[121]

In the latter half of the 1960s the statistics for the conduct of religious rites show a marked rise. This was explained, on the one hand, by more and better recording of rites performed by registered clergy and/or in the registered mosques and, on the other, by 'the greater democratisation of public life and existing opportunities for the free satisfaction of religious requirements.'[122] The burial figures continued to top the list. They ran into the hundreds for most oblasti in Kazakhstan[123] and exceeded 1,000 and in some cases 2,000 in some oblasti of Uzbekistan.[124] And they continued to rise into the 1970s by which time nearly all reported rites increased annually, burials still taking pride of place.[125] By 1973 all figures were ostensibly higher than in the late 1960s. They included by this time a fair number of circumcisions,[126] a rite for which, on the whole, data were rare and especially

121. A. A. Puzin to the CPSU Central Committee Department for Propaganda and Agitation, 7 June 1961; GARF, f.6991, o.3, d.1363, l.96.

122. CRA information, sent to the CPSU Central Committee, 22 May 1970; TsKhSD, f.5, o.62, d.38, l.5.

123. In 1966 there were 350 religious burials in Aktiubinsk Oblast', 22 in Alma-Ata, 368 in Gur'ev, 171 in Jambul, 174 in Karaganda, 519 in Kokchetau, 437 in Semipalatinsk, 6,161 in Chimkent; in none except Chimkent did the number of religious marriages exceed 100 – GARF, f.6991, o.6, d.28.

124. In Andijan Oblast' 2,500 religious burials were recorded in 1966, 2,002 in Tashkent Oblast' and 1,053 in Fergana Oblast'; in all three oblasti the number of recorded religious marriages was about one half of the number of burials –GARF, f.6991, o.6, d.29.

125. Burial rites increased from 22,730 in 1966 to 30,346 in 1970; marriage rites from 9,367 to 14,277 in the same period. By 1970, 6,004 circumcisions and 1,883 name-givings were also reported, as were 42,650 other – basically non-life-cycle rites – CRA information, sent to the CPSU Central Committee, 22 May 1970, and CRA information, sent to the Central Committee, 27 April 1971; TsKhSD, f.5, o.62, d.38, l.5, and o.63, d.89, ll.102-3.

126. In 1973 there were 2,474 religious burials in Kirgiziia, 1,913 religious marriages, 1,359 circumcisions and 2,129 Qur'an readings (*khatm-i Qur'ans*); in Kazakhstan 6,475 burials, 545 marriages and 3,929 other (unspecified) rites; in Uzbekistan 15,552 burials, 8,156 marriages, 4,482 circumcisions, 3,825 Qur'an readings, 926 *khuda'is*, 700 *iftars* and 21,050 other rites; in the city of Tashkent alone there were 2,791 burials, 2,243 marriages and 1,133 circumcisions – GARF, f.6991, o.6, d.557, ll.55,60,122,132. For a breakdown by oblast', see d.566 for Kazakhstan and d.567 for Uzbekistan.

uneven.[127] In parts of Azerbaijan at least, where clergy did not participate in circumcisions, none were reported.[128]

The data for the performance of circumcision are, however, only one aspect of the picture. They have to be supplemented by information on the percentage of the population who were actually circumcised. In the mid 1960s a check-up in two schools in Turkmenistan revealed that in each of them just one boy was not circumcised.[129] Towards the end of the decade, over 80 per cent in the rural areas of three of Uzbekistan's oblasti said they were circumcised.[130] In the early-mid 1970s the *upolnomochennyi* for Chimkent Oblast' was reporting that for those raiony for which he had data, 90 per cent of the indigenous population were circumcised.[131]

In addition to life-cycle rites and those connected with the *uraz* or Uraz-Bayram and Qurban-Bayram, at least two further rites were common in the Soviet Muslim community: the *mavlud* and the *khatm-i Qur'an*. Although often linked with rites of passage, they also stand in their own right. The *mavlud* is, in the first place, the festival of the birthday of Muhammad, but came also to refer to a recitation of traditional poetry in praise of the Prophet originally performed on the festival but in contemporary Islam often part of the ceremonial connected with rites of passage or other semi-religious occasions. The *khatm-i Qur'an* is, strictly speaking, the reading of the Qur'an from beginning to end, but the term came to be used for partial recitations as well. Apart from the first ten days of the *uraz* when the Qur'an would be recited in its entirety at the *tarawa-namaz*,[132] *khatm-i Qur'ans* would not in the Soviet Union be conducted in the mosque, but clergy

127. For example, in 1951 11,311 circumcisions were reported in Uzbekistan, as against 2,095 the previous year – Information, sent by V. Stepanov and V. Klochko to M. A. Suslov, 4 July 1952; RTsKhIDNI, f.17, o.132, d.497, l.54.

128. A. Galiev, Information, 30 May 1973; GARF, f.6991, o.6, d.537, l.188.

129. P. A. Solov'ev, undated, material prepared for CARC session No.10, 12 May 1964; GARF, f.6991, o.4, d.146, l.211. In one school the count was 74 boys out of 75, in the other 148 out of 149.

130. CRA information, sent to the CPSU Central Committee, 22 May 1970; TsKhSD, f.5, o.62, d.38, l.30.

131. Sh. Ospanov, Information for the Chimkent Obkom and Oblispolkom, 16 Nov. 1973; GARF, f.6991, o.6, d.633, ll.91-4.

132. That is, the recitations would be divided up over the ten days until the entire Qur'an was completed.

would be invited to private homes to conduct such readings. The *mavlud*, on the other hand, would be performed both in the mosque and in believers' homes and would be accompanied by collective feasting, becoming something of a social occasion. Reporting on the first quarter of 1950, for example, the *upolnomochennyi* for Osh Oblast' recorded that the fourteen registered religious societies under his jurisdiction all performed *mavluds* in their mosques, and all were well attended.[133] Furthermore, the clergy of eleven of these societies performed between them 241 *mavluds* and *khatm-i Qur'ans* in private homes,[134] with an attendance of from fifteen to fifty people at each one. The numbers performed in private homes were even larger in raiony without a registered mosque; just in one raion, for which he had data, there had been no less than 287.[135]

If the data for rite performance were very partial, the statistics regarding unregistered prayer-houses and clergy seem to have been totally arbitrary, although all sources concur that both were far more numerous than their registered counterparts, which – given the scarcity of the latter – is hardly surprising. The data in the documentation were arrived at by a variety of means, often completely random ones. The more reliable *upolnomochennye* reported simply that they had toured so-and-so many raiony in the area under their jurisdiction and that the numbers given reflected their findings in these raiony. In Kazakhstan in 1966, for instance, there were said to be ninety-four unregistered groups and twenty-five registered associations. But the former were all in eight of the republic's fifteen oblasti;[136] and just as there were no data at all for the remaining seven, so there were probably raiony in the first eight which had also not been covered for the purpose of gathering this information. Other *upolnomochennye* extrapolated at random or relied on hearsay from incidental sources.

The usual formula used in the *upolnomochennye's* reports was

133. Attendance ranged from 200 in one of the kishlaks which had a registered mosque to 3,000 in Osh's Ravat Abdulla-Khan mosque.

134. The *upolnomochennyi* believed the numbers the clergy gave to be an understatement, as they were interested in concealing part of their resultant income.

135. I. Halimov to CARC, 3 April 1950; GARF, f.6991, o.3, d.454, ll.55-7.

136. GARF, f.6991, o.6, d.28, *passim.* Similarly, the figures for Azerbaijan's unregistered clergy in 1969 covered three of its eight towns and 47 of 80 raiony –CRA information, 22 May 1970; TsKhSD, f.5, o.62, d.38, l.8.

that these were mosques or clergy which had been 'discovered' or 'exposed'. In some periods and places the local authorities were reasonably cooperative and would provide such information as they themselves might have. As a rule their own information was probably partial and poor, for both objective and subjective reasons. They tended whenever possible to turn a blind eye to religious activity, which might place a smear on their reputation with their superiors, and had a general inclination not to transmit such information as they did have to the *upolnomochennye*, who would be passing it on to the *oblispolkom* and *obkom* or the republican party central committee and council of ministers. The *upolnomochennye* themselves sought to show that they had been effective both in exposing and later in bringing about the closure of unregistered groups and would be reluctant to admit that a group they had dispersed had reappeared.[137] Nonetheless, since again these are the only available detailed statistics, they will be used, on the understanding that the numbers they provide constitute a considerable understatement. One 'historical-ethnographic' study claimed that over a period of thirty years the expedition which had conducted it had found more than 200 functioning mosques just in northern Tajikistan and a further 200 in other parts of Central Asia. Its author stated that each kishlak had at least one mosque, and some of the larger ones boasted one for each *mahalla*. In his view there were no fewer mosques in Tajikistan in the 1980s than there had been prior to Soviet rule, and in some places, because of the growth of population, even more.[138]

In 1947 there were said to be 843 unregistered Muslim prayer-

137. For example, a document entitled Information on the number of functioning unregistered groups of believers in the USSR on 1 Jan. 1952 (by faiths), prepared by the head of CARC's group of instructors, G. F. Frolov, sought to show the dynamic of the unregistered groups in the past year. It provided four columns: Taken stock of on 1 Jan. 1951; Ceased organised activity during 1951; Newly exposed groups in 1951; Included in reckoning on 1 Jan. 1952; GARF, f.6991, o.3, d.85, l.77. From the reports of the *upolnomochennye* it is evident that there were cases of groups which would be included both in columns 2 and 3. The figures for Muslim groups were: 313; 280; 403; 436. In 1949 the republican *upolnomochennyi* in Kirgiziia pointed out to the *upolnomochennyi* for Osh Oblast' in connection with his report that 93 unregistered communities had been disbanded, that he must pay constant attention that mosques which he reported as being closed were not re-opening, as had happpened in one raion – H. Akhtiamov to I. Halimov, 13 April 1949; GARF, f.6991, o.3, d.454, l.16.
138. Poliakov, *Everyday Islam*, p.96.

houses in the Soviet Union (as against 385 registered ones),[139] in 1951, 830 (as against 370), in 1957, 'over 1,000' (as against 398),[140] and in 1970, 645 (as against 315).[141] Certainly, the disproportion between the two categories was not constant. In periods and localities where religiosity was high and surveillance weak it might reach extreme dimensions. For instance, in Andijan Oblast' in the Fergana Valley, there were in the latter half of 1946 just seven registered mosques, whereas the *upolnomochennyi* knew of the existence of 183 illegal ones.[142] (Throughout most of the period under discussion an unregistered prayer-house was considered illegal.[143]) In the mid 1960s no less than 496 unregistered communities were reported to be operating in the Tatar ASSR and 295 in Kirgiziia (as against eleven and thirty-three registered ones respectively).[144] The majority of these unregistered religious groups were reported as functioning periodically or only on the major festivals.[145]

139. I. V. Polianskii to A. A. Zhdanov and K. E. Voroshilov, 22 July 1947; RtsKhIDNI, f.17, o.125, d.506, l.169. This number related to 1 April 1947, since which time Polianskii reported that 172 such mosques had been shut down in Uzbekistan; viz. his letter to G. F. Aleksandrov of 1 July 1947, where he reported 671 unregistered mosques. Earlier in the year G. Ia. Vrachev, head of CARC's inspectorial group at the time, said that 800 mosques were known to have opened without authorisation in Central Asia alone, and this was only a partial figure – Minutes, CARC session, No.4, 29 Jan. 1947; GARF. f.6991, o.4, d.19, l.81.

140. A. Puzin to V. P. Moskovskii, 14 Nov. 1957; GARF, f.6991, o.3, d.147, l.206.

141. See p.303.

142. N. I. Uzkov and G. Ia. Vrachev to Polianskii, 29 Nov. 1946; RTsKhIDNI, f.17, o.125, d.405, l.93. The *upolnomochennyi* had been informed by one *raiispolkom* that there were 29 unregistered mosques in the raion, but upon visiting it had found 79 – Polianskii to Zhdanov and Voroshilov, 22 July 1947; RTsKhIDNI, f.17, o.125, d.506, l.169.

143. There was, however, no absolute consensus on this score, see p.29.

144. Information on factually functioning religious associations as of 1 Jan. 1964, GARF, f.6991, o.4, d.431, l.97 and d.435, l.47. On this date in the entire country there were said to be 1,649 unregistered Muslim religious associations –Statistical data; GARF, f.6991, o.4, d.146, l.170. The assumption must be that the *upolnomochennye* for the Kirgiz SSR and the Tatar ASSR were more conscientious than their colleagues elsewhere in collating information and reporting to Moscow, rather than that there were major discrepancies in the actual existence of unregistered religious groups.

145. Not all data on these unregistered groups include a breakdown into the nature and extent of their activity, but some do specify 'functioning regularly, functioning periodically, only on major festivals,' e.g. Information on factually

This was not the case only in union or autonomous republics whose eponymous nationality was a Muslim one. Most areas in the RSFSR with significant Muslim populations also had more unregistered than registered associations: in 1966 in Stavropol' Krai, where Muslims were concentrated primarily, if not wholly, in the Karachai–Cherkess AO, there were fifty as against fifteen registered associations; in Gor'kii Oblast' thirteen as against four, in Kuibyshev Oblast' nineteen against thirteen, in Orenburg Oblast' twenty-six against four, and in Ul'ianovsk Oblast' twenty-one against five.[146] These numbers had fallen significantly by the early-mid 1970s.[147] The overwhelming majority of unregistered groups do not seem to have had prayer-houses, at least in the RSFSR's autonomous republics.[148] Of the 645 groups known to be functioning throughout the country in 1970, the CRA said that 127 operated regularly, had their own prayer premises and were 'in no way distinguishable' from registered associations.[149]

Very often the size of unregistered groups or associations was significantly smaller than that of registered ones,[150] although we have seen that some of the latter, especially in rural areas, could be very modest. Yet, there were unregistered prayer-meetings which were well attended. In at least one case, that of Leningrad, where the religious association struggled for a decade to obtain the right to recover the city's mosque, thousands came to the Tatar cemetery on the two major festivals to pray collectively.[151]

---

functioning religious associations (apart from sectarians) as of 1 Jan. 1965; GARF, f.6991, o.4, d.436, l.2, according to which only 23 of 429 such groups taken count of in the RSFSR functioned regularly.

146. GARF, f.6991, o.6, d.23, l.32, d.24, ll.60 and 126, d.25, ll.47 and 155.

147. See GARF, f.6991, o.6, d.557 and 558 (statistical reports for 1973).

148. Only one of the Bashkir ASSR's 74 unregistered groups had its own prayer-house in 1970 and none of the Tatar ASSR's 42, although all the latter and 25 of the former were said to function regularly – GARF, f.6991, o.6, d.302, ll.13 and 100.

149. CRA report, sent to the Central Committee, 27 April 1971; TsKhSD, f.5, o.63, d.89, l.97.

150. The 80 unregistered groups of which stock was taken in the late 1960s in the Bashkir ASSR had an aggregate membership of 3,000 believers – CRA report, 22 May 1970; TsKhSD, f.5, o.62, d.38, l.9. See also Chapter 5, n.7.

151. In 1953, for example, every Friday 300-400 people of all ages came to the cemetery to pray whatever the weather, and on Qurban-Bayram 7-8,000 came from all over the city, chanting the *takbir* on the way – V. I. Gostev to P. A. Tarasov, 4 Jan. 1954, also I. V. Polianskii to the CPSU Central Committee

In Samarkand Oblast' all ten unregistered religious societies, whose existence the *upolnomochennyi* reported at the end of the 1960s, had an attendance on festivals of between 200 and 700.[152]

The number of unregistered Muslim clergy was even higher than that of the unregistered religious associations. But again the figures provided varied tremendously and seem to have been influenced by incidental considerations and information. It may well be that one of the factors here was the policy of the powers-that-be regarding unregistered clergy and the energy with which their exposure was pursued. Theoretically, of course, they were constantly to be hunted out, but in practice the local officials, whose task it was to fulfil this function, often failed to act upon instructions.[153] The definition of unregistered clergy also varied from time to time: did it, for instance, include all the elders who performed rites for individuals in practically every aul or kishlak[154] but had no religious training and were not officially clergy by any criterion?[155] In the words of one official: 'It does not seem possible to make any accurate count of the number of unregistered mullas, for by Islam's very nature every believer who is able to read the prayers and is acquainted with the rules and procedure of conducting prayer-services and performing rites, can lead a prayer-meeting and conduct religious rites.'[156]

Be this as it may, there can be little doubt that throughout

---

and the USSR Council of Ministers, 20 Sept. 1955; GARF, f.6991, o.3, d.102, l.22, and d.114, ll.204-6.

152. T. Tashkenbaev, List of unregistered religious societies as of 1 Jan. 1970; GARF, f.6991, o.6, d.240, l.32. It is worth noting that none of these was closer than 25 km to, and some were as far as 120 km from, the nearest registered society and only two were in the same raion, so that they were also rather far from each other. The one with 600-700 was the sole urban society (in Katta-Kurgan), none of the others having more than 400 worshippers.

153. For the discrepancy between official policy and its implementation in the field, see pp.591-2 and Chapter 11 *passim.*

154. The rural settlement in which the indigenous population lived went by different names: in Uzbekistan and Tajikistan it was a kishlak, in Kazakhstan and the Northern Caucasus an aul.

155. The *upolnomochennyi* for Bukhara Oblast', for instance, noted in his report for the first half of 1954 that there were 250 kolkhozy in his oblast', each of which had at least one, and some two or three, mullas; he had taken stock of 300 in all – G. F. Frolov to I. V. Polianskii, 25 Feb. 1955; GARF, f.6991, o.3, d.112, l.8. For the characteristics of these unregistered clergy, see pp.325-30.

156. L. A. Prikhod'ko, Report, 2 June 1952; GARF, f.6991, o.3, d.81, l.134.

the period under discussion the number of unregistered clergy far outweighed that of the registered clergy. At the very end of the 1940s there were said to be about 3,500 in Tajikistan alone.[157] In the early 1950s CARC's *upolnomochennye* reported having exposed 800 of the former in Uzbekistan, 524 in Kirgiziia, 440 in Kazakhstan and 280 in Turkmenistan.[158] As of early 1965 in the country as a whole there were claimed to be 2,346 unregistered, as against 395 registered, clergy,[159] in 1971, 1,700 against 543,[160] and in 1983 over 10,000.[161] In some periods and areas, the figures for unregistered clergy seem to have corresponded exactly, or almost exactly, with those for unregistered religious groups, except in the Chechen-Ingush ASSR, where in 1970, for example, there were reported to be twelve of the latter and 150 of the former.[162] This did not necessarily signify that the real numbers coincided, but that these were the clergy who were exposed. In some places the data specifically computed people who were not clergy, but who performed and received income from the performance of religious rites.[163] Although by 1973 the number of unregistered

157. K. Hamidov, Report, Conference of CARC *upolnomochennye*, 17 Dec. 1949; GARF, f.6991, o.3, d.67, ll.53-4. It is not clear on what information this statement was based. In any event, a few years later CARC sources spoke of 700 unregistered mullas in that republic, many of whom operated at its numerous *mazars* – G. F. Frolov to I. V. Polianskii, 25 Feb. 1955; GARF, f.6991, o.3, d.112, l.8.

158. L. A. Prikhod'ko, Report, 2 June 1952; GARF, f.6991, o.3, d.81, l.134. One year later in Kazakhstan 515 unregistered clergy were taken count of – as against the 20 registered ones – and these were 'far from complete. figures'- L. A. Prikhod'ko, Report, 20 May 1953; GARF, f.6991, o.3, d.91, l.258.

159. Information as of 1 Jan. 1965; GARF, f.6991, o.4, d.436, l.1.

160. CRA information, sent to the Central Committee, 27 April 1971; TsKhSD, f.5, o.63, d.89, l.98.

161. CRA, Memo, 2 June 1983; TsKhSD, f.5, o.89, d.82, l.37. Another report said that in 1984 there were 3,114 unregistered Muslim clerics (against approximately 1,540 registered ones) – Corley, *Religion in the Soviet Union*, pp. 298-9. The source of this major discrepancy is not clear; perhaps the larger figure includes all those who performed rites and the smaller one those attached to religious groups.

162. Thus in the same year, 1970, 74 groups and the same number of clergy were accounted for in the Bashkir ASSR and 42 of each in the Tatar ASSR –GARF, f.6991, o.6, d.302, ll.13, 100 and 111.

163. The data for 1970, which are clearly partial, give 20 such people in the Ajar ASSR, 100 in the Bashkir ASSR, 60 in the Karakalpak ASSR and 18 in the Mordvinian ASSR – GARF, f.6991, o.6, d.302, ll.8, 13, 50 and 79. Throughout

groups had fallen, that of unregistered clergy had not: it was claimed that there were 664 of these in Azerbaijan, 533 in Kazakhstan, 229 in Kirgiziia, 251 in Turkmenistan, 564 in Uzbekistan and 150 in the Kabardino-Balkar ASSR.[164]

Again, it is impossible to tell whether the increase in unregistered clergy reflected an actual trend or whether it was the result of more precise and conscientious reporting.[165] (The two are not, of course, mutually exclusive, so that both may be true.) Even in the mid 1970s, after three decades of CARC and CRA activity and interaction between Moscow and the *upolnomochennye* in the republics and oblasti, one cannot help seeing the influence of subjective factors in the information which reached the centre. Thus, the numbers of unregistered clergy recorded in 1974 in Uzbekistan's oblasti of Fergana, Samarkand and Bukhara were 160, 159 and 120 respectively, while none at all were said to exist in Andijan and Khorezm, and just four in the Karakalpak ASSR and five in Namangan.[166]

In addition to mainstream Sunni Hanafi groups and clergy, there were also Muslims who belonged to other trends, schools and sects. Twelver Shiite associations existed in Azerbaijan, where some of them were registered,[167] in Turkmenistan, Dagestan and

---

the country this category was said to number 1,140 – CRA report, sent to the Central Committee, 27 April 1971; TsKhSD, f.5, o.63, d.89, l.99.

164. GARF, f.6991, o.6, d.557, ll.4, 54, 59, 114 and 131, and d.558, l.33. For a breakdown by oblasti, see *ibid.*, d.566 for Kazakhstan and d.567 for Uzbekistan. From time to time, however, these numbers, too, fell. For instance, in Kirgiziia the figure went down from 525 in early 1968 to 311 in mid 1969, partly because the earlier one included people who occasionally performed a burial rite and some who had been mistakenly counted twice, and partly because, as a result of taxes, fines, conversations with and warnings by the CRA *upolnomochennye*, local officials and the commissions of assistance, some ceased conducting prayers and other rites – K. Shabolotov to A. A. Nurullaev, 23 June 1969; GARF, f.6991, o.6, d.220, ll.150-1.

165. The *upolnomochennyi* for Bukhara Oblast', for instance, wrote in early 1974 that his report for 1972 made just a year previously had spoken of 80 unregistered clergy ('clerical people who in fact perform religious rites among the population, although many of them had not been ordained and are not clerics'), but in the past year they had been counted with greater accuracy and 120 had been discovered –S. Shamsutdinov to V. Kuroedov, 2 Jan. 1974; GARF, f.6991, o.6, d.567, ll.9-10.

166. Statistical report for 1974; GARF, f.6991, o.6, d.664, ll.8, 15, 36, 43, 65 and 72, and d.654, l.46.

167. Of 17 Muslim registered associations in Azerbaijan at the end of the 1960s,

Bukhara. These included two ethnic minorities, Kurds, who lived mostly in Azerbaijan and Turkmenistan, and Persians, who inhabited both these republics, as well as having a community in Bukhara, where they were known as Ironis. In Azerbaijan on Ashura, over 100,000 attended the registered Shiite mosques in the early 1970s.[168] The Chechen and Ingush basically pertained to Sufi groups, of which there were said to be more than 300 in that republic with a membership of over 15,000 at the end of the 1960s and more than 500 mullas, *tamadas* and *turkkhs*.[169] In Tajikistan's Gorno-Badakhshan AO much of the population belonged to the Shiite Ismaili sect and after considerable deliberation it was decided to register one *khalifa* (the Ismaili equivalent of a cleric) for each *sel'sovet*.[170]

Three further sets of figures seem to be relevant to our assessment of the dimensions of Islam. The first is of former mosques which remained in the various Muslim areas. All the evidence indicates, that the very existence of the building of a former mosque in a town or village stimulated concern for its recovery as a mosque. This was especially true for those edifices which were not in use as cultural or economic institutions of one sort or another and so both retained their original exterior[171] and were considered more easily available.

---

10 were Shiite and five mixed Sunni-cum-Shiite – CRA report, 22 May 1970; TsKhSD, f.5, o.62, d.38, l.19.

168. A. Barmenkov to the Central Committee Propaganda Dept., 17 June 1971; GARF, f.6991, o.6, d.361, l.40. Here, too, there were significant numbers of women and young people. On the morning of Ashura in 1974 at Baku's Taza-pir mosque 13,000 of the 22,000 people who assembled in the building and courtyard were women; in the evening 700 young men and women, 150 adolescents and 11 elementary school children gathered in the mosque and courtyard and a further 1,000 schoolchildren in the adjoining streets – V. Kuroedov to the Central Committee Propaganda Dept., undated; GARF, f.6991, o.6, d.622, l.41.

169. CRA report, sent to the CPSU Central Committee, 22 May 1970; TsKhSD, f.5, o.62, d.38, l.11. There may have been Sufi groups elsewhere in the Soviet Union, notably in Central Asia, but there is no indication of their existence in the archival material I have read apart from occasional reports on the activity of this or that *ishan*, notably in Tajikistan and in Uzbekistan's oblasti of Samarkand, Syr-Darya, Kashka-Darya and Surkhan-Darya – *ibid.*, l.13. For Sufi activity in both Central Asia and the Northern Caucasus, see Chapter 6.

170. *Ibid.*, l.17. For a more detailed discussion of the Ismailis, see pp.422-4.

171. This point was made by A. L. Alisov, *upolnomochennyi* for the Chechen-Ingush ASSR as of 1958, in his address at the all-union conference of *upolnomochennye* in November of that year. He noted that only two of the 83 non-functioning

In the 1920s and 1930s when large numbers of prayer-houses had been closed down, some had been destroyed outright, but the majority were transferred to other uses, which the Soviet sources refer to as cultural-educational (clubs, cinemas, schools, libraries, sport-facilities, clinics, and so on) and economic (mostly storehouses). A minority were under lock and key and simply remained empty; a few which had been assigned to other purposes had by the mid 1940s been vacated, probably because they were unsuitable for the end to which they had been designated, and become empty as well. According to one document, which claimed that 17,037 mosques had functioned prior to October 1917, 9,151 were still in existence in 1946. Of this number 4,265 served as cultural-educational institutions, fifty-nine as residential homes, 3,878 as storehouses and productive organisations and 1,252 stood empty.[172] In Uzbekistan alone at the end of 1944 there were 2,274 former mosques, of which just fourteen operated as mosques and 208 were empty.[173] Attempts were made by the secular authority to earmark some of the latter number for economic and other functions and from 1945-53, forty-eight former mosques were transferred to local organs of government.[174] In 1970 there were still considerable numbers of empty mosques: thirty-one in Dages-

---

former mosques were not in use as shops, schools, clubs, storehouses, etc., and so had not been refurbished and retained the appearance of mosques – GARF, f.6991, o.3, d.165, ll.107-8.

172. Statistical information as of 1 April 1946; GARF, f.6991, o.4, d.196, l.1.

173. Information as of 25 November 1944; TsGAUz, f.2456, o.1, d.3, ll.30-1. Over one half of the total number of former mosques were in Namangan Oblast' and the Karakalpak ASSR. (In Namangan, where 657 mosques remained, there had been 978 prior to the October Revolution, that is about one third had been destroyed – Statistical report as of 1 Nov. 1946; TsGAUz, f.2456, 0.1, d.5, l.4.) A year later, by which time there were 21 officially functioning mosques, there were said to be 2,259 non-functioning mosques, of which 750 were in use as cultural institutions, 1,299 as economic ones, and 203 were empty – I. Ibadov to N. Tagiev, Appendix, Report for Uzbek SSR, 3rd quarter of 1945, `5 Nov. 1945; GARF, f.6991, o.3, d.30, l.326. The total republican figure given here seems to be a serious underestimate, for in 1951 there were, in addition to the 653 in Namangan Oblast', 514 in Fergana Oblast', 574 in Samarkand Oblast', and 584 in Khorezm Oblast' – Report, 15 April 1952; GARF, f.6991, o.3, d.81, l.134. (Figures for the other oblasti are not given.) In 1966 there were reported to be just 34 empty mosques – undated report, GARF, f.6991, o.6, d.21, l.175.

174. L. A. Prikhod'ko, V. D. Efremov, P. A. Basis, Report, 8 May 1954; GARF, f.6991, o.3, d.100, l.34.

tan, fifty-one in Karakalpakiia, eighty in Mordoviia, 112 in Chechen-Ingushetiia,[175] and so on. Some of the empty mosques were not taken over for other purposes because they were in derelict condition, for instance almost one third of the 441 mosques which had operated before 1917 in the area that was to become the Turkmen SSR.[176]

The second group of figures relates to what Soviet jargon called the religious *aktiv*, that is those who were by definition engaged in activity connected with the religious associations. Basically, apart from the clergy, this group comprises the executive organs, the association's *revkomissiia* and sometimes the entire *dvadtsatka*. One document in the early post-Stalin period simply multiplied the number of mosques by twenty to reach the number of lay leaders.[177] Another report includes itinerant mullas in the *aktiv*.[178] From time to time, statistical data for this group are given in order to show that the numbers of potentially dangerous people with whom policy had to concern itself was relatively large.

And finally, there are statistics for what the documentary material terms 'so-called "holy places"' and those active there and making pilgrimages to them.[179] Just a few mausolea or *mazars* ('revered tombs' in Soviet terminology)[180] were registered in the late 1940s and into the 1950s in Uzbekistan and Tajikistan, and one in Azerbaijan.[181] In the mid 1950s there were said to be about 500 *mazars*

175. GARF, f.6991, o.6, d.302, ll.30, 50, 79 and 111.

176. M. A. Il'baev, Address, All-Union conference of *upolnomochennye*, 18-20 April 1960; GARF, f. 6991, o.3, d.208, l.104. Of the remainder, 47 were being used as cultural-educational institutions, 34 had been adapted as residential homes, 132 were storehouses or fulfilled other economic goals, and 76 had been destroyed by earthquake.

177. Information on the number of religious societies, clergy and *aktiv* of believers, undated (apparently early 1954); GARF, f.6991, o.3, d.102, l.63.

178. A. Puzin to K. U. Chernenko, undated, [1957]; GARF, f.6991, o.3, d.148, l.10. For itinerant mullas, see pp.326-33.

179. For these holy sites, see pp.363-82.

180. Most of the principal holy places were tombs, but there were also springs, caves, grottos, trees and so on.

181. Uzbekistan's four registered *mazars* drew 65,800 pilgrims and brought in an income of 287,297 rubles in 1951 – Kh. N. Iskanderov, Report for 1951, 15 April 1952, Table 4; GARF, f.6991, o.3, d.83, l.145. By the end of the decade nine mausolea were under the jurisdiction of SADUM and brought it an annual income of 4-5 million rubles – A. A. Puzin, Address, All-Union conference of CARC *upolnomochennye*, 18-20 April 1960; GARF, f.6991, o.3, d.208,

in Tajikistan alone[182] and 150 in Turkmenistan.[183] The most popular *mazar* in Central Asia, the Takht-i Sulayman in Osh, was said to have drawn at this same period as many as 100,000 pilgrims on some of the major festivals.[184] This was prior to the November 1958 legislation designed to curtail pilgrimages to holy places, following which even those that remained open drew a lesser flow of pilgrims.[185] In 1963, after several years of considerable activity to close them down, there were still 275 Muslim places of pilgrimage in the USSR; a year later their number was said to be down to 178.[186]

Although the campaign against 'holy places' – as distinct from the closure of prayer-houses – did not cease with Khrushchev's ouster, their numbers did not diminish. In 1966 we learn that there were nineteen holy places in Azerbaijan (of which four operated regularly and fifteen periodically on festivals), forty-three in Kazakhstan (of which two operated regularly and the rest just on festivals), 105 in Uzbekistan, thirty of which operated regularly, thirty-eight on festivals only and thirty-seven were non-functioning,[187] and so on, altogether 339 of these 'most revered "holy

---

1.21. Sh. Shirinbaev, the *upolnomochennyi* for Uzbekistan at the same conference, spoke of ten mausolea and an income in the peak year of 1958 of 3,117,600 rubles – *ibid.*, 1.77.

182. G. F. Frolov to I. V. Polianskii, 25 Feb. 1955; GARF, f.6991, o.3, d.112, 1.8. *Upolnomochennyi* for Tajikistan D. Ahmedov estimated their number at the beginning of 1959 as about 200 – Minutes, CARC session No.4, 25-26 Feb. 1959; GARF, f.6991, o.3, d.183, 1.61.

183. L. Prikhod'ko, Address, All-Union conference of *upolnomochennye*, 25-27 Nov. 1958; GARF, f.6991, o.3, d.165, 1.113.

184. For details, see pp.371-2.

185. N. I. Inogamov noted that in Uzbekistan's six best known *mazars* visitation on Uraz-Bayram decreased markedly from 1958 to 1959 – Address, Conference of Central Asian *upolnomochennye* in Tashkent, 5-6 June 1959; GARF, f.6991, o.3, d.186, 1.23. By June 1959, 138 of the republic's *mazars* were reported to have been closed down.

186. Statistical data as of 1 Jan. 1964; GARF, f.6991, o.4, d.146, 1.170.

187. Undated, apparently early 1967; GARF, f.6991, o.6, d.21, ll.2, 77 and 175. The 37 non-functioning ones are not explained in the document; when the campaign against pilgrimages to holy places began, the *upolnomochennyi* for Uzbekistan reported the existence in that republic of 177 holy places – Minutes, CARC session, No.4, 25-26 Feb. 1959; GARF, f.6991, o.3, d.183. 1.45. In 1973 the material tells us there were 442 holy places in Azerbaijan, 23 in Kazakhstan, 39 in Turkmenistan, 78 in Uzbekistan, 14 in Dagestan – GARF, f.6991, o.6, d.557, ll.4, 54, 114 and 131 and d.558, 1.26. The 39 in Turkmenistan

places"'.[188] In 1970 their number throughout the country was said to be 278,[189] and by early 1985 they still accounted for 'over 70 per cent' of the 332 holy sites of all denominations still active in the Soviet Union.[190] Some of these Muslim sites, moreover, continued attracting vast crowds on the major festivals.[191] Most of those they catered to were women and children, especially in areas where women were excluded from prayer-services in the mosques, many of them coming for healing. The data for these holy places seem particularly volatile, probably because they were constantly being closed and then re-opened for the next major festival. In addition, the less important ones continued functioning sporadically,[192] and so it was often difficult to assess whether in fact they were active.

The general picture which all the above data depict is one of considerable dynamism and vitality. Although the numbers do fluctuate considerably, especially in certain spheres, in response, among others, to changes in party and government policy,[193] the believer population of the Muslim nations was tenaciously adhering

---

had become 62 by 1974 – GARF, f.6991, o.6, d.653, 1.124. Some documents give details of the attendance at these places of pilgrimage, e.g. T. Tashkenbaev, List of so-called 'holy places' on the territory of Samarkand Oblast' as of 1 Jan. 1970; GARF, f.6991, o.6, d.240, ll.33-4.

188. CRA report, sent to the Central Committee, 27 April 1971; TsKhSD, f.5, o.63, d.89, 1.110.

189. CRA memorandum, 24 March 1971; TsKhSD, f.5, o.63, d.89, 1.88. Another report, also emanating from the CRA and said to be based on the same source of information – reports from the *upolnomochennye* – claimed there were 209 – CRA report, sent to the CPSU Central Committee, 27 April 1971; TsKhSD, f.5, o.63, d.89, 1.110.

190. Corley, *Religion in the Soviet Union*, p.297.

191. 40,000 visited the Shiite Goy-imam *pir* near Kirovabad in Azerbaijan in 1970 – CRA memorandum, 24 March 1971; TsKhSD, f.5, o.63, d.89, 1.88.

192. In Azerbaijan in 1970, apart from the 22 'actively functioning so-called "holy places", there are still over 300 different spots where unregistered clerics operate and organise pilgrimages of backward people' – CRA report, sent to the CPSU Central Committee, 27 April 1971; TsKhSD, f.5, o.63, d.89, 1.112.

193. These changes affected, as we have seen, the actual registration of mosques and clergy, applications to open mosques and register religious associations, attendance at registered mosques and the income which resulted from this attendance. The boost religious activity received in 1955 is unmistakable (see, for example, two reports by Uzbekistan *upolnomochennyi* Iskanderov, 28 May and 17 June 1955 – TsGAUz, f.2456, o.1, d.175, ll.1-12 and 13-21), as is the partial cooling down beginning 1959, which continued until about 1965.

to at least some of its customs and traditions. Moreover, although it was principally older people who attended prayer services and kept the fire burning, their numbers did not meaningfully decrease over the three decades for which we have extensive archival material. In other words, these were not a generation which was dying out, the remnants of those who had still attended religious educational institutions in their pre-revolutionary childhood and youth, but a static, stable stratum of pensioners, who, once no longer tied down to the workplace, considered it their obligation to their ancestors and their descendants to preserve their religion. Even prior to 1917 the older generation had been the bulwark of religion.[194] Those who became pensioners in the early 1970s had been very small children in 1917, most of their upbringing had been under Communism and they had gone through the socialist melting-pot. This meant that there was no reason to conclude that the believer population would diminish, let alone disappear. This seemed especially true given the high proportion and even growth in Central Asia of the rural population, which was significantly more religious than its urban counterpart (not only among the Muslims).[195] And approximately two-thirds of the country's Muslim population lived in Central Asia.

CARC Chairman Puzin was undoubtedly correct when he noted that it was impossible to estimate the size of the believer

194. See p.441.

195. Contradicting the countrywide trend, the great majority of the population of Central Asia's indigenous nationalities continued to reside in the countryside. In 1970, 77 per cent of Uzbeks, 76.5 per cent of Tajiks, 75 per cent of Turkmen and 86.6 per cent of Kyrgyz resided in rural areas – Saidbaev, *Islam i obshchestvo*, p.207. In the 1970s the rural population actually grew: in Tajikistan by 36 percent, in Turkmenistan by 28 per cent, in Uzbekistan by 21 per cent and in Kirgiziia by 18 per cent – *Islam v SSSR*, p.116. For the Central Asians' resistance to sovietisation by remaining not only in their native region, but even in their native villages, see Feshbach, 'Trends in the Soviet Muslim Population', pp.71-2. One of the reasons for the higher level of religiosity of this population, according to Soviet sources, was its lower level of education. While there was no difference between the level of education of the local urban inhabitants and their Russian neighbours, that of the indigenous nationals in the countryside, particularly among the older generation and among the womenfolk, was significantly lower – *ibid.*, pp.210-11. (For figures for female education, see *ibid.*, p.252.) Another reason was that the predominant majority of this group lived in mono-national communities; and a third was the extended family structure which still prevailed – *ibid.*, pp.222-3. For a discussion of the features and extent of Muslim religiosity, see Chapters 7 to 9.

population,[196] which the material indicates was significantly more numerous than those who actually attended prayer-services and conducted religious rites other than the life-cycle ones. On the other hand, those who observed the latter were almost certainly much more numerous than those generally identified as believers or who defined themselves as such.[197] Still in the late 1970s or early 1980s, 88 per cent of young people in Uzbekistan, even in the towns, considered parental consent essential when marrying,[198] which was manifest testimony to the continued influence of the older generation and the stability of tradition within the family framework.

Despite the manifest difficulties, attempts were made to estimate the dimensions of the believer population and as of the late 1960s recurrent sociological surveys came up with various figures. They covered all age groups and even when it came to the younger categories were not necessarily reassuring. In the extreme case of the Chechen-Ingush ASSR, surveys made in a few schools in the early 1970s revealed that no less than 40-50 per cent of the pupils were believers.[199] As far as can be learned, the surveys focused on special areas and there was no attempt to surmise the religiosity of the Muslim nationalities in the country as a whole. Yet, although they are not comprehensive, they provide some interesting data. Two surveys held apparently in the early 1970s revealed that in the Karakalpak ASSR 10 per cent of people employed in the work force were religious, 40 per cent of housewives and 70 per cent of pensioners; in Dagestan the figures were 20 per cent

196. A. Puzin to the CPSU Central Committee Department of Propaganda and Agitation, 7 June 1961; GARF, f.6991, o.3, d.1363, l.96.

197. According to one source, a doctoral dissertation on Uzbekistan, quoted by Saidbaev, they were almost four times as numerous as 'actual believers' – *Islam i obshchestvo*, p.218. See also p.433. This statement does not seem to be contradicted by the fact that in certain areas, at least in some periods, not all circumcised their sons or married according to religious custom. At one point Polianskii said anyone who practised any Muslim site must be considered a believer – see p.452.

198. *Islam i obshchestvo*, p.258.

199. A. Barmenkov to L. I. Matveev, 15 Jan. 1974; GARF, f.6991, o.6, d.622, l.3. The same source tells us that in one secondary school the predominant majority of pupils in the top classes said they believed in God, and that in Groznyi's teachers' training college 30 per cent of the indigenous nationalities' students considered themselves believers and 43 per cent admitted to observing the *uraz*.

among blue–collar workers, 30 per cent among kolkhozniki and 50 per cent among pensioners and those who did not work.[200] Religiosity among the Tatar population in two oblasti in the RSFSR (Penza and Gor'kii) was higher than among those who adhered to the Russian Orthodox Church and stood at 31.5 per cent in the former and at 40 per cent among men and 61 per cent among women in the latter.[201]

In short, the statistical information brought in this chapter cannot purport to provide a full picture of Muslim religious life and activity. It bears out, however, the statement made by Polianskii in 1947 that Islam, despite its few registered prayer-houses, was the most significant of all faiths in the Soviet Union after the Russian Orthodox Church from the point of view of the number of its adherents.[202] Moreover, the data indicate certain trends. They show that religiosity could no longer be gauged by traditional criteria, such as the observance of this or that pillar of Islam, let alone of all five, given the unquestionable secularisation that the Muslim population was undergoing under the Soviet regime.[203] They also show that the transformations which were taking place were not homogeneous. In the first place, they varied markedly from one region to another, and secondly, they did not all denote alienation from Islam or a steady decline in religious activity. These are weighty conclusions and serve as a valuable background to the study of the various components and aspects of Muslim life.

200. *Islam v SSSR*, p.31. The surveys covered approximately 5,000 people.

201. *Islam v SSSR,* p.66.

202. I. V. Polianskii to L. P. Beriia, I. V. Stalin, V. M. Molotov and K. E. Voroshilov at the Council of Ministers, and to A. A. Zhdanov, N. S. Khrushchev, A. A. Kuznetsov, N. S. Patolichev and G. M. Popov at the Central Committee Secretariat, 27 Feb. 1947; GARF, f.6991, o.3, d.47, l.92.

203. There can be no doubt that, even if in some areas this process was slower among the Muslims than among other sectors, it affected them as well. See my paper, 'The Secularization of Islam and the USSR's Muslim Areas'.

Part II. ESTABLISHMENT ISLAM

3

THE FOUR SPIRITUAL DIRECTORATES

Islam, unlike other religions with religious centres, did not have one centre, but four.[1] The Spiritual Boards or Directorates of the Muslims of Central Asia and Kazakhstan in Tashkent, of European Russia and Siberia in Ufa,[2] of the Northern Caucasus in Buinaksk in Dagestan,[3] and of Transcaucasia in Baku were officially independent of each other. Their separateness was highlighted by the fact that each used a different language in the conduct of everyday operations: Uzbek, Kazan' Tatar, Arabic and Azeri respectively.[4] The existence of four disparate centres was explained by 'historical circumstances and the national peculiarities of the Soviet Union's Muslims'.[5] This presumably meant the non-viability of subordinating Caucasian Muslims to a Tatar or Bashkir mufti and the incompatibility of customs and ritual between the Muslims of the RSFSR and of Central Asia, not to speak of the need to cater to the large Shiite community in Azerbaijan.

Autonomous bodies for the management of Muslim affairs had been set up under the tsars. The Orenburg Mahommedan Spiritual Assembly, headed by a mufti, had been established in Ufa under

1. For the religious centres, see pp.23–4.

2. Till 1948 called the Central Spiritual Directorate of the Muslims of Inner Russia and Siberia.

3. In 1974 this directorate was moved to the capital of Dagestan, Makhachkala.

4. The instructions and circulars the first two directorates sent out to their clergy would for the most part be in Arabic script – see I. V. Polianskii to Kh. N. Iskanderov, B. Jumashev, H. Akhtiamov, K. Hamidov and A. M. Komekov, 24 Sept. 1952; GARF, f.6991, o.3, d.86, l.23.

5. L .A. Prikhod'ko and N. A. Abushaev, Draft survey, 16 March 1950; GARF, f.6991, o.3, d.63, l.80.

Catherine the Great in 1788 to administer the affairs of the country's Muslims (except for those in the Crimea, who received a separate administration in 1794). Following the Russian conquest of new Muslim territories and populations in the subsequent decades, two other parallel organisations were instituted in Tbilisi, one for the Shiite, the other for the Sunni, community of the Caucasus. All these institutions were supported by and subordinated to the tsarist government.[6] It would appear that the creation of the Caucasian and Crimean regional administrations was motivated by apprehensions regarding the possible implications of subordinating all the country's Muslims to the central one in Ufa. Be this as it may, in 1879 Turkestan Governor-General Konstantin von Kaufman rejected the request of the mufti in Ufa for authority over Turkestan's Muslims on the grounds that the native religious authorities there were less 'fanatically religious' and 'more readily reconciled with our rule', so that such a step would be counter-productive.[7] In fact, the Russian Imperial government resolved not to establish institutionalised control of the Muslim clergy in Central Asia in the belief that the policy of ignoring Islam and its spiritual leadership would be the optimal way of precipitating their inevitable loss of influence over the population as the latter gave way before the onslaught of Russia's more progressive civilisation.[8]

By October 1917 only the original centre remained; the Tbilisi centres had been moved to Baku and subsequently shut down, and the one in Crimea met the same fate. The Ufa muftiate – renamed earlier that year the Central Spiritual Directorate of the Muslims of Inner Russia and Siberia (TsDUM) – continued to function under Soviet rule, apparently without interruption,

6. Landa, *Islam v istorii Rossii*, p.133; Saidbaev, *Islam i obshchestvo*, p.121; and Litvinov, *Gosudarstvo i islam v russkom Turkestane (1865-1917)*, p.14. According to one source, the original muftiate, the decision regarding whose opening was taken in 1788, was opened in fact a year later and moved to Orenburg in 1796 –Anwar Khairullin, 'Historical fate', *Nauka i religiia*, 1 (1990), p.12. This, however, seems to be inaccurate: the fact that the administration was called the Orenburg assembly or administration merely reflects the fact that Ufa was in Orenburg Guberniia. I am grateful for this information to Grigorii Kosach of Moscow State University.

7. Brower, 'Islam and Ethnicity: Russian Colonial Policy in Turkestan', p.120.

8. For the discussion within the Russian government regarding the optimal policy to be adopted *vis-à-vis* Islam in Central Asia following the conquest of the area in the third quarter of the 19th century, see Litvinov, *Gosudarstvo i islam v russkom Turkestane*, *passim*.

although there was a certain hiatus after the death in 1936 of its mufti, Rizaeddin Fakhreddin. A number of 'loosely organized, unconnected' administrations were set up in Uzbekistan as of 1923 in order to propagate 'revolutionary', 'reformist' and 'scientific' ideas, but they were closed down before the end of the decade. The decree ordaining their establishment spelled out their goal as constituting a 'connecting link between the government and the people', carrying out 'the reform of religious matters', and struggling 'with various unnecessary superstructures of Islam [and] with incorrect interpretations of Islam'.[9] A Bashkirian spiritual administration also existed from 1926, first in Sterlitamak, then in Ufa, until closed down in 1936,[10] and there may have been others. These attempts to take advantage of existing divisions between reform-oriented and traditionalist Muslim clergy must be seen against the backdrop of the Bolshevik regime's collaboration with the reform-minded Renovationist, or Living, Church in its struggle against the official leadership of the Russian Orthodox Church, which at first opposed the new order with all the means at its disposal.[11]

Terms of reference and raison d'être

When the Great Patriotic War broke out with the German invasion of the Soviet Union in June 1941, the Central Directorate under Mufti Abdurahman Rasulev[12] followed in the footsteps of the Patriarch of the Russian Orthodox Church[13] and sought to mobilise

9. Keller, *The Struggle against Islam in Uzbekistan, 1921-1941*, pp.10 and 220-3. Keller tells us that such administrations existed in Tashkent, Samarkand, Kokand, Andijan, Namangan, Margelan, Bukhara and Khiva. According to Saidbaev – *Islam i obshchestvo*, pp.159-60 – there was just one directorate, which had authority over the cities of Tashkent, Fergana, Andijan and Namangan and their outlying districts. It 'systematised' the appointment and replacement of clergy and took under its wing the old method (as against the jadid) Muslim schools. It is possible that the Tashkent administration was set up first and it was decided to create the others later.

10. I am grateful for this information to Grigorii Kosach.

11. Weakened as of the second half of the 1920s, the Living Church was finally and officially reintegrated into the patriarchal church in 1943 – Corley, *Religion in the Soviet Union*, p.147.

12. Rasulev was a Bashkir, the son of a shaykh and member of a well-known Muslim family – Foreign Office Research Dept., 'The Soviet Union and Islam', March 1947; PRO, FO371/66391, quoting *Soviet War News*, 20 May 1942.

13. For the activity of the Russian Orthodox Church during the war, see

the country's Muslims to demonstrate their support for the Soviet war effort.[14] That old scores were being forgotten and a rehabilitation process begun was evident from the publication in the Soviet press both of appeals by Rasulev to the country's Muslims to this end and of exchanges of telegrams between the mufti and the heads of state on important occasions.[15] In May 1942 TsDUM was able to hold a conference of clergy from the RSFSR which chose the composition of its leading body.[16] In the process of acquainting the Muslim population with TsDUM's appeal to provide assistance to the war effort, its representatives, who met with Muslim believers at meetings of kolkhozniki and even urban inhabitants, also sought to form religious societies. They sometimes delegated power of attorney to local unregistered clerics who, doing the rounds of the auls, would hold further meetings, some of which passed resolutions to elect 'the leading commission [presumably the *dvadtsatka* or executive organ] of a Muslim [religious] society'.[17]

Pospelovskii, *Russkaia pravoslavnaia tserkov' v XX veke*, Chapter 7.

14. According to a British Foreign Office report, 'old scores were quickly forgotten on both sides and a rapid process of rehabilitation took place' – Foreign Office Research Dept., 'The Soviet Union and Islam', *op. cit.* pp.8–9.

15. The first of the appeals to Soviet Muslims was issued on 18 July 1941 – *ibid.*; see also I. V. Polianskii, Information, 1 Oct. 1946; GARF, f.6991, o.3, d.34, l.13. These appeals engendered meetings of believing Muslims in various parts of the country to make their contribution to the war effort, and were then used in order to legitimise Muslim religious activity and reinstate a number of communities, see below. See, for example, Minutes No.3 of the general meeting of the Muslim society in a Tatar aul in Omsk Oblast', 15 June 1943; GARF, f.6991, o.3, d.4, l.109. The general meeting addressed itself to the Central Directorate's appeal of 29 Aug. 1942.

16. Foreign Office Research Dept., 'The Soviet Union and Islam', *op. cit.*, pp.8–9. Polianskii, Information, *ibid.* The exact nature of this conference is not clear; in a subsequent letter to Voroshilov, 13 Aug. 1948, Polianskii said TsDUM had held no conference since 1936; GARF, f.6991, o.3, d.54, l.177. The 1942 conference was probably the one mentioned by Saidbaev – *Islam i obshchestvo*, p.188 – convened for the purpose of an appeal to Muslims to take up the struggle against fascism, to enhance their contribution to the economy and to organise the collection of money for the war effort. Yet the opportunity seems to have been taken to discuss matters connected with the spiritual directorate. According to Saidbaev, this conference, of which he does not give an exact date, was attended by clergy from the country as a whole and not just the RSFSR. Saidbaev, too, brings some references to publication in the central press of Muslim declarations of support for the war effort.

17. P. D. Bezdel' to I. V. Polianskii, 7 Dec. 1944; GARF, f.6991, o.3, d.4,

In conjunction with Rasulev[18] a group of Muslim leaders in Central Asia approached Moscow with the suggestion to hold a conference, or *qurultay*, of Muslim clergy and believers from the five Central Asian republics with an eye to establishing a second spiritual directorate of Muslims in Tashkent. They contended in a letter addressed to USSR Supreme Soviet Presidium Chairman Mikhail Kalinin that the lack of such a centre, on the one hand, prevented the Muslim clergy of Central Asia from organising aid to the war effort and, on the other, enabled 'impostors' with 'little knowledge of Islamic dogma and ignorant of the Constitution of the USSR' to infiltrate the ranks of the clergy.[19] One can imagine that the first theme was included out of considerations of *Realpolitik* and what really concerned the authors of the letter was their own position within the local clergy, which they hoped to bolster in this way. At the end of July 1943 the Presidium of the Supreme Soviet of the USSR approved their request[20] and on 20 October the conference was opened in Tashkent.[21] It officially set up the new body, the Spiritual Directorate of the Muslims of Central Asia and Kazakhstan (SADUM), and elected its presidium headed by Ishan Babakhan Abdumajitkhanov who received, like

---

l.100. For the activity of TsDUM's representatives in Omsk Oblast' for example, see p.290.

18. In his opening address to the Tashkent conference (see below) Ishan Babakhan said the idea of the conference and the establishment of the directorate had arisen 'long ago' and at the end of 1942 letters had been dispatched to leading representatives of the clergy in all five Central Asian republics. After receiving positive replies, nine Muslim leaders had written to Rasulev, who asked the advice of lawyers and clarified the opinion of the USSR Supreme Soviet. On 9 July a reply from Rasulev had been received saying there was no objection on the part of either and giving some practical advice how to proceed – GARF, f.6991, o.3, d.6, ll.37-8.

19. The letter to Kalinin, sent on 12 July 1943, was signed by Ishan Babakhan Abdumajitkhanov, Abdurazak Ishan Muhammat Alimov, Akramkhan Gazikhanov and Mullasadyk Islamov; GARF, f.6991, o.3, d.6, l.32.

20. Decree of the Presidium of the USSR Supreme Soviet, No.55, 31 July 1943; GARF, f.6991, o.3, d.6, l.33. See also Babakhan's opening address at the conference – *ibid*.

21. Murat Khoja Domulla, 'The Great Qurultay', Sept. 1944; GARF, f.6991, o.3, d.6, l.44. This source tells us that 83 representatives were present from the five Central Asian republics and eight guests from Tatarstan, Transcaucasia and Moscow, including Mufti Rasulev. The proceedings were broadcast for the benefit of the local population.

Rasulev, the title of mufti.[22] The conference agenda included delegating to SADUM the management of religious matters among the Muslims of Central Asia and satisfying their needs in religious issues; the elaboration and approval of a charter; determining the spiritual directorate's sources of income and prescribing its expenses; confirming its personnel at the centre in Tashkent and delegating representatives to the union republics to satisfy believers' needs and establish a leadership for mosques in the more distant areas of those republics.[23]

This initiative was followed in the early summer of 1944 by two additional conferences. The first was held in Baku in May and elected a Shiite *cum* Sunni Spiritual Directorate of the Muslims of Transcaucasia (DUMZ), headed by a Shiite Shaykh-ul-Islam, Akhund Aga Mamed Jafar-ogli Ali-zade, and a deputy Sunni mufti, Ibrahim Efendi-zade.[24] The second was held in Dagestan in Buinaksk, which became the seat of the Spiritual Directorate of the Muslims of the Northern Caucasus (DUMSK) elected at the conference and headed by Hizri Gebekov.

The charters of the spiritual directorates, which were ratified at these *qurultays*, laid down the size of their governing bodies and their method of operation. Each had, in addition to its chairman, a presidium or governing board, an auditing commission elected by a convention of clergy and believers, and representatives in the territories under their jurisdiction.[25] These representatives –

22. Babakhan, like Rasulev, had a history of adaptation to and manifest sympathy for the Soviet regime. He, too, had in 1941 supervised patriotic activity among the Muslim clergy of Uzbekistan, Turkmenistan and Tajikistan – Polianskii, Information, 1 Oct. 1946; GARF, f.6991, o.3, d.34, l.13.

23. Z. Babakhanov, Information, sent to N. I. Inogamov, 17 Aug. 1956; TsGAUz, f.2456, o.1, d.184, l.59.

24. Like Rasulev and Babakhan, the Shaykh ul-Islam was the son of a leading religious figure. He had studied in Persia and returned to Baku in 1898 to serve as mulla in Baku's Taza-pir mosque – 'The Soviet Union and Islam', *op. cit.* Interestingly, the title Shaykh-ul-Islam had belonged to the head of the Shiite spiritual administration set up in the 19th century in Tbilisi (and later transferred to Baku), just as the Sunni administrations had each been headed by a mufti.

25. SADUM's territorial jurisdiction encompassed the four Central Asian union republics – the Uzbek, Tajik, Kirgiz and Turkmen SSRs – and the Kazakh SSR; that of DUMZ the three Transcaucasian union republics – the Azerbaijani, Armenian and Georgian SSRs; that of DUMSK the Dagestani, Kabardinian and North Osetian ASSRs and the Stavropol and Krasnodar krais, which included the Cherkess and Adygei AOs and Groznyi Oblast', as the Chechen-Ingush

called alternatively *muhtasibs*, qazis or *upolnomochennye* and described in one CARC memorandum as being equivalent to bishops in the Russian Orthodox Church[26] – were members of the governing board and/or auditing commission and served as intermediaries between the spiritual directorates and the individual registered religious societies whose activity they directed.

Each *muhtasib* had under his jurisdiction a single union or autonomous republic or, in the RSFSR and some parts of Central Asia, a number of oblasti. His tasks included the appointment and removal of clergy, the resolution of disputes which might evolve within a religious society, ensuring the transfer to the religious centre of a certain part of the funds received by the religious society from believers, and maintaining contact with CARC's *upolnomochennye*. In some parts of Central Asia, at least in certain periods, SADUM's representatives sought to control the activity of the religious societies given over to their jurisdiction independently of the centre[27] despite their official total subordination to it.[28] Altogether, while this link in the chain of control worked reasonably well in the RSFSR, the very concept of the *muhtasibat* was unacceptable to many of the clergy in Central Asia.[29] CARC noted that the Central Asian clergy were not in effect subordinate to SADUM, but as a result of the absence of a 'firm, canonically based, and so authoritative line' were anarchical, uncontrolled and detrimental.[30] Some CARC *upolnomochennye* were also opposed

---

ASSR had become following the deportation (see p.61); and that of DUMES the rest of the RSFSR.

26. N. I. Abushaev, Memorandum, 17 Nov. 1949; GARF; f.6991, o.3, d.61, l.120.

27. L. Prikhod'ko, Report, 20 May 1953; GARF, f.6991, o.3, d.91, l.263. And see below.

28. N. Abushaev, Information, 17 Nov. 1949; GARF, f.6991, o.3, d.61, l.120.

29. In a memo he prepared towards the end of 1946, Polianskii referred to the three-link system as having justified itself; he complained, however, that in Central Asia the clergy were opposed to it, apparently apprehensive that this would mean a curbing of their freedom of action, and the attempt to impose it there was encountering great difficulty. CARC, for its part, found this extra link beneficial, presumably because the spiritual directorates were unable to control effectively the entire territory under their jurisdiction – Memorandum, 11 Nov. 1946; GARF, f.6991, o.3, d.34, l.203.

30. Draft charter for a proposed all-union spiritual directorate (see below), undated (probably late 1946); GARF, f.6991, o.3, d.44, ll.79-80.

to the territorial *muhtasibats* on the grounds that the *muhtasibs* went from one mosque to another conducting 'religious agitation'.[31]

The charters of the spiritual directorates underwent changes in the late 1950s-early 1960s. *Inter alia*, the articles empowering them to appoint and dismiss the religious societies' executive organs, as well as the funds at their disposal which they used at their discretion, aroused concern in a period when efforts were being made to curb the influence of the religious leadership.[32] In October 1959 CARC informed its *upolnomochennyi* in Dagestan that the DUMSK charter contained a multitude of inaccuracies and contradicted Soviet law, as a result of which seventeen out of twenty-seven paragraphs required alteration. Drafts of an altered charter were twice sent to Moscow and each time CARC's legal advisor found errors requiring correction and it was only in May 1960 that a version was finally submitted which was basically acceptable.[33] The last to ratify its new charter was SADUM;[34] in 1961 CARC was complaining that SADUM and its republican qazis were still operating in accordance with the charters of 1948 and 1957, which by the criteria of Khrushchev's anti-religious campaign entailed undue interference in the affairs of the religious societies and their executive organs.[35] It was not until well into the 1960s that SADUM

31. N. I. Inogamov, Address, All-Union conference of CARC *upolnomochennye*, 26-27 Nov. 1958; GARF, f.6991, o.3, d.165, l.81.

32. A. A. Puzin, Address, All-Union conference of CARC *upolnomochennye*, 18-20 April 1960; GARF, f.6991, o.3, d.208, ll.11-12. In 1958, for example, CARC had recommended to DUMES to introduce changes in its charter in order to prevent the recurrence of incidents such as had occurred in Astrakhan', where it had remanned the *dvadtsatka* and thus interfered in the society's administrative and economic affairs in contradiction to the law (of 1931) – Minutes, CARC session No.18, 16 Sept. 1958; GARF, f.6991, o.3, d.164, ll.66-7.

33. Even now there were grammatical errors and a few small changes that had to be made. The new document was based on DUMZ's revised charter – N. Smirnov, Information, prepared for CARC session No.16, 10 June 1960; GARF, f.6991, o.3, d.205, ll.51-2. For the text of the revised charter, see *ibid.*, ll.53-7.

34. It seems, however, to have been the first to raise the question of updating its charter – see I. V. Polianskii to I. A. Shalaev, 13 Jan. 1956; TsGAUz, f.2456, o.1, d.191, l.29. In January 1960 Babakhanov informed CARC that SADUM had resolved to review its charter; he was told to present the draft of the new charter to CARC in Russian and to ensure that it corresponded in all its points to the law of the country – Proposals on questions raised by Ziyautdin Babakhanov at his reception by the CARC leadership in January 1960, prepared for CARC session No.3, 22 Jan. 1960; GARF, f.6991, o.3, d.204, l.20.

35. A. Puzin to First Secretary of the Tajikistan Communist Party Central

finally toed the line with a document which answered the new requirements. Its new articles were intended to regulate and spell out SADUM's basic functions and duties, and the nature of its relations with the religious associations, and to prevent the usurpation by the spiritual directorate of the rights of the associations' executive organs. They also authorised SADUM to remove 'the more fanatical clergy' and to curtail the distribution of funds for charitable purposes.[36]

From time to time, mostly long after the constitutional time period had lapsed, the spiritual directorates held conferences of clergy from the territories over which they presided.[37] In 1948 Rasulev asked for permission to hold such a conference in order to report on activity, ratify the charter of the Spiritual Directorate of the Muslims of the RSFSR, as TsDUM was now unofficially called, and elect a new spiritual directorate and auditing commission.[38] Each of the directorate's seven *muhtasibats* was split up into

Committee J. Rasulev, draft, August 1961; GARF, f.6991, o.3, d.1737, l.102. SADUM, for its part, complained that CARC's *upolnomochennye* throughout Central Asia were taking advantage of the deteriorating situation to encroach upon the responsibilities and privileges of SADUM – Memo of conversation of Z. Babakhanov with V. F. Riazanov, undated [1962]; GARF, f.6991, o.3, d.1738, ll.100-1.

36. M. Miragzamov to M. Kh. Khalmuhamedov, 22 Oct. 1966; GARF, f.6991, o.6, d.11, l.63. The charters of 1959-60 had no article on curbing the distribution of funds.

37. SADUM's original charter, for example, stipulated the convening of such a conference after three years, yet it was only in late 1948 that a second conference was convened – see below – i.e. over five years after the first, founding conference. This second conference changed SADUM's charter so that the subsequent conference need be convened only after five years. In 1953, as this period drew to a close, SADUM applied for permission to hold an expanded board plenum to prolong the term of office of its members, as well as to discuss its financial situation; this request was acceded to by CARC and the plenary meeting was held in February 1954 – N. Tagiev, Short survey, undated [early 1949], and L. A. Prikhod'ko, V. D. Efremov and P. A. Basis, Report, 8 May 1954; GARF, f.6991, o.4, d.23, l.11ob, and o.3, d.100, ll.27-8.

38. I. V. Polianskii to K. E. Voroshilov, 13 Aug. 1948; GARF, f.6991, o.3, d.54, l.177. The request spoke of a conference of 45 representatives of the clergy and believers, saying that since the last conference in 1936 – see n.16 above – the spiritual directorate's elected body had broken up and new people had been co-opted for auditing work; moreover, the charter confirmed in 1923 had been altered and added to by the spiritual directorate's presidium in 1946 and a conference was needed to ratify a new charter. A government instruction was issued on 11 September allowing the holding of a conference in October

small groups of three to five mosques, every group electing one delegate to the conference.[39]

At the end of the same year, SADUM, too, held its second conference which had an almost identical agenda.[40] It had already held two plenary sessions, in September 1945 and January 1947. These had heard reports of SADUM's activity in Tashkent and the periphery, the 1947 plenum also prolonging the authority of the directorate and its members, which had expired in October 1946, and postponed the convention of the next *qurultay* or conference. It also removed a number of officials for misdemeanours of various ilks[41] and reviewed the *fetwas* – official interpretations of dogma – issued by the presidium.[42] SADUM held two further

---

– *ibid.*, 1.178. The text of the address by CARC's representative at the conference, which opened on 25 October, made CARC's guiding role clear – *ibid.*, ll.210-1. For a short account of the conference, at which 35 delegates and 10 guests were present, including representatives from the three other spiritual directorates, see I. V. Polianskii to K. E. Voroshilov, 10 Nov. 1948; GARF, f.6991, o.3, d.54, 1.218.

39. Iu. V. Sadovskii to *upolnomochennye*, 22 Sept. 1948; GARF, f.6991, o.3, d.55, ll.54-7.

40. N. Inogamov, Information, 7 Dec. 1956; TsGAUz, f.2456, o.1, d.190, ll.20-27. The conference was attended by 96 delegates; the heads of the other three spiritual directorates attended as guests. Both conferences also authorised the presidium of the spiritual directorate concerned to call upon all Muslims in other countries to conduct a struggle against the instigators of war – N. Tagiev, Short survey, undated [early 1949]. For SADUM's request to hold this *qurultay* and for the proposed composition of the delegations from each Central Asian republic, see I. V. Polianskii to K. E. Voroshilov, 11 Aug. 1948, to CARC's republican *upolnomochennye* in the Kirgiz, Tajik, Kazakh and Turkmen SSRs, 13 Oct. 1948, and to K. E. Voroshilov and D. T. Shepilov, 29 Jan. 1949; GARF, f.6991, o.4, d.23, l.11ob., and o.3, d.54, ll.174-5, and d.61, ll.2-3.

41. It removed its qazi in Kazakhstan for inertia, violation of the Shari'a and undermining the authority of SADUM by his deeds, and resolved to recover from him 22,500 rubles belonging to SADUM; its qazi in Tajikistan who had been inactive and had requested to be relieved of his post for reasons of age; and a member of the auditing commission for Tajikistan for inertia and violation of the Shari'a and for Turkmenistan for total inaction. The session also decided to relieve Shafagat Khoja Khaliqnazarov of his post of chairman of the auditing commission and of imam for not carrying out the task of reviewing religious activity in all five republics, for appointing imams in mosques in Kirgiziia without SADUM's consent and for allowing the opening of illegal mosques in violation of SADUM's charter and his own commitments, although he was to remain a member of the commission for purposes of investigation – Minutes, the 2nd SADUM plenum, [20-27 Jan. 1947]; TsGAUz, f.2456, o.1, d.104, ll.1-3.

42. Z. Babakhanov, Information, 17 Aug. 1956; TsGAUz, f.2456, o.1, d.184,

plenary sessions, in 1952 and 1954. They too heard reports on the activity of the presidium and auditing commission, discussed and confirmed instructions and *fetwas*, heard reports on financial activity and ratified the budget for the coming year, and made changes in the composition of the presidium and auditing commission. Again, the 1954 plenum prolonged the authority of the presidium until the next *qurultay*, which was already overdue.[43] For plenary sessions, like conferences, permission had to be obtained from CARC or its apparatus,[44] CARC in turn, at least in the case of conferences, having to obtain the consent of the CPSU Central Committee.[45]

Formally, the election of a mufti or supplementing the composition of the directorate's presidium or governing board, for instance, required holding a conference. Given the complexity of the procedure and the doubts and hesitations of the parties concerned, particularly in the case of a mufti, an acting chairman would be chosen until it might be convened. When Rasulev died in 1950, a number of CARC officials opposed the idea of either a conference or the election of a successor on the grounds that this would animate the religious feelings of believers, which, they alleged, were dying out. In the final account, a conference was held and Shakir Khiyaletdinov, imam of the mosque in Chimkent and member of SADUM, was elected.[46] DUMSK chairman Gebekov also died in 1950, yet by 1954 no successor had been appointed, so acting chairman Mohamed Haji Kurbanov appealed for permission to hold a conference to elect a chairman, as well

ll.60-1. For the *fetwas* in question, see below.

43. Z. Babakhanov Information, 17 Aug. 1956; TsGAUz, f.2456, o.1, d.184, ll.64-6. By this time the presidium consisted of five members, the plenum of an additional eight and the auditing commission of seven. They were empowered to prolong their own authority until the next *qurultay*.

44. See Z. Babakhanov to Kh. N. Iskanderov, 14 Dec. 1955; TsGAUz, f.2456, o.1, d.174, ll.112-13.

45. See, for example, I. V. Polianskii to the Central Committee, 28 Oct. 1955; GARF, f.6991, o.3, d.115, ll.24-5. The occasion was a request from DUMZ to hold a conference in Baku to discuss its report, re-elect its members and inspection committee and choose a shaykh-ul-islam, Ali-zade having died in Dec. 1954. CARC deputy chairman Gostev noted on a copy of the letter on 10 Nov. that someone from the Central Committee apparatus, one Sakharov, had phoned to say that permission was being given to hold the conference.

46. L. A. Prikhod'ko, A short report, 11 April 1952; GARF, f.6991, o.3, d.81, ll.79-80.

as other board members in place of those who had for one reason or another quit their posts.[47]

Usually, however, critical questions, such as nominations or the ratification of the budget, would be resolved by convening a board plenary and inviting to it 'a restricted circle of religious figures'.[48] In 1954 Khiyaletdinov asked to be allowed to hold a conference in order to ratify the appointment of DUMES presidium and auditing commission members and to confirm the mufti's report. In order to obviate the necessity of a conference to which the delegates had to be elected by the various religious societies, he suggested convening representatives of the clergy and some individual believers from the major mosques under DUMES's jurisdiction; CARC was amenable to this proposal provided there not be over thirty delegates and the Bashkir Obkom party secretary and the chairman of the Bashkir ASSR Council of Ministers concurred.[49] In 1957, following the death of Ishan Babakhan, SADUM, too, asked to be allowed to hold a *qurultay* to choose a new mufti and renew the authority of its members, which had long since expired (they had been elected in 1948 for five years). CARC suggested that it might be worthwhile learning from the experience of DUMES and DUMZ regarding the composition of the conference; apart from which, all questions – the agenda, the conduct of the conference, the number and composition of participants and the procedure for their invitation – must be discussed with the Council's *upolnomochennyi* in Tashkent.[50]

The two purposes outlined in the 1943 letter to Kalinin served

47. L. A. Prikhod'ko, V. D. Efremov and P. S. Basis, Report, 8 May 1954, and I. V. Polianskii to the Central Committee, 17 Dec. 1954; GARF, f.6991, o.3, d.100, l.37, and d.103, ll.67-8. Kurbanov suggested a conference on lines similar to those proposed by Khiyaletdinov, see immediately below, and on 30 Dec. Polianskii received a telephone message that Agitprop gave its consent – *ibid.* For Kurbanov's eventual appointment as DUMSK chairman, see p.576.

48. L. A. Prikhod'ko, Report, 20 May 1953; GARF, f.6991, o.3, d.91, l.263.

49. I. V. Polianskii to G. M. Malenkov, 5 April 1954 and to N. S. Khrushchev, 6 April 1954; GARF, f.6991, o.3, d.102, ll.97-8 and 100-1. The major mosques mentioned specifically were those of Ufa, Kazan', Astrakhan', Moscow and Rostov-on-Don.

50. Reception by L. A. Prikhod'ko of Z. Babakhanov, 24 July 1957; GARF, f.6991, o.4, d.75, ll.109-10. SADUM contemplated inviting one delegate from each registered mosque, as well as delegates from the other three spiritual directorates and from the mosques of Kazan', Moscow and Leningrad, altogether 200-220 people – *ibid.*

as the guidelines for the activity of all four directorates. They were to ensure the homogeneity of the Muslim clergy from the point of view of both Islamic conformity and loyalty to the regime. This entailed supervision by the spiritual directorates of the clergy's strictly clerical activity and encouragement of 'patriotic' initiatives.

Indeed, all three *qurultays* held in 1943-4 passed resolutions on patriotic activity among the Muslim community. The charters of the spiritual directorates contained commitments to call upon believers to fulfil their obligations to the state.[51] It seems safe to presume that this aspect of their functions was seen by the Muslim leadership as a prerequisite for their continued existence or as an instrument to demonstrate their worth in the eyes of the powers-that-be, rather than as a major goal in its own right. It was indicative of the change in their status that this clause was omitted from the revised charters of the late 1950s.[52] At the same time, the spiritual directorates must have considered that their patriotic activity in the postwar years as well would be likely to enhance their authority among the local population, in addition to providing a pretext for them and their representatives to tour the various Muslim communities.[53] The spiritual directorates also clearly understood that their patriotic position would enable them to at least partly put an end to the isolation from the Muslim world in which the Soviet Union's Muslims had found themselves in the prewar period.

51. They were to urge them towards fraternal relations among themselves and with all the peoples of the Soviet Union and imbue in them 'an honest attitude to work', and 'unlimited devotion to their mother country' – I. V. Polianskii, Information, 1 Oct. 1946; GARF, f.6991, o.3, d.34. l.14. Polianskii went on to enlarge upon the emphasis that had been laid by the Muslim clergy in their sermons on the need to help the war effort and the personal donations of clergy and believers to that effort.

52. See, for example, the DUMZ charter, confirmed by that organisation in October 1959 and prepared as an appendix to minutes, CARC session No.31, 19 Dec. 1959; GARF, f.6991, o.3, d.185, ll.170-6.

53. At one of CARC's regional conventions of *upolnomochennye* in the early summer of 1946 it was pointed out that members of the spiritual directorates and their representatives had the right to travel only to raiony which had registered communities and to speak and collect funds for patriotic purposes solely within these communities – Draft of address, unsigned and undated, probably 31 May 1946; GARF, f.6991, o.3, d.36, l.10. This was noted in the context of information from the *upolnomochennyi* of Tiumen Oblast' that two people had been appointed by TsDUM to collect money for patriotic and other purposes.

Certainly the powers-that-be were quick to make use of the new directorates for domestic and foreign policy purposes, to gain the sympathies of both Muslim ethnic groups at home and Muslims abroad. This, of course, was not a peculiarity of their attitude towards the Muslim establishment, but a distinct component of overall religious policy.[54] In January 1944, Deputy People's Commissar for State Security Merkulov asked Central Committee Secretary Aleksandr Shcherbakov for instructions regarding SADUM's proposal to distribute an appeal in Kazakh and Uighur to Muslims in neighbouring Sinkiang.[55] In March the People's Commissariat for State Security was recommending the distribution through SADUM both abroad and in Tajikistan of an appeal by Ismaili leaders[56] and in June of an appeal by DUMZ to be disseminated in Azeri (in the Azerbaijani, Georgian and Armenian SSRs and in Iranian Azerbaijan), in Persian (in Iran), in Arabic (in the Arab countries) and in Turkish (in the Ajar and Abkhaz ASSRs and in Turkey).[57] The same organisation asked permission to circulate the Buinaksk conference 'patriotic appeal to the Muslims of the Northern Concasus' in the eleven languages of the region's 'main Muslim nationalities'.[58]

It was indeed contended that the publicity given to the Muslim clergy's patriotic activity was having a positive impact in the Muslim East.[59] In addition to written materials and broadcasts,[60] personal

54. See Pospelovskii, *Russkaia pravoslavnaia tserkov' v XX veke*, pp.191-3.

55. V. N. Merkulov to A. S. Shcherbakov, 21 Jan. 1944; RTsKhIDNI, f.17, o.125, d.261, l.1.

56. V. N. Merkulov to A. S. Shcherbakov, 4 March 1944; RTsKhIDNI, f.17, o.125, d.261, l.19.

57. Fedotov to Shcherbakov, 6 June 1944; RTsKhIDNI, f.17, o.125, d.261, l.27. For further details, see p.574.

58. B. Z. Kobulov to Shcherbakov, 15 July 1944; RTsKhIDNI, f.17, o.125, d.261, l.47. Similar approaches were made to publish through an Indian publishing house, which had asked Rasulev to write something on the topic of Soviet Muslim participation in the war – I. V. Polianskii to V. M. Molotov, 5 Aug. 1944; GARF, f.6991, o.3, d.1, l.15.

59. I. V. Polianskii to V. M. Molotov, *ibid.*

60. There are recurrent references in the documentation to broadcasts by Soviet Muslim clergy to various foreign Muslim countries, where possible in the languages of those countries. It was contended, for instance, that foreign Muslims often expressed the desire to extend and intensify their contents with Soviet Muslims, especially after radio broadcasts in which the latter told of the freedom of religion in the USSR – I. V. Polianskii to K. E. Voroshilov, 5 Aug. 1947; GARF,

contact was also encouraged. When Iranian Muslim leaders proposed a visit to Iran by DUMZ's Shaykh-ul-Islam, the Soviet ambassador in Tehran expressed himself in favour, saying it would have significance not only in that country but throughout the Middle East. Ali-zade in fast visited Tehran, as well as Tabriz and Qazvin; he met with a leading hierarch, Shaykh-ul-Islam Malayeri, and was received by the Shah.[61]

Apparently it was thought that at home, too, SADUM was likely to fulfil a salutary propaganda role, for its request for permission to publish a monthly journal in Uzbek in the Arabic script was granted by the authorities in Moscow.[62] Altogether SADUM was the most active of the directorates, perhaps because of Ishan Babakhan's considerable reputation and prestige within the Muslim community, perhaps because of the large concentration of Muslim nationalities in Central Asia and perhaps because of the distance between Tashkent and Moscow, which left it a freer hand. Throughout the 1950s SADUM remained the strongest, the most powerful and the most active of the spiritual administrations.[63] For relatively long periods during that decade DUMSK was incapacitated by the absence of an elected leadership (see below) and DUMZ by Ali-zade's ill health.

Yet even SADUM was not able to cope with the assignments it was expected to perform. The religious centres were designed to play a decisive role in the activity and direction of the various faiths and in the control of the believer population. However,

f.6991, o.3, d.48, l.9.

61. I. Sadchikov to I. V. Polianskii, 18 Nov. 1944 and I. V. Polianskii to V. M. Molotov, 23 Nov. 1944 – GARF, f.6991, o.3, d.6, l.65 and d.1, l.47. On 28 November Molotov passed the latter letter on to his deputy V. G. Dekanozov with a note that he had no objection to the proposed visit. The visit took place in the spring of 1945 and had 'exceptionally positive political results' – Polianskii to Molotov, 21 Nov. 1945; GARF, f.6991, o.3, d.10, l.154. For the visit, see also Lenczowski, *Russia and the West in Iran*, pp.214-5. Lenczowski stressed that whereas Soviet sources maintained that the visit was in response to an invitation by Malayeri, this was not confirmed by the Iranians.

62. For the request, see Izrail Ibadov to the Uzbek SSR SNK, 11 Sept. 1944, I. V. Polianskii to V. M. Molotov, 30 Sept. 1944, and Karl Pugo to Ibadov, 5 Oct. 1944 – GARF, f.6991, o.3, d.1, l.39 and d.6, ll.16-16ob. and 29. For the journal, see pp.167-8.

63. L. A. Prikhod'ko, V. D. Efremov and P. A. Basis, Report, 8 May 1954, and N. I. Inogamov, Address, Conference of CARC *upolnomochennye*, 25-27 Nov. 1958; GARF, f.6991, o.3, d.100, l.36, and d.165, l.34.

Polianskii and other CARC personnel point out, 'the religious movement' in Central Asia took its own course, beyond the bounds of SADUM's influence, leaving that institution isolated on the sidelines owing to its ineffectiveness in sytematising its operations and most of its leading figures' lack of what Polianskii termed 'a correct political orientation or, to be more praise, their political ineffectiveness'.[64] The implication of this was that since the political –administrative apparatus apparently held aloof from the directorate, envisaging it as essentially a religious institution, it was unable to exert any clout among the faithful.

The generally low 'cultural level' of the official Muslim clergy and the paucity of authoritative leaders among them, Polianskii explained to the Soviet leadership in 1948, was the reason for the abject working capacity of the Muslim spiritual directorates.[65] Their inability to control all the communities and groups which aspired to collective religious performance, in turn, led to the 'well-known spontaneity' (*stikhiinost'*) of the Muslim religious movement and the existence of a rather large number of unregistered but factually functioning communities and groups.[66] CARC was even concerned that SADUM's failure to work with its own representatives throughout the five Central Asian republics, with some of whom serious friction had developed, might actually lead to SADUM'S dissolution.[67] On occasions the Council found itself wondering whether, in view of the lack of authority of the leadership of the spiritual directorates, it was not backing the wrong horse. CARC Deputy Chairman Sadovskii pointed out in 1947 that even SADUM's prestige, instead of becoming enhanced, was diminishing daily as a result of squabbles within it own ranks; he suggested CARC might do better by cooperating with Ishan

64. I. V. Polianskii to K. E. Voroshilov, 11 Nov. 1946, and Minutes, CARC session No.11, 18-19 June 1947; GARF, f.6991, o.3, d.34, ll.197-200, and o.4, d.19, l.383, and Iu. V. Sadovskii to Kh. N. Iskanderov, 16 Jan. 1947 – TsGAUz, f.2456, o.1, d.82, l.2.

65. I. V. Polianskii, Report, sent to the Council of Ministers Cultural Bureau, K. E. Voroshilov, M. A. Turkin, M. A. Suslov and A. A. Kuznetsov, 9, 10 and 19 June 1948; GARF, f.6991, o.3, d.53, l.35. For the educational level of the clergy, see pp.243-4.

66. I. V. Polianskii, Memorandum, sent to K. E. Voroshilov and G. M. Malenkov, 23 April 1949; RTsKhIDNI, f.17, o.132, d.111, l.62.

67. I. V. Polianskii to Kh. N. Iskanderov, 8 Aug. 1947; TsGAUz, f.2456, o.1, d.82, ll.19-20.

Babakhan's two main critics, SADUM's representatives in Kirgiziia.[68]

Certainly, the rampant friction among the directorates' own leading élites was a major factor in the context of their general ineffectiveness. The intrigues within the spiritual directorates constantly interfered with prospects of their operating efficiently. This applied especially perhaps to SADUM and DUMSK, where the presidium was composed to a large extent on a territorial basis, so that each republic or territory had its own representative.[69]

DUMSK's jurisdiction, indeed, was barely felt in a number of the areas officially subject to its control. Its composition was dictated not by considerations of suitability and talent, but by inter-clan, inter-ethnic and inter-territorial interests. In addition, it suffered from the language barrier which plagued the North Caucasians, its chairman, always a representative of one of the leading Dagestani peoples, being unable to communicate with clergy belonging even to other Dagestani nationalities. While the natural focus of its activity was Dagestan, even there its authority was not felt in all parts or among all the registered clergy, some of whom totally refused to accept its hegemony. Outside of Dagestan in areas which were officially under its jurisdiction, – Stavropol' Krai, Groznyi Oblast' (as the Chechen-Ingush ASSR was known from 1944-57[70]), Krasnodar Krai and the Kabardinian and North Osetian ASSRs – it exercised no religious leadership whatever.[71] In the

---

68. Minutes, CARC session No.11, 18-19 June 1947; GARF, f.6991, o.4, d.19, l.392. Sadovskii was referring to Shafagat Khoja Khaliqnazarov and Alimkhantura Shakirkhojaev.

69. See, for example, Polianskii's comments on the report of CARC's *upolnomochennyi* for Dagestan, Minutes, CARC session No.7, 23-4 April 1947, and Akhtiamov's report, Minutes, CARC session No.9, 3 June 1947; GARF, f.6991, o.4, d.19, ll.185 and 253-7. Polianskii explained that DUMSK's presidium of eleven members had been chosen with an eye to their local specifications.

70. Except for a few areas of the Chechen-Ingush ASSR which were transferred to Dagestan and Georgia.

71. Report of CARC *upolnomochennyi* for Dagestan, I. Zakaryaev, Minutes, CARC session No.7, 23-4 April 1947; GARF, f.6991, o.4, d.19, l.167. In 1946 two DUMSK representatives were sent to Groznyi Oblast' to sell the brochure issued by its founding convention but returned without any success; the same lot befell a DUMSK member who went to Krasnodar Krai to take stock of functioning mosques and check up on clergy – *ibid*. CARC inspector N. Tagiev, commenting on Zakaryaev's report, confirmed the *upolnomochennyi's* remarks; he contended that DUMSK was basically inactive and did not even have

late 1960s DUMSK did not even have a qazi in the Kabardinian-Balkar ASSR or anyone to organise the collection of money in its mosques; Mufti Kurbanov contended that there was hardly a single cleric in that republic who met the minimal requirements demanded of a minister of religion, that he be literate and intelligent.[72] While this comment need not be taken at face value given the relations which pertained between the directorate and the clergy, it was probably not totally off the mark.

The Muslim spiritual directorates' organisational weakness and distance from Moscow, which made it hard for CARC to effectively control them,[73] and the contention that they were not coordinating their activities either in purely religious matters or in the fields of organisation and administration, became the rationale behind the suggestion to initiate the establishment of a single all-union spiritual administration.[74]

The proposals, however, which were tabled from time to time to this end were never sanctioned at the decision-making level.[75] The considerations in favour of coordinating all theological-doctrinal, administrative-organisational and propaganda activity under the auspices of a single umbrella organisation were not only recurrently elaborated in documents prepared by CARC from the end of 1944[76] until summer 1947[77] but they also apparently

information regarding the extent of 'the religious movement' outside Dagestan; not only had it not convened a single plenum in the three years of its existence, there was simply no means of communication between the mufti who knew only Kumyk and representatives of the other nine nationalities whose religious organisations he was supposed to direct – *ibid.*, ll.175-6. See also the report of M. Gajiev, Minutes, CARC session No.1, 7 Jan. 1964; GARF, f.6991, o.4, d.146, ll.18-19.

72. L. Aisov to the CRA, 11 June 1968; GARF, f.6991, o.6, d.153, l.138.

73. I. V. Polianskii to L. P. Beriia, I. V. Stalin, V. M. Molotov and K. E. Voroshilov at the Council of Ministers and to A. A. Zhdanov, N. S. Khrushchev, A. A. Kuznetsov, N. S. Patolichev and G. M. Popov at the AUCP(b) Central Committee, 27 Feb. 1947; GARF, f.6991, o.3, d.47, l.93.

74. I. V. Polianskii, Memorandum on the organisation of a Spiritual Directorate of Muslims of the Soviet Union, 11 Nov. 1946; GARF, f.6991, o.3, d.34, ll.201-6.

75. See, for example, an unidentified CARC official to I. Ibadov, 30 Jan. 1946 – TsGAUz, f.2456, o.1, d.90, l.4 – and I. V. Polianskii to G. F. Aleksandrov, 1 July 1947 – RTsKhIDNI, f.17, o.125, d.506, l.126.

76. The first time this matter was spelt out was in a draft letter to Molotov in which Polianskii wrote that CARC considered the establishment of a single

had the approval of the leadership of the spiritual directorates and
the government and party organs of the six Muslim union republics
and at least two of the Muslim autonomous republics.[78] The reasons
for the repudiation of these proposals are not known: in all prob-

---

centre expedient in order to coordinate the work of the four spiritual directorates
and extensively inform the outside world of the situation of Islam in the USSR.
The coordination was especially necessary in teaching Islamic dogma and
synchronising the practical aspects of managing the spiritual organisation of the
30-million strong Muslim population. Polianskii contended that the various contradictions which existed not only between Sunnis and Shiites but even within
each trend could be clarified and overcome were there a single centralised
religious leadership. He also insisted that this would enable uniform publication
activity, concerted action in establishing an effective organisation of religious
life and preparing and appointing clergy, and a united effort in disseminating
positive propaganda in foreign Muslim countries – I. V. Polianskii to V. M.
Molotov, handwritten draft, 21 Nov. 1944; GARF, f.6991, o.3, d.44, ll.65-72.
It is not clear whether this document was ever sent.

77. The last two documents relating in detail to this issue, to which considerable
attention had been paid in 1945 and 1946, are I. V. Polianskii to G. F. Aleksandrov,
1 July 1947 (RTsKhIDNI, f.17, o.125, d.506, l.121) and Appendix No.1 to
draft government decree dated July 1947 and apparently sent by Polianskii to
Minister of Culture S. Kaftanov, G. F. Aleksandrov and Minister of State Security
V. A. Abakumov on 26 July 1947 (GARF, f.6991, o.3, d.47, l.306 and
RTsKhIDNI, f.17, o.125, d.506, ll.184-5). It was probably the rejection of the
proposal by a commission comprising these three officials which to all intents
and purposes removed it from the agenda, although passing mention was made
in summer 1948 of the belief that the creation of a single coordinating centre,
if its authority were to be used skilfully, would be beneficial for regulating
Muslim activity – I. V. Polianskii, Report, ratified by CARC session No.8, 9
June 1948; GARF, f.6991, o.3, d.53, l.37. The report was sent to K. E. Voroshilov,
the Council of Ministers Cultural Bureau, M. A. Suslov, A. A. Kuznetsov, and
M. A. Turkin at the Central Committee Cadres Administration.

78. Memorandum signed by Polianskii, sent to K. E. Voroshilov, 13 Nov.
1946; GARF, f.6991, o.3, d.34, ll.197-206. According to Polianskii the initial
approach was made by the leaders of the four spiritual directorates, but since
CARC wrote to its various *upolnomochennye* to put out feelers among these very
same leaders to find out their reaction to the proposal – see Polianskii to I.
Ibadov, 25 Aug. 1945 and I. Ibadov to Iu. V. Sadovskii, 5 March 1946 (TsGAUz,
f.2456, o.1, d.37, l.23, and d.90, l.7), and B. Shahbazbekov to Polianskii, 14
March 1946, and I. Zakaryaev to Polianskii, 6 April 1946 (GARF, f.6991, o.3,
d.44, ll.5 and 7) – there is reason to doubt the veracity of this statement. It is
possible that certain members of the directorates raised the question, perhaps at
the prompting of CARC officials, but almost certainly not their chairmen.
Polianskii told Voroshilov of the appproval of the six union republic leaderships
and of the leading organs of the Bashkir ASSR, but we know from Zakaryaev's
letter that the Dagestan Obkom and Council of Ministers also agreed.

ability the opposition came from the propaganda and ideology apparatus of the AUCP(b) Central Committee which did not share CARC's desire to create a prestigious religious leadership and did not see any advantage in having concerted Muslim activity.[79] In 1947 Council of Ministers Deputy Chairman Voroshilov expressed his agreement with CARC's proposal, and said he would discuss the issue with the AUCP(b) Central Committee.[80] Yet in a conversation with Polianskii early in 1949, he gave a negative reply to the idea of establishing a single Muslim religious centre. First of all, he contended, once this was done for the Muslims, an analogous solution would have to be found for the Jews and the Old Believers. Secondly, there had never been such a centre and were one to be created, it would have to start from scratch and seek out a path for itself which would lead to a religious revival. Finally, it was already enough having one religious centre 'whose head had to be taken into account' (namely that of the Russian Orthodox Church).[81] Unquestionably, the decision was not Voroshilov's and there can be no certainty that the reasons he gave were the real ones.

The idea of creating a single Muslim religious centre under a grand mufti was broached again in the mid 1960s, but this time does not seem to have had much meaningful support. When SADUM Chairman Ziyautdin Babakhanov was asked his opinion, he expressed serious reservations, saying that it would be perceived by the heads of all spiritual directorates as an indication of lack of confidence in them. DUMZ in particular, representing principally, as it did, the Shiite community, was to all intents and purposes independent and would not be prepared to receive guidance from another, non-Shiite body.[82]

79. For further discussion of disagreements on policy between CARC and the ideologists, see pp.19 and 591.

80. Iu. V. Sadovskii's account of his meeting with Voroshilov, 4 Jan. 1947; GARF, f.6991, o.3, d.8, l.98.

81. Memorandum of Voroshilov's reception of Polianskii, 12 Feb. 1949; GARF, f.6991, o.3, d.8, l.177.

82. Reception by B. S. Rzhanov of Z. Babakhanov, 10 Nov. 1965; GARF, f.6991, o.4, d.171, ll.34-5. The idea was put to CARC by its *upolnomochennyi* in Tashkent, apparently after a conversation with SADUM deputy chairman, Ismail Sattiev, who seems to have hoped in this way to become mufti, for Babakhanov was the obvious candidate for the higher post. Sattiev had actually told a foreign delegation in October that this question was under review when

The spiritual directorates thus remained the primary link in the chain of command between the regime and Soviet Islam. This situation inevitably created a confluence of interests between them and the regime, both having a vested interest in the spiritual directorates monopolising all official and organised religious life. CARC evidently presupposed the fundamental loyalty of their leaders to the regime and their readiness to co-operate with it. Its officials dwelt frequently on SADUM's tendency to be pliant. The directorate's personnel, it was said, sought to violate the laws on religion as minimally as possible, and if a disagreement with the policy of the central authorities arose, CARC's *upolnomochennye* would draw their attention to this, and they would retract their previous positions.[83] As to DUMES, CARC's *upolnomochennyi* in Ufa noted in the second half of the 1950s that it was possible through DUMES Chairman Khiyaletdinov to carry through whatever measures might be in the state's interests. After many years of 'relations of confidence' with him, he was not even sure whether the mufti believed in God.[84] Both these factors notwithstanding, difficulties arose periodically between the spiritual directorates and CARC, and particularly its *upolnomochennye* in the Muslim areas who had to transmit to the directorates instructions or recommendations which were often not to their liking. The head office in Moscow was constantly endeavouring to remove friction between its representatives in the localities and the directorates, urging the former to show 'more tact' and not to hamper the directorates' smooth operation.[85]

Despite the very considerable constraints to which the spiritual directorates were subject, their activity was relatively variegated. In the first place, they were ultimately responsible for the religious life and activity of the communities in the territory under their jurisdiction. Strictly speaking, this centred on the registered

---

he knew this was not the case, with the intention, it seems, of trying to force the hand of the authorities – Minutes, CARC session No.24, 12-13 Nov. 1965; GARF, f.6991, o.4, d.169, l.167.

83. N. I. Inogamov, Address, All-Union conference of CARC *upolnomochennye*, 26 Nov. 1958; GARF, f.6991, o.3, d.165, l.77.

84. M. Sh. Karimov, All-Union conference of CARC *upolnomochennye*, 25-27 Nov. 1958; GARF, f.6991, o.3, d.165, l.94.

85. For instance, I. V. Polianskii to Kh. N. Iskanderov, 20 Feb. 1954; TsGAUz, f.2456, o.1, d.162, l.82. For the extent of mistrust between Rasulev and CARC's *upolnomochennyi* in Ufa, see n.141 below.

mosques, but, in fact, very often, especially in times when the regime was more lenient, it included links with unregistered clergy and some control of places of pilgrimage. Secondly, the spiritual directorates appointed clergy with all that this entailed, namely the verification of the candidate's knowledge of Islamic doctrine, the improvement of that knowledge where necessary, maintaining contact with the religious associations in regard to suggested candidates and, finally, the dismissal of clergy who in one way or another did not fulfil their task in appropriate fashion.[86] In addition, they issued *fetwas* interpreting dogma so as to facilitate the adaptation of their flock to the conditions of a communist society. They also concentrated in their hands rather large sums of money, collected from the mosques for their various activities. And, lastly, they sought to train cadres of new clergy, to publish religious calendars and other literature, and to enable some believers at least to perform the *hajj*.

At the same time, the dimensions and intensity of this activity depended very much on the circumstances of the times. In periods when it was possible to do so, the spiritual directorates expanded their activity; when the restrictions became more stringent they retreated, not always willingly. The first years, in the mid 1940s, were a period of trial and error and, on the whole, the Muslim religious centres took initiatives and tried their hand. Towards the end of the 1940s and in the early 1950s, their activities were low key, but by the middle of the decade were again on the upswing. By the turn of the decade, however, they were in retreat once more, only to push forward anew after the middle of the 1960s.

Relations with the registered mosques and religious societies

The basic function of the spiritual directorates was regulating the activity of the registered religious societies. These were their natural sphere of influence. This meant, in the first place, that the spiritual

---

86. The original DUMZ charter, for example, stipulated that DUMZ would dismiss 'preachers, imams and muezzins who operate contrary to the teaching of Islam and the instructions of the spiritual directorate' and people 'unworthy of clerical status or who operate in any way against the interests of the mother country'. The 1959 charter substituted for the last phrase 'those who violate the laws of the Soviet state' – GARF, f.6991, o.3, d.185, ll.77-8 and 172.

directorates were interested in the existence of as many such societies as possible, and in the early years, when conditions permitted, they made every effort to facilitate the registering of religious societies. When this was not a viable option, they devoted their attentions to trying to prevent the closure of mosques and the withdrawal of the religious societies from registration. Indeed, it appears that at least in the early years, the consent of the directorates was required in order to close mosques, especially if this was to be done by combining smaller communities with larger ones which operated nearby. In 1949, for instance, Ishan Babakhan gave his consent to the closure of six small mosques in Tashkent and transferring the religious societies attached to them to neighbouring mosques. But by the time the republican government discussed the matter two years had passed, attendance at the six mosques had grown and so too had SADUM's 'patriotic' activity on behalf of the peace movement, which apparently was seen by Babakhan as strengthening his position with the authorities. As a result, the mufti changed his mind and retracted his concurrence and it was decided to refrain from reviewing the issue of closure.[87]

Secondly, the directorates sought to guide the societies in a direction that they felt might be conducive to augmenting religious activity. This they did by sending them written instructions, holding conversations with individual clergy who might visit or be summoned to their head offices and travelling to the localities to issue verbal instructions and become acquainted with the situation in the field.[88] Obviously, the more believers there were and the higher the level of religiosity, the greater the potential impact of Islam's recognised leadership. The catch was that the directorates were the institutionalised instrument of the Soviet regime, and so they often found themselves walking a tightrope and in danger of losing some of the more genuine believers. In order to preempt this, the religious centres endeavoured to tie the religious societies to themselves in different ways.

A SADUM circular to all *imam-khatibs* and executive organ chairmen at the very end of the 1940s indicates how this was contemplated. The document began with an injunction to conduct

87. Kh. N. Iskanderov, Report, 2 June 1952; GARF, f.6991, o.3, d.83, l.137. See also Iskanderov to I. V. Polianskii, 24 Sept. 1951; TsGAUz, f.2456, o.1, d.132, ll.102-3.

88. N. Smirnov, Information, 8 Aug. 1962; GARF, f.6991, o.3, d.1390, l.23.

all rites and all contact with believers solely on the basis of SADUM's directives and to ensure that the registered clergy aim to acquire respect and authority. To this end, imams and *khatibs* had to coordinate the content of their sermons and readings from religious texts with the spiritual directorate. It was likewise incumbent upon them to inform SADUM of their exact revenues from the performance of rites. The chairmen of the executive organs, for their part, were to compose lists of the *mahallas* in the surrounding area, specifying which of them invited the registered clergy to perform rites for them; they must also present SADUM with a list of unofficial clergy who conducted rites without authorisation and without the knowledge of the powers-that-be. Such people had to be exposed in the eyes of believers, who must be made acquainted with their illegal activity. SADUM insisted that preaching, interpreting dogma and resolving religious questions were the sole prerogative of official clergy.[89] It is evident from this document that the spiritual directorates sought at one and the same time to exert stringent control of the activity of the registered clergy, to mobilise them in the struggle against unofficial clergy and to harness the executive organs of the registered religious societies to both ends.

A report on Islam in 1970 noted that the leaders of the religious centres tried not to miss any opportunity to issue instructions to the clergy. Wherever they met with them, whether the occasion be the opening of a new mosque, or the appointment, anniversary or funeral of a cleric, they would give them briefings. They would recommend to them, for example, to preach every Friday so as to lead their flock 'on the path of Islam and progress', and to bring their sermons into close rapport with their parishioners' daily lives. Many clergy accepted these guidelines from the spiritual directorates as directives from which they must not deviate.[90]

In addition to the registered mosques which were under their jurisdiction, the spiritual directorates were given the use and upkeep of a number of mausolea or *mazars*. In 1945 a special government instruction gave SADUM seven of the more important *mazars* for use as prayer-houses,[91] and in 1947 the Shiite *pir* of Goy-imam

89. Ishan Babakhan to all *imam-khatibs* and chairmen of executive organs, 30 Dec. 1949; TsGAUz, f.2456, o.1, d.127, l.4.

90. CRA, Information, sent to the Central Committee, 27 April 1971; TsKhSD, f.5, o.63, d.89, l.121.

91. SNK Instruction No.1324-r, 28 Jan. 1945; GARF, f.6991, o.4, d.1, l.13.

on the outskirts of Kirovabad was transferred to DUMZ.[92] (In the Caucasus these holy tombs were called *pirs*.) As of late 1956 SADUM was managing seventeen such mausolea,[93] and DUMZ too was acquiring more *pirs*.[94] (In 1960, in the course of Khrushchev's anti-religious campaign, thirteen of SADUM's mausolea were withdrawn from registration and returned to the Uzbek SSR Council of Ministers Committee for the Preservation of Monuments of Material Culture.[95]) The transfer to the spiritual directorates of some of the leading mausolea unquestionably enhanced their prestige in the eyes of believers, as well as being the source of considerable income, once the basic expenditures on repair work which most of them required after years of neglect had been undertaken. They were said to be visited by thousands of pilgrims from all over Central Asia, each such *mazar* receiving approximately 150 heads of livestock monthly as donations and on festivals 4–5,000.[96] Justifying the expenses in restoring the *mazars* given over

The seven mausolea, thought to be the most revered Muslim monuments, were all in Uzbekistan and had been under the jurisdiction of the Administration for Architectural Affairs at the Uzbek SSR SNK – *ibid.*, and I. V. Polianskii to K. E. Voroshilov, 5 April 1946; GARF, f.6991, o.3, d.34, l.45.

92. DUMZ was asking for its transfer already in 1946 – B. Shahbazbekov, Report, undated [June 1946]; see also I. V. Polianskii to K. E. Voroshilov, 2 Sept. 1947. The actual transfer was authorised by Instruction No.1543-rs of the USSR Council of Ministers, 20 Oct. 1947; GARF, f.6991, o.3, d.38, l.97, and d.48, ll.34-5 and 59.

93. Sh. K. Shirinbaev, Address, All-Union conference of CARC *upolnomochennye*, 18-20 April 1960. Some of these mausolea were in the Tajik SSR – Report, 8 May 1954. Nine *mazars* – eight of them with mosques – were transferred to SADUM by the Uzbek SSR Council of Ministers in Dec. 1956 – K. F. Tagirov, Information, 1 March 1957; GARF, f.6991, o.3, d.208, ll.74 and 76, d.100, l.39, and d.132, l.30.

94. See n.316 below. In 1956 DUMZ asked permission to open six *pirs* – G. F. Frolov, Information, 22 Feb. 1957; GARF, f.6991, o.3, d.132, l.78. For the registration of mausolea, see also p.94.

95. Minutes, CARC session No.9, 28 April 1960, and Sh. K. Shirinbaev, Address, All-Union conference of CARC *upolnomochennye*, 18-20 April 1960 – GARF, f.6991, o.3, d.204, l.92, and d.208, l.77.

96. The five *mazars* in the Uzbek SSR which were under SADUM's jurisdiction in 1956 brought in over 1 million rubles in that year – L. A. Prikhod'ko, Information, 18 May 1957; GARF, f.6991, o.3, d.146, l.99. The income from these *mazars* had climbed from 358,000 rubles in 1954 to 1,040,000 rubles in 1956. See also N.I. Inogamov, Address, Conference of CARC *upolnomochennye*, 25-27 November 1958; GARF, f.6991, o.3, d.165, l.36. For the expenses involved in repairing the Hakim al-Termezi *mazar* in Termez and restoring the Barak-Khan

to its management, SADUM explained to the clergy that these historical monuments were the glory of the Muslim world and 'we are bound to honour them as places where the ashes of our saints rest'.[97]

The charters of the spiritual directorates laid down that it was their responsibility to confirm the appointment of clergy and muezzins. (In the course of time the suggestion was put forward to remove the appointment of muezzins from the jurisdiction of the directorates on the grounds that they were not full-fledged clergy.)[98] The actual election of a cleric to a post in a particular religious society was to be carried out through its general meeting, but the mufti himself or his deputy had to sign the certificate of appointment. Sometimes the reverse might happen, that is the spiritual directorate would appoint a mulla, whom it had examined and determined which posts he was suited for, while the religious society retained the right to reject the appointee. The mosque in Troitsk, for example, appointed a cleric who was rejected by the mufti in Ufa, and the latter's choice was repudiated by the community, which therefore remained without a cleric.[99] Often the spiritual directorates' representatives in the localities would select candidates and examine their suitability for the suggested post, including their religious knowledge; they would then pass the matter on for approval to the spiritual directorate and to the local CARC *upolnomochennyi* who, after giving his consent, would transmit it to the *upolnomochennyi* immediately responsible for maintaining contact with the spiritual directorate.[100]

Medrese in Tashkent, see Z. Babakhanov to Kh. N. Iskanderov, 14 Dec. 1955; TsGAUz, f.2456, o.1, d.174, ll.112-3.

97. Z. Babakhanov and F. Sadyqkhojaev to members of SADUM and the *khatibs* of major mosques, 6 Nov. 1956; TsGAUz, f.2456, o.1, d.190, l.9. According to the CARC *upolnomochennyi* for the Uzbek SSR, these religious sites and monuments were transferred to SADUM in 1956 out of considerations of foreign policy – N. I. Inogamov, Address, Conference of CARC *upolnomochennye*, 25-27 Nov. 1958; GARF, f.6991, o.3, d.165, l.37.

98. Following CARC's ruling of 3 June 1950 that its *upolnomochennye* need not register muezzins since they were not in fact clergy, its *upolnomochennyi* in Tashkent suggested to the chairman of SADUM that it discontinue the issuance of certificates to them. The mufti asked, however, to be allowed to continue the practice in line with the SADUM charter – Kh. N. Iskanderov to I. V. Polianskii, 11 Jan. 1951; TsGAUz, f.2456, o.1, d.134, l.7.

99. V. Sitnikov to CARC, 6 July 1945; GARF, f.6991, o.3, d.25, l.142.

100. Iu. Sadovskii to I. Ibadov, 30 Jan. 1946; TsGAUz, f.2456, o.1, d.90, l.3.

In addition to the appointment, transfer and dismissal of clergy, the spiritual directorate frequently appointed and removed members of the lay leadership of registered religious societies.[101] Moreover, SADUM obligated the executive organs of official mosques to send quarterly reports to its qazis. It also sought to impose its authority on them by forbidding them to appoint people to levy moneys traditionally designed for charitable and communal purposes, the *sadaqa, fitr* and *zakat*.[102] In the late Stalin period, however, SADUM specifically prohibited clergy from intervening in the financial affairs of the religious societies, since legally their administration was the prerogative of the executive organ.[103] On the whole, however, the ongoing dispute between the clergy and executive organs as to who in fact predominated in the religious society found the spiritual directorates on the side of the former. When under Khrushchev the CARC *upolnomochennyi* for Kirgiziia pointed out to SADUM's qazi in that republic that the clergy were subordinate to the executive organ and not *vice-versa*, SADUM complained to CARC.[104]

In effect, the implementation of the right of appointment became an area of controversy between the spiritual directorates and CARC's *upolnomochennye* in the field. The latter took exception to the appointment of clergy whom they considered unworthy. Moscow pointed out to them, however, that the appointment by the mufti of clergy on the basis of personal acquaintance or as remuneration for some service, or the designation of people the *upolnomochennye* considered uneducated, were not valid reasons for refusing to register them. Only if clergy appointed by a spiritual directorate committed acts prohibited by Soviet legislation on religion did the *upolnomochennye* have the right to raise the issue of their withdrawal from registration.[105] The *upolnomochennye* also

101. A. A. Puzin, Address, convention of Central Asian *upolnomochennye*, 6 June 1959; GARF, f.6991, o.3, d.186, ll.224-5.

102. Minutes, session of SADUM's 2nd plenum, [20-27 Jan. 1947]; TsGAUz, f.2456, o.1, d.104, l.2ob-3. For these levies and the rationale behind the attitude of the religious leadership to them, see pp.128-9, 141, 153-4 and 486-8.

103. L. A. Prikhod'ko, Report, 20 May 1953; GARF, f.6991, o.3, d.91, l.249.

104. H. Akhtiamov, Address, All-Union conference of CARC *upolnomochennye*, 18-20 April 1960; GARF, f.6991, o.3, d.208, l.130. For the relations between the clergy and lay leadership of the registered religious societies, see pp.279-84.

105. I. V. Polianskii to Kh. N. Iskanderov, 20 Feb. 1954; TsGAUz, f.2456, o.1, d.162, ll.81-2.

complained that the directorates and their representatives sometimes held up appointments and delayed verifying the qualifications of candidates.[106] On the other hand, in Uzbekistan a re-registration of clergy in the late 1950s disclosed that six mosques had clergy who had been working for years without registration.[107] Occasionally, CARC *upolnomochennye* themselves usurped the right of appointing clergy.[108] More commonly, a representative of the spiritual directorates would dismiss clergy upon the recommendation of CARC's *upolnomochennyi*.[109]

From time to time, irregularities occurred for which the spiritual directorates were manifestly not to blame, but resulted from the ineffectiveness of their control. Their representatives in a republic or oblast', for instance, might appoint or remove clergy on their own initiative without obtaining the consent of the leadership of the religious centre,[110] or otherwise violate the established procedures for appointing and dismissing clergy. One SADUM representative called together 30-40 per cent of the believers of a religious society in Kirgiziia and then proceeded to remove the incumbent imam and replace him by another without any proper resolution being taken.[111]

106. H. Akhtiamov, Report, Conference of *upolnomochennye*, Alma-Ata, 30 Sept. 1946; GARF, f.6991, o.3, d.41, ll.107-8.

107. N. I. Inogamov, Address, Conference of CARC *upolnomochennye*, 26-27 Nov. 1958; GARF, f.6991, o.3, d.165, l.81.

108. For instance, in 1951 Kh. N. Iskanderov charged the *upolnomochennyi* for Namangan Oblast' with dismissing the SADUM representative in the oblast' and proceeding to appoint clergy; a decade letter SADUM Mufti Babakhanov contended that CARC's *upolnomochennye* had appointed and/or dismissed clergy in Tashkent, Samarkand, Chimkent and Tajikistan – Memo of conversation with V. F. Riazanov, undated (probably Dec. 1962); GARF, f.6991, o.3, d.1738, l.100.

109. E.g., Kirgiz SSR republican *upolnomochennyi* Akhtiamov initiated the removal of the imam of the religious society in Naryn who collected 'all possible donations' by travelling around the kolkhozy; but he was actually dismissed by SADUM's qazi – Report of H. A. Akhtiamov, 18 April 1960; GARF, f.6991, o.3, d.208, l.134.

110. The heads of SADUM told CARC's *upolnomochennyi* in Tashkent in 1946 that its qazi in the Kirgiz SSR, Shafagat Khoja Khaliqnazarov, was doing just this; he was also collecting large sums in the name of SADUM which he was expending on mausolea in that republic – I. Ibadov to I. V. Polianskii, 5 July 1946; TsGAUz, f.2456, o.1, d.90, ll.31-2.

111. N. Urumbaev to A. A. Puzin, Osh Oblispolkom Chairman Medetbekov and Obkom Secretary Eshmambetov, 20 Aug. 1957; GARF, f.6991, o.3, d.458, ll.4-5.

In the very late Stalin years, when the noose seemed to be tightening, SADUM in fact dismissed clergy who committed crass breaches of the legislation on religion. Whether its motivation was indeed, as was suggested by CARC, that it sought to demonstrate its negative attitude to clergy guilty of such violations or whether this was the consequence of the threat transmitted to Babakhan by the Uzbek SSR republican *upolnomochennyi* that he would in the future himself simply discharge clergy who transgressed the law, is not clear.[112] Towards the end of the 1950s with the advent of Khrushchev's anti-religious campaign, dismissals of clergy by the spiritual directorates in the context of religious over-enthusiasm which threatened to spill over into flouting Soviet law and established procedure, re-occurred.[113]

Nor were the antagonisms and disagreements with the religious societies and registered clergy conjured up by the activity of the spiritual directorates restricted to the field of appointments. The spiritual directorates' financial control of the registered communities was a further frequent bone of contention. From the outset, the directorates gave expression to their authority over the religious societies by levying money from and through them for a variety of purposes. DUMSK was said in the mid 1940s to have taken several thousand rubles for each mosque it opened. The directorates instructed the clergy to collect donations in money and kind from believers, part of which they assigned to charity, specifically for war invalids and orphans. At first they legitimised these collections as *zakat*, the tax traditionally given by believers to the communal treasury.[114]

By the end of the 1940s the directorates not only determined the salaries of the registered clergy,[115] but demanded that the lion's

112. L. A. Prikhod'ko, Report, 20 May 1953; GARF, f.6991, o.3, d.91, l.249.

113. See, for example, the address of the CARC *upolnomochennyi* for the Bashkir ASSR, M. Sh. Karimov, Minutes, CARC session No.21s, 22 July 1959; GARF, f.6991, o.3, d.184, ll.156-7. He brought as examples an *imam-khatib* removed by Khiyaletdinov who had gone around his raion, calling upon the Muslim population to observe the faith and organising the collection of money for the repair of his mosque, and the mulla in the town of Sterlitamak. And see pp.261-2.

114. I. N. Uzkov and G. A. Vrachev to I. V. Polianskii, Memorandum, 29 Nov. 1946; RTsKhIDNI, f.17, o.125, d.405, l.95.

115. In early 1947 SADUM fixed the salaries of *imam-khatibs* of official mosques at 500 rubles a month, of imams at 400 and of muezzins at 200, the money to be taken from the donations received by the mosques where they served –

share of the religious societies' income, specifically donations made on the major festivals, including the *fitr*, be earmarked for themselves. In the early 1950s the two leading directorates at least were taking measures to put their house in order and consolidate their financial situation. They brought in bookkeepers and inspectors and audited the finances of a number of mosques, revealing disarray in computing the sums received, as well as the unwillingness of certain religious societies to in fact transfer moneys to the directorates (see below), and the appropriation by clergy of moneys for the use of their own mosques and sometimes even for their personal needs. In order to rectify matters and ensure that they exercised effective control of the finances of the mosques and clergy, they resolved to stipulate in advance the sum which each religious society was to pay them. They also obliged the religious societies to enter into their accounts moneys received from the performance of rites by their clergy, which believers were to give to the society's treasurer in return for a receipt. This led to complaints from both clergy and ordinary believers, the latter fearing that they were designed to somehow register all who performed religious rites and subject them to taxation.[116]

In the course of the decade the directorates actually fixed the budget of each individual registered society under their jurisdiction, determining the size of its income and expenditure. The leadership of each mosque had to take every possible measure to fulfil the demands made of it and convey the requisite sums to the directorate, even if this sometimes entailed actions which jeopardised its position *vis-à-vis* the law-enforcement authorities, such as collecting donations in private homes. In some years SADUM sent representatives, notably students at the Mir-Arab seminary, to supervise the collection of these payments and their transfer to Tashkent. In 1959, when the situation was taking a turn for the worse, SADUM ordered the religious societies to inform believers at Friday prayers that those who lived nearby should bring the *fitr* to the mosque, whereas in the more outlying parts, where the clergy could no

---

Minutes, SADUM 2nd plenary session, [20-27 Jan.1947]; TsGAUz, f.2456, o.1, d.104, l.3.

116. Almaev to Tashkent Oblispolkom Chairman Mahkamova, Obkom Secretary Nazarov, Kh. N. Iskanderov and I. V. Polianskii, 19 Jan. 1952; TsGAUz, f.2456, o.1, d.142, l.46; and L. A. Prikhod'ko, Report, 2 June 1952; GARF, f.6991, o.3, d.81, ll.131-2.

longer go to collect it, believers in each settlement should appoint someone reliable to whom they would bring the *fitr* and who in turn would bring it to the mosque.[117] In periods when the spiritual directorates were feeling strong, they even removed imams who did not fulfil their monetary assignments.[118]

The rigid control of their purse-strings was particularly irritating for the registered mosques in view of the extravagant conduct of certain spiritual directorate officials. In Osh Oblast', which was the centre of activity of Shafagat Khoja Khaliqnazarov, originally SADUM representative in Kirgiziia and where the resentment of the clergy was acute, the lack of confidence in SADUM was attributed to the wasteful expenditure of the moneys it received from the religious societies.[119] As time went on, the registered societies in that oblast' became increasingly insistent that they did not wish to send SADUM the large sums of money it was demanding. Many representatives of these societies approached the local *upolnomochennyi* to ask whether they had in fact to send money for SADUM's upkeep. His superior, the Kirgiz republican *upolnomochennyi*, directed him to reply that the religious society itself disposed of its money, that this was their own affair in which no government organ could interfere. At the same time, the leaders of the religious societies should bear in mind that they were hierarchically subordinate to the spiritual directorate and must take into consideration its instructions.[120] Even Khaliqnazarov in fact fulfilled

117. I. Halimov to CARC, 23 May 1956, and H. Akhtiamov and B. Jumashev, Addresses, Conference of CARC's Central Asian *upolnomochennye*, 5-6 June 1959; GARF, f.6991, o.3, d.457, l.95, and d.186, ll.44-5 and 82-3.

118. Sh. O. Ospanov, Address, All-Union conference of CARC *upolnomochennye*, 18-20 April 1960; GARF, f.6991, o.3, d.208, l.120.

119. H. Akhtiamov to I. Halimov, 20 April 1950; GARF, f.6991, o.3, d.454, l.62. Akhtiamov instructed Halimov to verify whether this was the real reason and whether this was not a sign that the clergy sought to decentralise authority so that each religious society could operate autonomously. Already two years before, Khaliqnazarov was accusing SADUM of not expending the moneys it was receiving from the religious societies for the purposes for which they had been designated, and Ziyautdin Babakhanov, the mufti's son and deputy, personally for expending large sums on purchasing jewelery for his wife. SADUM's attempt in late 1949 to install a new representative in place of Khaliqnazarov was opposed by all the local clergy and believers – Halimov to CARC, 30 March 1948 and 14 Oct. 1949; GARF, f.6991, o.3, d.453, l.42, and d.454, ll.30-1.

120. H. Akhtiamov to I. Halimov, 11 Oct. 1950; GARF, f.6991, o.3, d.454, l.89.

SADUM's instructions when they did not threaten to have an adverse effect on his authority and the financial needs of his own mosque. For example, its 1949 directive to restrict the reading of *mavluds* just to one day, rather than throughout the month of Muhammad's birthday, and not to accompany the reading with festive fare in the mosque, was observed by all the registered mosques in Osh Oblast'.[121] In 1950 of eight mosques in his oblast', concerning whose festival donations the CARC *upolnomochennyi* in Osh had information, three gave the entire sum to SADUM, three approximately one half, and two nothing.[122]

Indeed, the financial procedures introduced by the spiritual directorates did not always operate smoothly. On the one hand, in some areas, notably in the Northern Caucasus, and in periods of greater repression, the clergy's salaries were simply not forthcoming, the community preferring the religious society to disband and the mosque to be closed rather than having to pay their clergy.[123] In a few places, where the clergy did not receive salaries from the mosque, for instance in Azerbaijan, their income continued to derive entirely from their performance of rites and from collections made at prayer-services and other ceremonies.[124] On the other hand, even when salaries were paid in accordance with the regular arrangements, the clergy were constantly aspiring to appropriate larger sums from the revenues of their mosques than the directorate assigned to the religious societies, both for themselves personally and for the needs of the community.[125] The spiritual directorates sought to mitigate the effect of their demands of the religious

121. I. Halimov to CARC, undated (probably April 1950); GARF, f.6991, o.3, d.454, ll.11-12. For SADUM's ruling on the Mavlud, see also pp.154 and 502.

122. I. Halimov to H. Akhtiamov, 4 Sept. 1950; GARF, f.6991, o.3, d.454, ll.82-3.

123. Minutes, CARC session No.19, Instructors' meeting, 20-22 Dec. 1950; GARF, f.6991, o.3, d.66, l.130. And see pp.200 and 213.

124. For example, in the case of the *akhund* and three mullas in the Shiite mosque in Kirovabad in the early-mid 1970s – A. Galiev, Information, 30 May 1973; GARF, f.6991, o.6, d.537, l.187.

125. In an effort to find a compromise, SADUM in 1951 agreed to raise the salaries of *imam-khatibs* from 700 to 900 rubles and of imams from 500 to 700 rubles, but left no loopholes for the clergy to appropriate any further sums for whatever use – Kh. N. Iskanderov, Report, 2 June 1952; GARF, f.6991, o.3, d.83, ll.136-7. Until 1947, the clergy had received one eighth of the *fitr-sadaqa* levied by the mosques – Saidbaev, *Islam i obshchestvo*, p.189.

societies by intervening from time to time to protect the clergy from exorbitant tax assessments, contending that these did not correspond to the clergy's real earnings.[126]

In addition to friction over appointments and finances there seem early on to have have been other foci of antagonism between the spiritual directorates and the registered mosques, especially in some of the Central Asian republics. Concern that the religious centres were not in effect controlling 'the Muslim religious movement' had been voiced by CARC since 1946.[127] In mid 1947 Polianskii reported to the Central Committee that in almost all faiths an opposition was forming to the religious centres encompassing both clergy and lay believers.[128] According to a CARC report in the early 1950s SADUM was struggling hard to enhance its influence among the religious societies in the Tajik, Kazakh and Kirgiz SSRs, where the clergy was demonstrating separatist tendencies and not always subordinating itself to the religious centre.[129] Even in Uzbekistan itself there were pockets of resistance to SADUM, notably in the Fergana Valley (see below); whereas in Turkmenistan SADUM's own representative complained in 1950 that it discredited the few registered clergy in that republic by not permitting them to perform rites in private homes and demanding that they condemn the activity of itinerant mullas. He compared its methods to attempts to swat flies with a sledgehammer.[130] In 1960 it was noted that in Kazakhstan, too, more and

126. Kh. N. Iskanderov, Report, 2 June 1952; GARF, f.6991, o.3, d.83, l.137. When Polianskii received Babakhan, then on a visit to Moscow, in 1951, the latter pointed out that the financial organs were including in the clergy's income for purposes of taxation moneys which were transferred to SADUM and as a result taxes were imposed on the clergy that they were in no position to pay – Information, 30 Aug. 1951; GARF, f.6991, o.3, d.8, l.254. For details, see letter from SADUM to Iskanderov, 11 May 1952; TsGAUz, f.2456, o.1, d.144, ll.42-3.

127. See pp.113-5 above.

128. I. V. Polianskii to G. F. Aleksandrov, 1 July 1947; RTsKhIDNI, f.17, o.125, d.506, l.113.

129. L. Prikhod'ko, Report, 20 May 1953; GARF, f.6991, o.3, d.91, ll.268-9. In this connection SADUM relieved its qazi in Kazakhstan of his post as *imam-khatib* in Alma-Ata in the latter half of 1951 (to enable him to devote more attention to directing the activity of the republic's religious societies) and a SADUM board plenum removed its *upolnomochennyi* in Tajikistan in 1952 (apparently because he was considered to have sided with the local clergy).

130. Minutes, CARC session, No.1, 13 Jan. 1951; GARF, f.6991, o.3, d.74, ll.13-4.

more voices were being heard among the clergy and lay leadership that they could manage without SADUM. Although there were difficulties in finding clergy – the cadres who had received a religious training before the regime's campaign against the Muslim educational system inevitably diminishing over time – Kazakhstan's mosques rejected SADUM's suggestion to 'inject' new mullas: they did not need mullas 'trained by the civil authority'.[131]

Undisputably, some of the disagreements between the spiritual directorates and the clergy under their jurisdiction – as well as among and between themselves – were ideological or theological. These emanated in part from the directorates' status as agents or representatives of the regime, in part from the tension which had developed in the nineteenth and early twentieth century between modernists and conservatives within the Muslim clergy. The former, to which category the leaders of the spiritual directorates belonged, were, Soviet commentators pointed out, the better acquainted with the achievements of science, the economy and culture and adapted to the conditions of a socialist society. One such commentator characterised these modernists as people who did not refute Qur'anic dogma and the prescriptions of the Shari'a or even admit that they were outdated, preferring simply to remain silent about 'the most archaic ones' and to interpret the others in a contemporary spirit. They were thus able simultaneously to maintain the basics of Islam and identify with the principal goals and slogans of the Soviet state.[132]

In their endeavour to enable believers to adapt to the new circumstances without relinquishing their faith, the directorates in fact seem to have perceived themselves as the heirs of what has been called the 'prestigious constellation of modernist and liberal theologians and philosophers' who sought in the nineteenth century to restore the *ijtihad*, the right to interpret the meaning of the Qur'an and 'more broadly, the necessity to replace "blind" faith by a "reasonable" faith, thus reconciling Islam with science and progress and guaranteeing its survival and revival in the modern scientific world'.[133] The difference between the jadid reformers

---

131. K. V. Ovchinnikov, Report, Minutes, CARC session No.16, 10 June 1960; GARF, f.6991, o.3, d.205, l.23.

132. Abdullaev, 'Za glubokoe kriticheskoe izuchenie ideologii islama', pp.26-7.

133. Bennigsen and Lemercier-Quelquejay, '"Official" Islam in the Soviet Union', p.155.

and the spiritual directorates of the post World War II period was that the former operated in accordance with their own understanding and upon their own initiative, whereas the latter were pressured to issue their interpretations of Islamic dogma in conformity with instructions from the Soviet regime. Neither their official position nor this ideological stance was likely to win the directorates favour among certain sections of the clergy, many of whom indeed rejected their *fetwas*.[134]

The spiritual directorates initiated their own counter-offensive against those clergy who levelled criticism against them. They complained to the secular authority that the clergy were not fulfilling their injunctions relating to the conduct of religious rites and eradicating superstition. Indeed, the clergy sometimes gave their *fetwas* the opposite meaning from that which was intended and otherwise mangled their sense on the contention that they affected customs which had existed from time immemorial and could not be changed.[135] A circular sent out by SADUM to the *imam-khatibs* and chairmen of the religious societies' executive organs in 1956 took to task the clergy and other personnel of the registered mosques for not conducting themselves in accordance with the Shari'a and with the regulations and procedures laid down by SADUM. They did not attend the five daily prayers, they travelled around to perform rites not permitted by the Shari'a and without being invited to do so by the mosques, sometimes even going outside the bounds of the territory under the jurisdiction of their mosque. Instead of being on the spot and caring for the needs of the mosque, they went from one wedding to another, as if they were mere *aksakals*, and believers who looked for them could not find them.[136] In pronouncing this critique, SADUM made no allowance for the fact that in a situation in which there was a major dearth of registered clergy, there was no way they could cater for the needs of all the faithful.

---

134. For these *fetwas*, see below, pp.140-55.

135. Z. Babakhanov to Kh. Iskanderov, 14 Dec. 1955; TsGAUz, f.2456, o.1, d.174, l.112.

136. Z. Babakhanov and F. Sadyqkhojaev to *imam-khatibs* and chairmen of religious societies, 19 Sept. 1956; TsGAUz, f.2456, o.1, d.191, l.5.

The spiritual directorates and non-establishment Islam

The spiritual directorates were officially designated to supervise the affairs of the registered mosques and clergy, *inter alia* in order to undermine the unofficially functioning religious associations. Nevertheless, they were accused recurrently of maintaining links with unregistered groups as well – to the point of actually directing their activity. These unregistered groups, for their part, made regular contributions to the coffers of the spiritual directorates,[137] which they seem to have perceived as protection money that they believed was likely to give them legitimacy and preserve them from being peremptorily shut down. In certain periods this practice was manifestly encouraged by some of SADUM's representatives in the various republics.[138] Indeed, it was legitimised by the inclusion in SADUM's budget, ratified at its January 1947 plenum, of a sum of 150,000 rubles from the unregistered communities of the city and oblast' of Tashkent.[139] Although formally refraining from all interference in the affairs of these groups, in 1949 SADUM officials requested the CARC *upolnomochennyi* for the Uzbek SSR to desist from closing fifteen unregistered mosques in Tashkent Oblast'.[140]

DUMES Mufti Rasulev, too, was said in 1949 to be maintaining contact with over 200 unregistered clergy from whom that directorate received contributions, and to have demanded of his *muhtasibs* to send DUMES moneys from all religious associations in their

137. N. Abushaev, Information, 17 Nov. 1949; GARF, f.6991, o.3, d.61, l.120. The CARC *upolnomochennyi* for the Mordvinian ASSR told a CARC session in response to a question that the heads of unregistered communities there had visited the mufti in Ufa – Minutes, CARC session No. 26, 1-2 Dec. 1949; GARF, f.6991, o.3, d.60, l.71.

138. SADUM's 2nd plenary session resolved to send members of its auditing commission to investigate 'the mobilisation of means from, and the organisation of, unofficial mosques' in Turkmenistan, Karakalpakiia and Tajikistan – Minutes, [20-27 Jan. 1947]; see also Minutes, Conference of the Uzbek SSR oblast' *upolnomochennye*, 9 Aug. 1948; TsGAUz, f.2456, o.1, d.104, l.3ob., and d.120, l.6. CARC *upolnomochennyi* for Kazakhstan Sabitov accused one of SADUM's delegates in Kazakhstan of actually instructing unregistered mullas to conduct collections of money for different purposes – N. Sabitov, Notes for address at conference of CARC *upolnomochennye*, Alma-Ata, 30 Sept. 1946; GARF, f.6991, o.3, d.41, l.85.

139. Minutes, CARC session No.11, 18-9 June 1947; GARF, f.6991, o.4, d.19, l.375.

140. Kh. N. Iskanderov, Address, Instructional conference of CARC's Central Asian *upolnomochennye*, Tashkent, 17-20 Dec. 1949; GARF, f.6991, o.3, d.67, l.59.

areas of jurisdiction, whether registered or not.[141] When Polianskii asked Rasulev point-blank whether he had ties with unregistered mosques and received money from them, he met with an ambiguous reply. DUMES, he was told, did not maintain regular contact with the many unregistered communities in the Tatar ASSR or even with those in the Bashkir ASSR, nor did it direct their activity. At the same time, there had been instances when individual elders had brought DUMES small sums (50-100 rubles) for its upkeep. Polianskii stressed that a spiritual directorate must not receive money from unregistered communities for in so doing it was recognising them, whereas the state did not do so, since, being unregistered, they did not have the right of legal existence. Voluntary donations from individual believers, on the other hand, were their own affair.[142]

Furthermore, in addition to ordaining clergy in the registered mosques, the spiritual directorates sometimes handed out documents to persons not employed in registered religious societies, attesting to their suitability to perform religious rites. CARC's *upolnomochennye* for both the Kirgiz and the Kazakh SSR complained that SADUM was providing such certificates to unauthorised people who were in fact simply itinerant mullas, thus augmenting the number of those qualified, as it were, to serve as clergy. This prerogative, the latter insisted, should be limited to just one mulla for each registered mosque.[143] In 1958 the SADUM *muhtasib* in Kazakhstan gave certificates and travel expenses to seven mullas in Kzyl-Orda – two of them members of the *mutawaliyyat* of the town's registered mosque, the other five itinerant mullas – authoris-

---

141. This was stated by CARC's *upolnomochennyi* in the Bashkir ASSR, Karimov, whose relations with Rasulev were clearly extremely bad. He accused Rasulev of conducting a dual policy, saying one thing and in fact acting quite differently –Minutes, Instructional conference of CARC officials together with its *upolnomochennye* in the RSFSR's autonomous republics and oblasti, 28-29 Oct. 1949; GARF, f.6991, o.3, d.60, ll.111-3. Karimov accused the mufti and his wife of haughty behaviour towards him, the latter presenting herself on the phone as the wife of the Patriarch of the Muslims.

142. Reception by Polianskii of Rasulev, 3 Dec. 1949; GARF, f.6991, o.3, d.8, l.203.

143. H. Akhtiamov, Report, Minutes, CARC session No.9, 3 June 1947; GARF, f.6991. o.4, d.19, ll.253-4, and N. Sabitov to Kh. N. Iskanderov, 28 April 1950; TsGAUz, f.2456, o.1, d.126, l.81.

ing them to collect the *fitr* during the *uraz* and to conduct festival prayer-services.[144]

In addition to authorising unregistered clergy to perform rites, the spiritual directorates also appointed incumbents as shaykhs at a number of unregistered *mazars*.[145] Given the popularity of these holy sites and the small number assigned officially to their care, this was a sure way of extending their influence. At the same time, certain *mazars* were not supported by SADUM, notably Central Asia's most important shrine, the Takht-i Sulayman in Osh, opened at the initiative of one of the directorate's chief critics and protagonists among the clergy, Shafagat Khoja Khaliq-nazarov. Ishan Babakhan specifically repudiated it,[146] although it is not clear whether he did so for personal reasons, or owing to its being in Kirgiziia, which was probably the most problematic area in the region from the point of view of SADUM, and so the likelihood of SADUM in fact exerting authority there was slight. In 1957 SADUM initiated an attempt to register the Takht-i Sulayman, maintaining that in this way the 'fanatical' *ishans* operating there would be replaced by more moderate clergy, who would be under SADUM's close supervision.[147] Once the regime began its major campaign against pilgrimages to holy places in 1958, the spiritual directorates tended to express reservations on the actual practice of pilgrimages to *mazars* as being 'repugnant to God'.[148]

The representatives of SADUM and TsDUM in a number of republics were also reported in the latter half of the 1940s to be actually opening mosques without recourse to the usual procedures and the permission of CARC.[149] The CARC *upolnomochennyi* for

144. B. Jumashev, Address, Conference of CARC's Central Asian *upolnomochen-nye*, 5-6 June 1959; GARF, f.6991, o.3, d.186, ll.82-3.

145. For example, CARC *upolnomochennyi* for Fergana Oblast', Hamidullin, to I. V. Polianskii, 31 Dec. 1946; TsGAUz, f.2456, o.1, d.72, l.65.

146. I. Ibadov to I. V. Polianskii, 5 July 1946 – TsGAUz, f.2456, o.1, d.90, l.31; and Kh. N. Iskanderov, Report, 2 June 1952 – GARF, f.6991, o.3, d.83, ll.137-8. Despite his reservations regarding the Takht-i Sulayman, Babakhan participated in the ceremonial Friday *namaz* which marked the opening in 1946 of the 16th century mosque at its foot, the Ravat Abdulla-khan – Kh. Iskanderov, Report, 8 Oct. 1946; GARF, f.6991, o.3, d.41, l.204.

147. N. I. Inogamov to L. A. Prikhod'ko, 18 April 1957; GARF, f.6991, o.3, d.458, l.2.

148. Ashirov, *Evoliutsiia islama v SSSR*, p.147. And see pp.146-9 below.

149. I. N. Uzkov and G. A. Vrachev to I. V. Polianskii, Memorandum, 29

Uzbekistan suggested that people, some of them claiming to be representatives of SADUM, were opening prayer-houses and *mazars* and attracting kolkhozniki to them, irrespective of whether the latter wanted this or not.[150] (According to established procedure, the opening of a prayer-house could take place only if a statutory group of believers took the initiative and filed a request to this effect.) And in the mid 1950s the chairman of SADUM's auditing commission accepted a petition to open a mosque in Fergana Oblast' that was in ruins and had not functioned for five to six years. If this tendency persisted, CARC's *upolnomochennye* feared it would obstruct their work, which was designed to hold back the growth of new religious formations and to regulate religious activity.[151]

This link with unregistered religious groups and associations was strongest when the general situation was most lax and it seemed to the spiritual directorates to be possible to establish and maintain such ties. In the years 1943-5 SADUM auditing commission member Shakir Khiyaletdinov was nominated responsible for Islam in Northern Kazakhstan. Styling himself oblast' imam, he appointed thirty-one mullas in its various kolkhozy and placed himself at the head of this 'network'.[152] In 1955 CARC noted that all four Muslim religious centres, especially SADUM, were developing organisational connections with unofficial religious groups and clergy and were receiving contributions from them. Indeed, they were extending their influence everywhere, including places where no registered religious societies existed, although this was in contradiction to their charters.[153] According to CARC,

Nov. 1946, and I. V. Polianskii to A. A. Zhdanov, 22 July 1947; RTsKhIDNI, f.17, o.125, d.405, ll.84-122 and d.506, l.173. Polianskii spoke specifically of SADUM's representatives in Fergana Oblast' and in the Kirgiz SSR and TsDUM's in Siberia. See also Minutes, SADUM 2nd plenary session, [20-27 Jan. 1947]; TsGAUz, f.2456, o.1, d.104, l.2. For the activity of SADUM's representative in Kirgiziia, Khaliqnazarov, see also n.110.

150. Report, undated (probably October 1946); GARF, f.6991, o.3, d.41, l.201. The document was presumably prepared by Kh. N. Iskanderov, who succeeded I. Ibadov as CARC *upolnomochennyi* in the Uzbek SSR in August 1946.

151. Usman Mangushev to Kh. N. Iskanderov, 30 Jan. 1954; TsGAUz, f.2456, o.1, d.170, ll.3-5.

152. Excerpts from reports of CARC *upolnomochennye* for the 1st quarter of 1945, undated; GARF, f.6991, o.3, d.12, ll.74-5.

153. V. I. Gostev, Theses of instructional address, Convention of *upolnomochennye* of the RSFSR, 25 July 1955, and Short report, discussed at CARC session

SADUM, for example, had issued instructions to its qazis in the republics to take over the direction of the activity of unregistered groups and *mazars*.[154] Still in the late 1960s some unregistered clergy were in regular contact with the spiritual directorates and transferring moneys to them either directly or through registered mosques. The eighty unregistered associations and groups taken count of in the Bashkir ASSR with their 3,000 believers, for instance, donated 9,500 rubles to DUMES in a single year.[155]

In certain periods, on the other hand, when the spiritual directorates' own situation seemed precarious, they conducted major campaigns against the unregistered clergy. They both sought – in accordance with the interests of the regime – to ensure that the establishment in fact controlled all religious activity, and by curbing the activities of former mullas and other unregistered religious personnel in the *mahallas*, to undermine believers' confidence in the unofficial, mosqueless clergy. The directorates would remind their *muhtasibs* and the registered clergy that all religious rites must be conducted solely by them without any participation whatever of unofficial persons. If an *imam-khatib* were not able for one reason or another (illness, infirmity, absence) to perform rites, he was to empower an appropriate member of the executive organ to do so. And where distances were great, that is, where believers resided a long way from the nearest registered mosque and there was no way of getting registered clergy to perform rites, no certificates or documentation were to be given to any unofficial clergy authorising them to conduct rites.[156] Apart from the spiritual directorates' apprehension that by endorsing the activity of the unregistered clergy they might be jeopardising their own position with the authorities, one of the reasons for this attitude was presumably the sense that these clergy were attracting too large

No.8s, 27 June 1956 – GARF, f.6991, o.3, d.110, l.115, and d.217, l.109.

154. L. A. Prikhod'ko, Information, 18 May 1957; GARF, f.6991, o.3, d.146, ll.101-2. Prikhod'ko contended that due to CARC's intervention the implementation of these instructions had been prevented.

155. M. Avdurvanov, Information, 25 June 1969; GARF, f.6991, o.5, d.220, l.307, and CRA report, delivered to the CPSU Central Committee, 22 May 1970; TsKhSD, f.5, o.62, d.38, l.9.

156. Ishan Babakhan to all *imam-khatibs* and mosque executive organ chairmen, 30 Dec. 1949, and to SADUM members and the *imam-khatibs* and executive organs of the major mosques, 6 Nov. 1953; TsGAUz, f.2456, o.1, d. 127, l.4, and d.144, ll.172-3.

a percentage of the believer population and that their very existence was a threat to the hegemony and prosperity of the religious centre. According to a CARC report in 1953, the struggle against unregistered clergy had for the last few years been one of the main foci of the activity of the spiritual directorates.[157]

The fetwa

Since the spiritual directorates were the sole go-between, the only institutionalised instrument for reaching out to the individual religious society, CARC worked through them to transmit messages and instructions to the organised community of believers. For instance, in the mid and late 1940s in order to put constraints on what it saw as Islam's most negative manifestations, it directed them to provide believers with the requisite explanations and justification for such restrictions, using citations from Islam's most authoritative sources. The spiritual directorates accordingly issued directives and dispensations clearly designed to assist believers to adapt to the conditions of a communist society. Some of these took the form of *fetwas* – official interpretations of dogma by a religious authority based on the Qur'an and the Hadith – in order to eradicate 'distortions of the Shari'a and the propagation of prejudices'.[158] These *fetwas* embodied in many ways the basic dilemma facing the spiritual directorates throughout the period under review, as they sought to walk the tightrope erected for them by the managers of the circus in which they had to perform.

The *fetwas* issued by the directorates would be read out by the clergy of the registered mosques in the course of their Friday sermons. They covered a wide range of controversial issues and touched upon some of the most fundamental practices of Islam. Several of them related to aspects of the fast and festivals which would be brought to the attention of believers on the Fridays preceding these occasions. In the words of one CARC official: 'Desiring to avoid any possible material damage to both the collective and private economy of kolkhozniki as a result of not going to work during the *uraz* and on festivals, of slaughtering livestock and paying the *fitr*, the spiritual directorates called upon believers

157. L. Prikhod'ko, Report, 20 May 1953; GARF, f.6991, o.3, d.91, l.263.
158. Ishan Babakhan to SADUM members and the clergy and executive organs of major mosques, 6 Nov. 1952; TsGAUz, f.2456, o.1, d.144, l.172.

to work honestly and not to permit absenteeism and explained to them that observance of the fast, the slaughter of animals and the payment of *fitr* were not obligatory. They maintained that the performance of the sacrifice, according to the Shari'a was purely voluntary, that the *uraz* was not compulsory for certain categories of people (pregnant women and nursing mothers, workers engaged in strenuous physical labour and the sick), and that the *fitr* in a socialist society had become meaningless, insofar as poverty had been eliminated in the Soviet Union 'and whoever works honestly is not in need of *fitr*'.[159]

The injunction limiting the observance of the *uraz* was repeated recurrently by all four spiritual directorates throughout the following decades, sometimes with slight variations.[160] The repetitions served presumably to indicate – at least, from the point of view of the directorates themselves – that while the heads of the establishment were loyal to the regime and had its economic and social success at heart, there were sections among the believer population who were unable, in Soviet terminology, to shake off the shackles of tradition. The recurrent endeavours of the directorates to transform,

159. N. Tagiev, Short survey, undated [probably early 1949]; GARF, f.6991, o.4, d.23, ll.12ob-13. The first *fetwa* issued by SADUM, on 20 Oct. 1944 laid down that the sacrifice on Qurban-Bayram was purely voluntary (*sunnat*). A further one, dated 28 Aug. 1945 related to *sadaqa*, the *fitr* and *zakat*, and apparently determined the conditions for their collection. In view of the voluntary nature of *sadaqa*, *fitr* and *zakat*, none of which was formally obligatory by Islamic law, the SADUM second plenary in January 1947, however, after ratifying the first *fetwa*, rescinded the second one. These payments, it claimed, had been collected from believers in pre-revolutionary times by both clergy and state officials and entered into the government's coffers, but under the Soviet regime taxes were levied directly from the population. In addition, there were, on the one hand, no poor to receive the *fitr* and *sadaqa*, nor, on the other, any rich people, *bais*, who received turnover from their capital, to pay *zakat*. The plenary also forbade executive organs to appoint collectors of *sadaqa*, *fitr* and *zakat* and abolished the procedure by which clergy received one eighth of voluntary donations – Minutes, SADUM 2nd plenary session, [20-27 Jan. 1947]; TsGAUz, f.2456, o.1, d.104, ll.2-3.

160. DUMSK, for example, issued such a *fetwa* in 1968. Commenting on this in his book on the evolution of Islam in the Soviet Union, N. Ashirov saw fit to point out that its content did not tally with the precepts laid down in the Qur'an which exonerated only those who were ill or on a journey, and they were to merely postpone the fast until such time as they could carry it out. A similar 'dispensation' was issued to believers in the Soviet Union by the spiritual directorates regarding another pillar of Islam, the five daily *salats* – Ashirov, *Evoliut-siia islama v SSSR*, pp.138-9.

rather than abolish, the sacrifice on Qurban-Bayram was evidently the outcome of similar motives and considerations and a yet further attempt to find a *modus vivendi* between the diktat of their masters in Moscow and the practices of the local believer population.[161] At one point, DUMSK issued instructions that it was sufficient to slaughter fowl rather than the customary sheep or lamb.[162] In 1952 DUMES, acting upon the recommendation of the *upol-nomochennyi* in Ufa, issued a *fetwa* to the effect that yet another rite which was anathema to the lay power, the chanting of the *takbir* in the streets on the way to the mosque on Qurban-Bayram, was not obligatory.[163]

Still in the 1970s the spiritual directorates were issuing *fetwas* in connection with the festivals. In 1973 SADUM promulgated two *fetwas* explaining some of the positions of the faith. One was designed to limit the conduct of the *iftar*, the collective repast at the end of each day of the month-long fast, and its attendant expenses. It also stressed the need to persist in the struggle against unregistered clergy in the context of the fast and the rites associated with it, recommending believers to conduct the evening *tarawa-namaz* and the festive prayer-service solely in the registered mosques. SADUM had issued an earlier *fetwa* (in 1966) in connection with the *iftar*, stipulating that only people who observed the fast might be invited to this ceremony. The second *fetwa* also pointed out, not for the first time, that worshipping at so-called holy places, which people tended to visit on festivals, contradicted Islam.[164]

Many *fetwas* were connected with different aspects of the status of women in Islam and Soviet society. One early *fetwa* shortly after the war sanctioned the marriage of women whose husbands were pronounced missing by the military authorities.[165] The SADUM plenary session of January 1947 resolved that according to the Shari'a women were allowed to appear in public without

161. *Ibid.* pp.142-3. And see pp.151-2 below.

162. I. V. Polianskii to G. M. Malenkov and N. S. Khrushchev, 2 Oct. 1953; GARF, f.6991, o.3, d.93, l.244.

163. L. Prikhod'ko, Report, 20 May 1953; GARF, f.6991, o.3, d.91, l.267.

164. A. Barmenkov to the Central Committee Propaganda Department, 13 March 1974; for Babakhanov's *fetwas*, see also K. Kulumbetov to A. A. Nurullaev, 28 June 1974 – GARF, f.6991, o.6, d.622, l.9, and d.629, l.30. For the earlier *fetwa*, see Ashirov, *Evoliutsiia islama v SSSR*, p.21.

165. Minutes, SADUM 2nd plenary session, [20-27 Jan. 1947]; TsGAUz, f.2456, o.1, d.104, l.3.

the *chador* or *paranja*, the robe worn outdoors by Uzbek and Tajik women that covered them from head to foot, and decided to issue a *fetwa* pronouncing the right of women to take part in public life.[166] In 1951 SADUM seems again to have issued a *fetwa* on the non-obligatory nature of the *paranja* as well as of the *dawra*, the ceremony at the end of the burial service for the expiation of the sins of the deceased, and of the sacrifice of Qurban-Bayram.[167]

The attitude to women was indeed a recurrent theme. Apart from the *paranja*, the relevant *fetwas* also dwelt on the right of women to be educated and to break away altogether from their centuries-long seclusion.[168] The status of women varied considerably from one area to another. Whereas, for example, in some parts, particularly in the RSFSR and Kazakhstan, women were now participating in collective prayer, DUMSK specifically forbade this.[169] Another question, pertinent to the status of women, which was the subject of several *fetwas*, was suicide or self-immolation. In 1950 and again in 1952, on the latter occasion apparently at the instigation of CARC's *upolnomochennyi* in Tashkent, SADUM issued *fetwas* condemning this custom, reminding people that those who took their own lives could not be given religious funerals.[170]

166. *Ibid.* For the status of women and relevant customs, see pp.535-49.

167. Kh. N. Iskanderov, Report, 2 June 1952; GARF, f.6991, o.3, d.83, l.136. In 1954 SADUM once more issued a *fetwa* concerning the *paranja*, or at least decided at a plenary session held on 1 Feb. to circulate the previous one. (It is not clear whether this was a new *fetwa* or not.) In any event, its text brought historical, doctrinal and pragmatic contemporary proofs against wearing the *paranja*. SADUM asked permission for the *fetwa* to be read out at the Friday *jum'a-namaz* throughout the five republics of Central Asia, but CARC considered it inexpedient to read it out in areas where the *paranja* was not worn – Iskanderov to I. V. Polianskii, Deputy Chairman of the Uzbek SSR Council of Ministers N. A. Mukhitdinov and Uzbekistan CP Central Committee Secretary Kamalov, 22 Feb. 1954; text of the *fetwa* 'The custom of Muslim women to wear the *paranja*', signed Ishan Babakhan (undated); and Polianskii to Iskanderov, 13 March 1954 –TsGAUz, f.2456, o.1, d.162, ll.65-73 and 110. In 1963 SADUM once again issued a *fetwa* on the *paranja* – Klimovich, *Islam*, p.297.

168. Ashirov, *Evoliutsiia islama v SSSR*, p.101.

169. Saidbaev, *Islam i obshchestvo*, p.240. Saidbaev noted, however, that even in Dagestan itself, where DUMSK was situated, there were instances of female participation in prayer-services in the mosques, not to speak of actual women clergy among the Sufi brotherhoods in the Chechen-Ingush ASSR. For women's participation in prayers, see pp.223-4; for their activity in the Sufi context, see p.410.

170. Kh. N. Iskanderov to Uzbekistan CP Secretary Kh. G. Gulamov, 20 July 1954; TsGAUz, f.2456, o.1, d.166, ll.46-7. For the context of self-immolation,

In early 1960 SADUM Mufti Babakhanov told CARC that SADUM intended issuing a *fetwa* regarding the *qalym*, or bride-money, which was still being practised in several regions of Central Asia.[171]

A host of other customs and traditions which had become an integral part of popular Islam, as practised in various parts of the Soviet Union, also became the theme of *fetwas*. In 1952 SADUM sent out to all mosques 'with CARC's knowledge' and the approval of the Uzbek SSR's executive organs, a *fetwa* on the incompatibilities between the Qur'an and the activity of the more 'reactionary' unregistered clergy (*ishans*, *duakhons*, 'and so on') and the impermissibility of exorcism, which was timed to be read out in the mosques of Uzbekistan and elsewhere on Qurban-Bayram.[172]

Many of these *fetwas*, too, like the one on the fast, failed to achieve the desired effect and had to be repeated several times. One report at the end of the 1940s noted that while the attempt of the spiritual directorates to abolish, or at least limit, religion's 'most negative' features was clearly praiseworthy, due to the inefficacy of their control the message was in many cases not even relayed to believers.[173] In theory, however, the *fetwas* would be read out on festivals or at Friday prayers in all registered mosques. Sometimes the *imam-khatib* would add his own explanations. Yet, many of the imams in registered mosques were of a low level of education, and so unable to explain SADUM's interpretations of

---

see pp.546-8.

171. It was proposed to ask Babakhanov to present CARC with a draft of the *fetwa* before it was issued to the mosques and to provide data regarding the actual taking of *qalym* – Proposals on questions raised by Babakhanov, prepared for CARC session No.3, 22 Jan. 1960; GARF f.6991, o.3, d.204, l.20. For the *qalym*, see pp.536-8.

172. Faizullin, The trip to Frunze and Alma-Ata, 15 Sept. 1952, Verses in honour of the *fetwa*, 20 Sept. 1952, and Resolution of believers at a Tashkent mosque, 22 Sept. 1952 – TsGAUz, f.2456, o.1, d.144, ll.84, 91-3 and 156; also L. Prikhod'ko, Draft report, 31 Jan. 1953, and Report, 20 May 1953, GARF, f.6991, o.3, d.91, ll.8 and 266. The SADUM plenum of 25 March 1952 discussed this *fetwa*, insisting that ishanism was impermissible from the point of view of the Shari'a, there being no precepts in Islam relating to 'ishanism' and 'muridism' –Z. Babakhanov, Information, 17 Aug. 1956; TsGAUz, f.2456, o.1, d.184, l.64.

173. N. Tagiev, A short survey, undated [early 1949]. A decade later it was pointed out again that clergy not infrequently ignored *fetwas* to the point of not passing them on to their congregants – A. F. Dobrokhotov, Address, Minutes, CARC session No.4, 25-26 Feb. 1959; GARF, f.6991, o.4, d.23, l.13, and o.3, d.183, l.123.

dogma in a way that would make it easy to understand their essence and significance. There may often have also been an element of unwillingness to do more than pay lip-service to a document with which the clergy did not identify.[174] In some cases, the clergy seem to have deliberately distorted or reversed the message of the *fetwas*.[175] The CARC session which discussed a request of clergy in the Tajik SSR at the end of the 1950s to re-issue the *fetwa* on self-immolation pointed out that it was not feasible to conduct the struggle against superstition solely through *fetwas*, which should be encouraged only in conjunction with other measures. It was also pointed out that not all clergy had read out the previous *fetwas* on this issue in their mosques and it was suggested that this time it might be promulgated in the Central Asian languages in 6,000 copies and that every effort he made to ensure that it be brought to the attention of as wide a public as possible.[176]

Sometimes the reading of a *fetwa* at services would be accompanied by questions from the worshippers. On the whole, it was reported that believers tended – at least *pro forma* – to accept the contents of the *fetwas*. Occasionally, they were even said to have expressed indignation at having hitherto been kept in ignorance of the actual teachings of the Qur'an and the Hadith.[177] This was

174. Kh. N. Iskanderov, Report, 6 June 1952; GARF, f.6991, o.3, d.83, l.136.

175. Ziyautdin Babakhanov wrote that the clergy reversed two *fetwas* in particular, the one that laid down that wearing the *paranja* was not obligatory, the other on the futility of holding weddings in connection with circumcisions when the child would be placed in a cradle, so as to disguise the performance of the circumcision, and distorted two others, against the holding of festive meals on the traditional memorial days of a deceased relative, and on ishanism and exorcism –Z. Babakhanov to Kh. N. Iskanderov, 14 Dec. 1956; TsGAUz, f.2456, o.1, d.174, l.112. For these *fetwas*, see pp.143 and 144 above and p.150 below.

176. K. F. Tagirov, Resumé, undated; prepared for CARC session No.22s, and Minutes, CARC session No.22s, 2 Sept. 1959; GARF, f.6991, o.3, d.184, ll.192 and 235-6.

177. SADUM Qazi Faizullin read out the *fetwa* on the absence in the Shari'a of any reference to ishanism and sorcerers in the Shaykh Zain ad-Din Mosque in Tashkent on Qurban-Bayram, 31 Aug. 1952. The believers there adopted a resolution stating that they understood that *ishans* had spread all possible superstitions and prejudices in their own personal interests. They asked that the *fetwa* be read out as often as possible in the mosque – Resolution of believers, 22 Sept. 1952; TsGAUz, f.2456, o.1, d.144, l.156. On behalf of SADUM, Faizullin took the text of the *fetwa* to Kirgiziia and Kazakhstan, where because of the great distances there was not sufficient time to assemble all the imams before the festival, and so it had to be read out on the following Friday. In one rural mosque in

not, however, always the case. When Khiyaletdinov abolished two *rak'as* (prostrations) in the Friday *namaz*, he provoked a dispute with the registered clergy in the Bashkir ASSR; and in Ufa itself, where the clergy supported the mufti, the believers disputed the *fetwa*.[178]

There were other occasions as well when the clergy, or some members of it, demonstrated their disagreement with a *fetwa*. Already in 1946 in Kazakhstan a number of registered clergy rejected SADUM's *fetwas* on the sacrifice and the *fitr*, which they saw as innovatory. (In Southern Kazakhstan, for example, where Islam was particularly strong, it had been profoundly affected by Sufism and tended towards conservatism in the old dispute between the reformist jadidists and the 'qadimists' who sought to preserve the status quo, and vestiges of this position remained.) In the Namangan area in the Fergana Valley a number of *ishans* incited their *murids*, or adepts, against SADUM's *fetwas*, for instance regarding the categories it claimed were exempt from observing the *uraz*. They demanded that SADUM either retract the *fetwa* or dismiss the imam of the local mosque who had read it out in the mosque. Unable to do the former, SADUM submitted to the latter demand and relieved the imam of his post, to which it had appointed him.[179] The clergy were also said to be concerned by the material implications of many of the *fetwas*, which deprived them of their traditional sources of income.[180]

Following the CPSU Central Committee resolution of November 1958 prohibiting pilgrimages to holy places, CARC's *upolnomochennyi* in Tashkent summoned Babakhanov to explain to him the need for measures on his part to terminate pilgrimages to, and all activity at, *mazars* and other revered sites. Otherwise, he cautioned, the government organs would take the strictest measures against those who were exploiting the ignorance of backward elements. This was sufficient to produce a condemnation

Kazakhstan, where Faizullin was present at its reading, the elders said to each other that they had been deceived by their mullas – Faizullin on his trip to Frunze and Alma-Ata, 15 Sept. 1952, TsGAUz, f.2456, o.1, d.144, ll.91-3.

178. M. Sh. Karimov, Report, prepared for CARC session No.16, 15 Aug. 1951; GARF, f.6991, o.3, d.75, l.210.

179. Minutes, Conference of CARC's *upolnomochennye* in the Uzbek SSR, 9 Aug. 1948; TsGAUz, f.2456, o.1, d.120, ll.15-16.

180. N. I. Sabitov, Synopsis of report, Conference of CARC *upolnomochennye*, Alma-Ata, 30 Sept. 1946; GARF, f.6991, o.3, d.41, ll.77-8.

of pilgrimages as contradictory to the basic teachings of Islam. The draft of a *fetwa* was presented by SADUM to the CARC *upolnomochennyi*, and, after being heavily amended and approved by the Uzbekistan Party Central Committee, was circulated as a *fetwa* to all qaziates, *muhtasibs*, and mosques. The *fetwa* stated that belief in *mazars* and the conviction that prostration at them could save people from misfortune was a manifest contradiction of the teachings of the Qur'an and the Hadith.[181] The *fetwa* was read out in mosques throughout Uzbekistan at Friday prayers in February, March and April 1959, often followed by further explanations warning believers against superstitions relating to the sanctity of *mazars*, and on the whole was said to have been positively received, the great majority of believers who heard it allegedly stating they would no longer visit these shrines.[182]

Similar instructions were circulated by the other spiritual directorates; DUMZ did so in the form of a special resolution,[183] although, according to one source, DUMZ was the only directorate never to condemn pilgrimages to holy shrines as contradictory to Islamic practice.[184] DUMSK issued a *fetwa* of its own,[185] whereas DUMES first issued an appeal to believers,[186] then a *fetwa* and finally in

181. Minutes, CARC session No.4, 25-26 Feb. 1959; GARF, f.6991, o.3, d.183, ll.41-4. For the original draft of this *fetwa*, see 'On restricting the activity of *mazars*', signed by Ziyautdin Babakhanov, and apparently handed to the CARC *upolnomochennyi* on 23 Dec. 1958; *ibid.*, ll.28-9. For further detail, see below.

182. N. I. Inogamov, Address, Conference of Central Asian *upolnomochennye* in Tashkent, 5-6 June 1959. Inogamov mentioned but one exception in one rural area, where people were back at the local *mazar* within a week. The *upolnomochennyi* for the Kirgiz SSR said on the same occasion that SADUM's representatives in that republic had also read out the *fetwa* on the holy places and distributed it to all the registered mosques, although it could not be said that all believers relinquished this custom of centuries. His colleague in Turkmenistan pointed out in an address to local party and soviet officials on 2 April 1959 that SADUM's qazi in that republic had sent the *fetwa* to the clergy of its four registered mosques but done nothing beyond that, as a result of which it had had no results – GARF, f.6991, o.3, d.186, ll.9-15, 30-1, and 74.

183. DUMZ discussed measures to be taken in connection with pilgrimages to holy places at its session on 15 Jan. 1959 – M. Shamsadinskii, Information, Minutes, CARC session No.4, 25-26 Feb. 1959; GARF, f.6991, o.3, d.183, ll.82-4.

184. Saroyan, 'Reconstructing Community', pp.205-7. Saroyan, however, visited Azerbaijan in the 1970s and it is possible that he was not given correct information regarding the period of Khrushchev's anti-religious campaign.

185. Makatov, 'Kul't sviatykh v islame', pp.173-4.

186. A. A. Puzin to CARC *upolnomochennye*, 25 March 1959; GARF, f.6991,

April 1959, at a convention of clergy (held upon the recommendation of CARC's *upolnomochennyi* in Ufa), the mufti spoke on
the need to put a stop to pilgrimages and other practices. This
convention adopted resolutions in which the participants expressed
their appreciation of the *fetwa* and promised to put an end to the
activity of former mullas who sought to organise pilgrimages to
holy places or practised other superstitions, such as faith-healing
and exorcising illnesses. Two clerics, however, took exception to
the sense of the convention. One, the *muhtasib* for Penza Oblast',
stated that his sermon against pilgrimages had been met with hostility
and that believers continued to organise pilgrimages and he asked
to be relieved of his post. A similar response had befallen a mulla
in Kuibyshev Oblast'.[187]

In addition to occasional opposition on the part of believers,
it was pointed out that there was a conspicuous indication of
'half-heartedness' in SADUM's position, for, while it censured
the worship of *mazars* in general, it continued to operate those
which had been given over to its own jurisdiction on the grounds
that these were memorials to prominent people in the fields of
science and religion.[188] It was suggested that this differentiation
made by SADUM between the smaller, local *mazars* and the major
ones under its auspices from which it derived financial profit,
rendered its *fetwa* meaningless.[189]

A decade later, one Soviet expert on Islam sought to analyse
the change of position of the spiritual directorates from support
for *mazars* and pilgrimages – prior to the 1958 decree – to their
negation. He attributed it to a variety of causes: the transformation
in the religious consciousness of the mass of believers who had
begun to repudiate the visitation of holy places; the activity at
the *mazars* of charlatans who 'speculated' upon the religious feelings
of ignorant believers and 'robbed' them, thus depriving the religious

---

o.3, d.187, l.50.

187. M. Sh. Karimov, Address, Minutes, CARC session No.21, 22 July 1959;
GARF, f.6991, o.3, d.184, ll.153-5.

188. H. Akhtiamov, Address, Conference of CARC's Central Asian *upolnomochennye*, 5 June 1959; GARF, f.6991, o.3, d.186, l.38. This perhaps was supposed
to he a more commendable version of the statement made in better times – see
pp.124-5 above.

189. This was the opinion of CARC's *upolnomochennyi* in the Karakalpak ASSR,
A. Irmanov, as expressed at the conference of Central Asian *upolnomochennye*,
5-6 June 1959; GARF, f.6991, o.3, d.186, ll.126-7.

associations of an important source of income; the opposition to
the religious establishment of those unregistered clergy who served
worshippers at holy places and the desire of the spiritual directorates
to deprive them of one of their main sources of strength; and,
finally, the desire of the Muslim establishment to present Islam
as a religion of progress taking issue with everything which constrained the forward movement of both society and the individual.[190]

In 1970 DUMSK issued a special *fetwa*, which the CRA recommended be circulated among all the registered mosques, censuring
those who spread false rumours that accounted for random misfortunes, such as the outbreak of a cholera epidemic, as divine
retribution for people's sins, and threatened more severe catastrophes
in the future if people, especially the younger generation, continued
to distance themselves from religion and if women went on dressing
immodestly. Instead of making sacrifices, the *fetwa* urged believers
to take an active part in eliminating the consequences of the
earthquake which had taken place in Dagestan that year.[191] In a
fetwa issued a few years earlier in connection with the earthquake
which destroyed much of old Tashkent in 1966, SADUM recognised that these events had natural causes. While stating that
earthquakes occurred from time to time in various parts of the
world 'at the will of Allah', it laid down that they also had natural
causes conforming to a certain law of nature (*zakonomernost'*).[192]

In one *fetwa* of 1952 SADUM provided an apologia for its
activity. As the organ of 13.5 million Muslims, it maintained, it
saw its duty as providing them with comprehensive assistance. In
order, however, to be able 'to guide the religious movement on
a desirable course and to resolve religious questions on the basis
of contemporary conditions and the Shari'a', SADUM needed
the assistance, sympathy and cooperation of the clergy, especially
of the qazis, *imam-khatibs* and *ulema* who, 'being persuaded of the
salutary nature' of steps taken by it, must help it 'eradicate religious
prejudices'. It was incumbent upon them to bring to SADUM's
attention abnormalities, distortions and generally undesirable
manifestations they had observed in the localities and to obtain

190. Ashirov, *Evoliutsiia islama v SSSR*, p.147.

191. CRA report, sent to the CPSU Central Committee, 27 April 1971; TsKhSD,
f.5, o.63, d.89, ll.107-8.

192. Quoted in Ashirov, *Evoliutsiia islama v SSSR*, pp.129-30, and in *Islam v
SSSR*, p.108.

from SADUM *fetwas* to eliminate them. Although, he contended, many ordinary believers indeed showed an aversion to customs that contradicted the Shari'a, Babakhan bemoaned the fact that not a few clergy, including even *ulema*, still adhered to the *dawra*, the *paranja* and similar falsifications of dogma. He focused in this document on the lavishness of wedding festivities, which cost so much that many young people either did not marry or postponed their marriage so as not to lose their basic security, whereas in fact Islam did not demand anything but the simplest of ceremonies. Wasteful spending of large sums on weddings or circumcisions was sinful. The same applied to sumptuous meals after the death of a relative and other rituals connected with mourning which frequently deprived survivors of their sustenance. It was sufficient simply to read the Qur'an in the mosque after a *namaz*. Nor were Qur'an readings to be ordered in return for payment. It was necessary to return to the simplicity of the original rites.[193]

To make visible efforts to adapt to the requirements of the regime and of society was often a paramount consideration for the spiritual directorates. In one of his public appearances Ziyautdin Babakhanov stated: 'Islam is an active adherent of the construction of socialism and communism in our country. The Spiritual Directorate of Muslims, indeed all the leaders of the religious organisations of Central Asia and Kazakhstan, see their chief assignment as caring for people's moral improvement and guiding Muslims on the path of Islam and socialism'.[194] Indeed, the heads of the spiritual directorates saw it as incumbent upon them to show the compatibility of the values of Islam and of the society in which they lived, such as the centrality of labour and the equality and brotherhood of nations.[195] DUMES issued a *fetwa* approving the use of musical instruments and visiting the theatre and cinema which taught 'edifying lessons', and insisting that nobody had the right to prohibit believers from so doing.[196] One deputy chairman of DUMZ, Mufti Sharif Veli-zade, said specifically that in a changing world it was impossible to adhere to all the norms of the Shari'a. Much in it had become antiquated and was alienating believers from religion, such as the procedure for divorce, which perpetuated the wife's

193. The *fetwa* was dated 16 May 1952; TsGAUz, f.2456, o.1, d.144, ll.23-30.
194. Quoted in Ashirov, *Evoliutsiia islama v SSSR*, p.77.
195. See, for example, *Islam v SSSR*, pp.109-10.
196. Ashirov, *Evoliutsiia islama v SSSR*, p.83.

inferior status. The mufti demanded that those positions of the Shari'a which were outdated should be rejected.[197] By the early 1980s about thirty *fetwas* and hundreds of injunctions were said to have been issued by SADUM alone which centred on a 'modernised interpretation of rites and rituals'.[198]

On the whole the spiritual directorates appreciated that they had perforce to accept directives from CARC, that their continued existence depended on their proving their usefulness to the regime and their assiduity in fulfilling its requirements. The result was that many of the *fetwas* were in fact the outcome of explicit or implicit instructions on the part of the authorities.[199]

From time to time, however, one of the muftis might show resistance. Thus, Rasulev was not prepared to include in his epistle to the mosques of the RSFSR prior to the advent of Qurban-Bayram any mention of the non-obligatory nature of the sacrifice, a characterisation which contradicted his own ruling in his book *Islam-dini*. He refrained from doing so in 1948, and in 1949 asked CARC whether in light of this he should desist altogether from sending a circular to the registered mosques under his jurisdiction. He maintained that were he to prohibit the slaughter of the sacrifice, as was suggested in the draft decree – which apparently had been presented to him by CARC's *upolnomochennyi* in Ufa – believers would not heed him and the result would be simply to undermine his authority.[200] It was perhaps to allay the negative impression of submission to the lay authorities in matters of religious dogma – in addition to the message they sought to convey to the secular

197. *Ibid.*, p.119. Ashirov noted that Veli-zade confined his criticism to the Shari'a which was composed by man, but refrained from even mentioning the Qur'an in this context.

198. *Islam v SSSR*, p.113.

199. One example was the *fetwa* on ishanism and exorcism, which seems to have followed upon a suggestion made by CARC's *upolnomochennyi* for the Uzbek SSR to SADUM that it take measures based on the Qur'an and the *hadith* to put an end to the activity of the *ishans* – Minutes, Conference of CARC *upolnomochennye*, 17-20 Dec. 1949; GARF, f.6991, o.3, d.67, l.60.

200. Reception of Rasulev by Polianskii, 3 Dec. 1949. Tagiev in an undated 1949 'Short survey' suggested that Rasulev had omitted all mention of sacrifices in his *fetwas*, apparently because he considered them obligatory. CARC sought to persuade the mufti to include a reservation regarding his original ruling, apparently to no avail – Minutes, CARC session No.17, 26 Aug. 1949; GARF, f.6991, o.3, d.8, ll.201-2, and d.60, l.37 and o.4, d.23, l.13.

power[201] – that in 1950 the spiritual directorates proposed a compromise. Believers, instead of bringing their sacrifice to the mosque
on Qurban-Bayram, would give it the animal's worth in money.
In later years this was apparently transmuted to a sum of money
equivalent to the value of its hide.[202]

The deliberations of the spiritual directorates and the ambiguities
of their position are also evident from the development of their
attitude to other questions. From its incipient days in 1943 up to
1947 SADUM encouraged believers to fulfil the obligation of
paying *fitr*. Then it changed course and issued a *fetwa* declaring
fitr to be voluntary. In 1951 SADUM asked CARC for permission
to collect *fitr* all the same and to channel all moneys received
from this payment to its own account, in light of its financial
difficulties and the need to repair the Mir-Arab Medrese and
other Islamic monuments under its jurisdiction. Ziyautdin Babakhanov, the mufti's son and deputy, explained verbally to the apparatus of CARC's *upolnomochennyi* in Tashkent that although there
were no indigent people in the Soviet Union, the *fitr* was a divine
precept and nobody could abrogate it. This meant that whatever
happened, believers would pay it, and if they did not donate it
to the imam of a registered mosque, they would give it to itinerant
mullas. So SADUM decided to concentrate all payments in its
hands. It had, however, refrained from stating this explicitly in
its request to CARC, as this reason was likely to lead to a refusal.
The official who received this clarification warned that in fact
SADUM's intention was not merely to solve its financial problems,
but also to legitimise the collection of the *fitr* in order to bolster
Islam.[203] Subsequently, SADUM issued instructions that the collection of the *fitr* was not obligatory, but desirable, and, somewhat
later, that it was not to be collected by going the rounds of
private homes, but that the clergy were to satisfy themselves with
whatever was brought to the mosque. In 1958, however, when
he was feeling sufficiently strong, Babakhanov, by now SADUM
Chairman, actually sent out telegrams to organise its collection in
private homes, which the registered mosques duly set about doing.[204]

201. See pp.141-2 above.

202. See p.497.

203. I. A. Shalaev, Information, 19 Nov. 1952; TsGAUz, f.2456, o.1, d.144,
ll.181-2. For SADUM's position on the *fitr*, see also pp.140-1.

204. H. Akhtiamov, Address, Conference of CARC *upolnomochennye*, 25-27 Nov.

Regarding other payments, notably *zakat,* the communal tax contributed to the community treasury, and *ushur,* the tithe, SADUM also changed tack in accordance with either its needs or its reading of the situation and consequent understanding of what it could get away with, or perhaps both. In the 1947 edition of its journal it published a *fetwa* elaborating the obligatory nature of the traditional payments made by the Muslim to the religious authority: *zakat, ushur* and *fitr-sadaqa,* and explaining how they were to be paid in practice. In the single issue of the journal which appeared in 1948 one of SADUM's qazis, however, wrote an article pointing out that, on the contrary, the first two payments were not obligatory. Presumably this second article was written in order to demonstrate to the powers-that-be that Islam, and SADUM specifically, aspired to adapt to the conditions of the new communist society. Unquestionably, the qazi had not written at his own initiative without making his opinions conform with the SADUM leadership. (The rationale behind the non-payment of *sadaqa, zakat* and *ushur,* was that they were not relevant in a socialist society, where people did not have any substantial wealth or property, and produce belonged to the kolkhoz.[205])

Nevertheless, in 1956 when SADUM was enjoying its heyday –and by which time the qazi in question had conveniently died –it rejected the viewpoint he had expressed as being unfounded. It demanded that the clergy collect the *ushur* and *zakat,* which, it explained, were traditionally assigned to religious ends, and transfer them to the coffers of the spiritual directorate. It was incumbent upon the clergy to ensure that believers appreciated the obligatory nature of these payments, concerning which SADUM was con-

---

1958; GARF, f.6991, o.3, d.125, 1.50. For the *fitr,* see pp.274-6 and 486-8.

205. See, for example, L. A. Prikhod'ko, Report, 20 May 1953; GARF, f.6991, o.3, d.91, 1.261. The *zakat* traditionally comprised a fortieth of one's income, *ushur* a tenth of one's crop. See also n.159 above. The *fitr* and *sadaqa* were traditionally two totally different payments. Soviet sources, however, frequently talk of them as though they were one – see, for example, Chapter 2, n.60 and n.125 above. The reason may have been that although the *fitr* was not eliminated by the regime, it and its representatives sought to denigrate it by associating it with *sadaqa,* the routine charity which the Soviet authorities prohibited. Alternatively, their coupling may have reflected the practice of giving other donations besides the *fitr* during the *uraz* and on Uraz-Bayram.

templating the preparation of a special *fetwa*.[206] Yet, it seems that in practice *zakat* and *ushur* were not levied.[207]

The equivocal nature of the spiritual directorates' doctrinal positions was reflected in their attitude to the Mavlud. In the first place, the various directorates expressed conflicting opinions regarding this festival and its celebration, which can only partly be explained by differences in local custom. Thus, whereas SADUM laid down that the celebration of Mavlud be limited to the actual day of Muhammad's birth and insisted that its accompanying ceremonies be performed solely within the precincts of registered mosques, DUMES and DUMSK ordained that it might be celebrated over the course of the entire month and the relevant rites performed in private homes.[208] Secondly, SADUM, at least, seemed to be trying to burn the candle at both ends. A *fetwa* it issued in 1949 declared the celebration of the festival obligatory, SADUM sending its people to the localities for the occasion to read texts devoted to the birth of the Prophet.[209] Just three years later later, it suggested that wherever possible the festival be marked in conjunction with the *jum'a-namaz* and in any case was not to be designated by communal feasting or other extravagances.[210] It must not, ofcourse, be ruled out that the latter position reflected the repressive atmosphere of Stalin's last months.

Apart from the *fetwas*, the spiritual directorates issued injunctions to the clergy under their jurisdiction in a variety of ways. They would send out circulars to the registered mosques, for example, requesting that festival prayers be held early in the morning and not be protracted, so that people could get to work on time, as, indeed, became common practice throughout

206. Z. Babakhanov and Fazil-Khoja Sadyqkhojaev to members of SADUM and the *imam – khatibs* of the major mosques, 6 Nov. 1956; TsGAUz, f.2456, o.1, d.190, ll.9-11.

207. CARC inspector K. F. Tagirov wrote: 'Issues concerning the levy of religious taxes (*zakat* and *ushur*) from believers on behalf of religion have not been elaborated upon by the spiritual centre and in effect have not been resolved' –Resumé, 1 March 1957; GARF, f.6991, o.3, d.132, l.32.

208. Ashirov, *Evoliutsiia islama v SSSR*, p. 22.

209. L. A. Prikhod'ko and N. I. Abushaev, A short survey, Draft, 16 March 1950; GARF, f.6991, o.3, d.63, l.84. For the Mavlud, see pp. 502-3.

210. Ishan Babakhan to members of SADUM, and *imam-khatibs* and executive organs of major (*sobornye*) mosques, 6 Nov. 1952; TsGAUz, f.2456, o.1, d.144, l.173.

the country.[211] Sometimes they would bring the clergy together: DUMZ, for instance, held a conference of clergy from all registered mosques in 1950 just before the month of Muharram, where it cautioned them against allowing instances of self-torture on the Ashura and the holding in private homes of illegal assemblies (*tekke*), neither of which, DUMZ insisted, being prescribed by Islamic teaching.[212] These initiatives, too, were necessarily synchronised with the lay power, if they did not actually originate with it. In 1960 CARC Chairman Aleksei Puzin, for example, suggested to the mufti of Central Asia and Kazakhstan that he send out instructions to clergy on the need to abide by the Soviet law on religion; otherwise the secular power would be obliged to take severe measures against transgressors.[213]

The spiritual directorates as leaders of Soviet Islam

The regime consented to the creation of the spiritual directorates in order that they might act as intermediaries between its representatives and the Muslim believer population and enable it in effect to control Muslim religious activity. Yet, although given a major role in policy implementation, the directorates were composed of leading religious personalities who despite their understanding, and *a priori* acceptance, of the assignment allotted them remained almost by definition suspect in the eyes of the powers-that-be. The attitude of the authorities to the directorates was therefore ambiguous; they sought to enhance their authority as the element within Islam closest to them, one fundamentally loyal to the Soviet state and generally pliant; strengthening the directorates meant buttressing the regime's leverage within a traditionally alien and uncontrolled sector among the country's citizenry. At the same time, Moscow was aware of the danger entailed in making its instruments too influential and powerful and acquired consid-

211. This held not only for rural areas, but for the cities and towns as well –K. F. Tagirov, Memo, 23 Aug. 1957; GARF, f.6991, o.4, d.73, l.83. And see p.498.
212. N. Abushaev, A short survey, 15 March 1951; GARF, f.6991, o.3, d.73, ll.7-8. For details of these customs, see pp.503-6.
213. Puzin was referring in particular to violations in light of the CPSU Central Committee resolution of 13 Jan. 1960 (see pp.43-4) –Reception by Puzin of Babakhanov, 17 Feb. 1960; GARF, f.6991, o.4, d.110, l.9.

erable skills in cutting them down to size or preventing their expansion. Seeing the mounting prestige of the directorates, especially SADUM, in the mid to late 1950s, CARC's *upolnomochennye* often sought ways to clip their wings. They kept close control of the directorates' activities to ensure no room for doubt as to where real power and authority laid. In this context CARC's *upolnomochennyi* in Tashkent suggested to Babakhanov to abolish the post of *muhtasib* in several oblasti of the Uzbek SSR on the grounds that they were revitalisng the clergy's activities, a request with which the mufti complied. At a certain point 'it became known' to this same official that the mufti had not transmitted to his fellow members of SADUM and its employees explanations and instructions he had received from the *upolnomochennyi* regarding the strict observance of Soviet legislation on religion. As a result, the *upolnomochennyi* met directly first with a number of SADUM personnel and then with all the *imam-khatibs* and *mutawalis* of Tashkent and Tashkent Oblast', whom SADUM convened to hear him enlarge upon the need for observance of the law.[214] Similarly, while encouraging the directorates' active participation in the World Peace Movement and ties with foreign Muslim countries, the regime feared that this gave an undue boost to their authority and helped them attract to the mosques many more worshippers than might otherwise have attended them.[215]

The directorates themselves were in an unenviable position. Just as Moscow perceived them as engaged in strengthening religion, the believer community viewed the concessions they were constantly making as a consequence of regime pressure. Delegated by the much-hated centre to control Muslim activity, they inevitably evoked mistrust and suspicion among those very groups which were subordinated to their authority. Aware of both the designs of their political patrons and the mood of their clientèle, however, the directorates seem to have believed that they might be able to take advantage of their importance to each of these to forge for themselves a status of prestige and even power. To this end

214. N. I. Inogamov, Theses of address, Conference of Central Asian *upolnomochennye*, 5-6 June 1959; GARF, f.6991, o.3, d.186, ll.15-6. The offending *muhtasibs* operated in the oblasti of Bukhara, Samarkand and Khorezm and in the Karakalpak ASSR.

215. K. F. Tagirov, Memorandum, 23 Aug. 1957; GARF, f.6991, 0.4, d.73, l.74. And see below, pp.175-7.

they aspired to acquire the traditional outward trappings of leadership in the Muslim regions. This applied in particular in years when policy towards religion was relatively lenient, when the directorates took advantage of the favourable political constellation and the large sums of money which came into their coffers to step up their requests from the authorities.[216]

Even in more difficult years, on the Muslim festivals and in the period preceding them the Muslim religious centres – together with the clergy – were said to buoy up their activity in order to elevate the religious atmosphere among believers. All members of SADUM, including the nonagenarian Babakhan, regularly attended prayer-services during the *uraz* in the early 1950s and read the Qur'an in private homes. One Tashkent mosque where the mufti conducted the service on Uraz-Bayram drew about 10,000 worshippers.[217] In addition to their public appearances, the spiritual directorates were the centre of intense activity on the eve of the fast and the festivals, when clergy and believers came to them to enquire how to conduct themselves on these occasions. The chairman of DUMES reported in 1954 that in the days prior to Qurban-Bayram about 100 mullas and representatives of believer communities visited him just from the raiony closest to Ufa to ask about procedures connected with the sacrificial rite and the chanting of the *takbir* in the streets, and to request assistance in opening mosques.[218] The following year, as the post-Stalin thaw set in, this number more than doubled; DUMES also

216. K. F. Tagirov, Information, 1 March 1957; GARF, f.6991, o.3, d.132, l.69. SADUM's demands in the mid 1950s were to enlarge the number of calendars it published from 4,000 to 10,000; to revive the publication of its monthly journal (5,000 copies) in Uzbek and Arabic; to enlarge the edition of the Qur'an put out in Tashkent from 3,000 to 10,000; to hand over to it 15 religious monuments and mosques in Tashkent, Bukhara, Samarkand and other towns in Uzbekistan; to increase the student body at the Mir-Arab Medrese by 20 and to open the *medrese* in Tashkent to raise the level of the clergy of the registered mosques; to enlarge the number of pilgrims allowed to go on *hajj*; to permit the construction of a mosque in Ashkhabad in place of the one destroyed by the 1948 earthquake; and to permit the opening of mosques in the oblasti of Kashka-Darya, Samarkand and Surkhan-Darya.
217. I. V. Polianskii to M. A. Suslov and K. E. Voroshilov, 29 Dec. 1950; RTsKhIDNI, f.17, o.132, d.285, l.258.
218. I. V. Polianskii to the CPSU Central Committee, 27 Sept. 1954; GARF, f.6991, o.3, d.102, l.29.

received some 150 letters with all kinds of questions on religious issues.[219]

Two weeks prior to the beginning of Ramadan in 1952, SADUM sent out a circular to all registered mosques on how to prepare and conduct the fast and subsequent festival, including rules for their observance and the time of the commencement and end of the fast. In order to attract a maximum number of worshippers to the festival prayers, the circular suggested that all clergy announce in advance that at their conclusion the appeal of the Zagorsk conference of churches and religious associations of the USSR to the World Peace Conference would be read out. SADUM dispatched officials to all five republics to keep an eye on preparations for and observance of the festival and, above all, to procure as many monetary donations as possible, superintend their assessment and ensure their transfer to SADUM's account. The three other spiritual directorates carried out similar activity although with less energy and efficacy, DUMSK, for instance, calling upon all believers to observe the fast in years when it did not coincide with urgent seasonal work in the fields.[220]

The motivation ascribed by CARC to this enhanced activity on the eve of festivals was the desire of the spiritual directorates to enlarge their financial resources. Undisputably, the two larger spiritual directorates had significant financial dealings. They received annually considerable sums from every registered mosque under their jurisdiction, as well as from the few registered holy places. There is considerable evidence that senior officials of SADUM and to a lesser extent of the other directorates enjoyed a rather

219. I. V. Polianskii to the CPSU Central Committee and the Council of Ministers, 20 Sept. 1955; GARF, f.6991, o.3, d.114, l.197.

220. L. Prikhod'ko, Memorandum, 31 Jan. 1953; GARF, f.6991, o.3, d.91, ll.5-7 and 17-18. A circular sent out by SADUM to all members of its board, and to the *imam-khatibs* and executive organs of the registered mosques a year earlier just prior to Qurban-Bayram (on 18 Aug. 1951) likewise suggested that the mufti's appeal concerning peace be read out at the festival *namaz*, and that the clergy speak of the need to aspire to a good harvest and urge believers to fulfil government assignments aimed at improving the general well-being. Moreover, believers were to go to work immediately after prayers. The *fetwa* on the impermissibility of prayer in the home after the *namaz* and the non-obligatory nature of slaughtering livestock was also to be read out, and it was to be explained to believers that they could make voluntary donations for the spiritual directorate and the *medrese*, all donations received at the mosque to be made over to SADUM's account – TsGAUz, f.2456, o.1, d.137, ll.31-2.

lavish life-style,[221] in addition to expending considerable sums on entertaining foreign guests and delegations, and that they were well aware of the power and prestige among their compatriots that the funds at their disposal brought them. SADUM further enhanced its authority by distributing money for the construction of new mosques and for charitable purposes (which contradicted the letter of the law) – in 1960, for example, it distributed tens of thousands of rubles to the needy in the city of Tashkent – and creating a mutual aid fund for its employees.[222] The situation of the two lesser directorates, however, was very different. In neither Transcaucasia nor the Northern Caucasus, for example, were monetary donations made to the religious societies on Qurban-Bayram and so there could be no transfer of such moneys.[223]

During the anti-religious campaign of the Khrushchev period, the *upolnomochennye* in the capitals of those republics where the spiritual directorates were situated sought to take drastic measures to curb their influence, laying stress on means to restrict their sources of income.[224] Even in the slightly laxer period of the late 1960s Moscow complained that SADUM continued to control the financial activity of the registered mosques, received quarterly reports from them and demanded that they transfer to it the entire *fitr* and moneys received on the festivals.[225]

---

221. This was particularly true of the chairmen of SADUM. In 1953 SADUM asked permission to be allowed to purchase a dacha on the outskirts of Tashkent in order to entertain foreign guests and to enable the aged mufti to relax there in the summer. After a while Babakhan changed his mind and resolved to buy a dacha at his personal expense for himself and his family – L. A. Prikhod'ko, V. D. Efremov and P. S. Basis, Report, 8 May 1954; GARF, f.6991, o.3, d.100, l.27. In the end, it appears that SADUM built a dacha. Valued at over three million rubles, it was said to be more luxurious than that of any state institution in the Uzbek SSR. The dacha was in fact used by the mufti as a place of rest and in order to meet with foreign guests – Sh. K. Shirinbaev, Address, All-Union conference of CARC *upolnomochennye*, 18-20 April 1960; GARF, f.6991, o.3, d.208, l.76.

222. Sh. K. Shirinbaev, *ibid.* ll.76-8; A. Puzin, Address, All-Union conference of CARC *upolnomochennye*, 18-20 April 1960 – GARF, f.6991, o.3, d.208, l.11; and Gitlin, *Natsional'nye otnosheniia v Uzbekistane*, p.223. For earlier criticism of Babakhanov's life style, see n.119 above.

223. L. Prikhod'ko, Memorandum, 31 Jan. 1953; GARF, f.6991, 6.3, d.91, l.22.

224. Sh. K. Shirinbaev, *ibid.*, p.79.

225. A. Barmenkov, Theses of lecture, sent to the Central Committee Department of Propaganda, 19 June 1968; GARF, f.6991, o.6, d.147, l.43.

At the same time, it seems that attributing the spiritual directorates' every initiative to monetary lust was somewhat simplistic, even if prescribed by Marxist doctrine. In the first place, they had major expenses: the repair and upkeep of holy sites, many of which were important historical monuments; the maintenance of one *medres*, and at certain periods two and, as of the mid 1950s, the maintenance of increasing foreign ties such as hosting delegations from abroad and trips of their representatives to Muslim countries. Secondly, ensuring and enhancing their incomes were a prerequisite for preserving and augmenting their status and authority among the population to which they catered. In the mid-late 1950s, SADUM pointed out to the clergy that they must broaden the scope of their collections in order to help cover its expenses, which, it insisted, were all undertaken in the name of consolidating the position of Islam in the country.[226]

When, in the mid 1960s CARC called the mufti of SADUM to task for sending a circular without permission from CARC to all religious societies, instructing them not to go on sending moneys to the peace fund but to direct all payments to SADUM, the mufti justified this step by saying that SADUM's coffers were empty owing to the considerable expenses it incurred in connection with its international activity. He also said he had received the consent of CARC's *upolnomochennyi* in Tashkent.[227]

Apart from the peace fund and other activity relating to the international arena, the spiritual directorates in fact fulfilled a number of representative functions which the secular authority and they themselves were persuaded enhanced their prestige among the believer population, specifically the preparation of new religious cadres, the publication of religious materials, and the organisation of the *hajj*. All these activities involved a great deal of uphill work, caused the directorates and their leaders major frustration and had rather meagre results, which inevitably subtracted from the prestige they might otherwise have engendered. Nonetheless,

226. Z. Babakhanov and Fazil-Khoja Sadyqkhojaev to members of SADUM and the *khatibs* of the major mosques, 6 Nov. 1956; TsGAUz, f.2456, o.1, d.190, ll.9–11. The Uzbekistan CP Central Committee noted that SADUM expended no less than 2.25 million rubles in 1958 and 1.5 million in 1959 on the construction and refurbishing of mosques and *mazars* in the republic – Gitlin, *Natsional'nye otnosheniia v Uzbekistane*, pp.223–4.

227. Reception by V. F. Riazanov of Z. Babakhanov, 19 Nov. 1964; GARF, f.6991, o.4, 148, ll.33–4.

the very position of the spiritual directorates as the only bodies empowered to negotiate with the authorities on these issues, served to strengthen their status.

One of the fields of activity of the religious centre in the Soviet Union was training cadres, and a number of religions were allowed to open and maintain special seminaries for this purpose. In 1945 SADUM was given permission to open two religious seminaries – in Tashkent and Bukhara – with thirty and sixty students respectively.[228] The Mir-Arab seminary, or *medrese*, in Bukhara opened in 1946 with twenty-six students and every year the number grew somewhat until by the 1949-50 academic year it had reached sixty-five.[229] Subsequently, the size of the student body fell off, not many people wanting to study there in Stalin's last years, so that SADUM had difficulty in composing the body of students.[230] But in the 1953-4 academic year the student body was up to seventy-four, including one or two students from areas under the jurisdiction of the other spiritual directorates.[231] At least ten people from Dagestan alone applied in 1953 for permission to study in

228. I. V. Polianskii to K. E. Voroshilov, 5 April 1946. The actual SNK instruction, No.14808r, of 10 Oct. 1945, did not mention numbers – GARF, f.6991, o.3, d.34, l.45, and o.4, d.1, l.15.

229. The majority of the students were Uzbeks (36). The others were Tajiks (14), Kazakhs (5), Karakalpaks (4), Tatars – presumably residents of Central Asia –and Kyrgyz (2 apiece), Turkmen and Uighur (1 each). The curriculum consisted of the study of Uzbek, Arabic (language and morphology), Hadith, *tafsir, fiqh,* the history of Islam, *akhlaq* (conduct), Qur'an, Persian, mathematics, geography, the Soviet constitution and the history of the peoples of the USSR. There were five lecturers (with inadequate qualifications) – L. A. Prikhod'ko and N. I. Abushaev, Draft, Short survey, 16 March 1950; GARF, f.6991, o.3, d.63, l.81.

230. At the beginning of 1951 there were 55 students, but quite a few did not return after the summer vacation and the student body for the 1951-52 academic year was made up of just 40 students. There was even talk of closing the *medrese* or transferring it elsewhere on the pretext that the building was in dilapidated condition, but CARC decided that this was a premature decision – L. A. Prikhod'ko, Report, 2 June 1952; GARF, f.6991, o.3, d.81, l.132.

231. L. A. Prikhod'ko, V. D. Efremov and P. S. Basis, Report, 8 May 1954; GARF, f.6991, o.3, d.100, l.38. The predominant majority continued to be Central Asians, the Uzbeks alone comprising 42 out of the 74. CARC thought the total number exaggerated and recommended that it be cut back to 60. It insisted, moreover, that this quota not be surpassed; CARC's *upolnomochennyi* in Bukhara was to keep an eye on the number of students and if it became too high he was to report this immediately – I. V. Polianskii to Kh. N. Iskanderov, 20 Feb. 1954; TsGAUz, f.2456, o.1, d.162, l.83.

Bukhara.[232] In 1956, although permission was given for seventy-five students, no less than 118 enrolled and began the academic year.[233] After further ups and downs, the student body stood at eighty-six in 1982, 60 per cent from Central Asia and the remainder from the areas under the jurisdiction of the other three spiritual directorates.[234]

In spite of the considerable publicity given to the *medrese*, and the major expenses involved in its upkeep, which were a serious drain on SADUM's budget,[235] its achievements were modest indeed. The level of instruction both in religious and secular subjects was low.[236] In all the years between 1945 and 1970 only eighty-five students graduated, not all of whom wanted to work as clergy; eighty students had dropped out for different reasons without finishing the full course of study.[237] Even under Gorbachev, after

232. Khabilov to I. V. Polianskii, 4 June 1954; GARF, f.6991, o.3, d.102, ll.128-9.

233. N. Achilov to I. V. Polianskii and Kh. N. Iskanderov, 16 Oct. 1956; TsGAUz, f.2456, o.1, d.190, ll.34. Achilov, CARC's *upolnomochennyi* in Bukhara Oblast', asked the director of the *medrese* to send home the extra 43 students.

234. Thrower, 'Notes on Muslim Theological Education in the USSR in the 1980s', p.178.

235. SADUM's anticipated expenses for 1947 were 1,930,080 rubles of which 940,000 were to go to the upkeep of the *medrese* – Minutes, SADUM 2nd plenary session, [20-27 Jan. 1947]; TsGAUz, f.2456, o.1, d.104, l.3. In 1960 Mufti Babakhanov was suggesting that the Bukhara *medrese* be closed, since its upkeep and repair cost SADUM dearly, leaving just the one *medrese* in Tashkent –K. Ovchinnikov, Information, prepared for CARC session No.9, 21 Feb. 1961; GARF, f.6991, o.3, d.1356, ll.13-4.

236. Among others, the textbooks were of pre-revolutionary vintage and totally inappropriate. SADUM expended considerable energy and effort in trying to persuade the powers-that-be to import textbooks from Egypt; see, for example, Reception by L. A. Prikhod'ko of Z. Babakhanov, 24 July 1957 – GARF, f.6991, o.4, d.74, ll.109-10. In addition, the academic year was very short – from 10 September to the beginning of May, and even during this period the students would be mobilised for an entire month, like all other students, to participate in the cotton harvest – cf. N. Achilov to I. V. Polianskii and Kh. N. Iskanderov, 16 Oct. 1956; TsGAUz, f.2456, o.1, d.190, l.3.

237. CRA information, sent to the CPSU Central Committee, 27 April 1971; TsKhSD, f.5, o.63, d.89, l.100. The poor turnout and the fact that not all who did complete their studies went on to serve as clerics had been evident already much earlier. See, for example, L. Prikhod'ko and N. Abushaev, A short report, 11 April 1952, and I. V. Polianskii to the Central Committee, 11 Jan. 1955; GARF, f.6991, o.3, d.81, ll.82-3, and d.113, l.8. (At first the period of study had lasted five years, then seven, and was finally fixed at nine.)

forty years of Mir-Arab's existence and twenty of the *medrese* in Tashkent, just 15 per cent of the clergy in Kirgiziia thirty-four mosques, for example, were graduates of one of them.[238] Nonetheless, since it was the sole institution of its kind, a large number of applicants asked to study there: in the late 1970s there were said to be 400 applications for thirty-four places.[239]

Knowing full well the lack of religious education of the clergy in the registered mosques, SADUM entertained thoughts about crash courses – in addition to the official *medrese* – to enable mullas and shaykhs to supplement their knowledge of Shari'a law and other fields relevant to their activity. This seems to have been the original intention of SADUM regarding the second, Tashkent *medrese* which it eventually opened in the building of the old Barak-Khan Medrese in 1956.[240] In a circular to Central Asian clergy in that year, it explained that creating conditions for the operation of its two colleges was designed to enlarge the body of people with theological knowledge, which was a precondition for the 'development and prosperity' of Islam.[241] At the beginning of the 1958-9 academic year there were ninety-six students in the two *medreses*, but the number declined in the subsequent years of the anti-religious campaign, in the process of which the Tashkent *medrese* was closed down again.[242] But in 1971, several years after

238. Doev, *Osobennosti islama v Kirgizii*, p.5.

239. *Novoe russkoe slovo*, 29 Sept. 1982.

240. Kh. N. Iskanderov, Report, 2 June 1952 – GARF, f.6991, o.3, d.83, l.136; Z. Babakhanov to Iskanderov, 14 Dec. 1955, and I. V. Polianskii to I. A. Shalaev, 13 Jan. 1956 – TsGAUz, f.2456, o.1, d.129, l.29, and d.174, l.113. In 1947 it was reported that the Tashkent *medrese* had not opened because the *gorispolkom* had not vacated it (it housed an artel of the blind) – Minutes, CARC session No.11, 18-9 June 1947 – and on 15 Aug. 1949 the USSR Council of Ministers rescinded the decision to open a *medrese* in Tashkent on the grounds that the one in Bukhara satisfied SADUM's needs – L. A. Prikhod'ko and N. I. Abushaev, Draft, 16 March 1950; GARF, f.6991, o.4, d.19, l.375, and o.3, d.63, ll.81-2.

241. Z. Babakhanov and F. Sadyqkhojaev to SADUM members and the *khatibs* of the major mosques, 6 Nov. 1956; TsGAUz, f.2456, o.1, d.190, l.9.

242. The Barak-Khan Medrese was closed on the grounds that it had been opened illegally, the Uzbek SSR Council of Ministers 1956 resolution having ignored the 1949 one of the All-Union Council of Ministers – Sh. K. Shirinbaev, Address, All-Union conference of *upolnomochennye*, 18-20 April 1960, and K. Ovchinninkov, Information, prepared for CARC session No.9, 21 Feb. 1961; GARF, f.6991, o.3, d.208, l.74, and d.1356, l.13.

Khrushchev's ouster, the Ismail al–Bukhari Medrese opened in Tashkant. Here, during the course of four years, students who had graduated from Mir–Arab were supposed to be able to become full-fledged *ulema*, doctors of Islamic law, a hope which seems not to have been fulfilled, at least as of 1982.[243] In the academic year 1979-80 the Tashkent institute boasted thirty-six students and was headed by Shamsutdin Babakhan, son of the Mufti of SADUM.[244] As of the mid 1950s, too, a handful of students from the Soviet Union were allowed to study at a number of Middle Eastern institutions of Muslim higher learning.[245]

In 1945 TsDUM also asked permission to initiate courses to prepare clergy,[246] and in the following year DUMZ too requested permission to open a *medrese*. The latter contended that there were not sufficient mullas and *efendis* to fulfil the role of clergy in the mosques that were being opened, compelling it to appoint laymen, and that it anticipated the closure of prayer-houses for lack of qualified personnel in the foreseeable future.[247] In December 1947 the USSR Council of Ministers authorised the inauguration of a *medrese* in Baku, but it did not open for lack of sufficient

---

243. Thrower, 'Notes on Muslim Theological Education in the USSR in the 1980s', pp.179-80.

244. Radio Moscow in Turkish, 28 Sept. 1979, and in English, 12 April 1980; SWB I, 6 Nov. 1979 and 10 May 1980.

245. The first time permission for this was given seems to have been towards the end of 1954, when a special instruction of the USSR Council of Ministers permitted SADUM to send three students to al-Azhar in Cairo – Instruction No.13010rs, 4 Dec. 1954. All requests to send even two or three students for study abroad were subject to protracted negotiation; see, for example, Reception by V. F. Riazanov of Ziyautdin Babakhanov, 31 July 1962; GARF, f.6991, o.3, d.113, l.35, and o.4, d.130, ll.30-1. Over time, a handful of Soviet Muslim students were allowed to study also in Morocco, Syria and Libya.

246. M. Sh. Karimov to I. V. Polianskii and Bashkir ASSR SNK Chairman S. A. Vagapov, 27 Sept. 1945; GARF, f.6991, o.3, d.26, l.3.

247. A letter from DUMZ to the CARC *upolnomochennyi* in Azerbaijan was quoted by the latter in his report for the first half of 1946. DUMZ had written that believers had approached it requesting permission to prepare clergy unofficially, but it had rejected such antiquated methods as unfitting to contemporary conditions. DUMZ would seek financial aid from believers, but needed the cooperation of the government in working out a curriculum of study that would be appropriate to the period – B. Shahbazbekov, Report, [June 1946]. A curriculum was eventually presented to the authorities and transmitted to the government – I. V. Polianskii to K. E. Voroshilov, 10 Dec. 1947; GARF, f.6991, o.3, d.38, ll.96-7, and d.48, ll.72-3.

applicants.[248] In 1946, at a conference held with representatives of Dagestan's functioning mosques, the issue of opening a *medrese* was raised also for the Northern Caucasus, but without any specification regarding the number of students, the duration of tuition, the syllabus, the provision of teaching staff and textbooks, or even the language of study.[249] When, however, DUMSK placed a proposal with CARC for opening a *medrese*, it was recommended to refrain from the attempt on the grounds that it would require means which were simply not at its disposal, and Mufti Gebekov concurred.[250] In the mid 1950s both DUMZ and DUMES were again endeavouring to open *medreses*, in Baku and Ufa respectively,[251] but their efforts remained without success. Eventually, arrangements were reached for sending students from the rest of the Soviet Union to Bukhara and Tashkent; to accommodate these students the language of tuition was changed from Uzbek to Russian. (The original intention of conducting studies in Arabic had still not been achieved by the mid 1980s.)[252]

Another sphere of activity of the two major spiritual directorates – SADUM and DUMES – was the publication of religious materials. Both issued lunar Muslim calendars in the Arabic script, the one in Uzbek, the other in Volga Tatar, for most years of the postwar period, although each time they had to file a special application to CARC, which passed it on to the powers-that-be.[253] Nor was there necessarily agreement among the latter. In 1949, for instance, the Council of Ministers Cultural Bureau agreed, but the Central

248. Instruction No.19447-r, 30 Dec. 1947, and N. Tagiev, Short survey, undated (probably early 1949); GARF, f.6991, o.3, d.54, l.1 and o.4, d.23, ll.12 and 12ob.

249. I. Zakaryaev, Report, Minutes, CARC session, No.7, 23-24 April 1947; GARF, f.6991, o.4, d.19, l.167.

250. L. A. Prikhod'ko and N. I. Abushaev, Draft, 16 March 1950, GARF, f.6991, o.3, d.63, ll.81-2.

251. I. V. Polianskii to A. Mikoian, 5 June 1956; GARF, f.6991, o.3, d.129, l.198.

252. Thrower, 'Notes on Muslim Theological Education in the USSR in the 1980s', p.180. Thrower speaks in this connection of the Tashkent Institute, but I assume that it holds, too, for the Mir-Arab Medrese.

253. The DUMES calendar was published in Kazan' because in Ufa there was no Arabic typescript. For this, special permission had to be obtained from the AUCP(b) Central Committee – I. V. Polianskii to G. F. Aleksandrov, 14 Sept. 1946; GARF, f.6991, o.3, d.34, l.187.

Committee Department of Propaganda and Agitation did not,[254] and no calendar appeared.[255] Sometimes by the time all the organisations which had to give their consent had done so, it was no longer feasible to issue the calendar for the beginning of the *hijra* year in question and so the permission that was granted would be made use of for the following year.[256] In the early stages the spiritual directorates sought to include in the calendar materials which were not considered intrinsic for such a publication – excerpts from the *hadith*, verses from the Qur'an, sayings of Muhammad, biographical sketches of Muslim figures, such as the founders of the Naqshbandi and Qadiri orders – but by the early 1950s the drafts they presented for approval contained only a few basic dates.[257]

Usually the number of copies the spiritual directorates were permitted to issue was less than actually asked for. In 1946 DUMES, then still the Spiritual Directorate of the Muslims of the RSFSR, asked to be allowed to publish 10,000 but was given permission to issue 3,000.[258] In 1948 SADUM issued 5,000 copies and DUMES 2,500;[259] by 1951 the numbers were up to 6,000 and 4,000 respec-

254. I. V. Polianskii to K. E. Voroshilov, 15 Dec. 1949; GARF, f.6991, o.3, d.61, l.215.

255. L. A. Prikhod'ko and N. I. Abushaev, Draft, 16 March 1950; GARF, f.6991, o.3, d.63, l.82.

256. This occurred, for example, with DUMES's application to edit a calendar for the year 1952-3 (the *hijra* year 1372) – L. Prikhod'ko, Report, 20 May 1953; GARF, f.6991, o.3, d.91, ll.241-2.

257. CARC inspector Tagiev together with *upolnomochennyi* for the Uzbek SSR Iskanderov excised the extra materials from the draft prepared in 1946; they were then reinserted by SADUM and given to the printer without being reviewed again by Iskanderov, who had to be alerted by telegram to look at the manuscript before it reached the typesetter – Minutes, CARC session No.11, 18-9 June 1947; GARF, f.6991, o.4, d.19, l.376. Some of the drafts of later years have been preserved in the CARC archives.

258. I. V. Polianskii to Deputy Chairman of the USSR Council of Ministers A. N. Kosygin, 26 June 1946; GARF, f.6991, o.3, d.34, l.101. Although the letter was directed to the government, permission was actually given by the head of the Propaganda Administration, G. F. Aleksandrov – by phone (*ibid.*). This same source tells us that SADUM had already issued a calendar in 1945.

259. N. Tagiev, Short Survey, [early 1949]; GARF, f.6991, o.4, d.23, l.12ob. According to a report sent to Voroshilov and Malenkov on 23 April 1949 –RTsKhIDNI, f.17, o.132, d.111, l.61; and GARF, f.6991, o.3, d.61, ll.36-61 –the numbers for the calendar of the lunar year corresponding to 1947-48 were 3,000 and 2,000 respectively. This seems to be a report based on Tagiev's document, but it is not clear whether his figures relate to the year 1947-48 or

tively,[260] but two years later SADUM was allowed to publish only 2,000 copies, as against DUMES's 4,000.[261] In 1953 SADUM asked permission to enlarge the edition of the calendar for the year 1953-4 from 2,000 to 8,000, and was permitted to put out 6,000 copies.[262] In 1957 and again in 1958 DUMES was given permission to issue a calendar in 6,000 copies (it asked permission for 10,000 copies); in 1959 it did not submit any application, but in the following year asked to be allowed to issue 4,000 copies and its request was granted.[263] From time to time, DUMZ also requested permission to publish a calendar.[264]

SADUM also published *The Journal of the Spiritual Directorate of the Muslims of Central Asia and Kazakhstan* in the 1940s and as of 1968 *Muslims of the Soviet East*. Originally intended to be a monthly publication, in Uzbek in Arabic script, only a very few issues of the former seem to have appeared in all (between 1945 and 1948).[265] In its original request, filed in September 1944 when the war was still waging, SADUM maintained that through the journal the Muslims' patriotic feelings would be enhanced.[266] It later sought to use it as a platform to propagate its resolutions and *fetwas*.[267]

1948-49. Possibly, too, there was a discrepancy between the number specified in the permit and the number actually issued.

260. L. Prikhod'ko, A short report, 11 April 1951; GARF, f.6991, o.3, d.81, l.83.

261. L. Prikhod'ko, Report, 20 May 1953; GARF, f.6991, o.3, d.91, l.242.

262. L. A. Prikhod'ko, V. D. Efremov and P. S. Basis, Report, 8 May 1954. It seems that the original application from both spiritual directorates had been for 15,000 copies, which CARC in its own approach to the Central Committee cut down to size, asking for 6,000 copies for SADUM and 4,000 for DUMES –Minutes, CARC session No.1, 30 Jan.1953, GARF, f.6991, o.3, d.92, ll.1-2, and d.100, ll.26-7.

263. N. I. Smirnov, Information, 19 May 1960, and Minutes, CARC session No.12s, 20 May 1960; GARF, f.6991, o.3, d.204, ll.177 and 186.

264. See, for example, L. A. Prikhod'ko to I. V. Polianskii, 5 May 1956; GARF, f.6991, o.3, d.217, l.54.

265. According to Prikhod'ko and Abushaev, Draft, 16 March 1950; GARF, f.6991, o.3, d.63, l.82, five or six double numbers appeared. See also Bennigsen and Lemercier-Quelquejay, ' "Official" Islam in the Soviet Union', p.54.

266. I. V. Polianskii to V. M. Molotov, 30 Sept. 1944; GARF, f.6991, o.3, d.1, l.38. SADUM said it would imbue readers with love for the mother country and for religion. For the content matter and division of the suggested journal, see K. Ia. Pugo to I. Ibadov, 5 Oct. 1944; GARF, f.6991, o.3, d.6, l.29.

267. Kh. N. Iskanderov to I. V. Polianskii, 11 April 1947. CARC had no

In the first issue or two the material was apparently not corroborated with CARC, but as of late 1946 that body instituted procedures to ensure that nothing appear in print which it had not first seen and approved.[268] In all, however, the journal seems to have had neither people who could contribute worthy material nor much in the way of content which it could safely publish. In the words of one CARC official, the journal in its early form simply dragged out a miserable existence.[269] The second journal, *Muslims of the Soviet East*, appeared at first in Uzbek in Arabic script and in Arabic and over time in several other languages as well (English and French as of 1974, Farsi and Dari, as of 1980 and 1984 respectively). The fact that its Uzbek edition was in Arabic script meant that it was not designed for the bulk of the local population, including the intelligentsia. Its subject matter, too, was clearly intended to convey to outsiders the impression of a normally functioning Islam in the Soviet Union. The journal appeared regularly four times a year until the end of our period and beyond.

In 1946 Rasulev put out a booklet entitled *Islam-dini* (The Islamic faith),[270] but was later prevented from issuing a second

objection to this request – Polianskii to Iskanderov, 25 April 1947. In an epistle dated 16 May 1952, Babakhan wrote that in the issue of 1 Jan. 1947 SADUM had shown the illegitimacy of a number of rites which contradicted the Shari'a and concerning which a *fetwa* had been published on the basis of arguments brought by *ulema* and legal experts – TsGAUz, f.2456, o.1, d.82, ll.8-9, and d.144, l.23.

268. I. N. Uzkov and G. A. Vrachev to Polianskii, 29 Nov. 1946; RTsKhIDNI, f.17, o.125, d.405, l.95. Uzkov and Vrachev stated that in an issue which had appeared in 1946 SADUM had published its ruling of August 1945 that *zakat* was obligatory for every Muslim, and insisted that CARC should not have permitted such a *fetwa* to appear in print. In the 1970s the CRA was still monitoring the manuscript of *Muslims of the Soviet East* with punctilious pedantry –A. Nurullaev, *Muslims of the Soviet East*, 1971, No.3 (11), undated; GARF, f.6991, o.6, d.370, ll.95-7.

269. N. Tagiev, Short survey, [early 1949]. Tagiev said permission had been given to publish 5,000 copies; in a subsequent letter to Voroshilov on 15 Dec. 1949, Polianskii spoke of 3,000 – the original request had certainly been for 3,000 – I. V. Polianskii to V. M. Molotov, 30 Sept. 1944; GARF, f.6991, o.4, d.23, l.12 ob, and o.3, d.1, l.38, and d.61, l.215.

270. I. V. Polianskii to K. E. Voroshilov, 5 April 1946; GARF, f.6991, o.3, d.34, l.45. The booklet was published in 5,000 copies, although Rasulev had asked permission to publish 10,000 copies, saying that the Muslims had no religious textbooks whatever and the need for them was great so that believers might become acquainted with some of their elementary rites and traditions

edition; nor was DUMES allowed to publish a *Haftiaq*, a selection of *suras* from the Qur'an (amounting in all to about one seventh of the Qur'an).[271] Commenting on DUMES's motivation in making these requests, CARC said that it wanted to 'broaden its material base' and extend the 'framework of religious propaganda'.[272] Rasulev's successor, Shakir Khiyaletdinov, applied for permission to distribute the 20,000 copies of a religious textbook published in 1918 which had been preserved in the archive of the spiritual directorate, or to put out new editions of a booklet entitled *Iman sharty* ('Duties of the Faith'), containing prayers in Volga Tatar for those who might have difficulty reciting them in Arabic, or that of Rasulev. CARC had these works translated from Tatar to Russian and decided that it was inexpedient to publish any of the three.[273] The chairman of DUMSK also raised the issue of publishing a journal, but it was explained to him that DUMSK lacked the wherewithal to overcome the difficulties involved in such a venture: the absence in Dagestan of typography in Arabic script and of educated correspondents, and the expense of printing a journal in the languages of the mountain tribes.[274]

By the mid 1950s SADUM and DUMES were asking to publish conjointly a new edition of the Qur'an in 2,000 copies to meet the requirements of believers, who were asking for new editions of 'The Basics of the Faith', the *Haftiaq* and the Qur'an;[275] there

–Polianskii to V. M. Molotov, 22 Dec. 1944; GARF, f.6991, o.3, d.1, l.52.

271. I. V. Polianskii to K. E. Voroshilov, 28 March 1949; GARF, f.6991, o.3, d.48, ll.22-3. Polianskii noted that a *Haftiaq* had been published in the Soviet Union in 1928 and was still available, as were pre-revolutionary editions of the complete Qur'an. See also a report sent to Voroshilov and Malenkov, 23 April 1949; RTsKhIDNI, f.17, o.132, d.111, l.61.

272. L. A. Prikhod'ko and N. I. Abushaev, Draft, 16 March 1950; GARF, f.6991, o.3, d.63, l.82.

273. L. Prikhod'ko, Report, 20 May 1953; GARF, f.6991, o.3, d.91, l.242. At the same time, CARC refrained from ordering the destruction of the approximately 75,000 books and pamphlets preserved at DUMES, but explained that they could not be disseminated among believers without permission. *Iman sharty* (or *Sharaitul-iman*) first appeared in the late 18th century. One of these three books seems, however, to have been published in 1956 or early 1957 –see p.438.

274. L. Prikhod'ko and N. Abushaev, Draft, 16 March 1950; GARF, f.6991, o.3, d.63, l.83.

275. Ishan Babakhan to I. V. Polianskii, 30 Sept. 1953. Babakhan also mentioned that foreign visitors asked to be given copies of a Qur'an issued in the Soviet Union. 'The basics of the faith' is probably a reference to Rasulev's book *Islam-dini*

had been no edition of the Qur'an since before 1917.[276] Since the spiritual directorates were publishing nothing except the calendar and in view of the recurrent questioning on the part of foreign visitors regarding Muslim publishing activities, and after verifying with Glavizdat at the Ministry of Culture that the publication of the Qur'an in Arabic script was technically feasible, CARC approved the request. Relaying the request to the CPSU Central Committee, Polianskii noted that the spiritual directorates were concerned primarily with supplying Qur'ans to clergy and foreigners rather than to regular believers, the great majority of whom did not know Arabic and so could not use them.[277] Permission for publication was given by the party,[278] and the Qur'an was eventually published in 3,000 copies in 1956.[279]

By 1958 SADUM was preparing a second edition of the Qur'an, using this time as its original a Qur'an published in Cairo, in order to avoid mistakes which had appeared in the first edition.[280] Babakhanov informed CARC that the amount of paper allotted for the second edition would suffice for the 2,000 copies which

(see above). The CARC official who prepared material for the discussion of the application at CARC session No.13, 5 Nov. 1953, noted that an edition of 2,000 copies of the Qur'an would enable the two muftis to provide some copies to members of the spiritual directorates and their *muhtasibs* as well as to leading clerics in mosques and some believers, to put some aside especially for presentation to guests from abroad, and to send a few to leading clerics in Egypt, Saudi Arabia and other countries – V. Efremov, Resumé, undated; GARF, f.6991, o.3, d.92, ll.62, 64 and 65-6.

276. For the publication of the Qur'an and other Islamic texts before 1917, see Saidbaev, *Islam i obshchestvo*, p.122.

277. L. A. Prikhod'ko, V. D. Efremov and P. S. Basis, Report, 8 May 1954, and I. V. Polianskii to the Central Committee, 15 May 1954; GARF, f.6991, o.3, d.100, l.28, and d.102, ll.118-20. After the Qur'an's publication CARC asked for a number of Qur'ans to be given to foreign visitors, as a result of which Khiyaletdinov was compelled to take back copies he had given to several clergy; the latter awaited the second edition in order to recover their Qur'ans –Reception by V. F. Riazanov of Khiyaletdinov, 9 April 1960; GARF, f.6991, o.4, d.110, l.17.

278. V. I. Gostev to CARC's *upolnomochennye* in Tashkent, Ufa and Kazan' (Kh. N. Iskanderov, M. Sh. Karimov and G. S. Safin), 1 June 1954; TsGAUz, f.2456, o.1, d.167, l.33.

279. I. V. Polianskii to A. Mikoian, 5 June 1956; GARF, f.6991, o.3, d.129, ll.197-8.

280. Reception by A. Puzin of Z. Babakhanov, 24 April 1958; GARF, f.6991, o.4, d.88, l.110.

SADUM needed, but not for the copies requested by the other spiritual directorates.[281] The second edition appeared in Tashkent in 1961, in 2,250 copies. Some of these had to go to the other spiritual directorates; moreover, Babakhanov was under pressure to send copies to SADUM's qaziates and to mosques which had contributed to the costs of publication, while 325 copies were designated as gifts to foreign delegations and religious figures.[282] Further editions of the Qur'an were said to have appeared in 1969, 1970, 1976 and 1977 in Tashkent and in 1984 in Kazan'.[283]

In 1956 the Uzbekistan Communist Party Central Committee permitted SADUM to publish, in addition to the 2,000 copies of the Qur'an, a calendar in 10,000 copies, 'A guide to the religious sites of Uzbekistan', 'An anthology of essays on the life of the Muslims' and a journal, *Islam haqiqati* ('The truth of Islam'), regularly once every two months, the last three items in 5,000 copies in Uzbek, Farsi and Arabic.[284] And in the following year SADUM was asking for the organisation of a small printing-press for the use of all four spiritual directorates, where it might be possible to print materials put out by them in the Arabic alphabet – calendars, journals, literature for religious instruction (in the two *medreses*), and guidelines and instructions distributed by the religious centres to the clergy. Needless to say, the response was not encouraging.[285]

The organisation of the *hajj*, too, fell within the jurisdiction of the spiritual directorates. After a long interval,[286] a small number

281. Proposals regarding questions raised by Z. Babakhanov, prepared for CARC session No.3, 22 Jan. 1960; GARF, f.6991, o.3, d.204, l.21.

282. K. Ovchinnikov, Information, prepared for CARC session No.9, 21 Feb. 1961, and Reception by Puzin of Babakhanov, 19 Dec. 1961; GARF, f.6991, o.3, d.1356, ll.16-7, and o.4, d.121, l.22.

283. Babakhanov, *Islam and the Muslims in the Land of the Soviets*, pp.64-5, and *Muslims of the Soviet East*, 1986, No.3, pp.14-15.

284. [Kh. N. Iskanderov?] to I. V. Polianskii, 2 Oct. 1956; GARF, f.2456, o.1, d.191, l.121.

285. Ziyautdin Babakhanov, who raised this on a visit to CARC, was told that he would do well to study the matter carefully, for it would entail considerable costs which would hardly be justified, especially since DUMSK and DUMZ were not likely to participate in the outlay – Reception by L. A. Prikhod'ko of SADUM acting chairman Z. Babakhanov, 24 July 1957; GARF, f.6991, o.4, d.75, ll.109-10.

286. In his letter to Molotov suggesting that a limited number of Muslims be allowed to perform the *hajj* in 1944, Polianskii said no Muslim from the Soviet Union had made the *hajj* for twenty years – I. V. Polianskii to V. M. Molotov,

of believers were allowed to make the pilgrimage to Mecca and Medina – another of the five pillars of Islam – in 1944 and again in 1945.[287] Polianskii, recommending to Molotov that the *hajj* be permitted, said it would have a positive impact first of all within the Soviet Union, as it would raise the authority of the spiritual directorates.[288] In the course of time, however, the impact at home came to be perceived as basically negative, since both during the preparation for the pilgrims' departure and even more so after their return, they became the focus of attention and a catalyst for demonstrating religious enthusiasm: prior to departure believers would bestow presents on the pilgrims and bring them money to help pay their expenses, and afterwards they would gather in the mosques and elsewhere to hear their stories.[289] As a result,

14 Sept. 1944; GARF, f.6991, o.3, d.1, l.22. According to the British Foreign Office Research Department, a Soviet delegation headed by TsDUM Mufti Rizaeddin Fakhreddin had participated in a Muslim congress in Jedda in 1926, which was the last time any Muslim ecclesiastic had been allowed to travel abroad – 'The Soviet Union and Islam', March 1947; PRO/FO371/66391. SADUM Mufti Ziyautdin Babakhanov, however, wrote that Muslims performed the *hajj* as of 1922 until it was forbidden in 1928 – Z. Babakhanov, Report, March 1970; GARF, f.6991, o.6, d.342, l.29. According to contemporary British sources, 1928 saw the largest Soviet contingent of pilgrims of any year, 749, whereas the last time Soviet citizens made the *hajj* until 1944 was 1929, when 207 made the pilgrimage. In each year there were also just a few Turkestanis who reached Saudi Arabia from India, 16 in 1928 and six in 1929, and in 1928 a further 1,987 'Bokharans'. (It is unclear where these Central Asians came from. Presumably, however, they were emigrés from the Soviet Union, who neither came on *hajj* from that country nor returned to it, large numbers of Central Asians having departed the Soviet Union in the 1920s) – *British Documents on Foreign Affairs*, Part II, Series B, vol.14, pp.29-30, 38, 54-5 and 65.

287. The first *hajj* was made by just six pilgrims, but as of 1945 the number was usually around twenty, a group small enough to fit into a single plane of the size allotted for the purpose. In 1945 the Soviet government allowed 22 pilgrims to go, but only 17 went; the delegation was led by the chairmen of TsDUM and SADUM and the deputy chairman of DUMZ – SNK Instruction No.14809rs, 10 Oct. 1945, and I. V. Polianskii to V. M. Molotov, 9 Nov. 1945; GARF, f.6991, o.3, d.10, ll.86-7.

288. Polianskii to Molotov, 14 Sept. 1944; GARF, f.6991, o.3, d.1, l.22. In addition, Polianskii pointed out, it would be an indication to foreign Muslims of the freedom of religion prevalent in the USSR.

289. For example, V. I. Gostev to P. A. Tarasov, 4 Jan. 1954, and L. A. Prikhod'ko, Information, 18 May 1957; GARF, f.6991, o.3, d.102, l.7, and d.146, l.102. CARC's *upolnomochennyi* in Tajikistan reported that when it became known that SADUM's qazi in that republic was going on *hajj* in 1945, kolkhozniki came to his home with rice, flour, money and presents, and upon his return

those favouring the *hajj* emphasised its importance for foreign propaganda, as it indicated to foreign Muslims that Islam was alive and permitted in the Soviet Union. Certainly, the very fact that the pilgrimage to Mecca and Medina took place led to a demand to go on *hajj* that far exceeded the quota of permits, which was usually about twenty. In 1946 and 1947 all four spiritual directorates received large numbers of requests from believers desirous of performing the *hajj*.[290] In the mid 1950s, when the atmosphere was again somewhat more easy-going, the numbers of requests mounted once more, not only to Mecca and Medina, but also to the Shiite shrines of Meshed and Kerbala.[291]

From time to time, suggestions were tabled to increase the number of *hajjis*, but it remained fairly static, since the authorities were interested in the pilgrims comprising an isolated and carefully supervised group.[292] Moreover, the circle of those who, it was felt, could be relied upon both to pray properly and to function in their contact with foreigners in a way that would be beneficial to the Soviet state was strictly limited. This meant that often it would be the same people who went on *hajj* year after year. In one of his conversations with Babakhanov, Puzin asked him to

---

he was visited even by high-ranking officials, and many non-believers invited him to their homes, feasted him and asked him to conduct readings from the Qur'an – Minutes, CARC session No.4, 29 Jan. 1947. The argument that the 1945 *hajj* had already had a negative impact at home and enlivened Muslim activity was brought by CARC as a reason not to permit the *hajj* to take place in 1950 - Iu. V. Sadovskii to K. E. Voroshilov, 15 May 1950; GARF, f.6991, o.4, d.19, 1.83, and o.3, d.68, 1.33. See also I. V. Polianskii to P. V. Kovanov, 23 June 1955, and Minutes, CARC session No.4, 25-26 Feb. 1959; GARF, f.6991, o.3, d.114, ll.29 and 35, and d.183, ll.116-17.

290. I. V. Polianskii to V. M. Molotov, 14 May 1947; GARF, f.6991, o.3, d.47, ll.157-8.

291. In 1956 DUMSK alone received 125 applications from people wanting to perform the *hajj* to Mecca and Medina, while DUMZ received 28 requests for permission to go to Meshed and 50 to Kerbala – G. F. Frolov, Information, 22 Feb.1957; GARF, f.6991, o.3, d.132, ll.77 and 79.

292. In 1946 Polianskii proposed doubling the figure from appproximately 20 to 40 – Polianskii to Voroshilov, [?] July 1946; GARF, f.6991, o.3, d.34, 1.117. (Agitprop chief Aleksandrov preferred 30 – G. F. Aleksandrov to A. A. Zhdanov, 29 July 1946; RTsKhIDNI, f.17, o.125, d.407, 1.59.) In 1956 Polianskii again sought to enlarge the number, contending that Muslims abroad could not understand why so few believers from the Soviet Union performed the *hajj*, which was obligatory for every Muslim with the requisite means – I. V. Polianskii to the CPSU Central Committee, 4 April 1956; GARF, f.6991, o.3, d.129, 1.84.

think about extending the circle of clergy who could be sent abroad, authorised to meet with foreigners – apparently in the Soviet Union – and appear in the foreign media.[293]

In 1947 and 1948, permission was given to perform the *hajj*, but the pilgrims did not set out, in the former year because of an outbreak of cholera in Egypt, in the latter because of the first Arab-Israeli war.[294] And it was only in 1953 that the *hajj* was resumed.[295] The procedure to obtain permission to perform the *hajj* was extremely cumbersome, involving a number of organisations at the republican and all-union level,[296] and several times a refusal was given on the grounds that there was insufficient time to process the request.[297] On a number of occasions the pilgrims committed misdemeanours which gave the powers-that-be in Moscow a pretext to withhold permission from would-be pilgrims to make the *hajj* in the following year.[298] The *hajjis* – usually headed

293. Reception by A. A. Puzin of Z. Babakhanov, 13 Feb. 1960; GARF, f.6991, o.4, d.110, 1.9.

294. Memorandum sent to Voroshilov and Malenkov, 23 April 1949; RTsKhIDNI, f.17, o.132, d.111, l.61. Deputy Foreign Minister Andrei Vyshinskii wrote to A. Ia. Chadaev on 5 June 1948 that the foreign ministry considered postponing review of the issue of sending pilgrims to Mecca until the end of hostilities in the Middle East – GARF, f.6991, o.3, d.54, 1.126.

295. For the *hajj* of 1953, see I. V. Polianskii to A. G. Zverev, 21 July 1953, and L. A. Prikhod'ko, V. D. Efremov and P. S. Basis, Report, 8 May 1954 – GARF, f.6991, o.3, d.83, ll.187-90, and d.100, 1.26.

296. These included the state security services which had to ratify the participation of each individual seeking to perform the *hajj*, as was common practice regarding any delegation abroad; the foreign ministry, which had to alert its embassies in the countries through which the pilgrims would be passing; the ministry of civil aviation which had to supply the aircraft and crew; and the ministry of finances, which had to provide some pocket money in hard currency for the pilgrims. See, for example, I. V. Polianskii to USSR Minister of Finances A. G. Zverev, 21 July 1953. Preparations for the *hajj* preoccupied the relevant CARC department for three months prior to the pilgrims' actual departure – L. A. Prikhod'ko, V. D. Efremov and P. S. Basis, Report, 8 May 1954; GARF, f.6991, o.3, d.83, ll.187-90, and d.100, ll.29-30.

297. For example, when DUMES chairman Khiyaletdinov asked to be allowed to perform the *hajj* at the head of a group of pilgrims in 1952, CARC considered it inexpedient, but explained its rejection as emanating from the late date the request was officially filed – L. Prikhod'ko, Report, 2 June 1952; GARF, f.6991, o.3, d.91, ll.242-3.

298. For instance, in 1964 the Uzbek members of the delegation sold honey they had brought with them for hard currency; in the following year three Uzbeks brought opium with them, were imprisoned in Saudi Arabia for the

by one or more of the four muftis – were mostly officials of the spiritual directorates or their immediate clientèle; they would include a few clergy and one or two believers from among the ranks who somehow had the necessary resources.[299]

The international relations of the spiritual directorates and the international aspects and implications of their domestic activity, indeed of their very existence, are beyond the scope of this work.[300] Note has, however, to be made of the major significance of this factor in the eyes of the authorities in Moscow, who were constantly seeking to impress upon the outside world that freedom of religion existed in the Soviet Union and that Islam specifically was prospering there. Moscow was also convinced of the influence of these relations on the directorates' prestige among the Muslim population at home.

The directorates' activity in the context of the peace movement was seen as the continuation of the 'patriotic activity' of the first years in connection with the war effort and was sometimes called by this name.[301] From 1950, when four Muslim clerics attended

---

duration of the pilgrimage and then expelled. Following these incidents, CARC decided in 1966 not to condone the *hajj* – B. S. Rzhanov to A. A. Puzin, 10 Nov. 1965, and Minutes, CARC session No.24, 12-13 Nov. 1965; GARF, f.6991, o.4, d.169, ll.167 and 176-9.

299. From the earliest years the expenses of the *hajj* were the concern of the individual pilgrim – I. V. Polianskii to V. M. Molotov, 14 May 1947; GARF, f.6991, o.3, d.47, l.158.

300. Although this activity increased markedly as of the mid 1950s, it was an important feature already in the late Stalin period, cf. L. Prikhod'ko, Report, 20 May 1953; GARF, f.6991, o.3, d.91, l.268. Prikhod'ko listed some of the foreign delegations received recently by Ishan Babakhan. After the relative opening of the Soviet Union to outsiders, especially from Third World countries, in the early Khrushchev years, ties with the Muslim countries increased in importance and in 1963 a department for international relations of the Muslim organisations of the USSR was established in Moscow. Among others, publications were initiated for foreign consumption on Muslim life in the USSR (including a film and picture album) and even an edition of the works of the medieval theologian Isma'il Bukhari – see Reception by A. Puzin of Z. Babakhanov, 20 Dec. 1963; GARF, f.6991, o.4, d.137, l.14. CRA Chairman Kuroedov told First Deputy Chairman of the USSR Council of Ministers Kirill Mazurov in 1970 that Babakhanov played a major role in the USSR's Muslim organisations' international ties, 'which are an important channel for our propaganda in the Muslim countries of Asia and Africa' – GARF, f.6991, o.6, d.284, l.71. For early contacts with abroad immediately after the establishment of the directorates, see pp.113-4.

301. For instance, Kh. N. Iskanderov, Report, 2 June 1952; GARF, f.6991,

the Moscow World Peace Conference (16-19 October), Muslim delegates to international forums which were initiated, or at least supported by, the Soviet government appeared in mosques to make their resolutions known to the Muslim public.[302] CARC ordered its *upolnomochennye* not to obstruct the public appearance of delegates to the All-Union conference of the adherents of peace so long as they restricted their reports to the precincts of registered mosques.[303] Describing these appearances in detail, CARC insisted that in all the mosques where they took place believers met them with great satisfaction, expressing their approval of the Soviet Union's policy in the struggle for peace and promising to work honestly.[304] One may safely assume that the believer population, whose mentality had been moulded by their own traditional respect for the secular power and by the Soviet regime's persistent 'mobilisation' and indoctrination, saw in the participation of their leaders in these activities a legitimisation of the existence and activity of the spiritual directorates and other establishment institutions and personnel and indirectly of Islam itself.

In 1952 DUMZ intensified its activity with the approach of the fast and festivals under the guise of disseminating among believers the appeals of the Zagorsk Conference (May 1952), and DUMES Chairman Khiyaletdinov travelled to Novosibirsk, Cheliabinsk and Kuibyshev oblasti to give exposure to the resolutions of that same conference among believers, taking advantage of the opportunity to call upon believers to celebrate the Muslim festivals.[305] The leaders of all four spiritual directorates appeared to be capitalising on their participation in conferences dedicated to the struggle for peace and, in general, their connections with foreign Muslim countries in order to enhance their own authority among believers at home.[306] CARC's officials were in two minds as to how to

---

o.3, d.83, ll.137-8. For the directorates' earlier patriotic position and activity, see pp.103-4 and 112-3.

302. N. Abushaev, A short survey, 15 March 1951; GARF, f.6991, o.3, d.73, ll.6-7. And see p.158 above.

303. L. Prikhod'ko, A short report, 4 April 1952; GARF, f.6991, o.3, d.81, l.80. Almost two pages are devoted to describing the large crowds who came to hear these addresses.

304. L. Prikhod'ko, Report, 2 June 1952; GARF, f.6991, o.3, d.81, ll.125-7.

305. L. Prikhod'ko, Memorandum, 31 Jan. 1953; GARF, f.6991, o.3, d.91, l.9.

306. L. Prikhod'ko, Report, 20 May 1953; GARF, f.6991, o.3, d.91, l.268. Prikhod'ko said this applied in particular to Ishan Babakhan and Khiyaletdinov.

react. On the one hand, it was suggested that activity in the localities should be limited, as it provided a context for stimulating religious activism.[307] The ardent involvement of officials of the spiritual directorates and some of the registered clergy in the peace movement not only enhanced their prestige, but was thought to attract increasing numbers of worshippers to the registered mosques on the Muslim festivals, believers asking to hear sermons devoted to this specific theme.[308] On the other hand, it was a major consideration in CARC's recommendation that Ishan Babakhan be granted a government decoration, Polianskii stressing the mufti's patriotic activity during the war, the *fetwas* he published as 'a progressive clerical figure', and his participation in the peace campaign.[309]

In the course of time, the increasingly frequent visits of foreign Muslim delegations, and specifically of religious personnel, and their contact with various Muslim religious societies were said to enliven the religious atmosphere among the autocthonous believer population.[310] SADUM itself explained to the clergy that it had extended its foreign connections in order to enhance its popularity;[311] it seems almost certainly to have been referring to its standing among the local population and not with the authorities, and the context was the justification of its demand for greater funding from believers. That these perceptions were well founded in the reality of Central Asian society can be seen by comparisons made between the first two muftis in Tashkent (Ishan Babakhan and his son Ziyautdin Babakhanov) with the emirs and beks of pre-revolutionary Bukhara and Khiva. The opinion was voiced in Tashkent that 'one of the principal reasons for the enlivened religiosity of the population' was what CARC's *upolnomochennyi*

307. Minutes, CARC session No.10s, 11-12 April 1952; GARF, f.6991, o.3, d.83, l.165.

308. I. V. Polianskii to the CPSU Central Committee and the USSR Council of Ministers, 20 Sept. 1955; GARF, f.6991, o.3, d.114, ll.197-8.

309. I. V. Polianskii to CPSU Central Committee, 18 Dec. 1954; GARF, f.6991, o.3, d.103, ll.76-8.

310. L. A. Prikhod'ko, Information, 18 May 1957; GARF, f.6991, o.3, d.146, l.102.

311. Z. Babakhanov and F. Sadyqkhojaev to members of SADUM and the *khatibs* of major mosques, 6 Nov. 1956; TsGAUz, f.2456, o.1, d.190, l.9.

in the Uzbek capital called the mufti's 'inordinately great popularity and authority'.[312]

Although the four spiritual directorates have been looked at together, there were important differences between them. The first was one of dimension, that is the number of registered religious societies subordinate to each of them and the approximate size of the population they served. There could be no doubt that in the eyes of all concerned, SADUM was the most important of the four, followed by DUMES as the spiritual directorate of the RSFSR. Both enjoyed a certain leadership position, at least among their respective subordinate clergy and their communities. DUMSK was clearly the most problematic from this perspective with its very heterogeneous clientèle. Perhaps the most interesting of the spiritual directorates, however, from the point of view of its composition and assignments, was DUMZ. The fact that it comprised Shiite and Sunni members, issued instructions which were binding on the two communities, and had a common budget for both was constantly stressed as an achievement of the regime, an example of its policy of 'friendship of the peoples'. The CARC *upolnomochennyi* in Baku reported regularly on the successful cooperation between the Shiite shaykh–ul–islam and his Sunni deputy.[313] Nonetheless, from time to time untoward incidents occurred between DUMZ's two leading persons, notably in the mid 1950s, when CARC and the republican authorities felt compelled to recommend that the mufti be pensioned off in order to restore a normal working relationship between the representatives of the two communities.[314] The official line continued to call for the further

312. Sh. K. Shirinbaev, Address, All-Union conference of CARC *upolnomochennye*, 18–20 April 1960; GARF, f.6991, o.3, d.208, l.76. For Babakhanov's proclivity for an extravagant life-style, see also pp.158-9 above.

313. For example, B. Shahbazbekov, Information, undated, Appendix to minutes of CARC session, 21 June 1949; GARF, f.6991, o.3, d.60, l.32. Shahbazbekov wrote that the two were working together in 'an atmosphere of mutual understanding and agreement' without any signs of tension.

314. L. A. Prikhod'ko to I. V. Polianskii, 5 May 1956; GARF, f.6991, o.3, d.217, ll.52-4. Prikhod'ko was reporting on his mission to Baku (as well as to Tbilisi and Batumi) in April, the first purpose of which was to acquaint himself with the bad relations which had developed between the two heads of DUMZ. Both the two men themselves and the chairman of the republican council of ministers and two representatives of the local KGB who were invited to take part in the deliberations agreed that there was no way the two could continue together. The main concern then became the appointment of a new mufti who

rapprochement between the two trends. One Azerbaijani cleric, a Sunni, called upon DUMZ in the late 1960s to convene a conference of all the region's clergy that would work out a common program for Shiites and Sunnis, designed eventually to eliminate the differences between them. He also called for the Mir-Arab *medrese* to adopt a syllabus that would be acceptable to Sunnis and Shiites alike.[315] At the same time, the emphasis placed by the shaykh-ul-islam as the leading representative of the Soviet Shiite community was on Shiite activity, and DUMZ seems to have made recurrent efforts to win recognition as an institution parallel in all aspects to the major Sunni spiritual directorates. In 1956 Hakim-zade was petitioning to be allowed to open a *medrese*, as well as a number of mosques and *pirs* (under the auspices of DUMZ), to publish a religious calendar, to vacate a former *medrese* in the courtyard of Baku's major mosque which was in use as a residential home, to perform the pilgrimage to Meshed (for 35–40 people) and to improve the living conditions of the shaykh-ul-islam and of the leading cleric in Baku's two mosques.[316]

Certainly, the spiritual directorates embodied the dilemmas both of the regime and of religious personnel. Each saw the necessity of cooperation and was fully aware that they were *a priori* mutually antagonistic. The regime recognised, at least as of World War II, that religion was there to stay for the foreseeable future. It therefore resolved to create an instrument from within the religious establishment which would be relatively reliable politically, as a result both of a carefully elaborated system of controls and of its own vested interest in collaborating with the state which gave it its *raison d'être*. In the early postwar years CARC constantly called for enhancing the prestige and authority of the Muslim spiritual directorates in order the better to contain and regulate Islam. Later on, during Khrushchev's anti-religious campaign, on the

would both be able to work with Hakim-zade and be acceptable to the Sunni community.

315. CRA report, handed to the CPSU Central committee, 22 May 1970; TsKhSD, f.5, o.62, d.38, ll.21-3.

316. L. A. Prikhod'ko to I. V. Polianskii, 5 May 1956, and G. F. Frolov, Information, 22 Feb. 1957. On 8 Dec. 1956, CARC resolved to transfer one such *pir* to the jurisdiction of DUMZ – Minutes, CARC session No. 16; GARF, f.6991, o.3, d.127, ll.54-5, and d.132, l.78, and o.4, d.55a, l.73.

other hand, it brought evidence to demonstrate that these centres were exceeding the bounds of their authority and sought to curb them.[317] The spiritual directorates, for their part, apparently appreciated from the experience of the fifteen or so years prior to the war that the regime had the wherewithal to physically eliminate all vestiges of institutionalised religion and would have no compunction in carrying this out if it considered it advisable. They accordingly strove to demonstrate to the authorities that this was not a viable policy. To make their point, they endeavoured to bring home to the party and government leadership both at the republican level and in Moscow that for the regime to ensure stability, it must mobilise its Muslim citizens, who were both myriad and economically important, and doing that meant making concessions to some of their basic religious needs. It is doubtful whether Islam in the Soviet Union would have remained so vital or so widespread had it not been for the existence and flexibility of the Muslim spiritual directorates, which provided an official framework for Muslim religious activity and in most periods were successful in engendering the sense among the population that people could safely participate in it.

At the same time, the partnership was fraught with perils for both sides. For the regime it entailed making compromises, which were problematic ideologically, and pandering to a group of clerics whom it manifestly despised. Not surprisingly, therefore, there were recurrent suggestions within the party apparatus to curb the power of the spiritual directorates. And for the spiritual directorates collaboration meant discrediting their authority among the more genuinely religious, their natural constituents, who could not accept the formulas which the muftis circulated among the flock in order to retain the goodwill of their lay patrons. As time went by and hostility to Moscow grew within the Muslim community, the opposition to the spiritual directorates among believers grew markedly and they found themselves severely, if not hopelessly, compromised.

317. In an address at an all-union conference of *upolnomochennye*, on 18-20 April 1960, Puzin pointed out that SADUM had distributed large sums of money for the construction of new prayer premises in contradiction to the stipulations laid down by the legislation. He also complained that both SADUM and DUMES had suggested disbanding all the executive organs of registered mosques which had been elected by believers – GARF, f.6991, o.3, d.208, ll.11 and 17.

4

THE REGISTERED MOSQUES
AND CLERGY

The registered mosques were the backbone of Soviet Islam just as the spiritual directorates were the showpiece, the living testimony of the reality of an Islam endorsed and condoned by the regime. Without the registered religious societies and the mosques to which they were by definition attached, the spiritual directorates would have been meaningless, for their primary *raison d'être* was directing the activity of these societies and forming a conduit belt between them and the regime. At the same time, the religious societies too endured a similarly difficult, often almost untenable, existence, subject, as they were, to pressures and constraints which sometimes jeopardised their very survival and often threatened to deprive them of the autonomy and vitality that should have been the essence of their being.

The 3-400 registered mosques[1] were spread out over a very large region and their distribution was extremely uneven. Mostly they were few and far between. In Kazakhstan, where there were at no time between 1944 and the Gorbachev period more than twenty-six registered mosques, the distance between mosques was mostly very great indeed. Even in the Uzbek SSR, the union republic where registered mosques were most numerous, there were communities which found themselves over 200 miles from the nearest one and at certain periods there were entire oblasti with not a single registered mosque.[2] Tashkent Oblast', on the

1. With the exception of a short period from the end of 1947 until some time in 1949, their number throughout the period from mid 1946 until 1989 fluctuated between 3-400; see pp.60-1.

2. In the early-mid 1950s, for instance, the two southernmost oblasti, Surkhan-Darya and Kashka-Darya, had no registered mosques – L. A. Prikhod'ko, Report, 20 May 1953. Still in 1974 the CRA *upolnomochennyi* for Kashka-Darya Oblast' pointed out that there were just two registered mosques in an oblast' with three towns, ten raiony, and four *poselki*, and part of the population lived over 100

other hand, had about one half of all the republic's mosques, nearly half of these being in the city of Tashkent itself.[3] In Kirgiziia, which had thirty-four registered mosques in 1957, there were in that same year thirty-one raiony with none, and the ones which did exist did not answer the needs of the believer population either from the purely numerical standpoint or from that of their geographical distribution, and not only in raiony with no mosque.[4] Thus large sectors of the Muslim population had in effect no registered mosque which they could feasibly attend not only for Friday prayers but even on the major festivals.

In the late Stalin period about two thirds of the registered mosques were in rural areas.[5] The proportion changed somewhat after the closures of the early 1950s and the anti-religious campaign of Khrushchev's latter years, both of which affected rural mosques much more than urban ones. The CRA reported in the early 1970s that the majority of registered mosques were in towns;[6] if this was true, this was a result not only of the closures, but also of the trend to officially term districts that were basically rural in nature as urban administrative units, presumably in order to demonstrate the country's proletarian orientation and general

---

km from the nearest mosque – P. Khidirov, Explanatory memo, undated (sent by K. R. Ruzmetov to V. A. Kuroedov, 15 Jan. 1974); GARF, f.6991, o.3, d.91, l.254, and o.6, d.567, l.20.

3. See p.62. Even in Tashkent however, the mosques which were opened were only a few of those for which applications were filed; see Chapter 2, n.38. Ziyautdin Babakhanov told I. A. Shalaev of the republican *upolnomochennyi's* apparatus that SADUM was refraining from recommending clergy to open mosques in Tashkent, where there were not a few mosques, so as not to create a disproportion between the various oblasti and republics – Minutes, Conference of CARC *upolnomochennye* in the Uzbek SSR, 9 Aug. 1948; TsGAUz, f.2456, o.1, d.120, ll.3 and 6.

4. K. F. Tagirov, Memo, 23 Aug. 1957; GARF, f.6991, o.4, d.73, ll.80-1.

5. The detailed lists which I have found for 1951, for example, contain 165 rural and 83 urban mosques, the first group being described as in some type of village: a *selo*, *selenie* or *derevnia* – GARF, f.6991, o.4, d.27. These were not in fact all the registered mosques for that year, the lists not including those subordinate to DUMZ and DUMSK or the mosques of Tajikistan. Although in Azerbaijan there were probably more urban mosques than in most union republics, their total number was small (16), and in Dagestan and Tajikistan rural ones predominated, so that the proportion of two-thirds to one-third was probably representative.

6. CRA Information, sent to the Central Committee, 27 April 1971; TsKhSD, f.5, o.63, d.89, l.97.

modernisation.[7] Nor were all urban communities in large cities; many were in rather small towns or *poselki*, 'settlements of urban type', of one sort or another, the distinction between them and some rural communities being purely juridical and administrative.[8] It is surely no coincidence that none of the documents which give statistics of the registered mosques provide data on the urban-rural divide.[9]

Even though much of the Muslim population had no easily accessible registered mosque, many of the mosques, particularly in rural areas, were poorly attended. Many of the larger, urban ones, too, were frequented by only a small proportion of the local Muslim inhabitants. The explanation of this fact is basic to the understanding of Islam in the Soviet Union in the postwar period. If, indeed, the reason was that religion was no longer strong in the Muslim areas, as the party ideologists sought to contend, then there were grounds to believe that Islam would disappear in the foreseeable future. If, on the other hand, it was that Muslims felt they could maintain their religion without and outside the mosque, and/or that it was physically impossible or politically perilous to attend mosque, it will be necessary to conclude that the registered mosques comprised only part of the picture.

The process and problematics of registration, 1944-48

According to the legislation on religious cults of 1929, every religious association had to register with the local authorities. This seems,

7. Thus, some of the mosques which had been opened in the mid 1940s in places described in the 1951 lists as villages of one sort or another were categorised in the 1960s as being in urban districts, usually *poselki*; e.g., Buzbash in Kuibyshev Oblast', see excerpt from Minutes, CARC session No.37, GARF, f.6991, o.3, d.1386, 1.91.

8. After changes in the law in the Khrushchev period, places were classified as urban if their population was at least 2,000 and the majority, usually two thirds, were not employed in collective farming – Shabad, 'The Urban-Administrative System of the USSR and Its Relevance to Geographic Research'. For a discussion of the tensions existing between the regime, with its urban proletarian orientation and focus, and the rural population, see Friedgut, 'Integration of the Rural Sector into Soviet Society'.

9. The few lists we have which enumerate the registered mosques in any given area almost invariably, however, indicate a preponderance of rural ones. For instance, in the Tatar ASSR in 1974 there were three urban and nine rural mosques – GARF, f.6991, o.6, d.558, 1.82.

however, not to have happened to all mosques and to have become a dead letter by 1941, whether for reasons of fear on the part of the communities or of apathy on the part of local government.[10] The fact that no official institution had any knowledge how many functioning mosques there were before CARC initiated registration apparently indicates that those mosques which opened in the war years did not register either, even those which did so with the blessing of the local authorities.[11] Most mosques which opened during the war probably commenced activity as of the end of 1943, following the establishment of SADUM. But there is evidence that some were opened prior to that event.[12] The majority of mosques, moreover, which registered in the first period of registration, at least in certain parts, had never ceased operating.[13]

While the process of registering 'factually functioning' prayer-houses began toward the end of 1944, it only gathered momentum in 1945[14] and continued officially until summer 1946 side by side

10. Of the mosques still open in Uzbekistan on 1 Jan. 1936 according to a survey commissioned by the republican Central Executive Committee close to 500 were said to have been registered as against some 2,500 unregistered ones –Keller, 'The Struggle against Islam in Uzbekistan, 1921-1941', pp.322-3. I have not been able to ascertain how many of each category fell victim to the closures of the following two years, but one must assume that the registered ones will have been more easily shut down, being under some degree of supervision on the part of the local authorities.

11. The Kirgiz republican authorities, for example, permitted the opening of mosques in 1942-43 in three towns – Tokmak, Osh and Frunze – but they were not registered. Nor were three others unofficially allowed to open in the town of Naryn and in two rural settlements – H. Akhtiamov to CARC, 10 July 1945; GARF, f.6991, o.3, d.29, ll.122 and 124.

12. CARC's republican *upolnomochennyi* for the Uzbek SSR, for instance, wrote in 1944 that there were some 200 functioning mosques in that republic, a 'considerable' number of which had been opened before SADUM was set up –I. Ibadov to I. V. Polianskii, undated; TsGAUz, f.2456, o.1, d.3, l.5. Ibadov was probably not including those mosques in more outlying parts which had never been closed.

13. 12 of the 13 mosques registered in the Bashkir ASSR in Sept. 1945, for example, had been functioning uninterruptedly since before 1917 – M. Sh. Karimov to I. V. Polianskii and Bashkir ASSR SNK Chairman S. A. Vagapov, 27 Sept. 1945; GARF, f.6991, o.3, d.26, l.4.

14. Nothing had been done to even start the process of regulating the activity of Kirgiziia's religious societies before Hakim Akhtiamov took office as republican *upolnomochennyi* in mid April 1945 – Akhtiamov to CARC, 10 July 1945; GARF, f.6991, o.3, d.29, l.122. By mid December 1945 he had registered eight mosques, and two prayer-houses of other denominations, as already existing ones, all of

with the opening and the inevitably concomitant registration of new mosques (and other prayer-houses).[15] As of late 1944, CARC's *upolnomochennye* began reporting the pace of registration, and the number of registered religious societies and clergy, as well as the tally of applications to open mosques and the fate of these applications.[16] And beginning from mid 1945 the documentation is very extensive, providing a fairly full general picture, from which it is clear that the dual process of registering already functioning religious societies and opening new ones engulfed most of the areas with any meaningful Muslim population.

There were, however, considerable differences from place to place regarding the actual tempo of registration and the success of applications. These variations depended on a variety of factors: local tradition, the position adopted by local officialdom, even the personalities involved. In Kazakhstan and Kirgiziia, for instance, where traditionally the population was largely nomadic and so had not had permanent communities or places of worship,[17] the urge to open and register mosques was much less than in the historically sedentary areas of Uzbekistan and Tajikistan[18] or in Dagestan where over 200 applications were filed between 1944 and 1948, although only twenty-six were approved.[19]

Moreover, since filing an application to register a religious society postulated the existence of a permanent prayer house and cleric, and in Kazakhstan and Kirgiziia there were very few buildings of former mosques outside the small number of settlements which had been towns in the tsarist period, the chances of doing so in these republics were slim.[20] In Kazakhstan most oblasti had just one or

---

them having operated before his appointment – H. Akhtiamov to I. V. Polianskii, 15 Dec. 1945; GARF, f.6991, o.3, d.30, l.248.

15. See p.20.

16. For example, B. Shahbazbekov to I. V. Polianskii, 24 Nov. 1944, and P. D. Bezdel' to Polianskii, 1 Dec. 1944 – GARF, f.6991, o.4, d.3, l.19, and o.3, d.4, ll.98-102; and I. Ibadov to Polianskii, undated – TsGAUz, f.2456, o.1, d.3, ll.4-5.

17. Interestingly some mosques were constructed in these parts in the 1920s – *Preodolevaia religioznoe vliianie islama*, pp.89 and 155. Unfortunately, I have no information regarding the dimensions of this construction activity.

18. For the speed with which all of Tajikistan's 38 official mosques were in fact registered, see K. Hamidov, Report, Minutes, CARC session No.4, 29 Jan. 1947; GARF, f.6991, o.4, d.19, l.71.

19. Khabilov to I. V. Polianskii, 4 June 1954; GARF, f.6991, o.3, d.102, ll.122-3.

20. In Osh Oblast', for example, four factually functioning religious societies

two mosques, except Southern Kazakhstan, which in the mid-1950s had seven, and Semipalatinsk, which had three.[21] The republican *upolnomochennyi* in Kazakhstan stated categorically that the Muslim groups which existed in almost every oblast' were not registered because there were no mosques; those mosques that had existed were being used for other purposes and could not be vacated, and there was no possibility to build new ones.[22] In one case the believers of a new town asked to have the building of the mosque of a nearby former town (now only a village) physically transferred to their community.[23]

Yet mullas existed in many areas of Kazakhstan and Kirgiziia, mostly itinerant mullas who performed the basic rites, without being attached to a registered mosque or operating within a delineated parish. SADUM's representatives in the localities sought in both republics to appoint mullas, hoping thus to enable in-stitutionalised contact with them, including the transmission of SADUM's instructions, and the continuation of their activities.[24] Similar considerations were almost certainly behind the suggestion of Kirgiziia's republican government that clergy be allowed to register in areas which were far away from any registered mosque; these would be *aksakals*, elders, chosen by the local believers to perform urgent rites and affiliated to the nearest mosque.[25] CARC

which were advised to register were unable to file applications for lack of buildings –I. Halimov to CARC, 7 Aug. 1946; GARF, f.6991, o.3, d.453, l.2.

21. K. F. Tagirov, Information, 1 March 1957; GARF, f.6991, o.3, d.132, ll.58-9.

22. N. Sabitov, Report, 10 July 1945, and Sabitov to Polianskii, 20 July 1945; GARF, f.6991, o.3, d.29, l.98, and d.21, ll.49-51.

23. These were the believers of Aiaguz in Semipalatinsk Oblast', which was just 5 km from the former uezd town of Sergiopol' – Sh. Nazirov, Report, 10 July 1945; GARF, f.6991, o.3, d.29, l.108.

24. Iu. V. Sadovskii to V. Liapunov, 12 Feb. 1945 and Liapunov to CARC and to N. Sabitov, 9 Oct. 1945, and Sabitov, Report, 10 July 1945; GARF, f.6991, o.3, d.23, l.7, d.30, ll.210-210a, and d.29, l.99. That this entire issue remained a problem for some time is clear from a letter from Polianskii to all five Central Asian republican *upolnomochennye*, of 22 May 1946, asking that they clarify to SADUM and its representatives the essence of the right of appointing clergy, specifically that it presupposed the existence of a prayer-house and religious society – TsGAUz, f.2456, o.1, d.90, ll.30-1.

25. H. Akhtiamov to CARC, 10 July 1945, and T. Kulatov, Chairman of the Kirgiz SSR SNK, to CARC, 18 July 1945; GARF, f.6991, o.3, d.29, l.124, and d.21, l.52.

was opposed to such practice in principle, and rejected these proposals out of hand. Its deputy chairman suggested rather that mosques be opened in several raiony in each oblast' in conformity with considerations of 'political expediency' and actual needs. The sense among CARC's oblast' *upolnomochennye* in Kazakhstan was also that applications to register a religious society should be indulged, since they appeared to correspond to a real need, especially in the south, in the centres of Uzbek population in Chimkent and Jambul. Here until 1930 there had been large networks of mosques, *mahalla* mosques for daily prayer and central ones for Friday and festival prayer-services, and the single mosque which had been opened in each of these towns could not cater for the entire believer population.[26] Because of the salience of the need, in fact, CARC's termination of the activities of the unregistered mullas led to the filing of applications. There were instances, for example, when believers of a number of communities joined forces and processed an application to open a mosque in one of them; insofar as a building was not available they would petition to be able to hold their prayer-meetings, at least provisorily, in a privately-owned house.[27]

This problem of populations which had transformed their lifestyle as a result of the Soviet policy of sedentarisation and collectivisation existed in not a few areas of Central Asia. In addition to the two above-mentioned republics, it held also for the Turkmen SSR, the Karakalpak ASSR and certain parts of Tajikistan. The CARC leadership was aware of its acuteness and sought to study its various aspects in order to attain some sort of satisfactory solution.[28]

The Turkmen SSR stood out as having especially few registered mosques. By mid 1947 their number was no more than three; it later rose to five and then fell to four.[29] CARC accused its *upol-*

26. For example, V. Liapunov to CARC and to N. Sabitov, 9 Oct. 1945, and Notes for address of N. Sabitov, Conference of CARC *upolnomochennye*, Alma-Ata, 30 Sept. 1946; GARF, f.6991, o.3, d.30, l.210, and d.41, l.78.

27. For example, in the oblast' of Northern Kazakhstan believers from three villages filed such a petition, asking that they also be given permission to construct a mosque; while both requests were agreed to by the *oblispolkom*, CARC acceded to the former, demanding further data from its *upolnomochennyi* before accepting the latter – Minutes, CARC session No.5, 5-6 April 1946; GARF, f.6991, o.4, d.15, l.21.

28. I. V. Polianskii to *upolnomochennye*, 6 Oct. 1945; GARF, f.6991, o.3, d.21, l.84.

29. This was due to the withdrawal of registration from the Ashkhabad religious

nomochennyi for that republic of specifically not wishing there to be registered mosques. He was reminded by Polianskii that religious organisations had adopted a generally 'patriotic position' and the state had to take into consideration the fact that a significant percentage of workers were still believers, and that performing their rites necessitated the existence of prayer-houses and clergy. This meant satisfying applications to open prayer-houses, handing them over to believers so that they might perform the necessary rites without obstruction, and monitoring religious procedures. This was impossible in a republic with, on the one hand, so few prayer-houses and, on the other, a considerable number of believers, whose existence was testified to by the large contingent of itinerant mullas. Polianskii recommended the opening of a further twenty or more registered mosques and instructed the *upolnomochennyi* to display greater tact and patience in dealing with believers in order to dispel the fear among them that his conduct had apparently engendered, deterring them from filing applications to register.[30] Not only were no additional mosques registered, but the four registered mosques did not gain in popularity, attendance remaining insignificant on ordinary weekdays and Fridays and not very large even on the major festivals. They were further discredited by the conduct imposed on them by SADUM's representative in the Turkmen SSR, who forbade them to perform rites in private homes and compelled them to speak out against the itinerant mullas.[31]

Another area which did not lend itself to the registration process was Stavropol' Krai, specifically the Cherkess AO, apparently because of the favourable attitude to religion, if not actual collusion with religious practice, of local officialdom. Here mosques had been transferred by raion and village *ispolkoms* to believers, who performed rituals and prayer-services 'officially, with the knowledge of the local soviet organs', yet without registering or concluding an agreement on the transfer of the building. Some auls even had more than one mosque.[32] In Central Asia there were also cases

---

society after the destruction of the mosque in the 1948 earthquake, see below. The number remained at four for several decades.

30. Comments on report of Babaev, Minutes, CARC session No.13, 10-11 July 1947; GARF, f.6991, o.4, d.19, ll.441-7.

31. P. A. Solov'ev, Report, Minutes, CARC session No.1, 13 Jan. 1951; GARF, f.6991, d.74, ll.1-2, 7-8 and 13-14.

32. V. Bulatov to I. V. Polianskii, 12 Feb. 1945; GARF, f.6991, o.3, d.33, ll.58-9. It is not clear from the available documentation how this description

of local organs handing over buildings of former mosques to groups of believers and registering them *de facto*, even though they did not fulfil all the formalities.[33]

In various types of settlement, too, requests to register religious societies were particularly unlikely to be complied with. A large number of kolkhozy set up in the prewar years were not situated on sites of former places of habitat, not to speak of settlements constructed in the postwar years on 'virgin lands', for example in Kashka-Darya Oblast'.[34] The new industrial towns which had sprung up in the Soviet period also had had no pre-revolutionary history. In all of these, there were necessarily no former mosques concerning which negotiations might even be initiated in accordance with established procedure.[35]

Sometimes actual pressure would be applied to make believers retract requests to open mosques,[36] or a *raiispolkom* would refuse to hand over a mosque to believers even though the republican government had issued a specific resolution to this effect.[37] There were instances, too, where the actual act of registration with the local government authority was implemented a year or more after CARC or the relevant republican government had given its ap-

---

related to the situation created as a result of the Nazi occupation, see Chapter 2, n.32.

33. H. A. Akhtiamov, Report, Conference of CARC *upolnomochennye*, Alma-Ata, 30 Sept. 1946; GARF, f.6991, o.3, d.41, l.106. Akhtiamov spoke specifically of a certain *raiispolkom* in Issyk-Kul' Oblast'. For local government and instances of its collusion with religious practice and with religious societies, see Chapter 11.

34. H. Akhtiamov, Report, Conference of CARC *upolnomochennye*, Alma-Ata, 30 Sept. 1946; GARF, f.6991, o.3, d.41, l.100.

35. For the tribulations of Tatar believers in Magnitogorsk, see reception by P. S. Basis of one of their representatives, 29 June 1956, and by N. I. Smirnov of another, 19 Aug. 1964; GARF, f.6991, o.4, d.57, l.82, and d.148, l.19. And see p.304.

36. In one such case in Kuibyshev Oblast' the *raiispolkom* secretary summoned the applicants to the raion NKGB, and together with that department's chief talked them into taking back their application; in another, in Batumi, the *raikom* secretary threatened a group of Muslim applicants with arrest if they did not withdraw their application – Minutes, All-Union conference of *upolnomochennye*, 20-26 May 1945; GARF, f.6991, o.3, d.12, ll.33-4. For the attitude of local officialdom in Ajaria, of which Batumi was the capital, see p.661.

37. This occurred in one of the rural raiony of Tashkent Oblast' – K. Mustafin to I. Ibadov, 25 June 1945; GARF, f.6991, o.3, d.30, l.258ob.

proval,[38] and not a few in which it took between six and twelve months.

In this way, a gap existed between theory and practice. According to the former, if a religious group sought to register and fulfilled the requisite requirements, an application to register could not be turned down unless its members refused to acknowledge and implement the laws of the state.[39] In reality, however, there were many instances in which this is precisely what happened, the government organ which rejected an application not always even taking the trouble to demonstrate that its position hinged on law.

Mostly, however, the local organs of government seem to have been nonchalant and not to have concerned themselves with the doings of those religious societies which began operating, often in large numbers, in the latter years of the war. As a result, these societies were neither enumerated nor registered, and the procedures so pedantically stipulated by the various laws and instructions simply ignored.[40] Religious societies were permitted to operate and no demands were made of them to register and legitimise their existence.[41] Often those that did apply to register ran into a brick wall, the local organs of government simply procrastinating and not addressing themselves seriously to the applications.[42] In some

38. Two mosques in Uzbekistan, one in Andijan and the other in Kokand, for example, waited 12 and 15 months respectively after the date of the Uzbek SSR SNK resolution in 1944 which stipulated their registration; a rural mosque in the Mordvinian ASSR waited 16 months after its registration was approved by CARC in Nov. 1946; three rural religious societies, one in Kuibyshev Oblast' and two in the Kabardinian ASSR, waited 17 months after CARC's decision; and one in Penza Oblast' waited three whole years, from July 1945 to July 1948 – Information on registered religious communities functioning in Fergana Oblast' as of 15 Sept. 1946; TsGAUz, f.2456, o.1, d.72, 1.3, and List of functioning registered mosques subordinate to DUMES as of 1 May 1951 and to SADUM as of 1 June 1951; GARF, f.6991, o.4, d.27, *passim*.

39. A. A. Puzin, 'Leninist principles regarding the attitude to religion, the church and believers', 5 Aug. 1965; GARF, f.6991, o.3, d.1483, 1.95.

40. H. Akhtiamov to CARC, 10 July 1945, and K. Mustafin to Tashkent Obkom Secretary Mavlianov, 19 July 1945; GARF, f.6991, o.3, d.29, 1.128, and d.30, 1.267.

41. K. Mustafin to Mavlianov and Tashkent Oblispolkom Chairman Turgunov, 10 Nov. 1945; GARF, f.6991, o.3, d.30, 1.286.

42. Aitlenov, Report, sent to Polianskii, 14 Nov. 1945; GARF, f.6991, o.3, d.30, 1.228. In the Tatar ASSR, too, the *upolnomochennyi* reported that 10 of the 60 applications which had been received to open mosques were of a positive character but the party *obkom* demanded that action be delayed – Report of

instances CARC's own *upolnomochennye* seem to have been responsible for delays in dealing with applications. One of the Council's inspectors, for instance, charged the *upolnomochennyi* for Dagestan in April 1947 with having dealt with a mere 13 out of 67 applications that he had received in the past fifteen months.[43]

In some areas believers themselves were reluctant to proceed with registration, temporising in order to see what happened to others who in fact registered. In the words of one CARC *upolnomochennyi*, they did not really believe in the opportunity to open and register prayer-houses, considering it a temporary measure,[44] perhaps even some sort of trap. This apprehensiveness was not surprising a decade or less after the purges of the 1930s when the clergy and religious associations had been among the categories singled out for retribution.[45] Thus, when CARC's *upolnomochennyi* in the Kabardinian ASSR approached a number of functioning religious societies with the demand that they register, some of them preferred to disband, declaring that they conducted no prayer-services and had no connection at all with any organised religious community. The mullas themselves entertained doubts about the existence in practice of free worship, believing that the policy of the immediate postwar years was intended to uncover those who were connected with religion, and would be followed by a return to the practices of 1937-8.[46] Representatives of Muslim inhabitants of the various raiony of Chkalov Oblast' told the CARC

Bagaev, Minutes, CARC session No.7, 23-4 April 1947; GARF, f.6991, o.3, d.30, l.228, and o.4, d.19, l.190. For the attitude of the Tatar ASSR leadership, see pp.609-10 and 626.

43. N. Tagiev on the report of I. Zakaryiaev, Minutes, CARC session No.7, 23-24 April 1947; GARF, f.6991, o.4, d.19, l.174.

44. K. Hamidov to I. V. Polianskii, 7 Dec. 1945; GARF, f.6991, o.3, d.30, l.364.

45. CARC's *upolnomochennyi* for the Turkmen SSR, Babaev, indeed retorted to the criticism by Polianskii (see above) that it was not his behaviour which aroused fear among clergy; the fear had been implanted beforehand and had not waned – Minutes, CARC session No.13, 10-11 July 1947; GARF, f.6991, o.4, d.19, l.452. In Sverdlovsk Oblast', too, the CARC *upolnomochennyi* was of the opinion that fear was a main reason – together with the dearth of people with religious training – for not filing applications to open mosques – Report to conference of CARC *upolnomochennye* in Novosibirsk, 31 May 1946; GARF, f.6991, o.3, d.36, ll.55ob-56.

46. Geshov to Polianskii, 26 June 1945, and report of Geshov to conference of CARC *upolnomochennye*, 14 June 1946; GARF, f.6991, o.3, d.25, ll.24-5, and d.38, ll.172-3.

upolnomochennyi that they would refrain from filing applications to open mosques until the mosque in Chkalov itself was registered.[47] In Taldy-Kurgan Oblast' in Kazakhstan, the Muslims dared to file applications only after Russian Orthodox churches actually began operating.[48]

Undisputably, even in instances where believers were not blatantly coerced into refraining from registration, they tended to be apprehensive of the supervision and control inherent in registration. In several localities believers were reported simply to have refused the registering of their communities.[49] The very act of filing an application inevitably drew the attention of the authorities, and this in itself sometimes entailed a certain risk. In Kazakhstan, together with some groups which did not register because they did not know how to fill in the necessary documentation or to whom to give it, there were those who said specifically that applying would 'expose' them and then they would either be persecuted or taxed.[50] Timidity on the part of those who filed the applications, and not mere illiteracy, may well have been behind recurrent instances in which surnames were omitted altogether from the application form or scribbled in such a way that they were undecipherable.[51] In one Kumyk aul in Dagestan the application to open a mosque was signed by women, although they did not attend mosque and so did not need one; they merely served as a screen for the menfolk, who were afraid of applying.[52] In some places, such as the Ajar ASSR, the pressure of the local authorities

47. Tsarev to CARC, 30 June 1945; GARF, f.6991, o.3, d.25, l.49.

48. Minutes, Conference of CARC *upolnomochennye*, Alma-Ata, 30 Sept.-2 Oct. 1946; GARF, f.6991, o.3, d.41, l.45.

49. For example, in Samarkand Oblast' – I. V. Polianskii to Kh. Iskanderov, 24 May 1947; TsGAUz, f.2456, o.1, d.82, l.11ob.

50. N. Sabitov to I. V. Polianskii, 25 Sept. 1945; GARF, f.6991, o.3, d.30, l.198.

51. Instances of this nature occurred apparently in rural areas throughout the country. See, for example, Menbariev to I. Ibadov and Andijan Oblispolkom Chairman Shadmonov, Report for the 3rd quarter, 1945, undated – TsGAUz, f.2456, o.1, d.16, l.25; and report of H. Akhtiamov, Conference of CARC *upolnomochennye*, Alma-Ata, 30 Sept. 1946. In the Bashkir ASSR, too, one group of believers refused outright to sign and several applications either had no signatures or far too few to make the application legitimate – M. Sh. Karimov to I. V. Polianskii and S. A. Vagapov, 8 Oct. 1945; GARF, f.6991, o.3, d.41, l.110, and d.26, ll.12 and 16.

52. I. Zakaryaev to CARC, 10 June 1946; GARF, f.6991, o.3, d.30, l.62ob.

was such that even after registration people were afraid of attending mosque. Fear was undoubtedly one of the reasons that in many areas only the old came to worship and attendance tended to be low.[53] Nor were apprehensions restricted to rank and file believers, but were shared by some clergy as well.[54]

These fears seem to have somewhat abated in the course of 1946-47 with the increased tempo of registration, which served in turn to accelerate the filing of applications. In the words of one *upolnomochennyi*, with the regulation of Muslim religious life, believers stopped concealing their attitude to religion.[55] In some instances, on the other hand, believers who encountered no obstruction to their activity from the *raiispolkom* or *sel'sovet* had no motivation to register and did not trouble to initiate the process.[56]

In addition to concern regarding possible molestation or persecution, believers seem to have been deterred from signing applications out of an unwillingness to take upon themselves the commitment and responsibilities this entailed. In the first place, many work-days and considerable expenses were usually required in order to repair and restore the building. Nor did material considerations end with its registration and opening, the costs involved in its upkeep and in maintaining a cleric falling upon the shoulders of the religious society.[57]

Certainly, many religious activists were ignorant of the requisite procedures; some were totally illiterate and many did not know how to read Russian. Most rural groups of believers in Kazakhstan's various oblasti were said not to know how to proceed with registration (to whom to address an application, how to fill in the forms, and so on).[58] There were cases in which the actual process of

53. B. Shahbazbekov, Address, Conference of CARC *upolnomochennye*, Rostov-on-Don, 14 June 1946; GARF, f.6991, o.3, d.38, ll.168-70.

54. For discussion of the clergy and their doubts, see below.

55. Report of H. Akhtiamov, Minutes, CARC session No.9, 3 June 1947; GARF, f.6991, o.4, d.19, l.249.

56. H. Akhtiamov to I. V. Polianskii, 15 Dec. 1945; GARF, f.6991, o.3, d.30, l.249.

57. See, for example, M. Sh. Karimov to I. V. Polianskii and S. A. Vagapov, 8 Oct. 1945, and Report of CARC *upolnomochennyi* for Sverdlovsk Oblast' prepared for conference of CARC *upolnomochennye*, Novosibirsk, 31 May 1946; GARF, f.6991, o.3, d.26, l.17, and d.36, l.58.

58. N. Sabitov, Report for 2nd quarter, 1945, 10 July 1945; GARF, f.6991, o.3, d.29, l.98.

registration lasted over a year because believers did not know how to supply all the necessary data or perhaps even what information they were expected to provide.[59] In some places groups desirous of registering ran into bureaucratic and technical obstacles which were not necessarily indicative of official policy. For instance, in the Kabardinian ASSR, the primary problem was the inertia and ineffectiveness of the DUMSK representative, which the clergy of the functioning mosques could not circumvent.[60]

Not infrequently the problems which arose regarding the actual procedure of registration emanated from obfuscation even among local government representatives and CARC's own *upolnomochennye*. The lack of clarity prevailed more in regard to the registration of already existing communities than to the opening of new ones. The first difficulty was the date by which a religious society had to have begun operating in order to qualify as having 'factually functioned beforehand'.[61] Another emanated from the lack of documentation, many local government institutions apparently not having noted the beginning of the activity of a local mosque, even if it had had their blessing, while the religious societies themselves seem not to have preserved such material. In spring 1947 CARC's *upolnomochennyi* in the Uzbek SSR reported that there were approximately fifty mosques in that republic which could not prove that they had in fact been operating three to four years prior to registration and as a result some *oblispolkoms* had begun shutting them down.[62] In addition to those spheres regarding which there might have been genuine uncertainty, other stipulations of established procedure were simply ignored. Thus in Uzbekistan, where there were at the time seventy-one registered

59. For example, in the town of Karkaralinsk in Karaganda Oblast' the procedure entered its second year – Notes for address of N. Sabitov, Conference of CARC *upolnomochennye*, Alma-Ata, 30 Sept. 1946; GARF, f.6991, o.3, d.41, l.84.

60. Geshov to I. Zakaryaev, 5 June 1945; GARF, f.6991, o.3, d.21, l.26.

61. See Chapter 1, n.55.

62. Kh. Iskanderov to I. V. Polianskii, 14 April 1947; TsGAUz, f.2456, o.1, d.82, l.10. Unfortunately, I have not found CARC's reply; nor is it clear to me why the criterion should have been that religious societies operated three to four years prior to registration. Possibly Iskanderov was referring to the requirement that they were functioning when CARC was formed, which was three years prior to the date of his letter. Certainly, the law laid down explicitly that it was illegal for a prayer house to be shut down by an *oblispolkom* without CARC's confirmation, see pp.21-2.

mosques, there were said to be only a few which actually boasted a *dvadtsatka*.[63]

The often arbitrary factors which influenced not only the pace but even the fact of registration, led many CARC officials both in Moscow and in the localities to press for the further registration of a number of religious associations, which they maintained were in no way distinguishable from those already registered. These had their own prayer-house and permanent contingent of believers who attended prayer-services regularly, seemed totally viable, and were situated at a considerable distance from the nearest registered mosque; the lack of proximity to another registered mosque was always a key consideration in remote rural areas where roads were poor and transport inadequate.[64] Moreover, these officials argued, registered religious societies were exposed to influence by the *upolnomochennyi* and other establishment institutions both directly and through the spiritual directorates and their *muhtasibs*.[65]

In mid-1947 Polianskii instructed the *upolnomochennyi* for Samarkand Oblast', where there were just two registered mosques, to register one or even two mosques in each of the oblast's twenty-two *raiony* rather than simply closing all of its 150 mosques indiscriminately; this, he pointed out, would enable the effective closure of the majority of factually functioning unregistered ones.[66] In order to eliminate unofficial Muslim activity, Polianskii wrote to the CARC *upolnomochennyi* for Uzbekistan that he should strive to register religious societies in raion administrative centres which had empty mosques and to extend their activity to the surrounding settlements. This would still leave some believers beyond the orbit of the Muslim establishment but would incorporate the main foci of activity.[67] This was just a month after Polianskii's statement

63. Iskanderov in answer to a question, Minutes, CARC session No.11, 18-19 June 1947; GARF, f.6991, o.4, d.19, l.367.

64. H. A. Akhtiamov, Report, Conference of CARC *upolnomochennye*, Alma-Ata, 30 Sept. 1946; GARF, f.6991, o.3, d.41, ll.105-7.

65. One CARC official pointed out that the opinion of the *upolnomochennyi* in the Tatar ASSR and that republic's leadership, that unregistered associations were preferable to registered ones, and that therefore it was expedient to procrastinate regarding registration, constituted a major error – Minutes, CARC session No.7, 23-24 April 1947; GARF, f.6991, o.4, d.19, l.199.

66. I. V. Polianskii to Baratov, 24 May 1947; TsGAUz, f.2456, o.1, d.82, l.11.

67. I. V. Polianskii to Kh. N. Iskanderov, 8 Aug. 1947; TsGAUz, f.2456, o.2, d.82, l.17. For the policy positions of CARC, see pp.552-8.

that the number of religious communities in all faiths had attained its natural limits, when he must have known that the possibility of opening new mosques was being significantly restricted by the powers-that-be; unless, perhaps, he hoped, or had reason to believe, that the general policy would not apply to Islam.[68]

Indeed, shortly before Polianskii had written to Molotov that CARC proposed to continue favouring the legal registration of factually functioning Muslim communities with the aim of enabling the four spiritual directorates to maximise control of Muslim religious activity.[69] He also urged his *upolnomochennye* not to delay applications to open mosques but to evaluate them positively, provided in each given case that it appeared 'politically expedient' and that all technicalities were satisfactorily met.[70] As a first step CARC planned opening nineteen mosques in various parts of the country, whose registration it had already consented to.[71] Several months later a CARC session approved the opening of a further twenty-one mosques.[72] But this seems to have been the last time the Council did so, for by February 1948 it was no longer merely approving resolutions of local government organs to reject applications, but it actually turned down two applications which regional *oblispolkoms* had endorsed.[73] Nonetheless, just as the registra-

68. For Polianskii's statement, see pp.32-3; for the possibility that greater leeway might he applied to Islam, see p.34.

69. I. V. Polianskii to V. M. Molotov, 10 June 1947; GARF, f.6991, o.3, d.47, l.198.

70. Minutes, CARC session No.11, 18-19 June 1947; GARF, f.6991, o.4, d.19, l.398.

71. The list was sent as an appendix to the draft decree Polianskii addressed to Kaftanov, Aleksandrov and Abakumov on 26 July 1947, see Chapter 1, n.79; RTsKhIDNI, f.17, o.125, d.506, ll.189-90. Not all of these mosques seem in fact to have been opened and officially registered. For toward the end of 1948 CARC passed a further resolution confirming the decision to open 15 of them, to postpone the opening of three, and to rescind the decision to open the last one, from which it would appear that there were difficulties even in opening some of the 15 – Minutes, CARC session No.20, 9 Dec. 1948. This impression is strengthened by a letter Polianskii sent to Voroshilov on 6 Jan. 1949 asking the Council of Ministers to approve the opening of 28 prayer-houses – 16 mosques and 12 of other faiths – which both CARC and the relevant republican or oblast' authority had consented to; 15 out of the 16 were included in the abovementioned 19 – GARF, f.6991, o.4, d.22, ll.246-51, and o.3, d.65, ll.1-7.

72. Minutes, CARC session No.18, 31 Oct. 1947; GARF, f.6991, o.4, d.19, ll.472-7.

73. Minutes, CARC session No.2, 10 Feb. 1948; GARF, f.6991, o.4, d.22, ll.75-8.

tion of factually functioning mosques continued in practice after mid 1946 – at least one CARC *upolnomochennyi* was dismissed from his post in 1947 for infringing instructions in this regard[74] – over twenty mosques were in fact registered in 1948 and two even as late as 1949.[75] In summer 1948 one CARC official was still pressing for the application of the old policy of allowing the opening of a prayer-house in places where there was a considerable believer population in order to provide a safety valve, and then later to take measures through the appropriate organisations to eliminate illegally functioning communities. Another pointed out that allowing the opening of registered mosques at considerable distances from each other entailed believers missing work in order to attend prayer-services.[76]

Very clearly the number of mosques registered in these first years, 1944-8, could not satisfy the religious needs of the country's Muslim believers. Some larger Russian cities with considerable Muslim populations – Leningrad, Gor'kii, Saratov – still had no registered religious societies despite incessant attempts by believers to obtain buildings of former mosques.[77] In the countryside, too,

74. Address of Kh. N. Iskanderov, Minutes, Conference of CARC *upolnomochennye* in the Uzbek SSR, 9 August 1948; TsGAUz, f.2456, o.1, d.120, ll.1-2. The person in question was Bekmuhamedov, *upolnomochennyi* for Tashkent Oblast'. He apparently also registered at least one mosque as having functioned earlier which, it later transpired, was not the case – *ibid.*, l.19. Apart from two mosques in Tashkent Oblast', at least seven other mosques were so registered in 1947: two in the Tatar ASSR, four in oblasti of the RSFSR, and one in Lithuania.

75. The registration of 13 of these mosques had been approved on 31 Oct. 1947; of the remainder, five had been approved before mid 1947, and two apparently in 1948; one was registered in connection with a change of address, and another without the documentation at my disposal giving any indication when it was approved for registration – GARF, f.6991, o.4, d.27, *passim*. Not all the mosques whose opening was approved in this late period, appear, however, to have actually started operating; the opening of a second mosque in the Kirgiz towns of Frunze and Tokmak, for instance, was suspended by a CARC instruction of Nov. 1948, for reasons that were not explained – H. Akhtiamov, Short report, Conference of Central Asian *upolnomochennye* in Tashkent, 17 Dec. 1949; GARF, f.6991, o.3, d.67, l.100.

76. Minutes, CARC session No.9, 10 June 1948; GARF, f.6991, d.22, ll.136 and 144.

77. CARC, too, sought to accommodate the believers in these three cities. In late 1948 it reconfirmed its earlier decision, spelled out in a letter to the Council of Ministers on 4 March 1948, concerning the need to gratify the recurrent requests of Saratov's Muslim believers to open a mosque in that city. This was

a number of settlements would sometimes combine to apply jointly for the opening of a mosque, and on occasion these petitions were successful. Of the seventeen rural mosques whose opening was ratified by CARC in autumn 1947, eight were designed to serve a number of neighbouring settlements in addition to the actual place in which they were situated.[78] Finally, even in oblasti with relatively large numbers of registered mosques, many communities had none. For example, Penza Oblast, which had fourteen registered mosques by 1948, had no less than forty-five settlements whose inhabitants professed Islam. At the same time, the registration of fourteen mosques was said to have curtailed the activity of religious groups in the other thirty-one places, their believers availing themselves of the services of those mosques which had been registered in order to satisfy their own religious needs.[79]

---

to no avail, for in 1956 the campaign for the recovery of a mosque in Saratov was still continuing. By this time Saratov's believing Muslims had filed over 40 applications to a whole range of bodies, including the All-Union and RSFSR councils of ministers and supreme soviets – Minutes, CARC session No.20, 9 Dec. 1948, and P. A. Solov'ev to V. I. Gostev, 31 July 1956; GARF, f.6991, o.4, d.22, l.247, and o.3, d.127, ll.164-73. In early 1949 Polianskii raised with Voroshilov the question of opening the mosque in Leningrad, to which the deputy prime minister was adamantly opposed on the grounds that the Tatar population of that city would not be able to maintain the mosque and it would have to be supported by collecting money from the Muslims of the RSFSR –Reception of I. V. Polianskii by K. E. Voroshilov, 12 Feb. 1949; GARF, f.6991, o.3, d.8, ll.176-7. In Gor'kii the *obkom* and *oblispolkom* sought to solve the problem by allowing the use of clubs as Muslim prayer-houses – Minutes, CARC session No.3, 10 April 1950 – while L. A. Prikhod'ko and N. I. Abushaev of CARC's Department for Eastern Religions both favoured the opening of a mosque in Gor'kii even in early 1952, although G. F. Frolov, head of CARC's group of inspectors, thought otherwise, having apparently been persuaded by local officialdom – Minutes, CARC session No.4s, 6 March 1952; GARF, f.6991, o.3, d.66, l.24, and d.83, ll.42 and 45. For the position of the local organs in these cities, see pp.652-3.

78. Minutes, CARC session No.18, 31 Oct. 1947; GARF, f.6991, o.4, d.19, ll.472-7. These eight mosques were spread over several oblasti: three were in oblasti of the RSFSR (one each in Astrakhan', Gor'kii and Molotov [Perm'] Oblast'), two in the Bashkir ASSR, one in Maryi Oblast' in Turkmenistan, one in South Kazakhstan Oblast' and one in Frunze Oblast'. The one in Perm' Oblast' was to serve Muslims of Perm' itself, where there was no registered Muslim community. Several of the others were opened in raiony where there was no other registered mosque.

79. Report of CARC's *upolnomochennyi* for Penza Oblast', Gorbachev, Minutes, CARC session No.9, 10 June 1948; GARF, f.6991, o.4, d.22, ll.113-14 and 152.

The first bout of closures

CARC, then, endeavoured even in Stalin's last, difficult years, at least in the first stages after the change in policy, to persuade the powers-that-be of the need to open more mosques. This was probably the consideration behind Polianskii's statement to Voroshilov in early 1949 that up to 500 mosques were functioning legally, i.e. had been registered – whereas the tally amounted in fact to 416 – and that it was essential to continue registering mosques in areas where the number of registered mosques was manifestly small, like Samarkand Oblast' or the Kazakh SSR. This, he insisted, would serve two purposes: it would contribute to regulating the situation regarding illegally functioning mosques and it would help extend the material base of the spiritual directorates.[80]

The Council's position notwithstanding, the period from mid 1948 to 1953 was, with very few exceptions, one in which mosques were no longer being opened,[81] but being shut down. Until mid 1947 CARC had basically been selecting applications in order to open and register mosques in places where it seemed expedient and appropriate, so that although more applications were refused than approved *in toto*, there was a sense of enlarging the number of registered mosques. As of mid 1947, the number of applications actually ratified fell markedly, and soon the principal trend was not just one of rejecting applications, but of closing mosques and withdrawing from registration the religious societies attached to

80. Reception of I. V. Polianskii by K. E. Voroshilov, 12 Feb. 1949; GARF, f.6991, o.3, d.8, ll.175-6. Polianskii's exaggeration of the number of registered mosques was perhaps intended to enable CARC to go on opening mosques without arousing the ire of the authorities. In fact, it backfired, giving Voroshilov grounds to compare the number of mosques with that of registered Russian Orthodox churches; the deputy prime minister contended, without sound arithmetical basis, that 500 mosques for 30 million Muslims were almost equivalent to the 2,700 churches for 100 million Russians in the RSFSR. (In addition to apparently underestimating the figure of functioning churches in the RSFSR, Voroshilov omitted mention of the far greater number in operation in the other union republics; cf. Chapter 1, n.113.)

81. A decree of the USSR Council of Ministers of 28 Oct. 1948 annulled a Council of Ministers instruction of 10 Aug., signed by Voroshilov, approving the opening of 32 prayer-houses of different faiths; from this point on and until early 1955 no prayer-houses of any religion were opened – Information on the applications of believers of the religious cults to open prayer-houses, attached to G. G. Karpov and I. V. Polianskii to the Council of Ministers, 5 Feb. 1955; GARF, f.6991, o.3, d.113, l.116. And see pp.34-5.

them. It should perhaps be noted that in not a few cases the local authorities closed mosques prior even to CARC's consideration of the matter and when the Council adopted a resolution to withdraw a mosque from registration, it was often merely putting its official seal on closures carried out in effect by the local authorities. One single closure was decided upon by CARC in mid 1947: a rural mosque in the Kabardinian ASSR, on the grounds that worshippers no longer wished to use the mosque for prayer;[82] and a further one occurred in mid 1948, again of a rural mosque in the Northern Caucasus, this time in the Adygei AO, where the 60-80 believers were unable to support a minister of religion and attended mosque in a neighbouring aul.[83]

The closures began in more meaningful numbers in the second half of 1949.[84] Not a few of these, too, were in the Northern Caucasus; for example, in the Cherkess AO, where the fall in mosque attendance was marked, CARC authorised the closure of six registered mosques at a single session in 1950.[85] The CARC *upolnomochennyi* for Stavropol Krai, which included the Cherkess AO, noted that of the remaining seventeen mosques only eight were functioning, the others no longer conducting organised prayer. Most of the mosques shut down were in rural areas, where the number of believers was often small and the religious society was for various reasons unable or unwilling to bear the yoke of paying for the upkeep of its clergy and prayer-house.[86] In Ul'ianovsk

82. Minutes, CARC session No.12, 3 July 1947; GARF, f.6991, d.19, ll.404-5.

83. Minutes, CARC session No.13, ? July 1948; GARF, f.6991, o.4, d.22, l.176. The decision spoke of disbanding the religious society and closing the mosque which had not functioned since February; CARC was in fact endorsing a decision of the Krasnodar Kraiispolkom of June 1948.

84. The number of registered mosques fell from 416 in early 1949 to 337 in early 1955; in 1949 alone it dropped by 31; see Chapter 2, n.18.

85. Minutes, CARC session No.6, 28 April 1950; GARF, f.6991, o.4, d.25, ll.41-2.

86. *Upolnomochennyi* V. V. Bulatov illustrated how the number of mosques had fallen from 62 at the end of the German occupation to 23 when the registration of factually functioning mosques was completed in January 1947 – see Chapter 2, n.32 – and how attendance at most of these was constantly dwindling. The Cherkess AO, he maintained, was no longer what it had been, as a result of the Stalinist nationalities policy and the major material and cultural achievements it had brought about. CARC senior inspector A. A. Murtuzov dwelt at length on the failure of the Cherkess communities to pay the salaries of their clergy, who for some years had been paying taxes on salaries they had not received

Oblast' two rural mosques were withdrawn from registration in 1949 on the grounds that there was another mosque in the same village, and three in 1950 on the grounds that the religious society attached to them had disbanded.[87]

The usual reason given for the withdrawal of registration was that the community had disbanded, ceased activity or refused to maintain its mosque and minister of religion; yet, on occasion, it was the violation of established regulations or the possibility of combining two or more religious societies which were in proximity to each other.[88] Here and there a religious society was closed because its prayer-house had been destroyed by some natural calamity. In Ashkhabad, for instance, the Muslim religious society had its registration withdrawn after its mosque was razed by the earthquake of October 1948. There being 'no possibility' of providing an alternative structure, it ceased activity.[89]

Not surprisingly, as always in periods when the local authorities felt they had state backing to shut down mosques (or other prayer-houses), there were instances of coercive closures despite CARC's admonitions, for example in the Bashkir ASSR and Ul'ianovsk Oblast'.[90] In one case, the local *raikom* secretary and *raiispolkom*

−Minutes, meeting of CARC instructors, No.17, 20-22 Dec. 1950. Three further mosques were shut down in this region in 1953 'in connection with the disbandment of the religious societies' attached to them − L. A. Prikhod'ko, V. D. Efremov and P. S. Basis, Report, 8 May 1954; GARF, f.6991, o.3, d.66, ll.123-4 and 128-30, and d.100, l.33.

87. Minutes, CARC session No.6, 1 March 1951; GARF, f.6991, o.3, d.74, l.85. See also pp.241-2 below.

88. For example, Kh. Iskanderov to I. V. Polianskii, 24 Sept. 1952; TsGAUz, f.2456, o.1, d.134, ll.102-3, and d.137, ll.45-6.

89. See, for example, Minutes, CARC session Nos.18 and 24, 30 Aug. and 2 Nov. 1949. Although the Ashkhabad religious society was said to have ceased activity, it held festive prayers in 1949 on Uraz-Bayram, conducted by eight clergy and in the presence of 200 worshippers, and on Qurban-Bayram when 150 worshippers participated; regarding the latter festival the CARC *upolnomochennyi* for the Turkmen SSR said specifically that prayers took place in the open − Report prepared for conference of Central Asian *upolnomochennye*, Tashkent, 17 Dec. 1949. According to this same source, all the premises of prayer-houses in the capital itself and in the two nearby raiony had been destroyed by the earthquake. Another mosque was shut down in the Tajik SSR in 1953 in similar circumstances − Report, 8 May 1954; GARF, f.6991, o.4, d.24, ll.84-5, 100 and 106, and o.3, d. 67, ll.144-6 and 149, and d.100, l.33.

90. For details, see below; also I. V. Polianskii to M. A. Suslov, 27 Dec. 1951; GARF, f.6991, o.3, d.76, ll.178-80, for a detailed description of the unacceptable

chairman came to a rural mosque, convened a meeting of believers, where they introduced a resolution to close the mosque, and began dismantling it in order to adapt the building as a school. All those who had voted in favour of closure then went to the republican capital to complain of the conduct of the local officials.[91] Of twelve decisions of local organs to close mosques which came before CARC at a single session in spring 1950, it removed three from the agenda in order to receive further information, not apparently being satisfied with the considerations provided.[92] One of these it agreed to shut down at its subsequent session and a second one it resolved not to close, contending that the reasons in favour of closing given in the decision of the local *oblispolkom*, namely undue proximity to children's institutions, schools and industrial enterprises, were not borne out by the verification it had carried out on the spot.[93] In 1950 Polianskii was still warning against closures in Central Asia other than in exceptional circumstances on the grounds that they merely served to strengthen the 'underground religious movement'.[94]

---

attempt of local officials to close a rural mosque in the Bashkir ASSR. CARC sometimes at least saw fit to point out to the respective authority that it had violated established procedure – e.g., Minutes, CARC session No.5, 21-22 Feb. 1950; GARF, f.6991, o.4, d.25, l.22.

91. Minutes, CARC session, No.26, 1-2 Dec. 1949; GARF, f.6991, o.3, d.60, l.104.

92. Of the three CARC decided to investigate further, two were in Kazakhstan – in Panfilov and Aktiubinsk – and one was in Andijan. Regarding the Panfilov mosque, the Taldy-Kurgan Oblispolkom maintained that the religious society had not conducted the repairs it had agreed to undertake in the agreement drawn up with it, and although it was an architectural monument; in Aktiubinsk the local *oblispolkom* contended that it was abrogating the lease agreement and had no other premises it could offer the religious society; while in Andijan the argument ran that there had been many applications to close the mosque, which was said to obstruct the normal activity of nearby schools, children's institutions and industrial enterprises. The closures with which the session concurred were in the Cherkess AO (six in a single raion) and three in Uzbekistan's Kashka-Darya Oblast' – Minutes, CARC session No.6, 28 April 1950; GARF, f.6991, o.4, d.25, ll.41-4.

93. Minutes, CARC session No.7, 30 May 1950; GARF, f.6991, o.4, d.25, ll.53-4. The one CARC agreed to close was in Panfilov; the one it declined to shut down was the one in Andijan, where it maintained that the mosque was not near to any children's institutions, schools or industrial enterprises and was isolated from residential dwellings by a 2 m – high fence.

94. I. V. Polianskii to K. E. Voroshilov, 27 May 1950; GARF, f.6991, o.3, d.68, ll.48-9.

The period of 'liberalisation'

In 1954 and even more so in 1955 the number of applications to open mosques began once more to increase. This was reported upon by almost all *upolnomochennye*. Moreover, numerous representatives of factually functioning religious groups were received by CARC officials in Moscow to ask that their associations be registered; most of them had but a meagre acquaintance with the intricacies of registration procedures, which dictated processing applications through local institutions.[95] And by the end of the latter year mosques were again being registered. The criteria for registration were that the religious society had to have its own prayer-house, which corresponded to the conditions laid down by law, as well as a reasonable number of believers, and to have been functioning prior to the Council of Ministers' decree of 17 February 1955.[96] Only a very few of the mosques opened in this period were those which had been closed in the previous years, presumably because this would have entailed acknowledging mistakes; one rural mosque which was re-opened in Ul'ianovsk Oblast' was said to have been closed because the raion organs had misled those of the oblast' level, telling them that the religious society there had disbanded.[97]

Not only were mosques being registered, but worshippers who had previously hesitated from committing themselves publicly by praying in registered mosques were now daring to move from unregistered to registered religious associations. This trend led to an increase in attendance at registered mosques.[98] At least, this was the interpretation of CARC officials for the growing number of worshippers in registered mosques, despite the generally accepted formula that the number of believers as a whole was declining. Thus, in the mid 1950s it was reported from Uzbekistan that, following upon SADUM's efforts to strengthen its image and its organisational capabilities, believers who had previously satisfied

95. See, for example, GARF, f.6991, o.4, d.75, *passim*.

96. See, for example, Minutes, CARC session No.1s, 4 Jan. 1956, which authorised the registration of three rural mosques in Tashkent Oblast'; GARF, f.6991, o.3, d.127, ll.3-4. For the decree, see pp.39-40.

97. A. S. Tazetdinov, Information, 28 Feb. 1957; GARF, f.6991, o.3, d.132, l.75.

98. K. F. Tagirov, Information, 1 March 1957; GARF, f.6991, o.3, d.132, l.69.

their religious requirements with the help of unregistered clergy were now turning to the registered mosques.[99]

CARC considered, as it had a decade previously when conditions were similarly auspicious, that where religious groups fulfilled the requisite criteria, the process of registration should not be impeded or held up.[100] It was of the opinion that refusal to register tended to strengthen the religious inclinations of believers and even to add to their numbers.[101] As one *upolnomochennyi* pointed out, un-registered associations should be registered wherever this might be necessary, for nothing bad came of registration. On the contrary, it meant enabling CARC to influence and supervise religious activity.[102] Often, however, the local government organs did refuse to register religious associations, for example in Samarkand Oblast', where, in the words of the CARC *upolnomochennyi*, they simply did not relate seriously to the decree of February 1955.[103] In other instances local officials transmitted false information to their superiors in order not to have to yield to applications by religious groups, as happened in one *poselok* in Ul'ianovsk Oblast'.[104] Or they sought to obstruct registration by taking administrative measures against a mosque or religious society.[105] In at least one case, in Dagestan, the republican government itself, after having given its consent to the opening of a mosque, forbade the registration of the religious society once it had been ratified by CARC, the *obkom* secretary

99. I. V. Polianskii to Kh. N. Iskanderov, 17 Aug. 1955; TsGAUz, f.2456, o.1, d.175, l.25. For the improved image of the spiritual directorates in this period, see pp.156-7.

100. V. I. Gostev to T. Tashkenbaev, 3 Feb. 1956, and to Kh. N. Iskanderov, 25 Feb. 1956; TsGAUz, f.2456, o.1, d.191, ll.40 and 57.

101. See, for example, P. A. Solov'ev to V. I. Gostev, 31 July 1956; GARF, f.6991, o.3, d.127, ll.165-70.

102. Sh. O. Ospanov, Conference of CARC *upolnomochennye*, 26 Nov. 1958; GARF, f.6991, o.3, d.165, ll.87-8.

103. Minutes, Instructional meeting of CARC *upolnomochennye* in the Uzbek SSR, 15-17 March 1956. Trying to follow this up, the *upolnomochennyi* for Samarkand wrote to the *oblispolkom* chairman to speed up matters – T. Tashkenbaev to R. Z. Artykov, 9 April 1956; TsGAUz, f.2456, o.1, d.183, l.54, and d.198, ll.38-9.

104. P. A. Solov'ev to V. I. Gostev, 24 May 1956; GARF, f.6991, o.3, d.127, ll.76-80.

105. In one village in Osh Oblast' the head of the raion department of people's education locked the mosque up – I. G. Halimov to CARC, 26 April 1956; GARF, f.6991, o.3, d.457, l.81.

for propaganda and agitation stating that he was categorically opposed to opening the mosque.[106] In other places things were easier. In a rural area in Kirgiziia's Jalalabad Oblast', where a functioning religious society was registered by CARC in October 1955, the building it used, which was situated in the cemetery precincts, underwent renovation with the participation of 'nearly all the believers' of the village.[107]

Khrushchev's anti-religious campaign

By 1958 the approach of CARC's *upolnomochennye* in the localities was undergoing a transformation. Those who thought that the leeway allowed to religious societies in the wake of the November 1954 resolution and the encouragement given to registration by the February 1955 decree were causing more harm than good were becoming increasingly vociferous.[108] This, of course, tallied with the new Central Committee line, expressed in its October 1958 resolution on strengthening atheistic work among the population. A number of CARC officials in Moscow, however, were still favouring the registration of religious societies in order to be in a position to control them and to know what was happening in them.[109] In some areas, too, the *upolnomochennye* were of a similar opinion.[110] Puzin himself said he supported the closure of mosques; the real question was how and when.[111] As in the last Stalin years, CARC sought to brake the enthusiasm of local authorities to close mosques.[112] In 1959, when the closures began,

106. Gasanov to V. I. Gostev, 19 March 1957; GARF, f.6991, o.3, d.145, ll.52 and 56. For the attitude of local officials in Dagestan, see also pp.647 and 670.

107. I. V. Polianskii to the CPSU Central Committee and the Council of Ministers, 16 Jan. 1956; GARF, f.6991, o.3, d.129, l.8.

108. For example, address of *upolnomochennye* for the Ajar ASSR Vanilishi, Conference of CARC *upolnomochennye*, 25-27 Nov. 1958; GARF, f.6991, o.3, d.165, l.83.

109. See, for example, L. A. Prikhod'ko, *ibid.*, l.112.

110. See, for example, address by CARC *upolnomochennyi* for Osh Oblast' Shadyev, Conference of CARC's Central Asian *upolnomochennye*, 5-6 June 1959; GARF, f.6991, o.3, d.186, l.175.

111. Address of A. A. Puzin, *ibid.*, ll.181-2.

112. For example, it rejected the decision of the Samarkand Oblispolkom to withdraw from registration the Palvan-Ata mosque on the Stalin kolkhoz, Mitan Raion, on the grounds that there was no legal ground for such a step – Minutes,

CARC was still simultaneously agreeing to register the odd mosque.[113] In the following year, while supporting the decision of the Ul'ianovsk Oblispolkom to close and dismantle a rural mosque which had fallen into disrepair and could not be repaired without being demolished, CARC refrained from withdrawing the religious society from registration with the intention of giving it an opportunity to find new premises.[114]

Nor did CARC change tack when the campaign reached new heights. As late as 1961, it protested that religious associations which had every right to register had not been allowed to do so by local authorities without any explanation being offered.[115] The Council also sought to impede what it considered unjustified closures. One mosque, in Samarkand Oblast', closed by 'administrative procedure' by the local authorities in 1959, was only finally withdrawn from registration in 1962.[116]

Fourteen requests by organs of local government to close mosques were rejected in the years 1960-3.[117] CARC likewise examined believers' complaints regarding acts of vandalism against their mosques and illegal closures. An attempt to tear down a mosque in the Bashkir ASSR had brought out over 1,000 believers to defend their prayer-house.[118] While agreeing that transgressions

---

CARC session No.22s, 2 Sept. 1959; GARF, f.6991, o.3, d.184, ll.187 and 204-5.

113. Ibid., ll.191 and 223.

114. N. I. Smirnov, Memo, Reception of representatives of the religious society of Elkhovyi Kust, 20 Feb. 1960; GARF, f.6991, o.4, d.110, l.26.

115. A. Puzin to J. Rasulov, First Secretary, Central Committee of the Communist Party of Tajikistan, draft, August 1961; GARF, f.6991, o.3, d.1737, l.100.

116. See decision of Shtykhan Raiispolkom, 30 June 1959, resumé of T. Tashkenbaev, 24 Feb. 1961, and Minutes, CARC session No.5, 22 Feb. 1962 – GARF, f.6991, o.3, d.1384, ll.57-9 and 65.

117. Information, 5 Oct. 1963; GARF, f.6991, o.3, d.1423, l.139. Some such requests which were postponed or rejected were later acceded to, e.g., in the case of the mosque in the town of Davlekanovo (the Bashkir ASSR) – Minutes, CARC sessions Nos.2 and 11, 20 Jan. and 26 April 1962; GARF, f.6991, o.3, d.1384, ll.15 and 138.

118. CARC instructed its *upolnomochennyi* in the Bashkir ASSR to verify the complaint that the heads of the local kolkhoz and *sel'sovet* had tried without authorisation to demolish the mosque, and the *upolnomochennyi* in Leninabad Oblast' to look into the complaint of the Muslim believers of Ura-Tyube concerning the illegal shutting down of their mosque – CARC session No.8, 14 Feb. 1961, and No.9, 21 Feb. 1961; and see also resumé by CARC inspector

against the legislation on religion had to be punished, CARC opposed retribution against entire communities by taking the ultimate step of withdrawal from registration or closure, especially if these measures were taken on the basis of violations of the law committed in the past and for which punishment had already been meted out.[119] It refused to accept at face value not only the conclusions of its own *upolnomochennye* when it considered them over-eager to take measures against certain religious societies; it even questioned the actual data they presented in justification of their recommendations, indicating that their considerations were short-sighted.[120]

CARC also took note of the report of its *upolnomochennyi* for Tajikistan that where mosques had been shut down by 'administrative' measures, this had been used by 'reactionary' unregistered clerics to enhance their activity.[121] Indeed, in those areas of Tajikistan where closure had been by such methods, attendance at festival prayers did not diminish, but went up markedly. In one such region prior to the shutting down of the registered mosque, 6,000 worshippers had gathered there for festival prayers and 4-5,000 in services organised by unregistered mullas. In the year following

---

K. Ovchinnikov, 14 Nov. 1961; GARF, f.6991, o.3, d.1355, ll.203-4 and 282, d.1361, ll.41-4, and d.1356, l.28.

119. Thus, CARC concurred with the decision of the Orenburg Oblispolkom that the mosque built without authorisation by the registered religious society of Novo-Musino should be expropriated, but took exception to its resolution to withdraw the community from registration. It similarly refused to withdraw from registration a mosque in a raion administrative centre in Cheliabinsk Oblast' where the mulla and some members of the executive organ had been withdrawn from registration early in 1959 for the same violation of the law which now served as a pretext for closure – Minutes, CARC session No.2, 12 Jan. 1961, and A. A. Puzin to V. G. Salov, draft prepared for CARC session No.15, 27 March 1961; GARF, f.6991, o.3, d.1361, ll.5-6, and d.1356, ll.134-5.

120. For example, in the case of the mosque in Karaganda, where the republican and oblast' *upolnomochennye* recommended closure, in line with the local *oblispolkom*, on the grounds that the mosque's revenues were continuing to grow annually and that its imam went to other towns in order to perform religious rites, frightened believers in his sermons and incited antagonism and even blows within the mosque. CARC stated that this information was simply incorrect and that closure would be inexpedient – Minutes, CARC session No.9, 21 Feb. 1961; GARF, f.6991, o.3, d.1361, ll.41-4. For CARC's reasoning, see pp.591-3.

121. Excerpt from CARC minutes, undated [probably session No.17, 25 April 1961]; GARF, f.6991, o.3, d.1737, ll.77-8.

closure, 22,000 worshipped in festival services conducted by the latter.[122]

Indisputably, the situation was becoming increasingly difficult for the registered religious societies, not a few of which were withdrawn from registration. Although there were several which could reasonably be argued to have genuinely disbanded,[123] even an authentic fall-off in attendance could have been the result of the general unease engendered by the new conditions. Sometimes it was a by-product of the withdrawal from registration or demise of the local mulla and the difficulty in finding a replacement.[124] In some instances the mosque required repair and the believers were not prepared to undertake the expense.[125] In others, the

122. D. Ahmedov to A. A. Puzin, 5 June 1961. According to another source, 22,000 attended festival prayers in the unregistered mosques of the entire republic —as against less than 10,000 who worshipped in its 29 remaining registered mosques – N. Smirnov and S. Fastoved, Information, 22 Aug. 1962. Be this as it may, it is clear even in the latter event that administrative closures did not reduce aggregate mosque attendance, but rather the contrary, the great majority of worshippers now reverting to praying in unregistered prayer-houses. It is possible that both sets of figures are incorrect: in 1963 on Uraz-Bayram 62,300 were said to have participated in prayer-services in the registered mosques and over 23,000 in prayers conducted by unregistered clergy – M. Kh. Hamidov to A. A. Puzin, 22 Oct. 1963; GARF, f.6991, o.3, d.1737, ll.81-2, and d.1390, ll.30-1 and 98.

123. For instance, one mosque which was withdrawn from registration in the Karachai-Cherkess AO had reportedly had a regular attendance of four to eight people for five years and had no executive organ or inspection committee long prior to its efendi and a few believers reporting the situation to the CARC *upolnomochennyi* – Excerpt, minutes, CARC session No.20, 11 July 1962; GARF, f.6991, o.3, d.1385, l.85.

124. In one village in Orenburg Oblast' the mulla had been withdrawn from registration for three months for not paying income tax, after which prayers were no longer held and the mosque ceased functioning; in another village, in Ul'ianovsk Oblast' the mulla had died and the executive organ declared they could find no one who could act as mulla and recite the Qur'an; in one aul in the Adygei AO, too, the mulla had died and there was no one to concern himself with the acquisition of a prayer-house after the expiry of the agreement on the old one – Excerpts, Minutes, CARC session No.20, 11 July 1962, and Minutes, CARC session No.15, 27 March 1961; GARF, f.6991, o.3, d.1385, ll.82 and 84, and d.1356, l.133.

125. For example, in one village in Penza Oblast' whose believers had the possibility of worshipping in a registered mosque in a nearby village just 1 km away – N. Smirnov, Information, prepared for CARC session No.21, 27 May 1961; GARF, f.6991, o.3, d.1356, l.209.

dvadtsatka and executive organ had disintegrated and noone could be found to fill the gap.[126]

Some of the closures were unquestionably the result of direct pressure by the local authorities. In fact, these organs seem frequently to have closed down mosques without troubling to have the step confirmed by CARC. Three mosques, for example, were shut down in the Bashkir ASSR in 1960 without CARC's *upolnomochennyi* in that republic even transmitting to Moscow the documentation announcing the decision to close them.[127] In 1959 four registered mosques were withdrawn from registration just in Leninabad Oblast' in Tajikistan; and two more were closed there in 1960, all apparently without CARC's consent.[128] CARC considered some of these closures to have been without justification and 'premature' (the word reflected the assumption that eventually, of course, all mosques would be closed down, so closure could not be wrong), especially since the mosques concerned drew over 1,000 worshippers apiece and closure had aroused manifest dissatisfaction.[129] In 1960 CARC withdrew from registration one mosque in Ul'ianovsk Oblast' and another in Penza Oblast' in accordance with the decision of the local authorities on the grounds that they were in a dilapidated condition, although both religious societies asked to be allowed to conduct repairs; one of them had actually prepared the requisite building materials.[130] In the following year the municipal *ispolkom*

126. This happened in the town of Kushva in Sverdlovsk Oblast', where eight of the 20 'founders' had quit their posts and seven more had left the town or died. Mosque attendance had also fallen off, with just five worshippers on Fridays and 25 on festivals, some of them from the nearby towns of Krasnoural'sk and Verkhniaia Tura – Memo prepared for CARC session No.23, 7 Aug. 1962; GARF, f.6991, o.3, d.1385, l.114.

127. A. A. Puzin to M. Sh. Karimov, draft, undated (apparently January 1961); GARF, f.6991, o.3, d.1355, ll.64-5.

128. Report of D. Ahmedov, Minutes, CARC session No.27, 15-16 Sept. 1960, and A. Azizbaev to A. A. Puzin, 10 Jan. 1961. In his annual report for 1960 Ahmedov said specifically that the local authorities had violated the law in at least some of these closures – D. Ahmedov to A. A. Puzin, 21 Feb. 1961; GARF, f.6991, o.3, d.206, l.132, and d.1737, ll.9 and 31.

129. Minutes, CARC session No.17, 25 April 1961; GARF, f.6991, o.3, d.1361, ll.115 and 139.

130. Minutes, CARC session No.11s, 17 May 1960, and No.19, 28 June 1960, and Reception by N. I. Smirnov of two believers from the former community, 27 April 1960; GARF, f.6991, o.3, d.204, ll.151 and 166-7, and d.205, ll.98 and 108-10, and o.4, d.110, l.20. The two representatives of the community

in Margelan decided to close down the registered mosque in the centre of the town – although, according to its executive organ, it boasted 5-6,000 worshippers – formally uniting its religious society with that of a mosque situated some 5 km away. The pretext was the not unusual one, that reconstruction work was being undertaken in the immediate vicinity of the mosque.[131] In a few instances, at least, mosques were shut down on the basis of dis-information provided by local officials.[132] In addition to those shut down as a result of blatant or indirect coercion by local government institutions, a number of mosques were withdrawn from registration on the grounds that they had in fact violated the law on religion, but these were a small minority.[133]

---

in Ul'ianovsk Oblast' maintained that 200 to 250 worshippers attended regular Friday prayers and that the request to conduct repairs had been signed by 65 believers, which would indicate that the community was far from being in the category of having disbanded; Smirnov himself admitted in the memo he prepared for the CARC session that over 200 had participated in prayers on Uraz-Bayram in the past two years. Nonetheless, it was resolved to demolish the mosque and not to allow it to be repaired.

131. A. Ivanov to A. Rahimov, 6 July 1961, A. Rahimov to Sh. Shirinbaev, 10 July 1961, and Members of the *mutawaliyyat* of the Khanaka mosque in Margelan to Mufti Babakhanov, undated [before 20 June 1961]; TsGAUz, f.2456, o.1, d.286, ll.76-7 and 22.

132. For instance, in the village of Tatarskii Baitugan in Kuibyshev Oblast'. The local organs had apparently contended that the religious society had but a few members. In early 1965 CARC senior inspector Smirnov received two representatives of the community who brought a statement signed by over 300 believers maintaining that the mosque had been closed unjustly. The CARC *upolnomochennyi* confirmed that the local officials had been in a hurry to shut it down and had given incorrect information. Consequently, permission was given for believers to conduct prayers on Uraz-Bayram in a private house – Reception by N. I. Smirnov of two representatives of the believers of Tatarskii Baitugan, 28 Jan. 1965; GARF, f.6991, o.4, d.171, l.12.

133. One was the mosque in Sol'-Iletsk, whose religious association was said to have held a prayer for rain, although it was also claimed that both the executive organ and the *dvadtsatka* had disintegrated, with one and seven members respectively. CARC officials expressed doubts about the justification for this step; see V. Riazanov to V. V. Opitin, two drafts, [25?] July 1962, and Draft resolution prepared for CARC session No. 23, 7 Aug. 1962, and see n.255 below. In a village in the Kirgiz SSR the community was similarly punished for having several years before, when times augured well, seized a plot to construct a mosque without authorisation – Excerpt, minutes, CARC session No.20, 11 July 1962. A third such case was in the village of Novo-Musino in Orenburg Oblast' – N. I. Smirnov, Information, undated [probably Jan. 1961]. According to CARC, whereas 43 mosques had been closed as having disbanded from Jan.

Given, however, the socio-political atmosphere of the Khrushchev period, the attempt was made to conduct closures with the approval and, where possible, with the actual participation of believers. This was a return to the practice regarding the closure of prayer–houses in the 1920s which was presented as 'the result of the mobilisation of social opinion'. This presumably was what one CARC *upolnomochennyi* termed 'appropriate preparation among the population for closure'.[134] The formal initiative for shutting down some rural mosques emanated from a general meeting of the villagers or of the local believers.[135] At one such general meeting in Dagestan, a member of the mosque council [sic] said that since it was the scene of constant violations of the law, which also contradicted religion, the mosque had to be closed.[136] The CARC *upolnomochennyi* for Uzbekistan reported that closure of the nine mosques withdrawn from registration in that republic between 1960 and 1964 had been guided by this principle of popular participation and so had not aroused any

1960 to 30 Sept. 1963, just two had been shut for violating the law – Information, 5 Oct. 1963; GARF, f.6991, o.4, d.130, ll.33-4, and o.3, d.1355, ll.36-7, d.1385, ll.86 and 112, and d.1423, l.139. (It is not clear which two CARC had in mind.)

134. D. Ahmedov to A. A. Puzin, 23 April 1962; GARF, f.6991, o.3, d.1738, l.21. For a 1929 instruction regarding popular support for closures, see Keller, *The Struggle against Islam in Uzbekistan, 1921 – 1941*, p.295. See also Luukkanen, *The Religious Policy of the Stalinist State*, pp.80-2.

135. In one village in Kuibyshev Oblast' 238 citizens participated in such a meeting, only three of whom voted against closure. The mosque had been without a mulla for two months, six people were lacking to complement the *dvadtsatka* and no one could be found to fill the void, and the chairman of the executive organ refused to fulfil his obligations. Two other mosques were closed in the same oblast' in 1962: in one instance the mulla himself had proposed the closure at a meeting of 21 believers, in the other the proposal was put at a similar meeting, of 13 members of the *dvadtsatka* and two rank-and-file believers, by a member of the executive organ, and in both the contention was that the religious society had so few believers it could not afford to undertake the requisite repairs in the mosque – Excerpts from minutes, CARC session No.37, 3 Dec. 1962; GARF, f.6991, o.3, d.1386, ll.88 and 90-91.

136. N. I. Smirnov, Information, prepared for CARC session No.21, 27 May 1961; GARF, f.6991, o.3, d.1356, ll.205-6. There were said to have been 375 villagers at the meeting. Nonetheless, a complaint was later lodged with 59 signatures, which contended that the decision on closure had been taken at a small meeting and that some believers who had been present had spoken up against closure.

'undesirable consequences'.[137] In Tajikistan mosques were closed 'at the decision of the believers themselves as a result of the ideological work carried out among the population', some of the religious societies amalgamating with nearby communities and the mosques being transferred to other uses.[138]

But these guidelines were not rigidly adhered to. Nor probably did most people, including officials, attribute serious significance to the outward expression of consent to closures on the part of believers, which even when it was formally forthcoming, was undisputably disingenuous. They must have known that reports of popular support did not necessarily reflect a truthful picture of what had occurred and that considerable social pressure was often applied in order to obtain the desired results, and sometimes even downright threats. (There had been such instances even in the earlier, 'better' years.[139]) CARC noted that even the large-scale shutting down of unregistered mosques evoked popular dissatis-faction;[140] so, surely it cannot have been deluded with reference to registered religious societies. Believers from at least four of the six mosques closed in Leninabad Oblast', including one where the closure had, according to the CARC *upolnomochennyi* for Tajikis-tan, been initiated by a general meeting of believers, complained to CARC about the shutting down of their mosques.[141] So, too, did believers in a rural area of the Karachai-Cherkess AO who claimed that the document entitling the local government to shut down their mosque was signed by its cleric and a number of elders who were illiterate in Russian and understood it poorly. The complaint also pointed out that the closure, which was rationalised by the dilapidated state of the mosque, had not been preceded by any warning about the need to repair it; that there was a Russian Orthodox church nearby, so why should they not be

137. Minutes, CARC session No.24, 27 Aug. 1964; GARF, f.6991, o.4, d.147, 1.88.

138. D. Ahmedov to A. Puzin, 21 Feb. 1961; GARF, f.6991, o.3, d.1737, 1.7. Ahmedov brought four specific examples, in two of which the believers themselves, and in two the *dvadtsatka* purportedly approached the local authorities with suggestions to close their mosque – *ibid.*, 1.8.

139. For example, in Osh Oblast', in 1956, see pp.664-5.

140. CARC, materials sent to the CPSU Central Committee, 27 Dec. 1960, draft; GARF, f.6991, o.3, d.210, ll.73-85.

141. Unsigned draft of letter to D. Ahmedov, prepared for CARC session No.9, 21 Feb. 1961; GARF, f.6991, o.3, d.1356, 1.26.

allowed their mosque; and that the elders now had to pray in the open, exposing themselves to the mockery of the younger generation.[142]

Measures were also taken to curb activity within the remaining mosques, so that there could be no doubt that the times were changing. Microphones were removed from nineteen mosques in the Uzbek SSR, which had enabled the relaying of prayers and sermons to the crowds who flocked to these mosques and could not get into the main building.[143] In Dagestan the women's sections in the registered mosques were closed.[144] In Nakhichevan, in the Azerbaijan SSR, workers of the *gorsovet* strew the main entrance to the mosque with rubble on the eve of Muharram in order to decrease visitation and on Ashura stationed a militiaman and a Komosmol member there to deter worshippers by enquiring about their prayer-mats. In Kirovabad in the same republic, as a result of municipal reconstruction, the religious society was given other premises and forced to close the mosque and transfer to the new building at once although it required repairing.[145]

In this period once again the number of applications to register decreased sharply. In Dagestan thirty applications had been filed in 1958, but in 1959 there were just nineteen and in 1960 only one.[146] A considerable number of clergy, too, were dismissed on various pretexts. In 1960 alone seven imams were withdrawn from registration just in Uzbekistan.[147] As in the last Stalin years, some also tendered their resignation. Now, however, the reason does not seem to have been so much the lack of financial support by believers, although here and there, as a decade before, the decrease in mosque attendance was so marked that some clergy complained they were not being paid their salary.[148] In the early

142. Minutes, CARC session No.17, 11 June 1962; GARF, f.6991, o.3, d.1385, l.3.

143. Minutes, CARC session No.27, 15-16 Sept. 1960; GARF, f.6991, o.3, d.206, l.128.

144. Minutes, CARC session No.33, 26-27 Oct. 1960; GARF, f.6991, o.3, d.207, l.40.

145. Minutes, CARC session No.3, 17-18 Feb. 1965; GARF, f.6991, o.4, d.168, l.29.

146. M. S. Gajiev, Report, Minutes, CARC session No.33, 26-27 Oct. 1960; GARF, f.6991, o.3, d.207, l.39.

147. Sh. Shirinbaev, Report, Minutes, CARC session No.27, 15-16 Sept. 1960; GARF, f.6991, o.3, d.206, l.128.

148. For example, in one raion just east of Dushanbe – D. Ahmedov to A. Puzin, 21 Feb. 1961; GARF, f.6991, o.3, d.1737, ll.8-9.

1960s there seems rather to have been something of a general retreat, the media publishing not a few statements by disillusioned clerics that they were renouncing religion altogether.[149] In not a few of these cases the repudiation of the post of cleric, which was sometimes accompanied by a declaration of total rejection of religion, was attributed to the children or grandchildren of the cleric concerned, who were generally of a higher level of education.[150] (This assertion for which no proof was brought rings rather hollow. On the one hand, it fits too neatly into the theory of the Soviet regime; on the other, it runs counter to the usual picture of the respect in which the younger generation held their elders. There may however, have been one or two such instances.) Those who left the ranks of the clergy included the director of studies at the Mir-Arab Medrese and some students at the same institution, all of whom announced their defection in the media, although apparently not overtly pressured to do so by the authorities. Their number also included five clerics and thirty members of executive organs in five mosques in the Bashkir ASSR.[151] Some resignations were undoubtedly the result of direct or indirect pressure applied by local officialdom. Equally certainly, some of the instances reported were purely pro forma or sheer disinformation designed to satisfy the authorities at the centre of power.[152]

'Normalisation'

By late 1964 the pendulum was showing signs of swinging back. Once more, the odd mosque was being allowed to register.[153]

149. One of the earliest examples seems to have been in Alma-Ata Oblast' at the beginning of 1960 – Address by B. Jumashev, All-Union conference of CARC *upolnomochennye*, 18-20 April 1960; GARF, f.6991, o.3, d.208, l.127. Altogether, eight imams resigned their posts in Kazakhstan between late 1959 and May 1960, explaining that they had been deceiving the people and wished henceforth to devote themselves to 'honest work'; some of them retired for reasons of age or because they had been 'influenced by their families', and most of them announced their resignation in the press – K. V. Ovchinnikov, Report, Minutes, CARC session No.16, 10 June 1960; GARF, f.6991, o.3, d.205, l.26.

150. Ashirov, *Evoliutsiia islama v SSSR*, p.12.

151. S. A. Shamsutdinov to A. A. Puzin, 30 June 1962, and A. Puzin to M. Sh. Karimov, draft, undated; GARF, f.6991, o.3, d.1388, l.156, and d.1355, l.264.

152. Cf. p.3.

153. For instance, in Stavropol' Krai – Minutes, CARC session No.31, 6 Oct.

And although there continued to be closures,[154] the pace was not the same and there was clearly no longer a policy to this end. In 1965 the CARC *upolnomochennyi* in Penza Oblast' allowed the continued functioning of a rural mosque, that the local authorities had designated for closure, contending that there were insufficient grounds for such a step. Meanwhile CARC asked the Orenburg Oblispolkom to review its decision not to re-open a mosque which had been shut down in 1962 'without sufficient cause' and on the basis of faulty information.[155] In summer 1966 the CRA *upolnomochennyi* for Tajikistan suggested re-opening five of the fifteen 'illegally closed' mosques in that republic: specifically those with a large membership.[156] And early in the following year the CRA was disputing the refusal of the Tatar ASSR Council of Ministers to register a factually functioning religious society in the town of Bugul'ma, contending that the refusal contradicted the law on religion, whereas the application to register fulfilled all the necessary requirements.[157] It similarly rejected the refusal of the Kuibyshev Oblispolkom to register the Muslim religious society in that city, returning the application for review, and of the Orenburg Oblispolkom to register the one in the town of Buguruslan. This produced a favourable outcome in both cases and the two religious societies were duly registered.[158]

1964; GARF, f.6991, o.4, d.147, l.137.

154. For example, in rural areas of Tiumen Oblast' and of the Karachai-Cherkess AO – Minutes, CARC session No.8, 9 April 1965, and CRA session No.6, 11 Sept. 1968; GARF, f.6991, o.4, d.169, l.10, and o.6, d.148, l.1.

155. S. Popov to A. Puzin, 20 Sept. 1965, and Minutes, CARC session No.24, 12-13 Nov. 1965; GARF, f.6991, o.3, d.1488, l.125, and o.4, d.169, ll.168-9 and 186. Regarding Orenburg Oblast' the reference is to the mosque in Sol'-Iletsk and the material was prepared following the visit of representatives of the Sol'-Iletsk community to CARC. For the closure of this mosque, see n.133 above.

156. The *upolnomochennyi* suggested simultaneously that the other ten which had been shut down be withdrawn from registration on the grounds that there was no need for them, that the number of their believers was small, and that there had been no complaints regarding their closure – U. Yuldashev, Information, 12 Aug. 1966; GARF, f.6991, o.6, d.8, ll.107-10. The situation in Tajikistan indeed seemed extremely complex. Officially just 17 registered mosques existed there, but the CRA figures spoke of 34, apparently not recognising the unlawful closures. (It is not clear how or why 17 and 15 amount to 34.)

157. Minutes, CRA session No.2, 7 Feb. 1967; GARF, f.6991, o.6, d.74, ll.20-1. For further details, see pp.654-6.

158. Minutes, CRA session No.5, 14 June 1967, No.8, 6 Sept. 1967, No.3,

Finally, the CRA persisted in calling for the registration of the larger functioning religious associations, which had been operating for several years and, having their own mosques and permanent mullas, were essentially indistinguishable from the registered religious societies. It also sought to register one mulla wherever there was a significant believer population, allowing him to perform religious rites and finding a way to link him to a registered mosque and through it to exert influence upon him.[159] Significantly, the last suggestion was identical with the policy which SADUM's representatives in Kazakhstan had recommended over twenty years earlier, in 1945, only to be rejected outright by CARC as contrary to the sense of the procedures established towards and immediately after the end of the war.

The CRA's line did not become accepted policy, and there was no large-scale registration of mosques, although in the five years 1978-82, fifty-seven mosques were registered. But the number of registered clergy did double from the early 1970s to the early 1980s,[160] so that this particular approach seems to have had some resonance.[161] It clearly constituted the rationale, for instance, behind the registration of a number of Ismaili *khalifas* in the Gorno-Badakhshan AO in the 1960s although the Ismailis had no mosques, and even of Sunni mullas in that region. Interestingly, these registered clergy were instructed not to permit the conduct of rites by unregistered clergy, to perform rites solely for the elderly

---

11 June 1968 and No.2, 27 Feb. 1969; GARF, f.6991, o.6, d.74, ll.59 and 77, d.148, l.20 and d.216, l.10. The Muslim believers of Buguruslan had been applying to register since 1947 and had sent no less than twelve delegations to CARC and the CRA for support – Reception by A. Barmenkov and A. Nurullaev of delegates from Buguruslan, 13 Nov. 1969; GARF, f.6991, o.6, d.221, l.73.

159. Theses of a lecture, 'The situation of the Muslim faith in the country and measures to strengthen control of observance of legislation on religion', sent by A. Barmenkov to the CPSU Central Committee Department of Propaganda, 19 June 1968; GARF, f.6991, o.6, d.147, ll.44-5. It seems that the latter suggestion was deleted from the lecture actually delivered by A. A. Nurullaev at the all-union conference of CRA *upolnomochennye* held in Tashkent on 30 July-1 August, presumably because it was expunged from the draft by the Central Committee; see excerpt from the lecture – GARF, f.6991, o.6, d.548, l.78. For the general context of the discussion on the registration of mosques see the discussion of the 24 July 1968 decree of the RSFSR Council of Ministers, p.50.

160. By the beginning of 1983 there were 374 registered mosques and 'about one thousand' registered clergy – see p.67.

161. For policy on these issues, see pp.593-4.

and in no circumstances to tolerate the performance of rites by young men and women.[162] In Azerbaijan clergy were registered with the sole purpose of conducting funeral rites, while in some parts of Kazakhstan itinerant mullas were registered and attached officially to one of the republic's registered mosques. Here, besides funeral rites, they were permitted to read the Qur'an at memorial ceremonies and perform the *tarawa-namaz* during *uraz* and prayer-services on the two main festivals.[163] At the same time, in certain areas at least, the practice of affiliating to registered mosques mosque-less clergy who performed rites in the localities was considered inappropriate.[164]

Mosque attendance

All believers were unquestionably conscious throughout the entire

162. M. Kh. Hamidov, Memo, 22 Oct. 1963, Arifov to A. A. Puzin, M. Kh. Hamidov, Obkom Secretary M. Nazarshoev, Ispolkom Chairman M. Shirinjanov and chief of the GBAO KGB Administration A. Iu. Salibaev, 25 Feb. 1964, U. Yuldashev, Memo, 'The Ismaili sect in the Pamirs', 10 July 1968, and address of Sh. N. Naimov, CARC *upolnomochennyi* for the GBAO, at a conference organised by the GBAO Obkom, 2 July 1973; GARF, f.6991, o.3, d.1739, l.97, and d.1740, l.15, and o.6, d.153, l.96, and d.545, ll.147-8. One cleric was to be registered for each of the area's 38 kishlaks and one in Khorog, its administrative centre. At first, in 1959, 47 *khalifas* had been registered, but in early 1961 the CARC *upolnomochennyi* resolved on his own to register 96 Ismaili communities with two to three clergy apiece, so that the oblast' had 250 registered *khalifas* and several dozen Sunni itinerant mullas. The new *upolnomochennyi*, however, cut the number down drastically, and by 1963 each *sel'sovet* had one registered cleric. These were to perform rites in private homes at the invitation of believers and there were to be no more registered religious societies – K. F. Tagirov, Information, 2 March 1964; GARF, f.6991, o.3, d.1740, l.22. For a more detailed discussion of the Ismailis, see pp.422-4.

163. In Kazakhstan's Taldy-Kurgan Oblast' there was not a single registered mosque in the 1970s. One of the mullas who functioned unofficially in one raion was registered as a mulla at the Alma-Ata mosque in an attempt to terminate the activity of the other mullas in that raion – T. Shaidildinov to V. A. Kuroedov, 20 July 1973. In Kokchetau Oblast', also in Kazakhstan, two itinerant mullas were appointed in 1973, one for each of two raiony which were 200 and 170 km respectively from the oblast's sole registered mosque. Their activities were carefully defined and monitored and coordinated with all the relevant parties –S. Eleusyzov to K. Kulumbetov, 11 Feb. 1974; GARF, f.6991, o.6, d.545, ll.60-2, and d.633, ll.24-9.

164. For one area where the suggestions were rejected totally, the Kabardino-Balkar ASSR, see below.

period under discussion of the implications for themselves of mosque attendance. Nevertheless, despite the fear, the number of worshippers who came to pray in registered mosques, especially in some of the larger ones, was considerable. At the same time, it appears that when the general policy towards religion was relatively lax, worshippers felt freer and attended mosque more regularly, and the converse when repression seemed more severe.[165] As of 1948 and until Stalin's death, for instance, people appeared to be attending in smaller numbers than in the first years of renewed religious activity;[166] true, in Uzbekistan attendance at a number of mosques seemed even then to be growing,[167] but this probably reflected the forementioned closure of a relatively large number of mosques and the participation of their congregants at prayer-services in the remaining mosques. The years 1955-8 saw a renewed growth of mosque attendance, which CARC's apparatus attributed to the 'religious propaganda' conducted among the population by the clergy and mosque *aktiv* with an end to strengthening Islam.[168] Attendance fell off again in the hard years of Khrushchev's anti-religious campaign, from the latter half of 1958 until 1964, except on the major festivals, although even then there seem to have been exceptions.[169] The data suggest that while attendance did not continue to fall as of the mid 1960s, it did not regain the

165. For some statistics on mosque attendance, see pp.71-79.

166. See, for example, B. Shahbazbekov, Information, undated [after 20 April 1949], and Information, 29 March 1952, both of which reported a slackening of mosque attendance, especially of young people. This included the Shiite attendance during Muharram. A similar trend was noted in this same period by the *upolnomochennyi* for Ul'ianovsk Oblast', P. F. Simonov, Minutes, CARC session No.6, 1 March 1951. In Dagestan, however, while mosque attendance fell off in the rural areas, it showed a certain growth in the towns – Khabilov to I. V. Polianskii, 4 June 1954; GARF, f.6991, o.3, d.60, l.30, d.83, l.79, d.74, ll.81-2, and d.102, l.124.

167. See a comparison of figures for attendance in Tashkent and Tashkent Oblast' for 1950 and 1951, which showed a marked increase in the latter year –Almaev to Oblispolkom Deputy Chairman Mahkamov, Obkom Secretary Nazarov, Kh. N. Iskanderov and I. V. Polianskii, 19 Jan. 1952; TsGAUz, f.2456, o.1, d.142, ll.43-4.

168. I. A. Shalaev, Information as of 1 Nov. 1955; TsGAUz, f.2456, o.1, d.174, ll.92-3.

169. For example in the mosque in Meleuz in the Bashkir ASSR, where it doubled from 300 to 600 from 1959 to 1960 – A. Puzin to M. Sh. Karimov, draft, undated; GARF, f.6991, o.3, d.1355, l.264.

heights of the previous decade.[170] CARC officials contended that the increased attendance of the mid 1950s did not denote a growth in religiosity, but reflected the closure of unregistered religious groups, whose members now attended the registered mosques.[171] Numerical data, however, relating to mosque attendance are, as has been noted, not always reliable and the picture was probably more complex than they would indicate.

In rural communities in particular, and even in towns which served nearby rural areas, there was a significant seasonal difference in mosque attendance. When a major festival fell during the height of seasonal work in the cotton fields, the numbers who came to collective prayer fell.[172] Mosques which might have considerable numbers of worshippers in the winter would have but a few elderly people in the summer.[173] Some clergy at least stated recurrently at Friday prayers that the daily *namaz* at times of seasonal agricultural work should be short and that attendance at them was not obligatory.[174] Altogether, the CARC *upolnomochennyi* for Kirgiziia noted, the registered Muslim communities tended to be stable, not experiencing any major changes in mosque attendance, beyond those that could be attributed to fluctuating economic circumstances.[175] The weather and the day of the week on which a festival fell also influenced attendance, especially since festival prayers were conducted largely in the open; in years when a

170. For example, in Chimkent Oblast' festival attendance in 1959 had been over 17,000. Ten years later it was approximately 8,000, with 1,800 on regular Fridays. While these numbers did not drop further, nor did they grow – Sh. Ospanov, 'Islam', material prepared for the *obkom*, 16 Nov. 1973; GARF, f.6991, o.6, d.633, l.92.

171. K. F. Tagirov, Information, 1 March 1957; GARF, f.6991, o.3, d.132, ll.68-9. And see p.203 above.

172. For instance, on Qurban-Bayram in Tajikistan in 1957 – K. F. Tagirov, Memo, 23 Aug. 1957; GARF, f.6991, o.4, d.73, l.80.

173. The *upolnomochennyi* for Osh Oblast' composed a table giving the attendance at the five daily prayers and the Friday *jum'a-namaz* in his oblast's 14 registered mosques in 1950; the data for all prayers in all mosques showed a higher attendance in winter than in summer – I. Halimov to H. Akhtiamov, 3 Jan. 1951. A report on Islam in Dagestan in 1953 also noted that mosque attendance was considerably higher in the autumn and winter than in the spring or summer – Khabilov to I. V. Polianskii, 4 June 1954; GARF, f.6991, o.3, d.454, l.95, and d.102, l.123.

174. I. G. Halimov to CARC, 6 June 1948; GARF, f.6991, o.3, d.453, ll.52-3.

175. H. Akhtiamov, Short report, Conference of Central Asian *upolnomochennye*, 17 Dec. 1949; GARF, f.6991, o.3, d.67, ll.101 and 103.

major festival fell on a rest-day it would be significantly larger than in years when festivals coincided with regular work-days.[176]

The performance of the five daily prayers was often not observed in registered mosques, especially in rural areas, but Friday and festival services were conducted regularly in all of them. Insofar as the weekday *namaz* was performed, it was usually in winter-time, when kolkhozniki had some free time, and the more 'fanatical' – presumably elderly – believers might be excused from work in the fields.[177] In the Bashkir ASSR believers gathered for prayer only once a week in the early 1950s, DUMES Mufti Rasulev having laid down specifically that believers need come together for collective prayer only on Fridays, and during the week the republic's rural mosques were actually closed.[178] No one attended the registered mosques in the Kabardino-Balkar ASSR on ordinary weekdays in the late 1960s.[179] The daily *namaz*, however, was observed throughout the postwar period in the more traditionally religious areas of Central Asia, sometimes with a large attendance. All of Tashkent's seventeen mosques conducted daily prayers in the early 1950s.[180] One of Andijan's mosques had 800-900 worshippers on average on ordinary weekdays in 1950 and two rural mosques in Andijan Oblast' 300 and 350 respectively.[181] In Bukhara's

176. I. V. Polianskii to P. V. Kovanov, deputy head, CPSU Central Committee Department of Agitation and Propaganda, 28 June 1955. In 1956 heavy rains fell in the Fergana Valley on Uraz-Bayram, as a result of which many worshippers were unable to attend prayer-services in the registered mosques in Osh Oblast' –I. G. Halimov to CARC, 23 May 1956; GARF, f.6991, o.3, d.114, l.63, and d.457, ll.95-6. In the oblasti of Andijan and Namangan attendance also fell from 1955 to 1956, probably for the same reason, but the *upolnomochennyi* for the Uzbek SSR who reported this did not give the reason – N. I. Inogamov to I. V. Polianskii, Z. R. Rahimbaeva and G. S. Sultanov, 30 May 1956; TsGAUz, f.2456, o.1, d.186, ll.102-3. And see K. F. Tagirov, Information, 1 March 1957; GARF, f.6991, o.3, d.132, ll.35 and 52.

177. N. Abushaev, Information, 17 Nov. 1949; GARF, f.6991, o.3, d.61, l.121.

178. M. Sh. Karimov, Report, prepared for CARC session No.16, 15 Aug.1951; GARF, f.6991, o.3, d.75, ll.209-10. When Khiyaletdinov succeeded Rasulev, he sought to restore the daily *namaz* in all registered mosques – *ibid.*

179. L. Aisov to the CRA, 11 June 1968; GARF, f.6991, o.6, d.153, ll.137-8.

180. Almaev to Deputy Oblispolkom Chairman Mahkamov, Obkom Secretary Nazarov, Kh. N. Iskanderov and I. V. Polianskii, 19 Jan. 1952; TsGAUz, f.2456, o.1, d.142, l.43.

181. I. V. Polianskii to A. I. Sobolev, Information, 15 March 1951; GARF, f.6991, o.3, d.76, l.14. These figures were unusually high. The same report said that the mosque in Fergana had 150 worshippers on average, the one in Margelan

three registered mosques, on the other hand, in 1955 only 30 – 50 people on average attended daily prayers,[182] although the following year a rough estimate said that on average 100 – 300 attended daily *namaz* in Uzbekistan's urban mosques and 30 – 120 in its rural areas.[183] Presumably, like all other figures, these too grew in the heyday of the mid 1950s.

On Fridays large numbers of worshippers came to the registered mosques in Central Asia.[184] Some mosques were so massively attended on regular Fridays that many had to pray outside the building and people brought their prayer-mats with them to that end.[185] In Uzbekistan young people, too, attended Friday prayers as well as festival services.[186] In one mosque in Osh Oblast', at the Kara-Suu raion centre, which was capable of accommodating 350 worshippers, 2,000 people attended *jum'a-namaz*; 400 were able to pray in the mosque courtyard and the rest had to pray in the street, obstructing the traffic.[187] The picture in other places, however, was often very different, for instance in the rural areas of some of the North Caucasian autonomous republics and regions. All of the Kabardino-Balkar ASSR's fourteen registered mosques

---

up to 250, in Kokand up to 200, in Osh and Jambul 60 apiece, in Kzyl-Orda 30, Karaganda 25, and so on.

182. I. A. Shalaev, Information, undated [after 1 Nov. 1955]; TsGAUz, f.2456, o.1, d.174, l.91.

183. K. F. Tagirov, Information, 1 March 1957; GARF, f.6991, o.3, d.132, l.32.

184. Polianskii wrote to Sobolev on 15 March 1951, that two to three times as many worshippers came on Fridays as on regular weekdays. The figures for Tashkent show that in some mosques it was five times as many, and sometimes more – Almaev to Mahkamov *et al.*, 19 Jan. 1952. Data provided in L. A. Prikhod'ko's report for 1951, of 2 June 1952, showed an even higher multiple – GARF, f.6991, o.3, d.76, l. 14, and d.81, l.118, and TsGAUz, f.2456, o.1, d.142, l.43.

185. Even Tashkent's relatively numerous mosques were unable to accommodate their worshippers, who had to pray in adjacent squares – V. Tatarintsev to A. A. Zhdanov, 15 Nov. 1946; RTsKhIDNI, f.17, o.125, d.421, l.108.

186. Almaev to Mahkamov *et al.*, 19 Jan. 1952; TsGAUz, f.2456, o.1, d.142, l.43.

187. I. Halimov to H. Akhtiamov, 22 April 1953; GARF, f.6991, o.3, d.94, l.60. The CARC *upolnomochennyi* considered this situation inappropriate and suggested transferring the mosque to the outskirts of the *poselok*, but the executive organ, fearing it would remain without a prayer-house, did not agree.

had a Friday attendance of less than forty at the end of the 1950s, and the five which remained a decade later had less than twenty.[188]

During the *uraz* the mosques registered a much higher attendance, both on Fridays and on weekdays, especially at the late evening *tarawa-namaz*, the service held on the first ten evenings of the *uraz*, in the course of which the entire Qur'an would be recited (*khatm-i Qur'an*). This ritual, which at the beginning of the postwar period was common practice in all registered mosques, was restricted over time to those whose regular clergy were able to perform it. When the attitude of the regime was more lenient, CARC approved the invitation of *qaris*, people trained in reading the Qur'an, provided they did not live outside the oblast' and were either known to the executive organ or recommended by the spiritual directorates.[189] At such times, too, mosque attendance during the *uraz* grew considerably, many believers apparently being prepared to attend prayers 'openly and officially' and to conduct religious rites.[190]

But the largest attendance, when the mosques often drew considerable crowds, was on the two main festivals – Uraz-Bayram and Qurban-Bayram,[191] or among the Shiites during Muharram, especially on the Ashura.[192] In the cities in particular this often meant again that large numbers had to pray in the courtyard or even in the adjacent street.[193] In the late 1960s one CRA official attributed the particularly large attendance in cities where the indigenous population did not profess Islam to the mosques having become a sort of national club, the sole meeting-place for the adult Tatar, or other Muslim, inhabitants. In 1968, 75 per cent

188. N. I. Smirnov and L. A. Prikhod'ko, Resumé, 28 July 1959, and L. Aisov to the CRA, 11 June 1968; GARF, f.6991, o.3, d.184, l.223, and d.153, ll.137-8.

189. Regulations prepared for discussion by CARC's groups of inspectors and approved by CARC session No.5, 1 April 1955; GARF, f.6991, o.3, d.110, l.56. For the *tarawa-namaz*, see p.473.

190. This, at least, was the interpretation put on this development by the *upolnomochennyi* for the Uzbek SSR – N. I. Inogamov to I. V. Polianskii, Z. R. Rahimbaeva and G. S. Sultanov, 30 May 1955; TsGAUz, f.2456, o.1, d.186, l.99.

191. See pp.74-6.

192. See, for example, Khabilov to I. V. Polianskii, 4 June 1954; GARF, f.6991, o.3, d.102, ll.126-7.

193. Polianskii wrote the CPSU Central Committee that on Qurban-Bayram in 1954 this was the case in Moscow, Tashkent, Kazan', Astrakhan', Ul'ianovsk 'and other cities' – 27, Sept. 1954; GARF, f.6991, o.3, d.102, l.300.

of Moscow's Tatars attended the capital's sole mosque on the major festivals.[194]

In Central Asia, except in Kazakhstan, it was chiefly the men who attended mosque, although women and children would flock to the precincts of the mosque or its surroundings on the two major festivals. Children under eighteen were not allowed into prayer-houses by Soviet law, although here and there believers did bring their children with them to prayer-services;[195] the opposition to the participation of women in the service, on the other hand, emanated from Muslim custom and the position of the clergy. Yet in certain areas of the Soviet Union women comprised a substantial proportion of the actual worshippers, especially on festivals. Apart from Kazakhstan, where female attendance at prayer-services had been a feature of religious life already in the 1920s,[196] this held chiefly for the urban areas of the RSFSR proper and the Tatar and Bashkir ASSRs.[197] When, however, the Kazan' mosque's executive organ was asked to provide a list of women who came to the mosque on Lailat al-Qadr (Kadar-Kich), the women refused to identify themselves and their attendance in the mosque declined markedly.[198] In certain mosques, notably in Moscow and, as of the time of its registration, in Leningrad, special

194. A. Barmenkov to the CPSU Central Committee, 27 May 1968; GARF, f.6991, o.6, d.147, l.22. The letter was delivered to the General Department.

195. Polianskii informed the CPSU Central Committee in 1954 that on Qurban-Bayram some believers ignored the prohibition of the clergy to bring children to mosques – 27 Sept. 1954. In two villages in Kuibyshev Oblast' children participated in festival prayer-services in 1956 – A. S. Tazetdinov, Information, 28 Feb. 1957; GARF, f.6991, o.3, d.102, l.300, and d.132, ll.73-4. Mostly the clergy tended to endeavour to enforce the legal prohibition on bringing children to prayers and not to jeopardise the well-being and peaceful operation of their mosques by frequently reiterating restrictions imposed by state law.

196. A report of the Turgai party *ukom* (the uezd party committee) on the expanding influence of the Muslim clergy in 1926 noted: 'The mullas have set out to attract women to the mosque... In a large number of religious communities women are beginning to attend mosque. For the Kazakh woman, from the standpoint of Kazakh custom, this is a major achievement of 'freedom'" – quoted in *Preodolevaia religioznoe vliianie islama*, p.119.

197. 1,500-1,800 women reportedly attended mosque on Qurban-Bayram in 1946 in the former republic – Minutes, Conference of CARC *upolnomochennye*, 11-13 [June?] 1946; GARF, f.6991, o.3, d.39, ll.110-11. It is not clear whether the number refers just to Kazan' – where the same source said that 25-30,000 attended mosque on the festivals, or to the republic's fifteen registered mosques.

198. I. Mikhalev to the CRA, 6 May 1974; GARF, f.6991, o.6, d.545, l.214.

prayer services were organised for the women, which attracted large numbers; first organised in Moscow in 1950, they continued throughout the period under study.[199] In Azerbaijan, too, especially among the Shiite community, female participation in communal prayers was common.[200] Even in Central Asia proper there were places and instances of female participation in collective prayer.[201] In the words of CARC Chairman Puzin, many Muslim clergy, realising that the womenfolk educated the younger generation, were attracting them to prayer-services in the mosques 'with a clear conscience, in spite of the teaching of the Qur'an and the tradition of centuries'.[202] Only DUMSK persisted throughout in prohibiting female participation in prayer-services.[203]

Again, while in most areas older men comprised the overwhelming majority of worshippers, among those who came to pray on festivals there would also usually be representatives of younger age groups, people of middle age, young men and women and even sometimes adolescents. Addressing himself to this phenomenon, the CARC *upolnomochennyi* for Kazakhstan in 1946 said these younger cohorts were mostly war invalids and a few blue- and white-collar workers, including even some party members; the children were brought to prayer-services by their parents.[204] Apart from written numerical data, some *upolnomochennye* provided CARC with photographs showing the crowds who attended prayers on Uraz-Bayram and Qurban-Bayram, in which young people

199. See pp.77-8.

200. Saroyan, *Reconstructing Community*, pp.239-40; and see p.78.

201. For example, a special place was allotted to women in at least one mosque in Tashkent – V. Tatarintsev to A. A. Zhdanov, 15 Nov. 1946; RTsKhIDNI, f.17, o.125, d.241, l.108. Sixty women were among 300 worshippers who took part in the *tarawa-namaz* in one of Bukhara's three registered mosques in 1956 –N. Achilov to I. V. Polianskii, Kh. N. Iskanderov, Oblispolkom Chairman N. Mahmudov and Obkom Secretary Namazov, 18 May 1956; TsGAUz, f.2456, o.1, d.198, l.49. Similarly, 70 women worshippers participated in the Uraz-Bayram prayer-service in Frunze in 1963 – Minutes, CARC session No.31, 6 Oct. 1964; GARF, f.6991, o.4, d.147, l.143. In Uzbekistan there had also been instances of clergy letting women attend mosque in the 1920s – Keller, *The Struggle against Islam in Uzbekistan, 1921-1941*, p.373.

202. A. A. Puzin, 'Some questions of state policy regarding religion and the church and the tasks of the Council', 1958, p.32.

203. See p.143.

204. Synopsis of report of N. I. Sabitov, Conference of CARC *upolnomochennye*, Alma-Ata, 30 Sept. 1946; GARF, f.6991, o.3, d.41, ll.80-1.

often comprised the great majority.[205] A generation after the end of the war, the situation was approximately the same. Observers remarked that while on ordinary Fridays there were very few young people, they still participated in festival prayers; and not only young adults, but children as well. This held especially for Uzbekistan, Dagestan and Kirgiziia, although there were even places in the heartland of the RSFSR where there was a significant contingent of young worshippers.[206]

While some clergy complied with the regime's position regarding the younger generation, as they did on most others, and did not try to reach out to it, this was not always the case. When local party officials informed an *imam-khatib* in the Fergana Valley of the November 1954 Central Committee resolution and added that despite its positive message to believers he should tell his congregation to keep their hands off the youth and not accustom them to fulfilling religious rites, the cleric replied that the officials themselves had not understood the resolution, otherwise they would not be giving instructions that contradicted it.[207]

Attributes and activities of registered religious associations

The great majority of mosques in the Soviet Union were inevitably Sunni, as were the predominant majority of Muslim believers. But in Azerbaijan and Dagestan a number of Shiite religious societies were registered. In addition, a few mosques in both republics served both Shiite and Sunni worshippers. In the three Dagestani towns of Makhachkala, Derbent and Khasavyurt the two communities held prayer-services in a single mosque.[208] Nonetheless, the good relations which were said to exist between the two

---

205. For instance, Kh. N. Iskanderov, Information, undated [probably Sept. 1954]; TsGAUz, f.2456, o.1, d.166, ll.79-80.

206. A. Barmenkov to the CPSU Central Committee Propaganda Department, 13 March 1974, and V. A. Kuroedov to the same department, undated; GARF, f.6991, o.6, d.622, ll.12-3 and 38; and see pp.78-9.

207. U. G. Mangushev to Fergana Obkom Secretary Kambarov, Oblispolkom Chairman Rizaev, I. V. Polianskii and Kh. N. Iskanderov, 10 Dec. 1954; GARF, f.6991, o.3, d.113, ll.83-4.

208. M. S. Gajiev to A. A. Nurullaev, 27 July 1973; GARF, f.6991, o.6, d.629, l.166.

communities in Azerbaijan, do not seem to have characterised the situation in Dagestan.[209]

Most mosques were nationalised property, for all prayer-houses had been nationalised by legislation in 1918; a few mosques, however, belonged to the local authorities.[210] In both instances, the mosque would be given to the religious society for use for an indefinite period and without payment.

Those religious societies, however, which had not been able to obtain the building of a former mosque were allowed to rent a privately-owned house.[211] In the city of Molotov (Perm') in the mid 1950s the Muslim community tried to recover a former mosque, which was being used as the party archive, but the municipal authorities were not prepared to concur, suggesting that the community register with a rented building, to which the Muslims did not at first agree.[212] Such an arrangement exposed these communities in particular to the whims of local officialdom. One religious society in the oblast' of Northern Kazakhstan was closed down in 1949 for conducting prayer-services in a privately-owned home on the grounds that it did not fulfil the accepted technical requirements and that the room was not suitably isolated from the residents of the house.[213] There were other reasons, too, why the arrangement was unsatisfactory from the point of view of the religious societies. The building was usually smaller than that of the mosque they were asking to acquire, and often could not accommodate all those who came to worship even on regular Fridays. In addition, the lease was likely to expire or even be

209. I. Zakaryaev, Conference of CARC *upolnomochennye*, 14 June 1946; GARF, f.6991, o.3, d.38, ll.153-5.

210. In Soviet terminology, were 'municipalised'. In Kirgiziia, at least, some buildings of former mosques were in the immediate postwar period also in the possession of the kolkhozy, and the republican *upolnomochennyi* initiated a republican government decree declaring all mosques to be nationalised property –H. Akhtiamov, Report, 3 June 1947; GARF, f.4, d.19, ll.249-50.

211. See p.25.

212. For the complexity of the negotiations, the number of organisations involved and the arguments brought by both sides, see A. A. Murtuzov to I. V. Polianskii, 28 July 1956; also Reception by L. A. Prikhod'ko of a representative of the city's Muslims, 23 Aug. 1956 –GARF, f.6991, o.3, d.127, ll.140-1, and o.4, d.57, l.135.

213. Minutes, CARC session No.18, 30 Aug. 1949; GARF, f.6991, o.4, d.24, l.85.

arbitrarily terminated by the owner and then their tribulations would re-commence, possibly ending in their being withdrawn from registration as not having a prayer-house. Finally, the building often required refurbishing in order to be adapted for use as a mosque, and since it belonged to someone who did not necessarily see it as a mosque in the long term, permission might not be given for far-reaching changes.[214]

In a few exceptional instances a registered society was permitted to purchase a building. For example, in the village of Sairam in Southern Kazakhstan, the local authorities allowed this in place of the buildings of two former mosques, which they refused to transfer to the religious society on the grounds that one of them was next to a school and the other was in use as a storehouse of the local kolkhoz. Even then, however, they heaped obstructions in the believers' path when it transpired that the building had to be repaired.[215] Just occasionally, too, when circumstances appeared particularly propitious, a religious society would ask permission to actually build its own mosque.[216]

Nationally or municipally owned buildings could also be summarily closed or expropriated, for example on the pretext of urban reconstruction, but this was unavoidable; such were the rules of the game. Moreover, all things being equal, the local authorities were theoretically at least obliged to offer the religious society a

214. For the hardships endured by one such community, in Ul'ianovsk, where the municipal authorities occupied the former mosque and the registered religious society rented private premises for festival prayers and some 700 believers gathered to pray in courtyards of believers' homes, see I. V. Polianskii to the CPSU Central Committee and the USSR Council of Minsiters, 20 Sept. 1955, and P. A. Solov'ev to V. I. Gostev, 24 May 1956; GARF, f.6991, o.3, d.114, l.199, and d.127, ll.80-2.

215. Khojaev and Aidarbekov, chairman and secretary respectively of the executive organ, to CARC, the CARC *upolnomochennye* in Alma-Ata and Chimkent, and SADUM's *muhtasib* in Kazakhstan, 18 Aug. 1959; GARF, f.6991, o.4, d.109, ll.38-9.

216. For instance, in 1955 two representatives of the Ul'ianovsk religious society asked CARC for assistance in obtaining a plot of land upon which to build a mosque. The religious society had been renting a house, and the proprietor was unwilling to prolong the lease, which was due to expire the following month. It was explained to the applicants that CARC could not give permission either to purchase a building for use as a prayer-house or to build such a prayer-house –Reception by P. S. Basis of two members of the Ul'ianovsk *mutawaliyyat*, 15 April 1955; GARF, f.6991, o.4, d.137, ll.75-6. For the conditions in which believers were operating in Ul'ianovsk, see pp.241-2.

substitute; the official formula stipulated that whether they did or did not provide one depended on 'concrete circumstances'.[217] Thus, even though the alternative premises would usually be smaller, less suitable and less centrally situated, the very existence of the religious society was not usually at stake. The understanding that if a mosque were demolished the local organs of government were obliged to find another site guided the Southern Kazakhstan Oblispolkom to allocate a plot to the Turkestan religious society on the grounds that its mosque was on the territory of Ahmed Yasawi's tomb, which was a major centre of pilgrimage and which it was resolved to neutralise.[218] Before, however, the *oblispolkom* had decided where this plot was to be, the religious society built a mosque in the centre of town capable of accommodating 500 worshippers, to which SADUM contributed 180,000 rubles. The local government thereupon expropriated it as having been illegally built and gave the religious society alternative, dilapidated, premises in its stead.[219] In Rostov-on-Don, too, the *oblispolkom* decided to appropriate the city's sole registered mosque and use it as a crèche, contending that the number of believers had diminished and that the mosque was situated between two military encampments which could be photographed from its windows; in this case, the *oblispolkom* suggested leasing another building to the religious society, nearer to the centre.[220]

A few registered religious societies were linked not to the usual mosque but to a holy place or *mazar* (or, in the Caucasus, *pir*), which had been handed over to the spiritual directorates and whose shaykh was appointed by them.[221] Thus, eight of the nine *mazars* transferred to SADUM by a decision of the Uzbek SSR

217. See, for example, reception by CARC senior inspector N. I. Smirnov of the chairman of the Rostov-on-Don religious society's executive organ, 6 July 1961; GARF, f.6991, o.4, d.121, l.14.

218. Minutes, CARC session No.26s, 16 Oct. 1959; GARF, f.6991, o.3, d.185, ll.84 and 114-6. For this mausoleum, see p.373.

219. All-Union conference of CARC *upolnomochennye*, 18-20 April 1960; GARF, f.6991, o.3, d.208, l.121.

220. Information prepared by N. I. Smirnov for CARC session No.38, 23-24 Nov. 1960, and reception by Smirnov of the chairman of the religious society's executive organ, 6 July 1961; GARF, f.6991, o.3, d.207, ll.125-6, and o.4, d.121, l.14. The original mosque was 408 sq.m., the other building just 50 sq.m.

221. See pp.123-5.

Council of Ministers in December 1956 had mosques attached to them.[222] Since these were places of traditional sanctity and the buildings around the tomb were generally large – most of them were officially registered as historical and/or cultural monuments –these religious societies tended to be among the biggest and most important ones, drew considerable attention and were a major source of income for the spiritual directorates. Describing the ten registered *mazars* in his republic, the CARC *upolnomochennyi* for the Uzbek SSR said in late 1958 that they had between them thirteen registered clergy and a forty-strong religious *aktiv*.[223]

Once registered, Muslim religious societies, especially in the cities and in the early postwar years, were keen to demonstrate their loyalty to the state and even the benefit they might bring it. They appeared to sense, correctly, that their support of the Soviet war effort had won them points in the eyes of the regime;[224] indeed, they were generally perceived as loyal to the regime, having given up the antagonism to the Soviet regime shown it in its early years.[225] Following the statutory registration of the mosque in Petropavlovsk, for instance, its imam, who was also a member of SADUM's auditing commission, asked to be received by the *oblispolkom* chairman to thank him for opening the mosque and promise that the patriotic activity, which the religious society had initiated prior to registration, would continue.[226] SADUM representative in Kazakhstan Abdul-Jafar Shamsutdinov instructed all mullas in mid 1945 to collect money for the country's defence fund.[227]

As of mid 1947 this theme began to disappear, probably in the wake of Polianskii's specific clarification that voluntary contributions on the part of religious societies could not serve as a criterion for demonstrating their patriotism; such contributions were the

222. See Chapter 3, n.93.

223. N. I. Inogamov, Address, Conference of CARC *upolnomochennye*, 25-27 Nov. 1958; GARF, f.6991, o.3, d.165, 1.36.

224. This was stated specifically by Polianskii – see pp.552-3 and 560.

225. See, for example, I. V. Polianskii to the Council of Ministers Cultural Bureau, K. E. Voroshilov, M. A. Turkin, M. A. Suslov, and A. A. Kuznetsov, 10 June 1948; GARF, f.6991, o.3, d.53, 1.13. Compare p.14.

226. V. Liapunov to CARC and N. Sabitov, 5 July 1945 [mistakenly dated 5 June]; GARF, f.6991, o.3, d.29, 1.81. A tank had in fact been built with the moneys provided by Petropavlovsk's Muslims – *ibid.*

227. N. Sabitov, Report, 10 July 1945; GARF, f.6991, o.3, d.29, 1.99.

internal affair of these societies and neither CARC's *upolnomochennye* nor local government or other organs were to apply pressure on them to make such payments.[228] In other words, apparently, they could not consititute a criterion for estimating the 'expediency' of the existence of any given religious society. Nonetheless, some imams continued encouraging their congregations to give money for war orphans and the needy, to give to state loans and to improve the kolkhozy's productivity. Presumably, they either hoped in this way to enhance their authority among the general population, as CARC believed, or they saw this as some sort of insurance policy for their continued existence and activity.[229] Indeed, in rural areas clergy often endeavoured to demonstrate their patriotism by organising work-brigades among elderly believers who were no longer in the work force to participate in seasonal campaigns in the fields, in the cotton harvest in Central Asia and the gathering of other crops elsewhere.[230] When the involvement of the clergy in the peace movement and its affiliated activities expanded as of the early-mid 1950s, the registered religious societies showed a manifest interest in, even identification with, these foreign policy objectives, apparently out of similar considerations.[231]

Their basic loyalty to the regime notwithstanding, the Muslim religious societies were under constant supervision and surveillance and subjected to a variety of constraints. In the first place, they were by definition subordinate to the spiritual directorates, which directed their religious activity through the *fetwas* and circulars they issued periodically, especially in the run up to the *uraz* and major festivals.[232] In addition to the indirect influence CARC

228. Letter of instruction No.5, 15 April 1947; GARF, f.6991, o.3, d.49, ll.22-3.
229. Report of CARC *upolnomochennyi* for Penza Oblast', Minutes, CARC session No.9, 10 June 1948; GARF, f.6991, o.4, d.22, ll.115-6 and 124. In the late Stalin period citizens were expected to contribute annually the equivalent of one monthly wage to a so-called voluntary state loan; the last of these loans was levied in 1951. For the favourable response of local government to the clergy's economic activity and initiatives, see pp.434-5 and 645.
230. For instance, I. G. Halimov to CARC, 25 Dec. 1947, and K. Hamidov to I. V. Polianskii, 14 Dec. 1949; GARF, f.6991, o.3, d.453, l.34, and d.67, l.98.
231. See pp.175-7.
232. Some CARC officials even proposed that the spiritual directorates be allowed to disseminate their interpretations of the Shari'a among the unregistered mosques so that they too might come under its influence and be brought within the framework of activity that was somehow impacted upon by the powers-that-be,

thus exercised over the registered religious societies through the spiritual directorates, it also exposed them to direct pressures. Its *upolnomochennye* visited them periodically and met with their clergy and other officials. The reports of oblast' *upolnomochennye* told of visits they had paid to registered mosques, sometimes to attend festival or Friday prayers, sometimes to meet with clergy or other members of the *aktiv*.[233] Both the CARC offices in Moscow and the *upolnomochennye* in the localities were constantly receiving representatives from the various registered communities who came to them with requests or complaints.[234] From time to time some *upolnomochennye* even held meetings of the clergy and religious *aktiv* in the area under their jurisdiction in order to convey a particular message, or as part of a campaign against violations of the law on religion and established procedure.[235] A few *upolnomochennye* actually took advantage of their position to interfere directly in the affairs of registered mosques, contrary to their instructions. One, for example, in the Udmurt ASSR, sought to influence the choice of a mulla.[236]

---

rather than continuing to operate as they themselves thought fit – see, for example, comments of P. A. Solov'ev on Kh. Iskanderov's report, Minutes, CARC session No.11, 18-9 June 1947; GARF, f.6991, o.4, d.19, l.382. The spiritual directorates had been established, it was said by K. Ia. Pugo, in order to influence 'the Muslim religious movement', yet a situation had been created by which three quarters of Muslim activity was outside their authority – *ibid.*, l.383. For the *fetivas*, see pp.140-55.

233. See, for example, quarterly reports of *upolnomochennyi* for Osh Oblast' Halimov, who regularly described visits to a number of mosques under his jurisdiction – GARF, f.6991, o.3, dd.453-4 and 457-8 *passim*.

234. Short report, Appendix to minutes, CARC session No.5, 1 April 1955. In 1954, CARC received 258 such memos relating to the religious societies of various faiths. By early 1956 the *upolnomochennye* had received special forms on which to report these conversations including the following data: date of the reception; full name of the visitor; from which religious society and on whose initiative he had come; his position within his religious society; the questions the visitor raised; the *upolnomochennyi's* replies; comments; date the report was sent to CARC – I. G. Halimov to CARC, 10 Feb. 1956, excerpt from reception book; GARF, f.6991, o.3, d.110, ll.60 and 62, and d.457, l.54.

235. The *upolnomochennyi* for the Azerbaijan SSR, for instance, held such a meeting in Dec. 1948 with the participation of the heads and members of DUMZ, the clergy of Baku and representatives of the city's mosques' executive organs – B. Shahbazbekov, Information, undated [after 20 Oct. 1949]; GARF, f.6991, o.3, d.60, ll.30-1.

236. V. G. Furov, E. A. Tarasov, A. A. Nurullaev, G. R. Gol'st *et al.*, The

The registered religious societies were also frequently exposed to pressure on the part of the local government, specifically the *gorispolkom, raiispolkom* and militia. Fear was not just a component of the registration process; it remained a permanent feature of their everyday existence, although its dimensions varied in accordance with the characteristics and exigencies of the period and the locality.[237]

The religious activity of the registered religious societies was not limited to collective prayer-services. It also entailed the performance of various rites, some of them by definition consummated within the mosque, but most of them in the believers' own homes. These were, for the most part, life-cycle rites: name-giving, circumcision, marriage, burial and memorial services, at all of which it was customary for a member of the clergy to officiate; but where this was unfeasible, rites could be conducted by any believer who was sufficiently acquainted with the ritual. While the extent of observance of these rites varied considerably by locality and period, they were an integral part of the life of the religious society. Although life–cycle rites were practised wherever there were Muslims, it seemed that their incidence was highest in places where there were registered mosques.[238] Funerals and, in many areas, circumcision, were widespread. Despite the separation the law made between the religious establishment and the cemetery, not a few registered mosques took the cemeteries under their tutelage, expending considerable funds in order to ensure that they be adequately equipped with all the necessary utilities.[239]

shortcomings in the work of the CRA *upolnomochennyi* for the Udmurt ASSR, P. S. Zubarev, undated [1969]; GARF, f.6991, o.6, d.220, l.342.

237. See pp.664-5.

238. See, for example, T. S. Saidbaev, Information, undated [1967]; GARF, f.6991, o.6, d.73, l.199. For life-cycle rites, see Chapter 9.

239. CRA, Information, sent to the CPSU Central Committee, 22 May 1970; TsKhSD, f.5, o.62, d.38, l.33. The mosques mentioned in this connection were a number of mosques in Kuibyshev Oblast', the mosque in Volgograd Oblast', the one in Moscow and those in the Udmurt ASSR. Instances of this nature had been occurring well before this date, e.g., in the Kabardino-Balkar ASSR, where this seemed to be a common feature of mosque activity. One rural religious society gave 15,000 rubles in the early 1960s for mending the cemetery fence, for which purpose it collected 80-100 rubles from each believer – L. Zh. Aisov to A. A. Puzin, 17 Jan. 1961, and CARC to the Central Committee, handed to one Dimitruk, 22 May 1961; GARF, f.6991, o.3, d.1605, ll.2-3, and d.1363, l.92.

Sometimes registered religious societies even posted a watchman or attendant at the cemetery and undertook his maintenance.[240]

The performance of some of these rites, particularly memorial services, would entail the recital of excerpts from the Quran or of *mavluds*, read or declaimed in private homes, not only on the day known as Mavlud, the festival denoting Muhammad's birthday. (Wherever these ceremonies took place the authorities tended to consider them religious propaganda.[241]) Various occasions, in addition to sites of passage, might be denoted by such recitals, for instance the purchase or construction of a home; or they might be a component of negotiations between the families of bride and groom who met to discuss wedding arrangements. In the year 1952 there were close to 200 instances of *mavluds* being recited in private homes in Chimkent Oblast'. In Jambul one believer invited a hundred guests to such an occasion, which cost him 3,000 rubles. Sometimes the clergy who conducted the ceremony might be accompanied by a choir and musicians.[242] Another ceremony which was also observed in private homes under the auspices of the registered religious society was the *iftar*, the collective evening repast at the end of each day of the *uraz*, and here, too, clergy would mostly be present and read from the holy texts.[243] This ritual was so popular that the clergy of the registered mosques were unable to be present at all the *iftars* to which they were invited. They therefore sent in their place their muezzins or members of the religious society's executive organ and *aktiv*. In some instances, the imam would go to a believer's home during the day to read the Qur'an and bless his *iftar* in advance.[244]

Indeed, all social activity of the religious societies was stringently repressed. Thus, for instance, the collective feasting which accompanied festival prayer-services was looked upon askance by the regime and its delegates in both centre and periphery. They saw in the traditional partaking of the sheep slaughtered at the

240. For a fuller discussion of the cemeteries, see pp.518-20.

241. Kh. N. Iskanderov to Uzbekistan CP Central Committee Secretary A. A. Stal', 9 April 1954; TsGAUz, f.2456, o.1, d.166, ll.39-41.

242. V.I. Gostev to P.A. Tarasov, 4 Jan. 1954 – GARF, f.6991, o.3, d.102, ll.16-7; and *Islam v SSSR*, p.74.

243. For the *iftar*, see pp.483-5.

244. A. Barmenkov to CPSU Central Committee Propaganda Department, 13 March 1974; GARF, f.6991, o.6, d.622, l.9.

mosque on festivals a manifest attempt to attract people to the prayer-house.[245] Not only did the mosques themselves no longer prepare the traditional repasts, which accompanied the celebration of Mavlud and other festivals, but believers were discouraged from bringing to the mosque the sweetmeats they had been accustomed to take with them on festive occasions as their contribution to these happenings. There were, however, occasional exceptions, for it took time for these traditions to be eradicated. Despite instructions to the contrary by the spiritual directorate, at the Mavlud festivities in Osh in 1949, those present partook collectively of the various dishes which had been brought to the mosque. In some mosques, too, livestock were slaughtered and prepared for collective repasts.[246] In the mid 1950s in Uzbekistan there were instances of the clergy organising communal meals after prayers.[247] Still in the 1970s believers partook of collective eating and tea-drinking on the precincts of a number of mosques, at least among Shiites, for whom the mosque served, according to the CRA *upolnomochennyi* for Azerbaijan, as a sort of meeting-place or club.[248]

Philanthropic activity, or charity, one of the traditional activities of the Muslim community (as of other religious organisations), was similarly prohibited in all its manifestations. Not only were alms in all forms inconceivable under communism where there could be no paupers – it was for this reason that *sadaqa* and *zakat* were not allowed to be levied[249] – all forms of material assistance were a clear example of 'religious propaganda'. The interpretation given by the religious societies to the term charity was extremely loose and it came to comprehend both aid to indigent individuals, the time-honoured recipients of charity, and any activity which might be construed as likely to benefit the community at large, the sequel, as it were, of the patriotic activity conducted by them in the mid 1940s. One of the main ways of attracting new adherents

245. I. V. Polianskii to P. V. Kovanov, 23 June 1955; GARF, f.6991, o.2, d.114, l.29.

246. I. Halimov to CARC, undated [early April 1949]; GARF, f.6991, o.3, d.454, l.12. For the Mavlud, see pp.502-3.

247. This happened in Fergana and in one of the mosques in Khorezm Oblast' –I. V. Polianskii to the CPSU Central Committee and the USSR Council of Ministers, 20 Sept. 1955; GARF, f.6991, o.3, d.114, l.203.

248. A. F. Ahhadov to V. Kuroedov, 10 Oct. 1969, and I. Bonchkovskii to E. I. Lisavtsev, 1 June 1973; GARF, f.6991, o.6, d.220, l.25, and d.537, l.175.

249. See pp.27 and 153-4.

to religious communities, Polianskii wrote to Zhdanov in 1947, was through financial or other material assistance. In the Cherkess AO rural Muslim communities collected money among believers and offered help to people. In Khorezm Oblast' clergy collected grain and other produce in the kolkhozy, distributing it, in particular, to war invalids.[250] Over a decade later Puzin complained that nearly all religious associations engaged in charity: in a single year SADUM was said to have expended over 180,000 rubles on material assistance to the needy, while DUMES and the mosques in Moscow, Leningrad and other cities similarly distributed such aid.[251] In the early 1950s, a SADUM representative who visited the mosque in Frunze found the courtyard and the area around the gates full of destitute women and children.[252] In the late 1960s in Bukhara on Fridays and festivals people gathered around the mosques in order to beg. In fact, this seems to have been a not uncommon phenomenon. I myself encountered beggars at the Leningrad mosque on a Friday in 1979.

In the mid 1960s money collected in mosques for the construction of a bridge or waterpipe in Dagestan's rural localities was daubed by the powers-that-be as philanthropy or charity. So, too, was the organisation of collective eating at the mosque on festivals or the hiring out of crockery for weddings and other celebrations. No distinction was made between this and money actually given to 'so-called needy', as was apparently done ubiquitously in the Northern Caucasus. In Dagestan, the Kabardino-Balkar ASSR and the Karachai-Cherkess AO moneys would be collected in the mosques on festivals for the poor, and religious figures would sporadically appeal to believers to distribute money to those around them.[253] These activities were probably more common in the

250. I. V. Polianskii to A. A. Zhdanov, 7 July 1947; RTsKhIDNI, f.17, o.125, d.506, ll.148-9.

251. A. A. Puzin, Address, All-Union conference of CARC *upolnomochennye*, 18-20 April 1960; GARF, f.6991, o.3, d.208, l.13.

252. Faizullin, The trip to Frunze and Alma-Ata, 15 Sept. 1952; TsGAUz, f.2456, o.1, d.144, l.91.

253. M. S. Gajiev to A. A. Puzin, 12 July 1965, A. Barmenkov to the CPSU Propaganda Department, 17 July 1971, Kh. Salahetdinov and I. Mikhalev, Report given to E. I. Lisavtsev, 26 Oct. 1971, and A. A. Nurullaev to M. S. Gajiev, L. Zh. Aisov and A. M. Narinskii, CRA *upolnomochennye* in Dagestan, the Kabardino-Balkar ASSR and Stavropol Krai respectively, 17 Jan. 1974; GARF, f.6991, o.3, d.1488, l.46 and o.6, d. 361, ll.40-1 and 107-8, and d.625, l.11.

Northern Caucasus than elsewhere because the mosques there did not give moneys received as *fitr* or other donations to the religious centre to which they were nominally subordinate.

A further rite practised by the registered clergy was collective prayer for rain, for which they collected donations from the population; this ceremony, too, would be accompanied by communal feasting.[254] Although this rite seems to have been performed particularly in Central Asia, it took place in other parts as well. In Orenburg Oblast' believers and their mullas held prayers for rain in an open field and slaughtered several animals to prepare for a collective repast on the occasion, for which their mosque was put under lock and key and their mulla's registration was revoked.[255]

The registered religious societies also transgressed against other established procedures, if not actual law – the dividing line between the two was not always clear. Thus, for instance, in the 1940s and 1950s a number of instances were recorded where religious societies assisted one another in carrying out repairs or actually building prayer-houses, whereas when permission was given for such ventures, it was specifically stipulated that they had to be implemented solely with the means of the community concerned. CARC's *upolnomochennyi* for the Kazakh SSR brought the example of the community in Pavlodar, which had donated 5,000 rubles to the Novosibirsk community for the construction of a mosque in that city.[256] The Moscow mosque, for its part, collected money to refurbish Muslim cemeteries in a number of rural areas in Moscow Oblast', which had no registered religious society, and to assist the mosque in Endovishchi in Gor'kii Oblast'.[257] In Osh Oblast', likewise, there were cases when believers of one raion proffered material aid to a registered mosque in another raion.[258] In Ural'sk in Kazakhstan the imam and *mutawaliyyat*, the executive organ of the religious society, helped an uregistered mulla restore

254. N. Urumbaev, Address, Conference of CARC *upolnomochennye*, 25-27 Nov. 1958; GARF, f.6991, o.3, d.165, l.41. See also below and p.317.

255. Reception by N. I. Smirnov of two of the community's representatives on 23 June 1962, and of a further two on 25 Aug. 1962; GARF, f.6991, o.4, d.130, ll.32 and 35. Interestingly, the religious society concerned was an urban one, from the town of Sol'-Iletsk – see above, n.133.

256. N. Sabitov to Kh. N. Iskanderov, 18 Oct. 1947; TsGAUz, f.2456, o.1, d.108, l.61.

257. L. A. Prikhod'ko, Report, 20 May 1953; GARF, f.6991, o.3, d.91, l.250.

258. I. G. Halimov to CARC, 20 Jan. 1956; GARF, f.6991, o.3, d.457, l.17.

a *mazar*, providing him with money, building materials and means of transportation, for which the imam was withdrawn from registration and the members of the executive organ replaced.[259]

A list of violations of the legislation on religion committed by the registered societies and their clergy drawn up by the CRA in 1968 included: establishing in advance the requisite dimensions of the *fitr* and inducing the mosque *aktiv* and sometimes even unregistered clergy to collect donations; engaging in charity; extending the dimensions of mosques without permission; continued clerical interference in the financial affairs of the religious society; and the regular performance of religious rites by the chairmen of the mosques' executive organs and other activists.[260]

The law stipulated that not only was the activity of religious associations to be strictly confined to the conduct of religious rites and prayer-services, but also that it should not exceed the limits of their various 'parishes'. Just as it was not always clear whether a certain action was an integral part of the performance of religious rites, so the boundaries of the community were not necessarily agreed upon. On the whole, CARC and its *upolnomochennye* endeavoured to restrict the activity of the religious societies not solely from the point of view of content, in particular in all that concerned the economic life of the local population; they strove to limit its geographical scope as well. At the same time, there was a clear tendency, especially in areas where registered mosques were few and far between, for them to seek to extend their sphere of activity beyond the confines of their defined parish. In Kazakhstan, where there would often be just one mosque in an entire oblast', its imam would in the immediate postwar period travel extensively to the rural raiony to conduct religious and 'patriotic' activity. This was a major bone of contention between the registered religious societies and the CARC *upolnomochennye*.[261]

In this way the ongoing debate regarding communities without a registered religious society saw one side insisting on the advantage of including in the parishes of rural mosques settlements where

259. B. Jumashev, Address, All-Union conference of CARC *upolnomochennye*, 18-20 April 1960; GARF, f.6991, o.3, d.208, l.125.

260. A. Barmenkov, Theses of lecture, sent to the CPSU Central Committee Department of Propaganda, 19 June 1968; GARF, f.6991, o.6, d.147, ll.42-3.

261. See, for example, V. Liapunov to CARC and to N. Sabitov, 9 Oct. 1945; GARF, f.6991, o.3, d.30, l.210a.

there were no registered mosques, on the grounds that this provided an opportunity for putting an end to unregistered organised activity in these places.[262] Consequently, the confines of the parish were often relatively flexible. This seems to have been the case especially in the historically sedentary areas of Central Asia, where every town or large village had traditionally been divided into quarters, each quarter or *mahalla*, having its own mosque for daily prayers, believers going to a more central – *sobornaia* or *jum'a* – mosque for Friday and festival prayer-services. Since now it was out of the question to re-establish so large a quantity of mosques, and it was illegal for a single community to be served by more than one mosque, the *mahallas* had to be included in the parish of the major mosques which might be opened.[263]

Yet there were instances where the parish limits were determined precisely, and apparently peremptorily. Thus, in Turkmenistan they seem to have been fixed for all four registered mosques at an exact number of kilometres in each direction; and even within this area, only SADUM's representatives, not the mosque's actual clergy, were allowed to conduct rites.[264]

Although the link with the Muslim world outside is beyond the scope of this study, it is relevant to note that a number of mosques were visited frequently by foreign guests, both official delegations and individual tourists. This was true, in particular, of the mosques in Moscow, Leningrand and Tashkent, and, to a lesser extent, in Baku, Kazan' and Bukhara.[265] The mosques which were on the established itinerary of foreigners were able to improve

262. See, for example, Report of CARC's *upolnomochennyi* for Penza Oblast', Minutes, CARC session No.9, 10 June 1948; GARF, f.6991, o.4, d.22, l.116.

263. See, for example, H. Akhtiamov, Report, Conference of CARC *upolnomochennye*, Alma-Ata, 30 Sept. 1946; GARF, f.6991, o.3, d.41, l.109. In an early circular to the republic's oblast' *upolnomochennye*, CARC's *upolnomochennyi* for the Uzbek SSR, I. Ibadov, wrote that they must list the *mahallas* which a mosque that believers were applying to open or register would serve – 6 Oct. 1944; GARF, f.6991, o.3, d.4, l.72.

264. Rahim Muhammadiev and Abdurahman Sharipov, SADUM's temporary representative in Turkmenistan and member of its inspection committee respectively, to Ishan Babakhan, 21 Nov. 1953 – TsGAUz, f.2456, o.1, d.162, l.56.

265. The mosque in Kazan', for example, was visited in 1956 by 12 groups of foreign tourists, in 1957 by 17, in 1958 by 19 and in 1959 by 9 – N. I. Smirnov, Information on the 'Marjani' mosque in Kazan' and the construction in its courtyard of a new building in September-October 1958, 16 Jan. 1960; GARF, f.6991, o.3, d.204, l.38.

their physical and material condition with greater ease than could most mosques. Indeed, the ground floor of the Kazan' mosque, which had been occupied as a storeroom by a local artel, was restored to it after a derogatory remark by the Turkish ambassador, who visited there in June 1955, on the appearance of the courtyard. Subsequently, in 1958, an additional building was constructed in the courtyard to serve as a cloakroom, office and reception centre for foreigners out of similar considerations.[266]

The clergy

In many areas there was from the beginning of the postwar period a serious dearth of Muslim clergy. The disinclination of potential candidates to serve as clergy for lack of financial incentive was only one of several reasons. In some areas no applications to open mosques were filed at all because there was no one fit to serve as mulla.[267] In Azerbaijan, where eighteen mosques were registered between mid 1944 and mid 1946, no clerics could be found for most of them; large numbers of clergy had been deported before the war and the republic simply had no cadres from whom to choose the appropriate personnel.[268]

There were also places where the mullas were apprehensive and the registration of religious societies could not proceed because they were unwilling to fulfil that role. The *upolnomochennyi* for the Tatar ASSR reported in 1947 that he had registered only fifteen of the republic's fifty functioning mosques because mullas were afraid of repeating the experience of 1937 when nearly all mullas were sent into exile. Those who had returned now worked in kolkhozy, had their own plots and cows and were not prepared to risk everything a second time.[269] One former mulla in the Bashkir ASSR seems actually to have been threatened that if he

266. *Ibid.*, ll.36–45.

267. For example, in Sverdlovsk Oblast', see F. Berezin, Report, 9 July 1945; GARF, f.6991, o.3, d.25, ll.170–170ob.

268. B. Shahbazbekov, Address, Conference of CARC *upolnomochennye*, Rostov-on-Don, 14 June 1946; GARF, f.6991, o.3, d.38, ll.96 and 168. Shahbazbekov said clergy could not be found for 8–12 of the mosques.

269. Report of Bagaev, Minutes, CARC session No.7, 23–24 April 1947; GARF, f.6991, o.4, d.19, l.188. For doubts entertained by mullas in the Kabardinian ASSR at this time, see p.191 above.

applied to open the local mosque, which was not in use, he would be excluded from his kolkhoz.[270] Such incidents and the fear rampant among the mullas, which not only deterred some from agreeing to serve in the registered mosques but persisted among those who concurred in filling the post of imam or *imam-khatib*, confirmed the impression of CARC's officials in Moscow that in certain areas government organs exerted administrative pressure in order to contain Muslim religious activity.[271]

At the same time, in a few places there seem to have been no lack of people both able and willing to serve as mullas or imams, including even younger cohorts. In Osh Oblast', for instance, in the immediate postwar years there were reported to be an ample number of candidates, especially among the Uzbeks. CARC's *upol-nomochennyi* there saw how SADUM's qazi in Kirgiziia examined four Uzbeks in their early to mid-thirties, who had learned the Qur'an by heart under the guidance of older mullas.[272] Similarly in 1946, eight of the twenty registered mosques in Tashkent Oblast' (excluding the city of Tashkent) boasted both an imam and a *khatib* or *imam-khatib*, as well usually as a muezzin.[273] Nor do there appear to have been difficulties in finding clergy for the registered mosques in Dagestan, where in the mid 1950s the twenty-six registered mosques boasted fifty-three clerical personnel (qazis and muezzins).[274]

Islam, however, does not require that those performing as clergy be in any way ordained, but simply that they know the basics of the faith and its ritual. As a result, at least among Sunnis, in areas where there were no trained professional clergy, the religious

270. M. Sh. Karimov to I. V. Polianskii and S. A. Vagapov, 8 Oct. 1945; GARF, f.6991, o.3, d.26, l.13.

271. N. I. Abushaev and V. G. Sokolov, commenting on Bagaev's report (on the Tatar ASSR) – CARC session No.7, 23-24 April 1947; GARF, f.6991, o.4, d.19, ll.196 and 199. For a further example, see n.279 below. For a further discussion of unduly antagonistic conduct by local government organs, see pp.651-75.

272. I. Halimov to H. Akhtiamov, 9 May 1947; GARF, f.6991, o.3, d.453, l.7.

273. K. Mustafin, List of registered mosques, 15 July 1946; TsGAUz, f.2456, o.1, d.81, ll.20-25. See also p.66.

274. Khabilov to I. V. Polianskii, 4 June 1954; GARF, f.6991, o.3, d.102, l.123. As we have seen, it was a moot question whether muezzins were to be considered clergy or not, see p.125.

society would elect someone from among its midst, an elder who had some knowledge of the Qur'an (parts of which he had learned by heart) and some idea how to conduct the *namaz* and other religious rites. In the Bashkir ASSR, where thirteen mosques were opened officially in 1944-5, six of the mullas had held that position before the mass closure of mosques in 1930 and seven were chosen by general meetings of worshippers and confirmed by examination by the mufti; seven of the thirteen were kolkhozniki.[275] As time passed, the proportion grew markedly of clergy who were not professionals but took up, or were appointed to, jobs as clergy as they became pensioners.[276] This did not apply among the Shiites (most of whom resided in Azerbaijan), for whom the *akhund* had to be a generally recognised authority, to be worthy of those who stood behind him in prayer; in their communites, if there was no such cleric there would simply be no collective prayer.[277]

In periods of religious repression, believers were less likely to pay for the clergy's upkeep, and members of the clergy – as a result both of financial constraints and social or official pressures – tended to renounce their jobs. Some seem to have done so specifically as a result of the lack of financial support.[278] The obvious risk of taking on a clerical post in such conditions, moreover, made it very difficult to find others to take the place of clergy who had resigned or died or left their jobs for any other reason. In Ul'ianovsk Oblast' in 1950 there were sixteen registered mosques, but just thirteen registered mullas. While the three which had no minister of religion, a CARC official pointed out, could not be closed summarily, but had to be given a specific time period in which to find a mulla, if they failed to do so by the end of this time they would be withdrawn from registration.[279] A year later,

275. M. Sh. Karimov to I. V. Polianskii and Chairman of the Bashkir ASSR SNK S. A. Vagapov, 8 Oct. 1945; GARF, f.6991, o.3, d.26, ll.7-9.

276. Ashirov, *Evoliutsiia islama v SSSR*, p.12.

277. A. F. Akhadov to V. A. Kuroedov, 10 Oct. 1969; GARF, f.6991, o.6, d.220, l.25.

278. CARC's *upolnomochennyi* for Osh Oblast' reported in 1948 that three clergy said they had left their posts for this reason – I. Halimov to CARC, 6 June 1948; GARF, f.6991, o.3, d.453, l.53.

279. P. F. Simonov, Report, and comments of N. I. Abushaev, Minutes, CARC session No.4, 4-5 April 1950; GARF, f.6991, o.3, d.66, ll.32-3 and 44. Simonov noted that of the 13 mullas, only five had served as mullas in the past, whereas the others had been chosen by the societies' believers, and all were over 60. It

by which time the three mosques had in fact been withdrawn from registration, two more were without clergy and the *upol-nomochennyi* considered that one of them at least had to be withdrawn from registration.[280] In the rural areas of the Tatar ASSR and in the Kabardinian ASSR and Stavropol' Krai a number of communities had no clergy for considerable periods in the early-mid 1950s.[281] Believers in not a few localities in the Soviet Union's European regions and in the Northern Caucasus, who refused to maintain a mosque, were asking to be allowed a registered cleric to perform rites in private homes and conduct collective prayer services on the two main festivals.[282]

The number of clergy attached to any single mosque was supposed to be the internal matter of its believers, who would decide in accordance with the size of the believer population that attended the mosque and whose religious needs the clergy had to meet, and with the extent of the territory given over to its jurisdiction. CARC did not favour an excess of clerical personnel, arguing that if the clergy were not fully preoccupied within the precincts of the mosque, they would indulge in propagating religion.[283] Presumably this was also the inclination of the registered society itself, since the believers were responsible for paying their clergy's upkeep. At the same time, CARC was of the opinion – certainly in the more lenient years – that in mosques where one minister of religion was physically incapable of satisfying the believers' religious needs, there were no grounds for refusing to register a second cleric.[284]

---

later transpired that the chairman of a certain *raiispolkom* had decided to shut down all the mosques in his raion and to that end had summoned their mullas and given them a choice between resigning their posts 'voluntarily' or being taxed with an 'unbearably' high tax. They chose the first alternative and all three informed the *upolnomochennyi* of their resignation – Minutes, CARC session No.6, 1 March 1951; GARF, f.6991, o.3, d.74, l.87. For a similar threat in another republic, see pp.664-5.

280. *Ibid.*, l.82. For the withdrawal from registration of Muslim religions associations in Ul'ianovsk Oblast', see pp.200-1.

281. L. A. Prikhod'ko, Report, 20 May 1953; GARF, f.6991, o.3, d.91, l.258.

282. *Ibid.*

283. I. V. Polianskii to Kh. N. Iskanderov, 13 Sept. 1950; TsGAUz, f.2456, o.1, d.131, l.74.

284. Regulations prepared for discussion by CARC's group of instructors and approved by CARC session No.5, 1 April 1955; GARF, f.6991, o.3, d.110, l.55.

All in all, while there were more registered clergy than registered mosques, the proportion differed from period to period: in the first two postwar decades their number usually exceeded that of the mosques by between 10 and 20 per cent; by the early 1970s, they were over 70 per cent more, and a decade later nearly three times as many.[285] Significantly, the number of clergy, which declined more than that of the mosques in the years 1948-52, picked up much more quickly.[286] The reason would seem to be that in the years of less religious oppression, for example 1955-7, there was more incentive for the individual to serve as a minister of religion and it was easier for the religious society to employ more than one cleric, while in harder times the opposite was true.[287]

The level of education, religious and secular, of most clergy in the entire postwar period was low, the lack of professional clergy being hardly made up for by the one, or later two, *medreses* which prepared new cadres, and their age was disproportionately high.[288] In some parts, such as the Cherkess AO, the level of literacy among the clergy was so low that they were said to be unable to fill in correctly the documentation necessary for their registration.[289] (It is possible that this referred specifically to illiteracy in Russian in which the forms were drawn up.) Despite the efforts of the spiritual directorates to ensure that clergy be appointed who were reasonably knowledgeable in dogma and to improve

285. For more precise data, see pp.66-7.

286. In 1952 there was reported to have been just one more cleric than there were mosques, whereas by 1957 there were 483 as against 398, or over 20 per cent more. Altogether in 1957, there were 513 registered clergy, but 30 of them seem to have been attached to the spiritual directorates without any direct affiliation to a mosque: in a report to the CPSU Central Committee CARC noted that there were 513 registered clergy, but someone added in pencil, 483 –A. A. Puzin to K. I. Chernenko, undated; GARF, f.6991, o.3, d.148, l.10.

287. Thus, by early 1955 even in Uzbekistan most mosques appear to have had just one minister of religion, so SADUM applied for permission to once again have two per every large mosque in order for the registered clergy to be able to cope with all the rites which had to be conducted – SADUM to Kh. N. Iskanderov, 25 Feb. 1955, and I. A. Shalaev to I. V. Polianskii, Chairman of the Uzbek SSR Council of Ministers N. A. Muhitdinov and Uzbekistan Party Secretary Kh. G. Gulamov, 28 Feb. 1955; TsGAUz, f.2456, o.1, d.178, ll.47 and 49.

288. For details, see pp.67-8.

289. V. V. Bulatov to I. V. Polianskii, 29 June 1945; GARF, f.6991, o.3, d.25, l.56. And see p.117.

the religious education of those already registered, the choice of candidates became increasingly limited as the years passed and the quality of the clergy deteriorated.[290] Not only were not a few clergy unable to recite the Qur'an by heart; in many cases their level of religiosity seems also to have been highly questionable. The reservations expressed by SADUM regarding some of the clergy's religious observance and devotion to their pastoral duties were surely well founded and not just the rantings of a religious centre trying to impose its authority.[291]

Their low level of education and advanced years notwithstanding, the registered Muslim clergy were thought to wield considerable influence, not only among believers, but even on some of the non-believing population. Most of them were inhabitants of the localities in which they officiated and had spent many years working in kolkhozy or low-grade administrative positions. Some of them were not yet pensioners and were still in employment.[292] Thus, the clergy knew the general mood and the views and interests of the population at large, as well as believers' spiritual needs. All these they took into consideration, adapting themselves to the changed conditions. They knew that although most of their active parishioners were old and illiterate or barely literate, they lived together with their children and grandchildren, who worked in collectives or studied in educational institutions, and were under the influence of the Soviet way of life. This awareness was manifest in their interpretations and sermons, which reflected the attitudes and concerns of their audience. Moreover, they met with their flock both in the mosque and in private homes, where many religious rites were performed. As a result of this, and of what the authorities perceived as their careful catering to the interests of their parishioners, the clergy were able to extend their influence to the womenfolk and youth as well, even if indirectly.[293]

290. CRA information, sent to the CPSU Central Committee, 27 April 1971; TsKhSD, f.5, o.63, d.89, ll.99-100. See also pp.133 and 163.

291. See p.134.

292. When registration of clergy began in the mid 1940s, those still in employment asked to be exonerated from work, as their religions duties caused them to arrive late at work or even to miss workdays – V. V. Bulatov to I. V. Polianskii, 29 June 1944; GARF, f.6991, o.3, d.25, l.58. It would appear that, at least in rural areas where communities were mostly small, these requests were not complied with.

293. CRA information, sent to the CPSU Central Committee, 27 April 1971; TsKhSD, f.5, o.63, d.89, l.98; and S. Agafonov to A. A. Nurullaev, 14 May

The ways the clergy were considered by the secular authority to exert influence were sundry. They read out in the mosques the letters circulated by the spiritual directorates before the advent of the festivals that called upon Muslims to observe the precepts of their religion and especially to attend mosque. They preached on Fridays, particularly as the festivals drew near, and on festive occasions. They invited prestigious *qaris* to recite the Qur'an in the mosques during the fast. They would spread the news that prior to the actual festival service an emissary from the spiritual directorates would be speaking on a theme that was of interest to the public. They participated in *tois*, the entertainment which accompanied circumcisions or weddings. Finally, they spread rumours to the effect that pilgrimages to Muslim shrines helped cure illnesses, would redeem a person from the difficulties of his or her everyday life and would bring about the fulfilment of people's wishes.[294]

An indicator of this influence was that, despite persistent constraints and deterrents, the number of people who approached registered clergy to perform rites of passage seems to have increased constantly as of the later 1960s. One report from 1970 said the rising statistics reflected not only improved reporting on the activity of the registered religious societies, but 'the further democratisation of public life and prevalent opportunities to satisfy one's religious needs'.[295] They were surely also a result of the growth in the number of registered clergy.

Occasionally, too, a registered cleric might be a charismatic personality, whose dynamism would impact upon the life of his community. The popularity and influence of Alimkhantura Shakirkhojaev was thought to be the reason that the Muslim community in Tokmak (Kirgiziia) which had had 2-300 believers when it began activity in 1943, reached 1,200 in 1946.[296] The *imam-khatib* of the Leningrad mosque, Abdulbari Isaev, who had

---

1974; GARF, f.6991, o.6, d.630, l.317. For the clergy's preaching activity, see below.

294. I. V. Polianskii to P. V. Kovanov, 28 June 1955; GARF, f.6991, o.3, d.114, l.63.

295. CRA report, sent to the CPSU Central Committee, 22 May 1970; TsKhSD, f.5, o.62, d.38, l.5.

296. H. Akhtiamov, Report, Conference of CARC *upolnomochennye*, Alma-Ata, 30 Sept. 1946; GARF, f.6991, o.3, d.41, l.103. Shakirkhojaev was a member of SADUM.

led the protracted struggle to register the city's Muslim religious community, seems to have been another such minister; he later became chairman of DUMES (1974-80).[297] The participation in prayer-services, particularly on festivals, of members of the spiritual directorates, the recognised leaders of the religious establishment, also drew large crowds and was thought to be a further indicator of clerical influence.[298]

Just as there were moot points in connection with the registration of mosques, so were there in regard to the clergy. Thus, for example, the *upolnomochennyi* for Osh Oblast' registered not only full-fledged clergy – imams, *khatibs* and *imam-khatibs* – but also muezzins or *sufis*, as they were called in Kirgiziia, for which the republican *upolnomochennyi* called him to order, instructing him to take back the certificates of the last category.[299] Some *upolnomochennye* entertained doubts about registering clergy who had been convicted by Soviet Courts and/or served prison terms.[300]

For the most part, the activity of the registered clergy was carried on within the confines of their mosques. Here they conducted *namaz* and preached, performed other rites, such as funeral services (although the majority of these were not held in the mosque), and collected money for the needs of the mosque and the spiritual directorate. At the same time, there were rites which registered clergy were allowed as standard practice to perform outside the mosque, even in certain periods beyond the confines or zone of service of their 'parish', provided that they received a specific invitation from believers[301] and, of course, that they

297. See account of celebrations held in honour of his fiftieth birthday shortly after registration of the religious society – Shahametov and Fakhrutdinov to L. A. Prikhod'ko, 4 Feb. 1957; GARF, f.6991, o.4, d.86, ll.9-12.

298. The nonagenarian Babakhan, for example, regularly led prayer-services in Tashkent during *uraz* in the early 1950s and visited private homes to recite the Qur'an – I. V. Polianskii to A. I. Sobolev, 15 March 1951; GARF, f.6991, o.3, d.76, l.15.

299. H. Akhtiamov to I. Halimov, 21 July 1947; GARF, f.6991, o.3, d.453, l.17. The muezzin was called *sufi, sopi* or *sopake* by common folk in Kirgiziia – I. Halimov to H. Akhtiamov, 19 Sept. 1947; GARF, f.6991, o.3, d.453, l.20.

300. Minutes, Instructional meeting of CARC *upolnomochennye* in the Uzbek SSR, 15-17 March 1956; TsGAUz, f.2456, o.1, d.183, l.60. When asked by one of the oblast' *upolnomochennye*, the republican *upolnomochennyi* said this did not present a problem. This was not necessarily true, see n.362 below.

301. See, for example, I. G. Halimov, Report, undated [April 1949?], and Reception by L. A. Prikhod'ko of the mulla of the Moscow mosque, Ismail

reported their resultant income. Basically, this related to life-cycle rites – marriages, funerals and circumcisions (although not all clerics performed circumcisions) – and the recital of excerpts from the Qur'an as part of the memorial rite conducted in the home of the deceased on certain fixed days.[302] Even in periods of relative leniency toward religion registered clergy were not supposed to go outside their oblast' or to take part in collective prayer in any locality they might visit in this connection.[303]

In certain periods and places, however, performance of rites further afield was not permitted. For example, in Turkmenistan in the mid 1950s registered clergy were strictly forbidden to conduct prayers at the graveside. This aroused protest at having to bring the body of the deceased long distances before burial so that the requisite prayers be recited in the mosque. The CARC *upol-nomochennyi* argued that allowing the conduct of prayers and the receipt of money outside the mosque was tantamount to opening a second mosque in the area.[304] CARC itself took exception to this, insisting that it differentiated between a registered cleric going on his own initiative to private homes and to different raiony, by which he artificially augmented the religious mood of believers, and being invited to perform a specific religious rite.[305]

The official subordination of the registered clergy to the spiritual directorates and their republican or oblast' representatives was the product of the system imposed by the central leadership which the former had perforce to accept. Yet this was one field where not a few clergy found the framework in which they had perforce to operate arbitrary and even unacceptable. Some clerics, especially in certain parts of Central Asia, were openly critical of the spiritual directorates and their leaders – especially with regard to their financial dealings and their directives on questions of dogma and ritual

Mushtareev, and the secretary of its executive organ, Hamza Aisin, 22 Jan. 1955 –GARF, f.6991, o.3, d.454, l.10, and o.4, d.137, l.12.

302. This was popularly referred to as *khatm-i Qur'an*, which literally meant completing the reading of the entire Qur'an; see p.84.

303. Regulation prepared for discussion by CARC's group of instructors, approved by CARC session No.5, 1 April 1955; GARF, f.6991, o.3, d.110, ll.55-6.

304. Rahim Muhammadiev and Abdurahman Sharipov, respectively SADUM's temporary representative and head of its inspection committee in the Turkmen SSR, to Ishan Babakhan, 21 Nov. 1953; TsGAUz, f.2456, o.1, d.162, l.56.

305. I. V. Polianskii to A. M. Komekov, 18 Jan. 1954; TsGAUz, f.2456, o.1, d.162, l.55.

–to the point of open recalcitrance.[306] Despite these reservations regarding the senior echelons of the establishment, the clergy in the registered mosques were generally regarded by the secular authority, at least in periods of relative goodwill on the part of the regime toward the religious establishment, as fundamentally loyal to the state and as aspiring to operate within the framework of the law. In addition to their connections with the spiritual directorates, they maintained regular contact, at least in theory, with the local CARC *upolnomochennyi*. In some parts, at least, they reported to him on a weekly basis to inform him how the Friday service had passed and to ask him about issues requiring clarification.[307] These ties with the CARC *upolnomochennyi* were designed to achieve agreement on, and solution of, issues connected with their practical work,[308] in acordance with the terms of reference of CARC's *modus operandi*.

Sometimes, too, an imam maintained such manifest links with the local organs of government as to be actually repugnant to the secular power. For instance, the imam of Kokand was dismissed by SADUM at the instigation of CARC's republican *upolnomochennyi* for highlighting his links with the MGB, as a result of which believers boycotted the registered mosque and went to prayer-services conducted by unregistered clerics.[309]

Inevitably, however, despite the intensity of their ties with the powers-that-be and their basic acceptance of the regime and its routine, the clergy tended to become involved in activity that could only be considered transgressive by anyone in the official world who might seek to implement the letter of the law. In periods when they sensed that the central power was comparatively lenient, it seemed that they were out to try their luck; in others, almost everything they did within the framework of their office was likely to be construed as unlawful.

Not a few of the misdeeds laid at the door of the religious

306. See pp.128-33.

307. I. V. Polianskii to all *upolnomochennye*, Letter of instruction No.7, Appendix, CARC Session No.15, 24-25 Aug. 1947; GARF, f.6991, o.4, d.22, ll.196-7.

308. N. Sabitov, Report, 15 Dec. 1949, prepared for conference of Central Asian *upolnomochennye*, Tashkent, 17 Dec. 1949; GARF, f.6991, o.3, d.67, ll.134-5.

309. Report of CARC *upolnomochennyi* for the Uzbek SSR, apparently prepared for conference of CARC *upolnomochennye*, 8 Oct. 1946; GARF, f.6991, o.3, d.41, l.196.

societies were linked directly with their clergy. One of the most frequent transgressions was exceeding the boundaries of their parish.[310] Another was the enlargement of their mosques, the original dimensions of which were often totally inadequate in light of the new needs: buildings which had, when they were built, been intended for the inhabitants of a small locality, perhaps even just a *mahalla*, and had been one of a large number of mosques in the town, now might have to serve not only the entire town but also neighbouring rural settlements. Many reports spoke of prayer-services which had to be conducted in the mosque courtyard or a nearby street because the mosque could not accommodate all the worshippers even on ordinary Fridays, not to speak of festivals. The clergy, therefore, with the help of the executive organ, would look for ways and means to enlarge the building. This was usually implemented in the process of repairing the mosque, sometimes embarked upon with official permission, in the course of which the building might be totally reconstructed. On occasion, the purchase or annexing of neighbouring houses or plots would be undertaken. In Tashkent Oblast' the capacity of three mosques was thus enhanced in 1947, two of them also adding minarets from which to summon worshippers to prayer (the *azan*).[311] In 1956 two mosques in Dagestan also extended their precincts.[312] And in subsequent years every single mosque in Tashkent, where there were twenty-two registered mosques, added to its premises. By 1960 eleven mosques in one raion of the city were said to have at their disposal an aggregate area four times as large as they had had when they registered in the mid 1940s.[313] So, too, did at least two mosques in Chimkent Oblast' in Kazakhstan[314] and two further

310. See below pp.270-1.
311. Nasretdinov to Obkom Secretary Nurudinov and Oblispolkom Chairman Isamuhamedov, 10 Sept. 1947; TsGAUz, f.2456, o.1, d.142, ll.55 ff. ob. Nasretdinov noted in passing the complaints of believers at the frequent collections of money for these works.
312. G. F. Frolov, Information, 22 Feb. 1957; GARF, f.6991, o.3, d.132, l.77. The two mosques were in the towns of Buinaksk and Khasavyurt.
313. Addresses of A. A. Puzin and of Sh. K. Shirinbaev, All-Union conference of CARC *upolnomochennye*, 18-20 April 1960; GARF, f.6991, o.3, d.208, ll.7-8 and 75. The 22 mosques included two *mazars* and the Barak-Khan Medrese.
314. A. Barmenkov, CRA resolution 'On the work of its *upolnomochennyi* for Chimkent Oblast', Sh. O. Ospanov', draft, Aug. 1969; GARF, f.6991, o.6, d.290, l.84.

mosques in Dagestan, one of which built two galleries, thus doubling its capacity, and the other a minaret. A third laid a new floor and built a terrace, where collective eating took place on festivals.[315]

Here and there clergy in registered mosques were thought actually to be *ishans*, belonging to Sufi brotherhoods. One of these, a mulla of a rural mosque in Kuibyshev Oblast', was said to have his own adepts, or *murids*.[316] Other clergy were said to practise and encourage a variety of superstitions. The mulla in Kirovabad, in the Azerbaijan SSR, was dismissed from his post for composing prayers against various ailments and diseases and taking money from believers for doing so.[317] The leading cleric at the Goy-imam *pir* in Azerbaijan was withdrawn from registration for letting various 'shady' characters settle on its grounds; these individuals had allegedly robbed pilgrims, taking advantage of their religions feelings, and 'surreptitiously' sold them sand from the *pir* precincts and hung portraits of saints on the grounds.[318] One imam sent three members of his mosque's *aktiv* to investigate a matter of inheritance according to Shari'a law, encroaching upon the functions of the Soviet court;[319] while in Dagestan a qazi was withdrawn from registration for performing a divorce according to the Shari'a in violation of Soviet legislation.[320]

A few clergy, especially apparently in the Fergana Valley, simply did not try to accommodate the regime. One mulla in Namangan told believers in the latter half of the 1950s that it was a sin to listen to songs broadcast over the radio as well as to other transmissions; this was said to have aroused expressions of dissatisfaction among those present and the imam was dismissed. In Andijan Oblast' two other imams advocated 'superstititous practices' in their sermons, and one of them, too, lost his job.[321]

315. Kh. Salahetdinov and I. Mikhalev, Report, given to E. I. Lisavtsev, 26 Oct. 1971; GARF, f.6991, o.6, d.361, ll.108-9.

316. See p.403.

317. M. M. Shamsadinskii, Address, All-Union conference of CARC *upolnomochennye*, 18-20 April 1960; GARF, f.6991, o.3, d.208, l.114.

318. N. I. Smirnov, Information, 8 Aug. 1962; GARF, f.6991, o.3, d.1390, l.20.

319. H. Akhtiamov, Address, All-Union conference of CARC *upolnomochennye*, 18-20 April 1960; GARF, f.6991, o.3, d.208, l.135.

320. M. S. Gajiev, Report, Minutes, CARC session No.24, 27 Aug. 1964; GARF, f.6991, o.4, d.147, ll.81-2

321. N. Inogamov, Address, Conference of CARC *upolnomochennye*, 26-27 Nov. 1958; GARF, f.6991, o.3, d.165, l.81.

The registered clergy were frequently accused of conducting 'religious propaganda' in order to attract non-believers, especially young people, to religion. This was an issue upon which there could hardly be agreement between the clergy and the secular power. The latter placed within this category a wide range of activities which the former could not but see as an integral part of their duties. One of CARC's letters of instruction to its *upol-nomochennye* defined the three most widespread forms of religious propaganda – not only in Islam – as group teaching, individual per-suasion and material assistance.[322] In the words of one CARC inspector in 1949, reading the Qur'an in private homes was not propaganda in the sense that it was tantamount to agitating against the Soviet regime in any way, yet it was religious agitation insofar as it evoked religious feelings among believers. Nonetheless, it was impossible to prohibit visits by clergy to private homes to perform urgent rites. It was therefore essential to differentiate be-tween agitation and propaganda, on the one hand, and the in-alienable components of the faith, on the other.[323] The practice of clergy in Tashkent Oblast' who held conversations with individual believers, telling them that if they did not fulfil all the precepts of the faith prescribed in the Qur'an, they would in the afterlife be tortured in hell clearly belonged to the former category.[324]

Even the reading of excerpts from the Qur'an at funerals, although this was standard practice and an official ingredient of the service, was sometimes said to comprise religious propaganda. One imam in Osh was reported to be taking advantage of funerals to preach on religious themes and the need for belief in God. Here he could reach out to people, including youth and children, who normally would not hear sermons because they did not attend mosque, and influence the minds of people at their time of mourn-ing.[325] A CRA report to the Central Committee in 1970 dwelt

322. Letter of instruction No.7, undated, Appendix No.3, CARC session No.15, 24-25 Aug. 1947; GARF, f.6991, o.4, d.22, l.201. For material assistance, i.e. charity, see pp.234-5 above.

323. N. I. Abushaev, Minutes, Instructors' meeting No.26, 1-2 Dec. 1949; GARF, f.6991, o.3, d.60, l.83.

324. Kh. N. Iskanderov to Uzbekistan Communist Party Central Committee Secretary A. A. Stal', 9 April 1954, and to Tashkent Obkom Secretary A. Alimov and Tashkent Oblispolkom Chairman Jalilov, 27 May 1954; TsGAUz, f.2456, o.1, d.166, l.39, and d.162, ll.174-5.

325. H. Akhtiamov, Address, All-Union conference of CARC *upolnomochennye,*

on the frequent use of ritual, specifically the burial service, to propagate 'religious ideology' as it was accompanied by the reading of prayers and passages from the Qur'an. Prior to the act of ritual purification, a prayer was read in the presence of believers. The ritual cleansing of the body was similarly accompanied by prayers, and yet another was read following its wrapping in a shroud. The deceased person was then brought to the mosque, where the *jinaz*, the burial rite, was performed in the presence of a large number of parishioners and relatives. Prayers were read at the cemetery as well before the actual burial. Finally, a mulla had to be present at the memorial ceremony conducted on the third, seventh, twentieth and fortieth day after death, and he would take advantage of these occasions to 'propagate Islamic ideology' among the considerable numbers who gathered to respect the memory of the deceased.[326]

The mullas' readings from the Qur'an and preaching at *iftars* were looked upon as a further instance of religious propaganda. The very presence of young family members and relatives at these collective feasts denoting the end of the day of fasting, by definition placed anything uttered at them by the clergy in the category of propaganda, for they were propagating religion among non-believers. This ceremony and its concomitant propaganda impact continued to be noted throughout the period under study. For, it was contended, the *iftars*, which were held in some Central Asian oblasti in every kishlak and *mahalla*, gave the clergy the opportunity to influence a meaningful section of the population.[327]

Finally, any enhancement of religions activity, for example on the eve of the *uraz* or festivals, was necessarily interpreted by the regime as an endeavour to augment Islam's popularity and therefore

---

18-20 April 1960; GARF, f.6991, o.3, d.208, ll.134-5.

326. CRA information, sent to the CPSU Central Committee, 22 May 1970, 22 May 1970; TsKhSD, f.5, o.62, d.38, l.29.

327. Kh. N. Iskanderov to Uzbekistan Communist Party Central Committee Secretary A. A. Stal', 9 April 1954, and to Tashkom Obkom Secretary A. Alimov and Oblispolkom Chairman Jalilov, 27 May 1954; TsGAUz, f.2456, o.1, d.166, ll.39-41 and d.162, ll.174-9. And A. Barmenkov to the CPSU Central Committee Propaganda Department, 13 March 1973 and 13 March 1974; GARF, f.6991, o.6, d.537, ll.15-6, and d.622, l.10. In the first of these documents Barmenkov noted that in the previous year the registered clergy of Tashkent participated in 662 *iftars*, those of Bukhara Oblast' in 100, and those of the Tatar ASSR in over 400. See also pp.81 and 483-5.

as religious propaganda, the manifest goal being to attract larger numbers of believers to the prayer-services in the mosque. It was within this context that CARC officials noted instances where registered clergy organised the playing of music from the roof of a mosque to draw people to the evening *tarawa-namaz* or to notify the population of the approach of a festival.[328]

The sermon

The ambivalence of the clergy's position, as they sought to find the golden path between manifest loyalty to the regime and observance of the basics of their faith, was epitomised in the sermon, the *khutba*, which was traditionally an integral component of the Friday and festival prayer-service. The clergy in their mosques faced the same basic dilemma as did the spiritual directorates. They could not simply allow believers to disregard the five pillars of Islam, notably the daily *namaz* and the *uraz*. At the same time, it was impossible to oblige them to adhere to them in a society where work discipline could not be breached in order to implement the precepts of one's faith. Unless they found an escape clause based on criteria recognised by Islam, they had no choice but to alienate believers from religion. Somehow, the diktat of communism and Islam had to be reconciled. The registered clergy were so eager to adapt to Soviet reality that, in the words of one CARC inspector in the early 1950s, they did not balk at pronouncing the radically false contention that the Qur'an's teachings concerning 'human society' in no way contradicted communism.[329]

As one Soviet expert on Islam, Nugman Ashirov, pointed out in the early 1970s, the Muslim clergy strove to show how Marx and Engels were tools of Allah who sought to attain socialism

---

328. In Bukhara during Ramadan the clergy of a registered mosque were reported to have organised the playing of music from the roof of the mosque to attract believers to the evening *tarawa-namaz* – N. Tagiev, A short survey, undated [early 1949]; also N. Abushaev, Information, 17 Nov. 1949; and I. V. Polianskii to the CPSU Central Committee and the USSR Council of Ministers, 20 Sept. 1955 – GARF, f.6991, o.4, d.23, l.17ob, and o.3, d.61, l.124, and d.114, l.201. For the enhanced religious activity on the eve of and during the *uraz*, see pp. 469-73.

329. N. Abushaev, Information, sent by Polianskii to A. I. Sobolev, 15 March 1951; GARF, f.6991, o.3, d.76, l.25.

and communism.[330] The imam of the Leningrad mosque dwelt on the plight of the workers before Marx and Lenin, making it appear that in the final analysis the latter had indeed implemented the will of Allah and the precepts of the Qur'an.[331] From here it was but a short step to the argument that there could be no contradiction between this world and the next and that believers were in no way restricted in their enjoyment of the good things of the former as long as they remembered that they were sent by Allah; or equally to the endorsement of their full participation in the construction of the new socialist society side by side with non-believers and their stringent adherence to work discipline.[332]

Perhaps in no sphere were the flexibility and adaptability of Islam so evident as in the sermon. The sermons, certainly those of most of the more centrally placed clergy, were usually carefully kept free of any references which might be construed as constituting religious propaganda. As time passed, sermons demonstrated the extent to which the registered clergy were prepared to go in order to conform to 'the contemporary conditions of social and technical progress' and to show the identity of the basic principles of communism and Islam.[333] CARC's *upolnomochennyi* in Osh noted in the mid 1950s that whereas a few years before the clergy had preached the need for a woman to cover her face, as in revealing it she lost her respect, honesty and dignity before God and man, they now contended that concealing the face was not obligatory. The clergy were similarly stating in their sermons that it was preferable to turn to official medical organisations rather than approaching them to cure the sick. In previous years the clergy had told their congregations that prostration at ancestral tombs or those of holy men was a sacred duty; lately they had begun explaining that this neither cured sickness nor brought well-being, since monuments and tombstones were not God, just the graves of dead people.[334]

330. Ashirov, *Evoliutsiia islama v SSSR*, p.40. Ashirov developed in considerable detail this theme preached by Muslim clergy that the socio-economic changes effected in the USSR were a fruition of the teachings of Islam – *ibid.*, pp.39-44.

331.CRA Information, sent to the CPSU Central Committee, 22 May 1970; TsKhSD, f.5, o.62, d.38, 1.25.

332. Ashirov, *Evolintsiia islama v SSSR*, pp.48, 51 and 65-6.

333. S. Zubarev, Report, undated (before 28 April 1973); GARF, f.6991, o.6, d.548, 1.85.

334. I. Halimov to CARC, 3 April 1956; GARF, f.6991, o.3, d.457, ll.72-3.

Many clergy tended to restrict their sermons to calls for greater personal and domestic morality: respect for parents and elders, the importance of marital ties and the need for men to show due honour to their wives, the responsibility of parents for the upbringing of their children. Often sermons comprised appeals to support the peace movement and other international activities sponsored by the Soviet Union, for which many among the official religious leadership were mobilised.[335] Some imams, 'the most politically educated and loyal' among them, devoted their sermons to supporting Soviet policy at home and abroad and appealed to believers to pray for its success.[336] The mulla in Izhevsk (the Udmurt ASSR) concluded a sermon in the early 1970s with the slogan: 'Long live Communism, the radiant future of mankind'.[337] CARC *upol-nomochennye* partly based their contention that the registered Muslim clergy were fundamentally loyal to the Soviet state and government on their sermons.[338]

The texts of a number of sermons, which had to be ratified in advance, have been preserved and they abound in admonitions to preserve the norms and criteria of everyday behaviour laid down in Soviet teachings.[339] By passing off Islam as the protagonist of a moral life – one Soviet authority wrote – the clergy in fact

335. See pp.175-7. Thus, a sermon delivered by the Moscow mosque's *imam-khatib*, Kamaretdin Salihov, on 16 Nov. 1956, condemned the 'triple aggression' against Egypt. And the letter sent out by the chairman of DUMES on the eve of Qurban-Bayram in 1957 to all registered mosques included a suggestion to the imams to tell worshippers in their sermons of the measures taken by the USSR in the struggle for peace – K. F. Tagirov, Memo, 23 Aug. 1957; GARF, f.6991, o.4, d.99, ll.37-8, and d.73, l.73.

336. L. A. Prikhod'ko, Memorandum, 25 July 1956, sent by V. I. Gostev to the CPSU Central Committee and the USSR Council of Ministers, 30 July 1956, and S. Agafonov to A. A. Nurullaev, 14 May 1974; GARF, f.6991, o.3, d.130, ll.26-34, and o.6, d.630, ll.319-20. Prikhod'ko referred specifically to the imam of Novosibirsk who called upon believers to take up the struggle against hooliganism and drunkenness, especially among young people.

337. C. Zubarev, Report, undated (before 28 April 1973); GARF, f.6991, o.6, d.548, l.85.

338. For instance, D. Ahmedov to A. A. Puzin, 21 Feb. 1961; GARF, f.6991, o.3, d.1737, l.17.

339. In the early period at least some leading clerics in Uzbekistan actually published their sermons – Minutes, Conference of CARC *upolnomochennye* in the Uzbek SSR, 9 Aug. 1948; TsGAUz, f.2456, o.1, d.120, l.14.

enhanced its influence.[340] Believers were enjoined to respect the elderly, strengthen the family and refrain from alcohol – on the basis both of the Shari'a and of their ruinous consequences in this world, where the Soviet state sought to eradicate this evil.[341] In one such sermon the imam of Moscow's sole mosque explained that in order to achieve happiness in this world and the next, one had to act honourably and scrupulously, to commit no amoral actions, to preserve domestic harmony and mutual respect between husband and wife, to honour one's parents, not to spread infectious diseases or live at other people's expense. A person must not loaf, drink, steal, lie or gossip or bring harm to the mother country. A Muslim had to perform pious deeds, which meant everything that was not prohibited by Soviet law, that was done in the name of God and brought benefit to human society. Above all, a Muslim had to learn, to seek education. As one imam put it:

> The essence of all our doings, of everything we do in God's name is composed of ten parts, nine of which are the creation of material goods through honest work, and one the performance of religious rites. That means that the creation of material goods and the wellbeing of the family through honest work at factories, plants and other enterprises are nine tenths of all that we do in the name of God. If in addition to this you pray to God, observe the fast and perform the pilgrimage, you will be doing God's work and become a person He loves.[342]

In this context, for example, the clergy would address themselves to civil holidays which were observed by the entire population irrespective of faith (the 7th of November, the 1st of May, Lenin's birthday), speaking of them in much the same way as was done at festive meetings in collective enterprises and institutions. They sought to respond to important events in Soviet life and even had resort to the terminology and concepts of Marxist sociology –social progress, the peaceful co-existence of opposing social systems, collectivism, imperialism, internationalism – although often using them in a different context. Individualism, for instance,

340. Saidbaev, *Islam i obshchestvo*, p.243.

341. A. Barmenkov to the CPSU Central Committee Propaganda Department, 13 March 1973; GARF, f.6991, o.6, d.537, ll.16–17.

342. Sermon by Imam Kamaretdin Salihov in the Moscow mosque on 'Id al-Fitr, 1 May 1957; GARF, f.6991, o.4, d.86, ll.38–47.

denoted aloofness from the mosque, collectivism those who were part of the community; solidarity was reserved for partnership with Muslims the world over. The bottom line of their message was that Islam had shaken off all the evil extremism of past centuries, bringing nothing but benefit to both the citizen and society as a whole. The clergy would bring passages from the Qur'an to show Islam's association with social progress, equality and justice and even its endorsement of revolution to attain certain social goals. In this same vein they reviewed Islam's traditional attitude to women and their economic, legal and social status.[343]

Often the *fetwas* and circulars of the spiritual directorates would provide the backbone, if not the sole content, of a sermon. Basing himself on *fetwas* issued by SADUM, an imam in Bukhara in the late 1960s encouraged believers not to hold extravagant *tois*, or celebrations, except in the event of the circumcision or marriage of a son, and not to accompany funerals with the customary repast, which was a major burden for a bereft family. He also insisted that the actual burial service, the *jinaz*, be conducted in the mosque, with only the reading of the Qur'an at the cemetery. Finally, he emphasised that Islam did not recognise pilgrimages, let alone bringing donations, to holy places; one was to prostrate oneself before Allah alone.[344] A few of the more prominent and educated clergy might even give their own interpretations of Shari'a law in the general line approved by the authorities or enlarge upon those given in the *fetwas*.[345] Just occasionally, however, clergy would give vent to opinions that ran contrary to Soviet law, such as approving polygamy in the event that one's wife was unable to have children,[346] or at least encourage circumventing it, for example exhorting parents, sometimes even threatening them, to

343. CRA information, sent to the CPSU Central Committee, 22 April 1971; TsKhSD, f.5, o.63, d.89, ll.124-6.

344. A. Barinskaia to V. A. Kuroedov, undated [late March or early April 1968]; GARF, f.6991, o.6, d.153, ll.108-9.

345. I. Halimov to CARC, undated [April 1949] – GARF, f.6991, o.3, d.454, l.13; and Faizullin, On the trip to Frunze and Alma-Ata, 15 Sept. 1952 – TsGAUz, f.2456, o.1, d.144, l.92.

346. This was expounded upon by SADUM's representative in Kirgiziia at the end of the 1940s – H. Akhtiamov, Short report, Conference of Central Asian *upolnomochennye*, Tashkent, 17 Dec. 1949; GARF, f.6991, o.3, d.67, l.105.

ensure that their children were circumcised and followed the precepts of their religion.[347]

Ashirov maintained that the clergy differentiated between various audiences as they constructed their sermons. They were far more stringent in the demands they made of their regular Friday 'contingent' than of those who came just twice a year on festivals. While enjoining the former category to pray regularly, some preached that 'he who comes to the mosque on festivals with a pure heart and performs his prayers will be vouchsafed paradise'.[348] When one analysed the 'renovationist process' in Islam, Ashirov insisted in the early 1970s, one could not but notice that the clergy aspired to strengthen the impact of the idea behind 'the transformed rite' and to buttress rituals which were either not stipulated at all or which were performed in practice otherwise than stipulated. Thus, one imam pointed out that the tradition of conducting a memorial ceremony on the third, seventh and fortieth day after death was a mistaken tradition, but insofar as a mulla was invited to perform such a ceremony he should go and do everything in accordance with custom: read from the Qur'an, preach, answer questions and pray.[349] The clergy went so far as to substitute their original antagonism to the performance of secular life-cycle rites, asking believers to perform the religious ritual after having registered in ZAGS.[350]

In an article published a few years later, Ashirov pointed out that the Muslim clergy preached in the local vernacular rather than in the traditional Arabic;[351] furthermore, the *khutba* or sermon now lasted not the customary five minutes but from twenty to forty, and it touched upon social, political and moral topics. Nor

347. Zh. Botashev to V. A. Kuroedov, 17 Nov. 1969; GARF, f.6991, o.6, d.220, ll.145-6.

348. Ashirov, *Evoliutsiia islama v SSSR* l.139, and 'Musul'manskaia propoved' segodnia', p.32.

349. Ashirov, *Evoliutsiia islama v SSSR* l.143.

350. *Ibid.*, ll.148-9. For the secular rites, see pp.513-4, 518 and 600-2.

351. Already in the 1920s a meeting of the *muhtasibat* of at least one uezd in what was then the Kirgiz ASSR resolved that sermons be delivered in Kazakh –From report of the Turgai party *ukom* on the expanding influence of the Muslim clergy, the 7th uezd party conference, 1926; *Preodolevaia religioznoe vliianie islama*, doc. No.86, p.119. According to popular tradition, Persian or its local version, Farsi, had served for centuries as the language of prayer and religious literature, among Tajiks – Rakhimov, 'O iazikovoi situatsii v Uzbekistane', p.113.

was it delivered solely in the mosque at prayer-services; any secular or religious festival, joyous or tragic event or life-cycle ceremony had become the occasion for a sermon. The preacher still interpreted dogma, as in the past, but he endeavoured to 'sidestep or couch in allegorical terms' those aspects which contemporary believers were unlikely to accept. Placing the concept of paradise in an earthly context, a cleric in Azerbaijan said that the Soviet state had come into being as a state of the poor and exploited. 'The poor who lived in tsarist Russia entered into the Soviet system like into a heaven granted by Allah'. Muslim preachers asserted that the principles of socialism were included in the Qur'an, giving the impression that by following the requirements of Islam, they were fulfilling the requirements of the moral code of the builders of communism (and vice versa).[352]

In the words of a 1970 CRA report, the transfer of the sermon from traditional spiritual themes to worldly ones enhanced, rather than diminished, its impact, for the clergy were now addressing themes close to their audience, issues which affected their daily lives. Examples of this were the appeal of imams to believers, including pensioners, to take part in the cotton harvest, or the insistence, given the harm caused to livestock by the difficult weather conditions of the last two years of the 1960s, that believers need not bring sacrifices on Qurban-Bayram. Moreover, in many ways the clergy highlighted the common ground on which the teachings of Islam and communism were based. Thus, the emphasis they laid on the need to give donations to the registered mosques, instead of to the needy, so as not to engender parasitism, in light of the fact that the regime provided everyone with a job and the old with pensions, brought home the common position of the two doctrines.

At the same time, the better trained clergy, such as the imams in Moscow and Leningrad, also tried to imbue in their flock a closer acquaintance with the principles of Islamic teaching and the most fundamental rituals, of which they were generally ignorant. They argued that the observance of Islam not only did not run counter to reason, it actually sprung from reason. A few seem to have even favoured the translation of the Qur'an into the languages spoken by the Muslim nationalities on the grounds that it had been given by Allah in order for men to study it and follow its

352. Ashirov, 'Musul'manskaia propoved' segodnia', pp.30-3.

precepts, which became difficult in an age when believers no longer knew Arabic.[353]

The sermons of the more authoritative clerics attracted large numbers of worshippers. Indeed, in some of the more reputed mosques worshippers came the evening before the festival or in the middle of the night in order to take up positions which would ensure their hearing the sermon.[354] By the late 1960s, however, it was noted that on the whole clergy were less and less capable of making theoretical presentations, and their sermons were increasingly taken up with mundane issues.[355]

Not infrequently, as a result of the advanced age and low level of education of so many clerics, their ability to come across to their audience was minimal.[356] The *upolnomochennyi* for Tselinograd Oblast' in Northern Kazakhstan reported that the only imam in the oblast', who was old and deaf, preached in the real sense of the word only on major festivals; on regular Fridays he would read and interpret the Qur'an and then appeal to the believers to pray for peace, work honestly and not steal, simply repeating himself every week.[357] The imam in nearby Pavlodar, who was even older, spoke on more religious themes, reminding believers of the significance of the mosque, the place for worshipping Allah, stressing that everything which happened to a person in this world and the next depended on Allah and so the believer must implement

353. CRA Information, sent to the CPSU Central Committee, 22 May 1970; TsKhSD, f.5, o.62, d.38, ll.24-8; and Ashirov, *Evoliutsiia islama v SSSR*, pp.120-4. Ashirov gives not a single example of a cleric who in fact advocated the translation of the Qur'an. It was not, indeed, until glasnost that the translation of the Qur'an into the languages of the main Muslim nationalities was undertaken.

354. I. V. Polianskii to the CPSU Central Committee and the USSR Council of Ministers, 20 Sept. 1955; GARF, f.6991, o.3, d.114, l.198.

355. CRA information, sent to the CPSU Central Committee, 22 May 1970; TsKhSD, f.5, o.62, d.38, l.24.

356. See, for example, the report of Faizullin on his visit to Frunze and Alma-Ata, 15 Sept. 1952; TsGAUz, f.2456, o.1, d.144, l.92. The imam in the latter city had talked in his festival sermon of life after death, paradise and hell, but he lacked a voice and had no speaking talent, so that 'the impression of his speech was paltry'.

357. A. Tishkov to A. A. Nurullaev, 16 July 1973; GARF, f.6991, o.6, d.545, ll.66-7. Tishkov was a Russian with but a poor knowledge of Kazakh and so attended the sole mosque in his oblast' in the company of Kazakh communists who translated the content of the imam's address for him. In the past, he explained, when the imams had been literate and preached frequently, he would ask for the text in advance and analyse it, but this was now superfluous.

the precepts of Islam and, above all, help propagate its ideology. But this imam, too, exonerated from mosque attendance those engaged in the work force, since their work constituted a substitute for prayer. Indeed, all the worshippers in his mosque were said to be above fifty-five and either illiterate or barely literate.[358]

On the whole, the content of sermons would be accepted with docility by the congregation or even incur open expressions of approval. In Uzbekistan in the early 1950s, where the clergy would stress the Muslim's religious obligations, such as the five daily prayers and the *jum'a-namaz*, their audiences related to these sermons as if they were God's own instructions, for any violation of which they would suffer punishment and torture in the next world.[359] But this was not always the case. The DUMES *muhtasib* for Penza Oblast' sought to bring across to believers at the end of the 1950s the need to rid themselves of unessential rites, in particular apparently the visitation of holy places. He was met with signs of dissatisfaction, almost hostility, and he asked to be excused from giving such sermons. Similarly an imam from Kuibyshev Oblast' wrote to Mufti Khiyaletdinov that when he read out the latter's *fetwa*, believers shouted out that the mufti had no business to prohibit pilgrimages to holy places.[360] Sermons of an opposite tendency might also arouse negative reactions. In the words of one study, 'contemporary believers do not appreciate the conduct of mullas who advocate the observance of antiquated precepts; they are impressed rather by sermons which correspond to their disposition and touch upon questions of contemporary life'.[361] The mulla in the town of Sterlitamak in the Bashkir ASSR complained to the mufti in Ufa toward the end of the 1950s that believers did not heed his sermons and that the *dvadtsatka* decided all the affairs of

358. S. Abenov to A. A. Nurullaev, 9 Aug. 1973 and 15 July 1974; GARF, f.6991, o.6, d.545, ll.91-2, and d.633, ll.31-2. The Pavlodar imam was 91 and, although he still had a loud voice, his age prevented him from conducting any meaningful religious activity.

359. Almaev to Deputy Chairman of Tashkent Oblispolkom Mahkamova, Tashkent Obkom Secretary Nazarov, Kh. N. Iskanderov and I. V. Polianskii, 19 Jan. 1952; TsGAUz, f.2456, o.1, d.142, l.43.

360. M. Sh. Karimov, Address, Conference of CARC *upolnomochennye*, 22 July 1959; GARF, f.6991, o.3, d.184, l.155. Karimov, CARC *upolnomochennyi* in the Bashkir ASSR, commented that evidently the imam had been unable to explain the *fetwa* and had fallen under the influence of charlatans.

361. *Islam v SSSR*, p.105.

the religious society without him. It transpired that the mulla had sought in his sermons to get believers to fulfil all the precepts of the Shari'a without missing a single rite, threatening them that otherwise they would burn in hell.[362]

Despite the general loyalty and conformity of the registered clergy, some of them in fact expressed dissatisfaction with the prevailing state of affairs. Unable to reconcile themselves with the secularisation of all aspects of the believer's life and of society as a whole, they sought to 'brake the movement of progress' and to apply all their authority in order to call for a literal interpretation of the precepts of Islam.[363] These clergy directed threats at apostates and, in the words of Soviet commentators, longed for the days when women were kept under lock and key and did not participate in public life. The extreme attacks against atheists and women's rights by an *imam-khatib* in Namangan led in 1969 to his dismissal. Another imam, in Bukhara, explained a series of natural calamities, which hit various regions in Uzbekistan, as being the result of people's break with Islam.[364] These dissenting voices apparently became more common and more vociferous towards the end of the period under study, in the late 1970s, early 1980s. By then clergy were not infrequently telling their audiences in their sermons: 'Whatever you may have become, however educated and cultured, you are Muslims by birth and it is incumbent upon you to fulfil your duty to your ancestors and your nation'.[365]

The attitude to non-establishment Islam

The registered mosques often conducted an uphill struggle to establish and maintain a position of authority among the population.

362. Divulging this at a conference of CARC *upolnomochennye*, Karimov added that the mulla, before serving in this capacity, had engaged in 'uncertain activities' and was accustomed to live off the work of others, had been known as a profiteer and even sat in prison. All this he had concealed when applying for the job of mulla. As mulla he had also violated the law on religion and as a result the mufti had dismissed him from his post and Karimov had withdrawn him from registration – Minutes, CARC session No. 21, 22 July 1959; GARF, f.6991, o.3, d.184, ll.156-7. See also Ashirov, *Evoliutsiia islama v SSSR*, p.11.

363. Saidbaev, *Islam i obshchestvo*, p.243.

364. CRA Information, sent to the CPSU Central Committee, 22 May 1970; TsKhSD, f.5, o.62, d.38, ll.24-8; and Ashirov, *Evoliutsiia islama v SSSR*, pp.120-4.

365. *Islam v SSSR*, p.50.

Among others, this manifested itself in a somewhat ambiguous attitude towards their unregistered counterparts. In many instances they regarded the unregistered groups and clergy in their vicinity with undisguised antagonism, as a result of which they could be expected to join hands with CARC and its representatives in the localities in the struggle against the unregistered mullas.[366] In Samarkand Oblast', for instance, registered clergy officially suggested to the *oblispolkom* to shut down unregistered religious associations.[367]

CARC and its *upolnomochennye* claimed that this hostility on the part of the registered clergy emanated wholly or mainly from their concern that the unregistered mullas were competing for revenues. True, registered clergy went on record as saying that all believers' donations during the *uraz* must be brought to registered mosques, as those given to unregistered mullas, invalids or needy did not reach Allah.[368] Certainly, there seems to have been a large measure of resentment among the registered clergy, a sense that they were disadvantaged in that they were taxed and controlled more than those who, for one reason or another, had refrained from registration. In the mid 1950s the imam of one of Baku's registered mosques complained to CARC that a cleric who had been withdrawn from registration had built up in that city a network of helpers with whose aid he performed a plethora of religious rites at the expense of the official establishment; moreover, taxes had not been imposed on his income. Whether merely in order to add insult to injury or to augment his own achievement, he dubbed the registered clergy as communists and discredited their legitimacy in the eyes of believers.[369] The fact that the unregistered

366. See, for example, H. Akhtiamov, Report, Minutes, CARC session No.9, 3 June 1947; GARF, f.6991, o.4, d.19, l.246.

367. Minutes, Instructional meeting of CARC *upolnomochennye* in the Uzbek SSR, 15-17 March 1956; TsGAUz, f.2456, o.1, d.189, l.54.

368. L. A. Prikhod'ko, Memo, 25 July 1956, sent by V. I. Gostev to the CPSU Central Committee and the USSR Council of Ministers, 30 July 1956; GARF, f.6991, o.3, d.130, l.31.

369. Reception by N. I. Smirnov of A. F. Temirbulatov, 24 Aug. 1957; GARF, f.6991, o.4, d.175, ll.124-5. The person about whom he was complaining had served as imam for ten years in one of Baku's registered mosques. Since his withdrawal from registration, the reason for which is not given, he had operated in the city with the help of ten men and ten women who 'agitate' among believers to invite him to perform rites. As a result, Temirbulatov had during a whole year performed just 20 weddings, 17 funerals and five name-givings although his religious society comprised 30,000 believers and every Friday 800

clergy were by definition outside the sphere of influence of the mechanisms designed to regulate religious activity was constantly being harped upon by the registered mullas. The latter stressed that paradoxically they were often more stringently and consistently repressed, although their transgressions against the law were manifestly less flagrant and less numerous. In the early 1960s in Tajikistan registered clergy, who were feeling the brunt of the anti-religious campaign, complained that SADUM was not operating against the far more frequent and serious violations of the law on religion committed by unregistered mullas, but expending all its energies on curbing their activities.[370]

During the anti-religious campaign of the early 1960s many registered clergy came out strongly against the 'itinerant mullas'. In Tajikistan, for example, they sought to deter believers from attending prayer-services held by the latter on the Muslim festivals, contending that the opening of mosques without authorisation contradicted both the law of the state and the Shari'a and that attendance at them was sinful.[371] However, the phenomenon of registered clergy engaging battle with unregistered mullas existed long before Khrushchev's anti-religious campaign. In 1947 the registered imam of the Pavlodar mosque passed on information to the oblast' *upolnomochennyi* concerning itinerant mullas, whose religious activity he sought to terminate 'in order to extend his own influence'.[372] In Tajikistan many itinerant mullas were exposed towards the end of the 1940s as a result of tensions between them and the registered imams, and the authorities took advantage of this to encourage the latter to act as informers.[373] The struggle

---

to 1,000 worshippers attended his mosque. He contended that he was complaining, not because he did not have sufficient income, but because the other person was not paying tax on the revenues he received from the rites he performed. Interestingly, he asked Smirnov not to mention his name to the *upolnomochennyi* for Azerbaijan as the source of the complaint.

370. D. A. Ahmedov to A. A. Puzin, 21 Feb. 1961, GARF, f.6991, o.3, d.1737, ll.11-13.

371. D. Ahmedov to A. A. Puzin, Tajikistan CP Central Committee Secretary N. Zaripova, and Tajikistan KGB Chairman S. K. Tsvigun, 2 June 1962; GARF, f.6991, o.3, d.1738, l.42.

372. I. V. Polianskii to all *upolnomochennye*, Instructional letter No.7, Appendix No.3, CARC session No.15, 24-25 Aug. 1947; GARF, f.6991, o.4, d.22, l.204.

373. K. Hamidov to I. V. Polianskii, 14 Dec. 1949; GARF, f.6991, o.3, d.67, l.97.

of the registered with the unregistered Muslim clergy, moreover, persisted long after the centrally-orchestrated campaign against religion had let up. Towards the end of the 1960s, the CRA *upolnomochennyi* for the Kirgiz SSR wrote: 'In the struggle against the anti-lawful activity of the unregistered clergy, we sometimes make use to an extent of the executive organs and clergy of the registered mosques, many of whom have an interest in this'.[374] In this same time period in the Kabardino-Balkar ASSR registered clergy were opposed to allowing the registration of unregistered mullas solely for the purpose of conducting funeral rites, on the grounds that after receiving a certificate authorising this, they would without doubt begin consolidating groups of believers in order to conduct collective prayer. Nor were either the registered or unregistered mullas in favour of the latter being placed under the authority of the registered mosques.[375] It was apparently not unusual for lists of mosqueless and itinerant mullas to be supplied to the local authorities by the imams of registered mosques for transmission to the financial organs for purposes of taxation.[376]

Altogether, on a countrywide level, the clergy and *aktiv* of the registered mosques tended to condemn the activity of the unregistered clergy; in their attempt to attract as many believers as possible to their own mosques they stressed that Friday and festival prayers should be conducted only in registered mosques.[377] Thus, in Tselinograd Oblast' the clergy and executive organ of the sole registered mosque appealed to believers and unregistered mullas not to hold collective prayers in localities where there was no registered mosque, but rather to attend the mosque bringing the donations, the *fitr-sadaqa*, collected in the nearby settlements to

374. K. Shabolotov to A. A. Nurullaev, 23 June 1969; GARF, f.6991, o.6, d.220, l.151.

375. L. Aisov to the CRA, 27 Aug. 1969; GARF, f.6991, o.6, d.220, l.326. There is an error in the document in the sentence explaining the opposition of both groups to this arrangement, so that it is not clear whether the unregistered mullas did not consider the registered ones to be an authority in questions of faith and therefore did not wish to be subordinated to them, or whether the registered clergy did not appreciate the religious qualifications of their unregistered counterparts.

376. For example in the Karakalpak ASSR – D. Erekeshov to V. A. Kuroedov, 10 July 1974; GARF, f.6991, o.6, d.634, ll. 81-2.

377. CRA, Information, sent to the CPSU Central Committee, 27 April 1971; TsKhSD, f.5, o.63, d.89, ll.97-8.

the mosque treasury. This was said to explain why, on Uraz-Bayram in 1970, over 1,200 worshippers attended the mosque, some of them coming from 2-300 km away.[378]

On the other hand, there were instances when hostility and apprehension gave way to a measure of cooperation. Sometimes registered clergy encouraged an unregistered religious group to apply for registration, conceivably out of a desire to increase the number of registered mosques.[379] Similarly, clergy in registered mosques would seek the participation of unregistered religious figures in their own prayer-services. The mulla of one mosque in Khorezm Oblast' invited a number of unregistered clergy who enjoyed prestige in the area to participate in festival prayer-services in his mosque allegedly in order to give them a more ceremonial character.[380]

Undoubtedly, a number of mosques, by virtue of their being the sole registered mosque in a major metropolis or in the administrative centre of an oblast' or raion, or in consequence of the particular sanctity of the site, served to consolidate the local believer population. One such instance was the mosque at the foot of Osh's holy mountain, the Takht-i Sulayman, which immediately on its opening in 1946 drew large crowds, including many who came from beyond the confines of the town, the oblast', or even the republic.[381]

A major document which sought in the early 1970s to describe and analyse Muslim life in the Soviet Union laid down that the registered urban mosques had perceptibly become centres of religious life for the surrounding settlements. Believers would often come from distant localities on the eve of festivals and spend the night on the grounds of the mosque.[382] There were also times and regions, especially in Central Asia, in which the registered mosques seemed to be extending a hand to unregistered religious

378. *Ibid.*

379. See, for example, U. Mangushev to Kh. N. Iskanderov, 30 Jan. 1954; TsGAUz, f.2456, o.1, d.170, l.4.

380. I. V. Polianskii to CPSU Central Committee and USSR Council of Ministers, 20 Sept. 1955; GARF, f.6991, o.3, d.214, l.203.

381. H. Akhtiamov, Report, Conference of CARC *upolnomochennye*, Alma-Ata, 30 Sept. 1946; GARF, f.6991, o.3, d.41, ll.101-3.

382. Information sent to the CPSU Central Committee, 27 April 1971; TsKhSD, f.5, o.63, d.89, ll.97-8.

groups, in the hope of overcoming the limitations imposed by the regime's endeavour to restrict their activity to the confines of their parish. CARC feared at one point that this might be a concerted effort initiated by SADUM, whose own attitude toward the unregistered communities seemed to be ambiguous and in a state of constant flux. SADUM's representatives were reported to have been behind a letter sent out by the executive organ of the Alma-Ata mosque to ninety-six religious figures in the various towns and villages of Alma-Ata Oblast' in 1952, asking for their cooperation in bolstering Islam.

Similarly, in Uzbekistan, registered mosques were maintaining a broad range of contacts with unregistered clergy and groups. In the early 1950s the executive organ of a mosque in Tashkent Oblast' authorised three unregistered mullas to perform religious rites in all the kishlaks within a radius of 10 – 25 km of it (those closer than 10 km were presumably considered as belonging to its legitimate parish confines), giving them receipts to register moneys that might be received, which would then be transferred to the mosque. Instances were also recorded in other oblasti of imams issuing certificates to unregistered clergy authorising them to perform rites. One mosque appointed an 'important religious figure' from Tashkent, who had just been released from a ten-year prison term, to collect moneys received by unregistered mullas in the local kolkhozy. This practice was said to have tied in with instructions given by SADUM officials that in kishlaks where the imam of a registered mosque was unable to conduct rites, local inhabitants might do so under the supervision of its executive organ.[383] In Bukhara Oblast' the clergy of the registered mosques were thought to be entertaining close links with unregistered clergy, instructing them how to conduct religious activity among the population and to conduct mass prayer-meetings. In one case an imam from Bukhara sent two clerics to one raion to conduct

---

383. I. V. Polianskii to CARC's five Central Asian republican *upolnomochennye*, 24 Sept. 1952, and Minutes, CARC session No.24s, 25-26 Sept. 1952, and K. F. Tagirov, Resumé, 1 March 1957; GARF, f.6991, o.3, d.86, ll.22-3, d.83, l.274, and d.132, l.42. It was probably the first of these documents which led to the demand by SADUM in a circular to its members and to *imam-khatibs* and executive organs, dated 6 Nov. 1952, that all rites be performed by official personnel, i.e. persons holding official positions in registered mosques; TsGAUz, f.2456, o.1, d.144, ll.72-3. For SADUM's attitude to unregistered religious associations, see pp.135-40.

khatm-i Qur'an during the *uraz*.[384] The *imam-khatib* of a registered rural mosque in Andijan Oblast' gave the imam of an unregistered mosque a document attesting his right to conduct prayers, on the grounds that without assistance from neighbouring raiony his mosque could not procure the sum fixed for it by SADUM.[385]

The registered mosques in Margelan and Kokand in Fergana Oblast' were also reported to be exerting considerable influence over unregistered religious societies, of which forty-eight had been counted throughout the oblast'. The former had organised 'mass prayer-services' in twelve unregistered mosques; it also summoned the imams of these mosques, apparently to coordinate with them the conduct of prayers, and probably also the collection of donations. On the eve of Qurban-Bayram in 1956 SADUM's *muhtasib* visited the oblast' and suggested to the registered mosques' executive organs to write to the raiony where unregistered mosques operated, proposing that they organise collective prayers and conduct a collection of funds for SADUM; thirty-eight such letters were sent. At the conclusion of one service a mulla from Kokand was stopped by the militia, to whom he showed a certificate from the Kokand mosque's executive organ demonstrating that he had been sent to organise and conduct the festival *namaz*; he was released after an hour but the militia 'suggested' to him that he put the nearly 5,000 rubles he had collected from over 3,000 worshippers in the state bank.[386]

Similar practices were recorded in other parts of Central Asia as well. Two mosques in Kazakhstan – in Turkestan and Kargaly, in the oblasti of Southern Kazakhstan and Taldy-Kurgan respectively – were likewise thought in the mid 1950s to have given unofficial mullas receipts so that they might hand over to them moneys they received for the performance of rites.[387] In Jambul in Southern Kazakhstan, the sole registered mosque was said in the late 1960s to be a '"methodical" centre for all the underground Muslim com-

384. Theses for instructional address at a conference of CARC *upolnomochennye*, 25 Sept. 1952; GARF, f.6991, o.3, d.83, l.263, and N. Achilov to I. V. Polianskii, Kh. N. Iskanderov, Bukhara Oblispolkom Chairman N. Mahmudov and Obkom Secretary Namazov, 18 May 1956; TsGAUz, f.2456, o.1, d.198, l.53.

385. M. Khalikov to I. V. Polianskii, Kh, N. Iskanderov, Obkom Secretary Kurbanov and Oblispolkom Chairman Rizaev, 19 May 1956; TsGAUz, f.2456, o.1, d.198, l.83.

386. K. F. Tagirov, Resumé, 1 March 1957; GARF, f.6991, o.3, d.132, ll.53-4.

387. *Ibid.*, ll.67-8.

munities of the oblast's towns and villages', a meeting-place for all the oblast's unofficial mullas.[388] In Chimkent, too, the registered religious societies had become the centres of religious life for all believers inhabiting a radius of 20 – 30 kilometres and maintained ties with unregistered associations and clergy.[389]

In Osh Oblast', too, donations given to local, unofficial clergy for *khatm-i Qur'ans* and *mavluds* read in private homes, were often passed on to the registered mosques, even if they were in another raion. The registered clergy not only did not protest, but on the contrary, appreciated this, giving receipts to the unregistered groups and mullas so that they would not be subjected to income tax for these moneys.[390] According to the CARC *upolnomochennyi*, the oblast's twenty-four registered clergy were the 'so-called leaders' of 402 unregistered clergy, giving them instructions and demanding that they collect money and donations among the population. Under the leadership of the clergy and executive organs of the oblast's sixteen registered mosques, they conducted organised, public *mavluds* and *khatm-i Qur'ans* in the mosques, as well as rites in private homes.[391] In the words of the CARC *upolnomochennyi* for Kirgiziia, many registered mosques were so closely linked with unregistered communities that the latter became a kind of branch of the former.[392]

In other regions, too, far removed from Central Asia, contacts of a similar character pertained between registered and unregistered clergy. In the Bashkir ASSR some mosques extended their jurisdiction by initiating smaller groups, which would be affiliated to them and bring them donations. One mulla organised prayer-houses in private homes in four settlements and appointed clergy who

388. E. Bairamov, Information, 13 Jan. 1969; GARF, f.6991, o.6, d.153, l.50.

389. A. Barmenkov, Draft CRA resolution on the work of its *upolnomochennyi* for Chimkent Oblast', Aug. 1969; GARF, f.6991, o.6, d.290, l.82.

390. I. G. Halimov to CARC, 20 Jan. 1956. The republican *upolnomochennyi* remarked in reply that there was nothing objectionable in this support for the registered mosques, as no regulations restricted the place of residence of those who gave donations, as long as the members of the mosque's own *aktiv* did not go far beyond the confines of their parish to collect the money – H. Akhtiamov to I. G. Halimov, 1 Feb. 1956; GARF, f.6991, o.3, d.457, ll.17-9 and 49.

391. N. Urumbaev, Address, Conference of CARC *upolnomochennye*, 25-27 Nov. 1958; GARF, f.6991, o.3, d.165, ll.41-2.

392. Report of H. A. Akhtiamov, All-Union conference of CARC *upolnomochen-nye*, 18-20 April 1960; GARF, f.6991, o.3, d.208, l.128.

conducted services and sent him moneys they collected.[393] In Azerbaijan there were examples of registered clergy telling itinerant mullas that in order to conduct rites in their raiony they must obtain their permission.[394]

Certainly, CARC and its representatives in the field, just as they took advantage of the element of rivalry in order to use the registered clergy in their struggle against the unregistered mullas, did not refrain, when it suited them, from coupling them together. Thus, CARC's republican *upolnomochennyi* in Uzbekistan at the end of the 1940s stressed the identity of interest and outlook of the registered and unregistered clergy in 'spreading religious propaganda', with the latter serving merely as accomplices of the former, for, although formally they trod different paths, their goal was the same.[395]

Economic activity

In the early and mid 1950s, there appear to have been not a few examples of clergy and executive organs of registered mosques in the Central Asian republics resorting to illicit practices in order at one and the same time to extend their influence to areas outside the reach of their official parishes and to enhance the revenues of their religious societies. True, the financial aspect of the activity of all religious figures and institutions was systematically highlighted by the Soviet regime from its inception in order to demonstrate the exploitation of the masses by religion in all its forms and shapes. At the same time, it is reasonable to assume that, in light of the constraints to which they were subject, the religious societies did all they felt they reasonably could in order to enhance their revenues. That they were frequently able to operate beyond the scope of their official mandate surely proves that the believer community was willing to comply. In some parts – according to reports – clergy and other members of the mosque *aktiv* collected the *fitr* openly in urban markets and it was common practice for them to make the rounds of believers' homes for the purpose of

393. A. Puzin to M. Sh. Karimov, draft, undated [probably Feb. 1961]; GARF, f.6991, o.3, d.1355, ll.265-6.
394. N. Smirnov, Information, 8 Aug. 1962; GARF, f.6991, o.3, d.1390, ll.19-20.
395. Kh. N. Iskanderov, Address, Instructional Conference of CARC's Central Asian *upolnomochennye*, 17-20 Dec.1949; GARF, f.6991, o.3, d.67, l.57.

soliciting donations, sometimes even exerting moral pressure on believers to give money by threatening them with punishment from Allah and exclusion from paradise in the event that they withheld payment.[396] In order to extend the scope of their economic activity and augment the mosque's sources of income, it was suggested, some religious societies elected to their executive organ people from different settlements on the assumption that they would as a result be able to attract donations from their inhabitants.[397] In the second half of the 1950s, the executive organs of religious societies in Kazakhstan collected moneys in localities which were at a considerable distance from their mosques.[398]

The economic activity of registered religious societies was carefully relegated to the receipt of voluntary donations from believers in money or in kind. Strictly speaking, these contributions had to be made within the precincts of the prayer-house and no compulsion was to be brought to bear on believers by the clergy or any other official of the religious society in order to augment these revenues. Such money as was received was to be used to pay the salaries of the clergy and any other personnel who might be on the pay-list of the mosque – service personnel[399] and sometimes the *mutawali* (the chairman of the executive organ) – and to cover all costs connected with the maintenance of the prayer-house and its religious articles and of the religious centre to which the prayer-house was subordinate.

The economic activity which the religious societies were permitted to conduct tended in periods of relative leniency toward religion to be considerably more substantial than in years of greater repression. By spring 1948, for instance, when the screws on religion were tightening, it was evident that the economic situation

396. L. A. Prikhod'ko, Report, 20 May 1953, and I. V. Polianskii to the Central Committee and the Council of Ministers, 20 Sept. 1955; GARF, f.6991, o.3, d.91, pp.245-6, and d.114, l.200. See also B. Jumashev, Address, Conference of CARC's Central Asian *upolnomochennye*, Tashkent, 5-6 June 1959; GARF, f.6991, o.3, d.186, ll.82-3.

397. I. G. Halimov to CARC, 20 Jan. 1956; GARF, f.6991, o.3, d.457, l.37.

398. K. F. Tagirov, Resumé, 1 March 1957; GARF, f.6991, o.3, d.132, ll.67-8.

399. Some registered mosques had not a few service personnel: cleaners, watchmen, and sometimes carpenters and other craftsmen who did repairs and maintenance. Uzbekistan's 75 registered mosques had in 1960 some 400 such personnel, Azerbaijan's 16 had 39 – N. I. Smirnov, Information, 8 Aug. 1962; GARF, f.6991, o.3, d.1390, l.13.

of the mosques and Muslim clergy in Kirgiziia's Osh Oblast' was deteriorating, the donations received by them not living up to expectations and the clergy having to forego their salary for several consecutive months.[400] The population was declining to give the material support to the clergy that it had given them the year before, nor was it continuing to give money for the religious needs of the community.[401] Although this situation changed drastically in the mid 1950s, it reversed itself at the very end of the decade, when measures were taken specifically to curtail the economic activity of the mosques.[402]

The dimensions of mosque attendance were reflected in the income they received. Where the number of worshippers was large, so too were the sums of money collected by the mosque officials, and when attendance mounted or fell, these sums tended to grow or decrease accordingly.[403] There were, however, some notable exceptions, for instance in 1956 in Central Asia when the revenue on Uraz-Bayram mounted steeply, while attendance actually decreased as a result of heavy rains throughout the region. CARC officials attributed this to the vigour with which the 'agitation' for the payment of the *fitr-sadaqa* had been conducted, to the clergy's insistence that moneys not go to mosqueless mullas but solely and directly to the registered mosques, and to the increasingly strict control and concentration of incoming funds, the growing efficiency of those responsible for the mosques' financial affairs and improved organisational work. The improved economic

---

400. CARC *upolnomochennyi* Halimov wrote to CARC on 30 March 1948 that at Friday prayers in Osh's major mosque Khaliqnazarov appealed to the over 2,000 worshippers to contribute money and products for the upkeep of the clergy. But the collection which ensued brought in no more than 520 rubles; the clergy's pay was already five months in arrears – GARF, f.6991, o.3, d.453, ll.41-2. And compare p.200 above.

401. *Ibid.*, l.42. Halimov reported that one cleric, in the *poselok* of Kara-Suu complained to Khaliqnazarov that not only were believers not sustaining him, but that he had received notification to pay 1300 rubles income tax for 1948 (to cover his income from both his religious work and his agricultural activity).

402. B. Jumashev, Address, Conference of CARC's Central Asian *upolnomochennye*, Tashkent, 5-6 June 1959; GARF, f.6991, o.3, d.186, l.83. If the religious societies continued to send their agents to outlying parts, Jumashev warned, the steps taken against them might include withdrawal from registration.

403. CARC's *upolnomochennye* usually reported simultaneously the dimensions of mosque attendance and the revenues of the registered mosques and, for the most part, the correlation is unmistakable.

situation in the country likewise enabled believers to enhance their payments.[404]

In any case, attendance and revenues alike were influenced by the general atmosphere surrounding religion at any given moment. Both for instance diminished, particularly perhaps the latter, during Khrushchev's anti-religious campaign, after the sharp rise in the mid 1950s, and income mounted markedly once it was over. Every single oblast' and republic registered a clear growth in mosque revenues in the second half of the 1960s and the aggregate income of all the registered mosques had topped the 2 million ruble mark by 1967 and was close to 3 million by 1970.[405] It was suggested that one of the reasons for this was the 'exposure' of itinerant mullas and the termination of their activity – pursued in the late 1960s with greater energy than before – which brought larger numbers of believers to the registered mosques; another was the improved material situation of the population; and a third, enhanced control of the activity of the executive organs and inspection committees, which apparently decreased errors in book-keeping.[406] As usual, the possibility of a rise in religiosity was ruled out *a priori*.

As of the early 1950s SADUM began insisting that the registered mosques keep receipt-books in which all revenue must be noted.[407] If previously, believers gave money to the mullas for the performance of rites, they now had to pay the mosque treasurer or the person responsible for its finances, from whom the mulla would get his own salary at the end of the month.[408] It was thought that this arrangement, which denied the clergy any income from responding to invitations by believers, would dampen their enthusiasm to

404. I. G. Halimov to CARC, 23 May 1956, L. A. Prikhod'ko, Report, 25 July 1956, and K. F. Tagirov, Resumé, 1 March 1957; GARF, f.6991, o.3, d.457, ll.95-6, d.130, ll.32-3, and d.132, l.65.

405. A. Barmenkov, A. Nurullaev and E. Tarasov, Information, sent by V. Kuroedov to the Central Committee Department of Propaganda, 14 Aug. 1968; GARF, f.6991, o.6, d.147, ll.121-2, and CRA, Information, sent to the CPSU Central Committee, 27 April 1971; TsKhSD, f.5, o.63, d.89, l.100. (For doubts regarding a similar trend in mosque attendance and difficulties in its assessment, see pp.75-6 and 218-9.)

406. *Ibid.*, l.101.

407. See p.129.

408. Almaev to Mahkamova, Nazarov, Kh. N. Iskanderov and I. V. Polianskii, 19 Jan. 1952; TsGAUz, f.2456, o.1, d.142, l.46.

perform rites in private homes,[409] yet there is no evidence that this was the case. Moreover, even after this date, not all income seems to have been registered in the books. The mosques under the jurisdiction of DUMZ and DUMSK were particularly remiss in this respect. At the mosque in Kirovabad in Azerbaijan in the early 1970s the income of the four clerics was derived entirely from the rites they performed and very little money indeed was recorded in the mosque's books.[410] The religious society in Nakhichevan kept no records at all of rites performed by its clergy, who in the 1970s were still receiving money directly from believers.[411] In some places, at least in the Northern Caucasus, and probably in many other rural areas as well, the members of the executive organs were not only old but uneducated, and so not in a position to keep any documentation of the religious society's financial activity.[412] In Dagestan in the early 1970s, however, the mosques' documentation was in the possession of the *akhund* or kept at the homes of members of the executive organs.[413]

The principal source of income was almost certainly the *fitr*, which even in the Soviet Union the religious authority did not exonerate the believer from paying.[414] The *fitr* would be paid in money or in kind (it had originally been fixed at a certain quantity of grain) and had to be paid for every adult member of the family. In the period prior to the fast the clergy reminded believers to conduct the traditional rites connected with it, notably to pay *fitr*, and not to be skimpy with other donations. In addition, those categories of people exonerated from fasting should bring supplementary expiatory gifts to the mosque.[415] Collections of the

409. D. Ahmedov to A. Puzin, 8 Aug. 1962; GARF, f.6991, o.3, d.1388, ll.143-4.

410. A. Galiev, Information, 30 May 1973; GARF, f.6991, o.6, d.537, ll.189-90.

411. I. Bonchkovskii to E. I. Lisavtsev, 1 June 1973; GARF, f.6991, o.6, d.537, ll.175-6.

412. L. Aisov to the CRA, 11 June 1968; GARF, f.6991, o.6, d.153, ll.137-8.

413. Kh. Salahetdinov and I. Mikhalev, Report, given to E. A. Lisavtsev, 26 Oct. 1971; GARF, f.6991, o.6, d.361, l.108.

414. For other traditional payments – *sadaqa*, *zakat* and *ushur* – which were not levied in effect, see pp.153-4.

415. L. A. Prikhod'ko, Memo, 25 July 1956; GARF, f.6991, o.3, d.130, ll.27 and 31. For the registered clergy's insistence that the *fitr* be paid to their mosques rather than elsewhere, see p.263 above. For the possibility of expiation, see p.479.

fitr in private homes were also carried out by unregistered clergy, sometimes at the behest of executive organs of registered religious societies, since they were too few to cope with the task.[416] At first the clergy determined the sum to be paid in each area, but at the end of the 1950s this was forbidden as undermining the concept of voluntary donation. Indeed, in this period the spiritual directorates agreed – in order to accommodate to the legislation on religion – that believers could not be forced to pay *fitr*, which had to be given voluntarily, and that representatives of the religious society were not to go the rounds of private homes to collect it.[417]

The *upolnomochennyi* for Osh Oblast' reported in early 1956 that believers supported the registered mosques, mainly through *fitr*. One mosque, in the *poselok* of Kara-Suu was doing so well that it exceeded the sum it was due to pay SADUM by 50 per cent. All the data – the number of rites performed by the clergy of registered mosques in private homes and the approximate attendance on Fridays and the two major festivals, as well as their revenues – are indeed impressive, both absolutely and when compared with the growth from 1954 to 1955.[418] The same *upolnomochennyi* maintained that mosque attendance had not changed and he, too, attributed the increased revenue of the registered mosques to a stricter and more effective control of incoming moneys and 'the conduct of propaganda' in the mosques to encourage payment of *fitr*.[419]

The *fitr* and other donations given on the festivals did not, however, remain in the coffers of the registered mosques, which were instructed to transmit to the spiritual directorates all revenues brought on the major festivals as *fitr* or other donations.[420] This

416. L. A. Prikhod'ko, Report, 20 May 1953; GARF, f.6991, o.3, d.91, ll.245 and 259.

417. Minutes, CARC session No.21, 22 July 1959; GARF, f.6991, o.3, d.184, ll.182-3. The Muslim religious societies in Astrakhan' Oblast' fixed a sum of five rubles per family member in 1959. When he heard of this CARC *uplnomochennyi* Gul'gazov talked with the clergy who then announced in the mosques that the amount would not be determined, each person bringing as much as he could.

418. I. G. Halimov to CARC, 20 Jan. 1956; GARF, f.6991, o.3, d.457, ll.26-8 and 35-7.

419. I. G. Halimov to CARC, 23 May 1956; GARF, f.6991, o.3, d.457, l.98.

420. See pp.128-9. Also, I. V. Polianskii to G. M. Malenkov, 8 Aug. 1953 –GARF, f.6991, o.3, d.93, l.183.

applied also to moneys received from unregistered groups of believers which in periods of relative laxity registered mosques and the spiritual directorates were permitted to accept, on the stipulation, of course, that they did not themselves initiate their collection outside the mosque's precincts.[421] Still in the late 1960s the executive organs of registered mosques were transferring to the spiritual directorates moneys received on the festivals from unregistered communities.[422]

Apart from the *fitr*, other rites performed in the mosques were occasions for making donations, notably the *khatm-i Qur'an* read at the *tarawa-namaz* during *uraz*. At the conclusion of these readings, as one *upolnomochennyi* wrote with a touch of cynicism, collections of voluntary donations were organised on behalf of SADUM.[423] In the process of Khrushchev's anti-religious campaign, the authorities put an end wherever they could to the performance by registered clergy of *khatm-i Qur'ans* and the recital of *mavluds* both in the registered mosques and in private homes.[424]

The religious societies were responsible for the maintenance of their prayer-houses, many of which had fallen into disrepair after a period of disuse or of use for other purposes, from the time of their closure in the 1920s or 1930s. Even mosques which were not branded as dilapidated or in danger of collapse and so qualified for registration tended to need considerable investment in order to ensure their continued operation as prayer-houses. The contracts drawn up with the local authorities included the upkeep of prayer premises in appropriate condition; disrepair was likely to provide a pretext for ill-wishers to threaten their existence. Moreover, a poor appearance was considered liable to alienate believers. This was a bone of contention between the registered mosques and the spiritual directorates, who sought to divert as much money as possible to themselves and to neglect the preferences of the religious societies. DUMES rejected the requests of six

421. Regulation prepared for discussion by CARC's group of inspectors and approved by CARC session No.5, 1 April 1955; GARF, f.6991, o.3, d.110, l.55.
422. M. Arduvanov, Information, 25 June 1969; GARF, f.6991, o.6, d.220, l.307.
423. N. I. Inogamov to I. V. Polianskii, Uzbekistan Party Central Committee Secretary Z. R. Rahimbaeva, and Deputy Chairman of the Uzbek SSR Council of Ministers G. S. Sultanov, 30 May 1956; TsGAUz, f.2456, o.1, d.186, l.98.
424. For instance, in Kirgiziia – Minutes, CARC session No.31, 6 Oct. 1964; GARF, f.6991, o.4, d.147, l.143.

rural mosques in the Bashkir ASSR to appropriate for themselves for purposes of mosque maintenance funds collected on Uraz-Bayram in 1951.[425] It was an indication of the insubordination of the mosques in Osh Oblast' *vis-à-vis* SADUM that in 1949-50 they began a major program of large-scale repairs. To this end they enlarged their executive organs, bringing in people who lived on the outskirts of the parish to expand possibilities of collecting funds, and sought to curb the influence of unofficial clergy for fear that they competed with the registered societies for funds. Moreover, the mosques received donations for this purpose in the form of construction materials, and in some instances believers volunteered work-days and took part in repairing their mosques.[426] In the relatively lax period of the mid 1950s even the poor communities of the Cherkess AO succeeded in collecting funds for the purpose of repairing their mosques.[427] Sometimes repair work motivated officials of registered mosques to tour the area of their jurisdiction, or even beyond it, in order to collect money from believers.[428] Just occasionally the impossibility of carrying out the repair work without the entire building collapsing provided a pretext for setting up an entirely new structure.[429] Sometimes, too, the religious society, having received permission to undertake major repairs simply proceeded to demolish the mosque and then build a new one; this naturally led to retribution from the local

425. M. Sh. Karimov, Report, prepared for CARC session No.16, 15 Aug. 1951; GARF, f.6991, o.3, d.75, ll.208-9.

426. I. G. Halimov to CARC, 3 Jan. and 3 April 1950, and to H. Akhtiamov, 4 Sept. 1950; GARF, f.6991, o.3, d.454, ll.42, 53 and 79-80. For the resentment of the registered mosques aroused by the financial demands of the spiritual directorates, see p.130.

427. G. F. Frolov, Information, 22 Feb. 1957; GARF, f.6991, o.3, d.132, l.79.

428. For example, in Andijan Oblast, in early 1955 – Majit Khalikov to Kh. N. Iskanderov, 12 March 1955; TsGAUz, f.2456, o.1, d.178, ll.55-8. While in principle opposed to the collection of money outside the precincts of the mosque, CARC did not think the imam in question should be dismissed for the offence –I. V. Polianskii to Kh. N. Iskanderov, 24 March 1955; *ibid.*, l.109.

429. For instance, in the town of Kyzyl-Kiya in Osh Oblast' in 1950 – I. G. Halimov to H. Akhtiamov, 3 Jan. 1951; GARF, f.6991, o.3, d.454, l.96. It is not clear from the document whether this was a pre-planned ruse or the consequence of technical incompetence. The republican and oblast' *upolnomochennye* not unexpectedly complained to the *oblispolkom* chairman about the unauthorised action of the *gorispolkom* in permitting the construction of the new mosque, a measure which was outside its authority.

authorities, who would either pull down the new building or take it over for their own ends.[430]

In the early period kolkhozy would pay the expenses of refurbishing and repairing mosques and provide the requisite labour force.[431] Endeavouring a decade later to explain where the registered religious societies found moneys to conduct repairs and purchase equipment, one CARC *upolnomochennyi* in Central Asia noted that although all their income on festivals was designated for SADUM and revenues from the conduct of rites went to the upkeep of the clergy and other personnel, mosques were being intensively repaired and refurbished. In his view, some income simply did not appear in the books and was used at the discretion of the executive organ and clergy; it was evident at this point that the religious societies were not suffering financial difficulties.[432] Polianskii, in a letter to the CPSU Central Committee and the USSR Council of Ministers bemoaned the unquestionably superior appearance of a number of rural mosques as compared with the local village clubs.[433]

On the whole, however, many mosques even in Central Asia were undoubtedly poor, if not positively dismal, with little in the way of furnishings or decoration; the three mosques in Bukhara combined, a Moscow visitor noted, had a much smaller income than the single Russian Orthodox church in the same town.[434] Not to speak of the unsatisfactory sanitary conditions which pertained in many mosques. In the central mosque in Buinaksk in Dagestan the lavatories and washstands were used by everyone who visited both the mosque – over 1,000 people every Friday –and the adjacent market.[435] In Nakhichevan the head of the republican sanitation department said in the 1970s that doctors

430. For example, in the village of Novo-Musino in Orenburg Oblast' – Reception by N. I. Smirnov of two representatives of its religious society, 15 May 1961; GARF, f.6991, o.4, d.121, l.5.

431. V. Tatarintsev to A. A. Zhdanov, 15 Nov. 1946; RTsKhIDNI, f.17, o.125, d.421, l.109.

432. I. Halimov to CARC, 10 Aug. 1956; GARF, f.6991, o.3, d.457, ll.119-20.

433. I. V. Polianskii to the CPSU Central Committee and USSR Council of Ministers, 20 Sept. 1955; GARF, f.6991, o.3, d.114, l.201.

434. A. Barinskaia to V. A. Kuroedov, undated [late March-early April 1968]; GARF, f.6991, o.6, d.153, l.109.

435. Kh. Salahetdinov and I. Mikhalev, Report, given to E. I. Lisavtsev, 26 Oct. 1971; GARF, f.6991, o.6, d.361, l.111.

were ashamed of going to the mosque and for twenty years nobody had inspected its sanitary conditions, which now reflected that neglect.[436] (It is not clear whether the doctors refrained from going to the mosque because they deemed it unfitting as men of free professions to be seen in a house of religious worship or because of the stench of the lavatories for which they were ostensibly responsible.)

The mosque's lay leadership

The lay leadership of the registered mosques – the *dvadtsatka*, the executive organ and the inspection committee – was habitually comprised entirely, or almost entirely, of people over sixty.[437] These elders often enjoyed considerable authority among believers and throughout the neighbourhood unit, the *mahalla*, or, as it was called in Soviet jargon, the *mikroraion*. The executive organ was usually composed of 'the most competent and experienced' members of the *dvadtsatka*, who were chosen by the registered mosque's general meeting.[438]

Despite the careful delineation of the spheres of activity of clergy and lay officials, there was theoretically no way of obstructing a minister of religion from being a member, even the chairman, of the executive organ or inspection committee.[439] For instance, in Chimkent Oblast' a second imam operated without registration in one mosque, having been sent there by the SADUM qazi for Kazakhstan to fill the post of executive organ chairman.[440] This, however, seems to have occurred only rarely.

436. I. Bonchkovskii to E. I. Lisavtsev, 1 June 1973; GARF, f.6991, o.6, d.537, l.175.

437. A few of these might still officially be working, usually as watchmen or in jobs of that nature. For instance, in Kashka-Darya Oblast', where in the mid 1970s all members of all the lay bodies were over 60, five were still working –P. Khidirov, [Jan. 1974]; GARF, f.6991, o.6, d.567, l.21.

438. CRA, Information, sent to the CPSU Central Committee, 27 April 1971; TsKhSD, f.5, o.63, d.89, l.98. In 1970 there were said to be 1,797 members in the executive organs of the registered mosques, 217 of whom (presumably all executive organ chairmen) received remuneration – *ibid*. It would appear that the aggregate number included members of the inspection committees.

439. I. V. Polianskii to Kh. N. Iskanderov, 13 Sept. 1950; TsGAUz, f.2456, o.1, d.131, l.74.

440. A. Barmenkov, CRA resolution on the work of its *upolnomochennyi* for

More frequently, the clergy sought to take advantage of their authority *vis-à-vis* believers to control the election of members of the executive organ and inspection committee, among other reasons in order – through the election of their associates or relatives – to keep their fingers on the purse-strings of the religious society. Nor were they alone in this. Since membership of a registered society's executive organ entailed the control of considerable funds and influence over religious activity, others, too, vied for election. Often, at least in the larger cities and more traditionally religious communities, significant pressure was exerted by elders wishing to be elected members, and especially chairman or *mutawali*, of the mosque executive organ. For it controlled the income of the imam and directed the activity of the religious society and its members participated, together with the imam, in all *ziyafat* (entertainment with food and drink) to which the former would be invited to recite a *mavlud* or verses from the Qur'an.[441] Sometimes, too, the spiritual directorates sought to influence the election of lay officials in an effort to introduce stronger personalities, who, they apparently believed, would be able to attract more worshippers to the mosques.[442] So did local organs of government, who sought to install people who might identify with, or be 'loyal', to their line.[443] Even CARC *upolnomochennye* thought in terms of having their confidants elected to these executive organs.

Members of the executive organ or inspection committee, who were often versed in religious practice, would be allowed by the clergy to perform religious rites in the event that the clergy could not answer all the needs of local believers.[444] This option they clearly considered preferable to leaving the task to unregistered,

---

Chimkent Oblast', Sh. O. Ospanov, draft, Aug. 1969; GARF, f.6991, o.6, d.290, ll.83-4.

441. Almaev to Tashkent Oblispolkom Deputy Chairman Mahkamov, Obkom Secretary Nazarov, Kh. N. Iskanderov and I. V. Polianskii, 19 Jan. 1952; TsGAUz, f.2456, o.1, d.142, ll.46-8.

442. Kh. N. Iskanderov to Tashkent Obkom Secretary A. Alimov and Oblispolkom Chairman Jalilov, 27 May 1954; TsGAUz, f.2456, o.1, d.162, ll.176-7.

443. Deputy Chairman of the Bukhara Gorsovet M. K. Barakatova, Address, All-Union conference of CRA *upolnomochennye*, 9 Sept. 1969; GARF, f.6991, o.6, d.217, l.93.

444. Ishan Babakhan to SADUM members and to *imam-khatibs* and executive organs of major (*sobornykh*) mosques, 6 Nov. 1952; TsGAUz, f.2456, o.1, d.144, l.173.

unofficial clergy. In Chimkent Oblast' people capable of performing religious rites tended to be elected to the lay leadership of the religious societies. In three of its five mosques at least two thirds of the members of the *dvadtsatka* at the end of the 1960s, and in one case all of them, belonged to this category and so in fact 'served as clergy'.[445] From the point of view of the authorities, this was no less a violation of the legislation on religion than the interference of the clergy in the administrative and financial affairs of the religious society.[446] In the town of Gur'ev in Kazakhstan, two members of the *dvadtsatka* of the oblast's sole registered mosque, one of them a former mulla, preached at burials on the need for strict observance of religious customs and told participants at memorial ceremonies that those who did not perform religious rites and attend mosque were doomed and would suffer in the next world.[447]

Officially, the minister of religion attached to any registered religious society was administratively subordinate to the executive organ. He was hired by it as representing the religious society which had elected it, as a specialist in the conduct of religious rites for the specific purpose of performing these rites although, according to Muslim tradition and the perception of the believers, the imam was the head, the leading person, in the community. So in practice the executive organ and inspection committee often became the *aktiv* of the clergy, and the entire *dvadtsatka* a sort of religious council which did their bidding. Especially in periods when official policy was to restrict the activity of the imams and the spiritual directorates who appointed them and to whom they owed allegiance, CARC's *upolnomochennye* sought to 'clarify the correct position' to the religious communities over whose lay representatives they had a certain leverage. They pointed out that a distinction should be made between questions of dogma and religious law and all other matters – administrative, financial and so on – leaving only the former within the authority of the

445. A. Barmenkov, CRA resolution on the work of its *upolnomochennyi* for Chimkent Oblast', Sh. O. Ospanov, draft, Aug, 1969; GARF, f.6991, o.6, d.290, ll.83-4.
446. Theses of lecture, sent to the CPSU Central Committee Propaganda Department, 19 June 1968; GARF, f.6991, o.6, d.147, l.43.
447. S. Irgaliev to A. Nurullaev, 8 May 1974; GARF, f.6991, o.6, d.633, ll.16-17.

imam.[448] Nonetheless, in practice this was not the case, the clergy's powers extending to all spheres of community activity. In places, moreover, where the local organs of government and, more specifically in the 1960s and 1970s, the commissions set up under their auspices to supervise the implementation of the legislation on religion, did not function as prescribed, there was no incentive for the clergy to relinquish their leadership role.[449]

Given the tenacity of tradition, on the one hand, and the contradictory inclination of Soviet legislation, on the other, it was not surprising that disputes arose between the clergy and lay officials of registered mosques which totally disrupted their effective operation. The background of these confrontations was sundry: sometimes the imam would be accused of being too close to the authorities, unduly lax in the observance of the precepts of Islam, or even an atheist.[450] At the other extreme, were occasional instances when believers reacted negatively to an imam's demands regarding their low level of religiosity.[451] For instance, in Leningrad at the very end of the 1960s or the beginning of the 1970s, a new *imam-khatib* was appointed who had studied at the Mir-Arab Medrese; he sought, as it were, to turn the clock back, forbidding women to participate in funerals and proclaiming it was sinful to go to the theatre. The mosque's believers filed complaints protesting his 'fanaticism', and the executive organ cautioned him that it was impermissible to 'distort the teaching of Islam and contravene resolutions of the mosque's executive organ'.[452] More frequently,

448. H. Akhtiamov and A. A. Puzin, Adddress, Conference of CARC's Central Asian *upolnomochennye*, Tashkent, 5 June 1959, and All-Union conference of CARC *upolnomochennye*, 18-20 April 1960; GARF, f.6991, o.3, d.186, ll.53-4 and 225, and d.208, l.130. The hold of the *upolnomochennye* over the religious societies' lay leaders emanated from their right to reject any one of them.

449. For example, in Nakhichevan – I. Bonchkovskii to E. I. Lisavtsev, 1 June 1973; GARF, f.6991, o.6, d.537, l.175.

450. This happened in Batumi, in the sole registered mosque in the Ajar ASSR, in the mid 1950s and a CARC official went there especially with orders to sort matters out. The deputy chairman of the local council of ministers favoured the imam – although the KGB did not – and the dispute was resolved in his favour – L. A. Prikhod'ko to I. V. Polianskii, 5 May 1956; GARF, f.6991, o.3, d.127, ll.56-9.

451. Such issues are reflected only rarely in the CARC documentation; see, for example, pp. 261-2 above; it is possible that CARC and its officials tended to highlight the more material aspects, in keeping with their perceptions.

452. Ashirov, *Evoliutsiia islama v SSSR*, p.10. The language used would imply

tensions developed in connection with the religious society's financial resources, and from time to time an imam would be withdrawn from registration for interfering in the financial affairs of his religious society. There were even instances where clergy were suspended for unauthorised appropriation of funds.[453] Seeking to analyse the resignation of a number of clergy in early 1960, the *upolnomochennyi* for the Kazakh SSR attributed it in part to endless disputes over material matters between the clergy, on the one hand, and the *mutawaliyyat* and the entire *aktiv*, on the other.[454] On one occasion in the Bashkir ASSR an imam was accused of organising a group of the more 'reactionarily-minded' believers, who concealed his income from the local financial organs. The group was exposed by other believers of the same religious society who informed DUMES and the imam was dismissed.[455] (In this particular case it seems that the financial aspect was a pretext for action against an imam who either took sides in an internal dispute between the believers or somehow preferred, and perhaps conferred benefits upon, one group at the expense of another.)

---

that here, too, it was not just a theological issue, but also a power struggle within the religious society between the clergy and the lay leadership.

453. For example, the mulla in the village of Novye Timersiany, Ul'ianovsk Oblast', in November 1963 – Reception by N. I. Smirnov of two believers from that village who sought to have him re-registered, 25 Aug. 1964. By this time, apparently unknown to the two visitors, the religious society itself had been withdrawn from registration for being without a minister of religion and having but few members – Minutes, CARC session No.15, 3 July 1964; GARF, f.6991, o.4, d.148, ll.200-21, and d.147, ll.21-2. In another instance in 1972 a qazi in a rural mosque in Dagestan had augmented his own salary by agreement with the mosque treasurer but without that of the executive organ; he had also performed a *mavlud* and *zikr*, distributed some of the money he received to several believers and appropriated the lion's share. The executive organ complained to the CARC *upolnomochennyi*, who withdrew him from registration. He also withdrew another qazi who insulted believers, refused to subordinate himself to the executive organ and interfered in financial matters, and the muezzin of the Khasavyurt mosque who had dismissed and appointed a watchman and cleaner without permission from the executive organ, performed various rites and not given the money he received for this to the mosque – M. S. Gajiev to A. Nurullaev, 27 July 1973; GARF, f.6991, o.6, d.629, ll.165-6.

454. B. Jumashev, Address, All-Union conference of CARC *upolnomochennye*, 18-20 April 1960; GARF, f.6991, o.3, d.208, l.127. For these resignations, see pp.213-4 above.

455. A. Tazetdinov, Information, 28 Feb. 1957; GARF, f.6991, o.3, d.132, l.72.

Certainly, misuse of finances led from time to time to internal disagreements and even disputes within the registered religious societies themselves, between believers and the lay leadership or among members of the latter. Sometimes the cause of trouble might be the alleged misdeeds, financial and otherwise, of the community's leadership. In one case, at least, doubts expressed by believers regarding the expenditure of the religious society's funds led to a brawl.[456] An executive organ or its chairman would occasionally be suspected of appropriating funds which belonged to the community as a whole. In Bukhara a *mutawali* was dismissed for not entering all donations in the books and pilfering some of them.[457] In one mosque in Baku the 'administration' (presuambly the executive organ) was changed because 'it answered to no one' regarding the mosque's revenues and the mosque was, indeed, moneyless; within three months of the change it was able to give DUMZ 10,000 rubles and still retain a reserve of 15,000 rubles.[458]

Instances were reported in which the executive organ would do all in its power to prevent the convening of a general meeting of believers where controversial issues might be aired.[459] The rank and file believers, for their part, having, in the words of one commentator, 'absorbed the democratic principles of the Soviet way of life', sought to further 'democratise' the conduct of affairs and to ensure that both the clergy and the lay leadership report regularly to them.[460]

Other quarrels within registered religious societies, which did not focus directly on financial matters, might centre on who should hold community positions, either as clergy or as lay leaders.[461]

456. I. Halimov to CARC, 20 Jan. 1956; GARF, f.6991, o.3, d.457, l.41.

457. Address by Deputy Chairman of the Bukhara Gorsovet M. K. Barakatova, All-Union conference of CRA *upolnomochennye*, 9 Sept. 1969; GARF, f.6991, o.6, d.217, l.90.

458. Reception by N. I. Smirnov of A. F. Temirbulatov, 24 Aug. 1957; GARF, f.6991, o.4, d.175, l.125.

459. For example, in Moscow where the chairman of the executive organ was suspected by believers of embezzlement – he seems not to have entered considerable sums in the religious society's books – and was accused of appointing clergy whom he could manipulate – Reception by N. I. Smirnov of three members of the Moscow religious society, 9 Dec. 1963, and of seven others, 25 Jan. and 15 April 1965; GARF, f.6991, o.4, d.137, l.12, and d.171, ll.11 and 14-15.

460. Ashirov, *Evoliutsiia islama v SSSR*, p.11. Ashirov does not bring examples.

461. For example, a dispute in the Kazan' community which was brought

Occasionally, such strife might have a national character, as the protracted dissension between Uighurs and Uzbeks at the 'Uighur' mosque in Andijan, the former not being willing to share the running of the mosque with Uzbeks.[462]

Despite the difficulties which many of them encountered, caught, as they were, between the spiritual administrations, on the one hand, and CARC's *upolnomochennye* and the organs of local government on the other, the registered religious societies and their clergy and lay personnel were often the object, not of the sympathy of those citizens they sought to represent, but of their criticism. On the whole, they were no less compromised in the eyes of the believer population than were the spiritual directorates. This was especially true if they received side benefits from the secular authority. The imam of one mosque in Namangan, for instance, who had previously been an authoritative figure and had attracted worshippers from outlying kishlaks, was branded as 'a Soviet mulla' after being allowed to make the *hajj* to Mecca.[463] In Tajikistan the registered imams in fact complained that their unregistered counterparts dubbed them and their mosques with the epithet 'Soviet'.[464] Unquestionably, the registered mosques and clergy, like the directorates, sailed with the wind and made concessions to the powers-that-be in their endeavour to ensure their well-being and sometimes very existence. Nonetheless, despite the somewhat miserable image some of them undoubtedly acquired, their ability to co-exist with the regime and their flexibility made it possible for the latter to condone the survival of a religion with which by definition it could have no common language. While it might be presumptuous to accept at face value the CRA's estimate that the mosques not only maintained their position among the population

---

before CARC – Reception by N. Smirnov of S. Timirkhanov, chairman of the mosque's executive organ, 12 Nov. 1963; GARF, f.6991, o.4, d.137, ll.16-17.

462. M. A. Khalikov to I. V. Polianskii, 19 May 1956; TsGAUz, f.2456, o.1, d.198, l.81. For the national factor and its influence on Islam, see Chapter 12.

463. Minutes, Instructional meeting of CARC's *upolnomochennye* in the Uzbek SSR, 15-17 March 1956; TsGAUz, f.2456, o.1, d.183, l.58.

464. D. Ahmedov to A. Puzin, 21 Feb. 1961; GARF, f.6991, o.3, d.1737, l.12.

but in some instances actually enhanced it,[465] there seems to be little doubt that they played a significant role in safeguarding the status of Islam throughout the period under discussion, their rather undignified conduct and sycophancy notwithstanding.[466] As one scholar who researched the history of the Tatar community of Orenburg Oblast', has pointed out, the mosque was never empty. On the contrary, it was attended throughout the period under study, despite the risks and difficulties mosque attendance entailed, especially for those still in the work force.[467]

The fluctuation of mosque attendance bore testimony to the sensitivity of clergy and worshippers alike to the opportunities which changing times provided. There was clearly a core of believers who were not to be daunted by the possibility of threats and repression, but there was also a shifting, wavering stratum which, when things were relatively lax, sought out the mosque yet tended to be deterred by indications of a worsening situation. (All this assumes that the statistical data for mosque attendance are basically reliable.) What is clear, however, is that on the all-union level there was no continuum testifying to a steady decline in mosque attendance. This was the litmus test, for it demonstrated that while older people comprised the nucleus of worshippers in most parts of the country, this was the result of convenience only. Old people have a tendency to die, yet this natural process, from which those who attended mosque were not spared, did not reduce mosque attendance. Those who died were always replaced by others, especially as they, in turn, left the labour force and became pensioners.[468] This meant that although the registered mosques were hardly centres of great spiritual edification, they did serve as an optimal framework, given the circumstances, for preserving Islam and Islamic tradition.

465. CRA, Information, sent to the Central Committee, 22 May 1970; TsKhSD, f.5, o.62, d.38, 1.5.

466. On returning from Bukhara, the CRA legal advisor described the registered clergy in that town as 'inclined to time-serving' – A. Barinskaia to V. A. Kuroedov, undated [late March–early April 1968]; GARF, f.6991, o.6, d.153, 1.108.

467. Kosach, *Gorod na styke dvukh kontinentov*, p.107.

468. This phenomenon was remarked upon by some of the more observant of the CRA's *upolnomochennye* who saw that the numbers of worshippers remained basically stable. One of them wrote that 'the natural decrease is being compensated for...by a new generation of believers, naturally elderly people, who 5-10 years ago were aged 45-50' – Sh. Ospanov, 16 Nov. 1973; GARF, f.6991, o.6, d.633, 1.92.

Part III. UNOFFICIAL, 'PARALLEL' ISLAM

5

UNREGISTERED ACTIVITY

The unregistered religious associations

It was generally agreed by all who observed the Muslim scene that the registered mosques and religious societies were too few and far between to cater to the religious needs of the believer population. It was similarly axiomatic that in these circumstances the creation and existence of unregistered associations and groups could not be prevented.[1] Indeed, such formations operated throughout the postwar period in all areas with Muslim inhabitants, for there were Muslim believers wherever people from the Muslim nationalities lived, dictating the ubiquitous performance of certain rites and customs. Moreover, in most areas they considerably outnumbered the registered societies, demonstrating that Muslim religious life was in fact developing spontaneously, beyond the influence of the religious establishment and the procedures stipulated by law. According to one source, in Central Asia registered mosques and religious societies comprised less than 1 per cent of all operating

---

1. The difference between an association and a group does not seem to have been clearly spelled out. The criterion was apparently neither the availability of prayer-premises nor the existence of a cleric. For example, in the Kabardino-Balkar ASSR in the early 1960s count was taken of 18 unregistered societies and 13 groups, all 31 of which appear to have had clergy and only four permanent prayer-premises – N. I. Smirnov to A. A. Puzin, 28 March 1963; GARF, f.6991, o.3, d.1607, l.18.

mosques and *mazars*.[2] As of the mid-1960s the regime's experts on Islam designed this non-establishment 'parallel Islam'.

That the size of the unregistered groups tended to be small was, like their aggregate quantity, a consequence of circumstances. The dangers involved in unofficial group existence in Soviet society required the taking of precautions and operating unobtrusively.[3] The principal exception to this rule were the few communities in some of the larger cities in areas where the indigenous population was not one of the Muslim nationalities, such as Leningrad or Gor'kii; the urge of these communities to formalise their existence was no secret, on the contrary, it drove them to demonstrative, almost provocative activity, whose effectiveness depended on it being large-scale.[4] At certain times there were also rather large communities in several of the towns and even raion centres in Uzbekistan which had no registered mosque, and just a few other big groups in other parts of Central Asia.[5] In some Tatar villages

2. Poliakov, *Everyday Islam*, p.95. Poliakov published his book in 1990, but his findings were based on thirty years of study by the Central Asian Expedition of Moscow State University's History Faculty – *ibid.*, p.6.

3. It is necessary to stress that information, and particularly statistical data, regarding the unregistered groups tended to be incomplete and questionable. (For statistical information, see pp.85-9.) In the words of one CARC *upolnomochennyi*, while clergy and believers in registered mosques generally had confidence in the *upolnomochennye* and so were prepared to provide them with information, and the latter could visit prayer-services in registered mosques with regularity, neither was true for the unregistered mosques. Since the latter knew that the authorities sought to close them down, they were not prepared to provide them with information that might comprise the basis for such action, and since they only met for collective prayer sporadically it was all the more difficult to find and visit them and to obtain data – H. A. Akhtiamov, Address, Instructional conference of CARC's Central Asian *upolnomochennye*, Tashkent, 17-20 Dec. 1949, f.6991, o.3, d.67, ll.122-4. I have sought in this chapter to provide only data which seem relatively reliable and without which the picture would be less complete, although aware that they, too, may not be completely correct.

4. See p.88. For the struggle conducted by these groups to register, see pp.652-3.

5. In Termez, for instance, one group met in a mosque from 1945 until well into the 1950s with an attendance of 70 at daily *namaz*, about 300 on Fridays and 2,000 on festivals. In Denau, also in Surkhan-Darya Oblast', a group had been operating since 1943 which had only a slightly smaller number of worshippers –Kh. N. Iskanderov to I. V. Polianskii, 4 Oct. 1955; TsGAUz, f.2456, o.1, d.193, l.132. (One of these groups was registered in 1956, the other in 1957.) One group in Osh Oblast', too, had about 400 believers at the beginning of the 1950s, 20-25 of whom attended daily *namaz* and 100-150 the *jum'a namaz* –I. G. Halimov to H. A. Akhtiamov, 10 March 1951; GARF, f.6991, o.3,

in the RSFSR, too, membership of the unregistered community might be quite considerable, for example in the Mordvinian ASSR, where in 1949 twenty of the sixty Tatar settlements were known to have unregistered groups.[6] Since, however, the unregistered groups tended on the whole to be small, the numbers involved in those groups which were accounted for, were in most areas far fewer than the ones who participated in prayer-services in the registered mosques.[7]

Although formally the destruction of the entire Muslim institutional network embarked upon in the 1920s had been consummated by the end of the 1930s, there is considerable evidence to suggest that Muslim activity persisted in a great many areas. In Tajikistan and Uzbekistan, especially in the rural sector, many mosques were never closed down and continued functioning.[8] Throughout the

---

d.454, l.102.

6. Manerov, Report, Minutes, Instructional meeting No.26, 1-2 Dec. 1949; GARF, f.6991, o.3, d.60, l.70. Manerov mentioned specifically two villages with 500 and 450 believers respectively. CARC inspector N .I. Abushaev, who had lived in one of the Mordvinian ASSR's rural areas, did not believe that just twenty villages had unregistered groups; he was convinced they existed in every Tatar settlement – *ibid.*, l.83.

7. In the Bashkir ASSR in 1948, for instance, there were 24 registered groups at which 8,840 worshippers prayed on Qurban-Bayram, and 23 unregistered communities with 684 worshippers. A year later there were said to be 22 unregistered groups with 1,500 believers; and in the Mari ASSR 17 groups with 2,500 people – N. Tagiev, A short survey, undated [early 1949], and M. Sh. Karimov and Nabatov, Reports, Minutes, No.27, Instructional meeting (CARC employees with *upolnomochennye*), 28-29 Oct. 1949; GARF, f.6991, o.4, d.23, l.16, and o.3, d.60, ll.110 and 114. (Interestingly, Karimov admitted that he had information concerning only 28 out of the republic's 63 raiony.) Similarly, while the 22 registered Muslim societies in the three Transcaucasian republics boasted 33,170 believers in the early 1960s, the 28 unregistered societies and one unregistered group had 2,200 – N. Smirnov, Information, 8 Aug. 1962. And, on the all-union level, the 374 unregistered groups taken count of in 1965 had 24,281 participants, and the 138 registered ones – 137,368 – Information handed to E. A. Tarasov at the CPSU Central Committee, 15 Nov. 1965; GARF, f.6991, o.3, d.1390, l.23, and d.1484, l.178.

8. K. Hamidov to I. V. Polianskii, 7 Dec. 1945; Minutes, CARC session No.13, 10-11 July 1947; and Keller, *The Struggle against Islam in Uzbekistan, 1921-1941*, pp. 326-9. Here and there other mosques were also said to have functioned throughout the years of repression, for example, in Rostov-on-Don, where one mosque functioned without interruption from 1924 up to the time of its registration in 1944 – Minutes, CARC session No.16a, 7-8 Sept. 1951; GARF, f.6991, o.3, d.30, l.364, and d.75, l.64, and o.4, d.19, l.428 (statement by N. Tagiev).

country, notably in the more inaccessible parts, prayer-services had been held in the open during the whole period of collectivisation, the purges and the war.[9] Finally, in 1942-3 with the initial signs of a changed attitude towards religion, including Islam, on the part of the leading organs in Moscow, a first batch of new religious associations came into being.

Most of the associations which sprang up during the war seem to have arisen spontaneously as a result of local initiative, but a few were the fruit of efforts on the part of representatives (*muhtasibs*) of TsDUM. In Omsk Oblast', for instance, where in the years 1942-4 these *muhtasibs* made the rounds of the localities appealing for help in the war effort and where there were no Muslim religious associations, they sought to influence believers to combine to create such communities. This they would do at general meetings of Tatar and Kazakh kolkhozniki, called to hear TsDUM's war appeal, and in Omsk itself at a special gathering of believers of these two nationalities.[10] In the two or so years after the establishment of SADUM, its representatives acted in similar fashion, touring the areas under their jurisdiction to encourage believers to initiate religious activity, although in Central Asia, too, a large number of religious associations were the product of moves by believers in the localities without any outside urging.[11] In Kazakhstan, even in the least religious parts, where Kazakhs mixed most with Slavs, 'old survivals' and religious traditions persisted,

9. N. I. Abushaev, Minutes, Instructional meeting No.26, 1-2 Dec. 1949. In some towns, too, unregistered groups functioned throughout, for example, in Bugul'ma in the Tatar ASSR, where a group operated since 1934 (presumably in the wake of the closure of the official mosque) – Reception by N. I. Smirnov of a representative of the believers of Bugul'ma, 23 April 1960. Most of the Chechen-Ingush ASSR's mosques seem also to have operated until the deportation in 1944 – A. Alisov to A. A. Puzin, 16 March 1962; GARF, f.6991, o.3, d.60, l.83, and d.1606, ll.15-16, and o.4, d.110, l.18.

10. P. D. Bezdel' to I. V. Polianskii, 7 Dec. 1944; GARF, f.6991, o.3, d.4, ll.100-1, and see p.103. TsDUM representative for the oblasti of Omsk and Novosibirsk M. Sadykov found that in some kolkhozy, where clergy had taken up management jobs, they used these posts as a cover to visit the homes of believers and perform religious rites there.

11. Reporting the existence in just three raiony of Tashkent Oblast' of 34 mosques which operated without registration, the CARC *upolnomochennyi* noted that 18 of them had opened since the establishment of SADUM – K. Mustafin to Obkom Secretary Mavlianov and Oblispolkom Chairman Turgunov, 10 Nov. 1945; GARF, f.6991, o.3, d.30, l.286.

and the *upolnomochennyi* who took up his post in Kokchetau, for instance, in early 1946 found more than thirty functioning communities in his oblast'.[12]

By 1945, when CARC's *upolnomochennye* began reporting on Islamic life in their areas of jurisdiction, they informed Moscow that most raiony, if not most settlements, boasted unregistered groups of believers. Some of them held collective prayers every Friday, but the majority were thought to do so just twice a year on the main festivals. While some were led by former mullas or muezzins, in others prayers were conducted by local *aksakals*, or elders, usually by turn. In all of them, however, the basic rites were performed, especially those relating to the dead (burial and memorial ceremonies).[13] The south-west part of Sverdlovsk Oblast', bordering the Bashkir ASSR, had some sixty settlements with a Tatar or Bashkir population, in almost all of which were people, 'more or less able to understand Muslim religious books', who fulfilled the task of mulla or muezzin. They performed ceremonies like name-giving, marriages and funerals illegally. Prayers were generally performed in private homes, sometimes in small groups. In industrial centres religious belief and activity were thought to be weaker, probably due to a dearth of people with any religious education capable of acting as mullas and to a greater caution among those who might be able or likely to lead community activity.[14]

Which of these groups did in fact register was often the result of untoward circumstances over which they themselves had no control. Some, even among those which had prayer premises and a minister of religion, for various reasons discussed in the previous chapter, did not file applications to register. One major consideration against doing so was that it put paid to chances of remaining undetected. Thus, in North Osetia there were quite a number of Muslim believers in the rural areas, who did not apply to open mosques. Yet, only one village was known in mid-1945 to be

12. Minutes, Conference of CARC *upolnomochennye*, Alma-Ata, 2 Oct. 1946; GARF, f.6991, o.3, d.41, ll.53-4.

13. For example, in the Bashkir ASSR – M. Sh. Karimov to I. V. Polianskii and Bashkir ASSR SNK Chairman S. A. Vagapov, 8 Oct. 1945; GARF, f.6991, o.3, d.26, l.10. Karimov based his information on conversations with believers and data in the possession of TsDUM.

14. Excerpts from conference of CARC *upolnomochennye*, Novosibirsk, 31 May 1946; GARF, f.6991, o.3, d.36, ll.55ob.-56.

actually conducting prayer-services; for it had sent representatives to the CARC *upolnomochennyi* to enquire as to the procedure for opening a prayer-house, although it, too, took no actual steps to process an application.[15] Moreover the great majority of those that did had their requests rejected, including many who filed repeated ones. They then had to decide whether to persevere in their activity in the hope either of one day changing the ruling against their opening a mosque or of escaping repression by somehow keeping a low profile. Most religious groups, having formed, did not choose to cease operating unless compelled or pressured to do so. It was not that most of the groups throughout the country, at least in the very early period (in the mid 1940s), sought to operate clandestinely, but rather that they apparently assumed that, so long as they were discreet, they would not be molested.[16] In two raiony in Penza Oblast' where there were a number of Tatar villages, believers persisted in conducting religious rituals in their mosques without processing any request for registration. And in those villages where there was no available mosque, they prayed at the cemetery.[17]

In most oblasti in Kazakhstan, where for reasons which have been discussed, registration tended to be particularly cumbersome and to have even less prospects of success than in most places, by mid 1945 groups of believers were gathering for prayer purposes on Fridays and festivals in private homes. These were chiefly older people who elected their own mullas, and most of the groups were not large. In Alma-Ata itself, where CARC had agreed to the opening of a mosque, believers were still meeting in a private home, because the mosque had not yet been vacated. Both in Jarkent, in Taldy-Kurgan Oblast', and in Kokchetau there was also a group which met in a private house, although the former

15. Kononov to I. V. Polianskii, 3 July 1945; GARF, f.6991, o.3, d.25, ll.144-144ob. The reason for their failing to follow up this enquiry is not known, that is whether they were deterred by what they heard or whether some outside factor influenced them.

16. A number of CARC *upolnomochennye* testified that the unregistered groups functioned quite openly. For example, A. Saltovskii, Report, Conference of CARC's *upolnomochennye* in the Kazakh and Kirgiz SSRs, 30 Sept. 1946; GARF, f.6991, o.3, d.41, l.96.

17. Gorbachev, Report, 28 June 1945; also M. Sh. Karimov to I. V. Polianskii and S. A. Vagapov, 8 Oct. 1945 – GARF, f.6991, o.3, d.25, ll.29-30, and d.26, l.10. For the use of cemeteries for collective prayer, see pp.300-1.

town had a vacant mosque (the latter had none). In Semipalatinsk there was a registered mosque, but groups existed in at least two of the city's suburbs and in a number of the oblast's raiony. So did they in some localities in the oblast' of Eastern Kazakhstan and in several towns in the oblasti of Karaganda and Akmolinsk, in none of which was there a single registered mosque, and in at least one kolkhoz in Pavlodar Oblast'.[18] In Kustanai Oblast' there were two groups, one with 'some kind of mosque'. Within two years people were performing rites in Eastern Kazakhstan in the open and in many raiony of Kustanai Muslims were being permitted to conduct rites, although not allowed to formalise their registration.[19] There were also groups in a number of places in the oblasti of Aktiubinsk, Western Kazakhstan and Kzyl-Orda[20] and another in the town of Gur'ev. Finally, there were a large number of groups in the two southern oblasti that were traditional centres of religious activity, Southern Kazakhstan and Jambul, neither of which had as yet a single functioning mosque; in the town of Jambul there was a large group which conducted prayer-meetings in the open.

This situation was thought to reflect the traditions of Kazakh nomad society, as it had been prior to collectivisation, which had never known a centralised clerical authority.[21] The CARC *upolnomochennyi* for the Kazakh SSR pointed out that since terminating the conduct of rites was possible only by administrative measures, which would arouse dissatisfaction among believers, he endorsed the request of SADUM's representatives to allow the operation in rural localities, and first of all in raion centres, of 'mosqueless mullas', who would serve as intermediaries between believers and the spiritual directorate and as 'organisers of all religious affairs', including the opening of mosques.[22]

18. In Pavlodar itself a decision had been taken to open a mosque, but implementation was not yet under way.

19. I. V. Polianskii to A. A. Zhdanov and K. E. Voroshilov, 22 July 1947; RTsKhIDNI, f.17, o.125, d.506, l.170.

20. In addition to the registered mosque which was due to open in the near future in the towns of Ural'sk and Kzyl-Orda.

21. A. Saltovskii, Report, Conference of CARC's *upolnomochennye* in the Kazakh and Kirgiz SSRs, 30 Sept. 1946; GARF, f.6991, o.3, d.41, l.87. And see pp.185-7.

22. N. Sabitov to I. V. Polianskii, 20 July 1945; GARF, f.6991, o.3, 21, ll.49-51. There was some discussion as to the use of terminology regarding unregistered clergy – see pp. 325-8 below – but the more pedantic preferred 'mosqueless mullas'

The Kirgiz SSR Council of People's Commissars took a similiar line. It argued that most of the population lived a long way from a registered mosque, that most settlements did not have a sufficient number of believers to maintain a mosque according to established procedure, that, moreover, it was neither expedient nor possible to open a dense network of registered mosques, and finally that obstructing the fulfilment of believers' religious needs would have negative consequences. Given these circumstances, it advised allowing groups of believers in localities where there was no registered mosque to in fact select an *aksakal* to perform the necessary rites and to register him as a cleric affiliated to the nearest official mosque.[23] In some of the more remote and mountainous areas registered mosques were situated well over 160 km from each other and were clearly inaccessible to most villagers in the oblast'. In Jalalabad Oblast', for example, some settlements were located as much as 350 km from the nearest registered community, and indeed it was thought at one time that this oblast' had as many as seventy unregistered groups.[24]

In the Turkmen SSR, with its minimal number of registered mosques, unregistered groups were inevitably also the rule rather than the exception. This referred, among others, to that republic's Shiite community, for SADUM did not at any time take Shiite communities under its wing.[25] Shiites, most of them so-called Ironis, the largely uzbekified descendants of Persian slaves captured in the seventeenth century and of Persian merchant communities, resided in Central Asia in Maryi Oblast' – formerly Merv – and in Ashkhabad in the Turkmen SSR, in the southern part of Garm Oblast' in Tajikistan, and in Bukhara, the latter two communities being likewise destined to an unregistered existence for the same

---

to 'itinerant mullas', which in most instances did not correspond to reality.

23. T. Kulatov, Chairman of the Kirgiz SSR SNK, to CARC, 18 July 1945; GARF, f.6991, o.3, d.21, ll.52-52ob.

24. H. A. Akhtiamov, A short communication, Instructional conference of CARC's Central Asian *upolnomochennye*, Tashkent, 17-20 Dec. 1949; GARF, f.6991, o.3, d.67, ll.109-12.

25. The head of CARC's Department for Eastern Religions, N. Tagiev, suggested in 1947 that the *upolnomochennyi* for the Turkmen SSR present proposals for bringing the Shiite communities under the auspices of SADUM, just as DUMZ catered for both Shiites and Sunnis – Minutes, CARC session No.13, 10-11 July 1947; GARF, f.6991, o.4, d.19, l.430.

reason.[26] Indeed, it appears that the Shiites tended to pray in extended family groups, which might be as large as 2-300.[27]

Yet even in localities where registered mosques existed, unregistered groups operated, often in considerable numbers. The phenomenon of opening actual prayer-houses without sanction – as distinct from prayer-meetings held in the open or in private homes – was paradoxically most widespread in the republic which also boasted the largest number of registered mosques, Uzbekistan. This was a reflection of it being a traditional centre of Islamic activity and having by far the largest Muslim population. In the city of Tashkent, with its abundance of registered mosques, there were dozens of unregistered mosques which opened without authorisation.[28] One of the reasons, apparently, was the existence in Uzbekistan of a plethora of abandoned former mosques, that is, mosques which had been shut down in the 1920s and 1930s, but not requisitioned for other purposes. Moreover, most of these abandoned or empty mosques, as they were called in Soviet terminology, retained the outward appearance of a mosque. Wherever the building of a mosque stood unused, there was a good chance of local believers seeking to renew religious activity there and re-open it as a functioning prayer-house. By September 1945 the authorities knew of thirty-one such mosques which had opened in Namangan Oblast', thirty-nine in Andijan Oblast', twenty-six in Fergana Oblast', forty-five in Tashkent Oblast', and so on. And these were just in those raiony for which they had information. In some areas, however, most former mosques were in use as cultural-educational institutions or as store-houses. Even in some of these a room might still be in use for collective prayer. For instance, one classroom in a kolkhoz school in Tashkent Oblast', which was housed in a mosque closed down in 1937, was being so used in 1946. An unregistered mulla conducted the *namaz* there five times daily, worshippers using the same entrance and

26. For the Shiites in Bukhara and Kagan, also in Bukhara Oblast', and kishlaks in the vicinity of these two towns, see A. Barinskaia to V. A. Kuroedov, undated [late March-early April 1968]; GARF, f.6991, o.6, d.153, l.110. Acording to one source, the Ironis of Uzbekistan number about 1 million – Fathi, 'Otines: the unknown women clerics of Central Asian Islam', n.39.

27. Minutes, CARC session No.26, 1-2 Dec. 1949; GARF, f.6991, o.3, d.60, l.96.

28. K. Mustafin to Obkom Secretary Mavlianov and Oblispolkom Chairman Turgunov, 10 Nov. 1945; GARF, f.6991, o.3, d.30, l.286.

corridors as did pupils, so that everyone was aware of what was going on.[29] In addition to these buildings of former mosques, which comprised the majority of the new unauthorised mosques, a number of mosques were actually built in the years 1944-5. Often these new constructions were on the site of mosques destroyed in the prewar period of repression. In Tashkent Oblast' mosques which had been built recently without permission were revealed in all those raiony where a check-up was conducted in the mid-1940s.[30] Still in the mid-1970s the authorities knew of eleven unregistered religious associations which operated there on a permanent basis and thirty more which functioned periodically, with a total membership of about 10,000 believers.[31]

Nor did the process of opening unregistered mosques ease up in 1946, when over 600 unauthorised mosques operated in just four oblasti in Uzbekistan;[32] no less than thirty-nine prayer-houses were taken count of in the single town of Kokand.[33] In the summer months of that year, according to Minister of State Security V. A. Abakumov, 150 mosques were opened without authorisation throughout the republic.[34] Although 172 were closed down in the second quarter of 1947,[35] and closures continued in the ensuing period, unregistered mosques continued to operate in large numbers, especially in rural areas, often initiating some sort of unofficial affiliation to registered religious societies, which they claimed to represent and to which they would transfer part of

29. Mustafin to Tashkent Oblispolkon Chairman Turgunov and to I. Ibadov, 19 April 1946; TsGAUz, f.2456, o.1, d.67, l.4.

30. *Ibid.*, l.2, and I. Ibadov to Chairman of the Uzbek SSR SNK Abdujabr Abdurahmanov, with a copy to Party Secretary Osman Yusupov, undated (translated from Uzbek by CARC inspector N. Tagiev, 11 Sept. 1945); GARF, f.6991, o.3, d.30, ll.355-6.

31. A. Barmenkov to the CPSU Central Committee Propaganda Department, 13 March 1973; GARF, f.6991, o.6, d.537, l.18.

32. Data prepared for conference of CARC *upolnomochennye* in Tashkent, 1 Oct. 1946 – GARF, f.6991, o.3, d.41, l.182; and A. Abdurahmanov to Seitov, Chairman, Council of Ministers, Karakalpak ASSR, 29 Dec. 1946 – TsGAUz, f.2456, o.1, d.82, l.1. The four oblasti were Khorezm, Andijan, Fergana and Tashkent.

33. Uzbek SSR Council of Ministers, Resolution No.850-45s, 1 July 1946; TsGAUz, f.2456, o.1, d.72, l.8.

34. V. A. Abakumov to K. E. Voroshilov, 12 Sept. 1946; GARF, f.6991, o.3, d.34, l.193.

35. See Chapter 2, n.139.

their revenue.[36] In the latter half of 1949 there were still fifty unregistered groups in Samarkand Oblast' with buildings, mullas, 'everything needed for registration', as against two registered ones.[37] In this same year, too, the *upolnomochennyi* for Osh Oblast' expressed his apprehension that the mosques which he contended still operated in nearly every kishlak in Andijan Oblast' might serve to arouse believers in his own adjacent fiefdom:[38] by 1945 mosques had been opened without authorisation in nearly all large settlements in Osh Oblast', some 130 in all. But 'almost all' of these were closed down during the next three years.[39] (Even so, over eighty unauthorised mosques were thought to be functioning in Kirgiziia at the end of 1949.[40])

In many areas where the influence of Islam was considered to be less incisive than in Central Asia, there were also more unregistered than registered mosques. In the Tatar ASSR, for instance, in mid-1947 there were thirty-four of the former against fifteen of the latter. (According to CARC, the reason was that the raion authorities obstructed the formalisation of their existence in line with established procedure, yet at the same time neither restricted nor put an end to their activity.)[41] Twenty years later the numbers

36. This practice was reported by the *upolnomochennyi* for Tashkent Oblast', Nasretdinov, at a conference of Uzbekistan's *upolnomochennye*, 9 Aug. 1948; TsGAUz, f.2456, o.1, d.120, l.6.

37. Iu. V. Sadovskii, Minutes No.26, Inspectors' meeting, 1-2 Dec. 1949; GARF, f.6991, o.3, d.60, l.96. In spring 1947 no less than 150 mosques had been reported in this oblast', just two of them registered – I. V. Polianskii to CARC *upolnomochennyi* for Samarkand Oblast' Baratov, 24 May 1947; TsGAUz, f.2456, o.1, d.82, l.11.

38. I. G. Halimov to CARC, 14 Oct. 1949; GARF, f.6991, o.3, d.454, l.27.

39. I. G. Halimov to H. A. Akhtiamov, 3 March 1951, GARF, f.6991, o.3, d.454, ll.100-1. Of the 130, 11 were newly built. According to Halimov, there were some 60-70 believers in every settlement, of whom 25-30 attended mosque regularly, and in large settlements and the towns up to 100 and more. This very stereotyped picture indicates that he was drawing conclusions and making generalisations on the basis of data gathered from just one or two cases, as CARC constantly accused so many *upolnomochennye* of doing.

40. H. A. Akhtiamov in reply to questioning, said there were approximately 80 excluding Talas Oblast' for which he did not have data – Instructional conference of CARC's Central Asian *upolnomochennye*, Tashkent, 17-20 Dec. 1949; GARF, f.6991, o.3, d.67, l.90.

41. Bagaev, Report, CARC session No.7, 23-24 April 1947; GARF, f.6991, o.4, d.19, l.188, and I. V. Polianskii to A. A. Zhdanov and K. E. Voroshilov, 22 July 1947; RTsKhIDNI, f.17, o.125, d.506, l.169. For the systematic

stood at sixty-one against twelve; according to the republican *upolnomochennyi*, their activity was in no way distinct from that of the registered communities: the mosques were well kept, had religious books, and, besides the mulla, there was an executive organ which ran the community's affairs.[42] In the Bashkir ASSR in 1951 there were thirty-two unregistered versus twenty-three registered mosques.[43]

Some, presumably most, of the mosques occupied by unregistered associations continued to be empty ones. Many were not locked, often even lacking doors, and so provided a convenient site for visitation by local believers.[44] In the early 1950s, four of Uzbekistan's oblasti had over 500 non-functioning mosques apiece, a fair number of which were not in use.[45] In the single year of 1950 itinerant mullas tried to occupy no less than twenty-two of Fergana Oblast's sixty-five empty mosques.[46] *Upolnomochennye* would seek to have these empty mosques requisitioned for other ends, precisely because they were the focus of 'enhanced religious activity'.[47] In Uzbekistan a meeting of CARC officials resolved to take account of all empty mosques in the kishlaks and raiony with the aim of their being used as clubs, schools and other cultural institutions.[48] In Tajikistan in the early 1960s, where most former mosques were said not to

---

obstructionism of the Tatar ASSR leadership regarding registration, see Chapter 4, nn.42 and 65, and pp.609-10.

42. T. S. Saidbaev, Information, undated [before 22 Nov. 1967]; GARF, f.6991, o.6, d.73, ll.199-200. A copy of this document was given to one Mamreev at the RSFSR Council of Ministers.

43. M. Sh. Karimov, Report, Minutes, CARC session No.16, 15 Aug. 1951; GARF, f.6991, o.3, d.75, l.205. The 32 associations had a total of 2,207 members.

44. Saroyan, *Reconstructing Community*, p.253.

45. L. A. Prikhod'ko, Report, 2 June 1952; GARF, f.6991, o.3, d.81, l.134. The oblasti were Namangan with 653, Fergana with 514, Samarkand with 574 and Khorezm with 584. In 1973, Fergana Oblast' still had 115 empty mosques, out of a total 1,050 former mosques – D. Malikov, Information, undated (probably late Aug. 1973); GARF, f.6991, o.6, d.548, l.68.

46. Minutes, Instructional meeting of Uzbekistan's oblast' *upolnomochennye*, 17-18 July 1951; TsGAUz, f.2456, o.1, d.134, ll.74-5.

47. For example, Musakhanov in Namangan, *ibid.*, l.69. In the period 1945-53, CARC agreed to transfer 48 buildings of former mosques to local government organs – see p.93.

48. Kh. N. Iskanderov to Deputy Chairman of the Uzbek SSR Council of Ministers Vahabov and Uzbekistan CP(b) Central Committee Secretary Tursunov, 19 July 1951; TsGAUz, f.2456, o.1, d.134, l.56.

have been requisitioned, seventy-three out of eighty-three listed unregistered mosques were former mosques, which retained the appearance of mosques.[49] In Azerbaijan in the early 1960s there were 124 empty mosques (out of a total of 882 buildings which still retained the appearance of mosques).[50] In cases where abandoned mosques were in dilapidated condition and unfit to serve as prayer premises, unregistered groups sometimes used them, as it were, as assembly points, holding prayer-services in the open in their vicinity.[51]

The republican governments and local officialdom were similarly inclined to find a lasting solution to the problem of empty mosques. Sometimes local *ispolkoms* asked oblast' or republican authorities for permission to demolish former mosques so that they might use the building materials.[52] This inclination of local authorities or kolkhozy to dismantle former mosques, which had no formal use and some of which were in various stages of disrepair, often aroused the ire of local believers, in some cases to such an extent that when demolition was initiated they renewed prayer-services in the mosque to prevent it being completely razed to the ground.[53] In one case in Dagestan in early 1971, believers occupied the mosque and refused to leave it for an entire month.[54] There were

49. N. Smirnov and S. Fastoved, Information, 22 Aug. 1962, and A. Puzin to the Tajikistan CP Central Committee, 26 Jan. 1963; GARF, f.6991, o.3, d.1390, l.30, and d.1739, l.2.

50. N. I. Smirnov, Information, 8 Aug. 1962; GARF, f.6991, o.3, d.1390, ll.12-14.

51. M. Sh. Karimov, report, 2nd quarter, 1951, undated (apparently Appendix to Minutes, CARC session No.16, 15 Aug. 1951). In a village in Gor'kii Oblast', where 408 believers signed an application to open a mosque and 30,000 rubles were collected for its repair, 700 people met in the square next to the building on Qurban-Bayram in 1953 – V. I. Gostev to P. A. Tarasov, 4 Jan. 1954; GARF, f.6991, o.3, d.75, ll.213-14, and d.102, l.23. In one case in Fergana Oblast' an unregistered group met for prayer on the site of a demolished mosque, which it asked to be permitted to rebuild – U. G. Mangushev to Kh. N. Iskanderov, 30 Jan. 1954; TsGAUz, f.2456, o.1, d.170, l.3.

52. For details see pp.660-1.

53. For example, I. G. Halimov to CARC, 20 Jan. and 11 May 1956; GARF, f.6991, o.3, d.457, ll.43-4 and 87. Here, too, the intention of the local authorities was to use the building materials within the kolkhoz.

54. Kh. Salahetdinov and I. Mikhalev, Report given to E. I. Lisavtsev, 26 Oct. 1971; GARF, f.6991, o.6, d.361, l.109.

also instances when a mosque which had been requisitioned was vacated for one reason or another and taken over by local believers.[55]

Sometimes unregistered groups might occupy or take over former mosques which had not been abandoned but were being used for other purposes, chiefly as storehouses. (In one raion in Andijan Oblast' in 1946 no less than forty-nine of seventy-nine unregistered mosques 'exposed' by the CARC *upolnomochennyi* had become storehouses which were used for drying cotton.) The two uses of a building were not necessarily mutually exclusive: it might serve to dry cotton immediately after the harvest, and for the rest of the year be used as a mosque; or part of the building would be a storehouse and part a prayer-house. Alternatively, religious associations might purchase former mosques from kolkhozy, or even build new ones, the necessary funds being provided by believers' donations.[56]

Islam, unlike, for example, the Russian Orthodox Church, did not, however, require a regular prayer-house in order to conduct a prayer-meeting, and it was common practice for services to be conducted in a variety of venues, in the open – in urban squares or parks, and, in the countryside, in fields or by a river – or in cemeteries, and even in private homes. Thus, groups which, for one reason or another, did not have access to the building of a former mosque, might also conduct Friday prayers, either at cemeteries, which in many ways seemed to serve as substitutes for mosques,[57] or in private homes. Yet most such groups were thought not to have gathered on Fridays, except perhaps in the summer; throughout most of the year their members tended to pray at home individually, meeting for collective prayer-services only on festivals.[58] Such use of cemeteries was very common and

55. Two former mosques which were used as schools, were vacated, one in 1952, the other in 1962; when the schools moved elsewhere prayer-services were resumed – I. G. Halimov to CARC, 11 May 1956, and L. Zh. Alisov to Kabardino-Balkar ASSR Obkom Secretary Sh. K. Mal'bakhov, 16 March 1963; GARF, f.6991, o.3, d.457, l.87, and d.1607, l.11.

56. I. V. Polianskii to A. A. Zhdanov and K. E. Voroshilov, 22 July 1947; RTsKhIDNI, f.17, o.125, d.506, l.171, and I. G. Halimov to CARC, Report for 1st quarter of 1949, undated [probably April 1949], and 3 July 1950; GARF, f.6991, o.3, d.454, ll.9 and 65.

57. L. A. Prikhod'ko, Report, 20 May 1953; GARF, f.6991, o.3, d.91, l.258.

58. See, for example, L. A. Prikhod'ko, Short report, prepared for CARC session No.10s, 11-12 April 1952; GARF, f.6991, o.3, d.81, l.85.

characterised unregistered activity in many parts. In Chimkent Oblast' in the early 1970s, all the approximately forty unregistered groups operated at cemeteries.[59] Not all groups which met for prayer at cemeteries prayed there in the open. Some used existing structures, originally put up for the performance of rites connected with the burial-service, or built small prayer-premises. At the beginning of the 1960s, seventeen out of the Kabardino-Balkar ASSR's thirty-one unregistered groups prayed in lodges at cemeteries.[60] In the Chechen-Ingush ASSR structures put up in cemeteries ostensibly to hold funeral equipment were actually called mosques by the Sufi groups who prayed in them.[61] In not a few places believers might in fact build mosques in cemeteries. In 1956 believers in Krasnoiarsk built a temporary structure at the cemetery with the permission of the chief town architect and the director of the municipal burial service trust for the purpose of ritual cleansing prior to burial and keeping burial equipment. The building was immediately used for prayer meetings, with the participation of 200 to 250 on regular Fridays and as many as 2–3,000 on festivals.[62] At another such prayer-house in Jizak (in Syr-Darya Oblast'), which was served in the early 1970s by three mullas, 120–150 worshippers came to pray on Fridays and 2,000 on festivals – more than in any of the oblast's registered prayer-houses; nor were measures taken to stop this activity as the nearest registered mosque was 120 km away.[63] This activity at cemeteries was particularly annoying to officialdom for by law they were supposed to be under the jurisdiction and supervision of the local authorities.[64]

The validity of the concern shown by those who preferred not to file an application to register their religious association lest it be rejected and they be exposed to retribution, was proven by the fact that as of 1945 very many unregistered groups were subjected

59. K. Kulumbetov to Kazakhstan CP Central Committee Secretary S. N. Imashev, 27 Nov. 1970; GARF, f.6991, o.6, d.290, l.48.

60. L. Zh. Aisov to A. A. Puzin, 12 Feb. 1962; GARF, f.6991, o.3, d.1606, ll.6-7.

61. A. Alisov to A. A. Puzin, 13 Jan. 1961; GARF, f.6991, o.3, d.1605, l.20.

62. Reception by N. I. Smirnov of a group of Muslim believers from Krasnoiarsk, 18 July 1960; GARF, f.6991, o.4, d.120, ll.29-30.

63. A. Galiev to V. A. Kuroedov, 5 Oct. 1972; GARF, f.6991, o.6, d.545, ll.162-4. Galiev reported that in no less than six cemeteries in his oblast' structures of various sorts had been set up to serve as prayer-premises.

64. For further discussion of the role of cemeteries in Muslim life, see pp. 519-22.

to harassment, to the point of being closed down. In Kashka-Darya Oblast' all fifteen mosques which began operating without sanction at the end of 1945 and the first half of 1946 were shut down by the CARC *upolnomochennyi*.[65] In some areas the same result was achieved when the local SADUM representative summoned the clergy of small religious groups, that had been established without authorisation and met in private homes, and cautioned them that their very existence was conducive to illegal activity.[66] The private home which was used for purposes of prayer might be that of the mulla or whoever served as the group leader, that of an ordinary believer, or simply the empty house of someone who had died or left the vicinity.[67]

Already in the early years the distinction was drawn between unregistered religious groups which prayed regularly, namely, conducted the *jum'a-namaz* on a regular weekly basis throughout the year, and those which merely held services on the major festivals, or perhaps also during the *uraz*. By early 1947 the top Soviet leadership was informed that there were in the country 'no less than' 800 mosques and *mazars* which had been opened without authorisation. This was apart from those groups which conducted prayer-services throughout the country on Uraz-Bayram and Qurban-Bayram in the open. The existence of so large a quantity of unregistered mosques was attributed to the fact that many of them were *mahalla* mosques which united a small number of believers, residents of a given town quarter (or *mahalla*).[68] These tended not

65. Samadov to CARC, 2 Aug. 1946; TsGAUz, f.2456, o.1, d.71, l.37.

66. I. G. Halimov to CARC, 23 Aug. and 23 Sept. 1947; GARF, f.6991, o.3, d.453, ll.26 and 30.

67. See, for example, I. G. Halimov to H. A. Akhtiamov, 3 Jan. 1951; GARF, f.6991, o.3, d.454, l.93.

68. In Kirgiziia there were thought to be over 100 such religious associations in 1946, most of them in areas populated by Uzbeks, and about 600 in the Uzbek SSR. Whenever the *upolnomochennye* would suggest that one of them cease activity, it indeed did so, but quickly renewed activity, holding prayer-meetings in private homes – H. Akhtiamov, Report, conference of CARC *upolnomochennye*, Alma-Ata, 30 Sept. 1946, and I. V. Polianskii to K. E. Voroshilov, 13 Nov. 1946; GARF, f.6991, o.3, d.41, l.109, and d.34, l.197. No less than nine such *mahalla* mosques were closed down in the small town of Uzgen in Osh Oblast' in the years 1946-48 – I. G. Halimov to CARC, 3 July 1950; GARF, f.6991, o.3, d.454, l.64. These mosques seem to have retained the characteristics of the traditional *mahalla* mosque, where people tended to pray on ordinary weekdays, going to the larger, *sobornaia*, mosque on Fridays and

to have clergy and to conduct simplified prayers and could hardly be regarded as permanently functioning prayer associations. Indeed, they existed primarily in the Uzbek and Tajik SSRs and the Kirgiz SSR's Osh Oblast', Central Asia's historically sedentary regions.[69] The aggregate numbers were not so different in the early 1970s, when 645 unregistered mosques were taken count of. Of these 127 operated regularly, had their own prayer-premises and were in no way distinct from registered mosques, while the other 518 held prayer-meetings periodically, basically only on the festivals.[70]

In the RSFSR as well there were not a few unregistered groups. While clearly not all were 'exposed' even here, since Muslims did not on the whole give up the practice of life-cycle rites and prayer-services at least on the two major festivals, those that were known gave the picture of rather considerable activity. In Penza Oblast' 5-7,000 gathered in villages without registered mosques in the year 1947.[71] In towns with a Tatar population, but where they were not allowed to register, believers met on Fridays in private homes and on festivals wherever feasible: in Kuibyshev at the Muslim cemetery, in Chkalov next to the mosque, in Saratov in fifteen to twenty different places.[72] In Ul'ianovsk Oblast' in 1949 there were twenty-seven known unregistered groups; a decade later there were thirty-nine such groups, none with its own prayer-house or comprising more than forty people (most of them comprised less than fifteen) and they held prayer-meetings every Friday,

---

festivals. For Halimov, speaking of one of these mosques which recommenced activity, described it as a small house, situated on the spot of a former, destroyed mosque, where 28-30 believers came for daily prayers, going, however, to the town's registered mosque on Fridays and festivals – *ibid.*, l.65.

69. I. V. Polianskii to Beriia, Stalin, Molotov and Voroshilov at the Council of Ministers, and to Zhdanov, Khrushchev, A. A. Kuznetsov, G. Patolichev and G. M. Popov at the AUCP(b) Central Committee, 27 Feb. 1947. One month later the number was broken down as follows: over 100 large mosques opened at *mazars* and other shrines, over 500 mosques whose 'continued existence' was under study and about 300 *mahalla* mosques, whose activity was being terminated –I. V. Polianskii to K. E. Voroshilov, 26 March 1947; GARF, f.6991, o.3, d.47, ll.92 and 112.

70. CRA, Information, sent to the CPSU Central Committee, 27 April 1971; TsKhSD, f.5, o.63, d.89, l.97.

71. Gorbachev, CARC *upolnomochennyi* for Penza Oblast, Minutes, CARC session No.9, 10 June 1948; GARF, f.6991, o.4, d.22, l.115.

72. I. V. Polianskii to A. A. Zhdanov and K. E. Voroshilov, RTsKhIDNI, f.17, o.125, d.506, l.170.

one half of them at cemeteries, the other half in private homes.[73] In addition to places of traditional Tatar habitation, Tatars had also settled in some of the new Soviet cities, many of which were in the RSFSR's centres of industrial development. Here naturally there were no buildings of former mosques and believers in such groups had to make good with provisory accommodation. In Magnitogorsk, for example, they purchased a house from a private citizen, which they adapted to their needs, adding to the building in the process; in 1961 it was closed down by the organs of local government and refurbished as a store.[74] In the mid-1960s 374 unregistered groups and 465 unregistered clergy were taken count of in the RSFSR, nearly 100 of the former and 150 of the latter in the Chechen-Ingush ASSR and over fifty of the former in both the Bashkir and Tatar ASSRs and in the Karachai-Cherkess AO.[75]

Indeed, when, beginning 1957, the deported nationalities started returning to their native territories, following their rehabilitation and the restoration of their administrative units, they were not allowed by the local government organs to register prayer-houses. The Chechen and Ingush, in particular, who were known for their religiosity even during the period of their exile, therefore began building prayer-premises without authorisation, which, however, were soon demolished or requisitioned for other ends. As elsewhere, they sometimes also adapted former mosques and whatever structures might exist on the precincts of cemeteries, which were described by the authorities as unequivocal centres of religious propaganda and influence. Sometimes, too, they conducted prayer-meetings in especially enclosed areas in the vicinity

73. P. F. Simonov, Report, Minutes, No.4, Instructors' meeting with oblast' *upolnomochennye*, 4-5 April 1950, and CARC session, No.21, 22 July 1959; GARF, f.6991, o.3, d.66, ll.32-3, and d.184, l.181. Simonov reported that in 1950 prayer-meetings were not held on a daily basis in any of these groups, either those that prayed in mosques or those which prayed in private homes. Moreover, although he still held by his figure of 27 groups, they showed less activity than in 1949, with prayer-services being held on Qurban-Bayram in just six groups, with a total of 775 worshippers and no youth (as against 1,120 worshippers, including 152 youth in 1949) – Minutes, CARC session No.6, 1 March 1951; GARF, f.6991, o.3, d.74, l.82.

74. Reception by N. I. Smirnov of a representative of this group, 19 Aug. 1964; GARF, f.6991, o.4, d.148, l.19.

75. Information, handed to E. A. Tarasov at the CPSU Central Committee, 15 Nov. 1965; GARF, f.6991, o.3, d.1484, ll.178-80.

of their villages, or a mulla might make available his own premises for this purpose. Certainly, they often seem to have had private homes at their disposal.[76]

Within the category of unregistered mosques which held regular prayer-services, the authorities tried to differentiate between those which in their opinion it was mandatory to register and legitimise and those whose activity ought to be stopped. Some of the former were difficult to distinguish from registered communities, even having an executive organ and inspection committee.[77] CARC's *upolnomochennyi* for the Kirgiz SSR explained in 1947 that selecting some unregistered mosques for registration would create the conditions necessary for the conduct of a decisive struggle against the others, especially since, given the interest of registered clergy in the income of the latter, they would co-operate in it.[78]

In the early-mid 1950s, prior to the post-Stalin thaw, the CARC *upolnomochennyi* for Osh Oblast' found groups of believers in almost every settlement he visited (eleven out of thirteen). In one kolkhoz of some 800 adults (above the age of sixteen) situated just 2 km from a registered mosque, believers met for daily prayers in a mosque built in 1944 and subsequently closed down. To be precise, after being used in the summer to store cotton and fulfil other economic functions, it was taken over in the winter of 1952-3 by the believers. On ordinary days ten to twenty people would come to pray and on Fridays up to 100; on festivals about 200 believers from the kolkhoz attended the registered mosque in the raion centre, to which also the wheat and corn collected as *fitr* during the *uraz* were brought. Prayers were led by a mulla, a person close to sixty without any religious education, who did not fulfil work days on the kolkhoz. Local officials and intelligentsia

76. P. A. Zadorozhnyi to A. A. Puzin, 30 Aug. 1960, A. L. Alisov to A. A. Puzin, 13 Jan. 1961 and 16 March 1962, and A. Asaulka to Chairman of the Chechen-Ingush ASSR Council of Ministers R. V. Vahaev, 10 Nov. 1971; GARF, f.6991, o.3, d.207, ll.50-1, d.1605, l.19, and d.1606, ll.15-16, and o.6, d.370, l.137. Most of the former mosques were in use for other purposes by the time the deportees returned; only seven were said to have retained the appearance of mosques. For the religious activity of the Chechen and Ingush, see pp.407-21.

77. For example, the religious associations in Gor'kii and Leningrad – Minutes, CARC session No.4s, 6 March 1952, and V. I. Gostev to P. A. Tarasov, 4 Jan. 1954; GARF, f.6991, o.3, d.83, l.45, and d.102, l.22. And see p.298 above.

78. See p.265.

alike kept a total silence regarding these activities, which were conducted quite openly for all to see. This was a typical case, the major variant being the venue for prayer; groups in places without an available mosque either built a small construct or used a private home. In some settlements, too, the *upolnomochennyi* gave information for the number of homes in which *mavluds* were read during the course of the past year.[79]

In the more lenient years (1955-7) many unregistered groups seem to have thought they could once again expand or initiate new activity.[80] Certainly, their situation seemed improved and they were less concerned about coming into the open. One CARC *upolnomochennyi* suggested that the catalyst was the Soviet Union's foreign policy and improved relations with states of the East, which dissipated the doubts of many believers regarding the possibility of in fact enjoying their constitutional right of freedom of worship and opening prayer-houses.[81] Whether this was the reason or not, there was a new spate of registration applications and of unauthorised mosque building, occasionally with the active assistance of local, especially kolkhoz, officials. In Andijan Oblast' alone seventeen such mosques were built in 1955-6, mostly on the sites of former mosques or in cemeteries. Occasionally, too, a mosque which had fallen into disrepair would be restored. For the first time, apparently, the number of worshippers who gathered for prayers in unregistered mosques was no smaller than those who attended the oblast's registered ones.[82] The republican *upolnomochennyi* for Uzbekistan specifically told his oblast' *upolnomochennye* that those groups which did not apply to register might continue functioning; information concerning them, which the *upolnomochennye* were supposed to supply to the relevant party and executive organs, was to be ac-

79. I. G. Halimov to H. A. Akhtiamov, 22 April 1953; GARF, f.6991, o.3, d.94, ll.56-68.

80. In late 1957 the Central Committee was told there were over 1,000 unregistered groups throughout the country – A. A. Puzin to CPSU Central Committee Department of Propaganda and Agitation head V. P. Moskovskii, 14 Nov. 1957; GARF, f.6991, o.3, d.147, l.206.

81. For this opinion of the *upolnomochennyi* for Dagestan, see p.437.

82. Minutes, Instructional meeting of CARC *upolnomochennye* in the Uzbek SSR, 15-17 March 1956, M. A. Khalikov to I. V. Polianskii, 19 May 1956, and U. Abdullaev to V. I. Gostev, 29 Nov. 1956; TsGAUz, f.2456, o.1, d.183, l.51, d.198, l.79, and d.190, ll.20-1, and G. F. Frolov, Information, 22 Feb. 1957; GARF, f.6991, o.3, d.132, ll.36-7.

companied by cautions against administrative measures, particularly closure.[83] In areas, such as the Cherkess AO, where believers had been wary of holding unauthorised collective prayers, they now gathered for festival services in the cemeteries.[84] In the Kabardinian ASSR, where believers did not endeavour to open mosques, the clergy began performing rites overtly and believers requested that their mullas be allowed to bury the dead without having to be afraid.[85] Even here eight mosques were put up at cemeteries between 1955 and 1959, some with up to three clergy.[86] Twelve such groups, each with 50 – 200 believers, still existed after the anti-religious campaign closures; they had their own clergy and held prayers at structures in the cemeteries during the *uraz* and on the festivals.[87]

In Dagestan by 1956 a large number of groups were using without authorisation prayer-premises which were generally un-suitable, being either semi-ruined mosques or private apartments that did not fulfil the requisite sanitary and fire regulations. Indeed, such groups existed in almost every settlement throughout the republic and were led by unregistered clergy who were subject to no control. Their membership comprehended almost the entire rural population, apart from those who attended registered mosques. Here applications to open mosques and register religious associations not only grew in number in the second half of the 1950s; their tone became increasingly assertive. The clergy in one village told the CARC *upolnomochennyi* that if their application did not receive a positive reply, their society would seize the village club, which was housed in a former mosque, throw its equipment into the street and refurbish the building as a mosque.[88]

83. Minutes, Instructional meeting of CARC *upolnomochennye* in the Uzbek SSR, 15-17 March 1956; TsGAUz, f.2456, o.1, d.183, l.59.

84. G. F. Frolov, Information, 22 Feb. 1957; GARF, f.6991, o.3, d.132, l.79.

85. *Ibid.*, l.80.

86. These constructs were apparently not considered permanent prayer-houses, for a count of unregistered associations in 1962 gave 18 societies and 13 groups, only four of which had permanent prayer-houses – N. I. Smirnov to A. A. Puzin, 28 March 1963; GARF, f.6991, o.3, d.1607, l.18.

87. L. Zh. Alisov, Explanatory memo, 16 Jan. 1967; GARF, f.6991, o.6, d.22, l.23.

88. G. F. Frolov, Information, 22 Feb. 1957, Gasanov to V. I. Gostev, Report, 19 March 1957, and M. S. Gajiev, Report, Minutes, CARC session No.33, 26-27 Oct. 1960. The last source spoke of over 40 unregistered groups.

When policy changed, with the advent of the anti-religious onslaught of the late 1950s and early 1960s, the unregistered groups were the first to be hit. CARC Chairman Puzin told an all-union conference of CARC *upolnomochennye* in November 1958 that believers might not organise clandestinely. The *upolnomochennyi* for Kirgiziia, who had been in the post since 1945, pointed out that while the law indeed laid down that a religious society might proceed to operate after registration, it did not stipulate what was to happen if such a society did so prior to registration. Surely the prohibition of administrative interference in the affairs of the church referred to all groups which incorporated followers of a single faith. If unregistered groups were not to be allowed to exist, they would be shut down, but this, he insisted, was a meaningless procedure, a Sisyphean labour.[89] In this period, however, clear steps were taken to make explicit that the very existence of an unregistered group was contrary to law. Apparently in 1959 the Kirgiziian CP Central Committee, for instance, adopted a resolution that measures be taken to forbid the activity of religious societies which were not appropriately registered.[90]

In the conditions of Central Asia in particular, this was no simple task. In the early 1960s unregistered groups persisted ubiquitously. Even in Turkmenistan there were still fifty (as against four registered ones).[91] Nevertheless, a large number were shut down: in Uzbekistan alone, just in the first months of 1960, no less than 130 unregistered mosques were closed, many of them in the course of prayer. According to the statistics provided by CARC, which certainly did not give the full picture for Central

---

Characteristically, statistical data for Dagestan spoke consistently of one or at most two unregistered mosques; e.g., Minutes, CARC session No.24, 27 Aug. 1964 – GARF, f.6991, o.3, d.132, ll.76-7, d.145, ll.51-2, and d.207, l.36, and o.4, d.147, l.79.

89. H. A. Akhtiamov, Address, All-Union conference of CARC *upolnomochennye*, 25-27 Nov. 1958; GARF, f.6991, o.3, d.165, l.49.

90. H. A. Akhtiamov, Report, All-Union conference of CARC *upolnomochennye*, 18-20 April 1960; GARF, f.6991, o.3, d.208, ll.131-2. As a result of this resolution steps were taken to terminate the activity of these groups. Of the 213 groups – of all faiths – in Osh Oblast', 46 Muslim groups ceased activity of their own accord and that of a further 59 was stopped by *rai*–and *gor-ispolkoms* and *sel'sovets*. By the end of 1960 the intention was to put an end to all 213. Akhtiamov gave data for other parts of the republic as well, which indicated a similar trend.

91. A. A. Puzin to the CPSU Central Committee Department of Propaganda and Agitation, 7 June 1961; GARF, f.6991, o.3, d.1363, ll.97-8.

Asia, 1,649 unregistered Muslim religious associations were operating as of 1 January 1963 throughout the country, 1,015 of them in the RSFSR. Of the former number, 324 had a permanent prayer-house and met regularly (that is, weekly, on Fridays), 407 came together periodically in private homes, and 918 held collective prayers just on the major festivals. Within one year, the numbers were down to 1,310 for the sum total (795 in the RSFSR), 281 of which fitted into the first category, 499 into the second and 533 into the third.[92]

CARC reported that in Kazakhstan in the early 1960s there were over sixty unregistered Muslim religious associations. These groups which performed religious practices and gathered for collective prayer in the open under the leadership of 'itinerant' mullas in every 'more or less large settlement with a compact mass of adherents of Islam' that lacked a registered religious society. (Neither the number of these settlements nor the criterion for a 'more or less less large settlement was specified.)[93] Indeed, just a year previously in the single oblast' of Northern Kazakhstan, for instance, small groups existed in every settlement with six, ten, fifteen members apiece, who observed the basic rites of collective prayer on festivals, religious burial and, in part, also the *uraz*. Of these, twenty-two groups were described as being the most active: led by local lay elders and numbering 15 – 150 believers, they conducted collective prayers in private homes. Their approach to the Qur'an and religious dogma was a simplified one: the old customs and traditions were simply adapted into their daily lives.[94]

In Tajikistan, where perhaps even more than in Uzbekistan and Kirgiziia the registered mosques and *mazars* were incapable of meeting believers' religious needs, the number of unregistered groups was by far the larger. In 1955 Polianskii reported to the CPSU Central Committee that religious activity in this republic centred around the mosques and *mazars* which operated without authorisation, the twenty-six registered mosques and four registered

92. Materials sent to the CPSU Central Committee, 27 Dec. 1960, and statistical data on church activity in the USSR as of 1 Jan. 1964; GARF, f.6991, o.3, d.210, ll.73-85, and o.4, d.146, ll.170-1.

93. Information (unsigned) handed to A. I. Aleksandrov at the CPSU Central Committee, 14 Feb. 1962; GARF, f.6991, o.3, d.1389, l.11.

94. K. V. Ovchinnikov, Resumé, 10 Jan. 1961; GARF, f.6991, o.3, d.1355, ll.7s-7sh.

mazars with their forty clergy being totally inadequate in light of the population's high degree of religiosity.[95] Two oblasti, Garm and the Gorno-Badakhshan AO, had no registered mosques at all. At the beginning of 1959, just prior to the repressions of the new anti-religious campaign, there were said to be 436 Muslim groups, the majority of which had about twenty members; 130 of these had their own, usually rather primitive, premises in which they held regular prayer-services. By early 1960 most of the mosques had reportedly been closed down and just seventy-five groups remained, and the clergy began holding prayers at *chaikhonas* – the traditional Central Asian tea-houses, which were supposed to be foci of atheistic propaganda – and *mehmankhonas*, where in wintertime the men in rural settlements would come together to spend their leisure time.[96] The numbers were apparently rather fluid, groups terminating and recommencing activity with relative frequency: whereas a report for 1963 mentioned 'no less than seventy-eight unregistered mosques' which were known to be operating, it was stated in 1964 that ninety-two had been shut down 'recently'.[97] (It is not clear whether this means that those which had been closed had re-opened, or that other mosques had commenced operating in the stead of those shut down – it is known that during 1962 some further *chaikhonas* and *mehmankhonas* began functioning as mosques and some former mosques re-opened[98]–or perhaps that the 1960 report was not accurate.) Certainly, the indiscriminate closure of registered mosques in this period significantly increased both the number of unregistered groups, which began meeting for collective prayer in private homes, and attendance at festival prayers organised by unregistered clergy at a variety of sites, including *mazars* re-opened for the purpose, which simply

95. I. V. Polianskii to P. V. Kovanov, 23 June 1955; GARF, f.6991, o.3, d.114, l.37.

96. D. A. Ahmedov to A. A. Puzin, 21 Feb. 1961, and N. Smirnov, S. Fastoved, Information, 22 Aug. 1962; GARF, f.6991, o.3, d.1390, ll.33-5, and d.1737, ll.9-10.

97. M. Kh. Hamidov to A. A. Puzin, Report for 1963, 24 Feb. 1964, Appendix 2, and Minutes, All-Union conference of CARC *upolnomochennye*, 25-26 June 1964; GARF, f.6991, o.3, d.1740, l.37, and d.1457, l.25.

98. M. Kh. Hamidov to A. A. Puzin, First Party Secretary J. R. Rasulev, Tajik SSR Council of Ministers Chairman A. K. Qahharov and KGB Chairman S. K. Tsvigun, undated (received at CARC, 19 April 1963); GARF, f.6991, o.3, d.1730, l.51.

soared. CARC officials attributed this to the fact that the closures had been implemented arbitrarily without due explanatory and propaganda work which, according to theory, would, if conducted correctly, induce the voluntary disbandment of the registered mosques and/or the abandoning of religion by believers. Such closures were therefore not just self-deception; they actually threw believers, who did not renounce their customs, into the arms of 'parasites, charlatans and all sorts of rogues who pose as mullas and derive profit therefrom'.[99] Most of the mosques closed in this period were transferred to kolkhozy for use as storehouses or schools, although a few remained empty.[100]

The difficulties which unregistered groups were enduring in this period can be gauged from the complaints of those of their representatives who appeared in CARC's offices in the hope of remedying their plight. They came from different parts, mostly from the oblasti or autonomous republics of the RSFSR; the dichotomy between the registered and unregistered societies and clergy which was so blatant in Central Asia seems to have been less prevalent elsewhere. Certainly, in Central Asia unregistered groups did not lodge complaints with the authorities about repression or encroachments on their rights.[101] The believers who came to Moscow related that lease agreements were not being renewed, that they were no longer being allowed to meet for prayer, and that when they nonetheless did so, they were forcibly dispersed and threatened with fines or other punishment were they to meet again.[102]

One group of believers, from the town of Bugul'ma in the Tatar ASSR, which had lodged a complaint in 1960, appeared again four years later; they contended that the landlord had been fined a considerable sum for not paying income tax on the rent, the annexe to his house had been demolished and they had been forbidden to hold collective prayers. They had nowhere to pray, the *uraz* was about to commence and they would have to pray

99. For closure of registered mosques in Tajikistan, see pp.207–8, 209 and 212.
100. U. Yuldashev to V. A. Kuroedov, 20 Dec. 1966; GARF, f.6991, o.6, d.11, ll.52–4.
101. M. Miragzamov, Information, 22 Oct. 1966; GARF, f.6991, o.6, d.11, l.66.
102. Receptions by N. I. Smirnov of representatives of unregistered communities in Bugul'ma and Kalinin, 23 April and 12 May 1960; GARF, f.6991, o.4, d.110, ll.18–19 and 23. See also pp.672–3.

in the cold and prostrate themseves in the snow.[103] (This happened in not a few places, reports coming in from various parts in 1964 that prayers were held at cemeteries in the open during the *uraz* and on Uraz-Bayram, which fell in mid-February.[104]) In Krasnoiarsk, where believers met for prayers in the precincts of a building erected at the cemetery – with the permission of the local authorities – they were simply told in 1960 they could not hold prayer-meetings until they had registered their society.[105]

A CARC official described how in Kazakhstan the public would mobilise to put an end to the activity of the unregistered groups and clergy. A group would form at the *raiispolkom* comprising a member of the local soviet, a number of atheistic propagandists, press correspondents, representatives of the Komsomol and KGB, and workers from the sanitary and anti-incendiary inspectorate. They would go to wherever believers gathered and find out the purpose of the gathering and who brought them together. The person from the soviet would talk with the organiser and the owner of the house, indicating that this activity was a violation of Soviet law and suggesting that they disperse. The propagandists would meanwhile speak with each individual believer, acquainting them, too, with Soviet legislation on religion. And the journalists would prepare an article for the local newspaper. At a kolkhoz meeting in Southern Kazakhstan the imam of a local unregistered mosque was severely criticised, a member of the party group of lecturers who knew both Arabic and the Qur'an demonstrating his ignorance and compromising him in the eyes of the believers. After the meeting and an article on it in the local paper the imam closed the mosque and began working in the kolkhoz.[106]

103. Reception by N. I. Smirnov of a representative of the Muslim believers of Bugul'ma, 14 Jan. 1964; GARF, f.6991, o.4, d.148, l.2. For further discussion of the tribulations of this group, see pp.654-6.

104. For example, L. Zh. Aisov to A. A. Puzin, 18 Feb. 1964; GARF, f.6991, o.3, d.1608, l.7. In Tajikistan 23,000 worshippers took part in services on Uraz-Bayram in unregistered mosques and in the open – M. Kh. Hamidov to A. A. Puzin, 24 Feb. 1964; GARF, f.6991, o.3, d.1740, l.11. How many of these in fact prayed in the open was not stated.

105. Reception by N. I. Smirnov of a representative of a group of Muslim believers in Krasnoiarsk, 18 July 1960; GARF, f.6991, o.4, d.110, ll.29-30. For the religious association in Krasnoiarsk, see p.301 above.

106. K. V. Ovchinnikov and Rumiantsev, Report, Minutes, CARC session No.16, 10 June 1960; GARF, f.6991, o.3, d.205, ll.28-9.

All the closures and other measures notwithstanding, Muslims continued to pray collectively, at least on special occasions. Although in 1964 there remained in the Tatar ASSR just twenty functioning mosques – eleven registered and nine unregistered – the CARC *upolnomochennyi* for that republic reported that prayer-meetings were held periodically in homes, in the open 'and elsewhere' in 487 settlements without mosques.[107]

This situation continued well into the Brezhnev period, indeed until perestroika. Reports to the CPSU Central Committee spoke of large numbers of unregistered associations and groups, the 'predominant majority' of which gathered for prayer just on the main festivals, during the fast and, in the case of the Shiites, in the month of Muharram. One of these said that eighty such groups were known to be operating in the Bashkir ASSR, forty-seven in the Karachai-Cherkess AO, sixty in Osh Oblast' (with 12,000 worshippers) and forty in Samarkand Oblast' (with 10,000 worshippers) in addition to ten unregistered mosques in the latter oblast'. Thirty-nine groups had been taken count of in Chimkent Oblast' and forty-six in Azerbaijan, eleven of which functioned regularly in former mosques. There had also been numerous attempts to build mosques without authorisation, notably in Tajikistan, Uzbekistan, Kirgiziia, Dagestan and the Karachai-Cherkess AO (most of which had been either demolished or transferred for cultural-educational and economic purposes).[108] In 1973, over 100 prayer-services were held on Uraz-Bayram in empty mosques, at holy places and at cemeteries in Uzbekistan with an aggregate attendance of approximately 20,000, and over 150 each in Kirgiziia and the Tatar ASSR; similar services took place in empty mosques in Azerbaijan and Tajikistan, and in fourteen settlements in Gor'kii Oblast'.[109] In the mid-1970s, too, over seventy structures at cemeteries were operating as mosques in the Kabardino-Balkar ASSR, some of them comparable in size with, and boasting all the accessories of, a regular mosque, possessing a *mihrab*, rugs and mats, and even electricity. At not a few of them, in the larger

107. F. S. Mangutkin, Report, Minutes, All-Union conference of CARC *upol-nomochennye*, 25-26 June 1964; GARF, f.6991, o.3, d.1457, l.30.

108. CRA, Information, sent to the CPSU Central Committee, 22 May 1970; TsKhSD, f.5, o.62, d.38, ll.8-10.

109. A. Barmenkov to the CPSU Central Committee Propaganda Department, 13 March 1974; GARF, f.6991, o.6, d.622, ll.11-12.

settlements, not only festival, but also regular Friday, prayers were held for groups of twenty to sixty worshippers. Moreover, new structures were in the process of being built.[110]

The groups which met only on the major festivals – in or around the buildings of former mosques, at *mazars* or cemeteries or elsewhere in the open – mostly expressed no interest in registration and becoming legalised. Nor did they have any permanent membership, coming together 'spontaneously' on festivals and otherwise praying at home in the family circle.[111] The number of these groups was unquestionably considerable. Certainly, in many oblasti in Muslim areas believers held festival prayers in every kolkhoz throughout the postwar period; attendance naturally varied, but, unlike the groups which met regularly, in the early 1950s it would often top the hundred mark, sometimes even reaching several hundreds, and occasionally a thousand and more.[112] Two decades later festival prayers were still taking place under the leadership of unregistered mullas in most settlements in the Dagestan, Chechen-Ingush and Kabardino-Balkar ASSRs. Such services were likewise recorded in 149 places in the Uzbek SSR and in 126 in the Tatar ASSR, as well as in many villages in Gor'kii, Kuibyshev and Ul'ianovsk oblasti.[113]

Some, primarily older men, also came together for the *tarawa-namaz* during the *uraz*, either in private homes,[114] or, at least in

110. L. Zh. Aisov to Deputy Chairman of the Kabardino-Balkar ASSR B. K. Chabdarov, 22 July 1974; GARF, f.6991, o.6, d.634, ll.75-6.

111. P. A. Solov'ev, Supplementary report, Minutes, CARC session No.9, 10 June 1948; GARF, f.6991, o.4, d.22, ll.120 and 122. Solov'ev was referring specifically to groups in Penza Oblast', but this applied equally to other areas. For *mazars*, see pp.363-82.

112. See, for example, I. G. Halimov to CARC, 27 July 1951; GARF, f.6991, o.3, d.454, ll.141-3. A CARC report for 1949 told of one prayer-meeting in a rural area of Tashkent Oblast' where 500 people came to pray on Qurban-Bayram in a square next to a metallurgical factory, and a report for 1950 told of at least two cases where as many as 1,000 attended festival service – undated report, sent by Polianskii to M. A. Suslov and Deputy Chairman of the Council of Ministers Cultural Bureau A. Ia. Sinetskii, 5 Sept. 1950, and Polianskii to Suslov, 29 Dec. 1950; GARF, f.6991, o.3, d.68, l.192, and RTsKhIDNI, f.17, o.132, d.285, ll.260 and 262.

113. V. A. Kuroedov to the CPSU Central Committee Propaganda Department, 22 Feb. 1971; TsKhSD, f.5, o.63, d.89, l.21.

114. See, for example, I. Halimov to CARC, 14 Oct. 1949, and to H. Akhtiamov, 5 July 1951; GARF, f.6991, o.3, d.454, ll.24 and 118-9.

certain oblasti, in empty mosques;[115] in the Karakalpak ASSR small groups of ten to fifteen people gathered around unregistered clergy in the mid-1970s to hold this service and observe the precepts of the *uraz*.[116] In Osh Oblast' in the 1940s unregistered clergy and believers asked to be allowed to temporarily open prayer-premises in areas without registered mosques so as to conduct the *tarawa-namaz*.[117] Such requests recurred in different places during the entire postwar period, among others, requests for permission to conduct this service at cemeteries.[118] In Tajikistan collective prayers during *uraz* would sometimes be held in *chaikhonas* or *mehmankhonas*.[119] The enhanced activity of the unregistered groups and clergy was likewise marked on Friday services during the month of Ramadan, when the number of worshippers would also be larger than on regular Fridays throughout the year.[120]

The predominant majority of unregistered groups, certainly in Kazakhstan and Kirgiziia and probably in many other places as well, seem not to have operated so much in actual buildings of former mosques as in private dwellings or small constructions erected specifically for this purpose on private plots of individual kolkhozniki or on kolkhoz farm-ground. These were small groups, usually ranging from ten to thirty people, who met daily and on Fridays; on festivals when numbers swelled to 100-200 worshippers and people's homes could no longer accommodate them, they would hold prayers in the open: on the street, on the outskirts of the village, at the cemetery, in the fields or at threshing-floors. In

115. For example, in Tashkent Oblast'- Almaev, Report, 18 July 1952; TsGAUz, f.2456, o.1, d.142, l.9. Almaev knew of three such instances and presumed there were more; in one place the local house management committee (*domkom*) forbade this and the believers went to a nearby registered mosque. Almaev also reported not a few unregistered groups which prayed collectively on Uraz-Bayram, either in empty mosques or in the open – *ibid.*, ll.17-18.

116. A. Barmenkov to the CPSU Central Committee Propaganda Department, 13 March 1974; GARF, f.6991, o.6, d.622, l.10.

117. I. G. Halimov to CARC, 5 July 1947; GARF, f.6991, o.3, d.453, l.14.

118. Applications to this end were filed in the early 1970s in the Kabardino-Balkar ASSR and in Jizak Raion in Syr-Darya Oblast' – A. Barmenkov to the CPSU Central Committee Propaganda Department, 13 March 1973; GARF, f.6991, o.6, d.537, l.15. For the *tarawa-namaz*, see p.473.

119. See, for example, N. Smirnov and S. Fastoved, Information, 22 Aug. 1962; GARF, f.6991, o.3, d.1390, l.33.

120. A. Barmenkov to the CPSU Central Committee Propaganda Department, 13 March 1973; GARF, f.6991, o.6, d.537, l.18.

the smaller kolkhozy at the beginning of the 1950s there might be three to four such groups, in the larger ones five to eight.[121] In later years, too, festival prayers continued to be held in Kirgiziia in most settlements, in the open wherever the local government did not prohibit it and clandestinely in the event that it did.[122] CARC's *upolnomochennye* reported in 1953 that one raion in Osh Oblast' which did not have a single registered community, had a plethora of unregistered groups that met for prayer in mosques and private homes, and no less than forty-three mullas; in another, which had one registered mosque, in the raion's administrative centre, unregistered mosques operated in almost every settlement.[123] In the towns, too, large prayer-meetings were held.[124] Still in 1964, the nearly 300 unregistered groups taken count of in Kirgiziia boasted 35,000 believers; clearly, many of them were quite large.[125] By the end of the decade the number of groups was approximately the same, but they were reported to consist of less than half that number of people; twenty-five of the groups functioned regularly (every Friday) and the rest just on festivals.[126] Nonetheless, in some parts at least the groups did become less numerous, both as a result of measures taken by the authorities to terminate their activities and of 'natural decline,' which led to some of them disbanding.[127]

Nor was activity confined to the holding of prayer-meetings and the performance of life-cycle rites. On one occasion in 1945

121. Minutes, CARC session No.11, 25 April 1951; GARF, f.6991, o.3, d.74, l.116.

122. V. I. Gostev to P. A. Tarasov, 4 Jan. 1954; GARF, f.6991, o.3, d.102, l.8. Gostev noted that in Issyk-Kul Oblast' the local organs of government endeavoured to prohibit collective prayers, but these were nonetheless held.

123. I. V. Polianskii to the CPSU Central Committee, 12 Jan. 1954; GARF, f.6991, o.3, d.113, ll.11-17. In the second raion 'incomplete data' revealed 20 mosques and 50 mullas.

124. For instance, in Gurev, where there was no registered mosque until 1957, 800 believers came to pray in the open at the cemetery on Uraz-Bayram and 1,000 on Qurban-Bayram in the year 1954 – I. V. Polianskii to P. V. Kovanov, 23 June 1955; GARF, f.6991, o.3, d.114, l.33.

125. Minutes, CARC session No.31, 6 Oct. 1964; GARF, f.6991, o.4, d.147, l.135.

126. K. Shabolotov to A. A. Nurullaev, 23 June 1969; GARF, f.6991, o.6, d.220, ll.149-51.

127. See, for example, I. Mikhalev, reporting from the Tatar ASSR, 6 May 1974; GARF, f.6991, o.6, d.545, l.215.

an unregistered community, which had been allowed to operate by the *oblispolkom*, openly conducted a procession at the local cemetery, where it performed ritual slaughter and prayed for rain. (When, shortly after, copious rain began to fall, the assumption that there was cause and effect was considered religious propaganda.)[128] On another such occasion a few years later, the entire village, including its officers, partook of the meat of the animals slaughtered at the ceremony.[129] In a kolkhoz in Andijan Oblast' in the mid-1950s a ceremony was held at which excerpts from the Qur'an were read and prayers held for a good cotton crop.[130] Altogether, natural phenomena were often perceived as having a religious message: earthquakes in particular were considered to be punishment for people's breaking with religion.[131]

Whether officially illegal or not,[132] the unregistered associations were, given Soviet conditions, a natural target of harassment almost by definition. For 'religious propaganda' and violations of law seemed to be an inevitable concomitant of the very existence of unregistered associations, the law, for example, not permitting the conduct of prayer-services either in the open or in privately-owned homes unless they were officially designated to this end. In most areas, apparently, even those groups which used the buildings of former mosques did so as a rule without permission. And if the local administration agreed to this, as sometimes happened, the agreement was not formalised by the requisite higher authority.[133] Nor was it formalised even in cases where mosques were actually transferred to believers by a local *ispolkom*, which thus knew that prayers and other rituals were conducted in them, but drew up no contract for the use of either the prayer-house or its furnishings.[134]

128. H. Akhtiamov to CARC, 5 Oct. 1945; GARF, f.6991, o.3, d.30, ll.243-4.

129. I. V. Polianskii to P. V. Kovanov, 23 June 1955; GARF, f.6991, o.3, d.114, l.29.

130. See p.652.

131. Compare pp.149, 262 and 458-9.

132. The general consensus was that they were indeed illegal, although from time to time a voice would be heard denying this; see p.29.

133. The CARC *upolnomochennyi* for Osh Oblast' reported at the end of 1948 a case of this nature, suggesting that, since there was no registered mosque in the raion in question, this group be registered – I. Halimov to CARC, 31 Dec. 1948; GARF, f.6991, o.3, d.454, ll.2-3.

134. This was the situation, for example, in Stavropol Krai – V. V. Bulatov to I. V. Polianskii, 12 Feb. 1945; GARF, f.6991, o.3, d.33, ll.58-9.

In localities where there were no registered communities the activity of unregistered groups seemed particularly unrestricted and the influence of unregistered clergy of various categories all the more resilient.[135] Whereas in places which found themselves in the proximity of a registered mosque believers at certain periods tended to stop having recourse to the services of unregistered clergy, unregistered groups persisted in localities which were further away or in which the nearby registered mosque was in the hands of a school or persuasion other than that of local believers.[136] In 1968 a programmatic lecture by the head of the CRA's Department for Islam and Buddhism laid down unequivocally that the very existence of a large number of unregistered Muslim associations and clergy constituted a 'most serious violation of the Soviet law on religion'.[137]

It was, thus, not surprising that the powers-that-be expended considerable effort in disclosing the existence of unregistered groups and then in curtailing and, where possible, terminating their activity. Even CARC, which advocated opening what seemed to it a reasonable number of mosques did so with the express intention of closing the others, and instructed its *upolnomochennye* to proceed to implement this line.[138] This position did not always enjoy the support of the local organs of government, which simply ignored injunctions to either formalise the registration of religious groups or disperse them.[139] So, when the Bukhara Oblast' authorities decreed in December 1949 that illegally functioning mosques be closed down, the oblast' *upolnomochennyi* was asked to verify implementation.[140]

135. This was the conclusion drawn by one CARC *upolnomochennyi* – I. G. Halimov to CARC, 3 April 1950; GARF, f.6991, o.3, d.454, l.52. Nor presumably was it his view alone.

136. L. A. Prikhod'ko, Report, 20 May 1953; GARF, f.6991, o.3, d.91, l.269.

137. Theses of lecture, 'The situation of the Muslim faith in the country and measures to strengthen control of observance of legislation on religion', sent to the CPSU Central Committee Propaganda Department, 19 June 1968; GARF, f.6991, o.6, d.147, l.43.

138. See pp.186-7, 191 and 195-7.

139. The CARC *upolnomochennyi* for Tashkent Oblast' complained that local officials and organs of government paid no heed whatever to *oblispolkom* resolutions to this effect – K. Mustafin to Obkom Secretary Mavlianov and Oblispokom Chairman Turgunov, 10 Nov. 1945; GARF, f.6991, o.3, d.30, ll.286-7.

140. Kh. N. Iskanderov to Jidirov, 5 April 1950; TsGAUz, f.2456, o.1, d.126,

Various methods, in addition to legislation, were employed in order to curb the activity of the unregistered groups. The *upol-nomochennyi*, after disclosing the existence of a group, would normally approach local government agencies, although well aware that, on the one hand, the likelihood of effective action was slight and, on the other, that local officials were not squeamish about reverting to 'administrative' methods, which CARC sought constantly to avoid.[141] In any case, since the unregistered mosques had no formal documentation, they could be closed down by the local organs of government without recourse to CARC. And although not only CARC, but also the CPSU Central Committee officially opposed the use of administrative measures against unregistered, as well as registered, mosques,[142] Moscow could hardly expect the intricacies of its policy toward religion's unofficial expression, which was even more obtuse than its general line on religion, to be appreciated and complied with by local organs of government.

In the very early postwar period the religious groups were apparently told to cease activity until they were formally registered, the assumption being that this was on the cards. This tactic seems to have met with little success.[143] Somewhat later, when it was evident that large numbers of religious associations would not be registered, the tendency becoming one of closing rather than opening mosques, the *upolnomochennyi* or the local *ispolkom* might invite the group's *aktiv*, or some of its members, to listen to an exposition on the illegality of their activity, their personal accountability for

---

l.10. A similar resolution was proposed in 1952 in Tashkent Oblast' – Resolution of Tashkent Oblispolkom on illegally functioning mosques, 25 July 1952; TsGAUz, f.2456, o.1, d.142, ll.4-5. For the position of local government, see Chapter 11.

141. For further discussion of these 'administrative' measures, see pp.663-8.

142. A. A. Puzin reported 16 instances of administrative closures in Tashkent Oblast' to the CPSU Central Committee on 26 Aug. 1961; GARF, f.6991, o.3, d.1363, ll.129-31 (see below). 'A Central Committee apparatus official telephoned CARC on 16 Sept. and told it instructions were to be given to the Uzbekistan CP Central Committee to eliminate the mistakes which had been committed and punish the guilty parties. CARC Deputy Chairman Riazanov, who wrote this on the copy of Puzin's letter which remained in the CARC files, added that the local authorities must receive explanations of the correct procedure for closing mosques and other prayer-houses.

143. See, for example, Kokand Gorispolkom Chairman M. Aliev, to A. Abdurahmanov, chairman, Uzbek SSR Council of Ministers, 14 June 1946; TsGAUz, f.2456, o.1, d.72, l.7.

all offences against the law, and the undesirability and risk of their course of action. On occasion the clergy of a registered mosque might be mobilised to make these explanations. Wherever possible, the proposition would be made to the members of unregistered groups to affiliate in some way to the nearest registered mosque, provided there was one in the proximity.[144] In some instances, the clergy and elders of the local registered mosque were cautioned that they would be held responsible if believers continued to pray in unregistered mosques.[145] Similarly, the spiritual directorates would be pressured from time to time to take action against the unregistered clergy, action which sometimes appeared to be solely *pro forma*.[146] Or the person who gave his home to the group for purposes of prayer-meetings, or its spiritual leader, might be fined.[147]

Despite their endeavours to shut down all unregistered groups and terminate all activity, CARC's *upolnomochennye* were constantly coming across new associations. According to one source, 313 such groups had been taken count of at the beginning of 1951; of these 280 terminated their activity during 1951, but in the course of that same year another 403 were exposed.[148] A similar number were exposed three years later, just over 40 per cent of them in the RSFSR, the rest in Central Asia.[149] Of the latter over two-thirds had mosques at their disposal, while the majority of the former had none and prayed in private homes or in the open. Most of the total number had been operating for five to ten years or even longer, had between 12 and 100 members

144. For these variants, see I. Halimov to CARC, 31 Dec. 1948, and M. Sh. Karimov, Report, minutes, CARC session, No.27, 28-9 Oct. 1949; GARF, f.6991, o.3, d.454, l.2, and d.60, l.111. Halimov claimed to have closed up to 100 unofficial communities since he had taken office in 1945 (see p.297 above). Karimov, on the other hand, said that he had not encountered great success, for which he blamed the mufti in Ufa, who, he claimed, gave support to 200 leaders of unregistered communities; see also p.135.

145. I. G. Halimov to CARC, 3 July 1950; GARF, f.6991, o.3, d.454, l.65.

146. For such attempts and the ambivalent attitude of the spiritual directorates to the unregistered associations, with which they sometimes seemed to be in actual co-operation, receiving contributions from them and giving them instructions, see pp.135-40.

147. For the fining of unregistered clergy, see p.350 below.

148. I. V. Polianskii to M. A. Suslov, 5 April 1952; RTsKhIDNI, f.17, o.132, d.569, l.94.

149. The fact that none were exposed in the Caucasus does not mean that there were none but that reporting there was faultier.

−some of whom prayed daily, the rest only on Fridays−and a mulla or lay leader.[150]

It is clear from their reports that since the *upolnomochennye* had no regular or systematic source of information regarding the unregistered groups, those which they did succeed in exposing were mostly brought to light by sheer accident, while the great majority were not discovered at all.[151] Moreover, an unregistered group which was reported to have terminated activity often re-appeared. Since so many of them operated sporadically, it was in fact extremely difficult to rely on an assurance that the group would cease functioning, let alone to verify its implementation.[152] This held true particularly in localities where local officials were either positively sympathetic or turned a blind eye to the activities of the unregistered groups. In one such place the CARC *upolnomochennyi* for Osh Oblast' secured a promise from the mulla and elders of an unregistered community that they would not continue praying in their mosque, but would go to pray in a registered mosque just 3 km away; as soon, however, as the *upolnomochennyi* left the scene, everything returned to the *status quo ante*.[153] In one raion in Tashkent Oblast' one unregistered mosque was closed thirteen times in the course of five years. Following each of the first twelve closures the believers complained, a promise was extracted from them not to pray in the mosque, upon which the lock was removed and gradually the believers returned to pray there. They approached the republican *upolnomochennyi* no less than sixty times over these five years in order to register their mosque, but to no avail.[154]

150. G. F. Frolov to I. V. Polianskii, 25 Feb. 1955; GARF, f.6991, o.3, d.112, ll.4-6.

151. The *upolnomochennyi* for Osh Oblast, for instance, would in each quarterly report inform his superiors of two, three or four such groups which he had come upon in the last three months.

152. This state of affairs is transparent from CARC's correspondence with its *upolnomochennye* or that of republican *upolnomochennye* with the oblast' ones under their jurisdiction, for example, H. Akhtiamov to I. Halimov, 10 July 1948 and 13 April 1949; GARF, f.6991, o.3, d.453, l.57, and d.454, l.16.

153. I. G. Halimov to CARC, 3 April 1950; GARF, f.6991, o.3, d.454, ll.48-9. The consent of the local authorities to the mosque's operation was blatant, for the *azan* summoned believers to prayer daily just 100 m from the local club. That everything returned to *status quo ante* was added to the letter by hand, not by Halimov.

154. A. A. Puzin to the CPSU Central Committee, 26 Aug. 1961; GARF, f.6991, o.3, d.1363, ll.129-31. For further details, see p.658.

This recurrent shutting down and re-opening of unregistered mosques – and *mazars* – occurred even in the period of Khrushchev's anti-religious campaign,[155] and persisted in subsequent years under Brezhnev as well. In Chimkent Oblast', for instance, the illegally constructed prayer-houses of unregistered associations were closed down and, according to reports received from the local authorities, transferred to kolkhozy and sovkhozy to be used for economic purposes, following republican legislation and an *oblispolkom* resolution in 1968. Yet they soon renewed activity, usually after standing idle for some time. One of them became a crèche, but after two children became ill, a decison 'motivated by superstition' was taken to close the crèche and the building reverted to its previous use as a mosque. In the single year 1973, for instance, fourteen associations terminated their activity 'with the agreement of the believers themselves' (they were all said to be small, with less than twenty members). Within less than a year, however, they were found to have resumed operations.[156]

The impasse regarding the unregistered religious groups and mosques thus remained largely unsolved. In the late 1960s the CRA in Moscow hoped to improve matters by enabling some of them to register.[157] While there is evidence that not a few unregistered associations contemplated applying to register, most seem to have been content with their situation. As one memorandum indicated, the majority of the over 900 groups which operated openly at the beginning of the 1970s in 'specially equipped prayer-premises' with permanent clergy – thus fulfilling the requisite conditions for registration – had not even raised the question of their registration as the 'anti-lawful activity' of their leaders had long gone unpunished.[158] On the other hand, local officialdom remained basically unresponsive to feelers put out by those desirous of registering; although it had no sound legal foundation for its position, there was clearly no meaningful pressure from the centre to act

155. N. Smirnov, Information, 18 Sept. 1962; GARF, f.6991, o.3, d.1390, l.73. Smirnov was referring specifically to Uzbekistan, but there is no reason to suppose that the phenomenon was restricted to that republic.

156. Sh. Ospanov to G. R. Gol'st, 21 Dec. 1973, Chimkent Oblispolkom, Resolution, 26 Sept. 1974, and K. Panzabekov, Information, 10 Oct. 1974; GARF, f.6991, o.6, d.633, ll.86–90, and d.637, ll.100-1 and 105-11.

157. See pp.215-6.

158. Memorandum, signed V. A. Kuroedov, 24 Aug. 1970; TsKhSD, f.5, o.62, d.137, l.174.

otherwise. And the result continued to be that the activity of the unregistered associations – their occupation with affairs 'not intrinsic' to religious associations, their 'interference in believers' lives', their 'incitement' of believers against atheists, their 'unbridled religious propaganda' – was subject to no control. This was all the more poignant, for such manifestations were easily discontinued when they occurred in registered mosques.[159]

A conference held in Tashkent in July 1968 with the participation of all those concerned with policy implementation regarding Islam gave 'special attention' to the issue of the unregistered religious associations and clergy in light of their large number (the former remained nearly ten times as numerous as the registered mosques in Kirgiziia, whereas there were about 700 of the latter versus sixty-seven registered clergy in Uzbekistan), the continued unauthorised opening of mosques and the ensuing deadlock, from which there was no obvious way out.[160] In the years following this conference and in light of a further spate of legislation and resolutions at the various decision-making levels, renewed efforts were made to shut down unregistered groups. The long-term effect of these measures, however, was no more impressive than had been that of earlier similar steps.[161]

The sense of frustration and ineffectiveness in dealing with the unregistered mosques and groups accompanied the CRA until the end of the period covered by this study. In a single *sel'sovet* in Andijan Oblast' fifteen recently repaired illegally functioning mosques were 'exposed' in 1982, and it was discovered they had been operating between ten and fifteen years. In Kurgan-Tyube Oblast' a year previously over seventy mosques were similarly 'exposed'. They had been erected by believers under the guise of *chaikhonas* on plots seized without permission from kolkhoz and sovkhoz land, and many of them had also been operating for fifteen to twenty years under the very eyes of the local *raikom* or *raiispolkom*.[162] Altogether, unregistered mosques were said to be

159. Theses of lecture, sent to the CPSU Central Committee Propaganda Department, 19 June 1968; GARF, f.6991, o.6, d.147, l.44.

160. V. A. Kuroedov to the CPSU Central Committee Propaganda Department, 14 Aug. 1968; GARF, f.6991, o.6, d.147, l.122. For this conference, see p.558.

161. For example in Chimkent, see above.

162. CRA memo, 2 June 1983; TsKhSD, f.5, o.89, d.82, l.39.

functioning in the early 1980s in over 200 settlements in Tajikis-tan.[163] And this was almost certainly a considerable underestimate.

The clergy

Just as Muslim collective prayer did not need to be held in a mosque, the leader of the prayer-service or the person who per-formed most religious rites did not have to be a professional minister of religion with any formal training.[164] In the pre-Soviet period, too, those who performed religious rites in Central Asia, for instance, knew very little about Islam apart from being able to recite a few prayers.[165] In spite of the marked improvement in general education, this patchy knowledge actually diminished over the Soviet period, when to all intents and purposes there were no Islamic schools. Yet, the minimal requirements demanded by the faith meant that although the quality of religious leadership of the unregistered, as of the registered, clergy, almost inevitably fell over the Soviet period, there was no quantative dearth of people able to fulfil them, especially in Central Asia. In the same way as its reports to the CPSU Central Committee apparatus and the Council of Ministers insisted that the data concerning the registered mosques did not tell the full story of Muslim religious activity, since these comprised but a small percentage of all religious associations and groups, so too CARC drew the leadership's attention to the fact that the number of unregistered clergy ministering to the needs of the Muslim believer population far exceeded that of the registered clergy.[166] Indeed, they also outnumbered the unregistered groups, for they were in need in areas where there was no tradition of collective prayer apart from the major festivals – in parts of Tajikistan and Kazakhstan and in Turkmenistan, for instance.[167] In 1970,

163. V. A. Kuroedov to the CPSU Central Committee, 16 Sept. 1983; TsKhSD, f.5, o.89, d.82, l.61. One scholar claims that by the close of the Soviet period there were over 1,000 such 'covert mosques' built ostensibly as clubs or tea-houses –Atkin, 'Islam as Faith, Politics and Bogeyman', p.251.

164. In a document dated 17 Nov. 1949 CARC inspector N. Abushaev attributed this feature to Islam's 'simplicity and adaptability' – GARF, f.6991, o.3, d.61, l.123.

165. Abashin, 'Sotsial'nye korni sredneaziatskogo islamizma', p.457.

166. For instance, I. V. Polianskii to the CPSU Central Committee, 11 Jan. 1955; GARF, f.6991, d.113, l.8. See also p.90.

167. G. F. Frolov to I. V. Polianskii, 25 Feb. 1955; GARF, f.6991, o.3, d.112,

count was taken of no less than 1,700 unregistered clergy, a number larger than existed for any other religion in the Soviet Union,[168] and by the mid 1980s they comprised over one half for all denominations.[169]

Not unlike the unregistered religious associations, the unregistered clergy could not be lumped together under a single heading. True, they were all by definition beyond the direct control of the establishment, falling within the jurisdiction neither of CARC's *upolnomochennye* nor of the spiritual directorates and their representatives. Even those among them who maintained contacts with the latter and/or with the registered clergy did so in the hope that this would somehow legitimise their activity or provide them with some protection. These ties did not imply an acceptance of the authority of the religious establishment, let alone a commitment to be guided by its injunctions or to act otherwise than they themselves saw fit at any given moment. Even such an arrangement, however, had advantages from CARC's point of view. Accepting, as it did, that the clergy traditionally enjoyed considerable influence among the Muslim population, the link between certain unregistered mullas and the registered clergy enabled the Council and its representatives in the localities to give maximum weight to that element among the unregistered mullas which it could reasonably hope to affect or manoeuvre and to isolate the more 'reactionary' component.[170]

Many of the unregistered clergy in the postwar years were, like the registered clerics, former mullas or sons of former mullas, who had been initiated by their fathers, it being a tradition in Central Asia and other parts for this calling to remain within certain families.[171] According to one source, the unregistered mullas

---

ll.7-8. And see pp.185-8.

168. CRA, Information, sent to the CPSU Central Committee, 27 April 1971; TsKhSD, f.5, o.63, d.89, l.98.

169. Even according to the lower estimate given in Chapter 2, n.161.

170. See, for example, report of K. Hamidov, Minutes, CARC session No.4, 29 Jan. 1947; GARF, f.6991, o.4, d.19, l.73.

171. In Osh Oblast', for instance, the CARC *upolnomochennyi* noted that many of the clergy who performed rites for the population, which was by and large religious, were either former mullas or their relatives – I. G. Halimov to CARC, 27 Dec. 1955 and 20 Jan. 1956; GARF, f.6991, o.3, d.457, ll.2 and 17. A similar situation prevailed in Bukhara Oblast' – I. A. Shalaev to Uzbekistan CP Central Committee Secretary Kh. G. Gulamov, 11 Nov. 1955; TsGAUz, f.2456,

and shaykhs 'with very few exceptions' came from such families, from whom toward the end of the period students would likewise be chosen for the underground religious schools. Many of these families seem to have been those popularly held to be descendants of Muhammad, *seids*, or of the regions's earliest Muslims and the Arabs who originally brought Islam to Central Asia, the *khojas*, who comprised a group which enjoyed considerable prestige and authority in Central Asian society, or, in Turkmenistan, of the six so-called holy tribes.[172]

The tendency, indeed, was to talk of all unregistered clerics as 'itinerant mullas', both in reference to clergy who in fact went from one place to another to perform religious rites[173] and to those who served as regular mullas at unregistered mosques[174] or catered to the needs of the population in their places of residence without recourse to any institutionalised prayer-premises. Indeed, while there were considerable numbers who rightfully fitted into the classification of itinerant mullas, the majority of the unregistered Muslim clergy were local people, who lived in a particular village or *mahalla* which did not have a registered mosque, or was not even in the proximity of one. They conducted occasional prayer-services in private homes or wherever they found it convenient, read *mavluds* and excerpts from the Qur'an at the invitation of believers on a variety of occasions, and performed the necessary life-cycle and other popular rites for the neighbourhood's believer population. In light of these activities they were said in the official documentation to be propagating religion and distracting people's attention from 'socially productive work'.[175]

o.1, d.174, l.94. For the situation in pre-revolutionary times, see Abashin, 'Sotsial'nye korni sredneaziatskogo islamizma', p.457.

172. Poliakov, *Everyday Islam*, pp.107 and 110. Poliakov actually says these families were *hajjis*, but he presumably means *khojas*. Poliakov discusses Central Asia, but it seems that the tendency for clergy to come from clerical families prevailed also in other areas with a concentration of Muslim ethnic groups. For the underground schools, see pp.353-8 below.

173. We have seen that the concept 'itinerant preachers' was a general one, not specific to Muslim clergy; see p.30.

174. For example, Polianskii wrote in 1949: 'The itinerant clergy serve illegally functioning mosques and open such mosques without authorisation, especially at the time of religious festivals... [and] they conduct regular prayer-meetings at *mazars*, which they also occupy without authorisation' – I. V. Polianskii to K. E. Voroshilov, 27 May 1950; GARF, f.6991, o.3, d.68, l.43.

175. T. Tashkenbaev to I. V. Polianskii, 28 April 1956; TsGAUz, f.2456, o.1,

Some of these 'mosqueless mullas', as they were sometimes described, who were former clergy, had in the past actually occupied important positions, even played leadership roles, within the religious community, as mullas, *ishans* and shaykhs.[176] Central Asia also had a rather large cohort of *qaris*, who would recite the Qur'an by heart during the *uraz*. Most of them were people who had acquired a religious education prior to the repression of the *mektebs* and *medreses*, but some belonged to a younger generation, who had been initiated by their elders.[177] Certainly, in the 1940s and 1950s there were still, especially in Central Asia, considerable numbers among the ranks of the unregistered clergy who had served as clergy prior to 1917, or until such time as the persecution of religion had put an end to their religious activity, and who, although they had afterwards become ordinary kolkhozniki, continued to serve the population unofficially.[178] A few of these one-time clergy had even become kolkhoz officials: one kolkhoz chairman in Omsk Oblast' in 1943 performed the festival service on Uraz-Bayram in kolkhozniki's private homes.[179] In the more outlying areas, where religious activity had persisted almost un-molested, for instance in some rural parts of Tajikistan, many unofficial clergy remained who had begun functioning prior to the regime's repression of Islam. It was these 'professional' clergy

---

d.198, ll.34-5. When the registered clergy began rejecting invitations to recite *mavluds* and excerpts from the Qur'an in private homes in view of the dis-couragement, if not actual prohibition, of this practice by the powers-that-be (see below), this assignment fell increasingly to the lot of the unregistered clergy —I. V. Polianskii to P. V. Kovanov, 23 June 1955; GARF, f.6991, o.3, d.114, l.34.

176. For example, in Bukhara Oblast' – Minutes, Instructional meeting of CARC *upolnomochennye* in the Uzbek SSR, 15-17 March 1956; TsGAUz, f.2456, o.1, d.183, l.63.

177. For example, K. Hamidov to I. V. Polianskii, 7 Dec. 1945, and I. G. Halimov to H. Akhtiamov, 9 May 1945; GARF, f.6991, o.3, d.30, l.364, and d.453, l.7. For the *qaris*, see also p.474.

178. Kh. N. Iskanderov to Tashkent Obkom Secretary A. Alimov and Oblispolkom Chairman Jalilov, 27 May 1954; TsGAUz, f.2456, o.1, d.162, l.175. Iskanderov suggested that they were 'fanatics' who had not given up any of their earlier tenets and refrained from serving in the registered mosques in view of the discrepancies between their point of view and the conduct of the contemporary registered clergy.

179. See n.10 above. Similar conduct was reported in other kolkhozy throughout the oblast' in both 1943 and 1944.

who sought to 'revive' religious rites which the spiritual directorates rejected.[180]

Most mosqueless mullas, however, particularly in rural areas, were not professional clergy by any criterion, but simply *aksakals*, elders, with a minimal knowledge of religious practice, or, as one source called them in Marxist jargon, 'fortuitous elements'.[181] In the late 1940s CARC's republican *upolnomochennyi* in Kazakhstan said that none of the nearly 400 'home-bred' mullas who had been exposed in his republic could be described as professional men of religion.[182] Most were unable to translate the Qur'an into their native tongue; some could not even read it at all.[183] Inevitably, as time passed, the number diminished of those who had any religious education or knew how to perform rites in accordance with custom. Often those who acted, or were branded, as un-registered clergy were simply people who engaged in ritual cleansing prior to burial (the most basic and menial of the cleric's tasks). They knew no Arabic and very little Qur'an except for a few *suras*.

The general ignorance of Islamic law or even custom held for most, if not all, areas inhabited by Muslim nationalities. It led, among other things, to mistakes in the actual conduct of ritual, which was duly taken advantage of by the authorities in order to compromise these mullas. Nonetheless, by leading prayers, they enabled those present to pray in conformity with the rudimentary requirements of the canon.[184]

CARC's *upolnomochennyi* for Northern Kazakhstan emphasised that the term 'itinerant mulla' by which they were generally known was singularly unsuitable for these lay elders.[185] So large a proportion of them were kolkhozniki that one report characterised all 'itinerant

180. V. I. Gostev to P. A. Tarasov, 4 Jan. 1954; GARF, f.6991, o.3, d.102, ll.3 and 13.

181. L. A. Prikhod'ko, Report, 2 June 1952; GARF, f.6991, o.3, d.81, l.134.

182. N. Sabitov, Report, Conference of CARC's Central Asian *upolnomochennye*, 17-19 Dec. 1949; GARF, f.6991, o.3, d.67, l.93.

183. Minutes, CARC session No.21, 22 July 1959; GARF, f.6991, o.3, d.184, ll.176-7. The speaker referred specifically to mullas in the Karachai-Cherkess AO.

184. T. Shaidildinov, CRA *upolnomochennyi* for Taldy-Kurgan Oblast', to A. A. Nurullaev, 29 April 1974, and I. Mikhalev to A. A. Nurullaev, 6 May 1974; GARF, f.6991, o.6, d.633, l.39, and d.545, l.215.

185. K. Ovchinnikov, on the basis of V. Liapunov's report for 1960, 10 Jan. 1961; GARF, f.6991, o.3, d.1355, ll.7s-7sh.

mullas' as kolkhozniki.[186] In Khorezm Oblast' in the mid-1950s many of the estimated 300 unregistered clergy were members of kolkhozy and industrial artels.[187] Some of these people, before becoming pensioners and taking up religious activity, had been 'village activists', had filled posts in the local apparatus, working in the *sel'sovet* or as chairmen of kolkhozy; some of them were relatives of contemporary officials.[188] Often mosqueless mullas still engaged in 'productive work', the kolkhoz or whatever other enterprise might employ them providing their main source of income.[189]

Although a very large proportion were kolkhozniki, the unregistered Muslim clergy seem to have comprised elements from a variety of social strata and groups. This is evident from a number of lists of clergy, for instance one for Tashkent Oblast' in the late 1960s which gave names and other data regarding eleven unregistered imams, who led prayers in unregistered mosques, as well as 24 itinerant mullas.[190] Some were described simply as rogues or "self-styled" mullas; often these might be members of non-indigenous Muslim groups in areas in which the eponymous nationality was Muslim. This was the case not only with Uzbeks in southern Kirgiziia, southern Kazakhstan or Turkmenistan's Tashauz Oblast', but also with Northern Caucasians who had been deported to Central Asia and Kazakhstan and even Crimean

---

186. L. A. Prikhod'ko, Minutes, No.4, Meeting of instructors with CARC *upolnomochennye*, 4-5 April 1950; GARF, f.6991, o.3, d.66, l.57.

187. I. V. Polianskii to P. V. Kovanov, 23 June 1955; GARF, f.6991, o.3, d.114, l.21.

188. K. Shabolotov to the Kirgiz SSR Council of Ministers, 26 Sept. 1969; GARF, f.6991, o.6, d.223, ll.70-1.

189. H. Akhtiamov to I. G. Halimov, 9 Oct. 1947; GARF, f.6991, o.3, d.453, l.22. The fact that they were not professional mullas, but engaged in other work and activity, and performed their religious duties only irregularly, made it all the more difficult to 'expose' them, let alone to assess their number – H. Akhtiamov to I. V. Polianskii, 15 Dec. 1945; GARF, f.6991, o.3, d.30, l.254. These people existed not only in Central Asia, but also in rural settlements in the RSFSR with a Tatar (or Tatar-Bashkir) population and in the Northern Caucasus; see, for example, report by CARC *upolnomochennyi* for Sverdlovsk Oblast' at conference of *upolnomochennye* in Novosibirsk, 31 May 1946, and L. Aisov to the CRA, 16 Jan. 1970 – GARF, f.6991, o.3, d.36, l.55ob, and o.6, d.232, l.43.

190. Iu. Bilialov, Information, undated (Dec. 1968 or early 1969); GARF, f.6991, o.6, d.173, ll.73-5. Of the 24, one was described as an *ishan* and another as engaging in 'muridism'.

Tatars in Abkhaziia, where most of the 3,000 people said to be professing Islam illegally were from other parts (particularly Crimean Tatars and some 'Turks').[191]

The basic assumption of the secular authority was that every settlement whose inhabitants were of one or another Muslim nationality, had at least one such person given the widespread adherence to the basic life-cycle rites;[192] in some parts there may have been two or three in each village. In many villages in certain areas each clan had its own *aksakal* who filled the role of cleric.[193] The statement made by Polianskii to Molotov in late 1945 that for the time being unregistered mullas 'operating sporadically' fulfilled the religious needs of most Muslims,[194] probably held for the entire postwar period right down to perestroika, when it finally became possible to register religious societies without any major difficulty. In the Kabardino-Balkar ASSR in the early 1960s, with its ninety-eight villages and four towns, there existed five registered mosques and thirty-one unregistered groups, but seventy-three unregistered clergy and an additional 205 people who catered to the population's religious needs – muezzins and

191. A. Lagvileva to V. A. Kuroedov, undated (received 25 July 1969); GARF, f. 6991, o.6, d.220, 11.83-4 and 86-7. 'Turks' probably referred here to different groups deported from the border with Turkey during the war, such as the Meskhetians. (In some areas Azeris were named Turks, but in this instance it seems unlikely.)

192. Many *upolnomochennye*, however, denied their existence, simply ignoring the facts as a result of the constraints under which they operated. Unable to go to all the localities under their jurisdiction – most oblast' *upolnomochennye* were single-person apparatuses (see p.620) and their oblasti were often large and included very inaccessible parts – the easy way out was to deny that there were unregistered clergy. See, for instance, H. Akhtiamov to I. Halimov, 10 July 1948. Over a decade later, when asked by Central Committee apparatchik K. I. Chernenko whether there were many itinerant mullas in Kirgiziia, Akhtiamov replied 'in nearly every kolkhoz' – All-Union conference of CARC *upolnomochennye*, 18-20 April 1960. The same held for the Northern Caucasus: 70 unregistered mullas were taken count of in the Kabardino-Balkar ASSR in the early 1960s – N. I. Smirnov to A. A. Puzin, 28 March 1963. In 1967 there were unregistered mullas in nearly all villages where Tatars resided – T. S. Saidbaev, Information, undated (before 22 Nov. 1967); GARF, f.6991, o.3, d.453, ll.57-8, d.208, l.137, and d.1607, l.17, and o.6, d.73, l.199.

193. For example in the Nakhichevan ASSR – I. Bonchkovskii to E. I. Lisavtsev, 1 June 1973; GARF, f.6991, o.6, d.537, l.171.

194. I .V. Polianskii to V. M. Molotov, 7 Dec. 1945; GARF, f.6991, o.3, d.10, l.139.

those who recited from the Qur'an at funerals.[195] Even in Groznyi Oblast', as the Chechen-Ingush ASSR had become in March 1944, from which the two eponymous nationalities were deported *en masse* just afterwards, unregistered mullas continued to operate, indeed were said to exist in nearly every kolkhoz. While the oblast' had not a single functioning mosque after the deportation and Muslims no longer came together for collective prayer, these mullas discharged all the population's religious needs, including the healing of the sick; by summer 1947 there were even unregistered communities.[196]

In at least some parts of Kazakhstan, too, 'itinerant mullas' were a common feature.[197] In the early-mid 1950s there were reckoned to be over 500 unregistered clergy throughout the republic, who performed religious rites among believers in raiony where there was no registered mosque, their number being especially large in the southern regions with their considerable Uzbek population.[198] At the beginning of the 1960s a similar number were accounted for. They were described as inciting the population to religious activity and sustaining 'feudal-bai vestiges', performing all rites, including circumcision and engaging in faith-healing.[199] And in the 1970s the numbers, if anything, grew. In Taldy-Kurgan Oblast', which had not a single registered mosque, there were about 100

195. L. Zh. Aisov to A. A. Puzin, 12 Feb. 1961, GARF, f.6991, o.3, d.1606, l.6.

196. Excerpt from a report of the oblast' *upolnomochennyi*, quoted by CARC member R. A. Tateosov at conference of *upolnomochennye*, Rostov-on-Don, 14 June 1946; GARF, f.6991, o.3, d.38, l.44. And I. V. Polianskii to A. A. Zhdanov and K. E. Voroshilov, 22 July 1947; RTsKhIDNI, f.17, o.125, d.506, l.169. According to the latter source there were 70 such mullas in one single raion. (It should be noted that Groznyi Oblast' was not completely identical with the Chechen-Ingush ASSR, some parts of which went to other administrative units; for example, the part in which the tomb of Kunta Haji's mother was situated became part of the Dagestan ASSR.)

197. For instance, in the oblasti of Eastern Kazakhstan and Kustanai – I. V. Polianskii to A. A. Zhdanov and K. E. Voroshilov, 22 July 1947; RTsKhIDNI, f.17, o.125, d.506, l.170.

198. V. I. Gostev to P. A. Tarasov, 4 Jan. 1954; GARF, f.6991, o.3, d.102, ll.17-8.

199. Information (unsigned), handed to A. I. Aleksandrov at the CPSU Central Committee, 14 Feb. 1962; GARF, f.6991, o.3, d.1389, ll.11-2. (Just half a year before, the number had been reckoned at 'over 300' – A. A. Puzin to the CPSU Central Committee Department of Propaganda and Agitation, 7 June 1961; GARF, f.6991, o.3, d.1363, l.98.)

people who performed religious rites. None of them had engaged in religious activity before becoming pensioners; they had worked in production, some had fought in World War II, some had filled posts in the lower echelons of the bureaucracy, a few were even former communists. Not only, in the view of the CRA *upol-nomochennyi*, did their large number constitute a serious violation of legislation, but they caused more harm than registered clergy, because they were subject to no control. When one of their number was officially affiliated to the mosque in Alma-Ata, thus obtaining permission to perform funeral services and depriving the others of this right, the latter, instead of renouncing their activity, as had been hoped would happen, wrote to the authorities requesting that their previous status be restored.[200] In many cases their age seems to have made them more complacent and liable to acquiesce to pressures to refrain from conducting prayer services, but this was not always the case. One elder who gathered over 100 old people at the local cemetery to hold a festival service in the late 1960s – despite, like others, being cautioned against this – told the authorities when they summoned him that he would soon die and so nothing mattered to him.[201] In other oblasti, too, so-called itinerant mullas sometimes led Friday, as well as festival, prayer-services.[202]

Uzbekistan, too, had a large contingent of unregistered mullas. At the beginning of the 1950s there were approximately 100 just in Kashka-Darya Oblast', where six mullas from the registered mosques recently shut down by the local authorities joined their ranks. (This oblast', which by now had not a single registered mosque, had thirty unofficial ones and ten functioning *mazars*.)[203] In 1953, there were close to 500 unregistered mullas in just six of the republic's oblasti, and at the beginning of the following decade and well into it over 1,000 throughout the republic.[204]

200. T. Shaidildinov to V. A. Kuroedov, 20 July 1973; GARF, f.6991, o.6, d.545, ll.60-2.

201. I. Isakov to V. A. Kuroedov and K. K. Kulumbetov, 6 Jan. 1969; GARF, f.6991, o.6, d.220, ll.223-4.

202. S. Abenov (in Pavlodar Oblast'), to A. A. Nurullaev, 9 Aug. 1973; GARF, f.6991, o.6, d.545, l.43.

203. I. V. Polianskii to K. E. Voroshilov, 27 May 1950; GARF, f.6991, o.3, d.68, l.43.

204. V. I. Gostev to Deputy Head of the CPSU Central Committee Department of Science and Culture P. A. Tarasov, 4 Jan. 1954, A. A. Puzin to the Department

These clergy were said to enjoy the support of the population in initiating new prayer-premises.[205] In parts of Uzbekistan the commissions set up in the 1960s at *ispolkoms* to assist in the observance of the legislation on religion actually designated a cleric in each kishlak to perform religious rites.[206]

The number of mosqueless mullas was particularly large in Tajikistan, where there were thought to be some 3,500 unregistered clergy at the end of 1949 and up to 4,000 in the early 1960s. These numbers, however, may have been exaggerated. In 1964, after what purported to be a careful check, 1,000 unregistered clergy were taken count of in the entire republic; and twenty years later a similar number – 'over 1,000' – was reported, dispersed over many hundreds of settlements.[207] Be the numbers as they may, and 1,000 such clergy for one of the smaller republics is also no mean figure, these were people who recognised no control and no law emanating from either the state or SADUM. Many of them, indeed, operated in inaccessible mountainous regions. Most of the population of Kulyab Oblast', for example, Polianskii explained in a report to the Central Committee, lived in such parts in close proximity to the Afghan border, so that the activity of the unregistered clergy was subject to no supervision.[208]

The abovementioned Tashkent conference of July 1968 came to the conclusion that in every settlement where believers lived, some form of organised religious life prevailed and people performed religious rites.[209] Nor did this hold only for rural parts. Mosqueless

---

of Propaganda and Agitation, 7 June 1961, and Minutes, CARC session No.24, 27 Aug. 1964; GARF, f.6991, o.3, d.102, 1.3, and d.1363, 1.98, and o.4, d.147, 1.89. (In 1953 Uzbekistan was divided into nine oblasti and one autonomous republic. Three oblasti – Tashkent, Andijan and Namangan – counted for over 100 unregistered mullas apiece.)

205. V. I. Gostev, *ibid.*, 1.4, quoting Kh. N. Iskanderov's report for the 3rd quarter, 1953.

206. D. M. Malikov and M. U. Aliev, Information, sent by K. Ruzmetov to A. A. Nurullaev, 24 June 1974; GARF, f.6991, o.6, d.634, 1.46.

207. M. Kh. Hamidov, Report, All-Union conference of CARC *upolnomochennye*, 25-26 June 1964 – GARF, f.6991, o.3, d.1457, 1.25; and V. A. Kuroedov to the CPSU Central Committee, 16 Sept. 1983; TsKhSD, f.5, o.89, d.82, 1.59.

208. I. V. Polianskii to P. V. Kovanov, 23 June 1955; GARF. f.6991, o.3, d.114, 1.39.

209. CRA report, sent to the CPSU Central Committee, 22 May 1970; TsKhSD, f.5, o.62, d.38, 1.8.

mullas existed in the towns as well, especially, but not solely, in those without registered mosques. Although they were now without functioning mosques, it was asserted that every *mahalla*, like every rural settlement, had its own religious figure who performed religious rites in private homes, a situation not basically changed since pre-revolutionary times. This was so even from the organisational point of view, except that a system which had previously been official, when Islam was the dominant religion, had become unofficial. Just as prior to the October revolution there had been thirty-five *mahallas* in Jambul, for instance, each with its own mosque (which, presumably, was somehow linked with the town's main mosque or mosques), so now every *mahalla* had its own *mulla-khoja*, and the 'activists' of the town's unregistered groups and those of the surrounding countryside attended its sole registered mosque, indeed composed almost its entire congregation.[210] The town of Osh with its three registered mosques was thought in the latter half of the 1940s to have about 100 unregistered clergy.[211] In some urban centres, where the Muslim community was particularly dynamic in its efforts to re-open a mosque, such as Saratov or Gor'kii, the clergy and religious *aktiv* were said to be composed of 'former kulaks, merchants and profiteers' who had undergone imprisonment for 'anti-state and criminal offenses'. [212]

This raises a basic question: what was it that attracted believers to unregistered clergy? While it is understandable that in places where there were no registered communities, they turned to unregistered mullas, what made them do so where there were registered mosques and clergy? It is conceivable that they shared the opinion that the registered prayer-houses by definition were compromised and so preferred mullas who seemed more authentic. It is similarly possible that they sought to evade the surveillance which was ubiquitous within the establishment mosques. Certainly, too, there were places and periods in which registered clergy refused invitations to perform rites in private homes, giving believers no option other than approaching unregistered mullas to conduct life-cycle rites,

210. E. Bairamov, Information, 13 Jan. 1969; GARF, f.6991, o.6, d.153, ll.49–50. And see also pp.187 and 268-9.

211. I. G. Halimov to H. A. Akhtiamov, 9 May 1947; GARF, f.6991, o.3, d.453, l.7.

212. Theses for an instructional address at a conference of CARC *upolnomochennye*, 25 Sept. 1952; GARF, f.6991, o.3, d.83, l.259.

recite *mavluds* or excerpts from the Qur'an and participate in *iftars*. Whatever the reasons, the existence and activity of unregistered clergy were not limited to places without registered mosques and there seems to have been some movement of believers between the two groups of clergy.[213]

There was also movement between the registered and un-registered clergy. Nor did the registered imams who from time to time reinforced the ranks of their unregistered brethren necessarily come from mosques which had been shut down. Sometimes they themselves had been withdrawn from registration for violating the legislation on religion. One such person set up an entire network of assistants in Baku in the mid-1950s with whose help he was able to almost monopolise the conduct of rites at the expense of the registered imams.[214] Another in Dushanbe (then still Stalinabad) refused in the early 1960s to heed SADUM's instruction to its qazi that he not be allowed to perform religious rites, declared himself a holy man and engaged in faith-healing.[215]

Unregistered mullas, in the words of one Central Asian *upolnomochennyi*, 'propagate religion and, after opening a mosque, organise public prayer'. It was not out of the question, according to this source, that even in places without a registered mosque the five daily prayers, as well as the Friday and festival *namaz*, were being conducted regularly and *mavluds* and *khatm-i Qur'ans* read.[216] Nor was the 'religious propaganda' of these mullas restricted to the holding of prayers. One mulla in Frunze Oblast' raised the question of religion at meetings in two kolkhozy devoted to the victory in World War II and had inserted in their minutes a resolution recognising the benefit of religion for mankind and calling for the inclusion of clergy in the local soviet.[217] In later decades mullas would introduce readings from the Qur'an to mark secular occasions, such as graduation from school or university, induction into or demobilisation from the army and receipt of

213. For the move toward the registered mosques in the mid-1950s, see pp. 203 and 218.

214. See p.263.

215. D. A. Ahmedov to A. A. Puzin, 21 Feb. 1961; GARF, f.6991, o.3, d.1737, l.14.

216. I. G. Halimov to H. A. Akhtiamov, 4 Sept. 1950; GARF, f.6991, o.3, d.454, l.75.

217. H. A. Akhtiamov to CARC, 10 July 1945; GARF, f.6991, o.3, d.29, l.127.

one's first pay.[218] Some of the more daring ones even accompanied induction into the army with a mourning ceremony.[219] Mullas would also appear in *chaikhonas*, where they would talk with those who frequented them,[220] perhaps even asking for the radio to be turned off so that they might read from the Qur'an or other religious texts.[221] Moreover, they took the opportunity, when holding prayer-services at cemeteries and other similar venues, to explain religious tenets to believers. In Nakhichevan mullas did this during Muharram, telling worshippers about Ali and Muhammad.[222]

Unregistered mullas also presided over *iftars* – the collective repasts at the end of the day during the *uraz* at which the presence of a cleric was obligatory – for the registered clergy could not attend them all. Indeed, often they participated in more of them than could representatives of the official mosques. These occasions provided an unusual opportunity to come into social contact with people who might not normally seek out a mulla.[223]

One report to the CPSU Central Committee in the early 1970s suggested that in practice the unregistered clergy exerted influence over believers in a variety of ways: besides their conduct of daily, weekly and festive prayer-services, and prayer-meetings on the

218. *Kommunist Tadzhikistana*, 28 April 1976; *Komsomol'skaia pravda*, 20 Jan. 1983.

219. John Soper, 'Unofficial Islam: a Muslim Minority in the USSR', p.227. The particular story relates to ceremonies held among Uighur rural inhabitants in Kazakhstan.

220. Kh. N. Iskanderov to Tashkent Obkom Secretary A. Jalilov, 27 May 1954; TsGAUz, f.2456, o.1, d.162, l.178.

221. The CARC *upolnomochennyi* for Tashkent Oblast' visited what was said to be a model *chaikhona*, in a workers' *poselok*. A mulla came in with a young man and the pair began praying there publicly. He then asked for a lamp to be brought to him and requested that the radio be turned off; when some young people protested the manageress rebuked them for lack of respect for their elders. Afterwards the mulla began reading aloud from a religious book about 'the lives of the prophets', interpreting it as he read, and a considerable group of people gathered around to listen – K. Mustafin to Obkom Secretary Mavlianov and Oblispolkom Chairman Turgunov, 10 Nov. 1945; GARF, f.6991, o.3, d.30, ll.286ob-287. And see p.310.

222. I. Bonchkovskii to E. I. Lisavtsev, 1 June 1973; GARF, f.6991, o.6, d.537, l.176.

223. In 1970, for instance, registered clerics attended 268 out of 1,169 *iftars* in Osh Oblast', in Astrakhan' Oblast' 112 out of 237, and so on – V. A. Kuroedov to the CPSU Central Committee Propaganda Department, 22 Feb. 1971; TsKhSD, f.5, o.63, d.89, ll.18-9. For the *iftar*, see also pp.233, 252 and 483-5.

occasion of natural disasters, their presence at life-cycle rites was taken advantage of so as to stress the obligatory nature of these customs and the need to make donations to a mosque, *mazar* or mulla in order, as it were, to pre-empt all misfortunes.[224] The unregistered clergy also re-opened mosques which had been closed down – whether in the 1920s and 1930s or in the postwar years – as well as initiating so-called *mehmankhona* and *alowkhona* mosques.[225] These religious figures went by a variety of names, which differed from place to place and performed many functions: the *bakhshi* in Kirgiziia would go into a trance as a holy spirit entered his or her body; the *folbin* would foretell the future (both these categories could be male or female), and so on. They practised exorcism, engaged in faith-healing, prayed at sick-beds, sold amulets and talismans, and proclaimed all kinds of miracles. Some declared themselves shaykhs and operated at *mazars*, even those that had been formally closed down. These unregistered clergy performed marriages where the brides were still adolescents (i.e. younger than the age stipulated in the republican criminal codes). Some also performed circumcisions. In short, in the eyes of CARC's officials, they encouraged 'religious fanaticism and superstition' among the 'backward section' of the population.[226]

As to the authentic itinerant mullas, who, indeed, went from place to place, either in response to an invitation or out of knowledge, or intuition, that in a certain locality their services might be needed, and performed rites there, their number, too, was considerable. The phenomenon of non-Sufi itinerant mullas seems to have dated from the second half of the 1930s when, on the one hand, many settlements remained without clergy and, on the other, significant numbers of ousted clerics sought to continue performing rites, but feared or were indeed unable to settle in a single location.[227] Almost 90 per cent of the country's 'exposed' itinerant clergy in the early 1970s (1,140 out of 1,276) were

224. CRA, Information, handed to the CPSU Central Committee Propaganda Department, 27 April 1971; TsKhSD, f.5, o.63, d.89, l.99.

225. The *alowkhona*, lit. house of fire, was a meeting-place for men in the mountain villages of Tajiksitan.

226. A. Azizbaev to D. A. Ahmedov, 2 Feb. 1962, M. Kh. Hamidov to A. A. Puzin, 22 Oct. 1963, and K. Kulumbetov to V. A. Kuroedov, 18 Dec. 1970; GARF, f.6991, o.3, d.1738, ll.49-52 and d.1739, l.99, and o.6, d.290, ll.39-41.

227. See Keller, *The Struggle against Islam in Uzbekistan, 1927–1941*, p.265. The Sufi orders and the *ishans* are discussed in the next chapter.

Muslim.[228] Some, probably the most active ones, continued to be Sufi *ishans*, but in most parts and in most years these almost certainly did not comprise large numbers. These itinerant mullas often had their own horses and travelled throughout, and beyond, their respective raiony. [229]

Some areas were more susceptible than others to the activity of itinerant mullas.[230] One of these was undoubtedly Kirgiziia, where 524 itinerant mullas were exposed in 1950,[231] notably Osh Oblast', where people came from nearby Uzbekistan, especially for the festivals; they were naturally attracted to Takht-i Sulayman, which drew large numbers of pilgrims from that republic.[232] Aside from this centre of pilgrimage, in just one raion in 1953 the CARC *upolnomochennyi* exposed no less than twenty unregistered clergy, including both local residents and people who came from outside, and three years later over 200 throughout the oblast'.[233] Another such area was Turkmenistan with its mere handful of registered mosques, where in 1947 the state security organs informed the CARC *upolnomochennyi* that forty-three communities were functioning illegally in the republic and supplied him with a list of 270 itinerant mullas, which he supplemented, providing the republican finance ministry with the names of 365 such people.[234]

228. CRA, Information, sent to the CPSU Central Committee, 27 April 1971; TsKhSD, f.5, o.63, d.89, ll.98-9. These 1,140 were in addition to the 1,700 regular unregistered clergy mentioned above.

229. Resolution, Eastern Kazakhstan Oblispolkom, 23 April 1969; GARF, f.6991, o.6, d.223, l.36. For activity of 'horseback *ishans*' in Uzbekistan in the mid-1930s, see Keller, *The Struggle against Islam in Uzbekistan, 1921-1941*, p.269.

230. Some areas were said to have no itinerant mullas at all, such as Ul'ianovsk Oblast' at the end of the 1940s – N. I. Abushaev, comments on report of P. F. Simonov, Minutes, No.4, Meeting of instructors with CARC *upolnomochennye*, 4-5 April 1950; GARF, f.6991, o.3, d.66, l.46.

231. Minutes, CARC session No.11, 25 April 1951; GARF, f.6991, o.3, d.74, ll.113 and 116.

232. For example, I. G. Halimov to CARC, 23 Sept. 1947; GARF, f.6991, o.3, d.453, l.28. For Takht-i Sulayman, see pp.371-2 below.

233. I. G. Halimov to H. A. Akhtiamov, 22 April 1953, and L. A. Prikhod'ko, Information, 18 May 1957; GARF, f.6991, o.3, d.94, ll.68-9, and d.146, l.101.

234. Babaev, Report, CARC session No. 13, 10-11 July 1947; GARF, f.6991, o.4, d.19, l.415. Nothing effective seems to have been done to terminate the activity of these wandering mullas, for in the early 1950s over 330 were taken account of – Minutes, CARC session No.9, 17 April 1951; GARF, f.6991, o.3, d.74, l.106.

A plethora of wandering mullas of various ilks operated in Uzbekistan. In the oblasti of the Fergana Valley and Samarkand, not a few instances of enhanced religious activity were noticed in 1946-7, behind which stood itinerant mullas, former imams, shaykhs and dervishes. They were described as residents of other localities, who sought out small groups (up to twelve believers) with neither an organised community nor a prayer-house of their own and, having found such supporters, they would open up prayer-premises and *mazars*.[235] Indeed, moving around from one republic or raion to another, even from kolkhoz to kolkhoz, gave the wandering mullas leeway and opportunities clergy could not enjoy in their places of residence. Many of the itinerant mullas who operated in Tajikistan at the end of the 1940s were said to have come from the Fergana Valley in Uzbekistan. They would visit kolkhozy, where they would speak on religious themes before small groups who gathered to hear them in private homes, and 'they enjoyed great respect and influence'. Sometimes, they took up jobs in the kolkhozy, chiefly as watchmen, which gave them a base from which to conduct their 'religious propaganda'. In some kolkhozy the administration encouraged the activity of wandering mullas in a variety of ways,[236] while the local government in parts of Central Asia was reported in some periods to have supplied them with certificates attesting to the legitimacy of their activities.[237]

A 1949 report on Islam in the country at large noted that itinerant mullas – apparently here the reference is to all unregistered, or 'mosqueless', mullas – stimulated a religious atmosphere. Although it went on to note that their main terrain was where there were no registered mosques, the report immediately remarked upon the 'agitation' they conducted in the city and oblast' of Tashkent to persuade people to attend festival prayers on Uraz-Bayram and pointed out that in Kazan', which had a registered

235. Kh. N. Iskanderov, Report, CARC session No.11, 18-19 June 1947; GARF, f.6991, o.4, d.19, ll.356-7.
236. K. Hamidov to I. V. Polianskii, 14 Dec. 1949, and report at Instructional conference of CARC's Central Asian *upolnomochennye*, 17-20 Dec. 1949; GARF, f.6991, o.3, d.67, ll.53 and 95-7. Some wandering mullas also came to Uzbekistan from other Muslim areas – see, for example, Kh. N. Iskanderov to Tashkent Obkom Secretary A. Alimov and Oblispolkom Chairman A. Jalilov, 27 May 1954; TsGAUz, f.2456, o.1, d.162, l.178.
237. For instance, one *raiispolkom* in Tashkent Oblast' in 1945 – see p.640.

mosque, prayers were conducted in six different venues, five under the leadership of wandering mullas. In the Kabardinian ASSR, too, believers came regularly to *tarawa-namaz* led by wandering mullas in unregistered mosques in six settlements which had no registered mosque, and mass prayer-meetings were held on Uraz-Bayram.[238]

The situation continued to be acute – from the point of view of the authorities – in many parts of the country. True, toward the end of the 1960s the number of unregistered clergy in Kirgiziia, for instance, seems to have been meaningfully cut back, partly because some mullas had previously been counted twice, partly as a result of 'extensive educational work' done with groups and individuals, including verbal and written warnings about the significance and seriousness of their activities, and partly as an outcome of the imposition of fines and taxes.[239] Even now, however, they remained far more numerous than their registered counterparts and their activity was relatively unperturbed. In one raion, where there were eighteen unregistered groups – as against a single registered society – one cleric performed the Friday *namaz* right next to the school and another built a mosque with moneys illegally collected from the population.[240]

Nor was it just in Kirgiziia that the unregistered clergy were still a major thorn in the side of the authorities at the turn of the decade. In Azerbaijan, too, in just forty-seven raiony and three towns (out of eighty raiony and eight towns) 496 unregistered clergy were taken count of, in the oblasti of Bukhara, Samarkand and Fergana 120, 160 and 350 respectively, in Dagestan over 200, in the Bashkir ASSR 170, and in Turkmenistan about 200. In one raion of Kzyl-Orda Oblast' in Kazakhstan, each extended family or clan had its own mulla, forty of whom had been taken count of[241]; the same was true in many villages in the Nakhichevan

238. N. Tagiev, A short survey, undated; GARF, f.6991, o.4, d.23, l.17.

239. K. Shabolotov to A. A. Nurullaev, 23 June 1969; GARF, f.6991, o.6, d.220, ll.150-1. Whatever the reason, the number was down to 311 (from over 500).

240. K. Shabolotov to the Kirgiz SSR Council of Ministers, 26 Sept. 1969; GARF, f.6991, o.6, d.223, ll.70-1.

241. CRA, Information, sent to the CPSU Central Committee, 22 May 1970 –TsKhSD, f.5, o.62, d.38, ll.10-11. Nor were these figures the bottom line; they continued to mount. By the second half of 1971, the number for Dagestan was up to 250 – Kh. Salahetdinov and I. Mikhalev, Report, 26 Oct. 1971; GARF, f.6991, o.6, d.361, l.105.

ASSR.[242] Indeed in Khorezm, the Karakalpak ASSR, Turkmenistan and parts at least of Kazakhstan, where the old social structures had largely been retained, each had its own mulla. Anthropologists in Khorezm Oblast' in the mid-1950s, who observed the life of the *elat*, or local community, noted that each too had its mulla who, together with the elders, controlled its everyday life.[243] In the early 1970s the CRA *upolnomochennyi* for the Kabardino-Balkar ASSR was maintaining that it was the unregistered clergy who were keeping religion alive there, by ensuring that rites were performed; he even noted that they had so augmented the price of the ritual of expiating sins, recited for every deceased Muslim, that some people were complaining.[244] In the mid-1970s there were still 150 unregistered clergy in the republic, fifty of them mullas who performed funerals and weddings and about 100 people who participated in the former and at memorial services as readers of the Qur'an (*dugashi*).[245] In Uzbekistan's Kashka-Darya Oblast' at the same time period fifty mullas and *ishans* met the needs of the population, many of whom lived 100 km and more from the closest registered mosque and could not go there in the harsh climatic conditions of either the winter or the summer.[246]

By the early-mid 1980s the situation had become yet more critical. The more than 10,000 unregistered clergy who were said to be operating monopolised religious activity in the great majority of settlements inhabited by people from Muslim nationalities, where their doings were subject to no control. Nor did they content themselves with fulfilling the needs of the population. They administered the cemeteries, organised pilgrimages to holy sites, initiated the construction of unlawful new mosques and assisted in violating the law, particularly in regard to transgressions connected with marriage.[247]

242. I. Bonchkovskii to E. I. Lisavtsev, 1 June 1973 – GARF, f.6991, o.6, d.537, l.171.

243. Snesarev, 'On some Causes of the Persistence of Religio-Customary Survivals among the Khorezm Uzbeks', pp.228-33.

244. L. Zh. Aisov to the CRA, 25 July 1971; GARF, f.6991, o.6, d.370, ll.134-6.

245. L. Zh. Aisov to the CRA, 14 Jan. 1974; GARF, f.6991, o.6, d.558, l.6.

246. P. Khidirov, Explanatory memo, undated (sent by K. R. Ruzmetov to V. A. Kuroedov, 15 Jan. 1974); GARF, f.6991, o.6, d.567, l.21.

247. CRA, Memo, 2 June 1983; TsKhSD, f.5, o.89, d.82, ll.37-8.

In the words of one study on Islam in Central Asia in the 1960s to the 1980s, the unregistered mullas were its main anchor. Even though they did not for the most part know Islamic dogma, the canonically approved rituals or even the prayers, they served Islam very well 'on the daily level'. As scions of clerical families, they enjoyed the respect of those around them. They knew what the people needed and preserved Islam in a form which satisfied their society. The author of this study speaks of the 'division of labour' between the registered and unregistered clergy; without the latter, in his view, the big official mosques of the cities would have been far emptier and poorer.[248]

The unregistered clergy were able to survive and even thrive despite all constraints not only because the population needed someone to perform basic rites, but because they were kith and kin to the society among whom they operated.[249] In some areas, at least, there were also female religious figures,[250] a fact which probably enhanced the resilience and attraction of popular Islam. These ladies were sometimes referred to in the documentation as 'women mullas', who would read or recite excerpts from the Qur'an and *mavlud*s among women. Apart from their roles as practitioners of popular folk Islam,[251] and the supervision and performance of ritual among women, their main job was the education of girls, to convey some basic knowledge of Islamic customs to the upcoming generation. In the traditionally sedentary areas of Central Asia these much respected 'elder sisters' exerted some sort of social control, exhorting the womenfolk to preserve their religion's age-old moral norms and observe such practices as pilgrimages to holy places. Known variously – depending on the area – as *otyn*, *atynbu*, or *bibiotun*, they existed in every *mahalla* of every settlement. These women were not qualified in the strict sense of the word, for they had undergone no official religious training and the occasional religious text that might have been saved was not sufficient to give them any formal or extensive

248. Poliakov, *Everyday Islam*, pp.106-7.

249. For their roots in the surrounding society, see p.329 above.

250. The jadidist movement had placed considerable emphasis on the equality of the sexes in Islam. In its wake Soviet Muslim reformists in the 1920s had maintained that women could serve as qazis or *mutawalis* and hold other religious posts – Keller, *The Struggle against Islam in Uzbekistan, 1921–1941*, p.374.

251. Women traditionally filled an active role in Sufi Islam – see p.393.

knowledge. (In the past their predecessors studied in special *mektebs* for girls.) Forced to lead a clandestine existence and with meagre means at their disposal to fulfil their duties, the form of Islam they preserved, to quote one Western scholar, was one of popular and oral traditions, based on the transmission of prayers and rites they had learned by heart and recited without understanding.

The *otyns* in the Soviet period, as before, seem to have come mostly or wholly from families of sufis, mullas, *seids* and *khojas* and acquired their knowledge of ritual and the Qur'an, such as it was, from their mothers and grandmothers. Usually the future *otyn* would be carefully chosen from among seven or eight-year old girls and she would go through stages of preparation not dissimilar from those of boys from traditional clerical families whom their elders destined to become mullas. Each *otyn* was responsible for the education of three to five girls, one of whom would ususally be her own daughter and one of whom would have to marry within the *mahalla*. From the age of twenty these girls became apprentices, who participated in collective ceremonies, until, at the age of forty, they might be allowed to practise as *otyns*.[252] Some women, too, indulged in a number of the more esoteric practices of the unregistered clergy, such as exorcism and faith-healing.[253]

The town of Uzgen had fourteen female religious figures in the mid 1950s.[254] One *otyn*, who lived in a *poselok* in Osh Oblast', had performed a variety of religious rites for some years before being exposed by the CARC *upolnomochennyi*. She would, according to one report, practice sorcery on sick children, bring husbands and wives together, exorcise all kinds of illness. Although she did not work, she dressed well and seemed to live in comfort, and her clientèle included the wives of local officials. When the *upol-nomochennyi* sought to find out concrete details about her activity from local inhabitants, among them raion officials, he got nothing but statements that they could give no information for they feared

252. I. G. Halimov to CARC, 5 Jan. 1956; GARF, f.6991, o.3, d.457, ll.10-11; Poliakov, *Everyday Islam*, pp.109-10; and Fathi, '*Otines*: the unknown women clerics of Central Asian Islam', pp.30-7. For women religious figures, see also p.544.

253. See p.337 above.

254. I. V. Polianskii to P. V. Kovanov, 23 June 1955; GARF, f.6991, o.3, d.114, l.26.

both her and her patrons.[255] In 1959 a mulla came from Kokand to Osh and set up three groups of women under the leadership of such women clergy, who met for daily and Friday prayers.[256] Nor was it solely in Central Asia that women performed rites. In the Tatar ASSR in the immediate postwar period the CARC *upolnomochennyi* reported the existence of 'women mullas'. Although he did not specify the nature of their activities, he indicated that they led women's prayer services.[257] During the *uraz* in Tomsk in the 1970s women were likewise reported to be acting as clergy, conducting small *iftars* and reading the Qur'an for groups of women.[258] On the whole, it seems that the Soviet authorities, for one reason or another, underestimated the significance of these female religious figures.

Since the sermons of unregistered clergy were by definition not handed in for approval before delivery, their texts have nowhere been preserved. This does not, however, necessarily mean that they did not address their congregations, although many of them apparently did not preach even on festivals, especially in the rural areas – where the imams of the registered mosques were also often unable to deliver sermons. Indeed, worshippers flocked from the countryside to the towns for the main festivals specifically in order to participate in prayer-services which would be sure to include a sermon.[259] Some unregistered clergy, however, did preach, stressing the importance of the *uraz*, of religious rites, of prayer for

255. I. G. Halimov to H. A. Akhtiamov, 22 April 1953; GARF, f.6991, o.3, d.94, l.63.

256. H. A. Akhtiamov, Report, All-Union conference of CARC *upolnomochennye*, 18-20 April 1960; GARF, f.6991, o.3, d.208, l.136.

257. Bagaev, Report, CARC seesion No.7, 23-24 April 1947; GARF, f.6991, o.4, d.19, l.191.

258. A. Barmenkov to the CPSU Central Committee Propaganda Department, 13 March 1974; TsKhSD, f.5, o.67, d.115, l.4. For *iftars* conducted especially for women in the Tatar ASSR, see p.484. Presumably here, too, female religious figures presided or recited from the Qur'an.

259. I. V. Polianskii to the CPSU Central Committee and the USSR Council of Ministers, 20 Sept. 1955; GARF, f.6991, o.3, d.114, l.198; and see p.260. Nearly two decades later CRA *upolnomochennye*, reporting one from Kazakhstan, another from the Tatar ASSR, noted that unregistered mullas rarely preached in the full sense of the word – A. Tishkov to A. A. Nurullaev, 16 July 1973, and I. Mikhalev to A. A. Nurullaev, 6 May 1974; GARF, f.6991, o.6, d.545, ll.67 and 215.

Allah's salvation so as to get into Paradise, and of understanding that life in the next world depended on the will of Allah.[260]

The unregistered clergy frequently went on record as exhorting believers not to attend 'Soviet' mosques or to heed the registered 'Soviet' clergy.[261] Many of the *fetwas* of the spiritual directorates, they pointed out, contradicted Islamic law and custom. This held, for example, for the *fetwas* which declared the sacrifice on Qur-ban-Bayram to be purely voluntary: CARC emphasised, in line with its basic thesis, that, since the tradition was that the hide of the slaughtered animal and a part of the meat went to the clergy, the unregistered mullas benefited from the continued practice of the sacrifice, especially where the registered clergy adhered to the mufti's ruling.[262]

In certain regions the unregistered clergy were so prestigious and influential that they completely undermined the position of the registered mosques and imams. In and around Kulyab in Tajikistan, for instance, some 30-40 wandering mullas operated in the early 1960s who refrained from attending the town's registered mosque and agitated against it systematically. They would go from one kolkhoz to another, and from kishlak to kishlak, and simultaneously with the conduct of rites, slander the town's registered mosque and clergy. God, they said, did not accept the prayers of 'Soviet clergy' and so it was incumbent upon believers to organise their own 'authentic' mosque where the imam would be a real Muslim. These itinerant mullas in fact established unofficial mosques in several settlements and some of them were even active in Kulyab, *inter alia* telling believers not to invite the registered clergy to their homes to perform rites as they would only bring them

260. S. Abenov, CRA *upolnomochennyi* for Pavlodar Oblast', to A. A. Nurullaev, 9 Aug. 1973; GARF, f.6991, o.6, d.545, ll.43-4.

261. K. Hamidov, Report, Instructional conference of Central Asian *upolnomochennye*, Tashkent, 17-20 Dec. 1949, N. Smirnov and S. Fastoved, Information, 22 Aug. 1962 and A. A. Puzin to the Tajikistan CP Central Committee, 26 Jan 1963; GARF, f.6991, o.3, d.67, l.53, d.1390, l.35, and d.1739, l.2. Unregistered clergy in the oblasti of Samarkand and Namangan contended that registered imams distorted the fundamentals of Islam and were not authentic men of religion – Minutes, Instructional meeting of CARC *upolnomochennye* in the Uzbek SSR, 15-17 March 1956; TsGAUz, f.2456, o.1, d.183, ll.55 and 58.

262. I. V. Polianskii to the CPSU Central Committee, 27 Sept. 1954; GARF, f.6991, o.3, d.102, ll.305-6. And see pp.151-2 and 496-7. This does not mean that the reservations regarding the *fetwas* were inevitably motivated by self-interest, although this was the general sense and implication of CARC's contention.

misfortune, as a result of which the local imam and *khatib* refused
to hold prayer-services and quit their posts.[263]

Some unregistered clergy were even more brazen, speaking out
unequivocally against conformity with Soviet law. In the immediate
postwar period one mulla resident in Namangan said Muslims
should not register marriages with ZAGS but perform them solely
in accordance with the precepts of the Shari'a, whereas a second
one in the same town contended that it was forbidden to purchase
produce of kolkhozy, which was 'more impure than pork', because
the kolkhozy had suppressed private lands.[264]

This basic attitude did not change over time at least not in the
Fergana Valley or in Tajikistan, where the unregistered mullas
seem to have become increasingly outspoken in their criticism of
both their establishment counterparts and of the state with which
they identified. In the 1980s they were calling openly upon believers
to boycott registered mosques and refuse the services of registered
mullas and appealing to the population not to buy meat, sweetmeats
and other products in government stores because they were
'unclean'. In Kulyab Oblast' they were even reported to have
came out with statements that 'it is forbidden to bury Soviet
soldiers killed in Afghanistan according to Muslim rites, as they
fought against true Muslims'.[265]

At the same time, not all unregistered clergy were outspoken
in their opposition to either the secular authority or the religious
establishment which cooperated with it. Indeed, in some areas
and periods the approach to each other of the unregistered and
registered clergy seems to have been somewhat ambiguous, involving an admixture of, on the one hand, antagonism and competition and, on the other, a degree of mutual dependence. Despite
the tension that, often characterised the relationship between the
two groups, there were recurrent instances of co-operation of various
sorts. Throughout the country there were many instances of unregistered clergy entertaining links with registered clergy and
religious societies. Some sought this as an insurance policy, as it

263. D. A. Ahmedov to A. A. Puzin and Tajikistan CP Central Committee
Secretary N. Zaripova, 17 Jan. 1962; GARF, f.6991, o.3, d.1738, ll.62-3.

264. I. Ibadov to I. V. Polianskii, 24 July 1945; GARF, f.6991, o.3, d.29,
ll.133-4.

265. V. A. Kuroedov to the CPSU Central Committee, 16 Sept. 1983; TsKhSD,
f.5, o.89, d.82, l.60.

were, against the likelihood of persecution and closure, believing that the vested interest of the religious establishment in their existence and even prosperity might save them. It was with this end in view that they contributed to the treasury of the registered mosques, depositing in them donations they had received from their own believers; received permission from them to conduct rites; and approached registered clerics and even the spiritual directorates with religious questions. Some such unregistered clergy desired, but were unable to obtain, registration, others feared to apply or thought that given the indifference and inefficacy of the local government organs it was unnecessary. But all in this category believed there were advantages in this unofficial affiliation, which seems to have been especially common in the kishlaks of Central Asia.[266]

Some unregistered mullas, moreover, sought direct legitimisation for their activities from the local organs of government. Particularly in the more stringent periods and in the RSFSR, there were instances of mullas actually refusing to conduct rites without obtaining express permission from the secular authority. One representative of the believers of the town of Yoshkar-Ola in the Mari ASSR, where he claimed there were 1,000 Muslim families (although the written statement he brought with him mentioned 500), asked permission in the early 1960s for a mulla and a number of other local inhabitants to perform rites, for without it they were not prepared to do so.[267]

The powers-that-be sought to restrict the activity of both groups, the sedentary and the itinerant, aware that the unregistered clergy's total elimination was not on the cards. In the words of one CARC *upolnomochennyi*, as long as there were significant numbers of believers in places without registered mosques and as long as the network of registered mosques remained negligible, mosqueless and wandering mullas would continue to exist.[268] The difficulty

266. For example, Kh. N. Iskanderov to Tashkent Obkom Secretary A. Alimov and Oblispolkom Chairman A. Jalilov, 27 May 1954 – TsGAUz, f.2456, o.1, d.162, ll. 177-8; theses of lecture, sent by A. Barmenkov to the CPSU Central Committee Propaganda Department, 19 June 1968 – GARF, f.6991, o.6, d.147, ll.43-4. For the relationship between the non-establishment clergy and the spiritual directorates, on the one hand, and the registered religious societies and clergy, on the other hand, see pp.135-40 and 262-70 respectively.

267. Reception by N. I. Smirnov of a representative from Yoshkar-Ola, 12 Feb. 1962; GARF, f.6991, o.4, d.130, l.21.

268. H. A. Akhtiamov, A short communication, Instructional conference of

in taking measures to put an end to the activity of the unregistered clergy, one *upolnomochennyi* wrote in the period of the anti-religious campaign of the early 1960s, was that the registered clergy were too few to satisfy the needs of all the republic's believers, for the customs and rules predominant especially in the rural areas meant that not a single funeral or marriage occurred without the participation of a mulla or a person knowing the ritual.[269] The CARC *upolnomochennyi* for the Tatar ASSR said at a conference in 1964 that the local organs of power in that republic were seeking to prohibit the practice of rites in private homes on the grounds that they contradicted the law. Yet, he contended, this was a centuries-old tradition, for believing Muslims did not conduct life-cycle rites in the mosque, so that to proceed from such a standpoint would evoke serious dissatisfaction among a significant mass of the indigenous population, most of whom buried their dead in accordance with Muslim custom.[270]

In order nonetheless to curb the impact of these clergy effectively and to lessen the number of violations of the law committed by them, a variety of means were employed. In the first place, these mullas had to be unearthed, 'exposed'. The *upolnomochennye* would go to some of the localities and try to procure information from the local organs of government. Frequently, names and other details were provided by the clergy and *aktiv* of the registered mosques.[271] Sometimes the mullas would then be summoned to the CARC *upolnomochennyi*, the imam of the registered mosque or officials of the local organs of power, who would seek to dissuade them from their activities. These attempts at deterrence were especially common as the *uraz* and festivals approached, these being the periods when the unregistered clergy, like their registered counterparts, were most active.[272] In the Mordvinian ASSR the *sel'sovet*

CARC's Central Asian *upolnomochennye*, Tashkent, 17-20 Dec. 1949; GARF, f.6991, o.3, d.67, l.113.

269. L. Zh. Aisov to A. A. Puzin, 17 Jan. 1961; GARF, f.6991, o.3, d.1605, l.6.

270. F. S. Mangutkin, Address, Minutes, All-Union conference of CARC *upolnomochennye*, 25-26 June 1964; GARF, f.6991, o.3; d.1457, l.30.

271. See, for instance, I. G. Halimov to CARC, undated [probably April 1949], and K. Hamidov to I. V. Polianskii, 14 Dec. 1949; GARF, f.6991, o.3, d.454, l.17, and d.67, l.97. And see pp.263-5.

272. See, for example, Arifov to A. A. Puzin, D. A. Ahmedov, Obkom Secretary G. Javov, Shirinjanov and Salibaev, 7 Feb. 1963; GARF, f.6991, o.3, d.1739,

chairmen warned them that they were not allowed to lead mass prayer-meetings; as a result they indeed refused to conduct services, but these were not undermined, regular believers being found who were prepared to substitute.[273] Such 'prophylactic' measures – summoning unregistered clergy to local organs of government to be cautioned – were still being employed in the 1970s, but probably not on a large scale.[274]

In the early 1960s atheistic propagandists seem to have directed their onslaught against the unregistered clergy both by means of direct discouragement and by inciting believers against them. Of five 'chiefly' unregistered clergy, who repudiated their work as mullas in the Kabardino-Balkar ASSR in the early 1960s, some were specifically said to have quit their posts following 'the onslaught of the atheists', while others did so under pressure from their adult children.[275] In the Chechen-Ingush ASSR, 112 Muslim religious figures – in Soviet terminology 'religious authorities' – were compromised at twelve raion mass gatherings in 1962; in 1963, thirty-eight religious 'authorities' announced publicly that they were repudiating their activity, thirty-two *murid* groups were paralysed and about 100 religious activists were 'compromised in the press, on the radio and on television'; and in 1964 'more than fifteen' public gatherings and assemblies discussed the cases of 100 mullas, *tamadas* and Muslim Sufi leaders. In this republic as of the early 1960s and into the 1970s, these meetings of villagers not only exposed the 'parasitical activity of these spongers' and of unregistered groups; they also adopted resolutions up to and including expulsion from the republic: twenty Muslim and clan leaders who engaged in illegal religious activty were banished in 1962, fifteen illegal Muslim preachers in 1963, and nineteen in 1964. (In each of the first two years two non-Muslim religious figures were also expelled.) In 1970-1 over 150 reactionary religious figures were subjected to such procedures and many of

ll.68-72. For this activity on the eve of the *uraz* and festivals, see pp.469-71.

273. Manerov, Report, minutes, No.26, Instructors' meeting of CARC workers and *upolnomochennye*, 1-2 Dec. 1949; GARF, f.6991, o.3, d.60, l.70.

274. For example, in the Nakhichevan ASSR, where there were unregistered clergy, *aksakals,* who performed religious rites in every settlement, the leadership of only one of five raiony did so – I. Bonchkovskii to E. I. Lisavtsev, 1 June 1973; GARF, f.6991, o.6, d.537, l.171.

275. For example, L. Zh. Aisov, Information, undated (received at CARC, 21 July 1962); GARF, f.6991, o.3, d.1388, l.170.

them declared they would cease their 'anti-social activity'; and a few 'parasite' clerics were convicted.[276]

Legislation against parasites had been adopted in 1961 and was clearly applicable to unregistered clergy, who had no official salary and engaged in illegal religious activity.[277] Not a few press articles attacked clergy as parasites.[278] Nor was parasitism the sole charge brought against some mullas, who found themselves standing trial, not only in 'popular courts', but periodically in official ones as well.[279]

In the mid and late 1960s in many areas the local organs were continuing to caution and call to book, often by the use of fines, the organisers and leaders of religious groups and those who conducted religious rites. For instance in the Bashkir ASSR, where evidence had been received from twenty-five of the republic's sixty-three raiony concerning 100 Muslim groups and associations and eighty-six people who illegally performed the duties of clergy, six such persons were warned and three fined in late 1968 and the first half of 1969.[280] Alma-Ata Oblast's thirty-two unregistered mullas were specifically prohibited from collecting *fitr* and *sadaqa* or conducting festival prayer-services and receiving renumeration for performing the *jinaz*.[281]

276. A. Alisov to A. A. Puzin, 15 Feb. 1963, 12 Feb. 1964 and 3 Feb. 1965, and A. Nurullaev, Information, 2 Feb. 1972; GARF, f.6991, o.3, d.1607, ll.26, d.1608, ll.25-6, and d.1609, l.27, and o.6, d.459, l.27.

277. See, for example, A. Alisov to A. A. Puzin, 16 March 1962; GARF, f.6991, o.3, d.1606, l.20, referring to the 4 May 1961 RSFSR Supreme Soviet Presidium decree 'On enhancing the struggle against people who evade socially beneficial work and lead an anti-social way of life'. The edict declared in its preamble that it was directed against persons 'living on non-labour income and enriching themselves at the expense of the state', who 'engage in forbidden businesses, private enterprise, speculation and begging'. The operative part of the edict provided that persons avoiding 'socially useful work' and committing 'other anti–social acts which enable them to lead a parasite way of life' could be tried by a court and subjected to 'resettlement' in specially designated locations for two to five years – Berman, *Soviet Criminal Law and Procedure*, pp.77-81. For the relevant articles in the criminal codes of some of the Muslim union republics, see Kuroedov and Pankratov (eds), *Zakonodatel'stvo o religioznykh kul'takh*, pp.197-202.

278. For example, *Serdalo*, the Chechen-Ingush ASSR republican newspaper and *Groznyi rabochii*, quoted by A. Alisov, ibid.

279. For these trials, see pp.577-82.

280. M. Arduvanov, Information, 25 June 1969; GARF, f.6991, o.6, d.220, ll.305-6.

281. R. Shaimardanov to A. A. Nurullaev and K. Kulumbetov, 14 July 1969;

The main weapon, however, in the struggle against the un-registered clergy was taxation. Despite reservations which were sometimes expressed regarding the imposition of taxes on un-registered clergy as this was, as it were, a form of recognition and even legitimisation of their status, their names would be trans-mitted to the financial authorities with the intention of their being taxed. Indeed, this led to some confusion among both local officials and believers, neither of whom distinguished between registered and unregistered clergy once the latter paid taxes.[282]

Early in 1951, by which time he had presented the financial organs with lists of nearly 300 mosqueless mullas,[283] the CARC upolnomochennyi for Osh Oblast' made a number of specific sug-gestions for somehow implementing a taxation policy which would fulfil the authorities' purpose of terminating the activity of the unregistered mullas.[284] The imposition of taxes indeed led to some unregistered mullas totally repudiating all religious pursuits, while others at least mitigated their open activity.[285] In Tajikistan, CARC's upolnomochennyi reported in the early 1950s, mullas who operated illegally had dispersed, quitting the mosques in a number of raiony, as a result of the imposition of income tax.[286] This was also demonstrated in Osh Oblast', for example, by one mosqueless mulla who, after being assessed for income tax, increased his working days in the kolkhoz from twenty in 1947 to 100 in 1948.[287]

Sometimes the local financial organs in fact imposed taxes on unregistered clergy. Often, however, they did nothing with the names and lists they received.[288] At times, this was simply the

---

GARF, f.6991, o.6, d.223, l.45.

282. For a further discussion of the taxation of clergy, ·including reservations of local government organs regarding taxation of unregistered clergy and the confusion it caused, see pp.22-3 and 595-9.

283. I. G. Halimov to H. A. Akhtiamov, 10 March 1951; GARF, f.6991, o.3, d.454, l.107.

284. For details, see p.598.

285. I. G. Halimov to CARC, 25 Dec. 1947 and 31 Dec. 1948; GARF, f.6991, o.3, d.453, ll.33-4, and d.454, l.3

286. Quoted in G. F. Frolov, Report, 28 Feb. 1952; GARF, f.6991, o.3, d.81, l.284.

287. I. G. Halimov to CARC, Report, undated [probably April 1949]; GARF, f.6991, o.3, d.454, l.17.

288. I. V. Polianskii to K. E. Voroshilov and G. M. Malenkov, 23 April 1949; RTsKhIDNI, f.17, o.132, d.111, l.62.

consequence of the difficulties involved.[289] In order to impose a tax the financial organs had to assess revenue, which the mullas concealed, sometimes even denying that they engaged in religious activity, while believers were reluctant to reveal anything and the lower level of local officials claimed ignorance. One possible way out of this impasse was to determine a fixed tax – as suggested by the *upolnomochennyi* in Osh – but there was no clarity regarding the criterion for so doing.[290] Still in the 1960s CARC's *upolnomochennye* were urging that the financial organs make greater efforts to reveal the income of unregistered clergy from the performance of religious rites in order to impose an appropriate income tax.[291] In some areas a number of unregistered clergy were said once again to have stopped functioning as such following their subjection to income tax. At the end of the 1960s thirty such cases were reported in the Kabardino-Balkar ASSR (as against 35-40 who continued activity despite taxation).[292] In the early 1970s a few clergy in the oblasti of Fergana and Samarkand also ceased operating following the imposition of higher taxes: in the former a number of shaykhs who operated at one of the *mazars* as well as five clergy and two unregistered mosques; in the latter an unspecified number made a written statement announcing that they were stopping activity in return for a reduction of the tax imposed upon them. Nonetheless, those taxed continued to constitute a small minority of all the unregistered clergy in light of the intricacies involved in establishing the identity of those who performed rites and their precise revenues.[293]

Here and there, 'administrative measures' were adopted against unregistered clergy. A mulla might, for example, be arrested while actually conducting prayers.[294] The justification for this was ap-

289. L. A. Prikhod'ko, Report, 2 June 1952; GARF, f.6991, o.3, d.81, l.135.

290. H. A. Akhtiamov, A short communiqué, Instructional conference of CARC's Central Asian *upolnomochennye*, 17-20 Dec. 1949; GARF, f.6991, o.3, d.67, ll.113-14.

291. K. Kulumbetov to A. A. Puzin, 13 July 1962; GARF, f.6991, o.3, d.1388, ll.97-8.

292. L. Zh. Alisov to the CRA, 27 Aug. 1969; GARF, f.6991, o.6, d.220, l.327.

293. K. Ruzmetov, Information, 14 June 1973; GARF, f.6991, o.6, d.545, ll.153-4. In Fergana Oblast' 177 such people were known as of 1 Jan. 1973, yet just 53 had been fined in 1969-70, 34 in 1971-2 and 18 in the first half of 1973.

294. N. I. Abushaev. Minutes, Inspectors' meeting No.26, 1-2 Dec. 1949; GARF, f.6991, o.3, d.60, l.84.

parently that other methods, particularly the enhancement of 'mass cultural and agitational work' among the believer population, was not effective and that the unregistered mullas violated the legislation on religion far more frequently and blatantly than did the registered clergy. They held prayers in the open, conducted 'religious propaganda' and 'took advantage' of shrines, 'revered tombs' as the Soviet documentation calls them, in order to conduct 'illegal activities'.[295]

More often, though, as has been noted, local organs of government tended not to take action against unregistered clergy.[296] For instance, CARC noted in 1952 that the number of *mavluds* read by them mounted markedly in certain areas of Uzbekistan (the city of Tashkent, the oblasti of Namangan and Andijan) because local officialdom was slack in taking the requisite measures against them.[297] The fact that the unregistered clergy were by definition beyond the control of the various mechanisms which had been established in order to regulate religious activity, notably the spiritual directorates, galled the registered mullas considerably.[298]

From the point of view of the Soviet authorities, the ultimate sin of the unregistered clergy was probably religious instruction, particularly of children. Immediately after the war there were at least two requests, in the Cherkess AO, to introduce the instruction of Islam and the Qur'an in regular schools, and another, in the Kabardinian ASSR, to open an elementary religious school or *mekteb*.[299] Direct approaches to the authorities, however, to actually teach Islam within a recognised school seem to have been extremely uncommon, even in this first period when believers were putting out feelers to gauge the measure of the new laxity.

More frequent were attempts, notably in Dagestan, Uzbekistan's Fergana Valley oblasti and Tajikistan, to teach children clandestinely in small groups. In 1946 USSR Minister of State Security V. A. Abakumov claimed that there were about thirty religious schools

---

295. L. A. Prikhod'ko, Report, 2 June 1952; GARF, f.6991, o.3, d.81, l.138.

296. For a systematic study of the position of local officialdom, see Chapter 11.

297. Minutes, CARC session No.9s, 2 April 1952, Appendix; GARF, f.6991, o.3, d.83, l.117.

298. In Tajikistan, for example, in the early 1960s – see p.264.

299. I. V. Polianskii to G. F. Aleksandrov, 31 Aug. 1945; RTsKhIDNI, f.17, o.125, d.313, l.180.

in Uzbekistan, where school-age children and young people learned religious topics. Three of these – two for boys and one for girls – were in Margelan, four in Kokand, and yet another in one of Fergana Oblast's rural areas; one in Andijan for people aged 18 –21, and another in Bukhara (both of these were said to have ten pupils), and one on a kolkhoz in Surkhan-Darya Oblast'. Although most of the pupils in these schools were children of clergy and 'former merchants', one or two were actually children of communists and local officials.[300] Another source reported that in 1946 in Bukhara alone fourteen schools had been exposed at which children were taught Qur'an by clergy or their wives and other relatives.[301] A report by the Uzbekistan CP Central Committee to that of the AUCP(b), referring to this phenomenon in early 1947, said there had been cases of the clergy opening 'illegal old-method religious schools',[302] in other words, schools where the entire curriculum focused on religious studies – as against the jadidist new method schools *(usul al-jadid)*, which included secular subjects. In Tajikistan there appear to have been at least three attempts at about the same time period to organise *mektebs* but they were duly thwarted, although parents continued sending their children to *qaris* for religious instruction.[303] In a rural community in Tashkent Oblast' an eight-year-old boy was not attending school in 1946 because he wanted to study only in Arabic and in accordance

300. V. A. Abakumov to K. E. Voroshilov, 12 Sept. 1946 – GARF, f.6991, o.3, d.34, l.194, and Hamidullin to I. V. Polianskii, 31 Dec. 1946 – TsGAUz, f.2456, o.1, d.72, l.65. One school operated in Andijan in 1947 – Kh. N. Iskanderov, Report, CARC session No.11, 18-19 June 1947; GARF, f.6991, o.4, d.19, l.368 – but it is not clear whether this was the same one as that mentioned by Abakumov. Polianskii also informed the decision-making level that 'the religious education of children is taking place in underground religious schools'; in one letter he mentioned schools in Andijan, Margelan and rural parts of the oblasti of Tashkent, Bukhara and Kokand [sic] – I. V. Polianskii to K. E. Voroshilov, 13 Nov. 1946, and to A. A. Zhdanov and K. E. Voroshilov, 7 July 1947; GARF, f.6991, o.3, d.34, l.198, and RTsKhIDNI, f.17, o.125, d.506, l.160.

301. V. Tatarintsev to A. A. Zhdanov, 15 Nov. 1946; RTsKhIDNI, f.17, o.125, d.421, l.109.

302. Quoted in Gitlin, *Natsional'nye otnosheniia v Uzbekistane*, p.216.

303. K. Hamidov, Report, CARC session No.4, 29 Jan. 1947; GARF, f.6991, o.4, d.19, l.73. This applied especially to Leninabad Oblast'. In the opinion of CARC member N. Tagiev, SADUM's qazi in Tajikistan, Salih Babakalanov, himself favoured opening *mektebs* in Tajikistan – *ibid.*, l.79.

with Islamic tradition. In the same oblast' at this time a *raiispolkom* employee was looking for an Arabic primer to teach written Arabic to his eleven-year-old son.[304] Describing these instances in a document written at the very end of the 1940s, one CARC inspector said that certain 'elements' had brought together small groups of children and youth and taught them the Arabic alphabet and how to read the Qur'an.[305]

Although every case of religious instruction in 'groups' was quashed as soon as it was exposed, and although those who engaged in this must have been aware of the gravity of the offence, the teaching of Islam was never totally eradicated. In the early 1950s in Dagestan a secondary school pupil who had received 'a secondary religious education' from his uncle was discovered to be instructing three other adolescents, while in Derbent a lady was found to be teaching Qur'an to three more adolescents (presumably girls). In the same period in Tajikistan, *ishans* and their *murids* reportedly organised religious schools for teaching Qur'an and the basics of the Shari'a.[306] Toward the end of the decade in some areas the younger generation was thought to be learning religion at home, parents who were unable to inculcate Islam in their children sending them to mullas to this end.[307] Instances were reported of teaching Qur'an to children in Kirgiziia, one teacher in a village in Osh Oblast' teaching Islam to more than ten children,[308] and children were being taught Islamic dogma in an outlying raion of Kurgan-Tyube Oblast'.[309] In 1962 three instances of religious instruction were discovered in Tajikistan in Hissar Raion, one of adults and two of adolescents, and three more in the same republic the following year, all of adults – in Leninabad, Kurgan-Tyube and Regar. In 1963 children were also being taught Qur'an in three

304. K. Mustafin to Tashkent Oblispokom Chairman Turgunov and I. Ibadov, 19 April 1946; TsGAUz, f.2456, 0.1, d.167, l.5.

305. N. Abushaev, Information, 17 Nov. 1949; GARF, f.6991, o.3, d.61, l.124.

306. L. A. Prikhod'ko, Report, 2 June 1952; GARF, f.6991, o.3, d.81, l.125. And see p.396.

307. H. A. Akhtiamov, Address, All-Union conference of CARC *upolnomochennye*, 25-27 Nov. 1958; GARF, f.6991, o.3, d.165, l.51.

308. H. A. Akhtiamov, Report, Conference of CARC's *upolnomochennye* in Central Asia, 5-6 June 1959, and All-Union conference of CARC *upolnomochennye*, 18-20 April 1960; GARF, f.6991, o.3, d.186, ll.42-3, and d.208, l.128.

309. N. Smirnov and S. Fastoved, Information, 22 Aug. 1962; GARF, f.6991, o.3, d.1390, l.34.

settlements in Dagestan, as well as in the town of Khasavyurt. A number of these instances were excoriated in the local press.[310] A woman faith-healer in Ashkhabad was also reported to be teaching 'the law of Allah' to children (again presumably girls) in the mid 1960s,[311] whereas at the very end of the decade Islam was being taught in the Fergana Valley. In one kishlak in Fergana Oblast' a school was discovered with twenty-three children, who also studied in a regular school. They were taught after school hours and were provided with religious books wrapped in covers of secondary school textbooks. In two raiony of Namangan Oblast' schools were organised which were attended by about fifty adults and more than twenty children. In addition to instruction in the basics of Islam, students were told not to go to the cinema or theatre or to let girls attend secular schools.[312]

In the 1970s this phenomenon seems to have become more widespread, presumably the result of growing concern at the general ignorance of the younger generation regarding all aspects of religion. In Dagestan early in the decade, the instruction of groups of children was known to be going on in four rural settlements, in one of them at a registered mosque.[313] Indeed, that seems to have been the one republic where registered clergy engaged in teaching children Qur'an in order to create new cadres. They also involved them in distributing leaflets of religious content.[314] In Nakhichevan two men from different raiony were tried for organising a night school to teach children Qur'an; such schools were said to crop

310. In one of the groups in Hissar there were seven pupils and in another six; the number in the third case is not specified – M. Kh. Hamidov to A. A. Puzin, 18 May 1963 and 24 Feb. 1964, and Minutes, CARC session No.24, 27 Aug. 1964; GARF, f.6991, o.3, d.1739, l.63 and d.1740, l.30, and o.4, d.147, l.81. The cases exposed in 1963 were of instruction by *ishans* and mullas to their *murids*. See also *Dagestanskaia pravda*, 20 Nov. 1960, quoted in Klimovich, *Islam*, p.232.

311. Minutes, CARC session No.3, 17-18 Feb. 1965; GARF, f.6991, o.4, d.168, l.41.

312. CRA, Report, 22 May 1970; TsKhSD, f.5, o.62, d.38, l.39.

313. Kh. Salahetdinov, I. Mikhalev, Report, handed to E. I. Lisavtsev, 26 Oct. 1971; GARF, f.6991, o.6, d.361, l.107. See also CRA, Information, sent to the CPSU Central Committee, 27 April 1971; TsKhSD, f.5, o.63, d.89, l.138.

314. CARC's *upolnomochennyi* in Dagestan reported that in 1972 clergy were instructing children in Qur'an. While he did not say so specifically, it is almost certain that he was referring to registered clergy – M. S. Gajiev to A. Nurullaev, 27 July 1973; GARF, f.6991, o.6, d.629, l.164.

up periodically in that republic.[315] In one single year (1972) incidents of teaching Islam to groups of schoolchildren were exposed in the city of Tashkent and the oblasti of Namangan, Andijan and Fergana. Moreover, students who applied to the Mir-Arab Medrese upon leaving school in this same time frame had already had some religious training, had a fair understanding of dogma and could read the Qur'an freely. Some claimed to have acquired these skills within the family circle, others from unofficial clergy.[316] At the Karl Marx Kolkhoz in Kurgan-Tyube Oblast' an unregistered cleric opened a school in a private home, where eighteen youngsters were reportedly given religious tuition.[317] Another mulla in Tajikistan was said to have taught twenty-two children, also in a private home, and both he and a third such teacher were brought to trial.[318] Sometimes young people would approach the cleric who performed burial services with questions on religion and learn the basics of Islam then and there at the cemetery.[319]

Towards the end of the decade an Islamic revitalisation took place in the Fergana Valley and Tajikistan, focusing on education. Small groups of young people, many from religious families, who had received some instruction at home, continued their education with older people, who had received their own education before 1917. The basic topics of study were Arabic language and script and Islam. Hundreds of youth studied in this way, beginning with two pamphlets by the jadidist reformer Munawwar Qari: *Adib-i awwal* (The First Teacher, *c.*1901), an Uzbek-language primer in Arabic script, with an introduction to the basics of Islam and excerpts from the Qur'an in Arabic; and *Adib-i thani* (The Second Teacher, 1903), containing more Islamic themes. The group in

315. I. Bonchkovskii to E. I. Lisavtsev, 1 June 1973; GARF, f.6991, o.6, d.537, l.172.

316. K. K. Ruzmetov, Memorandum, 14 June 1973; GARF, f.6991, o.6, d.545, l.159.

317. Kurgan-Tyube Obkom, Resolution, passed 24 Feb. 1978; TsKhSD, f.5, o.75, d.270, l.15. Unfortunately, the resolution gives no information whether the youth who studied here were still pupils at secondary school or older, or whether full-time or evening classes were being offered; nor do we know how long this school operated.

318. CRA, Information, sent to the CPSU Central Committee, 27 April 1971; TsKhSD, f.5 o.63, d.89, l.138.

319. Author's interview with a former CRA official who has asked to remain anonymous. For similar contentions regarding registered clergy, see pp.251-2.

Tajikistan led by Said Abdullo Nuri was the precursor of Tajikistan's Islamic Renaissance Party.

In 1979 one Rahmatulla, who had studied in the home of one of parallel Islam's prestigious figures Muhammad Hindustani Rustamov, called for a broader education programme that would enhance Islamic knowledge and awareness. He and Abduwali Mirzaev, who had studied with him, and their followers opened clandestine schools, each with five to ten pupils, whom they had recruited from a large number of towns and villages. The curriculum in these schools included the works of leading Islamic activists from other parts of the Muslim world, who had played a major role in radicalising and politicising Islam in the past generation or so: the Pakistani Abu–l 'A'la Maudoodi, and the Egyptians Hasan al-Banna and Sayyid Qutb.[320] By 1980 students in an underground *madrasa* in Namangan were reading Sayyid Qutb's *Ma'alim fi al-tariq* (Signposts on the Road) and Muhammad Qutb's *Shubhatun hawla al-islam* (Ambiguities Surrounding Islam).[321] The transmission of religious knowledge to the younger generation intensified throughout the Fergana Valley, young clerics forming groups of young people to instruct,[322] some apparently belonging to the older school, others to the more radical faction. (Rahmatulla himself was killed in a car accident in 1981, but his adherents did not let up.)

It is a moot point how far this movement was affected by the Iranian revolution, for it had roots in a manifest dynamic within the Fergana Valley. In the year 1982, no less than twenty-one underground schools for teaching Islam to children and adults were 'exposed' in Tajikistan, in some of which as many as fifty students of secondary and vocational schools were studying. This was not a phenomenon to which it was possible to put a stop and more of these schools were revealed in the following year.[323]

A small group of young unregistered clerics also came to light in Kulyab Oblast' in Tajikistan in the early 1980s who called themselves Wahhabis after the eighteenth-century trend in Saudi

---

320. Abduvakhitov, 'Islamic Revivalism in Uzbekistan', pp.81-3.

321. Olcott, 'Islam and Fundamentalism in Independent Central Asia', p.34.

322. Author's interview with an anonymous former member of the CRA.

323. CRA memo, 2 June 1983, and V. A. Kuroedov to the CPSU Central Committee, 16 Sept. 1983; TsKhSD, f.5, o.89, d.82, ll.38 and 60.

Arabia, which had sought to return to 'authentic' Islam. They reportedly circulated among believers theories about the "advantages" of the Islamic social system and the "equity of the Khomeini regime as distinct from the Soviet regime"'. A search in the home of one of the leaders of this group, who engaged in the regular teaching of religion, produced forty-four religious books and what was described as a 120-page 'anti-communist, anti-Soviet, Pan-Islamist' manuscript.[324] (As of the second half of the 1980s the Soviet authorities seem to have used the term Wahhabi to describe all Islamic activists in the Fergana Valley and Tajikistan who opposed the official Muslim establishment and sought to return to a pure, pristine form of Islam. It is nonetheless possible that the group in fact designated themselves as such, irrespective of the fact that they had no ties with Saudi Arabia.[325])

Another practice against which the authorities sought constantly to battle was faith-healing. There were not a few areas in the country where the sick, instead of turning to the state's medical insititutions and professionals, approached their mullas to find a cure. This appears to have applied particularly to women suffering from infertility, but it held also for a variety of illnesses. Nor was it only the illiterate or poorly educated who had resort to these practices. For instance, a teacher in Kirgiziia's Issyk-Kul Oblast' approached a mulla in the mid-1950s to cure her sick stomach by exorcism.[326] Some of the more famous faith-healers were reputedly 'living saints', who might be visited even by doctors and party functionaries.[327] One such person, charged in 1985 under Article 147-1 of the Uzbek SSR Criminal Code ('Infringement of Person and Rights of Citizens under the Guise of Performing Religious Ceremonies') had served a previous prison term; indeed, he had been taught Islamic principles and beliefs by a fellow

324. V. A. Kuroedov to the CPSU Central Committee, 16 Sept. 1983; TsKhSD, f.5, o.89, d.82, l.59. According to this document, the group comprised 22 unregistered clerics aged 22-45.

325. Nor is it to be excluded, even if they called themselves Wahhabis, that they found positive sides to Khomeini's Iran, for they were clearly not Wahhabis in the strict sense of the word.

326. I. V. Polianskii to P. V. Kovanov, 23 Feb. 1955; GARF, f.6991, o.3, d.114, l.30.

327. Kocaoglu, 'Islam in the Soviet Union: Atheistic Propaganda and 'Unofficial'' Religious Activities', pp.149-50.

prisoner and left jail as a self-declared mulla.[328] Although there were cases when the sick person's condition apparently deteriorated as a result of treatment received at the hands of the cleric and in spite of prayers and readings from the Qur'an on his behalf and the exorcism of evil spirits, the faith of the rural indigenous population in the achievements of Soviet medical science, at least as practiced in their localities, was apparently not enhanced and the popularity of their own traditional healers not usually impaired. (CARC and its *upolnomochennye*, not to speak of atheistic propaganda and the media, understandably dwelt at length on instances when sick people were hospitalised in critical condition or died, following, if not actually as a result of, treatment by faith-healers.[329])

A third manifestation of recalcitrance among the unregistered clergy was the dissemination of literature with a religious content. This form of *samizdat* literature was apparently mostly written by hand. But there were exceptions. In 1946 the distribution of a pamphlet drawn up at a convention of Muslim believers was held up by the local organs of government in rural parts of Dagestan and in Groznyi Oblast'.[330] In 1948 sermons of unregistered clergy were being propagated in two books in various parts of Uzbekistan. Indeed, the dissemination of unauthorized religious literature seems to have pertained in particular in Uzbekistan. Toward the end of the 1940s, leaflets were being distributed in Khorezm Oblast' containing the so-called testament of Ahmad Yasawi – an early Central Asian mystic, who had spread Islam among the nomad population and whose mausoleum in the town of Turkestan in Southern Kazakhstan was one of the region's best known shrines. These leaflets were disseminated even among party and soviet workers, and five teachers – in two schools and a teachers' seminary – were expelled from the party in connection with this affair. The testament bewailed the sins of the contemporary generation, which did not observe the fast, pray regularly or give charity, and contained a

328. Timur Kocaoglu, 'An 'Unofficial" Mullah Sentenced in Uzbekistan', RL 184/85; 5 June 1985.

329. For considerable detail on a number of cases disastrously dealt with by local faith-healers, see, for example, D. A. Ahmedov to A. A. Puzin, 21 Feb. 1961; GARF, f.6991, o.3, d.1737, ll.14-16. See also Petrushev, *Islam i ego reaktsionnaia sushchnost'*, pp.27-8.

330. Zakaryaev, Report, June 1946; GARF, f.6991,op.3, d.38, l.64. It was not stated when the pamphlet was composed and printed.

request by Muhammad himself that Yasawi seek to overcome these by distributing the Prophet's sermons. Anyone who passed on this testament to nine people in writing, or, if he be illiterate, orally, would have his sins forgiven and he would be able to enter Paradise when the time came.[331]

In the mid-1950s Ahmad Yasawi's 'testament' was again being copied and distributed in the towns of Margelan, Kokand and Fergana and a number of raion administrative centres in Fergana Oblast'. It was copied out by a girl student in a secondary school in Kokand, who had received it from a girl student in Margelan, and in her wake by eight other girls in the same school. The first girl was also responsible for the leaflet reaching one of the rural raiony, where she went for her wedding, and where, too, it was distributed among school students and others.[332]

The phenomenon of Islamic *samizdat* was sufficiently extensive for the Uzbek SSR Council of Ministers to include in its resolution in 1969 'On enhancing control of implementing legislation on the religious cults', a paragraph instructing the republican ministry of the interior to 'take measures to expose and pre-empt crimes on a religious basis'. The first of three crimes specified was 'the sale and distribution of religious literature (photocopies of sermons, extracts from the Qur'an, tapes and gramophone records of religious poems and songs)'.[333]

In the early 1970s and again in the early 1980s Muslim chain letters were circulating in Chimkent Oblast', notably among school students, and in schools in Kirgiziia. The former were said to have originated with 'self-appointed mullas' in the vicinity of the mosque in Turkestan. The latter included a letter, said to be actually written by God, which promised that whoever preserved, copied and transmitted it to others would be successful. It was reported that many parents, again under the influence of 'self-

---

331. Minutes, Conference of CARC *upolnomochennye* in the Uzbek SSR, 9 Aug. 1948; TsGAUz, f.2456, o.1, d.120, ll.9 and 14. For the mausoleum, see p.373 below.

332. Kh. N. Iskanderov to Deputy Chairman Uzbek SSR Council of Ministers G. S. Sultanov and Uzbekistan CP Central Committee Secretary Kh. G. Gulamov, 17 June 1955; TsGAUz, f.2456, o.1, d.175, l.14.

333. Kuroedov and Pankratov (eds), *Zakonodatel'stvo o religioznykh kul'takh*, pp. 156–9. The other two crimes were begging of people capable of working—on the precincts of prayer-houses and the 'activity of parasitic elements' among the itinerant clergy.

appointed mullas', urged their children to make several copies of these letters and distribute them in schools and other public places. In Turkmenistan, too, religious chain letters – in the form of a 'testament' – were circulating in various parts. They were received and passed on not only by 'ignorant and illiterate persons and naive secondary-school students', but even by well-educated people and university students.[334]

Some of these transgressions were attributed by the authorities to the more radically inclined *ishans*; it is not, however, certain that they belonged strictly speaking to this category, but simply that it was more convenient to accuse *ishans* of such extremities. Be this as it may, *ishans* in Urgut Raion in Samarkand Oblast' were said to be distributing – unidentified – 'religious leaflets' in twenty schools in the mid-1950s.[335]

By the late 1970s at the latest Qur'ans and books of religious commentary were being duplicated on rather primitive copying machines. These included pre-revolutionary religious primers, such as Munawwar Qari's two treatises.[336] In 1982 a court in Tashkent sentenced two men for printing and illicitly distributing religious books – both, incidentally, had been convicted previously for the same crime – and prosecuted eleven others for speculation, i.e. selling this literature in public places. The main item which focused attention was a thirty page booklet entitled 'About the Islamic Faith', containing information about Islam for people who had no knowledge of their religion, that appeared in thousands of copies and was being sold at a bazaar in Tashkent. It contained selections from Central Asia's classic poets and from Avicenna (Ibn Sina), which were intended to convey historical information about the faith and to describe Muslims' religious obligations, as well as *suras* from the Qur'an and prayers. While the first two pages were in Arabic, the bulk of the booklet was in Uzbek. Other literature was similarly produced, including copies of the Qur'an and cassette recordings of prayers.[337]

334. Kocaoglu, 'Islam in the Soviet Union: Atheistic Propaganda and "Unofficial" Religious Activities', pp.147-9. For chain letters in Dagestan, see p.356 above.

335. Minutes, Instructional meeting of CARC's *upolnomochennye* in the Uzbek SSR, 15-17 March 1956; TsGAUz, f.2456, o.1, d.183, l.54. For Sufi *samizdat* in the Northern Caucasus, see pp.417-8.

336. Olcott, 'Islam and Fundamentalism in Independent Central Asia', p.34.

337. Bess Brown, 'Profitable Religious Publishing Operation Uncovered in

Many of the other transgressions committed by the unregistered mullas were similar to those of the registered clergy. In some places after the war they sought to give material assistance to the needy. For example, in Kokchetau (Kazakhstan) itinerant mullas distributed potatoes and bread to families of soldiers killed at the front.[338] In the Northern Caucasus they continued to engage in charity throughout the period under discussion, collecting money and foodstuffs, mainly grain, from the villagers to give to their poor neighbours. They were also said to have sold hay gathered at the cemeteries to pay their income tax.[339] In some places village soviets farmed out the local cemetery to clergy to refurbish and they took advantage of this to build mosques and promote religious activity there. In the period 1968-70 in Kirgiziia fifteen cemeteries were taken over by unregistered clergy and *aksakals*, who opened prayer-houses in them, where Friday and festival prayers and the *tarawa-namaz* were held, *fitr* collected and rites performed for women twice a week.[340] Unregistered mullas were, in addition, constantly being accused of performing marriages which contradicted Soviet law, for instance where the bride was not yet of age, or the groom had other wives, and so could not be registered with the official civic registry office, ZAGS.[341]

Muslim holy places

The Muslim holy places with which certain Muslim areas, particularly in the Caucasus and Central Asia, abounded were a major focus of activity of unofficial clergy. Mostly these holy places were tombs of religious figures, called *mazars* in Central Asia, and *pirs* or *ziyarats* in the Caucasus. They might also be springs or trees or grottoes, to which supernatural attributes were similarly

Tashkent', RL 420/82, 20 Oct. 1982; Paksoy, 'The Deceivers'.

338. Eleusyzov, Address, Conference of CARC *upolnomochennye* for Kazakhstan and Kirgiziia, Alma-Ata, 2 Oct. 1946; GARF, f.6991, o.3, d.41, 1.54.

339. L. Zh. Aisov to A. A. Puzin, 14 Feb. 1963; GARF, f.6991, o.3, d.1607, l.3. Two years later Aisov said – rather more plausibly – that the hay was being sold to pay for the costs of fencing in the cemeteries, see Chapter 9, n.43.

340. S. Shafiqov, Information, 22 Jan. 1971, and S. Shafiqov to V. A. Kuroedov and U. D. Janybaev, 14 Oct. 1971; GARF, f.6991, o.6, d.370, ll.11-12 and 16.

341. See, for example, L. Zh. Aisov to A. A. Puzin, 17 Jan. 1961; GARF, f.6991, o.3, d.1605, l.3.

ascribed. Indeed, in Central Asia itself the term *mazar* had different connotations in various parts. Whereas in Turkmenistan it was used to refer specifically to a burial-place, in Tajikistan it served to denote the entire variety of sites to which special powers were imputed.[342]

Like faith-healing, the cult of holy men or saints was extrinsic to Qur'anic Islam. In Central Asia, at least, it was thought to be a leftover from shamanism, which had existed there prior to the region's conversion to Islam,[343] or from other non-Islamic belief systems, some of whose features had been adopted, with adaptations, by Islam, notably through its more mystical offshoots such as Sufism. In fact, saint veneration and the visitation of saints' tombs were common practice in all parts of the Muslim world which were affected by Sufism.[344] The Soviet regime's atheistic propaganda laid great stress on those elements within Islam that had been incorporated from earlier, paganistic practices. The intent was to demonstrate the superstitious component of popular Islam and to highlight the ignorance of the Muslim clergy who were unable to differentiate between the fundamentals of their faith and extraneous practices that had over time become part and parcel of Islamic tradition. Indeed, as a Western scholar has pointed out, the shrines frequently incorporated 'elements from former shamanistic practices, such as the adornment of the gravesite with traditional rams' horns or white standards of camel or sheepskin (frequently substituted by pieces of white cloth)'.[345] One Soviet writer stated that since, on the one hand, it required no complicated ritual and, on the other, had become an intrinsic part of people's lives, this particular aspect of Islam had persisted, while other less easily applied dogmas had disappeared. In many parts of Dagestan and the Chechen-Ingush ASSR, where the population had long since 'distanced itself from the mosque and official clergy' and ceased to observe many of the precepts of Islam, the belief in holy men was still widespread.[346] A Soviet ethnographer who did field work in Uzbekistan's Khorezm Oblast' and Karakalpak ASSR and among the Uzbeks of Turkmenistan wrote: 'the diverse complex of religious

342. Poliakov, *Everyday Islam*, p.99.

343. See Basilov, *Kul't sviatykh v islame*, pp.93-4.

344. Trimingham, *The Sufi Orders in Islam*, p. 26. For Sufism, see Chapter 6.

345. Subtelny, 'The Cult of Holy Places', p. 597.

346. Makatov, 'Kul't sviatykh v islame', p.164.

ideas and acts that existed alongside Islam: animistic, magical, the cult of ancestors and nature, the cult of saints and their graves...shamanism, etc.' was 'rooted in the very core of family life, one of the most conservative units of society'. It was this fact, in his opinion, which accounted for 'its significance in our day'. The cult of *mazars* had been perpetuated in particular by women as an integral component of the syncretistic religion that had taken root among them, the entire ritual conducted at these sites being permeated with animistic ideas and magical elements associated with the cult of nature.[347]

Almost certainly the importance of these holy places in the Soviet Union was enhanced by the fact that the *hajj* was not a viable option. A sociological survey conducted in Tashauz (Turkmenistan) in the late 1960s found that 27.8 per cent of male believers and 41.8 per cent of female believers accepted the miraculous power of the *hajj* and made pilgrimages to holy places 'of a local nature'. These apparently were people who made such pilgrimages regularly, for the same survey found that a further 58.8 per cent of male and 52.6 per cent of female believers 'doubt the value of the *hajj*, but still do it in some circumstances'. Their motivation, it was said, was 'not so much religious ideas' as the desire to make a trip to 'a healing spring, venerated by believers for purposes of healing' or to cemeteries 'for the purpose of venerating relatives buried there'. The survey also noted that among the women the idea of the pilgrimage as 'pleasing to God' had been 'replaced to a significant degree' by belief in the miraculous properties of these holy places.[348]

Some sites attracted pilgrims from far and wide. Other sanctuaries were of local significance and were unknown outside a particular locality. Indeed, a *mazar* or holy place existed in practically every settlement or kishlak,[349] at least in the traditionally sedentarised parts of Central Asia. The 275 *mazars* of which account had been taken in Uzbekistan by the end of the 1940s comprised only part

347. Snesarev, 'On some Causes of the Persistence of Religio-Customary Survivals among the Khorezm Uzbeks', p.218.

348. S. Begmedov, 'Particular Manifestations of Religious Survivals Among the Urban Population', *News from the Academy of Science of the Turkmen SSR*, Series: Social Sciences, 3, 1968, pp.34–40, quoted in *Religion in Communist Lands*, 2:4 and 5, July–Oct. 1974, pp.46–7. For the *hajj*, see pp.171–5.

349. Poliakov, *Everyday Islam*, p.99; Makatov, 'Kul't sviatykh v islame', p.165.

of the picture, according to Polianskii, for in addition to the better known ones, each settlement in the pre-revolutionary period had had its own holy place.[350] Clearly the assumption was that where these had existed in the past, they continued to operate. In Azerbaijan, too, the great majority of shrines were situated in rural areas, either just outside towns or, more ususally, in villages and remote locations, and almost every village had a holy place of some sort.[351] The sporadic registration of a small number of the more popular *mazars* in order to bring them under the control of the establishment, with all that this implied, did not therefore really address itself to the issue of terminating pilgrimages to those which remained in the hands of unregistered clerics.[352] One CARC official pointed out that although the Soviet government had permitted the opening of seven *mazars* in Central Asia, SADUM opened hundreds in the immediate postwar period; fifty-one operated just in Khorezm Oblast' at the beginning of 1947.[353] In Bukhara Oblast', where all three registered mosques were in the town of Bukhara, unregistered clergy developed an extensive activity in the multifarious *mazars* of the rural raiony, not a few of which were extremely popular.[354]

Most functioning *mazars* were visited primarily on religious festivals and in the summer and autumn. Some of the more famous ones might be visited daily during these seasons, and just a few of the most popular ones might even attract pilgrims every day throughout the year, except when snow made this impossible. Usually believers would come on a fixed day of the week, mostly on Wednesdays or Thursdays, in accordance with local custom.

Those who served at holy places were commonly called shaykhs.[355] Indeed, in Central Asia every holy place had its shaykh

350. I. V. Polianskii to K. E. Voroshilov, 27 May 1950; GARF, f.6991, o.3, d.68, l.41.

351. Saroyan, *Reconstructing Community*, p.215.

352. For *mazars* or mausolea brought under the control of the Muslim spiritual directorates, see pp.123-5.

353. These data were provided by the head of CARC's group of inspectors, G. Ia. Vrachev, CARC session No.4, 29 Jan. 1947; GARF, f.6991, o.4, d.19, l.81.

354. I. V. Polianskii to P. V. Kovanov, 23 June 1955; GARF, f.6991, o.3, d.114, l.21, and I. A. Shalaev to Uzbekistan CP Central Committee Secretary Kh. G. Gulamov, 11 Nov. 1955; TsGAUz, f.2456, o.1, d.174, l.94.

355. In the Caucasus they apparently had no special designation.

who conducted prayers and received gifts from pilgrims.[356] Some of the shaykhs who operated at *mazars* were, or asserted that they were, descendants of the holy men claimed to be buried there. They, like their saintly ancestors, were supposedly invested with supernatural powers.[357] It was not uncommon to find female shrine custodians,[358] which was hardly surprising given the predominantly female composition of pilgrims. Invocations made on behalf of pilgrims tended to combine Arabic with the local vernacular. These often took the form of rudimentary formulas, although shaykhs with greater knowledge of Arabic recited entire prayers, including verses and chapters from the Qur'an, and were able to write down phrases and invocations in Arabic that could be used as talismans.[359] The post of shaykh was – understandably – often hereditary, people inheriting the position from their fathers or other relatives.[360] Here and there the local authorities would agree to register one or two of these shaykhs in order to obtain some measure of control over what happened at a holy place and simultaneously to undercut those who continued to operate without authorisation.[361]

Indeed, the belief prevailed that the holy person protected first and foremost his own descendants and heeded the requests and appeals of his relatives more speedily than those of others. (This was the source of the custom of adding *ata* (father) or *baba* (grandfather) to the name of a saint.) In Turkmenistan, for example, each clan had its special saint, whose descendants would serve as

356. I. V. Polianskii to K. E. Voroshilov, 27 May 1950; GARF, f.6991, o.3, d.68, l.41.

357. Almaev to Deputy Chairman Tashkent Oblispokom Mahkamov and Obkom Secretary Nazarov, 19 Jan. 1952; TsGAUz, f.2456, o.1, d.142, ll.50-2.

358. Saroyan, *Reconstructing Community*, p. 217. Saroyan is speaking specifically of Azerbaijan, but the CARC and CRA materials give examples of this for Central Asia as well.

359. *Ibid.*, p.230.

360. Minutes, Conference of CARC *upolnomochennye*, 5-6 June 1959; GARF, f.6991, o.3, d.186, l.30.

361. For example, CARC's *upolnomochennye* in Kirgiziia registered two of the shaykhs at Takht-i Sulayman in Osh; the others continued to function, basically, however, receiving pilgrims in their homes, where, among other things, they would perform ritual sacrifices – H.A. Akhtiamov in answer to questions, Instructional conference of CARC's Central Asian *upolnomochennye*, 17-20 Dec. 1949; GARF, f.6991, o.3, d.67, l.89.

shaykhs at his tomb and the Turkmen would come to them to intervene on their behalf with their ancestor. Sometimes a saint might be considered the ancestor of an entire tribe. In some parts of Uzbekistan and Tajikistan certain saints were patrons of professions, but they, too, might be ancestors, as the area's traditional crafts would be passed on from father to son. People also tended to pray to the saint buried in proximity to their habitat, and he, in turn, would help all those who lived within a given distance of his tomb. Often, too, a cemetery would crop up around a *mazar*, the holy person whose tomb it was helping all those buried there to enter Paradise; among the Kyrgyz and the Karakalpaks clan cemeteries were customary.[362] Some of the most popular *mazars* were sought out as burial-places not only for those living in the vicinity, but from rather far afield. For instance, that of Sultan-baba, supposedly the tomb of the Yemeni Sufi saint Uwais al-Qarani, in the Karakalpak ASSR served as a burial-site for believers from other raiony in the republic and even from the neighbouring Khorezm Oblast'.[363]

Many *mazars*, therefore, were at cemeteries. For example, all ten of the *mazars* looked into in Turkmenistan in the early 1950s by a CARC inspector – out of forty-three said to be operating in the republic – were so situated.[364] In Bukhara Oblast', too, most of the *mazars* were at functioning cemeteries, and were included in the *upolnomochennyi's* annual report as unregistered religious societies rather than holy places.[365] Many of the better known *mazars*, indeed, had their own mosques and prayer-premises. Some *mazars* became to all intents and purposes permanently operating unregistered mosques, serving ongoing communities; others remained places of pilgrimage for those coming to pray sporadically, especially on the main festivals. Certainly, the visitation of *mazars* was at its highest during the *uraz* and on festivals. On these occasions those officiating at such shrines would conduct collective prayer-services, including sermons. At Sultan-baba on Uraz-Bayram in

362. Basilov, *Kul't sviatykh v islame*, pp.72, 75-6, 86-7, and 89-90.

363. K. Ruzmetov to V. A. Kuroedov, 15 May 1974; GARF, f.6991, o.6, d.634, l.37.

364. P. A. Solov'ev, Report, Minutes, CARC session No.1, 13 Jan. 1951; GARF, f.6991, o.3, d.74, l.7.

365. S. A. Shamsutdinov to T. S. Saidbaev, 4 Feb. 1967; GARF, f.6991, o.6, d.29, ll.16 and 19.

the mid-1970s clergy reportedly enjoined worshippers – 70 per cent of whom were women – to observe religious rites, threatening them with divine retribution if they did otherwise.[366]

A number of the more enterprising custodians of *mazars* would construct eating and sleeping facilities and receive often considerable donations.[367] Indeed, whereas donations given for the performance of rites normally went to the mosque, or at least should have been earmarked for it, those brought to shrines, except the few which were officially registered, would go into the pockets of the clergy. In addition, the general lack of control of what went on at *mazars*, the preference of many believers to go a few times a year to a holy place rather than every Friday, not to say every day, to a mosque, and the fact that scores of *mazars* were open to pilgrims throughout the year – all made these sites a natural choice of activity for many clergy.[368]

Not a few officials saw these holy places as a greater danger even than the unregistered mosque. On the whole, they were perceived by the regime as the epitome of fetishism and a main centre of evil practices, the 'seat of every kind of superstition', as they were called in one report.[369] Since people believed in their supernatural powers and made pilgrimages to them, bringing animal sacrifices and other donations, they became the focus for the practice of what the authorities perceived as the wildest and most repugnant fallacies.[370] Everything which was done in the mosque was done here, too, and more as well, one CARC *upolnomochennyi* pointed out. Whereas the believer spent half an hour in the mosque, he would stay six to seven hours or even an entire night at a holy place.[371] Moreover, those who visited the *mazars* and other holy

---

366. D. Erekeshov to A. Nurullaev, 7 May 1974; GARF, f.6991, o.6, d.545, ll.219-20.

367. V. I. Gostev to P. A. Tarasov, 4 Jan. 1954; GARF, f.6991, o.3, d.102, ll.14-15. For the hotal constituated at Sultan-baba, see p.372 below.

368. CRA, Information, sent to the CPSU Central Committee, 27 April 1971; TsKhSD, f.5, o.63, d.89, ll.115-16.

369. CARC report, sent to G. M. Malenkov, M. A. Suslov, V. S. Abakumov and the Council of Ministers presidium, 30 June 1951; GARF, f.6991, o.3, d.76, l.100.

370. See, for example, K. Hamidov, Report, CARC session No.4, 29 Jan. 1947, and L. A. Prikhod'ko, Short report, 4 April 1952; GARF, f.6991, o.4, d.19, l.74, and o.3, d.81, ll.96-7.

371. I. Zakaryaev, Report, Conference of CARC *upolnomochennye* in Rostov-

places were primarily women and children, so that they basically catered to groups within the population which the regular mosques did not reach.[372] At some *mazars* women actually participated together with the men in prayer-services.[373]

Finally, believers attributed to *mazars* the ability to heal disease, to cure infertility, to rid people of the difficulties and unpleasantnesses of life and to bring about the fulfilment of their wishes, and this encouraged faith-healers and 'sorcerers' of all kinds to install themselves there.[374] Infertility was particularly rife in Central Asia, perhaps, as has been suggested, as a result of child labour, which was widespread, and caused a variety of illnesses and diseases, especially in regions where tobacco was grown.[375] Indeed, each holy place had its own 'speciality', whether it be healing sickness, bringing children to the childless, or rain in times of famine. Some would be turned to for aid in working the land, others in building or animal husbandry.[376] Surveys carried out in both the Northern Caucasus and Azerbaijan indicate that in fact many, or most, pilgrimages were motivated by a specific request for which the intercession of the holy person buried at the shrine was sought. This lay behind the gift the pilgrim brought to the shrine, which was often rather an offering to the saint or sacred spirit inhabiting it, and the performance of devotional acts such as the tying of ribbons or strips of cloth at or near the site. These offerings generated considerable income for those who served at the shrines, particularly at the more renowned and popular ones.[377]

There is evidence that the visitation of these revered sites and holy places was revived and acquired considerable dimensions during World War II, when people came to ask for help for their relatives

---

on-Don, June 1946; GARF, f.6991, o.3, d.38, l.155.

372. For example, K. Hamidov to I. V. Polianskii, 14 Dec. 1949; GARF, f.6991, o.3, d.67, l.94.

373. For example, at one unregistered *mazar* in Turkmenistan on Uraz-Bayram in 1960 – M. A. Il'baev, Address, All-Union conference of CARC *upolnomochennye*, 18-20 April 1960; GARF, f.6991, o.3, d.208, l.107.

374. I. V. Polianskii to P. V. Kovanov, 23 June 1955; GARF, f.6991, o.3, d.114, l.39.

375. Poliakov, *Everyday Islam*, pp.61-2.

376. CRA, Information, sent to the CPSU Central Committee, 27 April 1971; TsKhSD, f.5, o.63, d.89, l.114. See also Saroyan, *Reconstructing Community*, pp.221-2. For one *mazar*, famed for healing the insane, see p.400.

377. Saroyan, *Reconstructing Community*, pp.222-7 and 231-3.

at the front. They would tie to twigs or poles shreds of the clothing of their husbands, fathers, sons, brothers, even photographs with their names, promising to make a sacrifice if they returned home safely.[378]

In Tajikistan worship at *mazars* was particularly widespread; according to one source, in the late 1940s there were 150 *mazars* in a single raion of Leninabad Oblast',[379] and 500 functioning ones throughout the republic in the middle of the following decade, served by some 700 mullas.[380] In Turkmenistan, with its total of four registered mosques, the population's religious inclinations were manifested at unregistered holy tombs. In early 1947 the chairman of the Turkmen SSR Council of Ministers sent CARC a list of twenty-three 'highly revered' *mazars*, which had been operating for many years despite attempts to repress them, and most of which had their own mosques, where prayers were conducted on Fridays and 'especially' on the two main festivals.[381] At the end of the following decade, CARC's *upolnomochennyi* there spoke of 400 'tombs and cemeteries, many of which are considered holy places for pilgrimage and the performance of rites'.[382]

The most popular of Central Asia's holy places was Takht-i Sulayman (lit. Solomon's Throne) in Osh, where as many as 60,000 pilgrims congregated on some of the festivals in the late 1940s, and up to 100,000 in the 1950s. About one-half crowded into the mosque and its courtyard, the others dispersed all over the mount. They came from all over Kirgiziia as well as from the neighbouring republics (Tajikistan, Uzbekistan and Kazakhstan), or, according to one report, from all over Central Asia.[383] Since

---

378. Klimovich, *Islam*, p.196.

379. K. Hamidov to I. Polianskii, 14 Dec. 1949; GARF, f.6991, o.3, d.67, l.94.

380. G. F. Frolov to I. Polianskii, 25 Feb. 1955; GARF, f.6991, o.3, d.112, l.8.

381. Minutes, CARC session No.13, 10-11 July 1947; GARF, f.6991, o.4, d.19, l.429.

382. Report, Conference of CARC *upolnomochennye*, 5-6 June 1959; GARF, f.6991, o.3, d.186, ll.63-4.

383. H. A. Akhtiamov, A short communication, Instructional conference of CARC's Central Asian *upolnomochennye*, Tashkent, 17-20 Dec. 1949, I. V. Polianskii to CPSU Central Committee, 27 Sept. 1954, I. G. Halimov to CARC, 20 Jan. 1956, and A. Puzin to V. P. Moskovskii, 14 Nov. 1957; GARF, f.6991, o.3, d.67, ll.102-5, d.102, ll.301-2, d.457, l.42, and d.147, l.207. Akhtiamov said there were disagreements as to the numbers of pilgrims who flocked to

the time of the October Revolution, when the *hajj* was no longer
a viable option, this site had been promoted as a second Mecca;[384]
according to one source, three visits to Takht-i Sulayman were
considered the equivalent of performing the *hajj*.[385]

Other *mazars* also drew large numbers of pilgrims. In 1949
10,000 worshippers gathered at the Baha ad-Din mausoleum – the
tomb of the founder of the Naqshbandiyya – in Bukhara Oblast'
on the popular spring festival of Gul-i Surh (lit. the ripening of
the red flower). Shortly afterwards the Uzbek Council of Ministers
decided to remove it and the Shoh-i Mardon *mazar* in Fergana
Oblast' from the jurisdiction of SADUM to which they had been
transferred in 1945. It contended that the repairs conducted at
Baha ad-Din by SADUM were insufficient to save it from falling
into disrepair and since it was included in the official list of his-
torical-cultural monuments, the state was responsible for its preservation. As to Shoh-i Mardon, SADUM was said not to have
exercised sufficient control over what went on at the shrine, and
it had become the scene of activity of 'a variety of "itinerant"
clergy and criminal elements'. Moreover, it was decided to build
a sanatorium close to the site of the Shoh-i Mardon mausoleum,
as well as a memorial to the revolutionary Uzbek poet Hamza
Hakim-zade, killed there at the instigation of clergy in 1929, and
it was out of the question that a functioning *mazar* be in the
proximity of either.[386] These measures did not, however, terminate
the pilgrimage to these two *mazars*, which were famous among
Muslims of the entire Soviet Union.[387] Baha ad-Din, also known
as a second Mecca, was still being visited secretly at the end of
the 1960s.[388] Another major *mazar* in Uzbekistan administered by

---

Osh, but did not give details. He also reported that the suggestion had been
put forward to turn the mount into a military observation point, in which case
pilgrimages would cease. Nothing seems to have come of this proposal.

384. H. Akhtiamov, Report, Conference of CARC *upolnomochennye*, 30 Sept.
1946; GARF, f.6991, o.6, d.629, l.168.

385. Poliakov, *Everyday Islam*, p.101.

386. I. V. Polianskii to K. E. Voroshilov, 27 May 1950, and Minutes, CARC
session No.7, 30 May 1950; GARF, f.6991, o.3, d.68, ll.45-8, and o.4, d.25,
ll.54-5. Polianskii had in fact gone to Uzbekistan at Voroshilov's request to
look into the Uzbek SSR Council of Ministers' decision to close the two *mazars*.

387. See I. A. Shalaev to Kh. G. Gulamov, 11 Nov. 1955; TsGAUz, f.2456,
o.1, d.174, ll.94-5.

388. S. Shamsutdinov, List of so-called 'holy places' in Bukhara Oblast' as of

SADUM was Sultan-baba in the Karakalpak ASSR, described by CARC's *upolnomochennyi* as 'a hotbed of religious prejudice', to which people came 'from far and wide',[389] so much so that a hotel was built there to accommodate pilgrims in the 1950s.[390]

Perhaps the most frequented of Uzbekistan's holy places was Shoh-i Zinda in Samarkand, the purported tomb of Muhammad's cousin, Qusam ibn Abbas, containing also several lavishly decorated fifteenth century mausolea and a Muslim cemetery. One Westerner, visiting the site in the Gorbachev period, witnessed how pilgrims from other parts of Uzbekistan 'almost invariably' touched the carved wooden screen in the tomb chamber of ibn Abbas and, 'much to the consternation of Intourist guides, who usher a steady stream of tourists past the tomb, frequently perform their prayers there'. The atheistic museum, which this and many other *mazars* had housed since the period of Khrushchev's anti-religious campaign, was by this time no longer in operation.[391]

In Southern Kazakhstan in the town of Turkestan the tomb of Ahmed Yasawi, the first great Turkic saint and mystic, was a centre of attraction not only for pilgrims from all over Kazakhstan, but also from other republics, especially Uzbekistan. Transferred to the jurisdiction of the Administration for Architecture in 1947, this large mausoleum underwent restoration as an architectural monument, and pilgrims were no longer allowed inside. But they continued coming to Turkestan, notably during the fast and on festivals. Local *khojas* succeeded in obtaining jobs at the mausoleum as caretakers, the Administration lacking the requisite permanent staff to appoint its own watchmen, and they enabled pilgrims to go in at night-time. Pilgrims from many oblasti of Kazakhstan and Uzbekistan were still coming here in the late 1960s.[392]

In the Caucasus, too, there were many *ziyarats* or *pirs*. In Dagestan, where almost no unregistered mosques were taken count of

---

1 Jan. 1969, undated; GARF, f.6991, o.6, d.173, l.18.

389. Minutes, All-Union conference of CARC *upolnomochennye*, 25-27 Nov. 1958; GARF, f.6991, o.3, d.165, l.106. For Sultan-baba, see also p.368 above.

390. Subtelny, 'The Cult of Holy Places', p.600.

391. *Ibid.*, pp.598-9.

392. I. V. Polianskii to P. V. Kovanov, 23 June 1955; B. Jumashev, Report, Conference of CARC's Central Asian *upolnomochennye*, Tashkent, 5-6 June 1959; and A. Barmenkov to the CPSU Central Committee, 23 May 1968 – GARF, f.6991, o.3, d.114, l.35, and d.186, ll.78-9, and o.6, d.147, l.24.

(reports spoke usually of no more than two), twenty-four of forty-four raiony had no registered mosque, and there were in the mid-1950s two registered and seventy unauthorised *ziyarats*, where people came with a variety of requests and problems, especially childless women. 10,000 pilgrims were said to come to these tombs during the course of a year. (This republic also had a host of 'false shaykhs, faith-healers and fortune-tellers'.)[393] In the Chechen-Ingush ASSR the return of the deportees in the late 1950s was accompanied by the re-opening and activisation of a large number of *ziyarats*, at some of which prayers would be held every week.[394] The most popular was probably the tomb of the mother of Kunta Haji, the founder of one of the most active and popular Sufi brotherhoods in the region. One of the very first reports from the republic related that pilgrims visited it every week in order to pray, the ceremony entailing collective incantation and stamping of feet.[395] Here, too, although the tomb was officially closed off by the local authorities in the early 1960s, pilgrimages continued; in 1962 'fanatics' broke the lock and no less than 500 pilgrims gathered to celebrate the Mavlud.[396] Every year in the month of May thousands of pilgrims came here not only from the Chechen-Ingush ASSR, but also from Dagestan, North Osetia and Georgia. In 1970, their number was reportedly about 10,000, and they came in a variety of vehicles, from tour buses to racing cars, and even a helicopter. (The appearance of pilgrims descending from the sky caused no little sensation.)[397]

In Azerbaijan there were a significant number of *pirs*. One report in the latter half of the 1950s spoke of 305, sixty-five of which were functioning ones and nineteen 'particularly active'.[398]

393. I. V. Polianskii, Information, undated (registered 21 Sept. 1954), and M. S. Gajiev, Report, Minutes, CARC session No.33, 26-27 Oct. 1960; GARF, f.6991, o.3, d.101, ll.107-14, and d.207, ll.35-6.
394. P. A. Zadorozhnyi to A. A. Puzin, 30 Aug. 1960, and A. L. Alisov to A. A. Puzin, 13 Jan. 1961; GARF, f.6991, o.3, d.207, l.56, and d.1605, ll.20-1.
395. A. Alisov to A. A. Puzin, 22 Jan. 1959; GARF, f.6991, o.3, d.596, l.1.
396. A. Alisov to A. A. Puzin, 15 Feb. 1963; GARF, f.6991, o.3, d.1607, l.27.
397. CRA, Information, sent to the CPSU Central Committee, 27 April 1971; TsKhSD, f.5, o.63, d.89, l.113. For detailed lists of holy places, most specifically, but not solely Sufi ones, in Dagestan, the Chechen-Ingush ASSR, Azerbaijan and Central Asia, see Bennigsen and Wimbush, *Mystics and Commissars*, Appendix A.
398. Minutes, All-Union conference of CARC *upolnomochennye*, 25-27 Nov. 1958; GARF, f.6991, o.3, d.165, l.89.

In 1970, the twenty-two 'better known' ones, three of them in the Nakhichevan ASSR, were said to be attracting thousands of pilgrims on the days of mourning in the month of Muharram. Another 300 *pirs* were also still operating on a minor scale. Sacrifices were brought and the believers would chant religious songs, at the peak of which they would inflict on themselves the traditional self-torture. The most important *pir* in Azerbaijan was Goy-imam, which in 1970 attracted no less than 40,000 pilgrims.[399]

Not all places of pilgrimage were old and established ones. Some dated from the Soviet period, even from the years under study. For instance tombs of certain leaders of the Qurbashi, or Basmachi, who fought the Soviet regime in the 1920s and 1930s became *mazars*.[400] In the Chechen-Ingush ASSR two *ziyarats* were erected in the 1950s, one of them at the beginning of the decade, the other towards its close, with the return of the deportees, and a third in the early 1970s.[401] In Dagestan, too, where most of the *ziyarats* were periodically closed down, attempts were made to open new ones, including one at the tomb of a Naqshbandi *murshid*, who had perished in a Soviet prison forty years before.[402] In the Karakalpak ASSR a *mazar* was established in 1953 in memory of an *ishan* who was arrested in the late Stalin years and died in prison two years previously.[403] And in Turkmenistan a structure which served as a mosque was erected near the tomb of the spiritual leader of the Tekke tribe's resistance to the Russians at Geok-Tepe fortress, whose population was massacred in 1881 at the culmination of the last large-scale effort to oppose the Russian

399. CRA, Information, sent to the CPSU Central Committee, 27 April 1971; TsKhSD, f.5, o.63, d.89, ll.111-12. For Goy-imam, which in the 1950s drew a similar number of pilgrims, see pp.123-4.

400. For instance a *mazar* in Tajikistan's Hissar Raion – Minutes, CARC session No.4, 25-26 Feb. 1959. Another tomb, also in Tajikistan, which was declared a holy place, was that of an *ishan* who died in 1942 – M. Kh. Hamidov to A. A. Puzin, 22 Oct. 1963; GARF, f.6991, o.3, d.183, l.70, and d.1739, l.102. For the Qurbashi, see also p.388.

401. P. Zadorozhnyi to A. Puzin, 30 Aug. 1960, and A. Asaulka to R. V. Vahaev, 10 Nov. 1971; GARF, f.6991, o.3, d.207, l.52, and o.6, d.370, l.137.

402. CRA, Information, sent to the CPSU Central Committee, 27 April 1971; TsKhSD, f.5, o.63, d.89, l.113. The document describes the *murshid* as 'a former kulak'.

403. Reception by K. Tagirov and A. Tiazetdinov of Idris Rahmatulla, 3 Oct. 1958; GARF, f.6991, o.4, d.88, l.211. For the ishan, see pp.399 and 404.

conquest of Turkestan.[404] These were undisputably actions of political content, intended to identify active opponents of the Russians and the Soviet regime as Islamic holy men. Yet, not all shrines initiated in this period were of this nature.[405] Here and there a miracle might be declared, or water discovered which was claimed to possess special healing qualities, and the site would open to pilgrims. In 1960, for instance, in a village in the Kabardino-Balkar ASSR a woman reported that Allah had appeared to her and informed her that a certain source of water had such traits, and hundreds of pilgrims began coming from all over the republic and even from Stavropol' and Kuban' to drink it and bathe in it. The local kolkhoz chairman sent a bulldozer to cover up the source, but believers dug up three new wells.[406]

The regime sought to curb, with an eye to eventually terminating, activity at 'so-called holy places' throughout the period under discussion. The republican governments addressed themselves to this problem several times – with but limited success – prior to the CPSU Central Committee resolution of November 1958.[407] Local

404. See *Turkmenskaia iskra*, 9 Jan. and 1 Sept. 1982.

405. For the tomb of an *ishan* who died in the Brezhnev years, which immediately became a place of pilgrimage, see p.401.

406. L. Zh. Aisov to A. A. Puzin, 17 Jan. 1961. A geyser discovered in Southern Kazakhstan in 1951 was similarly declared holy by the local inhabitants and pilgrimages to the site began forthwith – L. A. Prikhod'ko, Report, 2 June 1952; GARF, f.6991, o.3, d.1605, l.3, and d.81, l.36.

407. Nearly a decade previously towards the end of the 1940s the Uzbek SSR Council of Ministers required *oblispolkoms* to take steps to terminate activity at *mazars* and a number were indeed shut down. Yet, in at least three oblasti considerable numbers of shrines continued operating – I. V. Polianskii to K. E. Voroshilov, 27 May 1950; GARF, f.6991, o.3, d.68, l.42. This decision was quite apart from its specific resolution regarding the two abovementioned mausolea of Baha ad-Din and Shoh-i Mardon. Some of the more important *mazars* were transferred to the Administration for Architecture. As in the case of the mausoleum of Ahmed Yasawi – see above – this did not, however, terminate pilgrimages; one instance was recorded in Khorezm Oblast' where the Administration's watchman at a *mazar* substituted for a shaykh and received donations from pilgrims – Minutes, conference of Uzbekistan's *upolnomochennye*, 9 Aug. 1948; TsGAUz, f.2456, o.1, d.120, l.9. Descriptions of some of the more exasperating instances of healing at *mazars* were sent directly to the highest authorities well before the 1958 decree, for example, I. V. Polianskii to the CPSU Central Committee and USSR Council of Ministers, 13 Sept. 1955 (GARF, f.6991, o.3, d.114, ll.139-41) on the treatment of psychiatric illnesses at a *mazar* in Khorezm Oblast'. For the 1958 decree, see p.43.

officials had shown resourcefulness in obstructing pilgrimages.[408]
The head of CARC's Department for Eastern Religions, L. A.
Prikhod'ko, insisted in 1959 that an 'administrative' approach would
necessarily be counter-productive, that it was out of the question
to proceed to an indiscriminate closure of *mazars*. Those which
were just of local significance could be dealt with easily, as shown
by what had been achieved over the past ten years in Central
Asia, where a considerable number of *mazars* had already been
eliminated: in Namangan, for instance, on the site of one *mazar*
a clinic had been built, at another a school, at a third a residential
building, and so on, and the *mazars* had been forgotten. However,
shutting down the others, those with a broader, sometimes a
country-wide, importance, required protracted preparation, if they
were to be closed not merely on paper but once and for all; not
to speak of the risks involved in closures in Dagestan, where the
shaykhs and *murids* might foment actual opposition to such measures.
Prikhod'ko suggested trying to use the authority of certain unregistered clergy to disclose the deceitful activity going on at *mazars*.
He also proposed terminating burials at cemeteries at which holy
tombs were situated and opening up new burial grounds, where
the erection of new *mazars* would not be permitted.[409]
    In similar vein, the CARC *upolnomochennyi* for Kirgiziia expressed
his doubts as to the chances of success in the struggle against the
holy places. How, he asked, was the Takht-i Sulayman to be
closed, for it was merely a crag? Or again, he pointed out, militia
posts had been set up at one *mazar*, located just 2 km from the
border with Uzbekistan, and those going there had been turned
back, but they found other routes and performed the pilgrimage
nonetheless. He, too, emphasised that it was not possible to achieve
anything by resorting to administrative measures.[410]
    A variety of methods were in fact resorted to in order to attain
the cessation of pilgrimages to holy places. In the first place atheistic
propaganda focused on this particular aspect of 'obscurantism'.
Both the media and literature dwelt on the harm brought upon
society by the cult of holy places, which, it was maintained, not

408. For one such example, see p.667.
409. L. A. Prikhod'ko, Minutes, CARC session No.4, 25-26 Feb. 1959; GARF,
f.6991, o.3, d.183, ll.104-7.
410. H. A. Akhtiamov, Address, All-Union conference of CARC *upolnomochennye*, 25-27 Nov. 1958; GARF, f.6991, o.3, d.165, ll.50-1.

only perpetuated ignorance and superstition among the 'more backward' sectors of the population, but also encouraged parasitism and deceitful practices.[411] A plethora of lectures were given by scientists to disprove the authenticity of the sites themselves and of the stories and wonders ascribed to them. Registered clergy were mobilised to testify that the visitation of tombs had been introduced into Islam, not so that the living could obtain help from Allah with the help of the dead, but so that they might pray for the souls of the deceased.[412] Many *mazars* became the location of sanatoria and rest resorts, especially those situated in scenic spots or places renowned for their climate. Often, however, people found ways to continue making pilgrimages, coming, as it were, to take a cure and bringing their donations to the custodians or watchmen at these new institutions.[413] Sometimes, too, when a *mazar* was fenced off, pilgrims came to pray nearby.[414]

In the first period after the November 1958 decree most *mazars* were officially closed and access to them denied. One *upolnomochennyi* announced at a conference in spring 1960 that all fourteen *mazars* in his oblast' had been shut 'once and for all' and pilgrimages to them terminated.[415] In Dagestan, too, all seventy *ziyarats* had been closed down and pilgrimage to them 'almost terminated', although in a few places individual and group pilgrimage continued.[416] In Leninabad Oblast' many of the sixty *mazars* which had been exposed were closed in 1960, some of the older ones being transformed into local museums or handed over to the

411. See, for example, Kuliev, *Antinauchnaia sushchnost' islama i zadachi ateisticheskogo vospitaniia*, pp.106-11.

412. Minutes, Conference of CARC *upolnomochennye*, 5-6 June 1959; GARF, f.6991, o.3, d.186, l.39.

413. See, for example, M. Kh. Hamidov to A. A. Puzin, 22 Oct. 1963; GARF, f.6991, o.3, d.1739, ll.100-3. At one such place itinerant mullas 'received' 200-250 pilgrims every day from among 'the unorganised holiday-makers'. At another, the CARC *upolnomochennyi*, who visited the spot in the summer with one of SADUM's representatives and officials from Znanie and the KGB, found over 1,000 pilgrims (the day chosen was not a major festival). See also n.407 above.

414. This happened, for instance, in Ul'ianovsk Oblast' – Minutes, CARC session no.21, 22 July 1959; GARF, f.6991, o.3, d.184, ll.180-1.

415. Sh. O. Ospanov, Address, All-Union conference of CARC *upolnomochennye*, 18-20 April 1960; GARF, f.6991, o.3, d.208, l.120.

416. M. S. Gajiev, Report, CARC session No.33, 26-27 Oct. 1960; GARF, f.6991, o.3, d.207, l.39.

relevant administration for architectural monuments, although certain shaykhs persisted in their activity in the proximity of a few of them. In other instances public opinion had to be prepared before closure could be implemented.[417] There were instances where, as in the case of registered mosques, decisions were taken at presumably orchestrated meetings of 'village toilers' to request the closure of a nearby shrine.[418]

Over time, however, it became clear that this achievement of closing *mazars*, like so many other successes in the realm of the Soviet regime's policy toward religion, was temporary and even more partial than had at first appeared. Shrines given over to local sovkhozy or kolkhozy were often not put to use and continued to serve pilgrims. The authority for the preservation of cultural monuments, to which the major mausolea were transferred, sometimes sought to lease them out, but, in Bukhara Oblast' for example, demanded so high a rent that the transaction fell through and pilgrims persisted in visiting the sites and unofficial clergy in officiating there and performing all the customary rites.[419] In Kazakhstan the Administration of Architecture, which received jurisdiction over ten of the republic's twenty-three *mazars*, lacked the requisite permanent staff and gave the keys to shaykhs or khojas who lived in their vicinity and allowed pilgrims to go inside. By early 1962 CARC was reporting that verification in the field showed that nearly all of the seventeen *mazars* shut down in Kazakhstan were functioning and pilgrimages to them continuing.[420] A similar situation prevailed in Tajikistan, where the more popular *mazars* were again attracting large numbers of pilgrims.[421]

417. A. Azizbaev to A. A. Puzin, 10 Jan. 1961, and D. A. Ahmedov to A. A. Puzin, 21 Feb. 1961; GARF, f.6991, o.3, d.1737, ll.10 and 35.

418. M. S. Gajiev, Report, CARC session No.1, 7 Jan. 1964; GARF, f.6991, o.4, d.146, ll.9-10. For the 'mobilisation' of public opinion on behalf of mosque closures, see pp.211-2.

419. Sh. Shirinbaev, Information, sent to Deputy Head, Uzbekistan CP Department of Agitation and Propaganda K. G. Gulamov, 29 May 1961; TsGAUz, f.2456, o.1, d.290, ll.109-10.

420. B. Jumashev Lecture Conference of CARC *upolnomochennye*, Tashkent, 5 June 1959, and Information (unsigned), handed to A. I. Aleksandrov at the CPSU Central Committee, 14 Feb. 1962; GARF, f.6991, o.3, d.186, l.79, and d.1389, ll.11-12 and 14-15.

421. One mosque, in Regar, was said to have been visited by about 1,000 people weekly in 1962 – M. Kh. Hamidov to A. A. Puzin, 18 May 1963;

And in 1964, forty-nine holy places were reportedly operating in Uzbekistan.[422]

In other words, visitation of *mazars*, especially on festivals, persisted, constituting a massive demonstration of protest against regime policy, which was undoubtedly known to all and sundry. Pilgrims, moreover, were often brought there by public and state transport: reports to this effect reached Moscow from Turkmenistan and the oblasti of Samarkand and Osh. At Goy-imam in Azerbaijan the train made an unscheduled five-minute stop on Ashura for the convenience of pilgrims, while most of the 646 vehicles which brought pilgrims to the *pir* belonged to state enterprises and institutions and kolkhozy.[423]

At the end of the 1960s the CRA was still perturbed by and preoccupied with the re-opening of *mazars*. Hundreds of thousands of Muslims still made pilgrimages every year to over 300 illegally operating shrines.[424] Many of these places were in the mountains or other picturesque places and became the sites for collective holidays, which would be accompanied by the bringing of sacrifices and donations and the recital of prayers.[425] Sometimes 'itinerant shaykhs' settled in their vicinity and would invite believers who came there to their homes, where they conducted the requisite ritual. The CRA *upolnomochennyi* who reported such an instance, at a *mazar* in Tashkent Oblast', which attracted pilgrims from the other Central Asian republics as well as from all over Uzbekistan, mentioned no less than eight shaykhs who would stand at the bus-stop near the gates of the *mazar* and approach visitors. He commented that this was a 'new form of the clergy's adaptability to contemporary circumstances'.[426] At some *mazars*, the custodians placed there by the relevant authority for the preservation of cultural

GARF, f.6991, o.3, d.1739, l.64.

422. Minutes, CARC session No.24, 27 Aug. 1964; GARF, f.6991, o.4, d.147, l.89.

423. A. Barmenkov to the CPSU Central Committee, 23 May 1968; GARF, f.6991, o.6, d.147, l.25.

424. Theses of lecture, 'The situation of the Muslim faith in the country and measures to strengthen control of observance of legislation on religion', sent to the CPSU Central Committee Propaganda Department, 19 June 1968; GARF, f.6991, o.6, d.147, ll.42 and 45.

425. Saidbaev, *Islam i obshchestvo*, p.234.

426. Iu. Bilialov, Information, undated (apparently Dec. 1968 or early 1969); GARF, f.6991, o.6, d.173, l.73.

monuments actually organised pilgrimages.[427] In this period ten *mazars* were known to be operative in Bukhara Oblast' and another twenty in Samarkand Oblast' – seven of the former and two of the latter appeared in lists of unregistered religious societies.[428]

Altogether, at the turn of the decade, pilgrimages were known to be conducted regularly, especially but not solely on festivals and during Muharram, to no less than 198 holy places, nearly one half (ninety-five) of which were in Uzbekistan. There were instances when people who had occupied responsible posts in the local apparatus held sway at these *mazars*: at one place in the Karakalpak ASSR these included a former lecturer and kolkhoz chairman, and the current *sel'sovet* chairman 'colluded' with them. At another, in Azerbaijan, which the local *raiispolkom* several times reported to be closed, the administrative organs conducted successive raids, each time confiscating samovars, hides, pitchers, pots and other items.[429] In 1973 over forty holy places in Azerbaijan, which were officially preserved under the auspices of the state as cultural monuments, were still in use as holy places where 'self-styled mullas' operated.[430] The Turkmen SSR Council of Ministers showed its concern in the early 1970s at the large number of *mazars* still drawing pilgrims, particularly women with children of school and pre-school age. Among other reservations, it contended that conditions at these sites were unsanitary and that, rather than healing people, they were likely to be the source of contagion.[431] Believers in Dagestan were also still conducting pilgrimages to holy sites both within the republic and beyond its confines (Shiites presumably going to Azerbaijan, Sufis to the Chechen-Ingush ASSR).[432] In the Nakhichevan ASSR prayer-

427. A. Barmenkov to the CPSU Central Committee Propaganda Department, 5 Feb. 1969; GARF, f.6991, o.6, d.215, l.6.

428. S. Shamsutdinov and T. Tashkenbaev, Lists of so-called 'holy places' in Bukhara and Samarkand oblasti respectively as of 1 Jan. 1969, undated; GARF, f.6991, o.6, d.173, ll.18-20 and 47-9.

429. CRA, Information, sent to the CPSU Central Committee, 22 May 1970; TsKhSD, f.5, o.62, d.38, ll.11-12.

430. List, apparently attached to A. Galiev, Information, 30 May 1973; GARF, f.6991, o.6, d.537, ll.193-5.

431. Turkmen SSR Council of Ministers Deputy Chairman M. Mollaeva to *oblispolkom* chairmen and chairmen of *gor-* and *rai-ispolkoms* which were subordinate to the republican authorities, 17 Sept. 1971; GARF, f.6991, o.6, d.370, ll.57-60.

432. Kh. Salahetdinov and I. Mikhalev, Report, handed to E. I. Lisavtsev, 26

services were conducted regularly at a number of holy places, the deputy chairman of the KGB expressing the opinion that the 'evil of religion' emanated from them and that very often they were the centre of religious life.[433]

Nor did the situation change. If anything, it showed signs of returning gradually to the *status quo ante*. Toward the end of the period under discussion, less than two years before Gorbachev's appointment as General-Secretary, over 230 Muslim holy places were operating, still reportedly drawing hundreds of thousands of believers annually.[434] The CRA maintained that over fifty functioned just in Tajikistan and were visited by women and children, thus promoting the reproduction of superstitions among new generations, although the Tajikistan Communist Party insisted that pilgrimage to thirty-four of these had been stopped.[435] Altogether a wide variety of ways were found by believers to circumvent restrictions placed by the central and local authorities on their visitation of holy places. Often some sort of 'screen' concealed the real substance of a *mazar*, or even of an unregistered mosque. Many *mazars* had outside awnings, where in summertime prayers would be conducted, further concealed by the high thick walls that separate cemeteries from the outside world in many towns and villages. Often too the *mazar* would be made to look neglected so that it would be taken to be non-functioning.[436]

Nor was it only in relation to *mazars* that the believers seemed to have the upper hand. CARC and the CRA aspired to find a compromise, which would enable the registration of some of the larger and more permanent religious associations and some of the more moderate and flexible clergy in order the more effectively to terminate the activity of the multitudinous unregistered mosques and groups and to undercut the influence of the more 'fanatic'

Oct. 1971; GARF, f.6991, o.6, d.361, l.107.

433. I. Bonchkovskii to E. I. Lisavtsev, 1 June 1973; GARF, f.6991, o.6, d.537, ll.171-2.

434. CRA, Memo, 2 June 1983; TsKhSD, f.5, o.89, d.82, l.37.

435. V. A. Kuroedov to the CPSU Central Committee, 16 Sept. 1983, and Tajikistan CP Secretary G. Bobosadykova, Information, 11 Oct. 1983; TsKhSD, f.5, o.89, d.82, ll.61 and 68.

436. Poliakov, *Everyday Islam*, pp.102-3 and 109.

clergy. But this line did not find any resonance in the localities, where the organs of government continued systematically to conceal from their superiors the existence of illegally operating mosques and mullas and to ignore applications to register a few carefully selected religious groups. As a result of this dichotomy, the closure of illegally functioning groups by, for example, depriving them of their *chaikhona* mosques, simply led to the opening of new ones, while the ranks of unregistered mullas were filled with new generations of pensioners, some of them actually party members.[437] Moreover, believers were driven into the outstretched arms of 'rogues and rascals', and 'reactionary' clerics were encouraged to spread stories about the violation of believers' rights. Some unregistered mullas, together with their adherents, were by the early 1980s listening to broadcasts from the West, which, directed at this 'underground Islam', sought to inject into the Soviet Union 'the flame of an Islamic renaissance', implant among Soviet citizens a 'religious and nationalist mood', and exploit the thesis of the 'violation of the rights of Muslims' in the Soviet Union.[438]

The unviability of Soviet policy was probably nowhere more blatant than in the sphere of the activity of the unregistered mosques, groups and mullas. Many among these were in essence 'modernisers' who belonged by outlook, conduct and way of life to the category of their registered counterparts rather than to the more traditional or strictly orthodox Muslims who rejected registration out of principle.[439] Yet those who sought to become part of the establishment were thwarted by a host of obstacles. This left them with two basic options: some of them indeed chose to blend informally with registered religious societies, while others preferred to withdraw into the umbrage of their homes to pray and practise rites unobtrusively. But in many cases the frustration of the desire to register served rather to exacerbate dissatisfaction with the state

437. Cases of party members becoming men of religion occurred in both Azerbaijan and Kazakhstan – CRA memo, 2 June 1983; TsKhSD, f.5, o.89, d.82, ll.38-9.

438. V. A. Kuroedov to the CPSU Central Committee, 16 Sept. 1983; TsKhSD, f.5, o.89, d.82, l.62. The complexity of the attitude of local government is discussed in Chapter 11, the seeds of political discontent in Chapters 6 and 12.

439. Ashirov in one of his articles – 'Osobennosti ideologicheskoi i kul'tovoi deiatel'nosti musul'manskikh religioznykh organizatsii v sovremennykh usloviiakh', p.130 – pointed out that the traditional perception of the unregistered clergy in general as reactionary out of ideology was no longer correct.

of affairs and even to induce greater religious extremism. Those, on the other hand, who sought *a priori to* remain aloof, were often left to operate unperturbed, although this depended on the time period and the region. The pendulum swing of policy from relative laxity and readiness to meet some of the demands of the religious sector among the population to a greater stringency and even a measure of persecution, taught believers that in the latter periods they had basically to lie low until the situation improved once again, which it surely would. Considerable numbers in the Muslim areas were not ready to forego those few fundamentals of their faith to which they still clung, and when they agreed to yield under pressure, they clearly did so on the understanding that as soon as it might be possible they would resume their practices. True, rites were frequently performed in an over-simplified and sometimes even in erroneous form, and it is at best a moot point whether those who performed them were motivated mainly or solely by financial considerations, as the representatives of the Soviet regime suggested, or by more idealistic or social ones like the preservation of custom or belief. Be this as it may, the ubiquitous presence of people ready and able to perform rites, and the particular suitability of Islam to unofficial activity endowed the unregistered mosques, groups and clergy with a major role in enabling Islam to survive in however watered down a condition.

6

THE SUFI ORDERS AND THE SECTS

The registered clergy were basically controlled and supervised directly or obliquely by the Soviet regime, and they were oriented by definition towards identifying with the Soviet state. The unregistered clergy were in essence of a different category: they did not acknowledge any authority which might legitimately regulate their religious activity. Nor in fact were they generally recognised by the state. At the same time, the unregistered clergy were not on the whole actively antagonistic to the system, many of them actually seeking to co-exist, sometimes even to merge, with it. Yet there were among them some devotees – the more extremist offshoot, as it were, of 'parallel Islam' – who tended to be hostile. (This antagonism was not necessarily the consequence of an *a priori* position. It seems often to have been the result of the persecution to which they were subjected.)

Central Asia and the Northern Caucasus had both had long traditions of non-conformist Islam. In the former region the Muslim establishment had worked hand in glove with the rulers of the three khanates prior to the Russian conquest and subsequently.[1] It had, however, at least in certain periods, been offset by an opposition current, whose focus had been the Sufi *tariqas* (or orders). While these had not embarked on an openly confrontational course *vis-à-vis* the secular leadership, preferring rather a *modus vivendi* with it, the relationship between the two parties was often far from friendly. The most important *tariqas* in the Russian Empire after its conquest of the Caucasus and Central Asia, were the Naqshbandiyya and the Qadiriyya, the former actually native to

1. Originally, the area had boasted three khanates: Bukhara, Khiva and Kokand. As of 1848 the Khan of Bukhara adopted the title Emir. In 1876 the tsarist government abolished the Khanate of Kokand, incorporating its territory, as well as part of Bukhara and Khiva, in its Turkestan Krai. The Bukhara Emirate and the Khiva remained as distinct but dependent entities.

Central Asia.[2] Other orders, which require mentioning in the Central Asian context, are the Kubrawiyya, which had a strong following in Khorezm; the Yasawiyya, named after Ahmad Yasawi, whose stronghold was further north, in what was to become southern Kazakhstan; and the order of mendicant dervishes, the Qalandar, who lived on charity, and whose centre was in the Samarkand region.

The historic Sufi orders had over time been supplanted by a constantly multiplying number of splinter groups. By the early twentieth century, the link with the original orders was recognisable only with difficulty in Central Asia, traditional sufism having been superseded rather by 'ishanism', with each *ishan* of repute becoming the founder of a separate order. (The Sufi teacher or leader is called variously *ishan* or *ishon*, from the Persian plural meaning 'they', used as a term of respect; shaykh or *pir*, the Arabic and the Persian for elder or old man; *ustadh*, teacher; or *murshid*, guide.) In the Northern Caucasus the new sub-divisions of the older orders were known originally as *wirds*, each with its own leaders, adepts and rites.[3] The organisational framework of the Sufi orders, however, tended to be rather fluid and the distinction between *tariqa* and *wird* was often nebulous.[4]

In both the traditional orders and the new pattern, dervish shaykhs or *ishans* preached asceticism and abstinence, which, together with contemplation, were designed to bring man closer to God. In many respects their beliefs and practices were essentially animistic rather than Islamic in origin, tracing back to the rituals

2. The Qadiriyya, on the other hand, was imported from Baghdad, where it had been founded in the 12th century; the Naqshbandiyya had been founded in the 14th century. See Bennigsen and Wimbush, *Mystics and Commissars*. The Qadiriyya was important especially in the Fergana Valley. The *tariqa*, lit. the way or path, is conceived not as contradicting the injunctions of the Shari'a which are incumbent upon every Muslim, but as a narrower path, that of mystical education or experience, designed to lead the adept to attaining his goal, the perfect *tawhid*, 'the existential confession that God is One' – Schimmel, *Mystical Dimensions of Islam*, pp.98-9.

3. For Sufism in the Northern Caucasus, see Bennigsen, 'Muslim Conservative Opposition to the Soviet Regime: The Sufi Brotherhoods in the North Caucasus', and below. Strictly speaking, the *wird* is the 'special litany' given the adept by his *ustadh* (Schimmel, *Mystical Dimensions of Islam*, p.243); in this chapter I have used the term to describe the sub-divisions of the *tariqas*, each of the latter being in fact distinguished by some minor differences in prayer ritual.

4. I am grateful for this information to Moshe Gammer.

of ancient local cults.[5] They were traditionally popular preachers, faith healers, dispensers of amulets and talismans, and custodians of holy shrines. The *ishan*, who headed the Sufi community, received the right of mentorship by either descent or the blessing of his own mentor (*ustadh* or *murshid*). Everyone entering an order became an adept, a *murid*, renouncing his own free will and undertaking to keep no secrets from his mentor, to whom he also gave part of his income.[6] 'Throughout his life (even if he is only a "lay brother")', to quote two Western scholars, 'he must follow a complicated and compulsory spiritual rule in which permanent prayers, invocations and litanies [the *zikr*], accompanied by peculiar breathing and physical movements, play an important part and prepare the adept for a state of intense mental concentration'.[7] (The *zikr* might be either loud or silent depending on the *tariqa* and its origins.) The *zikr*, which 'takes place regularly at least once a week, and also at special occasions (births, marriages, funerals, etc.) is the central element in Sufi ritual'.[8]

Soviet Islam then, was principally conventional and fitted into the rubric of either establishment, in the form of the registered religious societies, or the new Soviet phenomenon of the unregistered groups, which were on the whole neither establishment nor opposition. Yet, in Central Asia and the Northern Caucasus there were throughout the Soviet period elements which the regime excluded a priori from the Islam it recognised and, at least post

5. For the connection between Sufism and shamanism in Central Asia, notably the common perception of the possibility of intercourse through ecstasy with the supranatural world, see Basilov, *Kul't sviatykh v islame*, pp.92-3. According to Basilov, who, in conformity with Soviet tradition, sought to demonstrate that many of the customs and beliefs which characterised the Soviet Muslim community were not in fact Islamic in origin, the very idea of the sanctity of various *khojas*, shaykhs and *ishans* was adopted by Islam from shamanism – *ibid.*, p.118. This thesis is not borne out by the history of Sufism in other parts of the Muslim world where shamanism had never existed, although inevitably local cultures and custom influenced the way Islam developed.

6. Originally, the *murid* intended to become a mystic himself, or even a *murshid*, but in modern, certainly in Soviet, usage the term refers to any follower of an *ishan*, shaykh or *murshid* who accepted his authority and his role as mediator between himself and God.

7. Bennigsen and Lemercier-Quelquejay, 'Muslim Religious Conservatism and Dissent in the USSR', p.155.

8. Bennigsen and Lemercier-Quelquejay, 'Islam in the Soviet Muslim Republics', p.148.

factum, legitimised and consequently defined as opposition, with all that this implied in the Soviet Union. (On occasion an establishment religious figure might even be suspected or actually accused of having *murids*; but this was a way of casting aspersions on his religious and also, by implication, his political correctness, and is not necessarily to be taken at face value.[9])

The reason for this perception – on both sides – of Sufism and its offshoots as opposition was partly historical and partly institutional. In both areas under discussion the *tariqas* and the type of religion they represented, generally described in Soviet literature as 'ishanism' or 'muridism', were associated with armed resistance not only to Russian Imperial rule, but also to the incipient Soviet regime. Sufi leaders had stood at the forefront of armed opposition first to the tsars and then to their successors. A Naqshbandi *ishan* had led the 1898 uprising in Andijan (probably the most violent revolt against Russian rule before that of 1916). And after 1917 Sufi figures played a prominent role in Central Asia in the uprising of the Qurbashi or, as they are more widely known, Basmachi,[10] and in the *gazavat* (holy war) conducted by the Chechen and Ingush *abreks*, or bandits of honour, in the Northern Caucasus.[11]

9. The CARC *upolnomochennyi* for the Bashkir ASSR, M. Sh. Karimov, for instance, claimed that DUMES Mufti Rasulev had his own *murids* or pupils, a charge which the latter denied categorically. A few people, he admitted, had approached him, desirous of becoming his pupils or adepts, but he had turned them down and would continue doing so in the future, for, as mufti, he could not permit this – Minutes, CARC session No.27, 28-29 Oct. 1949, and Reception by I. V. Polianskii of Rasulev, 3 Dec. 1949; GARF, f.6991, o.3, d.60, l.112, and d.8, ll.203-4. See also p.250 for a suspicion which seemed to be more well-founded.

10. For the Basmachi movement, see Fraser, 'Basmachi'.

11. This uprising was in the tradition of the previous century and a half, since the rebellion of the Chechen Shaykh Mansur Ushurma against Russian colonialism in the 1780s and the prolonged struggle against Russia of Shamil in the mid-19th century. For the 18th and 19th-century, rebellions against the Russians, see Zelkina, 'Islam and Politics in the North Caucasus', pp.115-18; for the post-1917 uprisings in the Northern Caucasus – the main one in 1920-21 and local ones in the following two decades, see Bennigsen, 'Muslim Guerilla Warfare in the Caucasus (1918-1928)', Avtorkhanov, 'The Chechens and the Ingush during the Soviet Period and its Antecedents', pp.157-84, and Zelkina, pp.118-19. One Western commentator summed it up: 'In the long run the war [of 1920-1] left a long heritage of anti-Russian xenophobia. From 1922 to 1943, the history of Chechnia and Daghestan was an almost uninterrupted succession of rebellions, counter-expeditions and 'political banditism'', of which the deportations of early 1944 were the outcome – Bennigsen-Broxup, 'The Last Ghazawat', p.143.

At the same time, on the institutional level, the discipline and hierarchical structure of the *tariqas*, which were implicit in their very essence and basic perceptions, seemed to pose a current threat. True, as one Soviet expert pointed out, it was strictly speaking, from the purely doctrinal point of view, a misnomer to designate the Sufi orders as sects, for they were primarily, certainly in the Northern Caucasus, Sunnis of the Shafi'i and Hanafi schools.[12] Nonetheless, given the fact that the *tariqas* were closed societies into which the adept was accepted after a ritual of initiation and remained under the control of his master, his *murshid* or *ustadh,* and that a similar fealty was required of the adherents of the *ishan,*[13] the new 'muridism' and 'ishanism' were looked upon by the Soviet authorities as 'sectarianism', just as the Sufi orders had been by the tsarist administration, with the attendant socio-political connotations.[14]

The Soviet government apparatus was particularly concerned by the existence and surfacing in the years following World War II of the 'extreme mystic manifestations of Islam' namely 'Sufism, dervishism and ishanism'. For the members of the orders belonging to this trend 'led a parasitical way of life, performed public mysteries and ecstasies, which stirred up fanaticism, as well as religious dances, and adhered persistently to the idea of the *gazavat*, the war against "infidels"'.[15] The *ishans* were reputedly the most extreme element within the Muslim clergy in their antagonism to the regime, many of them engaging in 'anti-Soviet activity'.[16] In the immediate postwar period, CARC at least seems to have believed that most of the differences within Islam could be smoothed over. In a memorandum of late 1946 CARC Chairman Polianskii wrote

Avtorkhanov gives a detailed description of the backdrop to the deportations.

12. Klimovich, 'Bor'ba ortodoksov i modernistov v islame', pp.66-7.

13. Bennigsen and Lemercier-Quelquejay qualify this by saying that the *tariqas* are not truly clandestine, in that the adepts do not hide their affiliation to them –'Islam in the Soviet Muslim Republics', p.147.

14. I. V. Polianskii, Address, Conference of CARC *upolnomochennye*, 11 [June] 1946; GARF, f.6991, o.3, d.39, l.70. For the attitude to sectarianism, see pp. 47 and 48.

15. I. V. Polianskii to K. E. Voroshilov, 26 March 1947; GARF, f.6991, o.3, d.47, ll.113-14.

16. CARC report, sent to G. M. Malenkov, M. A. Suslov, V. S. Abakumov and the Council of Ministers presidium, 30 June 1951; GARF, f.6991, o.3, d.76, l.102.

that the various trends in Islam had developed as a result of 'socio-political' circumstances and had over time acquired 'the traits of tribal and national religions', but with the transformations which had taken place in the relations among the Muslim peoples following the October Revolution, the concomitant antagonisms were abating. The one jarring note was the 'revival of muridism and dervishism', which was occurring outside the orbit of the spiritual directorates.[17]

From early on in the postwar period CARC's *upolnomochennye* were instructed to gather information about the existence and activity of *ishans* not only in Central Asia or Dagestan.[18] Some instances were exposed in Central Asia and in Armenia, but none – two years after the deportations – among the mountain peoples in the Northern Caucasus, the area where muridism had been 'most widespread',[19] except for a small group of women in a village in the Kabardinian ASSR who gathered to chant the *zikr* through the night.[20] The *zikrs* performed in some areas of the Caucasus, however, were not always connected with Sufi activity. In just one year in the latter half of the 1960s, for example, over 250 *zikrs* were reported to have been performed in Azerbaijan. These occurred not in Sufi prayer-services, but in the registered mosques, apparently in Northern Azerbaijan, where Muslims were Sunni and belonged to Dagestani ethnic groups, mostly Avars and Lezgin. They performed *zikrs* in memory of a deceased person or for a host of other individual occasions, from the blessing of a new house to a prayer for a son leaving for military service.[21]

17. I. V. Polianskii, Memorandum. 11 Nov. 1946 and Polianskii to K. E. Voroshilov, 13 Nov. 1946; GARF, f.6991, o.3, d.34, ll.198 and 202.

18. For example, I. V. Polianskii to a number of specified *upolnomochennye*, 13 Feb. 1954; GARF, f.6991, o.3, d.104, l.11. The letter was provoked by reports from the *upolnomochennyi* for the Tatar ASSR of the activity of an *ishan* in a village in Kuibyshev Oblast' who was attracting *murids* from his republic – see p.403 below.

19. I. V. Polianskii to K. E. Voroshilov, 26 March 1947; GARF, f.6991, o.3, d.47, l.114.

20. Geshov, Report, Conference of CARC *upolnomochennye*, 14 June 1946; GARF, f.6991, o.3, d.38, ll.178-9. Traditionally female religious figures, *otyns*, played a role in *zikr* ceremonies conducted by women Sufis in Central Asia as well – Fathi, '*Otines*: the unknown women clerics of Central Asian Islam', p.31.

21. M. Shamsadinskii to the CRA, 20 Jan. 1967; GARF, f.6991, o.6, d.21, l.4; Saroyan, *Reconstructing Community*, pp.253-4.

In some places in Dagestan as well a form of *zikr* was observed by CRA officials in the 1970s that was performed not by Sufi groups but in the registered mosques.[22]

Statistical data for the non-conformist elements, who were neither regular Sunnis nor Shiites, seem not to have been composed at all. The sole exceptions relate to the Ismaili sect in the Gorno-Badakhshan AO in the Pamirs, and to the Chechen and Ingush following their return to their national territory in the late 1950s, the only two instances in which the major indigenous population ascribed to 'sectarian' groups. Any precise information on the activity of the *tariqas* as a whole and individual *ishans* in particular was especially difficult to come by in light of the discipline that characterised them and the unmitigated allegiance of the *murids* to their mentors.[23] Their impact and weight can, however, be gauged from the interest they evoked and the description of their activities.

The picture is further obfuscated by the fact that in some sources the term *ishan* is used very loosely, as an apparent solecism for itinerant mullas in general, not necessarily for those with a Sufi orientation. In the words of one Western analyst, ishanism 'is sometimes used to describe Central Asian Sufism in general, as distinct from other forms of Sufism', sometimes for the 'largely autonomous, local networks of mystics whose activities were mainly associated with "popular" (i.e. folk, lay) religion', in contrast to the major orders (the Naqshbandi, Yasawi, Kubrawi or Qadiri). In addition, *ishan* 'has traditionally been used in Central Asia as an honorific for any revered religious teacher'.[24]

22. One report spoke of 941 *zikrs* which had taken place – GARF, f.6991, o.6, d.558, l.27. Two representatives of the CRA who visited Dagestan wrote that after the *jum'a-namaz* in the mosque, some 100 old men sat on rugs, recited the formula 'There is no God other than Allah', inclining by turn once to the right, once to the left – Kh. Salahetdinov and I. Mikhalev, Report, 26 Oct. 1971; GARF, f.6991, o.6, d.361, l.106. In another instance, which was reported to the CRA, a qazi of a registered mosque performed the duties of qazi in a second mosque as well, where he conducted the *mavlud* and *zikr* – M. S. Gajiev to A. A. Nurullaev, 27 July 1973; GARF, f.6991, o.6, d.629, l.165. For the *zikr*, as performed by the *tariqas* in the Chechen-Ingush ASSR, see below.

23. It is not impossible that some such information exists in the KGB archives, but, as has been noted, as of the time of writing, these have not been made accessible to the external researcher.

24. Akiner, 'Islam, the State and Ethnicity in Central Asia in Historical Perspective', p.95.

The confusion is evident in a report by Polianskii in which he pointed out that some itinerant mullas, taking advantage of the deep roots of ishanism in Central Asia, resolved to enhance their influence by declaring themselves *ishans* and enlisting *murids*.[25] Similarly, the CARC *upolnomochennyi* for the Uzbek SSR spoke of itinerant mullas and *ishans* who travelled around kishlaks and kolkhozy 'propagating and popularising religion', contending that all Muslims – men, women and children – were duty bound to fulfil religious rites as laid down in the Shari'a and Qur'an.[26] And the *upolnomochennyi* for Khorezm Oblast' enumerated together the mullas, shaykhs and *ishans* in some raiony in his bailiwick.[27] Shaykhs at *mazars* who were dubbed *ishans* were also often in fact probably not Sufi *ishans*, not a few sources speaking very generally of itinerant mullas, faith-healers, shaykhs and *ishans* operating at holy places.[28] It is not impossible that the jumble was intentional, or at least partly so, in order to discredit all mosqueless mullas by associating them with Sufism. Liutsian Klimovich, the doyen of Soviet atheist propagandists in the field of Islam, thus wrote in the mid-1970s that in Islam,

> [....] both Sunni and Shi'a, there exist two opposite trends: the official 'mosque' trend...and the unofficial, 'non-mosque' trend, led by *ishans*, *pirs*, shaykhs and *ustadhs*.[...]Everywhere the clergy of the 'non-mosque' trend are many times more numerous.[...]In some extensive areas – for instance in the Northern Caucasus and in particular in the Chechen-Ingush ASSR – almost all clergy belong to *murid*-dervish communities.[29]

Be all this as it may, it was indisputable that Sufism made an indelible mark on the development of Islam in both Central Asia

25. I. V. Polianskii to K. E. Voroshilov, 27 May 1950; GARF, f.6991, o.3, d.68, l.42.

26. Minutes, Instructional conference of CARC's *upolnomochennye* in the oblasti of the Uzbek SSR, 17-18 July 1951; TsGAUz, f.2456, o.1, d.134, l.65.

27. Quoted in K. F. Tagirov, Information, 1 March 1957; GARF, f.6991, o.3, d.132, l.57.

28. For example, the Turkmen SSR Council of Ministers chairman wrote to CARC in 1947 about *mazars* in that republic, at which wandering mullas, shaykhs and *ishans* operated – Minutes, CARC session No.13, 10-11 July 1947; GARF, f.6991, o.4, d.19, l.429. One doubts whether he or those who reported to that body were pedantic in their choice of terminology. See also below.

29. L. Klimovich, 'Bor'ba ortodoksov i modernistov v islame', pp.66-7.

and the Northern Caucasus. As a result, the local brand of Sunni Islam countenanced phenomena, which were generally not associated with it, and the dividing lines between Sufism and legal orthodoxy became somewhat amorphous. It was thus essentially Sufi influence which validated two of the manifestations of non-establishment Islam discussed in the previous chapter that had become an intrinsic part of Islamic life in the two areas. One was the cult of holy men, whose tombs were thought to be blessed with *baraka*, grace, a doctrine not consistent with the teachings of the Qur'an, but pleasing to a popular audience looking for magical mediation between man and God.[30] The other was the idea of women religious figures, similarly unaccepted in traditional orthodox Islam, many orders offering women a religious sphere of activity. Women could be enrolled as associates or even as leaders to organise women's circles, some even becoming dervishes.[31]

Central Asian 'ishanism'

The *ishans* in Central Asia were an inalienable part of the local social structure and they and their followers became part of an unofficial underground Islam following the outlawing of the *tariqas* and the mass persecution of the clergy as a class in the late 1920s and the 1930s. Traditionally they had enjoyed considerable political power – in the past every locality in the sedentary parts of Central Asia had had its own *pir*, spiritual leader or holy person, or *khalifa* (successor), the scion of a dynasty of *pirs*, who were supposedly endowed with the ability to perform miracles.[32] This power, however, had been largely usurped by the *ulema* who had become the mainstay of the regimes of the Bukharan emirs and the Khivan khans in the decades prior to 1917, although in the late nineteenth and early twentieth century the Sufis had tended to join hands with the religious establishment in opposing the jadidist trend,

30. Kefeli, 'Constructing an Islamic Identity', p.277.

31. Trimingham, *The Sufi Orders in Islam*, p.232; also Schimmel, *Mystical Dimensions of Islam*, pp. 426 and 432. For the worship of holy shrines – *mazars* or *pirs* – and the incidence of women religious figures, see pp.363-82 and 342-4 respectively.

32. Abashin, 'Sotsial'nye korni sredneaziatskogo islamizma', p.457. Indeed, each individual Muslim, certainly in the rural parts, had his own *pir*, in addition to the person who performed family and economic rites in the locality.

which had sought to adapt Islam to contemporary and changing conditions.[33] Yet, despite their loss of political status, the *ishans* continued, due to the clan and local ties which were the lifeblood of the region, to enjoy a special, privileged position. This gave them a degree of protection in the face of harassment and persecution, so that even though their numbers must have decreased in the pre-World War II period, some always remained.[34]

In the postwar period there were still said to be *ishans* with large followings, as many as 500 each and occasionally even more whose subordination and discipline were, as before, believed to be total. While the latter was indeed the theory, reality – according to eye-witness reports – was often rather different. And when an *ishan* died, he would be replaced by a relative, usually a son, whom he had initiated. An *ishan* from the town of Turkestan, who travelled around Kazakh auls in Tashkent Oblast' toward the end of the 1940s, enlisted new *murids* there and introduced his followers to his son and successor.[35] (Southern Kazakhstan, of which Turkestan was a major religious centre, had been traditionally impregnated with Sufism.[36])

In his report for the third quarter of 1945, the *upolnomochennyi* for the oblast' of Western Kazakhstan reported that two *ishans* were operating in his oblast'.[37] In Tajikistan, too, the republican

---

33. For Jadidism in Central Asia, see Zenkovsky, *Pan-Turkism and Islam in Russia*, Chapter 6; and Abduvakhitov, 'The Jadid Movement and Its Impact on Contemporary Central Asia', pp.67-71. See also pp.133-4 and 146.

34. For the particularly harsh attitude toward *ishans* and measures adopted to terminate their activities in Uzbekistan in the late 1920s, see Keller, *The Struggle against Islam in Uzbekistan, 1921-1941*, pp. 62 and 74. The same scholar has written elsewhere: 'Since Sufis were generally not dependent on institutional structures, the Soviets had to pursue them on a village-by-village and case-by-case basis, making complete eradication difficult. The Russians also did not realize how important or widespread they were' – Keller, 'Islam in Soviet Central Asia, 1917-1930', p.36.

35. L. A. Prikhod'ko and N. I. Abushaev, A short survey, 16 March 1950; GARF, f.6991, o.3, d.63, l.99.

36. N. I. Sabitov, Synopsis of report, Conference of CARC *upolnomochennye*, Alma-Ata, 30 Sept. 1946; GARF, f.6991, o.3, d.41, l.77. Even in Northern Kazakhstan, where Tatar influence had led to a more traditionally orthodox Islam, many Muslims were also 'not free' from Sufi influences – *ibid*. For the Yasawiyya, which originated and prospered in Southern Kazakhstan, see above; for the mousoleum of Ahmed Yasawi in Turkestan, see p. 373.

37. Kadyrbalin, Report, undated (sent by N. Sabitov to CARC, 5 Oct. 1945);

upolnomochennyi informed Moscow that dervishes and *ishans* with *murids* could be encountered, some of the *ishans* having actually approached SADUM's local qazi to appoint them shaykhs at *mazars*.[38]

The activity of *ishans* in both Tajikistan and Uzbekistan was sufficiently meaningful for State Security Minister Abakumov, writing about 'the religious movement' in the latter republic in 1946, to address himself to instances of it in a letter he sent to Voroshilov and Zhdanov. He maintained that the chairman and deputy chairman of one kolkhoz in Surkhan-Darya Oblast' were *murids* of an *ishan*, to whom they allotted a plot of over a hectare, which was cultivated for him by kolkhozniki. Abakumov likewise claimed that the head of the propaganda and agitation department in one *raikom* in the same oblast' gave an *ishan* a certificate testifying that he represented SADUM and requiring all kolkhoz and *sel'sovet* chairmen to give him every assistance in taking stock of mosques, *mazars* and 'the believing population', and in opening mosques.[39]

In several parts of Central Asia *ishans* went around rural areas in the latter 1940s enlisting *murids*.[40] One kolkhoz chairman in Tajikistan invited a well-known *ishan* from another oblast', offering him good conditions and even building him a house.[41] Two further *ishans* wielded considerable influence in the central parts of the republic in the early 1950s: one who was over seventy and did no travelling, but was visited at his kishlak by a large number of *murids*; and another who travelled around the Vakhsh Valley and was thought to have between 500 and 1,000 *murids*. The CARC *upolnomochennyi* for the Tajik SSR pointed out that in the past Sufism had been extremely widespread in Tajikistan, and although the population had meantime on the whole shaken off its influence,

GARF, f.6991, o.3, d.30, l.235.

38. K. Hamidov to I. V. Polianskii, 7 Dec. 1945; GARF, f.6991, o.3, d.30, l.365.

39. V. S. Abakumov to K. E. Voroshilov, 12 Sept. 1946; GARF, f.6991, o.3, d.34, l.194.

40. K. Hamidov, Report, Minutes, CARC session No.4, 29 Jan. 1947, and H. A. Akhtiamov to I. G. Halimov, 11 May 1948; GARF, f.6991, o.4, d.19, l.17, and o.3, d.453, ll.47-8. Hamidov spoke of the appearance of three *ishans*, but Tagiev, the head of CARC's Department for Eastern Religions, doubted whether there were just three and whether they were loyal to the USSR – *ibid.*, l.79.

41. K. Hamidov to I. V. Polianskii, 14 Dec. 1949; GARF, f.6991, o.3, d.67, l.96. The *ishan* referred to was known to have at least 200 to 250 *murids*.

it still remained here and there, particularly at *mazars*. Moreover, every day there was new evidence of the profound faith people in the rural areas had in *ishans* and faith-healers.[42] In the late 1940s and early 1950s, too, mendicant dervishes of the Qalandar order appeared in northern Tajikistan, as well as in Tashkent and other Uzbek cities, in places where people concentrated such as bazaars, bus-stops, trams, and *chaikhonas*. They would recite verses from the Qur'an, chant religious songs, and remind believers and non-believers alike of God's omnipresence, of death and life in the next world, of divine justice and the futility of worldly matters.[43]

Nor did the situation change over the following years and decades. A report from the mid-1950s saw fit to note that there were in Tajikistan, especially in its rural parts, 'significant cadres of the old Muslim clergy, including various sorts of *ishans*, shaykhs and former dervishes', who, in addition to performing rituals, 'incited a religious mood' among believers.[44] Two *ishans*, in particular, referred to in another document, lived and operated in central Tajikistan in the mid-1950s, the one allegedly with 3,000 *murids* and the other with 2,000. In 1953 the latter organised religious schools for teaching Qur'an and the basics of the Shari'a.[45]

At the very end of the 1950s the intensive activity of the *ishans* in Tajikistan led to a suggestion that SADUM be requested to re-activate its *fetwa* condemning ishanism and exorcism.[46] In the 1960s people engaging in ishanism and enlisting *murids* allegedly induced some believers to become 'fanatics' and gradually withdraw from all 'socially beneficial' labour and cultural undertakings.[47]

42. K. Hamidov, Report, delivered at CARC session No.18, 19-20 Dec. 1951; GARF, f.6991, o.3, d.75, ll.200 and 202.

43. N. Abushaev, Information, 17 Nov. 1949, and report, sent to G. M. Malenkov, M. A. Suslov, V. S. Abakumov and the Council of Ministers presidium, 30 June 1951; GARF, f.6991, o.3, d.61, l.125, and d.76, l.102.

44. V. Gostev to P. A. Tarasov, 4 Jan. 1954; GARF, f.6991, o.3, d.102, l.13.

45. I. V. Polianskii to P. V. Kovanov, deputy head, CPSU Central Committee Department of Propaganda and Agitation, 23 June 1955; GARF, f.6991, o.3, d.114, l.38. These may conceivably have been the above mentioned *ishans* or their successors.

46. K. F. Tagirov, Resumé, prepared for CARC session No.22s, 2 Sept. 1959; GARF, f.6991, o.3, d.184, ll.235-6. For further evidence of the activity of *ishans* – in Leninabad Oblast' – see A. Azizbaev to A. A. Puzin, 10 Jan. 1961; ibid., d.1737, l.35. For SADUM's 1952 *fetwa* on exorcism, see p.144.

47. B. Dodobaev, deputy chairman, Tajik SSR Council of Ministers, to all chairmen of oblast', municipal and raion *ispolkoms*, 25 Jan. 1961; GARF, f.6991,

Believers made pilgrimages to several major *ishans* in the Hissar and Vakhsh valleys and Kulyab Oblast', who were said to indulge in faith-healing and 'other superstitions'.[48] At the same time, it was reported in the early 1960s that thanks to intensive propaganda activity and the denigration of ishanism by SADUM Mufti Baba-khanov on a visit to Tajikistan, the activity of *ishans* and *murids* was showing signs of abating.[49] Some of them were exposed in the media and criminal proceedings were opened against a few;[50] one suspects that these were more effective than the various types of propaganda.

The imam of Osh's leading mosque, Shafagat Khaliqnazarov, lashed out at the *ishans* and their activity, which he prohibited, claiming they had no foundation in the Qur'an; he called them frauds and stated publicly that they were not to be shown the traditional signs of respect, nor were their prayers to be credited.[51] According to the oblast' *upolnomochennyi*, the campaign conducted by Khaliqnazarov and other registered clergy against them put an end to the *ishans'* activity. This did not, however, seem likely to his superiors. Perhaps, the republican *upolnomochennyi* for the Kirgiz SSR conceded, *ishans* who had previously come from Uzbekistan and Tajikistan had ceased coming, but this did not mean that ishanism had subsided in the oblast'. Once a person had become a *murid*, he lost all independence, became totally reliant on his patron, without whose approval he took no meaningful steps; such a relationship could not be disrupted by a few sermons. Either the *murid* now went to the *ishan*, or the latter found a substitute, a *khalifa*, to maintain contact with his *murids* in his stead.[52] Indeed, not long after, the *upolnomochennyi* for Osh Oblast' was again reporting the activity of two *ishans*, one of whom came from Andijan Oblast', accordingly cautioning the registered mullas

---

o.3, d.1737, l.2.

48. N. I. Smirnov and S. Fastoved, Information, 22 Aug. 1962 (transmitted to the CPSU Central Committee); GARF, f.6991, o.3, d.1390, l.35.

49. D. A. Ahmedov to A. A. Puzin, 23 April 1962; GARF, f.6991, o.3, d.1738, ll.27-8.

50. N. I. Smirnov and S. Fastoved, Information, 22 Aug. 1962; GARF, f.6991, o.3, d.1390, ll.35-8. For further instances of criminal proceedings, see pp.404-5 below and pp.577-82.

51. I. Halimov to H. Akhtiamov, 6 June 1948; GARF, f.6991, o.3, d.453, l.53.

52. H. Akhtiamov to I. Halimov, 10 July 1948; GARF, f.6991, o.3, d.453, ll.56-7.

and, where there were none, the local organs of government.[53] In the early months of 1953 this same *upolnomochennyi* unmasked an *ishan* who had been practising ishanism for many years (he had been initiated by his father-in-law), getting him to admit in front of a group of fellow-villagers not only the facts of his activity but also its basic fraudulence, and to promise not to continue engaging in ishanism.[54]

Nonetheless, in Kirgiziia's southern parts in particular, where there was a considerable Uzbek population, the activity of the *ishans* persisted.[55] The Long-Haired or Hairy Ishans, for example, traditionally centred around Osh, came into being as a radical branch of the Yasawiyya in the late 1920s. They resumed activities after World War II, after a respite following the major mass trial of 1935 which had sentenced thirty-two of their members. A second mass trial took place in 1952, at which the head *ishan* and his disciples were given various jail terms. Released in 1955, however, the head *ishan* attempted to reorganise the order, until he was forced in 1959 to announce that he was relinquishing his activities forever. Yet, the order did not disappear. At his trial in the early 1980s, the secretary of a sovkhoz in Kokand, who also belonged to the Komsomol, when asked about his membership in it, replied that he needed his Komosmol membership in this world, 'but my being a follower of religion is necessary in the next'.[56]

In Uzbekistan, too, ishanism kept up its activity. In Namangan Oblast' several *ishans* incited their *murids* against SADUM's *fetwas*, contending that from the point of view of dogma they were incorrect.[57] The prestige and ensconced status of the *ishans* in Uzbekistan can perhaps be further deduced from the fact that registered clergy sometimes referred in their sermons to the positive role filled by *ishans*, dervishes, *murids* and shaykhs and their hereditary

53. I. Halimov to H. Akhtiamov, 16 May 1951; GARF, f.6991, o.3, d.454, ll.111–12.

54. I. Halimov to H. Akhtiamov, 22 April 1953; GARF, f.6991, o.3, d.94, ll.61-3 and 69.

55. I. V. Polianskii to P. V. Kovanov, 23 June 1955, and H. Akhtiamov, Report, All-Union conference of CARC *upolnomochennye*, 18-20 April 1960; GARF, f.6991, o.3, d.114, l.25, and d.208, l.128.

56. Kocaoglu, 'Islam in the Soviet Union: Atheistic Propaganda and 'Unofficial" Religious Activities', p.151.

57. See pp.146.

authority among the population.[58] One *ishan* who travelled around Tajikistan in 1948 actually came from Urgut in Uzbekistan, with a retinue of no less than fourteen companions; in the following year his son came in his stead and large numbers of believers came to pay him their respects.[59]

In his address at a conference of CARC *upolnomochennye* in the late 1940s, the republican *upolnomochennyi* for the Uzbek SSR stressed that there were in the republic a group of clerics – *ulema*, *ishans* and dervishes – who considered themselves independent of SADUM and the registered mosques and took advantage of the freedom of worship offered by the Soviet constitution. These people saw themselves as sacrosanct and claimed to be descendants of Muhammad and other teachers of Islam. They surrounded themselves with a number of believers, including former clergy, and preached such 'supersititions' as predestination, by which God determined *a priori* a person's material well-being, and faith-healing, for only God's servants could heal sicknesses brought about by the divine will. They also taught that believers might take a second or third wife, if their wives were childless. Two *ishans* whom the *upolnomochennyi* singled out resided respectively in Tashkent and the Karakalpak ASSR, the former having about 100 *murids* and the latter 300. At his suggestion they had been summoned to SADUM and asked to cease their activity, but they refused, saying they were not subordinate to the spiritual directorate. Some *ishans* and shaykhs also performed the *chilla*, isolating themselves from the outside world for forty days in order to devote themselves solely to reading the Qur'an.[60]

Another *ishan* who resided in a kishlak in Tashkent Oblast' in the late 1940s had several hundred *murids*; he did not travel around –perhaps because of his age, perhaps so as not to incur the displeasure of the authorities[61] – but his adepts came to him from various parts of Tashkent Oblast', from Bukhara Oblast', and from Andijan, Margelan and Leninabad. He and his *murids* called upon the mullas

58. N. Abushaev, Information, 17 Nov. 1949; GARF, f.6991, o.3, d.61, l.125.

59. Instructional conference of CARC's *upolnomochennye* in Central Asia, Tashkent, 17-20 Dec. 1949; GARF, f.6991, o.3, d.67, l.54.

60. Ibid., ll.60-1. The *chilla* was 'a regular institution in the Sufi path' – Schimmel, *Mystical Dimensions of Islam*, p.103.

61. He had inherited an *ishan* who had been arrested by the MGB – I. V. Polianskii to K. E. Voroshilov, 27 May 1950; GARF, f.6991, o.3, d.68, l.43.

in the registered mosques to resign their positions on the grounds that SADUM had been set up by the Soviet regime.[62] A report on Islam a few years later noted that an influential *ishan* was performing religious rites on a kolkhoz in Samarkand Oblast',[63] where a number of *ishans* also distributed religious leaflets among schoolchildren.[64] Four further *ishans*, three of them young men, engaged in healing at the Yusup Hamadan-baba *mazar* in Khorezm Oblast',[65] which was famous for curing the mentally ill and retarded.[66]

The opening address at a conference of Uzbekistan's *upol-nomochennye* in 1951 ascribed the increase in religious activity in that republic in large measure to '*ishans* and shaykhs, dervishes and faith-healers'; there were said to be some twenty major *ishans*, about 100 shaykhs and 'a plethora of other obscurantists'. These people posed as the 'true scions of religion' and appealed to believers to observe rituals and festivals which had long ago been forgotten, including the teaching of religion to children and the reading of old religious works in auls, at bazaars and at assemblies.[67] From time to time imams of registered mosques were considered to be slipping into practices associated by the authorities with ishanism.[68]

In one raion in Khorezm Oblast' a group of ethnographers visited a 'congregation of female dervishes, led by women'. These *sopis* – as *murids* were called in those parts – periodically assembled to perform the *zikr*, described by one of the ethnographers as closely resembling shamanistic ceremonies which still persisted in

62. L. A. Prikhod'ko and N. I. Abushaev, A short survey, 16 March 1950; GARF, f.6991, o.3, d.63, l.99.

63. V. I. Gostev to P. A. Tarasov, 4 Jan. 1954; GARF, f.6991, o.3, d.102, l.5.

64. See p.362.

65. I. V. Polianskii to the CPSU Central Committee and the USSR Council of Ministers, 13 Sept. 1955; GARF, f.6991, o.3, d.114, ll.139–41.

66. 'Shaykh Yusuf Hamadani', *Nauka i religiia*, 12, 1984, pp.30-2.

67. Minutes, Instructional conference of CARC *upolnomochennye* in the oblasti of the Uzbek SSR, 17-18 July 1951. Just one day later, however, in a letter to the republican leadership, the speaker, CARC's *upolnomochennyi* in Tashkent, Kh. N. Iskanderov, said there were ten major *ishans* – Kh. N. Iskanderov to Deputy Chairman of the Uzbek SSR Council of Ministers Vahabov and Central Committee Secretary of the Uzbekistan CP Tursunov, 19 July 1951; TsGAUz, f.2456, o.1, d.134, ll.64 and 55.

68. For example, M. Khalikov to I. V. Polianskii, 19 May 1956; TsGAUz, f.2456, o.1, d.198, l.84.

the region and included whirling with a tambourine, making offerings to spirits and jumping barefooted on sharpened swords.[69]

In the second half of the 1950s the activity of several *ishans*,
who were designated by one senior CARC official 'Muslim
sectarians', was exposed in Fergana Oblast': these included four
inhabitants of Kokand, one who had been a *murid* of the organiser
of the insurgence of 1929-30[70] and had *murids* in Kokand; two
brothers, said to have 'inherited' 2,000 *murids* from their father
and to persist in enlisting new ones in several rural areas, taking
part in large prayer-meetings arranged by the oblast's leading
religious figures; and the fourth who had *murids* in Kokand, Angren
in Tashkent Oblast', and Kirgiziia; a fifth, who was an imam at
a registered mosque, and also had *murids* in Kirgiziia; and finally
a shaykh at a *mazar*, where he aspired to open a mosque, promising
SADUM to give its coffers 1,000 rubles annually. These *ishans*
had previously perceived all Communists as people who sought
to destroy religion and recommended that believers have no contact
with them, but some of them at least had mitigated their position,
saying some Communists could atone for their sins, that their
party membership must be seen as a blind, and if they were
apprehensive of praying publicly, they might do so at home within
their family circle.[71]

But although ishanist activity was occasionally exposed and even
punished, the phenomenon of ishanism did not disappear either
in Tajikistan or in Uzbekistan. In 1969 the death of an *ishan* in
Samarkand Oblast', who had *murids* in four oblasti, was followed
by a funeral with the participation of over 3,000 people who
came from various parts of the Uzbek SSR, and his tomb immediately became a site of pilgrimage.[72] In the early 1970s, twelve
ishans were exposed just in Samarkand Oblast',[73] while the thirty-five

69. Snesarev, 'On some Causes of the Persistence of Religio-Customary Survivals
among the Khorezm Uzbeks', pp.223-6.

70. The Basmachi revolt, of which the Fergana Valley had been the seat, flared
up anew in face of collectivisation, attaining the proportion of civil war in
certain areas – Fierman, 'The Soviet 'Transformation'' of Central Asia', p.18.

71. K. F. Tagirov, Information, 1 March 1957; GARF, f.6991, o.3, d.132,
ll.55-6.

72. CRA, Information, sent to the CPSU Central Committee, 22 May 1970;
TsKhSD, f.5, o.62, d.38, l.19.

73. CRA, Information, sent to the CPSU Central Committee, 27 April 1971;
TsKhSD, f.5, o.63, d.89, l.99.

vagrants of working age who engaged in begging, and who were
disciplined in this same period in the Karakalpak ASSR, probably
belonged to one of the mendicant dervish orders.[74] A decade later
100 'descendants of *ishans*' were still said to be conducting 'anti-legal
religious activity' in Tajikistan.[75]

In Turkmenistan, too, there were reported to be 20 – 25 *ishans*
in the early 1950s, each with at least ten *murids* (or *sopis*). Sufi
influence was especially felt in those areas which in the past had
been part of the Bukharan Emirate (Kerki and Charjou) and the
Khivan Khanate (Tashauz Oblast'); in the former the Naqshbandiyya
and in the latter the Kubrawiyya had been particularly strong.
Turkmenistan's *ishans* enjoyed considerable popularity, their *murids*
spreading stories about their sanctity and knowledge of Qur'an.
The funeral of one *ishan* in the early 1950s was attended by over
1,000 people, and about 2,000 gathered to mourn the grandson
of another *ishan* who had been killed in the town of Nebit-Dag.
Some of these *ishans* and their *murids* were accused of anti-Soviet
activity, and in 1950 three of them were tried and given prison
sentences of between six and ten years. Members of a dervish
mendicant order, their number unspecified, were said in this same
time period to have come to Turkmenistan from Uzbekistan in
the guise of wandering beggars and appeared in the bazaars and
chaikhonas in Ashkhabad and Charjou, where they engaged in
'praising Allah', reading Qur'an and faith-healing.[76] Later on in
the decade two young men allegedly 'declared themselves "new"
prophets', attracting dozens of people as *sopis*, through whom they
spread stories about the imminent 'end of the world' and the
'downfall of the infidels', and indulged in a series of 'malpractices'.[77]
A book dedicated to Sufism in Turkmenistan in the late 1970s
indicated the importance attached to this trend in the Brezhnev
period. Interestingly, it associated its leaders with the 'bandit regi-
ments of the Basmachi', demonstrating the threat the authorities

74. For their exposure and punishment, see p.582.

75. V. A. Kuroedov to the CPSU Central Committee, 16 Sept. 1983; TsKhSD,
f.5, o.89, d.82, l.60.

76. A. Atabaev to I. V. Polianskii, undated (before 30 Oct. 1945); Minutes,
CARC session No.1, 13 Jan. 1951; and N. I. Abushaev, A short survey, undated
[early 1951] – GARF, f.6991, o.3, d.21, l.72, d.74, ll.2 and 11, and d.73, l.24.

77. Kuliev, *Antinauchnaia sushchnost' islama i zadachi ateisticheskogo vospitaniia
trudiashchikhsia v usloviiakh Sovetskogo Turkmenistana*, p.110.

continued to perceive the Sufis as constituting.[78] Still in the early 1980s a Communist Party of Turkmenistan congress heard complaints that the raion party committees and primary organisations were indifferent to anti-religious work, and as a result 'self-appoined mullas and *ishans'* established themselves in holy places, spread absurd rumours and engaged in faith-healing.[79]

There were very occasional instances of Sufi activity in the RSFSR proper. In 1946, the *upolnomochennyi* for Molotov (Perm') Oblast' reported that the Naqshbandiyya were active in his oblast', conducting 'religious propaganda' in the kolkhozy.[80] In 1954 an *ishan* was said to be operating in a village in Kuibyshev Oblast' whose *murids* from various parts, including adjacent raiony of the Tatar ASSR, attended his prayer-meetings. (The *ishan* in question was none other than the mulla of the village's registered mosque.)[81]

A CARC official, stressing the 'reactionary' and 'anti-Soviet' activity of the *ishans* in the early 1950s, contrasted them with the registered clergy and the constant aspiration of the latter to adapt to Soviet conditions. The *ishans*, he pointed out, opposed modernisation and its concomitant manifestations. They preached predestination and the division of mankind into true believers and non-Muslims (both orthodox doctrines), laid great emphasis on the importance of *mazars*, and opposed the unveiling of women, whom husbands had to protect from the gaze of strange men. One *ishan*, he reported, had 'burst' into Shaykh Zain ad-Din *mazar* in Tashkent, which was under the supervision of the Administration of Architecture, creating a scandal, and proclaiming to the 100 or so believers present that nobody had the right to prevent them from visiting the tomb and prostrating themselves there.[82]

78. Rorlich, 'Islam and Atheism: Dynamic Tension in Soviet Central Asia', p.203. The book Rorlich quotes was S. M. Demidov, *Sufizm v Turkmenii: evoliutsiia i perezhitki*, Ashkhabad, 1978.

79. *Pravda*, 19 Jan. 1981. The republican party newspaper also carried an article on a history teacher in a kolkhoz and party member, who was the scion of a family of *ishans* and mullas, and after his work hours in school operated as an *ishan* – *Turkmenskaia iskra*, 17 May 1981.

80. Minutes, CARC session No.7, 23-24 April 1947; GARF, f.6991, o.4, d.19, ll.205-6.

81. Minutes, CARC session No.1s, 9 Jan. 1954, and I. V. Polianskii to CARC *upolnomochennye*, 13 Feb. 1954; GARF, f.6991, o.3, d.101, l.3, and d.104, l.11.

82. N. I. Abushaev, A short survey, 15 March 1951; GARF, f.6991, o.3, d.73,

On the whole, the authorities seem to have approached the issue of curtailing and terminating the activity of *ishans* somewhat gingerly. One rather cryptic entry in the minutes of a CARC session towards the end of the 1950s records a decision to write to Chairman of the Tajik SSR Council of Ministers Nazarsho Dodkhudoev saying that CARC considered the 'unlawful' conduct of a certain *ishan* 'impermissible' and asking that he be brought to book.[83] 'Administrative' measures taken against shaykhs, *ishans* and others who operated at *mazars* and were from time to time fined and called to account, were not considered to have had positive results. At least one major *ishan*, however, the above-mentioned *ishan* who operated in the late 1940s in the Karakalpak ASSR, was arrested in the late Stalin years and convicted and died in prison. When the *mazar* erected in his memory was closed in 1959, his family arranged a memorial service for him, which was attended by thousands of people bringing donations and sacrifices.[84] (A number of other *mazars* were tombs of former *ishans*, and their closure during the campaign against pilgrimages to holy places in the late 1950s was inevitably accompanied by the denigration of their personality and aspersions on their sanctity during their lifetime and after their death.[85])

Given the obvious difficulty in finding an effective solution to the question, the activity of the *ishans* troubled CARC considerably. In late 1958, in connection with the re-activated campaign against holy places, CARC Chairman Puzin noted that muridism had 'begun to revive' in Tajikistan and Uzbekistan. The activities had recently been exposed of several *ishans* who engaged in enlisting adepts, 'fanatical pupils who disseminated religious prejudices among the population'.[86] Indeed, CARC Deputy Chairman Riazanov

---

ll.25 and 27.

83. Minutes, CARC session No.8, 21 May 1958; GARF, f.6991, o.3, d.164, l.39.

84. Reception by K. F. Tagirov and A. S. Tiazetdinov of Idris Rahmatulla, former head shaykh of the Sultan-baba *mazar* in the Karakalpak ASSR and son of the *ishan*, 3 Oct. 1958, and Reports by N. Inogamov and A. Irmanov, Conference of CARC's Central Asian *upolnomochennye*, 5-6 June 1959; GARF, f.6991, o.4, d.88, l.111, and o.3, d.186, ll.24, 129 and 131. In 1958 the *ishan* was vindicated posthumously by a people's court. For the *mazar*, see p.372.

85. For example, Minutes, CARC session No.21, 22 July 1959; GARF, f.6991, o.3, d.184, ll.155 and 180 (regarding *mazars* in the Bashkir ASSR and in Ul'ianovsk Oblast').

86. Materials of All-Union conference of CARC *upolnomochennye*, 25-27 Nov.

and SADUM Mufti Babakhanov had recently discussed the issue of 'wandering mullas, shaykhs, *ishans* and other parasitical elements' who appeared at *mazars* and took advantage of believers' religious feelings.[87] The closure of *mazars* reportedly led to a number of the *ishans* who operated at these sites as descendants of those buried there ceasing their activity and repudiating their calling.[88]

As of the mid-1960s, with the fairly widespread repression of sectarians of all faiths, *ishans*, too, were subjected to persecution. One *ishan* was arrested in Kashka-Darya Oblast' with the collaboration of believers of the town of Shahr-i Sabz. For three weeks he had gone the rounds of his *murids* in local kolkhozy, collecting from them a considerable sum of money, as well as cloth and rugs, and the hides of over fifty sheep they had slaughtered in his honour.[89] Another, in Samarkand Oblast', was given three years' imprisonment in 1970 for 'posing as an ishan', spreading superstition and faith-healing.[90] Yet SADUM seems to have eschewed any outright attack on ishanism apart from the occasional *fetwa*, an indication that the authorities were not persistent in their antagonism and that the spiritual directorate did not believe that ishanism could be effectively eradicated by edicts or propaganda.[91]

The Northern Caucasus

The documentation provides very little information concerning the religious activity of the *tariqas* in the Northern Caucasus in the decade or so after the war, although there seems to have been some Sufi activity among the Avars, Dargin and Kumyks

1958; GARF, f.6991, o.3, d.165, l.24.

87. Reception by V. F. Riazanov of Ziyautdin Babakhanov, 22 Sept. 1958; GARF, f.6991, o.4, d.88, ll.166-7.

88. The CARC *upolnomochennyi* for Tajikistan, for example, told of one such instance in his republic – Minutes, CARC session No.4, 25-26 Feb. 1959; GARF, f.6991, o.3, d.183, l.69.

89. M. M. Miragzamov to M. Kh. Khalmuhamedov, 22 Oct. 1966; GARF, f.6991, o.6, d.11, l.66.

90. CRA, Information, sent to the CPSU Central Committee, 27 April 1971; TsKhSD, f.5, o.63, d.89, ll.136-7.

91. For one such *fetwa*, see p. 144. Interestingly DUMSK twice condemned 'apostates' from Islam and the Shari'a, apparently in reference to the brotherhoods, once in 1953, prior to the return of the Chechen and Ingush, and the second time in 1962 – Mamleev, *Nekotorye osobennosti islama v Checheno-Ingushetii*, p.30.

in Dagestan.[92] One report from the second half of the 1950s speaks of certain raiony in that republic where muridism remained active.[93] Even regarding later years the information concerning Dagestan is sparse. A report from the mid-1960s, spoke of 'religious fanatics, a large part of them simply charlatans', who adopted the title of shaykh and surrounded themselves with *murids*, whom they sometimes incited to actual crime.[94] An occasional newspaper article slashed out at the deeds and views of 'sectarians'. One such item noted in particular the *murids* of Shaykh Amay, who did not hear radio, watch television (that 'vanity of vanities'), go to the cinema, have resort to the services of regular doctors, or engage in productive and useful work.[95] One Western commentator has noted that until the late 1970s most Dagestani writers on religion concurred that the Sufi *tariqas* 'survived [there] only as unimportant "splinter groups"'. Yet from descriptions which appeared beginning with the advent of glasnost in 1987, it would seem that they operated clandestinely in the previous years and decades rather extensively.[96] Two other Western scholars have extrapolated figures for Sufi adepts in Dagestan. Relying on a survey carried out by a local 'expert', among whose sample 7.3 per cent were Sufi adepts, they believed there might have been as many as 95,000 *murids* in Dagestan in the 1970s. Moreover,

92. Minutes, CARC session No.7, 23-24 April 1947; GARF, f.6991, o.4, d.19, l.174. For a group of women in the Kabardinian ASSR who performed the *zikr* in 1945, see p.390 above. In 1926, prior to the assault on religion in the Northern Caucasus, there were said to have been some 60,000 *murids* in the Chechen and Ingush region (at the time both had autonomous oblasti, which were combined into the Chechen-Ingush ASSR in 1936), and just over that number in Dagestan – Bennigsen, 'Muslim Conservative Opposition to the Soviet Regime', pp.340-1. Both numbers must have been reduced drastically in the subsequent period of religious repression.

93. Gasanov to V. I. Gostev, 19 March 1957; GARF, f.6991, o.3, d.145, l.51; and N. A Smirnov, *Miuridizm na Kavkaze*, Moscow: USSR Academy of Sciences, 1963, quoted in Mamleev, *Nekotorye osobennosti islama v Checheno-Ingushetii*, p.20.

94. M. S. Gajiev, Report, Minutes, CARC session No.1, 7 Jan. 1964; GARF, f.6991, o.4, d.146, ll.15-16.

95. The article was sent by CRA *upolnomochennyi* in Dagestan M. S. Gajiev to A. Nurullaev, 27 July 1973; GARF, f.6991, o.6, d.629, l.168.

96. Broxup, 'Islam in Dagestan under Gorbachev', pp.216 ff. The article relates to activity in the Gorbachev period, but it is inconceivable that so broad a field of operations as it depicts could have emerged under perestroika without a meaningful long-standing infrastructure.

they noted that, according to the first secretary of the Dagestan Obkom in 1982, pilgrimages to holy places in that republic continued 'as before', despite all measures taken to curtail them.[97]

Nor is the documentation particularly illuminating regarding the deported Caucasian peoples in Central Asia in the years 1944 through 1957, when most of them were allowed to return to their native parts (the official names of which once again reflected their eponymous nationalities). However, it would appear that adherence to the Sufi orders actually increased among the Chechen and Ingush during their period of exile, perhaps as a way of demonstrating their protest against the deportation or of ensuring their group solidarity. The *tariqas* became a symbol of national affiliation and an effective instrument of community survival.[98] It has been argued that they were responsible for the very survival of the Chechen and Ingush nations during the period of exile.[99] During the deportation, according to one opinion, Sufi identity 'developed into feelings of national identity. The Sufi orders became extensively incorporated into the social structure, to the point where each individual had not only local, family and clan loyalties but also membership of a branch of one or another Sufi order'.[100]

In the oblast' of Northern Kazakhstan, where there were over 7,000 adult Chechen in the immediate postwar period, they were spread out in settlements with a primarily Russian and German population.[101] They did not have permanent places for collective prayer, and festival prayer-services were held in the open. Even in places where they comprised fairly large enclaves – in Alma-Ata Oblast', for instance, they constituted 9 per cent of the total population and 17 per cent of all Muslim inhabitants – they had no registered communities, for the process of registration was not applicable to 'special settlers'. Yet, the 'relevant organs' allowed their religious leaders to perform 'urgent rites' both in their own

97. Bennigsen and Wimbush, *Mystics and Commissars*, pp.55-6 and 125.

98. When they returned to their native parts, the *tariqas* boasted considerable numbers, probably far exceeding those of the pre-Soviet period; and see below.

99. Bryan, 'Anti-religious Activity in the Chechen-Ingush Republic of the USSR and the Survival of Islam', p.111.

100. Zelkina, 'Islam and Politics in the North Caucasus', p.120. Unfortunately, Zelkina brings neither sources nor evidence to corroborate this.

101. The ethnic Germans had themselves been exiled to Siberia and Kazakhstan and their autonomous republic on the Volga abolished in 1941, following the German invasion of the Soviet Union.

places of residence and in neighbouring villages. In exile, as at home, these clergy reportedly enjoyed undisputable authority, not only in strictly religious questions, but also regarding economic and political matters. Thus, their followers for the most part obeyed their injunctions to fulfil their duties to the state and work honestly, although, in the view of CARC's *upolnomochennye*, the clergy enjoined them to do so solely for tactical reasons and compliance was without enthusiasm. While not 'acclimatised' and undergoing a 'moral crisis' as a result of their deportation at least in the earlier years,[102] the exiles probably mixed more with the locals as the conditions of their existence gradually became less stringent.[103] Yet, still in the mid-1950s they did not attend the registered mosques of the indigenous Muslim inhabitants, even when these existed in the vicinity,[104] their own clergy continuing to perform the requisite rites for the community until their return home.[105]

Reports relating to the deportees noted that over 95 per cent of Chechen adults were 'believers', some of them to the point of 'fanaticism', and there is evidence that both the Chechen and the Ingush tended to be far more observant than most of the indigenous inhabitants in their areas of 're-settlement'. They endeavoured to perform the five daily prayers, whereas the four North Caucasian deported nationalities – the Chechen, Ingush, Balkars and Karachai – constituted the groups in Central Asia which allegelly observed the *uraz* most strictly and celebrated the festivals most actively.[106] But there is no more than a bare mention of their 'sectarian' activity,[107] one report from the mid-1950s referring

102. V. Liapunov and A. Saltovskii, Reports, Conference of CARC's *upol-nomochennye* in the Kazakh and Kirgiz SSRs, 30 Sept.-2 Oct. 1946; GARF, f.6991. o.3, d.41, ll.61-2 and 86-7.

103. For the legislation which between 1954 and January 1957 enabled them to move around more freely in the areas of their exile and eventually to return home and the size of the deported populations, of whom the Muslim nations accounted for about 800,000, see Zemskov, 'Massovoe osvobozhdenie spetsposelentsev i ssyl'nykh (1954-1960gg.)'. See also Chapter 2, n.22.

104. L. A. Prikhod'ko, Report, 20 May 1953; GARF, f.6991, o.3, d.91, l.269.

105. Interview with a former CRA official who has asked to remain anonymous.

106. N. Tagiev, A short survey, undated [probably early 1949]; V. I. Gostev to P. A. Tarasov, 4 Jan. 1954; and I. G. Halimov to CARC, 20 Jan. 1956; GARF, f.6991, o.4, d.23, l.14, and o.3, d.102, l.18, and d.457, l.23. See also Chapter 8, n.44.

107. Again, this may be available in the republican or all-union KGB archives.

to the fact that the religious activity of three Sufi *tariqas* – the Kunta Haji, Batal Haji and Golnar Haji – had been revealed among the Chechen and Ingush in Kazakhstan.[108] The Chechen and Ingush maintain that they persisted with their customary practices, particularly the *zikr*, throughout their period of exile.[109]

It is untenable to try to gauge the measure of influence of the deported nations on the populations among which they found themselves. True, muridism was said to have persisted in Kazakhstan into the 1960s after the return of the great majority of Chechen and Ingush to their homes.[110] Yet the reference is almost certainly to those Chechen and/or Ingush who remained behind, as some did in both the Kazakh and Kirgiz SSRs,[111] rather than to Kazakhs or other Central Asians.

Once, however, the majority of the Chechen and Ingush returned to their native lands, they became the subject of intense interest and study, although other ethnic groups who came back from exile seem likewise to have been of a stronger religious orientation than the population which had remained behind.[112] The report of a CARC official on his trip to the Chechen-Ingush ASSR in summer 1960 noted that not only was religiosity high – believers comprising over 90 per cent among both Chechen and Ingush –but that it was manifest primarily in the activity of a variety of Muslim 'sects': according to one source, over 95 per cent of believers were adherents of Sufism. The official reported the existence of some 200 religious figures, or 'authorities', belonging to the different sects, some of them descendants of well-known

108. I. V. Polianskii to P. V. Kovanov, 23 June 1955; GARF, f.6991, o.3, d.114, l.36. CARC suggested to its *upolnomochennyi* for Alma-Ata Oblast' that he include the study of the KuntaHaji in his workplan for 1956 – Minutes, CARC session No.2, 9 Jan.1956; GARF, f.6991, o.4, d.55a, l.6.

109. Oral testimony given to Moshe Gammer to whom I am indebted for this information.

110. Smirnov, *Miuridizm na Kavkaze*, quoted in Mamleev, *Nekotorye osobennosti islama v Checheno-Ingushetii*, pp.19-20. And see p.425 below.

111. CRA, Information, sent to the CPSU Central Committee, 22 May 1970 –TsKhSD, f.5, o.62, d.38, l.13; and S. Abenov to A. A. Nurullaev, 9 Aug. 1973 – GARF, f.6991, o.6, d.545, l.41.

112. The Karachai-Cherkess AO newspaper *Leninskoe znamia* noted on 9 Dec. 1958 that efendis and mullas were endeavouring to extend their influence in particular among the new Karachai settlers; the local *obkom* noted that the *qalym*, too, was still practised among the Karachai – quoted in Tsavkalov, *Prichiny zhivuchestva religioznykh perezhitkov i puti ikh preodoleniia*, pp.6 and 39.

spiritual figures of the past who posed as 'holy people'; by the beginning of 1963 this number had gone up to 500.[113]

The most widespread of the orders was that of the Qadiri Kunta Haji. The partial figures available at the beginning of the 1960s spoke of it having 2,000 *murids* in seventy odd groups, each headed by a *tamada*, or master-of-ceremonies. Their prayer-meetings, which took place regularly in private homes, were accompanied by the vocal *zikr*, consisting of going around in a circle, hand-clapping, chanting or yelling 'There is no God other than Allah', and dancing or capering. Describing the *zikr* in the Chechen-Ingush ASSR, which had been introduced by the Kunta Haji in the mid-nineteenth century, one source said it was reminiscent of a 'collective exorcism of the divinity – magical, rhythmic body-movements which not infrequently produce a collective religious trance or religious ecstasy of individual participants...Believers see in this ecstasy "a fusion with the divinity".' Non-*murids* might be invited to attend these *zikrs*, which would be followed by readings from the Qur'an and supplications for forgiveness of one's sins. Here and there Kunta Haji *murids* were strong enough to annul a kolkhoz administration nominated by the *raikom* and appoint new people from among their own ranks.[114] The Kunta Haji also had separate groups of women *murids*. This seems to have been a phenomenon which existed in several sects, Qadiri and Naqshbandi, both in the Chechen-Ingush ASSR and in Dagestan, where groups of women *murids* operated with women *tamadas*, shaykhs or *ustadhs*.[115]

Many of the other orders were sub-divisions of the Kunta Haji.

113. P. A. Zadorozhnyi to A. A. Puzin, 30 Aug. 1960, A. L. Alisov to A. A. Puzin, 15 Feb. 1963, and A. Asaulka to V. A. Kuroedov, 1 Nov. 1968; GARF, f.6991, o.3, d.207, ll.52-3 and 57, and d.1607, l.24, and o.6, d.153, ll.159-60. Compare also p.92. According to Zelkina, again bringing neither sources nor evidence, 'It was usual that in a village of about 500 people there would be about 25-30 active Sufi murids while the rest of the population consisted of non-active adepts of either the Naqshbandi or the Qadiri Sufi brotherhoods' –'Islam and Politics in the North Caucasus', p.120.

114. A. L. Alisov to A. A. Puzin, 5 March 1959 and 15 Feb. 1963, P. A. Zadorozhnyi to Puzin, and Zadorozhnyi, Information, 30 Aug. 1960 – GARF, f.6991, o.3, d.596, ll.5-8, d.1607, ll.24-7, and d.207, ll.53-5 and 71-2; and Mamleev, *Nekotorye osobennosti islama v Checheno-Ingushetii*, p.26. For the *zikr*, see also Mustafinov, *Zikrizm i ego sotsial'naia sushchnost'*, pp.18-19.

115. Saidbaev, *Islam i obshchestvo*, p.240; and Makatov, 'Kul't sviatykh v islame', p.177. Compare p.393 above.

Some of these had been formed in the 1870s, in the very early years after its establishment – its founder, Kunta Haji Kishiev having been arrested and exiled, he was succeeded not by one, but by three, shaykhs, each of whom established his own order. Others had sprung up in the Soviet period itself, when the number of orders actually increased. One commentator pointed out that the Qadiri *tariqa*, in the form introduced into the Caucasus by Kunta Haji and his successors, required no profound knowledge of Islamic dogma, but dwelt rather upon the ritual aspect, and so attracted the simple, illiterate mountainous population. Moreover, the Kunta Haji assimilated customs of the *adat* as practised by many of the local clans, and this in turn led to it constantly fragmenting into splinter groups.[116] Certainly in the period after their return from exile, a number of orders seem to have recruited adepts from specific clans, which, given the dual loyalty to order and clan, helped them preserve greater secrecy.[117] One report on the life of the Sufi communities stressed that each group combined fifteen or so families of the same clan, thus comprising a well-knitted group around which the entire existence of its members revolved.[118]

One order which attracted considerable attention among commentators was the Batal Haji, one of the three original offshoots of the Kunta Haji, described by a pamphlet devoted to it as 'the most reactionary' of them all and by the Western scholar Alexandre Bennigsen as the most 'puritan and fanatical' of the Sufi orders. Its leaders, all members of one family, had for a decade and a half before the war been engaged in active opposition to the regime, which culminated in attacks upon Soviet troops during the war. Back from deportation, the members of the Batal Haji and their leaders continued to commit purported crimes against society and the regime, for which many of them were charged and sentenced.[119] One of the orders which came into being in the Soviet period was that of Shaykh Amay. Founded in the

116. Mamleev, *Nekotorye osobennosti islama v Checheno-Ingushetii*, pp.27-8.

117. Bennigsen, 'Muslim Conservative Opposition to the Soviet Regime', p.341. According to Bennigsen, this applied specifically to the Naqshbandiyya.

118. S. Umarov, 'Muridism – A Close-Up', *Nauka i religiia*, 10, 1979, pp.30-2.

119. A. L. Alisov to A. A. Puzin, 16 March 1962; GARF, f.6991, o.3, d.1606, ll.19-20; Tutaev, *Reaktsionnaia sekta Khadzhi Batal*, p.5 and *passim*, and Bennigsen and Wimbush, *Muslims of the Soviet Empire*, p.188. Alisov quoted an article in the republican press on the activity of the leader of the Batal Haji.

1930s in Dagestan, it seems to have ceased operating with the arrest and execution of its leader in 1936. It was then re-activated in the 1950s, only to be repressed again with the arrest of the two people who initiated its re-appearance yet it re-surfaced from time to time[120] An additional order, the Vis Haji, came into being in the period of exile in Central Asia separating off from the Chim Mirza Haji, another of the three original offshoots of the Kunta Haji; Bennigsen wrote of it that it was the most popular of the Qadiri orders, the 'most modernist in its methods and the most conservative in its doctrine'.[121] The Vis Haji considered it sinful to wear clothes or shoes manufactured in state factories, to partake of food prepared by a non-Muslim,[122] or to speak Russian.[123] In reference to this group, one Soviet author wrote in the early 1970s that 'the melody of the violin, the rhythm of the drum-beat, and the spirited rites of people dressed in ritual clothes produce a strong effect even on a person who is indifferent to religion, but intellectually limited'.[124]

A further nine or ten orders operated in the Chechen-Ingush ASSR in the first five or so years after the return from exile, the largest with ten groups and over 800 members, the smallest with just one group and forty members. None of these seem to have met for prayer on a regular basis in this period, but they held prayer-services on the two main festivals and conducted prayers on Mavlud in private homes.[125] By 1966 the republican *upol-*

---

120. Broxup, 'Islam in Dagestan under Gorbachev', p.217. The Dagestan ASSR party organ *Dagestanskaia pravda* dedicated an article to this sect in 1963 – M. S. Gajiev, Report, Minutes, CARC session No.1, 7 Jan. 1964; GARF, f.6991, o.4, d.146, l.16. For another article on this sect, see p.406 above.

121. See Bennigsen and Lemercier-Quelquejay, 'Muslim Religious Conservatism and Dissent in the USSR', p.156 and n.11; and Bennigsen and Wimbush, *Muslims of the Soviet Empire*, p.188. The Vis Haji seems to have been the one order which in Central Asia recruited members of the indigenous nationalities into its ranks – see p.425 – and, after the return from deportation, spread westwards, gaining adherents from among other North Caucasian nationalities – I am indebted for this information to Moshe Gammer.

122. Mamleev, *Nekotorye osobennosti islama v Checheno-Ingushetii*, p.28.

123. Bryan, 'Internationalism, Nationalism and Islam', p.204.

124. Mustafinov, *Zikrizm i ego sotsial'naia sushchnost'*, p.31.

125. P. A. Zadorozhnyi to A. A. Puzin, 30 Aug. 1960. Some of the background and characteristics of these brotherhoods are depicted in Zadorozhnyi, Information, and A. L. Alisov to A. A. Puzin, 15 Feb. 1963; GARF, f.6991, o.3, d.207, ll.55-6 and 73-8, and d.1607, ll.25-6. It was only with the advent of glasnost

nomochennyi reported an aggregate of 4,000 *murids* and twelve 'brotherhoods', each with groups in a number of villages, but this, too, seemed to be an underestimate, for within two years, twenty 'brotherhoods' were known to be operating and 1,500 *murids* in over forty groups were discovered just in two *raiony*. In the early 1970s, it was said there were thirty 'brotherhoods', many of them offshoots of one another and virtually indistinguishable. According to contemporary Soviet documentation, none of the orders had any centralised leadership, each *tamada* being chosen from among the group and operating autonomously. Moreover, they were spread over the entire republic, there being hardly a settlement which did not have at least one or two groups of believers, the larger villages having representatives of almost every order. Altogether, by the turn of the decade the count was over 300 groups with an aggregate membership of over 12,000; and membership continued to mount. By this time, too, religious groups were once again building new mosques; in one single raion in 1969, mosques had been, or were being, built in ten out of twelve settlements. Groups which did not have new buildings prayed in former mosques or structures at the cemeteries. The *zikr* was conducted in private homes.[126] In the mid-1970s a further seventeen groups of *murids*, each with 18 – 20 members were exposed in the Prigorodnyi raion,[127] which had remained in the North Osetian ASSR after the return of the Ingush and the resuscitation of the Chechen-Ingush ASSR.

Western sources, on the other hand, believed the *wirds* to be 'well-structured hierarchies', each led, as it were, by a *vekil*, or representative, of Kunta Haji. The more widely diffused *wirds* had

---

that the press provided evidence of the vitality of the Sufi brotherhoods, see Irshad Makatov, 'To the detriment of the interests of society and the individual', *Sovetskii Dagestan*, No.6, 1987, pp.37-44, quoted in Marie Broxup, 'Islam in Dagestan under Gorbachev', pp.215-18.

126. A. Asaulka, Report, 14 Jan. 1967, A. Asaulka to V. A. Kuroedov, 1 Nov. 1968, and CRA, Information, sent to the CPSU Central Committee, 22 May 1970; GARF, f.6991, o.6, d.22, ll.88-88ob, and d.153, ll.159-60, and TsKhSD, f.5, o.62, d.38, ll.13-14. The *upolnomochennyi's* arithmetic is not clear, for later on the same document which speaks of 1500 *murids* in 40 groups talks of groups of 5 – 30 members each. The document of 1970 says that goups had anything from 10-15 to 100 or even 120 members. A similar report of a year later, dated 22 April 1971 – TsKhSD, f.5, o.63, d.89, l.108 – spoke of 150 groups with a membership of over 15,000.

127. F. Komarov to the CRA, 14 Feb. 1974; GARF, f.6991, o.6, d.558, l.74.

subordinate *vekils* to control and direct the *tamadas*, the elders who represented the order at the district level. Under the *tamada*, at the village level, were the *turkkhs* who led individual circles.[128] Contrary to the opinion of Soviet commentators, the *tamada* seems to have reported regularly to the *vekil* or shaykh of his *wird*.[129]

The activity of the orders consisted at first of restoring the mosques which in the past had operated in every aul, repairing sacred tombs and other constructs which had fallen into ruin over time, and setting up Shari'a courts.[130] Since mosques which were restored were closed by the authorities almost as soon as they were opened, holy places became the usual meeting places for *murids*. Here, it appears, they not only performed the *zikr*, but were also able to learn Qur'an and the rudiments of Islamic theology and Arabic.[131] These sites might be tombs of founders of *wirds*, local religious leaders, *ustadhs* and shaykhs, heroes who had been killed in wars against outside invaders and martyrs who had died for their faith. Sometimes they were ancient pagan sanctuaries, which Islam had adopted.[132]

According to the CARC official who toured the Chechen-Ingush ASSR in 1960, the *tariqas* also engaged in 'instigating national [anti-Russian] hatred and disagreements and deflecting young people from communist influences and participation in public life'. Some were actually lured away from the Komsomol. One mulla was quoted as saying that a young boy or girl who refused to pray and respect God must be physically forced to do so by the parents, even to the point of being beaten and intimidated with the threat of divine punishment. A later report noted that the *tamadas* enjoyed 'undisputable authority among their *murids*, in effect controlling their fate and that of their families'. They took upon themselves to resolve family and everyday questions in accordance with the requirements of the Shari'a and *adat*, in this way 'usurping the powers of the organs of government'.[133] Indeed,

128. Bennigsen, 'The Qadiriyah (Kunta-Hajji) Tariqah in North-East Caucasus', pp.74-5.

129. I am grateful for this information to Moshe Gammer.

130. P. A. Zadorozhnyi to A. A. Puzin, 30 Aug. 1960; GARF, f.6991, o.3, d.207, l.53; and see pp.304-5, 331 and 458.

131. Bennigsen, 'Muslim Conservative Opposition to the Soviet Regime', p.342.

132. Makatov, 'Kul't sviatykh v islame', pp.166-71.

133. P. A. Zadorozhnyi to A. A. Puzin, 30 Aug. 1960, and A. Asaulka to V.

they constituted a virtually autonomous social entity, with its own moral and legal code, its own leadership and hierarchy, and even its own sources of income, based on *zakat* and *sadaqa*.[134] It was, thus, not surprising that they were accused of meddling in social life and public affairs which did not bear on believers' religious feelings.[135]

Most Soviet sources which addressed themselves to the Sufi orders noted the total allegiance of their followers to these organisations and their leaders. The basic principle of the relationship between the *murid* and the shaykh-*ustadh* was the former's 'impersonal, unquestioning submission' to the latter,[136] whose authority, one writer pointed out, was not restricted to the conduct of collective prayer and the *zikr*, or even to personal censure. Some *murshids*, in addition to 'all available forms and methods of Muslim propaganda', actually meted out a variety of punishments to those of their adherents who violated the demands and requirements of the order.[137] The *murid* was taught self-abasement and self-denial, which meant first and foremost utter obedience to his shaykh or *ustadh*. Among other things, this was tantamount in the conditions prevailing in the Caucasus, to showing respect to one's clan and its honour and tradition.[138]

Nor, according to these same Soviet sources, had the orders given up the concept preached by the most famous opponent of the Russian conquest of the Northern Caucasus, Imam Shamil, concerning the *gazavat*, the holy war to achieve a 'military-theocratic state'; this militancy indeed characterised 'Caucasian muridism'.[139] In this vein the *tariqas* kept alive the struggle against the lay authority. Their leadership did not refrain from indicating the contradiction between Islam, on the one hand, and Soviet values and norms

---

A. Kuroedov, 1 Nov. 1968; GARF, f.6991, o.3, d.207, ll.53-4 and 57, and o.6, d.153, ll.159-60; also *Groznenskii rabochii*, 25 June 1958, quoted in Tsavkalov, *Prichiny zhivuchestva religoznykh perezhitkov i puti ikh preodoleniia*, p.6.

134. Bryan, 'Internationalism, Nationalism and Islam', pp.204-5.

135. *Ibid.*, p.206.

136. Mustafinov, *Zikrizm i ego sotsial'naia sushchnost'*, p.34.

137. Mamleev, *Reaktsionnaia sushchnost' miuridzma*, pp.37-8.

138. Mamleev, *Nekotorye osobennosti islama v Checheno-Ingushetii*, pp.21-3.

139. Mamleev, *Reaktsionnaia sushchnost' miuridizma*, pp.38-9, and Mamleev, *Nekotorye osobennosti islama v Checheno-Ingushetii*, p.19. Needless to say, this was not an accurate interpretation of the concept of *gazavat*.

of behaviour, on the other. They thus expressed their antagonism to atheistic lecturers and the authors of anti-religious articles in the press. They would shower curses upon them at their group meetings and send them anonymous letters requesting that they cease their activity. One mulla stated that the author of an article entitled 'Muridism, the enemy of everything progressive' should be killed or have his tongue cut out.[140] Some of the mullas and *murids* were said to have had a criminal past in the regions of their deportation, and now not only operated their prayer-houses illegally, but had no legal right to reside in their places of habitation.[141] One of them had been convicted in 1953 and sentenced to twenty-five years for anti-Soviet activity, which he had conducted 'under the guise of religion'.[142] The leader of the Kunta Haji himself was said to have collaborated with the Germans in World War II.[143] Some of the *tamadas* who engaged in illegal religious activity – the performance of religious rites in public places, the teaching of children in groups, the activisation of Shari'a courts –were indeed expelled from the republic.[144]

But such administrative measures had little effect. They do not seem to have in any way weakened the hold of the Sufi orders over various sectors of the republic's private and collective existence: Bennigsen mentions in this connection their infiltration and leadership of traditional Muslim professional gilds and of the aul assembly, the *jemaat*.[145] They certainly did not curb the hostility of the

140. P. A. Zadorozhnyi to A. A. Puzin, 30 Aug. 1960; GARF, f.6991, o.3, d.207, l.57.

141. *Ibid.*, ll.59-60.

142. A. L. Alisov to A. A. Puzin, 16 March 1962; GARF, f.6991, o.3, d.1606, l.18.

143. P. A. Zadorozhnyi, Information, 30 Aug, 1960; GARF, f.6991, o.3, d.207, ll.72-3. For the activity of the Chechen and Ingush in the context of the war, see also Zelkina, p.119. Collaboration with the Germans was the official pretext for the mass deportation of the Volga Germans in 1941 (see n.101 above) and of the North Caucasian Balkars, Karachai, Chechen and Ingush, the Kalmyks and the Crimean Tatars in 1943-4 and for the abolition of their administrative units – irrespective of the fact that in no case was there evidence of entire populations siding with the Germans. Moreover, members of all these peoples fought in the Soviet armed forces against Germany.

144. A. L. Alisov to A. A. Puzin, 16 March 1962, and A. Asaulka to V. A Kuroedov, 1 Nov. 1968; GARF, f.6991, o.3, d.1606, l.20, and o.6, d.153, l.159. And see p.349.

145. Bennigsen, 'Muslim Conservative Opposition to the Soviet Regime', pp.343-4.

population toward members of their own nationality who had joined the Soviet bandwagon. Individual Chechen or Ingush who spoke out against Islam were intimidated and even attacked physically. Two teachers threatened to kill a *sel'sovet* chairman who criticised them for performing religious rites.[146] The chairman of another *sel'sovet*, who obstructed pilgrims on their way to a holy place, was subjected to threats, blackmail and calumny, and eventually assaulted by 'hooligans'. The head teacher of a school, who published an article in the local press against the *uraz* received a signed letter from a pupil asking: 'Is such a man as you needed among the Chechen? He...should be expelled from the village. His nation does not need him'. The letter called him a goat, a dragon, a Satan who sullied Chechen honour and deserved to die. 'You want with the help of this article to become good in the eyes of the regime and the Russians, but you should know that the regime and the Russians think of people like you as good–for–nothings'.

The fact that not a single registered mosque was allowed in the entire republic for twenty years after the return from deportation became a cause célèbre, especially in view of the fact that there were two Russian Orthodox churches and a Baptist prayer-house. In all sections of society throughout the republic this was viewed not only as discrimination against Islam but as a violation of national rights.[147] It was only in 1978 that the first two registered mosques were opened in the Chechen-Ingush ASSR, to be followed in the following two years by five more.[148]

In early 1963 sect members in the Chechen-Ingush ASSR were discovered to be involved in a religious *magnitizdat*, the recording and/or transmission of illegal material on tapes. A 'primitive radio network' was eliminated which had helped ten families listen to recordings of religious verses, songs and *zikrs*, and the organs of government confiscated a hoard of thirty-nine recorded tapes of 500 metres each.[149] By the end of the decade technology was

146. For the phenomenon of schoolteachers who identified with religion, which was most irregular in the Soviet Union, see below.

147. CRA, Information, sent to the CPSU Central Committee, 22 May 1970; TsKhSD, f.5, o.62, d.38, ll.15-16. For further discussion of the national aspect of anti-Muslim discrimination in the Chechen-Ingush ASSR, see pp.704-5.

148. Bennigsen and Wimbush, *Muslims of the Soviet Empire*, p.187.

149. A. L. Alisov to A. A. Puzin, 12 Feb. 1964; GARF, f.6991, o.3, d.1608,

being widely used. Passages from the Qur'an were photocopied and distributed, as were records and tapes with religious content. Illegal transmissions of religious songs and sermons were especially popular. And 'holy letters' were circulated, calling on people to enhance their faith and strictly observe religious rites.[150] Here, as in Central Asia, some of these were chain letters reproduced by schoolchildren.[151] Muslim *samizdat* in the Chechen-Ingush and Dagestan ASSRs in ensuing years continued reproducing religious texts – classic authors such as al-Ghazali,[152] writings of Sufi shaykhs and Dagestani Arabist scholars of the sixteenth to nineteenth centuries, as well as of Tatar jadid theologians.[153] To all these had to be added the persistent activities of 'radio hooligans', some of them intelligentsia, who broadcast religious programmes.[154]

One of the concerns of the organs of government related to the influence of the *tariqas* on the school age and young adults. Their leaders did not allow *murids* to read books or the press, to listen to radio, go to the cinema or clubs and attend lectures. *Murids* were said to only barely let their children go to school; this held not only for the girls, but even for the boys, whom, according to one source, they did not wish to acquire knowledge which might lessen the educational impact of the orders on the younger generation. In no event would they allow them to become involved in the regime's instruments of socialisation, to join the Pioneers or Komsomol or participate in school social activity. In some schools the majority of children declared themselves believers

1.31. See also Mamleev, *Reaktsionnaia sushchnost' miuridizma*, pp.36-7.

150. CRA, Information, sent to the CPSU Central Committee, 22 May 1970; TsKhSD, f.5, o.62, d.38, l.14.

151. S. Murtazalieva, 'Uchitivaia mestnye osobennosti', *Sovetskii Dagestan*, 1982, No.5, p.47, quoted in Bryan, 'Internationalism, Nationalism and Islam', p.204. For chain letters in Central Asia, see pp.360-1.

152. Abu Hamid al-Ghazali, one of the early theorists of ethical mysticism, who contended, among other things, that the essence of Sufism could be attained only by 'direct experience, ecstasy and inward transformation' – quoted in Trimingham, *The Sufi Orders in Islam*, p.3.

153. Bryan, *ibid*. For a discussion of this literature, see M. A. Abdullaev, *Nekotorye voprosy teologii islama*, Makhachkala, 1973, pp.59-62 and 105-7, quoted in Bennigsen and Wimbush, *Mystics and Commissars*, pp.88-93.

154. A. A. Nurullaev, Information, transmitted to A. M. Vasil'ev at the CPSU Central Committee Department of Party-Organisational Work, 2 Feb. 1972; GARF, f.6991, o.6, d.459, l.27. Of 120 such 'radio hooligans' brought to book in the republic in 1970, 13 had made recordings of religious content.

and argued with teachers who sought to explain the bankruptcy of religion.[155] It is noteworthy in this context that in the Chechen-Ingush ASSR not all schoolteachers were avowed atheists, some actually declaring themselves believers. So, too, did 30 per cent of Chechen and Ingush students at the Groznyi Pedagogical Institute, when questioned in a sociological survey in the early 1970s, while 43 per cent of the students admitted to observing the fast.[156] The orders' religious leaders were also reported to have exhorted their adherents to make every effort to prevent their sons from being enlisted into the armed forces for fear that what they might learn there might contradict their traditions.[157] Despite their stringency, however, the orders boasted a considerable adherence among the younger generation. Sociological surveys conducted in the 1970s showed that over 50 per cent of young believers declared themselves 'adepts of a specific *wird*' and nearly 20 per cent participated in *zikrs*.[158]

Another cause of regime anxiety was the disruption of law and order that was a frequent concomitant of the unruliness with which the *tariqas* conducted their affairs. When the selection of a deceased *tamada's* successor, for example, deteriorated into a mass brawl, the matter came before a people's court and the four chief transgressors were fined.[159] The North Caucasians' traditional 'collective guarantee', it was contended, often led to harmful conduct of 'a criminal and on occasion of a political nature'.[160]

---

155. A. L. Alisov to A. A. Puzin, 16 March 1962; GARF, f.6991, o.3, d.1601, ll.20-1; Tutaev, *Reaktsionnaia sekta Batal-Khadzhi*, p.20, and Tutaev, *Protiv sektantskogo bezzakoniia*, pp.15-16. In one raion 98 children of members of the Batal Haji did not attend school, 83 of them not even appearing on the school lists.

156. A. Barmenkov to Komsomol Secretary L. I. Matveev, 15 Jan. 1974; GARF, f.6991, o.6, d.622, ll.3-4.

157. Mamleev, *Reaktsionnaia sushchnost' miuridizma*, p.33.

158. The percentage given was 50.9 – V. Iu. Gadaev, 'O kharaktere religioznosti sel'skoi molodezhi', in *Kharakter religioznosti i problemy ateisticheskogo vospitaniia*, published in 1979 by the Chechen-Ingush ASSR Institute of History, Sociology and Philosophy, quoted in Broxup, 'Islam and Atheism in the North Caucasus', pp.44-5.

159. A. Asaulka to V. A. Kuroedov, 1 Nov. 1968; GARF, f.6991, o.6, d.153, ll.160-1.

160. Deputy Heads of the CPSU Central Committee Departments of Propaganda and Party-Organisational Work, Iu. Skliarov and G. Lapchinskii, 4 May 1973; TsKhSD, f.5, o.66, d.139, l.34.

The central role played by the *tariqas* in the republic's rural society was demonstrated when the leader of one of them died on the last day of the *uraz* in 1964. Over 1,000 people participated in his funeral from a number of raiony and a large number of cars were deflected from the enterprises where they should have been in use. The local *sel'sovet* House of Culture did not operate for several days and for the course of nearly a week dozens of heads of livestock were slaughtered and cooked in the courtyard of the dead man's home exactly opposite the offices of the local *raikom* and *raiispolkom*, not a few communists taking part in this commemorative entertainment.[161]

The total disregard of the Chechen and Ingush religious leaders for the norms of the Soviet political and social system was reflected in an unofficial assembly of Ingushetiia's patrimonial and religious 'authorities', or, in their own terminology, of 'representatives of all Ingush settlements', i.e. including the Prigorodnyi raion. This gathering took place in 1969 with the participation, according to one source, of 180 persons. It discussed and passed resolutions on the basis of the Shari'a and *adat* on questions pertaining to regulating blood feuds, which still persisted in the republic and were an integral component of the collective guarantee, burial and betrothal arrangements, divorces, adjudicating cases of bridal abduction, and the like. It fixed the sums which were to be paid as retribution for murder (5,000 rubles), as *qalym* (1,000 rubles plus a sheep), for divorce and funeral expenses. These resolutions were then duplicated and distributed among the population, where they were said to have acquired the force of law, the document warning that anyone who violated them would lose the rights of 'mutual relations between people according to local custom and law'.[162]

161. A. L. Alisov to A. A. Puzin, 3 Feb. 1965; GARF, f.6991, o.3, d.1609, ll.30-1.

162. A. Asaulka to A. A. Nurullaev, 14 Aug. 1969, and CRA, Information, sent to the CPSU Central Committee, 22 May 1970; GARF, f.6991, o.6, d.220, ll.345-6, and TsKhSD, f.5, o.62, d.38, ll.14-15. The assembly had convened on 18 April at a rural cemetery. Its resolutions were said, among others, to have reduced the costs to the individual believer of the various practices and customs – perhaps in order to help ensure their continuance. According to Asaulka, only 50 to 60 people participated in the meeting. The local press devoted considerable attention to this gathering, making it the focus of a major anti-religious campaign; it was even the theme of an article in *Pravda*, 29 March 1970. For the persistence of the blood feud in the Chechen-Ingush ASSR after the return of the deportees, see P. A. Zadorozhnyi, Information, 30 Aug. 1960; GARF,

It was, then, little wonder that Soviet commentators dwelt at length on, and were duly concerned by, the unalloyed authority enjoyed among the *murids* by the *ustadhs* and shaykhs. The consolidating principle of the members of the *murid* community was the acknowledgement and study of the teachings of the *tariqa* of their shaykh. The 'conceptual pivot', one Soviet source pointed out, was the collective religious activity, whose aim was to prepare for eternal life and bliss. To achieve their goal the leaders of these groups endeavoured to distract their followers from all 'creative activity and isolate them from the collective, from society'. Within the orders their own value system prevailed, and they had their special 'group opinon' and religious aims. These exerted major influence, given the circumstances of the Chechen or Ingush aul, where vestiges of clan existence still pertained, and the leaders of the *murid* communities made every effort to ensure the strict observance of Islamic tradition among all their clan and extended family, believing that any digression would also weaken links within the clan. Indeed, sociological surveys demonstrated that 90 per cent of believers among the Chechen and Ingush received their religious education within the family.

The collective performance of religious acts, according to the same source, during which the adept 'experiences a tremendous emotional and psychological burden, becomes the goal and meaning of life'. The group leader cultivates a feeling of 'exclusiveness and isolation' among his adherents, based on their sense of superiority *vis-à-vis* not only non-believers and adherents of other faiths but also members of other *murid* groups. Thus, adherents of the shaykhs of the different *wirds* did not let their daughters marry followers of other *wirds*, let alone non-believers.[163]

Certainly, then, the conditions pertaining in the Chechen-Ingush ASSR dictated the politicisation of Islam in that republic following the return of the deportees. There was no way that a *modus vivendi* could be found between the Sufi *tariqas* and *wirds*, which continued to dominate the social and economic life of considerable sectors, if not the great majority, of the Chechen and Ingush population, and the Soviet authorities and their local representatives.

---

f.6991, o.3, d.207, l.78.

163. *Islam v SSSR*, pp.81–5.

The Ismailis

One of the sects about which some authentic information seeped through was the Shiite Ismaili Nizari sect in the Gorno-Badakhshan AO, which encompassed some 75 per cent of the oblast' population, with about 40,000 members shortly after the end of World War II,[164] and was subordinate to the authority of the Aga Khan in Bombay, the head of the Ismailis world-wide. The Ismailis were traditionally characterised by their discipline and secretive nature, each person on joining taking an oath not to divulge either the substance of the Ismaili dogma or his own membership in the sect; this custom reflected the centuries of persecution the Ismailis had undergone at the hands of the dominant Islamic denominations. It was thought in the immediate postwar period that the Ismailis of the Pamirs still paid the mandatory tithe to the Aga Khan, somehow transmitting it via Afghanistan.[165] The sect was divided into communities, each administered by a *pir*, and the local associations were headed by *khalifas* or elders.

Believing that God chose His own abode, the sect did not prescribe the construction of mosques for the performance of collective prayer. Its members performed two, not the standard five, daily prayers, which they conducted for the most part either in the seclusion of their homes or, in summer, in the fields.[166] Rites would be performed by the local *khalifa*, at the request of individual believers.[167] The Ismailis observed the festivals of Qurban-Bayram and the Nawruz, the Persian New Year, when they might indeed hold collective prayer-services in a variety of venues, and conducted regular pilgrimages to about twenty-five *mazars*, where they performed sacrifices. (By the mid-1960s these pilgrimages seem to have stopped, except at two sites.) According to one source, the Nawruz was celebrated in August with the ripening of the crops, according to another – from the mid-1970s – it was indeed

164. The figure, based on CARC sources, may be an underestimate, for an article written in the mid-1990s speaks of 340-350,000 Ismailis in the Pamirs –A. Niiazi, 'Islam i obshchestvo', *Aziia i Afrika segodnia*, No.7, 1996, p.28.

165. It was later conceded that payments to the Aga Khan had ceased as of 1932 – U. Yuldashev, Information, 10 July 1968; GARF, f.6991, o.6, d.153, l.96.

166. *Ibid.*, l.97.

167. K. Hamidov to CARC, 7 Dec. 1945, and I. V. Polianskii to K. E. Voroshilov, 26 March 1947; GARF, f.6991, o.3, d.30, l.365, and d.47, l.113.

celebrated in March, not necessarily, however, on March 21 (the equinox), but rather on different days in different places, so that the *khalifa* could perform the traditional ritual personally in each kishlak.[168]

Conflicts had existed up to approximately 1937 between the Ismailis and the Soviet state, as a result primarily of the subordination of large followings in the Pamirs to leading Ismailis in Afghanistan and what was to become Pakistan. (It is not clear whether these were religious figures who had fled the Soviet Union and settled in these parts, or local leaders.) These ties then ceased and the new *khalifas*, who headed the sect by the second half of the 1950s, were regular Soviet 'workers', basically kolkhozniki. The *zakat* had disappeared and their main religious occupation was linked with burial and memorial services, the *uraz* no longer being observed, and Qurban-Bayram being marked rather by collective repasts in the family circle than by the traditional sacrifice. An element of faith-healing, however, survived; medical assistance and the educational work which accompanied the introduction of better sanitary conditions in order to improve living standards in the country's backward areas were of such a low level in the Gorno-Badakhshan AO that, even according to CARC's oblast' *upolnomochennyi*, it was not surprising that the population persisted in giving credence to the healing powers of talismans and amulets. In addition, circumcision, a pre-nuptial betrothal ceremony and readings from the Qur'an for the dying and before and after the funeral service remained universal. Yet, the bottom line seemed to be that the substance of the faith had become more social than spiritual.[169]

By the end of the 1960s, there were not only no *pirs*, but most of the remaining *khalifas* were men without much religious education, their knowledge, such as it was, deriving primarily from individual study, usually probably with their fathers, and focusing on those parts of the Qur'an necessary for the conduct

168. I. V. Polianskii to P. V. Kovanov, 23 June 1955, Arifov to A. A. Puzin, M. Kh. Ahmedov, Obkom Secretary M. Nazarshoev, Ispolkom Chairman M. Shirinjanov and GBAO KGB Chief A. Iu. Salibaev, [25 Feb. 1964], and Lecture of the Gorno-Badakhshan AO Oblispolkom deputy chairman, 2 July 1973; GARF, f.6991, o.3, d.114, ll.40-1, and d.1740, ll.19-20, and o.6, d.545, ll.94 and 113.

169. Arifov to A. Puzin, D. Ahmedov and Gorno-Badakhshan Obkom Secretary G. Javov, 10 Dec. 1962; GARF, f.6991, o.3, d.1739, ll.11-17.

of the most vital rituals. While chosen by believers to be *khalifas* and perform rites for them, none had visited the Aga Khan, they had no *murids* even according to Soviet sources, and there were only a very few who persisted in zealously advocating the influence of religion and its representatives. Between twenty and thirty of these *khalifas* were officially registered (the number varied from time to time), one for each *sel'sovet*. There was no link between the *khalifas*, each one functioning entirely on his own.

The fundamental Ismaili approach to the Qur'an as allegorical, to the Shari'a as not requiring obligatory compliance, and to ritual as peripheral, alleviated the process of adapting to communist society and its values. The *khalifa* had no difficulty in accepting that Communism and Islam had a common purpose. By the late 1960s the rite connected with marriage consisted of a minimal ceremony conducted by a *khalifa* but without religious content, which would be conducted after the couple registered with ZAGS, and was not observed by all. Circumcision, which was performed by 'specialists', not by the *khalifas*, was not accompanied by reading from the Qur'an. Even memorial services were receding, so that it was only the actual burial rites and the religious readings held in the home of the deceased on the third night after interment which gave the *khalifa* scope for his activity. At the same time, since he did not have sufficient income from his religious functions, the *khalifa* was obliged to take part in 'socially beneficial' work. While this equated him with the ordinary believer, it also – in the words of Soviet sources – enabled him the better to know the latter's thoughts and to adapt his 'religious propaganda' accordingly. The *khalifas* were known to go the rounds of believers' homes to hold discussions, but the content of these talks was not divulged. Finally, the severe climate of the region was thought to be conducive to keeping religion alive, the population resorting to sacrifices in the face of avalanches and other recurrent natural disasters.[170]

170. U. Yuldashev, Information, 10 July 1968, and CRA, Information, sent to the CPSU Central Committee, 22 May 1970; GARF, f.6991, o.6, d.153, ll.84-105, and TsKhSD, f.5, o.62, d.38, ll.18-19. See also *Nauka i religiia*, No.1, Jan. 1982, pp.19-20.

Peripheral groups and sects

Other groups surfaced from time to time. In the late 1960s a number of them described in the Soviet documentation as the Ahl-i Qur'an (People of the Qur'an) appeared in Tashkent and its vicinity. Their main purpose was to attain the 'purity' of Islam. They demanded the universal observance of the five daily prayers. Maintaining that SADUM operated in conformity with orders from the regime, deviated from Islamic norms and made concessions to believers who did not observe the precepts of Islam, they inveighed against some of its instructions and called upon believers not to participate in prayer-services in registered mosques, whose clergy distorted and weakened religion. They also opposed the secondary and higher education of girls, which threatened to remove them from the authority of their parents, and stressed the need for *qalym*. In the course of the 1970s the organs of government took preventative measures to terminate the activities of this 'sect', cautioning its members that if they continued them, they would be prosecuted. In this process a search was conducted in the home of the leader of a group in the city of Tashkent which uncovered a large quantity of illegal religious material.[171] At approximately the same time, in Osh an unnamed 'sect' strove to convince believers to observe all Muslim rituals and, demanded that parents educate their offspring in the spirit of Islam.[172] In a rural area of Kazakhstan's Tselinograd Oblast' fifty members of 'the Muslim sect of "White Caps"' (*beloshaposhniki*) were uncovered in the mid-1970s. Those may have been Vis Haji, who were known by this name.[173]

It is highly probable that none of these groups, except perhaps the last one, was in fact affiliated to any of the recognised Muslim sects, representing rather – like the so-called Wahhabis a decade later[174] – Muslim zealots who sought to revive what they embraced as primordial Islam, an Islam unulliedly modernisation and constant compromises with the secular power.

171. CRA, Information, sent to the CPSU Central Committee, 22 May 1970 –TsKhSD, f.5, o.62, d.38, ll.28-9; P. Krivosheev, Survey, 25 Dec. 1972, and G. Gol'st to K. R. Ruzmetov, 19 April 1973 – GARF, f.6991, o.6, d.548, ll.49 and 56; and Saidbaev, *Islam i obshchestvo*, p.283, n.10.

172. Saidbaev, *Islam i obshchestvo*, p.283, n.10.

173. A. Tishkov to the CRA, 31 Dec. 1973; GARF, f.6991, o.6, d.566, ll.102-3.

174. Align See pp.358-9.

A few established sects, however, did survive in the Soviet Union. The Ahl-i Haqq (lit. the People of the Divine Truth), sometimes also known as Ali Ilahi (the Deifiers of Ali), survived in Turkmenistan and in Armenia (among the Karapapakhs). According to one Western source, this extremist, esoteric and syncretistic sect, which mixed Christian and Mazdean elements, numbered 20-30,000. There were also groups of Baha'is, chiefly in Azerbaijan and Turkmenistan, and Yezidis among the Kurdish population of Armenia.[175] Members of these sects tended to practise the Muslim custom of *taqiyya*, precautionary dissembling, in order to avoid discovery, although it was widely known that they existed in certain areas.[176]

The political implications of the activity of the *ishans* in Central Asia and the *tariqas* in the Northern Caucasus were becoming clear by the early 1980s in the context, in the domestic arena, of the resurgence of nationalism throughout the Soviet Union, and, on the international scene, of the Iranian revolution and the invasion of Afghanistan. A report sent by the CRA to the CPSU Central Committee noted that

> [....] the most reactionary element of the unregistered clergy (namely, over 200 descendants of *ishans* operating in Central Asia, the leaders of about 400 *murid* brotherhoods functioning in the North Caucasian republics, and a few more extremist mullas) are inciting the population to refuse to serve in the Soviet army and to prohibit their children joining the Pioneers and Komsomol. They are also setting up underground schools for the teaching of religion to children and adults, duplicating and distributing materials of foreign radio stations, and instigating religious fanaticism and a nationalist mood.

In Tajikistan a considerable number of schools had been discovered, as had many instances of reproducing and disseminating *samizdat* literature.[177] An entire section in a book on Islam in the

175. Bennigsen and Lemercier-Quelquejay, 'Islam in the Soviet Muslim Republics', pp.135-6.
176. I am grateful for this information to Michael Zand.
177. CRA memo, 2 June 1983; TsKhSD, f.5, o.89, d.82, l.38. For the schools and the reproduction and dissemination of materials, see pp.353-8 and 360-2.

USSR published by the CPSU Central Committee Academy of Social Sciences in 1983 dwelt on the strength of muridism among the Chechen and Ingush. It ascribed this vigour and power to the isolation of the rural surroundings in which most members of these two nationalities grew up and lived, and to the almost total identity which the shaykhs and *ustadhs* encouraged between religion, on the one hand, and nation and clan (*taip*) on the other.[178]

The unregistered Muslim clergy helped keep Islam alive in the areas not affected by the opening of the few official mosques. They had recourse to methods upon which the authorities could not but look with dispproval for they demonstrated that the clergy were not by and large subject to regime repression. But it was the traditionally oppositionist elements which were the cornerstone of resistance to Moscow's endeavour to bring religion into line, for they were not prepared even to put on a pretense of accepting the rules of the game. Deeply entrenched, as they were, in the social consciousness of the surrounding population and an intrinsic part of the local and national ethos, the *ishans*, or descendants of *ishans*, in Central Asia and the *tariqas* and *wirds* in the Northern Caucasus had the backing of the indigenous ethnicities. They were able to defy the powers-that-be, more quietly in the former case and more audibly in the latter, but with a similar determination and sense that history and God were on their side. These more extremist figures and groups, for whom surely considerations of financial profit were not a major factor, were risking all in order to maintain a cause in which they believed, and that was the essence of their existence. It was this, perhaps, that in the final event made the apprehension with which they were regarded by the regime a self-fulfilling prophecy.

178. 'Religious and national survivals in contemporary muridism' in *Islam v SSSR*, pp.79-86. The entire Chechen population comprises nine *taips*, so that the *taip* is rather larger than a clan; I have used the word for lack of anything more precise. For Islam and nationalism, see Chapter 12.

Part IV. THE SOCIAL ASPECT: THE PRACTICE OF ISLAM

7

THE SOCIOLOGY OF SOVIET ISLAM

General features

Islam in the Soviet Union differed from other religions in its substance, the tactics it employed in its relations with the regime and the historical, social and geographical circumstances in which it operated. While inevitably influenced by regime policy and general economic and social trends and developments, as was every other faith, it had its own specific features.

The essence of Islam is not to be found in the prayer-house and liturgy or even in its credo. It lies rather in law, the Shari'a, and in praxis, the latter consisting of two principal components, the one determined by the Muslim calendar, the other by the ordinary believer's life-cycle. The fast and festivals, on the one hand, and the rites of passage, on the other, comprised the axis on which Muslim religious life in the Soviet Union revolved.

As to its *modus operandi*, a former CRA official has noted that Soviet Islam was characterised by a basic, outward compliance coupled with obduracy in attaining its required goals. The Muslims, he said, would formally agree to implement the law and the instructions of local government organs, at the same time solving their problems their own way. Their situation was abnormal: an oblast' or republic with 1,000 settlements might have three or four official mosques, so the Muslims would build mosques without permission. When they were told that a mosque had to be destroyed since it had been illegally built, they demolished it and proceeded to construct another one in its immediate proximity. In other words, instead of protesting, like other faiths, they formally concurred

with the authorities, but in effect persisted in doing as they pleased.[1]
A CPSU Central Committee apparatchik reported in the early
1970s that Muslims tended to file complaints with the authorities
much more rarely than did representatives of other confessions;
yet, this in no way reflected a lower level of religiosity.[2]

The *mise-en-scène* within which Soviet Islam operated was the
product of two principle components: its own historical heritage
and the new Soviet circumstances. In most Muslim areas – certainly
in Central Asia and the Caucasus – Muslim awareness in the pre-
Soviet period was predetermined first of all by adherence to one's
family or kinship group. One was born into Islam and the religious
structure was built upon that of the social environment. Affiliation
to a mosque was a concomitant of membership of a kinship group
or economic union. People came together at the mosque not so
much in order to pray as to discuss their daily affairs within the
circle of their kinsfolk and friends and resolve urgent problems.
Islam was thus a mechanism for regulating relations within local
society, comprising entire groups of kinsmen and neighbours rather
than individuals and manifesting itself within the framework of
social events, in the conduct of family and economic ceremonies
in which participation was obligatory. In this way the observance
of Islam was linked to the structure of ritual roles laid down
primarily by one's sex and age.[3]

An inescapable concomitant of the totality of the hold of the
kinship group was antagonism to external authority on the part
of both the individual and the closed extended family and clan
community. This rendered legislation ineffectual and meant that
the average Muslim saw no obligation in surrendering to the
whims of the regime and that the local official in the Muslim
areas who came from indigenous ethnic groups had no problem
with transmitting false information to his bureaucratic superiors
in the oblast' centre or republican capital.

At the same time, Islam in the Soviet period inevitably bore
the imprint of what Soviet literature called modernising tendencies.
Not only the religious establishment (both the spiritual directorates

1. Author's interview with a former CRA departmental head, who has asked
not to be identified.
2. I. A. Bonchkovskii to E. I. Lisavtsev 1 June 1973; GARF, f.6991, o.6,
d.573, l.179.
3. Abashin, 'Sotsial'nye korni sredneaziatskogo islamizma', pp.455-6.

and the registered clergy) but also the rank and file could not be isolated from their Soviet surroundings. In the words of a book published in the early 1980s by the CPSU Central Committee's Academy of Social Sciences, all aspects of Islam's attempt to meet the challenges of a modern technological society in general and of the specific constraints of 'socialist construction' impacted on believers as a whole. This was reflected in modernist interpretations of the relationship between the teachings of Islam and those of contemporary science; in the re-interpretation of Islam's social teachings and moral and ethical norms in light of Soviet conditions; and in changes in traditional requirements on the plane of ritual practice. The mass of believers were loyal citizens and did not wish to be cut off from their own children and grandchildren, and so were unwilling to heed calls for 'fanatical' observance of the precepts of Islam. On the whole, believers had empathy with sermons and interpretations which suited and took into account Soviet conditions, and showed little patience for attempts to impose demands which ran counter to them.[4]

Muslim religious activity, like that of the Russian Orthodox Church, surfaced during the war throughout the Soviet Union. One Soviet expert on Islam noted many years later that the losses suffered in World War II helped strengthen the role of Islam among the population, for people found comfort in religion. 'War, like every misfortune, leads to an outburst of religiosity'. Both those who were unable to explain developments scientifically and those who endured material privations looked to God for protection and assistance. As a result of all this, the number of mosques grew, as did that of those who went there to pray; the role of the religious community was enhanced, and people began performing 'all kinds of rites'. In Central Asia the levirate was restored to secure the welfare of young children whose fathers had been killed at the front. There were attempts to organise the teaching of children in groups and to revive norms stipulated by the Shari'a. 'Acts of terrorism' took place against 'emancipated' women 'activists' and in the oblasti of Namangan and Bukhara some were actually killed. And 'elements hostile to the regime, especially among the clergy, became active'. Yet, this same expert insisted, all this did not spell a retreat from the achievements of the Soviet regime in

4. *Islam v SSSR*, pp.105-14. For further examples of Islam's adaptation to contemporary conditions in the context of sermons, see pp. 253-62.

the years of 'socialist construction', for the new recruits to religion did not come from the ranks of those who had previously acquired immunity from religion and embraced a 'scientific world-view'. They were people who had continued to believe and to practise religious rites in their homes.[5]

In many areas, indeed, especially in the more outlying regions, Islam had endured throughout the years of repression, simply going underground. In the words of CARC Chairman Polianskii in 1946, the institutionalisation of Islam in Uzbekistan and other areas as of 1942-3 had strengthened Islam organisationally; it had not induced a rise in religiosity. The collapse of its structures prior to the war had had, in his view, only a minor impact on the mass of believers, among whom Islam had struck deep roots. As a result, when circumstances changed favourably, it revived very quickly.[6] A similar opinion was voiced by the CARC *upolnomochennyi* for Kirgiziia, according to whom it would have been erroneous to speak of a resurgence of religion in that republic towards the end of the war; it had simply existed before behind closed doors. The mullas who served as clergy in the immediate postwar period had been there all along, they and their activity had just not been in evidence.[7] In some of the more out-of-the-way parts religion may have fallen off somewhat in the most difficult years, but there was probably little change in its practice. In certain areas of the Mordvinian ASSR, for instance, prayers had been conducted in the open and mullas had visited private homes to perform rites right up to the outbreak of war in 1941.[8]

Religion did not simply come to the fore during the war. Even before 1941, Polianskii wrote, Islam, together with other

5. Saidbaev, *Islam i obshchestvo*, pp.190-1.

6. I. V. Polianskii, Information, 1 Oct. 1946; GARF, f.6991, o.3, d.34, ll.12-13.

7. Minutes, Conference of CARC *upolnomochennye*, Alma-Ata, 2 Oct. 1946; GARF, f.6991, o.3, d.41, ll.45-6. In the rural areas of Tajikistan and Uzbekistan, too, large numbers of mosques had continued functioning, see p.289. A study of Islam in Uzbekistan in the prewar period reached the conclusion that the regime was unable to eliminate the Muslim clergy, in particular those who were 'not part of a regular Muslim establishment, such as many of the Sufi *ishans* and their followers, or people who knew just enough to lead prayers and conduct basic rituals, and therefore became *de facto* mullas' – Keller, *The Struggle against Islam in Uzbekistan, 1927-1941*, p.283.

8. Minutes, CARC session No.26, 1-2 Dec. 1949; GARF, f.6991, o.3, d.60, l.83.

faiths, had rejected the struggle against the Soviet state it had waged in the period of the civil war and the years of socialist construction.[9] Once war broke out religion in general and Islam specifically were given a measure of legitimacy. It was later claimed that the voluntary mobilisation of the spiritual directorates on behalf of the war effort, the publicity given in the central media to their expressions of loyalty and the support shown by local government organs for their *muhtasibs* and qazis created the impression that the state was giving Islam its support and actually caring for the work conditions of its personnel. People began discussing religion at their place of work, and resolutions were passed recognising the benefits of religion and calling upon local soviets to heed the advice of the clergy. One kolkhoz in Tajikistan held a general meeting to appoint a *domulla-imam*, whose candidacy it asked SADUM's representative, the Qazi-kalon (lit. the chief qazi), to confirm.[10]

The Muslim religious revival of the war years and the period immediately following the war was described by CARC as of a 'high level' and, especially in Central Asia, largely 'spontaneous'.[11] Continuing to expand in the initial postwar period, it probably reached its peak in 1946. At the end of 1945 Polianskii wrote to Molotov that the religious mood among the Muslims was on the rise and embraced 'a significant portion of the population', especially in Central Asia.[12] A year later two CARC officials confirmed that Islamic life was not abating; it had 'erupted', and was continuing to 'drift', beyond the framework of the law.[13]

The Islamic resurgence in Central Asia, Polianskii told the Soviet government, abounded in negative manifestations. In the first place, there were features which had distinguished it from its incipient

9. I. V. Polianskii to G. F. Aleksandrov, 1 July 1947, to A. A. Zhdanov, 7 July 1947, and to the USSR Council of Ministers Cultural Bureau, K. E. Voroshilov, M. A. Turkin, M. A. Suslov and A. A. Kuznetsov, 9 June 1948; RTsKhIDNI, f.17, o.125, d.506, ll.111 and 145, and GARF, f.6991, o.3, d.53, l.13.

10. Saidbaev, *Islam i obshchestvo*, pp.189-90.

11. I. V. Polianskii to K. E. Voroshilov, 5 April 1946; GARF, f.6991, o.3, d.34, l.44.

12. I. V. Polianskii to V. M. Molotov, 7 Dec. 1945; GARF, f.6991, o.3, d.10, l.139.

13. G. Ia. Vrachev and I. N. Uzkov to I. V. Polianskii, 29 Nov. 1946; RTsKhIDNI, f.17, o.125, d.405, l.93.

stages: mass prayer-meetings, especially on festivals, both in mosques and, where there were none, in the open; the unauthorised opening of former mosques, many of them *mahalla* mosques, which were taken over by clergy who were not subordinate to SADUM, and the clandestine building of new ones; and the opening of religious schools, *mektebs*, for school-age children. In addition, there was a plethora of itinerant mullas, who likewise, by definition, did not come into the orbit of SADUM's authority; a resurgence of 'muridism and dervishism', evidence of 'bigoted' Shiite activity in regions not subject to the control of DUMZ (the sole Muslim spiritual directorate which addressed itself to the Shiite community); and, in Uzbekistan, a return to the *chachvan* and *paranja*. There were also the *mazars*, 'places of mass pilgrimage, oblation and prayer', while 'vestiges of the tribal system, and rites and customs of the Shari'a and *adat*' were being resuscitated.[14]

Nor was the tenacity of these religious 'prejudices' the lot just of country folk; urban dwellers, too, including intelligentsia, local officials and even party members adhered to them as well, participating in religious ceremonies, visiting *mazars* and conducting rites.[15] These people, although non-believers, were reluctant to break with tradition. They visited relatives and friends on Uraz-Bayram, on the pretext that, if they refused, their kinsfolk would cease acknowledging them and would not forgive them; they circumcised their sons; their wives did not sit at table with men. While not trusting the mullas, they invited them to perform marriage and funeral ceremonies.[16] One sociological survey found that 20 per cent of those who considered themselves non-believers observed

14. I. V. Polianskii to K. E. Voroshilov, 5 April and 13 Nov. 1946, and to Beriia, Stalin, Molotov and Voroshilov at the Council of Ministers, and to Zhdanov, Khrushchev, A. A. Kuznetsov, N. S. Patolichev and G. M. Popov at the AUCP(b) Central Committee, 27 Feb. 1947; GARF, f.6991, o.3, d.34, ll.44 and 197-8, and d.47, l.92. In 1949 Polianskii was still attributing the 'well-known spontaneity' of Muslim religious activity to the organisational weakness of the spiritual directorates – see p.115. For the practical conclusions Polianskii drew from this situation, see p.117.

15. V. Tatarintsev to A. A. Zhdanov, 15 Nov. 1946; RTsKhIDNI, f.17, o.125, d.421, l.108, and I. V. Polianskii to the Council of Ministers' Cultural Bureau, K. E. Voroshilov, M. A. Turkin (the AUCP(b) Central Committee Administration of Cadres), M. A. Suslov and A. A. Kuznetsov, 10 June 1948; GARF, f.6991, o.3, d.53, l.35. And see pp.648-51.

16. E. Bairamov, 'Islam i 'natsional'nye traditsii'', *Agitator*, 24, Dec. 1966, p.43.

the festivals and performed other rites.[17] All kinds of rites which had been forgotten over the long years of repression were reviving. In the words of a mulla from the rural parts of the Tatar ASSR at the end of the 1940s, things were 'righting themselves': people were once again marrying according to religious custom, attending *jum'a-namaz*, expiating the sins of the departed and paying *fitr*.[18]

One of the manifestations of Islam's resilience, among both the people and the artistic intelligentsia, was its reflection in the national literatures of the period. The Kazakh writer Gabidin Mustafin in a novel he wrote shortly after World War II, *Chaganap Bertev*, presented the religious mood of Kazakh kolkhozniki in a positive light. He even composed a special prayer and made a number of references to Allah and Muhammad. The funeral of Chaganap, a leading agricultural worker in a kolkhoz, ended with the words: 'He who is esteemed [by men] is esteemed also by God. Your place is in Paradise. May you rest in peace'.[19]

The annual, indeed monthly enhancement of Muslim religious activity, to quote one CARC *upolnomochennyi*, inevitably impacted on economic and political activity. There was, for instance, an unmistakable falloff in work attendance on Muslim festivals. The AUCP(b) Control Commission representative in the Uzbek SSR visited eighty-six kolkhozy and seven sovkhozy in four oblasti in 1946 and reported to Zhdanov that not only were rites performed ubiquitously, but large crowds flocked to prayer-services, often absconding from the fulfilment of their agricultural work.[20]

Perhaps even worse in the long run, from the point of view of the authorities, were instances when local public and goverment organisations, unable to mobilise a work force to undertake urgent assignments, approached the clergy for assistance.[21] The fact that they were again being allowed to pray, one *upolnomochennyi* explained, was such a source of contentment for the elderly that

17. U. Arzuev, 'Umenie ubezhdat'', *Agitator*, 13, July 1980, p.51. The survey had been carried out in a single raion in the Karakalpak ASSR.

18. N. Abushaev, Information, 17 Nov. 1949; GARF, f.6991, o.3, d.61, l.125.

19. Memo of a group of officials of the Main Administration of Propaganda and Agitation, undated; RTsKhIDNI, f.17, o.125, d.311, ll.131-43.

20. V. Tatarintsev to A. A. Zhdanov, 15 Nov. 1946; RTsKhIDNI, f.17, o.125, d.421, ll.107-8. For the effect of Muslim festivals on productivity in the Muslim areas, see pp.80 and 498-501.

21. See p.645.

they took part in public life. In the Cherkess AO in the second half of the 1940s they actually helped the kolkhozy regulate work discipline; with the aid of the clergy, the local organs of government had recourse to the assistance of pensioners with excellent results.[22] Sometimes the initiative for economic activity originated with the clergy or the believer community. Groups of older believers – often rather large ones – recurrently mobilised to help with the cotton harvest.[23] During the harvest in Jalalabad Oblast' the clergy organised special brigades of older believers to assist the more backward kolkhozy.[24]

Defining the characteristics of 'the religious movement' within different faiths in the latter 1940s, Polianskii noted that Islam was the most significant of the faiths under CARC's jurisdiction – that is, excluding the Russian Orthodox Church – from the point of view of the number of its adherents. Although if one used the yardstick of registered communities, it was not one of the country's weightier religions, its large number of functioning, unregistered associations and its believers' intense craving to open new mosques made it one of considerable significance. At the same time, he pointed out, Islam was not a proselytising religion.[25] It had, however, its own special methods of conducting 'religious propaganda.' All sorts of superstitions were spread about by 'sorcerers, faith-healers, unclean forces...[and] evil spirits' in an organised endeavour to undermine and 'agitate' against science, the main instrument of the regime's anti-religious campaign.[26] Mullas would also conduct agitation to attract as many people as possible to mass prayer-services.[27]

22. I. V. Polianskii to A. A. Zhdanov, 7 July 1947; RTsKhIDNI, f.17, o.125, d.506, l.147.

23. See p.230.

24. I. V. Polianskii to A. A. Zhdanov, 7 July 1947; RTsKhIDNI, f.17, o.125, d.506, l.148.

25. I. V. Polianskii to L. P. Beriia, I. V. Stalin, V. M. Molotov and K. E. Voroshilov at the Council of Ministers, and to A. A. Zhdanov, N. S. Khrushchev, A. A. Kuznetsov, N. S. Patolichev and G. M. Popov at the Central Committee Secretariat, 27 Feb. 1947, and to K. E. Voroshilov, M. A. Turkin, M. A. Suslov, A. A. Kuznetsov, and the Council of Ministers Cultural Bureau, 10 June 1948; GARF, f.6991, o.3, d.47, l.92 and d.53, l.17.

26. Minutes, Conference of CARC *upolnomochennye* in the Uzbek SSR, 9 Aug. 1948; GAU, f.2456, o.1, d.120, l.14.

27. N. I. Abushaev, Information, 17 Nov. 1949; GARF, f.6991, o.3, d.61, l.124. Abushaev referred specifically to a number of such instances in the city

The Muslim believers' aspirations to inaugurate new mosques notwithstanding, Polianskii reported in spring 1949 that 'one of the most typical features' of contemporary Islam was that in areas where official mosques existed, the level of organised, public performance of the faith was 'relatively weak'. Thus, the *jum'a-namaz*, in the past one of the principal rites of the faith, was not as a rule attended by large numbers in rural areas (not to speak of the daily *namaz*), although there was a notable upsurge of activity on the two main festivals.[28] This low level of organised activity was presumably the outcome of the fear felt by so many of the possible consequences of mosque attendance and of visible pressures and constraints on the part of the authorities regarding those who nonetheless persisted in going to the mosque.

Yet, this reluctance to attend mosque did not spell the end of religious sentiment. In the words of one CARC *upolnomochennyi*, 'we have closed churches and mosques, but religion has remained unclosed'.[29] In some of the more traditionally religious oblasti of Uzbekistan (Andijan, Namangan, Fergana, Samarkand), where religious activity was particularly keen in the postwar years, the itinerant mullas, former imams, dervishes and shaykhs, who moved from one place to another, setting up small groups as they moved around, were frequently held responsible for this.[30] Indeed religious activity in the Uzbek SSR was said even in the late Stalin years to be growing daily. The clergy who led it had resort to various 'tricks' in order to strengthen it and attract new recruits. They sought to revive and promulgate traditional ceremonies and 'religious feudal-bai prejudices'. In this increased activity *ishans*, dervishes and faith-healers were still playing a major role, using old, abandoned mosques and *mazars*, where they could conduct rites and festivals secretly.[31]

28. I. V. Polianskii to K. E. Voroshilov and G. M. Malenkov, 23 April 1949; RTsKhIDNI, f.17, o.132, d.111, ll.59-60. And see pp.219-23.

29. Minutes, CARC session No.26, 1-2 Dec. 1949; GARF, f.6991, o.3, d.60, l.95.

30. Minutes, CARC session No.11, 18-19 June 1947; GARF, f.6991, o.4, d.19, ll.356-7. The groups, presumably for reasons of security, would usually be of less than twelve members, see pp.288 and 339.

31. Kh. N. Iskanderov to Deputy Chairman of the Uzbek SSR Council of Ministers Vahabov and Central Committee Secretary of the Uzbekistan CP Tursunov, 19 July 1951, GAU, f.2456, o.1, d.134, l.55. For the *ishans*, see Chapter 6.

In this context, the fundamental assumption that in Soviet conditions there could be no increase in religious activity was contested by a senior CARC official. Undisputably, he agreed, the roots of religious belief had been eliminated, a 'vast number of Soviet people have broken with religion completely, and their number is growing every day, yet in certain places in specific circumstances, the activity of the *religiozniki* can increase'. This appeared to be occurring in Uzbekistan, where it linked up with manifestations of nationalism.[32] Polianskii, however, reiterated the official assumption in a letter he sent the *upolnomochennyi* for Uzbekistan some years later. He reprimanded him for drawing the conclusion that the influence of religion was expanding in that republic. True, the figures for performance of rites and mosque attendance of the registered religious societies showed an increase, but these had to be attributed to SADUM's waxing prestige and improved organisation.[33] Yet the *upolnomochennye* on the spot stood their ground, continuing to report the enhanced activisation of religious life, as shown by the initiation of new religious groups and the legalisation of groups which had previously functioned unofficially.[34]

Nor was this the situation only in Uzbekistan. In Dagestan, too, religious activity was not receding in the second half of the 1950s, but on the rise. Here, the republican *upolnomochennyi* attributed this trend to the international situation. Many believers, he wrote, had been accustomed to regard their constitutional rights and the opening of mosques with scepticism, but that scepticism was gradually weakening in light of international events and the mutual relations which were evolving between the Soviet Union and the countries of the East, and religious activity was on the upswing. Similar reports about enhanced religious activity were reaching CARC from other areas in the Caucasus – Azerbaijan, Stavropol Krai (the Cherkess AO), the Kabardinian-Balkar ASSR, even the Ajar ASSR.[35] And the mass pilgrimage on the Muslim festivals to Takht-i Sulayman in Osh was one of a few manifestations

32. Minutes, CARC session No.10s, 11-12 April 1952; GARF, f.6991, o.3, d.83, l.164. For Islam and nationalism, see Chapter 12.

33. See pp.203-4.

34. M. A. Khalikov to I. V. Polianskii, Kh. N. Iskanderov, Andijan Obkom Secretary Kurbanov and Oblispolkom Chairman Rizaev, 19 May 1956; GAU, f.2456, o.1, d.198, ll.78-85.

35. G. F. Frolov, Information, 22 Feb. 1957; GARF, f.6991, o.3, d.132, ll.76-80.

of the dynamism of religious activity included by Polianskii in a survey of the situation within all the faiths under his auspices.[36]

Indeed, of all the years from the end of World War II until perestroika, 1955-8 were probably those in which 'the Muslim religious movement' made the most headway. The head of CARC's Department of Eastern Religions summed up the 1954-7 period, during which mosque attendance grew throughout the country, not only on the two major festivals, by noting that the religious mood was being reinforced from year to year. It was bolstered during the period of preparation for the annual *hajj*, although very few pilgrims were permitted to actually make the journey, and even more so upon the pilgrims' return.[37] It was given an additional boost by the visit to mosques of delegations, particularly religious ones, from the various Muslim countries and in connection with the trips of Soviet Muslim figures to these countries. It was further affected by occurrences such as the publication of the Qur'an in Tashkent, by the appearance in Ufa of the pamphlet 'Islam and its liturgy', and by the opening in Tashkent of the second *medrese*.[38] This was the sense, too, of a report to the Central Committee Propaganda Department in late 1957, which stressed not only the enlarged attendance at registered mosques and the abundance of unregistered religious groups, but also and especially the role of the *mazars*, their immense popularity and the variegated activity for which they served as venues.[39]

A decade later, when Islam, like other religions, had begun to recuperate from Khrushchev's anti-religious campaign, it was noted that although its position had been markedly weakened 'as a result of the radical changes which have taken place under Soviet rule', Islam continued to exercise influence upon 'significant strata of the population'. Religious ritual was still at a high level: in practically every settlement where Muslims lived there was some form of religious life, as well as a person who performed religious rites.

36. Minutes, Instructors' meeting, CARC session No.26, 1-2 Dec. 1949; GARF, f.6991, o.3, d.60, l.102.

37. Compare pp.171-3.

38. L. A. Prikhod'ko, Information, 18 May 1957; GARF, f.6991, o.3, d.146, ll.98-102. And see pp.163-4, 168-71 and 177.

39. A. A. Puzin to Head of the CPSU Central Committee Propaganda and Agitation Department V. P. Moskovskii, 14 Nov. 1957; GARF, f.6991, o.3, d.147, ll.205-10.

Over 300 holy places continued to attract pilgrims and a large number of unregistered religious associations and clergy engaged in matters which were by Soviet criteria not the concern of religious associations[40]

One of the characteristics of Muslim religious activity was its adaptation to changing circumstances. On the face of it, there could be no common denominator between Islam and communism. Yet, after its initial opposition to the Soviet regime, Islam changed tack. In the words of CARC's *upolnomochennyi* in Osh Oblast' in the mid-1950s, it stopped attacking Soviet rule, although the more 'reactionary' elements persisted in endeavouring to spread among believers dissatisfaction with the regime and in denigrating its actions. Realising that they were losing followers, the clergy stopped addressing public issues, confining their sermons to strictly religious questions; they rejected customs which were no longer acceptable, such as the *paranja*, the expiation of the sins of the deceased, faith-healing and prostration at ancestors' tombs and *mazars*, and put less demands on believers. The clergy even allowed believers to go to certain films. In this way, CARC officials reported, they apparently sought to retain their prestige and authority among the believer population, whose numbers were actually growing.[41]

This flexibility of the Muslim clergy in suiting its 'religious ideology' to circumstances continued to register successes and, therefore, to attract the attention of those within the bureaucracy whose task it was to evaluate the situation within Islam. By the end of the 1960s, this adaptability was reflected in the clergy's insistence that the observance of Islam's precepts was an expression of respect for one's national customs and traditions.[42] Interlacing religious 'prejudices' with 'the idea of national segregation' now appeared to be one of the most widespread and effective ways of propagating and bolstering religion.[43] Over time this became even more extreme. By the early 1980s the clergy were impressing upon

40. Theses of a lecture, sent to the CPSU Central Committee Propaganda Department, 19 June 1968; GARF, f.6991, o.6, d.147, ll.40-4. And see p.323.

41. I. G. Halimov to CARC, 3 April 1956; GARF, f.6991, o.3, d.457, ll.72-3 and 77-8.

42. V. A. Kuroedov to the CPSU Central Committee Propaganda Department, 23 May 1969; TsKhSD, f.5, r. 9849, o.61, d.32, l.105. For further discussion of Islam and nationalism, see Chapter 12.

43. CRA, Information, sent to the CPSU Central Committee, 27 April 1971; TsKhSD, f.5, o.63, d.89, l.120.

believers that their Islamic affiliation was in fact tantamount to their national definition.[44]

One CRA *upolnomochennyi*, reporting on the sermons of the 100 or so registered and unregistered clergy in his oblast' who engaged in propagating Islam, stressed that their primary premise was the believers' diminishing religious awareness. The clergy consequently expressed support for the foreign and domestic policy of the party and government, prayed for new achievements in the development of science and technology and for the successful implementation of economic and cultural construction plans. They also sought to demonstrate their loyalty to the Soviet regime and to impress upon believers the community of interests of Islam and the Soviet state.[45]

A report sent to the Central Committee in the early 1970s designated the various ways the clergy sought to imbue Islam with new life. They tried, it said, to 'rejuvenate' it and to make its customs more 'democratic' and more intelligible to the contemporary believer. But they were not compromising their positions. Thus, they insisted that the mosque was a school for inculcating the 'truths' of Islam, for instilling morals and for preparation for the next world.[46] In the words of one of the leading Soviet experts on Islam, these modernisers in their re-interpretations of 'dogmas, precepts and norms' and their adaptation to contemporary conditions, were operating under the banner of 'purifying' Islam from the layers artificially added over the ages by 'ignoramuses'. Although the result of this campaign was not in fact reproducing the primordial sense of the precepts in question, it would be erroneous to contend that these modernisers were discarding Islamic dogmas. At the same time, the clergy sought to strengthen the standing of the new, transformed rites and to uphold those ritual acts which were either not stipulated at all in Islam or practised differently than prescribed. Bearing in mind the rationalist approach of contemporary society, they provided new interpretations, ascribing 'worldly meaning' to such rites as the fast. They hoped to present Islam as a progressive religion which answered the pressing

44. *Islam v SSSR*, p.50.

45. Zh. Botashev to V. A. Kuroedov, 17 Nov. 1969; GARF, f.6991, o.6, d.220, ll.144-5. For the clergy's preaching activity, see pp.253-62.

46. CRA, Information, sent to the CPSU Central Committee, 27 April 1971; TsKhSD, f.5, o.63, d.89, ll.120-2.

issues that agitated the world around them and opposed anything that might put a brake on the movement toward progress of both society and the individual.[47]

The great majority of believers from the mid-1940s and until the 1980s were said in most areas to be elderly people, men and women who were no longer of working age. In the early-mid 1950s, CARC noted that the bulk of those who engaged in religious practice were in fact old people, pensioners or dependants, although some still worked as watchmen in a variety of enterprises, artels or other institutions. Most, too, were rural dwellers, kolkhozniki.[48] In the words of one CARC *uplnomochennyi*, people who all their lives behaved as loyal Soviet citizens, fulfilled their obligations at their workplace and elsewhere and were not even believers, upon retirement and having nothing to do, started going to mosque.[49]

Yet this, too, was no new phenomenon. Already toward the end of the nineteenth century students of Central Asia were asserting that only older men attended mosque, the younger generation being neither religious nor interested in religion. A young person could refrain from performing the daily prayer, the *namaz*, or observing the fast, without it being considered a violation of the rules of the game. But an elder person had to pray regularly, fast and take part in all religious events. In so doing he represented the younger members of his family as well. This change between generations, an 'enigmatic process' by which people who, when they were younger had paid no heed to religion, suddenly became believers as they aged, persisted into the Soviet era.[50]

Moreover, in the Muslim areas, particularly in the rural parts of Central Asia, the traditional way of life was, on the whole, preserved. This included, on the one hand, the co-habitation in a single home or courtyard of three generations, and, on the other, the respect shown to older people, as a result of both of which the grandparents continued to exert a meaningful influence

47. Ashirov, *Evoliutsiia islama v SSSR*, pp.23 and 143-5.

48. L. A Prikhod'ko, Report, 20 May 1953; GARF, f.6991, o.3, d.91, l.259.

49. Minutes, Conference of CARC *upolnomochennye*, 5-6 June 1959; GARF, f.6991, o.3, d.183, l.164.

50. Abashin, 'Sotsialn'nye korni sredneaziatskogo islamizma', p.456. It should be stressed that Muslim law made no distinction between the obligation to pray of different age groups.

on children and adolescents.[51] In the early 1980s the Komsomol newspaper of Tajikistan discussed a letter it received from the mother of a large family, one of whose sons, a teacher with two children of his own, sought to set up an independent household. She considered this a sign of disrespect for his parents. The paper concurred, condemning the young man severely.[52] Thus, although the traditional patriarchal family had officially broken up and with it the concentration of economic, social and religious functions in the hands of the patriarch, he frequently retained his authority, sometimes even to the extent of receiving and disbursing the wages received by family members. Nearly all sources dwelt on the respect still shown to the older family members, and to the *aksakals*, the older menfolk, in the community at large. The Soviet authorities in fact took advantage of the social status of the *aksakal* to initiate councils of elders with specific disciplinary functions in the areas of marriage and family life, education and labour, although these councils had to be kept under strict surveillance so as to ensure that they imparted the requisite norms and precepts.[53]

Given their position within the family, the older generation was able with ease and in natural fashion to transmit the traditional culture and values, in which religious rites played a central role. There was no need to propagate them actively. Children, even before they reached learning age, were exposed to Muslim rites, which they would witness at home and often inevitably internalise and imitate. Brought up in such an atmosphere, the prayers they recited when they were very small became part of their lives.[54] As one CRA *upolnomochennyi* pointed out in the mid 1970s, the life of the family, even when some of its younger members were educated, was frequently directed by its older, illiterate, or barely literate, members. Religious rites, widely perceived as popular (*narodnye*) traditional customs, were observed 'mechanically' even

51. Saidbaev, *Islam i obshchestvo*, p.224.

52. Quoted in Timur Kocaoglu, 'Propaganda against Religious Fasting in Soviet Central Asia', RL 246/83; 27 June 1983.

53. Dunn and Dunn, 'Soviet Regime and Native Culture in Central Asia and Kazakhstan', pp.162 and 166. In Osh Oblast', for instance, these committees operated 'under the direct guidance of party committees' – *Sovetskaia Kirgiziia*, 16 Sept. 1980.

54. Saidbaev, *Islam i obshchestvo*, p.224.

by non-believers, who were unable to overcome their 'false "fear" in face of the malevolent opinion' of their elders.[55]

The older generation thus moulded public opinion, especially in rural society, and filled the role of guardians of the community's 'morals', censuring those who rejected the traditions of their fathers and grandfathers.[56] A report on Islam in Kazakhstan at the beginning of the 1960s contended that the clergy inculcated religious views in the young through their elders.[57] The young women and girls who fasted on the *uraz* in the Kabardino-Balkar ASSR, although they could hardly be considered as belonging to the category of genuine believers, did so because they followed in the footsteps of their elders out of respect. Among the mountain-dwellers of the Northern Caucasus, the *gortsy*, the authority of older people in the family, the village and society as a whole, it was generally agreed, remained very high.[58] Other sources, discussing the transmission of Islamic customs in Kazakh and Kyrgyz families, noted that many adults not only preserved religious rites but passed them on to their children, which inevitably undermined the education they were receiving outside the home. 'The act of fasting, adherence to the rules [of the fast], and introduction to the history of Islam and its personalities', it was pointed out, were likely to have an adverse effect on children and impair their ability to understand what they were taught in school.[59] It is probably impossible to determine whether indeed it was correct to argue, as the regime inevitably tended to do, that the younger generation was actually being compelled to perform rites, or whether they did so out of custom or from a feeling of conscious identity. But the fact was undeniable that, at least in the rural sector, the phenomenon of rite performance by young people was common throughout the period under discussion, and perhaps especially so as of the 1970s.[60]

55. S. Irgaliev to A. Nurullaev, 8 May 1974; GARF, f.6991, o.6, d.633, l.14.

56. E. Bairamov, 'Islam i 'natsional'nye traditsii'', *Agitator*, 24, Dec. 1966, p.42.

57. Information, sent to A. I. Aleksandrov at the CPSU Central Committee, 14 Feb. 1962. For younger people's participation in prayer services, see pp. 78-9 (for some statistical data) and 224-5.

58. L. Zh. Aisov to CARC, 6 Jan. 1965; GARF, f.6991, o.3, d.1609, l.13. These young women and girls said explicitly that they fasted because their mothers, or mothers- and fathers-in-law did so.

59. Quoted in Timur Kocaoglu, 'Propaganda against Religious Fasting in Soviet Central Asia', RL 246/83; 27 June 1983.

60. See, for example, pp.707-8.

Moreover, even among the better educated in a city as russified and secularised as Kazan', only 38.9 per cent of first-year students at institutions of higher education asked about the role of religion in a socialist society gave the requisite reply that it was harmful, the others either not replying or considering it beneficial.[61]

Just as analysing the attitude of young people to Islam was crucial to evaluating the prospects of Islam eventually dying out with the demise of the older generation, so the role of women in Islam was no less central an issue. In contradistinction to the Russian Orthodox Church, of which women were thought to be the bulwark, Islam was perceived as having traditionally humiliated women and it was widely believed, or at least hoped, that the emancipated womenfolk of the Muslim nationalities would not only seek to break away from its shackles, but that they would be followed by the mass of women. As one Soviet expert on Islam wrote in the early 1970s, the process of liberating women from the constraints Islam had traditionally placed on their existence that had been started in the early Soviet period could not be halted.[62] At the same time, it was acknowledged that in the rural areas inhabited by Muslim nationalities, society was fundamentally conservative, and this was attributed first and foremost to the fact that many women did not go to work on a regular basis and so were exposed neither to the propaganda activity associated with the workplace nor to other socialisation agents. The role of women was so central since families tended to be large in the Muslim areas, particularly in Central Asia, a reflection in itself of Islam's influence on patterns of national behaviour,[63] so that women clearly had a major function as educators of new generations.[64] One report

61. RL 87/83; 21 Feb. 1983. Unfortunately, there is no breakdown here by religion; one may presume that the 38.9 would have been meaningfully lower were solely students from Muslim ethnic groups to have been polled.

62. Ashirov, *Evoliutsiia islama*, p.101. For the role of female emancipation in the regime's anti-religious campaign in Central Asia in the late 1920s and 1930s, see Massell, *The Surrogate Proletariat, passim.*

63. Saidbaev, *Islam i obshchestvo*, p.223.

64. A great deal has been written about women in particular and demography in general in the Muslim areas. In addition to Massell's pioneer study, *The Surrogate Proletariat*, see Murray Feshbach, 'Trends in the Soviet Muslim Population: Demographic Aspects', and Nancy Lubin, 'Implications of Ethnic and Demographic Trends', in Fierman (ed.), *Soviet Central Asia: The Failed Transformation*, pp.36–61.

from Fergana Oblast' in the mid-1950s stressed that Uzbek women were hardly represented in industry or in the economic, bureaucratic, party and Komsomol apparatuses. Rural women, in particular, tended still to cover their faces and did not enter social life, not attending clubs or the cinema or going to lectures, while many girls continued to drop out of school after 7th grade.[65] In Uzbekistan in the latter half of the 1970s women sat separately from their menfolk at family occasions.[66]

The failure of Soviet European observers to appreciate that women traditionally filled an important role in Muslim society was a reflection of the superficiality of their analysis of Muslim life, which emanated from their own preconceptions. True, women were isolated socially from the men, but their social existence had its own satisfactions, rules and hierarchies, which many women were probably loath to give up.

Not a few *fetwas* of the spiritual directorates addressed themselves to a variety of aspects of women's status in Islam, seeking to demonstrate that Islam in fact did not necessitate demeaning the woman in the family and society, and claiming that customs which had arisen over the centuries connected with her seclusion were not intrinsic to the teachings of the faith. It was in this connection that in some areas women were actually encouraged to attend mosque, although this ran counter to accepted custom. Similarly, Muslim clergy in their sermons frequently called upon believers to show respect for their wives.[67] Several leading figures within the Muslim establishment spoke directly about the irrelevance of certain traditional norms in the context of Soviet society, where women and men enjoyed equal rights. For instance, DUMZ Deputy Chairman Mufti Sharif Veli-zade said that neither the divorce procedure nor polygamy could any longer be upheld as valid.[68]

65. U. Mangushev to Kh. Iskanderov, 30 Jan. 1954; GAU, f.2456, o.1, d.170, ll.6-7. For further details on the position of women in the Muslim areas, see pp.535-49. All in all, there was no major difference in religiosity of men and women, see p.465.

66. Artykov and Nurmatova, 'Atheistic and Internationalist Education – A Single Process', *Kommunist Uzbekistana*, no.5 (May 1977), pp. 44–9, translated in *JPRS* 69643, 19 Aug. 1977.

67. For examples of such *fetwas*, see pp.142-4; for women's participation in public prayer, see pp.223-4; and for references in sermons to the centrality of the role of women and the need to show them respect, see pp.254-6.

68. Ashirov, *Evoliutsiia islama v SSSR*, p.119.

The predominant role filled by the rural sector in Muslim religious life was in itself a factor which seemed to guarantee Islam's continued strength and imperviousness to social change and regime policy. This was all the truer given the clear preference of the Central Asian and North Caucasian nationalities throughout the period under study for continuing to reside in the countryside.[69] One of the distinct features of Soviet rule was its neglect of the rural sector and Soviet history frequently highlighted the antagonism and persistent grievance harboured by the rural population for Moscow and everything it symbolised. The post-Stalin leadership took measures in order to close the widening gap between the country's urban and rural communities, but met with little success.[70] The clash of perceptions and outlook which characterised the relationship between the peasantry of the European part of the Soviet Union and the party with its intrinsically urban-based orientation was all the more pronounced in Central Asia and the Northern Caucasus. The geographic and physical remoteness of so much of the countryside in these regions made it difficult, if not impossible, to control, let alone to jerrymander. The rift between town and village was even greater in the Muslim areas than elsewhere and the resilience of Islam in the latter seems to have been both cause and effect: the traditional way of life that the indigenous population sought to retain was simultaneously a factor in its resolution to remain in the country – itself an act of passive resistance to the Soviet regime which believed in urbanisation as a method of mobilisation and modernisation – and in enhancing its adherence to Islam.[71]

Summing up the situation of Soviet Islam in the postwar period, one expert pointed out that on the one hand stood the unquestionable secularisation, encouraged first by developments of the war years – accelerated urbanisation and industrialisation, the massive influx of Russians and other Europeans into Central Asia, the increased participation of women in the labour force – and later by the momentum of the era of 'developed socialism'. On the other hand, Islam stood its ground. The authority of its leadership was enhanced by their participation in the World Peace Movement; the festivals continued to be celebrated and the *uraz* to be observed,

69. See p.97.
70. See Friedgut, 'Integration of the Rural Sector into Soviet Society'.
71. See Fierman, 'Central Asian Youth and Migration', pp.271-3.

people not going to work and the machines standing idle on the former and kolkhoz work days being curtailed and work in the fields interrupted on the latter. The individual believer, too, became secularised and his attitude to religion changed: he was no longer acquainted with Islamic dogma, he fulfilled its precepts selectively and he did not devote his life to the faith. Yet both he and the officially non-believing population in the areas where the indigenous nationalities had historically adhered to Islam retained many of its attributes. They clung to their traditional trades; they continued to be characterised by a respect for their elders; many of their womenfolk still remained in the home, unable to apply the perceptions and ideas of social awareness of a society whose ideals and values they could not understand. Moreover, the general sense of community focused in many ways on Islam, which in each such nation had acquired aspects of an openly ethnic character. In many places, each nationality or even clan had its own mosque, mulla, cemetery, place of pilgrimage. Often Muslims feared losing the unique features of their nation, its customs and traditions, and Islam personified their history and provided a framework for idealising that past.[72] In this sense Islam remained a major and potent force and retained a thrust suited to the conditions of contemporary society.

Intensity of Muslim religiosity

One of the questions CARC *upolnomochennye* were constantly asked to address was whether 'the religious movement' was expanding or contracting. This was, however, no easy task even on a local scale, let alone a country-wide one, not only on account of ideological constraints and pitfalls, but also because the criteria by which this dynamism was measured were both amorphous and subject to external influences. For instance, the republican *upolnomochennyi* for Kirgiziia wrote to one of his oblast' subordinates in the late 1940s that the latter had erred in concluding that Muslim religious activity in his oblast' was declining on the grounds that donations to mosques had dropped. The real reason for this was that the principal group of believers, the 'profiteers' who had accumulated large sums during the war and made meaningful

72. Saidbaev, *Islam i obshchestvo*, pp.191-227. For a more detailed discussion of this motif, see Chapter 12.

contributions, had been adversely affected by recent economic measures (the change of the ration system, the monetary reform and strengthening of the ruble).[73] Similarly, the upswing in religious activity and the concomitant growth of religiosity manifest in the second half of the 1950s in the increase in attendance at registered mosques and in the performance of rites by registered clerics did not necessarily reflect an objective trend. One CARC *upolnomochennyi* ascribed these to statistical information reflecting the greater concentration of believers in registered religious societies which was characteristic of this period.[74] Another source attributed the revival of religiosity in Uzbekistan to the excessive popularity and prestige of SADUM Chairman Babakhanov.[75]

Nevertheless, from reading the reports over the years, it appears that changes did take place, at least in certain parts. In the Cherkess AO, for instance, in the immediate postwar period there was said to be considerable 'religious fanaticism', people putting aside their work irrespective of what they were doing for ten or fifteen minutes when the time for prayer arrived. Clerics and believers even asked to switch the day of rest in their area from Sunday to Friday, and in two auls, at least, requests were made for permission to study Qur'an and to institute Islamic studies in Arabic (in one instance the suggestion was that the study of the Qur'an be included in the school curriculum).[76] This is not the picture which comes across in later years. By late 1949, when the euphoria of the end of the war and immediate postwar period had passed, and there was no longer a widespread belief in the positive attitude to Islam of the powers-that-be, the *upolnomochennyi* for Stavropol' Krai was reporting the disbandment of religious societies and the falling off of rite observance – even the traditional funeral being perceived as a national rather than religious ritual – although he agreed that many older individuals prayed five times a day at home and observed

73. H. A. Akhtiamov to I. G. Halimov, 11 May 1948; GARF, f.6991, o.3, d.453, 1.47.
74. I. G. Halimov to CARC, 3 April 1956; GARF, f.6991, o.3, d.457, 1.78. For the movement to the registered mosques in the years 1955-58, see pp.203 and 218.
75. See pp.177-8. This view was expressed by CARC's *upolnomochennyi* in Tashkent, Sh. K. Shirinbaev, who was quoting the opinion of a number of local party members.
76. V. Bulatov to I. A. Polianskii, 13 Dec. 1945; GARF, f.6991, o.3, d.26, 1.72. For the requests regarding schools, see Chapter 5.

the *uraz*.[77] Interestingly, a senior CARC official, who did not disagree with the facts brought by the *upolnomochennyi*, put an entirely different interpretation on them. In his view, there had not been a decline in religiosity; it was simply taking on a different form as a result of circumstances, specifically the lack of encouragement on the part of the authorities.[78] Certainly, there seem to have been few areas where regime policy had such ostensible resonance as in the Cherkess AO. Moreover, despite the pendulum of religious policy, the bottom line of its accumulative impact was basically negative. Thus, despite the temporary recovery of the early Khrushchev period, it seemed in the second half of the 1960s that over time Islam was being effectively eroded in this region, just a few rites being preserved, such as the charity which was characteristic of the Northern Caucasus and religious funerals.[79] An article in *Nauka i religiia* pointed out how the old customs had gradually been eliminated from the life of the population in this area – with the help of the community's own elders – and replaced by 'the new rites'.[80]

Drawing any conclusions regarding the evolution of Islamic life and activity on a country-wide scale was all the more difficult. There were clearly very major differences between the various regions. This held for the Islamic revival's initial spontaneous momentum as well as for its response to constraints imposed over the years by legislation and/or local government organs. It is, indeed, not clear whether the reporting on the resonance of these

77. Minutes, Instructors' meeting, CARC session No.17, 20-22 Dec. 1950; GARF, f.6991, o.3, d.66, ll.123-4. Just a year previously the *uraz* was reported to have been observed by the entire population of ten raiony, whose population was 'basically' composed of Cherkess, Nogai, Abazinians and Turkmen – see p.477.

78. *Ibid.*, l.132. A former senior qazi of the Cherkess AO told CARC Inspector Murtuzov that had the approach of the authorities been positive, there would not be a closure of mosques and he would not have resigned his post. Moreover, kolkhozniki had no possibility to perform the five daily prayers. Prikhod'ko, too, said that if Bulatov's data were correct and 80 per cent prayed, even if they prayed at home, this signified a high rate of religiosity. (This figure does not appear in Bulatov's report as recorded in the minutes; it may have been derived from another, written report.)

79. See, for example, CARC session No.31, 6 Oct. 1964; GARF, f.6991, o.4, d.147, ll.140-1.

80. A. Avksent'ev, 'The *aksakals* decide', *Nauka i religiia*, 2, 1967, pp.55-6. For the respite of the mid-1950s, see above; for the new, civil rites, see pp.600-2.

limitations reflected differing views within the bureaucracy itself, a heterogeneity of reactions among the population, or a gap between formal compliance and actual practice. Be this as it may, some officials gave glowing accounts of the achievements of their efforts at deterrence.[81] Others were more sceptical, insisting that 'individual extremist elements' took the path of 'consciously' violating the law on religious cults: in Kirgiziia, for instance, they even made the rounds of private homes during the *uraz* to collect the *fitr*.[82]

On the one side stood those areas which, in the words of the *upolnomochennyi* for Tajikistan when speaking of his own territory, were traditional centres of Islamic activity[83] Another such republic, which was a long-standing focus of religious activity, was Uzbekistan. Yet a third was Dagestan, the level of religiosity of whose inhabitants stood in sharp contrast to that of other North Caucasians. Although here, too, mosque attendance diminished between 1945-6 and 1950, the level of religiosity remained high, especially among the Avars, Dargin and Kumyks; still in the mid-1960s, 50 to 80 per cent of the population of a number of raiony – including non-believers – observed the life-cycle rites.[84] In the late 1950s, when CARC was preoccupied with terminating pilgrimages to, and activity at, holy places, it was anxious lest in Dagestan this might arouse organised opposition.[85] And, as of the late 1950s, there was the Chechen-Ingush ASSR, where, too, the influence and prevalence of religion were not in question.

There seemed to be no yardstick by which to compare let alone make valid generalisations for trends in these parts and those

81. The CRA *upolnomochennyi* for the oblast' of Eastern Kazakhstan, for example, in the late 1960s insisted that the low level of religious activity during the *uraz* and on Uraz-Bayram was the result of a well co-ordinated propaganda effort on behalf of local officialdom – I. Isakov to V. A. Kuroedov and K. K. Kulumbetov, 6 Jan. 1969; GARF, f.6991, o.6, d.220, ll.122-5.

82. Information on the quality and effectiveness of Znanie's atheistic propaganda in the Kirgiz SSR, unsigned and undated [first half of 1969]; GARF, f.6991, o.6, d.220, l.159.

83. K. Hamidov, Address, Instructional conference of CARC's Central Asian *upolnomochennye*, 17-20 Dec. 1949; GARF, f.6991, o.3, d.67, l.53.

84. Minutes, CARC session No.17, Instructors' meeting, 20-22 Dec. 1949, CARC session No.9, 17 April 1951, and CARC session No.24, 27 Aug. 1964; GARF, f.6991, o.3, d.66, l.129, and d.74, l.108, and o.4, d.147, l.81. See also V. I. Gostev to P. A. Tarasov, 4 Jan. 1954; *ibid.*, o.3, d.102, ll.21-2.

85. See p.377. They were nonetheless reported to have been closed down toward the end of 1960, see p.378.

in the areas at the other end of the spectrum: northern and central Kazakhstan, northern Kirgiziia, parts of Azerbaijan, and most of the territories inhabited by Tatars in European Russia. In these regions many of the earlier traditions, such as the seclusion of women, no longer prevailed – indeed, they had never been known in some of the formerly nomadic territories.[86] At the same time, here too, there were pockets of intense religiosity. 95 per cent of the inhabitants of some of the Tatar villages of the Mordvinian ASSR were said at the end of the 1940s to be believers.[87] In Azerbaijan the level of religiosity was allegedly high among the Shiites in the areas near the Iranian border, and among the Sunnis in proximity to Dagestan. The registered *akhund* in the town of Nakhichevan stated in the 1970s that just 5 per cent of the population of that autonomous republic were in fact atheists, although the crude administrative measures of the local government apparatus prevented Islam from revealing its true proportions. Regarding Azerbaijan as a whole, the CRA *upolnomochennyi* stated a few years previously on the basis of 'protracted observation' that at least 10 per cent of the adult population were believers in that they observed some religious rite. This figure encompassed about 250,000 people.[88]

In spite of these disparities, CARC was expected to provide a general picture. According to a report prepared in late 1949, the level of religiosity was indeed relatively high among Muslims. Not that, Polianskii insisted, the retention of religious rites meant that religiosity was proliferating – its highest rate of growth had been during the war – but neither was it falling.[89] A CRA report to the Central Committee over twenty years later spoke in a similar vein. 'Analysing the reasons for the conservation, in some instances even the consolidation, of the position of the mosques', it contended, 'it had to be borne in mind that among the peoples which had in the past professed Islam religiosity is, for a variety

86. Ashirov, *Evoliutsiia islama v SSSR*, pp.20-1.

87. Minutes, CARC session No.26, 1-2 Dec. 1949; GARF, f.6991, o.3, d.60, ll.69-70. And see p.476.

88. M. Shamsutdinov to the CRA, 20 Jan. 1967, A. Ahadov to V. A. Kuroedov, 10 Oct. 1969, and I. Bonchkovskii to E. I. Lisavtsev, 1 June 1973; GARF, f.6991, o.6, d.21, l.5, d.220, l.23, and d.537, l.177.

89. Minutes, CARC session No.28a, 23-24 Dec. 1949; GARF, f.6991, o.3, d.60, l.171. Polianskii was talking generally of all the faiths for which CARC was responsible.

of reasons, relatively high in comparison with other peoples'. If, for example, in Penza Oblast' religiosity among the adult population as a whole stood at just under 30 per cent, among the Tatars it was close to 50 per cent.[90] Although it was widely accepted that nobody knew the number of believers inhabiting any single administrative unit, let alone the country at large,[91] some CARC *upolnomochennye* occasionally supplied figures for the level of religiosity in their regions. Thus, in the early 1960s, the *upolnomochennyi* for Tajikistan reported that in certain raiony 60 to 70 percent of the population were believers.[92]

Nor was the problem merely one of determining the level of religiosity of a given area or administrative unit. It was not always clear how to evaluate the religiosity even of the individual citizen. One CARC republican *upolnomochennyi* asked in 1947 for the term believer to be defined. Was he a person who attended mosque regularly or sporadically, or was he a person who performed rites? The *upolnomochennyi* insisted that not all believers performed the requisite rites and not all of those who did perform them in fact believed.[93] One CARC inspector voiced the opinion that believers were all those who attended collective prayers, promoted religious activity and adhered to religious rites. Polianskii was even more specific: it made no difference from the point of view of the definition how many times a person attended mosque or invited a mulla to his home to perform a religious rite. Anyone who did either even once must be considered a believer.[94] Another CARC official, addressing himself to the same question a while later, noted that it was extremely difficult to know who was religious and who was not. True, some rites were more important than others, yet all the rites prescribed by Islam were in fact being performed in the Soviet Union. But data were faulty and incomplete. Certainly, for instance, it was irrelevant to look at lists in a *sel'sovet*

90. CRA, Information, sent to the CPSU Central Committee, 22 May 1970; TsKhSD, o.5, o.62, d.38, ll.5-6.

91. K. F. Tagirov, Information, 1 March 1957; GARF, f.6991, o.3, d.132, l.32.

92. D. A. Ahmedov to A. A. Puzin and N. Zaripova, 17 Jan. 1962; GARF, f.6991, o.3, d.1738, l.64.

93. H. A. Akhtiamov, Minutes, CARC session No.9, 3 June 1947; GARF, f.6991, o.4, d.19, l.249.

94. *Ibid.*, ll.270 and 281.

and draw conclusions from them.[95] The CARC *upolnomochennyi* for Kirgiziia, however, sought to reveal the measure of observance of the festivals by examining the work days performed in kolkhozy and the disparity between days on which festivals fell and ordinary days. Indeed, this method showed that large numbers did not work on festivals. Moreover, he was convinced that anyone who kept the festivals also performed other rites.[96]

Two principal criteria were used for evaluating the level of religiosity, each of which had serious pitfalls: mosque attendance and the performance of religious rites. In addition to the dubiousness of the statistical data for both, the former could not be used as a nation-wide yardstick for a number of reasons. On the one hand, entire areas had no registered mosques, and even where they did exist, the constraints exercised by the regime in order to discourage potential worshippers undoubtedly deterred large numbers, especially in the 30 – 50 age group. On the other hand, there were no satisfactory statistics for worship in unregistered mosques or groups. Moreover, in most parts women did not attend mosque. Finally, since it was not obligatory to pray collectively, individual prayer being totally legitimate in Islam, it was assumed that many believers in fact preferred this option. Certain nationalites and groups of people in particular had no tradition of or inclination for collective worship.[97] The dearth of registered mosques in Turkmenistan or northern Kazakhstan, it was pointed out, was not an indication of the passiveness of the population of these areas to religion. They simply had no predilection for collective prayer even on Fridays and they manifested their religiosity elsewhere: the Turkmen at *mazars*, the Kazakhs in their homes, where they conducted rites, which had not been performed by them in the past, such as the reading of *mavluds*. And among both peoples religious burials and circumcision were universal.[98] Even in other parts, mosque attendance tended to be low from

95. Minutes, Instructors' meeting, CARC session No.26, 1-2 Dec. 1949; GARF, f.6991, o.3, d.60, l.83.

96. H. A. Akhtiamov, Address, Conference of CARC's Central Asian *upolnomochennye*, 17-20 Dec. 1949; GARF, f.6991, o.3, d.67, ll.124-6.

97. Compare p. 184.

98. V. I. Gostev to P. A. Tarasov, 4 Jan. 1954, and K. I. Ovchinnikov on the basis of the report of CARC's *upolnomochennyi* for Northern Kazakhstan, 10 Jan. 1961; GARF, f.6991, o.3, d.102, ll.14-17, and d.1355, ll.7s-7sh.

the outset and to lessen over the years. The CARC *upolnomochennyi* for the Kabardino-Balkar ASSR warned that it would be erroneous to reach conclusions about a fall-off in religiosity from figures of mosque attendance: the true situation could be judged more correctly from the observation of festivals and family rites.[99]

Yet, rite observance was just as problematic. Non-observance of any of Islam's five pillars is considered in orthodox Islam a major deviation from the faith. But the four pillars connected with specific rites were extremely difficult to perform in an antagonistic authoritarian society: the five daily prayers were not an option for a person working in a collective or state-run enterprise in the Soviet Union; the month-long fast, the *uraz*, was similarly out of the question, given the pressure to attend work regularly and fulfil certain norms and quotas; the *hajj*, even in those years in which it was permitted, was restricted to a mere handful; and charity was illegal, and even when it was possible to pay the *fitr*, one knows only about those whose donation reached a registered mosque.[100] In order to observe a sense of proportion, it should be noted that in many Muslim countries, observance of the five pillars fell off significantly in the course of the twenteeth century. This included populations who unquestionably identified as Muslims. In the words of CARC's *upolnomochennyi* for Tajikistan in the early 1960s, 90 per cent of that republic's believers did not perform the basic rites,[101] although emigrants from Central Asia who left the Soviet Union in the late 1970s told a rather different story.[102] The fifth pillar, the credo or *shahada* (lit. testimony), could not be gauged, certainly not prior to the sociological surveys, which began to be conducted as of the mid 1960s and sought to investigate the extent of belief.

Nor was the sole problem how to decide which rites might be used as yardsticks of religiosity given the almost total relinquishment of the traditional pillars of Islam. An additional difficulty

99. L. Zh. Aisov to CARC, 6 Jan. 1965; GARF, f.6991, o.3, d.1609, l.13. For details of rite observance in the Kabardino-Balkar ASSR, see pp.476-8, 482, 496 and 518.

100. As a result of direct regime pressure/and/or of a desire to accommodate, the spiritual directorates issued a series of *fetwas* exonerating believers, or large groups among them, from performance of these rites, see pp.141 and 152.

101. D. A. Ahmedov to A. A. Puzin, N. Zaripova and S. K. Tsvigun, 31 March 1962; GARF, f.6991, o.3, d.1738, ll.12-13.

102. See below.

was that the only rites for which there were data were those performed in a registered mosque or through a registered cleric. And it was undisputed that most rites were performed by unregistered mullas, and that, wherever possible, registered clerics also refrained from reporting a certain portion of the rites they conducted, so as not to have to pay taxes on their income therefrom.[103]

A report on Islam in Central Asia from the second half of the 1950s, during the years when religious activity was at its climax, maintained that the only pillar to be strictly adhered to was the belief in Allah and His prophet, the *shahada*. The daily *namaz* was observed solely by old people, mostly in the privacy of their homes, although the Friday *jum'a-namaz* was another matter, mosques being visited for the occasion not only by the elderly, but also by younger age cohorts and women. The *uraz* and *fitr* were abided by 'quite zealously'. And the *hajj* by about twenty people from the entire Soviet Union.[104] That the picture which comes across here was not entirely representative or truthful can hardly be doubted. Interviews, for example, conducted with German emigrés from Central Asia repatriated in 1979, indicate a very different state of affairs. A large number of respondents noted that when the hour came, people 'throw everything down, even at work, kneel down, on the streets as well, they put down a cloth and pray'. Muslims might stop their cars to pray; others prayed in buses or trains. At the same time, respondents noted that this applied primarily to older people, young people being ashamed to pray openly.[105] (It is not clear whether the last remark indicated that there was concrete evidence that young people in fact prayed privately, or merely that this was inferred by their German neighbours.)

All in all, the general decline in the observance of the five pillars of Islam notwithstanding, there seemed to be a general consensus among observers that certain Islamic rituals ran in the blood of the peoples concerned, not just among believers but also

---

103. This issue has already been touched upon, see p.82.

104. K. F. Tagirov, Information, 1 March 1957; GARF, f.6991, o.3, d.132, ll.31-2.

105. Karklins, 'Islam: How Strong is it in the Soviet Union?', pp.67-8, and *Ethnic Relations in the USSR*, pp.186-7.

among non-believers. The reason, according to one source, was the 'centuries-long rule of Islam' in these parts.[106]

Consequently, despite the problems entailed in relying on the performance of rites as a criterion for estimating the level of religiosity, and of its rise or fall, this was common practice. In the mid-1960s CARC Chairman Puzin pointed out that the best indicator of religiosity was rite observance; he went on to state that in Stavropol' Krai 47 per cent of the dead were buried in accordance with religious rites, in the Tatar ASSR 69 per cent and in the Kabardino-Balkar ASSR 90 per cent.[107] (It should be pointed out that in none of these areas was the Muslim population a majority, and Puzin made no breakdown by faith.) In the words of a CARC inspector, rite performance was one of the main indicators of the dynamism of religious survivals among the 'most backward' sections of the Muslim population and constituted a major hindrance to the building of communism. 'The conservatism and vitality of these rites', he contended further, 'are explained not only by the believers' economic and social conditions, but also by the psychology and strength of opinion of those around them, who look with special jealousy upon their religious traditions, superstitions and prejudices.'[108]

The social factor was not expressed solely in the moral pressure exerted by one's surroundings. The strength of religious feeling and the resilience of traditional practices and 'superstitions' were evident in the rural milieu as a whole. It was generally postulated throughout the Soviet period that religion altogether was stronger in the countryside than in the towns, and this was thought to have applied in particular to those areas where a Muslim nationality comprised the eponymous national group, specifically in the Central Asian republics, in the Northern Caucasus, Tatariia, Bashkiriia and Azerbaijan. In all these areas, one authority reported in the early 1970s on the basis of sociological surveys, the majority of the rural population, 'believers and non-believers alike', circumcised their sons, religious funerals were performed for many of the

106. CRA report, sent to the CPSU Central Committee, 22 May 1970; TsKhSD, f.5, o.62, d.38, l.6.

107. A. A. Puzin, 'Leninist principles of the attitude to religion, the church and believers', 5 Aug. 1965; GARF, f.6991, o.3, d.1483, l.96.

108. N. I. Abushaev, Information, 17 Nov. 1949; GARF, f.6991, o.3, d.61, ll.121 and 123.

deceased and a 'significant number' observed the *uraz* and the two main festivals. The 'traditional esteem' for the authority of the older inhabitants, which was characteristic in particular in Central Asia and the Northern Caucasus, played a definite role in the preservation of these 'old customs'. Moreover, they comprised an accepted framework of social intercourse, helping to maintain ties within the extended family and among neighbours.[109] Nor were high levels of religiosity restricted to rural parts. One Central Asian *upolnomochennyi* insisted that religious practice and belief did not decrease in the decade following World War II in the towns as well, although their population by virtue of their employment patterns were supposed to have attained a 'higher cultural level'.[110] The CARC *upolnomochennyi* for Tajikistan in the mid 1960s pointed out that many officials, party members and intelligentsia throughout the republic, that is in both town and country, performed religious rites, claiming that if they acted otherwise, all their relatives and acquaintances would turn their backs on them and they would lose their authority among the population. Moreover, not a few among these groups maintained ties of friendship with clergy, even visiting in each other's homes.[111]

Undisputably, many of the rites had acquired a primarily social content, the religious wedding or circumcision providing an opportunity for merriment in which the entire village, as well as the extended family, took part, and the religious festivals being a time of socialising with neighbours and relatives. In the words of T. S. Saidbaev, the performance of Muslim rites provided the occasion for entertainment, leisure, general indulgence. They helped shake off the drabness and tension of the worker's everyday existence. Customs connected with marriage, such as the *qalym* or the giving off in marriage of young girls before the conclusion of their ten-year schooling also had clear social connotations, and they persisted in every town or aul in many Muslim areas.[112]

109. Filimonov, 'Sotsiologicheskie issledovaniia protsessa preodolevaniia religii v sel'skoi mestnosti', pp.71, 73 and 81. See also Chapter 2, n.195.

110. I. Halimov to CARC, 10 Aug. 1956; GARF, f.6991, 0.3, d.457, l.119.

111. A. A. Puzin to the Tajikistan CP Central Committee, 26 Jan. 1963; GARF, f.6991, o.3, d.1739, l.1. See also p.433 above.

112. Gasanov to V. I. Gostev, writing about Dagestan, 19 March 1957; a similar estimate was given for Northern Kazakhstan nearly four years later – K. Ovchinnikov, 10 Jan. 1961 – GARF, f.6991, o.3, d.145, l.50 and d.1355, ll.7s–7sh; and Saidbaev, *Islam i obshchestvo*, p.232.

Even funerals were social events. SADUM's representative in Tajikistan and his secretary frequently condemned large-scale entertainments on the occasion of weddings and circumcisions (*tois*) and extravagant funerals, at which cakes, sweets, cloth and money were distributed.[113] Certainly, in the Chechen-Ingush ASSR the most conspicuous religious vestiges were predominantly social in character: the collective guarantee, the blood feud, the so-called Shari'a court (or Khel), which was in fact an assembly of *aksakals*, and the various customs connected with marriage – the abduction of the bride, *qalym* and polygamy.[114] The fact that these rites had a social significance did not necessarily mean that their religious connotation was any less potent. One CARC *upolnomochennyi* said that they all remained in their essence religious rites and not popular customs.[115] Indeed, the modernisation or 'socialisation' of religion was demonstrated in recitals from the Qur'an or reading of *mavluds* to mark some of the events in the life of a Soviet citizen, which were an integral part of the communist ethos and had never had any religious connotation, such as graduation from school or university.[116]

Celebration of rites in kolkhozy was no different from other places, no exception to the rule. Individual and family rites were observed in the kolkhozy like everywhere else and they had the same Islamic tint. It was no secret that many kolkhozniki, like, indeed, other workers, could ill afford an expensive celebration of the birth of a child, a circumcision, marriage, funeral or memorial service. Yet, since they did not wish to risk condemnation or being otherwise put to shame by public opinion for not doing the right or accepted thing in accordance with the custom of their faith and nation, they often deprived themselves of their most elementary needs in order to pay for such ceremonies.[117]

In addition to these occasions for individual celebration, kolkhozniki also had resort to collective rites. Sporadic prayers for rain

113. M. Kh. Hamidov to A. A. Puzin, 22 Oct. 1963 and 24 Feb. 1964; GARF, f.6991, o.3, d.1739, l.98, and d.1740. l.28.

114. A. Alisov to A. Puzin, 12 Feb. 1964; GARF, f.6991, o.3, d.1608, l.30.

115. Nasretdinov, Address, Conference of CARC *upolnomochennye* in Uzbekistan, 9 Aug. 1948; GAU, f.2456, o.1, d.120, l.5.

116. For examples, see pp.335-6.

117. Doev, *Osobennosti islam v Kirgizii*, p.12; for further details of these celebrations, see pp.522, 526 and 530-1.

were organised in kolkhozy by both registered and unregistered religious associations.[118] Many kolkhozniki reacted to an eclipse of the moon in 1946 in traditional fashion, beating their copper utensils and other metal objects (with such zeal that some of them broke) in order to drive away the 'Evil Spirit'.[119] The chairman of a kolkhoz in Kazakhstan used a collective repast organised by mullas at his request to demand that the members of the kolkhoz take an oath on the Qur'an to improve their work habits and to cease stealing kolkhoz property.[120] Another kolkhoz chairman in the Chechen-Ingush ASSR, shortly after the return of the deportees to their native areas, demanded that all members of his kolkhoz swear by the Qur'an that they had not stolen two cows which had disappeared, on the grounds that 'our Muslim law is stronger than any other law'.[121] In the wake of an earthquake in Jalalabad Oblast' in late 1946 many kolkhozniki began interrupting their work in the fields in order to perform the *namaz*.[122]

Indeed, earthquakes, which periodically troubled Central Asia, were widely interpreted as punishment for a renegade population and led to a blatant upswing in religious consciousness and practice. Following the major earthquake in Tashkent in 1966, religious activity in the city and its surroundings witnessed a major revival and there was a large-scale return to rites not practised for a long while, such as the ritual slaughter of sacrificial animals in public places. There were similar manifestations following inundations in the Karakalpak ASSR in 1969 and an earthquake in Dagestan the following year.[123]

Interestingly, there did not seem to be any meaningful difference in the level of religiosity in registered and unregistered religious associations. One CARC *upolnomochennyi* compared the attendance of rural inhabitants at festival prayers in two villages, one of which

118. See pp.236 and 317.

119. V. Tatarintsev to A. A. Zhdanov, 15 Nov. 1946; RTsKhIDNI, f.17, o.125, d.241, l.110.

120. From a report by the CARC *upolnomochennyi* for Kazakhstan, 25 April 1946, used as documentation at the conference of CARC *upolnomochennye*, Alma-Ata, 30 Sept. 1946; GARF, f.6991, o.3, d.41, l.120.

121. A. L. Alisov to A. A. Puzin, 5 March 1959; GARF, f.6991, o.3, d.596, ll.6-7.

122. H. A. Akhtiamov, Report, Minutes, CARC session No.9, 3 June 1947; GARF, f.6991, o.4, d.19, l.253.

123. Saidbaev, *Islam i obshchestvo*, pp.212-13.

boasted a registered society, and he found that both the number of worshippers as a whole and that of young people was approximately the same.[124] Another compared places with religious societies, registered and unregistered alike, and those with neither, pointing out that there simply could be no figures for the latter, for here religiosity was confined to performance of rites by mosque-less mullas in private homes.[125]

Rite performance, too, varied from place to place and according to national tradition. The level of religiosity of the Kyrgyz, for instance, according to the CARC *upolñomochennyi* for that republic, could not be measured by the performance of rites stipulated by the Shari'a. For that reason the areas of Kirgiziia where official religiosity levels were highest were those inhabited by Uzbeks, Dungans and Uighurs and these groups had a disproportionately high number of representatives among the clergy and in registered religious societies.[126] In Kazakhstan, as well, the most profoundly religious oblast' was Southern Kazakhstan, which, likewise, had a large contingent of Uzbeks.[127]

A report by the CARC *upolnomochennyi* for Tajikistan in late 1949 revealed major differences even within that republic, which was known for its high level of religiosity, although, in his opinion, contrary to received wisdom, the divide was not between town and countryside, many urban inhabitants being observant Muslims. He saw fit to point out that religious activity was more vigorous in certain parts than in others, specifically in Leninabad and Kulyab, where 'prominent' figures conducted religious work among the population.[128] In the traditionally more religious areas even party members for the most part not only buried their dead in accordance

124. Minutes, Instructors' meeting, CARC session No.26, 1-2 Dec. 1949; GARF, f.6991, o.3, d.60, l.70. The speaker was *upolnomochennyi* for the Mordvinian ASSR.

125. H. A. Akhtiamov, Address, Conference of CARC's Central Asian *upolnomochennye*, 17-20 Dec. 1949; GARF, f.6991, o.3, d.67, l.126.

126. H. A. Akhtiamov, Report, Minutes, CARC session No.9, 3 June 1947; GARF, f.6991, o.4, d.19, l.251. For differences in rite performance according to nationality, see also p.691.

127. V. I. Gostev to P. A. Tarasov, 4 Jan. 1954; GARF, f.6991, o.3, d.102, l.17.

128. K. Hamidov to I. V. Polianskii, 14 Dec. 1949, and Address, Instructional conference of CARC's Central Asian *upolnomchennye*, 17-20 Dec. 1949; GARF, f.6991, o.3, d.67, ll.53 and 96.

with Islamic ritual and circumcised their sons; some of them participated in prayer-services in the mosques and performed pilgrimages to holy places. In the Chechen-Ingush ASSR party members
even belonged to *wirds*; some actually filed applications to open
mosques in their respective villages – there were such examples
in Uzbekistan as well. One party member from the Bashkir ASSR
requested to study at the Mir-Arab Medrese; while another, in
Namangan Oblast', 'fell under the influence of the clergy', returned
his party card, attended a clandestine religious school and forced
his wife and sons to pray.[129]

On the whole, Saidbaev pointed out, people performed religious
rites out of conformism, not wishing to behave in opposition to
their surroundings, their families and neighbours. A person could
feel a need for Islam irrespective of his individual convictions:
the rites to which he had been party before he developed any
awareness became a habit, an integral part of his life.[130]

Sociological surveys classifed Muslim believers into three somewhat arbitrary categories: profound believers, moderate believers,
and believers by tradition – who, 'in other words, equated religious
with national'. It should be borne in mind that the terms of
reference of those who conducted these surveys were to aid in
the conduct of atheistic propaganda.[131] The categories, therefore,
were not determined by objective criteria but by considerations
pertinent to the assignments of the atheistic propagandist. The
first group, said to be small, comprised those whose adherence
to religion was 'unconditional,' who believed in God 'blindly',
were 'actively religious' and were intolerant of atheists and representatives of other faiths. The second group were mostly elderly
people and a few of middle age, who genuinely perceived themselves
Muslims, were acquainted with the fundamentals of the faith and
conducted its rituals, but were not active in propagating Islam
and related with tolerance to the atheist viewpoint. The third
group was the largest. It, too, was composed chiefly of older
people or those of middle age, although it also comprised some
younger ones. This sector rarely burdened itself with strict observance of the Qur'an's basic precepts and for the most part

129. CRA, Report to the CPSU Central Committee, 22 May 1970; TsKhSD,
f.5, o.62, d.38, ll.7-9.
130. Saidbaev, *Islam i obshchestvo*, pp.227-8. Compare pp.442-3 above.
131. Anderson, *Religion, State and Politics*, p.39.

attended mosque only on the two major festivals. Its members had contradictory, and often very fragmentary, notions of God and science, and generally speaking took an interest in the affairs of their work collective and developments in the national and international arena. According to one work on Islam published in the early-mid 1980s, there was also a fourth category who, although not considering themselves believers, performed just a few rites, such as circumcision and the funeral service, which they identified with national custom.[132] Research carried out in Uzbekistan in the late 1970s was said to have shown that of those who performed Muslim rites 36 per cent did so under the influence of parents, relatives or their surroundings, 35 per cent out of habit, 19 per cent out of a lack of 'a worthy alternative' – according to the scholar who wrote up these findings in a lengthy article in the republican party organ, this was a snide reference to the inadequacy of the regime's secular rites – and just 10 per cent out of religious motivation.[133]

One source elaborated upon the situation which prevailed in Soviet Islam. On the one hand, the theological component was constantly undergoing depreciation; on the other, the complex of Islamic traditions and rituals was proving to be the most dynamic element in believers' daily lives. In this way, while a gradual curtailing of the fundamentals of Islam was in fact taking place, other, social, Islamic customs were proving their stability. Even mosque attendance was becoming a social event, people going there not so much to pray as to meet friends. The fall in religiosity had been brought about by the socio-economic transformations and the changes in people's concepts, feelings and notions which had occurred in the Muslim areas and mitigated the view of Islam and its representatives as the basic authority in the lives of the population. While the 'traditional interference of the Muslim clergy in all matters pertaining to the public and private lives of believers' and Islam's role as 'regulator of their political and socio-economic activity' had 'irreversibly become a thing of the past', the influence of the faith remained in their family and social activity.[134]

This pertained particularly in parts where Muslims lived in national isolation, as so many did, in mono-national urban quarters,

132. *Islam v SSSR*, pp.66-8.
133. *Pravda vostoka*, 20 Dec. 1979.
134. *Islam v SSSR*, pp.70-1 and 78-9.

townships or villages, in which the level of religiosity was meaningfully higher than in places where they mixed with other nationals.
Secularisation was higher in places where Muslims intermingled
with people of other nationalities: both in Tashkent and in Al'matevsk
(in the Tatar ASSR) religiosity was more marked in parts where
they lived in their old homes than in the new districts where
they resided together with other ethnics in vast apartment buildings,
and in Tashkent as a whole it was one-third less than in small
and medium-size towns.[135] These less secularised parts of the country
were also characterised by lower educational levels and inferior
professional achievement, many, moreover, still engaging in the
region's traditional trades.[136] As a result, they had minimal exposure
to the regime's persistent endeavour to create the elusive *homo
sovieticus* and the prospects of changing this situation were dim.
In some rural *raiony* – and in 1970 at least 75 per cent of Uzbeks,
Tajiks, Kyrgyz and Turkmen resided in the countryside – as many
as 25 per cent of the manpower were engaged either in housework
or working the small private plots allotted to *kolkhozniki*, and so
were totally isolated from the propaganda activity of the regime.[137]
Yet, even among the *dehqans* of Central Asia only 30 per cent
of older believers prayed five times a day, and this number was
halved in periods of urgent seasonal work in the fields.[138]

One of the most deeply ingrained feelings of people from the
traditionally Muslim ethnic groups is almost certainly a revulsion
from pork. Indeed, in areas where these nationalities were either
the eponymous nation or comprised a majority of the population,
pig-breeding was not introduced in settlements whose inhabitants
belonged to the indigenous peoples, despite the losses this 'irrational'
behaviour caused to the economy of the area as a whole and its
component *kolkhozy* in particular.[139] In the latter half of the 1950s
one CARC *upolnomochennyi* in Kirgiziia noted that the population,
including non-believers and the younger generation, persisted in

135. Saidbaev, *Islam i obshchestvo*, pp.197-8.

136. *Ibid.*, p.205. And see Chapter 2, n.195.

137. *Ibid.*, pp.207-8. Saidbaev stressed, in addition, that the 1970s saw a growth
of both the absolute numbers and the proportion of rural inhabitants among all
Central Asia's indigenous nationalities.

138. *Ibid.*, pp.197-8 and 201.

139. For a discussion of this issue in the context of the Northern Caucasus,
see Tsavkalov, *Prichiny zhivuchesti religioznykh perezhitkov*, pp.43-5.

disdaining pork.[140] While hardly a sign of religiosity, the attitude to pork indicated a very rudimentary identification with Islam, which seemed to be an integral part of the Muslim's identity, however secular he may have become. Two Tajik Ph.D. students at Moscow's Institute of Asian Peoples asked a fellow Central Asian in a Moscow restaurant in the latter half of the 1960s why he was eating pork. 'After all, you are a Muslim'.[141] Most Muslims were thought to see in this a cultural and social, rather than a religious, issue, and there is evidence of Uzbeks and Tajiks living in mixed areas of Central Asian cities expressing resentment at having to inhale pork fumes from their neighbours' kitchens, and of rural Central Asians' opposition to pig-breeding in their vicinity by Slavs for the Russian and Ukrainian inhabitants of nearby towns.[142] Certainly, one of the problems of the integration of soldiers from the Muslim nationalities in the Soviet armed forces continued till the break-up of the Soviet Union to be their unwillingness to eat pork. In 1964 DUMES Mufti Khiyaletdinov permitted Muslims to eat pork in certain circumstances, such as those serving in the military, but apparently not all Muslims relied on his dispensation.[143] Germans who lived in Muslim regions, however, noted that they had witnessed young people from the indigenous nationalities eating pork secretly or when there was no alternative, such as during military service.[144] (Other traditions, such as abstinence from alcoholic beverages, which had long been disregarded by significant sections of the Muslim community, and eating meat of animals slaughtered in accordance with certain regulations, were apparently more easily and readily discarded.)

A publication which appeared in the 1980s devoted to the 'situation of religiosity and atheistic education in regions where Islam traditionally prevailed' gives a notion of religiosity at the end

140. I. G. Halimov to CARC, 20 Jan. 1956; GARF, f.6991, o.3, d.457, l.19.

141. Dorzhenov, 'Musul'manin li ia?', *Nauka i religiia*, 4, 1967, p.50.

142. Wixman, 'Ethnic Attitudes and Relations in Modern Uzbek Cities', pp.163, 170 and 173.

143. Gabriel, 'The Morale of the Soviet Army', p.34; and Kosach, *Gorod na styke dvukh kontinentov*, p. 106. And compare the opinion of the mufti expressed by the CARC *upolnomochennyi* in Ufa, p.120.

144. Karklins, 'Islam: How Strong is it in the Soviet Union?', p.74.

end of our period of study.[145] This research reached the conclusion that although there were a number of indicators to show that the level of religiosity had been enhanced between the 1960s and 1970s, on the one hand, and the 1980s, on the other, the fieldwork was inconclusive as to whether one could speak of an unequivocal growth of religiosity in this period. At the same time it could be stated categorically that there had been no fall in religiosity.[146] Another major finding was that there was an evening out of the differences between the sexes and between the various age cohorts. Previous surveys had determined a considerably higher rate of religiosity among women than among men; by the 1980s the gap had closed markedly at least in Central Asia, where women were now just slightly more religious than men.[147] A similar picture emerged from a breakdown of the population by age, where the most important finding was probably the growth of religiosity among those under thirty. Whereas just over 10 percent of students in vocational schools (PTUs) defined themselves as believers or waverers in the Karachai-Cherkess AO, they comprised nearly 30 per cent in Uzbekistan, over 40 per cent in Dagestan and over 70 per cent in Tajikistan.[148] The study also examined the professional aspect: the percentages for kolkhozniki and blue-collar workers, for instance, topped 30 in the Karachai-Cherkess AO and Uzbekistan, 60 in Dagestan and 80 in Tajikistan. Altogether the data reflected 'a stabilisation of Islam's influence on the population and a halting of the secularisation process'.[149]

A further cause of concern was that the considerable growth in the level of education had not in fact been accompanied by a significant decrease in religiosity. This demonstrated that no linear correlation existed between the two and that 'social, historic, socio-psychological and other factors' had also to be taken into account. It meant, too, that the standard remedy of raising the 'cultural

145. This work, although published in 1989, was based on research carried out in 1985-86 and made extensive use of surveys conducted in 1982 – *Sostoianie religioznosti*, pp.2-3.

146. *Ibid.*, p.27.

147. *Ibid.*, pp.28-9. The surveys had been conducted in two raiony in Kurgan-Tyube Oblast' in Tajikistan, in one town and two raiony in Bukhara Oblast' in Uzbekistan, in four raiony in Dagestan and one in the Karachai-Cherkess AO. Altogether nearly 6,000 people had been interviewed – *ibid.*, pp.3-4.

148. *Ibid.*, p.30.

149. *Ibid.*, p.31.

level' of the population was not relevant. The 'traditional inter-pretation' of the situation was clearly contradicted by reality.[150]

Sociological fieldwork similarly refuted the hypotheses which had underlain the research, namely that as the level of religiosity stabilised, the proportion of those who adhered to the traditional fundamental precepts dwindled and that the number had grown of those who neither believed in Allah nor considered themselves believers but observed the festivals and rites as a result of 'a religious-ly-oriented public opinion'.[151]

The survey demonstrated that the number of non-believers who prayed daily, observed the *uraz*, and slaughtered sacrificial livestock or gave charity on Qurban-Bayram and Uraz-Bayram was in fact very small (in all cases and areas not exceeding 5 per cent); yet, the number of those who celebrated the two festivals in one form or another was considerably higher and that of those who participated in religious funerals or weddings greater still. Their motivation in so doing was that they perceived these rites not as an expression of religious belief but of ethnic identification. Their partaking in these ceremonies did not therefore justify reach-ing any conclusions regarding their level of religiosity.[152] Nor, however, did it signify that these rites had undergone a process of profanation and lost their religious connotation. The precepts of Islamic dogma constituted their ideological basis and were in-culcated among the population by the clergy, who saw in them an instrument for the strengthening of Islam's influence. Believers, too, interpreted them as Islamic precepts and connected them with belief in the after-life and predestination and endeavoured to transmit their observance to the younger generation as part of their tradition and 'the belief of their ancestors'. It was necessary to differentiate between the subjective perceptions and motives of individual participants in these rites and the rites' 'objective role in society'.[153]

The bottom line, then, of the findings of sociological research was that it was incumbent upon those who engaged in observing

150. *Ibid.*, p.32.
151. *Ibid.*, pp.32-3.
152. *Ibid.*, pp.34-6.
153. *Ibid.*, pp.36-7.

the situation in the Islamic areas to undertake a thorough re-evaluation of their perceptions and, in particular, to shake off the old conviction regarding inevitable processes as a whole and the dying out of religion in particular, certainly in all that concerned Islam. The outward trappings of Islam had been largely transformed, but its tenacity as a belief-system, however amorphous, and even more so as a way of life, albeit one that was generally flexible and compliant, was not open to question. Its very intangibility made all the more difficult the task of contending with its hold over the population and seemed to ensure that in one form or another it would continue to persist and stand its ground.[154]

154. One scholar pointed out that Islam was deeply embedded into the very speech of Central Asia's indigenous population, their greetings, dedications, curses –Saidbaev, *Islam i obshchestvo*, p.235.

8

RITES AND RITUALS: THE
YEARLY CYCLE

The practice of Islam divides naturally into two main parts, that which is determined by the Muslim calendar and that which reflects the daily existence of the individual believer and the main events in his life. Although in different periods and countries, where it was free to do so, Islam developed a rather sophisticated philosophy and its own system of ethics, it is first and foremost a religion of practical precepts. The study of their implementation in any Muslim society is basic to the understanding not only of its level of religiosity but also of its dynamism. In the case of an Islam which exists in a basically antagonistic political environment, the way it adheres to its customs and traditions and adapts them to the new conditions seems also to provide the clue to its ability to survive.

One Soviet student of Islam called Islamic practice, its cult, which encompassed nearly all aspects of the believer's life, its 'most conservative' dimension. It, too, he conceded, had been subject to moderation under the influence of the socio-economic transformations which had taken place in Soviet society, but this process had been slower than that which had occurred in the realm of ideology.[1] It is the object of this and the following chapter to observe these rites and their performance in the period under review and analyse the interplay between their dilution and the tenacity of tradition.

The fast of Ramadan

The month-long fast of Ramadan, known in the Soviet Union as *uraz* (from the Turkish *uruç*, 'fast'), is not just one of the five pillars of Islam. It is one of Islam's best-known attributes and has come to be regarded by many believing Muslims throughout the

1. Ashirov, *Evoliutsiia islama v SSSR*, p.133.

world as 'the most important religious act', observed even by those who neglect their daily prayers.[2] Study of its observance was important for the Soviet authorities, both as a litmus test of Muslim religiosity and as a requisite preliminary measure towards undermining a rite that was a major bane to the regime. For, in addition to its theological significance as a period of atonement and forgiveness – during which there seemed to be a tendency to observe the tenets of the faith more strictly than was usual[3] – the *uraz* was perceived as detrimental to the country's economy, preventing believing Muslims from fulfilling their work assignments for an entire month in whatever field of productivity they might be engaged.

CARC and in its wake the CRA called annually upon their *upolnomchennye* in areas with a significant Muslim population to report upon the fast and festivals. They sent out a series of questions which had to be addressed, relating both to the dimensions of adherence to the precepts connected with these occasions and the consequent violations of work discipline and legislation on religion. In addition, the fast and the festival denoting its conclusion, 'Id al-fitr – commonly known in the Soviet Union as Uraz-Bayram – were the occasion for the 'animation' of religious activity, which tended to be dormant in many parts throughout the year. This was reported regularly every year for four decades from the end of World War II down to the Gorbachev period from all parts of the Soviet Union with a Muslim population.[4] An upward swerve in the number of those observing the fast, which occurred from time to time, and other developments contradicting the theory of the inevitable decline and demise of religion, would be attributed to enhanced activity on the part of the clergy and other religious 'activists'.

The cycle of events connected with the fast was set in motion year after year by the spiritual directorates, which, given the dearth

---

2. Von Grunebaum, *Muhammedan Festivals*, p.51.

3. I. G. Halimov to CARC, 5 July 1947; GARF, f.6991, o.3, d.453, l.14.

4. For example, in the Kabardinian ASSR in 1945 – Geshov to I. V. Polianskii, 3 Oct. 1945; in Osh Oblast' in 1951 – I. G. Halimov to H. Akhtiamov, 5 July 1951; in Tashkent in 1955 – Kh. N. Iskanderov to I. V. Polianskii, Uzbekistan CP Central Committee Secretary Kh. G. Gulamov, Deputy Chairman of Uzbek SSR Council of Ministers G. S. Sultanov, Tashkent Obkom Secretary Popov, and Oblispolkom Chairman Jalilov, 28 May 1955; GARF, f.6991, o.3, d.26, ll.112-13, and d.454, ll.118-24, and TsGAUz, f.2456, o.1, d.175, ll.1-10.

of Muslim calendars,[5] annually informed all registered mosques of its advent. This was usually done in the form of a circular, which, apart from the actual dates and times, expounded for a congregation that, while literate, did not read – and one that had no access whatever to Islamic literature of any sort – upon the significance of the fast and its observance. It explained, for instance, that this was an effective way to atone for one's sins and provided information regarding the rites associated with the occasion. This document would be read out by the imam at Friday prayers, the *jum'a-namaz*, over a number of weeks, so that as many people as possible might be given the information contained in it.[6] During Khrushchev's anti-religious campaign the spiritual directorates were 'recommended' not to send these letters of instruction to the religious societies, as they 'evoke religious feelings among the believer population' and were a violation of the law on religion.[7] In subsequent years, however, the custom was revived, and in some parts the clergy and members of the *mutawaliyyat* would not just read out the circulars in the mosques but would go to the auls to inform people of the advent of the *uraz* and invite them to attend the festival prayer services in the mosque at its conclusion.[8]

Nor was it only the establishment which propagated information and directives connected with the *uraz*. Handwritten leaflets containing appeals by clergy to observe the fast and festivals were copied and distributed in Fergana Oblast in the mid 1950s. The leaflets called upon Muslims to pass on these communications and the knowledge they contained on the fast to their acquaintances; each believer was to transmit it to at least eight people.[9]

The general atmosphere of preparation which characterised the period prior to the advent of Ramadan would be marked in a

---

5. See pp.165-7.

6. For example, V. Kuroedov to the CPSU Central Committee Propaganda Department, 2 March 1970; GARF, f.6991, o.6, d.284, l.1.

7. Sh. K. Shirinbaev, Address, All-Union conference of CARC *upolnomochennye*, 18-20 April 1960, and M. S. Gajiev, Report, CARC session, No.1, 7 Jan. 1964; GARF, f.6991, o.3, d.208, l.79, and o.4, d.146, l.11.

8. A. Barmenkov to the CPSU Central Committee Propaganda Department, 13 March 1974; GARF, f.6991, o.6, d.622, l.9. (Barmenkov was speaking specifically of Tselinograd Oblast' in Kazakhstan.)

9. V. I. Gostev to Deputy Head, Central Committee Department of Propaganda and Agitation P. V. Kovanov, 3 Feb. 1956 – GARF, f.6991, o.3, d.129, l.24. For the dissemination of these and other leaflets, see pp.360-2.

variety of ways. The registered clergy would put their mosques in order: they would conduct repairs, plant greenery, and carry out a general cleaning up of the premises, including the courtyard.[10]

Furthermore, in connection with the *uraz* unregistered clergy and believers would request the opening of prayer-premises. Communities which had no official mosque and, insofar as they prayed throughout the year, did so mostly in private homes, whether collectively or individually, would often make the effort to acquire somewhere to pray communally during the fast. This occurred from the very first post-war years.[11] In periods when applications to open mosques were a regular occurrence, their number would increase with the approach of the fast. In years when applications were rare, they would be concentrated in this time-frame. Sometimes a community would actually ask for a former mosque to be opened temporarily so that prayers could be conducted in it during the *uraz*.[12] And when repression was at its height and the very idea of applying to obtain a building for the conduct of collective prayer was inconceivable, or in places where the local government was known to oppose the opening of mosques, believers would try inconspicuously to occupy former mosques, not necessarily empty ones, for the duration of Ramadan.[13] Some of these would continue operating after the conclusion of the fast.[14]

In many parts collective prayers, attended for the most part by older men, were held during the *uraz* in almost every settlement.

10. I. G. Halimov to CARC, 5 July 1947, and V. A. Kuroedov to the CPSU Central Committee Propaganda Department, 2 March 1970; GARF, f.6991, o.3, d.453, l.14, and o.6, d.284, l.1.

11. For example, Geshov to I. V. Polianskii, 3 Oct. 1945; GARF, f.6991, o.3, d.26, l.112.

12. See for example, p.315, and V. Kuroedov to the CPSU Central Committee Propaganda Department, 2 March 1970; GARF, f.6991, o.6, d.284, l.1.

13. In 1953 in one raion in Samarkand Oblast' which had no registered mosque, believers prayed every night during the *uraz* in a former mosque which was being used as a library –I. V. Polianskii to G. M. Malenkov, 8 Aug. 1953. Instances of opening former mosques were not infrequent in Tajikistan even in the early 1960s, whereas in the early 1970s this was reported from Khorezm, Samarkand and Syr-Darya oblasti and the Karakalpak ASSR (all in the Uzbek SSR), as well as in a number of raiony in Kazakhstan, Kirgiziia and Azerbaijan –M. Hamidov to A. A. Puzin, 18 May 1963, and A. Nurullaev, Survey [early 1969]; GARF, f.6991, o.3, d.93, ll.182-3 and d.1739, ll.60-1, and o.6, d.217, l.156.

14. For example, M. Hamidov to A. A. Puzin, 18 May 1963; GARF, f.6991, o.3, d.1739, l.61.

The great majority of unregistered groups were said to hold collective prayer only during the *uraz* and on the two major festivals, or, in the case of Shiites, during Muharram.[15] One report from Tashkent Oblast' in 1947 noted that in one raion every single kolkhoz had its unofficially functioning mosque during the fast.[16] Another from Tajikistan in the mid-1950s stated that in a large number of raiony without registered mosques collective prayer-services would be held during the *uraz* and on the two major festivals, when believers would gather in open areas around *mazars*, or near a local river, wherever in fact they found a suitable site.[17] In other places they gathered in the local cemetery.[18] This situation persisted. It was manifest, for instance, in the Kabardino-Balkar ASSR in the mid-1960s.[19] And in the early 1970s in places where there was no registered mosque, believers were still gathering to pray under the auspices of unregistered clergy at cemeteries, in *chaikhonas* and private homes, in ravines and other open places.[20] Shiite customs were different: on certain days of the *uraz* they would perform prayers almost round the clock. In Azerbaijan and Dagestan they also held collective readings from the Qur'an.[21]

Indeed, during the *uraz* mosque attendance would grow markedly.[22] Registered mosques which throughout the year only held the

15. CRA Report, sent to the CPSU Central Committee, 22 May 1970; TsKhSD, f.5, o.62, d.38, l.8; and see pp.307 and 315.

16. Nasretdinov to Tashkent Obkom Secretary Nurudinov and Oblispolkom Chairman Isamuhamedov, 10 Sept. 1947; TsGAUz, f.2456, o.1, d.182, l.56.

17. G. F. Frolov to I. V. Polianskii, 25 Feb. 1955; GARF, f.6991, o.3, d.112, ll.7-8. An analogous situation existed in Andijan Oblast', see M. A. Khaliqov to I. V. Polianskii, 19 May 1956; TsGAUz, f.2456, o.1, d.198, ll.78-83. For the conduct of prayer-services in places without registered mosques and the dilemmas that entailed, see pp.287-324, *passim*.

18. For example, see p.312.

19. L. Zh. Aisov to A. A. Puzin, 18 Feb. 1964 and 5 Feb. 1965, and L. Zh. Aisov, Explanatory memo, 16 Jan. 1967; GARF, f.6991, o.3, d.1608, ll.8-9, and d.1609, l.4, and o.6, d.22, l.23.

20. CRA, Information, sent to the CPSU Central Committee, 27 April 1971; TsKhSD, f.5, o.63, d.89, l.104. And cf. p.315.

21. V. A. Kuroedov to the CPSU Central Committee Propaganda Department, 22 Feb. 1971; TsKhSD, f.5, o.63, d.89, l.19.

22. For example, Nasretdinov to Tashkent Obkom Secretary Nurudinov and Oblispolkom Chairman Isamuhamedov, 10 Sept. 1947; TsGAUz, f.2456, o.1, d.142, ll.55ob.-56.

Friday *jum'a-namaz*, held daily prayers during Ramadan.[23] Friday prayers were especially well attended, as were the late evening prayers, the *tarawa-namaz*, following the breaking of the fast.[24] Attendance would be highest at those *tarawa-namaz* services, usually held on the first ten or twelve nights of the month, in the course of which the Qur'an would be read in its entirety, the *khatm-i Qur'an*. Traditionally, the *tarawa-namaz* was composed of twenty *rak'as*, or prostrations, and lasted longer than all five daily prayers together, but the Soviet Muslim establishment permitted curtailing the number as part of its recurrent attempts to attain a compromise between Islamic tradition and Soviet reality. It even stipulated that believers who had no time or lacked conditions for performance of the *tarawa-namaz* could simply manage without.[25] In some parts the *tarawa-namaz* took place every evening throughout the *uraz*; for instance, in all the registered mosques in the city and oblast' of Tashkent in the early 1950s.[26] This rite was thought by regime officials to wield considerable influence on the believer population, raising their level of religiosity, especially when accompanied by the *khatm-i Qur'an*, which observers considered 'one of the most effective ways of propagating Islam', one with a 'tremendous emotional impact'.[27] Apart from registered mosques, the *tarawa-namaz* would be held also in empty mosques, at cemeteries, even in private homes.[28]

23. L. Prikhod'ko, Memorandum, 25 July 1956; GARF, f.6991, o.3, d.130, l.32.

24. See, for example, L. Prikhod'ko, Short report, 4 April 1952; GARF, f.6991, o.3, d.81, l.87.

25. I. G. Halimov to CARC, 3 April 1956 – GARF, f.6991, o.3, d.457, l.72; Ashirov, *Evoliutsiia islama v SSSR*, p.142.

26. Almaev, Memorandum, 12 July 1952; TsGAUz, f.2456, o.1, d.142, ll.6-7.

27. For example, Zh. Botashev to Kzyl-Orda Gorkom Secretary A. I. Shebtsov and Gorispolkom Chairman M. Zhukusov, 20 Dec. 1967; and V. A. Kuroedov to the CPSU Central Committee Propaganda Department, 2 March 1970; GARF, f.6991, o.6, d.153, l.62, and d.284, l.3.

28. Almaev, Memorandum, 12 July 1952; TsGAUz, f.2456, o.1, d.142, ll.9-10. Among the Sunnis of the Pamirs, for instance, where there was not a single registered mosque, small groups of 7 to 10 people would gather in different homes every evening throughout the *uraz* for *tarawa-namaz* – Arifov to D. Ahmedov, GBAO Obkom Secretary N. P. Abdullaev, Oblispolkom Chairman G. D. Javov and head of the KGB directorate Kh. U. Valiev, 10 April 1961; GARF, f.6991, o.3, d.1737, l.75. For SADUM's *fetwa* recommending that the *tarawa-namaz* be held solely in registered mosques, see p.142; for the performance of the *tarawa-namaz* in registered mosques, see p.222, and in unregistered religious

Since many of the registered imams were unable to recite the Qur'an, special clerics, known as *qaris*, would sometimes be enlisted for the purpose. One of them would do the actual recital, another would stand by and supervise its correctness.[29] In parts where there was no registered mosque, these *qaris* would be invited to recite the Qur'an in private homes or other provisory premises.[30] In 1952 Ishan Babakhan instructed the *imam-khatibs* and *mutawalis* that they could perform the *khatm-i Qur'an*, contingent upon the wishes of their believers and the availability of *qaris*, but, if it was desirable from the point of view of seasonal work in the fields, the *tarawa-namaz* could be postponed to the latter part of the *uraz*. Moreover, it was not necessary to collect donations or hold communal meals on the occasion; the *khatmi-Qur'an* to be performed genuinely in the name of God and not for remuneration.[31] A year later SADUM forbade the invitation of *qaris* to registered mosques, ostensibly in order to economise on costs,[32] although this contention did not tally with the renewed permission to call in *qaris* when times became more lenient. The prohibition was accompanied of necessity by permitting registered mosques simply to manage without the *khatm-i Qur'an*. Over the years payments to the *qari* were indeed stopped in many mosques on the pretext that the state gave everyone adequate work and an ample salary or pension, so that they became, as it were, superfluous. This was said to reduce the *qari*'s motivation to perform the *khatm-i Qur'an*, not to speak of that of a new generation to even learn the verses of the Qur'an.[33]

During Khrushchev's anti-religious campaign the secular authority refused to allow the registered mosques to invite *qaris* at all, unless they belonged to their permanent staff. For it alleged that the *khatm-i Qur'an* gave the *tarawa-namaz* a ceremonious

associations, see p.315.

29. Ashirov, *Evoliutsiia islama v SSSR*, p.140.

30. H. Akhtiamov to I. Halimov, 21 July 1947; I. V. Polianskii, 27 Dec. 1951; GARF, f.6991, o.3, d.453, l.17ob., and d.76, l.182. And see p.327.

31. Ishan Babakhan to the *imam-khatibs* of the major (*sobornykh*) mosques and chairmen of their executive organs, [May 1952]; TsGAUz, f.2456, o.1, d.142, l.21.

32. I. V. Polianskii to G. M. Malenkov, 8 Aug. 1953; GARF, f.6991, o.3, d.93, l.182.

33. Ashirov, *Evoliutsiia islama v SSSR*, pp.140-1.

atmosphere which attracted to the mosque 'a large number of believers, including not a few young people'.[34] This measure was followed by a total prohibition of the *khatm-i Qur'an*, causing, according to SADUM Chairman Babakhanov, despondency among believers. The mufti therefore requested permission to conduct this rite, at least in places where there were *qaris* capable of doing so, in order to raise the level of spirituality during the *uraz*. This evoked an evasive reply to the effect that where the rite was no longer performed it should not be renewed and SADUM's *qazis* should reach an agreement with CARC's *upolnomochennye* in conformity with the circumstances prevailing in each locality.[35] One may assume that one of the religious establishment's concerns, if not the main one, regarding this issue was that the unregistered clergy continued performing the *khatm-i Qur'an*.[36]

The main feature of the *uraz*, however, was neither the plethora of prayer services nor the enhanced mosque attendance, nor even the attendant religious ebullience, but the fast itself. In spite of the extensive reporting on this subject, it was impossible to gauge with any accuracy the dimensions of its observance.[37] Certainly, there seems to have been no overlap between mosque attendance and observance of the fast, many of those fasting never going to mosque.[38] Results of a sociological survey in the early 1970s showed that in some parts more people admitted to observing the fast than to being believers.[39] Making estimates was all the more difficult as some people observed the fast in part, fasting just three, five or ten days.[40] Fasting the first, middle and last day of the month

34. Sh. K. Shirinbaev, Address, All-Union conference of CARC *upolnomochennye*, 18-20 April 1960; GARF, f.6991, o.3, d.208, l.79.

35. Memo, Reception by A. A. Puzin of Mufti Z. Babakhanov, 19 Dec. 1961; GARF, f.6991, o.4, d.121, ll.22-3.

36. M. Hamidov to A. A. Puzin, 24 Feb. 1964; GARF, f.6991, o.3, d.1740, l.10.

37. L. A. Prikhod'ko, Memorandum,' 25 July 1956; GARF, f.6991, o.3, d.130, l.31.

38. For example, S. Agafonov to A. A. Nurullaev, 11 May 1974; GARF, f.6991, o.6, d.630, ll.319-20. See also below.

39. See p.419.

40. L. A. Prikhod'ko, Memorandum, 31 Jan. 1953, and I. V. Polianskii to G. M. Malenkov, 8 Aug. 1953; GARF, f.6991, o.3, d.91, l.11, and d.93, l.182. This phenomenon of fasting for several days occurred elsewhere in the Muslim world, cf. p.454.

was, indeed, fairly common and at a certain stage was endorsed by the spiritual directorates in their attempt to preserve the fundamental structure of the fast.[41] One authoritative source, writing in the 1980s, claimed that whereas 40 per cent of the older generation of Central Asian *dehqans* observed the *uraz* fully, the majority of believers in the 16 – 39 age group fasted just three days.[42]

On the whole, it was generally agreed that observance was considerable among pensioners and housewives, comprising together what Soviet jargon termed 'the non-organised section' of the population, but that this was far from being the case among most of those engaged 'in production'.[43] It was only in a few of the more religious regions, such as Dagestan, or among some of the more traditionally inclined ethnic groups, like the Chechen and Ingush, that fasting was general and spread out fairly evenly among all age cohorts.[44] Nonetheless, sporadic reports showed that this was not the whole picture. In the Kabardinian ASSR shortly after the war many who never attended mosque kept the fast, including boys and girls who were Komosmol members.[45] At the end of the 1940s 95 per cent of the population in some *raiony* of the Mordvinian ASSR observed the *uraz*.[46] Although

41. Ashirov, *Evoliutsiia islama v SSSR*, pp.134 and 138.

42. Saidbaev, *Islam i obshchestvo*, p.201.

43. I. G. Halimov to CARC, 27 July 1951 and 23 May 1956; GARF, f.6991, o.3, d.454, l.137.

44. In 1951 the *upolnomochennyi* for Osh Oblast' reported that the Chechen, from the very young to the very old, all observed all the rites connected with the *uraz* – I. Halimov to CARC, 27 July 1951; and compare p.408. Two years later 50 – 60 per cent of the adult population were still said to be observing the fast in the Tatar ASSR, the Cherkess AO, and in villages in Kazakhstan and Kirgiziia with Dungan, Karachai, Ingush and partly also Uzbek populations – I. Polianskii to G. Malenkov, 8 Aug. 1953. Reporting on fast observance in Dagestan in early 1964, the CARC *upolnomochennyi* noted that most of the young people who observed the fast were women and girls – M. Gajiev, Report, CARC session No.1, 7 Dec. 1964; GARF, f.6991, o.3, d.454, l.136, and d.93, l.182, and o.4, d.146, l.11. Of a group of nearly 750 young people, believers and non-believers, interviewed in two villages in the Chechen-Ingush ASSR in the second half of the 1970s, just under 40 per cent observed the *uraz*, two-thirds of these fasting the whole month, the rest 3 – 5 days – V. Gadaev, 'The Character of the Religiosity of Rural Youth', quoted in Broxup, 'Islam and Atheism in the North Caucasus', pp.42-3. For some statistical data, see pp.80-1.

45. Geshov, Report, conference of CARC *upolnomochennye*, 14 June 1946; GARF, f.6991, o.3, d.38, l.172.

46. Minutes, CARC session No. 26, 1-2 Dec. 1949; GARF, f.6991, o.3, d.60, l.69.

in this period it was largely the elderly who fasted in Kazakhstan, Azerbaijan and the Adygei AO, according to a report by one CARC official, in the Tatar and Udmurt ASSRs and in Moscow young people aged 15 – 20 also fasted. Indeed, in some areas fast observance seemed to be on the increase, for instance in the ten raiony of Stavropol' Krai inhabited by Circassians, Nogai, Abazinians and Turkmen, where it was reported to have been kept by all believers, irrespective of age and sex, and in the Uzbek SSR oblasti of Bukhara, Kashka-Darya and Surkhan-Darya.[47] In Dagestan and the Kabardinian ASSR observance of the fast remained at over 70 per cent into the 1950s.[48] In the second half of the 1950s there were said to be people who observed the fast among the middle-aged and the young, for instance, in Kazakhstan in the Uzbek, Uighur, Dungan and Caucasian communities and in Azerbaijan as well. In the latter republic in one year the entire adult population of at least certain villages was reported to have fasted.[49] At the height of Khrushchev's anti-religious campaign, information supplied by CARC's *upolnomochennyi* in Tajikistan showed that the *uraz* was widely observed in many parts of that republic, sometimes even by party members.[50] In the late 1960s one report said that while the fast was observed by the majority of older people, it was also kept by a considerable number of middle-aged and young people, particularly women. It also stated that observance was higher in rural regions than in the towns.[51] Ethnic German emigrants from Central Asia, who left the USSR in 1979, reported overall fasting in various regions, especially among older people and women. Some of them also dwelt on such concomitant pheno-

47. N. Tagiev, Information, undated [early 1949]; GARF, f.6991, o.4, d.23, ll.37-8.

48. See p.80. Most of the figures seem to have related to the parishioners of registered mosques. For example, Polianskii noted that in Ufa's two registered religious societies approximately 1,200 fasted, as did some 2,000 in Chimkent.

49. L. A. Prikhod'ko, Memorandum, 25 July 1956; GARF, f.6991, o.3, d.130, l.31.

50. M. Hamidov to A. A. Puzin, Tajikistan CP Central Committee Secretary J. P. Rasulov, Tajik SSR Council of Ministers Chairman A. K. Qahharov, and KGB Chairman S. K. Tsvigun, [mid-April 1963]; GARF, f.6991, o.3, d.1739, ll.52-3.

51. A. Barmenkov to the CPSU Central Committee, 23 May 1968; GARF, f.6991, o.6, d.147, l.21. Barmenkov's conclusion was drawn from reports of CRA officials who had made trips to Kirgiziia, Azerbaijan and Uzbekistan's Andijan Oblast'.

mena as absence from work during the *uraz* and over-eating at
its conclusion, as a result of which many would be taken to the
hospital, some even subsequently dying.[52]

There were even places where school students observed the
fast. Cases were reported in certain oblasti in Uzbekistan at the
end of the 1940s, in the Kabardino-Balkar ASSR in the mid-1960s,
in Kirgiziia, as well as in the oblasti of Syr-Darya, Penza and
Kuibyshev in the late 1960s, and in Andijan in the 1970s.[53] In
the Chechen-Ingush ASSR in two raiony in the late 1960s as
many as 80 per cent of school pupils from both junior and senior
classes fasted from three to six days and missed school into the
bargain.[54] According to the journal *Nauka i religiia* in the latter
half of the 1960s it was not uncommon, in both towns and villages
in those republics and oblasti where 'the vestiges of Islam' had
been preserved, for parents to compel their school-age children
to observe the fast.[55] Just a few years previously when the anti-
religious campaign was at its height, the clergy – at least in Tajikistan
–were instructed to tell believers in their sermons not to obligate
adolescent children to observe the *uraz*.[56] Nonetheless, the fast
was observed almost everywhere in the republic by the 'backward
sector of the population', among them school pupils;[57] in some
parts of the country pupils who fasted included children of party
and other officials.[58] It is, of course, likely that many of the girls

52. Karklins, *Ethnic Relations in the USSR*, p.186.

53. N. Tagiev, A short survey undated [early 1949], L. Zh. Aisov to A. A.
Puzin, 5 Feb. 1965, K. Shabolotov to the Kirgiz SSR Council of Ministers, 26
Sept. 1969, V. Kuroedov to the CPSU Central Committee Propaganda Department, 2 March 1970, and K. Ruzmetov, Information, 14 June 1973; GARF,
f.6991, o.4, d.19, l.14, o.3, d.1609, l.4, and o.6, d.223, l.71, d. 286, l.1, and
d.545, l.158. Although there is no concrete evidence in the documentation I
have seen that this was a recurrent phenomenon, my sense is that this was
indeed the case, and that the incidents which were reported were indicative
rather than exclusive.

54. V. Kuroedov to the CPSU Central Committee Propaganda Department, 2
March 1970; GARF, f.6991, o.6, d.284, l.1.

55. A. Akliev, 'Uraza', *Nauka i religiia*, No.1 (1966), p.74.

56. D. Ahmedov to A. A. Puzin, Tajikistan CP Central Committee Secretary
N. Zaripova, and Tajik SSR KGB Chairman S. K. Tsvigun, 31 March 1962;
GARF, f.6991, o.3, d.1738, ll.10-11.

57. M. Hamidov to A. A. Puzin, 24 Feb. 1964; GARF, f.6991, o.3, d.1740, l.10.

58. N. Smirnov and S. Fastoved, Information, 22 Aug. 1962, and A. Alisov to A.
A. Puzin, 12 Feb. 1964; GARF, f.6991, o.3, d.1390, ll.40-41, and d.1608, l.32.

from age twelve up who fasted were no longer in school.[59]

The *fetwas* and other injunctions propagated by the spiritual directorates exonerating from the fast very broad categories of the population, particularly those employed in 'production', served as a pretext not to observe the fast for those who found themselves under serious pressure not to do so.[60] They were not, however, acceptable among certain sectors of the population, who saw in them yet a further indication, if one were needed, of the servility and sycophancy which characterised the religious establishment and, in particular, its leadership. The Shari'a in fact acknowledged the possibility that not everyone might be able to fast, stipulating that those who for reasons of ill health or travel, or pregnant or nursing women – the only categories it recognised as being absolved – should make a compensatory payment and observe the fast as soon as they were able to do so.[61] Between the devil and the deep blue sea, the spiritual directorates occasionally backed down, at least partially, from their own dispensations. In 1952, for instance, DUMSK called on all believers to observe the fast, for in that year it did not coincide with a period of seasonal work in the fields.[62] The following year SADUM laid down that those in categories excused from fasting need not fast at all, but in that case should pay the equivalent of 60 kg of wheat.[63] Altogether, the *fetwas* called upon those groups excused the actual fast to observe as far as possible the other precepts connected with the *uraz*.[64] In subsequent years many urban believers in Kazakhstan brought donations to the mosques instead of fasting or switched observance of the fast for other more convenient duties.[65]

59. CARC's *upolnomochennye* noted that girls fasted more than boys – for example, I. G. Halimov to CARC, 27 July 1951; GARF, f.6991, o.3, d.454, l.137 – and perhaps was one of the reasons was that in many parts, especially in the countryside, girls were taken out of school as soon as they reached puberty (see pp.541-2); another may have been that the girls followed the example of their housewife mothers.

60. For these *fetwas*, see p.141.

61. Von Grunebaum, *Muhammadan Festivals*, p.56.

62. L. A. Prikhod'ko, Memorandum, 31 Jan. 1953; GARF, f.6991, o.3, d.91, l.9. For pressures applied to the directorates, see p.146.

63. I. V. Polianskii to G. M. Malenkov, 8 Aug. 1953; GARF, f.6991, o.3, d.93, ll.181-2.

64. I. G. Halimov to CARC, 23 May 1956; GARF, f.6991, o.3, d.457, ll.94-5.

65. I. V. Polianskii to P. V. Kovanov, 23 June 1955; GARF, f.6991, o.3, d.114, l.34.

One Soviet Islamicist stated that the spiritual directorates sought to lay emphasis on, as it were, the substance, the true meaning, of the fast. In this way they preserved the skeleton of the rite without castigating as infidels those who did not observe it, which they could not afford to do in a society where observance was in constant decline. They maintained, according to him, that its most important aspect was the deepening of religiosity, a sincere comprehension of the truths of Islam. As one mulla pointed out, 'Allah obligates every Muslim, whatever his material situation, to experience the bitterness of deprivation and hunger. Allah obligates everyone who fasts to refrain from all sinful acts and for an entire month to cultivate good deeds'. The clergy sought in this way to show the positive aspects of the *uraz* from the viewpoint of a person brought up in Soviet conditions, contending that it educated people to self-restraint, teaching them to behave according to reason rather than desire, and to feel solidarity with the hungry wherever they might be.[66]

Most of CARC's *upolnomochennye*, at least in the first postwar years, reported instances of younger people observing the fast and, consequently, violating work discipline. Often these were people who did not attend mosque, including sometimes even party members and *komsomol'tsy*. Inevitably, according to the *upolnomochennye*, this entailed the non-fulfilment of their work norms and failure to perform their economic tasks as required.[67] Believers, for instance, would work half a day, until the noon break, and not return in the afternoon on the grounds that they had to rest until they might break the fast.[68] This, in fact, was the reason why in 1947 Polianskii initiated the approach to the spiritual directorates to instruct their *muhtasibs*, as well as the clergy and lay leaders of all registered religious societies, to explain to believers that their primary duty was the observance of kolkhoz discipline and that work in the fields must under no circumstance be interrupted.[69]

66. Ashirov, *Evoliutsiia islama v SSSR*, pp.134 and 136.

67. For example, Addresses of the *upolnomochennye* in the Tatar and Kabardinian ASSRs at conferences of CARC *upolnomochennye* in Moscow, 11 [June] 1946, and Rostov-on-Don, 14 June 1946; GARF, f.6991, o.3, d.38, l.172, and d.39, l.112. In the Tatar ASSR 60 to 70 per cent of young girls were said to observe the fast.

68. I. G. Halimov to CARC, 23 Aug. 1947; GARF, f.6991, o.3, d.453, l.23.

69. I. V. Polianskii to Kh. N. Iskanderov, 4 June 1947; TsGAUz, f.2456, o.1, d.82, l.13. Khaliqnazarov in Osh fulfilled this assignment assiduously – I. G.

By 1948 there was a marked decrease in violations of work discipline in connection with the *uraz*. The *upolnomochennyi* for Osh Oblast' reported that in contradistinction to previous years the fast had passed without any particular damage to productivity, since the large mass of workers, both urban and rural, no longer fasted. Field kitchens had served a similar number of meals during Ramadan as in previous months. Here and there one or two workers fasted the first few days, but they later succumbed to the agitation work conducted by their comrades or to pressure from the kolkhoz authorities. Only some older people who worked as watchmen were said by the heads of enterprises to have persisted in their fast.[70]

Compliance with the constraints imposed by the authorities in conjunction with the religious establishment was not, however, as total in all areas. A CARC report on Islam throughout the Soviet Union noted that there were in 1948 instances of material damage resulting from the *uraz*, particularly among the deported nationalities from the Northern Caucasus, but also in some of the RSFSR's national autonomous republics.[71] Summing up the situation countrywide at the end of the following year, a CARC official insisted that work productivity in the rural areas as a result of the *uraz* suffered enormously.[72] A report from Osh Oblast' in 1949 noted that four Uzbeks and three Kyrgyz had, because of the fast, refused the invitation of CARC's local *upolnomochennyi* to drink tea with him in a *poselok chaikhona*, and that in Uzbek kolkhozy both men and women fasted. Yet, it was not always easy to assess the harm done. According to both the kolkhoz chairmen and the team leaders who organised work in the fields, those who fasted filled their work norms no less well than did those who refrained from fasting. As the *upolnomochennyi* remarked cynically, 'the sheep remained whole and the wolf was satiated'. Indeed, there were instances when kolkhoz officials, just as they

---

Halimov to CARC, 23 Aug. 1947; GARF, f.6991, o.3, d.453, l.24.

70. I. G. Halimov to CARC and to H. Akhtiamov, 16 Aug. 1948 – GARF, f.6991, o.3, d.453, l.59; and Ivigin to Kh. N. Iskanderov, I. V. Polianskii, Fergana Oblispolkom Chairman I. B. Usmankhojaev, and Obkom Secretary Akramov, 23 July 1951; TsGAUz, f.2456, o.1, d.135, l.44.

71. N. Tagiev, A short survey, undated [early 1949]; and Manerov, Information, Minutes, CARC session, No.26, 1-2 Dec. 1949; GARF, f.6991, o.4, d.23, l.14, and o.3, d.60, l.69.

72. N. Abushaev, Information, 17 Nov. 1949; GARF, f.6991, o.3, d.61, l.122.

sometimes provided the finances or building-materials to repair or open a mosque, turned a blind eye to instances of slack work discipline. The leader of one group of 150 kolkhozniki sent to work at a road construction site, however, admitted that among them were nine people who fasted and failed to fulfil more than 70-75 per cent of their assignment.[73]

As the years passed, more and more people seem to have availed themselves of the permission granted by the religious establishment for those engaged in physical labour not to observe the fast. In the mid-1950s there were still violations of work discipline in connection with the fast in Central Asia and Kazakhstan, although not in great numbers, those who fasted being employed primarily in auxiliary jobs.[74] In 1955, apparently for the first time, restaurants were working as usual during the *uraz* even in Fergana Oblast'.[75] In the same period it was reported that in the Cherkess AO the number of those who fasted dwindled annually.[76] In Eastern Kazakhstan at the end of the following decade just a few older men and women in a small number of the larger auls and in the town of Zaisan still observed the fast.[77] Yet, there were people in the labour force who continued to fast. In the early and mid-1960s young women workers in factories in Nal'chik and elsewhere in the Kabardino-Balkar ASSR, for example, observed the fast.[78] Even in the Brezhnev years complaints were registered concerning people fasting on *uraz* who damaged both their own health and the economy. During the fast people forgot everything worldly, devoting themselves solely to God, and consequently productivity fell sharply, according to one report, for the fast was not observed only by the old but even by working people, including some Communists.[79] Another noted that in Dagestan and the Karachai-

73. I. G. Halimov to CARC, 14 Oct. 1949; GARF, f.6991, o.3, d.454, ll.25-30.

74. I. V. Polianskii to P. V. Kovanov, 23 June 1955; GARF, f.6991, o.3, d.114, l.20.

75. I. V. Polianskii to the CPSU Central Committee and the USSR Council of Ministers, 20 Sept. 1955; GARF, f.6991, o.3, d.114, l.204.

76. L. A. Prikhod'ko, Memorandum, 25 July 1956; GARF, f.6991, o.3, d.130, l.32.

77. I. Isakov to V. A. Kuroedov and K. K. Kulumbetov, 6 Jan. 1969; GARF, f.6991, o.6, d.220, ll.123-4.

78. L. Zh. Aisov, Report sent to A. A. Puzin, 14 Feb. 1963 and 18 Feb. 1964; GARF, f.6991, o.3, d.1607, l.3, and d.1608, l.9.

79. Kh. M. Mirzoshoev, Head of Gorno-Badakhshan AO Oblispolkom Cultural Administration, at Conference on Introducing new progressive traditions, rituals and rites, 2 July 1973; GARF, f.6991, o.6, d.545, l.131.

Cherkess AO many young people fasted, as well as workers in a number of enterprises in the former and in Izhevsk (in the Udmurt ASSR), lowering productivity rates.[80] One source in the 1980s, while noting the detrimental effect of the *uraz* on both the health and work capacity of those observing it, believed that its main harm was ideological.[81]

Two further rites connected with the *uraz* were the theme of major interest. One was the collective meal marking the end of the fasting day, known generally as *iftar*,[82] this was widely practised, for holding such a festive meal for other believers brought with it a pardoning of one's sins and the promise of a place in Paradise.[83] The *iftar* did not merely denote a religious act (ending the fast); it would be attended by a cleric, who would normally recite a prayer or excerpts from the Qur'an. In addition, he might tell legends from the life of Muhammad, and would seek to channel the conversation along religious themes, speaking, among other things, about the benefits which accrued from observing the fast and paying the *fitr* and other donations and encouraging those present to observe these and other precepts of the faith. Sometimes the *tarawa-namaz* would be held upon the conclusion of the *iftar* in the very same home.[84] Instances were reported where un-registered clerics took advantage of the occasion to incite believers to re-open empty non-functioning mosques or erect new ones without procuring the necessary authorisation.[85]

Because of both the *iftar's* content and the composition of its participants, the authorities claimed that it provided the clergy and religious *aktiv* with a broad audience for propagating religion.[86] Besides those who fasted, the master of the house in which it

80. V. Kuroedov to the CPSU Central Committee Propaganda Department, 2 March 1970; GARF, f.6991, o.6, d.284, l.1.

81. *Islam v SSSR*, p.73.

82. Again the name varied from place to place. In Turkmenistan, for instance, this repast was called *agyz-achar*.

83. Saidbaev, *Islam i obshchestvo*, p.232.

84. A. Barmenkov to the CPSU Central Committee, 23 May 1968 – GARF, f.6991, o.6, d.147, l.21; and V. A. Kuroedov to the CPSU Central Committee Propaganda Department, 22 Feb. 1971; TsKhSD, f.5, o.63, d.89, l.19.

85. *Ibid.*, l.21. These instances took place in Kirgiziia, Dagestan and the Karakalpak ASSR.

86. A. Nurullaev, A survey, undated [early 1969]; GARF, f.6991, o.6, d.217, l.155. And see p.252.

took place would invite his own children or grandchildren and those of his relatives, so that the younger generation, which in theory at least was far removed from everything that smacked of religion, came into direct contact with a religious event. Even intelligentsia and party members participated in these happenings.[87] In some parts women would participate in the *iftar*, although sitting apart from the men, in others separate *iftars* were held for women.[88] Frequently, the *iftar* thus had all the characteristics of a family feast, a social event which was pedantically prepared in advance.[89] One authoritative source commented that, while the *iftar* was no longer a totally religious event, it nonetheless wielded a considerable religious influence on those who participated in it, who were often not believers, but just friends, neighbours or fellow-workers of the host. Sometimes those present would split into two groups, one of which would read the Qur'an, discuss the deeds of Allah and Muhammad, the origins of the fast, the pleasures of Paradise and the torture of Hell, while the conversation in the other would be wholly secular. The religious content of other *iftars* would be restricted to a short prayer at the beginning and at the end.[90]

In many parts, in most of the years under discussion, the *iftar* was widely practised, although in years and places in which active opposition to Islam on the part of the secular authority was felt more acutely, it seems to have become rarer.[91] In the early 1950s

87. For example, Musakhanov, Address, Conference of CARC *upolnomochennye* in the Uzbek SSR, 9 Aug. 1948, and Almaev, Memorandum, 12 July 1952 –TsGAUz, f.2456, o.1, d.120, l.10, and d.142, ll.10-11; and V. Kuroedov to the CPSU Central Committee Propaganda Department, 2 March 1970 – GARF, f.6991, o.6, d.284, l.2. And see p.79.

88. V. Kuroedov to the CPSU Central Committee Propaganda Department, 2 March 1970 and 22 Feb. 1971, and A. Barmenkov to the Propaganda Department, 13 March 1974; GARF, f.6991, o.6, d.284, l.2, and d.622, l.12, and TsKhSD, f.5, o.63, d.89, l.18. In 1969 1,243 *iftars* were held for women in the Tatar ASSR, and in the following year in 15 raiony in the Tatar ASSR for which information was collated, *iftars* were held in 1,981 families, in 996 of them specifically for women.

89. A. Barmenkov to the CPSU Central Committee Propaganda Department, 13 March 1974; GARF, f.6991, o.6, d.622, l.9.

90. Saidbaev, *Islam i obshchestvo*, pp.232-3.

91. In 1949 in Osh, for instance, the number of *iftars* was reported to have decreased to 14, as against 50 the previous year – I. G. Halimov to CARC, 14 Oct. 1949; GARF, f.6991, o.3, d.454, l.28.

iftars were said to be held in every community in the city and oblast' of Tashkent, their number being greater in the towns than in rural parts.[92] In 1954 in Bukhara they were more numerous than in previous years, and their number grew yet again in the following year.[93] Two years later in one kolkhoz in Khorezm Oblast' three or four *iftars* took place every evening of the fast, even members of the kolkhoz *aktiv* taking part in them. Indeed, from time to time, kolkhoz chairmen actually held and organised *iftars*.[94] Certainly, as time passed, the incidence of the *iftar* seems to have increased considerably. In some areas *iftars* were held in the 1970s in every kishlak and every *mahalla*.[95] The clergy were so much in demand for these occasions that they would sometimes receive invitations to *iftars* even prior to the advent of the *uraz*.[96] In many parts so many were held that it was physically impossible for registered clergy to attend them all, even in places where they were to be found. As a result, the lay leadership of registered religious societies would be enlisted as well, and even more often unregistered clerics.[97]

92. Almaev, Memorandum, 12 July 1952; TsGAUz, f.2456, o.1, d.142, l.10.

93. I. A. Shalaev to I. V. Polianskii, 11 Nov. 1955; TsGAUz, f.2456, o.1, d.174, l.92.

94. Ishchanov to Khorezm Oblispolkom Chairman Rizaev, Obkom Secretary Rahmanov, Kh. N. Iskanderov and I. V. Polianskii, 31 May 1956 – TsGAUz, f.2456, o.1, d.198, l.91; also I. V. Polianskii to P. V. Kovanov, 23 June 1955, and V. A. Kuroedov to the CPSU Central Committee Propaganda Department, 2 March 1970; GARF, f.6991, o.3, d.114, l.30, and o.6, d.284, l.2.

95. A. Barmenkov to the CPSU Central Committee Propaganda Department, 13 March 1973; GARF, f.6991, o.6, d.537, ll.15-16.

96. A. Barmenkov to the CPSU Central Committee Propaganda Department, 13 March 1974; GARF, f.6991, o.6, d.622, l.9. In the mosque in Kazan' information about the incidence of *iftars* appeared a month before the beginning of Ramadan – V. A. Kuroedov to the CPSU Central Committee Propaganda Department, 22 Feb. 1971; TsKhSD, f.5, o.63, d.89, l.18. For the dimensions of this phenomenon, see p.81; for SADUM *fetwas* putting restrictions on the composition of invitees to the *iftar* and its cost, see p.142.

97. I. V. Polianskii to the CPSU Central Committee and the USSR Council of Ministers, 20 Sept. 1955 – GARF, f.6991, o.3, d.114, l.204; V. A. Kuroedov to the CPSU Central Committee Propaganda Department, 22 Feb. 1971, and A. Barmenkov to the CPSU Central Committee Propaganda Department, 13 March 1974 – TsKhSD, f.5, o.63, d.89, l.19, and o.67, d.115, ll.1-2. According to the second document, the fast had been broken collectively with the participation of clergy in no less than 6,000 homes in Osh Oblast', in 1,000 in the city of Tashkent and in another 2,000 in Tashkent Oblast'; and see p.81. For the

The second rite was the *fitr*, an obligatory expiatory payment without which the fast was incomplete. It had to be paid by the head of the household for every adult member of his family, whether or not he or she worked and had a source of income. The *fitr* was traditionally 2 kg of grain, but could be paid in money, the equivalent of the 2 kg usually being determined beforehand and often varying in a single year from one area to another. It had to be collected either during the *uraz* or, at latest, on the festival marking its conclusion, the Uraz-Bayram ('Id al-fitr). Once again, as with so many of the precepts of the faith, the spiritual directorates instructed the registered clergy under their jurisdiction that the *fitr* was not obligatory. Nonetheless, they did not seek to abolish its payment, both because of the outcry such a step would probably have evoked and because the *fitr* was their main source of income. In 1952 SADUM sent out no less than three circulars to all imams and executive organs insisting that all the revenues from the *fitr* be sent to it or paid into its account. CARC noted that SADUM was so eager to receive as large a sum as possible that it omitted mentioning in these instructions that the *fitr* had by law to be collected only inside the mosque, an omission which the clergy understood to indicate that it might be collected by itinerant mullas and believers in all settlements with a Muslim population.[98] In fact, however, the *fitr* was not ubiquitously given in its entirety to the registered mosque for the use of the spiritual directorates. In some places believers reserved for themselves the right given by Islamic tradition to give the *fitr* to the community's needy or even to their own poorer relatives.[99] And where there was no registered mosque, it was given to 'so-called "homebred"' mullas.[100]

Since Soviet law permitted voluntary donations by believers for the upkeep of the religious establishment, its personnel and buildings, special receptacles or boxes were placed in the registered

participation of the lay *aktiv* of registered mosques at *iftars*, see p.233, for that of unregistered clerics, see pp. 334-5.

98. I. V. Polianskii to Kh. Iskanderov, B. Jumashev, H. Akhtiamov, K. Hamidov and A. Komekov, 24 Sept. 1952; GARF, f.6991, o.3, d.86, ll.24-5. For *fetwas* issued by the directorates in connection with the *fitr*, see pp.140-1 and 152-3.

99. This applied particularly to the Northern Caucasus; see, for example, L. Zh. Aisov to A. A. Puzin, 5 Feb. 1965; GARF, f.6991, o.3, d.1609, l.5. For the central role of charity in this area, see pp.235-6 and 363.

100. N. Sabitov, Report, 15 Dec. 1949; GARF, f.6991, o.3, d.67, l.132.

mosques from the outset of the *uraz*. In some years at least students of the Mir-Arab Medrese were enlisted to supervise the payment of moneys toward the end of the *uraz*,[101] presumably to ensure that in fact they were given without any attempt at compulsion on the part of the clergy, and that the entire sum be transferred to SADUM. When the times were more favourable from the believers' point of view, clergy and members of the religious *aktiv* would go to believers' homes to collect the *fitr*. They could even be seen in some places collecting *fitr* in the market from people who came from the kolkhozy and surrounding countryside.[102] In 1957 it was said that the *fitr* was collected in believers' homes upon actual instructions from SADUM. The clergy of registered mosques would send members of the *mutawaliyyat* or itinerant mullas not only to nearby settlements but also to the more outlying parts to go to believers' homes for this specific purpose. But as times became more stringent, SADUM instructed the religious societies to inform believers that those among them who lived in the proximity of a mosque should give the *fitr* personally in the mosque. In the more distant localities believers should give it on their own initiative – under no condition at the instigation of clergy – to a reliable person, who would then bring it to the mosque.[103] In 1960 SADUM was informed in no uncertain terms that it must not permit the collection of *fitr* through compulsion,[104] it being left to the authorities to determine what constituted compulsion. Indeed, the sums which entered the coffers of the spiritual directorates during the years of Khrushchev's anti-religious campaign as *fitr* showed a marked decline. In the subsequent period, on the other hand, payment of the *fitr* seems to have made a considerable comeback.[105] The spiritual directorates were again

101. Kh. N. Iskanderov to Deputy Chairman Uzbek SSR Council of Ministers G. S. Sultanov and Uzbekistan CP Central Committee Secretary Kh. G. Gulamov, 17 June 1955; TsGAUz, f.2456, o.1, d.175, ll.13-14.

102. See p.270.

103. H. Akhtiamov, Address, Conference of CARC's *upolnomochennye* in Central Asia, 5-6 June 1959; GARF, f.6991, o.3, d.186, ll.44-5. See also pp. 274-5.

104. Sh. K. Shirinbaev, Address, All-Union conference of CARC *upolnomochennye*, 18-20 April 1960; DUMSK was similarly cautioned not to allow violations of the legislation on religion, especially in regard to collection of the *fitr*, and it instructed its members and all registered qazis accordingly – M. S. Gajiev, 7 Jan. 1964; GARF, f.6991, o.3, d.208, l.79, and o.4, d.146, l.11.

105. For the heights which the *fitr* attained in the years 1954-57, see, for example,

determining *a priori* the sum to be paid, and in a number of raiony in Kazakhstan, Kirgiziia and the Chechen-Ingush ASSR reports told once more of it being collected in private homes.[106]

In addition to the *fitr*, the *uraz* would be the occasion for all types of donations. Perhaps this explains why the Soviet documentation frequently speaks of *fitr-sadaqa* as though the two were synonymous or overlapped, although this has no basis in Islamic practice.[107] Believers paid sums of money at the conclusion of the *tarawa-namaz* and at *iftars*. The various instructions by the clergy on the eve of the fast, whether written or oral and whether issued by registered or unregistered clerics, would remind believers of the need not only to pay the *fitr*, but to be generous with other donations as well.[108] Nor was it apparently only in conjunction with the registered mosques that unregistered clerics went around the localities collecting donations during the *uraz*. They seem sometimes to have done so on their own accord and initiative.[109]

The *uraz* also provided occasion for other forms of what Soviet officialdom termed religious 'fanaticism'. This was reflected in the social conduct of the Muslim population. Thus, there was a general decrease during Ramadan in the number of marriages as compared with other months — in some areas it was reported that there were none at all — and of people frequenting places of entertainment and restaurants.[110] In some parts of Tajikistan, even in the years of Khrushchev's anti-religious campaign, restaurants and *chaikhonas* simply did not operate during the *uraz*.[111] In the Chechen-Ingush

K. F. Tagirov, Information, 1 March 1957 – GARF, f.6991, o.3, d.132, ll.33-5; for the decline during Khrushchev's anti-religious campaign, see p.69; for the increase in the Brezhnev years in revenues of the registered mosques, of which the *fitr* comprised the lion's share, see p.273.

106. Theses of lecture, 'The situation of the Muslim faith', sent to the CPSU Central Committee Propaganda Department, 19 June 1968, and A. Barmenkov to the CPSU Central Committee Propaganda Department, 13 March 1973; GARF, f.6991, o.6, d.147, ll.92-3, and d.537, l.19.

107. See, for example, Chapter 2, n.60, and pp.265 and 272.

108. See p.274.

109. For example, A. Nurullaev, Survey, undated [early 1969]; GARF, f.6991, o.6, d.217, l.156.

110. A. Barmenkov to the CPSU Central Committee, 23 May 1968, and draft CRA resolution on the work of its *upolnomochennyi* in Chimkent Oblast', August 1969; GARF, f.6991, o.6, d.147, l.25, and d.290, l.81.

111. N. Smirnov and S. Fastoved, Information, 22 Aug. 1962; GARF, f.6991,

ASSR the fast aroused more openly demonstrative behaviour. In one area, young people went past the offices of the local *raikom* and *raiispolkom* in state-owned cars chanting religious songs.[112] Here and there, too, some people, obviously concerned by the widespread erosion of religion, actually instituted a three-month-long fast,[113] while others undertook a seven-day preparatory fast as Ramadan drew near.[114]

The fast, then, was the major opportunity for the more genuinely religious Muslim to give expression to his religious sentiment, to at least seek an experience of spiritual elevation and a temporary respite from the chores and troubles of everyday life. Moreover, although not observed by large numbers of people in most Muslim areas, it did seem to have a presence and an impact even upon those who did not actually fast the full month as ordained.

The festivals

In contrast to the Ramadan fast, the two major festivals were the *mise-en-scène* for a large-scale popular demonstration of identity with traditions and customs which were being systematically undermined and eroded. Uraz-Bayram, which marked the end of the fast, and Qurban-Bayram, the Sacrificial Feast, when every free Muslim who has the means is bidden to sacrifice,[115] retained much of their customary character: the collective prayer-service (on this occasion individual prayer is precluded), the festive attire, the distribution and exchange of sweets and other dainties, the visit to the cemeteries where one's relatives are buried and recitations there from the Qur'an. The main difference was that instead of lasting three or four days, the two festivals in the Soviet Union were mostly celebrated just on the first day. Only in a few rural

o.3, d.1390, l.40.

112. A. P. Zadorozhnyi to A. A. Puzin, 30 Aug. 1960; GARF, f.6991, o.3, d.207, l.59.

113. A report on the *uraz* in 1969 noted that in Dagestan and Aktiubinsk Oblast' (Kazakhstan) unregistered clerics appealed to believers to observe such a fast, themselves setting the example. It stressed, too, that some believers in fact took up this appeal – V. Kuroedov to the CPSU Central Committee Propaganda Department, 2 March 1970; GARF, f.6991, o.6, d.284, l.1.

114. A. Barmenkov to the Propaganda Department, 13 March 1973; GARF, f.6991, o.6, d.537, l.15.

115. Von Grunebaum, *Muhammadan Festivals*, p.34.

settlements in Central Asia did people continue celebrating the second and third days.[116] As a whole, on a countrywide scale, the two festivals were observed much more extensively than the *uraz*, Uraz-Bayram especially drawing large crowds.[117] The aggregate of worshippers, which was estimated on different occasions at between 300,000 and 600,000, and usually around the half-million,[118] indicates that a considerable number of people were not prepared to forego marking the festivals in the traditional manner, in however truncated or emasculated a form. It should, in addition, be stressed once again that the numbers are almost certainly very much an underestimate.

The actual holding of collective prayers on the two festivals in officially legitimised prayer-houses was never called into question in the postwar period. Such services were conducted throughout the forty years covered in this study in all registered mosques, as well as in many other premises and outdoor sites. They took place in almost every urban and rural settlement with Muslim inhabitants, whether it had a registered mosque or not.[119] This held even for the years of Khrushchev's anti-religious campaign.[120] It was generally agreed that the unregistered clergy who performed such services, whether former clerics or 'fortuitous elements', were many times more numerous than the official clergy.[121] In certain parts and in certain periods it appears that the numbers of those who gathered for collective prayer on the festivals in unofficial

116. K. F Tagirov, Memo, 23 Aug. 1957; GARF, f.6991, o.4, d.73, l.72. And see below, p.500.

117. See, for example, N. Tagiev, Resumé, undated [early 1949]; in some years, however, Qurban-Bayram was said to have drawn to the mosques crowds which were no less than those that gathered on Uraz-Bayram – N. Abushaev, Information, 17 Nov. 1949; GARF, f.6991, o.4, d.23, ll.8-9, and o.3, d.61, l.122. In certain years, for a variety of reasons, there were actually larger crowds on Qurban-Bayram, if, for example, the latter festival fell on a rest day, or if the weather was particularly atrocious on Uraz-Bayram, compare pp.219-20.

118. For details of festival attendance at collective prayer, see pp. 74-6.

119. I. V. Polianskii to M. A. Suslov, 27 Dec. 1951; M. Hamidov to A. A. Puzin, 15 April 1965; GARF, f.6991, o.3, d.76, l.183, and d.1737, ll.15-16.

120. M. S. Gajiev, Report, Minutes, CARC session No.1, 7 Jan. 1964; GARF, f.6991, o.4, d.146, ll.12-13.

121. L. A Prikhod'ko, Report, 1 June 1952, and M. Hamidov to A. A. Puzin, Tajikistan CP Secretary J. P. Rasulov, Tajik SSR Council of Ministers Chairman A. K. Qahharov, and KGB Chairman S. K. Tsvigun, [mid-April 1963]; GARF, f.6991, o.3, d.81, l.133, and d.1739, l.54. And compare pp.324-5 and 330-4.

venues also far outnumbered those who attended the registered mosques. This was probably especially true in years of repression in areas where registered mosques were closed down.[122]

Many festival prayer-services, even some of the unofficial ones, were attended by large crowds, especially in the cities. This was particularly noticeable, according to one report, in the large cities of the RSFSR, where the Muslim nationalities did not comprise 'a compact majority'.[123] Many of the registered mosques were unable to accommodate their worshippers. People would sometimes take their place in the mosque the evening before, especially in mosques where popular speakers would be delivering the festival sermon.[124] Some mosques actually held their services outside the building, in the courtyard, where the precincts were sufficiently large, or, where they were not, in another appropriate location. In many places, the traffic would be held up for the duration of the service, as worshippers filled not only the mosque courtyard, but also adjacent streets, squares and open spaces.[125] In 1946 the sole official mosque in Kazan' was unable to accommodate the 25-30,000 who came to pray on festivals and prayers were held in five different places in the city, processions forming from the mosque to these sites.[126] One mosque in Tashkent held prayers

122. For example, the CARC *upolnomochennyi* for Tajikistan reported in 1964 that in that year in his republic, 41,300 had worshipped in the 17 registered mosques as against 23,000 who had prayed in unregistered mosques and another 23,000 who had participated in prayer-services held in the open – M. Hamidov to A. A. Puzin, 24 Feb. 1964. There can be no doubt that the two latter figures accounted for only some of all those who prayed in non-establishment prayer-meetings. The number for those who attended the registered mosques represented a big drop from the previous year, when there had been over 60,000, already far less than in previous years. A similar drop took place, for instance, in Ufa, where festival attendance at the registered mosque dropped in this period from 6,000 to 3,000 – M. Arduvanov to A. A. Puzin, 11 April 1964; GARF, f.6991, o.3, d.1740, l.11, and d.1466, l.16.

123. V. A. Kuroedov to the CPSU Central Committee Propaganda Department, 22 Feb. 1971; TsKhSD, f.5, o.63, d.89, l.20. Kuroedov mentioned specifically, besides Moscow, whose mosque drew an especially large number of worshippers: Astrakhan', Leningrad, Gor'kii, Irkutsk, Kuibyshev, Saratov, Ul'ianovsk and Cheliabinsk. And see pp.222-3.

124. See see p.260.

125. For example, T. Tashkenbaev to I. V. Polianskii, 14 May 1956 – TsGAUz, f.2456, o.1, d.198, l.44. See also p.499 below. For instances where this occurred even on regular Fridays, see p.221.

126. Bagaev, Address, Conference of CARC *upolnomochennye*, 11-13 June 1946;

in the early 1950s in an open square in the vicinity of a cemetery.[127] In the early 1960s, at the height of Khrushchev's anti-religious campaign, some 24,000 worshippers gathered for prayer on Uraz-Bayram in an open space near the sole registered mosque in the town of Kulyab (in Tajikistan). When the local militia warned them that they should be praying inside the building, 1,000 did their behest; the others, however, remained to pray in the square.[128]

All the evidence shows, too, that festival services in official prayer-houses were attended by hundreds of thousands who did not frequent registered mosques regularly, because they preferred to pray at home or did not pray at all, as well as by many who in the course of the year prayed in unofficial groups and/or prayer-premises. Even in small communities, with a regular membership of just a score or two, many hundreds would come to pray on the festivals.[129] In the more outlying parts unregistered clergy organised collective prayer, of groups of different sizes. In the towns and raiony of the oblast' of Eastern Kazakhstan, for example, they would take groups of over 100 older people to the cemetery, where they would conduct a short prayer-service. One mulla conducted prayers for some sixty or so people in his home.[130] At the same time, there was a major flow of believers from smaller to larger settlements for the occasion, from the countryside to the towns, from kolkhozy to raion administrative centres, from remote areas to towns with registered mosques.[131] In Central Asia on the eve of the festivals and on the festivals themselves there was very heavy traffic on the roads leading to the larger and more

GARF, f.6991, o.3, d.39, l.110.

127. Almaev, Memorandum, 12 July 1952; TsGAUz, f.2456, o.1, d.142, l.13.

128. N. Smirnov, S. Fastoved, Information, 22 Aug. 1962; GARF, f.6991, o.3, d.1390, ll.40-1.

129. In Aktiubinsk (Kazakhstan) with its hard core of 20-30 believers, 600 came to pray on Uraz-Bayram in 1946, including even children – N. Sabitov, Address, Conference of CARC *upolnomochennye* in Kazakhstan and Kirgiziia, 2 Oct. 1946; GARF, f.6991, o.3, d.41, l.42.

130. I. Isakov to V. A. Kuroedov and K. K. Kulumbetov, 6 Jan. 1969; GARF, f.6991, o.6, d.220, ll.123-4.

131. For example, Ivigin to Kh. N. Iskanderov, I. V. Polianskii, Fergana Oblispolkom Chairman I. B. Usmankhojaev, and Obkom Secretary Akramov, 23 July 1951; TsGAUz, f.2456, o.1, d.135, l.44, and V. A. Kuroedov to the CPSU Central Committee Propaganda Department, 22 Feb. 1971; TsKhSD, f.5, o.63, d.89, l.20. And see p.344.

popular mosques and *mazars*, many of the vehicles which transported people to prayer-services and traditional holy places belonging to official institutions and organisations.[132] In the towns themselves believers often went to the mosque in groups in high spirits, chanting the *takbir* as they went.[133] All this testified to the efforts that people were willing to make in order to be able to pray collectively at a service that might reasonably be expected to be ceremonious, festive and in accordance with tradition.

Moreover, if in most places the usual Friday prayers were attended primarily by older people, mostly men, the festival services attracted many young people and women. The former accounted, according to reports, for anything from 15 to 30 per cent of worshippers.[134] One *mutawali* said he was staggered by the number of adolescents and young people who accompanied their parents to the mosque, given the fact that they knew neither Qur'an nor the prayers. Perturbed lest the raion organisations think this was the result of any particular activity on the part of the mosque's executive organ, he accused the teachers in the schools of not undertaking explanatory work on the eve of the festivals.[135] The phenomenon of missing out on school on Muslim festivals was reported in several years and in a number of regions.[136] A report from Tajikistan in the period of Khrushchev's anti-religious campaign stated that in those parts where educational propaganda work had not been carried out effectively, young people participated in festival prayer-services even in those hard years.[137] In the middle

132. I. V. Polianskii to the CPSU Central Committee and the USSR Council of Ministers, 20 Sept. 1955; GARF, f.6991, o.3, d.114, l.198. And compare p.380.

133. L. A. Prikhod'ko, Memorandum, 25 July 1956; GARF, f.6991, o.3, d.130, ll.27-8.

134. I. V. Polianskii to M. A. Suslov, 27 Dec. 1951 – GARF, f.6991, o.3, d.76, l.184. Polianskii maintained that in 1951 young people, aged 15 to 25, comprised 30 per cent of worshippers in Osh, 25 per cent in Jalalabad and Kokand, 20 per cent in Astrakhan', and 10 per cent in Moscow and Semipalatinsk. And see pp.78-9 and 224-5.

135. Almaev, Memorandum, 12 July 1952; TsGAUz, f.2456, o.1, d.142, ll.12-13.

136. Materials prepared for conference of CARC *upolnomochennye*, 8 Oct. 1946, I. V. Polianskii to M. A. Suslov, 27 Dec. 1951, and to the CPSU Central Committee and the USSR Council of Ministers, 20 Sept. 1955, and K. Shabolotov to the Kirgiz SSR Council of Ministers, 29 Sept. 1969; GARF, f.6991, o.3 d.41, l.189, d.76, l.185 and d.114, l.202, and o.6, d.223, l.71. And see pp.79 and 501 below.

137. D. Ahmedov to A. A. Puzin, Tajikistan CP Central Committee Secretary

of the 1970s the CRA informed Komsomol Secretary L. I. Matveev that the number of young people and children who attended mosque on the two main festivals was increasing in all parts of Central Asia and the Northern Caucasus; this held, too, for Transcaucasia, where they came to holy places on the occasion of the Shiite services of mourning for Imam Husayn.[138]

In certain regions women actually took part in the usual services from a gallery or some other separated section.[139] In a few places special services were organised for women.[140] Even in those parts where women did not participate in the service, they would gather in the courtyard of the mosque or in adjacent streets, bringing their school-age and pre-school-age children with them. Sometimes they were able to hear the sermon, presumably relayed by loudspeakers. Women and children were also prominent in the ranks of pilgrims who flocked to Muslim holy places on the festivals.[141] These facts made manifest that the two major Muslim festivals were part and parcel of the existence of the populations concerned and were most unlikely to be eradicated either by forceful repression or by oral persuasion, let alone by any spontaneous development or trend within the ethnic groups concerned.

One aspect of Qurban-Bayram, in fact its central feature, the sacrifice of an animal, was a particular thorn in the side of the regime. Collectivisation and the concomitant upheavals had reduced the country's livestock by well over 50 per cent and sheep and goats by almost two-thirds. In Kazakhstan, traditionally a livestock economy, livestock was decimated. The situation had become even worse during the war, and for decades the population was manifestly short of meat and milk. (It was not until the mid-1950s that the Soviet Union was back to pre-1928 figures).[142] The un-

N. Zaripova, and Tajik SSR KGB Chairman S. K. Tsvigun, 2 June 1962; GARF, f.6991, o.3, d.1738, ll.40-3.

138. A. Barmenkov to L. I. Matveev, 15 Jan. 1974; GARF, f.6991, o.6, d.622, l.7. For the Shiite ceremonies on Ashura, see pp.503-6 below.

139. Goncharok to G. M. Malenkov, 8 Sept. 1949; RTsKhIDNI, f.17, o.132, d.258, l.77.

140. For these women's services and female participation in festival prayers, see also pp.77-8 and 223-4.

141. See p.369, and A. Barmenkov to the CPSU Central Committee Propaganda Department, 13 March 1973; GARF, f.6991, o.6, d.537, l.20.

142. See Hosking, *A History of the Soviet Union*, pp.166, 244 and 287.

controlled slaughter of large numbers of animals to fulfil a religious rite was anathema to a government which was strenuously striving to normalise this situation, in part by strict supervision of the provision of meat. From the immediate postwar years and throughout the period under discussion this was a major issue. The festival sacrifice was clearly widespread, even though its exact dimensions were very difficult to gauge.[143]

In 1946 the *upolnomchennyi* in Kokchetau (Kazakhstan) wrote to his superiors that, unless specifically forbidden, Qurban-Bayram would be accompanied by a mass slaughter of animals, bringing damage to the state.[144] Apparently, the dimensions of this phenomenon were particularly large in the first postwar years because many families had vowed that upon the safe return of their menfolk from the war, they would make such a sacrifice.[145] Although at the end of the 1940s in Kazakhstan, at least, this practice was said to be markedly less common than it had been in 'former times', being restricted solely to families where older men and women still 'adhered to the old (religious) viewpoint',[146] there was still hardly a settlement or town with a Muslim population throughout the entire country in which it was not observed in these and subsequent years.[147] In one year in the middle of the 1950s over 400 livestock were slaughtered in just two villages in Arzamas Oblast' and over 100 head in several kolkhozy in Turkmenistan.[148] In the Chechen-Ingush ASSR in 1959 over 44,000 beasts were slaughtered on Qurban-Bayram, as against a figure of less than 30,000 slaughtered for meat consumption in two regular months.[149] In some places, even officials of local soviets brought sacrificial animals. In one instance, a Znanie official, a professional atheistic-propagandist, asked permission to take a day off work in order to slaughter his horse in honour of the approaching

---

143. See pp.76-7.

144. Eleusyzov, Address, Conference of CARC *upolnomochennye* for Kazakhstan and Kirgiziia, 2 Oct. 1946.; GARF, f.6991, o.3, d.41, l.55.

145. See p.370.

146. N. Sabitov, Report, 15 Dec. 1949; GARF, f.6991, o.3, d.67, l.132.

147. N. I. Abushaev, Information, 17 Nov. 1949, and I. V. Polianskii to M. A. Suslov, 27 Dec. 1951; GARF, f.6991, o.3, d.61, l.122, and d.76, l.186.

148. I. V. Polianskii to the CPSU Central Committee and the USSR Council of Ministers, 20 Sept. 1955; GARF, f.6991, o.3, d.114, l.201.

149. A. Alisov to A. A. Puzin, 13 Jan. 1961; GARF, f.6991, o.3, d.1605, l.27.

festival.[150] Still in the late 1960s it was noted that, as the feast drew near, the price of livestock of all sizes and species rose notably. About 4,000 head were slaughtered just in the Kabardino-Balkar ASSR, and 1,500 in the oblast' of Northern Kazakhstan. In the Gorno-Badakhshan AO, where it was commonly held that a family which did not make a sacrifice on Qurban-Bayram would not enter paradise, enormous damage was said in the 1970s to be incurred by the state as a result of that festival. Yet not everywhere did Muslims continue to possess their own private animals, so that by this time some mullas and *khalifas* were suggesting that it was sufficient to make a monetary contribution to the mosque or clergy.[151]

The instructions given by the spiritual directorates to the clergy and by the latter to believers related recurrently to donations made in the course of festivals. In addition to the insistence of the spiritual directorates, especially SADUM, that all contributions given on these occasions, not just the *fitr*, be channelled to their account, they asked believers not to make donations of livestock. (Traditionally, donations would be brought in money, agricultural produce or animals, live or already slaughtered, depending presumably on the source of income of the individual believer and the resources at his disposal.) The faithful were now asked that instead of livestock, they bring the animal's value in cash; insofar as animals were brought, the clergy were requested to sell them and to transfer the money realised from the sale to the spiritual directorate.[152] While these directives did not put a stop to the slaughter of livestock on Qurban-Bayram, they led to many believers, who sought to abide by the dispensations and recommendations of the spiritual directorates, bringing the clergy the

150. E. Bairamov, Information, undated [January 1969]; GARF, f.6991, o.6, d.153, l.51, and see pp.649–50.

151. A. Barmenkov to the CPSU Central Committee, 23 May 1968; Kh. M. Mirzosheev, Head, Gorno-Badakhshan AO Ispolkom Cultural Department, Conference on Introducing new traditions, rituals and rites, 2 July 1973; GARF, f.6991, o.6, d.147, l.21, and d.545, l.132. (Earlier in the 1960s 8,000 head were reported to have been slaughtered on Qurban-Bayram in the Kabardino-Balkar ASSR – L. Zh. Aisov to A. A. Puzin, 1 June 1961; GARF, f.6991, o.3, d.1605, l.31.)

152. I. V. Polianskii to M. A. Suslov and K. E. Voroshilov, 29 Dec. 1950; RTsKhIDNI, f.17, o.132, d.285, l.261 and GARF, f.6991, 0.3, d.68, l.294. See also p.152.

cash equivalent of a hide, or, in some instances, live animals, which were duly handed over to the kolkhozy.[153] DUMSK's authorisation of the slaughter of fowl, rather than the traditional sheep, evoked the retort among believers that the mufti was evidently a communist, concerned primarily with assisting the authorities to fulfil the Five Year Plan regarding the projected increase in the quantity of livestock.[154]

The Muslim leadership seems to have sought to obtain regime approval of the celebration of the two festivals. On the first festival following the termination of World War II, Uraz-Bayram, when large crowds attended Ufa's two registered mosques, including people from the surrounding countryside, TsDUM Mufti Rasulev expressed gratitude to the government and Stalin, under whose leadership Germany and Japan had been finally defeated, and collected money for secular causes.[155] In Kazakhstan, too, at least in certain parts, moneys collected on this occasion were designated partly for the expenses of the local mosque, partly for SADUM and partly for war invalids.[156] In the conditions of the late Stalin period the acceptance by a government organ of contributions made in this fashion implied approval of the occasion on which they were made. In later years the messages of the various World Peace Movement organs and forums would be read out in the major mosques on the festivals[157] with much the same purpose. This was a proven method of signalling to the regime the Muslim establishment's willingness to collaborate and its identification with official policy and of demonstrating to the population that the festivals were recognised by the government as an appropriate framework for celebration.[158] These efforts met with a certain

153. I. V. Polianskii to the USSR Council of Ministers presidium bureau, 24 June 1952; GARF, f.6991, o.3, d.85, l.170.

154. I. V. Polianskii to G. M. Malenkov and N. S. Khrushchev, 2 Oct. 1953; GARF, f.6991, o.3, d.93, l.244. And see p.142.

155. M. Sh. Karimov to I. V. Polianskii and Chairman of the Bashkir ASSR SNK S. A. Vagapov, 27 Sept. 1945; GARF, f.6991, o.3, d.26, l.3.

156. For example, in Ural'sk in Western Kazakhstan – Kadyrbalin, Information, undated, sent by N. Sabitov to CARC, 5 Oct. 1945; GARF, f.6991, o.3, d.30, l.235. For such collections, see also p.230.

157. For example, Almaev, Memorandum, 12 July 1952; TsGAUz, f.2456, o.1, d.142, l.11.

158. For the World Peace Movement and the participation in it of the official Muslim leadership, see pp.156, 158 and 175-7.

success. Recognition of the legitimacy of the two festivals was implied in the permission given for moneys to be collected on them in the registered mosques.[159]

Simultaneously, however, the spiritual directorates took a number of measures, apparently at the specific bidding of the authorities, to make the celebration of the festivals palatable or at least acceptable to the regime. These were designed, first and foremost, to minimise the economic detriment they might cause, as well as to neutralise, if not actually eliminate, those elements which for ideological or other reasons seemed most obnoxious. One of the major measures in this direction was the instruction issued annually to the clergy to hold services early in the morning and to make them short so that worshippers could go to work on time at their conclusion. At one mosque in Bukhara, prayers on Qurban-Bayram not only commenced at 5.45 a.m., they lasted no more than 15 minutes.[160] Even at the mosque at the foot of the Takht-i Sulayman in Osh prayers finished before 8 a.m. so that people would not arrive late at work. Shafagat Khaliqnazarov, who served as imam at this mosque, explained beforehand to believers that this was being done to avoid any damage to productivity. The worshippers were in fact reported to have dispersed in haste immediately upon the conclusion of prayers.[161] One is left to wonder how tens of thousands could scatter so quickly, even bearing in mind that this presumably did not apply to the roughly 30 per cent of worshippers who came from outside the town, for whom it was not in any case feasible to appear at the workplace punctually.

With a similar end in view of pandering to the wishes of the regime when it felt the noose tightening around its neck, the Muslim establishment even attempted to minimise the donations given at the mosques on festivals. Thus in each of Bukhara's three registered mosques, for instance, the clergy – after being cautioned that only voluntary donations were to be permitted – placed just

159. I. V. Polianskii, Address, Minutes, CARC session No.9, 3 June 1947; GARF, f.6991, o.4, d.19, l.180.

160. Sh. Shirinbaev, Information, 27 July 1961; TsGAUz, f.2456, o.1, d.290, l.106.

161. I. G. Halimov to CARC, 16 Aug. 1948 and 27 July 1951; GARF, f.6991, o.3, d.453, l.61, and d.454, l.140. At first services ended at 7.50 a.m., in later years instructions were issued that they end at 7.25 a.m.

two collection boxes on festivals during the Khrushchev anti-religious campaign.[162]

Here and there prayer services did not finish early enough for worshippers to arrive at work in time, but these instances appear to have been exceptional. In 1955 in Samarkand, for example, where large numbers came from the surroundings, the prayer-service began at 7 a.m. and lasted an hour and a half. The town's single registered mosque was far from being able to accommodate the 5,000 worshippers, and they and the 8,000 onlookers spread into the adjacent streets, bringing all public transport to a standstill. The prayers over, the majority of the crowd went to the cemetery near the Shoh-i Zinda mausoleum to visit the tomb of Qusam ibn Abbas.[163] In some mosques, a second prayer-service was held for late-comers or simply to enable more worshippers to attend festival prayers; in one case, at least, a third service was also on the cards, but was dispersed following the intervention of CARC's *upolnomochennyi*.[164]

All the endeavours to encourage believers to attend their duties and obligations with regard to the workplace notwithstanding, there were recurrent instances of absenteeism on the two festivals. The very fact that Uraz-Bayram was the occasion for people from distant places to come together, according to one source, resulted inevitably in absenteeism, the non-fulfilment of work assignments and a fall in productivity.[165] From the very first year after the war these irregularities were reported recurrently. In Pavlodar in Northern Kazakhstan workers took time off in a number of enterprises on Uraz-Bayram in 1945.[166] In the following year on the same festival a group from one factory did not appear at work in Andijan Oblast', whereas in the Karakalpak ASSR kolkhozniki spent the entire day in the mosque instead of going to the fields to sow cotton.[167] In one kolkhoz in Kirgiziia in 1950 on the first half of

162. Sh. Shirinbaev, Information, 1 June 1961; TsGAUz, f.2456, o.1, d.290, l.120.

163. Kh. N. Iskanderov to G. S. Sultanov and Kh. G. Gulamov, 17 June 1955; TsGAUz, f.2456, o.1, d.175, ll.16-17.

164. Sh. Shirinbaev, Information, 27 May and 1 June 1961; TsGAUz, f.2456, o.1, d.290, ll.107 and 118.

165. Klimovich, *Islam*, p.232.

166. Gul'iaev, Information, undated, sent by N. Sabitov to CARC, 14 Nov. 1945; GARF, f.6991, o.3, d.30, l.229.

167. Report of CARC *upolnomochennyi* for the Uzbek SSR, apparently prepared

the first day of Uraz-Bayram nearly 70 per cent stayed away from work, on the second half of the day about 40 per cent; on the second day of the festival, however, everyone went to work.[168] Indeed, that year violations of work discipline were reported to be considerable, especially in the kolkhozy, 'despite the instructions of the spiritual directorates...to conduct prayer-services in the early hours of the morning before work'. Once again, in some instances the kolkhoz authorities were thought to have explicitly permitted people to arrive late at work or even take the day off.[169] The administration of one kolkhoz in Kazakhstan decided to celebrate Qurban-Bayram in 1951, as a result of which nobody, including party members and *komsomol'tsy* went to work for three days. In instances when people went to pray at holy places, too, they might well miss more than just the one day. In 1951 the members of one kolkhoz in Jalalabad Oblast' seem to have gone *en masse* to the Shoh Fazil *mazar* to celebrate Qurban-Bayram and not gone to work for four days.[170] Later on in the decade, when regime policy was relatively lenient, special lots would be assigned for the conduct of prayers in the proximity of the cotton-fields in the rural parts of Tajikistan, where it was not considered feasible to prevent people from participating in collective prayer-services on the major festivals in years when these fell in periods of urgent seasonal work. Neither the organs of local government nor the kolkhoz administrations obstructed this arrangement, tending rather to recommend it, so that at one and the same time there be neither violations of work-discipline nor disgruntlement among the population.[171] As time passed, however, it seems that absenting oneself from work on the two major festivals became increasingly common. Ethnic German emigrants from Kazakhstan in the late 1970s recounted that Muslims living in their native parts never went to work on these occasions.[172]

---

for conference of CARC *upolnomochennye* in Tashkent, 8 Oct. 1946; GARF, f.6991, o.3, d.41, ll.197 and 199.

168. I. G. Halimov to H. Akhtiamov, 4 Sept. 1950; GARF, f.6991, o.3, d.454, l.75.

169. I. V. Polianskii to M. A. Suslov, 29 Dec. 1950; RTsKhIDNI, f.17, o.132, d.285, l.261.

170. I. V. Polianskii to M. A. Suslov, 27 Dec. 1951; GARF, f.6991, o.3, d.76, l.185.

171. K. F. Tagirov, Memo, 23 Aug. 1957; GARF, f.6991, o.4, d.73, l.79.

172. Karklins, 'Islam: How Stong is it in the Soviet Union?', p.69.

There were also instances of absenteeism from school.[173] In a number of places in Kashka-Darya Oblast' in Uzbekistan in the late 1940s, it was reported that not only did the heads of some official institutions not work on the festivals, but classes were not held in the schools.[174] In the Chechen-Ingush ASSR, no work was done in many kolkhozy and sovkhozy for three or four days due to the celebration of Uraz-Bayram. In 1970 in one factory about two-thirds of the workers took off, while so many pupils failed to attend school that in some places classes were called off.[175]

In order to pre-empt violations of work-discipline local government officials occasionally intervened directly in the affairs of the religious community. To this end, in Andijan Oblast' in 1946, a *sel'sovet* chairman closed a mosque just prior to a festival, as a result of which 3,000 believers went to Osh to pray and as a result missed an entire workday.[176]

The clergy, both registered and unregistered, were undoubtedly active in attracting believers to festival prayer-services. When informing their flock about the *uraz*, they would also tell them to come to the mosque on Uraz-Bayram.[177] In some instances, they were said to have literally compelled people to attend prayers. For example, the clergy of Shahr-i Sabz (Kashka-Darya Oblast') were reported in 1946 to have forced kolkhozniki to attend mosque, including eighteen-year olds who were still in school with not an inkling how to perform rites, being completely ignorant of the *namaz* and not knowing a single letter of the Qur'an.[178] In various parts the clergy even visited private homes on the eve of Uraz-Bayram specifically to enlist them to observe the festival.[179]

173. See pp.79 and 493.

174. I. V. Polianskii to K. E. Voroshilov, the Council of Minsters' Cultural Bureau, M. A. Suslov, M. A. Turkin and A. A. Kuznetsov, 9 June 1948; GARF, f.6991, o.3, d.53, l.55.

175. V. A. Kuroedov to the CPSU Central Committee Propaganda Department, 22 Feb. 1971; TsKhSD, f.5, o.63, d.89, ll.21-2.

176. For details, see p.664.

177. See p.470 above.

178. Report of CARC *uponomochennyi* for the Uzbek SSR, apparently prepared for conference of CARC *upolnomochennye*, 8 Oct. 1946; GARF, f.6991, o.3, d.41, ll.202-3. It is not clear how this supposed compulsion occurred.

179. This was reported in the mid-1950s from Ufa, Astrakhan', Rostov-on-Don and other cities and *poselki* – L. A. Prikhod'ko, Memorandum, 25 July 1956; GARF, f.6991, o.3, d.130, l.27.

Two further occasions of collective prayer and other ritual need mentioning. The one was the festival of Mavlud (Mawlid an-Nabi), the birthday of the Prophet, which was celebrated widely in the late 1940s, although not marked by the same animation as were the two main festivals. Its celebration was not necessarily restricted to the actual day of Muhammad's birth, but might continue for an entire month. Appropriate readings of poetry in praise of Muhammad, also called *mavluds*, would be conducted in all registered mosques on the occasion, both by their permanent clergy and by *qaris*, invited especially for the purpose, as for *khatm-i Qur'ans* during the *uraz*. The worshippers who attended these services, however, did so as a passive audience, being no longer able to participate in the traditional chorus.

In the late 1940s SADUM instructed clergy, prior to the beginning of the month in which the Mavlud fell, that the recital of *mavluds* should take place only on the day of Muhammad's birth and that communal feasting should not take place at the mosques.[180] On the festival itself in 1949 about 6,000 men attended Osh's main mosque – about 20 per cent of them young people and about 25 per cent having come from outside the oblast', chiefly from Andijan – as well as a further 1,000 or so women with children who stood around as spectators. After the reading of the *mavlud* food brought by the worshippers themselves was shared out, everyone partaking of a little, and then the crowd dispersed. *Mavluds* were also recited in private homes, even in *mahallas* which boasted a registered mosque. In Kazakhstan in the early 1950s the Mavlud was celebrated in all registered mosques, and the *imam-khatibs* and muezzins would be invited to private homes. Here they recited a prayer prior to the repast, and in its wake the host would distribute money – *sadaqa* – to his guests, much of which allegedly found its way in to the pockets of the clergy. In the rural parts so-called itinerant mullas would be invited to the homes of believers, notably of non-Kazakhs (Uzbeks, Uighurs, Dungans and Chechen and other Caucasian deportees). Several *upolnomochennye* reported that the ceremonies connected with the festival were thought by the clergy to be important in order to initiate believers in the conduct of rites through the example of the Prophet.[181]

The other significant occasion related to the Shiite community, namely the month of Muharram, and particularly its three days of mourning, the most important of which was the tenth day, the Ashura, marking the death of Imam Husayn. In fact special prayers and rites lasted for fifty days, from the beginning of Muharram until the fortieth day after his death. In the words of one scholar, the 'principal and most characteristic festival of the Shi'a' has been built around the death of Husayn, son of Ali and grandson of Muhammad.[182] The customs associated with this occasion, the dramatisation of his death and the events leading up to it, the processions of men inflicting sword wounds upon themselves or dragging chains behind them and the re-enactment of Husayn's funeral procession, also irritated the Soviet authorities, especially the self-torture, called in Soviet literature and documentation, *shahsei-vahsei*. (This was a corruption of the cries or refrain of those participating in the procession who, as they beat or wounded themselves, would shout 'Shah Husayn, Wa-Husayn'.) A law specifically forbidding this practice had existed in Azerbaijan since 1931.

In the early 1950s DUMZ convened the entire clergy of Azerbaijan to tell them not to permit the holding of the Ashura service outside the registered mosques in *tekkes* – special meeting-places for the practice of religious rites, usually apparently in the Soviet period in private homes – and to explain the impermissibility of *shahsei-vahsei*.[183] Apparently, it was customary for the directorate to issue guidelines prior to the advent of Muharram for the public observance of the *taziyya*, the rites of mourning during this month, just as the Sunni directorates would do prior to Ramadan. They, too, included a calendar of dates and observances, among which was information regarding the *taziyya* services held in the evening of the first ten days of Muharram, especially the 9th and 10th

---

Feb. 1951 and 5 Jan. 1956 – GARF, f.6991, o.3, d.454, ll.11-12, 54-5 and 131-4, and d.457, ll.10-11; N. Sabitov to I. V. Polionskii, 13 March 1951 –quoted in Sultangalieva, *Islam v Kazakhstane*, pp.140-1; and Almaev to Tashkent Oblispolkom Deputy Chairman Mahkamov, Obkom Secretary Nazarov, Kh. N. Iskanderov and I. V. Polianskii, 19 Jan. 1952; TsGAUz, f.2456, o.1, d.142, l.46. For the celebration of the Mavlud in registered mosques, see pp. 233-4. For the recitation of *mavluds* by unregistered clergy, not necessarily in connection with the festival, see pp.326 and 334-5.
182. Von Grunebaum, *Muhammedan Festivals*, p.87.
183. N. I. Abushaev, A short survey, undated [approx. March 1951]; GARF, f.6991, o.3, d.73, ll.7-8.

days (the Tasu'a and Ashura) and the 40th day after the latter. These consist principally of singing elegies, *marsiyya*, recounting stories of the life and martyrdom of Husayn and his companions and the sufferings of Ali and other members of the Prophet's family. More than they give instructions how to carry out these rites correctly, DUMZ's guidelines stressed aspects that they proscribed as inappropriate, notably self-flagellation with chains, cutting the forehead with knives and other self-inflicted pain.[184]

The disapproval of the authorities notwithstanding, Shiite communities observed the Ashura wherever they thought it possible, even when they lacked registered mosques, including some of its more problematic practices. In 1946 Shiites in Bukhara Oblast' conducted prayers on Ashura and wounded themselves with 'cold weapons'.[185] In 1951, after four or five years in which this ceremony had not taken place in Dagestan at all, the *shahsei-vahsei* was performed in Derbent, outside the mosque, for all to witness.[186] In common with the other main events of the calendar year, the observance of Muharram enjoyed a tremendous boost in the mid-1950s. The republican leadership in Azerbaijan was undecided whether it might not be preferable to open for the first ten days of Muharram sufficient mosques to meet the needs of all believers, rather than tolerate Muharram street processions.[187] Even in the period of Khrushchev's anti-religious campaign the festivities connected with Muharram, including self-torture, took on a 'mass character' in Derbent, Shiites coming for the purpose from Azerbaijan, where these activities were subject to criminal proceedings.[188] Towards the end of the 1960s, the ceremony was again being performed in Azerbaijan, some 100,000 worshippers participating

184. Saroyan, *Reconstructing Community*, pp.256-7.

185. Testimony prepared for conference of CARC *upolnomochennye*, Tashkent, undated [Oct. 1946]; GARF, f.6991, o.3, d.41, 1.190.

186. L. A. Prikhod'ko, A short report, 4 April 1952; GARF, f.6991, o.3, d.81, 1.98.

187. M. Shamsudinskii at All-Union conference of CARC *upolnomochennye*, 26-27 Nov. 1958; GARF, f.6991, o.3, d.165, 1.88.

188. A. Daniyalov to CPSU Central Committee Secretay L. F. Il'ichev, 23 June 1964; CARC Chairman Puzin denied that self-torture was a mass phenomenon – A. A. Puzin, Information, given by hand to the CPSU Central Committee Ideological Department, 11 July 1964; TsKhSD, f.5, r.7732, o.55, d.72, ll.96 and 98, and GARF, f.6991, o.3, d.1459, ll.132-3.

in collective prayer on Ashura, the 'most fanatic element' among them indulging in self-torture.

At one mosque in Baku, the Taza-pir, Azerbaijan's largest and most prestigious mosque, two groups inside the building and another six in the courtyard were reported in one year during the late 1960s to have beaten their breasts during the service, and in one specific village, where 2,000 gathered for the collective prayer-service, four groups beat themselves with chains. A decade later a Western observer found this same mosque in Baku 'generously decorated with traditional black flags of mourning' and the mosque and its courtyard crowded with pilgrims, come to 'perform devotion throughout the day and into the night'. Sites for devotions had been set up in the mosque compound, 'similar to those observed at the shrines' with collection boxes for cash donations and poles to which silken scarves and other large strips of cloth were tied. According to this same source, the mutual accommodation of believers and establishment led to a compromise by which the former inflicted the customary forms of self-punishment, but did so at the registered mosques, under the supervision of the latter. In this way 'the flagellants are able to defy the clergy's instructions on legitimate forms of religious conduct, while integrating themselves into the realm of the mosque that operates under clerical authority'. By this time there were dozens of small groups of flagellants, five to ten per group, mostly aged 15 – 30, who, flagellated their bare backs with metal chains as others gathered around to chant and beat their chests in a rhythmic rite, one person narrating 'the formulaic chant...to which the rest of the crowd chants a fixed refrain'.[189] In just one happening in a rural part of southern Azerbaijan in 1970, some 10,000 witnessed a dramatisation of Husayn's death. The audience included many who came from other raiony in no less than 200 vehicles, party, soviet and kolkhoz officials and the pupils and teachers of the local village school.[190]

In addition to the purely religious, ceremonial aspect of the major festivals, they were also popular and social events. Even

189. A. Barmenkov to the CPSU Central Committee, 23 May 1968, and A. F. Ahadov to V. A. Kuroedov, 10 Oct. 1969 – GARF, f.6991, o.6, d.147, l.23, and d.220, ll.29-30; and Saroyan, *Reconstructing Community*, pp.258-62. Ahadov described in detail both the ceremonies connected with the Ashura and a number of other special dates in the Shiite calendar.

190. CRA, Information, sent to the CPSU Central Committee, 27 April 1971; TsKhSD, f.5, o.63, d.89, ll.105-6, and *Kommunist* (Baku), 4 Sept. 1970.

the vast gatherings in and around the mosques in the cities of the RSFSR were said to comprise many who came in order to meet people from their native parts and to become acquainted with members of their ethnic group, which, among other things, often led to the consummation of marriages.[191] Sometimes popular practices also entailed vestiges of religious custom. In some villages, for instance, at least in the early postwar years, believers of both registered and unregistered religious associations held prayer processions on Qurban-Bayram.[192] On occasion these practices were of a blatantly provocative nature. In a number of places in the Chechen-Ingush ASSR in the late 1960s–early 1970s young people went up and down the streets on horseback, motorcycles or tractors or in cars, carrying the green banner of Islam and greeting people in honour of Uraz-Bayram.[193]

Everywhere, as the festivals drew near, preparations for the great day became intense. The women cooked special dishes, cleaned up homes and courtyards, and bought new clothes for themselves and their children.[194] On the eve of Uraz-Bayram in 1950 in one kolkhoz in Kirgiziia three sheep were slaughtered. In the evening the kolkhozniki changed their clothes and invited each other to their homes, where they would read from the Qur'an. A group of older people in festive attire approached the chairman to ask permission to go to a nearby *poselok* the following morning to attend prayers in the registered mosque.[195] Around the mosques in the cities, towns and larger settlements, and the more popular *mazars* improvised markets sprang up on the festivals where people sold food and drink and all sorts of goodies (sweets, toys and the like). Sometimes even in places without a mosque these items would be hawked in the local *chaikhona* or restaurant.[196] On the

191. V. A. Kuroedov to the CPSU Central Committee Propaganda Department, 22 Feb. 1971; TsKhSD, f.5, o.63, d.89, l.20. For the authorities' endeavours to deprive the mosques of their traditional social role, see pp.233-4.

192. This was reported in regard to Tatar villages in the Mordvinian ASSR – Minutes, CARC session, No.26, 1-2 Dec. 1949; GARF, f.6991, o.3, d.60, l.69.

193. V. A. Kuroedov to the CPSU Central Committee Propaganda Department, 22 Feb. 1971; TsKhSD, f.5, o.63, d.89, l.22. And compare p.489 above.

194. L. A. Prikhod'ko, Memorandum, 25 July 1956; GARF, f.6991, o.3, d.130, l.27.

195. I. Halimov to H. Akhtiamov, 4 Sept. 1950; GARF, f.6991, o.3, d.454, l.76.

196. Ivigin to Kh. N. Iskanderov, I. V. Polianskii, Chairman, Fergana Oblispolkom I. B. Usmankhojaev, and Obkom Secretary Akramov, 23 July 1951 – TsGAUz, f.2456, o.1, d.135, l.43; and V. A. Kuroedov to the CPSU

other hand, the regular markets hardly operated at all on festivals.[197]

In conformity with traditional practice, many went to the cemeteries after the termination of prayers. At the Tatar cemetery in Moscow on Uraz-Bayram in the early 1950s there were a large number of cars by midday; in the late 1960s on this same occasion over 20,000 visited the capital's cemeteries 'where people are buried according to Muslim custom'.[198] At the cemeteries they would sometimes perform a short *namaz*, read excerpts from the Qur'an, and distribute bread, *halva* (sesame candy) and other sweetmeats.[199] (In Dagestan, at least, the visitation of cemeteries was customary throughout the *uraz* as well.[200]) From the cemeteries the men of a kishlak or *mahalla* would go in groups to visit the homes of people who had died during the past year, where the relatives of the deceased would hold memorial services.[201]

Above all, on both festivals people exchanged holiday greetings, visited each other's homes, often bringing gifts. In some of the smaller places older people came together for 'organised tea-drinking'. In Eastern Kazakhstan in the late 1960s these included 'repatriates' from China.[202] The festive atmosphere was somewhat marred, especially in urban areas, during the anti-religious campaign of the early 1960s.[203] Altogether, however, in more tranquil periods, the streets, parks and public squares took on a festive look, and

Central Committee Department, 22 Feb. 1971 – TsKhSD, f.5, o.63, d.89, l.20.

197. Almaev, Memorandum, 12 July 1952; TsGAUz, f.2456, o.1, d.142, l.12.

198. I. V. Polianskii to G. M. Malenkov, 8 Aug. 1953, and V. Kuroedov to the CPSU Central Committee Propaganda Department, 2 March 1970; GARF, f.6991, o.3, d.93, l.180, and o.6, d.223, l.3. The first report speaks of about 100 vehicles (cars and taxis), which in that period was undoubtedly a very considerable number.

199. M. S. Gajiev, Report, CARC session No.1, 7 Jan. 1964; GARF, f.6991, o.4, d.146, l.12.

200. *Ibid.*

201. Saidbaev, *Islam i obshchestvo*, pp.233–4.

202. I. Isakov to V. A. Kuroedov and K. K. Kulumbetov, 6 Jan. 1969; GARF, f.6991, o.6, d.220, l.124. The repatriates were presumably Uighurs, some 150,000 of whom migrated to Kazakhstan in the years 1953-63 – Roberts, 'The Uighurs of the Kazakstan Borderlands', p.513 and n.18.

203. See D. Ahmedov to A. Puzin, Tajikistan CP Central Committee Secretary N. Zaripova, and Tajik SSR KGB Chairman S. Tsvigun, 5 June 1961; GARF, f.6991, o.3, d.1737, ll.79-80.

restaurants and places of entertainment – cinemas, theatres, concert halls – were overcrowded with people in holiday attire.[204]

The fast and festivals, then, were year in, year out, major happenings in the lives of the Muslim community. For the *uraz* this was true especially in the rural areas, while the festivals were celebrated in the towns and cities as well. The *uraz* was of a purely religious significance, its symbolism being *a priori* one of a greater spirituality, a desire for, and identification with the more ephemeral side of Islam, although it, too, entailed social gatherings every evening during the course of the entire month. The major festivals, on the other hand, also had a blatantly societal aspect. True, the actual prayer-service remained the nodal point, bringing together at the mosque or *mazar*, or wherever, large numbers of people with a similar ethnic and social background, who for a brief spell found themselves united under the leadership of a religious figure. Yet, for the most part, ubiquitously throughout the Soviet Union, these services were abruptly curtailed in order to enable worshippers to hurry to work. The emphasis therefore tended to shift to the convivial coming together, to a general festive atmosphere, the inclusion in the celebration of this occasion of the womenfolk and children, even when – as was usually the case – they did not participate in the actual prayers. Through the festivals Islam thus retained a public hold on a population which in large measure no longer attended Friday prayers and did not perform the daily *namaz*, and helped it retain its Muslim identity in a world to which its mindset and way of life were fundamentally alien. In this way, the festivals became a kind of anchor, an assurance of stability, providing the Soviet Union's Muslim peoples with a feeling of safety and belonging with which they were loath to part despite all the pressures and constraints.

204. A. Barmenkov to the CPSU Central Committee, 23 May 1968, and V. Kuroedov to the Central Committee Propaganda Department, 21 Feb. 1970; GARF, f.6991, o.6, d.147, l.25, and d.284, ll.7-8.

9

RITES AND RITUALS: THE FAMILY
AND THE INDIVIDUAL

Just as the fast and festivals were the main events of the year in
the Muslim community, so Muslim custom and tradition made
their imprint on the milestones in the life of the family and the
individual. In the Soviet Union, the Muslim rites of passage were
more strictly observed than the pillars of Islam. Not only were
they less burdensome than, say, the five daily prayers or the *uraz*;
their retention and vitality were boosted by social and economic
circumstances, as well as by group psychology and the force of
opinion within a community which sought jealously to preserve
its traditions, or, in the words of one CARC inspector, its superstitions and prejudices. This official noted that while a person
would not be censured by his peers for not performing the *namaz*,
he would be subjected to severe social pressure were he not to
circumcise his son or bury his relatives in accordance with custom.
It was this pressure, combined with the need of every individual
to be an integral part of the community in which he lived, that
perhaps explains why even officials and party members of the
Muslim nationalities, especially in the regions where they comprised
the indigenous population, frequently observed these rites.[1] On
this score it made no difference whether the area in question was
or was not one where organised religious life had traditionally
been minimal and religious activity had inevitably focused on the
family circle.

The social constraints which made large sections of the population, who were declared non-believers, circumcise their sons and
bury their dead in conformity with religious ritual thus ensured
that in many of the areas inhabited by Muslim nationalities both

1. N. Abushaev, Information, sent by Polianskii to the head of the AUCP(b)
Central Committee group of lecturers, A. I. Sobolev, 15 March 1951; GARF,
f.6991, o.3, d.76, l.22.

customs were all but universal. It was manifest to that many non-believers adhered to these practices.[2] Throughout the period under study, life-cycle events had to be registered with the local registry office, ZAGS, but believers might also mark these by the performance of religous rites.[3] In the Brezhnev period, when official policy dictated the actual performance of civil rites, young couples who had registered in ZAGS would have their marriage consecrated by a mulla, and the coffin would be discarded and the *jinaz*, the Muslim funeral prayer, recited in the wake of the civic burial ceremony.[4]

Rites of passage

The principal rites connected with the life of the family and the individual related to the very formation of the family, the religious marriage, known in most parts of the Soviet Union as *nikoh*; to the birth of a son and particularly his circumcision, which was usually performed when the boy was already in school; and to death, specifically the *jinaz*, and the various memorial services, held on the seventh and fortieth days after death, and sometimes on the third and twentieth as well, and again on the first anniversary. It was perhaps an indication both of the tenacity of Islam and of the adaptibility of the Muslim population that these customs became in many ways the fulcrum around which its faith evolved in the Soviet period. They came to comprise the chief guarantee that Islam would continue to subsist, for they were so deeply rooted in society and the events they denoted so commonplace, regular and inevitable that their eradication was well-nigh out of the question.

In this way, while pressure to preserve these rites emanated from the Muslim's surroundings, from his social peers, it was the family which was the real focus of the Islamic faith in the Soviet Union. It was on the whole not in the mosque, but in the home, within the family, that a person received such knowledge of ritual

2. *Islam v SSSR*, p.76.

3. V. I. Gostev, Information, sent by A. Puzin to Novikov at the USSR Supreme Soviet, 29 July 1957; GARF, f.6991, o.3, d.146, l.125.

4. CRA report, sent to the CPSU Central Committee, 22 May 1970; TsKhSD, f.5, o.62, d.38, l.33, and Doev, *Osobennosti islama v Kirgizii*, p.12. For the introduction of the 'new rites', see pp.47-8 and 600-2.

as he may have acquired, and his attitude to Islam was frequently a projection of his upbringing and family background.[5] One frustrated *upolnomochennyi* (from Turkmenistan) voiced the opinion in the mid-1960s that 'the influence of the family on children and adolescents is sometimes so great that the entire system of public education seems powerless to correct the errors of the family upbringing'.[6] Here, the younger generation from its earliest years was exposed not just to the celebration of the festivals and the *uraz*, but to the everyday practice of religion. For instance, among the predominant majority of believers, especially in those households which included elderly family members, the *bata* or prayer of thanksgiving for one's food was recited after every meal.[7] In addition, as Polianskii pointed out in the late 1940s, a mulla inevitably participated in all family events in the Muslim areas,[8] performing the rites connected with them in the believer's home. This held for the funeral service (apart from that part which had to be read at the cemetery), memorial ceremonies, circumcisions, name-giving and weddings.[9]

There seems to have been considerable diversity between the different areas regarding the practice of life-cycle rites in the war and immediate prewar period. But, as religion in general and Islam specifically surfaced and received legitimisation towards the end of the war, it was noted by observers throughout the country

5. In the words of the republican *upolnomochennyi* for Kazakhstan in the immediate postwar years, Islam had a certain influence on the masses, especially within the family – N. Sabitov, Synopsis of report, Conference of CARC *upolnomochennye*, Alma-Ata, 20 Sept. 1946 (the conference took place from 30 Sept. to 2 Oct.); GARF, f.6991, o.3, d.41, l.81.

6. M. A. Il'baev, Address, All-Union conference of CARC *upolnomochennye*, 17 Feb. 1965; GARF, f.6991, o.4, d.168, l.40.

7. Information, signature illegible, transmitted by hand to Ivanov for I. I. Brashnik, 11 Feb. 1965; GARF, f.6991, o.3, d.1484, l.75. For the influence of the family, and particularly of grandparents, in the upbringing of the younger generation in the Muslim areas, see pp.441-3.

8. I. V. Polianskii to the Council of Ministers Cultural Bureau, K. E. Voroshilov, M. A. Turkin, M. A. Suslov and A. A. Kuznetsov, undated (ratified by CARC session No.8, 9 June 1948); GARF, f.6991, o.3, d.53, l.24.

9. V. I. Gostev to P. A. Tarasov, 4 Jan. 1954; GARF, f.6991, o.3, d.102, l.16. Even in the 1970s, by which time many circumcisions were performed in hospitals, the accompanying ceremony held in the boy's home would be attended by a religious figure, who would conduct a prayer and/or other ritual – K. Kulumbetov to A. A. Nurullaev, 28 June 1974; GARF, f.6991, o.6, d.629, l.15.

that the basic rites were ubiquitously observed. For the most part, given the dearth of registered religious communities and clergy, they would be performed by 'illegal mullas' or simply elders who were 'more or less competent in questions of religion and custom'.[10] The chairman of CARC informed Deputy Prime Minister Voroshilov and Central Committee Secretary Malenkov at the very end of the 1940s that the most widespread rites, apart from the *uraz* and the two major festivals, were the religious marriage, circumcision, burial and remembering the dead.[11]

Indeed, throughout the four decades from the end of the war down to perestroika, most reports from most Muslim areas confirmed that the life-cycle rites were observed by the overwhelming majority of the indigenous population. True, differences still prevailed. In the first place, observance was higher in the countryside than in urban centres, except perhaps in all that concerned the burial rite, which was the most generally practised. Secondly, circumcision seems not to have been performed in a few areas in the Northern Caucasus. And marriage, too, was not universal. Among the Kyrgyz shortly after the war the substance of 'Muslimness' was said to be a belief in God without the performance of ritual, apart from rites connected with burial, birth and, occasionally, marriage.[12] All in all, life-cycle rites were common, and were adhered to by all strata, including intelligentsia and party members.[13] In one single year in the late 1960s, the clergy of Osh Oblast's eighteen registered mosques met with believers on no less than 4,000 occasions in order to perform life-cycle rites.[14]

Legitimacy was given to the performance of these life-cycle rites, at least until Khrushchev's anti-religious campaign, by permitting clergy to go to private homes to conduct them, provided they received a specific invitation. This they might do, moreover, not only within the confines of their respective parishes, but even

10. H. A. Akhtiamov, Report, Conference of CARC *upolnomochennye*, Alma-Ata, 30 Sept. 1946; GARF, f.6991, o.3, d.41, l.100. And see pp.324-44 *passim*.

11. I. V. Polianskii to G. M. Malenkov and K. E. Voroshilov, 23 April 1949; RTsKhIDNI, f.17, o.132, d.111, l.60.

12. H. A. Akhtiamov, Report, Conference of CARC *upolnomochennye*, Alma-Ata, 30 Sept. 1946; GARF, f.6991, o.3, d.41, l.100.

13. See, for example, CRA report, sent to the CPSU Central Committee, 22 May 1970; TsKhSD, f.5, o.62, d.38, ll.6-7.

14. N. Alekseev, The work of the council on atheism, the Osh branch of Znanie, undated [June 1969]; GARF, f.6991, o.6, d.220, l.169.

in other raiony.[15] Such concessions, however, were not applied in all areas, the various republican and oblast' authorities clearly having considerable leeway to impose their own line. Thus, in Turkmenistan it was forbidden either to conduct the *jinaz* or to accept money for doing so outside the republic's four registered mosques, which created tremendous hardships for the families of people who died at any distance from one of these. (Turkmenistan had an area of over 400,000 sq.km.) Maryi Oblast', for example, had not a single registered religious society.[16]

The reasoning behind this permissiveness was that if registered clerics did not perform these rites, they would be conducted by unregistered mullas, for the population was not going to forego them, and it was clearly preferable from the point of view of the authorities that as many as possible be performed by the former, as this enabled some control by the organs of government.

Attempts were made to oblige clergy to conduct life-cycle rites only upon the presentation of a document certifying that the marriage, death or whatever, had previously been registered with ZAGS. In 1947 CARC Chairman Polianskii wrote to his *upol-nomochennye* in the four republics where the Muslim spiritual direc-torates were situated that the Ministry of the Interior, the MVD, had informed him that mullas were performing religious funerals in cases where death had not been duly registered with ZAGS (the law stipulated that death had to be reported within three days). The directorates were to instruct clergy in the interests of believers not being harassed by the militia to draw the attention of the deceased person's relatives to the desirability of registration prior to the actual performance of the religious rite.[17] There were localities where the local head of ZAGS appointed a mulla in each kolkhoz, from among its resident unregistered clergy, in order to perform marriages and funerals that had been so registered.[18]

Neither such measures, however, nor the major campaign to

15. I. V. Polianskii to A. M. Komekov, 18 Jan. 1954; TsGAUz, f.2456, o.1, d.162, l.55. And see pp.246-7.

16. SADUM's temporary *upolnomochennyi* in Turkmenistan Rahim Muhammadiev and its inspection committee member Abdurahman Sharipov to Ishan Babakhan, 21 Nov. 1953; TsGAUz, f.2456, o.1, d.162, l.56.

17. I. V. Polianskii to Kh. N. Iskanderov, M. Sh. Karimov, B. A. Shahbazbekov and I. Zakaryaev, 26 Aug. 1947; TsGAUz, f.2456, o.1, d.82, l.27.

18. For example, in one raion in Jalalabad Oblast' in 1954 – see p.667.

enforce civil rites as of the early 1960s scored any outstanding success. One CRA *upolnomochennyi* in Kazakhstan noted in the mid-1970s that, although Islam had been officially deprived of its position, in terms of daily routine and in people's consciousness and behaviour, everything remained as it had been before October 1917, especially among the rural population. In one aul in his oblast' not a single 'Komsomol wedding' had taken place in almost two years, and in two auls just a half of all marriages and births had been registered at ZAGS.[19]

Unquestionably, the population received encouragement from indications that in practice the authorities recognised its adherence to Islamic rites of passage and were prepared to make concessions to avoid confrontation. In addition to their leniency toward clergy who performed these rites, they thus allowed funeral processions, although all other religious processions required special permission.[20] The population, too, appears, like the powers-that-be, to have had an interest in having personal rites conducted by official clergy, probably to ensure that those adhering to them would not be subject to harassment or persecution. Immediately after the war, requests were made to register mosqueless mullas to conduct 'urgent' rites, such as funerals, recitals from the Qur'an for the dying, memorial prayers and weddings in settlements which had had no mosque in the pre-1917 period and so were not only without registered religious societies but had no prospects of acquiring one.[21]

In some parts the extent of observance was explained very early on by attributing these rites to national custom rather than to any religious precept.[22] Be this as it may, they were widely popular. Every settlement with inhabitants of a Muslim ethnic group had at least one person who knew how to perform the burial rite, and although in some parts not everyone seems actually to have been buried in accordance with Muslim tradition, it certainly was the general rule. Even in areas where the Muslim inhabitants

19. Zh. Botashev to the Kzyl-Orda Obkom, 24 Sept. 1974; GARF, f.6991, o.6, d.633, ll.72–3.

20. In the major cities such permission was necessary even for funerals – Minutes, CARC session No.28a, 23–24 Dec. 1949; GARF, f.6991, o.3, d.60, l.164. Regulations regarding funeral and other processions were not, of course, peculiar to Islam but applied to all faiths.

21. I. V. Polianskii to CARC *upolnomochennye*, 6 Oct. 1945; GARF, f.6991, o.3, d.21, l.84. See also p.186.

22. For instance, in the Cherkess AO – see p.448.

comprised neither the indigenous population nor a majority, these rites were practised – for example by 'russified Tatars' in various parts of the country, not only in the RSFSR, but also, for instance, in Belorussia, where there was still a fair-sized Tatar community after the war. Here, too, adherence to mono-ethnic marriages and burial in Tatar cemeteries was attributed as much to national sentiment as to religious conviction.[23] On the whole, among the Tatars rites connected with death were probably the most prevalent; the only other 'mass rites' in Moscow were said to be circumcision and the *fitr*. Ninety per cent of the capital's Tatars were thought to have been buried at the city's Muslim cemetery in accordance with Muslim ritual.[24] In the Tatar ASSR itself, the majority of the indigenous population was also buried in accordance with Muslim ritual (80 per cent in Kazan', for example, and 100 per cent in rural areas).[25] So were all Tatars 'without exception' in the rural parts of Kuibyshev Oblast',[26] and 'nearly all' of Kirgiziia's indigenous population, whether Kyrgyz or Uzbeks,[27] and similarly that of Kazakhstan.[28] Even in the mixed urban centres of Gur'ev and Petropavlovsk, the great majority of Kazakhs, nearly 90 per cent and over 70 per cent respectively, were so buried.[29] Among the Azerbaijanis, both Shiites and Sunnis, the burial ceremony was the most observed of all religious rites.[30]

The prevalence, often even the inexorability, of a religious funeral was best borne out by the fact that so many local officials and even communists were buried in conformity with religious tradition. Reports from the field constantly gave examples of officials

23. See p.694.

24. I. V. Polianskii, Information, 28 May 1955; GARF, f.6991, o.3, d.113, 1.184.

25. F. S. Mangutkin to A. A. Puzin, 20 April 1964; GARF, f.6991, o.3, d.1466, l.201.

26. Report, sent to the CPSU Central Committee, 22 May 1970; TsKhSD, f.5, o.62, d.38, 1.6.

27. N. Alekseev, The work of the council on atheism, the Osh branch of Znanie, undated [June 1969]; GARF, f.6991, o.6, d.220, 1.169.

28. P. Isakov to A. Nurullaev, 3 June 1974; GARF, f.6991, o.6, d.633, 1.20. (This particular report related to the oblast' of Eastern Kazakhstan.)

29. The precise figures given were 86 and 70.8 per cent – CRA report, sent to the CPSU Central Committee, 22 May 1970; TsKhSD, f.5. o.62, d.38, 1.6.

30. A. F. Ahadov to V. A. Kuroedov, 10 Oct. 1969; GARF, f.6991, o.6, d.221, ll.1-2 and 15. For details of the Shiite burial ceremony, see ibid., ll.15-16.

and party members who had resort to religious practices, in particular the burial service. These included people in all branches of the bureaucracy and the public sector. Just in one raion reports from the field told of religious funerals being held for a district attorney (*prokuror*), a passport office official, kolkhoz chairmen and teachers.[31] No work at all was done for an entire week in one kolkhoz in Kirgiziia owing to the funeral of its chairman's father.[32] When a former kolkhoz chairman died in Kazakhstan in the 1970s, the local *aksakals* led by unregistered mullas prevented the commission set up by the local party committee to arrange her funeral from even approaching her home, contending that she had been a Muslim and would be buried as one.[33] Occasionally, however, the clergy obstructed the interment in a Muslim cemetery of communists who were known propagandists of atheism, or of a person who did not belong to a Muslim ethnic group (for example, the husband or wife of one who did).[34] Sometimes the funeral of a government official would begin with a religious rite in the home of the deceased. Afterword would come the civil funeral ceremony, and finally the actual interment in accordance with religious custom.[35]

While life-cycle rites persisted, they seem to have undergone some change during the period under discussion. In particular, they underwent a process of simplification, often leaving just the barest essentials. For instance, the traditional burial service included, in addition to the *jinaz*, the *dawra*, or, as it was sometimes called,

31. The district attorney (*prokuror*) in one raion in Samarkand Oblast' organised a *jinaz-namaz* for his deceased father in his home, as well as memorial prayers on the third, seventh, twentieth and fortieth day after his death – Instructional conference of CARC's *upolnomochennye* in the Uzbek SSR, 17 July 1951 – TsGAUz, f.2456, o.1, d.134, l.73; while the parents of a kolkhoz chairman in Osh Oblast' invited to their son's funeral all the mullas from nearby kolkhozy and gave 100 rubles to each of the 23 clergy who attended the service, as well as slaughtering several heads of livestock to feast them and the nearly 400 worshippers who went straight from the *jum'a-namaz* in the mosque to participate in the funeral – I. G. Halimov to CARC, 3 April 1950; see also Halimov to CARC, undated [early April 1949]; GARF, f.6991, o.3, d.454, ll.14 and 57-8.

32. I. V. Polianskii to P. V. Kovanov, 23 June 1955; GARF, f.6991, o.3, d.114, ll.29-30.

33. Zh. Botashev to the Kzyl-Orda Obkom, 24 Sept. 1974; GARF, f.6991, o.6, d.633, l.73.

34. *Nauka i religiia*, No.12 (1974), p.21.

35. A. A. Puzin to the Tajikistan CP Central Committee, 26 Jan. 1963; GARF, f.6991, o.3, d.1739, l.1.

the *fidiyya*, the expiation of the sins of the deceased by mullas or shaykhs who read from the Qur'an, or even the entire Qur'an, and in some parts recited prayers as they stood at the four corners of the bier, prior to interment. This was frequently dropped in the postwar period, although a single *ayat* might still be recited. Here and there even the *jinaz* might be discarded, for example in the Karachai-Cherkess AO, although even there no funerals were held without the participation of an *efendi*. If the family of the deceased wished to have the Qur'an read in his memory, this might be done through the auspices of the nearest registered mosque.[36] Where the *dawra* was retained, however it persisted even when the civic rites were introduced in the late Khrushchev years. In the urban centres of the Kabardino-Balkar ASSR, for instance, the civic rite would be followed by the mulla performing the *dawra*.[37]

Moreover, funerals sometimes served as opportunities to hold collective prayers.[38] They also provided occasion for clergy to expound on religion before audiences to whom they normally had no access and for young people to approach them with questions on religion.[39] This was particularly pertinent in view of the fact that considerable numbers of people would attend funerals. Even funerals of simple people in rural areas would be attended by 100 people and more, or, in places where the clergy were 'particularly active', as many as 250 to 300.[40]

The Soviet regime had introduced its own life-cycle rites very

36. For example, in Osh Oblast' and the Karachai-Cherkess AO the *dawra* seems to have disappeared altogether – I. G. Halimov to CARC, 3 April 1956, and V. V. Bulatov, Report, CARC session No.21, 22 July 1959; GARF, f.6991, o.3, d.457, 1.72, and d.184, 1.177. For the *fetwa* issued by SADUM laying down that the *dawra* was not obligatory, see p.143. The arrangement for having the Qur'an read under the auspices of a registered mosque was introduced in Kokchetau (Kazakhstan) as part of the procedure to be followed by the itinerant mullas officially installed in 1973, see p.217.

37. L. Zh. Aisov to CARC, 6 Jan. 1965; GARF, f.6991, o.3, d.1609, 1.7.

38. Thus, for example, the CRA *upolnomochennyi* for Bukhara Oblast' noted in a list of unregistered religious associations in his oblast' that at one kolkhoz mosque, prayers were held on the two major festivals and on the occasion of burials – S. A. Shamsutdinov, A list of unregistered religious associations in Bukhara Oblast' as of 1 Jan. 1973, undated; GARF, f.6991, o.6, d.486, 1.16.

39. Author's interview with a former CRA official who has asked to remain anonymous. And see pp.251-2.

40. L. Aisov to A. Puzin, 14 Feb. 1963, and to T. Mal'bakhov at the Kabardino-Balkar Obkom, 16 March 1963; GARF, f.6991, o.3, d.1607, ll.4 and 10.

soon after 1917. But these had related in particular to marriage and the birth of a child, as part of the regime's endeavour to influence the shape of the family, to transmit its perception of sex roles, and to create the 'new Soviet man'. There had been very little effort to introduce a civil burial ceremony, except for public figures.[41] Indeed, at least in the Muslim areas, the local religious *aktiv*, in addition to monopolising burial ceremonies, also ran the cemeteries, although these were officially under the jurisdiction of the relevant municipality or *sel'sovet*.[42] In the Kabardino-Balkar ASSR, for instance, mostly as a result of the initiative of the village elders and religious *aktiv*, the rural cemeteries were fenced in and equipped by the local inhabitants at their own expense, each household contributing anything from one to five rubles.[43]

One report after another noted that the clergy and local religious *aktiv* had control of the cemetery and did there as they pleased. An attendant or watchman was often posted there by the local representative of the spiritual directorate or the *mutawaliyyat* of the nearest registered mosque,[44] or even by unregistered groups which would use the cemetery precincts for prayer purposes. These watchmen would see that the cemetery was kept in good shape and take upon themselves such repairs and refurbishing as might be necessary.[45] In some instances the local unregistered mulla actually

41. Lane, *The Rites of Rulers*, Chapter 5.

42. For local government and the cemeteries, see pp.628-9.

43. L. Zh. Aisov to CARC, 6 Jan. 1965, and to Deputy Chairman, Kabardino-Balkar ASSR Council of Ministers B. K. Chabdarov, 22 July 1974; GARF, f.6991, o.3, d.1609, l.12, and o.6, d.634, ll.75-6. The *upolnomochennyi* who reported this noted that as a result of this initiative all the republic's 150 cemeteries were in good condition, whereas previously only the urban ones were decently kept. In the process of fencing in the cemeteries, prayer premises were constructed in 70 of them, see pp.313-4. The elders, who took the initiative in this assignment, also sold the hay that grew in the cemeteries to help pay the costs.

44. Minutes, CARC session No.4, 25-26 Feb. 1959; GARF, f.6991, o.3, d.183, l.106.

45. For example, in Mozhga in the Udmurt ASSR, where there was a Tatar population of over 4,000. (This was an instance of a town which had had no Tatar inhabitants before 1930 and so had no former mosque) – I. Vasil'ev to CARC, 6 March 1956; GARF, f.6991, o.3, d.130, l.85. See also CRA Information, handed to the CPSU Central Committee, 22 May 1970; TsKhSD, f.5, o.62, d.38, l.33.

held the cemetery key, so that nobody could be interred without his participation.[46]

From the early postwar period, those who officiated at the cemeteries were not in effect subordinate to the local organs of government. And where the municipality or *sel'sovet* did appoint someone, he did not necessarily enjoy the confidence of the local believers.[47] In the words of one CRA *upolnomochennyi*, the latter had recourse to the elders and clergy whom they trusted as experts in religious ritual, traditions that had developed over the centuries.[48] The chairman of the Kokand *gorispolkom* noted in 1946 that at the central Uzbek cemetery in Kokand there were a number of shaykhs who did not belong to the staff of the municipal funeral office and to whose services that office did not have recourse. The town's inhabitants came to an *ad hoc* understanding with them as the need arose.[49] In the Karachai-Cherkess AO, too, the cemeteries were in the hands of the *efendis* and as soon as a person died, the body would be given into their care.[50] In the Kabardino-Balkar ASSR they were controlled by an *aktiv* of elders, usually headed by a cleric, and all decisions regarding cemetery facilities and maintenance were taken by them.[51]

The concern over the cemeteries and widespread interest in refurbishing them was only in part a consequence of their function as a burial-place. In many ways they also filled the role of substitute mosque.[52] Quite a few of the country's operating cemeteries had grown around a *mazar*, relegating them *a priori* to the orbit of influence of the shaykhs who operated it. People who came to bury their dead or visit the grave of relatives both encountered these shaykhs and happened upon a holy place. Indeed, the local authorities frequently suggested closing such cemeteries for burial

46. V. A. Kuroedov to CARC *upolnomochennye*, 2 Feb. 1972; GARF, f.6991, o.6, d.462, l.3.

47. For example, reception by V. I. Gostev of a representative of the Muslim believers of Sverdlovsk, 13 March 1958; GARF, f.6991, o.4, d.88, l.66.

48. A. F. Ahadov to V. A. Kuroedov, 10 Oct. 1969; GARF, f.6991, o.6, d.220, ll.37-8.

49. M. Aliev to Chairman of the Uzbek SSR Council of Ministers A. Abdurahmanov, 14 June 1946; TsGAUz, f.2456, o.1, d.72, l.7.

50. V. V. Bulatov, Report, CARC session, No.21, 22 July 1959; GARF, f.6991, o.3, d.184, l.176.

51. L. Aisov to the CRA, 11 June 1968; GARF, f.6991, o.6, d.153, l.138.

52. See pp.300-1, 304, 313-4 and 315.

in order to curtail the religious activity which went on in them. New burial grounds would be opened, at which it would be forbidden to erect *mazars*.[53]

It was not only cemeteries which had *mazars* that served as foci for religious ritual other than actual funerals. It was common practice for clergy to conduct prayer-services in cemeteries, especially in places which had no registered, or other available, mosque. These services were sometimes held in the open. Frequently, however, existing structures, built to provide funeral facilities and store funeral equipment, would be used for this purpose. There were even recurrent instances in which local believers and their unofficial clergy initiated the erection of a new structure, which, too, was officially designed to serve as a storehouse for funeral equipment, but was actually used for conducting collective prayers.[54] In Kirgiziia in the late 1960s – early 1970s cemeteries were in effect controlled by unregistered clergy, who conducted religious activity there – in addition to those rites which were strictly connected with the burial service.[55]

The existence of prayer premises on the precincts of the cemetery and their use for all religious rites implied, in the view of observers, that the religious association which operated them had in fact usurped the functions of the local authority in regard to the cemetery. In some places religious insignias or emblems, or even verses from the Qur'an, would actually adorn the cemetery entrance. One rural cemetery in Chimkent Oblast' had an inscription from a *sura* in both Arabic and Kazakh. At the entrance of another cemetery the rules of the burial procedure were written up.[56] Tombstones, too, were largely traditional, often retaining impressive dimensions and having a cupola reminiscent of a mausoleum.[57]

The 'Catch-22' of regime policy was manifest in relation to the cemeteries. Registered religious societies appear to have taken into consideration regime requirements, limiting the burial services they performed to those which they were invited to conduct.

53. See pp.368 and 377.

54. See Chapter 5, passim.

55. See p.363.

56. K. Kulumbetov to Kazakhstan CP Central Committee Secretary S. N. Imashev, 27 Nov. 1970, and Sh. Ospanov, Information, 15 March 1972; GARF, f.6991, o.6, d.290, ll.48-9, and d.633, ll.83-4.

57. Zh. Botashev, Information, 20 Sept. 1973; GARF, f.6991, o.6, d.548, ll.24-5.

This enhanced the position of the unregistered clergy, among whom there was no such deference.[58] Even in communities which boasted a registered mosque, its imam would only officiate at a small proportion of funerals,[59] so that all in all the unregistered mullas had a virtual monopoly of burial matters, religious funerals and memorial rites.[60]

While the lay authorities often resented the leading position of the clergy in burial affairs, despite the budgetary alleviance this brought to the local administration, believers, too, were often hard put to bury their dead as they would have wished. Communities, whether registered or not, whose mosques were closed down or whose clergy were harassed in one way or another, had a particularly hard time burying their dead in accordance with religious tradition. Nonetheless, they do not for the most part seem to have contemplated any alternative. Believers in a *poselok* in Tashkent Oblast' which had its mosque closed down contended that it no longer had an imam to whom to entrust burials: bodies would lie around for three days until someone could be found to perform the burial service. Or, to quote from the complaint they addressed to the CPSU Central Committee, 'Muslims die and are buried like dogs'.[61]

The population, or at least some elements among it, seems also to have occasionally borne a grudge against the clergy who performed the burial service. (Very naturally, government officials who reported on the religious situation selected and highlighted these grudges, so that they may perhaps be over-represented in the documentation.) Funeral expenses appear frequently to have been very large. In the first place came the payment to the clergy who officiated at the *jinaz* and read from the Qur'an, wherever the expiation ceremony was retained. In parts of the Northern Caucasus, for example, the fees for the *dawra* were considered

58. S. Shafiqov to V. A. Kuroedov and U. D. Janybaev, 14 Oct. 1971; GARF, f.6991, o.6, d.270, l.11.

59. In Karaganda, for instance, where there were approximately 70 Muslim religious funerals in the first eight months of 1952, the mosque's imam performed just 13 – Faizullin, The trip to Frunze and Alma-Ata, 15 Sept. 1952; TsGAUz, f.2456, o.1, d.144, l.93. See also Chapter 4, n.369.

60. K. Ruzmetov to A. I. Barmenkov, 20 Oct. 1972; GARF, f.6991, o.6, d.467, ll.181-2.

61. A. A. Puzin to the CPSU Central Committee, 26 Aug. 1961; GARF, f.6991, o.3, d.1303, l.129.

exorbitant and seem to have aroused discontent among the population.[62] In Azerbaijan, as well, testimonies accrued regarding extortionate demands made by the clergy at funerals.[63] In some communities, a fixed payment would be called for. Not all clergy, however, demanded payment, although even those who did not would not refuse a gift if it was offered, unless the family was particularly large or in financial straits. Nor did payment necessarily take the form of money; it could be made in produce, livestock, or chattels, sometimes even the clothing of the deceased person.[64] In some places it is doubtful whether the term payment is even appropriate. It was customary for the relatives of the deceased to simply distribute his belongings among the community *aksakals*, and the mulla would get his share.[65] In some areas of Kazakhstan whoever performed the *jinaz* would be presented with an animal or its worth.[66]

Secondly, there would be the collective repast which accompanied the funeral and marked each memorial service. SADUM sought to put an end to these banquets on the grounds that they constituted a major strain on the often slight resources of the bereaved family.[67] In certain rural regions as soon as a person died the community led by a mulla or *ishan* would kill a sheep and, after eating it, proceed to bury the deceased person. Following this, they would go to his home and, to use the terminology of the reports of the *upolnomchennye*, oblige the head of the house to kill yet another sheep and, after eating the meat, everything in the house would be placed into a single pile, which was divided into two equal parts, one for the family, the other to be distributed

62. L. Zh. Aisov to the CRA, 25 July 1971; GARF, f.6991, o.6, d.370, l.135. (This particular report related to the Kabardino-Balkar ASSR and see p.341.)

63. A. Galiev, Information, 30 May 1973; GARF, f.6991, o.6, d.537, l.188. (The report related specifically to the town of Kirovabad.)

64. B. Turtkarin and Z. Ibraev, respectively chairman and secretary, Eastern Kazakhstan *oblispolkom*, Report, 23 April 1969, and Zh. Botashev to V. A. Kuroedov, 17 Nov. 1969; GARF, f.6991, o.6, d.223, ll.36-7, and d.220, l.146.

65. Faizullin, The trip to Frunze and Alma-Ata, 15 Sept. 1952; TsGAUz, f.2456, o.1, d.144, l.93.

66. R. Shaimardanov to A. A. Nurullaev and K. Kulumbetov, 14 July 1969; GARF, f.6991, o.6, d.223, l.45.

67. Z. Babakhanov to Kh. N. Iskanderov, 14 Dec. 1955, and A. Barinskaia to V. A. Kuroedov, undated [late March-early April 1968]; TsGAUz, f.2456, o.1, d.174, l.112, and GARF, f.6991, o.6, d.153, ll.108-9. See also p.150.

among those who attended the funeral.[68] In the event of the
funeral of an important religious figure, the mourners themselves
would bring money and livestock.[69] When a well-known imam
died in 1970 in the Karakalpak ASSR, clergy were invited from
nearby oblasti in three republics; altogether some 6,000 people
attended the funeral, thirty-five *yurts* (the traditional tent of the
Central Asian nomads) being put up to accommodate them, and
300 livestock were slaughtered.[70]

The commemorative ceremonies held in private homes on a
number of fixed days following the death of a relative, were
likewise extremely widespread.[71] They consisted primarily of recitals
from the Qur'an, the *khatm-i Qur'an*, and a collective repast, which
again was often very sumptuous and its cost ruinous.[72] Despite
the reservations of SADUM, the clergy, in some parts at least,
were reported to have encouraged this practice,[73] which, it was
claimed, provided them with a further platform for propagating
religion.[74] In others, they at least condoned it. As one imam in
the Tatar ASSR pointed out to his flock, it was, strictly speaking,
a mistaken custom, but if invited to conduct such a ritual, the
clergy had no choice but to comply, and to perform it, as all
rites, 'with a reading from the Qur'an, a sermon, answers to
questions, and prayer'.[75]

The memorial service was such an accepted social custom that

68.   Arifov to Gorno-Badakhshan Obkom Secretary G. D. Javov, Ispolkom
Chairman M. Shirinjanov, head of the GBAO KGB Kh. U. Valiev, and CARC
upolnomochennyi for Tajikistan D. Ahmedov, 15 June 1961; GARF, f.6991, o.3,
d.1737, d.58.

69.   The funeral of the former imam of Karaganda drew people from several
raiony who, during the days of mourning, brought more than ten animals and
donated 4,000 rubles – Zh. Rahimov, Information, 27 Oct. 1969; GARF, f.6991,
o.6, d.223, l.47.

70.   Saidbaev, *Islam i obshchestvo*, p.107.

71.   For such rites in the Kabardino-Balkar ASSR, see L. Zh. Aisov to the
CRA, 25 July 1971, and in Nakhichevan, see E. Bonchkovskii to E. I. Lisavtsev,
1 June 1973; GARF, f.6991, o.6, d.370, l.135 and d.537, l.171.

72.   Zh. Botashev to the Kzyl-Orda Obkom, 24 Sept. 1974; GARF, f.6991,
o.6, d.633, ll.73-4.

73.   For example, in Kzyl-Orda – Zh. Botashev to V. A. Kuroedov, 17 Nov.
1969; GARF, f.6991, o.6, d.220, l.146.

74.   CRA Report, sent to the CPSU Central Committee, 22 May 1970; TsKhSD,
f.5, o.62, d.38, l.29.

75.   Ashirov, *Evoliutsiia islama v SSSR*, p.143.

it, too, was sometimes observed by people in the local government apparatus; for instance, the chairman of one *raiispolkom* in Osh Oblast' held such a ceremony for his son.[76] It was usual to invite mullas to one's home to conduct memorial ceremonies on the occasion of Qurban Bayram; so much so that the invitations would be issued weeks before the advent of the festival, and the few registered imams, who were unable to respond to all requests in time, would continue performing them two or even three weeks after the occasion.[77] Similar recitals from the Qur'an in memory of a deceased relative were commonly performed on the first Uraz–Bayram after his demise in the family home,[78] and on subsequent festivals in the cemetery and at *mazars*, where the shaykhs would read a number of *ayats* to groups of pilgrims in honour of their departed relatives.[79]

Also common was the reading of the *yasin-sura* for the dying. Even where there were no registered religious societies, unregistered mullas or elders would recite this special *sura* (XXXVI) from the Qur'an when the need arose.[80]

Second in line after the burial rite, from the point of view of its unversality, was circumcision, which frequently served as a symbol of Muslim identity. After a number of years in which it seems to have fallen into disuse in the 1930s and early 1940s as a result of the repression of religion, circumcision was resumed as soon as the situation began to improve. In some parts, as people began to sense that it was politically safe to perform circumcisions, the operation was carried out *en masse*, not only on smaller boys, but even on adolescents, whom it had not been considered salutary to circumcise when they were younger, even though these adolescents or young men sometimes apparently protested.[81] There is

76. I. G. Halimov to CARC, 3 April 1950; GARF, f.6991, o.3, d.454, l.57.

77. V. A. Kuroedov to the CPSU Central Committee, 21 April 1970; GARF, f.6991, o.6, d.284, l.6.

78. See p.507.

79. Almaev, Memorandum, 12 July 1952; TsGAUz, f.2456, o.1, d.142, l.13.

80. For example, in the Bashkir ASSR in the immediate postwar period and in Azerbaijan in the late 1960s – M. Sh. Karimov to I. V. Polianskii and Chairman SNK, Bashkir ASSR, S. A. Vagapov, 8 Oct. 1945, and A. F. Ahadov to V. A. Kuroedov, 10 Oct. 1969; GARF, f.6991, o.3, d.26, l.14, and o.6, d.220, l.37.

81. In the oblast' of Northern Kazakhstan, for instance, in late 1944 there was large-scale circumcision – I. V. Polianskii to G. F. Aleksandrov, 31 Aug. 1945;

evidence in the postwar years of parents declining to let their daughters marry someone who was not circumcised, of community elders forebidding children to befriend or socialise with boys who were not circumcised,[82] of boys scoffing at one of their number who might not be circumcised.[83] One atheist in the Karakalpak ASSR was obliged to leave the *mahalla* in which he lived after his uncircumcised son had gone bathing without trunks, as the other boys 'looked upon him with intolerance'.[84] An unregistered cleric in Kzyl-Orda explained to a group of believers that parents whose children did not follow the precepts of Islam and were not circumcised were grave sinners, for circumcision was Islam's highest quality.[85] It was often also perceived as a mark of respect for one's people, especially as of the 1970s, when the Muslim groups' national consciousness began growing.[86]

In most areas circumcision was well-nigh universal, certainly in Central Asia,[87] although according to some reports this was not ubiquitously true in Kazakhstan.[88] It was also the rule in those parts of the Northern Caucasus which were traditional centres of religion, such as Dagestan and the Chechen-Ingush ASSR, as well as in Azerbaijan. In Dagestan boys who had not been circumcised

---

GARF, f.6991, o.3, d.10, l.67.

82. E. Bairamov, 'Islam i natsional'nye traditsii', *Agitator*, No.24 (1966), p.43.

83. CRA report, sent to the CPSU Central Committee, 22 May 1970; TsKhSD, f.5, o.62, d.38, l.30.

84. Author's interview with a former CRA official who has asked to remain anonymous.

85. Zh. Botashev to V. A. Kuroedov, 17 Nov. 1969; GARF, f.6991, o.6, d.220, l.146.

86. See p.709.

87. For example, a report on Bukhara Oblast' maintained that circumcision there was observed by 100 per cent of the population – A. Barinskaia to V. A. Kuroedov, undated [late March-early April 1968], whereas one for Kirgiziia stated that in that republic the overwhelming majority of boys were circumcised –N. Alekseev, undated [June 1969]; GARF, f.6991, o.6, d.153, l.109, and d.220, l.149. See also p.84.

88. The CARC *upolnomochennyi* for Karaganda Oblast' reported in 1948 that the Muslim communities in his oblast' did not circumcise their sons – Letter of instruction, No. 7, Appendix No.3 to Minutes, CARC session No.15, 24-25 Aug. 1948; GARF, f.6991, o.3, d.55, l.38. Another report contradicted this, insisting that here, too, circumcision was practised by almost all, including communists – Goncharok to G. M. Malenkov, 8 Sept. 1949; RTsKhIDNI, f.17, o.132, d.258, l.76.

sometimes performed the rite themselves. In the Cherkess AO, on the other hand, circumcision was the exception rather than the rule.[89]

While the position adopted by those engaged in atheistic propaganda remained much the same as it had been before the war, namely that circumcision was a superstitious practice which needed to be totally eliminated, CARC took a more tolerant stand. It maintained that circumcision was not illegal provided that it was performed by competent people in sanitary conditions; in other words, that it be subject to some sort of control by the organs of local government.[90] Again, there were differences from place to place: in Turkmenistan, it seems to have been illegal until 1989.[91] Given the rather ambivalent attitude of the authorities to the practice of circumcision, on the one hand, and the tendency among the Muslim population not only to perform it, but to celebrate the event in the presence of relatives and friends, on the other hand, various ruses were employed in order to distract attention from its performance. For instance, it was common for circumcisions to take place at weddings, where the entire community gathered.[92] This practice was condemned by SADUM. After it had laid down in 1952 that circumcision was in any case not obligatory, but merely *sunnat*, a custom, it conceded three years later that there was some basis for it in the Shari'a. SADUM insisted, however, that it was not to be accompanied by major entertainment of guests and specifically not serve, as it were, as a pretext for holding ostentatious wedding festivities, it having become fairly common to circumvent problems by performing circumcisions at weddings, where the boy would be laid in a cradle and circumcised.[93]

89. Minutes, CARC instructional meeting No.17, 20-22 Dec. 1950; V. V. Bulatov, Materials, All-Union conference of CARC *upolnomochennye*, 25-27 Nov. 1958; N. I. Smirnov, Information, 8 Aug. 1962; and I. Bonchkovskii to E. I. Lisavtsev, 1 June 1973 – GARF, f.6991, o.3, d.66, l.129, d.165, l.91, and d.1390, l.19, and o.6, d.537, l.171.

90. Tajibaev and Eleusyzov, Addresses, Conference of CARC *upolnomochennye*, Alma-Ata, 2 Oct. 1946; GARF, f.6991, o.3, d.41, ll.43 and 55. For the complexities of policy toward the practice of Islam, see Chapter 10.

91. Poliakov, *Everyday Islam*, p.56.

92. Saidbaev, *Islam i obshchestvo*, p.234.

93. Ishan Babakhan, [apparently text of *fetwa*], 16 May 1952, Kh. N. Iskanderov to I. V. Polianskii, 11 July 1955, and Z. Babakhanov to Kh. N. Iskanderov,

In most places circumcision was not performed by regular clergy, but by 'professional people', 'specialists', or practitioners of folk medicine, *tabibs*.[94] Obviously, in view of the basic stance of the party that it was a harmful rite, which was likely to lead to complications, infection and even death, it was peremptory for every precaution to be taken to avoid unpleasantnesses. Nonetheless, accidents happened. Hardly a publication, which addressed itself to circumcision specifically or to the harmfulness of Islam in general, missed out on the opportunity to refer to instances of complications arising from this particular rite.[95] Government officials and the local media also regularly made an issue of every case where the operation misfired. In Eastern Kazakhstan in the late 1960s itinerant mullas and medics had circumcised a number of boys in unsanitary conditions, leading to serious illness and eventually hospitalisation; according to one report, the boys' lives were only just saved.[96] As of the mid 1970s doctors were allowed to perform circumcisions in medical institutions – usually those who did the job were Russian medical personnel who could not be accused of adhering to Islam – although in Central Asia most of them continued to be performed by *tabibs*. On one occasion a Russian Minister of Health in Tajikistan criticised the performance of circumcisions by uneducated people in unsanitary conditions; he was summoned to the party secretary, who recommended that he preoccupy himself with medical issues and not meddle in questions of world outlook and politics.[97]

It was not uncommon for circumcision to be performed on a number of boys at the same time. Many of the 'specialists', who performed circumcisions in Central Asia, would go from one settlement to another. Word of their arrival got around and they

---

14 Dec. 1955; TsGAUz, f.2456, o.1, d.144, ll.26-7, and d.174, ll.20 and 112.

94. V. I. Gostev to P. A. Tarasov, 4 Jan. 1954; M. A. Il'baev at All-Union conference of CARC *upolnomochennye*, 17 Feb. 1965, and U. Yuldashev, Information, 10 July 1968 – GARF, f.6991, o.3, d.102, l.16, o.4, d.168, l.53, and o.6, d.153, l.100, and Kuliev, *Antinauchnaia sushchnost' islama*, p.106. Gostev referred specifically to Kazakhstan, Il'baev to Turkmenistan, and Yuldashev to the Gorno-Badakhshan AO.

95. For example, Kuliev, *Antinauchnaia sushchnost' islama*, p.106; and Klimovich, *Islam*, pp.217-8.

96. B. Tutkarin, Z. Ibraev, Report, 23 April 1969; Zh. Botashev to the CRA, 20 Sept. 1973; GARF, f.6991, o.6, d.223, l.37, and d.548, l.23.

97. Author's interview with a former CRA official who has asked to remain anonymous.

would circumcise all the boys of a relevant age who had not yet been circumcised. Sometimes boys would run away to avoid the operation.[98] Others, however, prepared for the occasion in advance by a member of the family, usually a grandparent, were positively impressed by the ceremony and its implications and became interested in religion.[99] Although these group circumcisions seem to have happened throughout the postwar period, they were especially pertinent in the war's immediate aftermath after some years in which circumcision had not been practised. When a Bashkir girl refused to marry an uncircumcised member of her kolkhoz in Kuibyshev Oblast', the kolkhoz chairman summoned an 'expert' from Chkalov Oblast' who circumcised twenty-eight boys, including the chairman's two sons, and the young man. The kolkhoz chairman supplied him with a horse and he visited another seven villages, performing in all 255 operations.[100] In this same time period the head of a children's home in Tashkent had fifty boys circumcised at one fell swoop.[101] The director of one children's home in Samarkand Oblast' was dismissed from his post, excluded from the party and prosecuted for having seven boys circumcised in 1948.[102] Some years later Polianskii told of another case where seven boys had been circumcised collectively, in the home of the chairman of a kolkhoz inspection committee in Frunze Oblast', and of a teacher, in another oblast' of Kirgiziia, who was wont to circumcise boys, including his own pupils.[103] On one occasion in Southern Kazakhstan in the 1960s, where a mulla

98. Author's interview with a former CRA official who has asked to remain anonymous.

99. K. Kulumbetov to A. A. Nurullaev, 28 June 1974; GARF, f.6991, o.6, d.629, l.15.

100. Excerpts from reports by CARC *upolnomochennye* for the first quarter of 1945, undated (probably April or May 1945); GARF, f.6991, o.3, d.12, ll.67-8. The NKVD had meanwhile arrested the 'expert' despite his 78 years.

101. I. Ibadov to Chairman SNK Uzbek SSR Abdujabr Abdurahmanov (copy to Party Secretary Osman Yusupov), 11 Sept. 1945; GARF, f.6991, o.3, d.30, l.358.

102. Uzbek SSR Minister of Internal Affairs Babojanov to USSR Minister of Internal Affairs S. N. Kruglov, 23 Nov. 1948; RTsKhIDNI, f.17, o.132, d.56, l.103.

103. I. V. Polianskii to P. V. Kovanov, 23 June 1955; GARF, f.6991, o.3, d.114, l.30.

circumcised eighteen boys in a single day, one of them died from an infection.[104]

In some places, circumcision would be carried out covertly,[105] or under the guise of name-giving.[106] (Name-giving, which was a generally practised rite in the Muslim community, seems to have been considered relatively safe, since it was also a time-honoured Russian custom. Be this as it may, among some sections of the Muslim population it became a quasi-religious ritual in its own right conducted in the presence of a mulla.[107]) Some people circumcised their sons as part of the celebration connected by Soviet custom with a child's entry into the first class of school.[108] According to one report, it was only in the kishlaks and among the 'backward sectors' of the urban population that circumcision was performed openly.[109] In Jambul members of the commission of assistance attached to the local *ispolkom* soviet were told that all the town's children were circumcised. Everyone in town knew the two barbers who circumcised children, but all information about them was 'carefully hushed up even among the workers of the organs designed to control the activity of the religious organisations'.[110]

Where circumcision was general, party members and local officials could not allow their sons not to be circumcised for fear of the boys' social isolation. They tended, however, to perform circumcision secretly or to conceal it with some plausible excuse,

104. P. A. Solov'ev, undated, material prepared for CARC session No. 10, 12 May 1964; GARF, f.6991, o.4, d.146, l.211.

105. For example, in Karaganda Oblast' – Zh. Rahimov to the CRA, 27 Oct. 1969; GARF, f.6991, o.6, d.223, l.47.

106. Kh. N. Iskanderov to I. V. Polianskii, 11 July 1955; TsGAUz, f.2456, o.1, d.174, ll.21-2. The name-giving ceremony over, a barber who knew how to perform the operation, would be invited to circumcise the boy.

107. A. A. Puzin to the Tajikistan CP Central Committee, 26 Jan. 1963, and CRA report, sent to the CPSU Central Committee, 22 May 1970; GARF, f.6991, o.3, d.1739, l.1, and TsKhSD, f.5, o.62, d.38, l.6. In the rural areas of the Tatar ASSR, for instance, between 60 and 80 per cent observed this custom –F. S. Mangutkin to A. A. Puzin, 20 April 1964; GARF, f.6991, o.3, d.1466, l.199.

108. *Islam v SSSR*, p.75.

109. Kh. N. Iskanderov to I. V. Polianskii, 11 July 1955; TsGAUz, f.2456, o.1, d.174, l.21.

110. E. Bairamov, Information, undated [Jan. 1969]; GARF, f.6991, o.6, d.153, l.50. For the commissions of assistance, see pp.617-9.

saying it was being done for reasons of hygiene, or dubbing the ceremony as one of name-giving. A person who was not circumcised was not merely looked upon as an apostate, he was isolated and sooner or later would have to undergo circumcision.[111] Sometimes the rite would actually be performed in the father's absence.[112] On occasion an ill-wisher of a person appointed to a local party or government post whose son was circumcised might write to the local party committee, asking how so unprincipled a communist could occupy the post. The committee secretary, whose son was certainly also circumcised though no one had calumniated him for this, had no choice but to reprimand the person in question for conniving with religion and to insert a comment in his dossier.[113] Members of the intelligentsia, too, circumcised their sons, including teachers, who were supposed to set an example to others, especially those who upon concluding their studies returned to work in rural areas.[114]

Those who felt less need for caution, including party members and officials, often held ostentatious *tois*, or entertainment, to celebrate the occasion,[115] as was in fact general practice. In 1948 Polianskii reported the case of a kolkhoz deputy chairman who circumcised his son with great ceremony: he slaughtered a horse and four sheep for the occasion and during the festivities, which

111. Kh. N. Iskanderov to I. V. Polianskii, 11 July 1955; TsGAUz, f.2456, o.1, d.174, 1.21.

112. For example, a kolkhoz chairman in Osh Oblast' in 1950 had his son circumcised with a reading from the Qur'an and prayers, but he himself did not participate – I. G. Halimov to CARC, 3 April 1950; GARF, f.6991, o.3, d.454, 1.57.

113. Author's interview with a former CRA member who has asked to remain anonymous.

114. In Tajikistan, for instance, students at institutions of higher learning told people who conducted a sociological survey that they would be living in kishlaks among their fellow-villagers, relatives and acquaintances and so would circumcise their sons, although they agreed this was a backward and harmful practice – *Islam v SSSR*, pp.74-5.

115. Such instances were reported throughout our period: in the 1940s MGB Minister Abakumov's report mentioned eight cases of local officials who circumcised their sons, one of them at least, a member of the Tajikistan CP Central Committee apparatus, holding a *toi* which cost him 10,000 rubles – V. A. Abakumov to K. E. Voroshilov, 12 Sept. 1946 – GARF, f.6991, o.3, d.34, 1.195; and in the mid 1950s from a number of Uzbekistan's oblasti, Kh. N. Iskanderov to I. V. Polianskii, 11 July 1955; TsGAUz, f.2456, o.2, d.174, 11.20-2.

lasted three days, 300 kg of rice and 700 kg of flour were con-
sumed.[116] One Tajik father of three boys sold his car to be able
to hold a suitable celebration.[117] When done openly and with full
celebration of the ritual, a circumcision in the 1980s could cost
7-8,000 rubles.[118] Parents would save money for the celebration,
usually held with a large number of guests, from the time of their
son's birth and would continue paying off the debts they incurred
in connection with it for many years. This enabled representatives
of the regime to contend that circumcision entailed not only
possible damage to the health of the boy, but also economic hurt
to his family, as well as being ideologically harmful to society as
a whole.[119] In the words of one scholar, as a result of the blending
of religious and national custom and the desire not to invite shame
in their immediate surroundings, people deprived themselves of
all their needs in order to obtain the means for these galas.[120]

The incidence of religious marriage, *nikoh*, seems to have been
considerably lower than that of both burial rites and circumcision.
Undoubtedly, however, it was markedly higher in rural than in
urban areas – CRA *upolnomochennye* and local party and soviet organs
all reported that in the former the majority of couples had religious
weddings[121] – and in the traditionally sedentary parts of Central
Asia and in the Chechen-Ingush ASSR than in, for example, the
European regions of the RSFSR. In Bukhara, for instance, in the
late 1960s even student youth celebrated *nikoh*;[122] in Dagestan in
the late 1970s, 65 per cent of marriages were said to be conducted
in accordance with Islamic custom.[123].

On the whole, both the general trends which characterised
other rites and the manifestations which accompanied them per-

116. I. V. Polianskii to K. E. Voroshilov, M. A. Turkin, M. A. Suslov and A.
A. Kuznetsov, undated [approved by CARC session No.8, 9 June 1948]; GARF,
f.6991, o.3, d.53, l.35.

117. Karklins, 'Islam: How Strong is it in the Soviet Union?', p.71.

118. Poliakov, *Everyday Islam*, p.57.

119. *Islam v SSSR*, p.75.

120. See p.458.

121. CRA report, sent to the CPSU Central Committee, 22 May 1970; TsKhSD,
f.5, o.62, d.38, l.6.

122. A. Barinskaia to V. A. Kuroedov, undated [late March-early April 1968];
GARF, f.6991, o.6, d.153, l.109.

123. M. V. Vagabov, *Islam i sem'ia* (Moscow: Nauka, 1980), p.133, quoted in
Bryan, 'Internationalism, Nationalism and Islam', p.186.

tained also to marriage. In the first place, religious marriage ceremonies seem to have become rather frequent in the immediate postwar period, although not everywhere. For example, in the Bashkir ASSR, they were reported to be taking place only rarely.[124] Elsewhere, even party members were marrying and marrying their children in accordance with religious ritual.[125] In certain regions instances were recorded at this time of clergy calling upon believers to marry only according to the Shari'a, avoiding ZAGS and civil marriage altogether.[126]

The issue was particularly pressing in the context of the situation created by the exigencies of the war. In the first place, many soldiers were reported missing without their fate being known with certainty. Not a few scandals occurred as a result of men presumed dead returning home to find their wives re-married. The unregistered mullas who married them had simply not taken the trouble, as presumably the registry office sought to do, to find out whether the first husband had in fact been killed and duly buried.[127] SADUM issued a special *fetwa*, 'On marriage with someone else of wives of soldiers missing at the front', by which, in order to be re-married by clergy, a woman had to receive a document from the military authorities (*voenkomat*) ascertaining her husband's death and register the second marriage with ZAGS.[128] Secondly, the clergy appear to have conducted numerous marriage ceremonies for returning soldiers[129] and probably for others as well, whose marriages in the harsh pre-war years had presumably been registered with the civilian authority only and not consummated in accordance with Islamic law and custom. Just as many uncircumcised boys and young men now submitted to circumcision,

124. M. Sh. Karimov to I. V. Polianskii and Chairman SNK, Bashkir ASSR, S. A. Vagapov, 8 Oct. 1945; GARF, f.6991, o.3, d.26, l.14.

125. For example, V. A. Abakumov to K. E. Voroshilov, 12 Sept. 1946; GARF, f.6991, o.3, d.34, l.195.

126. See p.346.

127. I. G. Halimov, Address, Conference, CARC *upolnomochennye*, Alma-Ata, 2 Oct. 1946; GARF, f.6991, o.3, d.41, l.71.

128. This *fetwa* was ratified by SADUM's second plenary session, 20-27 Jan. 1947; see p.142.

129. Bagaev, Report, Conference of CARC *upolnomochennye*, 11-13 [June?] 1946; GARF, f.6991, o.3, d.39, l.111. Bagaev, who was CARC *upolnomochennyi* for the Tatar ASSR, contended that Muslim law demanded the renewal of marriage after a separation of over 40 days; I have found no source for this.

so too, a large number of couples took advantage of the more lenient atmosphere at the end of the war and in its immediate aftermath to regulate their married life.

Throughout the postwar period the authorities took pains to prevent the clergy of official religious societies from performing marriages of couples which had not previously been registered with ZAGS. (They had no way of exerting such pressure on unregistered mullas.) CARC's *upolnomchennyi* in Uzbekistan was asked to recommend to SADUM to oblige clergy to perform the rites of marriage and divorce – as of burial – only after being presented with evidence that the marriage or divorce had been legally registered. First, because, if performed solely according to religious ritual, these rites would not have juridical force (in other words they were considered illegal), and secondly, because this situation often engendered polygamy and other forms of what the regime saw as humiliation of women, as well as neglect of children.[130] Indeed, there were constant stories of people desirous of marrying an adolescent or taking a second wife turning to an unregistered mulla, who – unlike ZAGS – would not balk at bigamy or polygamy.[131]

Thus, at least in certain republics, those cases of religious marriage which were performed by registered clergy and reported by them, had all been registered beforehand by ZAGS.[132] In some parts all marriages were categorically said first to have been registered.[133] In Dagestan, on the other hand, instances occurred of marriages being performed by the leaders of an official religious society in accordance with the Shari'a, without recourse to the local *sel'sovet*. This was one of the pretexts for closing mosques and withdrawing religious societies from registration in that republic in the course of Khrushchev's anti-religious campaign.[134] Analogous violations of the laws on religion in regard to marriage and the status of

130. I. V. Polianskii to Kh. N. Iskanderov, 27 Aug. 1951; TsGAUz, f.2456, o.1, d.134, l.92. For polygamy, see below.

131. For instance, L. Zh. Aisov to A. A. Puzin, 17 Jan. 1965; GARF, f.6991, o.3, d.1605, l.3.

132. For example, in Azerbaijan – B. A. Shahbazbekov to I. V. Polianskii, 26 March 1952; GARF, f.6991, o.3, d.83, l.83.

133. For instance, in the Gorno-Badakhshan AO – U. Yuldashev, Information, 10 July 1968; GARF, f.6991, o.6, d.153, ll.99–100.

134. N. I. Smirnov, Information, 4 May 1961; GARF, f.6991, o.3, d.1356, l.205.

women served as pretexts for shutting mosques elsewhere as well.[135] Often couples would only trouble to register their marriage upon the birth of a fourth child, when they became eligible for the subsidy paid to large families. And in the Chechen-Ingush ASSR, at least in certain parts, it was reported that no marriages at all were performed according to Soviet law, but all solely in accordance with Muslim custom.[136]

Yet, if in many parts an increasing number of marriages, especially presumably in the towns and rural administrative centres, were registered according to law, this did not necessarily imply that the religious ceremony was abandoned. On the contrary. Of the 3,180 marriages registered in Tashkent in 1959, over 90 per cent of the couples, including students, academics and people in the government apparatus, also underwent a religious marriage.[137] One source noted in the 1980s that, whereas the majority of marriages consummated in the Muslim areas were duly registered in ZAGS, a considerable number of these were also sanctified by religious rite, even among the intelligentsia or when a Muslim took a non-Muslim wife. According to this same source, Muslim divorce procedures also persisted.[138]

A wedding could, like a circumcision, cost 7-8,000 rubles at prices of the mid-1980s; this did not include bride-money (see below) or the cost of the trousseau, both of which might also run into the thousands.[139] The spiritual directorates condemned sumptuous wedding feasts, as they did funeral banquets and circumcision celebrations. SADUM pointed out that it was not essential to spend all one's savings on one's marriage, for this was not stipulated by Islam, indeed contradicted Muhammad's own example. It emphasised that there were instances where men put

---

135. For example, in Tajikistan's Leninabad Oblast' – K. Ovchinnikov to A. A. Puzin, 2 Aug. 1961; GARF, f.6991, o.3, d.1737, ll.60-1.

136. P. A. Zadorozhnyi to A. A. Puzin, 30 Aug. 1960; GARF, f.6991, o.3, d.207, ll.60-1.

137. Sh. K. Shirinbaev, Address, CARC session No.27, 15-16 Sept. 1960; GARF, f.6991, o.3, d.206, l.128. (There is an outside possibility that Shirinbaev's figures relate to all marriages in Tashkent in the one year, and not only those of Muslims, but since the context in which he was speaking was Islam, he was probably referring just to Muslim couples.)

138. Saidbaev, *Islam i obshchestvo*, p.256.

139. Poliakov, *Everyday Islam*, p.57.

off marrying, or even refrained from marrying at all, because of the expenses involved.[140]

Some religious marriages were performed by proxy, without the participation of bride or groom, apparently because the parents insisted on consecrating the marriage according to custom, whereas the young couple itself had reservations, whether of principle or convenience.[141] All in all, however, the general preservation of religious marriage, the social prestige which accrued from the holding of ostentatious wedding and circumcision celebrations, and the expenses involved, profoundly affected the social pattern of Muslim society in the Soviet Union. They helped ensure the dependence of the married son on his father, with whom he continued to abide until it was felt that he had repaid these costs, often, in fact, until the father's death, or until his own son married, thus preserving the old family structure and life-style with all their ramifications and implications.

The role and status of the Muslim woman

Muslim custom, sometimes enhanced by local tradition, was responsible for the fact that the issue in regard to marriage was not merely the actual performance of a religious ceremony ratifying an act that the regime saw as essentially a civic one. The very idea of arranged marriages contradicted the spirit of Soviet thinking. Yet, these were of the essence in Muslim social custom, even though Soviet life had broken down many of the formal restrictions that had traditionally ensured sexual segregation. True, it was no longer legal to consummate a marriage without the consent of bride and groom, yet parents and grandparents continued to think about and prepare the marriage of their children and grandchildren while they were still at school. There can be no other explanation for the high rate of early marriages in the Muslim areas: in 1970

140. Ishan Babakhan, [Text of *fetwa*,] 16 May 1952; TsGAUz, f.2456, o.1, d.144, ll.24-7. See p.150.

141. Such instances were reported, for example, from Stavropol Krai (the Karachai-Cherkess AO) – Minutes, All-Union conference of CARC *upolnomochennye*, 25-27 Nov. 1958 – and from Azerbaijan, where in 1966 some 10 per cent of marriages took place in absentia – M. Shamsadinskii to the CRA, 20 Jan. 1967 and A. Galiev, Information, 30 May 1973; GARF, f.6991, o.3, d.165, l.91, and o.6, d.21, l.4, and d.537, l.188.

in Tajikistan over 40 per cent of girls were married by the age
of 18-19, and in Uzbekistan and Turkmenistan over one-third.[142]

Moreover, there were a considerable number of rites linked
with the Shari'a wedding which, at least to the outsider, seemed
degrading from the point of view of the emancipated woman. It
should be stressed that some of these were neither enjoined by
Islamic law nor Islamic in origin; yet they had become incorporated
in Muslim society – not only in the Soviet Union, but in many
Muslim countries – and were tolerated by Islam. The most important of these practices were the *qalym*, or bride-money, paid
by the groom and his family to the bride's parents as remuneration,
as it were, for the costs of her upbringing and education, for they
were now losing her to her husband's family; the *kaitarma*, by
which the groom returned his new wife to her family shortly
after the wedding until such time as his own family was able to
pay the full amount of the *qalym*; polygamy, the marriage by one
man with more than one woman; the levirate, a man's marriage
to the childless wife of his deceased brother, which was one of
the causes of polygamy; the abduction of the bride by her groom;
and the marriage of girls before they came legally of age. These
customs seemed to demonstrate that the woman was of lower
worth than the man, presenting her almost as a chattel to be
negotiated, bought and sold.

The most widespread of these were probably the first and the
last. *Qalym* was a general practice wherever Muslims lived, even
in the towns. Indeed, according to some sources, it was more
common in the 1960s to 1980s than it had been in the 1930s or
1940s, and was still continuing to grow in dimension at the end
of our period.[143] True, in order to avoid complications with the
law,[144] it became customary in the Soviet Union to make payment
to the bride's family in the form of presents or, in rural areas,

---

142. Kozlov, *The Peoples of the Soviet Union*, p.120. The exact percentages for
Uzbekistan and Turkmenistan were 34.3 and 33.6 respectively. Figures for the
Muslim population are undoubtedly higher, as the figures relate to the republic's
total population.

143. *Trud*, 29 April 1987; Poliakov, *Everyday Islam*, p.55.

144. The RSFSR Criminal Code prohibited: the purchase or receipt of payment
for a bride; forcing a woman to enter into a marriage or preventing a marriage;
concluding a marriage agreement with or concerning someone who had not
yet reached marital age; and polygamy – *Ugolovnyi kodeks RSFSR*, Articles 232-6,
pp.141-2.

livestock in lieu of money. Whatever the form of payment, brides, according to Mufti Babakhanov, were fetching tens of thousands of rubles in parts of Central Asia in the very early 1960s.[145] After the devaluation of that period, the bride-price inevitably went down, although in the 1970s it was still 5-6,000 rubles in the Karakalpak ASSR, where its practice, moreover, was kept in strict secrecy.[146] By the mid 1980s it was back to 10-12,000 rubles in Tajikistan and in Turkmenistan could reach 40,000.[147] Whatever form it took, *qalym* was presented in Soviet publications as being a serious economic burden on a family which had several sons, as well as having a deleterious moral effect on the bride whose value was negotiated.[148] The Soviet media and atheistic propaganda material maintained that *qalym* both led to girls being married off against their will, the agreement over the betrothal and marriage being conducted between the parents, and, alternatively, to young couples who wished to marry not being able to do so.[149] In addition, having bought her, the groom's family were in a position to impose 'intolerable conditions' upon her, which they frequently did, forbidding her to work in 'social production', i.e. outside the home, to study, or even to meet with her peers.[150] It was probably in order to avoid the degradation of being a bride for whom a lower price was offered or given that the 1969 assembly of Ingush religious leaders determined a fixed sum for a bride.[151] Still in the mid 1980s, 95 per cent of marriages in Turkmenistan were thought to entail *qalym*.[152]

As was the case with many traditions relating to marriage, there

145. L. A. Prikhod'ko, Proposals, undated, prepared for CARC session No.3, 22 Jan. 1960; GARF, f.6991, o.3, d.204, l.20. In Kazakhstan in 1962 the groom's family were still said to be paying anything from 10,000 rubles to 25,000 or even 30,000, the bride's parents giving the young couple a trousseau of approximately the same value – Information, sent to A. I. Aleksandrov at the CPSU Central Committee, 14 Feb. 1962; GARF, f.6991, o.3, d.1389, l.13.

146. D. Erekeshov to A. Nurullaev, 7 May 1974; GARF, f.6991, o.6, d.545, l.219.

147. Poliakov, *Everyday Islam*, p.55.

148. *Islam v SSSR*, pp.127-8.

149. For some of the concomitants of *qalym*, see, for example, *Turkmenskaia iskra*, 9 Jan. 1987.

150. Ashirov, 'Osobennosti ideologicheskoi i kul'tovoi deiatel'nosti', p.120.

151. See p.420.

152. *Trud*, 29 April 1987.

were major variations in local custom in this regard. For instance, the Balkars and Karachais observed a custom called *berne*, obligating the bride to give expensive presents to the groom's parents and other relatives, virtually dressing them from head to toe. As in the case of *qalym*, parents of young women, and sometimes the girls themselves, worked for many years in order to acquire a respectable *berne*, and sometimes tragedies ensued when a groom's family declared that it was unworthy or unacceptable.[153]

The second custom, *kaitarma*, was a consequence of the practice of *qalym*. Given the considerable sums which were fixed as bride-money, on the one hand, and the commonness of *qalym*, on the other, there were inevitably families which were unable to find the requisite payment. This custom, too, seems to have been practised particularly in Turkmenistan.[154]

Polygamy, too, was not uncommon in the rural parts of Central Asia, in particular. It was even legitimised by clergy in cases where a first wife was unable to have children.[155] But there seem to have been instances of polygamy even without such a valid excuse. A second wife was a sign of status, and certain people were clearly interested in having more than one wife. The bare fact that marriages were performed by unregistered clergy, who were subject to no control and were under no constraint to verify that a person was free to marry, was said to engender cases of polygamy.[156] Be this as it may, instances of polygamy were recurrently reported from Uzbekistan and southern Kirgiziia, the offenders even including party members and local officials.[157] In 1946 a number of party officials in Turkmenistan were dismissed from their posts for

153. L. Zh. Alisov to T. K. Mal'bakhov, the Kabardino-Balkar Obkom, 16 March 1963; GARF, f.6991, o.3, d.1607, l.11; Tsavkalov, *Prichinyi zhivuchesti religioznykh perezhitkov*, pp.39-43.

154. *Islam v SSSR*, p.128.

155. L. A. Prikhodko and N. I. Abushaev, A short survey, 16 March 1950; GARF, f.6991, o.3, d.63, l.100. The two officials who prepared this document attributed this opinion to the Shari'a as taught by *ishans*.

156. Minutes, CARC session No.9, 17 April 1951; GARF, f.6991, o.3, d.74, ll.108-9.

157. Kh. N. Iskanderov, Report, Minutes, CARC session No.11, 18-19 June 1947, and I. G. Halimov to CARC, undated [early April 1949] and 3 April 1950; GARF, f.6991, o.4, d.19, l.362, and o.3, d.454, ll.14 and 58; and Minutes, Conference of CARC *upolnomochennye* in the Uzbek SSR, 9 Aug. 1948 – TsGAUz, f.2456, o.1, d.120, l.16.

polygamy; a republican meeting of heads of party departments for work among women (*zhenotdely*) discussed this and other 'feudal survivals', such as wife-beating.[158] In Kazakhstan no less than 735 court cases aginst people who practised polygamy were heard in 1948 and the first quarter of 1949.[159] In the single year 1963, what was described as a partial enquiry revealed 800 instances of polygamy in the Chechen-Ingush ASSR, some of the men concerned having as many as five wives.[160] And polygamy still persisted in the 1970s, for instance, but not solely, in Kzyl-Orda Oblast' and the Karakalpak ASSR.[161]

Although polygamy was thought to be particularly offensive to, and degrading for, women, fifty women in Fergana Oblast' actually demanded it in the immediate postwar period, suggesting that men be allowed to marry two or three wives in light of the surplus of women created by the war. Some of them were wives of soldiers who had been reported missing several years before, others were women whose daughters had grown up, yet could not marry because there were too few men in the oblast'.[162] One Soviet writer noted in the late 1960s that for some reason women did not protest this custom, indeed, some actually insisted on its practice[163] – presumably senior wives who sought to shift household chores on junior or less favoured ones, or, among intelligentsia, younger wives who seemed to enjoy a privileged status with older husbands.[164] Saidbaev, an expert on Central Asia, also pointed out in the 1980s that in the Soviet Muslim areas polygamy was looked upon positively and that women entered such marriages of their own accord.[165]

158. *Turkmenskaia iskra*, 19 Sept. 1946.

159. Goncharok to G. M. Malenkov, 8 Sept. 1949; RTsKhIDNI, f.17, o.132, d.258, l.77.

160. P. A. Solov'ev, undated, Material prepared for CARC session No.10, 12 May 1964; GARF, f.6991, o.4, d.146, l.212.

161. Zh. Botashev, Information, 20 Sept. 1973, and D. Erekeshov to A. Nurullaev, 7 May 1974; GARF, f.6991, o.6, d.548, l.24, and d.545, l.219.

162. I. Ibadov to I. V. Polianskii, 24 July 1945; TsGAUz, f.2456, o.1, d.29, l.134.

163. Vagabov, *Islam i zhenshchina*, p.137.

164. A few years after the period discussed here, when people were freer to express themselves, an Uzbek woman with higher education wrote an article entitled 'I want to be a junior wife' – *Megapolis-Express*, No.6, 6 Feb. 1992.

165. Saidbaev, *Islam i obshchestvo*, p.255.

The levirate was, on the whole, less usual, after the first bout of the immediate postwar era. In the latter half of the 1940s, there were, indeed, not a few cases. In the oblast' of Southern Kazakhstan the secretary of a kolkhoz administration married the widow of his brother, who had been killed in the war.[166] Yet, the custom was not unknown in the ensuing decades as well.[167]

The abduction of brides from the home of their parents was also practised. Its relative frequency was probably dictated by a desire to avoid paying exorbitant sums as *qalym*. Once kidnapped, the bride had little· choice other than to agree to marriage with her abductor, for nobody would agree to marry her after such an occurrence. Several sources noted that abduction was sometimes carried out with the bride's consent, but this did not lessen the distress of her parents who were thus deprived of their bride-money.[168] In the four years 1969-73, no less than fourteen brides, some of them not yet of age, were abducted under the cover of night in the single oblast' of Kzyl-Orda.[169] In Turkmenistan several court cases resulted from this practice in the mid-1980s. In one of them the groom, the actual kidnapper, was sentenced to eight years' 'deprivation of freedom with a prison sentence in a colony of strict regime', his three brothers and sister who participated in the abduction received from two to six years, the mulla who performed the wedding ceremony was given a 'conditional' sentence of two years, and a teacher, whom the abducted bride had asked for help but advised her to surrender and then 'quickly departed the scene', was dismissed from his job as undeserving of educational employment.[170]

The marriage of adolescent girls remained extremely common practice. Although in some of the Muslim republics, the age of legal marriage was fixed at sixteen, rather than the usual eighteen,

166. I. V. Polianskii to K. E. Voroshilov, the Council of Ministers Cultural Bureau, M. A. Turkin, M. A. Suslov and A. A. Kuznetsov, undated (approved by CARC session No.8, 9 June 1948); GARF, f.6991, o.3, d.53, l.35.

167. Information, given to the CPSU Central Committee Propaganda Department, 11 Feb. 1965, and Zh. Botashev, Information, 20 Sept. 1973; GARF, f.6991, o.3, d.1484, l.80, and o.6, d.548, l.24; and Dunn and Dunn, 'Soviet Regime and Native Culture in Central Asia and Kazakhstan', p.163.

168. Poliakov, *Everyday Islam*, p.55.

169. Zh. Botashev, Information, 20 Sept. 1973; GARF, f.6991, o.6, d.548, l.24.

170. Iu Kuz'mina, 'Pozor', *Nauka i religiia* (1986), No.9, pp.28-31.

girls continued to be given away in marriage before reaching the required age. In a single year in the late 1950s no less than ninety-seven court cases took place in Turkmenistan against parents who had married off adolescent girls.[171] Nor was the problem solely those girls actually bestowed in marriage. The custom of marrying off young girls disrupted girls' education in most areas where the Muslims constituted the eponymous ethnic group. Due to this tradition, it remained normative in Muslim rural society for girls to be taken out of school on reaching puberty, or shortly thereafter. In some parts girls were only permitted to finish four classes of school, in others seven. Those who completed all ten or eleven classes in the countryside were apparently very few. The Central Asian party press and recurrent Central Asian republican party and Komsomol congresses discussed this issue: thus, we learn that in the 1947-48 school year just thirty-four Tajik girls completed their secondary school education, whereas 3,000 were taken out of school 'improperly'. In Kirgiziia in the early 1950s girls comprised 9.5 percent of the pupils in the top three classes and 8 per cent in institutions of higher learning and child-marriage was still occurring in three oblasti.[172] In Dagestan later on in the same decade it was common practice to give out in marriage girls who had not yet completed ten years' schooling.[173] Once again the situation appears to have been most extreme in the Chechen-Ingush ASSR, where girls of the indigenous nationalities simply had no opportunity to study. In one village, of seventy-five girls who should have been in school in the fourth to the seventh class, just four were in the former and none at all in the latter.[174]

The situation changed somewhat over the years, but was not

171. Minutes, Conference of CARC's Central Asian *upolnomochennye*, Tashkent, 6 June 1959; GARF, f.6991, o.3, d.186, l.209.

172. British Embassy, Moscow, to Foreign Office, Northern Department, 3 Feb. 1949, quoting *Kommunist Tadzhikistana*, 1 Dec. 1948; Sir Alvary Gascoigne to [Foreign Secretary Anthony Eden], 4 Jan. 1952; Paul Grey to Eden, 19 March 1952; and Memorandum, Komsomol Congresses in Kirghizia and Uzbekistan, undated – PRO/FO/371/77581 and 100817.

173. Gasanov to V. I. Gostev, 19 March 1957; GARF, f.6991, o.3, d.145, l.51.

174. P. A. Zadorozhnyi to A. A. Puzin, 30 Aug. 1960; GARF, f.6991, o.3, d.207, l.61. In 1962 there were 32,801 Chechen and Ingush girls in the first four classes, 5,678 in the fifth to eighth class, and 229 in the ninth to eleventh classes – A. Alisov to A. A. Puzin, 16 March 1962; GARF, f.6991, o.3, d.1606, l.21.

radically transformed. According to the Osh Oblast' newspaper, just 65 – 70 per cent of girls who completed sixth class in the school year of 1964-65 in urban and rural communities combined were still in school three years later.[175] In Gur'ev Oblast' in Kazakhstan both phenomena – taking girls out of school in the middle of their schooling and marrying them off – were likewise prevalent in the mid-1970s.[176] Nor was it only less educated parents who indulged in these practices: reports from the Muslim regions told of chairmen of kolkhozy and *raiispolkoms* and schoolteachers not letting their daughters study in the senior classes of secondary school. And in Turkmenistan one assistant head teacher gave his adolescent daughter away in marriage.[177]

All these diversions from customary Soviet legal practice demonstrate the tenacity of social custom and public opinion in determining what happened in effect in the realm of family relationships. Soviet writing refers to this 'reactionary' or 'philistine' side of public opinion, which compelled even non-believers to perform rites traditionally associated with Islam.[178]

Nor was it only in regard to marital matters and affiliated customs that Muslim society operated against the Soviet endeavour to emancipate its womenfolk. Several manifestations of women's traditional seclusion were retained in many parts of Muslim residence. The most apparent of these was, undoubtedly, the *paranja* or *chador*, the garment which covered the woman from head to foot, or, in some parts, the *chachvan* or *yashmak*, which covered her face or parts of it.[179] (Different areas had different names for a variety of garments all used to ensure female modesty. Moreover, in some parts, for example among the nomads of the Kazakh steppe or

175. The work of the council on atheism, the Osh branch of Znanie, undated [June 1969]; GARF, f.6991, o.6, d.220, l.170.

176. S. Irgaliev to A. Nurullaev, 8 May 1974; GARF, f.6991, o.6, d.633, l.15.

177. Minutes, CARC session No.3, All-Union conference of republican *upol-nomochennye*, 17-18 Feb. 1965; GARF, f.6991, o.4, d.168, ll.48-9.

178. Dunn and Dunn, 'Soviet Regime and Native Culture in Central Asia and Kazakhstan', p.163.

179. A CARC inspector who visited Turkmenistan in late 1950 reported that in the auls women and girls wore the *yashmak* – P. A. Solov'ev, CARC session No.1, 13 Jan. 1951; a decade later CARC's *upolnomochennyi* in Turkmenistan stated that it was still being worn – M. A. Il'baev, Report, All-Union confernece of CARC *upolnomochennye*, 17 Feb. 1960; GARF, f.6991, o.3, d.74, ll.6-7, and o.4, d.168, l.50.

the highlanders of Uzbekistan and Tajikistan, women had never had recourse to these means of seclusion.)

The elimination of the various forms of veil had been a major strategic objective of the *khujum*, or assault against female segregation of 1927-28,[180] but they began returning in the postwar period. Indeed, the fact that so many of the major themes of Soviet anti-Muslim propaganda in the late 1920s and through the 1930s were identical with those employed in atheistic propaganda half a century later indicates that the regime did not register any great success in this field.[181] In the words of a book devoted to the study of the status of women in Islam, printed in Moscow in the late 1960s, despite the 'profound changes...in the social, economic and spiritual life of the people of the Soviet East, among others in overcoming the old feudal-patriarchal attitude towards women, under the influence of long-outlived medieval traditions and customs, some men, primarily older ones with a backward world outlook, try to prevent women from participating in Communist construction and in the country's socio-political and cultural life'.[182] Not only were there still homes which were partitioned according to sex, but many men in the rural areas and even some urban dwellers considered it unseemly to appear in public places together with their wives.[183] Even young non-believers with higher education did not always sit down to table in their company.[184]

There is ample testimony that in certain parts the *paranja* was on its way back in the second half of the 1940s. State Security Minister Abakumov was informed in 1946 by the Uzbek SSR MGB that in Fergana Oblast' and other oblasti of Uzbekistan the wives of public officials wore the *paranja*.[185] Central Committee Secretary Zhdanov was advised that in Uzbekistan the number of women wearing the *paranja* was growing markedly, and that

180. For the *khujum* – a Russian adaptation of a word used in Turkish, Perisan and Arabic – see Massell, *The Surrogate Proletariat, passim*.

181. For the former period, see Bryan, 'Anti-Islamic Propaganda: *Bezbozhnik* 1925-35'; for the latter, see Ro'i, 'The Task of Creating the New Soviet Man: "Atheistic Propaganda" in the Soviet Muslim Areas'.

182. Vagabov, *Islam i zhenshchina*, pp.6-7.

183. *Ibid.*, pp.145-6.

184. E. Bairamov, 'Islam i "natsional'nye traditsii"', *Agitator*, no.12, Dec. 1966, p.43. See also p.445.

185. V. A. Abakumov to K. E. Voroshilov, 12 Sept. 1946; GARF, f.6991, o.3, d.34, l.195.

among their ranks were wives of kolkhoz chairmen and officials in the local government and even party apparatus.[186] CARC instructed its *upolnomochennyi* in Uzbekistan concerning the need to elaborate measures for an effective struggle against 'social abnormalities' like the *qalym* and *paranja*, which had almost disappeared after the October revolution, but had now re-surfaced.[187] And Polianskii mentioned the *paranja* specifically as one vestige of Islam with which SADUM was grappling with little success.[188] Nor was this true only for Central Asia. CARC's *upolnomochennyi* in the Ajar ASSR in Georgia reported in 1946 that most women covered their faces.[189]

In Tajikistan women were not simply wearing the *paranja* again –it was said to have become almost universal in a number of oblasti (Stalinabad, Garm, Leninabad and Kulyab) – but public opinion censured those who moved about without it, thus compelling them to return to it. In some parts of the republic women wore it even when receiving awards for their 'communist labour', for Stakhanovite achievements in the cotton harvest.[190] In Uzbekistan's three Fergana Valley oblasti (Namangan, Andijan and Fergana), as well as in Samarkand Oblast' and other parts of Uzbekistan, wearing the *paranja* was also widespread at the beginning of the 1950s.[191] In Namangan Oblast' a group of women who called themselves holy miracle-workers were arrested in 1947 for conducting rites among women and obligating girls to don the *paranja*. The chief of the Namangan militia himself forbade his wife, daughters and other relatives to remove their *paranja*; when

186. V. Tatarintsev to A. A. Zhdanov, 15 Nov. 1946; RTsKhIDNI, f.17, o.125, d.421, l.110.

187. Iu. V. Sadovskii to Kh. N. Iskanderov, 16 Jan. 1947; TsGAUz, f.2456, o.1, d.82, l.2ob.

188. I. V. Polianskii to Beriia, Stalin, Molotov and Voroshilov, Zhdanov, Khrushchev, Kuznetsov, Patolichev and Popov, 27 Jan. 1947; GARF, f.6991, o.3, d.47, l.93. For SADUM's *fetwas* pronouncing that women need not move about with a *paranja*, see pp.142-3.

189. Minutes, Conference of CARC *upolnomochennye*, Rostov-on-Don, 14 [June] 1946; GARF, f.6991, o.3, d.38, l.125.

190. P. Chepov to A. A. Kuznetsov, 27 July 1948; RTsKhIDNI, f.17, o.132, d.55, l.3. (Stakhanov was a coalminer in the 1930s who overfulfilled production norms and became a model for work achievement.)

191. I. V. Polianskii to K. E. Voroshilov, 27 May 1950; GARF, f.6991, o.3, d.68, l.45.

the Komsomol *raikom* secretary denounced him, he had her beaten up, after which he was dismissed from his post and expelled from the party.[192] A number of party members in other places, too, (kolkhoz party secretaries, the head teacher in a school) were charged with having compelled their wives to wear the *paranja*.[193] In Fergana Oblast' wives of local officials were wearing the *paranja* in the mid-1950s or concealed their faces 'some other way', and their husbands did not allow them to work in the fields, to participate in public life or to study.[194]

In Osh the leading cleric, Shafagat Khaliqnazarov, began as of 1948 to speak out against the use of the *paranja* by Uzbek women, contending that both the Qur'an and the Shari'a allowed them to move around with uncovered faces and to talk with men other than their husbands. At the same time, nearly all the registered clergy's own wives persisted in wearing that garment, so that ordinary believers concluded these were just words and did not even contemplate removing their wives' *paranjas*.[195] In a report of early 1951, the oblast' *upolnomochennyi* advised that the mass of Uzbek and Tajik women still wore the *paranja* and there were no signs that they were unveiling. (In Osh itself the Uzbeks comprised a majority of the population.)[196] However, just a few months later he wrote that the women in Osh were ceasing to wear the *paranja*, substituting head scarves or shawls. Khaliqnazarov's wife and daughter-in-law were by now walking about with uncovered faces and that cleric's sermons and other educational work by

192. Report of CARC *upolnomochennyi* in the Uzbek SSR, Minutes, CARC session No.11, 18-19 June 1947; GARF, f.6991, o.4, d.19, ll.358-9. For other officials in Namangan whose wives and daughters 'concealed themselves' behind the *paranja*, see Minutes, Conference of CARC *upolnomochennye* in the Uzbek SSR, 9 Aug. 1948; TsGAUz, f.2456, o.1, d.120, l.16.

193. L. A. Prikhod'ko and N. I. Abushaev, A short survey, 16 March 1950; the assistant to the first deputy chairman of the Osh *oblispolkom*, who had graduated a teachers' seminary, was likewise said to have forced his wife to wear the *paranja* – I. G. Halimov to CARC, 23 Aug. 1947; GARF, f.6991, o.3, d.63, l.102 and d.453, l.25ob.

194. U. G. Mangushev to Kh. N. Iskanderov, 30 Jan. 1954; TsGAUz, f.2456, o.1, d.170, l.6.

195. I. G. Halimov to CARC, 30 March 1948 and undated [early April 1949]; GARF, f.6991, o.3, d.453, ll.42-3 and d.454, l.13.

196. I. G. Halimov to H. Akhtiamov, 30 March 1951; GARF, f.6991, o.3, d.454, l.103.

people of their own nationality were showing results.[197] Yet, even at the end of the decade some still wore the *paranja* in Osh Oblast', despite the very severe methods which by now were being used to ban this dress: in one raion savings banks, post offices and stores were forbidden to serve women with *paranjas*, while women 'activists' tore off and seized forty-one *paranjas* at a bazaar in the fall of 1959; in Osh itself bus conductors were ordered not to let women with *paranjas* on the buses and sometimes simply tore them off their passengers.[198]

The most flagrant of all violations of Soviet law and order, however, was perhaps the self-immolation of women. Strictly speaking this custom could not in any way be portrayed as religious –Islam being unequivocal in its condemnation of suicide. The original logic informing this practice was, apparently, that to avoid compromising her clan or family, a woman or girl who had been dishonoured had no alternative to taking her own life.[199] SADUM, which issued repeated *fetwas* condemning self-immolation attributed it to grievances on the background of family scandals.[200] Here, too, the act may have taken on new meaning as a result of Soviet conditions. The CARC *upolnomochennyi* for Turkmenistan, where there were ninety-one instances of self-immolation in 1959, and another nineteen in a single oblast' in the first quarter of 1960, pointed out that most of these had not occurred for reasons connected with religion but as a result of the insulting attitude of husbands, parents and others to girls and young women, whom they did not let participate in public life or study.[201]

197. I. G. Halimov to H. Akhtiamov, 1[6] May 1951; GARF, f.6991, o.3, d.454, l.112.

198. Report, Conference of CARC *upolnomochennye*, 18-20 April 1960; GARF, f.6991, o.3, d.208, ll.136-7.

199. P. A. Solov'ev, Report, CARC session No.1, 13 Jan. 1951; GARF, f.6991, o.3, d.74, l.13.

200. Kh. N. Iskanderov to Kh. G. Gulamov, 20 July 1954; TsGAUz, f.2456, o.1, d.166, ll.46-7. SADUM issued such *fetwas* in 1950 and 1952 (*ibid.* –and see p.143) and again in 1955 –K. F. Tagirov, material prepared for CARC session No.22s, 2 Sept. 1959, see n.202 below. Iskanderov noted that there had been instances of self-immolation in at least four oblasti in Uzbekistan.

201. M. A. Il'baev, Report, All-Union conference of CARC *upolnomochennye*, 17 Feb. 1965; GARF, f.6991, o.4, d.168, l.51. Turkmenistan seems to have been one of the main regions where self-immolation prevailed: in the early 1960s several court cases were held in connection with self-immolation, presumably of those who had caused the woman or girl to commit suicide: 38 in 1961,

Whatever the precise background, the incidence of self-immolation was still sufficiently high in Central Asia in the late 1950s for CARC to suggest that SADUM issue yet a further *fetwa* on this theme. It was proposed that once again, together with the prohibition of taking one's life, the *fetwa* should stress that any person who took this step would be deprived of a religious burial and the regular memorial prayers.[202] Moreover, whether this was objectively justified or not, many of the intolerable situations from which women believed they could only escape by self-immolation were widely seen as having been imposed upon them by religious traditions sanctioned and perpetuated by Muslim law. This practice was, therefore, frequently enumerated among the Islamic rituals which it was incumbent upon the regime and its officials to eradicate.[203] In 1947 a CARC official pointed out a report from the *upolnomochennyi* in Turkmenistan, which spoke of forty-five cases of self-immolation in his republic and instances of Shiites wounding themselves with daggers on Ashura; these facts, it was stated, contradicted the *upolnomochennyi's* statement, in the very same document, that the population was indifferent to religion.[204] One Soviet writer noted in 1960 that self-immolation was primarily a religious act, resulting from the oppressed situation of women in a class, exploitative society. Phenomena such as betrothal before reaching maturity, *qalym*, *kaitarma*, and abduction pushed women to suicide. Masses of women were throwing themselves into rivers, pouring kerosene over themselves and burning themselves alive.[205]

Indeed, the large number of cases of self-immolation and its pervasiveness were frequently commented upon. Still under Gorbachev, CPSU Central Committee Secretary and Politburo can-

---

61 in 1962 and 22 and 31 respectively just in one quarter of each of the following years – Il'baev, ibid., ll.50-1.

202. K. F. Tagirov, Material prepared for CARC session No.22s, 2 Sept. 1959; GARF, f.6991, o.3, d.184, ll.235-6. And see p.145.

203. For example, M. A. Il'baev, Address, All-Union conference of CARC *upolnomochennye*, 18-20 April 1960; GARF, f.6991, o.3, d.208, l.107.

204. Minutes, CARC session No.13, 10 July 1947; GARF, f.6991, o.4, d.19, l.439. (For rites connected with Ashura, see pp.503-6.)

205. Kuliev, *Antinauchnaia sushchnost' islama*, p.86. Also in 1960, there were said to have been about 200 cases of self-immolation in Uzbekistan – N. Smirnov, Information, 18 Sept. 1962, delivered by hand to A. I. Aleksandrov at the CPSU Central Committee, 19 Sept. 1962; GARF, f.6991, o.3, d.1390, l.70.

didate member Aleksandr Iakovlev underscored at a Tajikistan Party Central Committee plenum, in his discussion of Islam and its clerics, the 'many instances' of self-immolation by women in that republic, 'including Komosmol members and schoolgirls'.[206] In the same year a central newspaper related five cases of brides in a single raion of Turkmenistan who had burned themselves to death in protest at having been given away to grooms they did not love and a further one of a bride who had committed suicide after being returned to her parents' home shortly after the wedding because the groom had not paid the entire *qalym*.[207] Also in 1987, 270 instances of self-immolation by brides in Uzbekistan were reported in the press, which, in the view of one student of Islam in Central Asia were far from representing the full figure, for they did not include those who drowned and poisoned themselves.[208] Many suicides too were attributed to the failure to bear children, which seems to have been a further stimulus for abasement at the hands of husbands and mothers-in-law. Certainly as timed passed these humiliations became increasingly incongruous and intolerable.

Given all the above, the situation of the woman in the traditionally Muslim areas was unquestionably complex. She was clearly subject to contradictory pressures and influences, on the one hand, from her family, and on the other, from the regime and its representatives and institutions. While many women obviously charted their path skilfully and successfully, the less flexible or the less lucky found themselves caught up in a web of intrigue and manipulation. One student of this intricate topic, who specialised on Azerbaijan, one of the USSR's more secular Muslim territories, came to the conclusion that 'the cultural characteristics attributed to an ideal Azeri woman, at times as rigidly stressed as in the Islamic-theocratic Iranian part of Azerbaijan, include: honor (*namus*), feminine shame (*haya*), chastity and modesty or prudery (*ismat*), virginity before marriage, beauty and tact, high education (especially in urban areas), self-sacrificing motherhood, docility and subservience towards the husband, home-making skills, endurance, ethnic loyalty

206. *Kommunist Tadzhikistana*, 8 April 1987.

207. *Trud*, 29 April 1987.

208. Poliakov, *Everyday Islam*, p.54. Even if we bear in mind that under Gorbechev Soviet officialdom was eager to play up for propaganda purposes such ills of Muslim, especially Central Asian, society as self-immolation, its incidence seems to have been sufficiently high to deserve serious attention and concern.

and endogamy'. She went on to analyze this dichotomy between the woman's private and public roles, the compartmentalization of public and private behaviour, concluding that, together with the Soviet regime's achievements in eliminating certain aspects of Islam, 'the *experimental, consequential,* and certain levels of the *ritualistic* dimensions of Islam, understood in a broad sense as a Muslim mode of life, have kept their vitality.'[209]

All in all, then, observation of some of the social aspects of Islam and the implementation of its rites at the level of the ordinary citizen's daily and family life left no doubt as to religion's deep roots throughout society wherever members of Muslim nationalities resided. It also made clear that any differentiation between the older generation which might be expected to die out and younger cohorts which were abandoning Islam totally was an ideological hypothesis that was not reflected in reality. Many of the rites were not merely adhered to by the latter, but were relevant for them only: the elderly did not have young sons to circumcise and for the most part did not marry young brides. Whatever the underlying reasons for the popularity of Islamic practices, whether, in fact, people sensed a social pressure to which they felt they had to succumb; or whether it was a question of their own feeling of identity to which they sought to give expression; or whether there was perhaps a subconscious consensus that this enabled them to withstand some of the constraints imposed by the Soviet regime, the evidence spoke for itself. It gradually dawned even on the most ideologically-minded party diehards that the campaign to extirpate religious vestiges in the Muslim sector was not just an uphill struggle, but one that had little if any prospects of success. For the most part, the elaboration of policy had no relation to what actually occurred in practice: Muslim religious life and activity and the policy-makers in Moscow, although operating in the same time period and 'space', revolving in two separate orbits.

209. Tohidi, 'The Intersection of Gender, Ethnicity and Islam in Soviet and Post-Soviet Azerbaijan', pp.151 and 154.

Part V. ISLAM AND THE REGIME

10

OFFICIAL POLICY

The attitude to Islam and policy implementation in the Muslim sector

It appears a moot question whether one can legitimately speak of a distinct regime policy towards Islam throughout the entire period under discussion. True, both the Council of Ministers and the CPSU Central Committee apparatus received throughout these decades recurrent reports on the situation within the Muslim community which stressed its specific features. Yet there is no evidence that until the late 1970s the country's leading bodies addressed Islam separately, as requiring distinct treatment or dictating the elaboration of different guidelines than directed their overall policy towards religion. It is not clear whether the reason was a general insouciance regarding religion as such, which, despite sporadic legislation and attempts to enhance atheistic propaganda, does not seem to have taken up a great deal of leadership attention,[1] or an underlying contempt for the Muslim nationalities as a whole and consequent disparagement of the danger they or their faith and traditions were capable of comprising to the Soviet body politic.

In many ways the attitude of the Soviet regime to Islam was reminiscent of that of the late tsarist period (following the conquest of Turkestan in the 1860s and 1870s). On the one hand, there

---

1. From time to time CARC sought to caution the CPSU Central Committee Department of Propaganda and Agitation that there was need for an enhanced alertness with regard to the influence of religion among the population. One such document brings a host of examples from the Muslim sector – A. A. Puzin to the Department of Propaganda and Agitation, 7 June 1961; GARF, f.6991, o.3, d.1363, ll.96-8.

was talk of Muslim 'fanaticism' and a conviction that Islam could never be at peace with an alien state. On the other hand, stood a resolve to tolerate, although not protect, the Muslim faith, which engendered administrative measures to weaken leading Muslim institutions, a general disregard of the practices performed by the individual believer, and attempts to secularise Muslim society with the help of material and technical progress.[2] Indeed, there was even a manifest overlap between the terminology used by the tsarist administration in the half century or so prior to the Bolshevik Revolution and that of the Soviet regime, just as there was in the ideological postulates which stood behind the attitude of both governments, founded, as they were, on a general appraisal of the goals and objectives of colonial rule, rather than on an understanding of the situation pertaining in the Muslim periphery. Nor did new motifs or concepts appear in the regime's attitude to Islam after 1945 when compared with the pre – World War II years.[3] Emphases, however, differed; so, too, did the general message the Muslim community was receiving from the main centres of authority in Moscow and the republican capitals. Both, moreover, changed several times in the course of the four decades under review, thus creating an impression of policy.

Only the establishment of an Islamic republic in Iran on the southern border of the Soviet Union and the backlash of the civil war in Afghanistan following the Marxist coup of 1978 and the Soviet invasion of that country at the end of 1979 seem to have compelled the Central Committee to address directly the situation within the USSR's own Muslim community. As a result, indeed, it passed a number of resolutions relating specifically to Islam in the domestic arena. Two of these was entitled 'Measures to counteract attempts by the adversary to use the "Islamic factor" for ends hostile to the Soviet Union' and 'Measures for the ideological

---

2. For a discussion of tsarist policy toward Islam in the last half-century of so prior to 1917, see Brower, 'Islam and Ethnicity: Russian Colonial Policy in Turkestan', pp.118-22. For the elaboration of the tsarist government's attitudes and policy toward Islam in Central Asia, see Litvinov, *Gosudarstvo i islam v russkom Turkestane (1865-1917), passim*. For use of the term 'fanaticism', see Chapter 1, n.84.

3. For the inter – war period there is no major overall study, but see for Kazakhstan, *Preodolevaia religionzoe vliianie islama*, and for Uzbekistan, Keller, *The Struggle against Islam in Uzbekistan, 1927–1941*.

isolation of the reactionary sector of the Muslim clergy'.[4] According
to one CRA official, these resolutions pointed out that 'imperialism
and reaction' were seeking to use 'the Islamic factor' to destabilise
the situation in the Soviet Union. It was therefore incumbent
upon the country's leading organs to reinforce atheistic propaganda
vis-à-vis the Islamic sector and to enhance efforts to ensure that
there be no violations of the legislation on religion by either
government officials or clergy.[5]

The lack of input in writing from either the Central Committee[6]
or the top leadership of the Council of Ministers and the inaccessibility of any written addenda or minutes of discussions at the
leadership level mean that this issue has to remain largely unresolved
for the time being. All that appears possible, therefore, within the
framework of this study is to examine the ideological and political
approach of those whose immediate task it was to deal with 'the
Islamic movement' and its representatives. Even though it is clear
from the material that their approach was not identical with that
of the upper élite – each organisation engaged in implementation
developed its own attitudes, had its clear vested interests and was
far more involved than the top party and government leadership
– one may safely assume that it somehow reflected that of their
superiors.

For instance, in the mid 1940s, CARC made considerable efforts
to encourage and reinforce the Muslim religious establishment.
CARC Chairman Polianskii reiterated many times that the regime

4. E. Ligachev and V. Stukalin to the CPSU Central Committee, 10 Nov.
1983; TsKhSD, f.5, o.89, d.82, l.74. The first resolution was dated 24 Sept.
1981, the second 5 April 1983. Unfortunately, it has not been possible to procure
the texts of these resolutions.

5. Author's interview with a CRA official who has asked to remain anonymous.

6. Mostly requests and recommendations made by CARC and the CRA would
lead to a reply by telephone, which would be added by hand to the copy of
the Council's letter to the Central Committee that remained in its archives; see,
for example, Chapter 3, nn.45 and 47, and Chapter 5, n.142. On occasion,
however, the party's directives were addressed directly to a local party organ.
For instance, in 1946 Polianskii wrote to Deputy Chairman of the Council of
Ministers Aleksei Kosygin that TsDUM Mufti Rasulev asked permission to issue
a calendar in Tatar in Arabic script. Kosygin transmitted the request to Aleksandrov
at Agitprop, who in fact gave the requisite permission directly to the Bashkir
Obkom, one of his aides informing CARC of his decision – I. V. Polianskii to
A. N. Kosygin, 26 June 1946, and to G. F. Aleksandrov, 14 Sept. 1946; GARF,
f.6991, o.3, d.34, ll.101 and 187. See also p.166.

could not ignore the patriotic stance of the Muslim clergy during the war and in the immediate postwar period and had, as a result, to adopt a 'positive' position toward the country's Muslim inhabitants.[7] The Council sought to encourage the registration of mosques in those places where this was deemed politically expedient and generally to maintain a sufficient quantity of mosques to answer the primary needs of the believer population. It was constantly urging its *upolnomochennye* not to shut down illegally functioning mosques indiscriminately, but rather to register those which answered the requisite criteria and were strategically situated.[8]

The reasoning behind this consistent pressure on the part of CARC and, later, the CRA for increased registration of religious societies was that this facilitated their supervision and control of Islam. As the government organisation whose primary task was policy implementation and the administration of religious life, CARC/the CRA was inevitably concerned first and foremost with practicalities. Since Islamic activity could not be stifled, they argued, some part of it must be legitimised. Altogether, the general impression from the documentation is that in the early years – 1944-47 – CARC and Polianskii specifically contemplated the opening and registering of rather larger numbers of mosques than were in fact given sanction. As Polianskii told the CARC *upolnomochennyi* for Dagestan, having just twenty-two official mosques in a republic which before the Bolshevik Revolution had had 1,600 was 'not normal'.[9] In mid-1947, when the leadership was moving towards a general curtailment of registration, he wrote to Molotov that as far as Islam was concerned, the registration of functioning religious associations should continue, in order to bring 'the Muslim movement' as much as possible under the auspices of the four spiritual directorates.[10] This, however, had to be done without transmitting the message to believers that the authorities were giving them encouragement to augment activity.

Polianskii wrote in a similar vein to the CARC *upolnomochennyi*

7. For example, I. V. Polianskii, Address, Moscow conference of CARC *upolnomochennye*, 11 [May?] 1946; GARF, f.6991, o.3, d.39, l.69. See also pp.32-3, 188 and 431-2.

8. For details, see pp.187, 191, 195-7, 215-6, 318 and 322.

9. Minutes, CARC session No.7, 23-24 April 1947; GARF, f.6991, o.4, d.19, l.185. Polianskii designated the number 'miserable'.

10. See pp.195-6.

for the Uzbek SSR. He suggested that, insofar as possible, mosques be opened in those raion administrative centres which had empty buildings of former mosques. These mosques were to extend their activity to the surrounding kishlaks, villages and *poselki* and their mullas should be 'used' in the struggle against unregistered religious societies and itinerant mullas. In no way were mosques to be opened wherever there were believers, although this meant that there would be Muslims who would not have resort to the services of a registered mosque and mulla.[11] In Kirgiziia, too, where believers were numerous and mosques few, Polianskii favoured a certain increase in the quantity of mosques in order to correct the dis-symmetry, although, he admitted, this sounded paradoxical.[12]

CARC and in its wake the CRA remained true to this policy of selective registration. At the end of the 1950s CARC took exception to the work of its *upolnomochennyi* in Dagestan, who maintained that registering mosques increased religiosity, whereas the Council held a diametrically opposite position – that refusal to register strengthened religious tendencies.[13]

The desire to bring Muslim religious activity to heel and exercise effective control over it was also behind CARC's policy of trying to strengthen the spiritual directorates and its suggestion to establish a single umbrella organisation to coordinate their activities.[14]

It must be assumed that CARC's position of constraining, regulating and controlling religious activity without suppressing it was inspired by people or bodies in the top leadership, if not directly and consciously, at least by default. CARC could hardly have taken such a line without receiving instructions or indications leading it to consider that this coincided with the general wishes and objectives of its superiors. In the final event, however, this course did not carry the day, either because it was frustrated by other, evidently more influential, individuals or interest groups, or because it evoked doubts and misgivings. Certainly the favourable

11. I. V. Polianskii to Kh. N. Iskanderov, 8 Aug. 1947; TsGAUz, f.2456, o.1, d.82, l.17.

12. Minutes, CARC session No.9, 3 June 1947; GARF, f.6991, o.4, d.19, l.276.

13. Minutes, CARC session No.4, 25-26 Feb. 1959; GARF, f.6991, o.3, d.183, l.105.

14. I. V. Polianskii to G. F. Aleksandrov, 1 July 1947; RTsKhIDNI, f.17, o.125, d.506, l.126. And see p.117.

signs emanating from Moscow in the mid-1940s merely led to a further strengthening of Islamic life and activity, in light of the understanding of the country's Muslim citizens that they were receiving backing from the all-powerful centre.

Thus, towards the end of the 1940s and in the early 1950s, in striking contrast to the earlier years, the main policy objective was the restriction, and, in parts, the termination of organised activity. CARC turned its efforts to the religious associations, registered and unregistered, with this objective in mind. A number of republics in traditionally Muslim areas actually passed resolutions to bring this policy into effect. The Uzbek SSR Council of Ministers, for instance, adopted a resolution in 1951 entitled 'Facts on the intensification of the reactionary activity of the Muslim clergy', which, among other things, stipulated measures to enhance 'natural-scientific propaganda'. Similar resolutions were taken by the Tatar and Dagestan ASSRs.[15]

CARC did not, however, seek in this period to restrain the conduct of religious rites by individuals. In the words of the republican *upolnomochennyi* in Kirgiziia, Islamic activity did not draw the attention of the *upolnomochennye* in places where there were no religious societies, either registered or unregistered, for here it consisted of the performance of rites by unofficial clergy in private homes. In the first place, believers would conduct these rites even if they were prohibited – the only way to put an end to this was through propaganda and education, by 'raising people's cultural level', which was not CARC's task; secondly, their prohibition would be a violation of the freedom of conscience guaranteed by the constitution. All that could be done in such localities was to wage a struggle against itinerant and other mosqueless mullas through taxation.[16]

The other main aspect of CARC's policy, seeking to restrict tenets of the faith and practices which it deemed believers might be prepared to give up while making compromises on issues over which the average Muslim appeared unlikely to agree easily to yield, also surfaced in a number of fields. In 1952, for instance,

15. V. Stepanov and V. Klochko to M. A. Suslov, 4 July 1952; RTsKhIDNI, f.17, o.132, d.497, l.35.

16. H. Akhtiamov, Address, Conference of CARC's Central Asian *upolnomochennye*, Tashkent, 17-19 Dec. 1949; GARF, f.6991, o.3, d.67, ll.126-7. For taxation, see pp.595-9 below.

the question of payment of the *fitr* arose, reaching the AUCP(b) Central Committee, where it was dealt with by Secretary N. A. Mikhailov. Polianskii explained, after what was described as 'a definitive review' of the problem, that collection of the *fitr* was not to be prohibited. If the registered clergy did not collect it in their mosques, the unregistered mullas would do so, for it was impossible to stop it. At the same time, collection was to be restricted to the precincts of the mosque and donation was to be totally voluntary: no compulsion whatever was to be exerted regarding either the actual payment or the sum to be paid.[17] Nor was the *fitr*, or any other money or produce collected from believers, to serve for charitable purposes.[18] Altogether, believers were permitted to collect donations twice a year – on, or in connection with, the two main festivals.[19]

In the mid 1950s policy changed again, following the Central Committee resolution of November 1954 and the decree of the Council of Ministers of February 1955, and the 'Muslim movement' attained new heights, reaching the acme of its activity for the entire period from the war down to perestroika.[20] In these years some of the republican leaderships, especially in republics where Islam was particularly assertive, manifested their concern at the leeway shown towards religion. In Uzbekistan, for example, CP First Secretary Nuretdin Muhitdinov dealt personally with questions concerning Islam personally.[21]

Toward the end of the 1950s and in the early 1960s CARC returned to the offensive. The Council was once more intent on cutting the spiritual directorates, especially SADUM, and the religious establishment, or to be more precise the entire 'Muslim movement', down to size. Even then, it took care not to meddle directly in religious activity or to provide an opportunity for people to lodge complaints that the authorities were interfering in the actual performance of religious rites. CARC Chairman Puzin ex-

17. L. A. Prikhod'ko, Notes, 20 Nov. 1958, and also Report, 20 May 1953; GARF, f.6991, o.3, d.164, l.86 and d.91, l.248.

18. Minutes, CARC session No.26s, 22 Oct. 1952; GARF, f.6991, o.3, d.83, l.286.

19. Minutes, CARC session No.9, 3 June 1947; GARF, f.6991, o.4, d.19, l.280.

20. See pp.203–5, 306–7 and 437–8.

21. See p.623.

plained to Mufti Babakhanov in 1961, for example, that he was not suggesting that Muslims refrain from observing the *khatm-i Qur'an* during the *uraz*, let alone prohibiting it, but sought ways to curb its expansion.[22]

Even more significantly, Puzin took issue with CARC's republican *upolnomochennyi* in the Kirgiz SSR two years previously, when the latter suggested that the republican criminal code include an article calling for the punishment of unregistered clergy. Why, he asked, should legislation be directed against them rather than against the organs of local government which refrained from registering them and enabling them to operate legally. Tens of thousands attended unregistered prayer services in Kirgiziia's mosques. Did the *upolnomochennyi* wish to wage war against all of them? In recent years hundreds of mosques had been illegally constructed. Everyone saw this, but no-one in local government did anything to oppose it; some actually helped. Believers knew this, and now that the party and government leadership had changed tack, it was not possible to simply close or burn down these mosques. In Kirgiziia alone ninety-nine mosques had been built without permission, and a further ninety-four empty mosques had been taken over by clergy and believers. To permit an error was easy, to correct one was more difficult, and it was unthinkable to commit a folly and embitter believers against the regime.[23]

Similar considerations guided CARC during the campaign against *mazars* in the late 1950s. Its officials insisted that it was inadvisable, under the guise of this onslaught, to endeavour to liquidate all unregistered mosques and demolish non-functioning ones. This was likely to lead to an enhanced religious mood and create a false impression among believers of party and government policy, which, in turn, would hinder the termination of pilgrimages to Muslim shrines. Nor was it possible to proceed indiscriminately to the closure of all *mazars*. Those of all-union significance, to which pilgrims came from all over the country, could be shut down only after careful and gradual work. Moreover, it was necessary to beware lest, when one holy place was put under lock and key, people move to another one in the vicinity. Otherwise,

22. Reception by A. A. Puzin of Z. Babakhanov, 19 Dec. 1961; GARF, f.6991, o.4, d.121, ll.22-3.

23. Minutes, Conference of CARC's *upolnomochennye* in Central Asia and Kazakhstan, Tashkent, 5-6 June 1959; GARF, f.6991, o.3, d.186, ll.200-8.

the outcome would be that *mazars* were closed merely on paper.[24] This opinion, however, was not shared by all *upolnomochennye*. One of them insisted that all *mazars* be closed, including the most important ones, for otherwise believers would ask why one was being closed and not the other. He also considered that the ar-gumentation being used by some people to denounce the *mazars*, namely that those buried there were not religious figures but leading scientists and philosophers, was counter-productive and that it would be preferable to contend categorically that the dead were unable to help the living.[25]

Although in the period of CARC's existence a number of conferences of *upolnomochennye* dealt with questions connected specifically with Islam, no resolutions seem to have been adopted which related to that faith alone. Nor does there appear to have been any legislation at the all-union level pertaining to Islamic issues. The first conference which was devoted solely to Islam took place in 1968 in Tashkent, with the participation of all organisations involved in policy implementation in the Islamic sector: all CARC officials and *upolnomochennye* who dealt with Islam, officials of the party agitprop apparatus at the centre and in the Muslim areas, and representatives of the executive branch. The resolutions it passed served as the guidelines for work among Muslims in subsequent years, its 'recommendations on enhancing control of the activity of the Muslim associations and clergy' being sent to the central committee of the republican parties and republican councils of ministers, as well as to the party committees and executive organs at the oblast', city and raion level.[26]

A number of statements were made asserting that the authorities did not differentiate between the various faiths, except for the Russian Orthodox Church, which undoubtedly 'enjoyed' special treatment.[27] One CARC official declared pointblank shortly after

24. Minutes, CARC session No.4, 25-26 Feb. 1959; GARF, f.6991, o.3, d.183, l.105. For the *mazars* and regime policy regarding holy places, see also pp. 376-8.

25. Minutes, Conference of CARC's Central Asian *upolnomochennye*, 5-6 June 1959; GARF, f.6991, o.3, d.186, ll.38-9.

26. CRA report, sent to the CPSU Central Committee, 22 May 1970; TsKhSD, f.5, o.62, d.38, l.36.

27. On the whole, the sense among the general public was that the Russian Orthodox Church received preferential treatment and that its leadership was closer to the regime than were representatives of other faiths. Indeed, CARC's

the war that that body related the same way to all religions under its jurisdiction, although endeavouring to take into account the different conditions in the various republics.[28] Certainly, there was an awareness of the need to avoid stereotyped attitudes to different Muslim republics: as early as the 1940s, Moscow's officials attributed great political importance to Tajikistan, which was at the 'juncture' of three countries with a predominantly Muslim population – India (before Partition), Western China and Afghanistan – whose 'gaze is fixed' on that republic, and could not be compared with territories such as the Tatar and Bashkir ASSRs.[29]

At the same time, different conditions prevailed in each faith as well: for instance, the Muslim religious centres, particularly SADUM, were further away from Moscow than other such centres, making them the more difficult to influence and control. Indeed, the very existence of four such centres was acknowledgement of the top leadership's awareness of the specifics of Islam, whether the reason for this decision was in fact consideration for the sensitivities of the different Muslim communities, or whether – as seems more likely – it was the result of a desire on the part of Moscow to 'divide and rule'.[30] The arguments brought for and against the formation of a single all-union Muslim centre demonstrated the two positions adopted by various components of the ruling élite. On the one hand stood those who considered that an umbrella organisation would facilitate the regulation of Muslim activity and make Moscow's control of it more effective; on the other were the party ideologists and, apparently, the MGB, the security apparatus, which was apprehensive of the strength and encouragement its creation and existence would give the leadership and the hard core of the believer community.[31]

---

upolnomochennye themselves complained that the discrimination between the Russian Orthodox Church and the other faiths made their work that much more difficult – for example, the *upolnomochennyi* for the Ajar ASSR, Minutes, All-Union conference of CARC *upolnomochennye*, 25-27 Nov. 1958; GARF, f.6991, o.3, d.165, l.84. At the same time, as has been pointed out, during the anti-religious campaign of the Khrushchev period, the Orthodox Church suffered a larger proportion of closures than did other religions – see p.42.

28. Minutes, CARC session No.7, 23-24 April 1947; GARF, f.6991, o.4, d.19, l.199.

29. Minutes, CARC session No.4, 29 Jan. 1947; GARF, f.6991, o.4, d.19, p.78.

30. See p.100.

31. For a more detailed discussion of the proposals to set up a coordinated

The clergy of the various faiths also differed in their basic attitude to the Soviet state, some being more generally loyal than others; in Islam the registered clergy were, on the whole, considered loyal, although this did not apply to rather large categories among the unregistered mullas, shaykhs and *ishans*.[32] In this context, Polianskii stated categorically in mid 1947 that 'we' could not relate in the same fashion to all the religions under CARC's jurisdiction. (It is not clear whether he was speaking for CARC or for his superiors in the party or government apparatus.) While the attitude to Roman Catholicism, for instance, was one of sufferance as a result of a variety of considerations, Islam required a more favourable attitude. During World War II the Muslims, including their clergy, had shown their patriotism. Consequently the state's position toward Islam was 'more positive' than toward the Roman Catholic or Greek Catholic churches. This had practical implications as well: review of applications to open or register mosques was not to be held up, indeed applications were to be evaluated 'positively' (although by this time applications regarding prayer-houses of other faiths were no longer being processed at all).[33] The recurrent references to Muslim loyalty to the Soviet state and patriotism during World War II stood in sharp contrast to the charges concerning Muslim collaboration with the Germans, notably in reference to the Crimean Tatars and the North Caucasian Muslim nationalities deported in 1943-4.[34]

To take another example, the closed mosques that retained the appearance of mosques seem to have been much more numerous than were former prayer-houses of any other religion, except the Russian Orthodox Church, and this spelled out a potential enticement for believers to seek to renew religious activity in them, especially since many of them stood empty. Considerable discussion focused on the relative advantages and disadvantages of each of the three alternative ways of dealing with these buildings: leaving them as they were, transferring them for use by cultural-educational or economic organisations, or demolition. Often voices were heard in favour of the first option on the grounds that the other two

Muslim centre and their rejection, see pp.117-9.

32. See pp.188, 248, 346-7 and 358-9 and Chapter 6 *passim*.

33. Minutes, CARC session No. 11, 18-19 June 1947; GARF, f.6991, o.4, d.19, l.398; and see Polianskii's abovementioned letter to Molotov.

34. See Chapter 6, n.143.

evoked negative reactions within the believer community. In Uzbekistan, however, where many instances occurred of believers simply taking over empty mosques and transforming them into functioning prayer-premises, CARC instructed its *upolnomochennyi* to broach with the republican government the possibility of using them for cultural or educational institutions.[35]

Although the diversity which pertained in different republics and regions, and which characterised different faiths did not oblige the regime to adopt a distinct position towards the country's various religions, it inevitably dictated, or at least suggested, divergent approaches to concrete situations and to policy implementation. For instance, it was declared policy, except perhaps in the mid-1950s, to try to reduce or weaken the material base of the religious centres and societies. The previous CARC leadership (Polianskii had died in 1956 and was succeeded the following year by Puzin) had erred, according to the *upolnomochennyi* for South Kazakhstan in 1960, in not obstructing the religious societies in the localities from fortifying their resources. As a result, the spiritual directorates, which annually budgeted each society's income and expenditures, also accumulated considerable wealth. One of the principal bulwarks of the mosques' income was the *fitr*. By limiting its dimensions in every possible way the authorities not only undermined a main tenet of the faith, which was still observed by so many Muslims, but also impaired significantly the flow of income to the Muslim establishment. The decision taken, the sums contributed fell accordingly.[36]

The Soviet leadership, moreover, was certainly conscious of the different reactions to its policy among the adherents of each religion. It must have known that among Muslims, for instance, the encouragement received from 'friendly' measures or legislation, such as the Central Committee resolution of November 1954, or, conversely, the discouragement from repressive enactments, almost certainly had more far-reaching impact on their actual conduct than on that of Baptists who were singularly unreceptive to regime signals and even pressure.[37] Voroshilov, the deputy chairman

35. L. A. Prikhod'ko, Report, 2 June 1952; GARF, f.6991, o.3, d.81, l.135. And see pp.295 and 298.

36. Minutes, Conference of CARC *upolnomochennye*, 18–20 April 1960; GARF, f.6991, o.3, d.208, ll.120-1 and 124. See also pp.486-8.

37. Certainly, the CARC material reflects the effect of the November 1954

of the Council of Ministers responsible for giving Polianskii his directives, thus opposed Polianskii's suggestion in early 1949 to continue opening and registering mosques on the grounds that this would not eliminate the 'underground, unofficial Muslim movement', but would rather encourage unofficial groups to intensify their demands to open mosques, kindling a flame that was currently merely smouldering.[38]

The documentation shows unequivocally that in periods when the freedom of worship promised them by the constitution seemed real, notably in the years 1944-6 or 1955-7, Islam became strengthened organisationally.[39] And when it was felt that regime pressure was mounting, believers in most parts tended to refrain from public identification with Islam, except in the more zealously Muslim pockets, such as the Fergana Valley. Here, on the contrary, the clergy told officials frankly that the sole anticipated effect of repressive measures was the alienation of the population. The *imam-khatib* in Margelan reacted to the November 1954 resolution by saying that were the authorities to have persisted with the mistakes mentioned in it (the situation which pertained in the wake of the July 1954 resolution), the population would have become antagonised; now, however, it would make common cause with the state. Indeed, although it was just an ordinary Friday, an unusually large crowd, of well over 10,000, attended *jum'a-namaz* on the Friday following the November resolution in order to hear its text being read out at the mosque.[40]

There is, however, no evidence that the diversity of the Muslim population was the reason for the lack of any tailored, specific

decree on Muslims, as a result of which the number of believers was said to have increased and people began performing rites openly – N. I. Inogamov, Address, All-Union conference of CARC *upolnomochennye*, 25-27 Nov. 1958; GARF, f.6991, o.3, d.165, l.35.

38. Reception of I. V. Polianskii by K. E. Voroshilov, 12 Feb. 1949; GARF, f.6991, o.3, d.8, ll.175-6.

39. Similarly, Polianskii contended that in the prewar period religiosity had not declined, but that its outward manifestations – most specifically mosque attendance – had been adversely affected – Information, 1 Oct. 1946; GARF, f.6991, o.3, d.34, ll.12-13.

40. U. G. Mangushev to Fergana Obkom Secretary Kambarov, Oblispolkom Chairman Rizaev, I. V. Polianskii and Kh. N. Iskanderov, 10 Dec. 1954; GARF, f.6991, o.3, d.113, ll.83-4. Polianskii sent the letter on to Agitprop Head V. S. Kruzhkov. For further detail regarding the reception of this resolution in the Fergana Valley, see p.225.

policy toward it or Islam. It was not a question of the party leadership hesitating between undue severity, which would arouse hostility among the more religiously inclined, and leniency, which would encourage a greater religiosity among those who were gradually becoming estranged from Islam. It seems just to have been the result of a general sense that what applied to one religion or religious community was valid for all, yet one further example of the general muddling through which characterised the Soviet regime in most periods on issues not demanding urgent attention. Moreover, from comparing the two periods, one cannot but sense that the tsarist administration's generally lackadaisical perception of its Muslim borderlands, particularly Turkestan, somehow affected the bureaucracy of the Soviet period, which made use first of the experts of the former regime and then, when they disappeared, of their books and reports, inheriting and internalising many, if not all, of their axioms and conclusions.

The ideological dimension

A further question which it behoves a study of Soviet policy toward Islam to address relates to the place of ideology in its elaboration. Even if, in fact, no conscious, separate policy was consummated, in theory, at least, ideological considerations might play a role in the practical, *ad hoc* decisions which were taken. This issue, too, is not easily resolved.

According to one analysis, made in 1948 by the Research Department of the British Foreign Office, although on the theoretical level there could be no congruence of Marxist-Leninist doctrine and the pillars and main tenets of Islam, 'sufficient tolerance' of Islam was shown by the Soviet government to win 'open support' from Muslim leaders. 'On the part of the Government, national unity has appeared to be a more pressing need than uniform acceptance of Communist doctrine, and on the part of the Muslim leaders [there has been] a readiness to give that support in exchange for toleration of their faith, rather than a genuine abandonment of principle on either side'. Despite this *Realpolitik*, the analysis rejected the feasibility of a permanent *modus vivendi* between the two parties, for the Soviet leadership saw Islam as a world system 'dividing the loyalty of the Soviet citizen' and thus presenting a threat to the Soviet regime not basically different from that posed, for instance, by Roman Catholicism. It was therefore necessary to differentiate between the attitude of tolerance to the Russian Orthodox Church, which was an instrument of Russian nationalism, and to Islam, which was its enemy, as clearly shown in 'a recent condemnation' of Islam as ' "a foreign religion"'.[41]

The logic of this argument notwithstanding, the materials available show that the medium and lower levels of the Central Committee bureaucracy at least tended, in relating to Islam, to give expression to stereotyped positions couched in Marxist-Leninist terminology and concepts. Thus, an inspector of the Administration Department who visited Tajikistan in 1948 reported that the generally unsatisfactory condition in that republic, where the hold of Islam was considerable and ubiquitously manifest, was the result of the inertia of the leadership of its party organs in the field of ideological and political education and the absence of any form of struggle against 'feudal-bai holdovers' and the clergy's 'anti-Soviet activity'.[42] An inspector of the Propaganda Department who toured Kazakhstan the following year prepared a draft Central Committee decree 'On strengthening the struggle against religious and feudal-bai holdovers in the Kazakh SSR' and spoke in similar terms: the Muslim clergy there were extending their influence and activity, aspiring to revive religious ideology and 'disseminate feudal-bai holdovers' among the more backward sector of the population.[43]

Even more striking, Polianskii himself relied on ideological postulates in relating to analyses of the situation which he received from his subordinates. He thus expressed reservations regarding conclusions drawn by CARC's *upolnomochennyi* in the Uzbek SSR based on data from the field, according to which Muslim activity in that republic was on the upswing in the mid-1950s. A growth of religion, he pointed out, 'cannot occur in Soviet reality', as this would necessitate an admission that there was no heightening of the workers' political consciousness. Therefore, the evidence had to be explained differently.[44]

41. Foreign Office Research Department, April 1948; PRO\FO371\71707A, pp.10 and 16. For the perceptiveness of this analysis, see pp.32-3.

42. P. Chepov to A. A. Kuznetsov, 27 July 1948; RTsKhIDNI, f.17, o.132, d.55, ll.3-4.

43. Goncharok to G. M. Malenkov, 5 Nov. 1949; RTsKhIDNI, f.17, o.132, d.258, l.99; for the draft decree, see *ibid.*, ll.106-10.

44. I. V. Polianskii to Kh. N. Iskanderov, 17 Aug. 1955; TsGAUz, f.2456,

Such utterances reflected the ideological backdrop of the party apparatus and senior government officials and the conceptual framework in which they thought and operated. Thus, while CARC rather naturally tended to reflect pragmatic aspects of policy implementation, its officials were all party members, and they were conscious of the ideological implications and impact of developments within the various religions. Moreover, while officially part of the government apparatus, CARC and the CRA were in fact subordinate to the party's central committee to whom they reported and from whom they received instructions. As a result of this dichotomy in their terms of reference, they had, together with their preoccupation with practical questions, to place their work in a broader perspective. This meant, especially in some of their more programmatic appearances, or at discussions which took place in proximity to party congresses, having to speak of the ideological significance of their assignment,[45] and of the fact that they were conducting practical work in the context of a major struggle with an alien ideology and its representatives. Some *upolnomochennye* in fact distinguished between measures which should be taken and those which should not, using the yardstick of their actual or anticipated effectiveness for this confrontation with Islamic practice. For instance, in the Kirgiz SSR in the mid-1950s they pointed out recurrently that the demolition of non-functioning mosques merely offended believers, on occasion even bringing them to renew prayer-meetings in them to prevent their being demolished, and had no connection to the principled struggle against religious ideology and so should be abandoned.[46]

In the words of Polianskii at a CARC session in 1947, the Council's officials as Marxist-Leninists were well aware that religion contradicted the official ideology; it was simply not their task to unmask religious ideology and dwell on the dangers inherent in it. CARC could not afford to lose the confidence of the clergy and the believer community and so had to approach them tactfully

---

o.1, d.175, l.25; and see pp.203 and 437.

45. For example, following the 21st party congress of January 1959, where Khrushchev laid down his programme and timetable for moving from the stage of socialism to communism, CARC's *upolnomochennye* sought to relate their own activity to this broader platform – M. A. Il'baev, Address, Conference of CARC *upolnomochennye*, 18 April 1960; GARF, f.6991, o.3, d.208, l.102.

46. See p.299.

and politely. In this connection Polianskii criticised the *upolnomochennyi* for the Tatar ASSR for his ideological approach to the unregistered mosques in his republic, as if he were still working in the League of the Militant Godless, where he had previously been employed. They had to be opposed by bringing argumentation demonstrating how in practice they violated the law on religion.[47]

At the same time, CARC's *upolnomochennye* maintained contact with the ideological workers in their areas of jurisdiction. Thus, the *upolnomochennyi* in Tajikistan spoke at a republican convention on ideology with the heads of cultural and educational departments and 'other responsible workers' about the correct ways to regulate Muslim activity.[48] Similarly, CARC and CRA officials on periodic visits to the Muslim periphery met with the local ideological apparatus so as to inform them of their findings and conclusions.[49]

According to the head of CARC's section for the Muslim, Jewish and Buddhist faiths in the late 1950s, CARC in fact operated with the ultimate aim of gradually eliminating religious ideology, but since its staff were not workers of the Society for the Dissemination of Political and Scientific Knowledge or the Ministry of Culture they could not condemn or attack it in public. The Council, he insisted, distinguished between clergy and ordinary believers. The latter were 'regular Soviet workers' who were 'infected' with an ideology foreign to Marxism-Leninism and were often, as a result of 'custom and tradition', under the thumb of the clergy. It was CARC's task to help all existing organisations in a general effort to persuade believers to wean themselves from the religious narcotic, but this had to be accomplished without offending their sensitivities. If, for instance, a mosque which had functioned for many years and maintained a normal existence as a religious society sought to register, its request had to be acceded to, for any alternative, such as pretending it did not exist, would

47. Minutes, CARC session No.7, 23-24 April 1947; GARF, f.6991, o.4, d.19, ll.207-9. The League of the Militant Godless had been dismantled during World War II, see p.36. For its activity in the context of Islam, see Bryan, 'Anti-Islamic Propaganda: *Bezbozhnik, 1925-35*', and Keller, *The Struggle against Islam in Uzbekistan, 1921-1941*, Chapter 3.

48. Minutes, CARC session No.18, 20 Dec. 1951; GARF, f.6991, o.3, d.35, l.200.

49. For example, CRA senior legal advisor Barinskaia, who travelled to Bukhara in March 1968 – A. Barinskaia to V. A. Kuroedov, undated [late March-early April 1968]; GARF, f.6991, o.6, d.153, l.116.

be an act of self-deception on CARC's part.[50] This same official attributed major political significance to the measures taken to terminate the activity of *mazars* and other holy places in the wake of the Central Committee resolution of November 1958, arguing that they would in the long run help in the onslaught on the religious ideology that was so strong in some of the Muslim areas, specifically Central Asia and Kazakhstan, Dagestan and Azerbaijan.[51]

CARC and CRA officials, moreover, often attributed the strength of Islam in a given area to the inadequacies of atheistic propaganda. Although the League of the Militant Godless had been disbanded, the regime's ideological arsenal was still in current use against all errant or non-conforming ideologies. While the context, dimensions and content of this propaganda are extraneous to this study,[52] it is necessary to mention some of the discussion surrounding its conduct in the Muslim milieu. Inevitably the officials of Agitprop insisted that improving atheistic propaganda would provide a satisfactory and effective reply to enhanced religiosity, as, indeed, they recommended in 1949 in the face of evidence concerning the vitality of Muslim religious life in the Tatar ASSR.[53] In the localities, party organisations were incessantly resolving to enhance the propaganda effort: in the early 1970s the Fergana Obkom discussed ways of strengthening atheistic propaganda three times in three years.[54] CARC and the CRA, too, encouraged their *upolnomochennye* to improve the information they supplied the republican and oblast' party leadership so as to enable atheistic propaganda to be more efficacious, apparently also on the assumption that this was a *sine qua non* for the ultimate success of anti-religious activity.[55] Both their Moscow personnel and the *upolnomochennye*

50. L. A. Prikhod'ko, Address, All-Union conference of CARC *upolnomochennye*, 25-27 Nov. 1958; GARF, f.6991, o.3, d.165, ll.110-13.

51. L. A. Prikhod'ko, Minutes, CARC session No.4, 25-26 Feb. 1959; GARF, f.6991, o.3, d.183, l.104.

52. For these, see, for example, Ro'i, 'The Task of Creating the New Soviet Man: "Atheistic Propaganda" in the Soviet Muslim Areas'.

53. Draft, AUCP(b) Central Committee resolution 'On strengthening party-mass and cultural-educational work in the Tatar ASSR', undated, [Nov-Dec. 1949]; RTsKhIDNI, f.132, d.109, ll.21-4. The document had in mind not just the Muslim but also the Russian Orthodox 'religious movement' in that republic.

54. D. Malikov, Information, undated [late Aug. 1973]; GARF, f.6991, o.6, d.548, l.46.

55. V. I. Gostev to F. V. Konstantinov, 31 May 1957; GARF, f.6991. o.3,

in the localities made constant reference to the urgency of intensive and effective atheistic propaganda in the Muslim areas.[56]

On the whole, the heads of CAROC and CARC stressed, atheistic propaganda was monotonous and unimaginitive and was usually directed at those who had long ago broken with religion rather than at the actual believer community. Moreover, it failed to bear in mind differences of local conditions and the audiences it addressed, although it was incumbent upon it to use different forms and methods for Russian Orthodox, Muslims and Roman Catholics.[57] Nor did atheistic propaganda manifest the requisite sensitivity for believers' feelings. From time to time, the believer community would lodge a complaint that propagandists trampled upon their susceptibilities, abusing them and their faith. One *raikom* secretary in Kirgiziia had told believers, whom he compelled the local imam to bring to hear him lecture, that Islam was a reactionary ideology and that they, like the 'Anglo-American imperialists', obstructed the construction of a communist society. The imam, passing on their complaint, said that insult had been added to injury in that his congregation had been forced to applaud at the conclusion of the lecture.[58]

Atheistic propaganda picked up somewhat during Khrushchev's anti-religious campaign, when major efforts were made to increase its intensity and ameliorate its content.[59] Following the November 1958 CPSU Central Committee resolution on the termination of pilgrimages to holy sites, the party central committees in the Muslim republics convened all the heads of *obkom* agitprop departments, editors of republican newspapers and the chiefs of other ministries and departments engaged in ideological work to discuss ways of improving it in light of that resolution. In Uzbekistan, for example, CARC's *upolnomochennye* prepared memoranda on religiosity in

d.146, l.88.

56. For example, Iu. Bilialov, Report, sent by K. Ruzmetov to V. A. Kuroedov, 18 June 1973; GARF, f.6991, o.6, d.545, ll.174-5.

57. G. Karpov and A. Puzin to the CPSU Central Committee, 27 Nov. 1957; GARF, f.6991, o.3, d.148, l.66.

58. H. Akhtiamov to I. V. Polianskii, 18 Sept. 1951; GARF, f.6991, o.3, d.454, ll.129-31.

59. See, for example, Report of the CARC *upolnomochennyi* for the Tatar ASSR, CARC session No.21, 22 July 1959; this tendency was augmented after the June 1963 Central Committee plenum on ideology – see Minutes, CARC session No.1, 7 Jan. 1964; GARF, f.6991, o.3, d.184, l.178, and o.4, d.146, ll.4-8.

the various oblasti so as to enable atheistic propaganda to relate to actual facts; while in Turkmenistan party resolutions obliged organisations in the localities to strive to convince workers to discontinue pilgrimages, as closures of holy places were to be accomplished with the approval of the local inhabitants.[60] In some parts, at least, special propaganda was conducted among women by women atheist propagandists.[61]

Atheistic propaganda among Muslims slackened or, in certain areas at least, actually disintegrated in the course of the decade after the anti-religious campaign let up. In the late 1960s a senior CRA official criticised atheist propagandists for not studying the information made available by the Council's *upolnomochennye* on such relevant themes as the content of sermons in the mosques, the celebration of the fast and festivals and the activity of the unregistered associations, as a result of all of which atheistic propaganda remained abstract and detached from reality.[62] Unquestionably, the councils had an interest in shifting responsibility for the failure to come to grips with religious activity onto the cadres who engaged in atheistic propaganda and were subordinate to other hierarchies (Znanie or the ideological apparatus), yet they seem to have had sufficient grounds for their contentions. Similar arguments were voiced periodically by other organs as well. Local government certainly remained aloof from the requirements and exigencies of the general propaganda effort. The Jambul Oblast' leadership, for example, explained the dearth of atheistic propaganda in that oblast' at the end of the 1960s by insisting that Islam did not exist there, and insofar as it did, was innocuous. Investigation of the situation in that region disclosed that Kazakh and Uzbek atheistic lecturers were literally fearful of conducting atheistic propaganda among their fellow nationals.[63] (It is self-evident that propaganda conducted among the indigenous nationalities of the Muslim areas by Russians in Russian was doomed to failure *a priori*.)

60. Minutes, CARC session No.4, 25-26 Feb. 1959; GARF, f.6991, o.3, d.183, ll.37 and 50. And see pp.378-9. (The closures of mosques in the period of the Khrushchev anti-religious campaign were similarly 'approved' by the local population, see pp.211-2.)

61. For example, in Dagestan, Minutes, CARC sessions No.1, 7 Jan. 1964, and No.24, 27 Aug. 1964; GARF, f.6991, o.4, d.146, l.7, and d.147, l.84.

62. V. A. Kuroedov to the CPSU Central Committee Propaganda Department, 23 May 1969; TsKhSD, f.5, r.9849, o.61, d.32, l.108.

63. E. Bairamov, Information 13 Jan. 1969; GARF, f.6991, o.6, d.153, ll.52-3.

The most serious problem connected with atheistic propaganda was perhaps against whom to direct it. The obvious adversary was clearly the Muslim establishment, yet by attacking the registered clergy and the spiritual directorates, the propagandist was tacitly endorsing the activity of the unregistered mullas. Given their very different, almost opposing, characteristics it was well-nigh impossible to turn the attention of the audience to both simultaneously.

The propaganda machine was well-oiled for denouncing the theories of the Muslim establishment regarding the compatibility of Islam and communism, as designed to strengthen Islam's position and prevent believers from breaking with religion,[64] and for high-lighting the corruption and immorality of the spiritual directorates. Here was an adversary who was more visible, whose activities and standpoints were more tangible and so perhaps easier to refute. Yet, rejecting or ridiculing the official clergy was totally irrelevant to the popularity of the more ubiquitous unregistered clergy, who were no less adamant in rejecting the co-habitation of Islam and the Soviet regime and the sycophancy, as they saw it, of the Muslim establishment with all its ideological, political and material implications. Thus, propaganda that pointed its arrows at those very clerics which the government supported and legitimised was letting off the hook, almost validating, those who constituted a more real danger or threat, who kept Islam alive in places without registered mosques and prevented the establishment from making far-reaching compromises.[65]

Hardly less poignant was the task of pinpointing the ideological threat of Islam. Many of the studies of this alleged danger rang decidedly hollow. One of the old ideological bogeys that loomed from time to time in these studies and in the documentation of the postwar period was Pan-Islam, which connoted that Muslim believers could not be trusted politically. Its origin dated back to pre-revolutionary times, when the Ottoman Sultan with whom Russia was recurrently at war claimed the title of caliph of the Sunni Muslims, so that a strengthened Islamic identity inside Russia might engender political disloyalty.[66] In the context of a discussion

64. *Islam v SSSR*, p.115.

65. See Ro'i, 'The Task of Creating the New Soviet Man', p.41.

66. 'The tsarist government', according to one scholar, 'judged the solidarity of Islam under the the leadership of the Ottoman sultan to be a menace to the unity and power of the empire' – Brower, 'Islam and Ethnicity: Russian Colonial

of Islam in Tajikistan in early 1947, CARC deputy chairman Sadovskii contended that that republic was a cause of constant concern, among other reasons because of signs that Pan-Islam, which had 'always been of major significance' was being revived.[67] CARC's *upolnomochennyi* in Turkmenistan maintained in the same time period that Pan-Islamic ideas and those of its ally, Pan-Turkism, were discernible among the itinerant mullas, a contention which seemed untenable to his superiors in Moscow.[68] Press reports from Komsomol congresses in Kirgiziia and Uzbekistan in the early 1950s likewise cautioned against manifestations of Pan-Islam and Pan-Turkism.[69] Given the atmosphere of the times, however, and the mounting campaign against symptoms of nationalism in Central Asian literature, some of which was specifically condemned for its Islamic content and connotations,[70] this can hardly be taken as valid testimony of the actual prevalence of these ideologies. There was little genuine evidence of Muslim believers sensing any real attachment to the *umma*, the universal community of Islam.

Works written on Islam in the Soviet Union, which were undoubtedly commissioned in order to serve political ends – as were so many allegedly academic books and papers in the Soviet period – inevitably dwelt, among other things, on its ideological dimensions. One such book, published in the early 1970s, maintained that the rites of Islam were designed to help spread its ideology and convince believers of the truthfulness of its teachings.[71] This, too, appears a somewhat meaningless and toothless statement, probably ensuing from the need for such a study to pay lip service to the ideological implications of enhanced Islamic practice.

Certainly, CARC and the CRA observed and attached considerable

---

Policy in Turkestan', p.119.

67. CARC session No.4, 29 Jan. 1947; GARF, f.6991, o.4, d.19, ll.89-90.

68. CARC session No.13, 10-11 July 1947; GARF, f.6991, o.4, d.19, ll.424-5. Pan-Turkism in the context of the international situation of the late 19th and early 20th century had similar implications to those of Pan-Islam from the point of view of the tsarist authorities, although its terms of reference were secular and based on ethnic and cultural, rather than religious, affinity.

69. One delegate, for example, at a congress of Uzbekistan's Komsomol in February 1952 called on that organisation to struggle against manifestations of bourgeois nationalism, Pan-Islam and Pan-Turkism – Memorandum sent by Paul Grey to Anthony Eden, 19 March 1952; PRO/FO371/100817.

70. See p.688.

71. Ashirov, *Evoliutsiia islama v SSSR*, p.133.

importance to changes which appeared to be occurring in the ideology of Islam as it modernised and adapted to Soviet conditions.[72] In some parts, too, *upolnomochennye* reported that the clergy were trying to initiate a 'process of integrating religious and tribal [or clan] ideology'.[73] Yet, while such observations clearly reflected an interest in, and awareness of, the ideological dimension of their object of study, one must beware of concluding that considerations of ideology constituted a major force behind decision making relating to Islam, even on the level of those *ad hoc* decisions which the Councils were empowered to make, or behind recommendations they periodically put to the Central Committee. Conscious of the necessity of conducting a struggle against Islam on an ideological as well as a practical level, the Councils' leadership was not oblivious to the basic irrelevance of this dimension and to the fact that it so often seemed to miss the mark and even sometimes actually aroused or exacerbated difficulties.

Questions of internal security

In addition to the ideological dimension, policy implementation toward Islam and the Muslim community entailed, at least by Soviet criteria, questions of security and the preservation of public order. True, the Soviet regime, or most of its representatives, apparently entertained doubts as to whether Islam constituted a real political, social or security threat – in any case, until the Khomeini revolution in Iran and the deterioration of the situation in Afghanistan, both in 1978-79. Nonetheless, the security organs were implicated in several aspects of the treatment of Muslim religious organisations and associations, as they were of that of other religions. In some years at least they received CARC's annual reports on the situation within the country's various religions. Moreover, they had special agents and collaborators to take part

72. For example, the CRA plan for its conference of *upolnomochennye* in the Muslim areas – A. A. Barmenkov to CPSU Central Committee Department for Propaganda, 19 June 1968; GARF, f.6991, o.6, d.147, l.47. One of the lectures at the 1968 conference was to be called 'Basic trends of the modernisation of the ideology and cult of Islam in the USSR'. For a further discussion of the adaptability of Islam, see pp.253-7.

73. Zh. Botashev to V. A. Kuroedov, 17 Nov. 1969; GARF, f.6991, o.6, d.220, l.147. The original used the term *rodovoi*. For a discussion of Islam and nationalism, see Chapter 12.

in 'the struggle with the reactionary part of the Muslim clergy'. One of these in 1980 was deputy chairman of SADUM and head of the USSR's Muslim organisations' Department of Foreign Ties Azam Alyakbarov[74]

Some of the documentation reveals the spectrum of NKVD/ KGB activity, even though the KGB archives are not open to researchers. Its staff engaged in investigating the level of religiosity by observing and looking into actual cases of religious practice, unstatutory examples of which they duly reported. For example, they would inform the authorities of instances of collective circumcision or of mullas performing funeral services in accordance with Islamic ritual for persons whose death had not been reported to ZAGS. They also intimidated believers into retracting applications to register their religious societies.[75] Attempts to threaten or frighten believers and clergy seem indeed not to have been uncommon. In Azerbaijan, for instance, believers lodged a complaint that the head of the raion MVD called in a muezzin and warned him not to perform the *azan*, summoning believers to prayer, from the mosque minaret.[76] In North Kazakhstan Muslim believers complained that NKVD troops had violated their cemetery.[77] In some parts, at least, the security organs provided CARC's *upolnomochennye* with lists of itinerant and other unregistered mullas, the *upolnomochennye* not possessing the means to undertake a task which necessitated an intimate acquaintance with all the settlements and localities in the entire area under their jurisdiction.[78]

In 1946 Minister of State Security Viktor Abakumov himself informed Voroshilov of the findings of an MGB report from

74. Corley, *Religion in the Soviet Union*, pp.366 and 369, quoting from a report on the work of the KGB 5th Directorate's 4th Department. For the role of the security organs in implementing policy toward religion in general, see pp.17-9.

75. Excerpts from reports of CARC *upolnomochennye* for the first quarter of 1945, undated, and I. V. Polianskii to Kh. N. Iskanderov, M. Sh. Karimov, B. A. Shahbazbekov and I. Zakaryaev, 26 Aug. 1947; GARF, f.6991, o.3, d.12, ll.67-8, and TsGAUz, f.2456, o.1, d.82, l.27. For the role of fear in deterring believers from filing applications to register religious societies, see pp.187-93.

76. Appendix, CARC session No.14s, 21 June 1949; GARF, f.6991, o.3, d.60, l.32.

77. V. Liapunov to N. Sabitov, 5 June 1945; GARF, f.6991, o.3, d.29, l.85. (The document should probably be dated 5 July.)

78. For instance, in Turkmenistan – Minutes, CARC session No.13, 10-11 July 1947; GARF, f.6991, o.4, d.19, l.415.

Uzbekistan, which gave details about how the official Muslim clergy in that republic had allegedly stirred up religious and anti-Soviet activity. Abakumov wrote that some of the more 'reactionarily-inclined' registered clergy were spreading rumours to the effect that religious rites were being permitted in the USSR as a result of British and American pressure, that soon demands would be put to Moscow to disband the kolkhozy and allow free trade, and that the establishment of British influence was imminent in Uzbekistan, which would be separated from the USSR.[79] In other words, Abakumov was suggesting that the Islamic revival in Central Asia was seen by the indigenous population as resulting from a serious weakening of the Soviet regime and was likely to lead to meaningful political discontent, which might threaten Soviet rule there. Unquestionably, the inference was that, in order to preempt any such development, steps had to be taken to restore law and order and the requisite measure of Soviet authority – or, to put it simply, a renewed repression was on the cards.

All activity that was connected with foreign countries or with the dissemination of literature emanating from the religions establishment inevitably fell under the jurisdiction of the security organs.[80] In 1944 the NKGB approached the AUCP(b) Central Committee Secretariat with a proposal to disseminate the 'patriotic' appeals of the founding conferences of DUMZ and DUMSK. It suggested that the former be put out in 10,000 copies: 6,000 in Azeri, of which 4,000 would be distributed in the Azerbaijan SSR, 500 each among Azerbaijanis in Georgia and Armenia, and 1,000 in Iranian Azerbaijan; 2,000 in Persian for distribution in Iranian Azerbaijan; 1,000 in Arabic for the countries of the Arab East; and 1,000 in Turkish for distribution among Muslims in the Ajar and Abkhaz ASSRs and in Turkey. The DUMSK appeal and congratulatory telegram to Stalin were to be translated into the languages of the North Caucasian nationalities and distributed in 5,000 copies.[81] Contacts between Muslim officials and foreign

79. V. A. Abakumov to K. E. Voroshilov, 12 Sept. 1946; GARF, f.6991, o.3, d.34, ll.195-6. Abakumov also informed Zhdanov of the report.

80. For their role in the system of formal censorship, see Knight, *The KGB*, pp.202-3.

81. Fedotov to A. S. Shcherbakov, 6 June 1944, and Deputy Commissar Kobulov to Shcherbakov, 15 July 1944; RTsKhIDNI, f.17, o.125, d.261, ll.27 and 47, see also p.113. For the founding conferences of DUMZ and DUMSK, see p.105.

delegations would regularly be reported to the security organs.[82] In one document Polianskii wrote to the deputy head of the MVD's 11th Administration of the undesirability of leaving in circulation a publication on Islam from the prewar period whose positions were no longer relevant, not corresponding to the current line of atheistic propaganda.[83]

Inevitably, the secret police had to acquiesce in the selection of believers allowed to make the *hajj*;[84] each year there would be candidates whom they did not endorse. On one occasion SADUM presented to CARC's *upolnomochennyi* in Tashkent a list of ninety-five candidates which he passed on to the republican KGB. Only thirteen were approved by the KGB.[85] Likewise, when the *hajjis* returned to the Soviet Union, the security organs heard of their doings and meetings and received their reports.[86] Almost certainly in each such delegation there was at least one person who, if not actually a KGB agent, collaborated actively with the security forces. The connection created with Muslim clergy who travelled abroad – in whatever capacity – had long term consequences, creating a group of people on whom the KGB had detailed information and often a certain leverage. A 1985 KGB report stated simply that 'a subsidiary card index had been created on representatives of the Muslim clergy in the USSR who have been abroad at some time, which will facilitate the conducting of better directed counter – intelligence work in this milieu'. In 1983 two actual KGB agents in the Muslim clerical establishment participated in the Soviet Muslim delegation to the 8th session of the World Peace Conference and, having returned via Saudi Arabia and Egypt,

82. For example, Kh. N. Iskanderov to I. V. Polianskii, N. S. Muhitdinov, S. K. Kamalov and Uzbek SSR KGB chief Hafizov, 8 June 1954; TsGAUz, f.2456, o.1, d.162, ll.191-2.

83. I. V. Polianskii to I. A. Isachenko, 21 May 1953; GARF, f.6991, o.3, d.96, l.58. This was the period when the MVD and MGB were amalgamated under Beriia; presumably, the 11th Administration was responsible for censorship and the dissemination of literature.

84. See Chapter 3, n.296.

85. Kh. N. Iskanderov to I. V. Polianskii, G. S. Sultanov and Kh. G. Gulamov, 1 July 1955; TsGAUz, f.2456, o.1, d.174, ll.14-16.

86. For example, I. V. Polianskii to G. M. Malenkov, N. S. Khrushchev, V. M. Molotov and Minister of Internal Affairs S. N. Kruglov, 30 Sept. 1953; GARF, f.6991, o.3, d.93, ll.231-8.

'presented information of operational value'.[87]

Appointments to senior posts in the Muslim hierarchy, notably in the spiritual directorates, whose leading officials met with foreign guests, or even to the post of imam or *imam-khatib* in some of the more 'sensitive' locations, i.e. in mosques frequented by foreigners, were subject to KGB endorsement. In 1954 over three years after the death of the first chairman of DUMSK, Dagestan Obkom Secretary Daniyalov consulted with the republican KGB chief as to whether his former deputy and acting successor was suitable for the job. After receiving a positive reply, he informed Polianskii that he had no objection to his appointment.[88] When a dispute broke out in 1956 between the Shaykh-ul-Islam and his deputy, the DUMZ Sunni mufti, the head of CARC's department for Islam, Judaism and Buddhism was dispatched to Baku to see if they could be reconciled. Among others whom he consulted were two KGB officials, who agreed with the view apparently held by everyone else that there was no alternative to the dismissal of the mufti.[89] This same official also consulted with the local KGB regarding the desirability of vacating the precincts of a former mosque in Batumi, the capital of the Ajar ASSR, where nineteen families resided, just one prayer-hall being at the disposal of the city's believers, and about the person who should serve as its imam. Eventually, after meeting with all concerned, the visitor from Moscow and the KGB chief were received together by the republic's *obkom* secretary.[90]

CARC officials touring the Muslim periphery would meet with KGB officials even when their missions were not connected to questions of personnel (such as appointments or dismissals). This held especially for areas which were considered particularly sensitive. When one CARC inspector visited the Chechen-Ingush ASSR shortly after the return of the deportees, he was briefed on the level of religiosity by the KGB.[91] A CRA official, who was sent

87. Quoted in Corley, *Religion in the Soviet Union*, pp.368 and 373.

88. I. V. Polianskii, Resumé, undated [21 Sept. 1954]; GARF, f.6991, o.3, d.101, l.114.

89. L. A. Prikhod'ko to I. V. Polianskii, 5 May 1956; GARF, f.6991, o.3, d.127, l.52. For the dispute between the Shaykh-ul-Islam and his deputy and Prikhod'ko's visit to Baku, see p.178.

90. *Ibid.*, l.57. And see Chapter 4, n.450.

91. P. A. Zadorozhnyi to A. A. Puzin, 30 Aug. 1960; GARF, f.6991, o.3,

to Bukhara Oblast' in 1968 to look into the situation of Islam there, discussed her findings with the *obkom* secretary for ideology and propaganda, the *oblispolkom* deputy chairman, the deputy head of the KGB oblast' administration and the head of its 5th department.[92] Another, visiting Nakhichevan in 1973, also met with KGB officials, who informed him that the region's so-called holy places were the focus of religious life and constituted the embodiment of the 'evil of religion'.[93]

During the period of Khrushchev's anti-religious campaign, when society organised to disband unregistered religious associations, KGB officials were included in groups which formed at *raiispolkoms* to terminate their activity and that of their mullas. Instances of such participation were reported from Kazakhstan in 1960; the task of the KGB representatives in these groups was to draw up lists of the members of these associations, which would then be sent through the *gor-* and *rai-ispolkom* to the relevant workplaces. These KGB officials would themselves speak at meetings held in the workplace to pass on information concerning the activity of the relevant offender.[94] In some places, at least, KGB employees were included in the commissions of assistance set up at local soviet executive committees to help ensure the implementation of the legislation on religion.[95]

Inevitably, too, the KGB and other organs connected with the preservation of law and order were involved in the discussion of criminal proceedings initiated against believers and religious associations in these same years.[96] Instigating criminal proceedings

---

d.207, l.44.

92. A. Barinskaia to V. A Kuroedov, undated [late March-early April 1968]; GARF, f.6991, o.6, d.153, l.116. See also above. The KGB's 5th Chief Directorate was created in the late 1960s to combat political dissent (replacing the 2nd Chief Directorate), its special operational departments including one for religious dissent and another for ethnic minorities – Knight, *The KGB*, p.123.

93. See p.381.

94. K. V. Ovchinnikov and Rumiantsev, Report, 10 June 1960; GARF, f.6991, o.3, d.205, ll.27-9. See also p.312.

95. For these commissions, see pp.45-6.

96. An all-union conference of CARC *upolnomochennye* convened in Moscow in 1964 was attended by representatives of the USSR Council of Ministers juridical commission, the supreme court and the procuracy (both all-union and RSFSR), the KGB and the RSFSR Ministry for the Defence of Public Order (MOOP) – Minutes, All-Union conference, 25-26 June 1964; GARF, f.6991, o.3, d.1457, l.1. Some, at least, of the crimes of which religious personnel were

against clergy and other members of the religious *aktiv*, which had been so common a procedure in the 1920s and 1930s, was not unknown in Stalin's last years despite the more favourable course followed by the regime. In 1946 the MGB arrested a former member of the executive organ of the Muslim religious society in Kokand, who was also the former *imam-khatib* of the town's registered mosque, on charges of anti-Soviet activity.[97] Criminal proceedings were launched against clergy accused of violating public order at the Shoh-i Mardon *mazar* in Fergana Oblast' in three consecutive years (1947–9).[98] And the Samarkand Oblispolkom passed a resolution in the early 1950s to initiate proceedings against a number of leading members of one of Samarkand's religious societies. The public prosecutor was asked to push forward with these on the grounds that the religious society lacked the requisite standard contract with the local administration allowing it to use the mosque for prayer-meetings; that some members of the clergy used the mosque for residential purposes; that the clergy engaged in charity as a means of religious propaganda, giving out to the 'needy' bread donated to the religions society; that religious rites were performed in the home of the imam, who refused to register; that contributions were collected by compulsion and part of them had been allotted to the imam and muezzin to pay their taxes; and that both clerics had performed religious rites beyond the confines of the religious society's established zone of activity, that is, outside the raion in which it was situated.[99] One prominent non-establishment Islamic figure was arrested in 1951 in the Karakalpak ASSR and died in prison.[100]

These instances seem indeed to have occurred mainly in Uzbekistan, although activities described as criminal on the part of religious personnel were recorded in other areas as well. In Saratov, for instance, a 'rogue' evoked 'artificial religious activity' among

---

frequently accused, such as anti-Soviet agitation and propaganda, came under the regular purview of the KGB – Knight, *The KGB*, pp.317-20.

97. Khamidullin to I. V. Polianskii, 28 Dec. 1946; TsGAUz, f.2456, o.1, d.72, l.59.

98. A. Abdurahmanov to K. E. Voroshilov, 24 March 1950; GARF, f.6991, o.3, d.68, l.37.

99. Samarkand Oblispolkom resolution, 2 Feb. 1951; TsGAUz, f.2456, o.2, d.135, ll.13-14.

100. See p.404. For the conviction of *ishans* in Turkmenistan in 1950, see p.402.

Muslim believers and slandered the local organs of government (who persisted in refusing to open a mosque there).[101] In the Abkhaz ASSR even in the mid-1950s, when in the country at large the situation regarding religion was at its most lenient, a believer was fined for committing deceitful deeds of a religious character and receiving remuneration, performing the *namaz* in his home and conducting rites – circumcision, *nikoh*, ceremonial washing of the dead and reading prayers for the deceased – despite being unregistered.[102]

Already prior to the expanded incidence of the use of the judiciary against religion as of 1961-2 there were a growing number of cases as Khrushchev's anti-religious campaign gathered momentum. CARC resolved to approach the Tajik SSR Council of Ministers in 1958 to ask that criminal proceedings be initiated against a certain *ishan*.[103] In Uzbekistan similar steps were taken sporadically against shaykhs, *ishans* and others who operated at *mazars*, and fines would be imposed on them (according to one source, at least, with little effect).[104] In early 1961 CARC endorsed a decision to undertake criminal proceedings against those guilty of constructing a new mosque in a village in Orenburg Oblast'.[105]

In mid-1964 Puzin pointed out that the Central Asian republics' criminal codes had special articles defining criminal responsibility for fraudulent acts intended to evoke superstition among the masses and extract material benefit therefrom. The CARC *upolnomochennyi* for Tajikistan suggested that these be applied by initiating criminal proceedings, for instance, against those who taught religion to children and opened prayer-houses without authorisation and called for adding articles to the republican criminal code to enable the punishment of transgressors in both such categories as criminals.[106] Indeed, court proceedings for offences in the realm of religion

101. Theses, Minutes, CARC session No.24s, 25 Sept. 1952; GARF, f.6991, o.3, d.83, l.259; see also p.334. For the position of the local authorities in Saratov, see pp.652-3.

102. Memorandum, Reception by L. A. Prikhod'ko of Haki Dmitrievich Tarba, 29 June 1955; GARF, f.6991, o.4, d.37, l.132.

103. See p.404.

104. Reception by K. F. Tagirov and A. S. Tazetdinov of Idris Rahmatulla, 3 Oct. 1958; GARF, f.6991, o.4, d.88, l.210.

105. Minutes, CARC session No.2, 12 Jan. 1961; GARF, f.6991, o.3, d.1361, ll.5-6.

106. Minutes, All-Union conference of CARC *upolnomochennye*, 25-26 June 1964; GARF, f.6991, o.3, d.1457, ll.26 and 47. For this conference, see n.96 above.

seem to have been most common in Uzbekistan and Tajikistan. In the former republic twenty-four people were brought to trial in 1963 and sixteen in 1964 for taking advantage of people's 'superstitions' and encroaching upon the rights of citizens under the guise of performing religious rites. In the latter republic twenty-one 'charlatans' were brought to justice in the year 1963 for a variety of crimes: parasitism, charlatanism, faith-healing, marrying off adolescents, polygamy, opening mosques without authorisation (and in one case organising an opium den there), and teaching children Qur'an. A further 106 people received prison-terms for engaging in 'feudal-bai survivals': seventy for giving out adolescent girls in marriage, twenty-nine for practising polygamy, and seven for paying or receiving *qalym*.[107]

In the Chechen–Ingush ASSR, too, a large number of criminal cases were initiated against believers connected with the various Sufi *tariqas* and *wirds* either in the courts or, in more outlying rural parts, at public meetings and 'citizens' assemblies'. In the year 1964, for instance, as a result of the discussion at, and resolutions adopted by, such assemblies, eight Muslim clergy repudiated their religious activity in the media, nineteen were banished from the republic and a further seven cautioned.[108]

Even after the Khrushchev anti-religious campaign subsided, 'deceiving the population with an end to evoking religious superstitions' or 'taking advantage of religious superstitions in order to extract material benefit' continued to be considered criminal.[109] The CRA *upolnomchennyi* in Azerbaijan called on the republican government to conduct criminal proceedings against people who engaged in self-torture on Ashura.[110] His colleague in Uzbekistan complained that the republic's administrative organs refrained from taking advantage of their privilege to punish charlatan itinerant

107. M. Hamidov to A. A. Puzin, 24 Feb. 1964, and Appendix No.1, and P. Krishoveev to Puzin, 3 July 1965; GARF, f.6991, o.3, d.1740, ll.26-7 and 34-5, and d.1490, l.51. For the relevant articles in the criminal codes of the RSFSR and some of the Muslim union republics, see *Zakonodatel'stvo o religioznykh kul'takh*, pp.197-202.

108. A. Alisov to A. A. Puzin, 3 Feb. 1965; GARF, f.6991, o.3, d.1609, l.27. See also p.349.

109. A. Ahadov, Information, undated [probably late Oct. 1969]; GARF, f.6991, o.6, d.220, l.21.

110. M. Shamsadinskii to I. I. Brazhnin, 19 Sept. 1966; GARF, f.6991, o.6, d.11, l.2.

mullas by legal means.[111] And a draft decree was drawn up by the CRA authorising the Kazakh SSR procuracy to take the necessary measures to enhance the struggle against criminal violations by the clergy and religious associations of the law on religion.[112]

Trials of unregistered clergy in fact continued in the post-Khrushchev period. One cleric, for instance, was tried in Samarkand Oblast' in 1966 and sentenced to three years' 'deprivation of freedom' for engaging in healing with 'holy water' at a place of pilgrimage. An *ishan* who visited *murids* in a number of kolkhozy in Kashka-Darya Oblast' was also brought to justice.[113] In Bukhara, at the solicitation of the CRA *upolnomochennyi*, criminal proceedings were instigated against the guard at the Baha ad-Din mausoleum, who organised pilgrimages there, reading excerpts from the Qur'an and telling 'cock-and-bull stories' about Baha ad-Din.[114] The activities of six clerics were discussed at meetings of *mahalla* committees in Namangan in 1971, with the participation of representatives from kishlak soviets: they had opened mosques illegally, treated the sick and taught children religion.[115] In the same year in Chust in Namangan Oblast', sixteen clergy were convicted for conducting rites in private homes – for which they had received remuneration – and in some cases for practising faith-healing as well.[116] A number of vagrants in the Karakalpak ASSR had criminal proceedings brought against them,[117] and in Fergana Oblast' and in Dagestan people who engaged in

111. M. Miragzamov to M. Kh. Khalmuhamedov, 22 Oct. 1966; GARF, f.6991, o.6, d.11, l.65. For the former, see p.405.

112. Signed by A. Barmenkov, A. Nurullaev and a third person whose signature is illegible, and dated 27 May 1969, it was sent by Kuroedov to CRA *upolnomochennyi* for Kazakhstan K. Kulumbetov; GARF, f.6991, o.6, d.223, ll.22-3.

113. M. Miragzamov to Khalmuhamedov, 22 Oct. 1966; GARF, f.6991, o.6, d.11, l.66. It is not clear whether the stories related to the powers of the *mazar* or of Baba al-Din Naqshbandi who was supposedly buried there.

114. A. Barinskaia to V. A. Kuroedov, undated [late March-early April 1968]; GARF, f.6991, o.6, d.153, l.111.

115. D. M. Malikov and M. U. Aliev, Information, sent by K. Razmetov to A. A. Nurullaev, 24 June 1974; GARF, f.6991, o.6, d.634, ll.45-6.

116. P. Krivosheev, Survey, undated [probably July 1973]; GARF, f.6991, o.6, d.548, l.50.

117. See below.

teaching Islam to children were tried in court.[118] Just the threat of criminal punishment was sufficient to put an end to the activity in Uzbekistan of the Ahl-i Qur'an 'sect', as the Soviet authorities insisted on calling them, in the early-mid 1970s.[119]

Toward the end of the 1960s the deputy head of the Investigation Administration of the Uzbek SSR MVD became a member of the coordinating council under the auspices of the republican CRA *upolnomochennyi* for carrying out and applying the legislation on religion.[120] The draft decree on enhancing implementation of these laws in the Kazakh SSR contained an article proposing that the republican MVD expose and forestall crimes committed in connection with religion and put an end to vagrancy and begging at prayer-houses.[121] In fact, the Uzbek SSR MVD succeeded in infiltrating groups of vagrants and beggars and people who sold and distributed religious literature at prayer-houses and holy places. The MVD reported that during the course of the year 1970 alone over 800 people were detained at prayer-houses for begging and vagrancy: of these 114 were placed in jobs, 112 'called to book administratively', and 532 cautioned to stop begging and find jobs. In the Karakalpak ASSR the MVD exposed in 1970 and the first half of 1971 thirty-five able-bodied men who engaged in begging at mosques and filled the role of shaykhs at holy sites. And the militia set up road blocks in order to prohibit the passage of all types of transport to such sites. The local MVD even prepared and sent in recommendations regarding the application of the Uzbek SSR Supreme Soviet decree 'On enhancing the struggle against vagrancy'.[122]

The role of the security organs in dealing with religious activity

118. CRA reports, delivered to the CPSU Central Committee, 22 May 1970 and 27 April 1971; TsKhSD, f.5, o.62, d.38, 139, and o.63, d.89, l.138.

119. See p.425.

120. Decree, Uzbek SSR Council of Ministers, Appendix No.1, 7 Feb. 1969; GARF, f.6991, o.6, d.223, l.87.

121. Draft decree, 27 May 1969 – see n.112 above.

122. CRA report, delivered to the CPSU Central Committee, 27 April 1971 –TsKhD, f.5, o.63, d.89, l.136; P. Krivosheev, Information, 30 July 1971, and Survey, 25 Dec. 1972, and D. Erekeshev to K. R. Ruzmetov, 14 May 1973 –GARF, f.6991, o.6, d.370, l.102, d.548, l.50, and d.629, l.170. 10 of the 35 were placed in invalid homes, 11 were found jobs, eight were given into the custody of relatives, four departed the republic and criminal proceedings were brought against two.

was institutionalised in other republics as well. In Kazakhstan the unsatisfactory monitoring of observance of legislation on religion was attributed by one *oblispolkom* resolution to a number of factors, one of them being the failure of the oblast' MVD to stop the clergy's anti-social conduct.[123] In Azerbaijan the CRA *upolnomochennyi* collaborated with the KGB and MVD and 'other organisations' in prophylactic work designed to prevent the turning of historical monuments preserved by the state into 'holy places'.[124]

In at least one union and one autonomous republic the KGB seems to have been particularly aware of a possible threat to local security from Islam. In Tajikistan, as of the early 1960s, CARC *upolnomochennye* reported regularly to the KGB chief on trends and developments within the republic's Muslim community, and not just to the republican first secretary and chairman of the council of ministers as was the custom.[125] It is not clear whether the danger was thought to be internal, given the vitality of Islam in Tajikistan and the physical inaccessibility of so many of its strongholds, or to have emanated from neighbouring Afghanistan, in view of the vulnerability of considerable sections of the border.

In the Nakhichevan ASSR, beyond any doubt, the KGB was blatantly concerned about the infiltration of Islamic influences from Iran, at least as of the early 1970s. It reported the persistent religious propaganda being broadcast by Iranian radio stations, inscriptions of a religious content which appeared on the hills in Iranian territory and were clearly visible on the Soviet side, and the demonstratively noisy performance of the *shahsei-vahsei* in the proximity of the Soviet border.[126] Needless to say, this apprehension was exacerbated by the events in Iran toward the end of the 1970s, by which time it attracted the attention of the Azerbaijani top leadership. At a meeting in December 1980 to celebrate the sixtieth anniversary of the Azerbaijan SSR's Cheka, republican

123. Aktiubinsk Oblispolkom resolution, 28 Dec. 1973; GARF, f.6991, o.6, d.637, l.3.

124. List, 'Cultural monuments preserved by the state as cultural monuments and in use as "holy places"', 30 May 1973; GARF, f.6991, o.6, d.537, l.195.

125. For the important role played by the security services in Tajikistan, see Rakowska-Harmstone, *Russia and Nationalism in Central Asia*, p.119. From 1958-63 S. K. Tsvigun was KGB chief in Tajikistan and was simultaneously a member of the Tajikistan CP Central Committee Bureau.

126. I. Bonchkovskii to E. I. Lisavtsev, 1 June 1973; GARF, f.6991, o.6, d.537, l.177.

first secretary Heydar Aliev stressed the need for more effective security measures in that republic in view of the 'increasingly complex international situation, especially in the region of the Near East in states immediately adjacent to the southern borders of our country'. The head of the republican KGB had been yet more specific in an article he published a few days before: 'In connection with the situation in Iran and Afghanistan', he wrote, 'the US special services are trying to use the Islamic religion as one of the factors in influencing the political situation in our country, especially in places with a Muslim population'. The ideological subversions currently subject to 'chekist' suppression in Azerbaijan included the 'anti-social activities of the sectarian underground and the reactionary Muslim clergy'.[127]

Considerations of foreign policy

One issue which kept cropping up in discussions of the attitude to be taken towards Islam, whose weight in actual policy-making is extremely difficult to gauge, was the importance of domestic Islam for Soviet foreign policy. While actual contacts with the Muslim world outside are extraneous to this study,[128] it is necessary to at least broach the question: how far did considerations of foreign policy influence decision making and practical measures relating to Soviet Islam?

From its earliest stages the Soviet leadership had been conscious of the criticism levelled against it on account of its treatment of Islam (and, indeed, religion as a whole). It has been suggested that the prime motivation behind concessions made to religion in the Soviet Union was the desire to conciliate foreign critics.[129] Be this as it may, from the time of the establishment of the spiritual directorates, voices were being heard at high levels of the political élite on the desirability of demonstrating to potential well-wishers in the Muslim world that the freedom of worship promised by the Soviet constitution was being realised in the

127. *Bakinskii rabochii*, 19 and 25 Dec. 1980, quoted in Ro'i, 'The Impact of the Islamic Fundamentalist Revival', pp.167-8.

128. Compare p.175.

129. See, for example, Pospelovskii, *Russkaia pravoslavnaia tserkov' v XX veke*, pp.192-3, relating to the improved situation of the Russian Orthodox Church towards the end of World War II.

Muslim areas.[130] Moreover, the Muslim faith – i.e. the official Muslim establishment – was 'not to be obstructed in extending and strengthening' links with co-religionists abroad with the purpose of propagating the existence of freedom of religion in the USSR and fulfilling other assignments given it by CARC.[131] These considerations engendered broadcasts and a few publications for Muslim countries – especially, but not solely, those in the Soviet Union's immediate proximity – and even the insertion of articles in their press.[132] Two officials who were employed by CARC, but seem to have come from either the party or the security organs, voiced serious criticism in 1946 of the Council's attitude towards Islam, which they contended was not sufficiently heedful. Among other things, they emphasised that a correct relationship between the Soviet government and Islam would help the Soviet Union in the conduct of its policy *vis-à-vis* the countries of the East.[133] A decade later the head of the CARC department which dealt with Islam believed that Islam in the Ajar ASSR should be considered no less, and perhaps even more, important than in the Tatar ASSR in view of the former's status as a border area and the presence in its capital, Batumi, of a Turkish consul.[134]

The importance of fruitful contacts with Muslims from other countries and transmission of the message to them that Muslims

130. See, for example, Draft decree, July 1947; GARF, f.6991, o.3, d.47, l.300.

131. Draft, Instructions to CARC, undated [apparently June 1948]; GARF, f.6991, o.3, d.53, l.41. Of all other faiths under CARC's auspices only the Armenian Church was to be allowed similar ties with abroad; all other religions were to restrict their activity to the confines of the Soviet Union, where they were to conduct an autonomous existence.

132. In 1944, for instance, the political administration of the Transcaucasian front published a newspaper in Azeri and Persian for Iran in which it sought to 'popularise' Soviet policy toward religion – Major-General Sorokin to I. V. Polianskii, 20 July 1947; GARF, f.6991, o.3, d.6, l.3. For broadcasts, see I. V. Polianskii to K. E. Voroshilov, 5 Aug. 1947 – GARF, f.6991, o.3, d.48, ll.9-11; and for articles inserted in the press of Arab countries, see Excerpt from supplement to report of Sovinformburo department of the press of France and the Near East, 12 July 1946 – RTsKhIDNI, f.17, o.125, d.389, l.9. See also pp.113 and 574.

133. I. N. Uzkov and G. Ia. Vrachev to I. V. Polianskii, 29 Nov. 1946; RTsKhIDNI, f.17, o.125, d.405, l.93. For the emphasis placed on Tajikistan in the 1940s out of similar considerations, see p.559 above.

134. L. A. Prikhod'ko to I. V. Polianskii, undated [5 May 1956]; GARF, f.6991, o.3, d.217, l.60. For the Turkish context of the registration of a mosque in Batumi, see p.661.

were being allowed to practise their faith was also a main consideration behind the re-institution of the *hajj* in the mid-1940s;[135]
as it was for the retention of the *hajj* in later years, although it
was agreed that the pilgrimage to Mecca had a manifestly deleterious
impact at home,[136] and for the actual selection of the pilgrims.[137]
It appears also to have been the motivating force behind the
granting of permission to open and operate a number of mosques
in the proximity of the Afghan border in Tajikistan and Uzbekistan.[138]

Regular visits of delegations from Muslim countries, as of 1954,
began to be adopted as a reason, or perhaps a pretext, for taking
measures to improve the situation of Islam in the purely domestic
context. (They had served the same purpose even in the late
Stalin years, but more rarely.) For instance, Polianskii used these
visits as an argument in 1954 in putting forward the case of
Leningrad's Muslims to get back their mosque.[139] He also dwelt
on this theme in letters he sent to CARC *upolnomochennye* and
to First Deputy Chairman of the Council of Ministers Anastas
Mikoian in 1956. In the latter Polianskii made proposals, based
on those of Chairman of the Uzbek SSR Supreme Soviet Presidium
Sharaf Rashidov for extending the ties of Muslim religious organisations with organisations abroad.[140] So, too, did his deputy,

135. Accordingly, the reports transmitted by the pilgrims on their return always stressed how faithfully they had fulfilled this mission – for example, Ishan Babakhan, Report, undated [Dec. 1945 –Jan. 1946]; GARF, f.6991, o.3, d.45, ll.17-18.

136. Appendix No.1, Draft decree, July 1947; I. V. Polianskii to G. M. Malenkov, N. S. Khrushchev, V. M. Molotov and S. N. Kruglov, 30 Sept. 1953; Appendix No.2, CARC session No.7, 14 March 1959; GARF, f.6991, o.3, d.47, l.306, d.93, l.238, and d.183, ll.146-50. And see pp.172-4.

137. Reception by A. A. Puzin of Mufti Babakhanov, 13 and 17 Feb. 1960; GARF, f.6991, o.4, d.110, l.9.

138. Report of K. Hamidov, CARC session, 19-20 Dec. 1951, and Minutes, Conference of CARC *upolnomochennye*, 25-27 Nov. 1958; GARF, f.6991, o. 3, d.75, l.200, and d.165, l.79. In the latter document the *upolnomochennyi* for the Uzbek SSR said three mosques were opened in Surkhan-Darya Oblast' so that traders coming from Afghanistan would have somewhere to pray.

139. I. V. Polianskii to D. M. Kukin, 4 June 1954; GARF, f.6991, o.3, d.114, l.52.

140. I. V. Polianskii to CARC's *upolnomochennye* in Tashkent, Frunze, Stalinabad, Ashkhabad, Alma-Ata, Baku, Ufa, Makhachkala, Kazan', Leningrad and Moscow, 16 March 1956, and to A. I. Mikoian, 5 June 1956 – GARF, f.6991, o.3, d.131, ll.3-4, and d.129, ll.197-9. The proposals in the latter document included enlarging the edition of the Qur'an being prepared for publication in the Soviet Union in order to be able to send copies abroad; increasing the number of people

who wrote to CARC's *upolnomochennyi* in Tashkent that his blue-prints for future work must bear in mind the Soviet Union's broadening international ties with the countries of the East; he asked for his thoughts on measures it might be expedient to take regarding Islam in order to dispel perceptions prevalent in these countries that Soviet Muslims were being denied freedom of worship.[141]

Polianskii pointed out that now that foreign delegations were more or less free to travel in the Soviet Union, propaganda directed at foreign delegations could achieve its purpose only insofar as it was based in fact. It was therefore essential to contemplate measures to demonstrate that the freedom of worship promised in the constitution was being implemented: for example, opening mosques in areas where foreign delegations visited, improving the *medrese*, even making it possible for believers to teach their children the basics of the faith.[142] (In the period of Khrushchev's anti-religious campaign, in conjunction with the general line that communism was raising the population's standard of living, the emphasis in propaganda to Muslim countries was placed not on the religious freedom enjoyed by the Muslims, but on their material achievements and welfare.)

The CARC material makes the impression that SADUM in particular took every advantage of its position as constituting the nexus of these links with Muslim organisations abroad to enhance its own status. In the words of CARC's *upolnomochennyi* in Tashkent, these extensive ties, which had made Tashkent 'the gateway to the East', indeed engendered a certain benefit in the realm of foreign policy; at the same time, however, they demanded a price

---

allowed to make the *hajj* and allowing them to spend time in foreign Muslim countries to dispel anti-Soviet calumnies; permitting pilgrimages of Shiites to Kerbala and Meshed; allowing DUMES and DUMZ to open *medreses* in Ufa and Baku respectively; importing textbooks from Egypt for use in the *medrese* in Bukhara; and enabling three additional students to go to study in Cairo at al-Azhar.

141. V. I. Gostev to Kh. N. Iskanderov, 25 Feb. 1956; TsGAUz, f.2456, o.1, d.191, l.58.

142. I. V. Polianskii to Kh. N. Iskanderov, 24 March 1956; TsGAUz, f.2456, o.l, d.191, l.136. It should be noted that despite the statement concerning freedom of travel for foreign delegations, most Muslim delegations visited just a very few cities in the Muslim republics – notably Tashkent, Bukhara, Baku, Kazan' – and hardly any rural areas.

in the domestic context, for they encouraged clerical activity and augmented the number of believers.[143] Mosques and clergy in other parts of the country maintaining ties with foreign delegations were also conscious of the leverage this gave them.[144] It seems too that CARC itself, with its vested interest in strengthening the organs subject to its jurisdiction and supervision, used the argument – in the context of its debates with other branches of the bureaucracy – that the USSR's Muslims with their 'versatile ties' with the Muslim population of a number of neighbouring countries were a potential trump card for use in the conduct of Soviet foreign policy. Indeed, the Muslim religious establishment brought only benefit to the Soviet state in the international arena.[145] This was given official endorsement with the creation in 1963 of the Department of Foreign Ties of the USSR's Muslim Organisations.[146]

On the weight of the available evidence it seems impossible to finally determine the influence of foreign policy considerations at the level of either decision making or policy implementation towards Islam inside the Soviet Union. However unlikely it may seem that any significant steps were taken without the relevant organs first calculating the implications for the domestic arena, or that in the final account foreign policy considerations were deemed

143. N. I. Inogamov, Address, Conference of CARC *upolnomochennye*, 25-27 Nov. 1958; GARF, f.6991, o.3, d.165, ll.34-5.

144. For example, the sole functioning mosque in Kazan' sought to extend its premises in order to create facilities that would make a favourable impression on foreigners, who began visiting it as of 1955 – N. Smirnov, Information, 16 Jan. 1960; GARF, f.6991, o.3, d.204, ll.36-45. For the extension of these premises, see p.239.

145. I. V. Polianskii, Address, Moscow conference of CARC *upolnomochennye*, 11 [May?] 1946, Polianskii to K. E. Voroshilov and D. T. Shepilov, 29 Jan. 1949, and A. A. Puzin, Circular, 14 Sept. 1960; GARF, f. 6991, o.3, d.39, ll.69-70, d.61, ll.2-3, and d.211, ll.82-110, *passim*. The Puzin circular relates to the various faiths under CARC's authority. For the Council's disputes within the government apparatus and with the party, see below.

146. The establishment of a Department for International Relations of the Muslim Boards (i.e. Spiritual Directorates) of the USSR was announced in October 1962 – TASS in English, 31 Oct. 1962; BBC/SWB I, 2 Nov. 1962 – but it seems that its office, in Moscow, was only opened the following year. Chaired by SADUM Mufti Babakhanov, the department's board comprised the heads of the four spiritual directorates and the *imam-khatib* of the Moscow mosque. (The name given in the text is a strict translation of the Russian title.)

more weighty by the top leadership than those of the domestic arena, it must be borne in mind that the various organisations within the party and state apparatus had different interests. Usually, those concerned with domestic security and with propagating the guidelines of party policy inside the country probably had the upper hand. The exception to this rule would seem to have been in the fifteen to twenty years between the mid-late 1950s and the early-mid 1970s, when the regime, in its eagerness to win allies in the Third World, apparently convinced itself that it could create an effective divide between its attitude to Islam abroad and at home and could afford to credit Islam with a positive social role in countries of a less 'progressive' character than the Soviet Union without producing any boomerang effect at home.[147]

By the latter half of the 1970s the Soviet establishment came to the conclusion that a backlash at home from such a dichotomous policy toward Islam in the domestic context and abroad was unavoidable. Moreover, there was little evidence that Moscow's courting of foreign Muslim dignitaries or permitting selected representatives of its own Muslim establishment to foster ties with their counterparts abroad had reaped any meaningful success. Consequently, it duly changed tack once more to demonstrate anew the fundamentally negative and reactionary essence of Islam wherever it might be[148] and to take up the cudgels again in its efforts to curb Islam at home.

Problems of policy implementation

One obvious conclusion from reading archival sources – not only those relating to questions of security – is that the authorities' treatment of Islam was inadequate and that the lacunae were manifest to a number of people and sectors. In part, these were the inescapable consequence of the contradictions inherent in CARC's terms of reference, of which its personnel were only too well aware. In

---

147. There is evidence that some people attributed the greater leeway given to domestic Islam in this period to Moscow's courting of the 'countries of the East', see pp.306 and 437.

148. For Moscow's different stance toward Islam at home and abroad and the dubious success of its overtures to foreign Muslim institutions and leaders, see Ro'i, 'The Role of Islam and Soviet Muslims in Soviet Arab Policy', and 'The Impact of the Islamic Fundamentalist Revival', *passim.*

the words of its chairman, it had at one and the same time to act as protagonist of the interests of the Soviet state and to secure for believers the practice of their religion to the extent to which they required it.[149] In part, the criticism levelled at those responsible for policy implementation was an inherent component of the political discourse of the period, especially in the late Stalin years, when criticism, certainly in writing, could be directed solely at those who carried out instructions and under no condition at those who laid down policy. Inevitably, given the context, fault-finding tended to focus rather on practical failures than on errors of judgement or principle, but sometimes it is possible to learn about these more profound issues from the censure of an individual official's particular conduct.

On occasion, too, disapproval was expressed in clichés or terminology which had meaning only in the atmosphere of the Soviet regime or of a certain time period in Soviet history. In one instance a CARC inspector accused the republican *upolnomochennyi* in Turkmenistan of not being guided by 'the principle of political expediency'.[150] Another such example was a warning by a CARC official in 1946 that pressure must not be applied to believers, as terror and fear, such as were employed, for example, in Dagestan and Ajaria, distorted party and government policy. The theory was always that 'administrative' measures must be avoided, for they evoked an inevitable negative reaction.[151] Unquestionably, however, 'administrative' meant very different things in the late Stalin period and in, for example, the years of the 'thaw' in the mid-1950s. During spells of repression methods considered administrative in more liberal years might no longer be so regarded. Even CARC did not necessarily reject all administrative measures in more rigorous years.[152]

Another unavoidable conclusion is that there were constant differences of opinion among those responsible for dealing with

149. Minutes, CARC session No.28a, Instructional convention, 23-24 Dec. 1949; GARF, f.6991, o.3, d.60, l.170. See also p.14.

150. Minutes, CARC session No.13, 10-11 July 1947; GARF, f.6991, o.4, d.19, l.423.

151. Minutes, Conference of CARC *upolnomochennye*, Rostov-on-Don, 14 [June] 1946; GARF, f. 6991, o.3, d.38, l.170. For the fear that pertained at this time in the Dagestan and Ajar ASSRs, see pp.192-3.

152. Compare pp.43-4.

the Muslim community. There were recurrent confrontations between CARC, or the CRA, and the Central Committee ideologists,[153] and between the Council and the KGB. One CARC
upolnomochennyi complained he had to obtain the opinion of the
KGB before deciding on the composition of the group going on
hajj in any given year, adding that this caused 'misunderstandings',
for that organisation's personnel 'have no faith in us' and reported
directly to the Central Committee.[154] There were also clashes
between the central bodies in Moscow and their people in the
field, whose reports highlighted the dilemmas of those who came
into daily contact with the religious communities. One such dispute
centred on the attitude to the registered clergy, whom CARC
mostly sought to co-opt in the struggle against itinerant mullas.
Some at least of its *upolnomochennye* were keen to avoid creating
illusions among the clergy themselves concerning their role or
the impression among believers that the clergy were allied with
the powers-that-be at a time – the late 1950s – when the regime
was intent on diminishing their influence and authority.[155]

Above all, the *upolnomochennye* were constantly at loggerheads
with the organs of local government. Their complaints against
them varied from area to area, but usually fell into one of two
categories: either that the local officials ignored the religious situation
altogether and turned a blind eye to violations of legislation on the
part of the clergy and the believer community, or that they resorted
indiscriminately to 'administrative' measures.[156] Even during the
anti-religious campaign of the early 1960s CARC's *upolnomochennye*
argued that the local authorities were too enthusiastic in their use
of administrative methods.[157] Sometimes, the Council in Moscow
took issue with the policy followed by a republican government
or party. One such instance was the persistent endeavour of CARC

153. One CRA official stated that the Council had constant discussions, which
often developed into sharp debates, with the Central Committee Propaganda
Department – Author's interview with a former CRA official who has asked to
remain anonymous. See also p.19 and above.

154. Minutes, CARC session No.4, 25-26 Feb. 1959; GARF, f.6991, o.3, d.183,
l.118.

155. *Ibid.*, l.122.

156. For example, Minutes, CARC instructional convention, 23-24 Dec. 1949;
GARF, f.6991, o.3, d.60, ll.160-1.

157. For example, Minutes, CARC session No.33, 26-27 Oct. 1960; GARF,
f.6991, o.3, d.207, ll.39-40.

and the CRA to open registered mosques in the Chechen–Ingush ASSR despite the obstinate opposition of the republican authorities. CARC took exception to the severity of the position adopted by local officialdom in this republic and in North Osetia, contending that it exploited the general anti-sectarian policy of the USSR leadership to prevent the registration of Muslim religious societies in these areas.[158]

These divergences were not mostly on issues of principle, but of tactics and practical conduct. Whatever the motivation, the consequence was usually the same: policy implementation became difficult and ineffective, for in the final account, especially in the rural sector, it was those on the spot who determined what steps were in fact taken. As one *upolnomochennyi* stressed in connection with the campaign against pilgrimages to holy places, the struggle to extirpate superstition and traditions which had taken root over long centuries was no easy one, but would eventually be successful if it were conducted thoughtfully and if all the 'relevant oranisations of the ideological front' cooperated.[159]

Believers and clergy, not to speak of the spiritual directorates, were acutely aware of discrepancies within the various branches of officialdom and naturally took every possible advantage of them. In spite of CARC's basic position, however, believers who came from all parts of the country to CARC's Moscow offices in the hope of rectifying wrongs that they maintained had been done them were usually told that the law was not, in fact, on their side. The eclectic nature of regime policy toward religion was indeed highlighted by CARC officials' reactions to believers' grievances. While systematically and persistently opposing administrative measures on the part of local government, they very rarely sided with the victims of these steps. They explained time and again that the conduct of prayer-services hinged upon permission from the local government organs. This was made explicit to representatives of various believer communities, who came to Moscow to complain that they were being forcibly prevented from con-

158. A. Puzin, Address, Minutes, CARC session, 17 March 1965 – GARF, f.6991, o.4, d.168, l.31; and author's interview with a CRA official who has asked to remain anonymous.

159. Minutes, Conference of CARC *upolnomochennye*, 5-6 June 1959; GARF, f.6991, o.3, d.186, l.41. For a further discussion of the positions adopted by local government and the attitude of CARC and the CRA to these positions, see Chapter 11, *passim*.

ducting collective prayers. They had either misinterpreted the legislation on religion or been allowed too long to indulge in practices
which should never have been tolerated in the first place.

This formal position was maintained throughout the ups and
downs of the postwar decades. Even at times when there was
relatively more chance of an amenable attitude on the part of
CARC and its *upolnomochennye*, there was little likelihood that
they would openly side with protests against the authorities in
the localities. And when believers continued complaining about
the inordinate behaviour of local officialdom during the years of
Khrushchev's anti-religious campaign, their grievances mostly fell
on deaf ears. The exigencies of the system, which led to CARC
adhering in essence to one policy, yet preaching another in its
contacts outside the establishment, underlined the anomalous nature
of its position. Moreover, its own personnel were not all of one
opinion, at least when it came to certain issues. Not all CARC
officials, for example, necessarily shared the views of its leadership.
Divergences sometimes took the form of a confrontation over
the substance of a particular line, and on other occasions over
the tactics employed to achieve a goal on which there was a
consensus.[160] There even appeared to be contradictions in CARC's,
or the CRA's, official line. For instance, the Councils sought on
the whole to sever all ties between the spiritual directorates and
the unregistered clergy and religious associations so as to curb the
influence of the directorates; yet, at times they strove to forge
such links in order to bring the unregistered clergy under some
sort of control.

One of the most controversial issues, which seems to have
permeated the entire period was the advisability of registering
mosques and clergy. In the course of a discussion on the situation
in Turkmenistan in 1947, a CARC official recommended that
one mosque be opened in every population centre and that the
most revered *mazars* be legalised. In this way, he maintained,
Muslim religious activity would be brought within the law and
regulated. CARC Deputy Chairman Sadovskii, too, polemicised
with the republican *upolnomochennyi*, saying that he was influenced

160. Perhaps the most blatant exmple was the above-mentioned criticism levelled
by two CARC officials at the Council's leadership, which included both elements
–G. Ia. Vrachev and I. N. Uzkov to I. V. Polianskii, 29 Nov. 1946; RTsKhIDNI,
f.17, o.125, d.405, ll.84-5, 93-8 and 105-22, *passim*.

by the republican authorities and sought to extinguish 'the religious movement', whereas CARC's policy was to create a safety valve for religious inclinations. Its officials were Marxists and were not out to protect religion; they were dealing with 'birth-marks which the state does not intend treating surgically'. Precisely because it did not wish to encourage religion, and at the same time was inspired by considerations of a practical nature, CARC believed that it had to register a certain number of mosques, but for every mosque it opened, ten unofficially functioning ones could be closed. A third official criticised the *upolnomochennyi* for not appreciating that the use of administrative measures – arbitrarily shutting mosques and forbidding the performance of rites – would evoke a negative reaction.[161]

While the registration of mosques was a complex procedure and easily stymied by one of the numerous links in the chain of those who had to consent to implementation, the registration of clergy was somewhat simpler. On this issue, the CRA seems to have found ways of outdoing its partners to policy implementation who had reservations in this regard. The Council's insistence on the need to increase the number of registered clergy in places where there was no registered religious society in order to enable some control and supervision of Islam, and its persistence in this position, led in fact to the doubling of the number of registered clergy from the early 1970s to the early 1980s, which by early 1983 was approximately three times as numerous as that of registered mosques and religious societies – although no hard and fast resolution to this end seems to have been taken by any of the decison-making bodies.[162]

Another question, over which there was constant disagreement within the Soviet bureaucracy, was the viability and desirability of imposing taxation on the clergy, and the application of other financial constraints. While the law was explicit regarding the subjection of registered religious personnel to taxation,[163] there

161. Minutes, CARC session No.13, 10-11 July 1947; GARF, f.6991, o.4, d.19, ll.436-7. See also pp.187-8.

162. For the numbers of registered clergy, see pp.66-7 and 243; for the CRA's policy of registering clergy in places without registered mosques by affiliating them to the nearest registered mosque and discussion of their terms of reference, see pp.216-7.

163. See pp.22-3; for clergy who refrained from applying to register in order not to expose themselves to taxation, see pp.30 and 192.

was no single coherent policy even within CARC on the issue of the taxation of unregistered clergy, which required recurrent clarification.

Polianskii himself was adamant that the sole effective method of fighting the itinerant mullas and the unregistered mosques was to subject them to taxation. Repressive measures – such as approaching the procuracy to have clergy brought to trial and arrested – were not to be used, he maintained, for the issue was not just the mullas but also the broad mass of the population, which, while participating in the building of socialism, still believed in God.[164] Polianskii did not spell out his meaning, but he was probably suggesting that repression would simply be counter-productive in that it would alienate the masses, push them to an antagonistic stance towards the state and in all likelihood also enhance their religious inclinations. One participant at a conference of CARC *upolnomochennye* in Kazakhstan and Kirgiziia in 1946 called for the imposition of taxes on unregistered mullas, contending this might put an end to their activity.[165]

Certainly in the more lenient years of the mid-1950s the policy of taxing unregistered clergy was considered the sole legitimate weapon to be used against them. As CARC's oblast' *upolnomochennye* in Uzbekistan were told unequivocally, if they had information that such clerics were receiving revenues from the performance of religious rites, it was incumbent upon them to inform the financial organs.[166] The usual procedure was for them to provide the relevant fiscal department, in most cases that of the *oblispolkom*, with lists of all unregistered clergy they had exposed, and it would pass on the information to the department at the raion level.[167]

Some CARC *upolnomochennye*, however, were of the opinion that taxes should be imposed solely on registered clergy, as taxation implied recognition of a person's income and legitimisation of his work.[168] It was so strange a conception in the Soviet context that

164. Minutes, CARC session No.13, 10-11 July 1947; GARF, f.6991, o.4, d.19, ll.444-6.

165. Minutes of conference, Alma-Ata, 30 Sept. to 2 Oct. 1946; GARF, f.6991, o.3, d.41, l.59.

166. Instructional meeting of CARC *upolnomochennye* in the Uzbek SSR, 15-17 March 1956; TsGAUz, f.2456, o.1, d.183, l.59.

167. Minutes, Conference of CARC *upolnomochennye*, 5-6 June 1959; GARF, f.6991, o.3, d.186, l.135.

168. Notes for address by N. Sabitov at conference of *upolnomochennye*, Alma-Ata,

unofficial clergy might be taxed that believers considered a cleric who they knew paid income tax must by definition be registered. Even republican organs of government and officials in the localities were of the opinion that a cleric who paid state taxes operated legally.[169] One CARC *upolnomochennyi* stated in the early 1960s that the predominant majority of unofficial clergy likewise understood the fact of their being subjected to taxation as evidence that they were being permitted to conduct religious activity without qualification. Since this meant that taxation, instead of curbing their activity, served in practice to enliven it, he wondered whether it was worthwhile.[170]

Despite the juridical advantages accruing to the clergy from the fact of being taxed, it was a very mixed blessing. The burden of taxation led to constant complaints on the part of clergy who felt they were being taxed unjustly, disproportionately to their actual incomes. Such instances were especially frequent in the Northern Caucasus and some oblasti of the RSFSR.[171] In a number of cases, taxation even led to clergy, both registered and unregistered, resigning their posts. For example, in the Cherkess AO, where believers did not provide their clergy with the 800 to 1,500 rubles which DUMSK had determined should be the salary of an *efendi* (as an imam was called in the Northern Caucasus), the financial

30 Sept. 1946. The financial organs in the Kirgiz SSR were at first of the opinion that whereas rural registered clergy were to be taxed like households with unearned income, namely 150 rubles, unregistered clergy should pay like kolkhozniki, i.e. 20 rubles – H. Akhtiamov, Short report, Conference of Central Asian *upolnomochennye*, Tashkent, 17 Dec. 1949. This position changed and in 1950 instructions were apparently issued ordering all local financial organs to tax registered and unregistered clergy by the same criteria – Draft circular of the head of Osh Oblast's financial department to all raion financial departments in the oblast', 5 Jan. 1951; GARF, f. 6991, o.3, d.41, l.85, d.67, l.114, and d.454, l.99.

169. Testimony to this effect was borne by CARC's *upolnomochennye* in Semi-palatinsk Oblast' and in the Uzbek SSR – Conference of CARC *upolnomochennye*, 5-6 June 1959, and M. Miragzamov to M. Kh. Khalmuhamedov, 22 Oct. 1966. This argument was used, for example, by the Dagestan ASSR Finance Ministry to reject the suggestion of CARC's *upolnomochennyi* for that republic to impose income tax on 'itinerant mullas' – Minutes, CARC session No.24, 27 Aug. 1964; GARF, f.6991, o.3, d.186, l.193, o.4, d.147, l.81, and o.6, d.11, l.65.

170. S. A. Shamsutdinov to A. A. Puzin, 11 July 1962; GARF, f.6991, o.3, d.1388, ll.87-9.

171. L. A. Prikhod'ko, V. D. Efremov and P. A. Basis, Report, 8 May 1954; GARF, f.6991, o.3, d.100, l.36.

organs imposed taxation on the assumption that they were indeed receiving this sum. And after several years religious personnel had no alternative but to quit.[172] Not infrequently money that had been collected from believers for special expenses of the religious society, such as repairs of the mosque, might be included by the financial organs in the revenues of the clergy or other officials of a registered mosque on the contention that they had, as it were, appropriated the funds.[173] Some complaints were so blatantly justified that they were even taken up by CARC's *upolnomochennye*.[174]

In fact, many of those who performed occasional rites were totally unable to pay the taxes imposed upon them; sometimes they offered to commit themselves to cease conducting rites in return for a cancellation of the tax. In certain instances, the situation was so unsatisfactory that the dead went unburied for long periods, because the clergy were unwilling to expose themselves to taxation by conducting the traditional funeral rites.[175]

At the same time, taxing clergy was no simple task. This applied even to registered clerics, whose income was mostly fixed, but who performed rites, particularly life-cycle ones, outside the mosque and had a manifest interest in not reporting all of these, precisely in order to evade taxation on the income that accrued from them. Since those for whom these rites were conducted had a similar interest in not reporting them, not wishing to be molested by the various organs of government, it was generally difficult, if not impossible, to learn the details (what rites had been performed, by whom, where, when, and how much the mulla had been paid) even in places where the financial organs were efficient and determined to pursue this.

172. Minutes, meeting of CARC inspectors, No.17, 20-22 Dec. 1950; GARF, f.6991, o.3, d.66, l.130. Cf. Chapter 4, n.86.

173. The documentation includes not a few complaints from the religious societies to this effect; for example, Kh. N. Iskanderov to Uzbek SSR Finance Minister M. Isametdinov, 26 March 1955, enclosing a letter to SADUM from the chairman of the executive organ of a registered mosque in Fergana Oblast', undated, and an official declaration of all the mosque's officials corroborating his story – TsGAUz, f.2456, o.1, d.178, ll.78-80. See also pp.130-1.

174. For example, Kh. N. Iskanderov to Deputy Chairman of the Uzbek SSR Council of Ministers G. S. Sultanov, Uzbekistan Party Secretary Kh. G. Gulamov and I. V. Polianskii, 14 May 1955; TsGAUz, f.2456, o.2, d.178, ll.151-2.

175. Minutes, Conference of CARC *upolnomochennye*, 5-6 June 1959; GARF, f.6991, o.3, d.186, ll.136-7.

When it came to unregistered mullas, the task was all the more formidable, as the constraints which existed regarding clergy who officiated in registered mosques were absent: they did not have to report on their financial dealings to a religious centre; they were not visited by the local CARC *upolnomochennyi*; they had no executive organ or inspection commission to keep tabs on their activities. When mullas denied performing religious activity, believers chose to give no information on payments for the performance of religious rites and local officials insisted there was no illegal religious activity in their region, taxing was to all intents and purposes impossible.[176] Early in 1951 the CARC *upolnomochennyi* for Osh Oblast' drew up a draft of a circular to be sent out by the head of the oblast' financial department to all raion financial departments. He suggested in this document that a tax of 150 rubles be imposed on all clergy, registered and unregistered, who performed religious rites and received income from them, be that income their sole source of revenue or just supplementary. In addition, the remuneration received by the clergy had to be assessed for purposes of imposing income tax. Nor were statements by *sel'sovet* chairmen that there were no unregistered mullas in their area of jurisdiction to be accepted, as such people existed in almost every kolkhoz, wherever there were believing Muslims and rites were performed.[177]

But the difficulties in formulating and implementing a policy of taxation remained considerable. In addition to the manipulations of all those who had an interest in forestalling the imposition of taxes and evading payment, the criteria for determining a fixed tax were abstruse.[178] The resolution of one *oblispolkom* in Kazakhstan noted simply that 'the financial organs do not expose the revenues of the unregistered clergy from the performance of religious rites and do not impose income tax on them', while a CRA *upolnomochennyi*, also in Kazakhstan, was categorical in stating that not a single Muslim unregistered cleric in his oblast' who violated the law had criminal proceedings initiated against him, was fined or subjected to income tax.[179] Throughout the period under study,

176. H. Akhtiamov, Report, Conference of CARC *upolnomochennye*, 17 Dec. 1949; GARF, f.6991. o.3, d.67, ll.112-14. See also pp.351-2.

177. Draft, 5 Jan. 1951; GARF, f.6991, o.3, d.454, l.99.

178. See p.352.

179. Zh. Botashev to the Kzyl-Orda Oblispolkom, 20 Sept. 1973, and Aktiubinsk

even when lists of unregistered mullas were given to the financial organs, the latter imposed taxes only on very few of those designated in them. In 1950 and the first half of 1951, taxes were imposed on just 25 per cent of the over 1,000 unregistered mullas whose names were given to the financial organs in Uzbekistan.[180]

Following the decision of the 1968 Tashkent conference to take count of all unregistered clergy in order to augment their income tax, the financial organs in the Kabardino-Balkar ASSR, together with the raion authorities, took stock of all of them and in fact increased their taxes.[181] Elsewhere the bureaucracy continued stalling or took up the challenge half-heartedly. The Kirgiz SSR Finance Ministry received a list of 229 functioning clergy. While it was able to look into 203 of these (the others had either died or left the republic), it imposed income tax on just twenty-eight: twenty were exempted for reasons of age or invalid status; the income of a further forty-eight did not attain the taxable minimum; sixteen had ceased their religious activity; while the remaining ninety-one whose income it had not been possible to establish were still being monitored.[182] The Finance Minister of the Nakhichevan ASSR simply contended that the clergy performed rites without remuneration.[183]

The various obstacles notwithstanding, taxation remained throughout the period under discussion the main weapon in the struggle against the clergy, in the endeavour to reduce its influence and cut it down to size. Yet the chief instrument used to undermine religious activity as a whole on the level of the individual believer, especially as of the early-mid 1960s, was probably the inculcation of secular rites.[184] The introduction of the 'new rites' seems, however, to have proceeded more slowly in the Muslim republics, especially in Central Asia, than elsewhere. Often they seem to have been

Oblispolkom, Resolution, 28 Dec. 1973; GARF, f.6991, o.6, d.548, l.23, and d.637, l.3.

180. Minutes, Instructional meeting of CARC *upolnomochennye* in the Uzbek SSR, 17-18 July 1951; TsGAUz, f.2456, o.1, d.134, l.60.

181. For the results of this activity, see p.352.

182. K. Shabolotov to A. A. Nurullaev, 23 June 1969; GARF, f.6991, o.6, d.220, l.151.

183. I. Bonchkovskii to E. I. Lisavtsev, 13 March 1973; GARF, f.6991, o.6, d.537, l.172.

184. See pp.47-8.

rejected because they had specifically Christian connotations.[185] A CRA official who visited Bukhara Oblast' in 1968 found that little had been done there to introduce them and as a result a high rate of religious ritual still prevailed.[186] The CRA *upolnomochennyi* in Azerbaijan bemoaned the fact that whereas the religious burial rites had developed over centuries and taken deep root, those who sought to structure civil funerals had to organise everything from scratch.[187] In many areas, indeed, the issue of burial rites remained the most crucial, with many organs of local government failing to equip cemeteries with facilities, organise civil funerals and prepare tombstones 'corresponding to contemporary needs'.[188]

Still in the mid-1970s a report on Azerbaijan noted that although some of the collective rites were becoming part of local tradition – such as the Day of Harvest or induction into the armed forces – the new rites were not having much success in supplanting the old life-cycle rites. The ritual of the new ceremonies lacked style, and the *sel'sovets* did not know how to adapt them to the needs of the population.[189] In some places more successful attempts appear to have been made, but even then there were clear limitations. In one oblast' in Kazakhstan, the CRA *upolnomochennyi* reported certain achievements, but continued to blame the local organs of government for not doing all that they should to override the old religious rites.[190] On the whole, it seems that the population, together with the clergy, came to accept a compromise situation, by which most of the rites of passage were marked by both ceremonies. (One suspects that this applied particularly in the urban areas.) One *akhund* in Azerbaijan explained: 'First, young people register at ZAGS, then ask us to perform a religious marriage,

185. Lane, *The Rites of Rulers*, p.232.

186. A. Barinskaia to V. A. Kuroedov, undated [late March-early April 1968]; GARF, f.6991, o.6, d.153, l.109.

187. A. Ahadov to V. A. Kuroedov, 10 Oct. 1969; GARF, f.6991, o.6, d.220, ll.37-8.

188. V. A. Kuroedov to CRA *upolnomochennye*, 2 Feb. 1972; GARF, f.6991, o.6, d.462, l.4.

189. I. Mikhalev to E. I. Lisavtsev, 2 June 1973; GARF, f.6991, o.6, d.537, l.181. On the ritual of induction into the armed forces, see Lane, *The Rites of Rulers*, pp.105-8.

190. Zh. Botashev to Chairman Kzyl-Orda Oblispolkom Sh. Bakirov, 22 Feb. 1971, and Botashev to the Oblispolkom, 20 Sept. 1973; GARF, f.6991, o.6, d.376, ll.5-10, and d.548, ll.22-3.

and afterwards organise a Komsomol wedding. We are in no way against such an arrangement. The main thing is that the marriage be ratified by Allah. Then it will be strong and the children born from it will be Muslims'. Observing this adaptability on the part of the registered clergy, one student of Islam who served the atheistic propaganda machine said this was not a genuine acceptance, for simultaneously with their acquiescence, the clergy detracted from the new rites, saying they were not those which 'came to us from our ancestors'.[191]

In certain areas at least, for example in the Karakalpak ASSR and the Gorno-Badakhshan AO, coordinating councils were set up under the auspices of the *obkom* and the *gor-* and *rai-koms* to promote the introduction of secular rites and rituals, although, as happened to so many similar bodies in the Soviet Union, they often existed on paper only, without actually doing anything or having any impact.[192] In some parts a plethora of organisations came into being to help ZAGS institute the new rites, but the figures for their performance showed only slow progress.[193] By late 1972 secular rites were being introduced in Uzbekistan and a republican council for propaganda and the inculcation of the new rites and rituals was trying to make their content more emotional and attractive so that they might become part of people's lives more quickly and smoothly.[194] In some places attempts were made to adapt the traditional spring and autumn festivals of the indigenous nationalities to the criteria of the new Soviet rites, such as the Nawruz in Tajikistan and Uzbekistan or the Saban-tui among the Volga Tatars and Bashkirs.[195] In at least one region in

191. Ashirov, *Evoliutsiia islama v SSSR*, pp.148-9.

192. P. Kirovsheev, Information, 30 July 1971; G. K. Kadamigoev, Lecture, 2 July 1973; and Oblast' conference of chairmen of commissions of assistance for the observance of the legislation on religion, 3 Sept. 1973 – GARF, f.6991, o.6, d.370, l.100, d.545, l.113, and d.548, ll.34-9.

193. The organisation and instruction department of the Kabardinian-Balkar ASSR Council of Ministers, Information, 2 Oct. 1974; GARF, f.6991, o.6, d.634, ll.70-4.

194. K. Ruzmetov to A. Barmenkov, [?] Oct. 1972; GARF, f.6991, o.6, d.467, l.180.

195. For such an adaptation of the Nawruz, see p.699, and of the Saban-tui in the town and raion of Lys'va, Perm' Oblast', see F. S. Eliseeva, V. P. Romanovskikh and L. F. Shapoval, Information, 1 Nov. 1974; GARF, f.6991, o.6, d.630, ll.287-8. For the evolution of the Saban-tui and the various ways in which it had been celebrated in different parts of the tsarist empire, and

the RSFSR, Kuibyshev Oblast', *raikoms* organised the Saban-tui, with all the traditional accompanying festivities, to coincide with Muslim religious festivals in order to detract the populace from attending mosque and participating in religious celebrations. This was also common practice in Central Asia[196]

CARC and the CRA, then, were first and foremost realists, a fact that probably reflected the general atmosphere among the government apparatus as a whole and perhaps even some of the party machine. Rather than be galvanised into action by hypotheses grounded in ideological stereotypes, they preferred to react to actual developments in the Muslim community. The situation, Puzin stated in the late 1950s, was more serious than CARC and its *upolnomochennye* contended. 'We make formal presentations, like reports on the cotton harvest', with statistical data and so on. (Puzin apparently did not know how unreliable statistical reports on the cotton crop could be.) But in fact, he went on, such information was irrelevant when it came to evaluating Muslim activity. The government organs closed mosques, yet believers continued praying at home, performing rites, burying the dead according to tradition, compelling their children to adhere to ritual. The reports insisted that children did not attend mosque, but forty years after the revolution the mosques were still full; if Islam did not affect the younger generation this would not be the case.

Puzin maintained that the issue at stake was people's world outlook. It had to be altered, and this could only be accomplished by stubborn and persistent effort, without, however, resorting to coarse methods. The closure of so-called holy places had to proceed, for this was a prerequisite for the building of communism. This did not apply to the unregistered mosques. In principle, he favoured their closure, but if this was done forcefully rather than tactfully, the *status quo* would be perpetuated for decades. CARC's chairman rejected the very idea of waging war against all those who attended unregistered mosques, which in Central Asia were so much more numerous than registered ones. This would simply embitter them against the regime. Even regarding the *mazars*, it was incumbent

continued to be celebrated under communism, see Urazmanov, 'Narodnyi prazdnik Saban-tui u tatar'. For the Saban-tui and other holidays of the agricultural cycle in the Muslim areas, see also Lane, *The Rites of Rulers*, pp.124-6.

196. L. A. Prikhod'ko, Report, 31 Jan. 1953; GARF, f.6991, o.3, d.91, l.6, and oral testimony of Michand Zand.

to use educational means, to mobilise the native intelligentsia to prove the harmfulness of 'holy places' for the population at large. Otherwise, people would simply exchange one shrine for another. As long as they were convinced that these sites could help them and saw in them their last hope, for example, to heal an incurable disease, they would go thousands of kilometres to reach one.[197] In the mid-1960s, Puzin was still talking of the need to carry on anti-religious work without causing harm and without adhering too adamantly to stereotypes. He insisted, for instance, that the fact that in the Chechen-Ingush ASSR there was not a single registered mosque did not make it a progressive republic.[198]

This was also the reason why it was so important to work among women, which was a *sine qua non* for an effective struggle against 'superstition' as a whole and in particular against pilgrimages to *mazars* and other revered sites, since – excluded from prayer in mosques by tradition – women comprised the main contingent among pilgrims and the main clientèle of faith-healers.[199] It was essential to appreciate that it was 'our own mothers, sisters and wives' the clergy were deceiving, and they must be told frankly that if they violated the law 'we shall stand in their way'.[200]

Even during the anti-religious campaign of Khrushchev's latter years, CARC sought not to be carried away by excessive zeal. It supported its *upolnomochennyi* in Uzbekistan who contended that to prohibit the conduct of rites in private homes until permission had been given by the local organs of government would merely cause dissatisfaction among the believer community and create difficulties for local officialdom.[201]

Realism, likewise, was behind the conclusion that even while persisting in their recurrent attacks upon unregistered mullas, the council must try to differentiate between those among them who were hostile to the regime and those who were loyal to it, especially

197. Minutes, Conference of CARC *upolnomochennye*, 5-6 June 1959; GARF, f.6991, o.3, d.186, ll.214 and 221.

198. Minutes, CARC session, 17 March 1965; GARF, f.6991, o.3, d.168, l.81.

199. Minutes, CARC session No.4, 25-26 Feb. 1959; GARF, f.6991, o.3, d.183, ll.127-8. See also pp.369 and 382.

200. Conference of CARC *upolnomochennye*, 5-6 June 1959; GARF, f.6991, o.3, d.186, l.183.

201. Minutes, CARC session No.44, 25 Nov. 1961; GARF, f.6991, o.3, d.1362, l.38.

in Central Asia, Azerbaijan and Dagestan, where the unregistered clergy far outnumbered the registered ones.[202] Some of the latter, those who could not in effect be distinguished from registered clergy, in that they served permanently functioning religious societies with their own prayer-houses, CARC and, subsequently, the CRA were insistent, should be registered. A CRA official stated categorically at the end of the 1960s, as he prepared the programme for the Tashkent conference on Islam, that in fact, if the law was strictly adhered to, many registered associations and clergy ought to be registered. Since, however, this would mean a massive opening of new mosques and a significant resuscitation of religious life, the Council favoured the registration just of the largest associations, which had already been operating for a number of years.[203]

The CRA was only too aware of the pitfalls of a situation in which, on the one hand, resolutions were constantly being passed at all levels, yet had no practical significance, remaining mere pieces of paper, and, on the other, Islam retained its dynamism, even acquiring, at least as of the early-mid 1970s, a new élan. Nowhere, its officials constantly reiterated, was there so much sensitivity to the actual capability and effectiveness of the regime as among the Muslim community. Moscow could not afford to play the game by its own rules without keeping in close touch with trends, indeed the very atmosphere, in the field. Otherwise, the game would be lost before it even began. The authorities must define their goals, determine their order of preferences, read the map pedantically and operate with maximum flexibility. Islam as an idea and a way of life was not an ordinary adversary and could not be fought without its specifics being borne in mind.

In a memorandum prepared for the CPSU Central Committee less than two years before Gorbachev came to power, the CRA summed up the state of affairs. Laying the blame, as usual, on the shoulders of the lower level of the bureaucracy, it stipulated: 'The work carried out for many years by party and soviet organs in the localities in order to curtail the activity of the unregistered Muslim religious associations and clergy is not having any permanent

202. Minutes, CARC session No.4, 25-26 Feb. 1959; GARF, f.6991, o.3, d.183, l.106.

203. A. Barmenkov, Theses of a lecture, 19 June 1968; GARF, f.6991, o.6, d.147, l.44. And see p.216.

results: in lieu of religious associations which have been closed down new ones spring up, while new generations of pensioners, some of them communists, continue to fulfil the functions of those unregistered mullas whose activity has been stopped'.[204]

Another document, addressing the critical situation which had evolved in Tajikistan, where Muslim activity was getting completely out of control, noted that the principle of freedom of conscience enunciated in the Soviet constitution was being violated there and the CPSU Central Committee resolutions on 'the Islamic factor' were being 'unsatisfactorily' implemented. It was adamant that the only solution was to organise a network of religious associations and clergy which would be able to reasonably serve the population, to ensure strict observance of the law by both clergy and officialdom, to terminate the use of *chaikhonas*, guest-houses and clubs as prayer-premises, and to elaborate and carry out effective measures 'for the struggle against religious extremism and the ideological isolation of the reactionary sector among the Muslim clergy'.[205] Pursuant to this, the CPSU Central Committee departments of party-organisational work and propaganda under-took the task of putting the situation aright in conjunction with the CRA and the Tajikistan party leadership.[206]

Given, on the one hand, the ideological constraints under which the CPSU had to operate and, on the other, Islam's vitality throughout the four decades covered by this study, no policy could be devised which might create a long-term *modus operandi* acceptable to both sides. Each saw in the working arrangement between them a provisory compromise which it hoped to erode in its own favour. The fact that Islam's main stronghold was in the family and the home – religious 'artefacts' which, as one Soviet source admitted, 'do not lend themselves to legal regulation' – meant that the 'difficulties of the ideological struggle' against it were 'con-

204. Memorandum, 2 June 1983; TsKhSD, f.5, o.89, d.82, l.38.

205. V. A. Kuroedov to the CPSU Central Committee, 16 Sept. 1983; TsKhSD, f.5, o.89, d.82, ll.62-3. For the Central Committee resolution in question, see pp.551-2 above.

206. E. Ligachev and V. Stukalin to the Central Committee, 10 Nov. 1983; TsKhSD, f.5, o.89, d.82, ll.74-5.

siderable'.[207] Be this as it may, towards the end of the period under study, the increasingly defiant stance of a growing number of young Muslim clerics and believers – especially, but not solely in Tajikistan, the Fergana Valley oblasti of Uzbekistan and the Chechen-Ingush ASSR – and the manifest bankruptcy of the Soviet system were bringing matters to a head.

207. *Sovremennaia kul'tura i byt narodov Dagestana*, p.211.

11

THE LOCAL ORGANS OF GOVERNMENT

Policy in all fields was thought out and laid down by the central authorities in Moscow. The nature and efficacy of its implementation, however, depended on the organs of local government: the republican leadership in the 'national' union and autonomous republics,[1] the party and administrative authorities at the level of the oblasti into which the former were divided,[2] the city bosses and their dependent bureaucracies in some of the larger urban centres, the raion organs of government, and, at the base of this pyramid, the party committee or organisation and the soviet of the village or group of villages, the *sel'sovet*,[3] and of the municipal raion.[4] For the purposes of this chapter, members of the kolkhoz administration are also included in local government, although formally they did not belong to this structure.[5]

1. Strictly speaking, the top organs in the union and autonomous republics – their councils of ministers and supreme soviets, as well as the party central committees in the former – were not considered local government. Nor do they appear frequently in the CARC and CRA documentation, so that the bulk of the material at our disposal related to what all agreed were local government bodies. For an account of the structure and intricacies of local government in the Soviet Union, see Jacobs, 'Introduction: The Organizational Framework of Soviet Local Government'.

2. Some of the smaller union republics were not divided into oblasti, but all six 'Muslim' union republics were so divided. The party machine in the autonomous republics was itself headed by an *obkom*.

3. Until the period of Khrushchev's administrative reforms, each village had its own soviet; from then on, the *sel'sovet* often represented two or more villages. The *sel'sovet*, as distinct from more senior soviets did not have departments and executive organs, but had a chairman and sometimes a deputy chairman and secretary – Jacobs, *op.cit.*, p.4.

4. For the hierarchy of local government and the party organisations' leverage over the administrative organs, see *ibid.*, pp.4-9.

5. For a study of the kolkhoz, its administration, and its relations with the local organs of government, party and other, see Bienstock, Schwarz and Yugow, *Management in Russian Industry and Agriculture*, chapters 10-17. Certainly, the

It was not sufficient for the centre, the republic or even the oblast' to pass resolutions or legislation if the municipal or rural raion or *sel'sovet* organs did not implement them, it being regular practice in the Soviet Union that a law be passed and not consummated. The co-operation of local officialdom was a prerequisite for effective action and its absence often tied the hands of the higher authorities. This official responsibility of local government organs for policy implementation in the areas under their jurisdiction applied to religion as well.[6] There was little the centre could do in face of decisive action or inaction on the part of a local leadership which did not always appreciate the niceties of Moscow's rather tortuous policy toward religion. In order, therefore, to understand the position of Islam in the republics and oblasti, it is necessary to look at the attitude towards it of the provincial bureaucracy and to see what factors influenced the patterns of behaviour of local officialdom in respect to Islam and how far these varied from one region to another and from period to period.

Even in the late Stalin period, when the chief occupation of the local bureaucracy was obedience to the centre,[7] CARC's *upolnomochennye* encountered cases of local officials misinterpreting the situation and/or ignoring the law, in that they believed that the constitutional right of freedom of worship entitled citizens to pray where and when they found it convenient.[8] CARC Chairman Polianskii reported recurrent cases of the leaders of local soviet organs in Central Asia not only misunderstanding, but actually distorting, regime policy toward Islam. Nor did the travesties of which they were guilty indicate a single, consistent line. They manifested an outward animosity to religion as a whole and to Islam in particular by turning down applications to open mosques, despite the manifest dearth of registered prayer-houses. At the same time, they were prepared to condone Islamic practice on the quiet, pretending not to notice mosques which operated without

---

power wielded by kolkhoz chairmen and administrations grew immensely as of 1950, when Khrushchev began implementing his policy of consolidating medium and small kolkhozy into large-scale production units.

6. See, for example, Chapter 1, *passim*.

7. Hill, 'The Development of Soviet Local Government since Stalin's Death', p.18.

8. For example, Guliaev, CARC *upolnomochennyi* in Pavlodar, to N. Sabitov, undated [probably July 1945]; GARF, f.6991, o.3, d.29, l.113.

registration. When pressured by their superiors to take steps against unregistered religious groups, local organs of government would initiate periodic campaigns to terminate their activity – although undoubtedly aware that closures, especially when conducted as a result of a specific campaign, comprised sheer deception, religious associations simply breaking up into smaller groups and coming together for prayers in a number of locations instead of one.[9] On one occasion, in a letter to the top leadership, Polianskii sweepingly maintained that the local bureaucracy in Central Asia did not merely ignore CARC's endeavours to legalise 'the Muslim movement', but stubbornly opposed it.[10]

Nor did this hold solely for Central Asia, but applied much nearer home as well. A year after the end of World War II Polianskii complained to Deputy Chairman of the USSR Council of Ministers Aleksei Kosygin that Chairman of the Tatar ASSR Council of Ministers Said Sharafeev, instead of following established procedures in dealing with applications to open mosques, referred them to the party *obkom*. This body, in turn, abstained from reviewing them, and the result was that mosques were simply not opened, Obkom Secretary Zinnat Muratov explaining that mosques and churches should not be opened so as not to 'promote the growth of religion'. The situation regarding Islam, however, was getting out of hand: in Kazan' on the Muslim festivals so many people thronged in and around the mosque that the militia had to be called in to restore order. When CARC's *upolnomochennyi* sought to review a number of applications despite the republican leadership's obstructionism, Muratov threatened to expel him from the party. CARC's efforts to get Muratov to accommodate to Moscow's position were unsuccessful and so Polianskii asked Kosygin to issue appropriate instructions to both Muratov and Sharafeev to ensure that they undertook to conduct themselves in accordance with official policy rather than following their own

9. I. V. Polianskii to the Bureau of the Ministry of Culture, K. E. Voroshilov, M. A. Turkin, M. A. Suslov, and A. A. Kuznetsov, 10 June 1948; GARF, f.6991, o.3, d.53, l.36. For various instances of closures of unregistered mosques and the termination of the activity of unregistered religious associations which re-appeared and re-commenced activity within a short period, see pp.321-2.

10. I. V. Polianskii to I. V. Stalin, L. P. Beriia, V. M. Molotov and K. E. Voroshilov at the Council of Ministers, and to A. A. Zhdanov, N. S. Khrushchev, A. A. Kuznetsov, N. S. Patolichev and G. M. Popov at the Central Committee Secretariat, 27 Feb. 1947; GARF, f.6991, o.3, d.47, l.92.

inclinations.[11] Fourteen years later the chairman of the council of ministers of the same autonomous republic showed a similar independent frame of mind when he dealt with a request of Kazan's registered mosque to construct an annexe without approaching CARC, maintaining that he did not know that its consent had to be obtained in order to give or refuse permission for such a step.[12]

Indeed, throughout the period, the concepts and goals that motivated the various decrees and resolutions of the centre were more often than not unknown to, or consciously ignored by, its satraps in the periphery.[13] They continued to show signs of failing to comprehend the principles behind the state's attitude to religion, tending to be guided rather by traditional norms of leadership conduct in their respective areas or by their own needs and interests. This held especially, but not solely, for the lower rungs of the hierarchy. It thus frequently occurred that the execution of policy in the localities was at total variance with the intent of its formulators.

The discrepancies that were evident throughout the Soviet Union between central and local organs of power were particularly manifest in Central Asia and the Northern Caucasus. Here the norms or criteria which directed the relationships between rulers and governed were least affected by the Russian Imperial conquest prior to 1917 and by the Soviet regime subsequent to that date. The Soviet policy of relying on indigenous 'cadres' to serve as the conduit between centre and periphery in the various national units into which the country was divided, led to a wide range of difficulties in policy implementation, and policy regarding Islam was no exception.[14] True, the higher echelons, at the republican

11. I. V. Polianskii to A. N. Kosygin, 16 May 1946; GARF, f.6991, o.3, d.34, ll.73-4. Kosygin in fact ordered the two officials to enable the *upolnomochennyi* to proceed to work 'normally'.

12. The issue was the construction of a two-storey annexe to the mosque, of which the top floor was to serve as an office and reception room and the bottom floor as a cloakroom. The republican council of ministers, after some deliberation, resolved to permit the building to be used for these purposes – N. I. Smirnov, Information, 16 Jan. 1960; GARF, f.6991, o.3, d.204, ll.39-45. For the issues connected with the construction of this building, see pp. 238-9.

13. Compare p.50.

14. This was a main reason for the pendulum quality of Soviet nationalities policy, which moved from the *korenizatsiia* – the promotion of national cadres – of the 1920s to an increased reliance on Russian personnel and then back, or partially so, to what was hoped would be a working compromise. Most of

level, were considerably more influenced by the winds blowing from the national capital than those at a further remove from the centre's leverage who did not come into constant, direct contact with its pressures. One expert on Uzbekistan has contended that Moscow adopted 'a bifurcated or two-tiered approach' in its dealings with that republic, by which the upper tier was geared to the centre's more streamlined and modern perceptions, while the mobilisation, elevation and equality of opportunity of the lower tier, consisting of the *mahallas* and kishlaks, were 'relegated to some indeterminate future'.[15] But even the republican leadership filled its mission on the basis of a general understanding with the all-union leadership that it must meet the latter's requirements while paying deference to the social and cultural habits of its constituency.[16]

It has been maintained, too, that the structural conditions of the Soviet system encouraged patronage networks to flourish that by their very nature undercut system performance and political effectiveness.[17] Indisputably, these had 'a special buoyancy' in the Central Asian and Transcaucasian republics as a result of cultural and institutional structures based on geographical and clan ties.[18]

---

the literature dealing with Soviet nationalities policy dwells at length on this quandary and its ramifications – see, for example, Simon, *Nationalism and Policy Toward the Nationalities in the Soviet Union, passim.*

15. Carlisle, 'Uzbekistan and the Uzbeks', pp.26-7.

16. Although probably never spelled out in so many words, this seems to have been one of the lessons of the Stalin period learned under Khrushchev. Some scholars insist that the republican élites in Central Asia were in fact appointed by Moscow precisely because they fitted its perception of a satrap, and filled the task of economic performer and/or propagandist – see Gleason, 'Sharaf Rashidov and the Dilemmas of National Leadership', pp.135 and 157. This, too, is surely the sense, the bottom line, of Carlisle's 'regional paradigm' as the key to political power in Uzbekistan and Tajikistan – Carlisle, 'Geopolitics and Ethnic problems of Uzbekistan and Its Neighbours'; also Vaisman, 'Regionalism and Clan Loyalty in the Political Life of Uzbekistan'.

17. See, for example, Voslensky, *Nomenklatura, The Soviet Ruling Class, passim.* It is worth noting here that the tsarist system had been famous for the corruption of its officials, especially in the provinces. The Soviet regime had not basically changed this, retaining, paradoxically, much of the traditional political amorality. (This was one of the many comparable features of the two body politics.)

18. Willerton, *Patronage and politics in the USSR*, pp. 13 and 191. This study concludes that the patron-client relationship rooted in geographic and clan ties in Azerbaijan transcended the political rivalries of the Soviet period – *ibid.*, p. 192. This clearly held for the other Muslim republics as well.

Close links existed among the occupants of public positions at the level of the republic, oblast' or raion, *mahalla,* kishlak or aul in each of the Muslim areas, every one of which had its own traditions, customs and interests, hierarchies and long-standing clan alliances and rivalries. This meant that loyalties were to the immediate reference framework, rather than to the distant overlord.[19] Moreover, the lower-rank officials in the localities were in every way indistinguishable from the masses of the population around them. People who filled positions in the *sel'sovet* and kolkhoz were ordinary citizens, often not even party members. Their loyalties tended to be first and foremost to their neighbours, relatives and local peer group, not even to the local or regional patronage system and network.

The situation regarding Islam was so unsatisfactory and the centre's condemnation of local officialdom in the Muslim areas in this context so sundry, massive and prevalent that a number of questions are in order. How far did this disapprobation represent an objective description? Or did it reflect rather the clash of interests or tension which unquestionably existed between the organs of government in the centre and the periphery?[20] Or was it perhaps an escape mechanism used by the responsible organisations in Moscow in order to exonerate themselves and their own apparatus from obvious inadequacies in the periphery?[21] Local government traditionally filled the role of lightning rod for bungling and mismanagement and failures in policy implementation.[22] In this context it is worth noting that Shepilov at Agitprop reacted to Polianskii's

19. For the intricacies of the system, see, for example, Carlisle, 'The Uzbek Power Elite: Politburo and Secretariat (1938-83)'.

20. This tension was not peculiar to issues relating to Islam and to religion. Polianskii sought to help overcome it by stressing the obligation of CARC's *upolnomochennye* to report to the oblast' and republican leadership no less regularly or fully than they did to Moscow, thus enabling local officialdom to become more aware of what was at stake – Minutes, Conference of CARC *upolnomochennye,* 11 [June] 1946; GARF, f.6991, o.3, d.39, ll.79-80. This, however, often proved to be a double-edged sword – see p.13. For these tensions between CARC and local government, see also pp.591-3.

21. For the systemic context of the ongoing dispute between CARC and the CRA, on the one hand, and the local organs of government, on the other, see Chapter 10, *passim.*

22. This, too, did not relate only to Islam but was a general phenomenon, dating back to tsarist times, when it was inappropriate, even inconceivable, to lay blame at the door of the *batiushka* tsar, the country's Little Father.

account of the distortions of policy and violations of the law on the part of local officials by blaming CARC itself for failing to issue regular instructions and guidance to the local government apparatus explaining the rights and obligations of religious organisations.[23] Further, can one speak of the attitude of local government to Islam, or did each official or perhaps administrative unit entertain its own standpoint? Altogether, was the issue an attitude to Islam or was it rather the relationship between a particular official and the local clergy or between officialdom and an individual mosque, mulla or religious society? How otherwise can one explain that the accusations hurled at the local organs of government ranged from connivance with violations of the legislation on religion by the clergy and underestimation of the political implications and significance of work regarding religion, to repressive measures or methods that contradicted the very spirit of the religious policy of the party and state and transcended the assignment the local organs of government were supposed to fulfil? Is it possible to extrapolate from a given action, or, more commonly apparently, instance of inaction, regarding a certain community and draw inferences or conclusions which will provide a broader picture?

Since Islam was in many ways the quintessence of local tradition, it inevitably comprised one of the crucial areas of conflict between centre and periphery. Almost certainly, the senior apparatchiki of the Muslim nationalities had discarded belief in God and imbibed, even internalised, some of the fundamental concepts of materialist thought. They considered Islam the epitome of that backwardness which it was incumbent upon them to help their co-nationals assign to the dustbin of history and were probably convinced that this was a prerequisite for their people's ultimate entry onto the path of progress. At the same time, they were fully conscious of the centrality of its rites for the indigenous population, especially in the social sphere, and of the obstacles that would have to be surmounted in order to meet this goal. The further down one descended in the hierarchy, the less evident was this conviction and the greater the pressure to indulge some of these rites and even to actively take part in them not only in the privacy of the home but in public places as well.

This chapter will look not so much at the perceptions of local

23. D. T. Shepilov to A. A. Zhdanov, undated [late July 1947]; RTsKhIDNI, f.17, o.125, d.506, l.180.

officials as at their deeds. True, the republican, and sometimes even the oblast', authorities did make policy decisions, and there were disagreements between Moscow and certain positions adopted by these higher local organs. Yet, the brunt of the criticism levelled by Moscow seems to have been directed first and foremost at the practice of the local organs of government and their general inefficacy. The atmosphere of mistrust which dominated relations between the organs of government in the centre and the periphery cannot be explained simply by a desire on the part of the former to find a scapegoat upon whom to lay the blame for blatant failures in policy implementation. The major attention paid by CARC and the CRA to local officialdom highlighted the latter's importance in the realm of executing policy towards the various faiths and Islam specifically – where its participation and cooperation were particularly crucial to, indeed prerequisites of, success – and the former's sense of acute frustration at its dependence upon so unreliable and uncontrollable a network.

CARC's *upolnomochennye*, whose apparatus was understaffed, had no choice but to maintain constant contact with, and rely upon, the local government apparatus, including the party organs of the kolkhozy, and the local press which it controlled, in order to gather information on, and expose, those who transgressed against the legislation on religion.[24] (It should be stressed in this context that the kolkhozy themselves underwent change in the 1950s: parallel to the process of amalgamating them, their links to the party became far more tenacious, Khrushchev being apparently convinced that the rural sector would thus become a more integral part of the Soviet body politic.[25]) The *upolnomochennye* also needed the local administration to fulfil another of their primary

24. Theses for instructional address at a conference of CARC *upolnomochennye*, approved by CARC session No.24s, 25-26 Sept. 1952; GARF, f.6991, o.3, d.83, ll.254, 261-2 and 269-70.

25. The number of kolkhozy was reduced from 93,000 at the end of 1953 to 39,500 at the end of 1963, partly due to the transformation of collective into state farms (*sovkhozy*), but mainly due to the amalgamation of farms, the average number of households per kolkhoz increasing in this same decade from 220 to 411. Between 1953 and 1958, too, tens of thousands of communists were transferred from the towns to rural administrative posts, party members were recruited in the agricultural sector and party cells were introduced in the 20 per cent or so of kolkhozy which were without them in the former year – Rigby, *Communist Party Membership in the U.S.S.R.*, pp.330-1. See also n.5 above.

assignments – taking stock of the unregistered religious associations and clergy and buildings of former mosques, which might be used as prayer-premises, and studying processes and changes in both the practice and consciousness of the believer community.[26]

Perhaps, in fact, the main task of the local organs of government was supplying information, and, precisely here, the fallibility of the system became evident. It almost seems as though this assignment was intended to make a laughing-stock of the very foundations of the Soviet body politic. It was not only that local organs and the centre in Moscow sometimes had conflicting interests, and therefore the former had a clear motivation for not unravelling the entire truth. It seems that they wanted at all costs to get Moscow off their backs, and so tended consistently to downplay the gravity of Muslim religious activity, except on those occasions where they had a patent interest in presenting it as threatening; for if Islam was disappearing in accordance with Marxist-Leninist theory, there was no need for constant surveillance and interference from the centre, which *ipso facto* no local officialdom desired. In the words of one report from the early-mid 1970s, statements of leading officials of municipal and raion executive organs that the public did not observe religious rites were without substantiation and were not confirmed by any concrete evidence.[27]

Local organs of government were likewise supposed to aid in taking repressive measures. Illicit religious activity could be effectively curtailed only through the systematic efforts of local government organs. Following the CPSU Central Committee resolution of January 1960 on violations of the law by clergy, CARC Chairman Puzin explained to SADUM Chairman Babakhanov the measures which would be taken by local officials in order to stop and correct these transgressions. He suggested that the mufti forestall these actions by instructing the clergy to implement legislation

---

26. For example, Draft CRA resolution 'On the work of the Council's *upol-nomochennyi* in Chimkent Oblast, the Kazakh SSR, Comrade Sh. O. Ospanov', Aug. 1969; GARF, f.6991, o.6, d.290, l.82.

27. I. Bonchkovskii to E. I. Lisavtsev, 1 June 1973; GARF, f.6991, o.6, d.537, ll.171-9. Bonchkovskii, deputy head of the CRA department of Muslim and Buddhist affairs, was reporting on a tour of Azerbaijan; the entire document is impregnated with doubts about the reliability of local officialdom in its attitude to Islamic practice. For the problems connected with the information transmitted by local officialdom, see also p.86.

with precision.[28] A decade earlier CARC insisted that it was the duty of local officialdom, for example, to summon people who engaged in holding unauthorised prayer-meetings or who put their homes at the disposal of believers for purposes of collective prayer, point out to them that this was illegal and ask them to desist. Leaders of religious groups who persisted should be warned by the local militia.[29] At the same time, CARC instructed its *upol-nomochennye* in the field, who were assigned simultaneously to the republican governments or oblast' executive organs, the *oblispolkoms*, to refrain from all manifestly anti-religious work. They, it insisted, had to be scrupulous in maintaining relations of confidence with the clergy and with the lay leaders of the religious societies, who were not subordinate to them and so could not, at least in theory, be given instructions by them. In this connection CARC's *upol-nomochennye* were not to create the impression that they were conducting a struggle against the unregistered clergy, leaving all 'educational and prohibitive' measures to the organs of local government.[30]

Undisputably, too, local officialdom was responsible for the conduct of atheistic propaganda, which it would be asked to augment as the fast and festivals approached in order to counter or pre-empt the animation of religion by the Muslim clergy and religious *aktiv*.[31] Guided by the decrees of the CPSU Central Committee and those of the local republican party, the party and Komsomol organs at the oblast' and raion level conducted scientific-atheistic work to form a material perception of the world in the minds of workers. In many parts, as of the 1960s, scientific-

28. Reception by A. A. Puzin of Ziyautdin Babakhanov, 17 Feb. 1960; GARF, f.6991, o.4, d.110, l.9.

29. I. V. Polianskii to K. E. Voroshilov, 4 Feb. 1950; RTsKhIDNI, f.17, o.132, d.285, l.22.

30. I. V. Polianskii, Letter of Instruction No.6, undated, ratified by CARC session No.6, 23 April 1948, and Minutes, CARC session No.4, 4-5 April 1950; GARF, f.6991, o.3, d.53, l.3, and d.66, l.61.

31. In 1952, for instance, the CARC *upolnomochennyi* in Andijan Oblast' noted the successful attempts of the local apparatus to keep young people away from the mosques on Qurban-Bayram – L. A. Prikhod'ko, Draft report, 31 Jan. 1953; GARF, f.6991, o.3, d.91, l.5. See also V. Kuroedov to the CPSU Central Committee Propaganda Department, 2 March 1970; GARF, f.6991, o.6, d.284, l.5. For the boost given to religious activity by the advent of the fast, see p. 469. For problems connected with the conduct of atheistic propaganda by local officialdom, see pp.567-70.

methodological councils of scientific atheism were established under the auspices of the oblast', town or raion *ispolkom*, and people's universities, as well as radio and television universities for atheistic education, were set up.[32]

The active co-operation of local officialdom, for example, which was a *sine qua non* for implementing the CPSU Central Committee resolution on terminating the activity of *mazars* and other shrines involved considerable propaganda activity. Thus, in Azerbaijan the republican party instructed party organs in the localities, the media and the various local executive organs to expose the anti-scientific and anti-social nature of those who exploited such holy places for their own interests. Letters and questionnaires were prepared for circulation to all the republic's forty-six *raiispolkoms* and *gorispolkoms* asking them to study the activity at the *pirs* in their areas of jurisdiction and to report to the special committee set up by the republican government. These included suggestions for the transfer of some of them to kolkhozy or sovkhozy as cultural institutions or their preservation as historical monuments.[33]

The commissions of assistance introduced in the early 1960s at the various local executive organs to ensure the implementation of the increasing number of anti-religious enactments were set up and implemented in the Muslim areas as well.[34] By late 1966, the CRA *upolnomochennyi* for the Uzbek SSR reported that in that republic there were 146 such commissions (with an average of seven members).[35] Yet, it seems that more often than not they existed on paper alone, to cite one report on the situation of Islam in Nakhichevan in the early-mid 1970s,[36] and new edicts were constantly being passed at various levels in order to activate them. In 1967 or early 1968 the Bukhara Oblast' executive committee, for instance, ratified new regulations concerning the commissions to ensure that they assist raion and municipal executive

32. For example, in the Karakalpak ASSR – P. Krivosheev, Information, 30 July 1971; GARF, f.6991, o.6, d.370, l.100.

33. M. M. Shamsudinskii, Information, 20 Feb. 1959; GARF, f.6991, o.3, d.183, ll.77-85.

34. For these commissions, see pp.45-6.

35. M. Miragzamov to M. Kh. Khalmuhamedov, 22 Oct. 1966; GARF, f.6991, o.6, d.11, l.65.

36. I. A. Bonchkovskii to E. I. Lisavtsev, 1 June 1973; GARF, f.6991, o.6, d.537, l.175.

committees and lower organs of local government – in the villages, *poselki* and *mahallas* – to expose unofficial clergy and religious societies and anyone else engaging in religious activity and to control and terminate the doings of itinerant mullas, *ishans* and *tabibs*. The members of the commission at the Bukhara Gorispolkom exposed eleven unregistered clergy, established personal control of their activity and sent their names to the municipal financial department in order that it impose taxes on them.[37] In Tajikistan the commissions' main task seems to have been the exposure of illegally operating mosques.[38]

Toward the end of the 1960s, apparently as part of the effort to implement the decisions of the Tashkent conference of July 1968, the union republics whose eponymous population was one of the traditionally Muslim peoples passed resolutions designating the terms of reference of the commissions of assistance. The Uzbek SSR Council of Ministers issued a special statute in early 1969 stipulating their obligations. They were to assist the local soviets in ensuring that citizens enjoyed their constitutional freedoms of the conduct of religious practice and anti-religious propaganda; to observe the activity of the religious associations and clergy and study its forms and methods, particularly in regard to the clergy's influence over the younger generation, adaptation to contemporary conditions and preaching; to help the local organs of government expose and eradicate vestiges of the past connnected with Islam, such as the marriage of adolescents, payment and receipt of *qalym*, and wearing the *paranja*; to take part in the verification of believers' complaints regarding violations of their rights; and to assist local officials in explaining the laws on religion.[39] In Dagestan such commissions were set up in most *sel'sovets*, which somewhat improved both the flow of information from the more outlying parts to the administrative centres and measures taken to curb religious activity.[40] A CRA report for the year 1970 noted some

37. A. Barinskaia to V. A. Kuroedov, undated [late March-early April 1968]; GARF, f.6991, o.6, d.153, l.114.

38. U. Yuldashev to V. A. Kuroedov, 20 Dec. 1966; GARF, f.6991, o.6, d.11, l.53.

39. Appendix No.2, Uzbek SSR Council of Ministers resolution, 7 Feb. 1969 (signed A. Azamov); on 15 May 1969 the Azerbaijan SSR Council of Ministers issued a similar document – GARF, f.6991, o.6, d.223, ll.88-91 and 3ob.-4.

40. Kh. Salahetdinov and I. Mikhalev, Information, transmitted by hand to E. I. Lisavtsev, 26 Oct. 1971; GARF, f.6991, o.6, d.361, ll.105-6.

of the positive results achieved by these commissions, namely in supervising the activity of the clergy and religious associations and controlling the observance of the laws on religion.[41]

Yet, many of the commissions were still not fulfilling their functions properly. They failed to study the situation pertaining in their area and to uncover most of the violations of the law committed by the clergy and religious *aktiv*, taking advantage of the fact that the local organs of government did not manifest much interest in their activity or urge them to be more effective.[42] In some parts of the country the unsatisfactory situation in respect to the implementation of the legislation on religion was actually blamed on the slackness of the commissions of assistance; for instance, in one raion in Eastern Kazakhstan toward the end of the 1960s, where itinerant mullas were not only not subjected to taxes, but travelled around openly on horseback completely undisturbed.[43]

Before looking at, interpreting and analysing the material itself, it is necessary to point out that the source was usually CARC's, or the CRA's, local – oblast' or republican – *upolnomochennyi*. He was himself often being hauled over the coals by his superiors in Moscow for not doing enough to investigate the situation in the field and for not actually visiting most of the territory under his jurisdiction and, consequently, for not being able to report with adequate precision; and for entertaining either an unduly partial or, alternatively, an overly antagonistic position regarding the Muslim community and its clergy. In the late 1960s, for instance, the *upolnomochennyi* in Chimkent Oblast' was blamed for not striving to procure the participation of local government in ensuring observance of the legislation on religion; for there being no commissions of assistance in the oblast'; for not giving instructions to, or holding seminars for, local officials, who, as a result, knew neither their rights nor their obligations in this respect, the various *raiispolkoms* having no documentation on the procedure for register-

41. CRA report, sent to the CPSU Central Committee, 27 April 1971; TsKhSD, f.5, o.63, d.89, ll.134-5.

42. Zh. Botashev to Sh. Bakirov, 22 Feb. 1971; GARF, f.6991, o.6, d.376, ll.7-11. The CRA *upolnomochennyi* in Kzyl-Orda Oblast' specifically asked the *oblispolkom* to compel the administration in the localities to activate the commissions.

43. Resolution, Eastern Kazakhstan Oblispolkom, 23 April 1969; GARF, f.6991, o.6, d.223, l.36. And see p.338.

ing religious associations or the standard forms for agreements regarding the handing over of prayer-houses. He was even accused of not interfering in the election of the executive organs and auditing commissions of the registered mosques, which he and the local organs of government left entirely to the clergy and mosque *aktiv*.[44] Although such elections were not within the jurisdiction of the *upolnomochennyi*, he was apparently expected to intervene opaquely – through persuasion and the use of his influence. (In other instances, indeed, both local officials and CRA *upolnomochennye* were berated for interfering in the election of lay officials of Muslim religious societies.[45])

As a result, in the communications he made to these same superiors, the CARC *upolnomochennyi* would seek to vindicate himself and lay all blame at other doors. He dwelt at length on the poor conditions in which he operated: lack of staff (an oblast' *upolnomochennyi* usually had no staff whatever), funds and means of transportation; on misinformation, or disinformation, on the part of local officials on whom he had perforce to rely; and on the inadequacies and misdeeds of these same people.[46] Unquestionably, much of the data supplied by local officials was sheer fabrication, such as the case of the second secretary of one Azerbaijani *raikom* who sought to impress the republican party agitprop department with the achievements of the local party in the field of religion.[47] Despite their vested interest in presenting local officialdom in a negative light, the *uplnomochennye's* own reports are so extremely insistent in presenting the shortcomings in the perceptions and actions of the representatives of local government, that their general content matter comes across as generally, even if not wholly, credible.

---

44. A. Barmenkov, Draft CRA resolution 'On the work of the Council's *upolnomochennyi* in Chimkent Oblast', the Kazakh SSR, Sh. O. Ospanov', Aug. 1969; GARF, f.6991, o.6, d.290, l.83.

45. See pp.231-2 and 280.

46. For example, H. Akhtiamov, Report, Conference of CARC *upolnomochennye*, Alma-Ata, 30 Sept. 1946; GARF, f.6991, o.3, d.41, ll.114-15. The lack of any auxiliary staff and minimal facilities was particularly onerous – or perhaps provided a particularly valid pretext for all the *upolnomochennyi*'s shortcomings – given the considerable size and the inaccessibility of many of the oblasti; compare Chapter 5, n.192.

47. For details, see pp.3-4.

Indifference to Islamic activity

The first accusation levelled against the organs of local government was that they disparaged the political significance of Islam and Islamic practice, and so, inevitably, the need to rectify the situation and prevent it from getting out of hand. In the words of CARC's *upolnomochennyi* for Kirgiziia in 1946, local officialdom, notably at the raion level, underestimated Muslim activity and did not treat its regulation as official policy.[48] This was in line with Polianskii's statement to AUCP(b) Central Committee Secretary Andrei Zhdanov in 1947 in connection with the widespread non-implementation of religious legislation in the localities to the effect that party and soviet organs underestimated the significance of questions connected with 'religious cults'. This was manifest in their arbitrary opening and shutting down of prayer-houses, their unwillingness to review and express an opinion regarding complaints and statements made by believers and clergy, and recurrent cases of intentional bureaucratisation.[49]

The widespread disregard for the political importance of Islam was one of the reasons why CARC's *upolnomochennye* in the Muslim areas, particularly at the oblast' level, were often allegedly chosen without due care and without anyone insisting that they have the necessary qualifications.[50] This continued to be true well beyond the formative period of the late war and immediate postwar years.[51] Moreover, once they were appointed, neither the *oblispolkom* chairman nor his deputy took any interest in their work.[52] Many of them complained, in addition, that they were being constantly sent on assignments which had nothing to do with their duties

48. H. Akhtiamov, Report, Conference of CARC *upolnomochennye*, Alma-Ata, 30 Sept. 1946; GARF, f.6991, o.3, d.41, l.115.

49. I. V. Polianskii to A. A. Zhdanov, 22 July 1947; RTsKhIDNI, f.17, o.125, d.506, l.167. While Polianskii spoke of religion in general, the first example he gave related to Islam in Uzbekistan. For a similar statement in this same time period, see pp. 13-14.

50. I. V. Polianskii to K. E. Voroshilov, 13 Nov. 1946; GARF, f.6991, o.3, d.34, l.199. For the appointment of CARC and CRA *upolnomochennye* by the republican governments and oblast' executive organs, see also p.13.

51. Nor did this apply solely to the Muslim parts of the country, although it seems to have been particularly acute there.

52. For example, Minutes, Instructional meeting of CARC *upolnomochennye* in the Uzbek SSR, 15-17 March 1956; TsGAUz, f.2456, o.1, d.183, ll.54 and 56.

in the field of religion and so these were perforce neglected.[53] Several documents testify to the lack of effective communication and common purpose of the CARC *upolnomochennye* and local officialdom in the Muslim areas. The latter disregarded information emanating from the former, especially when it contained data likely to present them in an unfavourable light and to lead to reprimands by their superiors. Nor were local officials forthcoming with the information they were supposed to provide the *upolnomochennye*.[54] According to one source, the clergy could not but notice the disdainful attitude of the local organs of government to the *upolnomochennye* and their work.[55] Sometimes, too, oblasti remained for considerable periods without an *upolnomochennyi*.[56] CARC Chairman Polianskii asked the USSR Council of Ministers to instruct the heads of government and *oblispolkom* chairmen in Central Asia to direct and supervise the work of the *upolnomochennye* and to select better people for the job, and sought to elaborate with the AUCP(b) Central Committee's Cadres Administration a procedure by which CARC would be authorised to consent to or reject the choice of *upolnomochennye*.[57]

Apart from the CARC *upolnomochennye*, most organs of government did not in fact have anyone who was specifically charged with dealing with questions of religion, even in those parts where Islam was particularly assertive.[58] One *upolnomochennyi* suggested that a specific official, ideally the *oblispolkom* chairman or his deputy, be statutorily defined as responsible for religion. He also proposed that the *oblispolkom* provide the facilities and finances to enable

53. See p.13.

54. H. Akhtiamov, Report, Conference of CARC *upolnomochennye* in Central Asia, 17 Dec. 1949; GARF, f.6991, o.3, d.67, ll.128-9. See also pp. 595-6 above.

55. Minutes, Conference of CARC *upolnomochennye* in the Uzbek SSR, 9 Aug. 1948; TsGAUz, f.2456, o.1, d.120, l.8.

56. At the very end of the 1940s, no less than six oblasti in Kazakhstan had no *upolnomochennyi* – N. Sabitov, Report, Conference of CARC's Central Asian *upolnomochennye*, 15 Dec. 1949; GARF, f.6991, o.3, d.67, l.141.

57. I. V. Polianskii to K. E. Voroshilov, 13 Nov. 1946; and to L. P. Beriia, I. V. Stalin, V. M. Molotov and K. E. Voroshilov at the Council of Ministers and to A. A. Zhdanov, N. S. Khrushchev, A. A. Kuznetsov, N. S. Patolichev and G. M. Popov at the Central Committee Secretariat, 27 Feb. 1947; GARF, f.6991, o.3, d.34, l.200, and d.47, l.97.

58. For the general lack of interest of local government in religion, see pp. 13-4.

its *upolnomochennyi* to make trips to the localities.[59] As early as 1945 the Tashkent Oblispolkom suggested to the *gorispolkoms* throughout the oblast' that they appoint a person to deal with religious affairs; but this was not done.[60] In the mid-1950s First Secretary of the Uzbekistan CP Nuretdin Muhitdinov himself took a personal interest in all that concerned Islam, but he was apparently an exception and he seems to have done so out of his own inclination rather than *ex officio*.[61]

Nor was it only on the issue of appointing someone responsible for religion that the local organs displayed their disinterest in Islam. The *raiispolkoms* in Tashkent Oblast' neither took the trouble to discuss religious matters nor to implement the decisions of the *oblispolkom*: in 1946 not a single raion executive organ made inventories of the functioning and non-functioning mosques on its territory or took any steps to register mosques which operated without authorisation, although they had at their disposal information concerning at least some of them; nor did any of the raion financial organs exact taxes even from registered prayer-houses and clergy.[62] In Kazakhstan at the end of the 1940s the financial departments at the local level were totally unable to raise taxes from the unregistered clergy, although the CARC *upolnomochennyi* informed the republic finance ministry of 382 'home-grown' mullas who operated in Kazakhstan.[63] In Kirgiziia the lowest rungs of the local hierarchy did not occupy themselves on an everyday basis with religious issues, so that the CARC *upolnomochennye* had to go to the raiony to ensure that measures be taken to disband

---

59. A. R. Saltovskii, Report, Conference of CARC *upolnomochennye*, Alma-Ata, 30 Sept. 1946; GARF, f.6991, o.3, d.41, l.96.

60. K. Mustafin to A. Mavlianov, 19 July 1945 – GARF, f.6991, o.3, d.30, l.267; and to Tashkent Oblispolkom Chairman Turgunov and I. I. Ibadov, 19 April 1946 – TsGAUz, f.2456, o.1, d.67, l.1.

61. N. I. Inogamov, Address, Conference of CARC *upolnomochennye*, 25 Nov. 1958; GARF, f.6991, o.3, d.165, l.37. Muhitdinov was First Secretary of the Uzbekistan CP from 1955-57 (before being summoned to Moscow to serve as Secretary of the CPSU Central Committee).

62. K. Mustafin to Tashkent Oblispokom Chairman Turgunov and I. I. Ibadov, 19 April 1946; TsGAUz, f.2456, o.1, d.67, ll.1-3. Mustafin does not draw a distinction in this connection between registered and unregistered prayer-houses and clergy, but the context leaves no doubt that this is his meaning.

63. N. Sabitov, Report, Conference of CARC's Central Asian *upolnomochennye*, 15 Dec. 1949; GARF, f.6991, o.3, d.67, l.135.

unregistered religious associations. Moreover, the steps taken were not long-lasting, for, since the oblast' and raion executive organs carried out campaigns rather than working on a systematic basis, religious associations that were closed down would within a short time re-commence their activity.[64]

Officials in the localities paid no heed to the distinction drawn by the centre between most mosques opened without authorisation which it demanded be closed, and the few, whose existence the local organs of government considered to be 'politically expedient', which it asked them to register.[65] (Thus this aspect of policy remained a dead letter.[66]) Polianskii wrote to Zhdanov that local officialdom was concerned solely or primarily with the political image of the territory under its jurisdiction, which it did not wish to spoil by having an official, registered mosque. Instances of *obkom* secretaries and *oblispolkom* chairmen being opposed in principle to the opening of mosques in their fiefdoms were constantly recorded. This lay behind the custom of giving permission to conduct prayer-services in the open or in a non-functioning mosque on an ad hoc basis in order to relieve pressure from believers.[67]

In Polianskii's considered opinion it was the failure of officials to appreciate the role of those mosques which functioned officially in eliminating 'the underground Muslim movement' that led to their obstructing the opening of mosques and the legal activity of Muslim clerics. Allowing just seventeen mosques to register in all Kazakhstan and six in Turkmenistan could in no way satisfy the needs of the believer community in those republics.[68] Writing to the head of Agitrop in 1947, Polianskii blamed the local party

64. H. Akhtiamov, Report, Conference of CARC's Central Asian *upolnomochennye*, 17 Dec. 1949; GARF, f.6991, o.3, d.67, l.126. Polianskii, it will be remembered, had spoken of all closures as fictitious, since religious associations tended to find ways to persist in their activity – see above.

65. See pp.318, 553 and 604.

66. I. V. Polianskii to Baratov, 24 May 1947; TsGAUz, f.2456, o.1, d.82, ll.11–12. The document related specifically to Samarkand Oblast', where the situation in this regard was particularly acute; see pp.195, 297 and 654.

67. I. V. Polianskii to A. A. Zhdanov, 22 July 1947; RTsKhIDNI, f.17, o.125, d.506, l.169; and see, for example, Hamidullin to I. V. Polianskii, 28 Dec. 1946; TsGAUz, f.2456, o.1, d.72, l.59. See also p.641 below.

68. I. V. Polianskii to K. E. Voroshilov, 13 Nov. 1946; GARF, f.6991, o.3, d.34, l.199. For the situation prevailing in these two republics in regard to mosque registration, see pp.185–8.

and government organs, especially in Central Asia, for the difficulties being encountered in the effort to bring Muslim activity into a legal framework and regulating it.[69] In places where local officials did not supervise the religious organisations and their activities, he contended in a letter to Zhdanov, 'religious propaganda' was conducted not only inside the mosques, but even beyond their confines. In Central Asia the leaders of the lower-level organs were notoriously indifferent, sometimes even giving protection to religious organisations.[70]

In late 1946 a resolution of the Uzbekistan CP Central Committee Bureau 'On the unsatisfactory situation of mass political work among the population of the Uzbek SSR', castigated the organs of local government for Islam's achievements. In its wake Chairman of the Uzbek SSR Council of Ministers Abdujabr Abdurahmanov specifically attributed the mass opening of unregistered mosques to the lack of interest on the part of the chairmen of oblast', municipal and raion executive organs in curtailing Muslim activity and to the non-observance of the all-union government's decrees on the procedure for opening prayer-houses, especially in all that concerned the preliminary review of applications. There was also a dearth of appropriate cadres to conduct agitation and educational work. He asked the *oblispolkom* chairmen to initiate discussion of the reports received from CARC's *upolnomochennye*, to control and guide the work of these *upolnomochennye*, and to transmit the necessary information to the relevant financial organs, so that prayer-houses which had been opened illegally be subjected to taxation.[71]

Whether as a result of its underestimation of the political implications of the growth of Muslim activity or out of other considerations, or – most probably – out of simple inertia,[72] local officialdom turned a blind eye to the recurrent violations of legis-

69. I. V. Polianskii to G. F. Aleksandrov, 1 July 1947; RTsKhIDNI, f.17, o.125, d.506, l.126.

70. I. V. Polianskii to A. A. Zhdanov, 7 July 1947; RTsKhIDNI, f.17, o.125, d.506, l.151.

71. Resolution of the Uzbekistan CP Central Committee Bureau, 21 Dec. 1946 –RTsKhIDNI, f.17, o.125, d.421, ll.131-2; and A. Abdurahmanov to Karakalpak ASSR Council of Minsters Chariman Seitov and all *oblispolkom* chairmen, 29 Dec. 1946 –TsGAUz, f.2456, o.1, d.82, l.1.

72. Apathy was generally thought to characterise Soviet local officials; see, for example, Friedgut, 'The Soviet Citizen's Perception of Local Government', p.127.

lation on the part of the clergy and the believer *aktiv*. Constant legislation and resolutions on the part of higher authorities did not in practice mean their being carried out by those who were formally subordinate to them. Decisions taken by the republican organs of government had no impact on the oblasti, while those taken by the latter were similarly disregarded by the raiony and so all resolutions had regularly to be repeated. Apathy and irresponsibility in all that concerned Islam were said to characterise local officials in a number of areas.[73] In Kokchetau, in Kazakhstan, itinerant mullas approached a group of *aksakals* in the presence of local officials to tell them to make offerings to God in order to ensure better weather for the harvest, without this evoking any negative reaction on the part of the officials.[74] In Osh Oblast' it was reported that local government did not initiate a single measure over a period of six years to curb the influence of religious communities on believers and the general population despite, on the one hand, the large number of unauthorised openings of mosques, and, on the other, a whole series of resolutions and instructions from superior organs of government.[75] In Khorezm Oblast', in Uzbekistan, the local organs of government knew of the existence of a *mazar* in the mid 1950s, but did nothing to curb its activity – not even imposing taxes on shaykhs who officiated there.[76] This did not hold only for Central Asia. Reports from the RSFSR's national republics were of the same purport. In the Tatar ASSR in the second half of the 1940s, local government and party organs were said neither to know anything about Islamic life nor to be interested in hearing about it.[77]

Nor did the situation change over the years. Similar complaints could be heard in the 1960s and 1970s. A report on Islam in Bukhara Oblast' in 1968 noted that the local organs of government neither controlled the activity of unregistered religious groups,

73. For example, in Taldy-Kurgan Oblast' in Kazakhstan – Conference of CARC *upolnomochennye*, Alma-Ata, 2 Oct. 1946; GARF, f.6991, o.3, d.41, l.45.

74. Conference of CARC *upolnomochennye*, Alma-Ata, 2 Oct. 1946; GARF, f.6991, o.3, d.41, ll.53-4.

75. I. G. Halimov to H. Akhtiamov, 10 March 1951; GARF, f.6991, o.3, d.454, l.105.

76. I. V. Polianskii to the CPSU Central Committee and the USSR Council of Ministers, 13 Sept. 1955; GARF, f.6991, o.3, d.114, l.141.

77. Conference of CARC *upolnomochennye*, 11 [June] 1946; GARF, f.6991, o.3, d.39, ll.111-12. See also pp.609-10 above.

nor made any effort to eradicate violations of the law and obstruct the performance of illicit religious rites. Despite endeavours to enhance the effectiveness of the commissions of assistance, local officialdom remained generally indifferent to most religious groups, not, for instance, taking any measures to oversee, let alone stop, the activity of the Shiite groups which operated in the oblast'.

In the single year 1967 the CRA *upolnomochennyi* in the oblast' sent twenty letters to local organs of government, as well as speaking at seminars before employees of the courts, procuracy and militia. A CRA emissary to the oblast', dissatisfied with the state of affairs, discussed her findings with the *obkom* secretary for propaganda and agitation, the *oblispolkom* deputy chairman and relevant KGB officials, suggesting that the commissions of assistance be revitalised, the activities of the unregistered groups and clergy studied, and explanatory work conducted among soviet and party workers, as well as clergy and believers, so that the legislation on religion and its implications could be fully understood.[78] In the Kabardino-Balkar ASSR, too, the overwhelming majority of village soviets did not pay the requisite heed to observance of the legislation on religion. Local officials took no initiative to introduce secular rites, and educational and propaganda activity left much to be desired, the pretext here being that religious rites were national custom.[79] Altogether local officialdom was reported to look with equanimity upon the activity of unregistered Muslim clergy in many areas of Uzbekistan, Kazakhstan and Kirgiziia, as well as in Dagestan and the Chechen-Ingush ASSR.[80]

There was a certain amount of discussion within the ranks of the central apparatus as to how far local officialdom knew of transgressions against the laws on religion. The dominant view seems to have been that they were well aware of the activity of the 'mosqueless mullas', but for a variety of reasons found it expedient to remain silent.[81] Often prayer premises operated and

78. A. Barinskaia to V. A. Kuroedov, undated [late March-early April 1968]; GARF, f.6991, o.6, d.153, ll.110 and 114-15. For Barinskaia's meetings with KGB officials, see p.577.

79. L. Zh. Aisov to the CRA, 25 June 1971; GARF, f.6991, o.6, d.370, ll.135-6.

80. A. Barmenkov to the CPSU Central Committee Propaganda Department, 17 July 1971; GARF, f.6991, o.6, d.361, l.41.

81. I. G. Halimov to CARC, undated [probably early April 1949]; GARF, f.6991, o.3, d.454, l.11.

sometimes mosques were actually built under the very noses of the local soviet. In one settlement in Osh Oblast' the call to prayer (the *azan*) in the building of a former mosque was performed openly.[82] In other parts, for instance in Nakhichevan, local officials simply endeavoured to evade all mention of Islam. For them, it was suggested, the most important thing was just not to see the processes which were taking place in the sphere of religion.[83]

One of the most significant areas in which the indifference of local government impacted upon Muslim activity related to the cemeteries. By law these fell under the jurisdiction of the municipal or village administration, the church having been deprived of the possession of, or the rights to administer, all property.[84] This meant that the maintenance of the cemeteries was a component of the local government budget and that the local authorities were responsible for their upkeep, for the provision and conservation of the necessary facilities and equipment, and for the appointment of any clergy who might officiate at them. In the Muslim areas the legal situation of the cemeteries was not reflected in reality. Either because their upkeep involved considerable expense or out of disinterest, or perhaps as a result of a sense that the cemeteries rightfully belonged to the sphere of religion, many *ispolkoms* in effect avoided taking them over. Their neglect of the cemeteries persisted even after a new bout of legislation in the late 1960s endeavoured to ensure that the local organs of government equip them with the requisite facilities and services.[85]

In this way it came about that the clergy or the religious com-

82. I. G. Halimov to H. Akhtiamov, 22 April 1953; GARF, f.6991, o.3, d.94, l.68.

83. I. Bonchkovskii to E. I. Lisavtsev, 1 June 1973; GARF, f.6991, o.6, d.537, l.178.

84. Decree of SNK RSFSR #23-24, 1929, quoted in Pospielovsky, *A History of Marxist-Leninist Atheism and Soviet Anti-Religious Policies*, vol.1, p.136. This decree was enlarged upon by an Instruction of the Standing Commission on Questions of Religion attached to VTsIK, 'On the Procedure for Setting Up, Closing and Liquidating Cemeteries and the Procedure for Demolishing Tombstones', 16 Oct. 1931 – *Zakonodatel'stvo o religioznykh kul'takh*, pp.126-30.

85. For the Uzbek SSR Council of Ministers' resolution 'On Measures for Improving the Maintenance and Refurbishing of Cemeteries in the Towns and Raion Centres of the Uzbek SSR', 4 Nov. 1968, see *ibid.* pp.165-7. See also S. Shafiqov, Information, 22 Jan. 1971; Resolution, Osh Oblispolkom, 24 Feb. 1971; and Sh. Ospanov, Information, 15 March 1972 – GARF, f.6991, o.6, d.370, ll.13-14 and 15-9, and d.633, ll.83-4. For the cemeteries, see also pp.518-20.

munity, who in effect controlled the cemeteries, tended to be unperturbed by the fact that this formally entailed encroaching upon the preserve of the local administration.[86] On the one hand, the takeover of the cemeteries by believers and/or clergy often saved them from neglect and disorder[87] On the other hand, it led to a series of violations of the law on the territory of the cemeteries, to which the relevant local government organ would close its eyes.[88] Often it seemed that officials at the local level were actually afraid of initiating any action that might be detrimental to those who administered the cemetery and its affairs.[89] Sometimes formal agreements were actually signed between the local administration and a religious society transferring the cemetery to the latter's jurisdiction. In one such case in Azerbaijan the religious society committed itself to surrounding the cemetery with a wall and paving an access road. It also planted trees there, the income from the fruit and from the hay which grew on the cemetery grounds going to the mosque.[90] A number of instances were recorded where local officials distributed plots of land in the vicinity of cemeteries to religious associations, whom they also authorised to equip the cemeteries with all the requisite facilities.[91] In some cases a *sel'sovet* or kishlak soviet would actually provide funds for a religious association and its clergy to equip a cemetery.[92] The anomalous situation created around the cemeteries thus provided the backdrop for a wide range of transgressions against the law by local government organs and officials.[93]

86. CARC Inspector L. A. Prikhod'ko, head of the Council's Department for the Affairs of the Muslim, Buddhist and Jewish faiths, insisted that equipping cemeteries was interference in the affairs of the municipal or raion administration –Report, 20 May 1953; GARF, f.6991, o.3, d.91, l.250.

87. For instance in Tashauz (Turkmenistan) – Resolution, Tashauz Oblispolkom, 29 Oct. 1973; GARF, f.6991, o.6, d.548, ll.44-5.

88. Interview with a former CRA official who has asked to remain anonymous.

89. For example, in the Kabardino-Balkar ASSR in the late 1960s – L. Zh. Aisov to the CRA, 11 June 1968; GARF, f.6991, o.6, d.153, l.139.

90. All-Union conference of CARC *upolnomochennye*, 18-20 April 1960; GARF, f.6991, o.3, d.208, l.114.

91. V. Kuroedov to CRA *upolnomochennye*, 2 Feb. 1972, and Sh. Ospanov, Information, 15 March 1972; GARF, f.6991, o.6, d.462, l.3 and d.633, l.83.

92. V. A. Kuroedov to CRA *upolnomochennye*, 2 Feb. 1972, and A. Galiev to V. A. Kuroedov, 5 Oct. 1972; GARF, f.6991, o.6, d.462, l.3, and d.545, l.162.

93. For a further such example, see p.669 below.

Sometimes, at least, local officials held aloof from involvement in religious affairs out of a realisation that this was a particularly sensitive issue, in which they could only burn their fingers. In one instance, where they sought to influence the appointment of a religious official – an imam at the mosque in Karaganda in the second half of the 1940s – a major scandal and friction between clans ensued. As a result, the *raikom* secretary and chairman of the raion soviet lost their posts, following which nobody was prepared to occupy himself with religious matters at all.[94]

The nonchalance of the local authorities seems to have been especially prevalent in rural parts, where in most periods no serious effort was made to undertake atheistic propaganda and disseminate scientific-materialist views. Frequently, too, local officials refrained from informing the financial organs of the existence and activity of unregistered clergy.[95] They similarly did everything to conceal from Moscow the existence of thousands of non-functioning mosques.[96] Nor were the local militia or procuracy an exception to the rule. In Namangan Oblast' in the early 1950s the latter failed to initiate proceedings against religious figures who perpetrated serious crimes – one cleric, for instance, who both committed rape and performed marriage rites for an adolescent went scot-free.[97]

The state of affairs was so worrisome that in 1953 the Uzbek SSR Council of Ministers passed a resolution stating that the increased activities of the unregistered mullas, especially in rural parts, were the consequence of the laissez-faire attitude, sometimes to the point of actual connivance, of the municipal and raion executive organs. This decree, like others of the republican government, engendered similar or identical ones by the oblast' executive organs (just as the union republic governments adopted resolutions in the wake of the all-union council of ministers – often couched in the very same language).[98] That of the Samarkand Oblispolkom

94. Conference of CARC *upolnomochennye*, Alma-Ata, 2 Oct. 1946; GARF, f.6991, o.3, d.41, l.50.

95. Conference of CARC *upolnomochennye* in the Uzbek SSR, 9 Aug. 1948; TsGAUz, f.2456, o.1, d.120, l.10. See also p.598.

96. Interview with a former CRA official who has asked to remain anonymous.

97. Minutes, Instructional meeting of CARC's *upolnomochhennye* in Uzbekistan, 17-18 July 1951; TsGAUz, f.2456, o.1, d.134, l.69.

98. The CARC *upolnomochennyi* for Southern Kazakhstan related how the local *obkom* adopted a resolution on the lines of that of the CPSU Central Committee, which had been sent to all *oblispolkoms,* and they in turn sent instructions to

pointed out that the permissiveness of the local organs of government *vis-à-vis* the Muslim clergy enabled them to open mosques without authorisation and to commit other offences. It also dwelt on the dearth of 'educational work' among the population and the meagre efforts of the financial organs in imposing taxes.[99] In other instances, the party and executive organs at the oblast' level issued general instructions to those of the raiony to implement policy, as in Surkhan-Darya in relation to the closure of *mazars* in the late 1950s.[100]

Yet, the legislation and fiats of the lower levels of the hierarchy were no more meaningful or effective than were those of the higher echelons. Complaints persisted throughout the period under discussion that the local organs of government were making only the most feeble attempts to curb the activities of unregistered religious associations and clergy. Even as far as registered religious societies were concerned, the law was being constantly infringed in consequence of the failure of local *ispolkoms* to pay heed to the composition of the 'founding members' (i.e. the *dvadtsatka*) and executive organs of the religious societies.[101]

In some areas it was maintained that the fault lay with the raion executive organs for not acquainting the lower levels with the relevant republic's legislation and resolutions. In Kirgiziia, for instance, the deficiencies in one raion were attributed to its executive organ not having informed either the commission of assistance attached to it or the various soviets, or even its own financial and administrative organs, of the decrees of the republican supreme soviet and council of ministers, as a result of which they could not be put into practice. This led to an attitude of incorrect indifference on the part of the executive organs of the *poselki* and villages. Many of them did not bother to find out the true situation in regard to the existence and activity of unregistered religious

the *raiispolkoms* – Minutes, CARC session No.4, 25-26 Feb. 1959; GARF, f.6991, o.3, d.183, ll.87-90.

99. Resolution, Samarkand Oblispolkom, 11 Sept. 1953; TsGAUz, f.2456, o.1, d.159, ll.66-7. The republican government resolution was also quoted in a report sent by V. I. Gostev to P. A. Tarasov, 4 Jan. 1954; GARF, f.6991, o.3, d.102, l.4.

100. Conference of CARC's Central Asian *upolnomochennye*, Tashkent, 5-6 June 1959; GARF, f.6991, o.3, d.186, ll.135-8.

101. Theses of lecture, sent to the CPSU Central Committee Propaganda Department, 19 June 1968; GARF, f.6991, o.6, d.147, l.42.

associations and clergy, adopting a stance of non-intervention in relation to the most serious violations of the law, perhaps because they feared to spoil their good-neighbourly relations with the local clergy and public. The financial and administrative organs, for their part, allowed red tape to snarl investigations of the income and activity of the clergy and religious *aktiv* and manifested undue leniency and tolerance towards those who committed, or were accomplices to, crimes.[102]

In the years of Khrushchev's anti-religious campaign Deputy Chairman of the Tajik SSR Council of Ministers M. K. Karimova conducted a seminar for *raiispolkom* deputy chairmen at which attention was drawn to the impermissibility of lavish festivities and the organisation of commercial transactions at mosques on Uraz-Bayram. Yet bazaars sprang up in their proximity throughout the republic. At one such venue the head of the local militia was present, but he was reported to have been preoccupied with keeping 'order' rather than arresting the speculators.[103]

The 1968 Tashkent conference of officials from all relevant branches of the central bureaucracy and CRA *upolnomochennye* in the Muslim areas noted that, while in some parts, there was a certain improvement in the observance of the legislation on religion and some local organs correctly combined atheistic work with the practical control of the activity of religious associations, in a number of towns and raiony the situation was the reverse. In particular, there was a widespread renewal of pilgrimages to holy sites. Moreover, the heads of collectives and public organisations failed to react satisfactorily to information concerning the participation at prayer-services and in other rites of party and Komsomol members and intelligentsia, sometimes even conniving in such goings-on. Yet again, it was decided that matters had to be taken in hand and local officials at the raion, *poselok* and village level made aware of the laws and of their own duties regarding their implementation.[104]

102. K. Shabolotov to the Kirgiz SSR Council of Ministers, 26 Sept. 1969; GARF, f.6991, o.6, d.223, ll.68-70.

103. M. Hamidov to A. A. Puzin, 24 Feb. 1964; GARF, f.6991, o.3, d.1740, ll.11-12.

104. A. Barmenkov, A. Nurullaev and E. Tarasov, Information, sent by Kuroedov to the CPSU Central Committee Propaganda Department, 14 Aug. 1968; also K. Shaimardanov to A. Nurullaev and K. Kulumbetov, 14 July 1969 – GARF, f.6991, o.6, d.147, ll.121 and 123-4, and d.223, ll.43-5. For the participation

As usual, decisions taken centrally were reflected in a plethora of resolutions at the republican and oblast' level. While the republican governments continued to be a main butt of Moscow's criticisms,[105] they passed the buck onto their own subordinate organs. In mid-1969 a decree of the Azerbaijani Council of Ministers thus insisted that the republican financial and administrative organs were taking part 'listlessly' in the struggle against illegal religious activity and that the various *ispolkoms* were not exercising the requisite control over the observance of the law and were directing the work of the commissions of assistance unsatisfactorily.[106] At the same time, the Tashkent conference resolutions were sent to all local government organs and served as guidelines for activity regarding religion over a period of several years. During 1969 and 1970, oblast' and raion executive organs, as well as councils of ministers in the union and autonomous republics, began discussing issues connected with religious activity, and the local organs studied religious life in their oblasti and republics with greater attention, with an eye to in fact putting an end to violations of the law by religious associations and clergy and undertaking prophylactic measures.[107] For example, the Tashkent resolutions were circulated to all raion and municipal party and soviet organs in Alma-Ata Oblast', where they were discussed at seminars held by the *obkom* for party and soviet workers and editors of local newspapers.[108]

Even now, however, the setting seemed to remain fundamentally unchanged. Letters and instructions from the republican governments or oblast' authorities notwithstanding, the organs of local government did not undertake effective measures to limit the activity of Muslim religious societies within the framework of the law. Such failures to take appropriate action were noted in particular in connection with the two major festivals and the days of mourning

---

of local officials and party members in religious ceremonies, see pp.648–51 below.

105. V. A. Kuroedov to the Kazakh SSR Council of Ministers, 20 May 1969; GARF, f.6991, o.6, d.220, ll.109-12.

106. Azerbaijan SSR Council of Ministers, Resolution No.193, 15 May 1969; GARF, f.6991, o.6, d.223, l.2.

107. CRA report, sent to the CPSU Central Committee, 27 April 1971; TsKhSD, f.5, o.63, d.89, l.134.

108. R. Shaimardanov to A. A. Nurullaev and K. Kulumbetov, 14 July 1969; GARF, f.6991, o.6, d.223, ll.43-4.

of the month of Muharram.[109] In Karaganda Oblast' local officialdom was said on the whole to have improved its activity in regard to Islam following the Tashkent conference, yet some *raiispolkoms* and commissions of assistance remained inactive. One *raiispolkom* had no data whatever on unregistered clergy and many soviets failed to respond to requests for lists of itinerant mullas. Of forty who were exposed by the CRA *upolnomochennyi* only sixteen were subjected to taxation, the others remaining 'under observance' by the financial organs until their incomes could be verified. No measures were taken by the relevant administrations or financial organs to curb the activity of a former imam of the Karaganda mosque who operated as an itinerant mulla in a number of smaller townships and their surrounding settlements, where he performed religious rites and engaged in faith-healing.[110]

This situation continued into the 1970s. In late 1973 the Aktiubinsk Oblispolkom adopted a resolution which addressed the 'unjustified complacency' of the municipal and raion administrations that considered Islam as having outlived its time. Consequently, despite testimony to the contrary, they maintained that it exercised no influence on the population. The resolution further censured the financial organs in the localities for not unmasking the income of unregistered clergy from the performance of religious rites and not assessing them for income tax; the departments of internal affairs for not putting a stop to the clergy's 'anti-social activities'; and the local administration for not controlling the cemeteries, where the clergy were in fact operating.[111] This inaction of the local bureaucracy led believers in Chimkent Oblast' to take over a village mosque they had previously transferred to the *sel'sovet* but which had not been used and had stood empty for a long period, and to begin praying in another rural mosque that had been under lock and key, collecting building materials and money in private homes to erect an awning. One raion administration had appointed a pensioner to tend three rural cemeteries, only to find he had become 'a veritable mulla', organising collective

109. V. A. Kuroedov to the CPSU Central Committee Propaganda Department, 21 April 1970; GARF, f.6991, o.6, d.284, l.9.

110. Zh. Rahimov to the CRA, 27 Oct. 1969; GARF, f.6991, o.6, d.223, ll.46-8. For the implementation of policy regarding taxation, see also pp. 596-9.

111. Aktiubinsk Oblispolkom, Resolution, 28 Dec. 1973; GARF, f.6991, o.6, d.637, ll.2-3.

prayer and performing rites at the prayer-houses which existed at these cemeteries.[112] A newspaper in the Tatar ASSR, commenting on the extensive practice of religion in the villages of that republic in the early 1970s, noted that the local authorities remained neutral, pretending to know nothing about it. The paper voiced the opinion that they simply did not want to quarrel with the villagers.[113]

One discussion of Islamic practice in the latter half of the 1970s condemned the stand adopted by officialdom in the various localities. It contended that the organs of local government claimed that, in giving a free hand to religious activists to operate beyond the limits of what strictly speaking fell under the category of performance of religious ritual, the latter were less free to engage in religious propaganda. In effect, however, this enabled them to extend their influence and authority among the population. Leaving to them, for instance, the entire range of activity connected with burial, including the upkeep of cemeteries, created the impression that those Muslim 'modernists' who preached the identity of interests of their religion and the regime represented Soviet reality.[114]

Connivance with and partiality for Islam

The general indifference to Islam of the organs of government in the localities was not only negative in itself in that it prevented the regime from taking full advantage of the powers given it by the legislation on religion to confine the activity of believers to a limited and clearly defined domain. It was thought to be conducive to actually enhancing religious activity,[115] a deduction appropriate to a body politic in which everything that was not actively repressed was undisputably permitted and probably condoned. Inertia was tantamount to leniency, which, according to one AUCP(b) Central Committee emissary to Kazakhstan in 1949, characterised both local government and the courts in that republic in their relation

112. K. Panzabekov, Information, 10 Oct. 1974; GARF, f.6991, o.6, d.637, ll.106-8.
113. *Sotsialistik Tatarstan*, 7 July 1972, quoted in RL 131/73, 21 April 1973.
114. Ashirov, 'Osobennosti ideologicheskoi i kul'tovoi deiatel'nosti musul'manskikh religioznykh organizatsii v sovremennykh usloviiakh', p.129.
115. K. Mustafin to Tashkent Obkom Secretary Mavlianov, 19 July 1945; GARF, f.6991, o.3, d.30, l.267.

to Islamic practice.[116] The CRA report on Islam for 1970 stated that municipal and raion administrations which did not wish to engage in controlling the activity of religious associations and clergy, were in practice adopting a position of concealing violations of the law on religion.

This applied specifically to instances of denying the existence of Islamic activity, even when it was known to have taken place, often on a large scale.[117] In Garm in Tajikistan one *raiispolkom* denied that people on its territory observed religion, although CARC's *upolnomochennyi* actually heard the *azan* calling people to prayer in two or three places in the town.[118] A *sel'sovet* chairman in Kirgiziia at the end of the 1960s similarly denied that there was a single believing Muslim in his bailiwick who participated in Friday prayers, although there were two known unregistered associations, each with a mulla and about twenty-five believers, as well as a *mazar* where several dozen people gathered every Friday.[119]

One report stated squarely that the reason the struggle against itinerant mullas was being conducted with little enthusiasm by local government and its financial organs was that not all local officials had broken with religious tradition. Moreover, whenever they thought they could do so with impunity, they were prepared to assist unregistered mullas in avoiding income tax assessments.[120] Some lower-level officials in the Muslim areas specifically expressed the opinion that the ideas of communism and religion should be synchronised.[121]

116. Goncharok to G. M. Malenkov, 8 Sept. and 5 Nov. 1949; RTsKhIDNI, f.17, o132, d.258, ll.77-8 and 99-105.

117. CRA report, sent to the CPSU Central Committee, 27 April 1971; TsKhSD, f.5, o.63, d.89, l.140. The report mentioned two such examples, one in the Bashkir ASSR, where one *raiispolkom* stated that there were neither unregistered religious associations nor unregistered clergy in the raion, although there were in fact a considerable number of the former and a plethora of the latter whose names were known to the village *aktiv*; the other in Syr-Darya Oblast' where the Jizak *raiispolkom* said there had been no collective praying on Uraz-Bayram, whereas the 'competent organs' reported that over 3,000 worshipppers had participated in such services.

118. L. A. Prikhod'ko, Report, 20 May 1953; GARF, f.6991, o.3, d.91, l.251.

119. K. Shabolotov to the Kirgiz SSR Council of Ministers, 3 June 1969; GARF, f.6991, o.6, d.223, l.53.

120. I. G. Halimov to CARC, undated [probably early April 1949]; GARF, f.6991, o.3, d.454, l.11.

121. N. I. Inogamov, Address, All-Union conference of CARC *upolnomochennye,*

A second principal accusation against local officials was that they actually aided and abetted 'the religious movement'.[122] In other words, they were guilty not just of sins of omission or transgressions that stood on the borderline between inaction and actual deeds, but also of sins of commission, of active violations of the law on religion or, at least, of established procedure. Indeed, it was common for reports on Muslim activities in the various areas to list infringements of the laws on religion committed by local organs of government together with those of the clergy. Moreover, it is evident that Moscow was in many ways more concerned by the former than by the latter.

While apathy seems to have characterised officials at all levels, active encouragement of Islam was probably more frequent among the lower ranks of the hierarchy. Polianskii informed the Soviet leadership that there were many instances of individual officials in the same 'soviet and party organs' in the localities which obstructed CARC's efforts to bring Muslim activity within the framework of the law, supporting the Muslim clergy and joining forces with it.[123] He stated officially that kolkhoz chairmen and the heads of lower level soviet organs often cooperated in opening mosques without due authorisation, initiating, encouraging and variously supporting such steps instead of officially granting or rejecting applications in accordance with the statutory 'considerations of expediency'.[124] One *raiispolkom* chairman brushed aside the instructions of a school principal, who forbade the conduct of the *namaz* in the kishlak school, permitting believers to use the school building for this purpose.[125] One *sel'sovet* chairman actually ordered a school headteacher to vacate his school in order

---

25-27 Nov. 1958; GARF, f.6991, o.3, d.165, 1.35.

122. Polianskii had coupled the indifference of local officials with the protection they gave religious organisations – see p.625 – while the Uzbek SSR Council of Ministers said specifically that their *laissez-faire* attitude sometimes reached the point of connivance – see p.630.

123. I. V. Polianskii to L. P. Beriia, I. V. Stalin, V. M. Molotov and K. E. Voroshilov at the Council of Ministers, and to A. A. Zhdanov, N. S. Khrushchev, A. A. Kuznetsov, N. S. Patolichev and G. M. Popov at the AUCP(b) Central Committee, 27 Feb. 1947; GARF, f.6991, o.3, d.47, 1.92.

124. CARC letter of instruction No.6, undated, ratified by CARC session No.6, 23 April 1948; GARF, f.6991, o.3, d.53, ll.1-2..

125. From materials prepared for a conference of CARC *upolnomochennye* in Tashkent, 8 Oct. 1946; GARF, f.6991, o.3, d.41, ll.189-90.

for it to be used as a mosque. (Presumably the building had once been a mosque.) Another gave a plot of kolkhoz land and provided building materials for the construction of a mosque, and a third supplied 18,000 bricks for a new mosque. A number of kolkhoz chairmen in Andijan Oblast' arbitrarily transferred to believers 'buildings of [former] mosques' or 'cotton-drying premises' (which may also have been former mosques) for purposes of prayer;[126] while in Tashkent Oblast' not one *sel'sovet* or kolkhoz chairman objected in the latter 1940s to the utilisation of cotton-drying premises, some of which were in fact former mosques, for the conduct of collective prayer during the *uraz*.[127] In Tashkent Oblast' the position seems to have been particularly acute in the early 1950s, one *oblispolkom* resolution pointing out that some chairmen of raion executive organs not only failed to draw attention to the violations of law on the part of unregistered religious groups, but were, themselves guilty of infringing it by actually submitting applications to SADUM to open mosques.[128]

Sometimes assistance in opening mosques took the form of confirming their inauguration without waiting for the completion of the entire and often protracted bureaucratic procedure of registration to take its full course – namely for the ratification of the republican authorities and of CARC – and often even without the religious community in question fulfilling all the necessary formalities.[129] In Tashkent Oblast' one chairman of a *mahalla* commission co-operated with a group of believers in aiding them to open a former mosque without receiving the requisite authorisation, and signed their application to activate the mosque and appoint a mulla; another, in Tashkent itself, both signed the application to open a mosque and actually assisted believers to conduct repairs in the building to make it serviceable. Altogether seventeen of over 100 applications processed in that city in the two years from

126. I. V. Polianskii to the Bureau of the Ministry of Culture, K. E. Voroshilov, M. A. Turkin, M. A. Suslov and A. A. Kuznetsov, 10 June 1948; GARF, f.6991, o.3, d.53, ll.36-7. See also p.300.

127. Nasretdinov to Tashkent Obkom Secretary Nurudinov and Oblispolkom Chairman Isamuhamedov, 10 Sept. 1947; TsGAUz, f.2456, o.1, d.142, l.56.

128. Resolution, Tashkent Oblispolkom, 25 July 1952; TsGAUz, f,2456, o.1, d.142, ll.4-5.

129. For example, H. Akhtiamov, Report, Conference of CARC *upolnomochennye*, Alma-Ata, 30 Sept. 1946; GARF, f.6991, o.3, d.41, l.106. For registration procedure, see pp.25-6, 29 and 183-95, *passim*.

mid-1943 to August 1945 were supported by *mahalla* commissions.[130]

In the late 1960s, when the CRA was trying to push the idea of partial registration, a considerable number of religious associations in Kazakhstan – both urban and rural – approached the local authorities with requests to register. Local organs frequently registered them provisorily, allowing them to meet for prayers and to celebrate the major festivals. A similar line of conduct was taken by local officials in Kirgiziia and the Tatar and Bashkir ASSRs.[131] Other functionaries continued in assisting believers in filing their applications. Nor did they bother to ask registered religious societies which expanded their premises or added on new prayer halls, whether they had received permission to do so. Indeed, in the oblasti of Tashkent, Surkhan-Darya and Bukhara in Uzbekistan local officials acquiesced and connived in the repair and construction of unregistered prayer-premises, just as their predecessors had done a generation before.[132]

This collusion with the local clergy, who did not aspire to register their mosques in accordance with established procedure, was said to have facilitated the existence of numerous unregistered mosques. CARC officials pointed out that in many instances local party and soviet organs supported the illegal activities of Muslim religious communities and clergy, manifested a 'compromising and liberal attitude' to Islam and joined forces with obscurantism.[133] The Kokand *gorispolkom* chairman was reported shortly after the war to have given permission to no less than thirty-nine mosques to operate without registration by the CARC *upolnomochennyi*, telling the latter into the bargain that no unofficial mosques were functioning in the town. In one kishlak believers had, with his agreement, dismantled a former mosque and built a new one, for

130. K. Mustafin to Tashkent Obkom Secretary [A.] Mavlianov, 19 July 1945, and to Gorkom Secretary Emtsov, 31 Aug. 1945 – GARF, f.6991, o.3, d.30, ll.265 and 273-273ob; and K. Mustafin, Resumé, undated [before 18 Sept. 1945]; TsGAUz, f.2456, o.1, d.47, l.47.

131. A. A. Nurullaev, Excerpts from lecture, 30 July 1968; GARF, f.6991, o.6, d.548, ll.78-9.

132. CRA report, sent to the CPSU Central Committee, 27 April 1971; TsKhSD, f.5, o.63, d.89, l.137, and A. Galiev to the Chimkent Oblast' Committee of People's Comptrol, 23 Jan. 1973; GARF, f.6991, o.6, d.545, ll.160-1.

133. G. Ia. Vrachev and I. N. Uzkov to I. V. Polianskii, 29 Nov. 1946; RTsKhIDNI, f.17, o.125, l.405.

which a kolkhoz had provided the building materials.[134] One *raiispolkom* chairman and administrative secretary in Tashkent Oblast' gave a mulla a document testifying that he was an official representative of SADUM; armed with this, he opened mosques in almost all of the raion's kolkhozy without encountering any obstruction.[135] A decade later local officials helped in the construction of several of the seventeen new mosques built in Andijan Oblast', and assisted in building mosques in the oblasti of Namangan and Fergana.[136] In neighbouring Kirgiziia one *gorispolkom* took a decision to build a mosque, although this was not within its jurisdiction and contradicted established practice, if not the law itself.[137] In Groznyi Oblast' in the Northern Caucasus, too, local officials tolerated unregistered Muslim (as well as Christian sectarian) communities and the activities of a large number of mullas.[138] Sometimes, these mosques would be allowed to open and function for a given occasion, usually the *uraz* or a festival, rather than on a permanent basis.[139]

   In Tajikistan local officials were constantly being charged with showing undue tolerance to Muslim religious activity. In the late 1960s two party officials were excluded from the party and two *raiispolkom* officials likewise punished for permissiveness toward religious officials (*tserkovniki*). In Kulyab the consumer service complex actually undertook the work of putting up an extra structure in the mosque courtyard, using materials which had been assigned for residential construction.[140] In the same republic local organs of government were reported to be tolerating, and in some instances

134. Materials prepared for conference of CARC *upolnomochennye*, Tashkent, 8 Oct. 1946 – GARF, f.6991, o.3, d.41, l.184; and I. V. Polianskii to A. A. Zhdanov, 22 July 1947 – RTsKhIDNI, f.17, o.125, d.506, l.167.

135. K. Mustafin to I. I. Ibadov, 25 June 1945; GARF, f.6991, o.3, d.30, ll.259-259ob.

136. K. F. Tagirov, Information, 1 March 1957; GARF, f.6991, o.3, d.132, l.37.

137. I. G. Halimov to Kyzyl-Kiya Gorispolkom Chairman Orozaliev, 11 Jan. 1951; GARF, f.6991, o.3, d.454, l.97.

138. I. V. Polianskii to A. A. Zhdanov, 22 July 1947; RTSKhIDNI, f.17, o.125, d.506, l.169.

139. For example, in Kustanai Oblast' in Kazakhstan in the second half of the 1940s – I. V. Polianskii to A. A. Zhdanov, 22 July 1947; RTsKhIDNI, f.17, o.125, d.506, l.170. For mosques which were allowed to operate on specific occasions, see also above p.624; for religious associations which operated solely during the *uraz* or on festivals, see pp.302, 307 and 314-5.

140. A. Barmenkov to E. I. Lisavtsev, 6 May 1969; GARF, f.6991, o.6, d.215, ll.25-6.

giving direct support to the appropriation of empty mosques, the organisation of prayer-services and the collection of contributions in money and kind.[141]

The laxity of local officials was not restricted to the actual opening of mosques. In Tajikistan chairmen of kishlak and *poselok* soviets and kolkhoz chairmen were said in the mid-1960s to pander to people guilty of other violations of the law on religion as well. Although they knew the identity of both the itinerant mullas and those unregistered clergy who inhabited their territory, these figures continued to operate without any constraints as a result of the 'liberal' attitude towards them by the local organs of government.[142] Local officialdom was reportedly refraining from taking measures to prevent or curb the conduct of prayer-services in unregistered mosques or even in the open, which was specifically prohibited by law, although this took on serious dimensions. *Sel'sovet* and kolkhoz chairmen in the Uzbek SSR and other republics, according to information from the early-mid 1950s, were helping the clergy, providing them with prayer premises, and permitting the collection of money for the clergy among kolkhozniki. Support of Islam also led to the taking of veiled bribes by the financial organs.[143] In Kirovabad in Azerbaijan the mosque paid neither for its water nor for its gas, and was charged less than the usual price for electricity.[144]

The performance of certain religious rites and ceremonies was attributed on a number of occasions to the explicit permission of local officialdom. Thus, in Fergana Oblast' individual believers who had the requisite means slaughtered livestock on Qurban-Bayram in 1946 with the permission of local officials.[145] Toward the end of the 1960s local government organs were said to connive at the conduct of *khatm-i Qur'ans* in empty mosques and at cemeteries

141. V. A. Kuroedov, Information, 24 Aug. 1970; TsKhSD, f.5, o.62, d.37, l.174.

142. M. Kh. Hamidov to A. A. Puzin, Information, 18 May 1963; GARF, f.6991, o.3, d.1739, l.63.

143. L. A. Prikhod'ko, Report, 20 May 1953; GARF, f.6991, o.3, d.91, l.251.

144. A. Galiev, Information, 30 May 1973; GARF, f.6991, o.6, d.537, l.190.

145. Hamidullin to Kh. N. Iskanderov, 25 Dec. 1946; TsGAUz, f.2456, o.1, d.72, l.53.

in a number of localities (specifically in the oblasti of Omsk and Bukhara and in Dagestan).[146]

Local government organs often indulged pilgrimages to *mazars*. In Tajikistan two holy tombs were said to have been renovated in the early 1950s as a result of this 'conciliatory' attitude.[147] In the same time period in neighbouring Uzbekistan, local officials participated in making the recently closed major *mazar* of Shoh-i Mardon accessible again to pilgrims, the chairman of the local *poselok* soviet, the head of the village school and the head of the *raikom* propaganda department organising guard duty at the site to enable its use for religious purposes.[148] Following the campaign to terminate the activity of holy sites in the late 1950s-early 1960s, which let up toward the end of the latter decade, believers took advantage of the permissive attitude of local officialdom to re-open some of them.[149] SADUM Mufti Babakhanov suggested that some *mazars* operated with the permission of local officialdom owing to the fact that they served as sources of revenue for the budget of the local administration.[150]

Another way of assisting religious practice was by providing transport to attend prayer-services or make pilgrimages. Frequently, worshippers attending the nearest registered mosque, not to speak of pilgrims to holy sites, had to cover considerable distances. Since these were not necessarily routes covered by public transport, and private vehicles were few and far between – certainly in the earlier years – they had to be given transportation. Sometimes, it was even necessary to obtain transport to reach the local cemetery. On Qurban-Bayram in the mid-1950s one kolkhoz chairman put ten carts at the disposal of clergy and believers for this purpose.[151] In 1955 thirty-two lorries, many of which belonged to state and

146. V. A. Kuroedov to the CPSU Central Committee Propaganda Department, 2 March 1970; GARF, f.6991. o.6, d.284, l.3.

147. Minutes, CARC session No.18, 20 Dec. 1951; GARF, f.6991, o.3, d.75, l.199.

148. Minutes, Instructional meeting of CARC *upolnomochennye* in Uzbekistan, 17-18 July 1951; TsGAUz, f.2456, o.1, d.134, ll.75-6. For this *mazar* and efforts to close it, see p.372.

149. A. Barmenkov to the CPSU Central Committee Propaganda Department, 5 Feb. 1969; GARF, f.6991, o.6, d.215, ll.4-7.

150. Reception by V. F. Riazanov of Z. Babakhanov, 22 Sept. 1958; GARF, f.6991, o.4, d.88, l.167.

151. I. V. Polianskii to G. M. Malenkov and N. S. Khrushchev, 2 Oct. 1953; GARF, f.6991, o.3, d.93, l.246.

local government organs, brought pilgrims to a *mazar* in Margelan.[152] Similar facts were noted throughout the period under discussion. In 1968 pilgrims were transported to Goy-imam near Kirovabad in hundreds of vehicles belonging to kolkhozy and government enterprises and institutions.[153]

In some cases the link between local officials and the Muslim clergy was very close. This applied in particular to the unregistered mullas, some of whom the former were instrumental in appointing. At one *mazar* in Jalalabad Oblast', which seems to have been especially lucrative, the local *sel'sovet* chairman helped have his own father-in-law appointed shaykh. Indeed, every time this post fell vacant the workers of the *sel'sovet* took an active part in replacing the outgoing incumbent. One shaykh was said to have been put in the job by the *raikom* secretary himself.[154] In the later 1960s the Bukhara cultural administration was said to have re-appointed as watchman at the Baha ad-Din mausoleum a person who had served three years for deceiving believers and inciting them to religious activity.[155]

Instances also occurred where clergy or members of the *mutawaliyyat* of a registered religious society transgressed against the law out of a feeling that they had nothing to fear since local officials supported them. In Dushanbe, the *mutawali* of one such society undertook major repairs of the mosque without the permission of the *gorispolkom* or any other authority, for, as he told fellow believers, he was afraid of nobody since the chairman of the raion executive committee was 'his man'.[156] In Kazakhstan fifteen years earlier the atmosphere of connivance was so strong that instances occurred of clergy using public places for collective prayer and what officialdom termed 'religious propaganda', such as readings from the Qur'an and 'other religious books'.[157]

152. I. V. Polianskii to the CPSU Central Committee and the USSR Council of Ministers, 20 Sept. 1955; GARF, f.6991, o.3, d.114, l.198.

153. See p.380. Compare also p.374.

154. I. V. Polianskii to the CPSU Central Committee and the USSR Council of Ministers, 16 Jan. 1956; GARF, f.6991, o.3, d.129, l.10.

155. A. Barinskaia to V. A Kuroedov, undated, [late March-early April 1968]; GARF, f.6991, o.6, d.153, ll.111-12.

156. M. Hamidov to Tajikistan Party Secretary N. Z. Zaripova, Deputy Chairman of the Council of Ministers M. K. Karimova, A. A. Puzin, and KGB Chief M. M. Miliutin, 24 Jan. 1964; GARF, f.6991, o.3, d.1740, ll.5-6.

157. Goncharok to G. M. Malenkov, 5 Nov. 1949; RTsKhIDNI, f.17, o.132,

Occasionally the collaboration between clergy and mosque lay officials, on the one hand, and the local bureaucracy, on the other hand, seems to have led to an actual overlapping of roles. In the early 1950s, before the amalgamation of kolkhozy under Khrushchev, when the kolkhoz chairmen and executive were local residents, over 100 instances were reported in Uzbekistan of members of kolkhoz administrations being elected to mosque executive organs. In Tashkent the warden of a mosque was actually proposed by the administrative secretary of the raion soviet as a candidate to that soviet and was chosen by a general meeting of its employees to be chairman of a *mahalla* commission.[158]

The line of action followed by a number of local financial organs of taxing solely registered clergy, even though this contradicted official policy, had a manifest impact. In the first place, it was said to encourage Muslim clergy to consciously evade registration, so as not to face taxation.[159] Secondly, in certain areas and periods it seemed to signify that the powers-that-be recognised only the activity of the registered imams, thus giving a green light to administrative measures against itinerant and other mosqueless mullas. In other parts or years, when the general line toward religion in general and Islam in particular was more favourable, it appeared to indicate that the latter category were receiving preferential treatment. There were even instances in which local officials actually helped the clergy evade the payment of taxes.[160] On the whole, however, taxation, like so much else, was not pursued on the basis of principle, but of arbitrary considerations or simple convenience. Thus, in many cases where long lists of mosqueless or itinerant mullas were presented to the local authorities for purposes of taxation, a few of these would in fact be taxed, while the great majority remained unmolested or managed somehow to keep out of harm's way.[161]

---

d.258, 1.99.

158. I. V. Polianskii to M. G. Kirichenko, 22 March 1951; GARF, f.6991, o.3, d.76, ll.37-8.

159. Materials prepared for conference of CARC *upolnomochennye*, Tashkent, 8 Oct. 1946; GARF, f.6991, o.3, d.41, l.186. For taxation policy and its ambiguities, see pp.595-9. And see p. 192.

160. Conference of CARC *upolnomochennye* in the Uzbek SSR, 9 Aug. 1948; TsGAUz, f.2456, o.1, d.120, l.10. And see p. 636 above.

161. See pp.351-2 and 599.

Sometimes officials at the local level went so far as to make use of the status enjoyed by the Muslim clergy in order to mobilise the population for recurrent economic campaigns and other urgent assignments, a phenomenon which necessarily served to enhance their authority even more and to give legitimacy to their public role. In the early years the registered religious societies sought to emphasise their 'patriotic' activity to show the regime or its local representatives their value to society.[162] Indeed, in Kazakhstan oblast' officials gave SADUM *upolnomochennye* a certificate testifying that they were empowered to collect money for war orphans. They were apparently so convinced of the capabilities of the Muslim clergy that they even suggested mobilising clergy to ensure that believers supply meat and deliver milk. One kolkhoz chairman took a loan of seventeen quintals of bread from a mulla to give to the needy until harvest-time.[163] In Osh Oblast' local officials proposed that the mullas participate in ploughing, sowing and harvesting.[164] Even in the late 1950s there was an instance where local officials in Uzbekistan instructed clergy to speak to a meeting of cotton-growers to speed up the harvesting process. In another case in the same republic a *raiispolkom* chairman summoned an unregistered mulla when an underground pipe burst and the town was in danger of inundation; he instructed him as to what had to be done and the mulla gathered people at night and the breakdown was fixed. The mulla was praised and soon came to request that a mosque be opened.[165]

Officials sometimes actually gave material assistance for the conduct of religious activity. Officials of one *sel'sovet* in Kirgiziia were reported in the late 1960s to be giving 'moral and material support' to those responsible for preserving 'vestiges of the [Islamic] past in peoples' consciousness'.[166] Over twenty years earlier, the chairman of the Kokand *gorispolkom* was said to have provided 20,000

162. See pp.229-30. For attempts by registered clergy to demonstrate their usefulness to the national and local economy and their mobilisation by local officials, see also pp.259 and 435.

163. Minutes, Conference of CARC *upolnomochennye*, Alma-Ata, 2 Oct. 1946; GARF, f.6991, o.3, d.41, ll.44 and 54.

164. Ibid., l.72.

165. Minutes, All-Union conference of CARC *upolnomochennye*, 25-27 Nov. 1958; GARF, f.6991, o.3, d.165, ll.79-80.

166. K. Shabolotov to the Kirgiz SSR Council of Ministers, 3 June 1969; GARF, f.6991, o.6, d.223, l.56.

rubles out of his municipal budget to refurbish a mosque. One kolkhoz chairman restored an old mausoleum building and put it at the disposal of believers. The administration of another kolkhoz also refurbished a mausoleum and constructed an awning for the conduct of prayer-services. The leading officials of one raion in Namangan Oblast', hearing that an imam had built a mosque, authorised the administration of a kolkhoz to undertake its interior decoration.[167] In another case a kolkhoz chairman organised a meeting of the entire kolkhoz administration – comprising forty-six people, including members of both party and Komsomol –which decided to dismantle an empty former mosque and give the building materials to the registered mosque so that it could construct an annexe.[168]

Throughout the period under study the situation appeared particularly critical in this, as in other, spheres, in the Fergana Valley, where the unofficial clergy enjoyed immense prestige among the population and local government alike. Here religious schools, where children were taught Islam, were opened with the aid of local officials. In some raiony, officials helped open illegal mosques in defiance of specific instructions and assisted believers in repairing them. One communist party primary cell secretary actually worked for an entire season at a *mazar*. (Many shrines operated only through the summer months.)[169] A Fergana Obkom resolution at the height of Khrushchev's anti-religious campaign detailed the irregularities which were going on in the oblast', attributing their persistence in no small part to the connivance of local officialdom, including specifically the judiciary, the public prosecutor's office, and the militia.[170] Between 1969 and 1973 the Fergana Obkom discussed no less than four times the unauthorised opening of mosques and the connivance of local officialdom in such actions.[171]

167. Materials prepared for conference of CARC *upolnomochennye*, Tashkent, 8 Oct. 1946; GARF, f.6991, o.3, d.41, ll.189-91.

168. Kh. N. Iskanderov to Tashkent Obkom Secretary A. Alimov and Oblispolkom Chairman Jalilov, 27 May 1954; TsGAUz, f.2456, o.1, d.162, l.178.

169. Hamidullin to I. V. Polianskii, 31 Dec. 1946; TsGAUz, f.2456, o.1, d.72, l.66.

170. Resolution of the Fergana Obkom Bureau, 11 Sept. 1962; TsKhSD, f.5, r.4820, o.33, d.215, ll.159-62. For the connivance with religion of these same branches of the local bureaucracy in Namangan, also in the Fergana Valley, see p. 630. For the punishment of offenders during Khrushchev's anti-religious campaign for violating the laws on religion, see pp.579-80.

171. D. Malikov, Information, undated [probably late August 1973]; GARF,

The state of affairs was equally acute in the Chechen-Ingush ASSR after the return of the deportees. Here the local organs of government seemed to identify totally with the believer population. In part this may have been the result of pressure and intimidation by the local inhabitants. Whatever the cause, in every raion private homes were given over to *murids* to use for clandestine prayer-meetings. The *raiispolkoms* knew this but neither provided the central authorities with any information whatever of goings-on nor conducted any struggle of their own against violations of the law. Some *sel'sovet* chairmen consciously endeavoured to conceal the true state of affairs in their localities.[172] Nor were matters very different in neighbouring Dagestan, where in the early 1970s a number of *raiispolkoms* were still supplying their superiors with formal answers to questions and questionnaires, contending that in the territory under their jurisdiction there were no religious associations, no holy places, no manifestations of religiosity. (Even the registered religious societies did not keep documentation of rites.) Only one single unregistered religious association was reported throughout Dagestan. There were no inventories of religious buildings; nowhere was there any documentation to record past work, so there could be no continuity or point of comparison. Religious associations repaired mosques without permission – obtaining 'scarce building materials' from private individuals, which was tantamount to 'participation in the plunder of socialist property' – and village minarets were reconstructed, yet the local organs of government did not react.[173]

In certain regions cases were reported of officials not working on the major Muslim festivals. In one raion in Uzbekistan's Kashka-Darya Oblast', neither raion nor kolkhoz officials went to work on Qurban-Bayram in 1946.[174]

f.6991, o.6, d.537, l.64.

172. P. A. Zadorozhnyi to A. A. Puzin, 30 Aug. 1960, and A. Alisov to A. A. Puzin, 13 Jan. 1961; GARF, f.6991, o.3, d.207, ll.58-9, and d.1605, l.21. For believers' threats against local officials in the Chechen-Ingush ASSR, see p.417.

173. Kh. Salahetdinov and I. Mikhalev, Information, presented to E. I. Lisavtsev, 26 Oct. 1971; GARF, f.6991, o.6, d.361, ll.105-12.

174. Materials prepared for conference of CARC *upolnomochennye*, Tashkent, 8 Oct. 1946; and see p.501.

Active participation in Muslim activity

The encouragement of Muslim activity on the part of local officials sometimes reached the level of active participation in rites and ceremonies. This was rather common when it came to life-cycle rites, especially in areas inhabited by a purely Muslim population, the offenders including not only officials of the soviet, but even of the party, apparatus.[175] They conducted religious burials and memorial services for their relatives and circumcised their sons.[176] Some officials even did so with great pomp; a kolkhoz chairman and bookkeeper in Bukhara Oblast' were brought to justice in the mid-1950s for misappropriating public funds, which they had expended on circumcising their sons with lavish entertainment.[177] In Dagestan members of village *aktivs* were reported in the early 1950s to be marrying in accordance with the Shari'a.[178] The secretary of one kolkhoz administration married his brother's widow in the late 1940s in conformity with the levirate and even forbade her to go to the Komsomol.[179]

In addition to performing religious rites for their own families, some local officials attended the life-cycle ceremonies of others. In Osh, for example, in the mid 1960s the *gorsovet* street committee chairman invariably took part in these occasions, the moneys collected at *tois* being divided among the mosque, the person who performed the circumcision and the street committee.[180]

There were also instances where local officials were party to ceremonies and rites other than those linked with the life-cycle. They held *iftars* during the *uraz*, and paid the *fitr*, some of them who did so were even party members (which not all local officials

---

175. I. V. Polianskii to K. E. Voroshilov, M. A. Turkin, M. A. Suslov, A. A. Kuznetsov and the Bureau of the Ministry of Culture, 10 June 1948; GARF, f.6991, o.3, d.53, l.35; and see p.433.

176. See, for example, V. A. Abakumov to K. E. Voroshilov, 12 Sept. 1946; G. Ia. Vrachev and I. N. Uzkov to I. V. Polianskii, 29 Nov. 1946; and P. A. Solov'ev, Statistical report, April 1964 – GARF, f.6991, o.3, d.34, ll.195 and 283, and o.4, d.146, l.210. See also pp.515-6, 523-4 and 529-30.

177. N. Achilov to Kh. N. Iskanderov, 29 June 1955; TsGAUz, f.2456, o.1, d.169, l.77. See also pp.530-1.

178. L. A. Prikhod'ko, A short report, 4 April 1952; GARF, f.6991, o.3, d.81, l.94.

179. See p.540.

180. P. A. Solov'ev, Statistical report, April 1964; GARF, f.6991, o.4, d.146, l.211.

were).[181] One kolkhoz chairman in Kirgiziia, who was a party member, planned the pilgrimage to a *mazar* of sixty kolkhozniki in two vehicles and took two rams for ritual slaughter, but was deterred from carrying this out when workers of the local sanatorium threatened to inform the *obkom*.[182] In the Tatar ASSR in 1946 a *sel'sovet* chairman and the head of a kolkhoz both performed ritual slaughter on Qurban-Bayram.[183] In Osh Oblast' a *sel'sovet* chairman slaughtered a sheep ritually every year on Uraz-Bayram in honour of his father's memory,[184] and in Andijan Oblast' a *gorkom* secretary performed memorial prayers for deceased relatives at a *mazar*. In Bukhara Oblast' a number of senior officials took part in the Shiite celebration of Ashura in the latter half of the 1940s, one employee of the procuracy actually inflicting knife wounds on himself.[185] Other instances were also reported of local officials attending communal prayer, especially on festivals. At one sovkhoz in Kazakhstan's Aktiubinsk Oblast', the entire Kazakh population took part in collective prayers – apparently on a festival – in the late 1940s, including the chairman of the *poselok* soviet and the secretary of the local Komsomol, whereas in Tajikistan two decades later a kolkhoz chairman and treasurer participated in prayer-services held in the local club.[186] Sometimes local officials had recourse to religious practice and custom in order to ensure their success in meeting the requirements made of them by the secular authority. One kolkhoz chairman in Kazakhstan, a party member, had his kolkhozniki vow on the Qur'an to fulfil their obligations to the collective, the chairman himself being the first to take this oath. The party secretary and chairman of the productivity council of a kolkhoz in Andijan Oblast' arranged a ceremony

181. Conference of CARC *upolnomochennye* in the Uzbek SSR, 9 Aug. 1948; TsGAUz, f.2456, o.1, d.120, l.10. See also p.485.

182. I. Polianskii to P. Kovanov, 23 June 1955; GARF, f.6991, o.3, d.114, l.27.

183. Conference of CARC *upolnomochennye*, 11 [June] 1946, GARF, f.6991, o.3, d.39, l.111. And see pp.495-6.

184. I. V. Polianskii to the CPSU Central Committee, 12 Jan. 1955; GARF, f.6991, o.3, d.113, ll.12-13.

185. Materials prepared for conference of CARC *upolnomochennye*, Tashkent, 8 Oct. 1946, GARF, f.6991, o.3, d.41, l.190. For participation of officials in Azerbaijan in Ashura celebration, see pp.505-6.

186. Goncharok to G. M. Malenkov, 5 Nov. 1949; RTsKhIDNI, f.17, o.132, d.258, l.99; and A. Barmenkov to E. I. Lisavtsev, 6 May 1969; GARF, f.6991, o.6, d.215, ll.24-5.

at which sacrifices were made and clergy invited to read the Qur'an and all the participants prayed for a good cotton crop and an abundance of produce.[187]

Usually officials as well as party and Komsomol members who participated actively in the conduct of religious rites contended that they did so not out of religious belief, but out of respect for family elders, whose wishes they were in no position to refuse or because they regarded these ceremonies as national, rather than religious, customs.[188]

The wives of local officials seem to have been even more 'remiss' than their husbands. Many of them adhered to religious practices. In some places the wives and children of officials attended mosque.[189] In Osh Oblast' the wives of leading personnel paid visits to women mullas who engaged in a variety of religious ceremonies, bringing them large presents and foodstuffs.[190] True, it is not always clear to what degree this was happening with the knowledge, let alone the active encouragement, of their menfolk, although in Muslim society the assumption must be that women with proclivities for religion consulted with their husbands and did their bidding. Undisputably, wives and daughters of local officials who wore the *paranja* could not have done so without their husbands, or fathers, being cognisant of it; indeed, it was probably worn at their instruction. In any case, officials in Namangan Oblast' whose wives, daughters and daughters-in-law concealed themselves behind *paranjas*, were brought before the 'investigating agencies' and duly removed from the *mahalla* committees.[191] The wife of the head of a raion financial department in Samarkand Oblast' visited the Shoh-i Zinda *mazar* on Uraz-Bayram in the early 1950s and asked the shaykhs there to pray for a deceased relative of her husband.[192] A few of the pupils attending religious schools in

187. For the first instance, see p.459; for the second, Minutes, Instructional meeting of CARC *upolnomochennye* in the Uzbek SSR, 15-17 March 1956; TsGAUz, f.2456, o.1, d.183, l.5.

188. See pp.433 and 457. For a discussion of the national factor, see Chapter 12.

189. For example in Ujara in Azarbaijan – see p.675.

190. I. G. Halimov to H. Akhtiamov, 22 April 1953; GARF, f.6991, o.3, d.94, l.63; and see p.343.

191. See pp.544-5.

192. Minutes, Instructional meeting of CARC's *upolnomochennye* in Uzbekistan, 17-18 July 1951; TsGAUz, f.2456, o.1, d.134, l.74.

Uzbekistan in the immediate postwar years were also children of local officials.[193] The families of local officials in Osh Oblast' were said to believe in and practise such superstitions as faith-healing.[194]

Altogether, it was difficult to know how many local officials (and party members) participated in the performance of Muslim rites, as they sought to cover up the traces of such deviations in order to avoid retribution from the party.[195] But the inference of most *upolnomochennye,* certainly in Central Asia and the Northern Caucasus, was that their number was considerable.

Antagonism to Islam and its practice

Just as an entire category of complaints addressed from Moscow to the local government related to its undue indulgence of Islam, so a further list recounted actions testifying to its hostility to Islam. Thus, local officials often did not accept, let alone review, applications to open mosques, even though they were properly formulated and the prerequisites for taking such a step existed. In the words of one CARC inspector, who reported that the activity of a certain functioning religious society had been declared illegal by the municipal organs, they were in this fashion 'overtly ignoring a factually operating religious association',[196] which was a violation of the law. In some instances these local organs of government did not even take the trouble to explain their opposition. In some parts the republican authorities themselves were adamant in refusing to open mosques.[197] In the late 1950s CARC's republican *upolnomochennyi* in Azerbaijan noted that two mosques in that republic which CARC had agreed to register ten years previously had not yet been opened as a result of the opposition of the local leadership.[198]

193. See p.354. Some officials' children also fasted on *uraz,* see p.478.

194. I. V. Polianskii to the CPSU Central Committee, 12 Jan. 1955; GARF, f.6991, o.3, d.113, ll.13-15.

195. I. G. Halimov to CARC, 3 April 1950; GARF, f.6991, o.3, d.454, l.56. Halimov was talking specifically of participation in *mavluds.*

196. A. Budov to A. A. Puzin, 12 June 1965; GARF, f.6991, o.3, d.1486, l.22.

197. For such a line in the Turkmen SSR and the Chechen – Ingush and Tatar ASSRs, see pp.594, 592 and 609-10 respectively.

198. Minutes, All-Union conference of CARC *upolnomochennye,* 25-27 Nov. 1958; GARF, f.6991, o.3, d.165, l.89.

One *oblispolkom* deputy chairman in Kazakhstan rejected an application to open an empty mosque in a particular kolkhoz on the grounds that if a mosque were to open in every kolkhoz, nobody would go to work.[199]

At least in the opinion of Polianskii, such an attitude did not serve to curb Muslim religious activity; on the contrary, it made the local situation more acute, actually heightening the religious mood among believers.[200] Over twenty years later the CRA adhered to a similar view, pointing out that refusing to register religious societies on the grounds that this reduced the population's religiosity ignored realities, and the indiscriminate rejection of all applications achieved the exact opposite.[201] CARC's *upolnomochennye* in the localities also pointed out that such a stance was counter-productive on two levels, both inducing the illegal performance of religious rites and breeding dissatisfaction among the believer population.[202] There is ample evidence of believers erecting prayer premises without permission, often without the knowledge of local officialdom, usually at the cemetery, in the wake of constant refusals on the part of local government organs to open a mosque.[203]

In a number of towns in the RSFSR, even in some of the major cities, where Tatars comprised a substantial percentage of the population, but were nonetheless a minority, the municipal authorities conducted a sustained struggle against attempts by the local believer population to open a mosque. The authorities in Saratov, for instance, refused to authorise the opening of a mosque, on the grounds that the town's former mosque was in use as a kindergarten. In Gor'kii the municipal authorities were similarly adamant, contending that the city had just a sprinkling of Tatars and that the recurrent applications to open a mosque were filed by a small group of 'speculators' interested in establishing a community in order to make personal profit. The same applied to

199. Minutes, Conference of CARC *upolnomochennye*, Alma-Ata, 2 Oct. 1946; GARF, f.6991, o.3, d.41, l.60.

200. I. V. Polianskii to L. P. Beriia *et al.*, 27 Feb. 1947; GARF, f.6991, o.3, d.47, l.92. See also p.554.

201. V. A. Kuroedov to the Kazakh SSR Council of Ministers, 20 May 1969; GARF, f.6991, o.6, d.220, ll.109-12.

202. For example, Vanishli, the *upolnomochennyi* in Ajaria, Conference of CARC *upolnomochennye*, Rostov-on-Don, 14 June 1946; GARF, f.6991, o.3, d.38, l.127.

203. For example, in Mozhg, in the Udmurt ASSR – I. Vasil'ev to CARC, 6 March 1956; GARF, f.6991, o.3, d.130, l.85.

Leningrad, where the municipal organs held out for almost a decade in the face of constant applications to re-open the city's mosque and resorted to such administrative measures as the use of militia to disperse worshippers, First Obkom Secretary Frol Kozlov and others opposing the opening of a mosque in the city which was the cradle of the October Revolution.

In all three cases CARC took an opposite stance, contending that the position adopted by the organs of local government was both unfounded and harmful. It pointed out that in Saratov the building had maintained the exterior and interior form of a mosque and was singularly unsuited to serve as a kindergarten. Moreover, the net result of the position of the municipal authorities was the conglomeration of thousands of worshippers in open places in the town centre on festivals and the performance of ritual in private homes. Regarding Gor'kii, CARC adopted the line that the unduly hostile posture of the relevant authorities merely provided occasion for Muslim 'fanatics' to incite believers to undesirable activity, including the slandering of the local government itself. And in 1955 CARC insisted that the measures taken against believers in Leningrad exacerbated believers' 'fanaticism', as well as the national sensitivities of the city's Tatar population, and caused an annual increase in the numbers of those attending prayer-services. Finally, in December 1955, the RSFSR Council of Ministers overruled Leningrad's local bosses.[204]

The persistent refusal of local authorities to respond positively to applications of Muslim religious associations and clergy to register continued to be a cause of concern in Moscow in later decades as well. The CRA was constantly seeking ways of obliging local organs of government to comply with requests of Muslim believers to legalise their position and activity, which it insisted in the late 1960s were being turned down without appropriate grounds in a number of areas, notably Tajikistan, Dagestan, the Chechen-Ingush

---

204. Iu. V. Sadovskii to K. E. Voroshilov, 18 Dec. 1946; Minutes, CARC session No.4s, 6 March 1952; Theses for instructional address, approved by CARC session No.24s, 25-26 Sept. 1952; I. V. Polianskii to D. M. Kukin, 4 June 1955; P. A. Solov'ev to V. I. Gostev, 31 July 1956; and Husain Kamaletdinov, Address, 26 Jan. 1957 – GARF, f.6991, o.3, d.34, 1.249, d.83, ll.39, 42-3, 254 and 259, d.114, ll.50-2, and d.127, ll.164-70, and o.4, d.86, ll.10-11. For the campaign to open mosques in these cities, see also p.197; for the national factor in the struggle to open the mosques in Leningrad and Gor'kii, see p.701.

ASSR, and the oblasti of Orenburg and Samarkand.[205]

Regarding Orenburg Oblast' the reference was presumably in particular to the town of Buguruslan, where, for over twenty years, the authorities inveterately refused requests to register a Muslim religious association. Their position was that this was an oil town, where cultural and educational institutions were functioning rather well and the construction of a mosque was 'inexpedient'. The opinion pertained among the believer community in the late 1960s that the reason was the dearth of Tatars in the organs of local government.[206] In most cases, unfortunately, there are no data to indicate that local officials who manifested negative attitudes to Islam belonged to non-Muslim nationalities or ethnic groups. Certainly, in the more outlying parts of Uzbekistan and Tajikistan, for instance, the likelihood of officials not being members of the autochthonous population was minimal. Even in the Stalin period, the bureaucracy in the localities in these two republics was manned almost solely by members of the indigenous nationalities, and this pertained yet more forcefully to the later period, when their domination was 'almost universal' among the 'highly visible party and government personnel' as well.[207] Nonetheless, Samarkand, for instance, had a long history of local authorities thwarting the legalisation of Muslim activity. When in the mid-1950s they refused to open the mosque and mausoleum of the well-known theologian Ismail al-Bukhari, CARC demanded that the oblast' organs review their decision. Similarly, when CARC resolved to open another important mosque in the same oblast' in 1956, the *oblispolkom* deputy chairman refused to open it or even to inform local believers of the decision, leaving CARC no option but to bring the matter via its *upolnomochennyi* to the republican council of ministers.[208]

In the town of Bugul'ma in the Tatar ASSR in the mid-1960s, the first secretary of the *gorkom*, who headed the opposition to restoring to the believer community a mosque closed in 1939, which they had been seeking to recover since the end of the war, was himself a Tatar. In 1960 the local organs had instructed

205. Theses of lecture, sent by A. Barmenkov to the CPSU Central Committee Propaganda Department, 19 June 1968; GARF, f.6991, o.6, d.147, ll.43-4.

206. Kosach, *Gorod na styke dvukh kontinentov*, p.100; and see pp.215 and 703-4.

207. Lubin, *Labour and Nationality in Soviet Central Asia*, p.89.

208. V. I. Gostev to N. I. Inogamov, 24 July 1956; TsGAUz, f.2456, o.1, d.191, ll.114-15. See also p.204.

the landlord of premises used for collective prayer to terminate the lease; when he replied that he would rent out to whomever he wished, local officials simply drove the believers away. They nevertheless returned to pray. Eventually, in November 1963, in the wake of pressure from the procuracy, the lease agreement was declared invalid and the landlord fined, and the municipal court resolved that the religious society's activity was illegal. The premises were then demolished, leaving the believers without anywhere to pray.[209] In the following year, the chairman of the *gorispolkom* and two other officials dispersed a prayer meeting held in a clearing near the Muslim cemetery, telling the worshippers: 'Go to Ufa, we will not let you pray here, you're transgressing Soviet law'. But the believers persisted in meeting for collective prayer and in requesting registration and the return of the mosque. In 1965 a CARC inspector, sent to look into the situation, informed the *gorkom* that according to the law, since this was a functioning, fully formed organisation, it had to be registered and given premises, only to be told in reply that this was a small group and that the situation was being exacerbated by the *dvadtsatka*, which was composed of 'scoundrels' seeking personal profit. The first secretary pointed out that just 35 per cent of the town population were Tatars and the majority ethnic Russians, so that the Tatars' demands were less justified than any which might have been put forward by Russian Orthodox believers. (Needless to say, this was sheer cynicism, because ethnic Russians who came to such a town in the Tatar ASSR presumably did so in the full knowledge that they had no chance of requesting a church and were probably *a priori* not religiously inclined.) In the view of the first secretary, the purpose of the law on religion was to affirm that religion existed in effect, but the local organs of government were in no way obliged to observe it. The CARC inspector insisted that the first pretext was harmful in that it was conducive to taking advantage of the nationality of Soviet citizens to trample their religious rights,[210] whereas the second amounted to a mockery of the law, emanating

209. Reception by N. I. Smirnov of Kurbangali Hafizov, 23 April 1960, and of Ya. Ya. Yakupov, 14 Jan. 1964, and A. Budov to A. A. Puzin, 12 June 1965 – GARF, f.6991, o.4, d.110, ll.18-19, and d.148, ll.2-3, and o.3, d.1486, ll.20-5; and see pp.311-2.

210. The text says the exact opposite: taking advantage of the religious affiliation of Soviet citizens to trample their national rights – but this seems to be erroneous.

from the conviction of medium-level party officials that anything they might do in respect to religion would go unpunished. This constituted a total negation of all public institutions, except the very practice of power, and reflected the impotence of atheistic propaganda in the face of religious ideology. Even the inspector, however, agreed that the mosque should not be transferred to the believers, since in a town of 75,000 with no cultural institutions except a single cinema, this would evoke a new wave of religiosity. The issue was brought before the Tatar ASSR Obkom,[211] and finally, in 1967, the religious association was registered.[212]

The disdain for the legislation on religion and established procedures among local organs of government was not restricted to refusals to open mosques and register religious societies. Both in the late Stalin period, 1949-53, and in the years of Khrushchev's anti-religious campaign they withdrew a number of mosques from registration without heeding the regular routine. In the former period the worst transgressors were probably the authorities in Ul'ianovsk Oblast', in the latter those of Leninabad Oblast' in Tajikistan.[213]

During 1960 and the first half of 1961 CARC received group complaints from believers regarding administrative actions, insults and the infringement of believers' rights on the part of the local organs of government in a number of towns and raiony in Tajikistan and Tashkent Oblast'.[214] A CARC inspector who visited Tajikistan in 1961 described the conditions under which mosques had been arbitrarily closed in that republic. Prior to the closure of one of them, in Ura-Tyube (in Leninabad Oblast'), party brigades studied cases of self-immolation, the wearing of the *paranja*, and the marriage of adolescents in the raion, as a result of which it was decided to stir up the public and unfurl a massive campaign for the closure of the mosque. Fourteen public meetings were then held, all of

211. A. Budov to A. A. Puzin, 12 June 1965; GARF, f.6991, o.3, d.1486, ll.20-5.

212. Tatar ASSR, Information, Factually functioning religious associations on 1 Jan. 1975; GARF, f.6991, o.6, d.654, l.97.

213. For details, see pp.200-2, 209 and 241-2.

214. Party statements frequently stipulated that offending believers' sensitivities and crude behaviour toward believers were totally impermissible – for example, G. G. Karpov and I. V. Polianskii to the CPSU Central Committee, 27 Nov. 1957; GARF, f.6991, o.3, d.148, l.67. Compare also p.44. This was one of Lenin's slogans as he launched his campaign against religion and the church.

which resolved to shut it down. This was carried out by a group headed by the *gorispolkom* secretary without any decision of either the *gorispolkom* or the *oblispolkom* or the consent of CARC, and the building became a Pioneer Club. Since that time a year had passed and the various organs of government – the *raikom*, the *gorkom*, the republican party Central Committee, the town and oblast' executive committees and the republican government – had unanimously agreed not to recant on the closure, but rather to register one or two mullas so that they might conduct life-cycle rites.

In the raion of Regar, the CARC inspector reported, 'nobody knows' when and in what circumstances the mosque had surfaced: from 1943 to 1952 there had just been a tent (*kibitka*); no organisation gave the believers land on which to build or construction materials, yet a mosque was erected and since 1956 touched up under the very nose of the local organs and the kolkhoz administration. By the end of the decade, on festivals approximately 5,000 worshippers crowded into the mosque, its courtyard and the adjacent roads, homes and courtyards. Following criticism and instructions 'from above', the kolkhoz chairman took a 'tough' decision – to close the mosque and use it as a library. The *gorispolkom* approved the decision and the republican council of ministers resolved that the mosque be closed. The kolkhoz chairman together with the *gorispolkom*, however, left the former *imam-khatib* as a watchman, and as a result believers continued to come there to pray. The local organs of government all concurred that it was inexpedient to re-open the mosque, but, as in Ura-Tyube, agreed, in view of the large number of believers in the town and raion of Regar, to register one or two mullas to conduct life-cycle rites.

In Leninabad itself the situation was rather different. The town party committee and executive organ decided to close one of two mosques, which had existed for 600 years, was situated in the town centre and catered to 2,000 believers on regular Fridays and 3,500 on festivals. Since, however, there were no legal grounds for such action, the *obkom* and republican Central Committee agitprop departments, as well as the republican council of ministers and the *oblispolkom* resolved not to decide on closure precipitously, but rather to prepare the ground carefully and not violate the law on religion.[215]

215. K. Ovchinnikov to A. A. Puzin, 2 Aug. 1961; GARF, f.6991, o.3, d.1737,

Complaints were lodged by believers in regard to the closure of unregistered mosques as well. One such mosque in Tashkent Oblast', which believers recurrently applied to register, had been closed down thirteen times between 1955 and 1960, when it was finally turned into a Pioneer Club. This was the last of sixteen mosques which had functioned in the raion in question since 1948, all of which had been closed by administrative measures. The *raikom* secretary was of the opinion that religion did not need churches and mosques; everyone should pray at home, he insisted, for 'God sees wherever believers pray'. According to the head of the raion agitprop department, only three or four believers remained in the entire raion. Officials of both the raion and oblast' party committee, as well as the republican party Central Committee agitprop and Council of Ministers, recognised that the closure of this mosque represented a violation of believers' rights, but refused to rectify the mistakes that had been made. CARC Chairman Puzin wrote to the CPSU Central Committee that similar instances of crass administrative measures against Muslim religious associations occurred in other raiony of Tashkent Oblast', indeed in various oblasti of Uzbekistan. Since most of the mosques operating in that republic had no documentation, local organs of government felt justified in closing them down without getting CARC's approval or even informing it, and mosques were being shut there on a 'mass' scale. CARC was informed by the Central Committee apparatus that the Central Committee of the Uzbekistan party was being instructed to take steps to 'eliminate mistakes which had been committed' and to punish the guilty parties. CARC, however, was to elucidate the regular procedure for closing mosques only in specific cases when this was explicitly called for, rather than issuing this information to all local organs indiscriminately.[216] This would seem to indicate that the Central Committee apparatus was not prepared to take sides in CARC's ongoing struggle with

---

ll.60-5. The involvement of both kolkhoz and municipal institutions in Regar indicates that here was a case of the extension of municipal jurisdiction over an area where a kolkhoz continued to operate. For the frequently arbitrary transformation of rural parts into urban ones for administrative purposes, see pp.182-3; for mosque closures in Leninabad Oblast' and their context and consequences, see pp.209 and 212.

216. A. A. Puzin to the CPSU Central Committee, 26 Aug. 1961; GARF, f.6991, o.3, d.1363, ll.129-31. For the Central Committee's instructions to CARC in this instance, see Chapter 5, n.142; for the mosque in question, see p.321.

the local organs of government, whose zeal in closing mosques in fact reflected the sense of the Central Committee's own enactments of this period.

Nor was the negative attitude and conduct toward the mosque on the part of local officialdom restricted solely to the issue of registration and withdrawal from registration or closure. In many parts the clergy and religious *aktiv*, sometimes even the entire believer community, lived in constant fear of local officialdom, which, out of a variety of motives, could be expected to relate to them with undisguised hostility. The situation in the Nakhichevan ASSR, for instance, was so acute in the early 1970s that, according to the local *akhund*, although only about 5 per cent of the population were atheists, Islam could not fully manifest itself. That was the direct result of the crude administrative actions of the local bureaucracy. (The cleric's estimate contrasted sharply with that of the first secretary of one of the republic's *raikoms* who said the raion could be considered essentially areligious, or with that of two other officials who maintained that there were no believers in the republic.)[217]

Elsewhere in Azerbaijan, in the town of Sheki, the CRA *upolnomochennyi* had DUMZ appoint a new *akhund* in the registered mosque in order to divert believers from illegal prayer-meetings and the influence of unregistered clergy and pre-empt the procession on Ashura to the Goy-imam *pir*. Some of the town's leading officials, however, led by the *gorkom* second secretary, expelled the new cleric from the town and directed a *rozakhan* to conduct the Muharram mourning ceremonies inside the mosque in accordance with the law. (A *rozakhan* was a person who knew how to recite the requisite elegies, but probably had had no religious training and was not really a cleric in any sense.) When the DUMZ deputy chairman pointed out to the second secretary that the new incumbent was to replace three clerics who had died, the latter retorted: 'Let all clerics die; that is what we want'. CARC reported that the mufti's feelings were deeply offended. The dialogue between these two personalities, the *upolnomochennyi* insisted, demonstrated bureaucratic tactlessness, and did not reflect the policy of the party and government regarding religion and its leaders. The second secretary explained his interference in the mosque's internal affairs by maintaining that the appointment of a new *akhund* would

217. See p.451.

mean that the entire effort of the party and soviet organs in the atheistic education of the workers would become meaningless. The *upolnomochennyi*, for his part, stated that his conduct was liable to evoke dissatisfaction with Soviet legislation among the believer community, brought no benefit to atheistic propaganda, and was illegal into the bargain. Eventually, the second secretary was summoned to the Central Committee of the republican party and severely reprimanded for misinterpreting party and government policy.[218]

Instances of an overtly antagonistic approach to Islam and its clergy were not necessarily an indication of consistent hostility or an opposition based on ideological considerations. They were frequently, as noted above, an expression of aspirations to build up the image of the oblast', town or raion. Perhaps no less often they were engendered by the material requirements of officials, who coveted the building of a mosque, which was frequently the only sound structure in a village. Former mosques were periodically transferred to organs of local government for use for either economic or cultural and educational purposes.[219] Presumably, some, at least, were mosques withdrawn from registration in the postwar period.

Alternatively, if the mosque was destined for demolition, the local authorities would have designs on the building materials, of which there was throughout the years under discussion a chronic dearth. One kolkhoz chairman in Astrakhan' Oblast' demolished the building of a former mosque in the immediate postwar period and used the building materials for a cowshed. So too, did another kolkhoz chairman in Osh Oblast' a decade later, at which the angered believers organised the collection of materials and began building a new mosque. [220] Following upon instructions from the Bashkir ASSR Council of Ministers in the early 1950s to use empty buildings of former mosques as cultural or educational institutions, some *raiispolkoms* asked to be allowed to dismantle them and use the building materials to construct clubs.[221] A decade

218. A. F. Ahadov to V. A. Kuroedov, 10 Oct. 1969; GARF, f.6991, o.6, d.220, ll.34-7.

219. See p.93.

220. A. Shadrin, Report, 30 June 1945, and I. G. Halimov to CARC, 11 May 1956; GARF, f.6991, o.3, d.25, l.151ob., and d.457, l.86.

221. M. Sh. Karimov, Report, 2nd quarter, 1951, Appendix to minutes, CARC session No.16, 15 Aug. 1951; GARF, f.6991, o.3, d.75, l.213.

later, at the height of Khrushchev's anti-religious campaign, a number of local government organs adopted resolutions to pull down non-functioning mosques, presumably with the same purpose in mind, although such decisions were not within their jurisdiction.[222] (It was this same lack of building materials which frequently led to reservations by local officials regarding the repairing of mosques. When, in the aftermath of very heavy rains, SADUM instructed that a number of mosques in Andijan Oblast' be repaired, necessitating the requisitioning of building materials, the local organs of government expressed their dissatisfaction. In one case they authorised an *imam-khatib* to seek the requisite materials beyond the confines of the oblast'.[223])

Sometimes refusal to review applications to register mosques was a purely tactical decision. In Ajaria, for instance, CARC's *upolnomochennyi* reported immediately after the end of World War II that he had perforce to reject all applications because of the opposition of the local leadership. Yet, when the question arose of possibly returning territory to Turkey in the process of negotiations over the renewal of the Soviet-Turkish treaty of friendship,[224] the *obkom* secretary instructed him to open a mosque. All of a sudden he not only agreed to opening a mosque, he was not prepared to brook any procrastination, the *upolnomochennyi* pointing out – to no avail – that there were established procedures which had to be followed.[225] .

That the stance adopted by local officialdom to Islam and its representatives was not on the whole the outcome of any position of principle can be learned too, from instances where it changed in accordance with conditions. There were examples of the same official or local organ first granting permission to believers to build a mosque and then, upon its completion, taking it away,

222. For example, in Penza Oblast', where a mosque in dilapidated condition was demolished in order to use the building materials for the construction of a hospital – Appendix, CARC session No.20, 11 July 1962; GARF, f.6991, o.3, d.1385, l.80.

223. M. A. Khalikov to Kh. N. Iskanderov, 12 March 1955; TsGAUz, f.2456, o.1, d.178, ll.55-7.

224. The treaty, signed in 1925, had been renewed in 1935 and was due for renewal again in 1945. In the event, the negotiations broke down and the treaty relapsed.

225. Minutes, Conference of CARC *upolnomochennye*, Rostov-on-Don, 14 June 1946; GARF, f.6991, o.3, d.38, ll.125-6.

or trying to take it away, from the community.[226] In 1947 the Novosibirsk *gorsovet* gave the town's Muslim community a plot in the neighbourhood of a former Muslim cemetery on which to erect a mosque. But work on the building was stopped in connection with large-scale construction plans. The community was then given a plot in a Russian cemetery, which it, however, rejected on the grounds that this contradicted Muslim tradition. Despite a favourable decision of the municipal soviet it in fact received no alternative plot, and so, in frustration, it proceeded to enlarge the building it was using for prayer purposes without obtaining permission, whereupon the *gorsovet* demolished the entire edifice and confiscated all the building materials.[227] In another instance, in Azerbaijan, a town council assigned a plot of land to an individual citizen, ostensibly to build a home – although he already had one – and believers collected money and began building a mosque. When the walls were two metres high the *raiispolkom* learned of it and resolved to transfer the building to its education department for use as a gym, empowering the chairman of the town council and head of the militia to halt further construction. This and other decisions of the *raiispolkom* were, however, not implemented and the building was completed under the very nose of the raion leading organs after the *raikom* secretary who had stopped work in its earlier stages took ill and died, his colleagues fearing a similar fate.[228]

It appears, too, that the measures adopted by local organs of government reflected their attitude not only to religion, but also to its practitioners and their anticipated response. In Ura-Tyube in Tajikistan, for example, local officials had no problem in the early 1960s taking administrative measures against Muslims, who were 'more obedient', and whose mosque they closed with ease, yet exhibited 'fear and uncertainty' when it came to carrying out the decision to close the local Russian Orthodox church. Indeed, the *gorispolkom* did not even adopt a resolution to this effect, since

226. For instance, in Tien-Shan Oblast' in Kirgiziia, Materials prepared for a conference of CARC *upolnomochennye*, Alma-Ata, 30 Sept. 1946; GARF, f.6991, o.3, d.41, l.122.

227. I. V. Polianskii to K. E. Voroshilov and M. I. Rodionov, 1 Dec. 1948; GARF, f.6991, o.3, d.54, ll.294-7.

228. All-Union conference of CARC *upolnomochennye*, 18-20 April 1960; GARF, f.6991, o.3, d.208, ll.115-16.

it was impossible to convince the community's believers, in accordance with accepted practice in this period;[229] and when the church was ultimately shut down – a year after the mosque – a 'scandal' ensued.[230] In the Chechen-Ingush ASSR, on the other hand, local officials feared Muslim religious figures. In one case both the first and second *raikom* secretaries refused to speak at a citizens' meeting convened to resolve the issue of a number of 'parasites', among whose ranks were several illegal Muslim preachers. Even the deputy chairman of the republican council of ministers, himself a member of one of the indigenous nationalities, who bravely suggested at the *obkom* to bring pigs to those places where Muslims met for prayers 'and they will never gather there again', was not prepared to speak before the local population on the unjustifiability and harmfulness of Islamic 'vestiges'.[231] One raion administration in Azerbaijan likewise took no action against an unregistered group of believers, who invited a blind dervish to recite the *marsiyya* prayer on the first ten days of Muharram, or to stop pilgrims visiting its mosque to see the saints who miraculously 'appeared' in its stained-glass windows, in order not to get into the bad books of the believer community.[232]

A large number of instances were recorded where local officials initiated 'administrative' measures against a religious community. These were so common that CARC's legal advisor commented that local officials knew no other way of dealing with religion.[233] As CARC Chairman Puzin wrote to the Tajikistan CP Central Committee, officials had to be instructed neither to tolerate violations by the clergy of the laws on religion nor to indulge in administrative measures against religious associations and believers. At the height of Khrushchev's anti-religious campaign, CARC was apprehensive that the existence of a large number of unregistered mosques and clergy in Tajikistan would be conducive to crude administrative measures, which would in turn be injurious to atheis-

229. For the practice of convincing believers and attempts to mobilise them to participate in the closure of prayer-houses in the Khrushchev period, see pp.211-2

230. K. Ovchinnikov to A. Puzin, 2 Aug. 1961; GARF, f.6991, o.3, d.1737, l.61.

231. A. Alisov to A. Puzin, 16 March 1962; GARF, f.6991, o.3, d.1606, l.23.

232. N. Smirnov, Information, 8 Aug. 1962; GARF, f.6991, o.3, d.1390, ll.21-2.

233. Minutes, CARC session No.28a, 23-24 Dec. 1949; GARF, f.6991, o.3, d.60, l.161.

tic propaganda activity and arouse legitimate dissatisfaction among the believer community.[234]

Administrative steps were taken in regard to both registered and unregistered religious societies. Even though CARC's position on local government's use of these steps to disband registered societies was 'severely negative', even in periods of repression,[235] this in no way deterred local organs, which had their own agenda. In Shahr-i Sabz a mulla was fined exorbitant sums in order to provide a pretext for closing a mosque, and when, as anticipated, he did not pay, the mosque was closed – on the festival of Qurban-Bayram. In another instance, in Andijan Oblast', a *sel'sovet* chairman, apprehensive that believers would not go to work on Uraz-Bayram, closed a mosque on the eve of the festival.[236] In a rural raion of Astrakhan' Oblast' the local organs decided to close a mosque just a few months after its registration: they summoned the members of the *dvadtsatka* to the *sel'sovet* and shortly afterwards received from each one of them an identical typed statement to the effect that he was illiterate, did not know how to sign his name and so should not appear on the *dvadtsatka* roll, from which he now, within months after submitting an application to open the mosque, asked to be removed. And the mosque was duly shut down.[237] One *raiispolkom* chairman in Osh Oblast' suggested to representatives of a rural registered religious society that they organise the signing of a petition by believers repudiating collective prayer and their mosque; otherwise he would see to it that their society be subjected to 'intolerable taxes'.[238] When CARC resolved to open a rural mosque in Andijan Oblast' in 1956, the *raikom* secretary ordered the local militia to disperse the believers and lock up the mosque. In Southern Kazakhstan in the same year the chairmen of a *sel'sovet* and a kolkhoz withdrew the registration

234. A. A. Puzin to the Tajikistan Communist Party Central Committee, 26 Jan. 1963; GARF, f.6991, o.3, d.1739, l.7.

235. Minutes, CARC session No.26, 1-2 Dec. 1949; GARF, f.6991, o.3, d.60, l.104; and see pp.43-4 and 206-7.

236. N. Tagiev, 'Violations of legislation on religion by clergy and connivance and interference of individual party and Soviet officials in the internal affairs of religious communities', [early 1949]; GARF, f.6991, 0.4, d.23, l.6.

237. Minutes, CARC session No.28a, 23-24 Dec. 1949; GARF, f.6991, o.3, d.60, l.160.

238. I. G. Halimov to CARC, 10 Aug. 1956; GARF, f.6991, o.3, d.457, l.132. For a similar threat of extravagant taxation, see chapter 4, n.279.

documents of a mosque CARC had recently permitted to register, imposed a tax of 13,000 rubles on the religious society, and induced its executive organ to sign a commitment not to permit the conduct of prayer-services.[239]

Not all administrative measures against registered mosques were directed at their closure. DUMSK complained shortly after World War II about local officials repressing believers for collecting money for the maintenance of their mosque. One *raikom* second secretary in Dagestan cautioned a qazi that he would have to quit his post unless he provided a list of those believers who contributed to the maintenance of the mosque and the spiritual directorate. In the same region a kolkhoz chairman confiscated maize and products which had been collected by believers for the upkeep of the mosque and clergy, whereas in one village clergy and their families were improperly deprived of their provisions.[240] In 1954 the head of the general department at a *raiispolkom* in Tien-Shan Oblast' in Kirgiziia, where the post of CARC *upolnomochennyi* had recently been discontinued, went to one rural mosque during prayers and announced that its fate was 'now in the hands of the *raiispolkom*', which would henceforth appoint and remove its imams. He thereupon proposed reinstating the imam whom SADUM had dismissed.[241] In 1961 a *raiispolkom* chairman in Azerbaijan sent for the two clerics of the local registered mosque in the middle of the Ashura service and kept them the entire morning in order to obstruct the conduct of this sacred rite; the official reason for the summons was to suggest that the morning *azan*, calling believers to prayer from the mosque minaret, be stopped.[242]

Cases of the use of administrative methods to fight religion were even more frequent when it came to unregistered religious associations. In 1945 the chairman of a *sel'sovet* in Andijan Oblast' dispersed a 'large group of believers' who gathered to hold prayers on Uraz-Bayram in the open, rejecting their offer to collect money for needy families of soldiers,[243] which was obviously intended to

239. K. F. Tagirov, Information, 1 March 1957; GARF, f.6991, o.3, d.132, ll.66 and 68.
240. I. Zakaryaev to CARC, Report, June 1946; GARF, f.6991, o.3, d.38, l.64.
241. I. V. Polianskii to P. V. Kovanov, 23 June 1955; GARF, f.6991, o.3, d.114, l.31.
242. N. Smirnov, Information, 8 Aug. 1962; GARF, f.6991, o.3, d.1390, l.21.
243. Menbariev to I. Ibadov and Oblispolkom Chairman Shadmanov, undated

convince him to change his decision. The secretaries of the party organisations in two villages in Dagestan threatened believers who performed rites in private homes.[244] In Osh Oblast' there were recurrent instances of officials interrupting services and driving worshippers out of unregistered mosques in the midst of prayers.[245]

Nor did the situation change noticeably in the more lenient years of the mid-1950s, when a multitude of similar actions were recorded. In the town of Jizak in Samarkand Oblast' an official sought to shut down the unregistered mosque in the middle of the Qurban-Bayram festival prayers.[246] Early in 1956 in Osh Oblast' a *raikom* secretary, accompanied by the *raiispolkom* executive secretary and a kolkhoz party organiser (*partorg*) went to an unauthorised mosque in the raion administrative centre in the midst of prayers and 'crudely' suggested to the worshippers that they stop the service, insulted them and cautioned them that if prayer-meetings recurred, criminal proceedings would be initiated against those who were guilty. The *raikom* secretary told the kolkhoz party organiser in the presence of the worshippers to remove their prayer-mats and take them to the kolkhoz and accommodate the kolkhoz livestock in the mosque. The mats were loaded onto a cart there and then and the building sealed. This behaviour led to the believers of the settlement and the nearby *poselok* demanding that their religious society be officially registered.[247] In the same year in Tashkent Oblast' a militia divisional inspector locked up a kolkhoz mosque which had been operating for an entire decade; the head of a *raikom* agitprop department ordered the closure of another kolkhoz mosque and subjected believers to criticism at a kolkhoz meeting; while a *raiispolkom* confiscated a private home rented by a religious society, although it belonged to an individual, not to the society, and forbade the conduct of prayers in it.[248]

[late Sept.-early Oct. 1945]; TsGAUz, f.2456, o.1, d.16, l.26.

244. I. Zakaryaev, Report, June 1946; GARF, f.6991, o.3, d.38, l.64.

245. For example, I. V. Polianskii to the CPSU Central Committee, 12 Jan. 1955 and 27 March 1956; GARF, f.6991, o.3, d.113, l.17, and d.129, ll.82-3.

246. Minutes, Instructional meeting of CARC *upolnomochennye* in the Uzbek SSR, 15-17 March 1956; TsGAUz, f.2456, o.1, d.183, l.54. In 1956 there were a number of similar instances in various oblasti of the Uzbek SSR - K. F. Tagirov, Information, 1 March 1957; GARF, f.6991, o.3, d.132, ll.65-7.

247. I. V. Polianskii to the USSR Council of Ministers, 27 March 1956; GARF, f.6991, o.3, d.129, ll.82-3.

248. K. F. Tagirov, Information, 1 March 1957; GARF, f.6991, o.3, d.132, ll.65-6.

Even within the framework of administrative measures, local government occasionally showed signs of recognising realities. Thus, for instance, the head of a raion department of ZAGS in Jalalabad Oblast' summoned fifteen unregistered clergy and informed them that in order to regulate burials and marriages at ZAGS he was appointing a mulla and assistant mulla in each kolkhoz, who would be authorised to conduct these rites for those providing documentary proof that they had duly registered them. Anyone who violated this regulation would be fined 300 rubles and a second offence would result in criminal proceedings.[249]

In the mid-1950s, at least, in spite of the fact that the operation of holy sites was consistently condemned by the central authorities, local officials were reprimanded for applying administrative measures against *mazars*. A group of officials, comprising an *obkom* instructor, two *raikom* secretaries, the *raiispolkom* chairman, the head of the raion MVD and officials of the raion financial department, appeared at the Shoh Fazil *mazar* in Jalalabad Oblast' on Qurban-Bayram in order to 'impede' believers from conducting a festival prayer-service at the site. They ordered the *chaikhona* which operated there to close so as not to provide conveniences for believers coming to the *mazar* and the militia impounded the sheep and goats brought by the pilgrims, which were taken to a nearby kolkhoz and returned to their owners on the conclusion of the service.[250]

Administrative measures sometimes took the form of rather dubious financial transactions. Employees of a *sel'sovet* financial department appeared at a mosque in Kirgiziia, did a re-count of moneys received as donations, confiscated part of them as 'income tax', without giving a receipt, and told the mulla that he must give the remainder to the mosque in Jalalabad (presumably the nearest registered religious society). One *sel'sovet* chairman summoned the shaykh of the Shoh Fazil *mazar* and proposed that he pay the *sel'sovet* 10,000 rubles. When he refused, he was summoned to the raion financial inspector, who demanded that he agree to pay 7,000 rubles and forced him to fill in two forms. A few days

249. I. V. Polianskii to P. V. Kovanov, 23 June 1955; GARF, f.6991, o.3, d.114, l.32.

250. *Ibid.*, l.31.

later the inspector visited the *mazar* with a policeman and received 1,500 rubles on the spot. On the same day the same inspector received further sums from three other *mazars*, giving no receipts for any of them.[251] Stressing in his report to the CPSU Central Committee that the local officials were not providing receipts, Polianskii was clearly insinuating that they were putting the money in their own pockets. Sometimes, too, they sequestrated for the use of local government moneys received or collected by the religious societies. For instance, one kishlak soviet in Bukhara Oblast' appropriated into its account moneys collected on Qur-ban-Bayram for refurbishurg the local cemetery.[252]

The total disregard of some local officials for Islamic practice and tradition was given expression in Tashkent Oblast', where it was suggested to move the celebration of Uraz-Bayram, which was due to fall on the Sunday that marked Aviation Day, to the day before. CARC's *upolnomochennyi* for Uzbekistan told AUCP (b) Secretary Mel'nikov that this was out of the question: it was impossible to curtail the *uraz* to twenty-nine days and re-arrange religious festivals in purely administrative fashion.[253] There were also instances when believers were coerced into attending, and applauding, lectures where local officials heaped insults on their faith.[254]

Similar contempt for believers' fealings was shown when, for example, in Astrakhan' Oblast' one *raisovet* deputy chairman allowed tombstones to be taken out of the Muslim cemetery by a local bigwig (the director of the motor-transport depot) in order to build himself a new house. This led to demonstrations by the believer population and he was obliged to return the tombstones. A similar incident occurred several years later in Kazakhstan when a kolkhoz chairman took tombstones to build a cowshed.[255] Some-times local officials simply took advantage of their authority to bridle

251. *Ibid.*, ll.31-2.

252. K. Ruzmetov to A. Barmenkov, [?] Oct. 1972; GARF, f.6991, o.6, d.467, l.182.

253. Minutes, CARC session No.7, 28-30 March 1951; GARF, f.6991, o.3, d.74, l.95.

254. For one such instance, see p.568.

255. I. V. Polianskii to A. A. Zhdanov, 22 July 1947 – RTsKhIDNI, f.17, o.125, d.506, l.176, and K. F. Tagirov, Information, 1 March 1957 – GARF, f.6991, o.3, d.132, l.68.

the Muslim believer community. In one case, in Nakhichevan, the town council used the occasion of street repairs to close the mosque main entrance with rubble on the eve of Ashura. The other, smaller, gate remained open, yet a militiaman and Komsomol member were stationed there who disconcerted believers by asking them about the prayer-mats they were carrying under their arms as they entered the mosque on the great day.[256]

Often local government organs obliged mosques to move from their regular precincts to less comfortable and less conveniently situated premises. The pretext or occasion was usually reconstruction or new building projects, which necessitated vacating the mosque. Not a few of the mosques closed in the period of Khrushchev's anti-religious campaign were shut down in the wake of construction projects – registered mosques, as distinct from unregistered ones, would usually be confronted with some real or imaginary pretext to justify closure even in these harsh years.[257] This was the rationale provided, for example, in the case of five of eight registered mosques which terminated their existence in Uzbekistan in these years. (The other three were closed by uniting their religious societies with those of nearby mosques.)[258] In Kirovabad in 1963 the decision to reconstruct the city's central square, where the mosque was situated, was the context for the town council's forcing the mosque's executive organ to move without prior notice to a building which was not fit for use.[259] Sometimes apparently local officials simply wanted the mosque to be situated in a less accessible and less conspicuous location. In one village in Dagestan they demanded that the mosque move away from the village centre.[260] In one instance in Southern Kazakhstan a religious society had its mosque taken away from it in order to distance it from a major *mazar*, when it built another one in the town centre without awaiting permission from the local authorities, the latter sequestrated the

256. Minutes, Conference of CARC's republican *upolnomochennye*, 17-18 Feb. 1965; GARF, f.6991, o.4, d.168, l.29.

257. For the withdrawal of registered mosques from registration in this period, see pp.205-13.

258. M. Miragzamov to M. Kh. Khalmuhamedov, 22 Oct. 1966; GARF, f.6991, o.6, d.11, l.65.

259. Minutes, Conference of CARC's republican *upolnomochennye*, 17-18 Feb. 1965; GARF, f.6991, o.4, d.168, l.29.

260. Minutes, CARC session No.24, 27 Aug, 1964; GARF, f.6991, o.4, d.147, l.82.

building for use as a club, substituting tumbledown premises else-where.[261]

In a few Muslim areas local government organs were particularly antagonistic to religious practice of any sort. In Dagestan, where there was a long record of opposition to religious activity on the part of the government, the republican leadership actually forbade CARC's *upolnomochennyi* to meet with believers, although this was part of his official duties, insisting that only local officials might converse with them to hear their problems. In the period following the CPSU Central Committee's November 1954 resolution, however, believers took courage to voice their dissatisfaction with the administrative conduct of local officialdom and lodge complaints with the *upolnomochennyi*. In two villages the mosques' lock had been broken in the middle of the night and replaced by a new one and religious articles thrown into the street; a mosque repaired in 1955 for use for prayer-services was taken from the religious society two years later and used as a club. In yet another village believers were constantly being harassed by local officials during prayers; while the person who officiated at a *ziyarat* was summoned to the local organs and threatened with arrest. The republican leadership ignored these doings altogether.[262] It should be noted that whereas the lower levels of the local bureaucracy seem to have operated in more persistent fashion – although this varied apparently from one region to another in this particularly hetergeneous republic – the attitude of the republican leadership was more composite, perhaps indeed because of the complexity of Dagestan's ethnic structure. A basic position of governmental antagonism also pertained in the Chechen-Ingush ASSR, where administrative methods were resorted to by bringing in *druzhinniki* to break up prayer-meetings.[263] (The members of these 'volunteer groups', activated and encouraged under Khrushchev, were supposed to help the police in patrolling streets and public places, combating hooliganism and drunkenness and coping

261. See p.228.

262. Gasanov to V. I. Gostev, 19 March 1957, and reception by N. I. Smirnov of Uzun Bashirov, Khalitbek Mukhtarov and Shamkhal Ramzanov, 15 Feb. 1958; GARF, f.6991, o.3, d.145, ll.52-3, and o.4, d.88, ll.19-20.

263. Draft, Materials sent to the CPSU Central Committee, 27 Dec. 1960; GARF, f.6991, o.3, d.210, ll.73-85.

with petty crime; needless to say, they were organised and directed by the party, and later, under Brezhnev, through the local soviet.[264])

CARC frequently found itself on a collision course with local officials in connection with their continual resort to administrative measures. The Council, and Polianskii personally, insisted that these measures achieved the exact opposite of their avowed intention and were detrimental to the state, and that the legislation on religion was no less binding for the bureaucracy than for the clergy. In those places where local organs of government resorted to 'administrative pressure', religious practice and 'prejudice', specifically, the activity of unregistered clergy and the observance of the fast and festivals, became enhanced.[265] One CARC inspector wrote that the administrative actions of local officialdom against a Tatar community in Ul'ianovsk Oblast' was being used skilfully by its *aktiv* to consolidate the entire Tatar population around the religious society.[266] Yet, even CARC did not totally exclude administrative action in harsher times. The CARC *upolnomochennyi* in the Mordvinian ASSR was told in the late 1940s that unregistered religious associations might be closed down by administrative measures, although such 'crude' ones as arresting a mulla at the cemetery in the middle of prayers could not be tolerated.[267]

As Khrushchev's anti-religious campaign developed momentum, and lines of conduct which had previously been censured as representing administrative measures became customary practice, CARC Chairman Puzin still contended that administrative measures might be employed only as a last resort, and then only after educational activity among the population.[268] Other CARC personnel were even more extreme in their reservations regarding the practices of local bureaucracies; they insisted that administrative measures contradicted the policy of the party and state and that they could

264. Fainsod, *How Russia is Ruled*, p.300; Friedgut, *Political Participation in the USSR*, pp.247 and 259-61.

265. I. V. Polianskii, Address, Conference of CARC *upolnomochennye* in Belorussia, 18-19 Nov. 1954, and L. A. Prikhod'ko, Memorandum, 25 July 1956; GARF, f.6991, o.3, d.101, ll.194-5 and d.130, l.33. For CARC's policy regarding administrative measures, see also pp.38, 43 and 590-1.

266. For details, see p.702.

267. Minutes, CARC session No.26, 1-2 Dec. 1949; GARF, f.6991, o,3, d.60, ll.83-4.

268. See p.43.

never achieve anything constructive.[269]

Even when a given religious society confessed to having committed transgressions against the law, CARC tended not to condone administrative measures against it. Believers in Sol'-Iletsk in Orenburg Oblast' admitted they were guilty of such violations: they had conducted collective prayer for rain in the fields. Nonetheless, CARC doubted the expediency of the mosque's closure by local officials who locked it up arbitrarily, forbidding the further conduct of prayers on the precincts.[270]

Certainly, there is ample evidence that the conduct of local government organs was characterized by a large measure of arbitrariness – even if we take into account that believers were prone to exaggerate. This applied particularly in periods when the provincial bureaucracy understood that such procedures were in line with regime policy. The believer community in the Azerbaijani town of Ujara, for example, had undertaken major repairs of their mosque which was in a state of semi-ruin and then began holding prayers in the building. Nobody, they maintained, had forbidden them to repair it or to pray in it. Indeed, the wives and children of local officials had been among the worshippers. Yet, all of a sudden, in mid-1960 the local administration closed it down and used it as a storehouse.[271] One rural group of Muslim believers in Gor'kii Oblast' complained that the local *raikom* and *raiispolkom* forbade the conduct of collective prayer in private homes and sought to appropriate the prayer-rugs and other objects belonging to unregistered religious associations, although in neighbouring *raiony* no such measures were taken.[272] A group in Kalinin had

269. For example, statements by CARC's *upolnomochennyi* in Kirgiziia, 25 Nov. 1958, and in Dagestan, CARC session No.33, 26-27 Oct. 1960; GARF, f.6991, o.3, d.165, l.51, and d.207, l.40. The former expressed apprehension several months later that if a CARC *upolnomochennyi* were to tell local officials to close an unregistered religious group by administrative measures, juridical procedures might be opened against him – Minutes, All-Union conference of CARC's Central Asian *upolnomochennye*, 5-6 June 1959; GARF, f.6991, o.3, d.186, l.50.

270. Reception by N. I. Smirnov of Jumad Apiev and Sarsen Ospanov, 23 June 1962, and V. Riazanov to V. V. Opitin, 25 July 1962 (draft); GARF, f.6991, o.4, d.130, ll.32-3. And see p.236.

271. Reception by N. I. Smirnov of A. I. Efendiev, 10 Nov. 1960; GARF, f.6991, o.4, d.110, l.55.

272. Reception by N. I. Smirnov of F. F. Ibragimov, 1 Sept. 1959; GARF, f.6991, o.4, d.100, l.81.

prayed for many years in private premises, before local officials finally gave them an ultimatum in 1960 that if they gathered again for purposes of prayer they would be fined.[273]

True to its position, in all these cases CARC backed local officialdom in its discussions with those who came to lodge compalints, however much it in fact disproved the steps taken by the bureaucracy in the periphery. The CARC inspector who received the believers was unequivocal in pointing out their digressions. He told the representative of the Ujara believers in no uncertain terms that it was they who had transgressed the law, since they should have required permission both to conduct repairs and to hold prayers. He similarly pointed out to the delegate from Gor'kii Oblast' that the believers were acting in defiance of legislation in that they gathered for prayer without registering with the organs of state power, and to the one from Kalinin that if they had managed for years without a mosque, this was not the appropriate time to seek one – there was no problem praying privately at home, but if they wanted to pray collectively, they must obtain permission from the local authorities.

By mid-1964, Khrushchev's anti-religious campaign began showing clear signs of letting up, and in June Puzin delivered a lecture at an all-union conference of CARC *upolnomochennye* on 'Eliminating administrative excesses towards believers and religious associations committed by local organs of power'.[274] In subsequent years under Brezhnev the CRA – into which CAROC and CARC had meanwhile amalgamated – was adamant that such legislation which the regime sought to impose not be enforced through administrative measures. Council officials stressed in this context that civil funeral rites must be introduced through harnessing public opinion rather than by administrative steps.[275] They continued to contend that organs of local government in many regions were resorting to excessive use of administrative measures.[276] And they

273. Reception by N. Smirnov of Osman Liuletbaev, 12 May 1960; GARF, f.6991, o.4, d.110, l.23.

274. Minutes, All-Union conference of CARC *upolnomochennye*, 25-26 June 1964; GARF, f.6991, o.3, d.1457, ll.40-92.

275. S. Shafiqov, Information, 22 Jan. 1971; GARF, f.6991, o.6, d.370, l.19.

276. For example, unsigned and undated report from Azerbaijan [probably between 30 May and 2 June 1973]; GARF, f.6991, o.6, d.537, l.196.

took exception to the recurrent extortion of statements from clergy that they were repudiating religious activity.[277]

It is evident from the documentation that local officials who had turned a blind eye to the activities of religious societies in the mid 1950s were a decade later becoming more pedantic and were rather eager to take advantage of slips on the part of these communities – either to gain buildings for public use or to prove their mettle to the centre. The sole complaint on the part of believers that was still likely to win approbation and perhaps even obtain results was that local officials had misled their superiors, providing them with faulty information in order to justify action against religious societies. Believers of one rural religious society in Kuibyshev Oblast', whose registration had been withdrawn after both the *oblispolkom* and CARC had given their consent, contended that these two authorities had been misinformed by lower organs of government as to the true state of affairs. Even then the mosque was not returned to them, but the *oblispolkom* compensated them partially by allowing them to conduct collective prayers on festivals on private premises.[278]

It has been suggested that some of the extreme cases of anti-Islamic sentiment and practice on the part of local government organs had the effect – and perhaps even the intention – of inciting the local population against the central authorities in Moscow, who were necessarily perceived in the periphery as the inspiration behind anti-religious policies. This applied especially to the Chechen-Ingush ASSR, where the republican authorities were insistent on not opening mosques following the return of the deportees in the late 1950s.[279] While the truth of the contention cannot be

277. There were, for example, a number of such instances in Semipalatinsk Oblast' – B. Korobaev to A. A. Puzin, 6 July 1965; GARF, f.6991, o.3, d.1490, l.107. See also p.214.

278. Reception by N. I. Smirnov of Islam Batretdinov and Normuhamed Bogout-dinov, 28 Jan. 1965; GARF, f.6991, o.4, d.171, l.12.

279. Interview with a former CRA official who has asked to remain anonymous; and see above. According to one report, there were differences of opinion among the local bureaucracy in the republic, some favouring the opening of mosques in order to acquire means of permanent control of Islamic activity, others opposing this on the grounds that the country was moving into the era of communist construction and so any talk of mosques was out of place – Minutes, All-Union conference of CARC *upolnomochennye*, 25-27 Nov. 1958; GARF, f.6991, o.3, d.165, l.107. See also p.417.

ruled out, it is by the very nature of things very difficult to prove. Whether true or not, the fact that this opinion was held by officials in Moscow punctuates their sense of frustration: their endeavours to impose a policy that would be acceptable to the population or, at least, mitigate its sense of resentment, were constantly coming up against a brick wall in the form of the local organs of government on which Moscow depended for policy implementation.

What seems more easily demonstrated is the position also held by officials of both CARC and the CRA that administrative measures were in the final event counter-productive, generally conducive not to reducing religious worship and practice but to augmenting them. A number of instances, for example, were recorded where local officials demolished an empty mosque which was not in use, and so angered believers, who had apparently entertained hopes that one day they might recover the building, that they initiated organised religious activity where before there had been none.[280]

Toeing the line

The general picture presented by the documentation is undisputably of a recalcitrant local government apparatus, guided by its own interests, inclinations and sympathies. Nonetheless, there were instances where it clearly and unequivocally accepted the line of the centre in Moscow and followed its instructions.

This was probably most manifest when it came to religious activity that threatened to affect adversely the economic performance of the administrative unit in question. In the early 1950s local party and soviet organs took measures to forestall the enhanced religious activity which normally accompanied the *uraz* and festivals, organising intensive 'political-cultural' work – specifically, talks on 'scientific-atheistic' themes – supposed to have a 'salutary' effect. The Osh Oblast' executive organ, for instance, instructed all municipal and raion *ispolkoms* to intensify activity so that the fasts and festivals not effect productivity in either the urban or rural sector.[281]

Not all initiatives taken by officialdom in the periphery to implement party and government policy seem, however, to have

280. See pp.299-300.
281. L. A. Prikhod'ko, Report, 31 Jan. 1953; GARF, f.6991, o.3, d.91, l.5. For an example of local government seeking to overcome possible violations of work discipline through administrative action, see p.501.

been directed at ensuring economic performance. In some parts measures taken to lessen the popularity of the major festivals were designed first and foremost to do just that, not necessarily being motivated by concern for work discipline. Steps were often taken in this connection reminiscent of the early 1920s, for instance, providing an alternative focus of attention for the public. In the early 1950s the Kazakhstan CP Central Committee ordered the *raikoms* to attract the population, especially the younger generation, to clubs, 'cultural palaces' and stadiums on Qurban-Bayram and not to allow prayer-meetings in settlements which had no registered mosque (of which in all Kazakhstan there were just over twenty). In the same time period in Kuibyshev Oblast' commercial organisations held fairs during the *uraz* and the *raikoms* organised the holding of the Tatar national holiday, the Saban-tui, entailing sporting events and competitions, which inevitably kept part of the believer population away from the mosques.[282]

In some parts, local organs of government put an end to the activities of clandestine religious groups on the specific recommendation or instruction of CARC's *upolnomochennye*. During 1951, for example, out of a total of 1327 such groups of all the faiths under CARC's jurisdiction which were shut down at their instance, 280 were Muslim.[283] In the early period of Khrushchev's antireligious campaign, in the wake of the republican government's resolutions, local organs of government – apparently in co-ordination with the *upolnomochennye* – not only withdrew registered religous societies from registration, but took steps to help close down considerable numbers of unregistered religious associations.[284]

Yet, even where the local government organs were prepared to proceed in conformity with directives from the centre, the

282. L. A. Prikhod'ko, Report, 31 Jan. 1953: GARF, f.6991, o.3, d.91, l.6. And see p. 602.

283. F. G. Frolov, Report, 28 Feb. 1952; GARF, f.6991, o.3, d.81, l.289. Over 60 of the 280 were in the Gorno-Badakhshan AO.

284. For instance, in Kirgiziia's Osh Oblast' they shut down 69 of 213 unregistered groups, 59 of them Muslim, and a further 46 Muslim groups disbanded 'of their own accord'; in Tien-Shan of 60 unregistered Muslim groups only 26 remained in early 1960; and in the former oblasti of Issyk-Kul, Frunze and Talas, which were now directly subordinate to the republican authorities, nearly all 99 groups had stopped activity – Minutes, All-Union conference of CARC *upolnomochennye*, 18-20 April 1960; GARF, f.6991, o.3, d.208, l.132. And see pp.308-13 for the disbandment of unregistered associations by local government in this period.

actions they took were often ineffective. It is unclear whether this was because they did so insincerely, merely going periodically through the motions without controlling the outcome, or whether they simply did not have the authority to undermine popular practice. In the period prior to the November 1958 resolution on terminating the activity of holy shrines CARC received reports, for example, that local officials would sporadically fine shaykhs and *ishans* who operated at *mazars* and even initiate court proceedings against them and drive away pilgrims who came to these sites – with little or no impact.[285] In the period subsequent to the passing of the resolution local organs took an active part in the closure of *mazars*.[286] Indeed, in Kirgiziia it was reported that in the first eighteen or so months after the resolution a number of *mazars* were formally shut down, although in effect pilgrimages to them continued.[287] In Uzbekistan the local bureaucracy was said not to know how to direct the work of the religious societies, in particular the unregistered ones, attempting to impose taxes and using the militia to keep *mazars* under control – all to no avail.[288]

Undisputably, without the active and watchful co-operation of local officialdom there was no chance of implementing the decrees of the centre regarding the termination of the activity of *mazars* and other holy places.[289] Puzin himself stated that SADUM could not be divested of its *mazars* nor could they be closed by decisions taken in Moscow: in each case it was necessary to speak with the party and soviet officials on the spot, look into the situation in the locality and then decide how to proceed.[290] In 1959, the Osh *gorispolkom* – according to one report, in response to 'the movement among the working masses to close holy places' – adopted a resolution 'On the application of the population to terminate pilgrimages to the so-called holy mount Takht-i Sulayman', in-

285. Reception by K. F. Tagirov and A. S. Tazetdinov of Idris Rahmatulla, 3 Oct. 1958; GARF, f.6991, o.4, d.88, l.210.

286. A. Irmanov, Report, Conference of CARC's Central Asian *upolnomochennye*, 5-6 June 1959; GARF, f.6991, o.3, d.186, ll.88-90.

287. Minutes, All-Union conference of CARC *upolnomochennye*, 18-20 April 1960 – GARF, f.6991, o.3, d.208, l.133.

288. N. I. Inogamov, Address, All-Union conference of CARC *upolnomochennye*, 25-27 Nov. 1958; GARF, f.6991, o.3, d.165, l.36.

289. See p.43.

290. Minutes, Conference of CARC's Central Asian *upolnomochennye*, Tashkent, 6 June 1959; GARF, f.6991, o.3, d.186, l.224.

structing the head of the municipal militia department to prohibit access of shaykhs to the site and expel from the town those who persisted in opposing this. The CARC republican *upolnomochennyi* in Kirgiziia told people at the Kirgiziian CP Central Committee and the republican council of ministers that this was in line with Puzin's statement of November 1958 that it was sometimes necessary in dealing with unregistered religious associations to combine administrative measures with educational work. These steps, combined with the actions of the Namangan, Andijan and Fergana *obkoms*, which, acting on the request of the Osh Obkom, spread the word that Osh was closed to pilgrimage, were said to have reduced the number of pilgrims who came to Takht-i Sulayman in 1959 to just 20 per cent of that of the previous year.[291]

On the whole, republican and oblast' authorities passed new resolutions and issued new instructions to the organs under their jurisdiction as the 1950s drew to a close and in the early years of the 1960s in keeping with those emanating from the centre. In Turkmenistan the republican ministry of finance ordered the financial organs at the oblast' and raion level to impose income tax on all clergy, itinerant mullas and other 'dubious people' who 'extort money from the population'. In that same republic local officialdom stepped up its atheistic propaganda activities, and as a result observance of the *uraz*, attendance at prayer-meetings and the visitation of *mazars* were said to have decreased.[292] (Presumably, as elsewhere, insofar as reporting mirrored reality, the reduction in pilgrimages was temporary here as well.[293])

While the general sense of legislation or resolutions and directives emanating from the centre was usually clear, there were from time to time issues which required clarification. Thus, for instance, local organs of government operated under a haze of uncertainty precisely as the anti-religious campaign unfurled. The new policy on religion coming, as it did, together, with a host of legislation on criminal law and procedure,[294] often found the bureaucracy

291. H. Akhtiamov, Report, Conference of CARC's Central Asian *upolnomochennye*, 5-6 June 1959; GARF, f.6991, o.3, d.186, ll.31-4.

292. A. M. Komekov, Report prepared for conference of CARC's Central Asian *upolnomochennye*, 5-6 June 1959; GARF, f.6991, o.3, d.186, ll.57-8.

293. For the long-term ineffectiveness of the steps taken to shut down shrines, see pp.378-83.

294. See Berman, *Justice in the U.S.S.R.*, pp.68-74.

in the localities groping to discover the extent of its powers to act against religious transgressors: which violations of the law, for instance, were liable to criminal procedure.[295] The form of contact which local party workers should maintain with the believer community was likewise unclear, even prior to the new repression of religious activity. The head of Margelan's agitprop read out the CPSU Central Committee resolution of 10 November 1954 before 10,000 worshippers in the town's registered mosque, evoking considerable disagreement among the bureaucracy itself as to whether a party worker should appear at all before believers during prayers, especially in cases where the groundwork had not been sufficiently laid.[296] In other words, there was a danger that his appearance would not have the desired result. In this particular case, however, the functionary in question probably sensed an unusual satisfaction at being able to announce a CPSU Central Committee decision favourable to religion that he knew would be welcome news to his audience and so undertook this rather unusual step.

From the above it appears that the local organs of government found themselves in a no-win situation. Islam was *a priori* a field in which the chances of the secular authorities making major headway were slim, particularly in the areas where it had a long history of predominance. Already in the interwar years the instructions issued from Tashkent, for example, to the more peripheral parts of Uzbekistan ignored the differences of conditions in remote, more outlying districts and set goals and timetables which could not be met, especially given the accompanying prohibition against using force.[297] In the postwar period this 'Catch-22' persisted. In those parts, for example, within the traditionally sedentary regions of Central Asia, where local officials effectively prohibited illegal mosques and there were no registered ones, people often travelled long distances (25 or 30 km) to attend regular Friday prayers.

295. The Stavropol' Krai Obkom, for instance, asked whether a person who took money from believers, for example for the conduct of a funeral service, could be brought to justice – Minutes, CARC session No.21, 22 July 1959; GARF, f.6991, o.3, d.184, ll.177-8.

296. U. G. Mangushev to I. V. Polianskii, 25 Jan. 1955; GARF, f.6991, o.3, d.113, ll.86-9.

297. Keller, 'The Struggle against Islam in Uzbekistan, 1921-1941', pp.35-6.

Festival prayer-services were conducted in most settlements, either in the empty buildings of former mosques or in the open, and if local officials forbade this and took administrative measures to prevent them, they would be held secretly. Such a situation was hardly conducive to major endeavours on the part of these same officials to fulfil the assignments imposed upon them from a distant centre, that had little understanding of the mechanisms of society in the Muslim areas and not much leverage in ensuring that its policy be implemented. Two further factors discouraged local organs of government from going to great lengths to carry out directives regarding Islam: their sense of commitment to the surrounding population, to which and to whose social culture, they generally belonged, and the fact that they entertained little, if any, sympathy for their superiors in the republican capital, let alone in Moscow, whose ideology and goals they formally represented.[298]

There can be no doubt that local organs of government frequently followed their own line in respect of Islam. Their approach, however, was often inconsistent for a number of reasons, some of them pertaining to circumstances in the different localities, others to the atmosphere of the period in question, for local officials, too, particularly in the higher rungs of the hierarchy, could not ignore the winds blowing from Moscow. As a consequence of the heterogeneity of the influences which impacted upon their attitude and conduct, it is impossible to characterise these by focusing on a single approach or pattern of behaviour. At the same time, there were on the whole a limited number of alternatives. A CRA report of the early 1980s summed up the situation succinctly:

> The work of local and party organs over many years to discontinue the anti-lawful activity of unregistered Muslim associations and clergy has not given lasting results: in place of religious associations which were closed down, new ones have arisen; the role of the unregistered clergy whose activity was cut short is being filled by new generations of pensioners. [...] The incorrect attitude of officialdom to the issue of regulating the network of religious associations has led to the desire to disregard the illicit activity of mosques and mullas, and has turned into connivance with religion.

298. For the hostility to Moscow of the party apparatus in the Fergana Valley, for example, see pp.5-6.

Preferring to ignore the instructions of the leading organs and the Council's recommendations, the bureaucracy in the localities failed to register the requisite number of religious societies, which, the CRA maintained, would have effectively brought Muslim activity under the control of the law and the authorities.[299]

In this way, the local organs of government made their own meaningful contribution to aborting the attempt of those of the central bodies which sought to find a *modus vivendi* or *modus operandi* with Islam. When, from time to time, they showed zeal in carrying out injunctions, one has the sense that it was more often than not perfunctory, and the Muslim believer community was quick to note this and draw the mandatory conclusions. The reasons and calculations of the local bureaucracies in keeping aloof from official policy seem to have been sundry. They included a conscious desire to promote their own national or local heritage, the hope of taking a ride on the back of regime policy to reap material and other benefits (buildings, taxes, enhanced power), a longstanding, inherent animosity towards Moscow, and an innate bureaucratic inertia. Whatever their motivation, the organs of local government thus filled a major role in Islam's survival as a viable presence, for which their non-cooperation with the centre of power was a *sine qua non*.

299. CRA report, 2 June 1983; TsKhSD, f.5, o.89, d.82, ll.37–40.

12

ISLAM AND NATIONALISM

The Muslim population of the Soviet Union was split up into a large number of ethnic groups: approximately forty in all.[1] Not all these *natsional'nosti*, nationalities or national groups appeared as such in the post-World War II population censuses, which enumerated the over one hundred ethnic groups that officially comprised the country's multinational body politic. The first full Soviet census, that of 1926, had listed a far larger number of ethnic groups – 194 – but many of the smaller ones had disappeared as separate entities having, according to Soviet theory, 'assimilated' into the larger nationalities around them in the process of 'nation-building' or national 're-unification'. Some of those which had been arbitrarily 're-identified' from the point of view of the census were nonetheless retained in the fifth rubric of the internal passports of individual citizens that denoted national affiliation.[2] Six of the major Muslim ethnicities constituted the eponymous population of union republics, while many of the others received

1. Feshbach, 'Trends in the Soviet Muslim Population: Demographic Aspects', Table 4.1; and Anderson and Silver, 'Demographic Sources of the Changing Ethnic Composition of the Soviet Union', Table. The number of groups varied from one population census to another. For example, the 1979 and 1989 censuses provided data for the Crimean Tatars and Turks (presumably the Meskhetian Turks departed during World War II and not allowed to return to their homeland in Georgia), whereas those of 1959 and 1970 mentioned neither. The 1989 census also included data for the Talysh, previously apparently included among the Azerbaijanis.

2. While official documentation – censuses, passports, etc. – described all recognised nationalities under the single denomination *natsional'nost'*, ethnographers engaged in recurrent theoretical debates as to how to categorise different groups of ethnicities. As of the mid-1960s, an ethnos after which a union or autonomous republic was named was considered a nation (*narod*), while a nationality lent its name to an autonomous oblast' and in some cases had no administrative-territiorial unity of its own. Even then, Soviet scholars did not agree completely as to who might be called a nation and who a nationality – Simon, *Nationalism and Policy toward the Nationalities in the Soviet Union*, p.14.

autonomous republics or oblasti,[3] in which they enjoyed their respective collective rights. These rights were first and foremost cultural, although, according to Soviet criteria, they related to the more formal attributes of their cultures, primarily the right to promote, preserve and use the national language in education, the arts and the media. The Soviet formula recognised and legitimised the culture of an ethnos only insofar as it was 'national in form and socialist in content'.

In its early stages, the Bolshevik regime had sought to ensure that each of the country's component national groups would identify with its respective nationality, although many of them had no such discrete collective affiliation. In some cases the nationality had, in fact, been created arbitrarily by the new order out of a variety of political considerations. Classification as a nationality involved accepting the RCP(b)'s norms for national existence, with language – the form – as the principal distinctive cultural feature, and the message transmitted by the party and its ideologues – the content – as the Trojan horse which would hasten the assimilation of all ethnic groups into the new internationalist Soviet people once they had attained the requisite level of development. In other words, the nationality, to which all had to belong, was to be a transient stage in the formation of the new socialist society; it was not a value unto itself. Paradoxically, it appears that nationality was not only given a boost by Soviet policies but also actually perpetuated by them, as occurred throughout the Third World, where an imperial presence and tactics served as a catalyst for crystallising national perceptions and movements.

Implicit in the Soviet design, in the division of the country's citizenry into ethnic groups, whose national attributes were severely restricted, was that Islam – and the other 'national' religions – would gradually be relegated to a past that was being consciously, even willingly, discarded in the process of the country's 'socialist construction'. However, the rank and file, the 'toiling masses' of the

3. As of the 1960s, eight of the country's 22 autonomous republics were called after autocthonous Muslim populations, two of them – the Chechen-Ingush and Kabardino-Balkar ASSRs – after two Muslim ethnic groups; while the Dagestan ASSR was also inhabited by Muslim nationalities, three of which (the Avars, Lezgin and Dargin) numbered over 100,000 and so fulfilled one of the official criteria for nationhood. In the prewar period there had also been national *okrugi* and raiony, but these no longer remained. For their disappearance, mostly between 1937 and 1939, see Simon, *Nationalism and Policy...*, pp.58-61.

peoples who had in the past professed Islam (to use the Soviet euphemism) all had their own mores, ethos and heritage. These constituted an obstacle no less serious than Moscow's reliance on local government in the implementation in the country's periphery of regime policies and postulates regarding Islam. This impediment, moreover, appeared increasingly insurmountable as the years passed, for these popular strata saw in the national religion, or in some of its features and rites, an integral part of their national culture, indeed were often unable to distinguish between the two. True, increasing quotas of cadres and the national intelligentsias went through the mill of Soviet education and imbibed the main teachings of the new secular, atheistic political culture. Yet the bulk of the population, especially in the rural sector, encountered *a priori* a rather watered down version of this culture and were neither persuaded by it at any stage nor saw any reason to identify with it. They retained as much as they could of their traditional social milieu and its concomitant customs and practices.

The broad masses of the nationalities concerned seem to have considered themselves Muslim throughout the Soviet period, as well as being Uzbek or Kyrgyz, Turkestani or Caucasian, members of a given clan or tribe and inhabitants of a certain locality. In this fashion Islam and the identification with the *umma*, the world-wide Muslim community, or the *millet*, the officially recognised Soviet Muslim community, encouraged, or threatened to encourage, an alternative to the internationalist aims of the CPSU: *sblizhenie* and *druzhba narodov*, the coming together or rapprochement of the country's many ethnic groups and their friendship or fraternity.[4] (At certain stages Soviet nationalities policy preached *sliianie*, the fusion of the various nationalities in one Soviet people, but as the likelihood of this happening seemed increasingly improbable,

4. From its very earliest stages the Soviet regime had sought to pre-empt any possible mélange of the Muslim peoples – see, for example, Bennigsen and Wimbush, *Muslim National Communism in the Soviet Union, passim*. Some Western analysts have argued that throughout the Soviet period the identification with the *umma* remained stronger and deeper than with the Soviet-created nationality –Bennigsen, 'Panturkism and Panislamism in History and Today', Lemercier-Quelquejay, 'From Tribe to *Umma*', and Wimbush, 'The Politics of Identity Change in Soviet Central Asia'. This does not, however, seem to be borne out by the history of the 1980s and 1990s, although it might conceivably be argued that the final page in this history has not yet been written. I myself discussed these issues in 'Religion as an Obstacle to *Sblizhenie*: The Official Perception', pp.171-5.

this slogan gave way to *sblizhenie*.) It seems, however, that to the Soviet citizen of a Muslim ethnicity more than meaning membership in a rather abstract universal fraternity or family,[5] being Muslim entailed particular conduct and mores,[6] although not necessarily any conscious, let alone declared, belief in Allah and Muhammad. An atheistic lecturer in Kirgiziia was asked by a member of his audience whether he was a Muslim; his reply that he did not believe in God and so was not a Muslim annoyed his interlocutor and evoked the retort: 'How can you speak this way? You are a Kyrgyz'. Two Tajik students in Moscow likewise told this same lecturer with conviction that being Tajik, they were naturally also Muslims.[7] A Uighur newspaper reproduced the dialogue between God and man supposed to take place on the Day of Judgment, which was recited by mullas as part of the regular funeral ceremony. It included the question, 'What is your nation?', to which the reply was: 'My nation is that of Abraham, the Friend of God.'[8] A Western correspondent visiting Baku in the late 1970s was told, when he stopped Azerbaijanis on the street and asked them if they were Muslims, 'Yes, but of course I am not a believer.' At the same time, they complained of a lack of Qur'ans, mosques and mullas, and of other restrictions on religious life.[9]

Apparently, it was not only the members of these ethnic groups who identified themselves as Muslims. They seem to have been so identified by others as well, without any implications regarding their level of religiosity. Even the regime and its representatives appear to have been confused by the somewhat loose usage of the term Muslim, referring recurrently, for instance, to the country's 'Muslim' population.[10] In other words, the term Muslim was not reserved for believers or people who performed any of the rites of Islam.[11] Despite the official separation between national affiliation

5. The issue of Pan-Islam has been touched upon on pp.570-1.

6. Such as not eating pork; and see pp.463-4.

7. S. Dorzhenov, 'Musul'manin li ia?', *Nauka i religiia*, 4, 1967, p.50.

8. Soper, 'Unofficial Islam: A Muslim minority in the USSR', p.227. The quote is from *Kommunizm tughi*, 13 Jan. 1979, which appeared in Alma-Ata.

9. *Newsweek*, 2 April 1979.

10. See p.57.

11. See also Abdullaev, 'Kritika kontseptsii nesovmestimosti sotsialisticheskogo obraza zhizni s prirodoi vostochnogo cheloveka', p.113. Abdullaev spoke of

and religion, the reports of CARC's *upolnomochennye* in the Muslim areas, too, contained statements such as: 'on the whole, the nationalities inhabiting the Kirgiz republic profess Islam', or 'a significant part of the republic's Kyrgyz, Uzbeks and Tatars are believers, even if they do not participate in any regular collective performance of religious rites'.[12]

The propaganda activity of the four spiritual directorates, in the early period after their establishment, directed, as it was, at defending regime policy,[13] sought also to adopt the slogans of, and vindicate, its nationalities policy. SADUM explained its desire to publish a journal by insisting that it would strengthen the patriotic feelings of Muslim believers, imbue them with love for their country as well as for their religion, acquaint them with the government's decisions relating to religion and the nationalities, and reproduce material on the history of the USSR's nationalities.[14] Such representatives of the Muslim establishment as were allowed to travel abroad to meet with co-religionists, whose ranks included émigrés from their own native parts and who were thus co-nationals as well, had to rebuff statements to the effect that the Soviet peoples must be allowed to practise their traditions.[15] In a 1947 letter to the Soviet leadership, CARC Chairman Polianskii distinguished between faiths that were loyal and those which expressed tendencies hostile to the Soviet state and Soviet society and were nationalistic.[16] Islam, in his view, belonged to the former category and so *ipso facto* entailed no nationalist connotations or innunedoes.[17] But many of the writers and other members of the artistic intelligentsia who identified with their national cultures and traditions tended to accept the importance of the rural hinterland which they represented

---

'eastern man' being a 'Muslim in general, *irrespective* of his national appurtenance, whether he be a Muslim Arab, Muslim Turk, Muslim highlander (*gorets*) of the Northern Caucasus, and so on'.

12. H. Akhtiamov to I. V. Polianskii, 15 Dec. 1945; GARF, f.6991, o.3, d.30, l.249. For the problems involved in defining believers, see pp.452-3.

13. See pp.112-4.

14. I. Ibadov to the Uzbek SSR Sovnarkom, 11 Sept. 1944; GARF, f.6991, o.3, d.6, l.16.

15. I. Ibadov to I. V. Polianskii, following conversations with returnig *hajjis* (the six people who had participated in the *hajj* in 1944 – see pp.171-2), 17 March 1945; GARF, f.6991, o.3, d.20, ll.84-5.

16. See pp.32-3 and 560.

17. See pp.552-3.

and to insist implicitly or explicitly on the place of Islamic customs and values. This was perhaps a corollary of the partnership resurrected during World War II between Russian nationalism and the Russian Orthodox Church which became its instrument and, in contrast to the stand adopted by Polianskii, portrayed Islam as its enemy.[18]

The regime and the 'Muslim' national intelligentsias thus perceived Islam very differently. The former still hoped to overcome it by a combination of suppression, mobilisation and assimilation. The latter, although they had for the most part become alienated from Islam as a faith, could not afford to reject it in its entirety lest they lose their own social base; perhaps, too, they genuinely perceived it as a necessary component of the national culture. The antithetical position of these mutually exclusive perceptions stressed the incompatibility between 'socialist construction' and Islam's survival and highlighted the non-viability of hopes for their peaceful co-existence. The role played by Islam in the evolution of nationalism within the Soviet Union's Muslim ethnicities, like that of other 'national' religions in the development of Russian, Ukrainian and Lithuanian nationalism, was a significant factor in the nationalist earthquake that eventually helped bring down the Soviet regime.[19] At the same time, it should be noted that none of the Muslim republics, except the Chechen – Ingush ASSR, had a particularly strident nationalism, of the type which concerned Moscow regarding, for example, Ukraine or Georgia. Manifestations of nationalism took similar, if not identical, forms in these areas as elsewhere: opposition to official Soviet historiography, especially as regards the 'joining' of their territories to the Russian Empire; a desire to rehabilitate 'repressed' writers and other artists; complaints concerning economic discrimination and subordination to the needs of the centre. But, for the most part, such protests

18. See, for example, Foreign Office Research Department, 'Islam and Communism', April 1948; PRO, FO371/71707A, p.16.

19. I have addressed some of these issues in 'The Islamic Influence on Nationalism in Soviet Central Asia', and 'Nationalism in Central Asia in the Context of *Glasnost* and *Perestroika*', pp.59–62. The discussion of Islam's role in the nationalist movements and organisations which formed in the Gorbachev period is beyond the scope of this study. For the role of religion in the evolution of Russian, Ukrainian and Lithuanian nationalism, see Dunlop, *The Faces of Contemporary Russian Nationalism*, *passim*; Markus, 'Religion and Nationalism in Ukraine', and Vardys, *The Catholic Church, Dissent and Nationality in Soviet Lithuania*, *passim*.

surfaced somewhat later than in other national republics and were not accompanied by political action.[20]

Islam as part of the national heritage

No less a person than Russia's prime minister, Petr Stolypin, noted just a few years prior to World War I that among the Volga Tatars, for example, a national revival was occurring that had a religious tinge. It was expressed in the buildings of mosques even in the smallest villages.[21] An authoritative Soviet islamicist wrote three quarters of a century later that Islam had for centuries been conducive to the formation of national communities from the tribes and clans of Central Asia. An important ingredient of ethnic self-awareness, it had served as an integrating factor, constituting an ethnic psychology and primordial values. Islam's dominance was reflected in the insertion of Islamic allusions in the Muslim areas' epics, which seminally predated Islam, such as the Kyrgyz *Manas*.[22] In the late Stalin period, in fact, the Turkmen national epic *Korkut-Ata* was denounced as 'a poem of religious fanaticism and of brutish hatred of non-Muslims', and the Uzbek *Alpamish* for being 'impregnated with the poison of feudalism and reaction, breathing Muslim fanaticism and preaching hatred towards foreigners'.[23] Interestingly, the period of liberalisation following Stalin's death saw a reversal of this trend: a conference of Uzbek intelligentsia in October 1956, their first gathering after World War II, for example, heard First Party Secretary Muhitdinov rehabilitate his nation's epic.[24]

The identification of religious and national affiliation among the peoples which had in the past professed Islam continued, indeed, to create a sense of community within the ranks of these

20. Willerton, *Patronage and politics in the USSR*, p.192; Ro'i, 'Nationalism in Central Asia in the context of *Glasnost* and *Perestroika*', *passim*.

21. Geraci, 'Russian Orientalism at an Impasse', p.142.

22. Saidbaev, *Islam i obshchestvo*, pp.96-7. In addition to the 'Manas', Saidbaev mentioned the Bashkir 'Zayatulak and Khiyakhulu' as also having incorporated Islamic references; I have not been able to find this epic and so cannot check the veracity of this assertion. For some of the implications of Islamic allusions in the 'Manas', see p.700 below.

23. Bennigsen, 'The Crisis of the Turkish National Epics, 1951-1952', pp.466-8.

24. Allworth, *The Modern Uzbeks*, p.253.

various ethnic groups. In so doing, it helped distinguish, even isolate, them from other non-Muslim ethnicities.[25] Furthermore, as peoples' interest in the past and its traditions grew — a characteristic of the enhanced national consciousness that was the lot of most if not all of the Soviet Union's ethnic groups as of the 1960s — all the components of the national patrimony came to be increasingly appreciated and valued. Certainly, Islam was one such component; if deprived of their Islamic heritage, the people concerned would have no past.[26] In this way, anyone who posed as the champion of Islam was presenting himself, among other things, as the guardian of an integral part of the patrimony of the Muslim nationalities, and, inevitably, those who denigrated or attacked it, became the adversaries of this heritage.

In the words of CRA Chairman Kuroedov in a report to the CPSU Central Committee, 'the Muslim clergy and religious organisations frequently appeal to peoples' national feelings and try to present religion as the "custodian" of the nation's national specificity and the mouthpiece of national interests, and portray many religious rites as national or popular'. They explained that by observing these rites, people demonstrated their national affiliation. Enjoying a marked resonance among a significant section of the believer population and even among non-believers, who regarded certain religious rites as national ones and considered their observance obligatory to members of their nation, these 'endeavours' were conducive to the retention of both 'religious and nationalist vestiges'. True, the registered clergy contended in their sermons that Islam had always preached 'the friendship of peoples', and called upon believers to co-exist and cooperate with adherents of other faiths and members of other nationalities, yet believers who were 'under the influence' of unregistered clergy perceived 'intercourse with adherents of other creeds as a deviation from the faith'.[27]

Increasingly, however, it was not only the clergy and believers who held the position that religion and nationality were analogous.

25. Saidbaev, *Islam i obshchestvo*, pp.216 and 229.
26. *Ibid.*, p.229.
27. CRA report, sent to the CPSU Central Committee, 22 May 1970; TsKhSD, f.5, o.62, d.38, ll.29-33. For the opposition of the more radical clergy to any formal link with regime institutions and with Russians and other Europeans, see pp.345-7 and 414.

Considerable sectors of the indigenous intelligentsias in the Muslim regions also shared it, although some dwelt on Islam being a relative latecomer and primarily alien to Turkic culture. The perception prevalent in society of identifying 'religious and national affiliation', according to one expert, enabled Islam to unite within a single nation both believers and non-believers, as well as creating 'a sense of community between the representatives of the nations which had professed Islam in the past'. Although the likelihood of such identification developing into yet another dissident political force caused some concern among the Soviet establishment as having 'nothing in common with the genuine community between the peoples of the Soviet Union',[28] it did not in effect materialise – probably a tribute to the strength of national sentiment, including considerable antagonism and even disputes between some of the Muslim ethnic groups.[29] Be this as it may, within the ethnos the difference between the perceptions of the religious *aktiv* and non-believers was not large, both emphasising the role of an Islam that was basically secular. Both, too, sought the preservation of national cultural monuments, which mostly consisted of mosques and Islamic shrines.[30]

The Soviet regime, however, persisted in its formal position that there could be no overlap between Islam and the national culture of its component Muslim ethnic groups. Yet, its officials

28. Saidbaev, *Islam i obshchestvo*, p.216. For Soviet discussion of the threat of Pan-Islam, see pp.570-1.

29. Some of these disputes were historical, such as conflict over land or water; others, such as that between the Tajiks and Uzbeks, were the result rather of developments in the Soviet period and have been attributed in part, at least, to Moscow's manipulations. For problems between Uzbeks and Tajiks, see the writings of a Tajik ethnographer based in St. Petersburg, Rahmat Rahimov, for example, 'O iazikovoi situatsii v Uzbekistane'.

30. Saidbaev, *Islam i obshchestvo*, p.229. Similar trends among other nationalities, especially among the Russians themselves and the Ukrainians, had led to the creation as of the second half of the 1960s of Societies for the Preservation of Historical and Cultural Monuments. For the prototype of these associations, VOOPIK – the All-Russian Society for the Preservation of Historical and Cultural Monuments – its background, context and activity, see Dunlop, *The Faces of Contemporary Russian Nationalism*, pp.64-87. For attempts by the Muslim establishment to take over some of the more popular Muslim shrines from the republican or local authorities charged with their preservation as historical and cultural monuments in the mid-1940s and mid-1950s and their return to the jurisdiction of the secular authorities during Khrushchev's anti-religious campaign, see pp.123-5 and 228-9.

accepted that different peoples related variously to Islam and that some were more 'fanatical' and more traditionally religious than others. The fact that this was not the sole *non sequitur* or ambiguity in official attitudes made it no less problematic or pertinent. Both in Dagestan and Kirgiziia, for instance, CARC's *upolnomochennye* recurrently reported that certain nationalities boasted a higher level of religiosity than others, implying, even when they did not say so outright, that Islam filled a major role in the national existence at least of the former. Thus, Dagestan's Avars were described as the most zealous of its many ethnicities;[31] in Kirgiziia the Uzbeks and Dungans were said to be more ardent in the observance of Islam's precepts than the Kyrgyz, who, while considering themselves Muslims, did not strictly observe Islamic rites.[32] And in both Kirgiziia and Kazakhstan in the decade or so after World War II, it was generally agreed, the Caucasian deportees, especially the Chechen and Ingush, were the most religious of all.[33] In Kazakhstan, as in Kirgiziia, areas with a dense Uzbek population, notably in the south around Chimkent and Jambul, Islam was more widely practised than in parts where the Muslim population was composed chiefly of Kazakhs and Tatars or where Kazakhs lived among Russians and Ukrainians, as they did, for example, in Kokchetau Oblast' in Northern Kazakhstan. In this way, the intensity of Islamic practice depended both on national affiliation and on conditions of national co-habitation or isolation.[34]

Nor were differences in observance necessarily a question of varying levels of religiosity. There were also disparities in the customs observed by different national communities. The Dungans, for example, did not recognise the calendar as predetermined by astronomic calculations and so reckoned the beginning of the month from the day they actually perceived the new moon. This often led to discrepancies in the timing of the fast and festivals, making it well-nigh impossible for them to use the same mosque as did other communities. It is not clear from the documentation whether this was the real or main reason for the request of Tatar

31. For example, I. Zakaryaev, Report, 10 June 1946; GARF, f.6991, o.3, d.38, ll.62-62ob. See also p.450.

32. See pp.460 and 512.

33. Minutes, Conference of CARC *upolnomochennye*, Alma-Ata, 30 Sept. to 2 Oct. 1946 – GARF, f.6991, o.3, d.41, l.61; and see p.408.

34. Compare pp.460 and 462-3.

believers in the Kirgiz town of Przheval'sk – where the sole registered mosque was that of the Dungans – to be allowed to maintain
a separate mosque. Officially, they attributed their motive to the
distance of the registered mosque from the Tatar quarter. But in
a number of towns, where in the past each national community
had had its own mosque, problems arose in the postwar years
around the issue of recognising the right of disparate ethnic groups
to have separate prayer premises.[35] Among the Pamiris, or Mountain
Tajiks, of the Gorno-Badakhshan Autonomous Oblast', those who
were Ismailis not only differed in their customs and traditions
from adherents of Sunni Islam; in raiony where Ismailis and Sunnis
co-habited, according to the CRA *upolnomochennyi*, there was
no intermarriage between the two communities, religion thus contributing to 'national alienation'.[36] (In fact, these small mountain
communities had been culturally autonomous for generations, even
speaking mutually incomprehensible dialects.)

Not surprisingly, the authorities were not prepared to recognise
or legitimise differentiations in religious practice based on nationality. CARC, which was interested in registering a significant
number of mosques for reasons that have been discussed, was
adamant that the believers' nationality should not constitute a
criterion for determining the establishment of a religious community, for this would be tantamount to encouraging a revival
of nationalism. The nationalities in question in the various Central
Asian republics had one religion and had to attend a single mosque.
Certainly, religion must not serve as a pretext for ethnic tension.[37]
Paradoxically perhaps, CARC nonetheless sought constant information regarding the nationality of believers who belonged to
minority religious groups within Islam, such as Shiites in Central
Asia,[38] or of people who sought to study in the Muslim seminary

35. Minutes, Conference of CARC *upolnomochennye*, Alma-Ata, 30 Sept. to 2
Oct. 1946; GARF, f.6991, o.3, d.41, ll.44, 53, 56, 101-3 and 105-6.

36. U. Yuldashev, Information, 10 July 1968; GARF, f.6991, o.6, d.153, ll.93-4.

37. Minutes, Conference of CARC *upolnomochennye*, Alma-Ata, 2 Oct. 1946;
GARF, f.6991, o.3, d.41, l.56. On one occasion CARC's republican *upolnomochennyi* in Kirgiziia admitted he was prepared to agree to the Dungans in the town
of Tokmak operating a separate mosque since they spoke Chinese – Minutes,
CARC session No.9, 3 June 1947; GARF, f.6991, o.4, d.19, l.251.

38. I. V. Polianskii to I. Ibadov, 8 April 1946; TsGAUz, f.2456, o.1, d.90,
l.15ob. Polianskii asked whether they were 'Ironis', i.e. of Persian descent, or
Azerbaijanis from the Caucasus or Northern Iran.

in Bukhara.[39] Similarly, its officials in the field noted that wor-shippers who came to pray in the precincts of the mosque destroyed by the 1948 earthquake in Ashkhabad, which the republican autho-rities refused to re-open, were non-Turkmen, but rather members of the republic's ethnic minorities (Uzbeks, Tatars, Kazakhs and Lezgin).[40]

CARC was also prepared to admit in internal correspondence that the different trends in Islam had been brought about by 'historical and socio-political' causes and had assumed over time features of 'national-tribal' religions, and that this was one of the reasons for antagonisms which still prevailed between certain ethnic groups, for instance between Uzbeks and Tatars, or between Kazakhs and Uighurs.[41] In Andijan the Uighurs and Uzbeks were at loggerheads for many years, the former not letting the latter into their mosque lay administration.[42] CARC officials attributed the existence of four distinct Muslim spiritual directorates to the historical circumstances and national specifics of the country's Mus-lim population.[43] This may have been a euphemistic allusion to the traditional mutual exclusivity, if not actual mistrust, of the country's various Muslim populations, which had not, however, been strictly speaking national, but related rather to the main areas of Muslim habitat: Central Asia, the Caucasus and the Middle Volga.[44]

There does not seem to have been unanimity among CARC's

39. I. V. Polianskii to Kh. N. Iskanderov, 1 Nov. 1946; TsGAUz, f.2456, o.1, d.92, l.88. Throughout the period reports on the composition of the seminary's student body never failed to mention their national affiliation; see, for instance, Chapter 3, n.229.

40. A. M. Komekov, Memorandum, Prepared for conference of CARC *upol-nomochennye*, 17 Dec. 1949; GARF, f.6991, o.3, d.67, ll.144-5.

41. I. V. Polianskii, Memorandum, 11 Nov. 1946; GARF, f.6991, o.3, d.34, l.202.

42. See p.285.

43. See p.100.

44. Even attempts by certain parties within the tsarist empire's Muslim community to take advantage of the winds of change blowing in 1905 and subsequently in order to initiate frameworks for Muslim solidarity, highlighted the differences between the various populations. Some major ethnicities were not represented at all at the Muslim congresses and conferences which took place in the years 1905-6 and again in 1917 – Zenkovsky, *Pan-Turkism and Islam in Russia*, especially Chapter 4.

personnel as to how to regard and categorise Islamic ritual. Its *upolnomochennyi* in Tashkent Oblast' in the late 1940s expressed his opinion unequivocally that the rites practised by the Muslim population in his area of jurisdiction were distinctly religious, not 'popular', ones. This applied equally to those connected with the life–cycle and to the *namaz*, the festivals or the *khatm-i Qur'an*.[45] One of the Council's *upolnomochennye* in Belorussia, on the other hand, noted in a closed meeting early in the 1950s that the Tatar population there retained both its national exclusivity and religious convictions: parents opposed their children marrying exogamously, burials were conducted solely in Tatar cemeteries, and almost ubiquitously Tatar homes were marked by the Muslim crescent moon.[46] Over two decades later a report from Kazakhstan's Gur'ev Oblast' noted that Muslim rites were widely perceived as popular traditions, and that people considered that in observing them they were showing respect for their nation and in rejecting them insulting it.[47]

In many places, throughout the period under study, the Muslim burial rite in particular was looked upon as a national custom rather than a religious rite.[48] In some instances it was adhered to solely out of national tradition.[49] In Chingiz Aitmatov's novel *The Day Lasts More than a Hundred Years* the funeral procession to the old Muslim cemetery is in effect an expedition into the Kyrgyz national identity; as are the efforts of the novel's hero to save the cemetery from destruction – it has been fenced off to serve a construction project for the space exploration authority – and to restore the traditional burial rites.[50] Indeed, according to CRA Chairman

45. Minutes, Conference of CARC's *upolnomochennye* in the Uzbek SSR, 9 Aug. 1948; TsGAUz, f.2456, o.1, d.120, l.5.

46. Minutes, Instructional meeting, CARC session No.17, 20-22 Dec. 1950; GARF, f.6991, o.3, d.66, l.112. It should be noted that the Tatars of Belorussia and Lithuania were not newcomers but had lived there for centuries – see Akiner, *Islamic Peoples of the Soviet Union*, pp.85-7.

47. S. Irgaliev to A. Nurullaev, 8 May 1974; GARF, f.6991, o.6, d.633, ll.14-15.

48. For example, in Uzbekistan – A. Barinskaia to V. A. Kuroedov, undated [late March-early April 1968] – GARF, f.6991, o.6, d.153, ll.109-10; and see pp.514-5.

49. Zh. Botashev to the Kzyl-Orda Obkom, 24 Sept. 1974; GARF, f.6991, o.6, d.633, ll.73-4.

50. It has been suggested that the story's leitmotif is rather animistic and based on pre-Islamic folklore, 'a combination of the cult of the earth, the ancestor

Kuroedov, all rituals connected with death and remembering the deceased were closely interlaced in people's consciousness with 'national exclusiveness'.[51] Certainly, it was usual in Soviet Central Asia to find cemeteries which were divided into Muslim, Christian and Jewish sections. The Muslim section was set aside for all persons belonging to nations which had in the past observed Islam, irrespective of whether the individuals concerned had been atheists or believers, and the same applied to the Christian part, sometimes popularly called the Russian or international section. The clergy or whichever religious body was responsible for the cemetery 'jealously' prevented Uzbeks from being buried in the Christian zone and Russians in the Muslim one. Thus, to cite one source, people who lived their entire lives in an 'international' family and toiled together 'for the triumph of the international ideals of communism, were separated after death into "national" cemeteries and their last journey [was] used to propagate religion and national exclusiveness'.[52]

Other Islamic ceremonies connected with rites of passage were similarly conceptualised as tributes to one's ethnic affiliation.[53] Yet, while indeed the family, a person's 'micro-milieu', contributed to consolidating the individual's perception of Islam as a moral value of national nature,[54] this overlap between the religious and the national did not apply solely to life cycle rites, but also to a number of other popular rituals and ceremonies.[55]

It was thus not surprising that the regime's renewed effort in the 1960s to impose secular rituals, including those connected with rites of passage, was particularly unsuccessful in the Muslim

---

cult, the mother cult and totemism' – Jeziorska, 'Religious Themes in the Novels of Chingiz Aitmatov', pp.51-7. While these themes are clearly present, they do not seem to me to detract from the contention that Aitmatov perceives Islam as one of the main elements in the national patrimony.

51. CRA report, delivered to the CPSU Central Committee Propaganda Department, 27 April 1971; TsKhSD, f.5, o.63, d.89, l.120.

52. CRA report, sent to the CPSU Central Committee, 22 May 1970; TsKhSD, f.5, o.62, d.38, l.32.

53. Saidbaev, *Islam i obshchestvo*, p.256; also the Kabardino-Balkar ASSR Council of Ministers Organisational and Instructional Department, Information, 2 Oct. 1974 – GARF, f.6991, o.6, d.634, l.73; and see pp.525 and 709.

54. Saidbaev, *Islam i obshchestvo*, p.225.

55. Theses of lecture, sent by A. Barmenkov to the CPSU Central Committee Propaganda Department, 19 June 1968; GARF, f.6991, o.6, d.147, l.41.

areas. According to one expert on Islam inside the Soviet Union, this was because these rites were formulated without any consideration for the population's national traits, which had been acquired over the centuries and because they were in essence European. Indeed, they achieved the opposite result, leading to an enhanced interest in the old traditions.[56] CRA, in its reports to the Central Committee, contended that the Muslim clergy refrained from openly denigrating the new secular ceremonies, yet inculcated the sense that side by side with these '"European" rites, it is necessary to remember our national rituals, bequeathed to us by our forefathers'.[57]

In the words of one author, it was generally difficult to draw the line between national and religious elements when it came to the life-cycle rites, which had been passed down from one generation to the next and took on an 'ethno-confessional form'. In his view, those who practised these rites regarded them as national-traditional, popular and primordial rather than Islamic, both believers and non-believers considering them, as well as the Muslim festivals and the Sunna itself, to be essentially national.[58] In many regions – in Tatar areas in Orenburg Oblast' or in Tatar villages of Penza Oblast', for instance, as well as in Leningrad, Omsk and Astrakhan' – a considerable portion of the student youth, who were totally estranged from religion, attended prayers on Muslim festivals to denote 'a Tatar festival'. In this way, religious festivals brought together people of a specific nationality, who participated in them out of a sense of national community.[59]

It was this understanding that made the authorities appreciate that atheistic propaganda, in order to be effective, had best be conducted by members of local Muslim ethnic groups. A decrease in wearing the *paranja* in Osh Oblast' with its large Uzbek population was attributed specifically to educational work by Uzbeks.[60] Over the years, however, as people's national awareness grew, this became increasingly problematic. Members of Muslim indigenous nationalities were repeatedly reported to be shying away from conducting

56. Saidbaev, *Islam i obshchestvo*, pp.229 and 274-5.

57. CRA report, sent to the CPSU Central Committee, 22 May 1970; TsKhSD, f.5, o.62, d.38, l.33. Compare also p.600.

58. Vagabov, *Islam i voprosy ateisticheskogo vospitaniia*, p.106.

59. Ashirov, *Islam i natsii*, pp.62-71.

60. I. Halimov to H. Akhtiamov, 1[6] May 1951; GARF, f.6991, o.3, d.454, l.112.

atheistic lectures among their co-nationals out of sheer fear of what might befall them at the hands of their audience, who regarded them as traitors.[61]

DUMES Mufti Khiyaletdinov, who came to Ufa in the early 1950s from Central Asia, maintained that if SADUM appointed an Uzbek as qadi in Kirgiziia or a Kazakh in Tajikistan, or the reverse, normal relations between it and the clergy and believer community in the republic in question would be untenable.[62] Often, in fact, the clergy were perceived as guardians of the national interest and of the integrity of the national culture. Sometimes they were looked upon as people who set the moral tone for the nation.[63] In some places not only each ethnic group but even each clan or tribe had its own religious leadership.[64] A report from Kazakhstan noted that the clans actually had their own mullas to perform the burial rite in accordance with clan tradition.[65]

By the mid-1950s it was clear to CARC that in dealing with Islam in Central Asia, at least, it was necessary to bear in mind the history, the geography and the national characteristics of each republic.[66] The rather different historical conditions of the various nationalities seemed to explain the specific features of Islam which pertained to each of them. One Kyrgyz scholar clarified that among his co-nationals knowledge of Islamic dogma was particularly poor, for until recently there had been no Kyrgyz clergy with a religious education. Prior to 1917 the Kyrgyz had had no written language and the clergy had been drawn from among the Uzbeks, Tatars or Uighurs; later Kyrgyz clergy were taken from among graduates of the elementary Islamic schools, *mektebs*, set up in the first years of Soviet rule, where the Arabic script had still been used. According to this same source, although Islam did not exist in its classic form among the Kyrgyz, it constituted for many believers and not a few non-believers as well, a system of moral, spiritual and

---

61. See, for example, p.569.

62. Reception by L. A. Prikhod'ko of Sh. Khiyaletdinov, 23 Feb. 1955; GARF, f.6991, o.4, d.137, ll.28-9.

63. Saidbaev, *Islam i obshchestvo*, p.246.

64. *Ibid.*, p.224. And see pp.330 and 340-1.

65. Zh. Botashev to V. A. Kuroedov, 17 Nov. 1969; GARF, f.6991, o.6, d.220, l.147.

66. Minutes, Operational meeting of CARC's central apparatus, 2 Aug. 1955; GARF, f.6991, o.3, d.112, l.1.

Islam and Nationalism

cultural values, a sort of popular psychology and traditional form of national self-awareness. Even people who were estranged from religion identified their affiliation to the indigenous nationality with the notion of being Muslim or linked it with the performance of circumcision.[67]

Nor was it only rites and customs which people associated with their national patrimony. This was true of the mosque itself, which was frequently regarded as a national attribute, and had therefore to be revered and insofar as possible supported. This was one of the reasons the mosque was looked upon favourably not just by its own parishioners. It was not solely a place for the performance of religious ceremonies but also, as it had traditionally been, for social intercourse.[68]

In order to undermine the possible identification of national and religious customs some of the more senior and perhaps also farsighted party chiefs in the Muslim areas suggested reinstating local popular festivals, which were fundamentally non-Islamic – even though some of them had during the course of the centuries acquired a partly religious connotation. The most important of these was probably the Nawruz, the traditional New Year, which Uzbek CP First Secretary Usman Yusupov and Chairman of the Uzbek SSR Council of Ministers Abdujabr Abdurahmanov recommended re-instating in 1949 together with the Kaun-sail, celebrated traditionally on the eve of the melon harvest. Despite the approval of the AUCP(b) Central Committee's Agriculture Department, however, the suggestion was overruled by the ideologists in Moscow on the grounds that, although these festivals lacked any religious foundation, the clergy had sought to endow them with religious nuances and they were sometimes marked by the visitation of local shrines. (The two leading Agitprop officials, including its chief, Dmitrii Shepilov, who rejected the proposal likewise refused the idea, also put forward by Yusupov and Abdurahmanov, of replacing the 'proletarian festivals' of the 1st of May and the 7th of November on the grounds that they fell at the peak of the most urgent seasonal agricultural work.)[69] Nonetheless, in the course

67. Doev, *Osobennosti islama v Kirgizii*, pp.4 and 6.

68. Saidbaev, *Islam i obshchestvo*, p.238; and see pp.429 and 462.

69. A. Abdurahmanov and U. Yusupov to I. V. Stalin, 6 Feb. 1949; A. Kozlov, head of the AUCP(b) Central Committee Agriculture Department, to G. M. Malenkov, 22 March 1949; and D. T. Shepilov and L. Slepov to Malenkov, 7

of time, the Nawruz made its way back into the calendar of the Central Asian republics as the Holiday of Spring and gradually received legitimisation as a popular festival. In 1964 the Tajikistan CP Central Committee Presidium resolved to reinstate it, decreeing, however, that it be celebrated on a Sunday at the end of March rather than on the day of the equinox; it also re-introduced the traditional harvest festival.[70] Three years later the Baku Gorkom also decided to reinstate the Nawruz in honour of the USSR's jubilee celebrations.[71]

The clergy, for their part, were said to be using national symbols to lure people to religious activity. In Jambul they organised the playing of Kazakh musical instruments in the streets on the eve of Uraz-Bayram, and again on the morning of the festival – this time from the mosque minaret.[72] Some clergy were said to try to appear as exponents of the national interests of the peoples of the 'Soviet East, artificially evoking such vestiges of the past as a disparaging attitude towards women and manifestations of a nationalist mood'.[73] According to reports from Central Asia, SADUM posed as the custodian of the unique national traits and culture of the region's peoples.[74] Nor was this identification of clerical activity with national custom reserved for the official clergy. The Uighur newspaper which appeared in Alma-Ata, referring to the mullas of that city's Uighur community, who were all unregistered, noted in the late 1970s that 'ten or fifteen years ago we conducted the ceremonies of our national customs and traditions without

---

April 1949 –RTsKhIDNI, f.17, o.132, d.114, ll.1-2, 5-6 and 6a-9.

70. Tajikistan CP Central Committee Presidium resolution, 20 March 1964 –GARF, f.6991, o.3, d.1740, l.44. For the discussion regarding the Nawruz, see also *Sostoianie religioznosti*, pp.33-4; Sadomskaya, 'New Soviet Rituals and Integration in the USSR', pp.103-6, who points out, among other things, that the festival was celebrated in different ways and on different dates in the various parts of Tajikistan and Uzbekistan where it was re-instated; and see p.602.

71. Lane, *The Rites of Rulers*, pp.136-7.

72. I. V. Polianskii to the CPSU Central Committee and the USSR Council of Ministers, 20 Sept. 1955 –GARF, f.6991, o.3, d.114, l.201; and see p.253.

73. A. Barmenkov, A. Nurullaev and E. Tarasov to the CPSU Central Committee Propaganda Department, 14 Aug. 1968; GARF, f.6991, o.6, d.147, l.124.

74. Iu. Bilialov, 'The influence of religion', sent by K. Ruzmetov to V. A. Kuroedov, 18 June 1973; GARF, f.6991, o.6, d.545, l.173.

mullas and qadis', clearly indicating that this was no longer the case.[75]

Islam as a source and inspiration of nationalist revival

The compromise that the Soviet regime made with religion in the course of World War II was accompanied by certain concessions in the field of its nationalities' policy as well: histories of the national republics depicted the Russian conquest of these territories as tsarist colonialism, national military units were re-introduced, and the union republics were formally allowed to take up direct relations with foreign states. In the last year or so of the war, however, as the tide of fortune changed and the need for a total mobilisation of forces for the war effort diminished, official ideology and policy reverted to identifying Soviet with Russian patriotism and other values. In the postwar period with the advent of Zhdanovism, the Soviet regime perceived nationalist tendencies, indeed, anything smacking of nationalism, among the non-Russian nationalities as a repudiation of Soviet patriotism and loyalty to the state. Nonetheless, the damage – from Moscow's point of view – had been done, and in many of the national areas there was a certain nationalist revival, which it took the repression of Stalin's last years to assuage. This first recrudescence led, among others, to the lionisation of old heroes and the reproduction of national epics.[76]

Some of the manifestations of nationalism in the postwar years in the Muslim regions took on a partly religious colouring. The attack on the Kyrgyz *Manas*, which included denunciations of its Muslim features, aroused a serious counter-attack in the Kyrgyz-language party press, according to which its 'Islamic character is no more shocking than the Christian character of the Russian *bylinas* [traditional heroic poems], the *Tale of Igor's Host*, or the Georgian *Hero in a Leopard's Skin*, all of which have remained

75. Soper, 'Unofficial Islam: A Muslim Minority in the Soviet Union', p.230.
76. As late as 1950 the official Soviet encyclopedia heralded the Caucasian Turks' national epic, the *Dede-Korkut*, as 'one of the most remarkable monuments of Azerbaijani culture, glorifying loyalty, heroism, gallantry and love of the Fatherland', and the Azerbaijan SSR Academy of Sciences published a Russian translation of long excerpts from it – Bennigsen, 'The Crisis of the Turkic National Epics, 1951-1952', p.465.

part of the accepted canon'.[77] One CARC department head had no doubt that the increasing activity of religious personnel in Uzbekistan in the early 1950s was linked with manifestations of nationalism in that republic.[78] More serious, perhaps, nationalist sentiment led to second thoughts about intermarriage which had been encouraged in earlier stages and which some, especially male urban intelligentsia, had embraced. Now, these men were reported to be turning against their Russian wives, in some cases – in Kazakhstan, for instance – even killing them.[79] This negative attitude to intermarriage among the Muslim population was retained throughout the period under study. A sociological investigation among the Tatars of Gor'kii and Penza Oblast' in the late 1960s revealed that the combination of religious and national affiliation led them to comprehend Muslim social rites as popular and national ones and that religious views continued to influence their inter-ethnic, personal, family and marital relationships.[80]

CARC personnel seem to have been convinced that in part this stimulation of Muslim nationalism was a reaction to negative attitudes among the Russian population and particularly in the ranks of Russian officials who restricted Muslim religious activity without justification. In Gor'kii, for instance, one of the cities where the local organs of government refused to register a single Muslim religious association, officials defended their position by maintaining that this was a Russian city and so there could be no place for a mosque.[81] Indeed, in Leningrad, CARC noted in a memorandum to the CPSU Central Committee, each year new forces were attracted to the Tatar struggle to register the city

77. *Kyzyl Kyrgyzstan*, 19 March 1952, quoted in Bennigsen, *ibid.*, p.469.

78. Minutes, CARC session No.10s, 11-12 April 1952; GARF, f.6991, o.3, d.83, l.164.

79. Goncharok to G. M. Malenkov, 8 Sept. 1949; RTsKhIDNI, f.17, o.132, d.258, ll.78-9.

80. Orlov, 'Opyt issledovaniia protsessa sekuliarizatsii v tatarskikh selakh', p.100. For the negative attitude to exogamy among the Tatars of the Belorussian SSR, see p.694 above.

81. G. F. Frolov, Memorandum, discussed at CARC session No.4s, 6 March 1952; GARF, f.6991, o.3, d.83, l.39. For the attitude of the local organs of government in Gor'kii and also in Bugul'ma in the Tatar ASSR, see pp.652-3 and 654-6.

mosque in which the Tatars' national, and not only religious, feelings were turned to account.[82]

In one *poselok* in Ul'ianovsk Oblast' the entire Tatar population, except for party and Komsomol members, was drawn into the struggle of the believer community to recover its mosque. Prior to 1949, when the mosque had been destroyed by a storm, the younger generation had taken no part in religious activity. By the mid 1950s they had become the most ardent advocates of their fathers' rights. A delegation of intelligentsia and young people asked CARC officials why their fathers were not being allowed to pray, pointing out that this was an insult to the entire Tatar population. According to CARC personnel, the local Muslim religious society had in fact become strengthened organisationally, its *aktiv* 'skilfully making use' of the administrative measures employed by local officialdom to consolidate all the local inhabitants of Tatar origin around it. The mulla of the believer community in the city of Ul'ianovsk, seeking to 'stir up national antagonisms on religious grounds', suggested giving the Tatars one of the city's three functioning Russian Orthodox churches, in the event that the *oblispolkom* persisted in refusing to return the mosque situated on the precincts of the Muslim cemetery. If that were impossible, because the local organs of government did not want to offend the Russians, the religious society should be given a crèche in the district inhabited by the Tatars.[83]

Frequently, in areas where the indigenous population belonged to a Muslim nationality there might be one or more Russian Orthodox churches and no mosque, a situation which inevitably aroused anti-Russian feeling and a sense among the eponymous nationality that they were being intentionally discriminated against. In Samarkand Oblast', for example, in the mid-1950s there were seven Russian Orthodox churches as against just one mosque and one *mazar*.[84] In Ashkhabad, as of 1948, there was no registered mosque – the only republic with a titular Muslim nationality whose capital had not a single mosque – yet it boasted a Russian Orthodox church. A similar situation prevailed in the Uzbek towns of Termez

82. I. V. Polianskii to D. M. Kukin, 4 June 1955; GARF, f.6991, o.3, d.114, l.52.
83. P. A. Solov'ev to V. I. Gostev, 24 May 1956; GARF, f.6991, o.3, d.217, ll.76–82.
84. V. I. Gostev to P. A. Tarasov, 4 Jan. 1954; GARF, f.6991, o.3, d.102, l.5.

and Denau.[85] A mosque was shut down in one *poselok* in Tashkent Oblast' in 1960, although the Russian Orthodox church there continued functioning without hindrance, leading Muslims to complain that the latter faith enjoyed a privileged position as compared with Uzbek believers.[86] In Karaganda in northern Kazakhstan there were three Russian Orthodox churches, and when suggestions were put forward to close the city's sole mosque in the early 1960s, the reaction of the Muslim inhabitants was very 'unhealthy'.[87] In the second half of 1961 Puzin prepared a letter for Tajikistan CP Central Committee First Secretary Jabbar Rasulov in which he addressed himself to instances where mosques had been closed, although Russian Orthodox churches continued operating, leading to 'serious dissatisfaction' among the Muslim believer community, and asking him to warn local organs of government against 'such errors'.[88] In one case, in the town of Davlekanovo in the Bashkir ASSR said to have an equal number of Orthodox and Muslim believers, a Tatar official first closed the Russian Orthodox church, exposing himself to accusations of nationalism, following which he proposed shutting down the mosque as well.[89]

Instances of discrimination against the indigenous population and its religion in Central Asia did not end with the conclusion of Khrushchev's anti-religious campaign, although their incidence seems to have diminished. In the town of Arys' in Southern Kazakhstan, where the Muslim believer community had by the end of the 1960s been trying for an entire decade to obtain permission to register, people were speaking openly of the unequal status of Kazakhs and Uzbeks *vis-à-vis* Russians and the existence

85. I. V. Polianskii to P. V. Kovanov, 23 June 1955; GARF, f.6991, o.3, d.114, ll.22 and 43.

86. See pp.521 and 661. For another instance – in the Karachai-Cherkess AO – where a mosque was closed down and a Russian Orthodox church remained intact, and the complaints on this score of the Muslim believers, see pp.212-3.

87. Minutes, CARC session No.9, 21 Feb. 1961; GARF, f.6991, o.3, d.1361, l.44.

88. A. A. Puzin to J. Rasulov, undated [probably August 1961]; GARF, f.6991, o.3, d.1737, l.103. For some reason, the letter was not sent. For discriminatory practices by the local bureaucracy in Tajikistan at this time, see pp.662-3.

89. N. I. Smirnov, Information, prepared for CARC session No.11, 26 April 1962; GARF, f.6991, o.3, d.1384, ll.161-4.

of discrimination against the former.[90] In the same time period the believers of Buguruslan in Orenburg Oblast' were attributing their failure to register to the fact that the local organs of government were staffed basically by Russians, who had no understanding of their needs; indeed, they pointed out in this connection, a Russian Orthodox church operated in the town without hindrance.[91]

The issue was probably most acute in the Chechen-Ingush ASSR, where in the period following the return of the deportees as of 1957, three churches operated officially and, until 1978, not a single mosque.[92] As CARC Chairman Puzin pointed out, this meant that the indigenous population was deprived of its right to perform its religious duties, whereas the Russians enjoyed this right.[93] Consequently, it was hardly surprising that the 200 or so 'religious authorities' who, in the early years after the return directed their activity to the reconstruction of mosques, that prior to the deportation had existed in every aul, were reportedly inciting national animosity and dissension in the process.[94] One *tamada* (the leader of a North Caucasian Sufi group) called upon the Chechen at prayer-meetings not to purchase homes from Russians as they would be throwing them all out in any case; those who might oppose this he recommended hounding out with threats and intimidation.[95] According to all accounts, the issue there became a national, not just a religious, one, questions being posed at public lectures and written and oral statements put out by intelligentsia and young people calling on the authorities to open mosques or to prohibit the activities of Christian religious societies. The editor of a local Komsomol paper received a letter asking why a church operated in the centre of Groznyi, whereas mosques constructed with the miserable kopecks of old people were pulled down. Was this not reminiscent of the Russian colonisation of

90. A. Barmenkov, Draft CRA resolution 'On the work of the Council's *upol-nomochennyi* in Chimkent, the Kazakh SSR, Sh. O. Ospanov', 15 Aug. 1969; GARF, f.6991, o.6, d.290, ll.82-3.

91. Reception by A. Barmenkov and A. Nurullaev of Shagmanov and Bibkov, 13 Nov. 1969; GARF, f.6991, o.6, d.221, l.73; and see p.654.

92. See pp.417 and 674-5.

93. A. A. Puzin, 'Leninist Principles regarding the Attitude to Religion, the Church and Believers', Lecture, 5 Aug. 1965; GARF, f.6991, o.3, d.1483, l.96.

94. P. A. Zadorozhnyi to A. A. Puzin, 30 Aug. 1960; GARF, f.6991, o.3, d.207, l.53; and see p.414.

95. A. Alisov to A. A. Puzin, 13 Jan. 1961; GARF, f.6991, o.3, d.1605, l.19.

the Chechen and Ingush in the previous century? On religious festivals young people proclaimed publicly the advent of national holidays, whereas national traditions were intertwined with religious rites at weddings, funerals and memorial services.[96] A CPSU Central Committee resolution in the early 1970s, 'On anti-social nationalist manifestations in Groznyi', led to enhanced party activity in the Chechen-Ingush and North Osetian ASSRs which stressed the role of the clergy and religious 'fanatics' in inciting nationalist 'extremism' and the large number of illegal mosques, where 'shaykhs and mullas conduct meetings of believers and indoctrinate them in a religious and nationalist spirit'.[97] One kolkhoznik, who insisted that there was no need to be apprehensive about the influence of the religious 'authorities' as the younger generation was becoming estranged from religion, added that there was nothing negative in religion's struggle for the preservation of old traditions and customs: 'If we repudiate old traditions, how will the Chechen nation's specificity be given expression?'[98]

Elsewhere, Muslim believers lodged complaints contrasting the assiduous care taken of the Christian/Russian cemetery and the neglect of their own. In the town of Orsk in Chkalov Oblast', Muslim believers protested to CARC's *upolnomochennyi* that whereas the Russian cemetery was well looked after, cattle grazed on theirs; he passed on their complaint to the local authorities, who agreed that a watchman he posted at the Muslim cemetery and a fence erected.[99] The CARC *upolnomochennyi* in Ajaria in the latter 1950s expressed concern over the difference in treatment of the Russian Orthodox Church, regarding which all was per-

96. CRA report, handed to the CPSU Central Committee, 22 May 1970; TsKhSD, f.5, o.62, d.38, l.15, and A. Nurullaev, Memorandum, handed to A. M. Vasil'ev, at the Central Committee Department of Party-Organisational Work, 2 Feb. 1972; GARF, f.6991, o.6, d.459, l.25. And see p.506.

97. Iu. Skliarov, deputy chief of the CPSU Central Committee Propaganda Department, and G. Lapchinskii, sector chief at the Department of Party-Organisational Work, to the CPSU Central Committee for its General Department, 4 May 1973; TsKhSD, f.5, o.66, d.139, ll.33-7. For the retention in North Osetia of a raion that had previously belonged to the Chechen-Ingush ASSR, after the return of the deportees and the resuscitation of the Chechen-Ingush ASSR, see p.413.

98. Chechen-Ingush Obkom, Information, 31 May 1973; TsKhSD, f.5, o.66, d.139, l.42.

99. Minutes, Instructional meeting of CARC *upolnomochennye* in the RSFSR, 26–28 July 1955; GARF, f.6991, o.3, d.110, l.179.

mitted, and of the other faiths, where all was forbidden.[100] Believers continued to contend throughout the period under discussion, indeed until perestroika, that failure to satisfy their religious demands was tantamount to infringing upon their national rights. They also maintained that measures taken against their religion were in effect a violation of their national sentiments and rights.[101] (It is perhaps worth noting that in Central Asia, the refusal of local officials to register the religious associations of certain Christian confessions occasionally evoked nationalist sentiment among them as well, notably in the case of Germans and Poles.[102])

Official policy as implemented in the various parts of the country and the ideological tenets on which it was based did not relate solely to specific instances of what Muslims perceived to be anti-Islamic discrimination. In the later 1950s in the wake of the 20th CPSU party congress, nationalist tendencies were coming to the fore among a number of the USSR's nationalities – led by the Russians. These were accompanied among the Tatar ASSR's indigenous artistic intelligentsia, for instance, by demands to review the accepted historiography regarding the nineteenth century jadidist reform movement. At a meeting of Tatar writers with the secretaries of the republican *obkom* in January 1958 writer Ahmat Fayzi said this 'popular scientific-enlightenment movement' had become a bogey, which people sought to link with Pan-Turkism and to present as counter-revolutionary because certain counter-revolutionary elements had joined it. In fact, he pointed out, half of those present at the meeting had graduated its *medreses.*[103]

100. Minutes, All-Union conference of CARC *upolnomochennye*, 25-27 Nov. 1958; GARF, f.6991, o.3, d.165, l.84.

101. CRA memorandum, 24 March 1971; GARF, TsKhSD, f.5, o.63, d.89, l.88.

102. V. Kuroedov to the Kazakh SSR Council of Ministers, 20 May 1969; GARF, f.6991, o.6, d.220, l.112.

103. S. Moshkin, *Sovetskaia Rossiia* correspondent in the Tatar ASSR, to the paper's chief editor P. P. Erofeev, 28 Jan. 1958; TSKhSD, f.5, r.5738, o.34, d.31, ll.7 and 11-12. Fayzi's presentation was not historically accurate: as of the 1920s the adherents of Jadidism were themselves considered counter-revolutionary on account of their views, social background and political choices. Jadidist thinkers Ismail Gasprali (Gasprinskii), Muhammad Ayaz Ishaqi and Fatih Kerim were labelled Pan-Turkists, and the regime took active measures against Mir-Said Sultan Galiev and Ahmed Zeki Velidi Togan, who later fled to Turkey. Fayzi himself had studied in a *medrese* in Ufa in 1911-15 – I am grateful for this information to Azade-Ayse Rorlich. For the Jadidist movement, see pp.133-4; for its schools, see p.354.

The sense of national consolidation which increasingly permeated Soviet society in the post-Stalin era and helped the Tatar population in a number of localities to persist, and in many cases to succeed, in its campaigns to officially re-open mosques, was evident also in Tatar religious activity in places where its mosques functioned without interruption or any particular obstruction. This seemed to hold in particular for cities where the indigenous population was not of Muslim origin and where members of Muslim nationalities were interspersed among peoples who traditionally professed other faiths. In Moscow itself no less than 75 per cent of the adult Tatar population were thought to have attended mosque on the two major festivals in the late 1960s.[104] The mosques in these cities were said to have become a sort of national club in the absence of any other national insititutions. The 100,000 or so Tatar inhabitants of Moscow city and oblast' had not a single library, club or theatre, no journal or newspaper, nothing in fact to bring them together apart from the capital's single registered mosque. This reliance on the mosque as a focus of national sentiment could only be circumvented, in the opinion of the CRA, if people's need for intercourse with their co-nationals were satisfied by cultural centres under the auspices of state or public organisations. It was maintained, too, that many of those who came to worship in Moscow on Uraz-Bayram did so out of the conviction that this was a national festival. In the Muslim areas, the annual growth of mosque attendance on festivals, particularly the presence there of significant numbers of young people, was likewise attributed to this enhanced national sentiment. It was noted time and time again that non-believers celebrated the two major festivals as a result of their understanding that these were national occasions.[105]

104. See p.223.

105. A. Barmenkov to the CPSU Central Committee, 23 May 1968; A. Nurullaev, Survey, undated [early 1969]; V. Kuroedov to the CPSU Central Committee Propaganda Department, 2 March 1970 and 22 Feb. 1971; CRA report, sent to the Central Committee, 22 May 1970; A. Barmenkov to the CPSU Central Committee Propaganda Department, 17 July 1971; and A. Nurullaev to CRA *upolnomochennye*, 2 Jan. 1973; GARF, f.6991, o.6, d.147, l.22, d.217, l.156, d. 284, l.3, d.361, l.38, and d.541, l.1, and TsKhSD, f.5, o.62, d.38, l.34, and o.63, d.89, ll.20-1. Summing up the activity of the sole registered mosque in Orenburg, one scholar stressed that it gradually became the centre of the Tatar population's national life, for which no 'preconditions' existed any longer either in the city or throughout the oblast'. Here people spoke Tatar and rites were performed without which the Tatar national and social association lost its meaning – Kosach,

In the Brezhnev years this identification by the intelligentsia and the younger generation of Islamic precepts with the traditional and popular customs of their fathers and grandfathers actually led to them 'idealising the past' and eulogising the virtues of Islamic teachings and their role in the development of the national culture.[106] Local organs of government, too, refrained from interfering in the doings of the clergy and religious *aktiv* out of an understanding that religious ritual was in fact nothing other than national custom.[107] The overlap between religious and national customs was so considerable and so organic that some officials in Azerbaijan 'in perfect conscience' saw nothing that was essentially Islamic in Muslim traditions and rituals, everything falling under the rubric of 'the national traditions of the Azerbaijanis'.[108] The Bashkir broadcasting authority received a letter from a professed atheist insisting that Islam helped preserve the national way of life, national traditions and the native tongue, all of which atheist youth tended to forget.[109] And Chairman of the Chechen-Ingush ASSR Supreme Soviet Presidium Khaksbikhar Bokov ascribed to similar views. The fact that most of the native population in his republic inhabited the countryside, in his opinion, helped preserve vestiges of religion and, consequently, obstructed 'the further internationalisation of their way of life'. Some believers, for whom Islam was associated with national self-consciousness, he pointed out in an article in the prestigious journal *Voprosy filosofii*, considered it an expression of national community, a common trait of a specific nationality, religion playing a significant role in 'regulating and standardising the conduct of members of a given ethnos'.[110]

In the post-Khrushchev period the regime's emphasis on the rapprochement and fusion of the country's nationalities evoked apprehension that the preservation and development of their na-

---

Gorod na styke dvukh kontinentov, p.107.

106. A. Barmenkov, Draft CRA resolution 'On the work of the Council's *upolnomochennyi* in Chimkent Oblast', the Kazakh SSR, Sh. O. Ospanov', Aug. 1969; GARF, f.6991, o.6, d.290, l.82.

107. See p.627.

108. I. Bonchkovskii to E. I. Lisavtsev, 1 June 1973; GARF, f.6991, o.6, d.537, l.178.

109. Ashirov, *Islam i natsii*, pp.87-8.

110. Bokov, 'Vzaimosviaz' internatsional'nogo i ateisticheskogo vospitaniia v usloviiakh razvitogo sotsializma', p.45.

tional specificity were being threatened. In this context Islam was thought to help people retain this ethnic uniqueness and the national customs and traditions.[111]

A report on Kirgiziia in the late 1960s remarked that the activity of the Muslim believer community was characterised by the inclination to modernise the content and practice of the faith and to identify national traditions with religion and national belongingness with religious affiliation.[112] It was claimed to be an indication of the clergy's flexibility that it was able to mould its 'religious propaganda' in accordance with circumstances, presenting the observance of Islamic rites and precepts as an expression of respect for national custom and tradition.[113] Thus, with the advent of Qurban-Bayram, for instance, the clergy explained to the populace in the early 1970s, that belonging to the Uzbek, Tajik, Tatar or any other formerly Muslim nationality meant affiliation to Islam as well.[114] By this time, the opinion was widespread that a person who was not circumcised was not an Uzbek, Kyrgyz, Kazakh, Tatar, or whatever.[115]

One official in the Gorno-Badakhshan AO Oblispolkom attacked Islam's 'ideologists' for inciting hostility between peoples by distinguishing between Muslims and non-Muslims. He also accused the Muslim clergy of exploiting the fact that communism had not eliminated all national customs, but retained and utilised those that were 'progressive', in order to pass off 'reactionary' practices, such as the sacrifice on Qurban-Bayram, as national tradition, although in fact these practices had nothing in common with national tradition. On the contrary, he noted, it was the clergy who were persistently intolerant of traditions that were purely national and contradicted the spirit of Islam, although they had always sought to imbue with Islamic content those customs of the Central Asian peoples which predated the Arab conquest of the region. They

111. Saidbaev, *Islam i obshchestvo*, p.228.

112. Information concerning Znanie's atheistic propaganda in Kirgiziia, undated, [first half of 1969]; GARF, f.6991, o.6, d.220, l.158.

113. V. Kuroedov to the CPSU Central Committee Propaganda Department, 23 May 1969; TsKhSD, f.5, r.9849, o.61, d.32, l.105.

114. V. Kuroedov to the CPSU Central Committee Propaganda Department, 21 April 1971; GARF, f.6991, o.6, d.284, l.6.

115. CRA report, sent to the CPSU Central Committee, 22 May 1970 – TsKhSD, f.5, o.62, d.38, l.30, and Sh. Ospanov, Information, 16 Nov. 1973 – GARF, f.6991, o.6, d.633, l.94; also *Islam v SSSR*, p.74.

had in this way presented the Nawruz as an Islamic festival, although this was historically without justification, and, consequently, communism had adopted it and it was currently widely celebrated.[116]

In an article on the solution of the nationality problem and the overcoming of religion in the USSR written in 1970, Uzbekistan Communist Party Secretary Rafik Nishanov noted that one of the components of the national question had since the early days of the Soviet regime been the struggle against 'vestiges of the past in people's consciousness, and above all the ideology of Islam'. He admitted, moreover, that this continued to be a problem, the struggle against religious ideology in Uzbekistan still being linked with overcoming nationalist as well as religious vestiges, and that the republic's party organisations considered that most of the indigenous population's traditions, customs and festivals had religious overtones.[117]

Indeed, atheistic literature in the Brezhnev period and its immediate aftermath abounded with allusions to the connection between Islam and the growing national awareness of the country's Muslim peoples and the obstacles it placed in the path of creating *homo sovieticus*. The more salient the nationalist feelings of the Soviet Muslim peoples, whether as Uzbeks, Tatars, Azerbaijanis, or as Muslims, the more perturbing became Islam's nationalist connotations and the common ground claimed by Islamic and national sentiment. 'The ideology of Islam', one article stated, 'contradicts the friendship of the peoples', bringing 'into our midst elements that are foreign to the spirit of proletarian internationalism – the hostility of Muslims toward non-Muslims'.[118] The fusion of 'religious and nationalistic prejudices', according to an Uzbek journal, was based on the affinities between nationalism and religion in their 'evaluation and distorted interpretation of the fundamental problems of the nation, its language, national culture, religious differences, and so forth'.[119]

116. Kh. M. Mirzoshoev, Lecture, Conference on 'Introduction of the new progressive traditions', 2 July 1973; GARF, f.6991, o.6, d.545, ll.132-4. For Nawruz and its celebration, see pp.698-9 above.

117. Nishanov, 'Razreshenie natsional'nogo voprosa v SSSR i preodolenie religii v svete leninskogo ucheniia', pp.174 and 184.

118. *Stroitel'stvo kommunizma i preodolenie religioznykh perezhitkov*, pp.52-3.

119. A. Artykov and S. Nurmatova, 'Atheistic and Internationalist Education –A Single Process', *Kommunist Uzbekistana*, no.5 (May 1977) pp.44-9, translated in *JPRS* 69643, 19 Aug. 1977. For a discussion of the implications of the link

It was against this background, apparently, that the Institute of Scientific Atheism of the CPSU Central Committee's Academy of Social Sciences and the CRA conducted a sociological survey in the early 1980s in a number of areas in Central Asia and the Northern Caucasus with the purpose of discovering, among others, Islam's 'links with nationalist and tribal survivals'. Its findings were that people characterised as 'internationalists' were far less likely to be believers and observe Muslim rites than were those defined as 'nationalists'. Among the former, for example, approximately 25 per cent said they were believers, among the latter about 60 per cent. The data thus testified that 'national narrow-mindedness and ethnic prejudices, on the one hand, and religiosity, on the other, are mutually nourishing and supportive'.[120]

Unquestionably, there were aspects of regime policy toward Islam which offended the national as well as the religious sentiments of the Muslim nationalities. In this way Moscow encouraged the intellectual élites of these ethnicities to stress the importance of Islam in helping to preserve their ethnic specificity and to identify Islam with their collective being and patrimony. This Moscow was doing at a time when these intelligentsias were becoming increasingly aware of the distinctiveness of their national heritage and were taking a growing interest in that heritage, as well as using every possible opportunity to manifest their pride in it. Each ethnicity in its turn was antagonised, whether because it was prevented from registering mosques in major centres (as in Turkmenistan) or at all (as in the Chechen-Ingush ASSR), or because its popular shrines were closed down, or its religious customs repressed, and they shared a general sense of humiliation and frustration. Thus, the events in Iran and Afghanistan in the late 1970s and into the 1980s turned into political dynamite, as they enhanced the understanding that Islam was not only an integral component of the ethnos's national culture, heritage and very existence that had to be defended against the encroachments of a foreign ruler, but also a potential instrument in the political struggle against Moscow for national assertion. The phenomena which surfaced

---

between Islam and the nationalism of the USSR's Muslim peoples, see my article, 'The Task of Creating the New Soviet Man', especially pp.34-8.

120. *Sostoianie religioznosti*, pp.3 and 44-5.

in conditions of glasnost and perestroika were not in any way new, except for the actual opportunity to organise and to air dissentient opinions publicly. It was only thanks to the fact that Islam and national sentiment had had a symbiotic relationship for a considerable period prior to Gorbachev's accession to power that their coincidence, or collaboration, became so worrisome to the regime in the late 1980s.

AFTERWORD

This study has sought to provide a picture of Islam in the Soviet
Union in the period from World War II down to the changes
wrought by Gorbachev which led to the dissolution of the Soviet
regime and empire. It has done so by looking at the various
aspects of Islamic life: its context within Soviet policy and legislation,
its dimensions, its two branches – the establishment and the non-
establishment – and the relations between them, its social framework, the level of observance and the rites and rituals which
were more frequently adhered to, and its links with and implications for the Soviet body politic on three levels: the central
authorities in Moscow, the organs of local government, and
the national movements which began to formulate among the
various traditionally Muslim ethnicities.

In preparing this survey, a number of questions have been at
the back of the author's mind. In the first place, was Soviet Islam
a phenomenon unto itself, existing in a sort of limbo created by
the artificiality and arbitrariness of the Soviet system, or did it
connect in integral fashion to what had come before 1917 and
what was to come after 1991 and to trends apparent in Islam in
other parts of the world? Secondly, what enabled Islam to survive
the Soviet experiment with its persistent animosity to religion in
general and to Islam in particular: was it establishment Islam or
was it perhaps the mosqueless and itinerant mullas and other religious
figures of 'parallel' Islam, or the interaction between the two? Or
was it not so much the religious structures and personnel as the
social infrastructure, the fact that Islam was an inherent ingredient
of society in all the Muslim nationalities, especially in the rural
sector, which, at least in Central Asia, included the great majority
of the indigenous population? Or may it even have been the
built-in weaknesses of the Soviet regime, namely the persistent
disagreement at the apex of the pyramid in Moscow and its hy-
pertrophic bureaucratism, which made its decision-making cumbersome and seemed often *a priori* to preclude implementation of
resolutions and legislation, especially in the more distant and in-

accesible peripheral regions and in spheres which were not of prime import or immediate urgency; and similarly the fundamental tensions and distrust that existed between the Russian/Slav leadership in the distant capital and its regional bailiffs in the Muslim republican capitals, not to speak of the local *nomenklatura* in the smaller towns and rural raiony? Thirdly, what stood behind Soviet policy towards Islam and how far was it successful, and if not, why not? Fourthly, can one legitimately talk of Soviet Islam, or were the differences between the areas of Muslim concentration in that vast country so great that they lacked any common features? Fifthly, what role, if any, did Islam play in the accelerated socioeconomic development of the USSR's many Muslim ethnicities as they became mobilised within the framework of 'socialist construction'? And, finally, how did the experience of the Soviet period proper lay the groundwork for what was to come under Gorbachev and in the first years of independence of the six Muslim nations which received their own eponymous states with the disintegration of the Soviet monolith?

In reply to the first question, it is clear that many of the main features of pre-1917 Islam were retained in the Soviet period despite the devastation brought upon the Islamic way of life by the regime, especially in the period 1927-38. In the first decade or so after the October Revolution the Bolshevik regime abolished a number of its main bulwarks: all religious educational institutions, which in their two forms – qadimist and jadidist – had an almost total monopoly of education in the Muslim regions; the Shari'a courts, which had controlled most litigation between members of the community and all problems linked to marriage relationships, inheritance, and similar juridical issues in most Muslim areas; and the *waqf*, the religious endowment, which provided the Muslim establishment the economic wherewithal not just to exist, to maintain its schools, prayer-houses and clergy, but often to expand and prosper. Toward the end of the first decade of its existence and throughout the second, the new regime harassed, persecuted and decimated the remaining symbols of Islam, notably the mosques and clergy, so that by the time of World War II – the Great Fatherland War – Islam, like most of the country's religions, was formally almost non-existent and its rites were not openly practised. Beneath the surface, however, Islam, which had a long history of survivalism in disadvantageous circumstances, persisted in men's consciousness and in their social mores, notably in the more distant and inaccessible areas, where many of its mosques had somehow escaped recurrent bouts of closures and continued to operate.[1] When it finally received official signals that it was being allowed to re-surface, as of 1943, it therefore made a vigorous comeback. Although it never revived its network of educational, juridical and economic structures, Islam became once again a recognised component in the lives of those of the country's nationalities whose cultural traditions and history were linked to that faith. Moreover, postwar Soviet Islam, though undoubtedly weakened, was characterised by many of the traits of pre-1917 Islam. It had an establishment which cooperated with the secular authority, although this was now a communist, militantly atheistic one and neither a tsar – himself bolstered by a Christian church, and so cognisant of the basic values of another monotheistic religion – nor a Muslim emir or khan. It also had non-establishment structures which sought to fight a rearguard action against modernisation and the compromises entailed in this collaboration, that they believed would imperil the very essentials of the faith. In the period under study these forces existed primarily in the Fergana Valley and much of Tajikistan in Central Asia, and in Dagestan and the Chechen-Ingush ASSR in the Northern Caucasus. In this way the historical confrontation between jadidists, who had aspired in the late nineteenth early twentieth century to introduce secular studies into the Muslim school curriculum and to bring Islam into line with late 19th- and early 20th-century scientific knowledge, and qadimists, who had dwelt on the need to preserve traditional frameworks and methods of study, was perpetuated. Islam, now as before,[2] at least in its central, official hierarchies, was an increasingly secular religion, that believed that it had to hold its own in the face of the new ethics and norms which were taking root in a society influenced by the boost of technology and the natural sciences, not by battling them and demonstrating unbending hostility to them, but by adapting to them and even partly assimilating them. Moreover, postwar Islam in the Soviet

1. For Islam in the inter-war period, see Keller, *The Struggle against Islam in Uzbekistan, 1927-1941;* and *Preodolevaia religioznoe vliianie islama.*
2. The Volga Tatars and the Azerbaijanis at least were undergoing a manifest process of secularisation by the end of the 19th century which necessarily impacted on their Islamic structures.

Union became again a major social force, interweaving its existence with that of the extended family, the village and the *mahalla*, in much the same way as it had done traditionally. Once more, it was primarily an Islam that was not based on erudition, but one that focused around local custom and tradition passed from father to son, as had been the case, too, in the nineteenth century – with the exception of just a few centres of Islamic learning. Finally, Islam again stood counterpoised to a distant colonial power that was convinced that its own cultural superiority and higher level of material achievement would not just bring Islam to its knees physically but also convince it that its day was past, its message archaic and irrelevant, and its content matter a contribution to the Muslim population's economic and technological backwardness and primitive outlook and way of life.[3]

Just as Soviet Islam retained its link to the historic past, so it was not totally severed from the geographic present. Completely cut off from the outside world in the prewar years, when no ties with Islamic communities beyond the Soviet borders had been permitted – no *hajj* (since 1929), no delegations in either direction, no receipt in the Soviet Union of foreign Islamic literature – these were renewed, albeit in very truncated form, after the formation of an Islamic establishment which was considered fundamentally reliable, and was under constant surveillance into the bargain. More, however, than Soviet Islam can have been influenced by the contacts maintained by the chosen few with co-religionists from outside, the similarity of the socio-political experience meant that Islam in the Soviet Union and in much of the Third World was undergoing identical challenges and inevitably reacted in ways that were not basically different. This tie, however ephemeral, to trends affecting foreign Islam was enhanced with the Islamic revolution in Iran and the Soviet adventure in Afghanistan. These brought the potential of a politicised Islam to the consciousness of the more radically Islamic activists inside the USSR. Previously Islam's politicisation or political role was rather a dialectical concomitant of the fundamental Marxist – Leninist position, by which every social phenomenon had political implications: every aspect of society

3. For Islam in the tsarist period, see Landa, *Islam v istorii Rossii*, especially Chapters 5 and 6; Litvinov, *Gosudarstvo i islam v russkom Turkestane*, *passim*; Abashin, 'Sotsial'nye korni sredneaziatskogo islamizma', and Brower, 'Islam and Ethnicity: Russian Colonial Policy in Turkestan'.

that was not a priori a component of 'socialist construction' was inevitably hostile to it and thus filled what was by definition a negative political role. By the 1980s this phantom was taking on concrete form. In 1983 the political organisation which led the resistance to Afghanistan's Marxist regime, Jemiat-e Islami claimed to have 2,500 card-carrying members in Tajikistan. Even if this number was exaggerated, which one may safely assume, the very idea of a militant Islamic party having any membership at all in the Soviet Union was clearly dynamite.[4]

Nor could Soviet Islam be isolated from what came later in the post-Soviet Commonwealth of Independent States, the CIS. As a major agent in the everyday life of the Muslim ethnicities of the Soviet Union and in the national movements which took shape among them – even if more slowly and hesitantly than other 'national religions' among some of the European national groups –Islam became incorporated as part of the national heritage of the new states. This new, post-Soviet Islam will be discussed briefly below; suffice it, at this point, to emphasise that it inescapably bore the imprint of the Islam that had been moulded in the previous half-century or so, especially since that Islam in turn had been a natural progeny of pre-revolutionary Islam.

Soviet Islam, then, was not an element divorced in time and place from what preceded it and what was happening around it. Nor did it merely survive, it developed a momentum of its own. The question thus begs itself – what enabled it to do so in face of all the adverse conditions and the omnipotent forces of compulsion at the disposal of the great atheistic power which was ideologically committed to its extinction, and made sporadic efforts to achieve this in practice? True, Moscow itself was instrumental in creating the Muslim spiritual directorates and formulating the subordination to them of the registered clergy and religious societies. In doing so, moreover, the regime was, as it were, legitimising the existence not only of the Muslim establishment, but of Islam itself, for in the Soviet context representative institutions of a prohibited and proscribed religion could not be thus affirmed and put under the supervision of the secular authority. True, it could conceivably be argued – as presumably certain groups in the party leadership must have done – that these organisations, obligated, as

---

4. Marie Broxup, 'Recent Developments in Soviet Islam', p.34, believes the number to have been fact.

they were by definition, to serving the Soviet state, augured their own downfall and with it that of the religion they headed. Nonetheless, it seems that even these time-serving factotums of a Marxist-Leninist regime filled a significant role in the persistence of Islam's existence. In the first place, they signified the possibility of a working relationship between what appeared on the surface to be two inexorably opposed competitors for the minds and souls of the country's Muslim population (if it is not a contradiction in terms to speak of communism's struggle to win over anybody's soul). Secondly, they inevitably became caught up in, and even identified with, some of the 'causes' of Muslim dynamism.

The contribution, however, of the spiritual directorates and the bulk of the registered clergy and religious societies to Islam's continued existence under conditions of communism could be significant on the formal level, but hardly on that of matter and content. Constrained upon by the regime to foster the adoption by the believer community of doctrinal interpretations of dubious authenticity, they had difficulty in claiming to be speaking for an Islam that was genuinely concerned with retaining its specificity and its historical religious mission. This could be accomplished solely by religious figures who were not contaminated by toadyism toward enemy forces, preserving rather their own independent spirit and remaining faithful through thick and thin to the message of Islam and their Islamic identity. It was thus the 'mosqueless mullas' who were prepared to conduct a minimum of religious rituals (festival prayer services and life-cycle rites) wherever Muslims resided, and the shaykhs who operated the Muslim shrines, who together ensured that the faith remained alive throughout the Muslim regions, that Muslims could retain a few elementary symbols of their way of life whatever the powers-that-be might think and do. These people operated mostly in very low profile, fulfilling their duties within their native communities without ado, certainly without any consciousness of fighting, or even representing, any 'cause'. While they might, moreover, be harassed and taxed, they on the whole ran little risk of major repression, given, on the one hand, the understanding of the regime that their activity was a prerequisite for political obeisance and, on the other hand, the general insouciance, if not active endorsement of their activity, on the part of the local organs of government. On another level, were the far smaller number of totally committed religious figures, some of them Sufi *ishans* or *murshids*, others former mullas or religious leaders within the run-of-the-mill Sunni community, and some younger men, usually scions of families in which a religious calling had been traditional. The members of this group were apparently prepared to jeopardise their freedom by undertaking intiatives which they clearly realised the authorities could not pretend to ignore, let alone condone, although they, too, probably relied on the apathy, if not actual sympathy, of local officialdom. At least in the four abovementioned regions, underground religious instruction was conducted throughout the period under study, or most of it, an instruction, moreover, that, in the Fergana Valley, acquired a new momentum, with manifest political connotations, as of the late 1970s. There was also a rather limited and sporadic Islamic *samizdat* – the printing and dissemination of religious litera- ture – again chiefly in these four areas. The more reactionary attitude towards Islam of this last category of activists seems to have put a brake on the tendencies of the establishment and its adherents to make far-reaching concessions to the regime and to 'modernisation'. This was probably not so much because the establishment was persuaded of the justness of the approach of the activists, as because it feared losing the believer community and thus endangering its power base, *raison d'être* and value to the regime.

Nor was this the sole connection between the Muslim estab- lishment and 'parallel' Islam. The two were evidently not totally dissociated. Indisputably antagonism often characterised their relationship – the former denouncing the unregistered clergy to the secular authority and informing on them to the financial organs for purposes of taxation, and the latter attacking the spiritual direc- torates and the registered clergy as Soviet agents. Yet there were sundry instances of co-operation. Unregistered clergy attended prayer-services in the registered mosques and even paid contribu- tions for their upkeep, and they approached the spiritual directorates for advice on the specifics of Islamic law and practice. The direc- torates and registered clergy for their part frequently sought to bring the unregistered mullas and groups under their tutelage. Worshippers, too, did not confine themselves to one particular category of religious association. When registered mosques were closed down, believers who had frequented them sought out un- registered religious associations and prayer-houses; when these were disbanded their congregants turned to the registered mosques. Or those who prayed in unregistered groups on regular Fridays might go to registered mosques on festivals. This interrelationship was a significant factor in enabling Islam to withstand regime pressure, and indeed highlighted its resilience in the face of this hostility.

Undoubtedly, then, both the spiritual directorates and the registered clergy and religious societies, on the one hand, and the various components of non-establishment Islam, on the other hand, played their part in preserving Islam's existence despite the hostility of the CPSU. Perhaps no less important a role was filled by society itself within the Muslim ethnicities. Islam was an integral component of these peoples' social infrastructure, was interwoven into their daily lives at the communal and family level. Society remained surprisingly static, many of its traditional structures and frameworks somehow untouched by the Soviet experiment, especially in the rural parts and in the mono-national *mahallas* of Central Asia's urban centres, the old parts of towns which had no European residents. So long as the indigenous populations of the Muslim regions remained in their natural surroundings – and they proved extremely loath to abandon them despite regime pressures to manipulate and jerrymander them – there was little chance that what had remained of Islamic practice would be whittled away or, indeed, any reason for that to occur. Nor did the rather artificial division made by the regime between believers and non-believers in Muslim society reflect any real divide. The community as a whole became accustomed to interpreting the signs it received from Moscow and taking its cue from them. When repression was active, it laid low, biding its time until things let up, which, after witnessing the pendulum nature of regime policy, it had valid grounds to assume would happen sooner or later. When the atmosphere was more relaxed, there was always a religious nucleus to take the lead, applying to register mosques, building, repairing and opening unregistered ones, holding prayer-services in the open. On the whole, this *aktiv*, however, was not left to hold the fort alone, but received considerable group support from its social peers.

Paradoxically, however, the regime too aided and abetted the survival of Islam in its own way. In the first place, its policy toward Islam was not hard and fast. Throughout most of the period, in fact, it might be contended that it had no policy towards Islam, aside from its line on religion as a whole. Since religion, too, does not seem to have been a major issue at most times, religious policy was followed lackadaisically and without resolution. There was no agreement at the apex of the Soviet hierarchy as to the optimal way of bringing about the disappearance of religion, which the ideology stipulated unequivocally was inevitable. While most were of the opinion that this historical process had to be actively promoted – this, surely, was the meaning of the dictatorship of the proletariat – there was no consensus whether this necessarily implied active repression, or whether it might not be preferable to make do with an intensive education programme and heavy-handed legislation which would permit only a very restricted religious activity. With the help of the regime's proven expertise in encouraging religionists (and other undesirables) to pull the noose around their own necks and in taking advantage of disagreements within the believer community to curb religion even further, the more gradual alternative might be expected to pre-empt the popular dissatisfaction that severer measures might evoke. Indeed, as far as Islam was concerned, those in government service whose prime field of action was implementing policy regarding religion contended that active repression tended, in addition, to actually arouse new waves of religiosity, thus impeding the slow but sure erosion that that faith was undergoing. At the level of the regime, then, Islam received indirect reinforcement from: the irresoluteness and lack of direction which characterised government policy towards Islam; the total ignorance among decision-makers of what in fact was taking place in the Muslim community, what forces were at play and what trends at work in the Islamic 'movement'; and the lack of professionalism in analysing the Muslim periphery. All this meant that when things came to a head following the Iranian revolution and the coup and subsequent civil war in Afghanistan, and the Soviet leadership decided that it had perforce to adopt an unambiguous and assertive policy regarding Islam, it was at its wits' end how to proceed.

It is not entirely clear what lay behind the inadequate treatment of Islam by the regime: whether it was sheer inefficacy in relation to matters that were not of prime import, which was certainly the category into which Islam fell prior to 1979; or whether it was part of Moscow's (and previously St. Petersburg's) inbuilt disdain for the Muslim population, particularly in Central Asia, which led it to underestimate Islam's impact; or whether it was yet another instance of the Soviet regime being stymied by its inability to bring its regional and local subordinates into line and to obligate them to fulfil its directives effectively. Certainly, the fact that most of the cadres in the republican capitals, not to speak of the bureaucracies which bestrode the public domain in the oblast' and raion administrative centres, belonged to the eponymous Muslim nationalities and were sensitive to the overbearing attitudes of their Russian/Slavic overlords, made them instinctively protective of Islam, which they knew was of the essence of their native culture and tradition, and its protagonists. Probably all three elements were present. What is certain, however, is that the all-powerful centre, side by side with its total disregard for domestic Islam, helped it persist as a major social force in the country's Muslim regions.

It was, almost certainly, not merely an ideological drive founded on eschatological perceptions that motivated policy towards Islam. There was also a sense that the repression of Islam, and above all, of what seemed to the regime its most obscurantist aspects, was a prerequisite for removing a major practical impediment to mobilising the Muslim *lumpenproletariat,* or, to be more precise, to transforming the masses of these peoples into such a body, and thus enabling their enlistment for the ends devised by the party leadership in Moscow. In light of the atmosphere, trends and tendencies dominant in society in the rural areas, semi-urban *poselki* and small towns in the Muslim republics, an inbred passive resistance to such mobilisation not only existed, but seemed to grow every time the regime augmented pressure. This included an obdurate adherence not so much to the time-honoured pillars of orthodox Islam as to some of its more ceremonial trappings, which helped consolidate a collective that was everything which from the standpoint of the Soviet worldview had no place in a modern, socialist or communist society: tradition-oriented, deprived of political awareness, with its own alternative value-system, norms and leadership. Indeed, analogies clearly exist between the lot which befell Islam in the Soviet Union and in neighbouring Turkey. Here, too, a secularising authoritarian regime, whose founder, Kemal Ataturk, took many a leaf out of Lenin's political dictionary, declared war on Islam as part of its attempt to modernise and bring a rather undeveloped country into the mainstream of the twentieth century. The Soviet regime likewise failed to purge the cultures of the

Muslim peoples of Islamic symbols and points of reference and substitute its own secular images and icons. Islam and Muslim identity thus became for both sides a theatre of conflict in the protracted struggle between the European, Western, colonialist power and the indigenous populations of Central Asia and parts of the Caucasus. (The fact that this was not to the liking of the local national intelligentsias carried little weight and they were compelled to take sides – and as time passed, they found themselves increasingly on the side of their co-ethnics.)

Clearly there is, then, a general picture, a single Islam which existed throughout the Soviet Union. It existed by definition within a single body politic and this polity – at one and the same time totalitarian, or authoritarian, and atheistic, propped upon a materialist philosophy – both provided a unique political framework with which Islam had constantly to contend and imposed its own special institutions to serve as a conduit between the regime and Islam. The constant challenge posed by the Soviet system in light of its structure and ideological commitment, could be dealt with in one of three ways – the one adopted by the Muslim establishment of showing the compatibility, if not actual overlap, of Islam and communism; the one chosen by radical Muslims of rejecting everything that smacked of, or was somehow linked to, the Soviet regime; and the one opted for by the great majority of Muslims, of turning a blind eye to potential confrontationism and hoping, and endeavouring, to peacefully co-exist with Marxism-Leninism and its representatives, without, however, accepting its postulates. Nor was it only the political implications of the Soviet system against which the Muslim community was matched. There was a more latent, but no less insiduous, danger – that presented by a modern, technological economy and society with their secular values and practical materialism (as distinct from the materialism of the dominant ideology), a threat which existed in every modernising, industrialising state. And, finally, there was an entire complex of everyday problems, which Islam had to cope with in all parts of the Soviet Union: a bureaucracy, which, although at times fundamentally friendly and sympathetic, might, out of considerations of its own economic or political advantage, turn nasty with little or no notice and put sticks in the wheels of all Islamic activity; economic hardship, as a consequence of the regime's persistent efforts to undermine religion's material base; and a population which, while largely unwilling to turn its back on all Islamic rites and practices and not rejecting its Muslim identity, neither knew anything about Islam nor was prepared by and large to rise up in arms on its behalf. All this came in addition to the permanent tension which existed between the genuine needs of the faith, as understood by its more independent representatives, and the total subservience of the spiritual directorates and the registered clergy to the diktat of the regime.

The common features of Soviet Islam notwithstanding, there were major differences from region to region. Islam in areas where a Muslim ethnicity was the titular national group and/or comprised a majority of the population was manifestly different from Islam in European-dominated regions. Within the former, too, there were significant variations, notably between territories sedentarised for centuries and those that until collectivisation had been largely nomadic, the latter never having boasted full-fledged Islamic institutions, including even mosques. Certain parts, moreover, had in the past been centres of activity of Sufi orders and the vestiges of their influence remained, including even some reputed *ishans* and shaykhs. Indeed, in the Chechen-Ingush ASSR and parts of Dagestan and North Osetia, Sufi influence remained paramount and most believers among the Chechen and Ingush were reportedly linked somehow to a Sufi order in the decades after the return from exile in Kazakhstan. In some parts worship at shrines had long been a focal feature of Islam, one of the marks of Sufi Islam. Aside from a number of major *mazars* in Central Asia which were famous throughout the Soviet Union and drew pilgrims from far and wide, both in that region and in the Caucasus almost every settlement had its holy site, where a variety of folk practices were indulged in – especially the sale of amulets and talismans and faith-healing. One of the striking regional disparities related to the place of women in religious worship: again areas with a history of Sufism had had in the past, and retained, women religious figures who performed rites, including prayer-services, for and among women. In other parts women were drawn in the Soviet period into the mosques: in Kazakhstan this occurred as early as the 1920s, and in the cities of European Russia and Siberia registered mosques began catering for women worshippers in the postwar years. Finally, while the far greater proportion of Soviet Muslims were Sunnis of the Hanafi school, Shafi'i Islam prevailed in Dagestan, while Azerbaijan was largely Shiite, especially in the south. Shiite enclaves also existed in parts of Central Asia and Dagestan. Finally, the Gorno-Badakhshan AO was in large part Ismaili.

The regime sought to emphasise and perpetuate these differences by preventing the establishment of a single religious centre for its Muslim citizens – Islam was the only faith which was allowed a recognised establishment leadership with more than one centre. This was almost certainly not motivated by consideration for variations in religious practice or such niceties as a desire to give every historically separate region its own accepted leaders, as Soviet officialdom maintained, but by apprehensions concerning a revived pan-Islam, the bogey that had haunted the tsarist government in the last generation or so before its fall or perhaps the creation of a paramount Muslim solidarity within the Soviet Union. In effect, the chances of any such consolidation of forces among the country's Muslim believer community were very dim. In addition to the abovementioned historical disparities, there was a great deal of antagonism within and between the various communities on almost every conceivable background: historical, social, cultural, ethnic and economic, and hostility between clans and tribes, not to speak of the divergences of opinion on how to relate to the regime and the trends and values which characterised it – secularisation, modernisation, 'socialist construction'.

One of the manifestations of the way in which Soviet Islam comprised a single, clearly defined unit was its relationship with the culture of the various Muslim ethnicities, for although the actual relationship was specific to each case, the form it adopted was common to most of these nationalities. As an integral component of the cultural heritage, Islam was inevitably a factor in the development of their cultures even under Soviet auspices. True, the official culture which the regime nurtured and promoted was to be disencumbered of all content matter that did not come under the rubric of socialism, for it had to be 'national in form and socialist in content'. Yet, the representatives of the 'artistic intelligentsias' found devious ways to cleave to all aspects of their cultural patrimony and Islam crept into their art, beginning in the latter 1940s and increasingly so as of the 1960s. Muslim religious figures, too, were insistent that Islam intertwined with the national, secular traditions of their ethnic group and was an inseparable ingredient in the national identity. The more developed the national culture – and some of the cultures of the major Muslim nationalities were able to boast rather impressive achievements – the more likely it was to display its spiritual independence from Soviet fiats and to embrace its Islamic connection.

Islam also contributed to the ethnos's social evolution. The Muslim holidays remained festive occasions for large numbers of citizens, especially but not solely in the rural sector. The ceremonies that traditionally marked the life cycle continued to be conducted by religious figures and to be accompanied by a short prayer or the recital of passages from the Qur'an. The secular ceremonies devised by the regime in order to serve as a substitute for the traditional religious ones took root with difficulty, if at all. The collective social consciousness within the national framework thus bore the indelible mark of the group's Islamic past and the Muslim identity was ubiquitously adhered to, even if it meant very little by strictly religious criteria. Moreover, the politicisation of Islam in other parts of the Muslim world enhanced the awareness of that identity, particularly as of the late 1970s. So, too, did the increasingly felt divide within the country between the Russian/Slav contingent and the Muslim/Asiatic one. Just as the policy of the Soviet regime and the character of its mechanisms helped keep Islam alive inside the USSR, so the growing identification of Soviet and Russian and the feeling that the Muslim nationalities were regarded and treated as second-grade citizens helped consolidate national and Muslim sentiment within them.

Islam did not make a similar contribution to the economic development of the Muslim nationalities. Religious institutions in the Soviet Union were forbidden by law to own property, and the economic wealth which had been sequestrated was at no stage returned to them. For the most part, the country's Muslim communities had great difficulty in maintaining themselves and their prayer-houses, and with the exception of SADUM's much-flaunted prosperity in the mid-late 1950s, the religious establishment had no riches to speak of. Nor did they manifest any involvement in economic activity beyond the administration of their own rather restricted affairs,[5] despite the constant harping of the Soviet media and documentation on the rapacity of mullas and shaykhs and on

5. The sole exception may have been in the Chechen-Ingush ASSR, where some of the *wirds* were reportedly influential in a whole host of activities which were normally beyond the scope of religious personnel.

the donations they received for every rite they performed.[6] The economic development of the Muslim nationalities – its forms and dimensions – depended, indeed, on what was decreed for, and allotted to, them by the country's central planning agencies.

The aggregate of all the characteristics of Soviet Islam was the dowry left by the Soviet regime to its successors. In this sense, Islam as it developed in the more liberal years of glasnost and perestroika was influenced by what had gone before, and became the stepping-stone for all that came later. Certainly, the Gorbachev leadership began by adopting a distinctly harsh line toward Islam, as evidenced by excerpts from Gorbachev's utterances in Tashkent in November 1986 and Igor' Beliaev's programmatic article in *Pravda* the following May, 'Islam and Politics'.[7] This changed as of 1989 – in the wake apparently of the changed attitude to the Russian Orthodox Church in the context of the 1988 millennium – when the regime switched to attributing a positive role to Islam, co-opting it in implementing some of its social goals, such as combating crime, alcoholism and drug abuse. This was accompanied by a large-scale re-opening of mosques; the publication of a religious journal in Uzbek, i.e. for a domestic audience, that gave useful information concerning Islam; and a re-vamping of the spiritual directorates, ignited by a mass demonstration against the incumbent mufti in Tashkent in February 1989. This last development, moreover, proved to be but a first step in the breakdown of the organisational structures created and supervised by the Soviet regime. Already under Gorbachev the regional spiritual administrations began disintegrating, the various national republics seeking their own independent organisations. Furthermore, the process of Islam's politicisation got underway with the formation in 1990 of the Islamic Renaissance Party, designed, according to its official spokesman, to revitalise Islam and protect the interests of the country's Muslims.[8]

6. This was a constant theme in Soviet propaganda regarding all religions and religious cadres from the very earliest years after the Bolshevik takeover in 1917 – religion being, by definition, one of the features of exploitative societies and seeking to extort moneys from the population by every possible means, its representatives were by definition rapacious.

7. *Pravda vostoka*, 25 Nov. 1986, and *Literaturnaia gazeta*, 13 and 20 May 1987. Unfortunately, my efforts to lay hands on the text of Gorbachev's Tashkent speech were unsuccessful.

8. For Islam under Gorbachev, see Anderson, *Religion, State and Politics*, pp.200-5,

Yet, the formal alteration that the directorates underwent did not herald any fundamental change in the relationship between the secular authority and the official Muslim establishment. The new independent Muslim states, now led by presidents of the eponymous Muslim nationality, sought similar arrangements to those brought into being by their Soviet predecessors, to enable them, as they hoped, to both identify with Islam and keep Islamic activity under control. They thought to justify their actions by dwelling on the 'threat of Islamic fundamentalism', intimated by Gorbachev as an apologetic for some of his rather savage repression of nationalist demonstrations in the Muslim republics,[9] and designed to win the support of Russians and assuage possible Western critics. Imomali Rahmonov, then speaker in Tajikistan's parliament and as of late 1994 head of state, described the power struggle in that country in 1993 as one between 'obscurantism, represented by Islamic fundamentalism, and the idea of progress and the democratic development of society',[10] the latter being represented by the communist or para-communist forces which he headed. Even some of the other states, where the new élites were somewhat less blatantly linked to the old Soviet system, developed similar attitudes to Islam. (It should, however, be noted that Nursultan Nazarbaev in Kazakhstan, Islam Karimov in Uzbekistan, Saparmurad Niyazov in Turkmenistan, all of them heads of state since independence, as well as Heydar Aliev who took over in Azerbaijan in 1993, were all former first party secretaries in their republics.) Karimov explained in no uncertain terms that his primary concern was the maintenance of law and order, and since giving free rein to Islamic forces meant anarchy and civil war – as happened in Tajikistan –he had no choice but to clamp down on independent Islamic groups such as surfaced in the Fergana Valley, particularly around Namangan. Thus, while there were mass openings of mosques (often with financial help from foreign Muslim states) and of Islamic educational institutions, including Islamic 'universities', and in spite

Bryan, 'Internationalism, Nationalism and Islam', and Ro'i, 'The Islamic Influence on Nationalism in Soviet Central Asia', pp.50-1.

9. The authorities constantly referred to pictures of Khomeini and the 'green flag of Islam' used by opposition elements in the disturbances that erupted in all the Central Asian republics and Azerbaijan in the Gorbachev era – Ro'i, 'Central Asian Riots and Disturbances, 1989-1990'.

10. Quoted in Atkin, 'Islam as Faith, Politics and Bogeyman in Tajikistan', p.247.

of the fact that Islam was declared officially to be an integral part of the national cultural heritage and patrimony, it continued to be carefully and closely supervised by an establishment that was hardly less docile and identified with the regime than in the Soviet period.

In all these ways, the Soviet period actively laid the groundwork for what was to come after independence or, in the case of the Muslim regions which remained in the Russian Federation, following the incidence of greater democratisation. Conceptually and in practice much remained the same, even though formally and on the surface a great deal changed. There was no longer a dearth of prayer-houses or repression of religious practice and Islam as a religion was not 'an enemy of the people'. But the new regimes preached the danger it entailed if allowed to get out of hand, if 'fanatics' were to take up leadership positions, and if it became politicised.

To the present author it seems that the great bulk of the Muslim population, while identifying with Islam, remains essentially moderate in its Islamic attachment, with the exception of a few enclaves; that secularisation is by and large – at least in the near and medium-term future – an irreversible process (this may change if the dream of Supreme Qazi Akbar Turajonzoda of giving a religious education to Tajikistan's population is realised);[11] and that the bugbear of Islamic fundamentalism is not on the whole relevant to the CIS (the Commonwealth of Independent States) except in Chechnia (Ichkeria), Dagestan and parts of Tajikistan and Uzbekistan's Fergana Valley. The Soviet regime was singularly unsuccessful in achieving its long-term objectives regarding Islam, which following World War II was revitalised and grew in strength – where it was unable to do this in registered religious societies, doing so as a popular, or folk, religion. But the new, post-Soviet leaderships are necessarily practical politicians and statesmen desirous of adjusting to the contemporary modern world and not wishing to become unduly identified with international Islam. Their orientation is therefore not sufficiently at variance with that of their Soviet progenitors to breed a totally different outlook or *modus operandi* regarding Islam. The great question remains whether the mass of the population among the Muslim ethnicities will go along with their leaders and opt for a secular existence

11. *Ibid.*, p.259.

in an industrialising society with a formal Islamic linkage or will prefer and even demand a more meaningfully Islamic existence. Either way the precedent of the Soviet period will long remain before the eyes of both élites and populations as an example not to be returned to – a regime oscillating in impractical and self-defeating fashion between repression and toleration; a citizenry fearing to rebel but unwilling to succumb and living its Islam in an undignified hide-and-seek way; and a largely ignorant clergy, partly collaborators, partly opponents, but mostly somewhere in-between, evoking but little respect for themselves and the faith they represented.

BIBLIOGRAPHY

Books in English

Aitmatov, Chingiz, *The Day Lasts More than a Hundred Years*, Bloomington: Indiana University Press, 1983.

Akiner, Shirin, *Islamic Peoples of the Soviet Union*, London: Kegan Paul, 1983.

────── (ed.), *Political and Economic Trends in Central Asia*, London: British Academic Press, 1994.

Allworth, Edward A., *The Modern Uzbeks from the Fourteenth Century to the Present: A Cultural History*, Stanford, CA: Hoover Institution Press, 1990.

Alstadt, Audrey L., *The Azerbaijani Turks: Power and Identity under Russian Rule*, Stanford, CA: Hoover Institution Press, 1992.

Anderson, John, *Religion, State and Society in the Soviet Union and Successor States*, Cambridge University Press, 1994.

Babakhan, Ziyauddin Khan Ibn Ishan, *Islam and the Muslims in the Land of the Soviets*, Moscow: Progress, 1980.

Bennigsen, Alexandre A. and S. Enders Wimbush, *Muslim National Communism in the Soviet Union*, Chicago University Press, 1979.

────── , *Muslims of the Soviet Empire: A Guide*, London: Hurst, 1986.

────── , *Mystics and Commissars: Sufism in the Soviet Union*, London: Hurst, 1985.

Berman, Harold J., *Justice in the U.S.S.R.: An Interpretation of Soviet Law*, Cambridge, MA: Harvard University Press, 1963 (rev. edn).

────── , *Soviet Criminal Law and Procedure*, Cambridge, MA: Harvard University Press, 1972 (2nd edn).

Bienstock, Gregory, Solomon M. Schwarz and Aaron Yugow, *Management in Russian Industry and Agriculture*, Ithaca, NY: Cornell University Press, 1948.

Bociurkiw, Bohdan R., *The Ukrainian Greek Catholic Church and the Soviet State (1939-1950)*, Edmonton and Toronto: Canadian Institute of Ukrainian Studies Press, 1996.

British Documents on Foreign Affairs, Part II: *From the First to the Second World War*. Series B: *Turkey, Iran and the Middle East, 1918-1939*, vol. 14: Robin Bidwell (ed.), *The Pilgrimage in the Reign of Ibn Saud, 1927-1939*, New York: University Publications of America, 1989.

Brower, Daniel R., and Edward J. Lazzerini (eds), *Russia's Orient: Imperial*

731

Borderlands and Peoples, 1700-1917, Bloomington: Indiana University Press, 1997.

Broxup, Marie Bennigsen (ed.), *The North Caucasus Barrier: The Russian Advance towards the Muslim World*, London: Hurst, 1992.

Corley, Felix, *Religion in the Soviet Union: An Archival Reader*, London: Macmillan, 1997.

Dunlop, John B., *The Faces of Contemporary Russian Nationalism*, Princeton University Press, 1983.

Ellis, Jane, *The Russian Orthodox Church*, London: Croom Helm, 1986.

Fainsod, Merle, *How Russia is Ruled*, Cambridge, MA: Harvard University Press, 1967 (rev. edn).

Fierman, William (ed.), *Soviet Central Asia: The Failed Transformation*, Boulder, CO: Westview Press, 1991.

Grunebaum, Gustave E. von, *Muhammedan Festivals*, London: Curzon Press (2nd edn), 1992.

Hosking, Geoffrey, *A History of the Soviet Union*, London: Collins, 1985.

Jacobs, Everett M. (ed.), *Soviet Local Politics and Government*, London: George Allen & Unwin, 1983.

Karklins, Rasma, *Ethnic Relations in the USSR: The Perspective from Below*, Boston: MA: Allen & Unwin, 1986.

Keller, Shoshana, 'The Struggle against Islam in Uzbekistan, 1927-1941: Policy, Bureaucracy and Reality', unpubl. Ph.D. diss., Indiana University, 1995.

Knight, Amy W., *The KGB: Police and Politics in the Soviet Union*, London: Unwin Hyman, 1988.

Kozlov, Viktor, *The Peoples of the Soviet Union*, London: Hutchinson, 1988.

Lane, Christel, *The Rites of Rulers*, Cambridge University Press, 1981.

Lane, David, *Politics and Society in the USSR*, London: Martin Robertson, 1978 (2nd edn).

Lenczowski, George, *Russia and the West in Iran; 1918-1948: A Study in Big-Power Rivalry*, Ithaca, NY: Cornell Univ. Press, 1949.

Lubin, Nancy, *Labour and Nationality in Soviet Central Asia*, Princeton University Press, 1984.

Luukkanen, Arto, *The Religious Polreg of the Stalinist State – A case Study: The Central Standing Commission on Religious Questions*, SHS (Finnish Historical Society): Helsinki, 1997.

Massell, Gregory J., *The Surrogate Proletariat*, Princeton University Press, 1974.

Poliakov, Sergei P., *Everyday Islam: Religion and Tradition in Rural Central Asia*, Armonk, NY: M. E. Sharpe, 1992.

Pospielovsky, Dimitry V., *A History of Marxist-Leninist Atheism and Soviet Anti-Religious Policies*, vol. I: *A History of Soviet Atheism in Theory and Practice, and the Believer*, London: Macmillan, 1987.

Powell, David, *Anti-religious Propaganda in the Soviet Union*, Cambridge, MA: MIT Press, 1975.

Rakowska-Harmstone, Teresa, *Russia and Nationalism in Central Asia: The Case of Tadzhikistan*, Baltimore, MD: Johns Hopkins University Press, 1970.

Rigby, T. H., *Communist Party Membership in the U.S.S.R., 1917-1967*, Princeton University Press, 1968.

Ro'i, Yaacov (ed.), *Muslim Eurasia: Conflicting Legacies*, London: Frank Cass, 1995.

———, *The USSR and the Muslim World*, London: George Allen & Unwin, 1984.

Saroyan, Mark Andrew, 'Reconstructing Community: Authority and the Politics of Islam in the Soviet Union', unpubl. Ph.D. diss., University of California, Berkeley, 1990.

Schimmel, Annemarie, *Mystical Dimensions of Islam*, Chapel Hill, NC: University of North Carolina Press, 1981 (4th imp.).

Simon, Gerhard, *Nationalism and Policy Toward the Nationalities in the Soviet Union*, Boulder, CO: Westview Press, 1991.

Trimingham, J. Spencer, *The Sufi Orders in Islam*, Oxford University Press, 1973.

Vardys, V. Stanley, *The Catholic Church, Dissent and Nationality in Soviet Lithuania*, Boulder, CO: East European Monographs, 1978.

Voslensky, Michael, *Nomenklatura: The Soviet Ruling Class*, New York: Doubleday, 1984.

Willerton, John P., *Patronage and politics in the USSR*, Cambridge University Press, 1992.

Zenkovsky, Serge A., *Pan-Turkism and Islam in Russia*, Cambridge, MA: Harvard University Press, 1960.

Books in Russian

Anufriev, L. and V. Kobetskii, *Religioznost' i ateizm*, Odessa: Maiak, 1974.

Ashirov, Nugman, *Evoliutsiia islama v SSSR*, Moscow: Politizdat, 1972.

———, *Islam i natsii*, Moscow: Politizdat, 1975.

Bairamsakhatov, Nursakhat, *Novyi byt i islam*, Moscow: Politizdat, 1979.

Basilov, V. N., *Kul't sviatykh v islame*, Moscow: Mysl', 1970.

Doev, Azgirei Batcherievich, *Osobennosti islama v Kirgizii*, Frunze: Znanie, 1988.

Gitlin, Semen, *Natsional'nye otnosheniia v Uzbekistane: illiuzii i real'nost'*, Tel Aviv, 1998.

Islam v SSSR: Osobennosti protsessa sekuliarizatsii v respublikakh sovetskogo vostoka, Moscow: Mysl', 1983.

Klimovich, Liutsian I., *Islam*, Moscow: Nauka, 1965.

Kosach, G. G., *Gorod na styke dvukh kontinentov*, Moscow: MGU, Institut stran Azii i Afriki, 1998.

Kuliev, Nedir, *Antinauchnaia sushchnost' islama i zadachi ateisticheskogo vospitaniia trudiashchikhsia v usloviiakh Sovetskogo Turkmenistana*, Ashkhabad: Akademiia nauk Turkmenskoi SSR, 1960.

Kuroedov, V. A. and A. Pankratov (eds), *Zakonodatel'stvo o religioznykh kul'takh*, New York: Chalidze, 1981 (appeared in Moscow 'for official use only', 1971).

Kuroedov, Vladimir Alekseevich, *Religiia i tserkov' v sovetskom obshchestve*, Moscow: Politizdat, 1981.

Landa, Robert Grigor'evich, *Islam v istorii Rossii*, Moscow: RAN, Vostochnaia literatura, 1995.

Litvinov, P. P., *Gosudarstvo i islam v russkom Turkestane (1865-1917), (po arkhivnym materialam)*, Elets, 1998.

Mamleev, Husiain Burganovich, *Nekotorye osobennosti islama v Checheno-Ingushetii*, Groznyi: Checheno-Ingushetskoe izdatel'stvo, 1970.

———, *Reaktsionnaia sushchnost' miuridizma*, Groznyi: Checheno-Ingushetskoe izdatel'stvo, 1966.

Mustafinov, M. M., *Zikrizm i ego sotsial'naia sushchnost'*, Groznyi: Checheno-Ingushetskoe izdatel'stvo, 1971.

O religii i tserkvi: sbornik vyskazyvanii klassikov marksizma-leninizma, dokumentov KPSS i sovetskogo gosudarstva, Moscow: Politizdat, (2nd [supplementary] edn.), 1981.

Petrushev, Dmitrii Ageevich, *Islam i ego reaktsionnaia sushchnost'*, Moscow: Znanie, 1960.

Pospelovskii, Dmitrii V., *Russkaia pravoslavnaia tserkov' v XX veke*, Moscow: Respublika, 1995.

Preodolevaia religioznoe vliianie islama, Alma-Ata: Kazakhstan, 1990.

Saidbaev, T. S., *Islam i obshchestvo. Opyt istoriko-sotsiologicheskogo issledovaniia*, Moscow: Nauka (2nd edn), 1984.

Sostoianie religioznosti i ateisticheskogo vospitaniia v regionakh traditsionnogo rasprostraneniia islama (Materialy sotsiologicheskogo issledovaniia), Akademiia obshchestvennykh nauk pri TsK KPSS, Institut nauchnogo ateizma, i Sovetskaia sotsiologicheskaia assotsiatsiia, Moscow, 1989.

Sotsiologiia, ateizm, religiia, Groznyi: Checheno-Ingushetskoe knizhnoe izdatel'stvo, 1972.

Sovremennaia kul'tura i byt narodov Dagestana, Moscow: Nauka, 1971.

Stroitel'stvo kommunizma i preodolenie religioznykh perezhitkov, Moscow: Nauka, 1966.

Sultangalieva, Alma Kadyrgalieva, *Islam v Kazakhstane: istoriia, etnichnost' i obshchestvo*, Kazakhstanskii institut strategicheskikh issledovanii pri Prezidente Respubliki Kazakhstana: Almaty, 1998.

Tsavkalov, Boris Khambievich, *Prichiny zhivuchesti religioznykh perezhitkov i puti ikh preodoleniia*, Nal'chik: Kabardino-Balkarskoe knizhnoe izdatel'stvo, 1959.

Tutaev, Amerkhan Maksharipovich, *Protiv sektantskogo bezzakoniia*, Groznyi: Checheno-Ingushetskoe knizhnoe izdatel'stvo, 1975.

———, *Reaktsionnaia sekta Batal-Khadzhi*, Groznyi: Checheno-Ingushetskoe knizhnoe izdatel'stvo, 1968.

Ugolovnyi kodeks RSFSR, Moscow: Iuridicheskaia literatura, 1986.

Vagabov, Makhsud V., *Islam i voprosy ateisticheskogo vospitaniia*, Moscow: Vysshaia shkola, 1984.

———, *Islam i zhenshchina*, Moscow: Mysl', 1968.

Articles and chapters in books (English)

Abashin, Sergei, 'Sotsial'nye korni sredneaziatskogo islamizma (na primere odnogo seleniia' in Martha B. Olcott, Valerii Tishkov and Aleksei Malashenko (eds), *Identichnost' i konflikt v postsovetskikh gosudarstvakh*, Moscow: Carnegie Endowment for International Peace, 1997, pp.447-67.

Abduvakhitov, Abdujabbar A., 'The Jadid Movement and Its Impact on Contemproary Central Asia' in Hafeez Malik (ed.), *Central Asia: Its Strategic Importance and Future Prospects*, New York: St. Martin's Press, 1994, pp.65-75.

———, 'Islamic Revivalism in Uzbekistan' in Dale F. Eickelman (ed.), *Russia's Muslim Frontiers: New Directions in Cross-Cultural Analysis*, Bloomington: Indiana University Press, 1993, pp.79-97.

Akiner, Shirin, 'Islam, the State and Ethnicity in Central Asia in Historical Perspective', *Religion, State and Society*, 24:2-3, 1996, pp.91-132.

Anderson, Barbara A., and Brian D. Silver, 'Demographic Sources of the Changing Ethnic Composition of the Soviet Union', *Population and Development Review*, 15:4, December 1989, pp.609-56.

Anderson, John, 'Islam in the Soviet Archives', *Central Asian Survey*, 13:3, 1994, pp.383-94.

Atkin, Muriel, 'Islam as Faith, Politics and Bogeyman in Tajikistan' in Michael Bourdeaux (ed.), *The Politics of Religion in Russia and the States of Eurasia*, Armonk, NY: M. E. Sharpe, 1995, pp. 247-72.

Avtorkhanov, Abdurahman, 'The Chechens and the Ingush during the Soviet Period and Its Antecedents' in Broxup (ed.), *The North Caucasus Barrier*, pp.146-94.

Bennigsen, Alexandre A., 'The Crisis of the Turkic National Epics, 1951-1952: Local Nationalism or Internationalism?', *Canadian Slavonic Papers*, 17:2 and 3, summer and fall 1975, pp.463-74.

———, 'Muslim Conservative Opposition to the Soviet Regime: The Sufi Brotherhoods in the North Caucasus' in Jeremy R. Azrael (ed.), *Soviet Nationality Policies and Practices*, New York: Praeger, 1978, pp.334-48.

------, 'Muslim Guerilla Warfare in the Caucasus (1918-1928)', *Central Asian Survey*, 2:1, July 1983, pp.45-56.

------, 'Panturkism and Panislamism in History and Today', *Central Asian Survey*, 3:3, 1984, pp.39-49.

------, 'The Qadiriyah (Kunta-Hajji) Tariqah in North-East Caucasus: 1850-1987', *Islamic Culture* (Hyderabad), 52:2-3, April-July 1988, pp.63-78.

------, and Chantal Lemercier-Quelquejay, 'Islam in the Soviet Muslim Republics' in Olivier Carré (ed.), *Islam and the State in the World Today*, New Delhi: Manohar, 1989, pp.131-58.

------, 'Muslim Religious Conservatism and Dissent in the USSR', *Religion in Communist Lands*, 6:3, autumn 1978, pp.153-61.

------, "Official" Islam in the Soviet Union', *Religion in Communist Lands*, 7:3, autumn 1979, pp.148-59.

Brower, Daniel, 'Islam and Ethnicity: Russian Colonial Policy in Turkestan' in Brower and Lazzerini (eds), *Russia's Orient*, pp.113-35.

Broxup, Marie Bennigsen, 'The Last Ghazavat: The 1920-1921 Uprising' in Broxup (ed.), *The North Caucasus Barrier*, pp.112-45.

------, 'Islam in Dagestan under Gorbachev', *Religion in Communist Lands*, 18:3, autumn 1990, pp.212-25.

------, 'Islam and Atheism in the North Caucasus', *Religion in Communist Lands*, 9:1-2, Spring 1981, pp.40-9.

Bryan, Fanny E., 'Anti-Islamic Propaganda: *Bezbozhnik*, 1925-35', *Central Asian Survey*, 5:1, 1986, pp.29-47.

------, 'Anti-religious Activity in the Chechen-Ingush Republic of the USSR and the Survival of Islam', *Central Asian Survey*, 3:2, 1984, pp.99-115.

------, 'Internationalism, Nationalism and Islam' in Broxup (ed.), *The North Caucasus Barrier*, pp.195-218.

Carlisle, Donald S., 'The Uzbek Power Elite: Politburo and Secretariat (1938–83)', *Central Asian Survey*, 5:3–4, 1986, pp. 91–132.

------, 'Geopolitics and Ethnic Problems of Uzbekistan and its Neighbours' in Ro'i (ed.), *Muslim Eurasia*, pp.71-103.

------, 'Uzbekistan and the Uzbeks', *Problems of Communism*, 40:5, Sept.-Oct. 1991, pp.23-44.

Corley, Felix, 'Believers' Responses to the 1937 and 1939 Soviet Censuses', *Religion, State and Society*, 22:4, 1991, pp.403-17.

Dunn Stephen P., and Ethel Dunn, 'Soviet Regime and Native Culture in Central Asia and Kazakhstan: The Major Peoples', *Current Anthropology*, 8:3, June 1967, pp.147-84.

Fathi, Habiba, '*Otines*: the unknown women clerics of Central Asian Islam', *Central Asian Survey*, 16:1, 1997, pp.27-43.

Feshbach, Murray, 'Trends in the Soviet Muslim Population: Demographic Aspects' in Ro'i (ed.), *The USSR and the Muslim World*, pp.63-94.

Fierman, William, 'Central Asian Youth and Migration' in Fierman (ed.), *Soviet Central Asia*, pp.255-89.

———, 'The Soviet Transformation of Central Asia', *ibid.*, pp.11-35.

Fraser, Glenda, 'Basmachi', *Central Asian Survey*, 6:1 and 6:2, 1987, pp.1-73 and 7-62.

Friedgut, Theodore H., 'Integration of the Rural Sector into Soviet Society', *Slavic and Soviet Series*, 3:1, spring 1978, pp.29-47.

———, 'The Soviet Citizen's Perception of Local Government' in Jacobs (ed.), *Soviet Local Politics and Government*, pp.113-30.

Gabriel, Richard A., 'The Morale of the Soviet Army: Some Implications for Combat Effectiveness', *Military Review*, 8:10, Oct. 1978, pp.27-39.

Geraci, Robert, 'Russian Orientalism at an Impasse: Tsarist Education Policy and the 1910 Conference on Islam' in Brower and Lazzerini (eds), *Russia's Orient*, pp. 139–61.

Gleason, Gregory, 'Sharaf Rashidov and the Dilemmas of National Leadership', *Central Asian Survey*, 5:3-4, 1986, pp.133-60.

Hill, Ronald J., 'The Development of Soviet Local Government since Stalin's Death' in Jacobs (ed.), *Soviet Local Politics and Government*, pp. 18–33.

Jacobs, Everett M., 'Introduction: The Organizational Framework of Soviet Local Government' in Jacobs (ed.), *Soviet Local Politics....*, pp.3-17.

Jeziorska, Irena, 'Religious Themes in the Novels of Chingiz Aitmatov' in Shirin Akiner (ed.), *Cultural Change and Continuity in Central Asia*, pp.45-70.

Karklins, Rasma, 'Islam: How Strong is it in the Soviet Union?', *Cahiers du monde russe et soviétique*, 21:1, Jan.-March 1980, pp.65-81.

Kefeli, Agnès, 'Constructing an Islamic Identity: The Case of Elyshevo Village in the Nineteenth Century' in Brower and Lazzerini (eds.), *Russia's Orient*, pp.271-91.

Keller, Shoshana, 'Islam in Soviet Central Asia, 1917-1930: Soviet Policy and the Struggle for Control', *Central Asian Survey*, 11:1, 1992, pp.25-50.

Khalid, Adeeb, 'Representations of Russia in Central Asian Jadid Discourse' in Brower and Lazzerini (eds), *Russia's Orient*, pp.188-202.

Kocaoglu, Timur, 'Islam in the Soviet Union: Atheistic Propaganda and "Unofficial" Religious Activities', *Journal of the Institute of Muslim Minority Affairs*, 5:1, 1983, pp.145-52.

Lemercier-Quelquejay, Chantal, 'From Tribe to *Umma*', *Central Asian Survey*, 3:3, 1984, pp.15-26.

Luchterhandt, Otto, 'The Council for Religious Affairs' in Sabrina Petra

Ramet (ed.), *Religious Policy jn the Soviet Union*, Cambridge University Press, 1993, pp.55-83.

Markus, Vasyl, 'Religion and Nationalism in Ukraine' in Pedro Ramet (ed.), *Religion and Nationalism in Soviet and East European Politics,* Durham, NC: Duke University Press, 1984, pp.59-81.

Olcott, Martha Brill, 'Islam and Fundamentalism in Independent Central Asia' in Ro'i (ed.), *Muslim Eurasia*, pp.21-39.

———, 'Women and Society in Central Asia' in Fierman (ed.), *Soviet Central Asia: The Failed Transformation*, pp.235-54.

Paksoy, H. B., 'The Deceivers', Central Asian Survey, 3:1, 1984, pp. 123-31.

Roberts, Sean R., 'The Uighurs of the Kazakstan Borderlands: Migration and the Nation', *Nationalitics Papers*, 26:3, 1998, pp.511-30.

Ro'i, Yaacov, 'The Impact of the Islamic Fundamentalist Revival of the late 1970s on the Soviet View of Islam' in Ro'i (ed.), *The USSR and the Muslim World*, pp.149-77.

———, 'The Islamic Influence on Nationalism in Soviet Central Asia', *Problems of Communism*, 39:4, July-Aug. 1990, pp.49-64.

———, 'Nationalism in Central Asia in the Context of *Glasnost* and *Perestroika'* in Zvi Gitelman (ed.), *The Politics of Nationality and the Erosion of the USSR*, New York: St. Martin's Press, 1992, pp.49-76.

———, 'Religion as an Obstacle to *Sblizhenie*: The Official Perception', *Soviet Union/Union Soviétique*, 14:2, 1987, pp.163-79.

———, 'The Role of Islam and the Soviet Muslims in Soviet Arab Policy', *Asian and African Affairs*, 10:2 and 10:3, 1974-75, pp.157-89 and 259-80.

———, 'The Secularisation of Islam and the USSR's Muslim Areas' in Ro'i (ed.), *Muslim Eurasia*, pp.5-20.

———, 'The Task of Creating the New Soviet Man: "Atheistic Propaganda" in the Soviet Muslim Areas', *Soviet Studies*, 36:1, Jan. 1984, pp.26-44.

Rorlich, Azade-Ayse, 'Islam and Atheism: Dynamic Tension in Soviet Central Asia' in Fierman (ed.), *Soviet Central Asia*, pp.186-218.

Sadomskaya, Natalia, 'New Soviet Rituals and National Integration in the USSR' in Henry R. Huttenbach (ed.), *Soviet Nationality Policies: Ruling Ethnic Groups in the USSR*, New York: Mansell, 1990, pp.94-120.

Shabad, Theodore, 'The Urban-Administrative System of the USSR and Its Relevance to Geographic Research' in George J. Demko and Roland J. Fuchs (eds), *Geographical Studies on the Soviet Union*, University of Chicago, Dept. of Geography Research Paper No.211.

Snesarev, G. P., 'On Some Causes of the Persistence of Religio-Customary Survivals among the Khorezm Uzbeks' in Stephen P. Dunn and Ethel Dunn (eds), *Introduction to Soviet Ethnography*, Berkeley, CA: University of California Press, 1974, pp.215-38.

Soper, John, 'Unofficial Islam: a Muslim Minority in the USSR', *Religion in Communist Lands*, 7:4, winter 1979, pp.226-31.

Subtelny, Maria Eva, 'The Cult of Holy Places: Religious Practices among Soviet Muslims', *Middle East Journal*, 43:4, autumn 1989, pp.593-604.

Thrower, James, 'Notes on Muslim Theological Education in the USSR in the 1980s' in Shirin Akiner (ed.), *Political and Economic Trends in Central Asia*, pp.175-80.

Tohidi, Nayereh, 'The Intersection of Gender, Ethnicity and Islam in Soviet and Post-Soviet Azerbaijan', *Nationalities Papers*, 25:1, March 1997, pp.147-67.

Vaisman, Demian, 'Regionalism and Clan Loyalty in the Political Life of Uzbekistan' in Ro'i (ed.), *Muslim Eurasia*, pp.105-22.

Wimbush, S. Enders, 'The Politics of Identity Change in Soviet Central Asia', *Central Asian Survey*, 3:3, 1984, pp.69-78.

Wixman, Ronald, 'Ethnic Attitudes and Relations in Modern Uzbek Cities' in Fierman (ed.), *Soviet Central Asia*, pp.159-85.

Zelkina, Anna, 'Islam and Politics in the North Caucasus', *Religion, State and Society*, 21:1, 1993, pp.115-24.

Articles and chapters in books (Russian)

Abdullaev, M. A., 'Kritika kontseptsii nesovmestimosti sotsialisticheskogo obraza zhizni s prirodoi vostochnogo cheloveka', *Nauchnyi kommunizm*, 5, 1978, pp. 123–32.

——, 'Za glubokoe kriticheskoe izuchenie ideologii islama' in *Sotsiologiia, ateizm, religiia*, Groznyi: Checheno-Ingushskoe knizhnoe izdatel'stvo, 1972, pp.23-35.

Ashirov, Nugman, 'Musul'manskaia propoved' segodnia', *Nauka i religiia*, 12, Dec. 1978, pp.30-3.

——, 'Osobennosti ideologicheskoi i kul'tovoi deiatel'nosti musul'manskikh religioznykh organizatsii v sovremennykh usloviiakh' in *Aktual'nye voprosy ateisticheskogo vospitaniia*, Alma-Ata: Kazakhstan, 1976, pp.110-31.

Bokov, Kh. Kh., 'Vzaiosviaz' internatsional'nogo i ateisticheskogo vospitaniia v usloviiakh razvitogo sotsializma', *Voprosy filosofii*, 4, 1985, pp.42-53.

Filimonov, E. G., 'Sotsiologicheskie issledovaniia protsessa preodoleniia religii v sel'skoi mestnosti: itogi, problemy, perspektivy', *Voprosy nauchnogo ateizma*, 16, 1974, pp.71-84.

Klimovich, L. I., 'Bor'ba ortodoksov i modernistov v islame', *Voprosy nauchnogo ateizma*, 2, 1966, pp.65-88.

Makatov, I. A., 'Kul't sviatykh v islame', *Voprosy nauchnogo ateizma*, 3, 1967, pp.164-82.

Nishanov, R. N., 'Razreshenie natsional'nogo voprosa v SSSR i preodolenie religii v svete leninskogo ucheniia (na primere Uzbekskoi SSR)', *Voprosy nauchnogo ateizma*, 10, 1970, pp.167-86.

Orlov, A. M., 'Opyt issledovaniia protsessa sekuliarizatsii v tatarskikh selakh', *Voprosy nauchnogo ateizma*, 16, 1974, pp.89-102.

Rahimov, Rakhmat, 'O iazikovoi situatsii v Uzbekistane' in *Mezhnatsional'nye otnosheniia v usloviiakh sotsial'noi nestabil'nosti*, St. Petersburg: RAN, 1994, pp.109-32.

Urazmanova, R.K., 'Narodnyi prazdnik Sabantui u tatar', *Sovetskaia etnografiia*, 1, 1977, pp.94-100.

Zemskov, V. N., 'Massovoe osvobozhdenie spetsposelentsev i ssyl'nykh (1954-1960gg.)', *Sotsiologicheskie issledovaniia*, 1, 1991, pp.5-26.

INDEX

Abakumov, Viktor, 296, 353, 395, 543, 573
Abazinians, 477
Abdurahmanov, Abdujabr, 625, 698
Abkhaz, 57n.
Abkhaz ASSR, 113, 329-30, 574, 579
absenteeism, *see* work ethic
Abushaev, N. I., 324n.
adat, 411, 414, 420, 436
Administration of Architecture, *see* historical monuments
administrative measures (*administrirovanie*), 35, 38, 38n., 39, 40, 43, 44, 48, 204, 206-7, 240, 242n., 293, 307, 319, 352, 376-7, 404, 416, 451, 590, 591-3, 594, 644, 656, 658-9, 663-75 *passim*, 678, 702
adolescents, *see* children; marriage of adolescents; youth
Adygei AO, 200, 208n., 476-7
Afghanistan, 423, 551, 559, 572, 583, 584, 711, 717, 721; border with Tajikistan and Uzbekistan, 333, 586; Soviet invasion of, 346, 426, 551, 716; *see also* Jemiat-e Islami
Ahl-i Haqq, 426
Ahl-i Qur'an, 425, 582
Aiaguz, 82n., 186n.
Aitmatov, Chingiz, 694
Ajar ASSR, 77nn., 81, 90n., 113, 189, 437, 544, 574, 585, 590, 661, 705; *see also* Batumi; Ajar Obkom, 576
Ajars, 57n.
Akhtiamov, Hakim, 184n., 377, 397, 431, 447, 452, 557, 621, 678
Akmolinsk, 72, 77, 293
aksakals, 54-5, 134, 186, 213, 214, 241, 279, 291, 294, 320, 328-9, 330, 332, 341, 349n., 363, 434-5, 441-2, 449, 456-7, 512, 516, 518, 519n., 522, 626; *see also* pensioners

Aktiubinsk, city and oblast', 83n., 202n., 293, 489n., 492n., 634, 649
alcohol, 464
Aleksandrov, Georgii, 173n., 552n., 624-5
Aliev, Heydar, 584, 728
Ali Ilahi, *see* Ahl-i Haqq
Alimov, Abdurazak Ishan Muhammat, 104n.
Ali-zade, Akhund Aga Mamed Jafarogli, 105, 110n., 114
All-Russian Society for the Preservation of Historical and Cultural Monuments (VOOPIK), 690n.
All-Union Society for the Dissemination of Political and Scientific Knowledge, *see* Znanie
Alma-Ata, city and oblast', 72, 77, 78, 82n., 83n., 214n., 267, 292, 332, 350, 407, 633, 699
Al'met'evsk, 463
alowkhona, 337
Alpamish, 688
Alyakbarov, Azam, 573, 575-6
Andijan, city and oblast', 59n., 72, 73n., 77, 78, 79n., 83n., 87, 91, 102n., 190n., 202nn., 220n., 220, 250, 268, 277n., 285, 295, 296n., 297, 300, 306, 323, 333n., 354, 357, 397, 399, 436, 472n., 477n., 478, 499, 501, 502, 544, 616n., 638, 640, 649, 661, 664, 666, 678, 693
Andropov, Iurii, 51
Angren (Tashkent Oblast'), 401
animism, 365, 386, 695
anti-Muslim discrimination, *see* discrimination, anti-Muslim
anti-religious campaign (1958-64), 10, 41-48, 61, 65, 69, 70, 75, 95, 107, 128, 160, 179, 205-15, 218, 264, 308, 322, 348, 373, 438, 470, 474,

741